INDEX TO THE 1830 CENSUS OF GEORGIA

Transcribed and Compiled by
MRS. ALVARETTA KENAN REGISTER
Certified Genealogist

Baltimore
GENEALOGICAL PUBLISHING CO., INC.
1982

First Printing 1974
Second Printing 1982
Library of Congress Catalogue Card Number 73-22267
International Standard Book Number 0-8063-0609-2
Made in the United States of America

INTRODUCTION

Records of the first three censuses of the population of the United States for the state of Georgia, taken in 1790, 1800, and 1810, were apparently destroyed in the British attack on Washington during the War of 1812. Names contained in the 1820 and 1840 censuses of Georgia have been published, but these publications do not identify the original census page on which the name appears. This present work, however, is keyed to the original census page, and is, therefore, the only Georgia census index with complete finding apparatus.

The only names listed in the 1830 census were those of heads of families. The composition of the family is shown as the number of free white males and females in 5-year age groups to 20, 10-year age groups from 20 to 100, and 100 years and over. The number of slaves and free colored persons is indicated in six broad age groups.

Census enumerators spelled names exactly as they sounded, a practice which tends to create problems for the researcher. To obviate such problems, this Index groups together all names of like sound as the same surname, regardless of spelling. Names are transcribed verbatim from the original census records, except that colonial spellings, such as the long s which appears as f, are modernized. All names have been checked against the 1830 census records in the National Archives to insure the greatest accuracy possible, and difficult, unusual, or hard-to-read names have been checked against various published records of Georgia.

Anyone wishing a xerox copy of a census page should submit a written request to: Census Records (NNC), National Archives (GSA), Washington, D.C. 20408. The letter should specify the following: 1830 census of Georgia, name of county, page number of census, and name of individual on whom data is desired. Do not send money, as you will be billed $ 2.00 for the search and photocopy.

The Compiler wishes to express appreciation to Mrs. Jacqueline C. Limerick for the many hours she spent verifying names against published Georgia records; to Mr. Herbert B. Kimzey, Dr. James C. Bonner, Dr. H. S. Shearouse, Mrs. Horace L. McSwain, and Mrs. G. L. Swan for checking names in individual counties; to Mr. J. Hobart Bartlett of Arlington, Virginia for checking names in census records in the National Archives when they were illegible on microfilm, and to Mrs. Anna K. Parrish for typing a rough draft and assisting in correcting filing errors and in regrouping variant spellings of the same surname.

ABBREVIATIONS OF COUNTIES
MICROFILM REEL AND PAGE NUMBERS FOR COUNTY

County	Abbrev.	Pages
Microfilm Reel M-19-16		
Appling	App	5- 13
Baker	Bak	15- 20
Baldwin	Bal	28- 45
Bibb	Bib	49- 77
Bryan	Bry	84- 89
Bulloch	Bul	92-103
Burke	Bke	117-155
Butts	Bts	158-179
Camden	Cam	181-192
Campbell	Cpb	194-211
Carroll	Car	214-234
Chatham	Cht	240-283
Clarke	Clk	291-328
Columbia	Col	334-364
Coweta	Cow	367-392
Crawford	Crf	393-415
Microfilm Reel M-19-17		
Decatur	Dec	3- 19
DeKalb	DeK	25- 73
Dooly	Doo	78- 89
Early	Ear	91-100
Effingham	Eff	104-116
Elbert	Elb	119-160
Emanuel	Em	164-178
Fayette	Fay	181-207
Franklin	Frk	210-258
Glynn	Gly	264-269
Green	Gre	272-305
Gwinnett	Gwn	308-379
Microfilm Reel M-19-18		
Habersham	Hab	6- 66
Hall	Hal	68-134
Hancock	Han	148-173
Harris	Har	175-192
Henry	Hry	199-251
Houston	Hst	261-296
Irwin	Irw	298-304
Jackson	Jks	311-349
Jasper	Jsp	352-398
Jefferson	Jef	401-424
Jones	Jns	428-475

County	Abbrev.	Pages
Microfilm Reel M-19-19		
Laurens	Lau	4- 24
Lee	Lee	26- 35
Liberty	Lib	42- 56
Lincoln	Lin	58- 75
Lowndes	Lwn	79- 83
Madison	Mad	98-118
McIntosh	McI	121-132
Marion	Mar	137-144
Meriwether	Mwr	150-169
Monroe	Mon	172-229
Montgomery	Mtg	231-236
Morgan	Mor	238-272
Muscogee	Mus	277-292
Microfilm Reel M-19-20		
Newton	New	5- 55
Oglethorpe	Ogl	62-103
Pike	Pik	106-132
Pulaski	Pul	138-163
Putnam	Put	172-219
Rabun	Rab	222-235
Randolph	Ran	241-250
Richmond	Rch	253-292
Screven	Scr	299-319
Talbot	Tlb	322-348
Taliaferro	Tfo	354-369
Tattnall	Tat	371-380
Microfilm Reel M-19-21		
Telfair	Tlf	2- 12
Thomas	Tms	16- 30
Troup	Trp	32-55
Twiggs	Twg	60- 89
Upson	Up	95-121
Walton	Wal	123-174
Ware	Ware	183-189
Warren	Wrn	192-233
Washington	Wsh	239-276
Wayne	Wyn	281-285
Wilkes	Wil	287-324
Wilkinson	Wks	331-358

POPULATION DISTRIBUTION BY COUNTIES AS SHOWN IN CENSUS RETURNS

County	Names	Free White			Slaves			Free Colored			Grand
		Males	Females	Total	Males	Females	Total	Male	Female	Total	Total
Appling	217	652	632	1,284	88	91	179	5	0	5	1,468
Baker	161	494	483	977	140	135	275	0	1	1	1,253
Baldwin	468	2,223	1,915	4,138	1,640	1,339	2,979	14	12	26	7,143
Bibb	766	2,228	1,932	4,160	1,637	1,362	2,999	15	7	22	7,181
Bryan	138	385	338	723	1,170	1,232	2,402	9	5	14	3,139
Bulloch	312	1,000	933	1,933	325	324	649	3	1	4	2,586
Burke	1,017	2,654	2,412	5,066	3,341	3,301	6,642	56	69	125	11,833
Butts	552	1,676	1,549	3,225	824	856	1,680	3	4	7	4,912
Camden	311	752	706	1,458	1,523	1,563	3,086	20	14	34	4,578
Campbell	464	1,426	1,268	2,694	305	313	618	4	7	11	3,323
Carroll	503	1,430	1,293	2,723	244	244	488	111	97	208	3,419
Chatham	1,035	318	285	603	3,142	3,060	6,202	13	9	22	6,827
& Savannah		1,887	1,733	3,620	1,394	1,885	3,279	169	235	404	7,303
											14,130
Clarke	929	2,735	2,701	5,436	2,298	2,411	4,709	16	13	29	10,174
Columbia	822	2,266	2,202	4,468	4,091	3,940	8,031	53	54	107	12,606
Coweta	634	1,939	1,695	3,634	665	707	1,372	0	0	0	5,006
Crawford	593	1,919	1,672	3,591	864	854	1,718	4	0	4	5,313
Decatur	456	1,363	1,178	2,541	654	648	1,302	2	3	5	3,848
DeKalb	1,372	4,301	4,087	8,388	786	883	1,669	8	9	17	10,074
Dooly	312	914	873	1,787	166	170	336	5	7	12	2,135
Early	267	776	729	1,505	246	294	540	3	3	6	2,051
Effingham	298	903	837	1,740	650	569	1,219	1	4	5	2,964
Elbert	1,129	3,336	3,165	6,501	2,837	2,928	5,765	45	43	88	12,354
Emanuel	374	1,080	1,088	2,168	233	251	484	12	17	29	2,681
Fayette	744	2,198	2,070	4,268	562	610	1,172	24	27	51	5,491
Franklin	1,297	3,925	3,787	7,712	1,138	1,242	2,380	29	14	43	10,135
Glynn	147	338	259	597	1,992	1,976	3,968	2	0	2	4,567
Greene	921	2,603	2,421	5,024	3,822	3,650	7,472	23	30	53	12,549
Gwinnett	1,839	5,597	5,341	10,938	1,156	1,118	2,274	6	2	8	13,220

County	Names	Free White			Slaves			Free Colored			Grand
		Males	Females	Total	Males	Females	Total	Male	Female	Total	Total
Habersham	1,657	5,025	4,701	9,726	377	443	820	5	0	5	10,551
Hall	1,729	5,294	5,279	10,573	598	580	1,178	3	1	4	11,755
Hancock	779	2,323	2,284	4,607	3,729	3,455	7,184	16	19	35	11,826
Harris	485	1,519	1,312	2,831	1,184	1,085	2,269	4	1	5	5,105
Henry	1,366	4,091	3,900	7,991	1,212	1,358	2,570	3	3	6	10,567
Houston	925	2,666	2,495	5,161	1,069	1,125	2,194	10	4	14	7,369
Irwin	178	551	515	1,066	51	63	114	0	0	0	1,180
Jackson	1,050	3,133	3,047	6,180	1,387	1,396	2,783	25	16	41	9,004
Jasper	1,186	3,509	3,258	6,767	3,195	3,127	6,322	24	18	42	13,131
Jefferson	672	1,827	1,776	3,603	1,801	1,846	3,647	34	25	59	7,309
Jones	1,186	1,768	1,627	3,395	1,907	1,883	3,790	10	8	18	7,203
Laurens	557	1,645	1,543	3,188	1,162	1,214	2,376	7	7	14	5,578
Lee	247	715	652	1,367	171	133	304	3	0	3	1,674
Liberty	384	783	805	1,588	2,789	2,836	5,625	8	13	21	7,234
Lincoln	495	1,470	1,352	2,822	1,614	1,662	3,276	19	24	43	6,141
Lowndes	340	1,071	1,043	2,114	156	179	335	2	3	5	2,454
Madison	567	1,685	1,680	3,365	592	667	1,259	2	0	2	4,626
McIntosh	228	557	538	1,095	1,924	1,870	3,794	53	56	109	4,998
Marion	218	684	643	1,327	58	51	109	0	0	0	1,436
Meriwether	538	1,610	1,408	3,018	723	673	1,396	7	3	10	4,424
Monroe	1,488	4,584	4,252	8,836	3,614	3,741	7,355	6	5	11	16,202
Montgomery	154	474	460	934	168	167	335	0	0	0	1,269
Morgan	923	2,695	2,451	5,146	3,499	3,366	6,865	8	4	12	12,023
Muscogee	396	1,274	987	2,261	669	577	1,246	0	1	1	3,508
Newton	1,326	4,186	3,945	8,131	1,465	1,534	2,999	8	16	24	11,154
Oglethorpe	994	2,945	2,609	5,554	4,058	3,928	7,986	15	3	18	13,558
Pike	733	2,237	2,125	4,362	829	845	1,674	9	11	20	6,056
Pulaski	541	1,605	1,512	3,117	911	850	1,761	11	7	18	4,896
Putnam	1,042	2,831	2,680	5,511	3,890	3,813	7,703	25	16	41	13,255
Rabun	328	1,081	1,034	2,115	26	33	59	2	0	2	2,176
Randolph	275	807	701	1,508	354	328	682	1	0	1	2,191
Richmond	1,065	2,738	2,425	5,163	3,105	3,141	6,246	123	112	235	11,644

County	Names	Free White			Slaves			Free Colored			Grand
		Males	Females	Total	Males	Females	Total	Male	Female	Total	Total
Screven	415	1,212	1,175	2,387	1,185	1,183	2,368	8	13	21	4,776
Talbot	697	2,011	1,828	3,839	1,050	1,049	2,099	2	0	2	5,940
Taliaferro	405	1,138	1,024	2,162	1,352	1,383	2,735	18	19	37	4,934
Tattnall	264	767	752	1,519	249	257	506	9	5	14	2,039
Telfair	269	808	761	1,569	289	276	565	2	0	2	2,136
Thomas	382	1,126	1,001	2,127	580	585	1,165	4	0	4	3,296
Troupe	618	1,909	1,698	3,607	1,053	1,135	2,188	4	0	4	5,799
Twiggs	791	2,310	2,185	4,495	1,773	1,734	3,307	17	12	29	8,031
Upton	736	2,263	2,181	4,444	1,310	1,247	2,557	9	3	12	7,013
Walton	1,313	3,967	3,796	7,763	1,494	1,670	3,164	1	3	4	10,931
Ware	187	584	548	1,132	28	31	59	3	0	3	1,194
Warren	1,081	3,085	3,067	6,152	2,403	2,290	4,693	37	64	101	10,946
Washington	1,026	3,015	2,780	5,795	2,059	1,950	4,009	6	10	16	9,820
Wayne	125	339	337	676	124	152	276	5	6	11	963
Wilkes	983	2,670	2,595	5,265	4,511	4,449	8,960	2	10	12	14,237
Wilkinson	746	2,438	2,165	4,603	1,068	883	1,951	3	1	4	6,558
	52,168	152,343	142,516		106,748	106,199		1,228	1,209		
				294,859			212,947			2,437	510,243

Note: Indians in Carroll County included with Free Colored Persons

INDEX TO THE 1830 CENSUS OF GEORGIA

Name	County	Page
AARON/aarons		
Aaron, Jesse	Frk	235
______, Mary Ann	Mad	105
______, Sarah	Jsp	398
______, William	Frk	257
Aarons, William	Em	174
ABBOTT/ABBOT/ABBET		
Abbott, Abraham	Pik	122
______, Bennet	Tms	25
______, G. W.	Cht	278
______, Mary	Gly	266
______, Sarah	Bib	58
______, Sarah	Rch	280
______, Thomas	Pik	127
______, William	Frk	246
______, William	Wrn	220
______, William W.	Tms	17
Abbot, Abner A.	Lau	15
______, Ezekiel	Bts	178
______, Frances	App	6
______, John	Gwn	329
______, Mrs.	Cht	243
______, Robert	Cpb	211
Abbet, Obediah	Gwn	320
ABELL/ABELS/ABLES		
Abell, Joseph	Gre	292
Abels, Abraham	Frk	245
Ables, Ezekiel	Rab	231
ABERCROMBIE/ABBERCROMBIE/ ABERCUMBEE/ABERCROMBER		
Abercrombie, Anderson	Han	145
______, Edmond	Han	144
______, James	Hal	115
______, John	Hal	115
______, Martin	Han	144
______, William	Hry	232
______, Young	Hal	126
Abbercrombie, Eliza	Put	218
______, Nancy	Wrn	196
Abercumbee, Hugh	Wal	138
Abercromber, Charles	Jns	450
ABERNATHA, Samuel	DeK	45
ABERNATHY, Buckner	Hab	65
ABERHART, Adams	Ogl	76
______, Cinthy	Ogl	81
______, Mathew	Ogl	76
______, Thomas	Ogl	96
ABNEY, Benjn.	Jks	333
______, Hez.	Jks	338
______, James	Mwr	159
______, John	Jks	339
______, Lucy	Jns	428
______, Lucy	Jns	429

Name	County	Page
ABRAHAMS/ABRAHMS/ABRMS/ ABRAHAM		
Abrahams, Isaac	Gly	264
______, Isaac	Wyn	285
______, Jacob	Rch	264
Abrahms, A. D.	Cht	281
Abrms, Samuel	Gwn	372
Abraham, B.	Rch	256
ACHOLS: see Echols		
ACHORD, John	Wsh	245
______, John F.	Wsh	273
______, L. H.	Wsh	272
ACKER, William S.	Frk	244
ACOCK, Bardon	Wks	340
______, Burrel	Ogl	94
______, Jesse	Bul	102
______, Jesse	Mon	214
______, Joel	New	28
______, John	Mwr	163
______, Redrick	Wal	162
______, Richard	New	17
______, Zachariah	Ogl	93
ACRE/ACREE/ACEE		
Acre, Allen	Frk	256
______, Elizabeth	Tfo	368
______, Frances	Tfo	362
______, John	Tfo	354
______, Sterling	Tfo	361
______, William	Frk	249
______, Willie	Tfo	359
Acree, Hardy H.	Bak	15
______, Leonard F.	Bak	15
Acee, Alfred L.	Tlb	327
ADAIR/ADARE/ADER/ADIR		
Adair, Bozeman	Car	214
______, Danny	Col	351
______, Geo. R.	Gwn	350
______, Hiram	Ran	250
______, Isaac	Gwn	344
______, J. F.	DeK	27
______, James	Hry	241
______, James L.	Car	214
______, John	Gwn	327
______, Jones	Mor	250
______, Joseph	Jks	332
______, R. S.	Gwn	319
______, Samuel	Gwn	378
______, Waller	Gwn	377
______, William	Hry	207
______, William	Mad	99
______, William R.	Mor	252
Adare, James	Hab	56
______, John B.	Mad	100

Name	County	Page
Adare, W. H.	Mad	101
Ader, Thos. B	Gwn	378
Adir, James	Put	200
ADAMS/ADAM		
Adams, Abel	Tms	24
______, Abner	Elb	148
______, Absalom	Car	217
______, Absalom	Frk	232
______, Absla	Put	198
______, Alexander	Mar	139
______, Allen	Tms	25
______, Allen	Wal	138
______, Anthony	Crf	405
______, Arnold	Wsh	268
______, Asa	Mtg	232
______, Baker	Pul	153
______, Benjamin	Jns	443
______, Benjamin	Lau	6
______, Benja.	Wrn	199
______, Benja. Jr.	Wrn	219
______, Benja of Arthur	Wrn	210
______, Braxton	Wal	136
______, Briant	Tlf	10
______, Britain	Mwr	162
______, C. B.	Jsp	361
______, Caleb	Mon	177
______, Charlotte	Jsp	361
______, Daney Sr.	Col	356
______, Daniel	Twg	79
______, David	Doo	82
______, David	Hab	43
______, David	Hry	232
______, David	Hst	273
______, David	Jsp	359
______, David	Mar	144
______, David	Tlb	331
______, David	Wrn	215
______, Edward	Clk	317
______, Edward	Jks	312
______, Edward Jr.	Jks	313
______, Edwin	Mwr	164
______, Eleazer	Mon	182
______, Elizabeth	Col	356
______, Elizabeth	Tms	16
______, Elizabeth	Tms	20
______, Ezekiel	Hst	278
______, Frances	Hry	226
______, Franklin	Pul	159
______, Garry	DeK	28
______, George	Hab	66
______, George Z. B.	Hab	7
______, Gillisiah	New	10
______, Harriet	Cht	262
______, Heartwell	Wal	132
Adams, Henry	Col	356
______, Henry	Hab	32
______, Henry	Wrn	214
______, Hiram	Elb	124
______, Hopwell	Wsh	259
______, James	DeK	42
______, James	Elb	139
______, James	Elb	143
______, James	Elb	189
______, James	Hab	66
______, James	Jef	408
______, James	Jsp	354
______, James	Jef	408
______, James	Jns	428
______, James	Jns	455
______, James	Ogl	103
______, James	Wsh	263
______, James B.	Elb	143
______, James C.	Hab	27
______, James E.	Put	190
______, James M.	Wal	166
______, James W.	Hab	7
______, Jesse	Cow	392
______, Joel	Wal	162
______, John	Car	222
______, John	Clk	294
______, John	Cow	377
______, John	DeK	41
______, John	Elb	148
______, John	Hab	34
______, John	Har	181
______, John	Hry	199
______, John	Jks	325
______, John	New	50
______, John	Tlb	344
______, John	Tms	16
______, John	Trp	38
______, John	Trp	38
______, John	Twg	68
______, John	Twg	80
______, John	Wrn	219
______, John	Wil	321
______, John C.	Elb	158
______, John G. B.	Hab	6
______, John W.	Wsh	244
______, Johnathan	Hab	10
______, Jonathan	Pik	119
______, Joseph	Wil	298
______, Joshua	Mon	177
______, Lamack	Lau	12
______, Larkin	Pik	111
______, Laurence	Elb	159
______, Leon	Lee	30
______, Levi M.	Mwr	152

Name	County	Page
Adams, Levin	Lau	14
______, Louissa	DeK	49
______, Lucy	Clk	306
______, Martin	DeK	25
______, Martin	Mon	209
______, Mathias	Mtg	232
______, Miles	Irw	301
______, N. A.	Clk	325
______, Nancy	DeK	34
______, Nancy	DeK	38
______, Nancy	Tms	20
______, Nathaniel	Car	230
______, Nathaniel	Hab	66
______, Nipper	Mon	177
______, Norval	Jef	408
______, Orpah	Jef	408
______, Peter	Lau	7
______, Phabean	Tms	24
______, Reb^{a}.	Wrn	219
______, Reubin	Crf	403
______, Reuben	Mon	174
______, Reuben Sr.	Wal	145
______, Reuben Jr.	Wal	145
______, Richard	Clk	295
______, Richard	Jns	455
______, Rich^{d}.	Jsp	389
______, Richard	Rab	223
______, Richard	Wil	321
______, Richard C.	Elb	144
______, Robert	Bib	59
______, Robert	Wal	149
______, Rowel	Wrn	212
______, Rubin	Wrn	197
______, Samuel	Elb	143
______, Samuel	Twg	70
______, Samuel	Wal	166
______, Sarah W.	Lwn	80
______, Sarah E. E.	Rch	255
______, Shad	Wks	335
______, Solomon	Wal	138
______, Stephen	Put	210
______, Thomas	Cht	252
______, Thos.	DeK	71
______, Thomas	Elb	159
______, Thomas	Jks	311
______, Thomas	Jks	347
______, Thomas	Pul	159
______, Thomas	Tms	26
______, Thomas F.	Elb	149
______, Varnal	Pul	154
______, W. B. P.	Gre	297
______, Wiley	Mtg	232
______, William	Car	223
Adams, Wm.	Cht	279
______, William	Elb	159
______, William	Hal	92
______, William	Tlb	326
______, William	Tlb	345
______, William A.	Fay	198
______, William A.	Mon	177
______, William E.	Put	184
______, William R.	Wre	184
______, Willoughby	Wre	186
Adam, Amos	Crf	397
_____, David	Mon	183
_____, Kenching	Col	349
_____, William	Col	341
ADAMSON, Augustus Y.	Hry	221
________, George W.	Hry	229
________, Greenberry	Hry	239
________, James J.	Hry	239
________, William C.	Hry	220
ADCOCK/ADDCOCK		
Adcock, Anderson W.	Har	184
_______, Edmond	Frk	216
_______, Edmund	Wal	129
_______, George	Wal	143
_______, James	Wal	143
_______, John	Fay	202
_______, John C.	Mwr	156
_______, Joseph	Car	230
_______, Stinson	Wal	126
Addcock, William	Gwn	335
ADDERHOLD/ADDERHOLT		
Adderhold, Abraham	Frk	238
______, John C.	Frk	235
______, Lewis	Frk	245
Adderholt, George	Car	222
______, John J.	Hal	91
ADEL, James R.	Wsh	275
ADDISON/ADISON		
Addison, Ann	Frk	243
________, Brassel	Hab	33
________, Christopher	Frk	216
________, Hester	Hab	36
________, L. B.	Wks	346
________, Mark	Wre	184
________, Thomas	Hal	95
________, William	Hry	222
Adison, Elizabeth	Wal	157
ADFORTIN, Salva	Hal	84
ADKINS, Aron	Wrn	221
_______, Artamistia	Bib	49
_______, Burrel	Hal	131
_______, Chas.	Up	121
_______, Daniel	Wrn	223

Name	County	Page
Adkins, David	Jef	408
______, Helory	Gwn	315
______, Jesse	Jns	446
______, John	Up	103
______, Jno.	Up	121
______, Jno.	Wrn	223
______, Joseph	Hal	128
______, Joseph C.	Pik	122
______, Lewis	Twg	73
______, Lewis D.	Hry	215
______, Thomas	Twg	63
______, William	Gwn	336
______, William	Trp	46
______, William	Twg	62
ADKINSON: see Atkinson		
ADRIAN, David	Frk	218
______, Fleming F.	Car	220
AGERTON/ADGERTON		
Agerton, Thomas	Bke	154
_______, Willis	App	9
Adgerton, Sabra	Hal	84
AGETY, P.	Cht	270
AGNEW, Polley	Wal	167
AGSDEL, Richard	Hab	58
AINSDAY, James	Har	186
AINSWORTH, James	Wsh	239
AITHY, Francis W.	Wal	171
AJON, Eli	Cht	250
AKELS, Elisabeth	Hab	40
_____, Robert	DeK	47
AKEHEART, Ann	Lib	42
AKERS, John	Gre	299
_____, Mary	Gre	299
_____, Samuel	Gre	299
AKINS/AIKINS/AIKENS/AIKIN/		
AIKEN/AKIN/AKEN		
Akins, Benjamin	Tfo	358
_____, Elijah	Hry	220
_____, Elijah	Irw	299
_____, Jas.	Cpb	206
_____, James	DeK	66
_____, James	Gre	274
_____, Joel	DeK	27
_____, John	Gre	291
_____, John	Mor	257
_____, John T.	Mor	265
_____, Joseph	Gre	274
_____, Lucy	Mor	248
_____, Milton	Mor	264
_____, Robert	Tfo	363
_____, Stephen M.	Mor	264
_____, Thomas	DeK	30
_____, Thomas	Tfo	363

Name	County	Page
Akins, Thos. J.	DeK	40
_____, William	Har	182
_____, William Sr.	Mor	272
_____, William G.	Lwn	88
_____, Winifred	Tfo	364
Aikins, Frances	Lwn	88
______, George	Frk	243
______, Randal	Wsh	266
______, Sally	Frk	245
______, William	Bts	165
______, William	Frk	225
______, William	Hst	269
Aikens, Lewis	Bul	103
______, Thomas	Frk	251
Aikin, James	Jsp	395
_____, Jno.	Jsp	398
_____, Samuel	Tms	22
_____, Thos.	Jsp	395
Aiken, Daniel	Jsp	380
_____, James	Jsp	395
_____, James	Mon	191
_____, Samuel	Tms	22
Akin, Edward R.	Clk	318
____, Elizabeth	Clk	305
____, Hilla	Fay	184
____, James	Clk	294
____, James	Fay	204
____, John	Clk	313
____, John	Pik	117
____, John	Pik	118
____, Johnson	Elb	156
____, Samuel M.	New	26
____, William	Clk	318
____, William	Fay	205
____, William E.	Mon	197
Aken, Thomas	Elb	152
AKRIDGE/AKRIDG/AKERIDGE		
Akridge, Ab.	Bal	38
_______, Hardy	Bak	19
_______, Samuel	DeK	25
Akridg, Ezekiel	Clk	301
______, Levy	Clk	298
______, Levy	Clk	298
Akeridge, Abel Sr.	Doo	79
ALAIR, James	Cam	185
ALBERT, Abner	Wil	296
______, Frances	Tfo	356
ALBRIGHT/ALLBRIGHT/ALRIGHT/		
ABRIGHT		
Albright, Jacob Sr.	Mad	107
________, Jacob Jr.	Mad	107
________, Jeremiah	Jks	327
Allbright, John	DeK	46

Name	County	Page
Allbright, Michael	DeK	31
Alright, Henry	Hab	35
_____, William	DeK	26
Abright, Henry	Hab	35
ALBRITTON/ALBRITON/ALLBRITTON		
Albritton, Elizabeth	Han	145
_____, Isaac D.	Frk	229
_____, Joel	Wsh	256
_____, John	Frk	226
_____, Lanear	Wrn	226
_____, Matthew	Bke	123
_____, Matthew	Hst	285
_____, Peter	Wsh	271
_____, Robert L.	Bke	123
_____, Thomas	Bry	88
Albriton, Henry	Lwn	79
_____, William	Lwn	79
_____, Henry	Lib	42
Allbritton, James	Lwn	84
_____, Matthew	Lwn	84
ALDEN, Augustus	Ogl	95
ALDERMAN, George	Bak	19
_____, George	Tms	27
_____, James	Tms	27
_____, James	Tms	29
_____, Samuel	Bul	98
_____, Thomas	Tms	28
_____, Timothy	Bul	97
_____, William	Lwn	80
ALDRED/ALRED/ALLRED		
Aldred, James	Wrn	216
_____, William	Wrn	220
Aldred, Jno.	Gwn	309
Alred, Elias Sr.	Hal	99
_____, Elias	Hal	98
_____, William	Hal	99
Allred, William	New	48
_____, William B.	New	47
ALDRIDGE/ALDREDGE/ALREGE		
Aldridge, Absalom	Fay	182
_____, Aaron	Rch	285
_____, Henry	Cpb	210
_____, Isaac	Hst	296
_____, James	Tlb	332
_____, Mathias	Tlb	331
_____, Nathan	Mor	253
_____, Reuben	Tlb	330
_____, Thomas	Mon	200
_____, Thomas B.	Mon	175
_____, William	Wil	318
Aldredge, Aron	Wrn	216
Aldrege, Elizabeth	App	12
ALDRICH's Plantation	Cam	181
ALESBERRY, Jno.	Gwn	341
ALEWINE/ALERVINE		
Alewine, David	New	32
_____, Nanul or Dancel	New	50
_____, Reuben	New	31
Alervine, Elijah	Tlb	327
ALEXANDER/ALLEXANDER/ ALEXANDRIA		
Alexander, Abraham	Jns	455
_____, Adam	Jsp	354
_____, Adam, Estate	Lib	42
_____, Adam L.	Wil	289
_____, Albert	Jsp	353
_____, Albert J.	Fay	199
_____, Alford R.	Fay	203
_____, Allen	Elb	155
_____, Arthur	Car	224
_____, Benj.	Tat	378
_____, Cullen W.	Jns	467
_____, David	Jef	412
_____, Elam	Elb	138
_____, Eli O.	Hry	225
_____, Elone	Bib	53
_____, Feriby	Tfo	365
_____, George	Jsp	354
_____, George L.	Jsp	353
_____, James	Bry	86
_____, Jas.	Gwn	314
_____, Jas.	Gwn	347
_____, James	Wil	288
_____, James B.	Elb	122
_____, James S.	Frk	217
_____, Jas. W.	Ear	96
_____, John	Clk	319
_____, John B.	Hst	262
_____, John H.	Jef	419
_____, John N.	New	9
_____, Johnathan	Mon	223
_____, Joseph Y.	Ogl	98
_____, Louisa	Jsp	381
_____, Margaret	Jsp	356
_____, Mary	Elb	124
_____, Moses	Wrn	201
_____, Nathaniel G.	Gre	298
_____, Peter	Elb	153
_____, Rebecca	Pul	141
_____, Sally	Hab	40
_____, Sarah	Bts	159
_____, Sarah	Gwn	362
_____, Silas	Hab	28
_____, Smith	Clk	294
_____, Tabitha	Elb	156
_____, Thos. W.	Gwn	359

Name	County	Page
Alexander, Uriah	Put	196
_____, William	Clk	292
_____, William	Elb	124
_____, William	Frk	230
_____, William	Gre	301
_____, William	Hal	78
_____, William	Har	188
_____, William	Wsh	258
_____, William D.	Mwr	153
_____, William G.	Elb	152
_____, Willis	Elb	152
Allexander, William	Jns	443
Alexandria, M.	Bak	15
ALFORD/ALLFORD		
Alford, Aseneth	Tfo	368
_____, Bias	Wsh	244
_____, Britain	Pik	109
_____, Bryant	Pul	154
_____, Clinton	Tlb	343
_____, Cullen	Fay	184
_____, E. C.	Mus	277
_____, Handy	Hst	276
_____, Henry	Put	175
_____, Isom	Mwr	161
_____, Jacob	Han	145
_____, Jephthal	Jsp	358
_____, Job	Tlb	342
_____, Julius C.	Tlb	342
_____, Lodwick	Trp	46
_____, Obadiah	Han	144
_____, Owen	Han	144
_____, Peyton	Jns	450
_____, Sippy	Bts	158
_____, Spier	Pik	109
_____, Thos.	Gwn	378
_____, Turner	Tlb	342
_____, William	Mor	243
_____, William	Twg	64
_____, Willie	Tfo	358
_____, Wyatte	Twg	61
Allford, Isaac H.	Har	190
_____, James	Cow	389
_____, Julious C.	New	14
ALFRED, Arthur	Cam	191
_____, B. E.	Col	362
_____, Getson	Col	352
_____, John	Gwn	309
_____, Julius C.	Gre	305
_____, Needham	Wrn	196
ALFRIEND, Abraham	Han	144
_____, Edward D.	Gre	276
ALGIERS, William D.	Hst	276
ALLA, William	Hab	56

Name	County	Page
ALLCORN, James	Jks	317
ALLCUT, Thomas	Doo	87
ALLDAY, Benj.	Wks	342
_____, John P.	Bke	133
_____, Josiah	Bke	133
_____, Nancy	Bke	133
_____, Peter	Bke	133
ALLEN/ALLIN		
Allen, Abraham	Jns	430
_____, Adam	Ran	244
_____, Alexander	Jsp	354
_____, Alexander M.	Jef	423
_____, Anderson	Bak	20
_____, Andrew	Lin	72
_____, Andrew Y. J.	Bke	118
_____, Asa W.	Frk	214
_____, Barnabus	Jef	423
_____, Benjamin	Bib	69
_____, Benjamin	Frk	246
_____, Benjamin	Hab	65
_____, Benja.	Wrn	203
_____, Beverly	Elb	150
_____, Beverly	Jks	315
_____, Binet	Mar	144
_____, Boler	Jns	464
_____, Bryan	Lau	23
_____, Carter	Hab	55
_____, Champion	Wil	310
_____, Charles	Bke	155
_____, Charles	Clk	319
_____, Charles	Mon	206
_____, Charles	Mor	260
_____, Charles	Up	104
_____, Churchwell	Pik	114
_____, Clement	Pik	124
_____, Cloe	Put	218
_____, Coleman	Hab	65
_____, Cynthia	Jns	464
_____, Cyrus	Cpb	199
_____, Darling R.	Hst	270
_____, David	Hab	16
_____, David	Lib	42
_____, David	Mar	140
_____, David	Tlf	12
_____, David	Wsh	240
_____, David P.	Gwn	341
_____, Dennis	Tms	18
_____, Eason	Lau	23
_____, Edward	Elb	145
_____, Edward	Wrn	230
_____, Edwin	Han	144
_____, Elijah P.	Fay	182
_____, Eliza	Bal	29

Name	County	Page
Allen, Elizabeth	Jsp	361
______, F. A.	Gwn	344
______, Fanny	Mad	118
______, Frances	Jks	344
______, Frances	Jns	434
______, Frances D.	Rch	288
______, George	Tfo	362
______, George A. F.	Put	215
______, George S.	Tfo	358
______, Gideon	Twg	74
______, Gillum	Lau	16
______, Greene	Put	190
______, Green B.	Put	216
______, Grey	Mad	107
______, Henry	Ogl	68
______, Henry	Tms	18
______, Hezekiah	Hry	247
______, Howard	Mad	104
______, Hugh	Bke	135
______, Ira	Trp	41
______, Isaac	Tms	24
______, J. W.	Bak	17
______, James	Bke	132
______, James	Clk	319
______, James	Col	358
______, James	Fay	196
______, James	Frk	253
______, James	Gwn	366
______, James	Hab	16
______, James	Han	144
______, James	Lwn	83
______, James	Mwr	162
______, James	Mwr	162
______, James	Pul	154
______, James	Up	110
______, James P.	Bke	120
______, James P.	Bke	135
______, James S.	Bke	132
______, James S.	Har	186
______, Jeremiah	Bke	119
______, Jeremiah	Wal	125
______, Jesse	Fay	199
______, Job	Bib	59
______, Jno.	Bal	32
______, John	Bul	92
______, John	Frk	231
______, John	Gre	287
______, John	Gre	296
______, John	Mus	288
______, John	Trp	50
______, John	Twg	80
______, John	Wal	139
______, John E.	Mon	173
Allen, John M.	Jns	464
______, John R.	Mon	176
______, John S.	Hal	111
______, John W.	Crf	406
______, Jordan	Put	215
______, Joseph	Elb	132
______, Joseph	Frk	216
______, Joseph	Jef	420
______, Jos.	Rab	222
______, Joseph	Wrn	203
______, Joseph	Wsh	244
______, Josiah	Mwr	158
______, Larkin W.	Mor	252
______, Larken W.	Mor	271
______, Leland	New	6
______, L. Samuel	Hab	65
______, Martha	Han	145
______, Mary	Cht	269
______, Mary	Fay	182
______, Matthew	Frk	215
______, Mathew	Trp	39
______, Meshire	Bib	69
______, Nancy	Gre	296
______, Nathan	Tfo	369
______, Nathaniel	Mor	250
______, Nat. B.	Mad	103
______, Nazareth	Lau	16
______, Parham	Han	144
______, Phillip	Clk	308
______, Reuben	New	35
______, Richard	Frk	238
______, Richard	Jns	433
______, Richard	Rch	267
______, Riley	New	8
______, Robert	Col	345
______, Robert	Col	354
______, Robert	Frk	216
______, Robert	Jks	311
______, Robert	Mon	210
______, Robert	Pik	120
______, Robt.	Rab	232
______, Robert A.	Bke	140
______, Sarah	Bke	155
______, Sarah	Elb	152
______, Sarah	Jsp	390
______, Sary	Frk	257
______, Sherwood	Jef	419
______, Singleton W.	Elb	156
______, Stephen	Gre	296
______, Stephen	Ogl	96
______, Stokes	Ogl	101
______, Susan	Rch	283
______, Thomas	Bke	135

Name	Co.	Page
Allen, Thomas	Clk	303
______, Thos.	Gwn	318
______, Thos. A.	Gwn	344
______, Thomas J.	Up	111
______, Thomas V.	Mor	264
______, Tilman	Han	145
______, Waddle	Jef	423
______, Welcome	Rch	262
______, William	Cpb	199
______, William	Elb	135
______, William	Frk	250
______, William	Gre	272
______, William	Hry	220
______, William	Jsp	380
______, William	Jns	464
______, William	Mor	257
______, William	New	48
______, William	Rab	232
______, William	Scr	317
______, William	Twg	77
______, William	Wal	142
______, William	Wal	154
______, William D.	Mwr	163
______, William F.	Hry	202
______, William P.	Bke	124
______, William W.	New	24
______, Willie	Han	144
______, Willie	Tfo	364
______, Woodson	Wal	159
______, Wyak	Pul	139
______, Wyatt	Mad	105
______, Yond D.	Pik	132
______, Young	Bak	20
______, Young S.	Fay	189
______, Young S.	Gre	304
Allin, Absalom R.	Gwn	366
______, George W.	Clk	295
______, James	Gwn	366
ALLEY, Frederick F.	Cpb	202
______, Geo. W.	Gwn	361
______, N.	Rch	271
ALLGOOD/ALGOOD/ALAGOOD/ ALIGOOD		
Allgood, Edward	Wal	127
________, John	Elb	141
________, John Y.	Wal	127
________, Mary	Elb	151
________, William	Elb	151
Algood, Samuel	Wal	126
_______, William	Cpb	195
Alagood, Write	Dec	12
Alligood, Hillery	Lau	15
ALLISON/ALISON/ALLSON/ ALLISAN		
Allison, A. H.	Jsp	360
________, David	Mon	219
________, Elias	Mor	242
________, Henry	Jsp	360
________, John	Elb	135
________, John	Mor	267
________, William	Bts	167
________, William C.	Wil	288
Alison, Elenor	Clk	323
_______, Martha	Gre	277
_______, Wyley	Car	230
Allson, Alex^r.	Mwr	155
Allisan, James	Mus	284
ALMAND/ALMOND/ALLMOND/ ALLMAN/ALMAN/ALMON		
Almand, Ann	Elb	146
_______, Isaac	Elb	146
_______, John	Elb	119
_______, Sarah	Elb	160
_______, Simeon	Elb	146
Almond, Daniel H.	Gwn	370
_______, William	Mon	178
Allmond, John	Bke	151
Allman, John	New	8
_______, Thomas	New	8
_______, William	Ear	92
Alman, Burwell	Hst	288
______, Nelson	New	5
Almon, James	Mor	267
______, Richard V.	Mor	268
______, William	Frk	248
______, William	Mtg	236
ALLUMS/ALLUM		
Allums, Briggs	Cow	370
_______, Britain	Trp	39
_______, Edmund	Hry	218
_______, Hopson	Hry	237
_______, John	Tlb	325
_______, William	Trp	50
Allum, Jeremiah	Wks	357
ALNE, Lucresa	Hab	54
ALRUY, Henrietta C.	Cht	258
ALSABROOK/ALSABROOKS/ ALSIBROOKS		
Alsabrook, Amos	Jns	443
__________, Asa	Tlb	342
__________, Lewis	Tlb	339
__________, Wilson C.	Jns	443
Alsabrooks, Howel	Jns	438
___________, Landon	Jns	438
Alsibrooks, Clabin	Lee	26
___________, Howell	Lee	26
ALSTON/AWLSTON/ALSTEAD		
Alston, Christian L.	Elb	156

Alston, Gilly Elb 155
______, James Y. Elb 156
______, Joshua Sr. Doo 88
______, Joshua Jr. Doo 78
______, P. Mus 288
______, P. B. Bal 39
______, P. H. Mus 285
______, Robert W. Han 144
______, William Tlf 6
______, William H. Mus 285
Awlston, Ann Bib 63
______, James Bib 63
Alstead, Harvy Ogl 97
ALTMAN, David Hst 267
______, Thomas Ware 187
AMBROSE, David Eff 113
______, Elizabeth Eff 113
______, Hezekiah Eff 112
______, Marcus Gwn 316
______, Warren Jsp 357
AMBURN, Martha Bke 155
AMES, Thomas Ogl 95
____, William Jns 436
AMISON/AMERSON/AMASSON/
AMMASON/AMBERSON
Amison, Cullen Wsh 274
______, Edward Wil 306
______, Henry Wsh 273
______, John Wsh 255
______, Josiah Wsh 268
______, Nathan Wsh 255
______, Warren Wsh 254
Amerson, Britton Han 144
______, Jesse Mar 144
______, Josiah Han 145
Amasson, Abraham Bak 19
______, C. Bak 15
Ammason, James Jks 324
Amberson, Mathew Mor 266
______, William Wal 165
AMMONS/AMMOND/AMMONDS/
AMONS
Ammons, Elizabeth Wyn 282
______, Jessee Hst 296
______, John Wyn 282
______, Johnson Up 108
______, Joshua Wal 139
______, Sarah Mor 269
______, Stephen Hst 296
Ammond, Jesse Mor 269
Ammonds, Sterling Mor 238
Amons, Sarah Twg 84
AMOS, Casper M. Bts 164
Amos, Daniel Han 144
_____, George Han 144
_____, James Put 181
_____, James Trp 39
_____, Jonathan McI 125
_____, Maulden Jns 437
_____, William Jns 435
_____, William M. Pik 127
ANCIAUX, Lydia Bul 101
ANDERS/ANDES
Anders, Frederick Pul 155
______, Joel Lau 21
______, John Crf 395
Andes, Tuttle H. Han 144
ANDERSON, A. Gwn 308
________, Abraham Hst 272
________, Alfred F. Bts 165
________, Alle Scr 307
________, Amos Tat 376
________, Arrimonis Hab 49
________, Aug. H. Bke 127
________, Charles Jef 414
________, D. D. DeK 56
________, D. R. Jks 321
________, David S. Wrn 203
________, Edward A. Wil 290
________, Elijah Gre 274
________, Elijah Gwn 336
________, Elijah Twg 66
________, Elizabeth Put 212
________, Evan Wsh 266
________, George Cht 253
________, Geo. Plantation Cht 279
________, George Rch 290
________, George W. Cht 253
________, Geo. W. Plan-
tation Cht 279
________, Godekia Hab 52
________, Henry Frk 241
________, Henry Ran 242
________, Henry Tms 17
________, Isaac Hab 50
________, Jacob Mad 99
________, Jacob Ran 242
________, James Bke 129
________, James Bts 175
________, James Cow 383
________, James DeK 35
________, James Hab 12
________, James Hal 80
________, James Har 186
________, James Jef 419
________, James Lwn 87

Name	County	Page
Anderson, James	Mad	99
________, James	Mwr	165
________, James	Tat	371
________, James	Tlb	340
________, James C.	Clk	323
________, James C.	Clb	139
________, James M.	Wil	287
________, Jane	Bke	125
________, Joel	Cpb	198
________, John Sr.	Hab	62
________, John Jr.	Hab	62
________, John	Bul	92
________, John	Gly	264
________, John	Gwn	353
________, John	Gwn	354
________, John	Hab	11
________, John	Hab	42
________, John	Hry	200
________, John	Lee	28
________, John	Pul	138
________, John	Rab	233
________, John	Tfo	355
________, John	Tat	376
________, John	Twg	66
________, John	Twg	72
________, Jno. C.	Mon	216
________, John G.	Lau	15
________, John L.	Rch	268
________, John M.	Rch	282
________, John R.	Wil	287
________, John S.	Cow	384
________, John V.	Elb	130
________, Joseph	Tms	23
________, Joseph	Rab	230
________, Joseph	Tms	23
________, Joseph	Scr	307
________, Joseph S.	New	15
________, Joshua	Hab	29
________, Lewis	Tat	378
________, M. L.	DeK	56
________, Mariah	Wsh	271
________, Martha E.	Jef	412
________, Mary	Pul	138
________, Mathew	Hry	201
________, Moses	Hab	11
________, Tms	23	
________, Moss G.	Rab	234
________, Nancy	Wil	304
________, Nelson	DeK	32
________, Noble	Rab	227
________, Obadiah	Hry	250
________, Philip	DeK	32
________, Richard	Tfo	358
Anderson, Robt.	DeK	56
________, Robert	Hab	46
________, Robert	Mon	209
________, Rubin G.	Hab	29
________, Samuel	Hab	46
________, Samuel J.	DeK	62
________, Samuel	Hab	46
________, Sarah	Bib	49
________, Sarah	Wrn	197
________, T. J.	Lee	32
________, Thomas	Bts	176
________, Thomas	Cow	378
________, Thomas	Gre	285
________, Thomas	Wil	291
________, Thomas F.	Frk	218
________, Thomas W.	Twg	78
________, Vincent	Tlf	11
________, W. C.	Col	350
________, Wesley A.	Tlb	322
________, Wiley	Hab	31
________, Will	Bal	30
________, William	Col	348
________, William	DeK	55
________, William	DeK	56
________, William	DeK	63
________, William	Hab	42
________, William	Hab	64
________, William	Hal	133
________, William	Lau	14
________, Wm. dec'd estate	Lib	42
________, William	Mon	218
________, William	Rab	226
________, William	Tfo	358
________, William H.	Bts	174
________, William L.	Tfo	365
________, William P.	Hal	81
________, William Q.	Wil	290
________, Wyllie	Tat	371
________, Zedekia	Hab	52

ANDREWS/ANDREW/ANDRES/
ANDRUS/ANDRESS/ANDRUCE

Name	County	Page
Andrews, Abisha	Twg	66
________, Adam	Frk	230
________, Adam	Gre	301
________, Allen	Tfo	364
________, Ann	Bts	175
________, Charles	Elb	153
________, David	Pik	120
________, David	Cpb	196
________, David	Gwn	342
________, Davis R.	Put	206
________, Edward	Lib	42
________, Enoch	Frk	212

Name	County	Page
Andrews, Green	Wsh	274
______, Harvey	Bke	133
** ______, J.	Rch	274
______, Jacob	Pik	116
______, James	Pik	119
______, Jesse	Gwn	342
______, John	Bke	132
______, John	Bts	177
______, John	Han	144
______, John	Ogl	72
______, John P.	Rch	260
______, Joseph	Lib	42
______, Joseph B.	Twg	66
______, Joseph W.	Har	182
______, Lunsford L.	Tfo	354
______, Marcus	Tfo	354
______, Mark	Ogl	73
______, Marsillar	Han	144
______, Martha	Ogl	68
______, Mary	Wrn	196
______, Micajah	Lib	42
______, Nancy	Wrn	203
______, Nicholas S.	Wil	302
______, Nimrod	Frk	220
______, Owen	Gwn	337
______, Owen	Gwn	342
______, Peter	Wks	352
______, Richard	Tfo	359
______, Robbins	Twg	77
______, Richard	Tfo	359
______, Robert	Bts	170
______, Samuel	Bke	132
______, Samuel R.	Mus	278
______, Sterling	Mon	192
______, Susan	Em	169
______, Thomas	Doo	89
______, W., Heirs of	Wrn	193
______, Wiley	Frk	249
______, William	Gwn	342
______, William	Hry	218
______, William G.	Up	100
______, William H.	Bib	58
______, Wyatt	Pik	117
Andrew, Beesley	Elb	142
______, Benjamin	Elb	133
______, James O.	Clk	325
______, Mary	Clk	300
______, Mary	Wil	317
______, Sterling	Mon	192
______, Willis	Em	165
Andres, Loderic	Scr	317
______, Martin	Wil	308
______, Rachel	Scr	315

Name	County	Page
Andrus, John	Wil	317
______, William	Wil	317
Andress, John	Cpb	195
Andruce, Lunsford L.	Tfo	354
ANGLIN/ANGLE/ANGLEN/ ANGLING/ANGELLY		
Anglin, Elijah	Twg	73
______, Henry	Clk	318
______, Henry	Jks	328
______, Henry	Twg	62
______, John	Gwn	330
______, John	Jks	337
______, John	Twg	66
______, John A.	Jks	344
______, Susan	Pik	126
______, William	Cow	375
Angle, Charles	Frk	249
______, John	Fay	202
______, Thomas	Cpb	203
______, Thomas	Frk	249
Anglen, Peter A.	Jks	337
Angling, David	Mor	259
Angelly, Benjamin	Twg	89
ANSLEY/ANSLY		
Ansley, Gilbert	Jns	438
______, Jesse	Rch	288
______, Tilmon	Up	108
______, Marlin	Crf	408
______, William	Gre	280
Ansly, Asa	Put	206
______, Isaiah	Put	206
ANSON, M. D.	Bal	28
ANTHONY/ANTONY		
Anthony, Ann	Jsp	356
______, Ann	Wil	289
______, Ansolem	Gwn	367
______, David	Elb	156
______, David	Frk	221
______, Elijah	Elb	156
______, Free	Jns	442
______, James	Jns	436
______, John	Crf	400
______, John	Fay	187
______, John	Jks	341
______, John A.	Cpb	203
______, Joseph	Fay	182
______, Joseph B.	Tlb	340
______, Mark	Lin	65
______, Micajah T.	Wil	290
______, Nelly	Elb	156
______, Tabitha	335	
______, William	Wil	317
______, Willis	Jks	342

Name	County	Page
Antony, Lewis	Mus	287
______, Mary	Jks	336
______, Martin	Jks	336
______, Milton	Rch	263
______, Samuel	Mus	289
______, Wiley	Jks	336
ANTIGNAC: see D'Antignac		
APLEDGE, William G.	Cpb	202
APPISON, James	Har	179
APPLEBY, James	Jks	314
______, William	Jks	326
APPLING/APLING		
Appling, Ellearander	Col	353
______, Joel	Wil	308
______, John	Ogl	99
______, Rebecca	Col	345
______, Walter A.	Clk	299
______, William	Clk	297
Apling, Burwell	Wil	295
APPLEWHITE, John	Bke	117
__________, John	Mor	258
__________, Peter	Bke	117
__________, Robert	Mor	255
__________, Stephen	Bke	117
__________, Thomas B.	Ran	244
ARANS, Peter	Cow	388
ARCA, Mary	Frk	237
____, Thomas	Frk	237
ARCHER, David	Clk	318
______, David	Scr	299
______, Elias S.	Han	144
______, Elihu	Scr	299
______, Frederick	Han	145
______, Harvy A.	Jks	333
______, James	Han	144
______, James K.	Tat	377
______, Lodowick	Hry	199
______, Milton	Clk	305
______, Thomas	Hab	63
______, Thomas	Tat	375
______, William	Han	144
______, Williamson	Han	145
ARD, George	Lau	23
___, John	Twg	77
___, Jno. S.	Wks	339
___, Neil	Hst	283
___, Seaborn M.	Hry	216
ARDIS, John	Mus	289
ARENDALL, John	Frk	230
________, Susannah	Frk	247
ARGO, David	DeK	33
___, Edmund	Hry	219
___, Nimrod	DeK	32
ARLEDGE, Samuel	DeK	43

Name	County	Page
ARLINE, Henry	Dec	16
______, James	Wsh	267
______, Jesse	Lau	20
______, Jethro	Lau	6
ARMAND, Samuel	Gwn	372
ARMOUR/ARMOR		
Armour, James	Jks	314
______, John	Hal	129
______, Richard H.	Har	183
______, Robert	Hal	128
______, William	Hal	124
Armor, Newton D.	Wil	306
_____, Robert	Wil	307
_____, William	Gre	294
ARMS, Seth	Jsp	371
ARMSTEAD/ARMISTED/AMSTED		
Armstead, A.	Jsp	371
_________, John	Wal	149
_________, John	Wal	149
_________, William	Wal	144
Armisted, H.	Jks	345
Amsted, John	Gwn	317
ARMSTRONG, Alex^{r}.	Wsh	267
__________, Alex^{r}. Jr.	Wsh	267
__________, Edward	Wsh	254
__________, George	Gre	279
__________, Golden	Wrn	216
__________, Hugh	Col	361
__________, J. H.	Bal	37
__________, James	Bal	49
__________, James	Hst	271
__________, James	Wil	291
__________, James	Wrn	207
__________, James W.	Cam	185
__________, Jesse	Wrn	209
__________, Jesse	Wsh	249
__________, John	Gre	279
__________, Larkin S.	Hst	262
__________, Margaret	Gre	279
__________, Martin W.	Hal	79
__________, Mary	Wrn	207
__________, Samuel	Hry	204
__________, Sarah	McI	123
__________, Wily S.	Twg	88
__________, William	Gly	264
__________, William	Gwn	339
__________, William	Jsp	356
__________, William	Wyn	285
ARNETT, Henry W.	Up	98
_______, Mary	Frk	238
_______, Meradeth	Wrn	230
_______, Peter	Scr	309
_______, Seaborn	Wil	304
_______, Thomas	Wrn	230

Name	County	Page
Arnett, Timothy	Scr	305
_____ , William	Scr	309
_____ , William	Wil	304
_____ , Wyley	Jns	441
_____ , Zabel	Wrn	233
ARNOLD/ARNALD/ARNOLA/ ARNAURD/ARNOW/ARNEL		
Arnold, Allen J.	Wil	297
______, Arnet	Wsh	247
______, Chas.	Lee	33
______, Charles	Tat	378
______, Chesley	Ogl	71
______, Davis	Elb	119
______, Edmond	Gwn	376
______, Elijah B.	Wal	130
______, Elizabeth	Elb	156
______, Elizabeth	Ogl	84
______, Elizabeth	Wil	323
______, Greene	Han	144
______, George	Irw	302
______, Harison	Gwn	359
______, Harrell	Wsh	247
______, James	Frk	249
______, James	Ware	186
______, James B.	Mor	272
______, Jesse H.	Wal	123
______, John Sr.	Han	144
______, John	Elb	139
______, John	Han	144
______, John	Trp	50
______, John	Twg	75
______, John	Wil	312
______, Joseph	Ogl	65
______, Keziah	Rch	267
______, Laughlin	DeK	29
______, Lewis	New	54
______, Lock	Hab	28
______, Mary	Hry	244
______, Moses	Wil	298
______, Owen	Tfo	366
______, Park	Ogl	67
______, Peter	Han	144
______, R. J.	Bry	84
______, Randol	DeK	59
______, Reason	Tlb	336
______, Samuel	Gwn	356
______, Solomon	Gre	295
______, Solomon	Wks	344
______, Stephen	Jks	321
______, Stephen	Ogl	64
______, Tabitha	Pul	145
______, Thomas	Rab	224
______, Thomas	Tlb	347

Name	County	Page
Arnold, Thomas	Wsh	259
_____ , Wiley	Han	144
_____ , William	Elb	157
_____ , William	Gwn	360
_____ , William	Gwn	361
_____ , William	Han	144
_____ , William	Ogl	64
_____ , William	Put	179
_____ , William	Tlf	2
_____ , William P.	Mad	115
_____ , William	Twg	87
_____ , William	Wal	162
_____ , William W.	Mon	197
_____ , Zephemiah	Han	144
Arnald, William	Clk	306
_____ , William	Wal	162
Arnola, W. P.	Bal	39
Arnaurd, P.	Cht	261
Arnow, Jo	Cam	183
_____ , Peter	Cam	184
Arnel, Elizabeth	Scr	317
ARNSDORPH, Christian	Eff	105
________ , George	Eff	112
________ , Godlieb	Eff	113
________ , Israel	Eff	114
________ , John	Eff	107
________ , Jonathan	Eff	113
________ , Solomon	Eff	114
ARRANT, Allen	Up	109
_____ , Cornelius	Lin	67
_____ , Nimrod	Lin	62
_____ , Peter	Up	110
_____ , William	Up	116
ARRINGTON/ARINGTON		
Arrington, Agnes	Har	183
________ , Charles	Car	227
________ , Ely	Mwr	163
________ , Ezekiel	Jef	416
________ , Henry	Jef	411
________ , Henry	Jef	417
________ , Isom	Cpb	206
________ , James	Jef	417
________ , John	Jef	415
________ , Martha	Twg	85
________ , Peter	Up	112
________ , Rex	Twg	62
________ , Samuel	Mor	267
________ , Sherrod	Jef	411
________ , Silas	Jef	415
________ , Syrus	Har	183
________ , William	Jef	417
________ , William	Mor	267
Arington, William	Jsp	397

Name	County	Page
ARROWOOD, Polly	Frk	218
ARTHUR/ARTHER/ATHOR/ARTER		
Arthur, Caleb	Clk	308
______, Gideon	Pul	157
______, Lewis	Hal	132
______, Luois	Clk	307
______, Martha	Rch	253
______, Richard F.	Hal	101
Arther, Felix	Hab	66
______, Mathew	Hab	53
______, Thomas	Ogl	103
______, William	Hab	53
Athor, Barnabos	Hab	65
Arthor, Burdith	Ogl	102
Arter, John	Ogl	102
Arthy, Francis W.	Wal	170
ARWOOD, Jesse	Pik	130
ASBELL/ASBEL		
Asbell, E.	App	12
______, Elisha	Twg	76
Asbel, John	Twg	64
ASH, Alexander F.	Frk	229
___, Geo. A.	Cht	249
___, Susan	Cht	267
___, Thomas	Hab	10
___, William	Frk	220
___, Ash	Frk	239
ASHBURN, Allen	Ran	250
_______, Miles	Up	114
ASBURY/ASBERRY/ASBERY/ ASHBERRY/ASHBY/ASBY		
Asbury, John	Mon	173
______, Richard Sr.	Tfo	357
______, Thomas P.	Tfo	358
Asberry, Jesse	Gre	284
Asbery, Henry	Gre	295
Ashberry, Jonathan	Mar	142
Ashby, George	Ear	99
_____, William	Tlf	4
Asby, David	Jns	467
____, James	Bib	69
ASHFIELD, Jane	Put	177
________, Johnson	Up	107
________, Mrs.	Rch	277
ASHLEY/ASHLY/ASLEY		
Ashley, Allen	Lau	11
______, Cornelius R.	Tlf	11
______, Edward	Elb	120
______, James	Put	185
______, John	Elb	129
______, John	Han	145
______, John	Tlf	7
______, Jno.	Wks	344
Ashley, Laudaick	Cam	187
______, Nathaniel	Tlf	11
______, Robert	Col	341
______, Robert H.	Tlf	5
______, Thomas	Hab	21
______, Thomas H.	Tlf	11
______, William	Cam	186
______, William	Col	359
______, William	Han	144
______, William	Mad	114
______, William	Tlf	4
Ashly, Thomas	Crf	396
Asley, Jesse	Dec	8
ASHMORE, Joel	Hry	226
_______, John	Hry	239
_______, John	Lib	42
_______, John L.	Hry	226
_______, Joseph	Lib	42
_______, Penton	Mus	282
_______, Peter	Lin	62
_______, William	Hry	211
ASHTON/ASTON		
Ashton, John	Gre	284
______, Nathaniel	Frk	248
______, William L.	Gre	297
Aston, Robert	Gre	299
ASHURST, Josiah	Put	172
_______, Martha	Put	204
ASHWORTH, Elisha	Elb	159
________, Jeremiah	Frk	231
________, Joah	Hal	134
________, Job	Frk	247
________, John	Elb	126
________, Martha	Frk	257
________, Noah	Elb	125
ASKEW/ASKA/ASKU		
Askew, Ann	Cht	248
______, Benj.	Bal	37
______, Betsey	Han	145
______, Elisha	Hab	43
______, Elizabeth	Han	145
______, Frederick	Lau	7
______, Irwin	Jsp	387
______, James	New	54
______, Jas.	Ran	246
______, James D.	Har	177
______, John	Jsp	362
______, Josiah	Hab	43
______, Josiah	Hry	214
______, Julius A.	Gre	288
______, Perry	Car	217
______, Thomas	Cht	240
______, Uriah	Pik	124

Name	County	Page
Askew, William	Cow	386
______, William	Han	172
______, William	Jsp	388
______, William	Mon	182
Aska, Jeremiah	Frk	241
Asku, William	Cow	386
ASKILL, William H.	Mon	180
ASLIN, David	Mon	184
ASPINWALL, Elijah	Bul	101
ASPLEY, Elizabeth	Jns	447
ATCHINSON/ATCHISON		
Atchinson, Chs.	Bal	31
________ , John	Wrn	200
________ , William	Cow	380
Atchison, Benjamin H.	Wil	313
________, James A.	Jsp	381
________, Jno. P.	Gwn	332
ATERS, Peter	Pik	107
ATHEN/ATHON		
Athen, Barnabos	Hab	65
Athon, Nathan[l].	Tlb	326
ATHY, George W.	Gwn	361
ATKINS, Abram	Jks	334
______ , C. J.	Har	177
______ , Hannah	Tlb	346
______ , Hiram	Dec	17
______ , Ica	Pul	150
______ , Jeremiah	Pik	116
______ , John	Wsh	258
______ , John C.	Mon	182
______ , Joseph	Hry	199
______ , Joseph	Wsh	271
______ , Nancy	Jns	471
______ , Robert	Tlb	345
______ , Spencer J.	Har	177
ATKINSON/ADKINSON/ATKISON/ ATKERSON/AKINSON		
Atkinson, Alexr.	Cam	191
_________, Archibald	Mor	242
_________, Armstace	Tfo	364
_________, Burrell	Cam	190
_________, Cornelius	Bts	174
_________, Dan[l].	Cam	191
_________, Dixon	Rch	282
_________, Edmond	Cam	192
_________, Henry	Tms	20
_________, John	Bke	130
_________, Katharine	Pul	152
_________, Lemuel	Pik	121
_________, Lossbye	Wks	353
_________, Robert	Cow	375
_________, Robert	Pul	150
_________, Samantha	Pul	146
Atkinson, Samuel W.	Mad	110
_________, Sarah	Bke	131
_________, Shedrick	Tms	19
_________, Thomas P.	Bts	164
_________, Volentine	Ogl	69
_________, Washington G.	Bts	168
_________, William	Cow	379
Adkinson, Burrel	Hal	87
_________, James	Hal	88
_________, Jno.	Gwn	345
_________, William	Gwn	330
Atkison, Littleton	Bib	49
________, Stephen	Bib	59
Atkerson, James	Gre	292
_________, James	Gre	294
_________, Lazarus	Gre	286
_________, Nathan	Gre	280
_________, R. R.	Bke	140
Akinson, Thomas	Mor	264
ATTAWAY, Candacy	Bke	117
________, Daniel	Hst	272
________, David	Bke	153
________, David Jr.	Bke	154
________, Elijah	Bke	122
________, Elisha	Wrn	231
________, Elizabeth	Frk	248
________, Harley	Bke	152
________, Isaac	Hal	86
________, Isaiah	Twg	62
________, James	Frk	236
________, James	Wrn	233
________, Jesse Sr.	Bke	153
________, Jesse Jr.	Bke	153
________, John T. C.	Frk	236
________, Joseph	Cow	373
________, Joseph	Frk	230
________, Robert	Cow	380
________, Susan	Wsh	273
________, William	Cpb	204
________, William	Frk	235
ATWATER, Edmund	Jns	444
ATWELL, James	Hal	80
_______, James	Har	188
_______, James	Rch	290
_______, P. P.	Bib	53
_______, Richard Y.	Trp	33
_______, Ridden	Rch	290
ATWOOD, Agnes	DeK	46
_______, Berry	Gwn	315
_______, Henry	McI	126
_______, James	DeK	44
_______, Jesse	Pik	130
_______, John C.	DeK	25

Name	County	Page
Atwood, Judson	Bul	98
______, Thomas	DeK	31
AUBART, Eli	Bal	28
AUBRY/AUBREY		
Aubry, Benjamin	Wal	125
Aubrey, Thomas	Trp	48
AUDOLPH, Henry	Ran	243
AULGER, Isaac	Hst	295
AULMAN/AULTMAN		
Aulman, Green	DeK	52
Aultman, James	Crf	403
AURICK, James	Up	112
AUSBORN/AUSBON		
Ausborn, Harrison	New	45
______, Jane	New	9
______, Roling	New	38
Ausbon, John	New	26
AUSLEY, Alfred	Wrn	211
______, Amey	Lin	63
______, James Jr.	Wrn	214
______, Jesse	Wrn	209
______, John	Wrn	209
______, Joseph	Wrn	211
______, Lydia	Wrn	212
______, Samuel	Pik	127
______, Thos. Jr.	Wrn	213
______, William Jr.	Wrn	213
AUSTIN/AUSTINS/AUSTON		
Austin, Allen J.	Mus	290
______, Ann	Jef	419
______, Ann	Scr	306
______, Charles	Fay	188
______, Dickerson	Car	218
______, Mrs. Elizabeth	Bry	84
______, Ethreldrid	Wal	160
______, Isaac	Wal	126
______, James	Gwn	373
______, James	Scr	311
______, James M.	New	22
______, Jno	Bal	32
______, John	Gwn	314
______, Jno	Gwn	342
______, John	Wal	153
______, John G.	Hal	76
______, John J.	Gwn	315
______, Jno. J.	Gwn	318
______, John H.	New	34
______, Joseph	Lib	42
______, Mary	Lib	42
______, Nat.	Gwn	320
______, Rachael	Hab	19
______, S.	Gwn	316
______, Thomas	DeK	47

Name	County	Page
Austin, Thomas	Gwn	342
______, Thompson	Gwn	357
______, Walter	Gwn	361
______, William	Car	218
______, William	DeK	61
______, William	Gwn	359
______, William	Mus	286
______, William	Wal	161
Austins, Daniel	Wrn	223
Auston, William	Wal	160
AUTRY, John	Wal	145
______, William	Wal	143
AUVICE, Susan	Cht	245
AUSBORN: see Osborn		
AUZIE, Joseph	Cht	263
AVENT/AVANT/AVONT		
Avent, Benjamin	Tlb	337
______, J. B.	Wsh	247
______, John	Tlb	324
______, R. D.	Wsh	249
______, William	Tlb	338
Avant, L. S.	Wsh	262
______, Thomas	Lin	75
Avont, Thomas	Lin	75
AVERETT/AVERITT/AVARETT		
Averett, Albert	Mus	292
______, David	Put	199
______, James	Twg	71
______, Jesse	Rch	289
______, Jo	Gwn	342
______, John	Twg	74
______, Silas	Bal	31
______, Sol	Gwn	341
Averitt, Alexander	Rch	283
______, Mathew	Ran	241
______, William	Ran	248
Avarett, Wyley	Jns	440
**Averill, T.	Rch	269
AVERY/AVEREA/AVERA/AVARY/ AVORY/AVREA/AVREY/AVRY		
Avery, Alexander	Hst	295
______, Alexander	Jsp	382
______, Ann	Clk	322
______, Archer	Col	339
______, Benjamin B.	DeK	52
______, Daniel	Wks	331
______, Daniel	Wks	355
______, David	Crf	402
______, Jacob	Hal	81
______, James	Bal	30
______, James	Crf	402
______, James	Frk	242
______, James C.	Jsp	352

Name	County	Page
Avery, Jesse	Hal	115
______, John	Tlb	335
______, Moon	Wks	350
______, Robert	Hal	115
______, Samuel	New	47
______, Mrs. Sarah	Wsh	244
______, Thomas	Rch	288
______, William	Col	340
______, William	Crf	402
Averea, Ingram	Put	187
_______, John	Put	187
_______, John Jr.	Put	189
_______, Needham	Put	187
_______, William	Put	188
Avera, Bradley	Put	187
______, Samuel	Wsh	265
Avary, Jane	Wrn	222
______, Jane	Wrn	226
______, Thomas	Wrn	206
______, William	Wrn	226
Avory, Absalom	Hal	81
______, Jesse	Hal	115
______, Robert	Hal	115
Avrea, William H.	Fay	189
Avrey, George	Hab	41
Avry, Polley	Wal	170
AVIN, Joseph B.	Up	112
AWALL, William	Hry	231
AWBRY/AWBREY		
Awbry, William	Trp	49
Awbrey, Thomas	Trp	48
AWLSTON: see Alston		
AWTRY/AWTREY		
Awtry, Elbert	Hry	228
______, Eldridge	Hry	227
______, George R.	Mor	261
______, Greenberry	Hry	228
______, Isaac	Hry	220
______, John	Hry	227
______, William	Trp	49
Awtrey, Absalom	Mor	263
_______, Alexander	Mor	262
_______, Isaac	Mor	263
_______, Jacob	Car	215
_______, Jacob	Mor	261
AXSOM, Richard L or S	Lib	42
AYCOCK, Elias	Lau	7
_______, Milton E.	Wil	302
_______, Presley	Wil	291
_______, Richard D.	Elb	138
_______, Richard M.	Ogl	104
AYERS/AYRES/ARYERS/ARES		
Ayers, Baker	Frk	216
Ayers, Baker	Frk	254
______, Daniel	Frk	245
______, Dudley	Frk	231
______, Godwell	Hal	128
______, Jedediah	Frk	245
______, Larkin C.	Frk	243
______, Nancy	Col	362
______, Nathaniel	Hab	12
______, Obadiah	Frk	229
______, Thomas	Col	338
______, Thomas	Lin	72
______, William	Frk	215
______, Zacharia	Scr	300
Ayres, A.	Bal	34
______, Abram	Mon	219
______, Dread	Hst	274
______, Frances	Jks	346
______, Ishmael	Pul	160
______, John	Car	216
______, John	Col	358
______, John	Pul	160
______, John B.	DeK	60
______, Martin	Gwn	355
______, Moses	Frk	215
______, Orvill	Hal	114
______, Thomas	Col	338
______, William	Ran	242
Aryers, Godwell	Hal	128
Ares, Jese	Hab	56
BABB, Joel	DeK	29
_____, John	DeK	29
_____, William Sr.	DeK	29
_____, William	Bal	29
BABER, Ambrose	Bib	53
______, Johnston	Tlb	342
______, Thomas	New	18
______, Washington	Mor	256
BACHELOR/BATCHELOR/BACHLOTT/ BATCHALDER/BACHELDER/ BACHELLOR/BASHLER		
Bachelor, Berry	Put	179
_________, Corda	Put	182
_________, Cor.	Wks	347
_________, Eliza	Put	186
_________, Jesse	Put	181
Batchelor, Alex[r].	Jks	337
__________, John	Jks	331
__________, Sarah	Wal	145
__________, William	Wal	128
Bachlott, Alexr.	Cam	182
_________, John Sr.	Cam	182
_________, John Jr.	Cam	183

Name	County	Page
Batchalder, Bennet	Dec	4
Bachelder, Josiah W.	Har	175
Bachellor, Archibald	Jns	438
Bashler, Charles	Bry	85
BACKLEY, Mary	Eff	113
BACKUS, Thomas	Mor	264
______, William	Cow	380
BACON, Charles	Jks	312
** ______, E.	Rch	271
______, Egene	Lib	42
______, Eliza	Tat	379
______, Francis	Crf	395
______, Henry	Cam	183
______, Henry W.	Lib	44
______, John	Lib	42
______, Jonathan	Lib	43
______, Joseph, dec'd Est	Lib	43
______, Joseph	New	36
** ______, Mrs.	Rch	259
______, Mary	Col	356
______, Nathaniel	Bry	86
______, Nicholas	Jks	315
______, Thomas	Lib	44
______, Thomas D.	Lau	6
______, William	Jks	333
______, William	Rch	253
______, William Sr.	Jks	346
BADELET, Mary	Cht	261
BADGER/BADGERS		
Badger, Levin	Put	198
Badgers, John B.	DeK	58
BADULY, John G.	Bke	150
BAGBY/BIGBY		
Bagby, Elizabeth	Bib	53
______, Elizabeth	New	15
______, George W.	New	17
______, James	New	42
______, James H.	Gre	282
______, John	New	33
Bigby, John	Cow	378
BAGGETT/BAGGET/BAGGOT/ BAGGOTT		
Baggett, Allen	Hry	225
________, Andrew B.	Hry	233
________, Asa	Cpb	202
________, Bennett	Wal	133
________, Elias	Col	351
________, Irwin	Fay	201
________, Larry	Hry	225
Bagget, Burton	Cpb	202
_______, Elizabeth	Wal	141
_______, Josiah	Doo	85
_______, Randal	Gwn	357

Name	County	Page
Baggot, Stephen	Cpb	195
_______, Uziah	Cpb	200
_______, William	Cpb	209
Baggott, Elias	Tms	17
________, Peter J.	Tms	17
BAGGS, Archibald	Cow	374
______, Archa. G.	McI	131
______, James	Jef	419
______, John	Bib	63
______, William	McI	131
BAGLEY, Benjamin	Ware	183
_______, Henry	Gwn	349
_______, Hy Sr.	Gwn	362
_______, James	Put	174
_______, John	Gwn	345
_______, Thomas	Put	179
_______, W. P.	Rch	254
_______, Willa	Gwn	361
_______, William	Mus	281
_______, William	Put	175
BAGWELL/BAGGWELL		
Bagwell, Hinson	Gwn	357
________, John	Elb	143
________, Larkin	Gwn	351
________, Littlebury	Frk	228
________, Rebecca	Gwn	341
Baggwell, Kindred	DeK	30
_________, William	DeK	30
BAILEY/BALEY/BAILY/BALY/ BAELY/BAYLEY		
Bailey, Absalom	Gwn	310
_______, Albern	Jks	318
_______, Anna	Hry	230
_______, Azariah	Mor	255
_______, Benjamin H.	Mor	255
_______, Bryant	Hst	293
_______, Burrel	Tms	27
_______, Charles	Elb	130
_______, Charles	Bts	161
_______, Charles C.	Trp	54
_______, David	Bke	134
_______, Edmond	Pik	132
_______, Elijah	Hry	201
_______, Elizth	Cam	186
_______, Elizabeth	Rch	272
_______, Ephraim	Wil	289
_______, Esachiah	Elb	152
_______, Francis E.	Hry	249
_______, George	Ear	99
_______, George R.	Wil	309
_______, Green	Up	106
_______, H. C.	Gwn	316
_______, Hannah	Mon	205

Name	County	Page
Bailey, Henry	Col	349
______, Henry	Elb	158
______, Henry B.	Ogl	85
______, Henry J.	Bts	161
______, Hezekiah	Rch	271
______, Horatio C.	Gwn	363
______, Isaac	Cam	186
______, Isaac	Up	117
______, Jacob	Col	336
______, James	Bts	176
______, James	Cow	387
______, James	Gwn	360
______, James	Hal	77
______, James	Jks	325
______, James	Jsp	396
______, James	Jef	402
______, James	Jef	417
______, James	Mon	182
______, John	Bib	72
______, John	Cam	186
______, John	Frk	234
______, John	Hst	279
______, John	Jks	311
______, John	Wal	140
______, John D.	Gwn	328
______, Jonathan	Frk	244
______, Jordon	Frk	245
______, Joseph	Gwn	334
______, Joseph	Gwn	367
______, Joseph	Trp	51
______, Joshua	New	18
______, Julious	New	27
______, Mary (W)	Mor	264
______, Mathew	Bak	19
______, Nathaniel	Col	361
______, Nath[l].	Gwn	334
______, Nathaniel	Gwn	367
______, Olive	New	52
______, Peter K.	Tms	24
______, Philips	Hst	279
______, Ralph	Jks	330
______, Richard	Bts	162
______, Richard P.	Jns	471
______, Robert	Rch	286
______, Russell	Wil	309
______, Samuel	Jks	320
______, Samuel A.	Trp	35
______, Samuel N.	Elb	158
______, Sarah	Jef	421
______, Stephen	Mon	221
______, Stephen	Pik	119
______, Thomas	Hal	89
______, Thomas	Hst	279
Bailey, Thomas	Jef	418
______, Tolly	Hry	250
______, Urbin C.	Bib	69
______, W. M.	Wks	355
______, Wesley S.	Elb	148
______, William	Elb	121
______, William	Elb	144
______, William Sr.	Hal	77
______, William	Jsp	367
______, William	Mon	185
______, William J.	Hal	77
______, Williamson	Mor	254
Baley, Anderson	Clk	319
______, David	Put	197
______, Jacob	Ogl	68
______, James	Twg	79
______, James W.	Trp	50
______, Moses P.	Fay	201
______, Nancy	Put	197
______, Pierce	Wrn	199
______, Peter	Twg	81
______, Robert S.	Cpb	198
______, W.	Rch	270
______, William	Clk	318
______, William	Tms	22
______, William	Ogl	65
______, William	Wal	173
Baily, Abram	Mwr	150
______, Absalom	Gwn	345
______, Dawson	Mwr	152
______, Geo. W.	DeK	30
______, Jacob	Mwr	151
______, John	Wsh	257
______, John	Wil	309
______, William	Wsh	253
______, Zachariah	DeK	55
Baly, Isham	Dec	13
______, Joel	Bts	166
Baely, Ferdinand	Gwn	377
Bayly, Henry	Lau	8
BAINS/BANES		
Bains, Westly	DeK	42
Banes, Robert	Put	194
BAIRD, Absalom J.	Frk	226
______, John	Scr	310
______, John Sr.	Frk	213
______, John P.	Frk	251
______, Nelson	Rch	270
______, Robert M.	Frk	229
______, William W.	Frk	211
BAISDEN, J. S.	Cam	189
______, Josiah	Lib	43
______, McGregor	Gly	267

BAITY, David K. Hab 44
______, Hugh DeK 53
______, Thomas Gwn 349
BAKER, Abigal Bib 49
______, Abner Trp 45
______, Absalom Frk 213
______, Amos Elb 150
______, Anderson Wal 123
______, Ann W. Wal 123
______, Archibald Mwr 167
______, Artemus Lib 43
______, Austin Wrn 200
______, Beal Hal 105
______, Benj. Gwn 320
______, Benj. Irw 302
______, Charles Hab 13
______, Charles Frk 216
______, Charles Crf 414
______, Chalote Hab 39
______, Christopher Gwn 312
______, Christopher B. Frk 211
______, Cyrus O. McI 121
______, Daniel Cht 265
______, Daniel D. DeK 65
______, Dempsey Bib 72
______, Dennis Wal 173
______, Dennis B. Wal 148
______, Edward B. McI 128
______, Edwin Wrn 198
______, Elias Hal 105
______, Elias Gwn 353
______, Elijah DeK 43
______, Elijah Lib 43
______, Francis Jns 450
______, Gab Bal 30
______, Greenberry DeK 37
______, Greene Wrn 204
______, Guilford Jns 450
______, Harley Wal 123
______, Henry Hal 92
______, Henry H. Fay 201
______, Hugh Cow 372
______, Isaac DeK 40
______, Isaac Mus 285
______, J. T. DeK 40
______, James Frk 237
______, James F. Lib 43
______, James Jr. DeK 40
______, James W. Wyn 283
______, Jeremiah Han 148
______, Jeremiah Irw 302
______, Jeremiah Jr. Irw 302
______, Jeremiah Lib 42

Baker, Jeremiah Crf 401
______, Jesse Hab 23
______, Jesse Up 99
______, Jesse L. New 9
______, Jethro DeK 43
______, Joel Hab 13
______, John Hab 106
______, John Hry 244
______, John Gwn 349
______, John Gwn 353
______, John Jns 455
______, John Trp 40
______, John Put 199
______, John G. Lib 43
______, John Jr. Wsh 252
______, John O. Lib 42
______, John Q. Lib 42
______, Johnathan Lin 61
______, Jonathan Pik 113
______, Jonathan Pik 123
______, Jonathan Sr. Wsh 254
______, Jordan Lau 9
______, Jordan New 10
______, Joseph Hal 105
______, Joseph Hry 244
______, Joseph Hst 295
______, Joseph Jsp 378
______, Joshua Hal 114
______, Joshua Gwn 344
______, Joshua Gwn 356
______, Laurense New 30
______, Mary Trp 42
______, Mary Cht 248
______, Mary Ann Up 111
______, Morrel Wks 337
______, Nancy Gwn 310
______, Nathaniel Bib 54
______, Nathaniel Cow 385
______, Nicholas Irw 302
______, Polly Gwn 330
______, Prescilla Wal 173
______, Racheal Cht 241
______, Richard F. Lib 43
______, Richard S. Lib 42
______, Ryley S. Wal 134
______, Samuel Mor 258
______, Silas Gwn 356
______, Silas S. Hab 22
______, Solomon Jns 455
______, Stephen Frk 227
______, Stephen Wrn 200
______, Tabitha Pik 109
______, Terry Car 229

Name	County	Page
Baker, Thomas	Irw	302
______, Thomas	Lib	43
______, Thos. dec'd Est.	Lib	43
______, Thomas	Gwn	343
______, Thomas	New	10
______, Thomas B.	Bry	84
______, Thomas H.	Wsh	261
______, Wiley	Gwn	368
______, William	Bts	158
______, William	Crf	393
______, William	DeK	71
______, William	Gwn	355
______, William	Hst	267
______, William	Pik	113
______, William	Tlb	329
______, William	Tfo	366
______, William C.	DeK	38
______, William S.	Lib	42
______, William S.	Lib	42
______, W. P.	Mus	288
______, Wilson	Wal	138
BALCOMB, Ichabod	Jns	459
BALDWIN/BALDIN		
Baldwin, Anderson	Mon	186
________, Augustos	Ran	244
________, Catherine	Clk	324
________, Christopher	Ran	242
________, Cyrus G.	Gre	296
________, David	Jns	434
________, Demaris C.	Clk	324
________, Dr.	Rch	255
________, Edmund	Jsp	370
________, Edward	Mad	107
________, Elisabeth	Ogl	66
________, Frederick	DeK	35
________, John	Jsp	371
________, John C.	Mon	172
________, John R.	Mor	248
________, Joseph	Han	147
________, Joseph	Hst	288
________, L.	Cht	253
________, Larkin	Wal	152
________, Nancy	Gre	283
________, Rachel	Col	358
________, Samuel	Gre	287
________, Samuel	Ogl	66
________, Thomas	Frk	229
________, W. A.	Col	358
________, William	Ran	242
Baldin, Lewis	Wal	142
BALES, Burwell	Cow	372
_____, John	Wks	352
_____, William	Wrn	217

Name	County	Page
BALEW/BALOO/BALYEW/BELUE		
Belew, Isiah	Hal	74
Baloo, Lenard	Hab	14
Balyew, Thomas	Tlb	344
Balue, James H.	Frk	253
BALL, Anson	Wks	331
_____, Eliza	Wil	289
_____, Harvey	Col	343
_____, Henry Sr.	Ear	97
_____, Henry Jr.	Ear	92
_____, James G. N.	Mon	190
_____, James H.	Cow	383
_____, Jesse	Gwn	328
_____, Jesse	Jsp	395
_____, John	Gwn	328
_____, Johnathan	Jsp	395
_____, Peter	DeK	46
_____, Sarah	Irw	304
_____, Sarah	Twg	87
_____, Stephen	Frk	224
_____, Tuscan H.	Mus	278
_____, Wade H.	Twg	84
_____, William	Bal	39
_____, William	Clk	295
_____, William B.	Hst	261
_____, Zilpha	Mor	245
BALLARD/BALLAD		
Ballard, Benjamin	Mor	253
________, Charles	Cam	189
________, Edward	Dec	3
________, Edward R.	Fay	195
________, Elias	Hst	281
________, Elijah	Gre	283
________, Elizabeth	Doo	84
________, Gardner	Ogl	62
________, James	Cow	380
________, James	Jns	450
________, James	Up	103
________, James	Wks	353
________, Jarvis	Rch	268
________, Jesse	Mor	253
________, John	DeK	54
________, John	Hry	199
________, Lewis	Frk	258
________, Mary	Bke	121
________, Milley	Bke	119
________, Nancy	Gre	295
________, Phillip	New	49
________, Reddick	Bke	151
________, Sarah	Jns	437
________, Thomas	Gwn	365
________, Wesley	Cow	375
________, Whorton	Cow	379

Name	County	Page
Ballard, Wyly	Rab	234
Ballad, David G.	Lau	20
______, Ransom	Put	181
BALLENGER/BELLINGER/BELENGER/ BELANGER/BALENGER		
Ballenger, Eli	New	31
_________, John	Elb	134
_________, William	Elb	133
Bellinger, Margaret	Cht	245
Belenger, Peter C.	DeK	62
Belanger, William	Bke	126
Balenger, Rebecca	DeK	71
BALSAM, Elizabeth	Crf	406
BANDY/BANDRY		
Bandy, Absalom	Mor	253
_____, James	Mor	253
_____, Jesse	Cht	280
_____, Luke	McI	131
_____, Mary	McI	124
_____, Mary	Mor	253
_____, Samuel	Cht	280
_____, Thomas	Mor	272
Bandry, Augusta	Rch	253
BANISTER, Alexander	Hst	281
________, Harmon	Rab	226
________, Jarott	Cpb	199
BANKS/BANKES		
Banks, Allen	Hal	125
_____, Allen	Gwn	323
_____, Benjn.	Jsp	390
_____, Charles	New	14
_____, Chesley	Fay	190
_____, David	Lin	74
_____, Dunston	Jsp	362
_____, Drewry	Fay	205
_____, Eaton	Jsp	386
_____, Edmund	Jsp	386
_____, Eli	Jns	434
_____, Elizabeth	Ogl	86
_____, Henry	Elb	137
_____, J. C.	Jsp	386
_____, James	Ogl	86
_____, James Jr.	Elb	148
_____, James Jr.	Elb	150
_____, James J.	Mon	183
_____, John	Bul	93
_____, John	Ogl	98
_____, John	Elb	127
_____, John	Jsp	386
_____, John H.	Wal	125
_____, Joseph	Fay	187
_____, Joseph	Wal	172
_____, Joseph Sr.	Wal	129
Banks, Rachel	Gwn	366
_____, Ralph	Hab	34
_____, Richard	Elb	132
_____, Simeon	Em	173
_____, Solomon	Put	209
_____, Thomas A.	Elb	152
_____, William	Hal	120
_____, William	Fay	188
_____, William	Wal	136
Bankes, George	Ran	249
BANKSTON, Abner	Bts	165
________, Abner	Fay	185
________, Alfred	Bts	171
________, Elijah	DeK	32
________, Isaac	New	27
________, Jacob	Fay	197
________, James	Bts	169
________, James S.	Bts	165
________, John	Trp	49
________, John	Bts	177
________, John	Gwn	320
________, John Jr.	Gwn	350
________, Joseph	Cow	392
________, Lawrance	Gwn	361
________, Lawrence	Wil	314
________, Nathan	Cow	379
________, Sally	DeK	36
________, Willborn H.	Tfo	367
________, William	Tms	26
________, William	Wal	168
________, Willsby	Tfo	367
BANON/BANION		
Banon, John O.	Wks	332
Banion, John O.	Bke	142
BARBARY/BARABURY		
Barbary, Ellis	Mon	225
_______, Peter	Up	116
_______, William	Up	100
Barabury, James	Col	351
BARBEE/BARBAREE/BARBY		
Barbee, F.	Cht	243
______, Jesse	Wal	140
______, Matthew	Bts	163
Barbaree, Stansel	Hst	285
Barby, James	Wsh	247
_____, Nimrod	Crf	408
BARBER/BARBOUR/BARBAR/ BABER		
Barber, Allen	Clk	322
______, Asa	Dec	12
______, Catherine	Clk	320
______, Charles	App	12
______, Christopher	Cow	387

Name	County	Page
Barber, Cornelius	Wyn	281
______, Elisha	Car	227
______, Elizabeth	Doo	79
______, George	DeK	55
______, George W.	Bts	163
______, George W.	Col	362
______, Griffin	Clk	302
______, Holding	Bke	125
______, Isaac	Bry	86
______, Israel	Cam	188
______, James	Clk	291
______, James	Wks	335
______, John	App	12
______, John	Bul	92
______, John	Bul	93
______, John	Car	222
______, Moses	Lib	43
______, Moses	Fay	189
______, Robert	Clk	321
______, Roda	Jef	410
______, Samuel	Lib	43
______, Samuel	DeK	55
______, William	Clk	293
______, William	Hal	123
______, William Sr.	Lib	43
______, William	Lib	43
Barbour, Frederick	Hst	284
______, Sampson	Frk	238
______, Samuel Sr.	Jsp	365
______, Samuel Jr.	Jsp	365
______, Wiley	Tlb	326
______, William A.	Frk	225
Barbar, William	Scr	303
Baber, Barnabas	Gwn	352
______, George	Gwn	351
______, James	Gwn	352
BARCLAY/BARCLEY		
Barclay, A.	Cht	266
** ______, A. slaves	Cht	282
______, William	Jsp	357
Barcley, David	Twg	61
BARCO, Dan[1].	Cam	192
BARDEN/BARDIN		
Barden, A. G.	Col	343
______, Arthur	Hst	284
______, Bronson	Hst	291
______, John	Trp	42
______, William J.	Har	177
Bardin, Simon	Pul	138
BAREFIELD/BAIRFIELD		
Barefield, Cullen	Bke	134
______, Jama	Mor	251
______, James	Wrn	217
Barefield, Jesse	Bke	130
______, Jesse	Wks	344
______, John	Bke	131
______, John	Jns	459
______, John C.	Mon	224
______, Levy	Lee	26
______, Luke	Han	148
______, Richard	Jns	471
______, Sarah	Jef	414
______, Solomon	Han	147
______, Vinson	Bke	134
______, W. W.	Wks	347
______, Winney	Pik	124
Bairfield, John	Jns	436
______, Mary	Jns	440
BARFIELD, Sampson	Bib	59
______, William	Hry	205
______, Zachariah F.	Lau	9
BARFOOT, Miles	Pul	153
______, William	Pul	153
______, William	Pul	154
BARGE, Abel	Hry	220
BARGERON/BARGONER/BARGAIN/ BARGAINERN		
Bargeron, Abigail	Bke	134
______, Elijah	Bke	147
______, Elisha	Bke	134
Bargoner, Margarett	Jns	471
Bargain, Michael	Jef	402
Bargainern, William	Jef	405
BARHAM, Edward	Col	351
______, Jane	Rch	287
BARKER, Alsiph B.	Hab	42
______, Burwell	Jns	432
______, David	Trp	48
______, E. M.	Gwn	330
______, Edward	Crf	394
______, Eldridge	Trp	40
______, Elijah	Pul	138
______, Elizabeth	Wks	354
______, Ephriam	Gwn	330
______, Henry	Mwr	158
______, Hester	Put	200
______, Isham	Hal	120
______, John	Gre	279
______, John	Jks	317
______, John	Up	106
______, John	Wal	131
______, Joseph	Crf	395
______, Killingsworth	Wal	164
______, Lewis	Fay	181
______, Samuel	Lwn	81
______, Senar	Ogl	85

Name	County	Page
Barker, Susanna	Gre	279
______, William	Gre	279
______, William Sr.	Hst	265
______, William Jr.	Hst	289
______, William	Jsp	368
______, William	Wal	168
BARKLEY/BARKELEY		
Barkley, Andrew	Mon	202
_______, William	Mor	265
_______, William	Trp	48
_______, William D.	Jns	464
Barkeley, Jane	Bts	173
BARKSDALE/BARKESDALE/BARKESDEL		
Barksdale, Hor.	Bal	36
_________, Hor.	Bal	41
_________, Nicholas G.	Lin	64
_________, Samuel	Wrn	202
Barkesdale, Daniel	Han	147
__________, Jeffery	Han	145
__________, John	Han	146
__________, Mary	Put	183
__________, Stith	Lin	65
__________, William	Han	148
__________, William C.	Han	148
Barkesdel, John	Hab	23
BARKWELL, John W.	Pul	138
________, Major	Fay	207
________, Stephen	Pik	106
BARLEY, Celia	Bke	148
______, John	Bke	148
______, William	Hry	238
BARLOW, Anderson	Lau	16
______, Archibald	Mtg	231
______, Eddy	Wks	341
______, Elias	Mtg	231
______, Elisha	Wks	342
______, Henry	Wsh	240
______, James	Lau	8
______, John	Wks	342
______, Mash.	Mtg	231
______, Richard	Lau	13
______, Thomas	Lau	4
BARNARD, Jesse	Hry	232
_______, John B.	Cht	281
_______, Lucy	Bib	49
_______, Nancy	Tat	379
_______, Timothy	Cht	281
_______, William	Bal	36
BARNES/BARNS		
Barnes, Absalom	Mor	252
______, Alford	Mor	253
______, Amos	Mon	181
______, Amy	Rch	269

Name	County	Page
Barnes, Andrew A.	Cam	190
______, Benjamin	Han	146
______, Benjn.	Jsp	380
______, Betsey	Rch	267
______, Charles	Mus	291
______, Danil D.	Hab	36
______, David	Bke	121
______, David H.	Wsh	239
______, Dempsey	Bke	121
______, Dempsey	Jef	414
______, Ellenor	DeK	51
______, Enos	Hry	246
______, George	Han	145
______, Henry	Elb	146
______, Isaac B.	Mwr	163
______, Jacob	New	11
______, (or Burns) Jacob	Wsh	242
______, James	Dec	7
______, James	Han	147
______, James A.	Frk	240
______, James B.	Wal	131
______, James P.	DeK	68
______, Jessee	Hst	286
______, Jethro	Hry	219
______, John	Col	359
______, John	Elb	132
______, John	Hab	42
______, John Sr.	Twg	73
______, John	Twg	83
______, John	Wsh	265
______, John A.	Rch	287
______, John M.	DeK	32
______, Joseph	Col	362
______, Joshua	Han	148
______, Lewis B.	Han	146
______, Mary	Col	335
______, Micajah R.	Trp	42
______, Michael	Jsp	388
______, Noah	Han	147
______, Phillip	Wal	145
______, Rosanah	New	18
______, Sarah	Scr	309
______, Sollomon	Hab	42
______, Soloman	Hst	277
______, Susan	Lib	43
______, Thomas	Han	147
______, William	Trp	38
______, William	Twg	78
______, William	Bke	121
______, William	Mon	189
______, William H.	Wil	299
Barns, Abel	Put	176
_____, Absalum	Mad	105

Barns, Benjamin Crf 402
______, Edward Put 193
______, Eleas Wks 335
______, Gideon Pik 128
______, Hiram Wks 341
______, Isaac Jks 341
______, James Jns 436
______, James Put 192
______, John Hal 115
______, Jordan Pik 127
______, Joseph Put 204
______, Nathaniel Put 188
______, Ransom Hal 115
______, Samuel Jks 317
______, Thomas Jks 337
______, William Jks 330
______, William Jns 444
______, William Put 218

BARNETT/BARNET/BARNETTE

Barnett, Calvin Rab 230
_______, Caroline Clk 312
_______, Daniel Frk 245
_______, Elizabeth Put 175
_______, Francis M. Ogl 67
_______, G. D. Jsp 362
_______, James Frk 253
_______, Jeherda Hal 115
_______, Joel Ogl 67
_______, John DeK 58
_______, John DeK 67
_______, John Gre 290
_______, John Gwn 373
_______, John Put 204
_______, John Trp 51
_______, John Wsh 263
_______, John F. Clk 312
_______, John G. Hry 200
_______, John J. Mor 267
_______, John L. Jsp 361
_______, Jonathan Gwn 373
_______, Joseph Hal 121
_______, Larkin Fay 181
_______, Martha Ogl 76
_______, Miles J. Mor 271
**_______, Mrs. (slave) Rch 254
_______, Nathan B. Bts 158
_______, Nathan C. Clk 299
_______, Nathaniel Ogl 71
_______, Samuel Jks 321
_______, Samuel Wil 288
_______, Sebon Jsp 361
_______, Solomon Frk 227
_______, Susan Wal 162

Barnett, Thomas Jks 328
_______, Uriah Hal 124
_______, William Col 358
_______, William Gre 296
_______, William Ogl 102
_______, William Ran 241
_______, William Up 112
_______, William B. Clk 323
_______, William C. Put 202
_______, William H. Ogl 76
Barnet, Clarky Wks 342
______, James Mon 203
______, James T. Cpb 201
______, John Hab 65
______, Wale Jsp 378
Barnette, David Ogl 76
________, James Ogl 76
________, William Ogl 76

**BARNEY, Doctor (slave) Rch 261
______, Job S. Rch 291
______, John W. Jsp 371

BARNHART/BERNHARD

Barnhart, Charles Gre 276
________, George Gre 302
________, John Gre 302
________, Juda Gre 301
________, Rachael Put 213
Bernhard, Jacob Hry 200

BARNWELL/BARNAWELLS

Barnwell, David Car 220
________, George Hal 118
________, John Hry 211
________, Michael Hst 281
________, Robert Hal 101
________, Robert Hry 237
________, Robert M. Gwn 355
________, William Gwn 348
________, William Hal 101
Barnawells, Henry Gre 277

BARR/BARS/BARRS

Barr, George J. Elb 137
____, Isaac Jsp 355
____, James Jks 335
____, John Bib 49
____, John Hry 214
____, John G. Dec 10
____, Robert S. Elb 139
____, Roger D. Hst 274
____, Samuel M. Jef 418
____, Sidney Hab 18
____, Thomas G. Dec 10
Bars, Arthur Twg 76
____, Dempsey Twg 77

Name	County	Page
Barrs, Gideon	Pik	128
_____, James	Twg	88
BARRARD, Allen	War	192
BARRENTINE/BARRINTINE/ BARENTINE/BARINTINE/ BARRANTINE/BARRINGTON/ BARINGTON		
Barrentine, Jess	Fay	193
__________, Samuel	Hst	283
__________, Sary	Fay	205
__________, William	Wsh	244
Barrintine, Jacob	Fay	197
__________, Jacob	Irw	298
Barentine, Elizabeth	Irw	300
Barintine, Elizabeth	Crf	402
Barrantine, Jacob	Hry	205
Barrington, Elbert	Cow	386
__________, Isaac	Jns	436
Barington, John	Put	198
BARRETT/BARETT/BARRATT/ BARROTT		
Barrett, Ann	Rch	279
_______, Elisha C.	Hal	94
_______, Elizabeth	Jks	322
_______, James	Hal	103
_______, James	Rab	232
_______, James H.	Jsp	397
_______, John	Gre	295
_______, John	Hal	71
_______, John	Wal	174
_______, Lewis	Wil	297
_______, Niman	Mor	252
_______, Reuben	Hal	94
_______, Richard	Wal	165
_______, Robert T.	Wil	297
Barett, Agnes	Cow	372
______, Robert	Cow	382
______, William F.	Gwn	345
______, William W.	Cow	367
Barret, William	Pik	119
______, William	Put	188
Barratt, Bernard	Cam	183
Barrott, E. D.	Jsp	372
BARRON, Ann	Cht	266
______, Barnabas	Wsh	264
______, Barnabas	Jks	312
______, Bevely	Rab	227
______, Edwd.	Jsp	378
______, Henry	Up	101
______, Henry	Bts	167
______, Hiram	Up	115
______, Joannah	Jns	444
______, Jomes	Wsh	269
Barron, John	Pul	143
_______, John	Bts	171
_______, John	Fay	200
_______, Jonathan	Mon	207
_______, Joseph	Bts	167
_______, Joseph	Jks	349
_______, Samuel	Up	95
_______, Samuel	Tlb	341
_______, Silas	Hry	206
_______, Smith	Bts	167
_______, Thomas	Up	107
_______, Thomas	Har	191
_______, Thomas	Mon	181
_______, William	Up	120
_______, William	Bts	167
_______, William	Wsh	264
_______, William	Jns	439
_______, William Jr.	Bke	133
_______, William Sr.	Bke	151
_______, Willis	Mon	207
BARROW, Aaron	Bke	141
_______, Clementine	Jef	403
_______, Cullin	Bul	101
_______, Green	Hst	277
_______, Isaiah	Bke	141
_______, Henry	Hst	265
_______, James	Mwr	151
_______, James	Up	110
_______, John	Bke	123
_______, John G.	Tms	18
_______, Joseph	Tlf	4
_______, Josephus	Put	206
_______, Josiah	Put	206
_______, Lucy	Mon	189
_______, Nancy	Put	207
_______, Michael	Wrn	198
_______, Richard	Fay	191
_______, Samuel	Bke	152
_______, Thomas	Hst	271
_______, Thomas C.	Jks	321
_______, Warren	Mon	226
_______, Wiley	Mon	191
_______, William	Hst	281
_______, William	Mor	241
_______, William	Pul	157
_______, William	Put	207
BARRY, D[d]. D.	Up	96
______, George L.	Tms	29
______, Nicholas	Scr	311
BARSE, John	Hst	285
BARTHELMASS, John	Cht	266
BART, John H.	Pik	127
BARTEE, A. M.	Jns	432

Name	County	Page
BARTLETT, Abner	Jsp	370
________, Allen	Put	183
________, B. B.	Col	347
________, Blake	New	12
________, Lainda	Wsh	260
________, James	Mad	109
________, John	Han	146
________, John Jr.	Han	146
________, Richard	Ear	91
BARTLEY, William	Bib	72
BARTON/BARTEN/BARTIN		
Barton, Benjamin	Rch	274
______, Campbell	Har	177
______, David	Bke	143
______, David	Hal	123
______, David	Rch	290
______, Elias	Frk	243
______, Elizabeth(W)	Mor	238
______, Henry	Hal	114
______, James	Hal	126
______, James	Rch	271
______, James	Wrn	223
______, James H.	Clk	303
______, John	Hab	38
______, John	Mor	271
______, John	Hal	117
______, Joseph	Hal	89
______, Larkin	Mwr	165
______, Lewis	Frk	231
______, Martha	Twg	60
______, Olliph	Hal	126
______, Presley	Wal	144
______, Rebeca	Hal	95
______, Stephen	Bke	139
______, Stephen	Hal	126
______, T.	Cht	265
______, Thomas B.	Clk	326
______, W. C.	Cht	256
______, William	Jks	345
______, William H.	Ran	246
______, Willis	Hal	96
Barten, John Sr.	Hal	100
______, Lewis	Hab	58
Bartin, Samuel	Gwn	349
*BARTOW, T. slaves	Cht	282
______, William	Twg	76
BARWICK, Benjamin	Wsh	245
_______, John	Wsh	246
_______, Nathan	Em	171
_______, Samuel	Wsh	241
_______, William	Wsh	248
BASKIN/BASKINS/BASKEN		
Baskin, James	Car	223
Baskin, John	Gwn	323
______, Robert	Frk	236
Baskins, James G.	Hst	265
_______, Robert	Hst	280
Basken, William	Gwn	325
BASS, Andrew	Trp	49
____, Andrew Jr.	Trp	49
____, Benjamin	Hst	290
____, Buckner	Wrn	204
____, Burwell	Mon	188
____, Christopher	Wal	140
____, Colin	New	26
____, Drewry	Twg	78
____, Eaton	Trp	53
____, Edmond S.	Han	147
____, Edward	Har	180
____, Elizabeth	Han	145
____, Elizabeth	Jsp	384
____, George	Wal	165
____, George G.	Jef	410
____, Hamlin	Put	180
____, Hartwell	Put	199
____, Henry	Wal	164
____, Henry	Rch	277
____, Ingraham	Cpb	197
____, James	Bke	124
____, James	Han	145
____, John	Bke	124
____, John	New	49
____, John	Wal	163
____, John	Har	183
____, John H.	Put	180
____, Larkin	Han	147
____, Lewis	Up	113
____, Mary	Wrn	214
____, Obediance	Wrn	208
____, Persons	Mon	195
____, Phillip	Wal	165
____, Phillip	Wal	163
____, Rebecca	Eff	116
____, Richard	DeK	34
____, Rowel	Wrn	215
____, S.	Bal	33
____, William	DeK	34
____, William	Jns	467
____, William	New	26
____, William H.	Trp	46
BASSETT/BASSET		
Bassett, John	Bib	66
_______, Richard	Bib	66
_______, Richard	Har	185
_______, Richard	Har	185
_______, Thomas	Twg	64

Name	County	Page
Basset, Ezekiel	Clk	300
______, John	Trp	37
______, Stephen	Hst	266
BASTIN, Mrs. Ann	Col	336
______, William	Col	346
BATEMAN, Benjamin	Hst	292
______, Bryant	Crf	402
______, Claiborn	Crf	402
______, Claborn	Mon	182
______, David	Mon	182
______, David	Wsh	255
______, Jason	Wsh	265
______, Jesse	Twg	69
______, John	Bib	63
______, John	Fay	202
______, Joshua B.	Up	95
______, Micajah	Hst	292
______, Simon	Hst	263
______, Thomas	Hst	275
______, William	Twg	61
BATES, Albert	DeK	68
______, Anderson	Wil	313
______, Asa	Mus	280
______, Elias E.	Hal	71
______, Fleming	Lwn	88
______, George	Hal	69
______, Horace J.	New	13
______, James	Jks	315
______, James A.	Jks	317
______, James M.	Lwn	88
______, Jesse	Hab	30
______, John	Bke	148
______, John	Cpb	210
______, John	Fay	205
______, John	Gwn	324
______, John	Hal	125
______, John	Hry	247
______, John H.	Wil	315
______, John W.	Hal	102
______, Julius	Hal	102
______, Julius R.	Hal	102
______, Mary	Hab	7
______, Mathias	Gwn	325
______, Mathias	Hal	122
______, Matthew	Cpb	210
______, Nancy	Lin	62
______, Nancy	Wal	163
______, Robert	Gre	276
______, Selathiel	Hab	12
______, Selathel	Hab	58
______, Thomas G.	Bib	49
______, William	Gre	275
______, William	Wsh	248
Bates, William	Wks	354
______, William C.	Bke	148
______, Willson	Lwn	87
BATEY/BATTY/BATY		
Batey, James	Jef	414
______, John	Twg	73
______, Rachael	Twg	85
______, William S.	Twg	72
Batty, Joseph S.	Put	181
______, Sarah	Cht	254
Baty, David	Gwn	349
BATSON, John	Lau	18
______, Thomas	Up	113
______, Zachariah	Up	113
BATTISE/BATISE		
Battise, Polly	Cht	261
Batise, Betsey	Cht	242
BATTLE, Andrews	Pik	118
______, Cullen	Han	148
______, Elisha	Han	148
______, Hartwell	Tlb	328
______, Isaac	Up	103
______, Isaac	Tfo	363
______, Jesse	Mwr	169
______, Jesse B.	Han	147
______, John	Tfo	359
______, Joseph A.	Tfo	356
______, Joseph J.	Up	120
______, Lazarus W.	Tfo	358
______, Matilda	Han	148
______, Reuben T.	Han	148
______, Sarah	Tfo	358
______, Thomas	Mon	225
______, Thomas W.	Col	354
______, William	Tfo	358
BATTON/BITTON		
Batton, Isom M.	Tlf	3
Bitton, Edward	Dec	3
BATTS, John	Jef	407
______, Nathan	Wsh	258
______, William	Jef	410
BAUGH/BAUGHN		
Baugh, Absalom	Gre	290
______, Daniel	Jks	332
______, Darcas	Frk	219
______, John A.	Gre	285
______, John H.	New	13
______, Jonathan	Jks	328
______, Martin	Jks	330
______, Moses	Lin	74
______, Peter	Gre	303
______, Peter	Put	176
______, Pleasant	Gre	290

Baugh, Richard Han 146
______, Sarah Jks 345
______, William Frk 218
______, William Put 176
Baughn, Edmond Mwr 169
______, John Ogl 96
BAXLEY, Aaron Jsp 360
______, Caleb Jef 418
______, John Hry 239
______, Joshua Jef 418
______, William Lib 43
BAXTER, Charles Bke 118
______, Eli H. Han 146
______, James DeK 29
______, James Hry 239
______, Mad 104
______, James M. Mwr 150
______, James W. Gwn 349
______, John Car 223
______, John Cow 389
______, Joshua Hry 230
______, Nathaniel Mad 109
______, Ruben DeK 29
______, Stephen Tat 379
______, Terza DeK 29
______, Thomas W. Bal 39
______, William Mad 99
BAYARD, N. J. Cht 261
BAYBY, Henry Lau 8
BAYLIS/BAYLESS
Baylis, John T. Rch 287
______, Thomas J. Col 361
Bayless, William H. Col 342
BAYNES/BAYNE/BAYNS/BAYS
Baynes, James V. Jsp 382
______, William Wrn 232
Bayne, Charles Mon 194
______, John Jns 446
______, John Jr. Jsp 392
______, John H. Jsp 384
______, William Mon 225
Bayns, Jonathan W. Ogl 86
Bays, John R. Trp 38
BAZDEN, Thomas Tlb 336
BAZE, Joseph Cpb 210
BAZEMORE/BASEMORE/BASMORE/
BAYMORE
Bazemore, N. T. Tat 373
________, Reddick Jns 467
________, Thomas Jns 467
________, Thomas Tlb 339
Basemore, B. H. Crf 404
________, Humphry Scr 310

Basemore, Starke Scr 309
Basmore, James Hal 74
Baymore, Watkins Jks 321
BEACH, Jonathan Doo 86
______, Thomas G. Up 109
BEACHAM, Henry Doo 79
_______, William Mwr 153
BEACHAMP/BEAUCHAMP
Beachamp, Labon Crf 407
________, Levi Hry 231
Beauchamp, Daniel Bts 160
_________, John Bts 167
_________, John DeK 68
_________, Nathan DeK 40
_________, Nathaniel DeK 40
_________, Sabard DeK 73
_________, William DeK 40
BEALL/BEAL/BEALE
Beall, A. R. Col 344
______, Alpha Wks 334
______, Charles C. Wks 333
______, Charlie F. Col 337
______, Daniel Har 182
______, Egbert B. Wal 123
______, Eleas Mon 195
______, Elias Tlb 329
______, Eliza Wrn 229
______, Erastus Wrn 228
______, Frederick Frk 210
______, Frederick Wks 331
______, George New 17
______, Hannah (W) Mor 246
______, Henry Tlb 348
______, Hez. Col 336
______, Hillarey Jsp 387
______, Horatio Frk 252
______, Isaac Jns 441
______, James Hry 217
______, Joel Mon 186
______, John W. Jsp 385
______, Mrs. L. Col 338
______, Nathan H. Put 190
______, Marquis D. F. Ogl 88
______, Mrs. Rch 253
** ______, Mrs. (slaves) Rch 253
______, Nathan Wrn 204
______, Nathaniel Bke 144
______, Noble P. Frk 231
______, Nyal Lin 60
______, Phereby Wks 331
______, Robert Car 229
______, Robert A. Twg 60
______, Robert A. Wrn 192

Name	County	Page
Beall, Samuel	Wks	334
______, Samuel	Wrn	227
______, Spencer	Twg	71
______, Thadius	Wal	126
______, Thomas	New	39
______, Thomas	Tlb	348
______, Thomas	Up	95
______, William	Frk	231
______, William	Frk	251
______, William	New	16
______, William A.	Rch	287
______, William H.	Lau	23
______, William P.	Rch	284
______, Zephariah	Mon	187
Beal, Alice	Mor	267
_____, Ann	Rch	288
_____, James	Rch	291
_____, Nathaniel	Rch	289
_____, Reason D.	Doo	84
_____, Richard H.	Jef	410
_____, William	Mor	248
Beale, W. B.	Col	343
BEAMAN/BEAMON/BEEMAN/BEMAN		
Beaman, Robert	Crf	412
Beamon, Nathan	Mar	142
Beeman, Lancing	Gre	278
Beman, Carlile P.	Han	147
BEAN, Alexander	Wal	155
_____, John	Jsp	387
_____, John	Jsp	392
_____, John	Wal	160
_____, Johnson	Hry	210
_____, Viney	Gwn	375
_____, Walter	Bts	162
_____, Wiley J.	Bts	162
BEARD/BIERD		
Beard, Alexander	Mor	262
______, Archibald	Wal	143
______, Benjamin W.	Mor	240
______, Chs.	Cam	183
______, Edmond	Mor	262
______, Edmond C.	Ran	243
______, James	Hst	292
______, James	Wal	150
______, John	Mad	113
______, Jonathan	Clk	325
______, Joseph	Jns	459
______, Moses	Clk	327
______, Robert	Hry	238
______, Robert B.	Hry	238
______, Samuel F.	Mad	110
______, Thomas	Bib	53
______, Thomas	Mad	106
Beard, William	Ran	245
______, William	Wal	158
Bierd, James A.	Hab	46
BEARDEN/BEARDIN		
Bearden, Aaron	Clk	304
________, Ansel	Hab	42
________, Aquilla	Put	194
________, Edward	Clk	298
________, Elijah	Jks	342
________, Humphrey	Clk	298
________, Jacob	Hal	127
________, James	Jns	428
________, John	Clk	299
________, John	Clk	301
________, Richard	Clk	298
________, Soloman	Clk	298
________, William	Put	190
________, Williby	Har	184
Beardin, Rolin	Hab	42
________, Sarah	Wal	132
________, Thomas	Hab	42
________, Wilaba	Hab	41
________, William	Hab	41
BEASLEY/BEASLY/BEESLEY/BEESLY		
Beasley, Adam	Mon	217
________, Berry W.	Jns	450
________, Chapman	Mor	266
________, Charles	Gwn	357
________, David Sr.	Crf	412
________, Elijah	Em	171
________, Henry	Wal	166
________, Hiram	Mor	265
________, Isaiah	Bul	101
________, Jacob	Wal	141
________, James	Clk	300
________, James	Mwr	157
________, James	Tlb	327
________, James Jr.	Clk	301
________, Jarrel	Jsp	363
________, John	Clk	299
________, John	DeK	29
________, John	Hab	54
________, John	Ogl	88
________, John H.	Mad	110
________, John J.	Jns	464
________, Lucretia	Mor	266
________, Morris	Wal	142
________, Nancy	Ogl	91
________, Nancy	Ogl	92
________, Richard	Clk	299
________, Richard	Wal	155
________, Robert	Jns	464

Name	County	Page
Beasley, Robert	Wal	137
________, Robert C.	Jsp	352
________, Royland	Wil	288
________, Sarah	Cam	191
________, Stephen	Jsp	353
________, Thomas	Bul	92
________, William	Bul	96
________, William	Em	170
________, William	Em	171
________, William K.	DeK	29
Beasly, Abraham	Jef	418
_______, David Jr.	Crf	393
_______, James	Em	170
_______, John	Jef	415
_______, John	Ware	188
_______, William	Gwn	353
Beesley, James	Lwn	82
_______, Mary	Bry	85
Beesly, Elijah	Lwn	81
______, John T.	Gwn	331
BEATY/BEATTY/BEATIE/BAYTY		
Beaty, Francis	Jks	326
______, James	Mad	98
______, James	Put	213
______, James	Wal	157
______, John	Jsp	397
______, Robert	Hst	262
Beatty, Thomas	Tlb	331
Beatie, John	Tms	26
Bayty, George	Hab	25
BEAUFITELL, J. P.	Cht	253
BEAULARD, John A.	Cht	253
BEAVERS/BEVERS/BEAVER/ BEEVER/BEAVIS		
Beavers, John F.	Cpb	199
________, Polly	DeK	68
________, Robert	Cpb	203
________, Silas	Mor	260
Bevers, James M.	Clk	311
_______, Thomson	Hab	25
_______, William	Clk	318
Beaver, R. M.	Crf	399
Beever, Thomas	Gwn	365
Beavis, John	Hry	221
BECK, Absolem	Pik	122
_____, Andrew	Hry	203
_____, Gedion	Hab	32
_____, Isaiah Sr.	Car	226
_____, Isaiah Jr.	Car	226
_____, Jacob	Trp	50
_____, James	Rab	232
_____, Jeffrey	Fay	192
_____, Jeffrey	Frk	242
Beck, Jesse	Fay	192
_____, John	Elb	157
_____, John	Hst	271
_____, John D.	Mon	205
_____, John G.	Gly	268
_____, Samuel	Mus	286
_____, Samuel	Rab	228
_____, Solomon	Rab	230
_____, William	Hry	201
_____, William	Hry	220
_____, William A.	Elb	156
BECKHAM/BECKCOM/BECKEN/ BECKOM/BECKUN		
Beckham, Abel	Wsh	273
________, Albert G.	Pik	113
________, Daniel	Pik	113
________, John S.	Har	184
________, Laban	Pik	113
________, Osborn	Wsh	273
________, Polly	Rch	291
________, Sherwood	Mon	222
________, Simeon	Gly	267
________, Solomon	Mon	203
________, Solomon	Mon	225
________, Thomas	Wyn	283
________, William	Twg	83
________, William C.	Mon	187
Beckcom, Sherwood H.	Twg	76
Becken, William	Gre	291
Beckom, Ann	Twg	87
Beckun, John	Crf	403
BICKLEY, Samuel	Bib	59
BECKTON, Micajah	Scr	304
________, Rachel	Jef	407
BECKWORTH, Hansel	Wrn	231
__________, Izreal	Mor	254
BEDDINGFIELD/BEDINGFIELD		
Beddingfield, Gideon	Twg	63
____________, Hardy	Twg	86
____________, John	Jef	407
Bedingfield, Bryan	Wks	333
___________, Hardy	Wal	170
___________, Martha	Bke	154
BEDDINGTON, Mary	Gwn	325
BEDELL, Absylum	Har	190
_______, Charles	Tlb	329
_______, Charles E.	Tlb	337
_______, Nancy	Jns	453
_______, P. T.	Har	192
_______, Thomas J.	Har	176
BEDDISH, Drury	App	9
BEDENBOCH, Joshua	Eff	105
__________, Mary	Eff	114

Name	County	Page
BEDGOOD, John	Wsh	255
_______, Matthew	Bke	151
_______, Richard	Wsh	269
_______, Samuel	Wsh	269
BEDIFORD, William	Rch	282
BEDSILL, Godfrey	Fay	191
BEDSOLE, Amos	Wrn	230
BEE, Ann	Cht	257
___, William	Cht	252
BEECHER, Samuel T.	Mon	172
BEEDLE/BEEDLES		
Beedle, Isaac	Gre	283
______, John	Gre	299
______, Micajah	Gre	278
Beedles, Joseph	Trp	38
_______, William	Cow	381
BEEKS, Sarah	Bts	164
BEELAND, James	Jsp	381
BEERS, William P.	Bke	150
BEESON, Richard D.	Gwn	344
BEEZE, Warren	Em	168
BEGGARLY, David	Mon	227
________, Henry	Mon	173
BEGGS, Thomas	Elb	126
BELCHER/BELSHER		
Belcher, Abner	Dec	18
_______, Ann	Cht	248
_______, Daniel	Dec	3
_______, Frances	Wil	300
_______, Francis	Mon	189
_______, John	Har	187
_______, John	Jef	402
_______, John	Trp	41
_______, Littleton	Mon	174
_______, Matthew Sr.	New	32
_______, Mathew	New	31
_______, Mathew	Put	189
_______, Mourning	Bke	128
_______, Obediah	Jsp	393
_______, Phillip	Jef	411
_______, Robert	Twg	65
_______, Sarah	Scr	304
_______, William	Jsp	388
Belsher, C.	Col	345
_______, John	Pik	127
BELDAM, Elizabeth	Scr	317
BELDING, Nelson S.	Han	146
BELK, James	Tfo	357
____, Thomas	New	24
____, William	Tfo	361
BELKNAP, M. P.	DeK	71
BELL, A. H.	Jsp	371
____, Abner W.	Hal	68

Name	County	Page
Bell, Adam	Frk	221
____, Archibald	Bke	133
____, Asa	Tms	20
____, Bailey	Jns	434
____, Bailey	Wil	309
____, Bartholemew	Wil	309
____, Bartholemew Jr.	Wil	309
____, Bartlet	Wks	342
____, Basil	Hst	291
____, Bradley	Cpb	205
____, David	Cht	253
____, David	Elb	149
____, Delany	Bke	132
____, Dempsey	Bke	132
____, Duncan	Dec	18
____, Elias	Bke	132
____, Elizabeth	Elb	157
____, Elizabeth	Mad	108
____, Frederick	Bke	132
____, George	Cpb	195
____, Green	Bke	151
____, Henry	Bke	151
____, Henry	Cam	190
____, Hiram	Bke	133
____, Hiram	Up	97
____, Hugh	Hry	218
____, Ira	Jks	329
____, James	Cow	371
____, James	DeK	65
____, James	Elb	137
____, James	Frk	220
____, James	Hal	69
____, James	Mad	98
____, James	Mon	187
____, James	Rch	285
____, James	Tlb	333
____, James	Wal	130
____, James Jr.	Elb	151
____, James	Bke	151
____, Jarrett	Clk	303
____, Jeremiah	Dec.	17
____, Jesse	Jns	459
____, Jesse	Ogl	101
____, John	Frk	219
____, John	Gwn	356
____, John	Hal	131
____, John	Lib	43
____, John	Mad	109
____, John	Mad	112
____, John	Ogl	72
____, John	Ogl	87
____, John	Put	212
____, John	Wil	297

Name	County	Page
Bell, John B.	Mad	112
_____, John C.	McI	121
_____, John N.	Gwn	371
_____, Jonathan	Clb	139
_____, Jordan	Bke	131
_____, Joseph	Hab	15
_____, Joseph	Elb	150
_____, Joseph	Mtg	234
_____, Joseph J.	Tat	376
_____, Joshua	Tfo	357
_____, Lloyd	Wil	321
_____, Montgomery	Hab	51
_____, Margret	Dec	9
_____, Mary	Elb	149
_____, Mary	Wil	322
_____, Mathew	Ogl	80
_____, Nancy	Elb	152
_____, Nathaniel	Gly	265
_____, Noble	Gly	265
_____, Pheba	Frk	247
_____, Pierce	Frk	232
_____, Polly	Jns	459
_____, Riddick	Ran	247
_____, Robert	Cow	388
_____, Russel	Trp	35
_____, Sampson	Ran	247
_____, Samuel	Ogl	72
_____, Silas	Hab	16
_____, Silas	Hab	17
_____, Simeon	Bke	133
_____, Sylvanius	Cow	374
_____, Tandy	Wsh	260
_____, Thomas	Clk	307
_____, Thomas	Elb	150
_____, Thomas	Gwn	335
_____, Thomas	Hab	16
_____, Thomas	Hab	15
_____, Thomas	Hab	52
_____, Thomas	Jns	459
_____, Thomas	Rch	273
_____, Thomas C.	Col	343
_____, Thomas Sr.	Elb	151
_____, Tolbert	Wks	243
_____, Wallace	Col	353
_____, Waller	Dec	8
_____, William	Bul	103
_____, William		
_____, William	Ear	96
_____, William	Frk	233
_____, William	Gre	289
_____, William	Hst	291
_____, William	Jks	329
_____, William	Mad	109

Name	County	Page
Bell, William	Mon	174
_____, William	Up	114
_____, William	Wal	130
_____, William A.	Mus	292
_____, William B. Jr.	Clk	318
_____, William M.	Hal	69
_____, William S.	McI	128
BELLAH, John	Mor	253
_____, Samuel	Bts	170
BELLAMY/BELOMY/BELONY/BELEMY		
Bellamy, Alexander	Mon	216
_____, John	Put	215
_____, John F.	Mon	220
_____, Lucy	Frk	229
_____, Richard	Frk	231
_____, William	Frk	228
_____, William	Mon	213
Belomy, John	Fay	197
Belony, John	Cht	256
Belemy, Joney	Put	215
_____, Martha	Put	215
BELLAS/BELLES		
Bellas, Nathan	Cow	371
Belles, Elijah	Cpb	197
BELLER, James	New	21
_____, Morgan	New	38
BELLFLOWER/BELFLOWER/BELFLOUR		
Bellflower, John	Doo	86
_____, Robert	Lau	16
Belflower, William	Wks	355
Belflour, Homer Milton	Pul	140
BELLINGS, Sarah	Col	360
BELOME, Nicholas	Hab	24
BELOTE, Alford	Lwn	82
_____, Edmond	Hab	38
_____, Thomas	Doo	80
BELWICH, William	Cht	271
BENCE, William	New	49
BEND, Micajah	Col	344
BENDER, Parker	Lau	16
_____, Thomas W.	Jsp	361
BENEDICT, A.	Cam	184
_____, R.	Cht	269
BENEFIELD/BENNIFIELD		
Benefield, Andrew	Lau	15
_____, Hardy	Wal	138
_____, James K.	New	38
Bennifield, Neadom	New	8
BENFORD, Henry	Jsp	394
_____, John	Mon	212
_____, John K.	Jsp	393
BENNETT/BENNET/BENNIT/BENNT		

Name	County	Page
Bennett, A.	Cht	255
______, A. S.	Bib	58
______, Alexander	Tfo	364
______, Barnabas	Bul	95
______, Cooper	Trp	37
______, Daniel	Hal	128
______, Dotson	Wal	149
______, Edmund	Tlb	343
______, Elijah	Hal	83
______, Eliza Mrs.	Bry	85
______, Elizabeth	Jns	464
______, George	Trp	32
______, Green	Hal	84
______, Henry	App	7
______, Henry Sr.	Hal	84
______, Hiram	Frk	225
______, Israel	Hal	71
______, James	Frk	241
______, James R.	Bib	49
______, Jane	Gre	299
______, Jeremiah	Tlb	325
______, Joel	Hal	84
______, Joel J.	Hal	84
______, John	App	7
______, John	Gwn	358
______, John	Jns	464
______, John	Lwn	85
______, John	Lwn	88
______, John	Tlb	344
______, Joseph	Crf	394
______, M.	Mus	282
______, Mark	Hal	84
______, Matthew, Estate	Lib	44
______, Micajah	Fay	194
______, Peter	Wil	301
______, Polly	Hal	84
______, Randall	Hst	285
______, Sarah	Lee	28
______, Tarpley W.	Hal	128
______, Thomas	Cpb	205
______, Thomas	Jks	319
______, Widow	Rch	261
______, William	App	7
______, William	Bke	120
______, William	Fay	182
______, William	Hal	85
______, William	Lee	32
______, William S.	Jns	464
______, William S.	Ware	183
______, Winston	Wal	140
______, Wyllie S.	App	7
______, Zecheriah	Bul	95
______'s (family of color)	Wrn	233

Name	County	Page
Bennet, Benjamin	Em	174
______, Eli	Up	109
______, Elisha	Dec	19
______, Emanuel	Em	173
______, Ira L.	Gwn	319
______, John	Em	174
______, John L.	Gwn	343
______, Jonal	Wks	331
______, Margaret	App	9
______, Mary	App	9
______, Mitchel	Gwn	314
______, R.	Gwn	308
______, Richard	McI	131
______, Thomas	Gwn	344
______, William	Bts	178
______, William	Gwn	350
______, William	Gwn	346
______, William	Up	111
Benitt, William	Rab	223
Bennt, William	Gwn	313
BENNYFIELD/BENNIFIELD		
Bennyfield, James	Irw	301
______, John	Irw	301
______, Judah	Rch	253
______, Thomas	Lee	31
Bennifield, C.	Col	348
______, Lewis	Jns	450
BENNING, P. M.	Col	339
______, Thomas	Col	339
______, Thomas C.	Hry	120
BENNISTER, James	Hab	39
BENNOCH, Peter	Rch	268
______, Peter	Rch	292
BENNODICT, Eli	Mad	111
BENRICK, William	Lin	69
BENSON, Eli	Pik	108
______, Enoch	Gwn	316
______, James	Wil	300
______, John	Lin	64
______, John B.	Gwn	315
______, Levi	Car	224
______, Lewis	Wsh	240
______, Penelope	Put	201
______, Reuben	Gwn	331
______, Robert	Trp	35
______, William	Bts	172
______, William Sr.	Wil	300
BENTLEY/BENTLY		
Bentley, Abi	Wil	292
______, Hiram	Elb	160
______, Isaac	New	12
______, Jack	Fay	193
______, James	Elb	153

Name	County	Page
Bentley, James	Mon	227
_______, James	Wal	140
_______, James	Wal	148
_______, James	Wal	164
_______, James	Up	106
_______, Jesse	Elb	140
_______, John	Cht	255
_______, John	Fay	195
_______, John	Fay	197
_______, John	Lin	70
_______, John T.	Hry	220
_______, Josiah	Har	185
_______, Samuel	Elb	131
_______, William	Wal	129
Bently, Benjamin	Lin	74
_______, John	Jns	450
_______, James	Frk	240
_______, James	Ogl	62
_______, Sol.	Gwn	368
BENTON, Abe	Jsp	378
_______, Eli	Wal	140
_______, David	Lib	43
_______, Francis	Jns	459
_______, James	Hst	295
_______, James	Jks	331
_______, James	Wks	336
_______, Jessee	Jsp	397
_______, John	Cow	388
_______, John	Crf	396
_______, John	Jks	343
_______, John (R.S.)	Lib	43
_______, John	Mon	222
_______, John	Wal	162
_______, Jonathan	Trp	53
_______, Joseph	Bts	174
_______, Levi	Jks	332
_______, Lewis	Tlf	2
_______, Martha	Lau	21
_______, Nelson	Col	342
_______, Powell	Crf	396
_______, Reason	Jks	332
_______, Samuel	Jsp	391
_______, Sarah	Jks	340
_______, Thomas	Jks	344
_______, Warren M.	Col	342
_______, William	Cow	374
_______, William	Wal	163
_______, Willis	Har	179
BERDELL, Robert	Clk	299
BERGMAN, C. F.	Eff	106
BERNARDY, Margt.	Cam	181
BERRIEN/BERIENS		
Berrien, Thomas M.	Bke	150

Name	County	Page
**Beriens, Jno. M. slaves	Cht	277
BERRY/BERY		
Berry, Andrew J.	Cow	367
** ______, D.	Rch	277
______, Dabney	Rch	272
______, David	Bts	164
______, David	Fay	200
______, Edmond	New	45
______, Elijah	Elb	155
______, F.	Gwn	309
______, Frances	Tfo	363
______, George W.	New	18
______, Gilson	Wrn	228
______, Henry	Fay	200
______, James	Bib	66
______, James	Cht	248
______, James	Trp	36
______, James	Gwn	358
______, James H.	Bib	58
______, Jessay	Hab	20
______, Jessee	Har	190
______, John	Clk	314
______, John	Gwn	322
______, John	Gwn	324
______, John	New	51
______, John	Twg	67
______, John B.	Eff	109
______, John J.	Han	145
______, Lewis F.	Hry	204
______, Martin	Hab	22
______, Robert	Gwn	375
______, Robert	Jns	434
______, Samuel	Bib	72
______, Samuel W.	Hry	209
______, Sarah	Bib	75
______, Sarah	Jks	338
______, Simon	Gwn	334
______, Thomas	Trp	40
______, Thomas	Wil	294
______, Thomas D.	New	25
______, W. G.	Cht	266
______, William	Cam	191
______, William	Gwn	333
______, William	Gwn	324
______, William	Har	191
Bery, Little	Hab	60
BERRYHILL/BERRIHILL		
Berryhill, James	Wsh	266
______, John	Jef	422
______, Thomas	Doo	87
______, William	Mwr	159
______, William	Pul	144
Berrihill, James	Bal	34

Name	County	Page
BERRYMAN, Charles	Mad	118
_____, John	Mad	115
BERTHETOTT, J. A.	Cht	264
_____, John	Cht	266
BERTON: see Burton		
BESHEARS, Sarah	Put	180
BESSENT, Ann	Cam	182
BESSINGER/BESINGER/		
BEASINGER/BEISSINGER		
Bessinger, Gabriel	Cht	244
_____, Thomas	Cht	249
Besinger, William	Lib	43
Bessinger, Edward	Bak	17
Beissinger, Jacob	Cht	255
BEST/BESS		
Best, Absalom	Scr	300
_____, George	Scr	307
_____, Jacob	Scr	300
_____, John	Scr	300
_____, John G.	Gly	268
_____, Thomas	New	49
_____, William	Scr	300
Bess, Mary	Wil	306
BETHELL, Thomas F.	Up	95
BETHUNE, Daniel	Gre	284
_____, John	Bal	42
_____, Malcolm	Fay	206
_____, William M.	Pik	123
BETTERTON/BETTERSON/BETTON		
Betterton, Joshua	Fay	201
_____, John	Hry	229
_____, Levi	DeK	66
_____, Nathan	Fay	192
_____, Thomas	Fay	201
_____, William	Fay	202
Betterson, Thomas	Eff	112
Betton, Joseph R.	Tms	16
BETTS/BETTIS		
Betts, Elisha	Wal	124
_____, Isaac	Wal	129
_____, Jacob	Wal	149
_____, James	Jsp	367
_____, John	Wal	149
_____, John W.	DeK	56
_____, Joseph	Jsp	385
_____, Lorie	Wal	168
_____, William	DeK	39
Bettis, Aaron	Gwn	318
BEVERAGE, James	Wil	297
BEVERLY, Abner	Up	97
_____, John	Up	97
_____, William	Ware	183
BEVILLE/BEVEL/BEVILL		
Beville, Claibourne	Scr	306
_____, Granville	Scr	308
_____, Robert	Scr	306
_____, Mrs.	Scr	310
Bevel, Thomas	Elb	153
_____, Zachariah	Put	187
Bevill, Paul	Eff	112
BEVINS/BEVIN/BEVAN/BEVANS		
Bevins, Benja.	Up	100
_____, Milley	Bal	43
_____, Polly	Wks	332
_____, Shadrack	Bal	28
_____, Stephen	Jns	471
_____, Mrs.	Bal	40
Bevin, William H.	Cow	382
Bevan, John	Lin	61
_____, Thomas	Tms	26
Bevans, W. H.	Cht	279
BIBB, John H.	Hal	84
BIBBY, Moses	DeK	73
_____, Nathaniel	Har	185
BICKERS, John	Gre	293
BICKERSTAFF, Robert	Jsp	368
BIDDEAU, J.	Cht	248
BIDDY, Masach	Hal	78
BIERS, James	Hab	63
_____, Joseph	Hab	63
BIFFLE, Goldman	Fay	193
_____, John	DeK	32
BIGGERS, John	Clk	312
_____, Joseph	Mus	290
_____, Nathan	Clk	316
_____, Robert	DeK	56
BIGGS, Freeman	Clk	297
_____, Jesse	Wsh	239
_____, John	Wrn	205
_____, Polly	Clk	315
_____, Sarah	Cht	255
_____, Thomas	New	33
_____, William J.	Mad	113
BILBO/BILBRO		
Bilbo, James	Cht	282
_____, William G.	Wal	137
Bilbro, Thomas	Gre	281
BILLINGS/BILLING		
Billings, Bardwell	Jsp	369
Billing, Samuel A.	Har	176
BILLINGSLEA/BILLINGSLY/		
BELLENGILEA		
Billingslea, Cyrus	Tfo	360
_____, Francis	Tfo	361
_____, Francis B.	Tfo	355
_____, James	Mor	247

Billingslea, Winston Tfo 363
Billingsly, Howell Trp 49
Bellengilea, Elizabeth Jns 464
BILLUPS, John Hst 290
_______, John Ogl 98
_______, Joseph Clk 320
_______, Richard R. Wal 135
_______, Robert R. Mor 265
_______, Thomas C. Ogl 68
BINE, Louis Jef 423
BING, Edward Frk 251
BINGHAM/BIGHAM
Bingham, Elijah Cow 390
_______, Hillisman Cpb 207
_______, William New 29
Bigham, James Jr. Jef 420
______, John Jef 414
______, Josh A. Bal 34
______, Samuel Jef 420
BINION/BENIEN
Binion, Joab DeK 62
______, John B. Col 357
______, Mary Han 147
______, Noel W. Col 357
______, Robert Han 146
Benien, Margrett Col 352
BINNS/BINS
Binns, Augus-in Wil 320
_____, Burwell Sr. Wil 291
_____, Burwell Jr. Wil 291
_____, Sarah Wil 324
_____, William M. Wil 290
Bins, C. H. Jsp 359
____, Zachariah Up 98
BIRCH, Gerard Mus 279
_____, Jarrat Rab 226
_____, John Rab 226
_____, John Rab 226
_____, Reuben Y. Jef 408
BIRD, Adam Har 192
____, Allen Han 148
____, Andrew Bry 88
____, Archibald Rch 290
____, Billings B. DeK 58
____, Braxton Mon 185
____, Buford Tfo 355
____, Burrel Elb 144
____, Ebenezer Wrn 203
____, Elijah DeK 31
____, Fitzgerald Mus 277
____, Francis Hab 65
____, George L. Mor 243
____, Henry C. Cpb 198
Bird, Hiram Mwr 155
____, Jacob Eff 110
____, James Dec 10
____, James Lwn 83
____, James Mad 98
____, James C. Gwn 355
____, Jeremiah Mon 204
____, Jinsey Rch 283
____, Job S. Put 187
____, Joel Em 176
____, John Frk 213
____, John Gre 273
____, John Hab 18
____, John Sr. Hal 103
____, John Hal 117
____, John Hal 123
____, John Han 146
____, John Jns 468
____, John Lee 33
____, John A. Clk 325
____, Jonas Mtg 233
____, Joseph Trp 33
____, Josiah Cht 248
____, Lee Put 189
____, Marguett Wil 294
____, Mary Wal 173
____, Parker Bul 97
____, Philip Hal 116
____, Samuel DeK 62
____, Sarah Mrs. Bry 86
____, Sarah Bul 99
____, Sarah Cht 270
____, Sarah Mad 112
____, Susan Put 186
____, Sutton Fay 181
____, Thomas Hab 45
____, Thomas Sr. Hal 73
____, Thomas Hal 119
____, Thomas New 28
____, Thomas Wal 139
____, Wiley N. Mon 179
____, William Bul 98
____, William Eff 106
____, William Ogl 91
____, William Wal 172
____, William D. Gwn 360
____, Williamson Tfo 363
____, Wilson Mad 98
____, Wilson Wrn 228
____, also see BYRD
BIRDSONG/BIRDSON
Birdsong, Edwin F. Han 146
________, Freeman Up 116

Birdsong, George W.	Ogl	65
________, Harrison	Trp	44
________, James	Up	100
________, Joseph	Up	100
________, Rebeccah	Han	148
________, Rebecca	Twg	79
________, Robert	Bib	49
Birdson, John	Ogl	96
BIRGE: see Burge		
BISHOP/BUSHOP		
Bishop, Abner	Dec	9
______, Abner	Hal	93
______, Absalom	Hab	18
______, Asa J.	Han	145
______, Benjamin	Trp	54
______, Clabourn	Cpb	211
______, Dudley	Hry	202
______, Elijah	New	29
______, Eliott	New	23
______, Elizabeth	Hry	216
______, Ephraim	Put	207
______, Ephram	Wrn	206
______, Fanny	Gre	296
______, George	Dec	16
______, Greer	Put	208
______, Henry	Fay	190
______, Ira	Mwr	163
______, J. B.	Rch	268
______, James	Tat	380
______, Jeremiah	New	27
______, John	Mus	291
______, John	Rab	233
______, John	Wal	126
______, Joseph	Cpb	209
______, Joseph	New	13
______, Littleberry	Mon	191
______, Matthew T.	Fay	195
______, Philip	Hry	202
______, Purnell	Mor	242
______, Rodah	Hal	68
______, Rubon	DeK	58
______, Samuel	Dec	9
______, Simeon	Pul	149
______, Thomas D.	Mon	182
______, Thomas R.	Pik	120
______, Wiley	Hal	103
______, William	Em	165
______, William N.	Hal	73
______, Wilson	Gre	290
______, William S.	Tlb	326
Bushop, David	New	41
______, Mathew	Mar	142
BISSELL/BESSELL		
Bissell, Leonard	Wal	123
Bessell, William	Jns	464
BIVINS, Elizabeth	Bts	175
_______, James	Bal	34
_______, Roland	Bib	63
_______, Thomas	Bal	32
_______, William	Bib	54
BLACK, Absalom	Bal	32
______, Alfred	Twg	75
______, Allen	Hab	56
______, Augustus	Jns	472
______, David	Hab	52
______, Douglass	Tms	26
______, Edward	Wil	292
______, Edward W.	Rch	272
______, Finly	Hab	57
______, Gavin	Car	224
______, George	Hab	51
______, Isaac	Cow	373
______, Isaac	Hab	48
______, James	Cpb	202
______, James	Frk	225
______, James	Gwn	373
______, Jane	Hab	51
______, Jane	Scr	299
______, Jesse	Wal	156
______, John	Gwn	370
______, John	Hab	53
______, John	Mus	286
______, John	New	13
______, John	Rab	223
______, John L.	DeK	56
______, John W.	Ogl	81
______, Mary	Clk	324
______, Mary	Scr	299
______, Mary	Tlb	326
______, Mary A.	Ogl	81
______, Matthew J.	Elb	142
______, Moses	DeK	52
______, Nathaniel	Put	178
______, Peter	Han	147
______, Polly	Gwn	373
______, Richerson	Put	213
______, Robert	Jef	408
______, Robert	Jks	344
______, Robert	New	11
______, Ryel	Han	146
______, Sampson	Hab	49
______, Samuel Sr.	Up	101
______, Samuel	Up	116
______, Thomas	Cpb	205
______, Thomas	Elb	158
______, Thomas	Hab	57

Black, Thomas New 17
_____, Thomas Put 215
_____, Thomas Up 105
_____, Thomas J. Mad 101
_____, William Hab 52
_____, William Rab 231
_____, William Scr 299
_____, William Up 112
_____, William Wrn 229

BLACKBURN/BLACKBURNE

Blackburn, D. J. Ware 189
_________, Jesse Wil 304
_________, John Lin 74
_________, John Mus 290
_________, John Wks 344
_________, John L. Pik 119
_________, Lewis Gwn 374
_________, Nancy Wil 305
_________, Nathan Wil 305
_________, Owen Jks 344
_________, William Mor 258
Blackburne, Aron Scr 307
_________, John Scr 303
_________, Stephen Scr 307
BLACKLEDGE, Joseph G. Jks 318

BLACKMAN/BLACKMON

Blackman, Amos Lib 42
________, Burrel Har 183
________, Edmund Hry 229
________, Jimpsey Scr 304
________, John Har 190
________, John Mus 290
________, Joseph Har 183
________, Jonathan Har 182
________, Nathan Har 185
________, Waitman Mon 212
________, William Har 184
________, William R. Har 178
Blackmon, John Mad 109
________, John P. Tlb 335
BLACKMORE, James Gwn 336

BLACKSHEAR/BLACSHEAR

Blackshear, Amy Tms 19
__________, David Lau 18
__________, Enoch Hst 286
__________, Isaac Twg 81
__________, James Lau 14
__________, James Tms 19
__________, John Lwn 81
__________, Joseph Lau 20
__________, Joseph Twg 63
__________, Lewis Lwn 80
__________, Thomas E. Tms 19
Blacshear, Jacob Hst 285
BLACKSTOCK, Ashly DeK 38
__________, Daniel Hal 70
__________, James Sr. DeK 38
__________, James Jr. DeK 39
__________, James Jr. DeK 48
__________, John DeK 55
__________, John Hal 104
__________, Joseph DeK 42
__________, Kindred DeK 39
__________, Richard Hal 104
__________, William Hry 213
__________, William Jks 327

BLACKSTON/BLACKSTONE

Blackston, F. Mrs. Col 337
_________, John Crf 393
_________, John B. Fay 193
_________, Richard Rab 224
_________, Zephariah Rch 282
Blackstone, James Rch 281
BLACKWELDER, Jacob Up 107
BLACKWELL, Ambors New 25
_________, Banks Elb 157
_________, David Gwn 355
_________, Dunston Elb 155
_________, Gedder Hal 109
_________, Hardy Elb 131
_________, Jesse Car 230
_________, Joseph Elb 137
_________, Josiah Hal 124
_________, Nancy Hal 72
_________, Park Elb 156
_________, Ralph Elb 152
_________, Royal Hal 127
_________, Samuel H. Jsp 393
_________, Wiley Hal 115
_________, William Frk 213
_________, William Hab 6
_________, William Hal 80
_________, William Hal 116
_________, William Mar 143
BLACKWOOD, Cornelius Tlb 323
BLAIN, George Rab 230
_____, Silas Hab 21
_____, Thomas Jsp 368

BLAINY/BLANEE

Blainy, Thomas W. DeK 73
Blanee, Joseph G. Eff 106

BLAIR/BLARE

Blair, Allen Elb 135
_____, George Hab 35
_____, George Wsh 272
_____, James Sr. Hab 38

Name	County	Page
Blair, James Jr.	Hab	35
______, James	Wal	151
______, James	Wsh	272
______, John D.	Wsh	274
______, Joseph	Jks	333
______, Levi C.	Frk	243
______, Middleton	Elb	135
______, Nancy	Wsh	274
______, Powel	Hab	35
______, Thomas	Hab	21
______, Thomas	Mon	218
______, Thomas H.	Tlf	12
______, William	Lwn	82
______, William Sr.	Mon	218
______, William Jr.	Mon	217
______, William	Wal	161
Blare, Simeon	Hab	34
BLAKE, Amy	Eff	113
______, Archibald	Tlb	325
______, Calvin	Cam	186
______, Dan[l]. plantation	Cht	279
______, E. M.	Up	114
______, John	DeK	42
______, Moses	Bib	72
______, Moses	Gwn	316
______, Sarah	Cow	373
______, Thomas	Car	216
BLAKELY/BLAKEY/BLAKLEY		
BLECKLEY		
Blakely, Churchill	Wil	316
______, David	Bal	28
______, Samuel	Clk	304
______, Thomas	Wil	316
Blakey, Fountain T.	Put	202
______, John	Jns	455
______, William	Tlb	348
Blakley, Elizabeth	Wsh	273
Bleckley, Jos.	Rab	223
BLALOCK/BLAYLOCK/BLAILOCK		
Blalock, David	Hal	100
______, Ellender	Jns	442
______, Harris	Lee	30
______, James	Up	110
______, John	Hal	91
______, John	Hal	133
______, John	Mwr	152
______, John L.	Lin	69
______, Millington	Gwn	369
______, Thomas	Mwr	162
______, William	Hal	88
______, William	Jns	443
______, Zadek	Mwr	166
Blaylock, Giles	Jks	333
Blailock, John	DeK	49
BLANCH/CLANCE		
Blanch, John	Cht	254
Blance, John C.	Mus	277
BLANCHARD, Bellington	Col	338
______, Benjamin	Mar	137
______, James	Col	338
______, Mary Mrs.	Col	338
______, Sarah	Col	338
______, Sarah	Hst	275
______, Thomas	Hst	275
______, Uriah	Col	341
______, William	McI	121
BLANCHET/BLANKETT		
Blanchet, William	Twg	84
Blankett, William	Bib	49
BLANDFORD, Clarke	Har	176
BLANKENSHIP, Daniel	Tlb	322
______, James	Pik	118
______, James	Tlb	323
______, John	Jks	330
______, Solomon	Hry	248
______, William	Frk	214
______, Woodson	Frk	225
BLAND/BLANN		
Bland, Arthur	Tlf	10
______, George	Tlb	348
______, Richard	Rch	256
______, William	Bul	102
______, William	Fay	185
Blann, Elisha	Wsh	246
______, John	Wsh	255
______, Michajah	Wsh	244
______, Simeon	Wsh	244
BLANKS, James	DeK	46
______, James	Jks	324
______, Littleberry	Jns	454
______, Nancy	Gre	292
______, Thomas	Jns	437
______, William H.	Gre	298
BLANSELL/BLANSET		
Blansell, Thomas	Bib	54
Blanset, James	Dec	18
BLANTON, Alexander	Bul	102
______, Benjamin	Ogl	103
______, David	Lwn	84
______, William	Tlb	338
BLASSINGAME/BLASSANIGAME/		
BLASSAMGAME/BLASENGIN/		
BLOSINGAME		
Blassingame, Benjamin	Trp	52
______, James	Crf	406
______, Wiatt	Crf	409

Name	County	Page
Blassanigame, James	Wal	130
Blassamgame, John	Wal	143
_____, Powell	Wal	131
Blasengim, Thomas	Car	228
Blosingame, William	Mor	262
BLEACH, Abraham	Tms	22
_____, Willis	Tms	22
BLEDSOE, Bailey	Cow	375
_____, Benjamin	Cpb	198
_____, F.	Cht	254
_____, Harvey G.	Bts	168
_____, Jane	Han	148
_____, Jane	Put	218
_____, John Sr.	Ogl	99
_____, John Jr.	Ogl	99
_____, Joseph	Gre	285
_____, Margarett (w)	Mor	272
_____, Miller	Ogl	89
_____, Morton	Bts	160
_____, Peach	Pik	123
_____, Robert	Put	219
_____, Thomas W.	New	21
_____, Tramy G.	Bts	168
BLESSIT/BLESSET/BLESORET		
Blesset, Benjamin	Bts	169
_____, Mary	Bts	171
_____, Reason	Bts	171
Blesset, Stephen	Bts	169
Blesoret, John	Dec	9
BLISS, E.	Cht	259
_____, James	Cam	184
BLITCH, Benjamin	Eff	106
_____, Spier	Eff	110
_____, Thomas	Eff	112
BLITHE/BLYTHE/BLIETH		
Blithe, Charles	Hab	55
_____, George	Hab	55
_____, Matha	Hab	50
_____, Robert	Hab	48
_____, Robert C.	Hab	48
Blythe, Jonathan	Car	221
_____, Leroy	Gre	275
Blieth, John	Hab	31
BLIZARD, Levy	Bal	40
BLOCKER, Jacob	Tat	379
_____, Joseph	Mar	141
_____, Redden	Gwn	342
_____, Timothy	Mar	142
BLOIS, James	Cht	264
_____, Peter	Cht	251
BLOME, Cesaire	Rch	273
BLOODWORTH/BLUDWORTH		
Bloodworth, Arnold E.	Ran	241

Name	County	Page
Bloodworth, Henry	Wks	354
_____, Hiram	Mon	212
_____, James	Wks	354
_____, John	Crf	404
_____, John W.	Wks	356
_____, Junious	Fay	193
_____, Slomon	Pik	132
_____, Thomas	Mus	281
_____, Timothy	Wks	335
_____, William	Wks	355
Bludworth, Thomas	Mar	144
BLOUNT/BLUNT		
Blount, Benjamin	Twg	70
_____, Brittian	Har	190
_____, Daniel	Wks	352
_____, Greene W.	Han	146
_____, Isaac	Han	146
_____, Jacob	Pul	144
_____, James	Wsh	259
_____, Joseph	Twg	74
_____, Major	Mon	198
_____, Marshall	Jns	436
_____, Mary	Put	186
_____, Moab	Han	147
_____, Peter	Put	193
_____, Richard	Jns	443
_____, Richard A.	Wsh	269
_____, Stephen M.	Bke	122
_____, Thomas	Jns	450
_____, William	Mon	208
_____, William	Twg	70
_____, William H.	Wrn	193
Blunt, Freeman	Mwr	162
_____, Isaac	Gwn	345
_____, Jane	Cht	272
_____, Luke	Gly	268
_____, N. L.	Col	339
_____, Stephen	Col	348
BLOW, John Sr.	Jns	471
_____, John Jr.	Jns	471
_____, Micajah	Jns	453
_____, Samuel	Jns	444
BLUE, Daniel	Gly	267
_____, Daniel Jr.	Cam	192
_____, James	Gly	268
BLUFORT, John	DeK	71
BOATRIGHT/BOATWRIGHT		
Boatright, Drewrey	Frk	217
_____, Eliza	Gwn	322
_____, George	Wsh	242
_____, James	Crf	415
_____, James	Wsh	242
_____, James	Wil	318

Boatright, John Wsh 247
_____, Rolly Wsh 246
_____, William Fay 182
Boatwright, Daniel Elb 130
_____, Reuben Em 165
BOBBET, Thomas Sr. Twg 76
BOBLEY, Bird App 12
BOBO, Benjamin Elb 136
_____, Burwell Elb 130
_____, Dempsy Frk 238
_____, Lewis Elb 144
_____, Sampson Jr. Frk 237
_____, Spencer Gwn 372
_____, Tilman Gwn 360
BODDIE/BODDY
Boddie, Nathan V. Trp 44
Boddy, Jane Rch 276
BODIFORD, Stephen Rch 281
BOGAN, George J. Hst 277
_____, J. W. Rch 272
_____, John Jsp 384
_____, S. Gwn 308
BOGERS/BAGGER
Bogers, Silas Put 196
Bagger, John Lee 33
BOGGS/BOGS/BOOGS
Boggs, Aaron Clk 318
_____, Archibald Rch 267
_____, James Tlb 342
_____, John M. Mwr 156
_____, Joseph Car 225
_____, Joseph Twg 73
_____, Sally Bal 30
_____, Violett Jks 343
_____, Z. L. Tat 372
Bogs, John Ogl 66
Boogs, James Wks 335
BOGGUS/BOGGUST/BOGGESS/
BAGGUS
Boggus, Elisa Ogl 98
_____, Jeremiah New 31
Boggust, Robert Gre 273
Boggess, Giles S. Car 215
_____, Jeremiah Mor 264
Baggus, Thomas Hal 97
BOHANNON/BOHANNAN/
BOHANAN/BOHAN
Bohannon, Alexander Lin 59
_____, Beverly B. Hry 209
_____, Duncan Wyn 285
_____, Henry Lau 8
_____, John Lau 14
_____, John Wyn 284
Bohannon, Joseph Lau 20
_____, Milledge Mor 258
_____, William Lau 5
Bohannan, B. Mus 279
_____, Buddy Mus 285
Bohanan, Kinchin Car 224
Bohan, Joseph Bke 146
_____, Nancy Put 218
BOHLER/BOKCHER
Bohler, William Rch 286
Bokcher, Tilison Hab 51
BOIRCLAIR/BOISCLAIR
Boirclair, Michael F. Rch 278
Boisclair, Peter F. Rch 278
BOLAN/BOLAND
Bolan, John Gwn 310
_____, Joseph Gwn 313
_____, Joshua Gwn 362
_____, Martin Gwn 362
_____, Richard Rch 272
Boland, Benjamin Crf 415
_____, David Gwn 337
_____, J. W. Gre 301
_____, William Pik 108
BOLCH, George A. Frk 242
BOLDER, Isaac Tat 380
BOLER, Absalom Lin 61
_____, Leroy Wrn 193
_____, Rhoda Lin 72
BOLING/BOLINGS/BOLIN/
BOLEN/BOLLING/BOLEY
Boling, Daniel Hry 217
_____, John Hal 98
_____, John Twg 77
_____, John W. D. Trp 48
_____, Shuble Hal 98
_____, Smith Bts 159
_____, Thomas Rab 223
_____, Waney Hab 16
_____, Wiley Hry 242
_____, William Hab 16
Bolings, Merrel Hab 16
_____, Stephen Hab 16
_____, Williby Hab 16
Bolin, Joseph Rch 292
_____, Reubin Jks 315
Bolen, Richard Doo 80
_____, William Dec 8
Bolling, Thornberry Ogl 103
Boley, James W. Trp 50
BOLTON, Archibald Hry 201
_____, Charles L. Wil 311
_____, Elizabeth Wil 308

Name	County	Page
Bolton, Harmon	Mar	137
Bolton, Isaac	Elb	149
______, James	Scr	315
______, John	Crf	413
______, John	Wil	311
______, Lanck Stone	Mar	142
______, Leonard	Ogl	69
______, Mary	Col	364
______, Mathew	Gwn	351
______, Minoah	Ogl	62
______, Reubin	Scr	305
______, Robert	Col	357
______, Samuel	Col	364
______, Solomon D.	Dec	3
______, Thomas C.	New	23
______, Thomas W.	Car	214
BOMAN/BOWMAN/BOMON		
Boman, George R.	Cow	377
______, Greenberry	Wal	168
______, Harris	Wal	169
______, Isaac	Hab	41
______, Joel	Twg	72
______, John	Cow	379
______, John	Pik	122
______, Levi	Trp	40
______, Thomas	Mor	253
______, Thomas	Wal	168
______, William	Mor	254
______, William O.	Hab	37
______, Winna	Hab	44
______, Zachariah	Elb	124
Bowman, Charles	Rch	262
______, Drury M.	Gwn	337
______, Ezekiel	Gwn	318
______, Gilbert	Gwn	338
______, Gilbert	Gwn	338
______, Peter	DeK	42
______, Ralph	Eff	115
______, Robert	Eff	111
______, Sherod	Gwn	377
______, Vincen	Gwn	377
______, Wald. H.	Gwn	318
Bomon, Harris	Wal	142
BOND/BONDS		
Bond, Ann	Cht	266
______, Ann Moriah	Lin	59
______, Benjamin	Twg	79
______, Charles W.	Frk	214
______, Chappell	Lee	27
______, Daniel	Elb	141
______, Dudley	Fay	184
______, Edward	Bry	84
______, Edward H.	McI	121

Name	County	Page
Bond, Esom	Mad	109
______, Gabuel	Mad	98
______, George T.	Frk	218
______, James	Wil	296
______, Joel	Bib	53
______, Joel	Elb	121
______, John	Hry	225
______, John M.D.	Bts	160
______, Joseph	Hal	78
______, Joseph B.	Hal	78
______, Joseph M.	Cpb	204
______, Leonard	Frk	233
______, Lewis A.	Bal	39
______, Lewis	Wks	358
______, Lindsay	Frk	236
______, Luke	Jns	437
______, Mark	Lin	58
______, Nancy	Hal	100
______, Peyton	Pik	111
______, Richard	DeK	59
______, Richard C.	Frk	214
______, Robert	Wsh	262
______, Samuel	Jns	447
______, Samuel	Lee	32
______, Samuel M.	McI	124
______, Thomas R.	Pik	116
______, William	Elb	139
______, Willis	Elb	121
______, Whitfield W.	Hab	8
Bonds, Andrew B.	Gwn	368
______, Dudly	Gwn	331
______, James	Gwn	329
______, James	Gwn	373
______, John	Hal	97
______, John Peter	Twg	66
______, Luke	Jns	453
______, Mary	Gwn	366
______, Nancy	Gwn	324
______, Nathan	Elb	143
______, Richard	Cow	380
______, Richard	DeK	60
______, Thomas	Hry	220
______, Vardy	DeK	59
______, W.	Gwn	308
BONE/BONES/BONEY		
Bone, Bailey	Mad	105
______, Elizabeth	Mad	116
______, George	Mad	105
______, James	Mad	111
______, John	Mad	104
______, Johnston	Bib	66
______, Mahala	Elb	129
______, Rachael	Bib	49

Name	County	Page
Bone, William Jr.	Mad	102
______, William Sr.	Mad	106
Bones, John	Rch	260
Boney, Cullin	Tlf	9
BONNELL, Archibald	Bke	135
______, Archibald	Bke	147
______, Mary	Scr	311
______, Tapley	Jks	319
BONNER/BONER/BONNOR		
Bonner, Alley	Up	110
______, Bedford B.	Up	102
______, Everitt	Jns	473
______, Hamilton	Han	148
______, James	Bal	29
______, Jonathan	Up	112
______, James S.	Mon	222
______, Lavicey	Hry	228
______, Lucy	Clk	309
______, Richard	Put	179
______, Smith	Fay	194
______, Thomas	Car	214
______, Thomas	Han	147
______, Thomas	Mor	259
______, Thomas M.	Put	179
______, Thomas S.	Mor	246
______, William	Hry	226
______, Uriah	Jns	471
______, William	Mon	200
______, Wyatt	Mon	191
______, Zadoc	Fay	189
______, Zadoc Jr.	Fay	194
Boner, James	Jsp	396
______, William H.	Gre	285
Bonnor, Robert H.	Jsp	357
BONUM, Isom	Cpb	197
BOOKER/BOOKOUT		
Booker, John	Tfo	361
______, Mary	Wil	316
______, Richarson	Wal	154
______, Richeson	Wil	306
______, Thomas	Lin	73
______, William	Wil	306
Bookout, Charles L.	Wal	134
BOOLEFORD, Vincent G.	Dec	15
BOON/BOOWN		
Boon, Alsey	Bal	42
______, Benjamin	Mor	238
______, Bollan	Wyn	283
______, George	Lwn	87
______, Jacob	Wks	353
______, James	Jsp	396
______, James	Wks	334
______, Jesse	Cpb	197

Name	County	Page
Boon, Jesse	Gre	283
______, Joshua	Dec	12
______, John	Tlf	11
______, Kincheon	Cow	376
______, Lewis	Han	147
______, Lydia	Mon	227
______, Ratleff	Wks	351
______, William	Cpb	197
______, William	Crf	407
______, Willis	Crf	407
Boown, Larkin	New	9
BOOTH/BOOTHE		
Booth, Benjamin H.	Clk	292
______, Edward	App	7
______, Hugh	App	6
______, Gabriel	Elb	138
______, James	App	5
______, James	Mor	250
______, John	Elb	147
______, John	Wal	134
______, John T.	Tlb	339
______, Joseph J.	Elb	123
______, Nancy	Elb	119
______, Prudence	Elb	160
______, Robert	Elb	123
______, Tapley	Tlb	338
______, Thomas	Clk	322
______, Victor E.	Elb	119
______, William	Ogl	78
______, William	Tlb	341
______, William Jr.	Tlb	341
______, William S.	Elb	141
______, Zachariah	Tlb	347
Boothe, Edward	Wrn	216
______, James	Wal	133
______, Joel	Mad	113
______, John	Lib	42
______, Robert	Gre	288
______, Theophilus D.	Pul	139
______, Zacheriah	Mar	140
BOOTY, Benjamin S.	Tlb	329
______, John L.	Mon	195
BOOZER, John	Gwn	344
______, John Jr.	Gwn	359
BORDEN, Michael A.	Jks	330
BORDERS, Isaac	Jks	312
______, John	Jks	332
______, John	Pik	112
______, John	Pik	124
______, John H.	Clk	297
______, Lewis	Pik	113
______, Stephen	Clk	327
BORELAND, John	Han	146

Name	County	Page
BOREN/BORING/BORAN/ BORAM/BOREM/BORUM		
Boren, James	Gwn	346
______, John, Esq.	Gwn	329
______, John	Wil	287
______, John D.	Wal	138
______, Joseph	Bib	49
______, Joseph	Wil	309
______, Thomas D.	Tfo	358
______, William	Mus	282
______, William E.	Bib	49
______, William E.	Bib	58
Boring, David	Jks	322
______, Isaac Jr.	Jks	322
______, Isaac Sr.	Jks	322
______, Robert	Fay	190
______, Quincy	Jks	317
Boren, Nancy	Gre	302
Boram, Sarah	Mad	104
Borem, Margeritt	Wil	295
Borum, Nathaniel	Ogl	85
BORN/BOURN		
Born, John M.	Hry	229
______, Samuel	Gwn	321
Bourn, Katharine	Tlf	4
______, William	App	11
BOSBY, Bartholomew	Lib	43
BOSTICK/BOSTWICK		
Bostick, Charles H.	New	28
______, Garland	Lin	63
______, George W.	Twg	70
______, Helony	Lin	63
______, Hillery	Jef	410
______, John Sr.	Jef	401
______, John	Jef	408
______, Joshua D.	Twg	74
______, Littlebury	Dec	5
______, Littleberry	Jef	407
______, Nancy	New	28
______, Nathan	Jef	406
______, Rebecca	Clk	324
______, Rhesa	Twg	68
______, Stephen	Jns	459
______, Tilman	Jef	424
______, William D.	Twg	70
Bostwick, Ann	Bal	45
______, Azariah	Mor	266
______, Berry	Mor	265
______, John	Gwn	356
______, Levi C.	Dec	3
______, Mary (W)	Mor	266
______, Nathaniel L.	Pul	161
______, Rhesa	Bke	120

Name	County	Page
Bostwick, Richard	Gwn	356
______, Thomas	Bke	133
** ______, William (slave)	Rch	270
BOSTON/BOSTAIN		
Boston, Jacob	Hry	223
______, James	Scr	309
Bostain, Matthew	Trp	51
BOSWELL, Charles	Wil	322
______, Henry	Jsp	381
______, John	Up	112
______, John	Wil	313
______, Johnson	Tfo	366
______, Joseph	DeK	43
______, Josiah	Mor	243
______, Levi	Put	190
______, Mrs. Mary	Col	336
______, Richard	DeK	28
______, Sarah	Tfo	366
______, Thomas	Jns	439
______, William	Frk	221
______, William	Frk	233
______, William	Tlb	327
______, Williamson	Jsp	381
BOSWORTH, James	Mus	278
______, Jane	DeK	34
______, Josiah R.	Fay	189
______, Philip	Car	218
______, Richmond	Bib	69
BOTHWELL, Ebenezer	Mon	207
______, John W.	Jef	401
______, Samuel Sr.	Jef	414
______, Samuel Jr.	Jef	414
BOTSFORD, Theophilus	Dec	12
BOTT, James	Fay	193
BOTTOM, David	Rch	264
BOTTOMS, James	Pik	107
______, John	Pik	108
______, Robert	Put	194
______, Thomas	Hal	125
BOULINEAU, George	Rch	257
______, Joseph	Rch	277
______, Oliver T.	Rch	254
BOURQUIN, B.	Cht	279
______, Ed.	Cht	280
______, Robert H.	Cht	280
BOUTEN, John	Jef	403
BOUTWELL, C.	Bal	36
______, Robert	Pul	151
BOWDEN, Dangerfield	Gre	275
______, Daniel W.	Put	209
** ______, H. (slave)	Rch	270
______, James	Mon	228
______, Jesse	Bib	59

Name	County	Page
Bowden, Jesse	Hry	218
______, John	Mon	221
______, Joshua	Mon	216
______, Lot	Gwn	314
______, Reading	Jns	455
______, Travis	Put	205
______, Turner	Mon	220
______, William	Bib	59
______, William	Mon	220
______, Willis	Put	205
______, Willis	Put	206
BOWDRE, Edward	Col	343
**______, H.	Rch	257
**______, H.	Rch	275
**______, H.	Rch	276
**______, H.	Rch	277
______, Hays	Rch	277
**______, Hays	Rch	288
______, Preston, E.	Up	95
______, Thomas	Col	362
BOWEN/BOWIN/BOIN		
Bowen, Alanson	Wal	150
______, Christopher	Car	227
______, Dickson	Hry	223
______, Drewry	Mad	98
______, Durham	Hst	263
______, Edward	Jns	446
______, Edward	Tlf	6
______, Elizth	Cam	182
______, Harman	Gwn	313
______, Harrod	Wsh	241
______, Hezekiah	Bul	92
______, Hiram	Jks	339
______, Horatio	Jns	464
______, Horatio C.	Elb	132
______, James	Wrn	213
______, Jesse	Bal	40
______, John Sr.	Doo	79
______, John	New	6
______, John F.	DeK	56
______, Levi	Bal	32
______, Mark	Bul	96
______, Matthew	Fay	204
______, Parra	Jks	339
______, Penelope	Bul	100
______, Samuel H.	Wil	313
______, Sary	Fay	199
______, Session	Doo	80
______, Sparkman	Doo	79
______, Stephen	Fay	190
______, Stephen	Hry	221
______, Stephen	Tat	375
______, Susan	Jns	464

Name	County	Page
Bowen, Thomas J.	Jks	325
______, W. P.	Cht	264
______, William	Bke	123
______, William	Elb	135
______, William	Wil	293
______, William P.	Lib	42
______, William U.	Elb	137
______, Windol	Jef	408
Bowin, Isaac	Col	345
______, James W.	Gwn	326
______, John C.	Jns	444
______, Mary	Hab	23
______, Mary	Put	204
______, Richard	Hab	28
______, Thomas	Hab	32
Boin, Andrew	Hab	47
BOWERS, B.	Bal	38
______, Benjamin	Bal	30
______, Benjamin	Hst	267
______, George	Hab	66
______, John	Frk	236
______, John	Mus	290
______, John G.	Rch	291
______, Jonathan	Gly	266
______, Samuel	Elb	153
______, Sealy	Fay	198
BOWIE, B.	Rch	256
______, James W.	Scr	317
BOWLS/BOWLES/BOLES/BOOLES/ BOLLS/BOLL/BOLOS		
Bowls, Benjamin	Gwn	350
______, Benjamin H.	Gwn	311
______, John	Bak	15
______, Nathaniel	Jks	330
______, William	Jks	320
Bowles, Benjamin B.	Tfo	366
______, Henry H.	Mon	224
______, Henry P.	Tfo	367
______, Nelson	Mwr	169
Boles, Benjamin	Clk	301
______, Henn	Crf	409
______, Sarah	Bts	169
______, Sarah	Wal	162
Booles, Allen	Gre	274
______, Bevin	Gre	288
______, Jackson	Gre	279
______, John	Gre	279
______, Thomas	Gre	278
______, Turner	Gre	272
Bolls, Richard	Frk	223
Boll, Alen	Hab	30
BOWLIN/BOWLING		
Bowlin, Edward	Clk	316

Name	County	Page
Bowlin, William D.	Clk	314
Bowling, Henry	Clk	309
______, John	Ogl	94
BOX, Ann	Cht	245
______, Jonathan	Car	222
______, Lemon	Jns	471
______, Michael	Frk	219
______, William B.	Car	230
BOYCE, Brinkley	Wal	125
______, Cyrus	Hry	208
______, George	Dec	9
______, Joseph	Jks	337
BOYD/BOYT		
Boyd, Adin	Lwn	86
______, Alston	Gwn	325
______, Andrew	DeK	48
______, Andrew	Wal	136
______, Bane J.	Lwn	86
______, Bruce	Hal	128
______, C. C.	Jsp	356
______, E. A.	Cht	257
______, Edward	Scr	304
______, Elbert	Bke	121
______, Elenor	Jef	414
______, Elias	Trp	55
______, Elijah	Rch	272
______, Elizabeth	Cht	281
______, Elizabeth	Pul	146
______, Fanny	Jsp	394
______, Fleming	Col	343
______, Henry	Lwn	86
______, Henry	Trp	40
______, Hez.	Col	352
______, Hugh	Mwr	151
______, James	Col	353
______, James	Gwn	357
______, James	Hal	128
______, James	Scr	304
______, James	Up	117
______, Jane	Wrn	226
______, Jeslice	Hst	279
______, John	Col	339
______, John	Doo	82
______, John	Hab	10
______, John	Jsp	390
______, John	Jsp	394
______, John	Jef	414
______, John	Mwr	150
______, John	Mwr	151
______, John	Pik	115
______, John	Scr	304
______, John	Wsh	242
______, John B.	Wrn	196
Boyd, Joseph	Mwr	158
______, Joseph	Trp	39
______, Mary	Gly	267
______, Mary	Pul	162
______, Nathan	Pik	115
______, Noah	Tms	23
______, Richard	Jsp	395
______, Robert	Jef	412
______, Robert	New	53
______, Robert	Tlb	335
______, Samuel	Jsp	395
______, Samuel	Jef	424
______, Sarah	Col	349
______, Seth	Scr	303
______, Spruce	New	11
______, Thomas	Pul	160
______, William	Jef	413
______, William	Mwr	152
______, William	Mus	286
______, William W.	Cow	369
Boyed, Philip	Dec	9
Boyt, Abraham Sr.	Bke	141
______, Elbert	Bke	121
______, James	Bke	140
______, John	Twg	70
______, Josiah	Lau	12
______, Stephen	Bke	122
BOYER/BOUYER/BOYET		
Boyer, Elias	Han	148
______, William	Han	147
Bouyer, Balthagen	Rch	276
Boyet, Isaac	Dec	8
BOYNTON/BOYINGTON		
Boynton, Elijah S.	Hry	250
______, James	Jns	439
______, John C.	Tlb	340
______, Stoddard	Jns	438
______, Willard	Twg	60
Boyington, A. F.	Bal	37
______, Moses	Bal	44
BOYKIN/BOYACON/BYKIN		
Boykin, Burwell	Jns	459
______, Florid	Scr	308
______, Henry	Car	225
______, James	Ran	248
______, John	Scr	308
______, Samuel	Bal	34
______, Scion	Scr	307
Boyacon, George	Irw	301
Bykin, John T.	Jsp	378
BOYLE/BOYLES		
Boyle, Charles	Hal	99
______, Enoch	DeK	43

Name	County	Page
Boyle, Hugh C.	Hab	16
______, John	Cpb	211
______, Peter	Jks	317
______, Robert	Jks	317
______, William	DeK	48
Boyles, Charles	Tlf	7
______, William	Hry	246
BOZEMAN, Amos	Hal	110
______, Eli W.	Mon	197
______, J. N.	Lee	29
______, James	Lwn	90
______, James R.	Tlb	340
______, John	Pul	160
______, Luke	Hst	272
______, Ralph	Hst	280
______, Thomas	Wks	333
______, William A.	Hst	266
BRABBIN, James	Hry	228
BRACEY, William	Bib	53
BRACK, Eleazer	Wks	338
______, James	Wks	337
______, John	Scr	302
______, William	Lau	14
______, William	Wks	337
BRACKETT/BRACKET/BRACKIT		
Brackett, John	New	23
______, Polly	Hal	73
Bracket, Betsey	Hal	105
Brackit, Benjamin	Hal	132
BRACKMAN/BRACKEN		
Brackman, John H.	DeK	62
Bracken, Andrew	Twg	85
BRADBERRY/BRADBERY/ BRADBURY		
Bradberry, Eli	Clk	294
______, James	Gwn	325
______, James	Ogl	81
______, Lewis	Clk	295
______, Robert	Hry	233
______, Spencer E.	Mad	109
______, Thomas	Cht	245
______, William	Clk	295
______, William	Mad	114
______, William	Ogl	81
______, William H.	Mad	108
Bradbery, Ambrose	Hab	58
______, James	Hab	57
Bradbury, Edmond	Jks	336
______, Joseph	Col	334
______, Joseph	Cpb	201
______, William	Pik	110
BRADEN, Harvey	Hal	108
______, Rhoda	Gwn	338
Braden, Richard	Hal	114
BRADER, Enoch	Hab	32
______, Lewis	Hab	32
BRADFORD, Abe	Jsp	353
______, Ann	Put	218
______, Arch^{d}.	Jks	327
______, Batholomew	Wal	159
______, Charles	Gwn	329
______, David	Jks	319
______, Elizabeth	Wil	320
______, Futowig	Rch	261
______, Henry	Col	348
______, James	New	17
______, James S.	Jks	316
______, Joseph	Ogl	86
______, Joshua	Gwn	361
______, Lucy	Hab	66
______, Nathaniel	Crf	398
______, Nathaniel	Wil	319
______, Randolph	Rch	289
______, Richard	Wil	316
______, Robert	Gwn	328
______, Sarah	Jef	410
______, Seabourn	Irw	303
______, Thomas	DeK	35
______, Thomas	Irw	303
______, Timothy	Wal	140
______, Timothy	Wal	160
______, William	Hal	77
______, William	Irw	303
BRADLEY/BRADLY		
Bradley, Abdou	Ogl	63
______, Abner	New	8
______, Asa	Doo	83
______, Asa	Frk	256
______, Azeriah	New	41
______, Dennis	Jns	435
______, Drury	Mor	268
______, Eli	Lib	43
______, Ellis	Put	201
______, Ira	Hst	286
______, James	Mad	113
______, James	Put	200
______, James J.	New	46
______, Jessee	Hst	286
______, John	Cht	253
______, John	Jks	349
______, John	Lib	42
______, John	New	9
______, John	Put	201
______, Joseph	New	39
______, Joshua	Pik	121
______, Josiah	Hst	286

Name	County	Page
Bradley, Josiah	Jks	323
______, Newman	Lib	42
______, Patrick	Rch	269
______, Presley	Mor	270
______, Thomas	Wal	126
______, Thomas	Wal	149
______, Willard	Bts	161
______, William	Hal	89
______, William	Jsp	379
______, William	Wks	356
______, William D.	Wil	303
Bradly, Benjamin	Hal	134
______, Bryant	Pul	146
______, Charlotte	Em	167
______, Elizabeth	Ogl	81
______, John L.	DeK	32
______, William	Cow	367
BRADSHAW, Clayton	Pul	161
______, Elijah	Gre	289
______, Elizabeth	Pul	162
______, James	Hal	90
______, John	Bke	138
______, John	Pul	161
______, Justus	Trp	50
______, Lucy	Clk	317
______, Peter	Clk	292
______, Shad.	Wrn	220
______, Woodson	Wrn	225
BRADWELL/BRADNELL		
Bradwell, James S.	McI	124
Bradnell, Joseph J.	Pul	159
BRADY/BRADDY		
Brady, Elijah	Rab	230
______, Enoch	Hab	14
______, Isaac	Mus	285
______, James	Bts	174
______, Jared J.	Ran	247
______, John	Lee	32
______, John	Ogl	75
______, Joseph G. W.	Ran	247
______, Mills L.	Crf	408
______, Molten	Em	176
______, Nathan	Doo	79
______, Nathan	Ran	247
______, Nathan	Up	102
______, Nermon	Cow	367
______, Robert	Jef	424
______, Samuel	Lee	32
______, Samuel	Lee	32
______, Samuel	Wks	338
______, William	Hst	288
Braddy, Alford	Bib	58
______, Charles	Wsh	245
Braddy, Cullen L.	Wrn	217
______, Delila	Bib	75
______, Elizabeth	Ear	91
______, James	Wrn	232
______, John	Bib	58
______, John	Mor	240
______, John	Wsh	276
______, John Sr.	Bib	75
______, Luten	Jns	447
______, Miller	Ear	91
______, Richard	Mon	224
______, Willie G.	Wrn	217
BRAGG/BRAG		
Bragg, Elijah Sr.	Bul	97
______, Enoch	Up	113
______, George	Mad	111
______, Humphrey A.	Mad	114
______, John	Scr	305
______, Joseph	Mad	111
______, Matthew	Wks	345
______, Samuel	Wks	345
______, William	Bul	99
Brag, Joseph	Ogl	78
______, Mary	Ogl	78
BRAILSFORD, Daniel H.	Gly	266
______, Daniel H.	McI	128
______, Mrs.	Gly	266
BRAING, Edmon	New	34
BRAKE, Elizabeth	Han	146
BRALEY, John	Lau	17
BRAMBLET/BRAMBLETT		
Bramblet, Elizabeth	Elb	135
______, Enoch Sr.	Hab	10
______, Enoch Jr.	Hab	10
______, Garnet	Hab	82
______, Henry	Hab	10
______, Jesse	Rab	225
______, John	Hab	55
______, John B.	Hal	130
______, John W.	Hab	42
______, Miles	Gwn	326
______, Nathan	Hal	121
______, Reuben	Rab	225
Bramblett, Henry	Frk	236
______, Henry	Gwn	328
______, James	Frk	227
______, John	Frk	225
______, Reuben	Gwn	319
______, Wiley	Frk	240
BRAMER, J. H.	Jks	314
BRANCH, Armstead	Bts	170
______, Burten	Lwn	87
______, David	Lau	11

Name	County	Page
Branch, Elias	Lau	24
______, George C.	Hab	19
______, Hester	Tat	376
______, James	Lau	24
______, James C.	Gre	282
______, John	Gre	288
______, Needham	Lib	43
______, Peter	Tms	18
______, William S.	Gre	305
BRAND, Benjamin	Gwn	326
______, Isaiah C.	Wal	137
______, Jonas	Gwn	327
______, Malikiah	Mor	258
______, Thomas	Wal	137
______, William	Wal	173
______, Zachariah	Mor	259
BRANDON, Alexander	Jsp	354
______, F. L.	Gwn	308
______, James	Jsp	355
______, James	Rch	278
______, John	Rch	282
______, Mary	Gwn	332
______, Thomas W.	Gwn	369
______, William	Gwn	309
BRANER, William	Jsp	378
BRANHAM, Alexander	Jns	472
______, Eli S.	Pik	119
______, Fanny	Wil	287
______, Ishmall	Put	188
______, Isom	Put	215
______, Harris	Frk	224
______, James	Tlb	332
______, Joel	Har	177
______, Joseph	Put	182
______, Martha	Ogl	81
______, Mary	Ear	95
______, Thomas	Ear	95
______, Wiley	Put	177
BRANNEN/BRANNAN/BRANNON/ BRANAN/BRANOM/BRENAN/ BREMAN/BRANNUM		
Brannen, Alexander	Bul	92
______, Edmund	Bul	97
______, Hugh P.	Bul	102
______, John	Bul	101
______, Solomon	Bul	96
______, William	Bul	96
______, William	Scr	313
Brannan, Calvin	New	42
______, Elizabeth	Scr	313
______, Hope	Scr	313
______, John	Hry	246
______, Leroy	Hry	245
Brannan, Thomas	Lwn	84
Brannon, James	Hab	18
______, James	Hal	111
______, James A.	Mad	109
______, William	Wal	150
Branan, Adam	Wks	348
______, Harris	Wks	348
______, James	Wks	348
______, John	New	42
______, John	Wks	358
______, Jonathan	New	42
______, Littleberry	New	7
______, Wiley	New	42
Branom, Michael	Hal	113
Brenan, Thomas	Bts	173
Breman, Joseph	Cht	262
Brannum, William C.	Wrn	230
BRANT, Starling	Hab	56
BRANTLEY/BRANTLY		
Brantley, Aaron	Wsh	241
______, Ann	Cht	277
______, Benjamin	Cht	257
______, Edward	Wsh	255
______, Edwin	Wsh	240
______, Elijah R.	Han	146
______, Frances	Han	145
______, Green	Wsh	248
______, Green D.	Jsp	370
______, Harris	Wsh	240
______, Harris	Wsh	256
______, James	Car	230
______, James	Col	344
______, James	Ear	93
______, James	Jns	437
______, James	Wsh	240
______, Jeptha	Mon	187
______, John	Cht	278
______, John	Jns	468
______, John	Wsh	240
______, John F.	Wsh	240
______, John H.	Jsp	355
______, Joseph	Jns	467
______, Joshua	Wal	154
______, Joshua	Mor	269
______, Mary	Wrn	207
______, Rebecah	Wrn	206
______, Spencer	Wsh	240
______, Thomas	Wsh	272
______, William	Cht	278
______, William	Wsh	251
______, Z.	Wsh	246
Brantly, (blank)	Bal	35
______, Aaron	Tlf	4

Brantly, Benjamin Han 147
_____, Benjamin Lau 11
_____, Benjamin Mon 187
_____, James Cht 268
_____, James Tfo 358
_____, Jeremiah Lau 9
_____, Joseph Em 167
_____, Larken Wrn 206
_____, Louis DeK 57
_____, William Lau 21
BRANSFORD, John Tlb 322
BRASWELL/BRASSEL/BRASELL/
BASEL/BRAZWELL/BRACEWELL/
BROSWELL
Braswell, Benjamin Tlb 347
_____, David Crf 411
_____, David Lau 18
_____, David Wal 160
_____, Isaac D. Wal 160
_____, James Gwn 343
_____, Jesse Tlb 347
_____, Jesse Up 116
_____, John Tat 375
_____, Kindred Lau 9
_____, Redding Lau 24
_____, Sampson Sr. Lau 7
_____, Sampson Jr. Lau 7
_____, Samuel Clk 300
_____, Timothy Crf 411
_____, Valentine Wal 135
_____, Wesley New 12
_____, William Clk 304
_____, William Crf 411
_____, William Lau 8
_____, Williamson M. New 10
_____, Wilson Lau 19
Brassel, Arthur Wsh 240
_____, James Fay 185
_____, William Fay 185
Brasell, Arthur Crf 399
Brassell, William Mad 101
Brasel, Lide Hab 53
Brazwell, Allen Pik 114
Bracewell, James Pul 146
_____, James M. Pul 146
_____, Wiley Hst 265
Broswell, Solomon Twg 74
BRAUARD, Allen Wrn 192
BRAWLEY, Daniel Frk 255
BRAWNER/BRAUGHNER
Brawner, Ceely DeK 50
_____, Henry Elb 147
_____, Henry P. Elb 147
_____, James M. Elb 146
Brawner, Jesse Frk 237
_____, Joel Hry 200
_____, John Frk 228
_____, John Gwn 350
_____, Joseph Elb 147
_____, Middleton Elb 137
_____, Tilman Mon 211
_____, William T. DeK 54
Braughner, William M. Mor 252
BRAXTON, Holinger Bib 69
BRAY, Bannister R. Mad 101
_____, Benjamin Mon 211
_____, David Elb 134
_____, George Har 191
_____, Jarod Wsh 265
_____, John Elb 134
_____, John Ogl 71
_____, John Wsh 256
_____, Joseph Wsh 273
_____, Lewis Elb 140
_____, Lucy Wrn 207
_____, Michael Bul 101
_____, Peter Mon 211
_____, William Mon 202
BRAZEL/BRAZIL/BRAZEAL/
BRAZELL/BRAZZELL/BRAZILE
Brazel, Bird Han 148
_____, Blainey Up 113
_____, Nathan Wrn 232
_____, Robert Tms 24
_____, Samuel Tms 23
_____, Sarah Cam 190
_____, Simeon Tms 23
_____, William Up 97
Brazil, Also Han 148
_____, Benjamin Up 119
_____, Betsy Jef 404
_____, Blainey Up 119
_____, Isom Mwr 167
_____, James Up 114
_____, James Up 119
_____, Henry Jef 422
_____, Kindred Jef 404
Brazeal, Britain Cpb 200
_____, Darial Cpb 208
_____, George R. Jks 331
_____, John M. Jks 322
_____, William Cpb 206
Brazell, Jane Wil 298
_____, Jane Wil 307
Brazzell, James Trp 49
Brazile, May Wks 334
BRAZELTON/BRASILTON
Brazelton, Jacob Sr. Jks 315

Brazelton, Jacob Jr. Jks 315
_____, Reuben Jks 311
Brasilton, Amos Hal 89
_____, Job Hal 83
BREED/BREAD
Breed, John Hry 207
_____, William Fay 187
Bread, Nathan Hry 207
BREEDLOVE, John H. Han 147
_____, John DeK 35
_____, Leonard P Tlb 343
_____, Rebecca Put 175
_____, Richard F. Wal 141
_____, William W. Mon 206
BRESSIE/BRASIE
Bressie, Murrell Hry 222
Brasie, Harris Hal 118
BREWER/BRUER/BRUOR
Brewer, Allford New 44
_____, Alsey Jef 422
_____, Archibald Tel 10
_____, Arthur Tlf 2
_____, Betsey Cam 185
_____, Drury Mor 257
_____, Edmund H. Elb 155
_____, Ely Mar 140
_____, English Mar 138
_____, Ethen New 44
_____, George Mor 247
_____, Henry Frk 255
_____, Henry Mon 195
_____, Hopkins W. Wil 287
_____, Hundley Wal 151
_____, James DeK 27
_____, James Han 146
_____, James Lib 43
_____, James Wal 125
_____, Joel Wks 341
_____, John Clk 295
_____, John Mar 139
_____, John Mon 199
_____, Mary Eff 112
_____, Mary Gre 301
_____, Robert Lib 43
_____, Samuel Mar 137
_____, Simon Wks 347
_____, Solomon Pul 153
_____, Susan Elb 154
_____, Thomas A. Ogl 97
_____, William Mar 138
_____, William Ogl 94
_____, William B. Elb 151
_____, William F. Elb 151
Bruer, Benjamin Gwn 352
_____, Britton Gwn 338
_____, Jesse Gwn 356
_____, Jesse Gwn 372
Bruor, Randal Gwn 362
BREWSTER/BRUSTER/BRUCESTER
Brewster, Hugh Sr. Gwn 316
_____, Hugh Gwn 329
_____, Hugh Gwn 347
_____, John Gwn 318
_____, John D. Wal 149
_____, Jonathan D. Cpb 207
_____, Sheriff Har 178
_____, Sheriff Trp 50
_____, Sheriff Wal 126
_____, William Gwn 313
_____, William B. Har 184
Bruster, James Hab 57
Brucester, James DeK 39
BREWTON/BRUTON
Brewton, Benjamin Tat 372
_____, John Dec 18
_____, Nathan Tat 378
Bruton, Emanuel Bul 94
_____, Isaiah Rch 266
BRICE/BRISE
Brice, Daniel Hal 104
_____, John Jsp 387
_____, Thomas Hal 104
Brise, James Car 214
_____, Thomas Car 216
BRICKLEY, William Bib 69
BRIDGEMAN, Frances Twg 60
BRIDGER/BRIDGERS
Bridger, Bartlett Twg 68
_____, Joseph Wks 342
_____, William F. Cht 279
Bridgers, Derrel D. Ran 246
_____, Jonathan Ran 249
BRIDGES, Abner Gwn 352
_____, Benja. Hal 107
_____, Berry J. Ogl 75
_____, Bolan J. Gwn 328
_____, Burwell Bts 172
_____, Corban Hry 217
_____, Daniel Tlb 343
_____, Hardy Gre 276
_____, Herod Put 207
_____, Isaac Ogl 69
_____, Jacob Wal 130
_____, James Frk 245
_____, James Gre 274
_____, James Gwn 333

Bridges, James Hry 217
______, James Ogl 62
______, James Up 109
______, John Bib 63
______, John Frk 245
______, John Gwn 352
______, John Mor 264
______, John R. Gwn 332
______, John W. Jns 464
______, John W. Rch 271
______, Jonathan F. Jns 447
______, Joseph Jns 433
______, Joseph Wsh 249
______, Joshua Hal 124
______, Lewis Gwn 312
______, Moses Ogl 69
______, Nancy Ogl 62
______, Nathaniel New 49
______, Peter S. Mon 172
______, Radford Wal 129
______, Reuben Bal 34
______, Sealas Wsh 240
______, Simon Mon 202
______, Sol. Gwn 369
______, Solomon Wal 142
______, Susan Tfo 369
______, Thomas Jns 434
______, Wiley Gwn 325
______, Wiley J. Cow 389
______, William Bts 171
______, William Lau 12
______, William Mtg 231
______, William Ogl 62
______, William G. Wrn 230
______, Willis Mwr 169
______, Wilson Frk 236
______, Wiseman Jsp 352
BRIDWELL, Henry L. Mad 105
BRIGDON, William Scr 303
BRIGG/BRIGGS
Brigg, Molly Rch 278
Briggs, John Bib 58
BRIGGET, Sarah Rch 282
BRIGHAM, John Bke 146
BRIGMAN, Thomas Bib 49
BRIGNON, Joseph Rch 264
BRIGHT, Absalom Bke 127
______, Meley Wsh 269
______, Samuel Hab 10
BRIGHTWELL, John Clk 291
______, Samuel Jks 336
BRIMER, James Gwn 334
______, W. N. Gwn 334
BRINBURY, Mathias Mor 249
BRINKLEY, Abram Wrn 229
______, John Wrn 226
______, Simeon Jsp 390
______, William Jef 402
______, William Wrn 229
______, Wylie Ear 91
BRIMM/BRIM
Brimm, Minor W. Hal 73
** ______, W. (slave) Rch 254
Brim, William Hst 269
BRINSON, Adam Scr 304
______, Benjamin Bke 130
______, Cyprian Bke 130
______, David Jef 413
______, Isaac Jef 419
______, Jeremiah Bak 20
______, John Sr. Bke 131
______, John Jr. Bke 128
______, Mary Bke 130
______, Moses Sr. Jef 422
______, Moses Jr. Jef 418
______, Shepherd Bke 128
______, Stephen Bke 130
______, Stiring Bke 127
______, William Bke 117
BRINTLE, Oliver Hal 101
BRIREAU, Phillis Cht 256
BRISCOE/BRISCO
Briscoe, John Col 360
______, Ralph Wal 130
______, Waters Wal 123
Brisco, John Ogl 91
______, Nathan Clk 309
BRISKY, Nicholas Har 192
BRISTER, Chesley Tfo 355
BRITT/BRIT
Britt, Alsey Bib 58
______, David J. Mus 287
______, Edw[d]. J. Mus 287
______, Elisha D. Mon 179
______, Henry Wsh 262
______, Hugh Gwn 368
______, James Wsh 252
______, Joel Gwn 368
______, John Hst 279
______, John New 27
______, John J. Tlb 340
______, Mary Jef 409
______, Obed. Wsh 262
______, William Ran 250
Brit, Agnes Clk 310
______, Ephrem Wal 173

Brit, John W.	Cam	182
______, Mathew	Put	180
______, William A.	Bts	173
BRITTENHAM/BRITTAINHAM		
Brittenham, Elijah	Mon	206
Brittainham, Nicey	Tlb	336
BRITTON/BRITON/BRINTON/ BRITAIN		
Britton, George	Bts	167
______, Henry	Clk	313
______, Henry	Ogl	98
______, John	Bts	167
______, John	Jsp	382
______, Stephen	Cht	257
______, William	Clk	317
Briton, Govey	Jsp	383
Brinton, James	Jks	311
Britain, Emanuel	Mus	287
______, Santford	DeK	61
BROADAWAY, William	Jns	442
BROACH, Charles	Wal	140
______, George	Jns	468
______, George	Mad	116
______, James	Mad	102
______, Sarah	Mad	116
______, William H.	Gre	279
BROADNAX, Edward B.	New	29
______, John H.	Trp	46
______, Robert	Han	148
______, Robert E.	Bke	150
______, William	Han	147
BROADUS/BRODDUS		
Broadus, Robert E.	Bal	38
Broddus, Thomas	Jsp	370
BROADWELL, Needham	Jks	318
______, William	Jks	332
BROCK/BRACK		
Brock, Benjamin	Fay	206
______, David	Dec	15
______, Elizabeth	Hal	107
______, Elizabeth	Hry	242
______, George	Hab	21
______, George	Hab	23
______, George	Hal	120
______, Henry	Cpb	202
______, Isaac	Dec	8
______, Isaac	Hab	46
______, James	Hab	25
______, James	Hab	46
______, Jessey	Mtg	231
______, John	Cpb	199
______, John	Hab	46
______, John	Hab	46
Brock, John	Hab	53
______, John	Pul	151
______, Martha	Dec	15
______, Moses	Hab	46
______, Rubin	Hab	21
______, Rubin	Hab	46
______, Thos.	Hab	26
______, William	Cow	368
Brack, Thomas	Lin	59
BROCKINGTON, Daniel	Gly	269
______, Samuel	Cam	190
BROCKMAN, Bledsoe	Gre	285
______, Elijah	Ogl	90
______, Elizabeth	Ogl	90
______, Moses	Ogl	91
BROCKWELL/BOCKWELL		
Brockwell, Daniel	Put	190
______, William	New	7
BROGDON/BRAGDEN/BRAGON		
Brogdon, George	Gwn	309
______, Gideon G.	Bts	168
______, John	Fay	185
______, Welea	Gwn	360
Bragden, John	Ble	129
Bragon, Richard	Ogl	97
**BRONSON, S. (slaves)	Rch	277
______, Zenos	Rch	278
BROOKER, Joseph	Tlf	2
______, William	App	5
BROOKING/BROOKINGS/ BROOKINS		
Brooking, Ann H.	Han	148
______, Charles V.	Han	147
______, Frederick E.	Han	148
______, Rebeccah A.	Han	148
______, Robert N.	Han	146
______, William	Han	146
Brookings, Samuel	Bke	129
______, William	Bke	152
Brookins, Benjamin	Wsh	252
______, Edwin	Lau	16
______, Haywood	Wsh	246
______, Nancy	Lau	23
BROOKS/BROOK/BROOKE		
Brooks, Aaron	Hry	199
______, Abel	Cpb	209
______, Abm. L.	Up	116
______, Alford	Jks	321
______, Alfred	Mon	195
______, Allen	Jns	433
______, Allen	Tlb	347
______, Amos	Gwn	324
______, Asberry	Cow	387

Name	County	Page
Brooks, Balam	Crf	402
______, Benjamin	Wrn	224
______, Benjamin F.	Mon	203
______, Bevin	Trp	50
______, Caty	New	47
______, Charles H.	Jns	455
______, Chieves	Mor	269
______, Christopher	Wil	306
______, Delily	Wrn	232
______, Edward	Hst	277
______, Edward	Ogl	99
______, Elijah	Hry	244
______, Elisha	Crf	393
______, Elisha	Hry	204
______, Elizabeth	Jns	435
______, Elizabeth	Jns	445
______, Esau	Gwn	341
______, Esau	Wil	306
______, Hamilton	Bts	162
______, Hannah	Wrn	228
______, Henry	Gre	279
______, Hillary	Hry	203
______, Isaac	Cpb	198
______, Isaac	Hst	267
______, Isaac	Wrn	224
______, Isaac P.	Tms	19
______, Isam	Put	190
______, Ivey	Mon	200
______, J. L.	Jsp	354
______, Jabez	Wal	135
______, Jacob	Jks	330
______, Jacob R.	DeK	47
______, James	Bts	178
______, James	Hab	57
______, James	Hal	100
______, James	New	46
______, James	Up	106
______, James	Wsh	256
______, Jefferson	Mwr	167
______, Jesse	Gre	278
______, Joel	Crf	402
______, John	Car	223
______, John	Col	350
______, John	Gwn	325
______, John	Mad	104
______, John	New	46
______, John	Trp	40
______, John	Trp	46
______, John	Wks	336
______, John B.	Hst	267
______, John S.	Hst	276
______, John S.	Jns	453
______, Jonathon	Hst	281
Brooks, Joseph	McI	121
______, Joseph C.	Mar	137
______, Josiah	Mar	138
______, Jourdan Jr.	Up	109
______, Maguire	Jks	343
______, Mary	Crf	415
______, Mary	Gre	293
______, Mary	Twg	76
______, Mary	Wrn	218
______, Matthew	Mad	114
______, Mathew	Ran	248
______, Maxey	Trp	54
______, Micajah	Hry	216
______, Middleton	Jks	330
______, Middleton	Jks	337
______, Moses	Hry	200
______, Oliver	Gwn	314
______, P. L. W.	Up	102
______, Paschal	Jsp	360
______, Philip H.	Jns	468
______, Robert	Gwn	363
______, Robert	Hst	276
______, Robert	Mwr	167
______, Robert	Ogl	102
______, Robert	Tlb	334
______, Robert	Wsh	245
______, Samuel	Hst	276
______, Samuel	Jns	455
______, Samuel	Wil	303
______, Samuel Jr.	Wil	303
______, Silas	Bts	167
______, Silas	Trp	36
______, Simon	Mon	200
______, Thomas	Hry	200
______, Thomas S.	Mwr	153
______, Vollenlin	Ran	248
______, Waddy	Cow	387
______, Walker	Ogl	99
______, William	DeK	51
______, William	Gre	297
______, William	Hal	100
______, William	Hst	291
______, William	Lee	30
______, William	Ogl	96
______, William	Mon	189
______, William	Tlb	341
______, William	Wal	125
______, William	Wal	135
______, William	Wks	345
______, William B.	Mar	144
______, William C.	Ran	241
______, William W.	Mar	140
______, Williamson	Tlb	337

Name	County	Page
Brooks, Willie	Pik	111
______, Wilson	Cam	187
______, Wilson	Ogl	99
______, Zemri	Gwn	341
Brook, Abijah	New	8
______, Ignitious R.	New	41
______, Jarvis	Wil	306
______, John	Wil	297
______, Jonathan	Ogl	90
______, Joseph	Wil	292
______, Little J.	Ogl	88
______, Preston	Ogl	91
______, Rachal	Ogl	88
______, Samuel	Ogl	90
______, Thomas P.	Ogl	93
______, William	Wil	296
Brooke, John P.	Hal	72
______, Wyatt	Har	178
BROOM, Adam	Wrn	202
______, Ezekiel	Wrn	199
______, Ishmel	Wrn	195
______, Nancy	Wrn	198
______, Rufus	New	32
______, Soloman	Wrn	208
______, William	Bke	142
BROUGHTON/BROTTON		
Broughton, Daniel S.	Lib	43
______, Edward	Gre	290
______, Eliza	Cht	248
______, James	Jef	416
______, James B.	DeK	52
______, John C.	Lib	43
______, John H.	Gre	300
______, Mary	DeK	53
______, William	DeK	53
______, William	Mor	255
Brotton, Joshua	Hry	215
BROWER, Eliza	Cht	251
______, Lucy	Cht	240
______, Robert	Cht	242
______, William	Cht	240
BROWN, A. D.	Bib	49
______, A. H.	Up	99
______, Aaron	Gwn	318
______, Abel	Mor	254
______, Abraham	Elb	133
______, Abraham	Jns	446
______, Absalom	Bib	59
______, Agnis	Cht	268
______, Alexander	Col	346
______, Alexander	Gwn	347
______, Alexander M.	Mor	264
______, Alfred	Fay	191
Brown, Allen	Mor	261
______, Allen W.	Ogl	90
______, Ambrose	Hab	62
______, Ambrose	Hal	82
______, Amos	Jsp	395
______, Amos	Hal	106
______, And.	Bal	31
______, Andrew	Elb	120
______, Andrew	Wal	141
______, Andrew M.	Hry	219
______, Ann	Doo	88
______, Aron	Hal	73
______, Aron	Mon	207
______, Asa	Pul	155
______, Asa A.	Elb	137
______, Augustus J.	Jks	331
______, Barthena	Wil	288
______, Bazele	Up	116
______, Benjamin	Bke	126
______, Benjamin	Elb	122
______, Benjamin	Gwn	348
______, Benjamin	Hry	239
______, Benjamin	Mad	109
______, Benjamin	Mor	241
______, Benjamin	New	51
______, Benjamin	Pik	120
______, Benjamin H.	Ran	241
______, Benori	Pul	159
______, Brinkly	Pul	162
______, Britain	Bul	102
______, Burrel	Bke	126
______, Burwell	Han	147
______, Candess W.	Up	113
______, Cath.	Bal	36
______, Charity	New	35
______, Charles	Bke	128
______, Charles	Cht	256
______, Charles	Ogl	87
______, Christopher	Cam	182
______, Christopher B.	Cow	384
______, Clark	Hst	296
______, Clary	Wrn	225
______, Collins	Mus	290
______, Coward	Bal	31
______, Cowen	Jsp	370
______, Cyntha	Mad	115
______, Daniel	Clk	313
______, Daniel	Trp	42
______, Daniel	Twg	74
______, Danil	Hab	64
______, David	Cam	190
______, David	Crf	403
______, David	Twg	86

Name	County	Page
Brown, David D.	Put	198
______, Dempsey	Mad	103
______, Dempsey Sr.	Twg	83
______, Dempsey Jr.	Twg	61
______, Diana	Cht	246
______, Douglass H.	Jef	407
______, Dozier,	Elb	157
______, Easter	Jef	408
______, Edmond	Gwn	323
______, Edmond	Pik	110
______, Edmund M.	Pul	143
______, Edward	Bib	58
______, Edward	Doo	84
______, Edward	Elb	149
______, Edward	Gwn	347
______, Edward G.	Hst	272
______, Elbert	Elb	157
______, Elias	Wrn	229
______, Elias	Hst	286
______, Elijah	Clk	302
______, Elijah	Jef	408
______, Elisha	Tlb	335
______, Elizabeth	Bib	59
______, Elizabeth	Bke	123
______, Elizabeth	Bke	141
______, Elizabeth	Cam	191
______, Elizabeth	Jef	419
______, Elizabeth	Wil	297
______, Elizabeth E.	Han	147
______, Ellenor	DeK	55
______, Emanuel	Wsh	247
______, Enoch G.	Mon	189
______, Ephram	Hab	83
______, Ephraim	Jks	339
______, Ervin	Hst	265
______, Evin	Cpb	202
______, Ezekiel	Har	179
______, Ezekiel	Har	186
______, Ezekiel	Mwr	154
______, Ezekel	Cam	186
______, Ezekiel	Trp	48
______, Ezekiel	Wal	141
______, F. Mrs.	Col	346
______, F. B. T.	Rch	270
______, Fadius	Hst	290
______, Fanning	DeK	52
______, Fanon	Fay	190
______, Fanny C.	Jsp	394
______, Federick D.	Twg	67
______, Fielding J.	Bke	150
______, Franklin	Up	102
______, Fredick	Col	356
______, Fredick	Irw	300
Brown, George	Wsh	267
______, George A.	Mon	173
______, George R.	Wal	156
______, Green	Pul	153
______, H. C.	Bal	45
______, H. T.	Cht	246
______, Handley	Wsh	243
______, Hardy	Gwn	355
______, Hardy	Twg	61
______, Hen.	Bal	31
______, Henry	Bul	102
______, Henry	Col	350
______, Henry	Em	166
______, Henry	Mor	241
______, Hezakiah	Wsh	249
______, Hezekiah	Hal	115
______, Hezekiah	Hst	264
______, Hiram	Lin	68
______, Hiram	Mad	111
______, Hiram	Pik	115
______, Holden	Twg	88
______, Hollinger	Jns	450
______, Hubbard	Tlb	323
______, Hugh	Cam	191
______, Hugh	Crf	407
______, Hugh	Hab	14
______, Ichabod	Jks	343
______, Irby	Pul	159
______, Isaac	Cow	382
______, Isaac	Hst	291
______, Isaac	Mon	219
______, J. Q. W.	DeK	53
______, J. R.	Jsp	372
______, James	Bib	49
______, James	Bul	101
______, James	Bke	126
** ______, James (slaves)	Cht	280
______, James	Clk	300
______, James Sr.	Dec	10
______, James	Dec	3
______, James	DeK	53
______, James	Elb	121
______, James	Gwn	358
______, James	Gwn	359
______, James	Hab	14
______, James	Hab	26
______, James	Irw	301
______, James	Lin	71
______, James	Mtg	236
______, James	Pul	151
______, James	Wks	338
______, James B.	Bke	138
______, James B.	Jef	409

Brown, James B. Put 187
______, James D. Elb 130
______, James E. Up 96
______, James L. Frk 252
______, James M. Mor 253
______, James N. Bul 100
______, James N. Elb 146
______, James S. Pik 122
______, James V. Mon 209
______, Jane Ogl 93
______, Jemima Hab 41
______, Jeptha Gwn 338
______, Jesse Bul 100
______, Jesse Col 347
______, Jesse Crf 403
______, Jesse Ear 98
______, Jesse Elb 140
______, Jesse Em 175
______, Jesse Frk 251
______, Jesse Lau 16
______, Jesse Pik 109
______, Jesse Wks 335
______, Jesse Wks 352
______, Jesse D. Wks 353
______, Joel Hry 203
______, John Bul 100
______, John Cam 184
______, John Cow 375
______, John DeK 35
______, John Doo 84
______, John Elb 131
______, John Frk 233
______, John Gre 281
______, John Gwn 330
______, John Hal 76
______, John Han 147
______, John Har 185
______, John Har 192
______, John Mon 206
______, John Mon 207
______, John Mor 261
______, John Tlb 335
______, John Sr. Trp 54
______, John Wal 155
______, John Wal 161
______, John Wsh 253
______, John Wyn 282
______, John E. Cam 187
______, John G. Jns 456
______, John M. Pik 116
______, John R. Pik 126
______, John S. Han 146
______, John S. Up 107

Brown, John U. New 37
______, John U Hst 268
______, John W. Hry 234
______, John W. Pik 118
______, Jonathon Hst 295
______, Joseph Hal 76
______, Joseph New 9
______, Joseph New 17
______, Joseph Rab 235
______, Joseph Tlb 339
______, Joshua Bib 58
______, Joshua Bib 75
______, Joshua Gwn 361
______, Josiah Rch 272
______, Judy Cht 269
______, Jules K. Elb 156
______, Keller DeK 50
______, Kilbey Crf 411
______, Larkin Gwn 324
______, Larkin Gwn 340
______, Lemuel Clk 297
______, Levi Hry 213
______, Lewis Elb 160
______, Lewis Gwn 316
______, Lewis Sr. Mon 186
______, Lewis Mon 205
______, Lewis Wal 151
______, Lewis L. Wil 287
______, Loam Hst 262
______, Loami Doo 83
______, Margret Hab 33
______, Mark M. Hst 268
______, Martha Gwn 323
______, Martha Hry 232
______, Martha Hst 296
______, Martha Tlb 328
______, Martin H. Bib 63
______, Mary Bul 99
______, Mary Cht 247
______, Mary Cht 247
______, Mary DeK 50
______, Mary Hry 234
______, Mary A. Wyn 283
______, Mary D. Mor 256
______, Mary D. Wsh 271
______, Mary G. Hry 230
______, Mathew Gwn 329
______, Mathew Hry 230
______, Matthew Rch 278
______, Meredith DeK 43
______, Mildred Mon 205
______, Milly Rch 257
______, Morgan Wsh 239

Name	County	Page
Brown, Moses	Han	146
______, Moses M.	Mon	208
______, N.	Bal	44
______, Nancy	Elb	159
______, Nancy	Hry	241
______, Nathan	Bak	19
______, Nathaniel	Tlb	345
______, Neal	Hal	75
______, Nicholas	Frk	238
______, Noah	Irw	300
______, Odam	Lee	31
______, Parthina (w)	Jsp	384
______, Patrick Sr.	Rch	286
______, Pearson	Pul	159
______, Peter	DeK	43
______, Philip	Irw	301
______, Rachel	Frk	257
______, Rachel	Hab	10
______, Rebecca	Cht	261
______, Rebecca	Hry	218
______, Reuben	Mon	175
______, Reuben E.	Hst	270
______, Rich.	Bal	31
______, Richard	Jef	401
______, Richard	Rch	258
______, Richard S.	Jef	410
______, Rigden	Cam	189
______, Riley	Hal	105
______, Robert	Bts	161
______, Robert	Bts	170
______, Robert	Cam	186
______, Robert	Gwn	319
______, Robert	Gwn	334
______, Robert	Hab	14
______, Robert	Hab	14
______, Robert	Hst	282
______, Robert	Jks	323
______, Robert	Jns	453
______, Robert	Jns	471
______, Robert	Jsp	361
______, Robert	Lin	71
______, Robert	Mon	226
______, Robert	Ogl	78
______, Robert	Rab	227
______, Robert	Twg	86
______, Robert	Up	106
______, Rowland	Hry	219
______, Sally	Hab	13
______, Samuel	Bts	176
______, Samuel	Car	221
______, Samuel	Clk	318
______, Samuel	Clk	326
______, Samuel	DeK	71
Brown, Samuel	Doo	85
______, Samuel	Irw	300
______, Samuel	Mad	103
______, Samuel	Wal	133
______, Samuel	Wsh	241
______, Samuel J.	Bke	138
______, Sarah	Hab	9
______, Sherrod	Fay	190
______, Silas	Twg	63
______, Solomon	Wsh	242
______, Spencer	Mwr	150
______, Stark	Wal	130
______, Stephen	Hal	75
______, Stephen	Hst	270
______, Stephen	Lin	62
______, Stephen	Wks	350
______, Stephens	Twg	68
______, Tanner	Wsh	267
______, Thomas	DeK	71
______, Thomas	Fay	199
______, Thomas	Hal	98
______, Thomas	Hry	242
______, Thomas	Jns	467
______, Thomas	Lwn	80
______, Ogl	64	
______, Thomas	Mor	241
______, Thomas	Wal	141
______, Thomas A.	Ogl	102
______, Thomas C.	Tfo	357
______, Thomas P.	Hst	279
______, Thomas P.	Jef	422
______, Turner T.	Wsh	254
______, Vincent	Hal	76
______, Vollentine	Ogl	79
______, W.	Bal	35
______, Wade	Bke	139
______, Washington	Wrn	199
______, Whitfield	Hab	23
______, Wiley B.	Elb	135
______, William Sr.	Bul	100
______, William Jr.	Bul	100
______, William	Cam	191
______, William	Clk	322
______, William	Crf	413
______, William	Dec	11
______, William	Dec	17
______, William	Doo	88
______, William	Elb	158
______, William	Frk	230
______, William	Frk	244
______, William	Gwn	330
______, William	Gwn	330
______, William	Hab	40

Name	County	Page
Brown, William	Hab	62
______, William	Hry	200
______, William	Hry	212
______, William	Hry	213
______, William	Hry	244
______, William	Jns	456
______, William	Mwr	166
______, William	Mon	192
______, William	Mor	269
______, William	New	15
______, William	Pik	106
______, William	Pik	110
______, William	Pul	140
______, William	Pul	156
______, William	Pul	159
______, William	Put	204
______, William	Trp	46
______, William	Twg	65
______, William	Up	95
______, William	Wsh	254
______, William	Wsh	274
______, William	Wil	323
______, William	Wks	332
______, William	Wks	344
______, William	Wks	348
______, William A.	Elb	120
______, William B.	Han	147
______, William B.	Up	96
______, William H.	Jns	468
______, William R.	Bib	49
______, William S.	DeK	50
______, William S.	Twg	88
______, William T.	Crf	394
______, William W.	Up	100
______, William W.	Wks	348
______, Wilson	Gwn	327
______, Wyatt	Hry	212
______, Zelous	New	9
______, Ziba	New	15
BROWNFIELD, John	Jsp	378
______, Robert	Jsp	379
BROWNING/BROWIN/BROWNIN		
Browning, Andrew	DeK	65
______, Benjn.	Jks	333
______, Daniel	Mtg	235
______, Daniel	Tms	24
______, Eli B.	Mon	224
______, George	Mtg	235
______, Henry T.	Elb	128
______, John	Clk	295
______, John	Lwn	81
______, John	New	37
______, Joshua	Lwn	81
Browning, Joshua R.	Mor	252
______, Josiah	Lwn	80
______, Laney	Mtg	235
______, Margaret	Clk	302
______, Nathan P.	Trp	32
______, Radford	Tms	24
______, Robert M.	Trp	35
______, Solomon	Jks	339
______, Washington	Trp	41
______, William	Tms	26
______, Wyley	DeK	28
______, Wyley	DeK	63
______, Young	DeK	58
Browin, John	Hab	31
Brownin, John	Wrn	229
______, William	Hab	31
BROWNJOHN, William	Cht	262
BROWNLOW, John A.	Frk	234
BROWNWELL, John	Lee	35
BROXTON, James	Pul	153
______, John	Bke	149
______, Sarah	Bke	149
______, Thomas	Bke	141
BROYERS, Henry	Clk	313
BRUCE, Archibald	Up	111
______, Aquiler	Hab	61
______, Aziel	Gre	300
______, Bryant	Mwr	168
______, Daniel	DeK	25
______, Elizabeth	Wil	315
______, Ephraigm	Gre	288
______, George	Hal	106
______, George	Han	146
______, Hugh C.	Hal	106
______, James	DeK	50
______, James	Gre	277
______, James	Hab	48
______, James Jr.	Hab	48
______, John	DeK	69
______, John	Gre	283
______, John	Hal	106
______, John	Mwr	164
______, John A.	Gre	284
______, John L.	Gre	277
______, Jonathan	Hab	50
______, Laburn	Hab	61
______, Robert	Frk	253
______, Thomas	Jks	316
______, Thomas	Wil	296
______, Walter H.	Mad	102
______, Ward	Pik	128
______, William	DeK	29
______, Wilson	Gre	276

Name	County	Page
BRUEN, William	Cht	252
BRUMBLES, Stephen	Mar	143
BRUMBALO/BRUMBALOW/		
BRUMBOLO/BRUMLO		
Brumbalo, Isaac Jr.	Twn	354
______, Volantine	Gwn	354
Brumbalow, Edwd.	Gwn	354
______, James	Cpb	203
Brumbolo, David	Bib	66
______, Isaac	Gwn	354
Brumlo, Edward	Mon	183
______, Edward G.	Mon	183
BRUMLEY/BRUMLY		
Brumley, James	Car	218
______, Vincin	Gwn	342
Brumly, Steven	Gwn	337
BRUNE, Thomas	Rch	253
BRUNER/BRAUNER/BREWNER		
Bruner, A. C.	Bak	16
______, Jacob	Hab	65
______, Thomas	Bak	16
Brauner, Simeon	Elb	146
Brewner, William	Wks	333
BRUNDAGE, Jesse	Han	145
BRUNSON, Daniel	Hst	287
______, Daniel	Lin	70
______, David	Hst	287
______, Duncon	Lin	69
______, Jarrott D.	Hst	287
______, Joseph	Lin	69
______, Matthew	Lin	69
______, Nathaniel D.	Tms	16
BRUNT, John	Gre	291
______, Nancy	Gre	304
______, Richard	Twg	85
BRUSHELL, John	Wil	297
BRUTON: see Brewton		
BRYAN/BRYANT/BRIANT/BRIAN/		
BRIEN/BRYEND/BRIAND		
Bryan, Alexander	Bib	54
______, Alexander	Rch	275
______, Alfred	Tms	22
______, Anna	Pul	154
______, Asberry	Gre	292
______, Benja.	Hal	72
______, Benjamin Sr.	Twg	65
______, Blackshear	Pul	141
______, Clement	Mtg	233
______, Council S.	Twg	84
______, David	Frk	251
______, David	Tlb	327
______, David R.	Lwn	87
______, Edmon	New	45
Bryan, Edward	Hst	286
______, Edward	Lau	10
______, Edward	Tms	29
______, Elender Jane	Dec	18
______, Elias	Mon	207
______, Ezekiel	Hst	288
______, Federick	Wyn	283
______, Felix	Mor	249
______, George H.	Har	192
______, Hardy	Tms	30
______, Israel	Eff	115
______, J. H.	Rch	272
______, James	Bul	96
______, James	Eff	115
______, James	Twg	84
______, James A.	Hst	294
______, James C.	Twg	76
______, James H.	Hry	214
______, Jesse	Gre	300
______, Jessie	Har	176
______, Jesse	New	21
______, Joel	Frk	213
______, John	Bib	59
______, John	Frk	235
______, John	Gre	292
______, John	Hst	278
______, John	Jsp	393
______, John	Lwn	79
______, John	Mon	190
______, John Jr.	Pul	154
______, John N.	Pul	141
______, Joseph	Han	147
______, Joseph	Tms	24
______, Joshua	Hst	269
______, Lary V.	Pul	158
______, Lewis	Wal	167
______, Little	Mon	189
______, Loverd	Mtg	233
______, Mary	Cht	241
______, Micajah	Frk	242
______, Nathan	Mon	189
______, Needham R.	Ran	244
______, Penelope	Twg	78
______, Reddick	Hst	274
______, Robert	Han	145
______, Royal	Frk	213
______, S. J.	Cht	257
______, Samuel	New	31
______, Stephen	Hst	283
______, T. M. F.	Cht	281
______, Theophilus	Mus	284
______, Thomas	Frk	254
______, Thomas	Gwn	368

Name	County	Page
Bryan, Thomas	Hab	29
_____, Thomas	Twg	66
_____, Thomas P.	Mus	285
_____, Tilman	Frk	210
_____, Torrence	Frk	242
_____, W.	Lee	32
_____, William	Bke	119
_____, William	Dec	18
_____, William	Frk	254
_____, William	Frk	256
_____, William	Gre	292
_____, William	Hst	278
_____, William	Mon	194
_____, William	Pul	139
_____, William	Twg	70
_____, William B.	Mon	205
Bryant, Almon	Gwn	369
_____, Anna	Bke	123
_____, Arch[d].	Wil	318
_____, Benjamin	Gwn	371
_____, Benjamin	Han	146
_____, Benjamin	Pik	123
_____, Caleb O.	Rab	234
_____, Duncan	Gwn	376
_____, Elizabeth	Pik	129
_____, Hardy	Jsp	356
_____, Harison	Gwn	335
_____, Hugh	Hal	81
_____, Isaac	Col	345
_____, Isaac	Scr	311
_____, Ittai	Gwn	335
_____, Jacob	Scr	316
_____, James	Jks	323
_____, James	Rch	282
_____, James Sr.	Cam	192
_____, James Jr.	Cam	186
_____, Jarnt	Bts	165
_____, Jason	Wsh	252
_____, Jesse	Put	188
_____, Joel	Pul	157
_____, John	Hry	248
_____, John	Jns	450
_____, John	Jns	467
_____, John	Mad	107
_____, Lawry	Clk	295
_____, Mary	Crf	404
_____, Mason	Mad	118
_____, Mary	Put	172
_____, Mary	Wyn	283
_____, Nancy	Gwn	335
_____, Nancy	Jsp	398
_____, Nancy	Wil	291
_____, Nathan	Pik	129
Bryant, Needham	Bke	124
_____, Osborn C.	Crf	410
_____, Osten	Cpb	196
_____, Richard	Wil	307
_____, Richmond	Wil	306
_____, Rodisa		*
_____, Ransom	Hry	217
_____, Sally	Em	164
_____, Sally	Wil	291
_____, Samuel	Wal	128
_____, Sarah	Bke	139
_____, Selina	Bke	141
_____, Solomon	Scr	313
_____, Susanah	Ear	97
_____, Thomas	Bib	54
_____, Thomas	Lau	24
_____, Timothy	Bul	96
_____, Wiley	Put	183
_____, William	Gwn	337
_____, William	Hry	231
_____, William	Ogl	67
_____, William	Ogl	91
_____, William	Rch	281
_____, William	Scr	313
_____, William L.	Jks	311
Briant, Benjamin	Jef	421
_____, Elias	Doo	82
_____, James	Put	176
_____, Pleasant	Clk	312
_____, Stephen	Hal	68
_____, Thomas	Put	176
_____, Wiley	Put	174
_____, William	DeK	60
Brian, Daniel	Dec	11
_____, John O.	Gre	304
_____, Newton	Dec	77
Brien, John	Bal	37
Bryend, John	Hab	66
Briand, James	Hab	26
BRYSON, Daniel H.	Fay	203
_____, William	Bts	173
_____, William	Rch	267
BUCHANNON/BUCHANAN/BUCKHANNON/BUCKHANAN/BUCHAN		
Buchannon, Benjamin	Lau	20
_____, George	Jsp	388
_____, George H.	Jsp	387
_____, Isaac	Jks	323
_____, James	DeK	51
_____, James	Mad	99
_____, James E.	Jsp	389
_____, Joseph	Tlb	323
_____, Martha	Mon	212
_____, Martin	Mon	212

* County and page inadvertantly omitted from index card.

Buchannon, Martin Mon 212
______, Peggy Mad 116
______, Sarah Put 197
______, Thomas Tlb 336
______, William Mtg 234
Buchanan, A. R. Jsp 370
______, Benjamin Bal 34
______, Benjamin New 35
______, George D. Wil 310
______, James New 35
______, Joseph Wil 297
______, Silas B. Hry 246
Buckhannon, James Jsp 379
______, John Wal 153
______, John W. Jsp 395
______, Micajah Jsp 387
______, William B. Jsp 392
Buckhanan, George Gwn 350
______, R. H. L. Q. Bal 34
Buchan, John Pul 151
BUCK/BUCKS/BUCH
Buck, Charles Bal 44
______, Charles Rch 286
______, Hardy Hst 265
______, John Jsp 352
______, William Wsh 246
Bucks, Charly Wil 318
Buch, Maria Rch 260
BUCKHOLTS, Peter Hry 218
______, P. Wks 347
______, Silas Wks 343
______, William Hry 218
BUCKLEY/BUCKNEY
Buckley, Gasta Cht 271
______, Hiram DeK 25
Buckney, Daniel Wks 354
BUCKALOW/BUCKALOO/BUCKLER
Buckalow, Federick Twg 74
______, James Lee 27
______, John Dec 4
______, William Hry 199
Buckaloo, Joel Bke 145
Buckler, Samuel E. Mus 280
BUCKNER/BUCKNEY
Buckner, Appleton Jns 440
______, Averea Put 209
______, Claib. Bal 39
______, Daniel Wil 207
______, Daniel Jr. Wil 317
______, Eli Put 202
______, H. Bal 38
______, Henry M. Mon 208
______, John Put 202

Buckner, John S. Mon 199
______, Leonard Mon 199
______, Lester Crf 404
______, Lucresa Put 209
______, Mary Put 210
______, Meredith Mar 138
______, Parham Mon 215
______, Peter Gre 277
______, Richmond Put 209
______, Thomas Wal 133
______, Wiley Tlb 344
Buckney, Daniel Wks 354
BUCY, Sarah Bts 164
BUDWELL, Moses Mad 117
BUFFETT, A. Cht 265
BUFFINGTON, Absalom New 47
______, Alfred Mon 210
______, Audin Pik 132
______, Ellis Hal 102
______, Ezekiel Hal 73
______, John Cpb 202
______, John Pik 121
______, Johnathan Cpb 196
______, Joshua Gwn 375
______, Oburn Hal 93
______, Samuel Bal 42
______, Samuel Pik 120
______, Thomas Hal 102
______, William Elb 124
______, William C. Mor 249
BUFORT, Henry Scr 315
______, John Scr 315
BUGG/BUGS
**Bugg, Ansel (slave) Rch 254
______, Anselm Rch 281
______, Benjamin Col 342
______, Charlotte Rch 284
______, Edmond Mus 279
______, Jacob C. Rch 285
______, Peter Mus 286
______, Sarah A. Col 360
______, Stephen Wyn 284
______, Thomas J. Tlb 333
______, William Ogl 101
Bugs, James DeK 66
BUISE/BUICE/BUIS/BUIAS/BICE
Buise, John Jns 433
______, Joseph Wal 173
Buice, Thomas Wal 173
Buis, Caswell Mon 188
______, John Up 99
Buias, Elbert Tlb 347
Bice, James Hal 111

Name	County	Page
BUIE, Archibal	Scr	303
______, John	Dec	14
______, Margret	Dec	14
______, Neal	Bul	96
BULENEAU, Augustus	Cht	244
BULGER, John	Tlb	322
BULL, Edmund	Ear	99
______, Robert	Pik	114
______, William	Wil	293
BULLARD/BULARD		
Bullard, Amos	Bke	126
______, Ann	Elb	150
______, Daniel	Twg	77
______, James	Bke	126
______, James	Jsp	353
______, Jeremiah	Bts	175
______, Middleton	Cow	376
______, Parthena	Twg	77
______, Richard	App	8
______, Robert S.	Wal	149
______, Sion R.	Pik	121
______, Thomas	Elb	151
______, Thomas	Hst	263
______, William	Cow	375
______, William	DeK	25
______, William	Hab	59
______, William	Jns	433
BULLINGTON, Reuben	Han	146
BULLION, Thomas	Car	223
BULLOCH/BULLOCK/BULLOUGH		
Bulloch, A. S.	Cht	251
______, Elizabeth	Cht	244
______, James S.	Cht	243
______, W. B.	Cht	251
**______, Wm. B. slaves	Cht	279
______, Wyatte	Ogl	67
Bullock, A. G.	Mad	100
______, Batson	Bib	66
______, Baylock	Mus	284
______, Carter	Doo	88
______, Daves	Wrn	195
______, Eliza	Mus	279
______, Hardy	Wil	296
______, Hawkins	Mad	111
______, James	Col	356
______, James	Wks	348
______, Mitchell	Han	146
______, Reuben	Mwr	165
______, Richard	Crf	405
______, Shadrack	Hry	243
______, Thomas	Cpb	206
______, Thomas	Mon	217
______, Uriah J.	Bib	66
Bullock, William G.	Mad	99
______, Willis	Wks	341
Bullough, James	Cht	246
BULMAN, Thomas	Up	110
BUMBGARNER, Absalom	Gwn	309
______, Melger	Gwn	309
BUNCE, C. F.	Bul	99
______, William J.	Rch	261
BUNCH, David	Wil	317
______, Permelea	Gre	284
______, William	Mtg	231
BUNKLEY/BUNCKLEY		
Bunkley, Albert G.	Wrn	203
______, Elizabeth	Gre	283
______, James	Bts	161
______, John	Up	111
Bunckley, Briton R.	Cam	187
______, Thomas P.	Cam	181
BUNN, Henry	Twg	74
______, Jesse	Hry	219
______, Moses	Bke	126
______, William	Gre	303
BUNT, Edward	DeK	54
BUNTEN/BUNTIN/BUNTYN		
Bunten, Benjamin	Pik	117
Buntin, Jeremiah	Jef	419
Buntyn, Elcy	Pik	116
BURAN, Henry	Lee	32
BURBIDGE, George	Col	352
BURCH, Allen	Gwn	338
______, Benjamin	Lau	7
______, Blanton	Rch	282
______, Charles	Lau	19
______, Charles	Rch	289
______, Charles C.	Tlb	332
______, Edward	Pul	158
______, Edward	Rch	290
______, Edward A.	Pul	157
______, Elizabeth	Elb	139
______, James J.	Elb	157
______, John	Gre	296
______, John	Lau	19
______, John	Wil	287
______, John N.	Clk	323
______, L. B.	Bke	130
______, Littleton	Lau	19
______, Morten N.	Fay	186
______, Rebecca	Rch	291
______, Reuben	Lau	18
______, Sarah	Han	148
BURCHSTEINER, Jaines A.	Eff	108
______, Matthew	Eff	105
______, Samuel	Eff	108

Name	County	Page
BURDEN/BURDIN/BURDINE/ BUDINE		
Burden, Archibald	Elb	141
______, Archibald	Rch	282
______, Henry	Elb	121
______, Joel	Car	217
______, William	Elb	141
______, William	Twg	71
Burdin, James	Trp	36
Burdine, Samuel	DeK	27
______, William B.	Jns	464
Budine, Nancy	Bib	69
BURDETT/BURDITT/BERDUTT		
Burdett, Benjamin	Wil	306
______, Benjamin	Wil	311
______, James	Wil	310
______, John	Wil	310
______, John C.	Wil	291
______, John Jr.	Wil	311
______, Henry	Jsp	391
______, Margerett	Wil	306
______, Samuel	Wil	311
______, William	Mus	289
Burditt, Samuel L.B.	Hry	208
Berdutt, Humphry	DeK	45
BURDICK, Elam C.	Lau	4
BURFORD, P. H.	DeK	33
______, Samuel P.	Bts	168
______, Thomas	Hal	83
______, Thomas B.	Bts	168
______, Thomas M.	Trp	53
______, Thomas W.	Hal	70
______, William	Bts	168
______, William	Gre	277
BURGAMY/BERGAMY/BERGANY		
Burgamy, Nathaniel	Wil	322
______, Tobias	Wsh	272
______, Tobias	Wsh	272
______, William	Wsh	268
Bergamy, William	Hst	290
Bergany, John	Wks	344
BURGAY, John	Mon	174
______, Levin	Mon	192
BURGE/BIRGE		
Burge, Hambleton	New	14
______, John	Jsp	367
______, John D.	Bib	58
______, Mathew	Mon	194
______, Nancy	New	34
______, Nathaniel	Gwn	363
______, Thomas	Gwn	310
______, Winny	Twg	88
Birge, David	Gwn	353
Birge, John F.	Gwn	311
______, William	Gwn	312
BURGEAU, U.	Cht	246
BURGER, Ann	Clk	315
______, Charles	Clk	293
______, Charles	Clk	297
BURGESS/BURGES		
Burgess, Abner	Frk	241
______, Dempsey	Up	114
______, Elias	Frk	217
______, Ezekiel	Frk	240
______, J.	Gwn	308
______, James	Cow	376
______, James	Frk	228
______, Joel	Frk	239
______, Joel	New	35
______, John	Frk	241
______, John C.	New	46
______, John H.	Cow	377
______, Josiah	Doo	85
______, Linsey	Cow	376
______, Mary	Gwn	325
______, Moses	McI	131
______, Robert	Doo	81
______, Roland	Cow	377
______, Thornton	Frk	242
______, W.	Gwn	309
______, William	Doo	78
Burges, Edward	Hab	10
______, Josiah	Jsp	362
______, Jonathan	Ogl	88
______, William	Put	203
BURGLOSS, John	Cht	271
BURKE/BURK/BURKS,BURKES/ BOURKE		
Burke, Abraham	Scr	305
______, Calaway	Car	214
______, David	Scr	305
______, Henry	Hry	226
______, John	Car	216
______, John	Mor	263
______, John B.	Hab	18
______, Jonathan	Hry	239
______, Matthew	Bke	130
______, Michael	Jef	424
______, Nathaniel	Gwn	352
______, Richard E.	Clk	322
______, Robert B.	Rch	290
______, Thomas Sr.	Bke	132
______, Thomas S. Jr.	Bke	150
______, Willey	Mor	263
______, William	Mor	263
______, William	Mor	270

Name	County	Page
Burke, William	Scr	304
______, William M.	Mor	264
Burk, Charles	Gre	284
______, Charles J.	Gre	278
______, Daniel	Wks	358
______, Edward	Tlf	9
______, Francis	Ogl	86
______, Hope H.	Clk	326
______, Isaac	Gwn	373
______, James	Gwn	357
______, James	Gwn	373
______, James	Mad	103
______, John	Fay	189
______, John	Tms	19
______, Joseah	Gwn	358
______, Jordan S.	Put	172
______, Littleton L.	Trp	35
______, Robert Sr.	Mon	175
______, Robert Sr.	Mon	211
______, Thornton	Mon	175
______, Wiley P.	Wil	322
______, William T.	Tlb	346
______, William	Wks	334
______, William B.	Bts	158
Burks, James L.	Tlb	327
______, John	Lee	30
______, John	New	37
______, John	Trp	53
______, John	Wil	290
______, Joseph H.	Wil	317
______, Shiels	Wil	294
______, William	New	37
______, William	New	43
Burkes, Brinkley	New	43
______, Elisha	Hry	231
______, Nimrod	Bke	145
______, William	Hry	223
Bourke, Ann	Cht	246
BURKHALTER/BUCKHALTER		
Burkhalter, Christiana	Tlf	8
______, David	Wrn	192
______, Isaac	Pul	141
______, Jacob	Wrn	192
______, Jeremiah	Wrn	214
______, John Jr.	Wrn	218
______, John R.	Wrn	215
______, Joshua	Jns	446
______, Michael	Jns	446
______, Richard H.	Pul	143
Buckhalter, Isham	Wrn	229
______, John	Har	183
______, Peter	Scr	299
BURKETT/BURKITT/BERKET/		
BURKET/BURKIT		
Burkett, Hugh G.	Twg	78
______, Solomon	Twg	62
______, Uriah	Twg	78
Burkitt, John	Tlf	3
______, William	Tlf	4
Berket, John	Up	100
Burket, T.	Wks	346
Burkit, Alexander	Dec	16
BURNAM/BURNHAM		
Burnam, Canna	Lwn	91
______, James W.	Han	145
______, Lewis	Twg	85
______, William	Lwn	81
Burnham, Benjamin	Hst	281
______, Elijah	Hst	281
______, Elisha B.	Wal	128
______, Thomas	Wal	135
BURNEL, Anthony	Em	173
BURNLEDGE, Henry	Col	349
BURNETT/BURNET		
Burnett, Alexander	Bib	54
______, Charlotte	Bib	63
______, Christopher	Gly	269
______, Daniel	Lwn	83
______, Daniel M.	New	19
______, Isaac	Mon	176
______, Isma	Bke	125
______, James	DeK	72
______, James	Lwn	83
______, Jeremiah	Bib	66
______, Jeremiah	Elb	134
______, Col. John	Gly	264
______, John Jr.	Gly	269
______, John	Wil	297
______, Littleberry	Clk	294
______, Molsey W.	Lwn	84
______, Nicholas M.	New	13
______, Rachael	Clk	292
______, Richard	DeK	53
______, Samuel	Mor	270
______, Sarah	Bib	66
______, Thomas	Wsh	247
______, Washington	Jns	455
______, William	DeK	67
Burnet, Anthony	Mon	198
______, Berry	Hab	60
______, S. B.	Crf	412
______, Thomas	Pik	127
______, Thomas M.	Mwr	153
______, Valentine	Car	230
BURNEY, G. B.	Wks	341
______, John	Cht	267

Burney, John M. New 12
______, Randol New 12
______, Susan Wyn 285
______, Thomas J. Mor 249
______, William Clk 296
______, William Gly 268
BURNLEY, Richmd. Wrn 202
______, Stephen W. Wrn 221
______, Stephen G. Wrn 202
BURNS/BURNES
Burns, Andrew Mar 138
______, Benjamin Cpb 197
______, Darius Tlb 323
______, David Jks 328
______, George W. Wal 168
______, Gilliad Pik 131
______, Jack Col 345
______, James Pul 138
______, James Cow 383
______, Jinney Hry 247
______, Joseph Twg 77
______, Leander Tlb 324
______, Mijamin Fay 202
______, Nancy Gwn 339
______, Robert Hal 103
______, Saml. Jks 320
______, Samuel T. Wil 323
______, Scillus O. Gre 293
______, Thomas Hal 122
______, William Car 217
______, William Cpb 194
______, William DeK 46
______, William Elb 142
Burnes, Andrew Mor 265
______ (or Barnes) Jacob Wsh 242
______, James Twg 83
______, James Wsh 241
______, John Gwn 338
______, Thomas Scr 310
______, William Scr 313
BURNSIDE/BURNSIDES
Burnside, David Up 95
______, Eleanor Up 102
______, James Hst 266
______, Mathew Up 101
______, William Bul 93
Burnsides, Edmund Bul 97
______, James Bul 97
______, James Col 342
______, John Bul 97
______, Thomas Col 347
BURR, Jason Mon 222
BURRINGTON, Willis Hry 222

BURREL/BURRELL/BURWELL
Burrel, Hardy Gwn 332
Burrell, Jessee Gwn 312
Burwell, Lua Clk 294
BURROUGHS/BURROWS/BURRUS/
BURRIS/BURIS/BURROW
Burroughs, Benjamin Cht 249
______, George N. Frk 228
______, James Mad 100
______, James Jr. Col 335
______, James W. Col 335
______, Jos. H. Cht 249
______, Lemuel Wyn 284
______, Reubin Bib 49
______, Rozel Mad 100
______, Sarah Scr 309
______, Thomas P. Frk 235
______, W. H. Cht 277
______, William Frk 232
Burrows, Alfred Cam 181
______, James Har 186
______, Joseph DeK 43
______, Joseph Har 185
Burrus, Jacob Wsh 242
______, James Wsh 241
Burris, Alfred Wsh 240
Buris, Mary Dec 17
Burrow, Philip Pik 111
BURRY, Benj. Col 336
BURSON, Brookfield Jks 323
______, Elisha Jks 335
______, Elizabeth Wal 167
______, Isaac Cpb 204
______, John Wrn 209
______, Mary Wrn 223
______, Nancy Wrn 210
BURT, Anderson Mon 177
______, Elisha Mus 282
______, Henry Wal 130
______, James Put 176
______, James G. Put 177
______, John Crf 415
______, John Hab 7
______, John Hab 44
______, Oliver Hab 44
______, Richard Sr. Put 177
______, William Cow 386
______, William Hab 44
______, William Hal 115
______, Zacheus Put 178
BURTON/BURTEN/BIRTON
Burton, Abraham Elb 154
______, Amos Jks 318

Name	County	Page
Burton, Blackman	Elb	154
______, Charles	Bke	127
______, Elizabeth	Lin	59
______, German	Lin	64
______, Henry A.	Eff	112
______, Ira	Rch	287
______, Jacob	Mad	107
______, Jacob	Trp	52
______, James	Hab	54
______, James	Mar	139
______, James S.	Jks	320
______, John	Bts	177
______, John	Frk	253
______, John	Ran	250
______, Leroy	Elb	154
______, Nancy	Bts	159
______, Nancy	Elb	152
______, Rebecca	DeK	70
______, Robert	Eff	112
______, Robert F.	Bts	158
______, Samuel W.	Ogl	78
______, Thomas	Elb	141
______, Thomas W.	Han	147
______, William	Bke	135
______, William	Elb	153
______, William	Jks	345
______, William B.	Col	346
______, William C.	Gre	297
______, Willis	Jns	464
Burten, Jacob	Trp	38
Birton, Alanson	Bib	63
BUSBIN/BURBIN		
Busbin, Benjamin	Ogl	69
______, Isaac	Ogl	67
______, Jacob	Ogl	66
______, John	Ogl	66
______, Lucinda	Ogl	66
Burbin, Isaac	Mad	108
BUSBY/BUSBEE/BUSBEY		
Busby, Allen	Hst	267
______, Elias	Clk	307
______, Jacob	Hst	268
______, James	Bib	72
______, Jeremiah	Hst	267
______, Nathan	Hst	267
______, Reace	Bib	72
Busbee, Elisha	Crf	399
______, Fredrick	Crf	399
______, Kinchen	Hry	212
______, William H.	Crf	399
Busbey, Sampson	Crf	408
BUSH, Abram	New	24
______, Andrew	Wrn	214
Bush, Charles	Tlf	8
______, Daniel	Frk	220
______, David B.	Tlb	340
______, Dorcas	Twg	77
______, Elizabeth	Pul	162
______, Jackson	Mon	176
______, James	Ear	93
______, James	Lau	23
______, James	Pik	107
______, James	Pul	154
______, Jasper	Ogl	84
______, John	Frk	220
______, John	Hst	293
______, John	Wks	334
______, John B.	Bke	142
______, John B.	Pul	140
______, Jordan	Wks	333
______, Joseph	Bke	139
______, Josiah	Lau	19
______, Levi	Pul	141
______, Mary	Lau	22
______, Mary	Wil	293
______, N.	Wks	347
______, Sanders	Doo	78
______, Solomon	Pul	140
______, Thomas	Hst	269
______, Thomas	Frk	224
______, William	Doo	89
______, William	Frk	222
______, William	Lau	6
______, William	Wks	337
BUSHELL or BUSKELL, Jesse C.	Clk	328
BUSSY/BUSSEY		
Bussy, Benjamin	Put	174
______, Benjamin P.	Put	189
______, Flemin	Put	176
______, James	Put	217
______, Malakiah	Pik	130
______, Nathan	Put	176
______, Wade	Lin	69
Bussey, B.	Bak	16
______, Charles	Mon	179
______, Joshua	Lin	69
______, Mary	Rch	261
______, Zadoc	Lin	70
BUSTIN, Christopher	Put	176
______, Elisha	Up	95
______, James	Scr	309
______, John	Put	213
______, John	Up	98
______, Thomas	Up	98
______, Thomas	Up	103

Name	County	Page
Bustin, William	Pik	124
BUSTLE, Isaac	Han	148
______, James	Han	148
______, Priscilla	Han	148
______, Solomon (of Col.)	Wrn	217
BUTCHER, Henry P.	Tlb	343
BUTLER, Abel	Tlb	327
______, Booker	Col	353
______, Chas.	Lee	31
______, Ch.	Wks	346
______, Daniel	Hal	86
______, David C.	Elb	139
______, Davis	New	23
______, Dempsey	Pik	119
______, Edmund M.	Gre	302
______, Edward	Bts	161
______, Elenor (w)	Mor	268
______, Elisha	Dec	7
______, Elizabeth	Pik	126
______, Eliz^{a}.	Up	118
______, Ford	Cow	381
______, George	Mad	102
______, George S.	Elb	142
______, Gilbert	Cht	246
______, Greenberry	DeK	48
______, Haley	Elb	124
______, Hudson	Hab	57
______, Isaac	Doo	86
______, Isaac	Har	184
______, J. B.	Col	346
______, James	Bib	72
______, James	Bry	89
______, James	Bts	171
______, James	Elb	151
______, James	Elb	153
______, James	Hry	248
______, James	Ogl	97
______, James	Tms	23
______, James P.	Mor	243
______, Jefferson	Bry	86
______, Jesse	Bry	87
______, Jesse	Put	191
______, Joel	Mad	107
______, Joel	Wks	343
______, John	Bry	85
______, John	Hal	86
______, John	Hry	227
______, John	Hst	277
______, John	Jsp	379
______, John	Lee	32
______, John	Lib	43
______, John	Twg	60
Butler, John G.	Cht	278
______, John G.	Pik	120
______, John W.	Mor	268
______, John W.	Wil	295
______, Joseph	Har	177
______, Joseph	Rch	290
______, Joshua	Cpb	203
______, Larkin	Jks	328
______, Mal.	Wks	339
______, Mancil	Tlf	10
______, Martha	DeK	52
______, Martha	Elb	149
______, Martin	DeK	57
______, Mary	Mon	193
______, Mary	Ogl	81
______, Mary	Put	213
______, May	Wks	335
______, Micheal	Cht	240
______, Nathan	Wal	127
______, Patrick	Wal	135
______, Pearce, Estate of	Gly	266
______, Peter P.	Elb	149
______, Peter P. Jr.	Elb	141
______, Peter P. Sr.	Elb	140
______, Richmond	Wal	155
______, Robert	Lee	27
______, Sally	Gwn	337
______, Stephen	Scr	317
______, Thomas	Cht	265
______, Thomas J.	Mor	250
______, Whitiker	Hal	72
______, William	Cht	272
______, William	Ogl	94
______, William	Pik	126
______, William	Wks	337
______, William B.	Mor	249
______, Zacheus	Put	186
BUTTERWORTH, Isaac	Hal	95
______, Stephen	Hal	73
______, Stephen H.	Hal	95
BUTTON, Walton	Gly	267
BUTTRELL/BUTRELL		
Buttrell, Margarett	Wrn	205
______, Thomas	Trp	52
______, Thomas S.	Wrn	205
Butrell, William	Bts	160
______, William	Cow	385
BUTTS/BUTT/BUTS		
Butts, Azariah	Han	145
______, E. P.	Cht	245
______, Federick A.	Trp	50
______, Frederick	Han	145
______, Henry	Up	121

Name	County	Page
Butts, Henry	Wal	140
_____, Jacob C.	Mor	271
_____, James	Han	145
_____, James R.	Bibb	49
_____, Jesse G.	Han	147
_____, Martha W.	Han	145
_____, Mary (w)	Mor	241
_____, Matt. C.	Han	146
_____, Sarah	Bib	75
_____, Spiers	Mon	182
_____, Thomas C.	Han	145
_____, Wilson	Bak	19
_____, Zachariah	Mwr	153
Butt, Jeremiah	Wrn	192
_____, John	Wrn	192
_____, Moses	Mus	279
_____, Noah	Jns	439
_____, William	Cpb	205
_____, William	Wrn	192
Buts, Allen	DeK	33
_____, David	Doo	83
_____, Edmund	Put	176
_____, James	Dec	19
_____, Sarah	Put	174
BUXTON, Benjamin	Bke	148
_____, William	Bke	146
BYARS/BYERS		
Byars, David	Bts	179
_____, George Sr.	Bts	166
_____, George Jr.	Bts	166
_____, Henry	Bts	175
_____, Joel	Bts	166
_____, John D.	Bts	179
_____, Josiah	Bts	178
_____, Thomas	Cow	388
_____, William	Bts	166
Byers, Robert	Rab	231
BYNE, Ann Jane	Bke	152
_____, Elijah	Bke	122
_____, Enoch	Bke	155
_____, Henry	Bke	155
_____, Mary	Bke	136
_____, Richard	Bke	137
_____, William	Bke	137
BYNUM/BYNAM/BYRAM		
Bynum, Drewry	Wrn	231
_____, James	Hst	283
_____, John	Hst	283
_____, Mary	Put	203
_____, Reuben	Hst	283
_____, Sugars	Hst	282
Bynam, Henry	Wsh	267
_____, John	Col	347
Bynam, Tarver	Wsh	251
Byram, Bevely	Pik	108
BYRD, Eleanor	Wil	295
_____, Henry	Rch	275
_____, Mahala	Rch	265
_____, Mariah	Twg	83
_____, Nancy	Twg	83
_____, Nathan	Bke	117
_____, Philemon	Wil	304
_____, Wiley	Hst	286
_____, William	Hst	283
_____ ALSO SEE BIRD		
BYTHEWOOD, Matthew	Jsp	369
CABEEN, Alexander	Up	120
CABELL, John	Tms	16
CABINESS/CABANIS		
Cabiness, George	Mus	284
_____, H. B.	Jns	438
_____, Sarah	Jns	444
_____, William	Wal	138
Cabanis, Elbridge G.	Mon	196
CABLE, Ann	Clk	320
CABUS, John	Cht	251
CADE, Bedford	Wil	319
_____, Drury B.	Wil	317
_____, James	Wil	302
_____, Robert	Hry	215
_____, William	Wil	317
CADLE, Jesse	Up	105
CADENHEAD/CADDENHEAD		
Cadenhead, Alex^{r}.	Tlb	340
_____, Edmund	Jns	432
_____, James	Up	106
_____, John	Up	106
_____, Martin	Up	107
_____, William	Jns	431
CADY, Alexander	Col	358
CAESAR, O.	Cht	250
CAGLE, Benjamin	Hry	207
_____, David	Hry	220
_____, George	Hry	225
_____, Henry	Jns	446
_____, Honor	Hab	16
_____, Jacob	Hry	204
_____, Jeptha	Hry	229
_____, Joseph	Hry	203
_____, Leonard	Hry	204
_____, Leonard	Hry	229
_____, Zachariah	Cow	385
_____, ALSO SEE KAGLE		
CAIN/CANE/KAIN/KANE		
Cain, Abel	Doo	82

Name	County	Page
Cain, Allen	Doo	79
______, Andrew	Gwn	343
______, Benemi	Hab	6
______, Elisha	Jef	403
______, James	Col	364
______, James	Gwn	359
______, James	Jef	403
______, James B.	Hry	217
______, John	Gwn	309
______, John	Lee	29
______, John	Mon	181
______, John R.	Hal	103
______, Joseph	Hal	88
______, Lidia	Wsh	245
______, Lucinda	Gly	267
______, Magee	Hal	91
______, Michael	Doo	82
______, Nancy	Gwn	342
______, Richard	Bib	72
______, Richard	Jks	335
______, Robert C.	Hal	91
______, Sutherland	Up	98
______, William Sr.	Doo	82
______, William Jr.	Doo	81
______, William	Hab	6
______, William W.	Hal	88
Cane, James	Hab	23
______, Jonathan	Ear	96
______, Jos.	Wrn	223
______, Ransom	Hab	52
______, William N.	Mus	291
Kain, Eugenia	Rch	269
Kane, Flora	Rch	269
CAHILL, John	Tms	16

CALAHAN/CALLAHAN/CALLAHAND/
CALLIHAN/CALIHAN/CLANAHAN/
KALLAHAND

Name	County	Page
Calahan, David	Lin	61
______, James	Clk	304
______, Josiah	Rab	231
______, Nathaniel	Trp	55
______, Sarah	Jks	329
______, William	Hal	122
Callahan, Edwd. S.	DeK	31
______, Jacob	Wal	132
______, William	DeK	54
______, William	Ogl	90
Callahand, Briant	Doo	78
Callihan, Joshua	DeK	54
______, Pierce	Lau	17
Calihan, Sterling	Gwn	326
Clanahan, Robert	Cow	379
Kallahand, James	Dec	7

CALDWELL/CAULDWELL/COLDWELL/
CALWELL/COLWELL/CULWELL

Name	County	Page
Caldwell, Alexander	Hry	231
______, Allen	Jns	456
______, C. M.	Cam	185
______, Chas. Y.	Mon	225
______, Creed	Mwr	164
______, David	Hab	65
______, David	Mwr	157
______, Eleaner	Gre	302
______, Eliza	Up	121
______, Garland	Hal	74
______, Glenn	Mon	211
______, M. T.	Mon	203
______, Isabella	McI	128
______, James	Hry	231
______, James	Jns	435
______, John	Car	224
______, John	Cow	369
______, John	Gre	275
______, John	Rch	273
______, John	Up	112
______, John E.	Mad	98
______, Joshua	Gre	290
______, Josiah	Gre	275
______, Littleton	Gre	293
______, Marcus	Mwr	154
______, Mary	Gre	285
______, Matthew	Up	107
______, Peter	Mor	262
______, Richard C.	Mon	211
______, Robert	McI	128
______, Robert	Jns	428
______, Rosaline	McI	131
______, Samuel	Gre	301
______, Samuel	Lau	6
______, Whitfield	DeK	25
______, William	Gre	275
______, William	Mwr	158
______, William R.	Bke	150
Cauldwell, Matthew	Trp	47
Coldwell, A. C.	Rch	260
______, Chas.	Gwn	339
______, James	Cow	390
______, James	Gwn	315
______, James	Gwn	338
______, Robert	Gwn	338
______, Sarah	Lin	61
______, William	Han	149
______, Curtis	Gwn	319
Calwell, James	Clk	326
Colwell, Green	Jsp	360
______, Harvin	Lee	33

Colwell, Margaret Pik 108
______, William L. Dec 11
Culwell, Andy Cpb 209
CALHOUN/CALHOON/CALHUNE/
COLGAHOUN
Calhoun, Adam Doo 85
______, Alexander Tlb 340
______, Allen Wsh 276
______, Archibald Tlb 341
______, Axiom Hst 283
______, D. W. Crf 395
______, Dugald Tlb 332
______, E. N. DeK 27
______, Elbert Bib 63
______, Ephraigm Gre 276
______, J. L. Bal 45
______, James Wsh 271
______, John Jns 468
______, John Hal 112
______, John E. Hst 284
______, John M. Put 186
______, Joseph Doo 78
______, Joseph Hst 284
______, Levi Bib 67
______, P. M. Crf 399
______, Samuel Wsh 275
______, Samuel Doo 88
______, Samuel Up 107
______, Vincent Hst 279
______, William Wsh 275
______, Williamson Wks 347
Calhoon, Burrel R. Mtg 232
______, Elizabeth Jef 404
______, Isaac Cpb 198
______, James Mar 144
______, John Cpb 196
______, Mary Mtg 233
______, Rosannah Mtg 234
______, William Jef 408
______, Winiford Mtg 236
Calhune, Thos. M. Ran 247
Colgahoun, Duncan Hry 245
CALIFF, Pugh Jns 450
CALLAM/CALLUM: see KELLAM
CALLEY/CALEE/CALLESS/
CAULLEY
Calley, Leanna M. Gre 305
Calee, James DeK 50
Calless, James L. Hab 40
Caulley, George Lau 4
CALLIN/CALLING
Callin, Peter Mor 249
Calling, Sarah Col 344
CALLOWAY/CALLAWAY/CALAWAY/
CALLEWAY/CALIWAY/CALOWAY/
CALWAY
Calloway, Abraham B. Wil 322
______, Barthena Wil 307
______, Burham Wil 324
______, David Wil 319
______, Drury Wil 323
______, Edward Mon 174
______, Elijah M. Hry 218
______, Enoch Wil 307
______, Francis Ogl 73
______, Jesse Wil 290
______, Joel Pik 116
______, John Ear 98
______, Jonathan Mon 204
______, Joseph Wil 320
______, Joseph M. Wil 319
______, Joshua S. Hry 209
______, Josiah Mon 184
______, Laurence Elb 140
______, Marten K. Jsp 389
______, Martha Ogl 94
______, Martha H. Wil 324
______, Mary Wil 297
______, Mary A. Wil 324
______, Noah Jsp 373
______, Parker Wil 323
______, Peter Jsp 398
______, Seabon Wil 323
______, William Mon 204
______, William A. Hry 208
______, Wineford Clk 324
______, Woodson Wil 291
Callaway, Daniel Up 114
______, David Irw 301
______, Elisha H. Hry 218
______, Henry Up 114
______, James M. Gre 278
______, Jesse M. Up 98
______, John Hry 238
______, Joshua Wal 159
______, Leroy Jsp 379
______, Levin Hry 233
______, Lewis B. Gre 275
______, William Hry 239
Calaway, Mary Mwr 169
______, William New 54
______, William T. Mwr 157
Calleway, Isaac Mad 112
Caliway, Jonathan Har 187
Caloway, John Bal 35
______, John Bal 36

Name	County	Page
Calway, Jas. A.	Mwr	157
CALVERT/CAVORT		
Calvert, John M.	Jsp	353
Cavart, Thomas G.	Doo	88
CALVRY, Thomas	Wal	144
CAMBY, Leroy	Wsh	271
CAMEL/CAMMEL		
Camel, Mr. (no name)	Put	191
______, Adam	Frk	242
______, Isaac	Frk	241
______, Margaret	Gwn	356
______, Robert	Frk	244
Cammel, Jesse	Hab	41
______, W.	Gwn	309
______, William Sr.	Ogl	101
______, William Jr.	Ogl	101
CAMERON/CAMRON/CAMBRON		
Cameron, Benjamin	Trp	35
______, David B.	Trp	46
______, Duncan	Tlf	7
______, James	Mor	256
______, John	Gwn	362
______, John	Pik	115
______, Malcome B.	Wal	134
______, Murdock	Up	97
______, Robert	Clk	313
______, Robert R.	Hry	209
______, Thomas	Trp	47
______, Thomas	Up	105
Camron, Allen	Tat	378
______, Allen	Tat	378
______, Duncan G.	Frk	243
______, George	New	42
______, Henry	New	39
______, Henry	Rab	231
______, James	Jsp	394
______, John	Jks	328
Cambron, Allen	DeK	60
______, Allen D.	Hry	243
CAMP, Abner	Wal	141
______, Abnor	Hal	118
______, Alsa	Gwn	357
______, Andrew	DeK	32
______, Arthur T.	Pik	122
______, Berryman S.	Jks	313
______, Burwell	Hry	216
______, Claiborn	Car	215
______, Edmund K.	Wal	134
______, George B.	Cpb	206
______, Harrison	Wal	167
______, Henry	New	45
______, Hiram	Wal	152
______, Hope H.	Wal	168

Name	County	Page
Camp, Hosea	Wal	127
______, Ira	Gwn	357
______, Ira	Wal	154
______, Jarrard	New	43
______, John	Hry	210
______, John	Car	215
______, Joseph	Wal	130
______, Joseph T.	Mus	280
______, Littleberry	Hry	237
______, Martin	Hal	118
______, Martin	Hab	39
______, Mary	Wsh	275
______, Merada	Wal	173
______, Osamas	Bak	17
______, Pyramus	Jks	346
______, Robert B.	Gwn	315
______, Samuel	Wrn	229
______, Shirrod	Fay	204
______, Starling	Bts	165
______, Thadeus	Wrn	228
______, Thomas	Wal	153
______, Westley	Cpb	197
______, Wilea	Gwn	358
______, William	Bak	17
______, William	Hry	215
______, William	Wal	138
CAMPBELL, Adison H.	Mor	239
______, Alexander	Lwn	81
______, Andrew	Gre	289
______, Ann	Cht	272
______, Archibald	Tlf	10
______, Archibold	Jef	401
______, Burrel	Jef	422
______, Catlett	Bts	163
______, Charles A.	Mon	206
______, Charter	Mor	250
______, Daniel	Frk	233
______, Daniel	Jns	429
______, Daniel	Tlf	10
______, Dugan	Rch	265
______, Duncan	Hal	75
______, Duncan	Wal	133
** ______, E. F. (slave)	Rch	269
______, Edward F.	Rch	287
______, Elias	DeK	28
______, Elisha	Doo	88
______, George	Mor	239
______, Griffeth	Har	187
______, Harriet	Cht	264
______, Henry S.	Hal	74
______, Isaac	Wyn	282
______, James	DeK	48
______, James	Gwn	311

Campbell, James Hry 222
_____, James Hry 249
_____, James Jns 468
_____, James Mor 270
_____, James A. Pik 119
_____, James H. Mor 238
_____, James P. H. Fay 181
_____, Jarriott Jsp 373
_____, Jehu Bib 58
_____, John App 6
_____, John Cam 192
_____, John Cpb 204
_____, John Lin 63
_____, John Mon 181
_____, John Mor 255
_____, John New 12
_____, John C. Cow 374
_____, John S. Rch 273
_____, Joseph Wil 293
_____, Levi Jef 407
_____, Mary Bib 54
_____, Murdock Hal 69
_____, Nicholas DeK 40
_____, Obediah Elb 138
_____, Peter Mor 255
_____, Ransom Bib 66
_____, Randle Mtg 235
_____, Robert Rch 267
_____, Robert Rab 229
_____, Samuel P. Hry 222
_____, Thomas Bib 54
_____, Thomas Mon 186
_____, Thomas Rch 262
_____, Thomas Clk 299
_____, Walter L. Hst 274
_____, William Jsp 390
_____, William Jns 456
_____, William Wyn 281
_____, William Scr 317
_____, William B. Elb 132
_____, William D. Elb 147
_____, William L. Fay 191
_____, William S. Cht 277
CAMPFIELD, Edward Rch 272
_____, Joseph Bts 169
_____, N. Cht 261
CANADA/CANEDA
Canada, James N. Hab 39
_____, William Hab 47
Caneda, Elizabeth New 34
CANADY/CANNADY/CANADAY/CANNIDAY
Canady, Allen Lau 11
Canady, Andrew Gre 273
_____, Caleb Cpb 208
_____, John Cpb 208
Cannady, Thomas DeK 37
Canaday, David Mar 138
_____, John Bry 86
_____, Thomas Bry 86
Canniday, John Dec 5
CANNANT/CANANT
Cannant, Jeremiah Har 182
_____, William L. Har 180
Canant, Burwell Tlb 328
CANAMORE/CANEMORE
Canamore, David Hab 52
Canemore, Obadih Gwn 341
CANDLER, Henry Mon 226
_____, Henry A. Bib 49
_____, William Jns 428
_____, William S. Har 184
CANDRY, John B. Cht 257
CANAFAX/CANIFAX/CANNIFAX
Canafax, Benjamin Trp 41
_____, Elijah Trp 41
Canifax, Benjamin Mus 281
Cannifax, John Har 191
CANNON/CANON/CANNAN/CANNEN
Cannon, Allen Wks 338
_____, Archibald Hst 282
_____, Dempsy Bul 101
_____, Elisha Hab 53
_____, Ellis Rab 231
_____, George P. Up 108
_____, Hiram Rab 224
_____, Isaac F. Rab 223
_____, Jackson Tlb 323
_____, James Jns 453
_____, James P. Lau 10
_____, James W. Hst 282
_____, John Hal 114
_____, John Mus 288
_____, John B. Hst 265
_____, Joshua Gre 280
_____, N. Wks 356
_____, Polly DeK 29
_____, Reddick Ware 183
_____, Samuel Jns 453
_____, Spires Jef 409
_____, Thomas Hst 282
_____, Wiley Wks 335
_____, Wiley Wks 338
_____, Wiley Wks 358
_____, William Wsh 242
_____, William J. McI 126

Name	County	Page
Canon, Basel	Hab	53
______, Richard	Hab	53
______, Simson	Clk	316
Cannan, Alen	Wks	337
Cannen, Henry	McI	128
CANTELOU, L. C.	Rch	258
CANTER, Richard D.	Wsh	274
CANUEL, William	Cht	241
CANOP/CANUP/KANUP		
Canop, Frederick	Car	222
Canup, Alsey	New	31
______, Fredrick	Hab	57
Kanup, Thomas	Hab	11
**CANTELOUS, Mrs. (slave)	Rch	253
CANTRELL/CANTREL		
Cantrell, James	Hal	71
______, Moses	Hab	52
Cantrel, Jesse	Car	216
______, John	Hab	43
CAPE, Brinkley	Elb	120
______, Hiram	Hal	96
______, Lewis	Mad	118
______, Merimon	Gwn	362
______, Thomas	Frk	219
CAPEHART/CAPEHEART		
Capehart, Jacob	Rab	231
Capeheart, John	Mor	249
CAPERS, Gabriel	Bib	54
CAPETER, John	Jns	460
CAPLE/KOPPELL		
Caple, Sterling	Jns	444
Koppell, M. J.	Cht	245
CAPPS/CAPS		
Capps, Cason R.	McI	124
______, Eda	Jns	431
______, Eli	Bts	163
______, James	Mar	140
______, John	Hry	200
______, John	Bts	174
______, Mariah	Gly	265
______, Randol	Jsp	353
______, Sampson	Rab	235
Caps, Jesse	Em	172
______, Robert B.	Hab	65
CARA, Ann	Cht	240
CAREKER/CARACTER/CHARACTER		
Careker, Jacob	Lau	5
Caracter, Moses	Up	113
Character, Daniel	Cow	377
CARAWAY/CARRIWAY		
Caraway, Ezekiel	Mon	206
______, John	Up	95
______, Robert	Up	95

Name	County	Page
Caraway, William	Mus	277
______, William	Up	108
Carriway, Thomas	Ran	246
CARD, Abraham	Jns	433
______, Benson	Frk	245
______, Richard	Jns	428
______, William	Jns	428
CARDEN/CARDIN		
Carden, Benjamin D.	Pik	127
______, Cohn	Pik	129
______, Charles	Elb	129
______, Charles	Twg	65
______, David	Jsp	360
______, James	Hry	250
______, James	Jsp	364
______, Jesse	Fay	191
______, William	Tlb	344
Cardin, Freemon D.	Ran	245
______, Lucy	New	8
______, Thomas M.	Ran	246
CARDWELL/CARDELL/CADWELL		
Cardwell, John	Trp	50
______, John W.	Ogl	97
______, Thomas	Car	224
Cardell, Peter	Jsp	363
Cadwell, James	Lau	17
CAREY/CARY/CARRIE/CARIE		
Carey, Edwd.	Bal	40
______, James	Frk	248
______, James P.	Rch	265
______, Rebecka	Up	113
Cary, George	Col	344
______, James	Wrn	200
Carrie, John	Rch	276
**______, John (slave)	Rch	276
______, Joseph	Rch	273
Carie, D.	Rch	274
CARGILE/CARGIL/CARGILL/ COGIL/CARGEL/CARGOL		
Cargile, Charles	Jsp	371
______, John	Mwr	164
______, John R.	Bts	163
Cargil, John	Pik	109
______, Thomas	Pik	120
______, William	Pik	111
Cargill, Tunison	DeK	33
Cogil, George H	Rch	290
Cargel, Charles	Cpb	210
Cargol, James	Crf	399
CARLETON, Stephen	Elb	133
CARLEW, Elias B.	Gre	278
CARLISLE/CARLILE/CAROLISLE		
Carlisle, Edward	Doo	89

Name	County	Page
Carlisle, Eli	Doo	89
______, Elizabeth (w)	Mor	258
______, Hosia	Jks	317
______, James W.	Trp	40
______, James	Jks	316
______, John	Jks	316
______, Robert	Han	150
______, Thomas C.	Up	105
______, William	Tlf	6
______, William	Lwn	79
______, Willis	Gre	275
______, William W.	Trp	43
______, Robert	Hal	83
Carlile, M.	Crf	403
______, Mathew	Wsh	258
______, W.	Jks	316
______, William	Crf	404
Carolisle, Robert W.	Wal	139
CARLSON, Cartis	Crf	411
CARLTON, Alderman	Tms	27
______, Archibald	Gre	280
______, Archibald	Trp	35
______, Benjamin	Cow	381
______, Blake	Cow	382
______, Elizabeth	Crf	412
______, Elizabeth	Ogl	68
______, George	Ogl	89
______, Isaac B.	Lwn	89
______, Isaac	Tms	27
______, James	Cow	372
______, James	Gre	291
______, James Jr.	Gre	273
______, John	Tms	28
______, John W.	Gre	284
______, Mildred	Wil	304
______, Samuel	Scr	315
______, Shedrack	Tms	27
______, Stephen	Tms	25
______, Thomas	Tms	28
______, William	Tms	22
CARMACK/CAMAK		
Carmack, William	Tlb	344
Camak, James	Bal	29
CARMICHAEL/CHARMICHAEL/ CARMICAL		
Carmichael, James M.	Bts	170
______, John	New	18
______, John	Tlf	8
** ______, John (slave)	Rch	271
______, John	Rch	276
______, Joseph	Bts	172
______, William	Clk	306
______, William	Cow	371
Charmichael, James	Wal	141
______, Margy P.	Jks	334
______, William	Wal	159
Carmical, Richard	Ogl	94
CARNES/CARNS		
Carnes, David	Car	222
______, Edwoord	Hab	33
______, Hubbard	Rab	234
______, John	Car	223
______, Joseph	Car	220
______, Lydia	Car	230
______, Peter	Car	230
______, Peter	Jks	349
______, Richard	Frk	235
______, Robert W.	Han	149
______, Ruth	Rab	235
______, W. W.	Bal	33
Carns, Lucy	Rch	275
______, Patrick H.	Rch	285
______, Sarah	Rch	254
______, Thos.	Hab	44
CARNEY, Elis	Cht	256
CAROLINE, Daniel	Rch	255
CARPENTER, Absalom	Elb	129
______, Archabald	Hal	126
______, Bailey Sr.	Bke	132
______, Bailey Jr.	Bke	133
______, George	DeK	31
______, Jacob	Wal	161
______, James	DeK	63
______, James	Elb	146
______, John	Frk	250
______, John	Bke	150
______, John	Put	179
______, Joshua	Frk	245
______, Joshua S.	Elb	127
______, Josiah	Tat	376
______, Thomas	Hry	206
CARPER, Phillip	Hab	29
CARR, Ann	Hst	288
______, Aron	Wks	344
______, Bayless	Wks	343
______, Benjamin	DeK	58
______, Catharine (w)	Mor	238
______, David	Frk	235
______, Gibson D.	Gwn	334
______, Henry	Gre	304
______, Isaac	Hal	117
______, Jesse	Han	149
______, John	Gwn	318
______, John	Elb	132
______, John	Wrn	208
______, John P.	DeK	58

Name	County	Page
Carr, Joseph	Jns	445
______, Kinchen	Hab	27
______, Nancy	Gre	289
______, Peter	Wrn	208
______, Radford M.	Gwn	334
______, Radford M	Gwn	363
______, Robert	Jks	326
______, Samuel	Elb	126
______, Samuel	Hst	272
______, Samuel	Put	204
______, Thomas D.	Col.	353
______, Wiley M.	Gwn	333
______, William	Wal	123
______, William	Wks	343
______, William A.	Clk	319
______, William S.	Gwn	350
CARRINGTON/CARAGAN		
Carrington, Daniel	Wil	306
______, Henson	Mad	109
______, John	Cow	378
______, M. (Guardian for estate of J. Powell	Cow	368
______, Nancy	Han	150
______, Ozbon	Mad	113
______, William	Ogl	76
Caragan, William F.	Ear	95
CARROLL/CARROL/CARREL/ CARRELL		
Carroll, Abnor	Wal	169
______, David	Hry	214
______, David	Ear	96
______, Ellen	Cht	272
______, Ellis	New	20
______, Geo.	Gwn	356
______, Geo	Gwn	357
______, Hartwell H.	Gre	276
______, James	Col	349
______, James B.	Hry	227
______, Jesse	New	16
______, Jesse W.	New	19
______, John	Jsp	362
______, John	Wrn	221
______, Rigdon	Crf	398
______, Rowan	Hry	250
______, Sterling	New	20
______, Thomas	Jsp	355
______, Thomas	Fay	190
______, William	Col	348
______, William	Wrn	208
Carrol, Benjamine	Cpb	195
______, Britton	Wrn	225
______, Daniel	Mon	178
______, Elisha	Hab	8
______, Elisha	Wks	341

Name	County	Page
Carrol, Gideon S.	McI	128
______, James	Hab	34
______, James W.	Wrn	201
______, Jno.	Gwn	338
______, John	Hab	64
______, John	Hal	88
______, Leonard	Pik	117
______, Lucy	DeK	34
______, Mary	Wil	324
______, Patrick	Jef	402
______, Robert E.	Wrn	208
______, Sally	Hal	88
______, Thomas	Gwn	338
______, Thos.	Hab	34
______, William	Hab	64
______, William	Pik	112
Carrel, Clemond	Frk	226
______, Edward	Frk	225
______, Sarah	Gwn	326
Carrell, John	Frk	225
______, Thomas	Twg	70
CARRUTH/CARUTH		
Carruth, Adam	Mad	106
______, Alford	Mad	105
______, Iredell	Mad	109
Caruth, Leroy	Hal	120
______, Robert	DeK	65
CARRUTHERS/CARUTHERS		
Carruthers, James	Mad	103
______, James L.	Pul	144
______, James S.	Pul	146
______, Samuel	Gwn	345
______, Thomas	Gwn	345
______, William C.	Mad	100
Caruthers, James	Bke	119
______, Jane	Jns	445
______, John	Hst	284
______, Nancy	Bke	119
______, Samuel	Bke	120
______, Temperance	Ogl	76
CARSON, Adam	Jns	444
______, Adam	Mon	181
______, Andrew	Bke	120
______, David	Frk	230
______, James	Frk	244
______, James W.	Fay	186
______, John	Tlb	346
______, John E.	Frk	213
______, John	Rab	232
______, John	Wal	127
______, Joseph P.	Trp	40
______, Lydia	Cht	261
______, Robert	Jns	472
______, Robert H.	Bke	153

Carson, Sarah Cow 382
_____, William Hal 105
CARSTARPHIN/CARSTAPHER
Carstarphin, James Put 212
_____, Joseph J. Put 178
_____, Oran D. Put 212
Carstapher, Thomas Crf 413
CARTER/CARDER/CARTOR/
CARTIER
Carter, Abner Up 114
_____, Abraham Put 203
_____, Anthony Hst 277
_____, Austin Frk 243
_____, Benjamin D. Wil 290
_____, Benona Clk 312
_____, Cader Pik 110
_____, Charles Ogl 74
_____, Charles Cow 371
_____, Charles C. Bib 72
**_____, Charles (slave) Rch 260
_____, Christopher A. New 20
_____, Cyrus B. Cht 243
_____, Daniel Hry 215
_____, David Wsh 259
_____, David Sr. Frk 245
_____, David Jr. Frk 245
_____, Edward Ogl 74
_____, Edward Rab 233
_____, Elisha Clk 317
_____, Elizabeth DeK 67
_____, Elmore Em 171
_____, Ezekiel Em 168
_____, Farish Bal 41
_____, Frances DeK 58
_____, Frederick Lau 14
_____, George Elb 140
_____, George Lwn 85
_____, George McI 131
_____, George Put 175
_____, George W. Mon 225
_____, Geo. W. Mus 292
_____, Hartwell Cpb 209
_____, Henry Bib 50
_____, Henry Jns 464
_____, Henry Wrn 210
_____, Hiram Pul 146
_____, Isaac App 5
_____, Isaac App 13
_____, Isaac Bts 175
_____, Isaac Hst 262
_____, Isaac Lwn 85
_____, J. E. App 8
_____, Jacob App 6
Carter, Jacob Bib 60
_____, Jacob Jef 405
_____, James App 11
_____, James Bib 59
_____, James Bts 159
_____, James Elb 121
_____, James Gwn 347
_____, James Hal 129
_____, James Put 191
_____, James Wil 318
_____, James Jr. Wrn 209
_____, James Jr. Wrn 210
_____, James H. Up 98
_____, James M. Rch 277
_____, Jarrerd Han 150
_____, Jesse Ogl 74
_____, Jesse Rab 233
_____, Jesse Tlb 329
_____, Jesse Sr. Lwn 85
_____, Jesse Jr. Lwn 87
_____, Joel Crf 409
_____, John Cow 373
_____, John Crf 409
_____, John DeK 45
_____, John Hab 12
_____, John Jns 464
_____, John Lee 28
_____, John Lwn 85
_____, John Mtg 236
_____, John Ogl 68
_____, John Put 184
_____, John Wal 126
_____, John A. Mon 214
_____, John C. Hab 27
_____, John J. Bib 63
_____, John L. Ogl 84
_____, John T. Fay 204
_____, John T. Mwr 159
_____, John T. Wil 322
_____, John W. Elb 136
_____, Jonathan Bts 173
_____, Joseph Gre 286
_____, Joseph Jr. Gre 296
_____, Joseph Mon 202
_____, Joseph A. Wil 309
_____, Josiah Rab 232
_____, Josiah H. Bib 60
_____, Josiah H. Rab 226
_____, Lewis Elb 127
_____, Levy H. Clk 301
_____, Magnus Ogl 68
_____, Martin Cow 373
_____, Mary Cht 240

Name	County	Page
Carter, Micajah	Frk	245
______, Michial	Dec	4
______, Moore	Mon	220
______, Moses	Cht	280
______, Mumford	Ogl	75
______, Nathan	Bib	59
______, Nathan	Gwn	347
______, Nelson	Rch	277
______, Obadiah	Jks	333
______, Paul	Ogl	77
______, Presley	Hal	99
______, Rich^{d}.	Jsp	356
______, Robt.	Gwn	342
______, Robert	Hab	15
______, Robert	Hst	266
______, Robert	Lau	19
______, Robt. D.	Jks	349
______, Samuel	Har	185
______, Samuel	Hst	294
______, Samuel	Lwn	85
______, Silas	Em	168
______, Silas	Wsh	244
______, Sivility	Fay	205
______, Solomon	App	9
______, Starling	Ogl	62
______, Sterling	Wil	295
______, Thomas	Em	168
______, Thomas	Fay	207
______, Thomas	Frk	252
______, Thomas	Hal	99
______, Thomas	Hry	237
______, Thomas	Ogl	68
______, Thomas	Ogl	74
______, Thomas	Pik	129
______, Thomas	Put	199
______, Thomas A.	Wil	288
______, Thomas S.	Elb	142
______, Thomas	Gwn	310
______, Tilman	Hab	23
______, Wiley	Ogl	75
______, Wilie	Wrn	214
______, William	App	6
______, William	Wsh	269
______, William	Wsh	275
______, William B.	Twg	84
______, William	Gwn	85
______, William	Ogl	68
______, William	Pik	109
______, William H.	Rch	284
______, William P.	Wil	305
______, Willis	Mtg	234
______, Wilson	Hab	10
______, Winefred	Wil	309

Name	County	Page
Carder, Iverson	Hab	10
______, Thomas	Hab	27
Cartor, Secratory	Wal	141
Cartier, Peter	Cht	243
CARSWELL, Alexander	Bke	137
______, Alexander	Tlf	11
______, Allexander	Twg	68
______, Beniah S.	Jef	412
______, Edward	Rch	290
______, James A.	Jef	419
______, James B.	Har	190
______, Matthew	Bke	137
______, Samuel M.	Wks	342
______, Sarah	Wks	341
______, William E.	Wks	341
CART, Sarah G.	Rch	268
CARTAN, Dorothy	Jsp	385
CARTLEDGE/CARTLAGE		
Cartledge, Benjamin	Col	341
______, Edmond	Col	341
______, James	Col	343
______, James	Dec	5
______, James Sr.	Col	341
______, Jeremiah	Col	341
______, John	Col	340
______, John	Rch	289
______, Samuel	Jks	318
______, Thomas	Col	341
Cartlage, John	Lin	60
CARTWRIGHT/CARTRIGHT		
Cartwright, James	Gre	272
______, Jonas	Gre	272
______, Martha	Gre	300
______, Milus	Gre	295
______, Samuel	Gre	294
Cartright, Polly	Twg	80
______, Wilson	Car	223
CARVER, Jessee	Ware	189
______, John	Hab	38
______, Sampson	Ware	186
______, Sampson B.	Ware	184
______, Thomas	Hal	74
______, Thomas	Rab	228
______, William	Rab	227
______, William	Ware	184
CASE, Daniel	Mar	144
CASEY/CASSEY/CAISEY/ CASSEY/CASY		
Casey, Absalom	Jns	447
______, Henry	New	37
______, Hiram	Wal	151
______, Jane	Cam	188
______, Joel	Hal	100

Name	County	Page
Casey, John	Hal	100
______, John	Mtg	236
______, Ozburn J.	Wal	168
______, Vincent R.	Wrn	228
______, William	Em	177
______, William	New	22
Cassey, Phillip	Ran	248
Caisey, Robert	DeK	64
______, Uriah	DeK	63
Cassey, John	Ran	248
Casy, Elisha	Wal	168
CASH, Briant	DeK	52
______, Coward	Elb	126
______, Daniel	Col	341
______, David	Lib	44
______, Dawson	Col	360
______, Henry	DeK	64
______, Henry C.	Frk	240
______, Howard	Hab	13
______, Howard	DeK	64
______, James	Frk	234
______, James	DeK	64
______, James	Cpb	201
______, James	Jks	326
______, Jesse	Elb	126
______, Joel F.	Mwr	153
______, John	Jks	345
______, Moses	Elb	123
______, Nealy C.	Hab	32
______, Nelson	Hab	13
______, Patrick	Jks	320
______, Patrick	Rch	278
______, Peter	DeK	64
______, Ruben	Hab	13
______, Silas W.	Jks	327
______, Stephen	Elb	126
______, Stephen P.	Hal	80
______, William	DeK	64
______, William (colored)	Cpb	196
CASHIN/CASHON		
Cashin, Catherine M.	Rch	275
______, William	Wal	158
Cashon, Elzay	Up	99
CASON/CASONS/CASEN/		
CASSANS/CASASON		
Cason, Benj.	Wal	172
______, Connor	Lwn	79
______, Dennis	Wsh	260
______, Edward	Elb	145
______, Eli	Ware	189
______, Frederic	Ware	187
______, Henry	Wsh	247
______, Jas.	Wrn	220
Cason, Jesse	Crf	399
______, John	Elb	145
______, Joseph	Fay	189
______, Lewis	Hry	237
______, Mathew	Wrn	224
______, Michael S.	Mon	172
______, Seth	Crf	401
______, Silas	Lwn	81
______, Triplet	Wal	166
______, Whitehouse	Pul	162
______, William	Wsh	247
______, William	Wrn	224
______, Willis Sr.	Pul	162
______, Willis Jr.	Pul	162
______, Willis	Ware	187
______, Willoughby	Ware	187
______, Wyeiat	Jef	401
Casons, Jas.	Rab	229
Casen, Abner	Hab	25
Cassans, Green	Up	102
Casason, Abraham	Jks	331
CASPER, George H.	Car	214
______, Joel H.	Car	222
______, William	Car	222
CASSADA/CASSIDY		
Cassada, Sella	Hab	20
______, William	Har	176
Cassidy, Hugh	Cht	254
CASTLEBERRY/CASTLEBERY/		
CASSELBERRY/CASTLEBERREY/		
CASTLEBURY/CASTLERRY		
Castleberry, Allen	Jsp	390
______, Asa	Ear	98
______, David	Gwn	319
______, Edward	Jsp	387
______, Elizabeth	Han	150
______, Henry	Lwn	89
______, James	Mar	140
______, Jehu	Hst	279
______, Jerimiah	Put	181
______, John	Bts	171
______, Labun	Hst	276
______, Mark Jr.	Hal	110
______, Odum	Hal	112
______, Peter	Crf	401
______, Thomas	Hst	276
______, Thos.	Jsp	396
______, Warren T.	Tlb	323
______, William	Hst	276
______, Zachariah	Car	229
Castlebery, David	Hal	109
______, Mark	Hal	109
______, Robert	Hst	274

Castlebery, Timothy Wrn 216
_____, William Wal 149
_____, Williams Hal 110
Casselberry, James DeK 48
_____, Lucinda DeK 44
_____, Samuel DeK 65
Castleberrey, William Wal 168
Castlebury, William Wrn 219
Castlerry, Ezra Wrn 227
CASSLEY, Oliver Wal 172
CAST, William Gwn 375
CASTELOW/CASTELLOW/
CASTLELOW
Castelow, Surhen Dec 15
_____, Thomas New 40
Castellow, H. Cht 267
Castlelow, Amy Jsp 359
CASTER, James W. Fay 183
CASTIN, Robert J. Bib 54
CASTLES/CASSELS/CASELS
Castles, Henry Fay 204
_____, William H. Dec 3
Cassels, Samuel J. Rch 283
Casels, Absalom Mor 256
CASWELL, Isham Mus 284
_____, Mathew Put 211
_____, William Dec 14
CATCHINGS, Frances Jns 473
_____, Joseph Hry 224
_____, Joseph Gre 297
_____, Martha Gre 297
_____, Phillip Jns 473
CATER, Benj. F. Gly 266
_____, H. W. Rch 266
_____, Thomas Frk 233
CATES, Charles Mus 288
_____, Charles Jr. Gwn 353
_____, James Bke 120
_____, John Gwn 371
_____, John Bke 153
_____, John Gwn 362
_____, John Gwn 351
_____, Joseph Bke 122
_____, Richard Jsp 394
_____, Robert Gwn 334
_____, Thomas Bke 153
_____, William Mwr 166
_____, William Hry 213
CATHERS, Robert Ogl 76
CATLETT/CATLET
Catlett, Alsey Mad 110
_____, John Frk 223
_____, Labun Frk 256
Catlett, William Frk 256
Catlet, Clark Hab 24
CATHY, James H. Jsp 369
CATLIN, Samuel Wal 138
_____, Willis Rch 268
CATO/KAPTO
Cato, Ailey Wsh 273
_____, Butt C. Gre 276
_____, George Wks 348
_____, Green Han 149
_____, James W. Han 150
_____, James Wsh 254
_____, William Crf 403
_____, William Tlf 2
_____, William Tms 28
_____, William Wil 321
_____, William P. Tms 28
Kapto, Charles Tfo 363
CATON/CATTON
Caton, John D. Ran 242
_____, Williba Hab 28
Catton, James R. Clk 326
_____, William Ran 246
CATONET, P. Cht 262
CAUDEL/CAUDLE/CAUDAL
Caudel, Benj. Hab 31
_____, Benj. Hab 59
_____, Jese Hab 57
_____, Stephen Hab 59
_____, Stephen Sr. Hab 59
Caudle, Benjamin Frk 250
_____, Elijah Trp 40
_____, Elizabeth Frk 256
_____, John Frk 251
_____, Joseph Twg 62
Caudal, David Hab 59
CAULDEN, Martin Mus 282
CAULDER, Alexander H. McI 121
_____, Henrietta McI 130
_____, James McI 128
_____, John McI 128
_____, John M. McI 128
CAUSEY, Absolom Wyn 281
_____, Allen Jef 411
_____, Elizabeth Jef 411
_____, Israel Jef 413
_____, Lemon Crf 407
_____, Lothey Wyn 283
_____, William Trp 50
CAVANNAH/CAVENAH/CALVENOR
Cavannah, Thomas Cht 255
Cavenah, Charles Bke 132
Calvenor, William Em 171

Name	County	Page
CAVEN/CAVIN		
Caven, Alexander	Hal	70
Cavin, Forgus	Jks	332
CAVENDER, Clemeth	Hal	121
_____, George	Jsp	389
_____, Griffin D.	Jsp	389
_____, James B.	New	20
_____, Joseph	Fay	186
_____, William	Hab	9
CAVER, David	Rch	273
_____, Jacob	Lin	68
_____, Jacob F.	Lin	67
CAWLEY, Amos	Rch	284
_____, Chaney	Mon	217
_____, Jacky Montainvell	DeK	59
_____, James	Bke	138
_____, Samuel	DeK	67
_____, Tubal C.	DeK	46
CAWTHORN: see Cothern		
CEARS: see Sears		
CECIL, James B.	Mon	173
CECITY, Mary	Lau	24
CECOPELY, John C.	Cht	241
CELLARS, John	App	8
_____, Samuel	App	9
_____, Solomon	App	8
_____ (also see Sellers)		
CELMON: see Selman		
CEMORE: see Seamore		
CENTAL/CENTIL/CENTRAL		
Cental, Samuel	Cpb	196
_____, William	Cpb	196
Centil, Britam	DeK	29
Central, Nathan	New	54
CENTER/CENTERS/CENTRE		
Center, Abner	Hab	50
_____, John	DeK	32
_____, John	Mon	197
_____, Nathaniel	DeK	57
_____, William	DeK	56
Centers, Stephen	Hab	51
Centre, Coy	Hab	57
CENTREFIT, John	Hst	264
CERBORO/CERBOW/CURBOW/ CARBOW		
Cerboro, John	Bib	69
Cerbow, Robert	Bib	75
Curbow, Henry	Cpb	198
_____, Zekiel	Cpb	201
Carbow, Daniel	Gwn	348
CESSIONS: see Sessions		
CESSNA, Robert	Mor	239
_____, Samuel	Mor	239
CESSOMS: see Sessions		
CHABONIER (no 1st name)	Rch	276
CHACEN, Reuben	Dec	9
CHADBOURN, Jacob	Cht	257
CHAFFIN/CHAFIN		
Chaffin, Amos	Hab	31
_____, Amos	Hab	50
_____, Elijah	Hab	40
_____, Jno.	Jsp	380
_____, Lemuel	Mor	268
_____, Mary	Wil	315
_____, Moses	Jsp	383
_____, Thomas	Tfo	357
Chafin, Joel	New	53
_____, John	New	27
_____, Robert	Wal	137
_____, Terry	New	53
CHAGHUNE, Mrs. Martha	Col	336
_____ also see Cleghorn		
CHAIN, Isaiah	Hst	261
_____, Levin F.	Hst	262
_____, Sarah	Jns	450
CHALKER, Hodges	Wrn	226
_____, Nath[1].	Wrn	222
_____, Samuel	Col	350
CHALMERS, Andrew	Hal	98
_____, James	Hal	97
_____, John	Frk	219
_____, John	Hal	98
CHAMBERLAIN/CHAMBERLIN/ CHAMBLAIN/CHAMBLIN/ CHAMBLEE/CHAMBLY		
Chamberlin, Washington	Gwn	318
_____, Thomas C.	Lin	67
_____, William	Up	98
Chamberlin, Remembranc	Mor	243
Chamblain, Thomas	Hal	74
_____, William	Hal	100
Chamblin, Asa	Dec	17
Chamblee, Martin	Hal	85
Chambly, William H.	Frk	221
CHAMBERS, Alexander	Fay	205
_____, Andrew D.	Jns	468
_____, Henry	Wks	337
_____, James	Mon	205
_____, James M.	Put	184
_____, John	Fay	203
_____, John	Hst	272
_____, Joseph	Jns	432
_____, Joseph S.	Fay	203
_____, Nathan	Wil	297
_____, Robert	Fay	199
_____, Samuel	Fay	200

Name	County	Page
Chambers, Simon P.	Wsh	262
______, T. J.	Gwn	308
______, William	Ear	99
______, William	Fay	193
______, William	Wks	349
______, William	Hab	15
______, William J.	Hry	206
CHAMBLESS/CHAMBLISS/ CHAMBLES/CHAMNESS/CHAMBRIS		
Chambless, Christopher	Bib	59
______, Dicy	Wrn	232
______, Henry	Bib	60
______, James	Jns	460
______, Jeptha	Bib	69
______, John D.	Tlb	323
______, Samuel	Bib	69
______, William	Jns	460
______, William	Trp	32
Chambliss, Abram	Ear	92
______, John	Ear	92
Chambles, Jesse	Jns	435
Chamness, John	Mon	174
______, Zachariah	Mon	180
Chambris, Hardin	Han	150
CHAMPION/CHAMPAIN		
Champion, A.	Cht	255
______, Abel	Mon	214
______, Abner	Fay	197
______, Eli	Han	148
______, Elias F.	Lau	9
______, F.	Cht	272
______, Hannah	Mon	214
______, Henry	Bib	63
______, Henry	Bib	69
______, Henry	Crf	406
______, Henry	Jns	456
______, Israel	Crf	415
______, Jeremiah	Hst	272
______, Jesse	Gre	282
______, John	Wrn	225
______, John	Jns	456
______, Martin	Tlb	343
______, Micajah	Lau	7
______, Moses	Jsp	369
______, William G.	Jns	443
______, Willis	Lee	27
Champain, Henry	New	21
CHAMPS, Rachel	Rch	254
CHANCE, Cannon	Hry	233
______, Edna	Twg	83
______, Henry S.	Crf	394
______, Isaac	Hst	280
______, Henry	Bke	129
Chance, James	Bak	20
______, James	Bke	152
______, John	Bke	126
______, Nancy	Doo	84
______, Reuben	Bke	152
______, Simpson	Hst	280
CHANCEY/CHANCY/CHANCELY		
Chancey, Amos	Hst	287
______, C.	App	9
______, Elizabeth	Lwn	87
______, Hugh	Lwn	85
______, John	Hst	283
______, Nathan	Hst	287
______, Samuel	App	10
______, Solomon	Pik	108
Chancy, John	Clk	294
Chancely, William	Mon	206
CHANDLER/CHAMBLER		
Chandler, Abram	DeK	25
______, Allen	Wal	151
______, Ambrose	Frk	235
______, Bailey	Jks	324
______, Bailey	New	12
______, Daniel	Frk	226
______, Daniel	Frk	250
______, Daniel	Wil	289
______, David	Mus	282
______, Frances	Wks	352
______, George	Bke	141
______, Green	Frk	240
______, Henry	Jns	468
______, Henry F.	Frk	210
______, Hezechia	Hab	26
______, Hy	Gwn	325
______, Isaac	Jks	325
______, James	Frk	220
______, James R.	Mad	111
______, Joel	Hry	229
______, Joel	New	12
______, John	Cht	249
______, John Sr.	Gwn	336
______, John Jr.	Gwn	336
______, John Sr.	Gwn	369
______, John Jr.	Gwn	369
______, John C.	Gwn	336
______, John C.	Gwn	369
______, John F.	Frk	211
______, Joseph	Frk	232
______, Joseph	Tlb	346
______, Lewis	Frk	240
______, Lusendy	Col	353
______, Mordecai	Elb	148
______, Parks	Frk	210

Name	County	Page
Chandler, Parks	Jks	330
______, Richard	Wal	174
______, Richard	Frk	227
______, Robert	Gwn	340
______, Robert	Frk	229
______, Robert J.	Car	219
______, Soloman	Jks	325
______, Stephen	DeK	32
______, Sterling	Mad	117
______, Tebetha	Jks	348
______, Thomas	Car	215
______, William	Dec	4
______, William	Frk	226
______, William	Frk	235
______, William C.	Mwr	167
______, William J.	Gwn	340
______, Wyatt	Gwn	319
______, Zachariah	Frk	212
Chambler, William	Hal	85
CHANEY/CHENEY/CHAINEY/ CHANAY		
Chaney, Aquilla	Mon	198
______, James	Mtg	234
______, Jerh.	Ware	186
______, John	Hal	118
______, John	Ware	187
______, Peter	Jks	339
Cheney, John	Tfo	367
______, John	Wil	314
______, John	Wil	315
Chainey, Thomas B.	Mor	258
______, William M.	Mor	258
Chanay, Edmund	Hst	264
CHANNELL/CHANNELL/CHANEL		
Channel, Harman	DeK	73
______, Henry C.	DeK	39
______, Isham	Gre	302
______, John	Gre	290
______, Micael	Han	150
______, William	Gre	277
Channell, Thomas	Gre	304
Chanel, Hannah	Put	184
CHAPMAN/CHIPMAN		
Chapman, Abner	Jsp	361
______, Abner	Jsp	370
______, Abner	Mwr	166
______, Abner	Pik	119
______, Allen	Put	180
______, Ambrose	Cow	386
______, Ambrose	Mon	225
______, Anderson	Mor	258
______, Amos H.	Hal	76
______, Benj.	DeK	46
Chapman, Benjamin	Mon	197
______, David	Elb	137
______, Deberry L.	Up	101
______, Elijah	Pik	120
______, Elijah M.	Hry	221
______, Elizabeth	Bts	170
______, Enoch	Hal	118
______, Ezereal	Gwn	370
______, Francis J.	Lib	44
______, Giles M.	Jns	456
______, Hannah	Bib	49
______, Henry	Mwr	166
______, Hinson	Hal	125
______, Isaac	Hal	125
______, Isaih	Bal	32
______, J. H.	Jks	325
______, James	Pik	122
______, Jessee	Hst	287
______, John	Mar	138
______, John	Tfo	357
______, John P.	Bib	54
______, Joseph	Hal	124
______, Margaret	Cht	280
______, Mary	Bib	54
______, Moses	Pik	117
______, Nathan	Tfo	355
______, Randle	Gre	277
______, Robert	Bts	174
______, Robert A.	Wrn	200
______, Samuel	Hal	130
______, Samuel	Jns	456
______, Sanford	Jns	468
______, Sintha	Wrn	201
______, Solomon	Har	178
______, Solomon	Jns	440
______, Solomon D.	Bib	58
______, Turner	Jns	441
______, William	Har	192
______, William	Jsp	382
______, William	Wks	343
______, William W.	Fay	202
Chipman, Joseph	Mon	175
CHAPPELL/CHAPPEL/CHAPELL		
Chappell, Abraham	Cpb	197
______, Easterlin	Gwn	339
______, Edward T.	New	10
______, Henry	Mwr	163
______, James G.	Har	175
______, Jefferson	New	10
______, John	Wal	169
______, Joseph J.	Twg	70
______, Js. N.	Cam	183
______, Nancy	Wal	140

Chappell, Obadiah Wal 152
_____, Samuel Wal 167
_____, Thomas Twg 73
_____, Thomas S. Twg 62
_____, Wilks E. Wal 138
_____, William Wal 134
_____, Wyley Jns 437
Chappel, Abram H. Mon 200
_____, George Cpb 204
_____, Jesse F. Pik 126
_____, John H. Tlb 330
_____, Thomas Fay 206
_____, Thomas Mon 191
_____, William Mon 201
_____, Willson Cpb 196
Chapell, Allen Up 116
_____, Isaac New 6
CHAPPELEAR/CHAPPELLAR
Chappelear, Henry Frk 250
_____, Richard F. Frk 237
Chappellar, Thomas J. Frk 214
CHARLES, James G. Hab 26
_____, Melchisidich Hab 54
CHARLOTTE, Adams Jsp 361
CHARLTON, Arthur M. Wil 308
_____, John Eff 105
_____, John Eff 116
_____, R. M. Cht 268
_____, T. U. P. Cht 264
CHARRY, Samuel Dec 3
CHASE, Zach[r]. Jns 473
CHASON, John Dec 13
_____, Mrs. Bal 41
CHASTAIN/CHASTEEN/CHASTINE/
CHASTION/CHASTAN
Chastain, Abner H. Hal 94
_____, Edney Bak 19
_____, Edward Hab 32
_____, John Hab 19
_____, John Hab 20
_____, John Hal 116
_____, John B. Hab 19
_____, Joseph Hab 10
_____, Jonathan D. Hab 27
_____, Rainey Hab 27
_____, William Hal 103
Chasteen, Edward Rab 230
_____, Elijah Rab 225
_____, Hannah Rab 225
_____, Jolingh Rab 232
Chastine, John Tms 21
Chastion, Abner Hab 41
Chastan, Abraham Hal 72
CHATFIELD, Geo Mus 278
_____, John Bib 69
CHATHAM, Chafan Frk 228
_____, George N. Har 175
_____, Josiah Bts 171
_____, Obediah P. Bts 174
_____, William Frk 235
CHAVIS/CHAVERS/CHAVOS
Chavis, Mary Rch 278
Chavers, Moses Cht 280
_____, William Cht 280
Chavos, John Lee 29
CHEELY/CHEALEY
Cheely, John Han 150
_____, Lewis L. Han 149
_____, Thomas Han 150
Chealey, Mary Jks 349
CHEATHAM, Ann Clk 305
_____, Anthony R. Clk 318
_____, Arthur R. Jef 413
_____, Charles Clk 311
_____, Isham Ogl 69
_____, Nancy DeK 37
_____, Thomas H. Jks 314
CHEAVES/CHIEVES
Cheaves, Thomas Cpb 206
Chieves, Grief Mor 243
_____, James Wal 138
_____, Sarah Put 188
CHEEK, Austin M. Cow 392
_____, Burgess Frk 241
_____, Ellis Frk 236
_____, Isaiah Frk 235
_____, James Frk 236
_____, James Mad 111
_____, James B. Wal 144
_____, John Frk 236
_____, John Sr. Mad 114
_____, Robert Wal 148
_____, Rolon Wal 158
_____, Silas Cow 378
_____, William Elb 131
_____, William Frk 244
_____, William Jsp 362
_____, Willis Frk 236
CHENAULT, Abram Lin 65
CHENKINS/CHINKINS:
see Jenkins
CHERLY, Aaron Hab 30
CHERRY, Abner Bib 63
_____, David C. Hab 21
_____, Frederick Hst 280
_____, Howell Mon 181

Name	County	Page
Cherry, Jesse	Jsp	354
_____, Job G.	Bib	63
_____, John V.	Ran	244
_____, Smith R.	Ran	241
_____, William	Wsh	249
_____, William T.	Mon	185
CHESHER/CHESSER/CHESHIRE/ CHESER		
Chesher, John	Mon	214
_____, John	Tat	375
_____, Thos. S.	Tat	378
_____, Turban	Mon	225
Chesser, Thomas	Lib	44
_____, W. W.	Gwn	318
_____, Willis C.	Wal	159
Cheshire, Philip	Crf	398
_____, Richard	Bib	60
Cheser, Ester	Clk	293
CHESNUT/CHESNUTT		
Chesnut, Charles	Tms	30
_____, James	Hst	293
_____, Jesse	Tms	25
_____, Nedum	Bak	19
_____, Needham	Hst	293
_____, William	Hst	289
_____, William R.	New	47
Chesnutt, Alexander	Cow	376
_____, David	New	36
_____, Joseph	Cpb	206
_____, Polly	DeK	34
CHESTER, A.	Wsh	239
_____, Abel	Dec	6
_____, Abner	Dec	7
_____, E. W.	Gwn	351
CHESTINE, John	Wal	167
CHEVERS/CHEVIRS/CHIVERS		
Chevers, Larkin	Wsh	243
Chevirs, Sarah	Tfo	358
Chivers, Elizabeth	Tfo	365
_____, Larkin	Ear	98
_____, Robert	Wil	295
_____, Thomas	Twg	67
CHEVALEIR/CHEVRIER		
Chevaleir, John	Cam	185
Chevrier, M.	Cht	250
_____ Also see Crevillier		
CHEW, B. F.	Rch	260
_____, John	Gre	277
CHEWNING/CHEWING		
Chewning, David	Gre	301
_____, William J. V.	Gre	301
Chewing, John J.	Mon	206
CHILDERS/CHILDRES/CHILDRESS		
Childers, A. Dr.	Ear	96
_____, Catherine	Clk	313
_____, Douglass	Hry	227
_____, Drury	Bib	72
_____, Henry	Pik	107
_____, Isaac	Mon	199
_____, Jesse	DeK	39
_____, Jesse C.	Pik	132
_____, John	Jns	431
_____, John A. D.	DeK	39
_____, John S.	Bib	54
_____, Malinda	Twg	88
_____, Martin	Wal	145
_____, Martin	Wal	157
_____, Nathan	Crf	412
_____, Nicholas	Bib	54
_____, Richard	Wsh	264
_____, Thomas	New	5
_____, Thomas	Wal	157
_____, William	Frk	220
_____, Willie	Pik	117
Childres, Edmund	Lin	67
_____, John	Elb	156
Childress, Holman	Elb	155
CHILDS/CHILES		
Childs, Benjamin	Frk	253
_____, Elijah	Jns	431
_____, Elizabeth	Jns	431
_____, Jeremiah	Mon	182
_____, Joel	Mar	140
_____, John	Jns	432
_____, John S.	Jns	434
_____, Mathew	Mon	204
_____, Michael S.	Jns	432
_____, Nimrod	Cow	384
_____, Thomas M.	Jsp	357
_____, William	Jns	432
_____, William	Mon	222
_____, Zach. B.	Mon	204
Chiles, Daniel	DeK	50
_____, John	Hry	213
_____, John	Rch	277
_____, Jonathan	Tlb	328
_____, Lewis G.	Elb	154
_____, Seaborn	Elb	150
CHISOLM/CHISLOM/CHISEN/ CHISAM		
Chisolm, Ann	Elb.	127
_____, George W.	Wal	158
_____, John	New	34
_____, Silvia	Jef	405
_____, Thomas A.	Wal	144
Chislom, Murdock	Bib	54

Name	County	Page
Chislom, William	Mor	259
Chisen, Ester	Clk	293
_____, Matthew	Tat	378
Chisam, Robert J.	Dec	5
CHITTY, Henry K.	Bak	17
CHITWOOD, Daniel	Hab	17
_____, James	Hab	56
_____, Margaret	Hab	17
_____, Moses	Hab	20
_____, Pleasant	Hal	119
CHOAT, Isham	Jns	472
_____, Thomas	Jns	459
CHOCHEVAL, Moses	Bts	178
CHOICE, John	Gwn	337
_____, Tully	DeK	35
_____, Tully	Han	149
_____, William	Han	149
CHOLSTON, John	Mad	108
_____, N. B.	Mad	108
CHOSLEY, Theophilus	Hab	60
CHRISTWELL: see Criswell		
CHRISTIAN/CHRISTIN/CRISTIAN		
Christian, Charles	Mad	104
_____, Charles W.	Elb	119
_____, Elijah	Elb	153
_____, Elijah W.	Mad	105
_____, Elijah W.	New	35
_____, Gabriel	Mon	196
_____, Gideon	Mwr	151
_____, George M.	Mad	101
_____, Ira	Elb	140
_____, Isaac	New	51
_____, Joannah	Mad	117
_____, John	Crf	411
_____, Marshal	Jks	322
_____, Mary	Elb	160
_____, Melton	New	43
_____, Nancey	Mad	112
_____, Ransom	Pik	109
_____, Robert B.	Elb	160
_____, Simeon	Hal	127
_____, Thomas J.	Elb	131
_____, Turner	Elb	142
_____, William P.	Elb	131
_____, William	Hal	70
_____, William B.	Hry	224
Christin, Ann	Col	345
Cristian, Reuben	New	22
CHRISTIE, Allen	Han	150
_____, Elihu	Up	108
_____, George	Cht	262
_____, Josiah	Up	111
_____, Nathan G. Jr.	Jef	406
Christie, Sarah	Jns	428
CHRISTLER, Jonathan	Jks	333
CHRISTOPHER, Cory	Wal	137
_____, David	Clk	299
_____, Edwd. R.	Tlb	332
_____, John	Ogl	102
_____, Richard	Ogl	103
_____, Seaborn	Mor	259
_____, William	Gre	301
_____, William	Hab	43
_____, William	Hry	211
CHUMLEY, Mason	Frk	219
CHUNN, Amos Sr.	Mwr	160
_____, Amos Jr.	Mwr	160
CHURCH, Alonzo	Clk	327
_____, Benjamin	Cpb	200
_____, Charles	Rch	265
_____, George B.	Jks	337
_____, Lemuel	Cam	183
_____, Mary	Wil	288
_____, Mary Ann	McI	121
_____, Robert	Cam	181
_____, Timothy	Hab	56
CHURCHILL/CHURCHELL/CHURELL/ CHURCHWELL		
Churchill, John	Rch	291
_____, William	Rch	290
Churchell, John	New	12
_____, Samuel B.	New	10
_____, Simon	New	12
Churell, William	New	12
Churchwell, Henry	Twg	74
_____, James	Twg	83
_____, John	Twg	74
CITROWER: see Zitterour		
CISOM, Vardiman	Hab	42
CISON, David	Hab	31
CLACK, John	New	22
CLACKLER, Henry	Fay	195
_____, Jacob	Fay	184
CLAGHORN: see Chaghune		
CLAIBORN/CLAYBRN		
Claiborn, Henry	Tlb	333
Claybrn, James	Han	150
CLANAHAN: see Callahan		
CLANCE/CLANCY		
Clance, Martin S.	Wks	332
_____, Wiley	Twg	62
Clancy, James	Cpb	210
CLANTON, Daniel	Bul	99
_____, David	Hab	36
_____, Gillim	Hab	39
_____, John P.	Tfo	362

Name		
Clanton, Samuel B.	Hst	288
______, Turner	Col	334
CLARDY, A. N.	Mon	206
______, Elliot	Rab	224
______, Wadworth	Hab	27
CLARK/CLARKE		
Clark, Aaron	New	28
______, Abigal	McI	121
______, Alfred	Crf	414
______, Anna	Frk	252
______, Archibald	Cam	185
______, Arthur	Mon	177
______, Benj.	Hab	31
______, Benjamin	Crf	410
______, Benjamin W.	Up	97
______, Betsey (colored)	Bke	148
______, Caleb	Hal	113
______, Catharine	Cht	269
______, Charles	Bke	137
______, Charles	Mus	281
______, Christopher	Bke	133
______, Christopher	Elb	138
______, Coy	Hab	28
______, Cullen	Mus	291
______, Daniel Sr.	Hst	261
______, Daniel Jr.	Hst	269
______, David	Elb	150
______, David	Hst	295
______, David	Jns	440
______, David	Wrn	221
______, Drury	Hst	268
______, Drury	Mus	292
______, Edwd	Up	98
______, Eli	Cht	254
______, Eli	Tms	28
______, Elijah	Hab	47
______, Elijah	New	9
______, Elijah	Wal	172
______, Elisha	Jns	440
______, Eliza	McI	121
______, Elizabeth	Hst	284
______, Elizabeth	Mtg	235
______, Ely	Crf	406
______, Emily	Lau	20
______, Frances	Hab	59
______, George	Hab	20
______, George	Hab	54
______, George	Jsp	357
______, George W.	Wal	154
______, Henry	Hal	129
______, Henry	Mtg	231
______, J. C. F.	Bal	41
______, Jacob Sr.	Cam	189
Clark, Jacob Jr.	Cam	189
______, James	Cam	189
______, James	Gre	286
______, James	Hst	267
______, James	Hst	286
______, James	Mar	142
______, James	Put	175
______, James A. D.	Bib	54
______, James O.	New	13
______, Janet	Up	115
______, Jeremiah	Put	217
______, Jesse	Wil	294
______, John	Cam	189
______, John	Frk	229
______, John	Hab	41
______, John	Hab	63
______, John	Hry	229
______, John	Hst	297
______, John	Jef	420
______, John	Jks	335
______, John	Irw	304
______, John	New	53
______, John J.	New	19
______, John	Wrn	205
______, John H.	Put	210
______, John L.	Cht	245
______, John M.	Put	203
______, John M.	Wal	128
______, Joshua	Lau	17
______, Joshua B.	Jns	472
______, Joshua R.	Jns	433
______, Josiah H.	Eff	111
______, Larkin	Elb	156
______, Leonard H.	Tlb	337
______, Lewis	Hab	19
______, Lewis H.	Twg	74
______, Mary	Elb	156
______, Mary D.	Bib	63
______, Michael N.	Mon	196
______, Nancy	Gre	286
______, Olive (colored)	Bke	148
______, P.	Cht	283
______, Peter	Put	183
______, Rebecca	Mon	203
______, Rebecca	New	55
______, Samuel	Bts	166
______, Samuel	Cam	184
______, Samuel	Hry	229
______, Samuel	Jsp	390
______, Samuel	Jef	402
______, Samuel	McI	131
______, Samuel	Mtg	231
______, Sandford C.	Fay	183

Name	County	Page
Clark, Savier	Hal	114
______, Silas	Twg	67
______, Thomas	Cam	182
______, Thomas	Cht	264
______, Thomas Sr.	Frk	228
______, Thomas	Jef	420
______, Thomas	Put	203
______, Thomas J.	Hab	55
______, Thomas J. G.	Mon	218
______, Warren	Bak	20
______, Warren	Bke	142
______, Wiley	Frk	250
______, William	Bke	120
______, William	Bke	142
______, William	Cht	267
______, William	DeK	60
______, William	Hab	33
______, William	Hab	41
______, William	Hab	55
______, William	Jef	413
______, William	Jef	416
______, William	Jef	424
______, William	Mwr	163
______, William	Mtg	231
______, William	Mus	285
______, William	New	47
______, William	Put	210
______, William	Wal	128
______, William	Wal	141
______, William	Wal	173
______, William B.	Gre	293
______, William B.	Mon	198
______, William D.	Elb	150
______, William F.	Bib	72
______, Williamson	Elb	133
______, Zachariah	Frk	216
______, Zachariah H.	Elb	139
Clarke, Agnes	Rch	269
______, Allen	Gwn	334
______, David	Hab	17
______, Elizabeth	Mor	254
______, Gabriel	Rch	271
______, George W.	Rch	269
______, Isaac	Clk	302
______, James	Bry	85
______, James	Pul	146
______, John	Rch	276
______, John M.	Rch	262
______, Joseph	Clk	305
______, Josiah	Ogl	69
______, Lewis	DeK	69
______, Littleberry	Car	222
______, Lucy (w)	Mor	254
Clarke, Oliver	DeK	27
______, Samuel	Elb	132
______, U. B.	Rch	269
______, William Sr.	Clk	305
______, William	Clk	304
______, William H.	Mor	257
** ______, Mrs. (slave)	Rch	277
CLARKSON/CLARKSTON		
Clarkson, John	Frk	247
Clarkston, Joseph	New	25
CLARY, Daniel	Lin	62
______, James	Dec	9
CLAXTON, Mrs. C.	Col	335
______, Mrs. C.	Col	337
______, James	Wrn	202
______, Nathaniel	Col	335
CLAY, Adam	Crf	396
______, Augustus	Col	340
______, Charles	Col	340
______, Edmond	Up	99
______, Greenberry	Tlb	330
______, James	Hab	60
______, Jesse	DeK	51
______, Jesse F.	Jsp	369
______, John	New	12
______, John	Wsh	270
______, Lewis	Wks	349
______, Mary Ann	Up	108
______, Mastin	Up	108
______, Peyton	Wks	351
______, Pirce	Wsh	271
______, Robert	Wks	354
______, Ryal Jr.	DeK	48
______, Samuel	Bts	161
______, Thomas	Jsp	370
______, Thomas S.	Bry	84
______, Upton	App	9
______, William	Wsh	249
CLAYTON/CLATON		
Clayton, Augustin S.	Clk	326
______, Dempsey W.	New	46
______, George R.	Bal	44
______, Isaac	Tlb	344
______, James	Bts	160
______, James	Bts	173
______, James	Mon	221
______, Jesse	Hal	74
______, Jesse	Hal	105
______, John	Hal	86
______, Josiah	Hal	120
______, Lemuel	Hal	95
______, Middleton	Car	226
______, Milton	Jsp	352

Name	County	Page
Clayton, Nelson	Pul	143
______, Newman H.	Tlb	347
______, R. C.	Jsp	352
______, Richard	DeK	67
______, Ryal	DeK	61
______, Samuel	Car	215
______, Samuel	Mwr	165
______, Seward	Hal	88
______, Stephen	Hal	94
______, Stephen Sr.	Hal	94
______, Thomas	Han	149
______, Warren	Hal	131
______, William	Car	226
______, William	Rch	291
Claton, Thomas B.	Pik	127
CLAYBROOK, William	Han	149
CLEAVES/CLEVES		
Cleaves, John	Hry	224
Cleves, George	Tms	29
CLEFF, Zachariah	Clk	317
CLEGG/CLEIG		
Clegg, Charles D.	Wal	143
______, James	Wal	137
______, John P.	Pik	109
______, Jonathan	Wal	144
______, Thomas	Wal	144
Cleig, Archy	Rch	255
CLEGHORN, Avington	Hab	34
______, Charles	Cow	374
______, James	Hal	80
______, John	Mad	109
______, William	Cow	370
______, William	Mad	105
______: see Chaghune		
CLEM, Henry	Bib	59
CLEMENTS/CLEMMENTS/CLEMENT/ CLEMANT/CLEMANTS/CLEMONTS		
Clements, Bish	Bal	43
______, Charles	Fay	194
______, Clem	Bib	69
______, Clem	Bib	69
______, David	Hry	208
______, Doct. P. B.	Crf	415
______, Eleanor	Hal	93
______, Ellis	Gre	297
______, Gabriel	Bib	69
______, Henry	Wil	293
______, Isaac	Wil	293
______, Jacob	Pul	149
______, Jacob	Tlf	8
______, James	Car	229
______, James	Mwr	156
______, James	Tlf	6
Clements, James	Wil	293
______, James L.	Jef	414
______, Jephthah	Jsp	354
______, Jesse	Mor	265
______, John	Hst	288
______, John Sr.	Jef	412
______, John	Tlf	4
______, John	Tlf	11
______, John A.	Mad	114
______, Marth	Lau	20
______, Mary	Jsp	353
______, Mary	Mor	264
______, Mary	Rch	278
______, Mary Ann	Twg	72
______, Matthew	Jns	450
______, Nancy	Hal	93
______, Nelson	Hst	292
______, Peyton	Gre	280
______, Peyton	Jns	434
______, Samuel	Jef	412
______, Sarah	Doo	79
______, Sarah	Jef	414
______, Sarah M.	Mad	112
______, Thomas	Jef	412
______, Thomas	Jns	437
______, W. L.	Jsp	353
______, Wiley	Bib	60
______, Wiley	Bib	67
______, William	Bib	69
______, William	Car	229
______, William	Crf	399
______, Mrs.	Rch	255
Clemments, Aron	Hal	96
______, Gabriel	Pik	120
______, Noble	Mad	103
Clement, Adam	Hal	72
Clemant, Richard B.	Har	179
Clemants, William	Wyn	281
Clemonts, Joseph	Em	170
CLEMMONDS/CLEMMONS/CLEMONS/ CLEMMINS		
Clemmonds, A.	Gwn	308
______, George	Gwn	322
______, George	Gwn	367
Clemmons, Ann	Put	175
______, Henry	Wrn	200
______, Malcolm	Lee	28
Clemons, Mary	Wks	338
______, Meriwether	Frk	218
______, William	DeK	52
Clemmins, William	Tms	22
CLENSY, Sarah	McI	128
CLEVELAND/[illegible]VELAND/CLELAND		

Name	County	Page
Cleveland, Aaron A.	Wil	287
______, Albert J.	Hab	35
______, Allen	Bts	175
______, Benjamin	Frk	225
______, Benjamin	Frk	253
______, Benjamin	Hab	11
______, Jacob	Hry	219
______, Jacob M.	Elb	124
______, James	Elb	126
______, James	Hab	35
______, Jeremiah	Hab	35
______, Jesse	DeK	26
______, John	Frk	232
______, Josh	Hab	32
______, Larkin	Frk	244
______, Malachi	Ear	94
______, Moses	Cht	254
______, Oliver	Trp	52
______, Reuben	Elb	148
______, Reuben	Frk	240
______, Rhody	Elb	156
______, Robert H or A	Frk	234
______, Temperance	Frk	218
______, Washington C.	Mwr	155
______, William	Rab	231
______, William L.	Han	149
______, Willie	Pik	130
Cleaveland, William	Hab	54
______, William	Jsp	371
Cleland, James	Cht	259
CLEWIS, John	Dec	15
CLIATT, Gehue	Col	335
______, Isham	Col	347
______, Isaac	Jsp	389
______, Isaac	Rch	287
______, Jessee	Jsp	389
______, John	Col	337
______, Jonathan	Col	337
______, Mrs. P.	Col	334
______, Sarah	Col	337
______, Thomas H.	Fay	184
CLIFTON, A. S.	Mus	282
______, Aaron	DeK	52
______, Betsey	Cht	261
______, Clement F.	Trp	49
______, Daniel	Gre	298
______, Daniel	Jns	456
______, Ezekiel	Jns	456
______, Ezekial	Tat	380
______, George	Clk	310
______, George	DeK	52
______, Henry	Lwn	83
______, John	Clk	310

Name	County	Page
Clifton, John	Em	174
______, Levin	DeK	52
______, Nathan	Wsh	246
______, Polly	Gre	300
______, Richard	Mor	252
______, Thomas	Scr	304
______, Thomas	Trp	37
______, William	Gre	300
______, William	Tat	380
______, William	Trp	48
CLINCH, Elizabeth	Lau	20
CLINE, Daniel	Rab	229
______, Joe	Rab	230
______, John	Car	216
______, Thomas	Gwn	376
CLINTON, David	Hab	37
______, William P.	Cpb	198
CLISSEN, Nathaniel	Ear	92
CLODFELLER, Peter	Hry	227
CLOPTON, Alford	Put	217
______, Pleasant P.	Mwr	160
______, Thomas	Put	176
CLOUD, Elisha	Mar	141
______, Ezekiel	Hry	220
______, James	Crf	401
______, Jeremiah	Hab	64
______, Joel	Wrn	205
______, John	Dec	4
______, Love	Hry	200
______, Reubin	Dec	3
______, William	Mar	143
______, Zilpha	Dec	14
CLOWER/CLOWERS		
Clower, Daniel P.	Gwn	341
______, George	Mon	226
______, Jessee	Mon	228
______, John	Gwn	347
______, Morgan	Jsp	361
______, Peter	Jns	468
______, Simeon	Mon	226
______, Stephen	Jns	468
Clowers, David S.	Mor	243
______, George	Bak	17
______, Green A.	Mwr	163
______, Jacob	Mwr	152
______, Martin	Mwr	158
______, Thomas	Har	188
CLUBB, Jas. A.	Cam	181
______, Sarah	Cam	184
______, William	Cam	192
CLYATT, J.	Har	185
______, Samuel M.	Lwn	89
COACH, Drury Jr.	Jsp	362

Coach, Polley Jsp 362
COATS/COATES/COATE/COTES
Coats, Calvin Wil 313
______, Delaney Doo 81
______, Henry Put 210
______, Jane Jsp 368
______, John Har 190
______, John Jsp 369
______, Lemuel Hal 126
______, Morgan Jsp 368
______, Penelope Put 210
______, Robert Lau 16
______, W. Lee 30
Coates, James Mor 243
______, John Jsp 381
______, William Ogl 64
Coate, Nathaniel J. Hab 23
______, William Lee 35
Cotes, John Cht 267
COBB/COB/COBBS
Cobb, Abraham Jef 415
______, Ammon Tfo 360
______, Benj. Wks 347
______, Betsey Gwn 351
______, Billy Rch 265
______, Briant Tlf 6
______, Curtis Bke 125
______, Daniel Bal 36
______, Daniel Tlb 335
______, Darling Hst 277
______, David G. Hal 86
______, Dawson S. Hst 290
______, Edward Doo 79
______, Ellison Frk 242
______, Enoch Gwn 347
______, Ezekiel M. Tfo 356
______, Garrison Wks 340
______, Henry B. Hal 69
______, Horatio Tat 373
______, Howell Hst 261
______, Jacob Han 150
______, Jacob Hry 203
______, Jacob Lee 34
______, Jacob Jns 472
______, Jacob McI 124
______, James Crf 398
______, James Elb 144
______, James Frk 241
______, James Tat 375
______, James M. Frk 217
______, John Jks 314
______, John Pul 162
______, John Wal 137

Cobb, John A. Clk 326
______, Joseph E. Crf 404
______, Joseph Fay 201
______, Lemuel DeK 51
______, Levi Bts 165
______, Lewis Tat 374
______, Lucrecia Wrn 232
______, Mark Jns 472
______, Martha Car 225
______, Nancy Wal 165
______, Nathaniel Crf 409
______, Nathaniel Frk 228
______, Nathaniel Twg 79
______, Samuel Car 228
______, Samuel DeK 52
______, Samuel B. Trp 52
______, Seth Up 118
______, Stephen Hab 20
______, Thomas Col 353
______, Thomas Doo 83
______, Wiley Doo 83
______, Wiley Twg 86
______, William Mus 291
______, William A. Up 95
______, William Hal 93
______, William F. Hst 277
Cob, Turner Ogl 94
Cobbs, John Mad 117
COBLER, John Gwn 312
______, Samuel Gwn 312
COCHERAL, Martha Fay 195
COCK/COCKE/COCKS
Cock, Allen Jks 322
______, John Bke 124
Cocke, Mrs. Rch 273
Cocks, Caleb Twg 86
COCHRAN/COCKRAM/COCKRUM/
COCKRON/COKRON/COKERHAM/
COKHAM/COUGHRAN
Cochran, Benjamin Up 114
______, Charles Hal 100
______, Christopher Crf 400
______, Elijah Gwn 342
______, James Hab 16
______, James Scr 300
______, James Gwn 337
______, John DeK 40
______, John Hal 82
______, John Jns 445
______, John McI 131
______, John Pik 130
______, John J. Col 342
______, John L. Car 218

Name	County	Page
Cochran, Mathew	Scr	300
______, Prudence	Gwn	343
______, Robert	Hal	100
______, Robert	Tlb	328
______, Shedle	Cpb	197
______, William	Gwn	342
______, William A.	Gwn	344
______, William	Hab	10
______, William	Hal	86
Cockran, Abram	Hal	112
______, Alexander	Hal	107
______, Alexander	New	38
______, Allen	Mon	197
______, David	Har	187
______, Henry	Hal	110
______, Jacob	Hal	110
______, James	Hab	13
______, James	Hab	40
______, James	Hal	133
______, James	Jks	315
______, James	New	43
______, Martin	Jsp	355
______, Matilda	DeK	33
______, Matthew	DeK	60
______, Seabrum	Wal	149
______, Susannah	Jsp	357
______, Thomas	Har	179
______, William	Hab	40
______, William	New	38
______, William	New	53
Cockram, Elisha	DeK	42
______, Jacob	Hal	108
Cockrum, Banister	Mor	246
______, Banister	Mor	248
______, Mathew	Mor	244
Cockron, Samuel	Ogl	77
Cokron, Jesse	Wrn	199
Cokerham, Peter	Frk	232
______, Susannah	Frk	228
Cokham, Robert	Han	15
Coughran, John	Bts	165
COCKBURN, Arachabal	Hal	78
______, George	Frk	234
______, George	Hal	104
______, James	Hal	104
______, Jeremiah	Frk	257
COCKRELL/COCKREL/COCKERAL		
Cockrell, George	New	45
______, George	New	52
______, Mary	New	52
______, Thomas	New	17
Cockrel, Jesse	Har	177
Cockeral, William	Cow	385
COCROFT, Henry	Gre	282
CODY, Absolum	Col	336
______, D.	Jks	335
______, David	Wrn	213
______, Edm^{d}.	Wrn	219
______, Edmond Jr.	Wrn	198
______, Eliza	Wrn	219
______, Elizabeth	Wrn	201
______, Harnett	Wrn	226
______, James	Wrn	214
______, James	Rab	232
______, Jesse	Jks	348
______, M.	Cht	271
______, Michael	Wrn	214
______, Peter	Wrn	194
COE/CLOE/CLORE		
Coe, George W.	Cht	263
______, Joseph	Wsh	272
______, William H.	Cht	246
Cloe, Elijah	Jks	339
Clore, Abner	Mad	102
COFFEE, Abner	Gwn	321
______, Cleveland	Rab	225
______, Edmond	Gwn	321
______, Edward	Rab	233
______, Elijah	Rab	225
______, Elisha	Rab	226
______, Jessee	Gwn	312
______, Joel	Rab	222
______, Joel	Rab	225
______, John	Tlf	12
______, Lewis	Gwn	321
______, Lewis	Hab	56
______, William	Cpb	208
______, William	Gwn	321
COFER/COFFER		
Cofer, John	Wil	323
______, Joseph B.	Wil	314
______, Simon	Jks	328
______, Thomas B.	Wil	316
Coffer, Chany	Hal	92
COFIELD/COFFIELD		
Cofield, Gresham	Trp	37
______, John	Pul	139
______, Nelson	Bts	170
______, Uriah	Put	193
Coffield, John	Wsh	251
______, Thomas	Cpb	200
COFFIN, H.	Rch	256
COFFMAN, John	Jsp	394
______: see Kofeman also		
COGBILL, Edward	Gre	295
COGBURN/COBOURN		

Name	County	Page
Cogburn, Allen	Put	187
_____, Benjamin	Clk	296
_____, Cyrus	Tlb	344
_____, Moses H.	Clk	303
Cobourn, M.	Cht	254
COGGIN/COGGINS/COGAN		
Coggin, Asa	New	24
_____, Burrel	Pik	106
_____, James	Gwn	327
_____, James	New	24
_____, John	Pik	123
_____, Silas	Pik	107
_____, Thomas	New	13
_____, William	Wal	172
_____, Zilphy	New	13
Coggins, Andrew	Hal	119
_____, Isaac	Tlb	341
_____, Peter	Hab	45
_____, Richard	Hab	30
_____, William	Tms	20
Cogan, Dennis	Mwr	161
COGSWELL, John B.	Gwn	363
_____, John B.	Gwn	368
_____, William	Hal	117
COHEN/COEIN		
Cohen, G. P.	Cam	186
_____, Isaac	Cht	256
Coein, Eli	Hry	242
COHORN/COHRON		
Cohorn, Cornelius	Tfo	366
_____, George	Scr	300
_____, Isaac	New	50
_____, Seabron	Wal	163
Cohron, Felix	Mon	203
_____, James	Tlb	336
COILE/KOIL		
Coile, Elizabeth	Bke	147
_____, James	Mad	103
_____, Mary	Mad	117
Koil, John	DeK	34
COKER, A.	Wks	351
_____, Alsey	Elb	119
_____, Arlan	Mus	278
_____, Carlton	Frk	244
_____, Daniel	Wsh	276
_____, Elisha	Hry	243
_____, Elizabeth	Frk	245
_____, Elizabeth Jr.	Frk	245
_____, Frances	Mar	141
_____, Hardaman	Wal	167
_____, Henry	Hry	243
_____, Hiram	Wal	166
_____, Isaac	Hry	243
Coker, Jacob	Elb	119
_____, James	Hry	223
_____, John	Cow	381
_____, Larkin	Frk	214
_____, Malachi	Elb	132
_____, Newel	Elb	131
_____, Pleasant	Ran	247
_____, Robert	Wal	129
_____, Solomon	New	5
_____, Thomas	Hal	89
_____, Thomas	Pik	110
COLBERT/COLBORN/COLBOTT		
Colbert, Frederick G.	Gre	304
_____, James	Mon	219
_____, John	Han	150
_____, John	Mon	173
_____, John G.	Mor	248
_____, Larkin	Tlb	330
_____, Lindsey G.	Mad	106
_____, Nicholas	Ogl	76
_____, Philip	Ogl	76
_____, Richmond	Han	150
_____, Susan	Mon	219
_____, Thomas	Elb	137
_____, William	Col	346
_____, William	Mon	191
Colborn, Thomas	Col	345
Colbott, Jonathan	Crf	415
COLBY, Jno.	Wks	355
_____, John	Gre	305
_____, William	Wks	332
COLCLOUGH, Charity	Tfo	368
_____, John	Gre	296
_____, William	Tfo	361
COLDWELL: see Caldwell		
COLDING/CAULDING		
Colding, Henry	Scr	310
Caulding, William	Mor	241
COLE/COLES/COAL		
Cole, Allen J.	McI	121
_____, Benjn.	Wsh	262
_____, Bud	Scr	305
_____, Charlton B.	Bib	49
_____, Ezekiel	Wal	158
_____, Grovey	Put	215
_____, Hoesea	Fay	197
_____, Isaac	Han	149
_____, James D.	Clk	316
_____, John M.	Pul	161
_____, Jesse	Hry	213
_____, John	Bke	119
_____, Lorenzo D.	Wal	129
_____, Lydia	Cam	186

Name	County	Page
Cole, Mark	Bts	160
______, Nancy Ana	Pik	122
______, Reuben	Jns	460
______, Richard	Cow	389
______, Samuel	Lin	65
______, Stephen	Wal	132
______, Tilman	Gwn	343
______, William	Gwn	343
______, William	Hst	275
______, William	Mon	175
______, William	Wil	291
______, Winney	Hry	238
______, Wright	Scr	302
Coles, Jerry	Bib	54
Coal, John	Col	340
COLEMAN/COLMAN/COALMON		
Coleman, Abner	DeK	41
______, Abner	Hal	83
______, Allin	Gwn	373
______, Charles	Bke	125
______, Charles	Han	150
______, Charles	Mon	217
______, Clarissa	Lau	21
______, Daniel	Hry	248
______, Daniel T.	Mor	254
______, David	Bts	164
______, David	Mon	224
______, David	New	27
______, David	Wsh	263
______, Elijah	Lau	10
______, Elisha	Bke	125
______, Elizabeth	Gre	305
______, Ephraign	Hab	15
______, Hezekiah	Cpb	195
______, Isaac	Ear	91
______, Isaac	Ran	250
______, J. B.	Lee	26
______, James	Doo	79
______, James	Put	204
______, James L.	Rch	285
______, Jesse	Bak	18
______, Jesse	Bke	123
______, Jesse H.	Fay	188
______, John	Gre	273
______, John	Jef	403
______, John	Jef	407
______, John	Lau	7
______, John	Lib	44
______, John	Mus	281
______, John	New	11
______, John	Rch	288
______, John	Wil	321
______, John G.	Han	149
Coleman, John M.	Bts	172
______, Jonas	Elb	154
______, Jonathan	Em	164
______, Jos. L.	Cpb	207
______, Joseph	Mus	285
______, Joseph	Tfo	359
______, Josey	Lau	7
______, Lucy	Em	173
______, Matthew	Cow	379
______, Matthew	Gre	290
______, Mathew W.	Mor	253
______, Nancy	App	6
______, Phil.	Gwn	378
______, Philip	Hal	81
______, Pleasant P.	Jsp	388
______, R.	Gwn	308
______, Resa	Jef	407
______, Richard	DeK	73
______, Richard	Pul	162
______, Robert	Bibb	54
______, Samuel	Mwr	162
______, Stephen	Pul	160
______, Thomas	Bak	19
______, Thomas	Fay	188
______, Thomas	Han	149
______, Thomas	Fay	181
______, Thompson	Wil	322
______, Washington	Han	149
______, William	Hal	133
______, William	Jef	407
______, William	Wal	127
______, Willis	Put	207
Colman, Harriett	Col	340
______, Wade W.	Tat	378
______, William	App	9
Coalmon, Jacob	Tms	29
COLEEN, Thomas (Collens in 1820)	Gwn	370
COLINSWORTH, John	Put	216
COLINTINA, J.	Cht	266
COLLARS/COLLER/COLLA		
Collars, Elijah	Lin	60
______, George	Lin	60
______, Matthew	Lin	59
______, Rich	Lin	60
Coller, Margaret	Hst	284
Colla, James	Hab	50
COLLEDY, William	Elb	153
COLLET, Green	Hal	83
COLLEY/COLEY/COLLY		
Colley, Anderson	Ogl	64
______, Edward	Hry	236
______, Francis	Wil	312

Name	County	Page
Colley, Joel	New	27
______, John	Mad	103
______, Jonathan	Wil	296
______, Martha	Wil	297
______, Sarah	Wil	323
______, Zachariah	Pik	117
______, Zacherias	Mad	107
Coley, David	Mtg	235
______, Dollinson	Twg	70
______, Gabriel	Hal	104
______, Gemima	Ear	91
______, John	Gre	303
______, John	Pul	141
______, Morgan	Hal	104
______, Rowland	Pul	138
______, Turner	Pul	153
______, William	Gre	276
Colly, A. M. D.	Mon	226
______, David	Ogl	63
______, Mary	Clk	292
______, Spain	Wil	296
______, Zack	Col	364
COLLIER/COLIER/COLLEAR		
COLYER/KOLYER		
Collier, Benj.	Crf	406
______, Benj.	Ear	91
______, C. C.	Gre	293
______, Charles	Ogl	88
______, Charles P.	Fay	194
______, Charles W.	Han	150
______, Cuthbert	Mon	175
______, Cuthbert L.	Ogl	88
______, Edward W.	Rch	275
______, Edwin	Gre	294
______, Henry	Ear	93
______, Isaac	Ogl	88
______, James	Frk	226
______, James	Gre	299
______, Jesse	Ear	91
______, Jessee	Twg	82
______, John J.	Dec	7
______, Nathaniel H.	Ogl	88
______, Richard	Wks	340
______, Robert	Hry	201
______, Robert	Twg	71
______, Robert	Up	117
______, Sarah	Lau	24
______, Sarah	Rch	269
______, Sterling	Mor	265
______, Thomas	Gre	298
______, Thomas	Pul	146
______, Thomas W.	Bts	158
______, William	Clk	303
Collier, William	Frk	257
______, William	Car	229
______, Williamson	Up	109
Colier, John	Hal	85
Collear, Robert	Pul	160
______, William	Ogl	64
Colyer, Meredith	DeK	25
______, Morrel	DeK	56
______, Tahos	Hab	34
Kolyer, John	Hab	39
COLLINGEN, Sarah	Pik	115
COLLINS/COLLENS/COLINS/		
CULLINS/CULLIN/CULLERS		
Collins, A.	Bal	30
______, A.	Bal	33
______, Mrs. A. L.	Col	340
______, Abysha	Wks	345
______, Albert	Col	340
______, Alfred	Lin	68
______, Alfred	Pul	161
______, Andrew	Bib	59
______, Andrew	Bib	69
______, Andrew	Bke	125
______, Andrew	Fay	196
______, Andrew	Jks	312
______, Briant	Cow	387
______, C.	Col	336
______, Charles	Bib	49
______, Charles	Hal	68
______, Christopher W.	Twg	69
______, Dav.	Bal	37
______, David	Irw	299
______, David K.	Tat	373
______, Eli	Har	181
______, Enoch	Lwn	89
______, Enoch	Put	187
______, George	Bib	63
______, George	Gwn	310
______, George W.	Mon	176
______, George W.	Rab	228
______, George W.	Tlb	331
______, Gibson	Wil	299
______, Hardy	Tat	373
______, Harvey	Tlf	3
______, Henry	Hry	247
______, James	Bul	97
______, James	Col	354
______, James	DeK	72
______, James	Gwn	354
______, James	Hal	68
______, James	Mar	140
______, James W.	Twg	71
______, James	Wks	344

Collins, Jesse	Cpb	202
_____, Jesse	Lee	28
_____, Jesse	Tat	373
_____, John	Bke	149
_____, John	Col	353
_____, John	Cow	374
_____, John	Hab	39
_____, John	Hal	68
_____, John	Mad	106
_____, John	Mon	227
_____, John	Rch	292
_____, John B.	Frk	252
_____, John G.	Wsh	267
_____, John S.	Wsh	251
_____, Jonath	Bal	33
_____, Jones	Ogl	103
_____, Jonus	Rch	274
_____, Joseph	Twg	82
_____, Joseph	Mor	245
_____, Joseph Sr.	Mor	246
_____, Joseph Sr.	Tat	373
_____, Joseph Jr.	Tat	374
_____, Joshua	Wsh	251
_____, Josiah	Tat	374
_____, Lewis	Doo	86
_____, Lewis	Rch	290
_____, Littleton	Har	176
_____, Lydia	Car	223
_____, M. C.	Wks	335
_____, Mahaly	Jef	409
_____, Miol	Tat	373
_____, Moses	Bib	75
_____, Peter H.	Col	353
_____, Philip	Hal	108
_____, Riley	Har	182
_____, Robert	Bib	54
_____, Samuel	Bts	165
_____, Samuel	Elb	152
_____, Sarah	Bke	132
_____, Seaborn	Har	189
_____, Stephen	Mon	198
_____, Thomas	Bib	63
_____, Thomas	Bib	72
_____, Thompson	Hab	8
_____, Timothy	Wal	153
_____, Watson	Rab	225
_____, William	Lee	29
_____, William	Mor	249
_____, William K.	Tat	373
_____, William	Car	220
_____, William	Ogl	72
_____, William	Pik	107
_____, William	Wks	334

Collins, Williamson	Wks	344
_____, Wilson	Mar	141
_____, Zilpah	Tat	375
Collens, Absalam	New	22
_____, Jesse	Dec	5
Colins, Ezekiel	Dec	7
_____, William	Dec	7
Cullins, Fred	Wsh	276
_____, M. D.	Wsh	242
_____, W. W.	Wsh	249
Cullen, H.	Cht	272
Cullers, Chas.	Doo	88
COLLIS, John	Hab	41
COLLUM, Henry	Hal	123
_____, Peggy	Hal	130
_____, Polly	Ear	99
_____, Solomon	Mon	178
COLON/COLUN		
Colon, James B.	Wal	124
Colun, James	Rch	266
COLQUITT/COLQUIT		
Colquitt, James	Ogl	86
_____, John H. H.	Cpb	194
_____, Robert	Ogl	73
_____, Thomas	Gre	275
_____, William T.	Cpb	204
Colquit, Henry P.	Ogl	66
_____, John	Ogl	73
_____, Jonathan	Up	112
_____, William	Ogl	71
COLSON/COULSON/COALSON		
Colson, Abraham	Elb	153
_____, B. M.	Tat	375
_____, Henry	Lwn	82
_____, James	Elb	155
_____, Paul	Scr	306
_____, Sanders	Pul	140
_____, William	Bke	143
Coulson, Abram	Wks	332
_____, Elizabeth	Tms	29
_____, William S.	Hst	263
Coalson, John	Pul	157
COLSTON, Dennis	Bak	17
COLVARD/CULYARD		
Colvard, John S.	Elb	137
Culyard, Jonathan	Hab	58
COLVIN, Mary	Hry	242
COMBS/COMB/COMBY		
Combs, Bud	Tlb	323
_____, Enoch	Wil	321
_____, Hannah	New	55
_____, James	Twg	60
_____, John	Wil	309

Name	County	Page
Combs, Mary	Wil	313
______, Nathan	Jsp	389
______, Nathan	New	55
______, Patsy	Wil	315
______, Permelia	Put	218
______, Phillip	Wil	309
______, Phillip	Wil	321
______, Reuben	Mwr	156
______, William	Mon	185
______, William	Mon	194
Comb, William	Jks	334
Comby, Terrey	Wal	140
COMER, Alfred H.	Jns	450
______, Anderson	Jns	437
______, Hugh M.	Jns	453
______, James	Jns	447
______, James	Mon	188
______, Joseph F.	Gwn	361
______, Marquis L. F.	Tlb	335
______, Thomas J.	Tlb	333
COMMANDER, Elias	Crf	409
______, Patsey	Rch	257
______, Samuel	Crf	408
COMPTON/COMTOM/CROMPTON/ CUMTON		
Compton, Elizabeth	Jsp	369
______, Jane	Gwn	321
______, Jane	Gwn	344
______, Jesse	Gwn	344
______, John	Fay	191
______, Jordan	Jsp	366
______, Thomas	Frk	221
Comtom, Isham	Bak	16
Crompton, Joel	Cpb	208
Cumton, John	Put	202
CONAWAY/CONEWAY/CONNAWAY		
Conaway, Charles	Eff	115
______, Henry	Wrn	208
______, John	Hal	110
______, William	Hal	110
Coneway, John	New	45
______, John	New	55
______, Sarah	New	55
______, William	New	49
Connaway, Epm.	Cam	189
CONDON/CONDEM		
Condon, J. P.	Cht	269
Condem, Caleb	Bib	49
CONE/COANS/COON		
Cone, Aaron	Bul	93
______, Abel	Wsh	262
______, Archabald	Wsh	272
______, Archulas	Wsh	267
Cone, Asa R.	Gre	296
______, Bazil	Mwr	161
______, Benjamin	Jsp	370
______, C. L.	Col	334
______, Edmund L.	Rch	287
______, Francis H.	Gre	281
______, Gardner	DeK	70
______, Gilbert	DeK	40
______, Henry H.	Bib	49
______, James	Bul	93
______, James	Wsh	267
______, James	Bal	31
______, Jeremiah	Frk	239
______, John	Bal	36
______, John	Tms	30
______, John D.	Wsh	268
______, Jos.	Bal	30
______, Joseph	Mwr	152
______, Joseph	Tms	26
______, Levi	Wsh	262
______, Margaret	Gre	287
______, Mary	Bal	31
______, Midd.	Bal	30
______, Robert	Bul	92
______, Samuel	DeK	33
______, Stephen	McI	124
______, Thomas	Wsh	262
______, William	Cam	187
______, William	Gre	278
______, William B.	Bib	54
Coans, Umphrey	Col	339
Coon, Henry L.	Jks	327
CONELY/CONERLY		
Conely, Nathaniel	Gwn	311
______, T.	Gwn	308
Conerly, Briant	Clk	322
______, George H.	Clk	311
CONEY, Jeremiah	Pul	159
______, Joel	Lau	6
CONGER/CONGOR		
Conger, Amos	Bts	164
______, Benj.	Gwn	309
______, Eli	Bts	161
______, James	Hab	22
______, John A.	Hry	234
______, Simeon	Gwn	311
______, Zachariah	Gwn	324
Congor, O.	Cht	256
CONGHAM, John	Bts	165
CONGLETON, Allen	Mon	188
CONYERS/CONIERS/CUNYERS		
Conyers, John	Scr	313
______, Rachel	Wsh	253

Name	County	Page
Conyers, Sarah	Scr	313
______, William D.	New	16
Coniers, Benett	Cow	370
______, John E.	Cow	368
Cunyers, Henry	Hst	266
______, William	Hst	266
CONINE/CONIN		
Conine, John	Gwn	330
______, Nancy	Jks	347
______, Richard	Put	180
Conin, William	Jks	344
CONKLE, Henry	Hry	221
CONLEY, Henry	Hab	7
______, John	Hal	128
______, William	Hal	128
CONN, George	Gwn	333
______, John	Hal	98
______, John	Rch	279
______, Joseph	Hal	12
______, Penelope	DeK	29
______, Samuel Sr.	DeK	45
______, Samuel	DeK	70
______, William	DeK	42
CONNALLY/CONNELLY/ CONNELY/CONOLLY		
Connally, Abner	DeK	49
______, David	DeK	39
______, Dempsey J.	DeK	33
______, George W.	Frk	246
______, Patrick B.	Jef	411
______, Susannah	Frk	226
Connelly, Christopher	Cpb	208
______, Michael	Lau	12
______, Samuel W.	Frk	231
______, Thomas	Mad	105
Connely, Charles	New	14
Conolly, Constantine	Cht	272
CONNARD, John	Jsp	388
CONNELL/CONNEL/CONNOL		
Connell, Benjamin	Mor	267
______, Daniel	Gre	275
______, Green	Mor	272
______, John	Han	150
______, John	Hry	240
______, John	Mtg	232
______, William	Jsp	389
Connel, Hy	Gwn	371
______, Mary	Han	150
Connol, Thomas	Jef	417
______, Weyse	Jef	417
CONNER/CONNOR/CONOR/CONER		
Conner, Benjamin	Mon	185
______, Christopher	Mwr	168
Conner, Daniel	Hry	202
______, David	Scr	310
______, Earley	Wal	144
______, Edward	Clk	307
______, Edward	Tat	378
______, Elijah	Wrn	227
______, Fedrick	Mwr	168
______, Fredrick	Put	188
______, Garaway	Wal	161
______, Henry	Hab	36
______, Henry	Wal	161
______, Isaac	Scr	300
______, James	Clk	303
______, James	Gwn	354
______, James	Lin	67
______, James	Pul	161
______, James	Put	217
______, James	Scr	306
______, Jesse	New	34
______, John	Bke	153
______, John	Clk	308
______, John	Lin	67
______, John	Tat	372
______, Louis	Scr	310
______, Lucretia	Eff	111
______, Martin	Lin	66
______, Sarah	New	33
______, T. C.	Bib	54
______, Thomas	Clk	308
______, Thomas Jr.	Clk	296
______, Thomas	Put	190
______, Thomas	Scr	302
______, William	Lin	58
______, William	Tat	372
______, Willis	Dec	5
______, Wilson	New	33
______, Wilson	Scr	307
Connor, James G.	Mtg	234
______, John	Hab	26
______, Wilson	Mtg	233
Conor, James H.	Hal	116
______, John	Hal	103
Coner, Miggelly	New	33
CONROY, J.	Cht	249
CONSTANTINE, B.	Cht	267
COODY, Clayton M.	Bts	165
______, Lewis	Bul	101
______, William	DeK	64
COOK/COOKE		
Cook, Mrs.	Cht	269
______, A. M.	Lee	28
______, Abraham	Elb	137
______, Allen	Mwr	159

Name	County	Page
Cook, Allen	Wsh	274
______, Amos	Cht	278
______, Anie	Rch	263
______, Asa B.	Hst	289
______, Augustin	Mon	217
______, Barbara	Twg	83
______, Benjamin	Han	149
______, Benjamin	Pik	130
______, Benjn.	Wsh	268
______, Benj. T.	Hab	47
______, Beverly C.	Elb	153
______, Burrel	Gwn	309
______, Caleb	Cow	382
______, D. A.	Jsp	355
______, Daniel	Fay	184
______, David	New	28
______, Dempsey	Ran	248
______, Dicy	Jsp	366
______, Edward	Wsh	252
______, Elijah	Mus	291
______, Elisha	Frk	239
______, Ephraim	Jks	334
______, Farhinatus S.	Mus	279
______, Fenton	Pik	125
______, Frances	Hry	223
______, Frances T.	Frk	244
______, Frederick W.	Ogl	97
______, George	Elb	157
______, George	Hal	104
______, George	New	40
______, George W.	Jns	453
______, Grief	Mon	228
______, Harbard	Fay	196
______, Henry	Tms	29
______, Henry H.	Rch	268
______, Hugh	Tlf	7
______, Issacher	Elb	147
______, James	Clk	309
______, James	Gwn	331
______, James	Gwn	347
______, James	Hry	225
______, James	Jns	453
______, James	Wsh	245
______, James C.	Mor	249
______, James H.	Jef	423
______, James H.	Tlb	341
______, James S.	Wsh	253
______, Jesse	Fay	196
______, Jesse	Hry	224
______, Joel	Dec	15
______, John	Cow	375
______, John	Cow	385
______, John	Crf	413
Cook, John	Dec	6
______, John	Elb	139
______, John	Elb	149
______, John	Fay	204
______, John	Hal	117
______, John	Han	150
______, John	Hry	226
______, John	Jef	406
______, John	Jef	423
______, John	Jks	349
______, John	Jns	428
______, John	New	20
______, John	New	28
______, John	Ran	247
______, John G.	Jns	464
______, John W.	Gwn	371
______, Johnson	Dec	15
______, Jonathan	New	19
______, Joshua	Gre	272
______, Julius	Put	187
______, Lydia	Eff	111
______, McKeen	Wsh	264
______, Martha	Hal	117
______, Martha	Jns	456
______, Martha	Wrn	203
______, Mary	Cam	191
______, Mary	Ran	249
______, Nathan	Clk	310
______, Nathan	Han	149
______, Nathan	Lee	33
______, Nathaniel	Mon	204
______, Neverson	Hal	96
______, Pernall	Clk	308
______, Phil.	Bal	41
______, Philip	Hry	202
______, Ransome	Jks	335
______, Rebecca	Jks	348
______, Robert	Mor	251
______, Rowland B.	Fay	196
______, Samuel	Wsh	257
______, Sarah	Hry	224
______, Sarah E.	Jns	450
______, Sheeland	Han	149
______, Shem	Fay	196
______, Sidney	Wks	358
______, Silas	Hal	105
______, Smith	Elb	147
______, Sterling	Wsh	242
______, Theodosius Sr.	Elb	136
______, Theodosius Jr.	Elb	147
______, Thomas	Bts	159
______, Thomas	Hal	105
______, Thomas	Hry	221

Name	County	Page
Cook, Thomas	Pik	130
______, Thomas	DeK	52
______, Thomas	Hab	24
______, Thomas S.	Mad	112
______, Wesley	Hry	243
______, Wiley	Har	186
______, William	Col	337
______, William	McI	128
______, William	Rab	222
______, William	Twg	73
______, William	Wks	348
______, William	Wal	155
______, William A.	Mon	214
______, William B.	Wal	165
______, Willis	Dec	6
______, Zadock	Clk	311
Cooke, Abram	Bke	144
______, Arthur S.	Bke	144
______, James	Bke	144
______, John D.	Bke	139
COOKSEY/COOXSEY		
Cooksey, John	Wal	156
______, Pharaby	Jef	401
______, Robert	Wal	134
Cooxsey, Hannah	Wil	312
______, Thomas	Wil	295
COOLEY/COOLY		
Cooley, John	New	50
______, Sarah	Jns	435
Cooly, John	Cpb	211
______, Nancy	Hab	42
COOMBS/COOMS		
Coombs, John S.	Rch	273
Cooms, Martha	Rch	253
COONER, Mary	Bul	92
______, Mary	Bul	92
COOPER/COUPER		
Cooper, Abner	Hry	213
______, Alice	Wyn	283
______, Arther	Clk	317
______, Benj.	Bal	30
______, Beverly	Up	115
______, Blake J.	Wal	138
______, C. C.	Gly	267
______, Daniel	Pul	154
______, David	Col	363
______, David	Put	183
______, Davis	Hry	233
______, Eli	Bts	164
______, Elijah	Up	117
______, Elizabeth	Mad	117
______, Elizabeth	Tms	17
______, F.	Cht	258
Cooper, George	Mtg	236
______, George W.	Mtg	232
______, Gideon	Wil	309
______, Guilford	Up	104
______, Henry	Lau	4
______, Henry	Put	174
______, Henry H.	Mtg	232
______, Humphrey	New	30
______, Isaac	Bal	44
______, Isaac	Up	105
______, James	Clk	313
______, James H.	Gly	264
______, James W.	Trp	52
______, Jessee	Lib	44
______, Joel	Jsp	397
______, Joel M.	Jsp	398
______, John	Cht	244
______, John	Col	334
______, John	Col	363
______, John	Mon	201
______, John	Ran	247
______, John G.	Bak	19
______, John M.	Rch	255
______, John W.	Har	176
______, Jonathan	Mad	108
______, Joseph	Doo	82
______, Joseph	Wil	308
______, Joseph M.	Wil	310
______, Josiah	Up	111
______, Kennon	Clk	317
______, Lewis J.	Tms	17
______, Lloyd	Har	182
______, Lydia	Cht	264
______, M. C.	Rch	260
______, Mark A.	Put	218
______, Martha	Wrn	217
______, Mary	Hry	232
______, Mary	McI	121
______, Micajah	Put	180
______, Milton	Mad	102
______, Ransom	Gwn	313
______, Robert	Car	223
______, Sherrid K.	Hab	30
______, Salome	Cht	260
______, Samuel	Put	172
______, Samuel	Wks	332
______, Thomas	Cow	382
______, Thomas	Frk	214
______, Thomas	Gwn	309
______, Thomas	Hry	232
______, Thomas	New	49
______, Thomas	Put	217
______, Thomas	Wil	321

Name	County	Page
Cooper, Uriah	Car	226
_____, Vincen	Gwn	317
_____, Vining	Gwn	359
_____, W. A.	Tms	17
_____, William	Hst	293
_____, William	Lau	24
_____, William	Mus	285
_____, William	Ran	243
_____, William	Scr	304
_____, William	Wal	159
_____, William J.	Jef	405
_____, William W.	Trp	35
_____, Willis	Wal	166
_____, Willougby	Ware	187
Couper, John Sr.	Gly	266
_____, John Jr.	Gly	264
COPE/COPP/COPPEE		
Cope, Adam	Cht	266
_____, Adam	Cht	280
_____, Lewis	Cht	260
Copp, B. A.	Cam	183
Coppee, Edward	Cht	249
COPELAND/COPLAND/COPELAN/ COPELIN/COAPLIN/COOPLIN		
Copeland, Archibald H.	Hry	213
_____, Coalson	Gre	281
_____, Coleston	DeK	68
_____, Coulson	Hst	296
_____, Elijah	DeK	31
_____, Gilbert	Cpb	204
_____, Isaac	Mon	174
_____, Jesse	Tat	380
_____, John	Gre	294
_____, John	Jsp	386
_____, John D.	Gre	302
_____, John H.	Gre	305
_____, M. M.	Rch	279
_____, Peter	Mor	251
_____, Robert	Hry	249
_____, Thomas	DeK	34
_____, William	DeK	64
_____, William	Har	187
_____, William	Rab	234
_____, William Sr.	Hry	248
_____, William Jr.	Hry	249
_____, William R.	Car	229
Copland, Henry C.	Crf	396
_____, John	Put	193
Copelan, William	Gwn	358
Copelin, Sam.	Gwn	376
Coaplin, Thomas	Bib	66
Cooplin, Thomas	Bib	66
COPLEY, Elizabeth	New	19
Copley, John	New	19
_____, Pierce Sr.	New	19
_____, Pierce Jr.	New	19
COPPAGE, Carter	Pik	106
_____, Lewis	Hst	263
_____, William	Hst	263
COPPER/COPER		
Copper, Lewis	Hal	78
_____, Warren H.	Fay	190
Coper, James A.	New	10
CORAM/CORAN		
Coram, Thomas	Wrn	211
Coran, John	Mwr	167
CORBET/CORBETT		
Corbet, Elizabeth	Mon	227
_____, James	Jef	424
_____, John	Bib	69
_____, Marshall	Ware	184
_____, Sarah	Wsh	271
Corbett, Jesse	DeK	59
_____, John	App	8
_____, L. D.	Cht	246
CORBIN, Elizabeth	Wil	319
_____, James	Hab	9
_____, Richard	Hab	50
_____, Sarah	Hst	282
CORDEMAN, Frederic	New	48
CORDER/CORDERY/CORDRY		
Corder, Betsey	Jns	468
_____, Morgan	Hst	268
Cordery, David	Gwn	374
_____, Sharlot	Gwn	374
_____, Thomas	Gwn	374
Cordry, Daniel	Wsh	257
_____, Jonathan	Wsh	242
CORDLE, William H.	Trp	52
CORK, Allen	Hal	89
_____, William T. C.	Elb	140
CORKER, Drewry	Bke	129
_____, James V. L.	Lib	44
_____, Stephen	Bke	125
CORLEY/CORLEE		
Corley, Allen	Mwr	159
_____, David	Tlb	339
_____, Elijah	Up	102
_____, Gor^{t}.	Cow	371
_____, Hollis	Jsp	371
_____, Isham	Tlb	343
_____, James	Tlb	328
_____, Jeremiah	Cow	370
_____, Overton	Rch	264
_____, Willis	Rch	288
Corlee, Jesse	Tlb	322

Name	County	Page
Corlee, Meredith	Har	182
______, William	Tlb	329
CORMERY, Peter	Cam	184
CORN, John	Hab	10
CORNEGE/KORNEGA		
Cornege, Bazel	Lwn	79
Kornega, Daniel	Tms	21
CORNELIUS, Benjamin	Lwn	85
______, William	DeK	53
CORNETT, Cullen	Rab	234
______, George	Put	184
______, Henry S.	Put	181
______, Joel	Lib	44
______, Uriah D.	Put	184
CORNWALL, Daniel	Pul	146
______, Elijah	Hry	209
CORNWELL/CORNWEL/CONWELL		
Cornwell, Cathrine	Jsp	397
______, George W.	Jsp	397
______, Hiram	Jsp	392
______, Mahala	Jsp	398
______, Mary	Cht	259
______, Obediah	Jsp	397
Cornwel, Martin	Hab	61
Conwell, Daniel E.	Elb	147
CORRY, James	Gre	274
______, Margaret	Gre	273
______, William	Gre	291
CORTES, William B.	Gre	288
COSART/COSSORT/COZART		
Cosart, James	Gwn	379
Cossort, Jesse	Gwn	376
Cozart, Anthony	Mon	213
COSBY, Austin W.	Frk	229
______, Chales R.	Wal	123
______, David	Wil	301
______, Hickason	Put	183
______, John	Hry	235
______, Philip B.	Hst	290
______, Thomas H.	Jsp	382
______, William	Wrn	207
______, Wingfield	Wrn	207
COSNAHAN, Thomas	Bke	142
COSNARD, H.	Bal	32
COSTIN/COSTON		
Costin, Francis	Jef	408
Coston, John	Wsh	259
______, Thomas	Wsh	243
COTHERN/COTHRON/COTREL/ COTHRELT/CAWTHON/CAWTHORN/ CAUTHRON		
Cothern, James	Mor	239
______, John	Mor	248
Cothern, Samuel	Mor	239
Cothron, E.	App	10
______, Elizabeth	Han	149
Cotrel, Jacob	Car	220
Cothrelt, Jehu	Hal	69
Cawthon, Ashley	Tlf	6
______, Chesley	Frk	226
Cawthorn, Orval	Frk	238
______, William	Frk	238
______, William	Tfo	359
Cauthron, Jesse	Tfo	359
COTTER, David	Jef	412
______, George	Jef	414
______, John R.	Hal	101
______, Samuel	Col	340
COTTLE, Ebenezer J.	Jef	407
______, James	Mon	222
______, John J.	Jef	409
**______, Paul G. (slave)	Rch	276
______, Peggy	Mon	197
COTTON/COTTEN/COTTIN		
Cotton, Charles	Bib	54
______, Cyrus	Bib	69
______, Cyrus W.	Bib	69
______, David	DeK	25
______, Elijah	Bib	69
______, George	Wrn	197
______, Henry	Gre	277
______, John H.	Fay	203
______, Leonard	Mus	281
______, Mary	Mon	223
______, Richard	Har	188
______, Seth	Ran	245
______, Smith	Put	215
______, Stephen G.	Crf	401
______, Thomas	DeK	35
______, Weaver	Wil	315
______, William	Lwn	79
______, William	Mon	190
______, William G.	Trp	54
______, William P.	Bib	69
Cotten, George W.	Mor	269
______, John	Mon	224
______, Josiah	Mor	259
Cottin, Cary	Cow	390
______, Tiptin White	Hab	46
COUCH/COUTCH		
Couch, Benjamin	Frk	242
______, Drury	Jsp	360
______, Elijah W.	Frk	240
______, James	Frk	236
______, Nathan	Frk	236
______, Reuben	Frk	241

Name	County	Page
Couch, Samuel	Elb	128
_____, Samuel	Gwn	322
_____, Watson	Bib	63
_____, William	Frk	249
_____, William	Jsp	360
Coutch, Terry	Hal	70
COUDY, A. B.	Bke	130
COUEY/COUY/COVEY/COURIE		
Couey, Absalom	Col	334
_____, James	Lau	11
_____, John	Lau	15
Couy, Andrew	Gwn	314
_____, Andrew	Gwn	346
_____, Joseph	Gwn	346
_____, Samuel	Gwn	314
_____, Samuel	Gwn	346
Covey, John	Bal	43
_____, William	DeK	40
Courie, Alexander	DeK	26
COUGH, Hiram	Gwn	322
COULTER/COULTEAU		
Coulter, Moses F.	Bts	172
_____, William	Jns	428
Coulteau, Mary	Bke	146
COUNCIL/COUNSEL		
Council, Joshua	Ear	98
Counsel, Robert M.	Wks	354
COUNTRYMAN, Andrew	Hab	57
_____, Elias M.	Hab	57
_____, James F.	Hab	57
COURSEY/COURSAY/CORSEY/ CORSSEY/CURSEY		
Coursey, Absalom	Scr	299
_____, Charles	DeK	36
_____, Charles	New	15
_____, Christopher	Jsp	358
_____, James	Jsp	359
_____, John	Lau	18
_____, Sarah	Tat	376
_____, William	Hry	251
Coursay, James	Jef	408
Corsey, Levi	Bib	54
Corssey, Alfred	Wsh	267
Cursey, Bud	Dec	14
COURSON, John	Mon	191
_____, Thomas	App	10
COURTER, Harman	Cam	184
COURTNEY/COTNEY		
Courtney, Ann	Cht	263
_____, E.	Cht	281
_____, Emanuel	Mon	200
Cotney, James	Har	183
COUSINS/COZENS		
Cousins, John	Jsp	372
_____, Sarah	Clk	318
_____, Thomas	Clk	317
_____, Thomas	Jsp	359
Cozens, Williams	Wil	310
COVINGTON, Cloe	Wsh	265
_____, Edward	Pik	128
_____, Isaac	Jef	421
_____, John	DeK	32
_____, Laver	Mar	143
_____, Marshel	Pik	129
_____, Newbill	Cow	336
_____, Noah	Jef	404
_____, Silas	Jef	404
_____, Thomas	Cow	379
_____, William	Pik	130
COWAN/COWEN/COWIN/COWN/ Cowden		
Cowan, Ann	Gwn	329
_____, Chambers	Mus	278
_____, Elijah	Hry	243
_____, John	DeK	52
_____, Middleton	Jks	317
_____, Stephen	Jks	314
Cowen, Alexander	New	42
_____, George	Jks	325
_____, John	Jef	413
_____, Martha	Jks	347
_____, Robert	New	42
_____, William	Hal	114
_____, William A.	Twg	80
Cowin, Edward	Hal	116
_____, John	Ran	241
_____, John C.	Ran	249
Cown, William T.	DeK	32
Cowden, David	New	31
_____, Mary	Cow	384
_____, William	Cow	385
COWARD, Abel	Tat	373
_____, Eliburgh	Rab	233
_____, James	Hab	47
_____, John	Ware	184
_____, John W.	Lee	33
_____, Sarah	Lwn	83
_____, William B.	Lwn	85
COWART, Abraham	Em	173
_____, Augustus M.	Em	175
_____, Cullen	Tat	376
_____, David	Ear	92
_____, Eleazer L.	Em	176
_____, Elias	Doo	78
_____, Hardy	New	47
_____, James	Em	176

Cowart, James	New	53
______, Jesse	New	51
______, John	Tat	376
______, John H.	New	32
______, Lewis	Mon	189
______, Lewis Jr.	Mon	190
______, Malachi	Ear	92
______, Michael	Jef	409
______, Nathaniel	Em	173
______, Penny	Jef	406
______, Stephen	New	47
______, Wiley	New	47
______, William	Jef	406
______, Zachariah	Bib	72
______, Zachariah	Ear	94
COWLES, Asbury	Mon	216
______, Samuel	Put	176
______, Thomas	Put	179
COWLING, Mrs. U.	Rch	256
COWSER, Thomas	New	55
COWSET, Ann	Put	203
COX, Mrs.	Rch	255
______, Aaron	Wsh	271
______, Aaron B.	Wks	357
______, Absalom	Up	100
______, Amos	Frk	248
______, Asa	Bke	152
______, Asa	Jns	430
______, Asa	Mon	222
______, Bartley M.	Jns	472
______, Benjamin	Gwn	351
______, Bobo	Gwn	371
______, Cary	Jns	439
______, Carey	Put	206
______, Chappel	Tlb	324
______, Charles	Mon	181
______, Charles	Up	97
______, Cullen	Wsh	266
______, Damaris	Pul	162
______, David	Trp	50
______, David	Wsh	256
______, Derious	Wsh	243
______, Drury M.	Mon	222
______, Edward	Ogl	98
______, Edwin F.	Clk	303
______, Elisabeth	Hab	47
______, Elizabeth (w)	Mor	272
______, Elizabeth	Rch	257
______, Ephraim	Hry	241
______, Esther	Bke	117
______, George	Elb	134
______, Henry	Hry	204
______, Henry	Wsh	256
Cox, Ichabod	Tlb	346
______, J. Westly	DeK	50
______, James	Bke	132
______, James	Doo	80
______, James	Jef	409
______, James	Jns	443
______, James	Mor	262
______, James	Mus	289
______, James	Wsh	245
______, James R.	Up	114
______, Jeremiah	Put	208
______, Jesse	Bke	125
______, Jesse	DeK	28
______, Jesse	Jns	459
______, John	Hab	56
______, John	Hal	71
______, John	Hal	120
______, John	Jef	422
______, John	Lee	34
______, John	Mar	140
______, John	Wsh	247
______, John	Wsh	270
______, John H.	Bke	152
______, John M.	Ogl	101
______, John R.	Fay	195
______, John T.	Hal	85
______, Johnathan	Hab	19
______, Joseph	Cht	240
______, Joseph	Jns	450
______, Joshua	Fay	184
______, Levi	Doo	79
______, Lewis	Trp	44
______, Malone	Gwn	372
______, Mary	DeK	50
______, Mary	Frk	219
______, Mathew	Wrn	232
______, Moses	Hry	243
______, Moses	Wsh	273
______, Phebe	Hal	96
______, Phebe	Mar	143
______, Pleasant	Mwr	160
______, Reuben	Frk	217
______, Richard	Clk	316
______, Richard	Hab	19
______, Richard	Wal	140
______, Robert	Gwn	372
______, Robert	Ogl	85
______, Robert M.	Hst	289
______, Robert R.	Fay	188
______, Samuel	Em	173
______, Sarah	Jsp	363
______, Terry	Hab	33
______, Thomas	Fay	184

Name	County	Page
Cox, Thomas	Gwn	353
______, Thomas	Gwn	372
______, Thomas W.	Mus	277
______, Thomas W.	Trp	40
______, Venson	Gwn	372
______, William	Frk	251
______, William	Hab	14
______, William	Hab	25
______, William	Hab	49
______, William	Hry	241
______, William	Jns	441
______, William	Jns	450
______, William	Mor	252
______, William	Wsh	272
______, William	Wil	308
______, William B.	DeK	50
______, Williamson	Doo	86
______, Willis	Bts	171
______, Willis	DeK	44
______, Willis	Tlb	337
______, Z	Up	97
______, Zilphy	Tlb	332
COXON, Mary	Han	149
COXWELL, Benjamin Jr.	Wrn	230
______, James	Wrn	231
______, John	Wrn	230
______, Mitchell	Bib	66
COYLES, James	Tlb	344
CRABB, Asa	New	44
______, Benjamin	Wil	304
______, Burton	Hry	248
______, Elizabeth	Mwr	168
______, Robert	Wsh	240
______, Sarah	Col	353
______, Stephen L.	Pul	162
CRABTREE, John	Put	212
______, William	Cht	244
CRABY, Jacob	Mon	220
CRADDOCK/CRADUK		
Craddock, David	Wal	130
______, John A.	Car	221
______, William	Gwn	317
Craduk, John A.	DeK	72
CRAFFORD: see Crawford		
CRAFT/CROFT		
Craft, Anderson	Elb	138
______, Benjamin	Pul	156
______, Daniel Sr.	Clk	296
______, Daniel Jr.	Clk	308
______, David	Hal	101
______, Edward	Clk	308
______, Garrett	Clk	303
______, Jese	Hab	52
Craft, John Jr.	Elb	126
______, Pleasant	Gwn	343
______, Pleasant	Gwn	364
______, Samuel	Elb	123
______, Selia	Wsh	271
______, Washington	Elb	124
______, William	Elb	122
Croft, Samuel	Har	189
CRAFTON, Bennet	Rch	289
______, John H.	Put	185
______, Mathew	Wsh	250
______, William	Wsh	250
CRAIG/CRAIGE/CRAGG/CRAGE		
Craig, Alexander	Hry	211
______, Andrew	Fay	198
______, Ann	Cht	251
______, Elbert	Cht	240
______, H. K.	Gwn	332
______, Loddrick	Tlb	344
______, Robert	Gwn	365
______, W. M.	Cht	269
______, William	Cht	259
Craige, Allen	Rch	269
Cragg, James	Gwn	356
Crage, William	Clk	321
______, William D.	Hab	44
CRAMER/KRAMER/CREMER/		
CREAMA/CREAMER/CREMEEN		
Cramer, Samuel	Ogl	87
______, Solomon	Eff	107
Kramer, David	Bal	34
Cremer, Benjamin	Hst	285
______, Hugh S.	Lin	68
______, Robert	Pik	114
Creama, A.	Cht	260
Creamer, James	Hal	117
Cremeen, James	Tlb	332
CRANDAL, Smith	Jks	331
CRANE, Coalba	Hab	50
______, David	Hry	236
______, Eleanor	Jsp	366
______, Elijah	Rab	224
______, Elizabeth	Jsp	373
______, George	Mwr	155
______, James	Cht	270
______, James	Eff	114
______, Jemima	Hry	221
______, Jesse	Rab	233
______, John	Rch	256
______, Joshua	Wil	297
______, Josiah	Bts	160
______, Spencer	Jsp	373
______, Warren	Jsp	366

Name	County	Page
Crane, Wiley	Hry	237
______, William H.	Hab	62
CRANFORD, Elias	New	32
______, James	Jsp	356
______, Jesse	Jsp	356
______, Jesse	Mwr	151
______, John	Twg	71
______, Leonard	New	32
______, William	Twg	67
CRANSON, Felia	Lin	61
______, John	Lin	62
CRAVEN/CRAVAN/CRAVENS		
Craven, Balum	Clk	307
______, John	Hab	26
______, Thomas	Clk	309
______, Thomas W.	Hab	26
Cravan, John	Cow	370
Cravens, Isaac	Hab	27
CRAVER, Andrew	Mor	244
______, Phillip	Mor	249
CRAVEY/CRAVY		
Cravey, David	Tlf	9
______, Henry	Tms	20
______, James	Doo	80
Cravy, Joshua	Dec	8
______, Lewis	Har	191
CRAWFORD/CROFFORD/ CRAFFORD/CRAFORD		
Crawford, A. L. Mrs.	Col	343
______, Aaron	Hry	211
______, Alexander	Hal	94
______, Alexander P.	Twg	60
______, Andrew	Pik	118
______, Ann	Col	349
______, Arthur	Hal	92
______, Arthur	Hry	208
______, Charles	Bib	54
______, David	Mon	201
______, David Sr.	New	34
______, David	New	10
______, Dorothy	Bib	50
______, Edward	Col	334
______, Elijah	DeK	25
______, Elijah D.	Jsp	386
______, Elisha	Frk	229
______, Elza	Col	337
______, George	Mon	178
______, George	Mon	210
______, George W.	New	10
______, George W.	Rch	277
______, Gideon	Lwn	86
______, Hardy	Pik	118
______, Henry	Elb	154

Name	County	Page
Crawford, Henry	Jks	343
______, Hinton	Gre	288
______, Hugh	Frk	242
______, James	Han	150
______, James	Lwn	88
______, James	New	28
______, James	Tlb	328
______, Joel	Han	148
______, Joel	Mor	252
______, John	Eff	106
______, John	Lin	70
______, John	Mon	201
______, John	Wks	348
______, John	Wks	358
______, John M.	Jks	343
______, Jos.	Jks	327
______, Leonard	New	31
______, Lerry	Lin	71
______, Levy M.	Clk	316
______, Lucy	Elb	121
______, Margaret	Rab	231
______, Mariah	Clk	292
______, Mary	Cht	269
______, Nancy	Trp	43
______, Nathan	Col	334
______, Nathan	Col	361
______, Noel	Gre	297
______, Peter	Col	337
______, Reuben	Lwn	86
______, Riley J.	Mon	203
______, Samuel	Jsp	380
______, Semers	Col	343
______, Silas	Clk	323
______, Syntha	Pul	149
______, Thomas Sr.	Gre	288
______, Thomas Jr.	Gre	288
______, Thomas	Lin	72
______, Thomas	Lin	73
______, Thomas	Lwn	88
______, Thomas	Tms	24
______, Thomas	Twg	66
______, Thomas	Wal	161
______, Thomas	Wsh	276
______, Uriah P.	Tlb	326
______, W. L.	Col	337
______, William	Col	346
______, William	Elb	158
______, William	Gre	297
______, William	Hry	213
______, William	Hry	225
______, William	Lee	28
______, William	McI	131
______, William	Mon	218

Crawford, William B. Tms 28
_____, William H. Ogl 94
_____, William S.P. Frk 242
_____, William W. Hry 215
_____, Williamson Hst 266
Crofford, Bennet Dec 12
_____, Charles Cpb 209
_____, Milton Dec 16
Crafford, George Hab 62
Craford, Hardy Dec 19
CRAWLEY/CRAWLY/CROLEY
Crawley, Charles Mor 257
_____, Darcus DeK 61
_____, Genethan Pik 106
_____, James Pik 117
_____, Robert Mor 259
_____, Simon Wal 155
_____, William Mor 258
Crawly, Kern Pik 115
Croley, Abraham Clk 318
CRAWMAN, Mary Wrn 223
CRAY, Scott Bib 54
CRA YTON/CREYTON/CREIGHTON
Crayton, John Cam 182
_____, Sylvester Wil 291
_____, William L. Hry 214
Creyton, John Jks 345
Creighton, Mary Ann Wil 299
_____, William W. Mar 140
CREACH, Charles Lau 16
_____, Joshua Lau 15
CREAL, John New 31
_____, Joseph Hry 244
_____, William New 32
CREDELLE/CRIDDLE
Credelle, Gray Gre 286
_____, Sarah Gre 290
_____, William Gre 290
_____, William Sr. Gre 303
Criddle, Abigail Hry 208
CREDLETON, Eleanor Rab 225
CREEMY, Rebecca App 11
CREMER: see Cramer
CRENSHAW/KRENSHAW
Crenshaw, Benjamin Wrn 204
_____, Duke R. Lee 29
_____, Fortune W. Frk 218
_____, James Pik 128
_____, James J. Clk 326
_____, Joseph Jsp 355
_____, Levi Mon 202
_____, Margaret Wrn 202
_____, Micajah Lee 29
Crenshaw, Micajah Lee 29
_____, Robert Cpb 210
_____, Sus. Bal 41
Krenshaw, Nathaniel DeK 72
CREVILLIER/CRUVILLEIR
CRevillier, Hager Cht 250
Cruvilleir, Justine Cht 253
_____, also see Chevaleir
CREWS/CREW/KREWS
Crews, Alexander Cam 191
_____, Benedicta Wil 308
_____, David Frk 243
_____, Edward Ware 185
_____, Hannah Eff 113
_____, Isham Wyn 282
_____, Isaac Cam 183
_____, James Tfo 367
_____, John Cam 187
_____, Joseph Sr. Cam 185
_____, Joseph Jr. Cam 187
_____, Mary Cam 191
_____, Nancy Ann Gre 302
_____, Peter Fay 204
_____, R. J. Up 95
_____, Richard Wil 297
_____, Stephen Ware 185
_____, William Gwn 347
_____, William Ware 185
Crew, Carter Hry 211
_____, Elisha Hry 219
_____, John Mus 292
_____, Penny Wrn 217
_____, William Mus 290
_____, William F. Hry 251
Krews, Phillip J. Wsh 273
CRIBB, Covington Bul 95
_____, Jeremiah Jns 456
_____, John Lib 44
_____, Jonathan App 11
_____, Thomas Wyn 282
CRIDER, Barbary Frk 248
_____, David Frk 214
_____, Jacob Frk 248
_____, Jacob Mad 106
_____, John Frk 214
_____, Mary (w) Mor 250
CRIM/CRIMM
Crim, Mrs. Clary Col 340
_____, James Lin 71
Crimm, David Hry 211
CRISLER/CRISTLER
Crisler, Benjamin Elb 146
_____, Julius Elb 159

Cristler, Absalom	Jks	335
CRISP/CRISS/CHRISP/CRISSOP		
Crisp, Moses P.	Col	352
Criss, John	Frk	245
Chrisp, Jane Lane Marian	Rch	258
Crissop, Jarrerd	Han	150
CRISWELL/CHRISTWELL/ CHRESTWELL		
Criswell, John	DeK	60
Christwell, Sarah	Wks	353
Chrestwell, Whit	Wks	348
CRITTENDEN/CRITTENTON/ CRITENTON/CRIDDENTON		
*Crittenden, Edward	Car	234
_____, Robert G.	Tlb	327
Crittenton, Edney	Fay	197
Critenton, Elijah	Elb	133
Criddenton, Pryor	Mad	104
_____, William	Mad	102
CROCKER, Elijah E.	Hst	266
_____, John	Frk	221
_____, John	McI	128
_____, John	Twg	74
_____, William	Twg	62
_____, William W.L.	Hst	265
CROCKET/CROCKETT		
Crocket, David	Wal	123
_____, Joseph	Car	218
_____, Joseph	Mwr	151
_____, Samuel	Car	217
_____, Wilson	Bts	177
Crockett, Daniel	Rch	260
_____, Floyd	Bke	142
_____, James W.	Hry	245
_____, Joseph	DeK	65
_____, Nancy	Hry	245
CROFFORD: see Crawford		
CROMBIE, James B.	Hry	234
_____, James B. A.	Fay	198
_____, William A.	Fay	198
CRONAN, James	Hab	9
_____, James S.	Hab	11
CRONIC/CRONICK		
Cronic, Hasell	Wal	173
Cronick, John	Wal	174
CRONVOISE, Estate of F.	Cht	279
CROOK/CROOKS		
Crook, Griffin	Pik	107
_____, Hugh	Hal	73
_____, Jeremiah	Car	220
_____, John	Ogl	83
_____, Lewis	Wil	306
_____, Osborn	Har	179
Crook, Valentine	Ogl	80
Crooks, Robert	Jef	401
CROOM, Emmara	Wsh	261
_____, Jinnett	Wsh	273
_____, Major	Wsh	262
CROP, Silas	Jks	314
CROPPER, Cornelius	Hal	131
CROSBY/CROSBEY/CRAUSBEY		
Crosby, John	Wil	301
_____, Levi	App	6
_____, Nancy	Col	351
_____, Thomas	Col	349
_____, Urial	Wil	313
Crosbey, Thomas	Bul	98
Crausbey, Sally	Twg	80
_____, Spencer	Twg	80
CROSS, Ann E.	Jsp	365
_____, Betsey	Gre	280
_____, Cullin	Lau	14
_____, Dawson	Dec	4
_____, Edward	Hst	283
_____, Featherston	Ogl	92
_____, Harris	Jsp	373
_____, Isaac	Bke	123
_____, Jese	Hab	29
_____, John	Elb	140
_____, John	Irw	299
_____, John	Wks	338
_____, Joseph	Bke	124
_____, Joseph	Fay	197
_____, Nemrod	Hal	82
_____, Richard	Jsp	369
_____, Robert	Mus	288
_____, Sardis E.	Bke	124
_____, Thomas	Bke	125
_____, Thomas	Hab	29
_____, Thomas Jr.	Hab	57
_____, William	Bke	118
_____, William	Hal	82
_____, William	Lau	14
CROSSLEY/CROSLEY		
Crossley, Edward	Gre	301
_____, Issabella	Jef	410
_____, John	Mon	225
_____, Lemuel	Gre	276
Crosley, Robert	Col	344
CROSSON/CROSSIN		
Crosson, Lewis	Fay	186
Crossin, James	Cow	383
_____, Manna	Jns	464
CROTWELL, Adam	Gwn	311
_____, George	Gwn	311
CROUCH/CROUTCH		

Name	County	Page
Crouch, George	Put	185
______, George	Tlb	340
______, James	Tlb	341
______, John	Wal	130
______, Joseph	Hry	247
______, Thomas	Jsp	388
Croutch, John Jr.	Jsp	388
CROW/CROE		
Crow, Aaron	Clk	291
______, Abel	Wal	167
______, Abner	DeK	49
______, Austin	DeK	42
______, Burney	Cpb	210
______, Carlile B.	Hal	78
______, Casey	Frk	211
______, Colemon M.	Frk	248
______, Dennison	DeK	43
______, Devron	Pik	113
______, Elisha	Jsp	373
______, Elizabeth	Wal	163
______, Henry	Pik	116
______, Isaac	Clk	291
______, Jacob	Cpb	209
______, Jacob	Fay	182
______, James	Car	226
______, James	Hab	6
______, James	Hal	88
______, James	Rab	233
______, John	Hab	19
______, Jonathan	Hal	88
______, Joshua	DeK	45
______, Larton	Hal	88
______, Lewis	Hal	88
______, M.	Bal	38
______, Malinda	Frk	257
______, Martin	Clk	311
______, Randolph	Frk	210
______, Randolph Jr.	Frk	257
______, Reuben	Jsp	356
______, Samuel	Hal	77
______, Samuel B.	Hal	79
______, Sarah	Frk	248
______, Stephens	Clk	302
______, William	Cpb	210
______, William	Mwr	167
______, William L.	Hab	59
______, William T.	Frk	246
Croe, William	Hab	57
CROWDER, Fredric	Mon	215
______, George W.	Ogl	94
______, George W.	Hry	213
______, H. C.	Bal	31
______, John M.	Bib	63

Name	County	Page
Crowder, Nancy	Ogl	67
______, Nancy	Ogl	93
______, Sterling	Jns	472
______, Thomas	Han	150
CROWELL/CROLL		
Crowell, Henry	Crf	398
______, Nancy	Gwn	354
Croll, Samuel K.	Tlb	322
CROWLEY, Mrs.	Rch	263
______, George	Trp	43
______, Sarah	Rch	263
______, Thomas	Tlb	342
______, also see Croley with Crawley		
CROWN, Lurence	Rab	233
CROXTON, Gidean H.	Mus	290
______, James	Clk	306
CROZIER/CROSIER		
Crozier, John	Bke	132
______, John	Hry	203
______, John	Lin	74
______, Thomas	Bke	133
Crosier, A.	Bal	32
CRUCE/CRUSE/CRUISE		
Cruce,Jesse	Lee	34
______, Rich.	Gwn	338
______, Stephen	Gwn	346
______, William	DeK	64
Cruse, Hiram	Mwr	159
______, John	Bke	126
______, Samuel S.	Hal	94
Cruise, Samuel	Cht	278
______, William	Cow	383
CRUM, Benjamin	Pul	146
______, David	Cam	190
______, Harmon	Lwn	83
______, Henry W.	Bry	84
CRUMLEY/CRUMBLEY/CRUMLY		
Crumley, Benjamin	Gwn	324
______, Benjamin	Hab	64
______, Robert	Hab	64
______, Robert H.	Hab	64
______, William	Hab	60
Crumbley, Anthony	Hry	241
______, Anthony Jr.	Hry	242
______, George	Hry	251
______, John	Hry	241
Crumly, Henry M.	Hab	56
______, Thomas	Hab	60
CRUMP, John C.	Em	165
______, Philip	Rch	257
______, Richard	Frk	234
______, Robert	Elb	144

Crump, Robert Frk 216
_____, Samuel Col 338
CRUMPLER, John Doo 85
CRUMPTON, John Bul 103
_____, Richard Cpb 200
_____, William Twg 85
CRUTCHFIELD, George Gre 283
_____, John Wks 335
_____, Joab Pul 158
_____, Joseph Gwn 376
_____, Philip Fay 196
_____, Stapleton Jns 431
_____, Thomas Crf 415
_____, Thomas P. Wks 336
_____, Ulyses Pul 158
_____, William Jsp 362
CRYE/CRYER
Crye, William Sr. Hal 94
_____, William Jr. Hal 94
Cryer, Patty Cam 186
CUBBAGE, John Cht 258
CUDD, John DeK 41
CULBERSON/CULBESON/
CULBERTSON
Culberson, David B. Trp 46
_____, Green Trp 50
_____, J. F. Up 104
_____, James New 53
_____, Martin Rab 223
_____, Thomas Jsp 383
Culbeson, James Trp 35
Culbertson, William P. Mad 112
CULBREATH/CULBRETH
Culbreath, Alexander Mar 138
_____, James Col 336
_____, James Col 347
_____, James Rch 283
_____, Lewis Tlb 327
_____, Joel Wal 150
_____, Obedeoh Col 352
_____, Thomas Col 338
_____, Thomas Col 339
_____, Thomas Col 345
_____, William Wal 130
_____, William L. Col 345
Culbreth, Anguish Elb 119
_____, John Gre 279
CULPEPPER/CULPEPER
Culpepper, Allison Hst 275
_____, Benjamin Wrn 199
_____, Catharine Lau 24
_____, Chadwell Lau 19
_____, Charles Hst 285
Culpepper, Christopher Jns 468
_____, Daniel Crf 394
_____, David Lau 12
_____, David Mus 291
_____, Dickerson Wrn 193
_____, Edey Lau 21
_____, Edward Jns 468
_____, Elijah Lau 21
_____, Francis G. Tlb 339
_____, H. Jks 338
_____, Isiah Ran 248
_____, James Wrn 199
_____, James J. Crf 399
_____, Jeremiah Jns 468
_____, Joel Crf 410
_____, Joel Jks 338
_____, Joel Jns 464
_____, Joel Wks 336
_____, John Mon 194
_____, John C. Lau 8
_____, John J. Up 110
_____, John S. Mon 197
_____, Joseph Hst 280
_____, Joseph Wrn 199
_____, Joseph R. Pik 113
_____, Lemuel Jsp 365
_____, Malliciah Cow 382
_____, Mariner Mon 173
_____, Mary Mon 194
_____, Mary Wrn 198
_____, Nancy Jks 339
_____, Owen Jks 339
_____, Sampson Hst 294
_____, Simon Jks 339
_____, Wilson Jns 468
Culpeper, Benjamin Doo 84
_____, Jane Col 354
CULVER, Augustus Han 149
_____, Eliza Put 176
_____, Elizabeth Han 150
_____, Hardy C. Han 149
_____, Isaac Han 149
_____, Joseph Han 149
_____, Joshua Han 149
_____, Levin E. Han 149
_____, Nancy Han 149
_____, Obadiah Han 148
CULVERHOUSE, Charles Wrn 202
_____, John Crf 400
_____, Mildred Han 149
_____, Polly Han 172
CULWAT, John Put 186
CUMBO/CUMBER

Name	County	Page
Cumbo, Uriah	Tms	17
Cumber, Peter	Han	150
CUMMING/CUMMINGS/CUMMINS/		
CUMINS/COMMINS		
Cumming, A	Bal	45
_____, David	Wsh	263
_____, Elijah	Ogl	103
_____, Elizabeth	Rch	259
_____, Henry H.	Rch	277
_____, John	Cht	249
_____, Joseph	Cht	249
_____, Sophia	Cht	241
_____, Thomas	Gre	289
_____, Thomas	Rch	274
_____, William	Rch	264
Cummings, Ann	Lwn	89
_____, Benjamin	Fay	199
_____, Eli	Wsh	254
_____, George	Tlf	9
_____, James	Fay	193
_____, Luther	Rch	274
_____, Robert	Wsh	250
_____, William	Bib	49
Cummins, Elijah	Gre	298
_____, Francis	Gre	278
_____, Stephen	Put	193
_____, William	Mus	278
Cumins, Gideon	Put	179
_____, Harmon	DeK	42
Comins, Robert	Twg	60
CUNNINGHAM/CUNNIGAN/CUNNING		
Cunningham, A.	Rch	260
_____, Andrew	Jks	317
_____, Ann	McI	121
_____, Ann P.	Jef	420
_____, Ansel	Jks	326
_____, Charles	Jef	420
_____, David	Mad	107
_____, Drury	Wil	307
_____, Franklin	Elb	145
_____, George	New	15
_____, Harry	Cht	241
_____, J. T.	Jks	317
_____, James	Jks	315
_____, James	Mon	207
_____, John	Gre	282
_____, John	Mor	242
_____, John A.	Elb	124
_____, Joseph	Elb	158
_____, Joseph B.	Mwr	156
_____, Joseph H.	Fay	195
_____, Joseph L.	Har	190
_____, M.	Cht	261
Cunningham, Philip	Up	113
_____, Robert	Jns	442
_____, Robert E.	Jef	420
_____, Sophia	Jks	334
_____, Tabitha	Jef	419
_____, Thomas	Gre	305
_____, Thomas	Wsh	276
_____, William	Mon	190
_____, William	Mon	225
_____, William	Pik	119
Cunnigan, William	Ogl	80
Cunning, John	Jef	414
CUPP, Henry Sr.	DeK	72
_____, Henry Jr.	DeK	72
_____, Michael	DeK	44
_____, Ralleigh	Cow	371
_____, Thomas	DeK	44
_____, Walner	DeK	44
_____, William	Gwn	319
CURAUR, Charles	Bul	96
CURD, Edward	Put	209
_____, John	Hry	231
_____, Nancy	Hry	231
CURETON, Dickson	Tlb	326
_____, Hannah	Up	119
_____, James	Up	106
_____, John	Mon	188
_____, William	Up	99
CURINGTON/CURINTON/CURRINGTON		
Curington, John	Hst	293
Curinton, Rison	Crf	398
Currington, Robert	Bib	60
CURKINDOL/CURKINDOLL/		
KURKINDOL		
Curkindol, Abraham	Hab	49
_____, Peter	Hab	59
Curkindoll, Jese	Hab	25
Kurkindol, James	Hab	63
_____, Joseph H.	Hab	63
CURL, John	Em	172
_____, Jordan	DeK	55
_____, Mathew	Em	172
_____, Mathew	Em	172
_____, Willson	Lee	35
CURLEY/CURLEE		
Curley, Arthur Sr.	Bul	94
_____, Benjamin	Em	172
_____, Zekiel	Cpb	210
Curlee, Mary	Wal	158
CURRY/CURRIE/CURRAY/CURREY		
Curry, Allen	Lin	71
_____, Ann	Cht	269
_____, Arburthy	Cht	247

Name	County	Page
Curry, Daniel	Gre	273
______, David	Wsh	257
______, Duncan	Dec	11
______, Duncan	Tlf	11
______, Ebenz.	Wks	337
______, Frances	Lin	64
______, George	Wsh	251
______, Henry	Bib	69
______, Jacob	Up	121
______, Jacob	Wks	337
______, James Jr.	Gre	272
______, James	Wks	337
______, James S.	Cow	377
______, John	Eff	110
______, John	Har	185
______, John	Wsh	251
______, John	Wsh	267
______, John S.	Gre	273
______, Joseph	Tat	377
______, Leroy	Mwr	152
______, Nancy	Em	177
______, Nathaniel	Lin	74
______, Peter M.	Bib	63
______, Robert	Cow	377
______, Robert M.	Bts	169
______, Russel	Tat	374
______, Samuel S.	Mad	103
______, Sarah	Lin	73
______, Thomas	Bal	37
______, Thomas	Hry	212
______, Thomas	Lin	70
______, Thomas C.	Lin	71
______, Thompson	Jsp	389
______, W. L.	Bal	41
______, Whitmel	Wks	350
______, Wiley	Wil	317
______, William	Eff	107
______, William	Lin	70
______, William	New	26
______, William	Tlf	8
______, William S.	Lin	65
______, Willis	Wil	317
______, Wyley	Wil	302
Currie, Alexander	Mtg	231
______, John	Lib	44
______, Malcom	Mtg	232
Curray, William	Mor	263
______, Currey, Grace	Mtg	235
CURTIS, David	Scr	303
______, Henry	Car	217
______, John	Crf	411
______, Mary	Han	150
______, Robert	Crf	393
Curtis, Thomas G.	Crf	414
______, William	Cam	182
CURTON, Henry	DeK	61
______, Hily	DeK	61
CUSEN, Martha	Col	335
CUSHIN/CUSHING/CUSHAN		
Cushin, Elisha	Ran	250
Cushing, J. T.	Bal	29
Cushan, James	Mwr	152
CUSHMAN, Ira	Ear	95
CUTHBERT, Col. Alfred	Jsp	378
______, Alfred	Lib	44
______, John	Cht	257
______, John A.	Mon	196
______, Molly	Cht	270
CUTHRELL/CUTHRILL/CUTHRIELL		
Cuthrell, Moses	Hal	105
Cuthrill, Thomas	Bak	16
Cuthriell, Joshua	Pul	138
CUTLIFF, Benjamin	Crf	409
CUTTER, Henry S.	Bib	58
CUTTS, Elijah	Lwn	91
______, Elijah	Wsh	267
______, Elisha	Hst	290
______, Major	Hst	282
CUWILLS, James	Mwr	164
CUYLER, J.	Cht	261
______, Jeremiah	Eff	112
______, R. R.	Cht	266
______, W. H.	Cht	261
CYRUS, Nimrod	Hry	246
______, William	Hry	245
DABA, L.	Cht	271
DABNEY/DABNY		
Dabney, Garland	DeK	64
______, Hannah	Jsp	393
______, Tiry G.	New	33
Dabny, William D.	Ogl	77
DACUS, Thomas	New	21
DAGNALD/DAGNALL		
Dagnald, John	Col	343
Dagnall, Ambrous	Col	340
DAILEY/DAILY/DALY		
Dailey, James	Frk	230
______, John Sr.	Hry	214
______, Mary	Bke	118
______, Mary	Rch	288
______, Samuel C.	Hry	214
Daily, Martha	Jks	338
______, Vince	Bul	96
______, William	Frk	246

Name	County	Page
Daly, John	Eff	116
DAMPEER/DAMPERS/DAMPIER/ DAMPIERE		
Dampeer, John	Lwn	80
______, William	Lwn	81
Dampers, James	Scr	306
Dampier, Mary	Eff	113
Dampiere, Daniel	Eff	112
DALBY, Elizabeth	Rch	258
DALE, John	Mtg	233
______, Stephen	Hal	101
______, Thomas P.	Gre	278
DALLAS, Dennis B.	Elb	154
______, Lee	Lin	58
______, Thomas	Lin	58
______, William	Lin	58
DALMEYDA, David	Bib	50
DALTON/DAULTON		
Dalton, Baley T.	Put	202
______, James	Wal	139
______, Jesse	Ogl	79
______, John	Clk	304
______, Ollive	Put	203
Daulton, George	Hab	12
DALRYMPLE/DALRYAMPLE		
Dalrymple, Edmond	Hal	97
______, Thomas	Hal	97
Dalryample, Isaac	Hal	97
DAME, George	Em	171
______, John	Jns	428
DAMRON, Uriah	Jks	311
DAMSON, Edward	New	44
DANAH/DANAHA		
Danah, John	Crf	410
______, Joseph T.	Crf	409
Danaha, O.	Cht	251
DANARD, Isaac	Wil	319
DANCE, Mathew	Ogl	101
DANDY, William	Mor	250
DANFORTH/DONFORTH		
Danforth, Jacob	Rch	260
______, Mary	Pul	147
______, Samuel	Wil	316
______, Thomas B.	Rch	273
______, Thomas L.	Rch	266
______, William	Cpb	205
Donforth, Joshua	Rch	253
DANGER, Nathan	DeK	45
DANIEL/DANIELS/DANIELL/ DANEL/DANNELL/DANIL/DANNILS		
Daniel, Aaron	Irw	303
______, Aaron	New	43
______, Abel	Crf	407
Daniel, Abraham	Lib	44
______, Alexander	Irw	304
______, Alexander	Wsh	248
______, Alexander M.	Fay	186
______, Asa	Hal	113
______, Asbury	Mor	255
______, Asy	Lee	34
______, Beaton	New	8
______, Beverly	Hal	70
______, Bevely	Pik	113
______, Bryant	Rch	281
______, Burgess	Fay	200
______, Catherine	Jsp	382
______, Clara	Rch	278
______, Cordiel N.	Gre	283
______, Cordy	Clk	301
______, Cunningham	Wil	314
______, David	Cow	375
______, David	Elb	123
______, David	Gwn	325
______, David	Mor	256
______, David	Mor	266
______, David	Tfo	366
______, David	Wks	332
______, David	Wrn	210
______, David M.	Pul	151
______, Eckels	Crf	406
______, Edmund	Tfo	364
______, Edmund	Mon	227
______, Elizabeth	Hal	104
______, Elizabeth	Pul	147
______, Elizabeth	Ran	245
______, Elizabeth	Tat	379
______, Egbert P.	Pik	119
______, Enoch	Lib	44
______, Ephraim	Twg	77
______, Ezekiel	Wal	162
______, Ezekial	Wsh	257
______, Fedrick	Pik	119
______, Gen. Allen	Mad	104
______, George	New	37
______, George W.	Lau	5
______, Hannah	Tfo	369
______, Hopkins	Mon	183
______, Isaac	Jsp	365
______, Isaac	Ran	249
______, Isaac H.	New	37
______, Isham	Hst	285
______, J. W. G.	Bal	35
______, James	Lau	4
______, James	Mad	106
______, James	Mon	180
______, James Sr.	Mor	266

Name	County	Page
Daniel, James	New	43
______, James	Mus	281
______, James	Pik	121
______, James	Wal	162
______, James	Wil	291
______, James K.	Gre	305
______, James L.	Elb	122
______, James L.	Han	151
______, James W.	Mon	183
______, Jane	Tfo	366
______, Jesse	Fay	200
______, John	Bib	72
______, John	DeK	31
______, John	Elb	124
______, John	Elb	144
______, John	Har	192
______, John	Jns	456
______, John	Lau	6
______, John	Mor	255
______, John Sr.	Mor	271
______, John	Pul	149
______, John	Wsh	241
______, John D.	Jsp	352
______, John K.	Gre	286
______, John L.	Tfo	357
______, John M.	DeK	27
______, John R.	Em	175
______, Jonas	Twg	61
______, Joseph	Wsh	247
______, Josiah	Clk	293
______, Josiah	Hab	7
______, Josiah	Twg	61
______, Kenith	Wsh	243
______, Lewis	Pik	113
______, Levi	Har	185
______, Littleton Sr.	Cow	385
______, Magers	Rch	283
______, Martha	Han	151
______, Mary	Gre	284
______, Mary	Gre	295
______, Mary	Tat	380
______, Mary	Wsh	275
______, Mary K.	Gre	295
______, Master	New	8
______, Moses	Pul	149
______, Moses	Tms	16
______, Needham	Rch	283
______, Obadiah	Tlb	339
______, Owin D.	Crf	408
______, Peter	Lau	18
______, Reuben	Gwn	375
______, Rejoice	Mon	215
______, Richard	Fay	200
Daniel, Robert H.	Jsp	363
______, Russel J.	Mad	98
______, Sarah	Hst	288
______, Seth	Hst	287
______, Thomas	Mus	284
______, Thomas	New	39
______, Thomas B.	Pik	119
______, Timothy	Mus	287
______, W. C.	Cht	259
______, William	Bal	37
______, William	Bib	55
______, William	Clk	293
______, William	Em	176
______, William	Gre	284
______, William	Hal	104
______, William	Lau	7
______, William	Tlb	329
______, William	Wks	355
______, William H.	Tfo	357
______, Wilson	New	21
______, Young	Bal	37
______, Zachriah	Wsh	263
Daniels, James	Hal	131
Daniell, Alfred	Clk	294
______, Christopher	Bke	137
______, David	Bke	143
______, Ezekiel	Mor	268
______, Isaac	Clk	311
______, Jeremiah	Clk	302
______, Matthew	Bke	148
______, Moses	Bke	117
______, Nathanuel	Clk	315
______, Robert C.	Bke	136
______, Thomas	Clk	312
______, Zachariah	Bke	148
Danel, Allen	Mar	141
______, Joseph	Mar	141
Dannel, Robert C.	Ogl	79
Danil, William	Hab	28
Dannils, Hamilton	Tms	27
DANILEY/DANIELY/DANIELLY/ DANILY/DANELEY		
Daniley, Sarah	Bib	50
______, William J.	Bib	54
Daniely, Margaret	Mtg	236
Danielly, Elizabeth	Jsp	363
Danily, Arthur	Wrn	215
Daneley, John	Wrn	227
DANNER, Abraham	Wil	310
______, Bryant	Wil	294
______, John	Lin	59
______, Joseph	Wil	292
DANSBY, John C.	Ogl	63

D'ANTIGNAC, Hannah Rch 263
_____, W. M. D. Rch 275
DARBY/DERBY
Darby, A. E. Rch 264
_____, Charles Sr. Frk 218
_____, Cusbeth Mon 204
_____, Isaac Twg 74
_____, J. Col 335
_____, Jeremiah Twg 77
_____, Julus G. Wal 144
_____, Mary Wal 141
_____, Micajah Hst 277
_____, Oliver Jef 421
_____, Thomas Fay 202
Derby, James Tfo 358
DARDEN/DARDAN/DARDIN
Darden, C. B. Jsp 367
_____, Elisha Wal 161
_____, Elisha Wrn 200
_____, Elizabeth Jsp 369
_____, George W. Mwr 158
_____, Hezekiah Wil 294
_____, James Wrn 200
_____, Jethro Mon 214
_____, Jethro Wrn 200
_____, Jonathan Wrn 201
_____, Josiah Tlb 329
_____, Micajah Wrn 200
_____, Reuben R. Tlb 328
_____, Samuel Wil 301
_____, Stephin Wsh 262
_____, William Mon 192
_____, William Tfo 359
_____, Willis Wrn 201
_____, Wilson Mon 216
_____, Zachariah Mon 215
Dardan, Elisha Mar 142
Dardin, James H. Trp 32
DARK, Thomas Mwr 153
_____, William L. Mwr 153
DARLEY, James Jef 403
_____, John W. Jef 406
_____, Thomas Jef 406
_____, Thomas Mtg 232
DARLING, Massa Cht 270
_____, Ralph Col 334
DARNELL/DARNEL
Darnell, A. Bal 37
_____, Benjamin New 31
_____, Joseph Mor 261
_____, Samuel New 31
_____, William Mor 262
Darnel, Sarah Rab 229

DARRAGH/DARRAH/DOURROUGH
Darragh, James Wil 314
_____, Richmond Wil 314
Darrah & Townsend Bib 50
(a group: 30 white males, 3 white females, 11 slaves)
Dourrough, Thomas Mor 268
DARRICOAT/DERRICOTE
Darricoat, William Gre 285
Derricote, James B. New 34
DARSAY: see Dorsay
DART, Ann Gly 265
DASHER, Benjamin Eff 113
_____, Benjamin Jr. Eff 107
_____, Christian Eff 105
_____, Christian H. Eff 107
_____, Gideon Eff 105
_____, Gottlieb Eff 107
_____, John Eff 108
_____, Joshua Tat 380
_____, Martin Eff 104
_____, Samuel Eff 107
_____, Solomon Eff 104
_____, Thomas Eff 107
DAUGHTRY/DAUTRY
Daughtry, Bryant Hst 261
_____, Edmund Put 212
_____, Jacob Em 176
_____, Joshua Ear 94
_____, Joshua Hst 281
Dautry, Joseph Scr 304
_____, Michael Scr 304
_____, Samuel Scr 304
_____, William Scr 304
_____, also see Dougherty
DAVENPORT/DEVENPORT/DAVENPOT
Davenport, David S. Hry 237
_____, Henry Gre 296
_____, John Clk 300
_____, John Jsp 354
_____, John Han 151
_____, John Put 183
_____, Joseph DeK 63
_____, Jouett Clk 308
_____, Moses Clk 306
_____, Richard Gwn 348
_____, Sarah Cht 246
_____, Smith Jsp 364
_____, Stephen Bke 119
_____, William Clk 298
Devenport, Rebecah C. Mor 244
_____, Susan Ogl 81
Davenpot, Booker G. Wrn 203

Name	County	Page
DAVID, Berry M.	Mad	117
______, Henry	Frk	229
______, Henry F.	Frk	239
______, Isaac Sr.	Mad	107
______, Isaac	Mad	115
______, J. H.	Jks	340
______, Jacob	Elb	146
______, Lucy	Mad	116
______, Mary	New	6
______, Morefelt	Mad	101
______, Peter	Mad	112
______, Samuel	Elb	149
______, William A.	DeK	56
______, William B.	Trp	34
DAVIDSON/DAVISON/ DAVISSON/DAVESON		
Davidson, Allen	Wks	348
______, Asa	Wsh	274
______, Delila	Jns	473
______, Elijah	Mon	180
______, Fontaine	Tlb	334
______, Grune	Jns	450
______, H.	Jks	346
______, Hugh	Frk	219
______, Isham	Twg	82
______, J.	Cht	255
______, James	Jns	437
______, James	Mon	199
______, James C.	Jns	437
______, John	Car	226
______, John	Jsp	394
______, John	Twg	72
______, John	Wrn	196
______, John	Wrn	215
______, Joseph	Mwr	150
______, Joseph	Mon	199
______, Joseph	Pik	109
______, Joseph	Wks	344
______, Nancy	Twg	76
______, Oliver	Put	183
______, Robert	Jsp	382
______, Samuel J.	Jns	460
______, Sarah	Cht	260
______, Talbot	Jns	450
______, Thomas	Jsp	390
______, Thomas	Jsp	398
______, William	Lin	67
______, William	Tms	25
______, William	Wks	344
Davison, Cary	Jns	447
______, William	Twg	76
Davisson, James H.	DeK	47
Daveson, Washington	Cpb	197

Name	County	Page
DAVIE/DAVY		
Davie, Nancy	Lin	68
______, Randolph	Lin	73
Davy, Jonathen	Mus	288
______, Joseph	Mus	288
DAVIS/DAVES/DAVIES		
Davis, (blank)	Lin	67
______, Mrs.	Scr	311
______, A. B.	Mus	281
______, A. H.	Col	364
______, Aaron	Hst	268
______, Aaron	Wks	337
______, Abner	Hry	227
______, Abraham	Crf	415
______, Abraham	Twg	66
______, Absalom	Frk	257
______, Adam	Frk	254
______, Alexander	Hry	245
______, Alexander	Lau	24
______, Alford	Hab	14
______, Alfred B.	Wal	139
______, Amos	Bul	98
______, Archi.	Mon	100
______, Arter	Wal	156
______, Arthur	Bke	139
______, Arthur	Mtg	235
______, Arthur	Mor	243
______, Baldwin	Mon	223
______, Benjamin	Clk	312
______, Benjamin	Fay	206
______, Benjamin	Gwn	362
______, Benjamin	Mon	177
______, Benjamin E.	Mar	140
______, Britain	DeK	41
______, Champion	Ogl	95
______, Charity	Mon	210
______, Charles	Fay	196
______, Charles	Jns	445
______, Charles	Lib	44
______, Charles D.	Wal	123
______, Chrispin	Bts	170
______, Clary Ann	Frk	242
______, Clement	Mon	220
______, Cross R.	Crf	399
______, Cullin	Hal	78
______, Daniel	Hal	132
______, Daniel Sr.	Mtg	236
______, Daniel	Tms	28
______, Daniel C.	Fay	201
______, David	Bts	171
______, David	Em	167
______, David	Han	151
______, David	Han	173

Davis, David A. Hab 28
______, David D. Mon 186
______, Dolphin Up 103
______, Drury Mor 256
______, E. A. Wsh 272
______, Early Mtg 233
______, Edward T. Bry 85
______, Elias Crf 408
______, Elias Jks 324
______, Elijah Gwn 332
______, Elijah Hab 44
______, Elisha Bib 75
______, Elisha Crf 394
______, Elisha Wks 344
______, Eliza Cht 241
______, Elizabeth Put 181
______, Elizabeth Wal 173
______, Eliz. Wks 353
______, Elnathan Hry 202
______, Ely Mwr 165
______, Emberson Col 363
______, Enoch Hab 52
______, Enoch McI 126
______, Esau Jns 472
______, Evans Col 364
______, Featherston Tlb 324
______, Finch Lee 34
______, Flemin Put 206
______, Francis Mon 206
______, Franklin Mwr 164
______, Fredrick Hab 45
______, G. H. Up 97
______, Gary Hal 71
______, Gaz. Col 352
______, George Fay 184
______, George Ware 188
______, George C. New 21
______, George W. Fay 186
______, Rev. Geo. Washington Lib 45
______, Goodrum Wsh 242
______, Grant Mor 253
______, Greenvil Hab 60
______, Hansford Wks 334
______, Harman Gwn 344
______, Henry Crf 412
______, Henry Fay 196
______, Henry Frk 235
______, Henry Hab 14
______, Henry H. Frk 231
______, Hez. Wks 337
______, Hickman Jsp 362
______, Hiram Mon 215
______, Hozias L. Pul 149

Davis, Hugh Mon 187
______, Hugh Mon 227
______, Ichabod Up 98
______, Isaac B. Jef 424
______, Isaac C. Elb 136
______, Israel P. Frk 254
______, J. G. F. Cht 260
______, J. S. DeK 59
______, J. T. Col 364
______, Jackson Hab 60
______, Jacob Tlf 6
______, James Cpb 200
______, James Cow 376
______, James Elb 125
______, James Elb 149
______, James Fay 199
______, James Frk 240
______, James Jef 405
______, James Jef 408
______, James Lee 27
______, James Pik 125
______, James Pul 160
______, James Put 203
______, James Rch 286
______, James Wal 166
______, James (P.S.) Ware 186
______, James (Satilla) Ware 189
______, James Wil 301
______, James G. Fay 203
______, James G. Hst 287
______, James J. Cow 385
______, James J. Hry 202
______, James J. W. Bke 145
______, James L. Hal 92
______, Jane Lee 32
______, Jane Pul 141
______, Jane L. Cht 247
______, Jeptha V. Gre 283
______, Jeremiah Tlf 6
______, Jeremiah Wrn 195
______, Jesse Dec 4
______, Jesse Eff 113
______, Jesse Frk 232
______, Jessee Gwn 324
______, Jessee Mon 202
______, Jesse Twg 67
______, Jesse H. Dec 7
______, Jo Gwn 331
______, Joel A. Wsh 248
______, John Car 224
______, John Cpb 202
______, John Cht 243
______, John Cht 280

Name	County	Page
Davis, John	Clk	317
______, John	Eff	111
______, John	Elb	122
______, John	Elb	143
______, John	Fay	190
______, John	Gly	267
______, John	Gwn	332
______, John	Hab	36
______, John	Hal	126
______, John	Hry	215
______, John	Jns	446
______, John	Mon	216
______, John	Mtg	233
______, John	Pik	121
______, John	Rch	278
______, John	Tlf	6
______, John	Twg	88
______, John	Wal	126
______, John	Wsh	268
______, John	Wrn	192
______, John A.	Frk	254
______, John C.	Ogl	95
______, John F.	Bke	128
______, John G.	Lwn	85
______, John J.	Frk	221
______, John J. H.	Ware	188
______, John L.	Cpb	210
______, John S.	Hal	92
______, John T.	Fay	205
______, John T.	Jks	337
______, John T.	Mon	211
______, John W.	Jks	319
______, Jonathan Sr.	Crf	414
______, Jonathan Jr.	Crf	408
______, Jonathan	DeK	72
______, Jonathan	Hab	60
______, Jonathan	Tfo	355
______, Jonathan R.	Car	221
______, Jonathan W.	Car	221
______, Joseph	Bul	99
______, Joseph	Dec	3
______, Joseph	Dec	6
______, Joseph	Doo	88
______, Joseph	Jks	313
______, Joseph	Mon	221
______, Joseph O.	Tat	371
______, Joseph W.	Elb	151
______, Joshua	Car	229
______, Joshua Sr.	Jns	447
______, Joshua Jr.	Jns	465
______, Josiah	McI	131
______, Jourdan	Trp	55
______, Judith	Col	361

Name	County	Page
Davis, Julus	Hab	40
______, Keziah	Tlf	6
______, Lawson	Mus	287
______, Lewis	Crf	406
______, Lewis	Frk	217
______, Lewis	Hry	207
______, Lewis	Tlf	2
______, Lewis L.	Wil	313
______, Lewis Q.	Mus	277
______, Levi	Bul	98
______, Levi	Lau	13
______, Littleberry	Wrn	204
______, Louis	Em	166
______, Luvicy	Hal	78
______, Lydia	Tms	27
______, Madison	Cow	382
______, Margarett	Wrn	207
______, Margery	DeK	51
______, Mark	Tat	375
______, Martha	Bib	67
______, Mary	Col	357
______, Mary	Eff	105
______, Mary	Ran	250
______, Mary	Rch	284
______, Mary Ann	DeK	30
______, Mason	Gwn	329
______, Micajah W.	Wil	298
______, Miles	Hab	48
______, Milton	Hab	31
______, Moses	Bke	155
______, Moses	Elb	134
______, Moses	Jns	460
______, Moses	Mor	250
______, Moses	Twg	64
______, Moses	Wrn	216
______, Nancy	Elb	157
______, Nancy	Wsh	259
______, Nathan	Trp	33
______, Orange	Jns	429
______, Owen	Jns	436
______, Peter	Tlb	330
______, Pleasant	Elb	147
______, Pleasant	Hst	287
______, Price	Wrn	206
______, Ransom	Lin	63
______, Reason	Gwn	349
______, Redding	Ware	186
______, Reubin	Col	362
______, Richard	Gwn	328
______, Richard	Jns	445
______, Richard	Mon	200
______, Richard	Up	96
______, Richard C.	Tlb	344

Name	County	Page
Davis, Robert	Han	151
______, Robert	Hry	240
______, Robert F.	DeK	26
______, Robert H.	Cow	376
______, Roblin	Bke	134
______, Rubin B.	Crf	398
______, Russel	Hab	14
______, S. F.	Bry	85
______, Samuel	Bul	92
______, Samuel	Bke	154
______, Samuel	Crf	415
______, Samuel	Fay	185
______, Samuel	Gre	272
______, Samuel H.	Tlb	343
______, Sarah	Cht	264
______, Sarah	Jsp	358
______, Seburn	Clk	320
______, Sheridan Y.	Mon	182
______, Shurry	Hab	60
______, Silas N.	Gre	293
______, Sollomon	Hab	12
______, Soloman	Hst	269
______, Stafford	Mtg	232
______, Sterling	Jks	334
______, Susanna	Em	167
______, Terry	Elb	150
______, Terry	Jns	473
______, Thomas	Bke	137
______, Thomas	Col	345
______, Thomas	Crf	403
______, Thomas	Fay	194
______, Thomas	Frk	217
______, Thomas	Gwn	331
______, Thomas	Gwn	334
______, Thomas	Hab	20
______, Thomas	Hab	51
______, Thomas	Hal	115
______, Thomas	Jks	331
______, Thomas	Jns	460
______, Thomas	Mar	138
______, Thomas Sr.	Mon	207
______, Thomas	Mon	190
______, Thomas	Mor	254
______, Thomas	Mus	284
______, Thomas	New	6
______, Thomas	Ogl	78
______, Thomas	Wrn	229
______, Thomas C.	Up	97
______, Thomas E.	Eff	106
______, Thomas F.	Elb	157
______, Thomas H.	Up	106
______, Thomas W.	Mon	196
______, Thomas W.	Wal	170
Davis, Underhill	Wks	356
______, Uria	Hab	11
______, Uriah	Hab	43
______, Van Sr.	Frk	251
______, Vincent	Wrn	231
______, W. J.	Bal	35
______, Wadkins	Wrn	229
______, Warrin	Gwn	368
______, William	Clk	320
______, William	Cow	382
______, William	DeK	36
______, William	Em	172
______, William	Fay	186
______, William	Fay	196
______, William	Gre	289
______, William	Gwn	311
______. William	Gwn	371
______, William	Hal	112
______, William	Har	187
______, William	Hry	207
______, William	Hry	240
______, William	Jef	404
______, William	Mwr	164
______, William	Mtg	233
______, William	Mor	245
______, William	Rab	222
______, William	Twg	62
______, William	Up	97
______, William	Wsh	244
______, William	Wil	304
______, William Sr.	Wil	320
______, William Jr.	Wil	320
______, William	Wks	348
______, William C.	New	55
______, William E.	Hal	91
______, William J.	Cow	368
______, William J.	Wal	137
______, William L.	Ogl	94
______, William N.	Bul	102
______, William N.	Car	221
______, William W.	Bke	153
______, Wiley	Cpb	200
______, Wily	Lee	30
______, Wyley	DeK	54
______, Zadoc	Fay	183
______, Zacriah	Ran	249
______, Zion	Cam	188
Daves, Green	Rab	224
______, Joel P.	Han	151
Davies, Thomas W.	Bke	151
______, Mrs.	Cht	282
DAWKINS, Absalem T.	Pik	114
______, Daniel	Pik	106

Name	County	Page
Dawkins, Garland	Jsp	354
______, George	Jsp	359
______, John	Put	206
______, Reuben	Jsp	354
DAWSON/DORSON		
Dawson, Benjamin	Rab	231
______, Charles	Mad	104
______, Davis	Up	101
______, Easley	Hab	6
______, Enoch	Rab	232
______, George	Gre	293
______, Gibson	Up	112
______, Henry C.	Mus	279
______, Henry T.	Ogl	98
______, John	Hst	281
______, John	Hst	294
______, John	Jsp	391
______, John E.	Mor	255
______, Jonas	Rab	223
______, Jonas	Rab	228
______, Jonas B.	Car	226
______, Jonathan	Jns	450
______, Joseph	Bts	173
______, Joseph	Jsp	378
______, Lemuel G.	Up	96
______, Martha	Tfo	364
______, Mary	Bke	121
______, Mary	Jks	349
______, Philip H.	Put	202
______, R.	Cht	261
______, Reuben	Cpb	204
______, Robert Tooms	Wil	314
______, Thomas	Wrn	192
______, Thomas J.	Wrn	192
______, William	Mad	108
______, William A.	Rab	228
______, William C.	Gre	305
______, Wilson	Wrn	197
Dorson, John	Clk	327
______, John	Hab	46
DAY/DAYS		
Day, David	Mus	292
______, Dollison	Mor	257
______, Isham	Mor	257
______, Jesse	Trp	46
______, John	Col	346
______, John	New	16
______, Jonathan	New	34
______, Joseph	Jns	443
______, Joseph	Ran	246
______, Lewis	Jns	441
______, Lewis	Jns	473
______, Lewis	Wal	148
Day, Moses	Mon	200
______, Nimrod	Twg	73
______, Polly	Tlb	328
______, Richard B.	Rch	278
______, Robert	Wal	142
______, Samuel	Wal	142
______, Sarah (w)	Mor	257
______, Stephen	Twg	73
______, William	Cpb	205
Days, F.	Cht	267
______, Robert	Wal	164
DEACON, John	DeK	39
DEADMAN/DEDMAN		
Deadman, Sinaca	Hab	42
Dedman, William	Rab	234
DEADWILDER/DEADWILER/ DEADWALER/DEADWYLER/ DEDWILDER		
Deadwilder, Lindsey	Fay	193
Deadwiler, Joseph	Cpb	195
Deadwaler, Marten	Elb	160
Deadwyler, Joseph	Elb	146
Dedwilder, Christopher	Jsp	360
DEAL/DEALL/DEEL		
Deal, Argent	Em	174
______, Furney	Em	174
______, James	Em	174
______, James S.	Gwn	339
______, John	DeK	30
______, John	Em	174
______, Simon	Em	173
______, William	Bib	60
______, William	Hab	21
Deall, Ezekiel	Bke	119
______, John	App	12
Deel, William	Hab	28
DEAN/DEEN/DEANE		
Dean, Alsey	Mon	202
______, Alvan	Frk	210
______, Benjamin F.	Rch	263
______, Charles	Elb	130
______, Charles	Frk	252
______, David	Mus	284
______, Edward	New	55
______, Elijah	Hst	271
______, Elisebeth	Hab	64
______, Frederick	Frk	214
______, Frederick	Mor	240
______, Gabriel C.	Trp	47
______, George	Mor	242
______, Gidion	Lib	45
______, Henry	Gwn	329
______, Henry	Har	181

Name	County	Page
Dean, Henry	Lwn	79
_____, J. J.	Cht	280
_____, James	Wks	355
_____, Jeremiah	Hab	61
_____, Jethro	Wks	333
_____, John	Cht	267
_____, John	Elb	143
_____, John	Hab	53
_____, John	Hal	100
_____, John	Lau	12
_____, John	Mwr	165
_____, John	Mon	196
_____, John W.	Mon	201
_____, Joseph	Mor	242
_____, Kinnard	Lau	12
_____, Lucy	Jsp	357
_____, Martin	App	10
_____, Mathew	Mor	240
_____, Moses	Lau	23
_____, Nathan	App	10
_____, Robert	Hab	60
_____, Samuel	DeK	32
_____, Seaborn L.	Mon	172
_____, Shadrack	Hal	103
_____, Smith	App	11
_____, Thomas	Jns	434
_____, Thomas C.	Trp	55
_____, Wiley	Crf	406
_____, William Sr.	Hab	44
_____, William	Hab	42
_____, William	Up	99
_____, Williamson	Doo	84
_____, Willis	Cpb	204
Deen, Howel	Bak	19
_____, Jacob	Mad	111
_____, James	Wsh	260
_____, Jesse	Wsh	266
_____, Joel	Wsh	260
_____, Silas	Bak	19
_____, Thomas	Mad	106
Deane, John	Clk	311
DEARING, Blakely	Wil	324
_____, Elijah	Wil	313
_____, Jesse	Hry	237
_____, Parky	Jsp	398
_____, Reuben	Hry	220
_____, Simeon	Bts	174
_____, William	Clk	326
_____, William	Hry	219
DEARMON/DEARMOND/DEAMOND		
Dearmon, Elizabeth	Jef	413
Dearmond, William P.	Rch	287
**Deamond, W. P. (slave)	Rch	274

Name	County	Page
DEASON/DISON		
Deason, John D.	Bts	173
_____, Joseph	Pik	124
_____, Micajah	Car	207
_____, Polley	Wal	156
_____, Thomas	Wks	332
_____, Zachariah	Bts	168
Dison, Isham	DeK	37
DEATON, Elijah	Hal	75
_____, Joseph	Hal	80
_____, Thomas	Gwn	367
_____, William	Hal	73
DEAVERS/DEVERS		
Deavers, John	Hal	116
Devers, Isaac B.	Up	104
DEBORCE, Reubin	Dec	15
DEBROTH, John	Cam	184
DEBROUGH/DEBRO/DUBOURG		
Debrough, Samuel	Dec	19
Debro, William	DeK	37
Dubourg, Andrew	Bal	28
DEBUSH, John	Bal	28
DECKER, Young A.	Elb	144
DECKIN, Richard	Clk	292
DECY, Nathaniel	Tfo	356
DEDGE, Isaac S.	App	8
DEES/DEAS		
Dees, Benjamin	Doo	83
_____, Bolan	Jks	338
_____, Bythum	Pul	138
_____, Calvin	Twg	61
_____, Daniel	Pul	150
_____, James	Cam	189
_____, James	New	52
_____, John	Hab	40
_____, John	Lwn	86
_____, John	Pul	138
_____, Jourdan	Doo	87
_____, Leonard	Lwn	87
_____, Mark	Wks	336
_____, Moses	Lwn	87
_____, Ransom	Jns	460
_____, Richard	Hry	218
_____, Tabitha Ann	Up	113
_____, William	Lwn	87
Deas, Anthony	Han	151
_____, Sarah	Mor	256
DEFNAL, Bush	Pul	157
DEFUR/DEFOR/DEFORE/DEFOOR/ DEFURR/DUFORE		
DeFur, James	Gwn	361
_____, John	Gwn	347
Defor, James	Hab	31

Name	County	Page
Defore, John	Twg	68
Defoor, Robert	Cpb	205
Defurr, John	DeK	72
Dufore, Lewis	Cam	183
DEGRAFFENREID/DEGRAFFENRUDT		
deGraffenreid, E. L.	Mus	277
Degraffenrudt, B. B.	Clk	326
DEGREYTENNIA, John	Dec	7
DEKLE/DEEKLE		
Dekle, Leonard	Tms	21
______, Thomas	Tms	19
______, William G.	Tms	29
Deekle, George	Em	175
______, William	Em	178
DELAFIELD, Nicholas	Hal	69
______, William	Hal	70
DELAMAR/DELIMER		
Delamar, Churchill	Bts	159
______, Francis	Doo	81
______, Selden J.	Pul	144
Delimer, Francis	Mon	221
DELAMOTTA/DELAMATER/ DELAMAT		
DeLamotta, E.	Cht	266
DeLamater, William H.	Cht	245
Delamat, Francis	Mon	172
DELANY/DELANCY/DELANNAY		
Delany, Martha	Mon	221
DeLancy, Mary	Cht	247
Delanny, F. V.	Bal	29
DELEGAL/DELAIGH/DELAIGLE		
Delegal, Jane	McI	128
______, William	McI	128
DeLaigh, Nicholas	Rch	279
Delaigle, D.	Rch	259
DELAPRIER, Ange	Jks	330
DELESLINE, F. G.	Gly	264
DELESPILEN, William E.	McI	124
DELIAC, Antoine	Rch	278
DELK/DELKS		
Delk, David	Crf	395
______, David	Gwn	356
______, David (R.S.)	Lib	44
______, Elisha	Wks	333
______, John	Lib	44
Delks, Joseph	Ran	242
DELL, John	Bul	94
______, John	Ear	98
DELOACH/DELOATCH		
Deloach, A.	Gly	267
______, John	Bul	95
______, Leacy	Jns	460
______, Mary	Lib	44

Name	County	Page
Deloach, Samuel	Mon	222
______, Sandy	Lee	30
______, Simeon	Tlb	341
______, Thomas	Mon	226
______, William	Up	116
Deloatch, Abraham	Tat	372
______, Elizabeth	Tat	379
______, Sarah	Tat	376
______, General	Tat	372
______, William	Tat	372
DELONG, James A.	Jns	473
DELONY/DELONEY		
Delony, Edward	Ear	93
Deloney, Robert	Cam	181
DELT, Thomas	Cow	389
DELYON/DELIONS		
DeLyon, A.	Cht	259
______, Isaac	Cht	251
______, L. S.	Cht	263
Delions, Mary	App	8
DEMERE, Joseph	Gly	269
______, M.	Cht	266
______, R.	Cht	265
______, Raymond P.	Bry	84
______, Ramond	Gly	266
DEMMING, David	Mor	250
DEMOTT, Garrott	Cam	182
DEMPSEY/DEMSEY		
Dempsey, Barnett	Cpb	202
______, Chapley W.	Gwn	346
______, Eli	Gwn	363
______, Jesse	Gwn	347
______, Larkin	Gwn	343
______, Levi Jr.	Gwn	363
______, Levi	DeK	46
Demsey, Henson	Car	219
DENCE, Elizabeth	Twg	65
DENDY, Yongeset	Pik	122
DENICK, John	Rab	229
DENMARK, Malachi	Bul	99
______, Nancy	Bul	100
DENMAN/DENMON/DEMON/ DUNMAN/DANMAN/DENNAN		
Denman, Blake	Hab	11
______, Christopher	Frk	214
______, James	Hab	39
Denmon, Felix G.	Frk	232
______, Moses H.	Frk	212
______, William S.	Frk	213
Demon, Chapel A. R.	Hab	34
Dunman, John	Hal	92
______, Thomas	Hal	92
Danman, Michael	Jks	320

Name	County	Page
Dennan, Kennady	Rab	250
DENNARD, Alexander	Pul	139
______, Bird	Twg	68
______, Green	Bak	15
______, Hugh	Har	177
______, Isaac	Twg	85
______, Jarrard	Har	192
______, John	Bak	15
______, John	Elb	132
______, John	New	8
______, John J.	Pul	141
______, John E.	Twg	63
______, Shaderick	Twg	67
______, William	Bak	19
______, William E.	Twg	85
DENNIS/DENIS		
Dennis, Allen	Lin	67
______, Benjamin	Gwn	378
______, Daniel	Mon	185
______, Daniel	Wrn	207
______, Elizabeth	Lin	66
______, Hiram	Lin	66
______, Isaac	Crf	402
______, James	Mon	211
______, John	Cht	242
______, John	Jns	464
______, John	Jsp	387
______, John Sr.	Put	179
______, John Jr.	Put	179
______, John	Put	212
______, Johnson	Put	173
______, Josiah	Mor	258
______, Martha	Gwn	379
______, Michael	Put	174
______, Nancy	Wal	174
______, Peter	Put	212
______, Reuben	Mon	200
______, Richmd.	Wrn	204
______, Samuel	Trp	41
______, Simion	Mon	183
______, William	Gwn	378
______, William Jr.	Put	212
______, William	Put	212
______, William H.	Han	151
Denis, Emery S.	Cow	380
______, Samuel	Cow	370
DENNY/DENNEY		
Denny, David	Elb	133
______, Edward	Elb	131
______, Elrood	Rab	233
______, Irby	Jsp	389
______, Samuel	Jef	420
Denney, Thomas	Mad	115

Name	County	Page
DENSLER/DENSLOW		
Densler, Ann	Cht	250
______, F.	Cht	252
______, H.	Bal	41
______, Joseph	Cht	269
______, Thomas L.	Bal	41
Denslow, Allen	Cht	262
DENSMORE, Abner Y.	Hab	45
______, David	Hab	32
______, Samuel	Hab	26
______, William	Gwn	339
DENSON/DENISON		
Denson, Colley	Put	199
______, Eli	Fay	182
______, Frances	Han	151
______, Francis (widow)	Jsp	394
______, Joel	Twg	63
______, John Jr.	Twg	61
______, John Sr.	Twg	83
______, John Jr.	Twg	81
______, Joseph	Har	190
______, Joseph	Put	201
______, Mary	Fay	187
______, William	Wal	131
Denison, William P.	Ware	186
**DENT, Dennis (slave)	Rch	272
______, Elizabeth	Put	215
______, Fred	Rch	272
______, Jacob	Rch	272
______, James	Cht	242
______, James T.	Rch	262
______, John	Fay	204
______, John	Lau	20
______, John	Rch	275
______, Joseph M.	Wil	323
______, Michael L.	Wil	323
______, Richard	Ogl	66
______, Thomas	Put	181
______, Thomas	Tlf	5
______, William B. W.	Cow	392
DENTON, Allen B.	Han	151
______, Aron	Wrn	225
______, Elijah	Rab	224
______, James	Jsp	358
______, John	Hal	95
______, John	Han	151
______, Jonas	Rab	223
______, Samuel	Gwn	341
______, Samuel	Tlf	3
______, Sarah	Bib	58
DEOCHNG, Darkis	Hab	30
DEPEAU, Charles	Cht	243
DERARKIN, Lucy	Bal	38

Name	County	Page
DERISE, Michael	Jef	409
______, Stephen	Jef	409
______, Stephen	Jef	424
DERRETT/DERRITT		
Derrett, Andrew	DeK	38
______, Francis	DeK	38
Derritt, Rice	Bibb	58
DESALEAYE, Mark	Bke	121
DESCLOUX, Margt.	Cam	192
DESEBLEAU, Maria	Cht	241
DESHAZO/DESHARO		
Deshazo, Richard	Twg	69
______, Robert	Twg	70
______, Ross	Twg	76
Desharo, John	McI	124
DESHIELDS, William	Mor	251
DESIRE, Dominick	Cht	255
DEUCE, Elizabeth	Twg	65
DEUVILLE, Rebecca	Cht	254
DEVANN/DEVANE/DEVINE		
Devann, Freeman	Fay	189
______, Isham	Fay	203
______, Samuel	Fay	194
______, Visa	Pik	108
DeVane, Benjamin	Lwn	81
______, Francis	Bul	97
Devine, William H.	Pik	109
DEVANT, James	Wil	301
DEVANY, John	Gre	286
______, Samuel	Gre	276
DEVEREAUX/DEVAUX/DEVORE/ DEVOW/DEVEAURE		
Devereaux, Samuel M.	Han	151
Devaux, William	Wil	287
Devore, Eleas	Up	95
Devow, John	Ogl	68
Deveaure, Catharine	Cht	247
DEVERGER, James	McI	128
DEWBERRY/DUBERRY		
Dewberry, Giles	Jsp	380
______, Giles	Mon	197
______, Irby	Tfo	362
______, James	Wrn	200
______, John	Jsp	383
______, John	Mon	197
______, John	Tfo	359
______, Richard	Mon	197
Duberry, Hopson	Jsp	369
______, Thomas	Pik	115
DEWEY, Robert	Elb	140
DEWITT, Zilpha	Pul	147
DEWS, John J.	Cht	264
DIAL, Isaac	Wal	149

Name	County	Page
Dial, John	Hab	39
______, John	Wal	142
______, Martin	Wal	142
______, Tempey	Mad	115
DIAMOND/DIMON		
Diamond, James	DeK	60
Dimon, Abel	Tlb	329
DIBBLE, Samuel	Cht	241
DICK, T.	Wks	347
DICKENS/DICKINS/DICKIN		
Dickens, Elijah	Wrn	231
______, Elizabeth	Wil	322
______, Gillum	Wsh	253
______, Isaac	Wsh	272
______, James T.	Wrn	199
______, Susannah	Wil	324
Dickins, Ephraim	Jns	472
______, James	Wsh	268
______, John	Wsh	272
______, Joseph	Wsh	272
______, Robert	Wsh	274
Dickin, John W.	Wal	152
DICKERSON/DICKESON		
Dickerson, Abraham	Hab	17
______, David	New	22
______, George	Hab	17
______, James	Clk	295
______, James	Hab	17
______, James	Jks	319
______, James M.	Eff	113
______, Jessee	Gwn	339
______, John	Elb	159
______, John Sr.	Gwn	338
______, John	Gwn	338
______, John	Put	203
______, Joseph	Hab	17
______, Levi	Jks	338
______, Levi	Tfo	368
______, Michael C.	Jks	332
______, Nelson	Hal	71
______, Obediah J.	Rab	229
______, Phillipping	Hab	17
______, Robert	Elb	123
______, Robert P.	Elb	142
______, Thomas	Hab	19
______, Thompson	Gwn	338
______, William B.	Gre	276
______, Zachariah	Elb	152
Dickeson, John	Hab	25
DICKERT, Adam	Frk	212
______, Michael	Frk	225
DICKINSON/DICKENSON		
Dickinson, Alphens	Han	151

Dickinson, Clark Han 151
______, Corley Rch 277
______, D. F. Rch 291
______, Francis Dec 10
______, Hiram Hal 89
______, Isaac Han 151
______, John Wal 125
______, Roger Q. Tfo 357
Dickenson, John P. Hry 238
DICKSON/DIXON/DIXSON
Dickson, Anna A. Fay 181
______, Benjamin Han 151
______, Charles A. Trp 36
______, Curry Han 151
______, Elizabeth Pul 158
______, Ellenor Lau 6
______, Enich Hab 55
______, Guen Doo 81
______, Hampton Tlb 346
______, Henry Rch 287
______, Hickman Wrn 217
______, James Car 220
______, James Han 151
______, James Scr 303
______, James Scr 304
______, James Twg 88
______, James J. Hst 266
______, John Bib 60
______, John Cow 379
______, John Han 151
______, John Han 152
______, Joseph H. Hst 277
______, Josiah Bib 60
______, Josiah Trp 55
______, Mary Scr 304
______, Micajah Crf 395
______, Michael Trp 36
______, Moses Twg 85
______, Pleasant Twg 85
______, Robert Bib 60
______, Roland Tms 24
______, Thomas Bib 60
______, Thomas Han 151
______, Thomas G. Cow 381
______, William DeK 36
______, William Hab 35
______, William Han 151
______, William Han 153
______, William Han 172
______, William H. Fay 185
______, Wilson M. Cpb 200
______, Wimburn Tfo 362
Dixon, A. Cht 269
Dixon, Allen Bul 101
______, Bryant Put 194
______, Erwin Jks 344
______, Hickman Put 201
______, James Bul 98
______, Jeremiah Ear 98
______, John Ear 100
______, John Em 167
______, John Jr. Frk 254
______, John Lee 27
______, John L. Mwr 167
______, Lanny Jks 346
______, P. Cht 255
______, Polly Wks 356
______, Robert Bke 118
______, Robert Elb 154
______, Robert H. Irw 298
______, Robert H. Tlb 326
______, Robert J. Bke 148
______, Robert L. Irw 298
______, Sampson Wks 336
______, Shaderick Wsh 259
______, Stephen Cow 390
______, Thomas Fay 182
______, Thomas Wsh 256
______, Thomas Wsh 273
______, Thomas J. Bke 149
______, William Ear 98
______, William Lee 27
______, William Wks 341
Dixson, Benjamin Crf 405
______, Isaac Jns 429
DICKY/DICKEY/DICKIE
Dicky, Henry Gwn 348
______, John Bke 151
______, Joseph Bke 130
______, Owen Put 207
______, Samuel Put 206
______, Shadrack Tms 21
Dickey, John Hry 238
Dickie, John Elb 142
DIEMER, Clement Jsp 352
DIER, Allen Gwn 320
______, Joshua T. Clk 306
DIGBY, Berry Jsp 379
______, Rebecca Pik 112
______, William Crf 400
DIGGS, David Wal 143
DIGMAN, William Cht 249
DIKES, Daniel App 9
______, John Twg 70
______, Joshua Jns 431
______, Solomon Hab 39

DILDA/DILDY
Dilda, Polly Rab 222
Dildy, Elias Rab 232
DILL, Alsa Hab 17
______, Andrew J. Rch 261
______, Daniel Rch 275
______, Jacob Rch 261
______, John Ear 95
______, Job Frk 254
______, Joseph Scr 310
______, Philip Lin 75
DILLARD/DILLIARD/DILARD
Dillard, David Hst 275
______, Edmond Gwn 327
______, Edmond Sr. Gwn 333
______, Edmond Gwn 333
______, G. W. Mus 277
______, James Elb 149
______, James Gwn 333
______, James Rab 232
______, John Bke 137
______, John Rab 232
______, John Wal 151
______, John G. Bke 145
______, Joseph Ogl 71
______, Owen Bib 50
______, Philip Pul 156
______, Sampson Pul 155
______, Susan Mus 291
______, Theophilus Jef 423
______, Thomas Gwn 327
______, Thomas Gwn 333
______, Thomas Jns 436
______, Tolliver Bke 154
______, William Wal 140
Dilliard, Allen Wsh 256
______, Arthur Mon 221
______, Mrs. B. Wsh 246
______, Dempsey Wsh 260
______, John Mon 197
Dilard, Sameson Em 172
DILLINGHAM/DELINGHAM
Dillingham, George M. Jns 464
Delingham, Hiram Rab 232
DILLON/DILLION
Dillon, C. Cht 272
______, Elizabeth Cht 240
______, J. Cht 266
______, John Cht 255
______, M. Cht 272
** ______, Robert (slave) Rch 255
______, Thomas Cpb 207
______, W. C. Rch 255
Dillon, William C. Rch 274
Dillion, Henry Jsp 371
DILLPORT/DILPORT
Dillport, Catharine Wal 170
Dilport, James Frk 240
DINGLER, Henry Hry 224
______, John Bts 173
______, Johnathan B. Jsp 383
______, Jsp 388
DINKINS/DENKIN
Dinkins, Horace R. Hst 268
______, Isham Hst 275
______, Manning Hst 271
Denkin, Frederick Tat 375
DIPTON, Benjamin Dec 3
DISHAROON/DISHEROON
Disharoon, Jese Hab 50
______, John E. Tlb 343
______, Samuel Hab 13
______, Timothy Hab 50
Disheroon, Isaac Hab 12
______, Waitmon Hab 12
______, William Hab 12
______, William Hab 13
DISMUKES/DISMUKE/DISMUK/
DISMICK
Dismukes, Elizabeth Hry 236
______, Finny Put 172
______, James Bal 44
______, James Put 174
______, James Put 208
______, Jeptha V. Jsp 378
______, Reuben Rch 283
______, William Pik 122
______, William H. Ran 247
Dismuke, James Har 191
______, John Jsp 381
______, Joseph T. Han 152
Dismuk, Bethena Jns 438
Dismick, Edmond Har 185
DIX, Elisabeth Ogl 91
______, James T. Ogl 90
______, Tandy Cam 191
DIZE, John Bib 69
DOBBINS, Amy Rch 255
______, James Hal 130
______, John M. Hry 226
______, Joseph Frk 219
______, Moses W. Clk 326
______, William DeK 48
______, William C. Clk 297
DOBBS/DOBS/DABS/DABBS
Dobbs, Asa Elb 145

Name	County	Page
Dobbs, Burrell	Frk	215
______, David	Elb	138
______, Elijah	Elb	138
______, James	Gwn	309
______, James G.	Frk	103
______, Jesse	Elb	143
______, Jesse	Gwn	360
______, John	DeK	25
______, John	DeK	41
______, John	DeK	69
______, John	Mad	108
______, John H.	Gwn	360
______, Lott	Frk	215
______, Martin	Car	220
______, Mormon	Hal	78
______, Morton	Frk	215
______, Nathaniel	Gwn	367
______, Nathaniel	Har	192
______, Peter	Frk	251
______, Samuel	DeK	41
______, Samuel	Har	180
______, Silas	Car	217
______, Silas	Elb	126
______, Siras	Cpb	208
______, Solomon	Frk	211
______, William	Frk	217
______, William	Mus	278
Dobs, Alexander	Cpb	198
______, Boleram	Hab	30
______, Jesse	Hal	114
______, Lewis	Hab	44
Dabs, Sulser	Hal	112
Dabbs, James	Wal	123
DOBSON, Alexander	Scr	307
______, Andrew	Mar	141
______, Henry	Hal	73
______, John	Twg	80
______, Joseph	Hab	21
______, Joseph	Hab	29
______, Neely	Hal	112
DOBY, John	Jsp	389
______, William	Wal	150
DOCKEY, Thomas	Hry	237
______, William	Hal	104
DODD/DODDS/DOD/DODS/DOOD		
Dodd, Mrs.	Bal	40
______, Aaren	Col	356
______, John M.	Gwn	366
______, John S.	Fay	192
______, Patterson	Hal	97
______, Sarah	Elb	159
______, Thomas	Elb	120
______, William	Gwn	323

Name	County	Page
Dodd, William	Hal	100
______, William	Tms	29
______, William P.	Hab	66
Dodds, James	Gwn	345
______, John	Gwn	345
______, John F.	Gwn	347
Dod, Cammel	Hab	22
Dods, William	Elb	145
Dood, Edward	Fay	188
______, James	Hab	31
DODGE, Charles	McI	121
______, Theodore	McI	121
DODGINS/DODGIN		
Dodgins, Larkin	DeK	65
______, Olomon Sr.	DeK	65
______, Olomon Jr.	DeK	65
______, William	DeK	65
Dodgin, Eli	Hal	133
DODSON, Armisted	Jsp	390
______, Asop	Jsp	391
______, Daniel	Fay	201
______, David	Cht	278
______, Edmond	Fay	201
______, Elijah	Fay	201
______, Elijah	Jsp	390
______, George W.	Wil	323
______, Isaiah	Hry	229
______, Joel W.	Jsp	393
______, John P.	Hry	230
______, Joshua	Car	220
______, Joshua	Hry	228
______, Lott	Har	187
______, Samuel	DeK	46
______, William	Cht	278
______, William	Hry	228
______, William	Hry	230
DODWELL, Hezekiah S.	Put	188
DOGAN, Henry	Bib	50
DOGGETT/DOGGET		
Doggett, Garner	Jsp	352
______, Mark	Hry	206
______, Thos. J.	Jsp	368
Dogget, John R.	McI	126
______, Thomas	Clk	299
DOKES, Alex.	Wks	354
DOLES/DOLE/DOYLE/DOYLES		
Doles, Benjamin	Bal	31
______, Herod	Ear	96
______, Jesse	Bal	31
______, John M.	Gwn	361
______, Willis	Ear	96
Dole, John	Gwn	346
______, John M.	Pik	108

Name	County	Page
Doyle, Dennis	Han	152
_____, Jesse	Wrn	206
_____, William	Rch	288
Doyles, John	Hst	268
_____, Thomas	Hst	268
DOLLAR/DOLLARS		
Dollar, John	Doo	85
Dollars, William	New	38
DOLLERSON, Giles	Cpb	207
DOLLY, J.	Cht	247
_____, Nelly	Cht	241
DOLVIN, James	Gre	275
_____, John	Gre	275
_____, John	Gre	294
DOMINY/DOMINI/DOMONY		
Dominy, John Jr.	Irw	302
_____, John Jr.	Irw	301
Domini, Fred.	Wks	355
_____, John	Wks	355
Domony, Willis	Lee	35
DOMINGO, Emanuel	Rch	290
DONALD, John	Bib	67
DONALDSON/DONNALDSON/ DONNALSON/DONELSON/ DOLANSON		
Donaldson, Anna	Dec	16
_____, George	Scr	306
_____, Hugh	Tms	21
_____, James	Bul	100
_____, James	Dec	10
_____, James	Hal	68
_____, James	Mon	211
_____, John	Dec	10
_____, John	Jef	413
_____, John	Tms	26
_____, Johnathan	Dec	16
_____, Nancy	Dec	18
_____, Robert	Bul	94
_____, Robert	Jef	402
_____, Robert	Tms	23
_____, William	Dec	6
_____, William Jr.	Dec	3
_____, William	Jef	414
Donnaldson, Betsey	DeK	45
_____, Eli	DeK	45
_____, Scission	DeK	31
_____, William	DeK	46
Donnalson, Jacob	DeK	47
_____, James	DeK	31
Donelson, William	Tlb	322
Dolanson, John L.	New	17
DONALLY/DONNELLY		
Donally, James	Jks	318

Name	County	Page
Donnelly, M. D.	Mon	181
_____, William	McI	126
DONE, Isaiah	Cam	183
DONEY, Louden	Fay	189
DONOVAN, Abel	Rab	232
DOOLING/DOOLIN		
Dooling, Dennis	Lwn	88
_____, William	Lwn	88
Doolin, Michael	Scr	315
DOOLITTLE, Abram	Clk	293
_____, Alfred	Cam	183
_____, Mary	Clk	302
DOOLY/DOOLLY/DOOLEY		
Dooly, Bennet	Elb	145
_____, James	Hab	30
_____, James W.	Hab	37
_____, Jese	Hab	37
_____, John	Hab	30
_____, Thomas	Col	353
_____, Thos.	Hab	29
_____, William	Elb	126
_____, William W.	Elb	127
Doolly, Thos.	Hab	30
Dooley, William	Mar	139
DOPSON, Averilla	Mar	140
DORCH/DORTCH		
Dorch, David	Wsh	248
_____, John	Wsh	253
_____, Mary	Tlf	5
Dortch, Lewis	Frk	229
_____, Newman R.	Frk	242
DORMAN, Alfred	Fay	202
_____, Allen	Twg	83
_____, Hiram	Fay	194
_____, John	Fay	194
_____, John	Lin	71
_____, Wiley	Har	181
DORRIS, James	Jks	313
_____, John M.	Car	229
_____, William	Car	225
DORSETT, James	Pik	121
_____, John	Pik	124
_____, Thomas	Pik	121
_____, William	Pik	121
DORSEY/DARSEY/DAWSEY/DORCY		
Dorsey, Daniel	Jsp	386
_____, Henry	Hst	264
_____, Isaac	Hal	72
_____, Isam	Up	95
_____, James	Lib	44
_____, John	DeK	38
_____, John	Gre	289
_____, John	Hry	212

Dorsey, John L. Hry 204
_____, Joseph New 18
_____, William Tfo 366
_____, William B. Lib 45
Darsey, Benjamin Lau 4
_____, George Col 357
_____, James M. Col 358
_____, Joel Col 359
_____, Joel Dec 13
_____, Joel Lau 20
_____, Joseph Col 359
_____, Joseph Lau 19
_____, Leodicey Lau 16
_____, Seth Lau 7
_____, Thomas Lau 11
_____, Willis Lau 18
Dawsey, Thomas Ogl 101
_____, W. Ogl 103
Dorcy, Andrew Hab 26
_____, Basil Hab 25
_____, Joshua Hab 47
DORTIC, G. T. Rch 277
DORTON, Benjamin Pik 117
_____, John Hry 207
DOSS, Azariah Hry 211
_____, Clabon Bts 159
_____, Edward Gwn 321
_____, Edward Hal 81
_____, George Gwn 321
_____, James Gwn 321
_____, James New 21
_____, Jeremiah Hry 233
_____, Jo. C. Gwn 321
_____, John Car 216
_____, John Hry 206
_____, Mark Jks 338
DOSSET/DOSSETT/DOSSIT
Dosset, Elijah Cpb 209
_____, John Cpb 199
_____, Joseph Cpb 200
Dossett, James Jns 441
_____, John Jns 436
Dossit, William Rch 287
DOSTER/DOSSITER
Doster, Elisha Jks 339
_____, Henderson Jns 433
_____, James Clk 303
_____, James Gwn 324
_____, James Gwn 330
_____, James Jsp 395
_____, James W. Jsp 394
_____, Jonathan Jks 314
_____, Mal Wks 332
Doster, Stephen Jns 443
_____, Thomas Jks 314
_____, Thomas Tfo 360
_____, William Gwn 330
_____, William Tfo 360
Dossiter, Thomas Cow 372
DOTHARD, Samuel Fay 182
DOTSON, Charles Ogl 98
_____, Daniel Clk 325
_____, Matthew Cht 279
_____, Richard Cht 279
_____, Thomas Cht 279
_____, Thomas Rab 231
DOTTERY/DOTTY
Dottery, William G. Lib 45
Dotty, Mary Cht 252
DOUBERLY, John Tat 377
DOUGLAS/DOUGLASS/DUGLAS/
DUGLASS
Douglas, Alexander App 11
_____, Benjamin Cht 278
_____, Eaton App 11
_____, Elbert Wal 134
_____, Frederick Tat 372
_____, George Hab 14
_____, John Bts 173
_____, John Cht 278
_____, Jonathan M. Hry 200
_____, Joseph Mon 184
_____, Michael Tat 380
_____, Philip R. Cht 279
_____, Thomas Cht 279
_____, Wright Tat 377
Douglass, Catharine Cht 240
_____, Elizabeth Rch 274
_____, James Bib 64
_____, John Em 169
_____, John Tlf 3
_____, John Wil 319
_____, John M. Jef 412
_____, Jonas Gwn 348
_____, Josiah Bry 88
_____, Robert Tlf 3
_____, Thomas Wil 298
_____, William Em 167
_____, William Jns 465
_____, William B. Bke 118
_____, William S. Up 96
Duglas, Asa Put 185
_____, Daniel B. Dec 12
_____, James Put 189
_____, Robert M. Crf 406
Duglass, Alexander Dec 19

Duglass, Frances Bts 176
DOUGHERTY/DAUGHARTY/
DAUGHERTY/DOHERTY/
DORITY/DORITHY
Dougherty, Charles Clk 322
_____, Charles Sr. Jks 317
_____, James Jks 316
_____, John Cow 367
_____, Patrick Col 360
Daugharty, Dempsy Ware 185
_____, Dennis Ware 185
Daugherty, Michall Col 343
Doherty, Elizabeth DeK 61
_____, James DeK 67
_____, Mason DeK 47
Dority, Elias Wal 129
_____, John Put 206
_____, Thomas Up 120
Dorithy, James New 30
DOUTHIT, Thomas Fay 206
_____, William Fay 206
DOVE, Baily Rab 222
_____, Jacob Rch 262
_____, Jane Pul 152
DOVER, Anderson Hab 29
_____, Francis Hab 29
_____, Johnson Hab 30
_____, Simpson Hab 29
_____, Thomas Gly 264
DOWD/DOUD
Dowd, John Ran 243
Doud, Burton W. Mar 137
DOWDELL, Lewis Jsp 363
DOWDEN, Johnathen Twg 82
DOWDER, James Har 187
DOWDY/DOWDE/DOWDLE
Dowdy, Aaron Hry 235
_____, Amos Hal 92
_____, Armstead Frk 252
_____, Balaam Hal 131
_____, Benjamin Hry 235
_____, Henry Ogl 85
_____, James Car 225
_____, John Scr 308
_____, John M. Ogl 68
_____, Marchant Ogl 86
_____, R. Cht 267
_____, Richard Ogl 75
_____, Robert Hal 84
_____, Robert Hal 92
_____, Sally Hry 242
_____, William Hal 93
_____, William Mon 175
Dowdy, William Pik 118
_____, Willis Sr. Ogl 86
_____, Willis Ogl 86
Dowde, John Wrn 223
Dowdle, Lewis Har 190
DOWELL, E. Cht 251
_____, Thomas Cht 252
DOWERS, James Elb 140
DOWLING, Darling Ware 187
_____, Jabez L. Ware 187
_____, James Ware 187
DOWNER, John Elb 139
_____, Joseph Sr. Elb 137
_____, Joseph Jr. Elb 133
_____, William W. Elb 147
DOWNIE/DOWNEY
Downie, Charles P. Tlb 322
_____, Joseph Gwn 310
Downey, Joseph Fay 203
DOWNING/DOWNIN
Downing, Benjamin Mon 184
_____, Edmund Wks 331
_____, George Tfo 355
_____, Matthew Gre 289
_____, Thomas Gre 291
_____, Wa^{t}. Gwn 375
Downin, William Gwn 377
DOWNMAN, Beverly O. Hst 263
_____, William P. Hst 263
DOWNS, Allen Hab 6
_____, Ambrose Frk 241
_____, Barnett DeK 53
_____, Barrett Bry 88
_____, Elias C. Gwn 346
_____, Mrs. Eliz. Col 334
_____, George G. Frk 211
_____, Isaac Col 335
_____, Isaac Har 181
_____, Isaac Trp 53
_____, Isaac Wrn 230
_____, James Mad 118
_____, James New 52
_____, Jesse Elb 133
_____, Jesse Mad 118
_____, Richard Mor 268
_____, Richard New 44
_____, Seaborn Eff 115
_____, Shadrack Hry 223
_____, Shelley New 43
_____, Silas Har 179
_____, Silas Wrn 231
_____, William Eff 115
_____, William Wrn 231

Downs, William W. Gwn 316
_____, Willy DeK 47
_____, Winiford Cam 181
DOWSE/DOWES
Dowse, Samuel Bke 153
_____, Samuel Rch 283
Dowes, William Hal 117
DOWSTER, Benja. Wrn 203
DOYLE: see Doles
DOZIER/DOZER/DOSIER
Dozier, Adolph Cht 263
_____, Augustus Col 363
_____, B. Cht 240
_____, James Wil 321
_____, James C. Twg 69
_____, James F. Col 363
_____, John Wrn 205
_____, John M. Tlb 343
_____, John W. Wrn 205
_____, Lemuel Twg 75
_____, Nancy Wrn 207
_____, Richard Wrn 205
_____, Richard Jr. Wrn 208
_____, Richmond Hst 287
_____, Seaborn Wrn 206
_____, Thomas Col 363
_____, Thomas Twg 72
_____, Thomas J. Jsp 367
_____, William Col 359
_____, Woody Jsp 368
_____, Woody Trp 41
Dozer, Green Col 353
_____, William DeK 53
Dosier, James P. Mon 180
DRAKE, Alfred Crf 408
_____, Archibald Ogl 79
_____, Berry Mad 115
_____, Cargal Han 142
_____, Dudley E. Rch 291
_____, Elisha Han 151
_____, Epaphroditus Han 152
_____, Etheldred Ogl 87
_____, Frances Wsh 249
_____, James Tat 374
_____, John Wil 321
_____, Meredeth Mad 102
_____, Patrick H. Han 151
_____, Pleasant Bts 166
_____, Robert Doo 81
_____, Sarah Bke 123
_____, Turner New 25
_____, Vines Han 151
_____, William Pik 111
DRANE/DRAIN/DRAND
Drane, Benjamin Col 351
_____, Hiram Col 351
_____, Stephen Col 351
_____, William Sr. Col 348
_____, William Col 351
Drain, Elias Gwn 365
Drand, James Col 347
DRAPER, James Wrn 209
_____, Joshua Wrn 209
_____, Josiah Bts 172
_____, S. A. Cht 271
_____, Thomas Mar 139
DRAW, James Hst 262
DRAWDY, Daniel Irw 299
_____, James Tat 372
_____, Thomas Irw 298
_____, William Wyn 284
DRAWHORN/DRAHORN
Drawhorn, James Jns 445
_____, Joseph Jns 445
_____, Joseph Jns 468
_____, Richard Jns 468
_____, Thomas Twg 81
Drahorn, Thomas J. Jns 468
DRENNAN/DRENNON/DRENON
Drennan, David Fay 201
_____, William Tlb 323
Drennon, JOseph W. Elb 127
_____, William Car 217
Drenon, William Wal 162
DREW, Hugh Mwr 153
_____, Jesse B. Wsh 248
_____, John S. Lau 17
_____, John S. Jsp 373
_____, Kenyon Em 164
_____, Levi Em 176
_____, Mary Bke 127
_____, Newitt Jns 460
_____, Sary Fay 207
_____, Thomas Bak 18
_____, Thomas Em 164
_____, Wilson Em 164
DRICKARD, Smith New 47
DRIGGERS/DRIGORS/DREGORS
Driggers, Daniel Up 97
_____, Dennis Bul 100
_____, Drury New 41
_____, Elizabeth Bul 103
_____, Ephraim Bul 101
_____, James New 41
_____, Joel DeK 55
_____, John Bul 99

Name	County	Page
Driggers, John	Fay	187
______, Moses	Fay	197
______, Nancy	Bul	101
Drigors, Ann	McI	131
______, John	McI	131
______, Jonas	McI	131
______, Nancy	McI	131
Dregors, Henry	Lib	44
______, Jonas	Lib	44
______, Matthew	Lib	45
______, Naan	Lib	44
______, William	Lwn	86
______, William K.	Lib	44
DRINKWATER, John	Mar	144
DRISCALL/CRISKEL/DRISKAL		
DRISKIL/DRISKILL/DRESKELL		
Driscall, Beecham	Gwn	348
______, Elgat	Mon	213
______, George	Mon	215
Driskel, Jacob	Wks	346
______, Tilman	Hal	69
Driskal, Joshua	Put	208
Driskil, Nancy	Jks	346
Driskill, William	Jsp	385
Dreskell, Christopher	Jsp	366
DRIVER, Benjamin	Jns	434
______, Elizabeth	Mar	141
______, Giles	Jns	435
______, Goodridge	Jns	434
______, Jacob	Hry	250
______, James	Hab	36
______, John	Mon	213
______, Jordan	Pik	107
______, Leonard	Up	113
______, William	Tlb	330
______, William G.	Wil	288
DRUMGOLD, Julia	Cht	262
DRUMMOND/DRUMMON		
Drummond, Daniel	Gwn	342
______, James	Mor	248
______, John	Mor	248
______, Martha	Cam	188
______, Moses	Wal	164
______, W. L.	Bal	32
______, William	Wal	163
Drummon, William H.	Gwn	316
DRURY/DREWRY		
Drury, Charles	Cam	191
______, Edwin	Pik	106
______, John	Han	151
Drewry, James	Mon	192
DRYDEN/DRYDON		
Dryden, John	Ware	189
Dryden, William	Ware	187
Drydon, John	Lib	45
DUAWA, William	Hab	48
DUBERLY, Joseph	Tat	371
DUBIGNON, Henry	Gly	269
______, Mrs. Joseph	Gly	269
DUBOSE/DEBOSE/DELBOSE		
Dubose, David	Col	335
DuBose, Edwin	Wil	312
______, James R.	Wil	311
Debose, Peter	Tms	16
Delbose, John F.	Tat	378
DUBUEICH, Clara	Cht	260
DUBULIN, Geo. N.	Wrn	226
DUCK, David	Jsp	393
______, Jonathan	Gwn	335
______, Leroy	Cpb	209
DUCKED, Jacob	Hab	43
DUCKER, Nimrod E.	Hst	284
DUCKWORTH, Elizabeth	Han	152
______, Jeremiah	Crf	408
______, John	Up	113
DUDLEY/DUDLY/DUDNEY		
Dudley, Anderson	Car	220
______, Daniel Sr.	Hal	108
______, Daniel	Hal	118
______, David	Hal	81
______, Edan	Wsh	244
______, Edward	Put	184
______, Elam	Wsh	248
______, George M.	Ogl	97
______, Guildford	Eff	110
______, Ignatues	Elb	131
______, James	Bts	163
______, James	Bts	176
______, James L.	Elb	140
______, John B.	Frk	251
______, John T.	Elb	141
______, Peter	Trp	46
______, Robert	Mus	285
______, Thomas	Han	151
______, W. J.	Cht	256
______, Wiley	Mad	108
______, William	Gre	274
______, William B.	Clk	291
______, William J.	Eff	110
Dudly, Mrs.	Scr	310
______, Oliver	McI	124
______, Robert	Gwn	331
Dudney, Arthur	Wsh	253
DUE, Jno. R.	Wrn	215
______, William J.	Wrn	216
DUFF, Darcas	Hab	54

Name	County	Page
Duff, Polly	Hab	55
_____, Richard M.	Jsp	391
DUFFY/DUFFEE/DUFFIE		
Duffy, Fedric	Mon	194
_____, Nancy	Hal	94
_____, T.	Cht	272
_____, Thomas	Rch	268
_____, William	Mon	192
Duffee, John	Bts	169
_____, John M.	Car	217
_____, Thomas	Crf	402
Duffie, Edith	Hry	240
_____, Margaret	Hry	250
_____, Robert S.	Hry	244
DUFFIL/DUFFLE/DUFFEEL		
Duffil, Austmus	Hst	271
_____, Nathaniel	Hst	280
_____, Thomas	Hst	282
Duffle, Luckey	Ogl	82
_____, Thomas H.	Fay	201
Duffeel, Lucy	Ogl	82
DUGAS, L. P.	Rch	272
_____, Mrs. V.	Rch	256
DUGGAN/DUGAN/DUAGAN		
Duggan, A. C.	Wsh	274
_____, Asa	Wsh	267
_____, Jessee J.	Mon	206
_____, John	Wsh	254
_____, John H.	Wsh	254
_____, William	Mon	204
Dugan, James	Cht	257
Duagan, Hiram	Hab	50
DUGGAR/DUGGER		
Duggar, John	Tms	25
_____, Sampson	Pik	118
_____, William Sr.	Tms	26
_____, William	Tms	18
Dugger, Chesley	Eff	109
_____, David	Bul	99
_____, John	Eff	110
_____, John	Eff	110
_____, Nathaniel	Eff	115
DUKE/DUKES		
Duke, Aristottle G.	Bts	168
_____, Azariah	Bke	117
_____, Baily C.	Tlb	342
_____, Charles	New	8
_____, Christiana	Bke	118
_____, David	New	40
_____, David	New	44
_____, Edmond	Mor	263
_____, Edmond	Trp	53
_____, Edward S.	Fay	187
Duke, Elijah	Lwn	79
_____, Elisha	Bke	117
_____, Epps	Wal	143
_____, Ferdinan	New	25
_____, Francis	Cow	378
_____, Gibson	New	51
_____, Green	Mon	177
_____, Green R.	Jks	311
_____, Hamilton	Tlb	338
_____, Hardy	Jsp	368
_____, James	Bke	117
_____, James	Wal	148
_____, James H.	Trp	54
_____, Jesse	Gwn	354
_____, Joel	Tat	372
_____, John	Tat	376
_____, John	Trp	40
_____, John T.	New	39
_____, Joseph	Up	109
_____, Kranshaw	Gwn	354
_____, L. B.	Gwn	354
_____, Mary Sr.	Bke	118
_____, Mary Jr.	Bke	118
_____, Massa	Clk	310
_____, Moses S.	Har	184
_____, Nancy	Bke	118
_____, Robert	Tlb	340
_____, Sander	Hry	210
_____, Seaborn	Tlb	342
_____, Seaborn J.	Put	204
_____, Stephen	Up	111
_____, Stephen H.	Jsp	361
_____, Thomas	Car	227
_____, Thomas	Cow	382
_____, Thomas	Trp	51
_____, Turner	Bke	117
_____, William	Cpb	201
_____, William	Har	176
_____, William	Jsp	390
_____, William	Wsh	242
Dukes, Benjamin	Lee	33
_____, Charles	Mor	262
_____, David	Cow	370
_____, David	Mwr	168
_____, Drury	Crf	397
_____, Fred	Jsp	373
_____, Green	Crf	397
_____, Henry	Mor	256
_____, Isam	Lee	33
_____, James	Up	104
_____, Jessee	Bul	99
_____, John	Bry	87
_____, Joseph	Hry	247

Dukes, Kezeah Wil 304
_____, Mary A. Mus 277
_____, Nancy Lwn 82
_____, Richard Hry 225
_____, Robert Hry 234
_____, Samuel Crf 397
_____, Shadric Lee 33
_____, William Bry 86
_____, William Hry 233
DULIN, John C. Hry 216
DUMAS, Benjamin Mon 224
_____, David Frk 211
_____, David Mon 189
_____, Jeremiah Jns 440
_____, John Jns 440
_____, Moses Mon 174
DUMPLUY, L. Cht 259
DUNAGAN/DUNAGEN/DUNNAGAN/
DONAGAN
Dunagan, Ezekiel Hal 73
_____, Isaah Hal 91
_____, John Hal 116
_____, Joseph Hal 71
Dunagen, Joshua Hal 111
Dunnagan, Abner Hab 37
Donagan, Ezra Hab 34
DONAHOO/DUNAHOO/DUNNAHOO
DUNNEHOO/DONAHO/DUNAHO
Donahoo, Cornelious Frk 213
_____, Cornelius K. Frk 253
_____, John H. Frk 225
Dunahoo, John W. Cow 380
Dunnahoo, James DeK 37
Dunnehoo, James Ogl 71
Donaho, W. Cht 283
Dunaho, John Hal 77
DUNAVANT, Mann Wrn 211
DUNAWAY/DUNNAWAY
Dunaway, Benjamin Wil 311
_____, Edward Jks 325
_____, James Lin 67
_____, John Wal 131
_____, Johnston Lin 68
_____, Joseph Wil 316
_____, Mary Wrn 212
_____, Samuel Wil 316
_____, Timothy C. Lin 68
_____, William Lin 68
_____, William Wrn 195
Dunnaway, Benjamin Ran 244
_____, James W. Ran 244
DUNBAR, Alexander Gwn 358
_____, G. W. Gwn 358
Dunbar, George Rch 264
_____, Harriet Cht 261
_____, John Gwn 357
_____, Ninean H. Gwn 358
_____, Thomas S. Jns 441
_____, Wash. P. Gwn 359
DUNCAN/DUNKIN/DUNKEN/DUNKION
Duncan, Absalom Gwn 309
_____, Alexander Hab 63
_____, Allen Pik 115
_____, Ben Gwn 371
_____, Charles R. Gwn 355
_____, David Hry 239
_____, Daniel Jns 460
_____, Dennis Jks 340
_____, E. Gwn 308
_____, Edmond Jns 460
_____, Edmond Jr. Jns 472
_____, Edmund Hry 200
_____, Elbert Lau 15
_____, Elisha Hab 63
_____, Elizabeth DeK 72
_____, George Jns 472
_____, George Wal 172
_____, Henry Bal 36
_____, Henry Elb 133
_____, Hinton Jns 460
_____, J. Cht 263
_____, James Bal 39
_____, James Jsp 396
_____, James Tfo 365
_____, James E. Hst 261
_____, John Elb 120
_____, John Gwn 310
_____, John Har 190
_____, John Hry 212
_____, John Jks 340
_____, John Mus 286
_____, John Tlb 323
_____, John T. Mwr 164
_____, Lee Jns 472
_____, Mary Mwr 164
_____, Maple Hab 66
_____, Moses Elb 140
_____, Moses Hst 285
_____, Nathaniel Frk 236
_____, Peasion Elb 120
_____, Peter Clk 311
_____, Robert Gwn 354
_____, Robert Tlb 323
_____, Samuel New 40
_____, Thomas Jks 339
_____, Thomas N. Mwr 159

Name	County	Page
Duncan, Wiley	Hal	125
______, William	Gre	291
______, William	Jns	460
______, William	Tfo	366
Dunkin, John C.	Mar	142
______, John H.	New	12
______, Wilson	Wal	135
Dunken, Samuel	Gwn	331
Dunkion, Matthew	Cow	374
DUNFORD, Susannah	Bke	128
DUNHAM/DENHAM		
Dunham, Daniel	Up	112
______, Davis	Put	186
______, Rev. Jacob H.B.	Lib	45
______, Leonard	Lib	45
______, Nancy	Put	185
______, Nathaniel	Put	191
______, Samuel	Rch	278
______, Thomas	Lib	48
______, William	Cht	256
______, William A.	McI	124
Denham, David	Hry	203
______, John A.	Bke	155
______, Marget	Car	222
______, Patrick G.	Car	225
DUNLAP, David	New	31
______, Elizabeth	DeK	38
______, James	DeK	39
______, John	DeK	38
______, Jonathan	Rab	234
______, Joseph	Mwr	153
______, Matthew	Rab	231
______, Samuel C.	Gwn	317
DUNN/DUN		
Dunn, A.	Mus	289
______, Abner	New	52
______, Abraham	Frk	226
______, Alfred J.	Col	360
______, Augustus B.	Han	151
______, Chorlott	Crf	402
______, David	Hst	276
______, David	Ogl	100
______, Eph.	Bal	39
______, Gatewood	Jsp	357
______, Henry	Bib	60
______, Henry	Gwn	353
______, Hiram	Gre	294
______, Hy. Jr.	Gwn	352
______, Isaac	Bib	60
______, Ishmael	Fay	205
______, Jacob		
______, James	Frk	255
______, James	Gre	295

Name	County	Page
Dunn, James	Twg	
______, James M. Plantation	Put	1
______, James M.	Put	2
______, Jane	Bke	1
______, Jeremiah	Up	1
______, Joel	Jsp	3
______, Joel	Pul	1
______, John	Elb	1
______, John Jr.	Elb	1
______, John	Fay	1
______, John V.	Mwr	1
______, John	Mus	2
______, John	Up	1
______, Josie	Mon	1
______, Lemmon	Bke	1
______, Levisa	Rch	2
______, Michael	Cow	3
______, Rebecca	Rch	2
______, Stephen	Hry	2
______, Thomas	Ogl	
______, Thomas	Pul	1
______, Thomas	Tms	
______, Uriah	Trp	
______, Waters	Col	3
______, William	Bib	
______, William	Col	3
______, William	Hry	2
______, William	Mwr	1
______, William	Mon	2
______, William S.	Col	3
Dun, John	Cpb	1
______, John	Rab	2
______, John	Rab	2
______, John T.	Clk	3
______, Waters	Ogl	
______, William	Cpb	1
DUNNING/DUNING		
Dunning, Charles	Crf	4
______, S. C.	Cht	2
______, Thomas	Hal	1
Duning, Lucy	Put	2
DUNNAGHER, John	Jns	4
DUNSEITH, James C.	Bts	1
DUNSTON, Betsy	Jks	3
______, John	Hry	2
______, Walker	Frk	2
______, William	Jks	3
DUNWODY/DUNWOODY		
Dunwody, James	Crf	4
______, James	McI	1
Dunwoody, John Esq.	Lib	
DUPOISTER, Lewis C.	Up	1
DUPRIEST/DUPREAST/DEPRIEST		

Dupriest, Martin Mor 260
Dupreast, James A. Ogl. 82
Depriest, Joseph Gwn 321
DUPREE/DUPREY
Dupree, Arthur Hry 225
_____, Burges Put 188
_____, Charles L. Mor 239
_____, Curtice Clk 293
_____, D. Jsp 367
_____, Daniel Hst 269
_____, Daniel P. Ogl 97
_____, Gee Gly 266
_____, Herod Tlb 339
_____, Ira E. Twg 76
_____, James Wsh 248
_____, James Wsh 265
_____, Jeremiah Hst 269
_____, Jesse Hst 264
_____, John Lau 11
_____, John Mor 239
_____, John Tlb 339
_____, Lewis Put 215
_____, Lewis Wsh 260
_____, Lewis Jarrel DeK 68
_____, Patsy Twg 84
_____, Simon Hst 272
_____, Sterling Twg 89
_____, Synthia Lau 22
_____, T. R. Wsh 260
_____, Thomas R. Tlb 339
_____, William H. Hst 291
_____, William N. Tlb 343
Duprey, Daniel Ogl 66
_____, Daniel Ogl 75
_____, Joseph Ogl 68
_____, Lewis J. Ogl 97
DURANT, Francis McI 126
DURDEN/DURDIN/DURDAN/
DIRDEN/DERDAN
Durden, Asa Hry 237
_____, David Cow 388
_____, Dennis Em 176
_____, Eleazer Em 171
_____, Frances Wsh 270
_____, Henry Em 175
_____, Jacob Em 175
_____, Jane Twg 62
_____, John Capt. Mor 256
_____, Josiah Twg 65
_____, Miles Bak 15
_____, Mills Wks 346
_____, Richard M. Twg 62
_____, Stephen Hst 286
Durden, Stephen Mor 254
_____, Stephen Wsh 261
_____, Washington Bib 72
_____, William Em 176
_____, William Tlb 338
Durdin, William Wks 346
Durdan, Abner Jns 442
Dirden, John Wrn 216
Derdan, Mathew Wsh 273
DURE/DURR
Dure, F. Cht 253
Durr, Larkin Cow 380
DUREN/DEUREN/DURIN
Duren, Delila Wal 157
_____, John Wal 156
_____, Lemuel Wal 156
Deuren, George Wal 137
_____, George Wal 137
Durin, Jesse Hry 233
DURHAM/DERHAM/DURRAM
Durham, A. V. Col 346
_____, Abner Mwr 155
_____, Alse Jsp 362
_____, Anderson Jks 325
_____, Arthur Fay 183
_____, Daniel DeK 35
_____, Hardy Twg 64
_____, Howell J. Hal 90
_____, Isaah Fay 201
_____, John Irw 300
_____, Joseph Clk 303
_____, Joshua Gwn 339
_____, Matthew Mon 222
_____, Polly Mon 186
_____, Sanders Mon 222
_____, Seaborn Mon 187
_____, Seth Hst 289
_____, Shelman Mon 219
_____, Silas M. Gre 304
_____, Singleton Mon 187
_____, Stephen Jks 346
_____, Thomas DeK 63
_____, William Gre 284
_____, William Jks 325
_____, William A. Rch 278
_____, William M. Gre 273
Derham, John Dec 10
_____, Lindsey Clk 305
Durram, Stephen Frk 244
DURICE, Margaret App 12
DURINGER, Peter Cht 240
DURKEE, Malinda Frk 210
DURNS, James Hab 57

Name	County	Page
DURRENCE, James	Tat	373
______, Jesse	Tat	372
______, Joseph	Tat	374
______, William Sr.	Tat	378
______, William Jr.	Tat	372
DUSENBERRY, Susannah	Hry	233
DUSKIN, Michael	Crf	413
DUTTON/DOUTTON		
Dutton, Henry	Bul	92
______, James	Elb	128
______, James	Elb	152
______, Thomas	Elb	121
______, Thomas Jr.	Elb	124
Doutton, John	Bib	50
DWIGHT, H.	Bib	60
DYALL, Elisabeth	McI	128
______, George	McI	124
DYAN, Thomas	Cow	368
DYAR, Elisha	Frk	234
______, Nicholas	Cow	368
______, Washington	Cow	373
DYAS/DYASS/DYESS/DYUS		
Dyas, George	Bib	72
______, John	App	13
______, Lucy	Tat	379
Dyass, Thomas	Mon	205
______, William	Mon	205
Dyess, Aquilla	Crf	403
______, Henry	Ware	184
Dyus, John	Bke	144
______, Moses	Bke	143
DYE, Abram	Wrn	193
______, Avery	Bke	138
______, Burwell	Elb	149
______, David	Elb	124
______, Jane	Elb	150
______, Martin	Wrn	250
______, Martin M.	Bke	138
______, Martin P.	Bts	166
______, Margaret	Rch	263
______, Silas	Mon	190
______, Stephen	Hal	130
______, William	Elb	150
______, William	Hal	130
______, William	Twg	63
DYER/DYRE		
Dyer, Anthony	Jsp	369
______, David	Mor	250
______, Edm^{d}. H.	Jns	472
______, Edwin	Gwn	315
______, Elisha	Hab	9
______, Elizabeth	Tlb	332
______, Jacob	Put	189
Dyer, Joel H.	Elb	144
______, John	Bal	43
______, John	Mor	270
______, Micajah	Ogl	80
______, Richard H.	Mor	268
______, Thomas	Bal	44
______, William	Bib	54
______, William	Wil	312
______, Wyley	Car	219
Dyre, Charity	Em	178
______, James	Twg	80
______, Susannah	Twg	87
______, Thomas	Wrn	205
DYKES/DYKE		
Dykes, Allen	Wal	159
______, Elias	Pul	153
______, George Sr.	Wks	347
______, George	Wks	335
______, Henry	Hst	265
______, Isaiah	Dec	7
______, Jacob	Pul	153
______, James Sr.	Pul	154
______, James Jr.	Pul	153
______, Jesse	Eff	106
______, Jourdan	Hst	271
Dyke, Warrin	Wks	339
DYSON, Ann	Wil	312
______, Effee	Lee	28
______, Isaer	Lee	28
______, James	Mwr	150
______, Thomas	Mon	192
______, Thomas	Trp	44
EADES/EADS/EDES		
Eades, Randolph	Jks	319
______, William	DeK	49
Eads, Ruben	Ogl	81
______, William	New	30
Edes, Harriet C.	Rch	271
EADY, Benjamin	Lin	67
______, Henry	Pik	115
______, Henry	Wks	331
______, James	Lin	67
______, John	Lin	66
______, John R.	Pik	115
______, Johnathan J.	Fay	191
______, Jno.	Wks	353
______, Samuel	Mwr	158
EAGLE/EIBLE		
Eagle, George	Clk	295
Eigle, Mathew	Cht	257
EAKIN/EAKINS		

Name	County	Page
Eakin, William	Put	184
Eakins, Henry	Hab	63
EANS, John	Twg	65
**Earbob (no other name: Indian)	Car	233
EARGIN, Coleman	Cpb	200
EARICK, Ann	Rch	292
EARLY/EARLEY		
Early, George	Tms	17
_____, James	Col	351
_____, Joel	Gre	305
_____, Jesse	Wsh	264
Earley, Enoch	Hal	104
_____, Simeon	Ogl	64
EARP, Daniel	Ogl	91
EART, Silas	Clk	295
EARWOOD, Burd	Hab	36
_____, George	Hab	37
EASLEY, William P.	Wal	135
EASON/ESON		
Eason, Abraham	App	5
_____, Abraham	New	25
_____, Alfred	Bke	154
_____, Edmond	Fay	188
_____, Edmonds	Jef	408
_____, Elijah	Pul	159
_____, Elisha H.	Ogl	91
_____, Henry	Wal	126
_____, Isaac	Wsh	271
_____, Isaac	Wil	298
_____, John	Ogl	101
_____, Lucy	Fay	188
_____, Messock	Twg	71
_____, Milly	Hry	236
_____, Moses S.	App	5
_____, Parker	Hry	236
_____, Rice	Fay	182
_____, Rice	Ogl	102
_____, Seth	Bke	127
_____, Sterling D.	Jef	410
_____, Thomas	Cow	392
_____, Iredell	Tms	21
_____, Whitmel	Tlb	336
_____, Whitmel	Trp	36
_____, William	Tat	373
_____, William	Twg	60
Eson, Joseph	Mor	261
EAST, Benjamin	Trp	41
_____, Beryamin	Hal	128
_____, Dancel	Hal	126
_____, Ezekiel	Cht	279
_____, Jesse	Trp	40
_____, Stephen	Hal	129
EASTERLING/EASTERLIN/EASTIN		
Easterling, Bennet	Doo	82
_____, Henry	Cow	370
_____, Henry	Wal	142
_____, Joel	Wal	144
Easterlin, James	Tat	371
_____, Shaderick	Twg	64
Eastin, Philip	Fay	182
EASTERS/EASTER		
Easters, Allen	Hry	211
_____, George	Lwn	83
_____, James	Put	193
_____, John	Ogl	80
_____, John	Ogl	81
_____, John	Ran	243
_____, Miles H.	Trp	36
_____, Zachry	Trp	36
_____, Zephariah	Hry	239
Easter, John C.	Jsp	352
EASTES, John	DeK	56
_____, Miles	Gwn	327
EASTRIDGE/EASTRIGE		
Eastridge, Charles	Fay	199
Eastrige, David	Put	181
EASTWOOD/EASTERWOOD		
Eastwood, Daniel	Cow	378
_____, Gideon	Cow	388
_____, John	Wsh	265
_____, Lawrence	Cow	388
_____, Marium	Wsh	265
Easterwood, Lawrence	Car	224
EATON/EATTON		
Eaton, Charles R.	Jns	460
_____, James	Jks	327
_____, John	DeK	49
_____, John	Hab	34
_____, Polly	Hab	59
_____, Reubin	Gwn	375
_____, Samuel	Hab	7
_____, William	Hab	7
_____, William	Hab	59
_____, William	Hab	61
_____, William	Jns	456
_____, William	Rch	286
Eatton, Ansel	Jks	346
EATRIS, Peter	Hab	24
EAVES, Burrel	Cpb	209
_____, Guilford	Hal	111
_____, Lewis P.	Jks	325
_____, Rhoday	Elb	141
EBERHART, Frances P.	Mad	101
_____, George	Mad	105

Name	County	Page
Eberhart, Jacob	Hal	74
_____, Jacob	Mad	101
_____, James	Mad	116
_____, John	Hal	75
_____, Robert	Mad	102
EBORN, John	Lau	17
ECHOLS/ECKLES/ECKELS/		
ECHOLES/ECHOLDS/ACHOLS/		
ACLES		
Echols, Abraham	Hab	13
_____, Absalom	Mus	287
_____, Benjamin	New	54
_____, Elijah	Lin	61
_____, Elijah	Wil	307
_____, Elijah	Wil	317
_____, James	Hab	12
_____, James	Wil	296
_____, John	Hab	62
_____, Joshua	Mor	250
_____, Miller	Wal	125
_____, Nan Allen	Wil	297
_____, Nathaniel J.	Wil	307
_____, Obediah (Rev.)	Jsp	383
_____, Obediah	Lin	71
_____, Obediah	New	11
_____, Reubin	Cow	378
_____, Robert	Wal	142
_____, Robert M.	Wal	125
_____, Samuel B.	Wal	132
_____, Samuel D.	Cow	373
_____, Sarah	Wil	298
_____, Thomas	Clk	291
_____, William	Tlb	333
_____, William S.	New	11
_____, Zelphia	Wsh	275
Eckles, James	Cow	390
_____, James C.	Tfo	363
_____, Joel	Mad	101
Eckels, Ratliff	Hst	271
Echoles, Joshua	Frk	254
Echolds, Thomas	Put	180
Achols, Davis	Hab	34
_____, Margaret	Gwn	367
Acles, Elizabeth	Rch	288
ECKLEY, Levi	Bib	55
ECTOR, Hugh W.	Mwr	154
_____, Joseph	Clk	301
_____, Wiley B.	Mwr	154
EDEN/EDDINS		
Eden, Thomas	Cht	255
Eddins, Mary	Hal	121
_____, William	Frk	255
EDENFIELD, David	Em	176

Name	County	Page
Edenfield, David	Tlf	
_____, Jesse	Em	17
_____, Richard	Em	17
_____, Thomas	Em	17
EDGAR, Abraham	Hry	22
_____, Hugh	Wal	16
_____, John	Wal	17
EDDLEMAN, Elizabeth	New	1
_____, Moses	New	1
_____, John	New	1
_____, Reuben	New	1
EDGE, Alexander	Bib	7
_____, Ellen	Jsp	35
_____, Ezecal	Hab	3
_____, Garland	Mon	19
_____, James	Tfo	35
_____, Jehu	Bal	3
_____, John C.	New	5
_____, Jonas	Hab	4
_____, Joseph	Wil	29
_____, Joshua	Wil	30
_____, Marlin	Mon	21
_____, Obedeah	Mon	19
_____, Sean	Mon	17
_____, Simpson	Mon	19
_____, Thomas	Hry	20
_____, Thomas	Hab	3
_____, William	Hab	3
EDINS, William D.	Pul	14
EDMONDS/EDMOND/EDMONS/		
EDMON/EDMUNDS/EDMUND		
Edmonds, Amos	Mwr	16
_____, Anthony	Ogl	7
_____, Nathan	Pik	12
_____, Winifred	Wil	31
Edmond, William	New	4
Edmons, Sarah	Wil	31
Edmon, James	Hab	2
Edmunds, Asa	Wal	12
_____, Aurilla	Wal	15
_____, William	Tlf	
Edmund, Samuel	Hal	10
EDMONDSON/EDMUNDSON/EDMONSON/		
EDMUNSON/EDMUSON/EDMONSTON		
Edmondson, Bryant	Trp	4
_____, Eli	Fay	20
_____, Humphrey	Mor	25
_____, James	Lwn	9
_____, James	Gwn	34
_____, John	Lwn	7
_____, John	Up	10
_____, Mary	Ogl	9
_____, Thomas	Jsp	37

Name	County	Page
dmondson, Thomas	Mor	264
_____, Willey	Mor	265
_____, William	Wrn	195
_____, William G.	Wrn	220
_____, Zacheus	Put	212
dmundson, Demoval	Lin	70
_____, Edmund	Put	218
_____, James	Put	212
_____, John	Put	213
dmonson, Elijah	Clk	307
_____, Hannah	Jsp	385
_____, James	Frk	210
_____, Joseph	Cow	374
_____, Mahalah	New	43
_____, Martha	Jsp	393
_____, Phillip	Ogl	90
_____, Richard	Ogl	90
_____, Samuel	Elb	134
_____, Thomas	Elb	134
_____, William	Gre	285
dmunson, Hannah	Twg	82
dmuson, George	Hab	18
dmonston, James	Hal	77
DSON, Calvin	Doo	89
DWARDS/EDWARD		
dwards, A. F.	Up	95
_____, Abel H.	Frk	254
_____, Alfred	DeK	46
_____, Alfred B.	DeK	48
_____, Amber	New	50
_____, Ambrose	Tlb	334
_____, Andrew	Han	152
_____, Asa	Trp	51
_____, Aulston W.	Hab	62
_____, Beal	Eff	109
_____, Benjamin	Jef	416
_____, Benjamin	Ogl	100
_____, Berry	Tlb	336
_____, Charles	Eff	115
_____, Daniel	Eff	107
_____, David	Trp	49
_____, Edward	Clk	295
_____, Edward	Gwn	378
_____, Elisha	Cow	386
_____, Elizabeth H.	Ran	244
_____, Ehich	Hab	55
_____, Etheldred	Ran	245
_____, Etheldred	Tfo	359
_____, Henry	Hal	124
_____, Henry L.	Clk	313
_____, Isaac C.	Elb	139
_____, J. C.	Clk	325
_____, Jacob	Wal	161

Name	County	Page
Edwards, James	Eff	106
_____, James	Jsp	362
_____, James	Tms	28
_____, James	Twg	75
_____, James H.	Hry	222
_____, Jesse	Elb	138
_____, Jesse	Up	115
_____, John	Col	363
_____, John	Cow	368
_____, John	Elb	133
_____, John	Eff	105
_____, John	Har	185
_____, John	Jns	445
_____, John	Mon	201
_____, John	New	7
_____, John	Put	186
_____, John	Tlb	334
_____, John	Wal	127
_____, John	Wsh	243
_____, John S.	Jns	445
_____, Joseph	Frk	254
_____, Joseph	Jns	456
_____, Jourdan	Wal	150
_____, Lemuel	Ogl	93
_____, Ledpa	Cow	382
_____, Loxla	Tlb	334
_____, Lucky	Mon	195
_____, Mary	Col	363
_____, Morriss	Jsp	379
_____, N. U.	Bib	75
_____, Nancy	Frk	255
_____, Nathan	Car	227
_____, Nathaniel	Jef	417
_____, Obediah	Eff	106
_____, P. H.	Ran	245
_____, Penelope	Bib	69
_____, Peter	Hal	120
_____, Polly	Han	152
_____, Precious C.	Tfo	362
_____, Prior	Trp	48
_____, Reubin	Hry	224
_____, Reubon	Jsp	382
_____, Robert	Bak	18
_____, Robert L.	Elb	153
_____, Ruel	Hry	237
_____, Sherrards	Tms	18
_____, Simeon	Hry	224
_____, Simon	Wal	149
_____, Solomon	Clk	294
_____, Sturling	Col	341
_____, Susanah	Jsp	398
_____, Thomas	Hab	62
_____, Thomas	Ogl	86

Edwards, Thomas Ogl 93
_____, Thomas Tfo 357
_____, Thomas G. Frk 250
_____, Thomas H. Mon 210
_____, William Clk 312
_____, William Elb 149
_____, William Eff 112
_____, William Eff 115
_____, William Hab 19
_____, William Hry 199
_____, William Mon 227
_____, William Tlb 334
_____, William Tlb 342
_____, William Wal 157
_____, William Wsh 262
_____, William H. Bry 89
_____, William P. Jns 453
_____, William S. Bib 73
_____, William W. Wal 155
_____, Young Tlb 335
Edward, Isac Mtg 234
_____, Joel Jsp 361
_____, Lemuel DeK 69
EDY, Henry Tlb 325
_____, Thomas Har 182
EARWOOD: see Yearwood
EELLS, Nathan Bib 50
EGBERT, Peter M. Rch 285
EGGERTON, Noah Mus 281
EGLETREE, Edwin Jsp 382
EGNEW, William Jsp 361
EIDSON, Boyce Wal 136
_____, Boyd Mor 262
_____, David C. Hry 205
_____, James Gre 274
_____, James Ogl 101
_____, James Mon 179
_____, John Mor 263
_____, Lewis Clk 293
_____, Shelton Mor 261
_____, Thomas Gre 274
_____, Thomas R. Wil 308
_____, William Up 97
_____, William Wil 321
EILANDS/EILAND
Eilands, David McI 124
_____, Francis M. Jns 450
_____, Lydia McI 124
_____, Nancy Jns 450
_____, Stephen Jns 450
_____, William McI 121
Eiland, Rutha Jns 460
EIVEY, Thomas Hab 23

Eivey, Viles Hab
***EKOAH (Indian) Car
ELSBERRY/ELLSBERRY
Elsberry, Benjamin Ogl
Ellsberry, Michael Ogl
ELAM/ELIM
Elam, George DeK
_____, William DeK
Elim, Hodyah Put
ELBERT, Harriett A. Cam
ELDER, Ann Clk
_____, David Clk
_____, David Jr. Clk
_____, Doctor W. Clk
_____, Edmonds Clk
_____, Edmund Wal
_____, Edward A. Mon
_____, Harison W. Clk
_____, Hartewell M. Clk
_____, Howell Clk
_____, James P. Clk
_____, Jeremiah Ogl
_____, John P. Clk
_____, Joseph Clk
_____, Joseph M. Clk
_____, Joshua Clk
_____, Joshua Fay
_____, Littleberry Har
_____, Thomas Clk
_____, Wyck W. J. Pik
ELDRIDGE, Daniel Mwr
_____, Peter Mwr
_____, William Twg
ELEBEE/ELIBY/ELLIBY/
ELLERBEE
Elebee, James Bul
Eliby, William Bib
Elliby, Dick (colored) Bke
Ellerbee, John Hst
ELEY/ELY/ELLEY/ELI
Eley, Bennett H. Gre
_____, Charles A. Wrn
_____, John Tfo
_____, Michael Tfo
_____, Osbern Gre
_____, Samuel Gre
_____, William Gre
Ely, John Wsh
_____, Seaborn Mus
Elley, James Han
Eli, Thomas DeK
ELHANNON, John W. Jks
ELISBERRY/ELSBURY

Name	County	Page
Elisberry, Lindy	DeK	25
Elsbury, Benjamin	Clk	321
ELKINS/ELKIN		
Elkins, Alexander	Eff	106
______, Eli	Gwn	310
______, Elvira	Eff	115
______, Ervin	Ogl	68
______, John	Dec	13
______, John	Eff	112
______, Thomas	Eff	108
______, William	Dec	13
______, Young	Dec	13
Elkin, David	Wil	297
ELLARD, Amos A.	Rab	224
______, James Jr.	Rab	224
______, James Sr.	Rab	233
ELLEN, Nancy	DeK	61
ELLENBURGH, Hezekiah	Hal	83
ELLER, Joseph	Rab	232
ELLERSON, Moses	Wal	169
______, Rachel	Wal	170
______, Watson	Wal	170
ELLINGTON/ELINGTON/ELLETON		
Ellington, David	Wil	301
______, David B.	DeK	45
______, Hezekiah	Tfo	361
______, James	New	27
______, John	Mon	202
______, John S.	Lau	21
______, John T.	Wsh	275
______, Josiah	Hal	115
______, Josiah	Lau	13
______, Leonard	Hal	90
______, Martha	Bal	39
______, Nancy	Pik	112
______, Rice	Elb	153
______, Richard C.	Fay	182
______, Simion	Lau	9
______, Stephen	Tfo	355
______, Tyre	Tfo	362
Elington, William	Hab	65
______, William	Hab	66
Elleton, Elizabeth	Put	199
ELLIOTT/ELIOTT/ELLIOT/ ELLETT/ELLOT/ELLIT/ELIT		
Elliott, Alexander	Mor	268
______, And^{W}. W.	Up	99
______, Benjamin	Pik	130
______, Benjamin	Wsh	258
______, David	Mon	179
______, Drewry	Bke	132
______, Edward F.	Har	180
______, G. W.	Mus	279
Elliott, George	Jks	336
______, Dr. H. slaves	Cht	280
______, James	Hry	249
______, James Sr.	Rch	280
______, John	Bke	132
______, John	Col	352
______, John	Hal	102
______, John	Hry	210
______, John; dec'd. Est.	Lib	45
______, M.	Cht	251
______, Martha	Lib	45
______, Mary	Bke	134
______, Mary	Hry	249
______, Robert H.	Hry	220
______, Heirs of S.	Cht	280
______, Sarah	Hal	82
______, Silas	Bts	166
______, Stephen	Cht	280
______, Thomas C.	Elb	150
______, Sarah A.	Tfo	366
______, Thomas	Mor	256
______, Thomas	Wal	156
______, William	Mon	185
______, William	Ran	245
______, Zachariah	Jns	432
Eliott, James	Wrn	200
______, James S.	Hal	77
Elliot, Ephraim	Rab	231
______, Harriet	Tat	372
______, George H.	Mon	177
______, James	Wal	144
______, John	Gwn	378
______, Thomas	Lin	73
______, William	DeK	59
______, William	Lin	61
______, William	Pik	129
Ellott, Cornelious	Ogl	87
______, Davis	Ran	244
Ellot, Andrew	Hab	56
______, Arther	Hab	56
______, James	Hab	56
Ellet, Henry	Ear	99
Ellett, Mary	Clk	298
Ellit, Robert	Ran	245
Elit, Ebin T. J.	Hab	53
ELLIS/ELLISS/ELLICE		
Ellis, Benjamin	DeK	66
______, Benjamin	Jns	465
______, Benjamin	Put	180
______, Benjamin	Tlb	341
______, Calvin H.	Frk	232
______, Edward	Put	176
______, Edwin	Hst	285

Ellis, Elijah Rab 230
_____, Elisha Wal 140
_____, Ephraim Twg 79
_____, Evan New 42
_____, George Up 101
_____, George W. Bib 55
_____, George W. Hst 262
_____, Green B. Han 152
_____, Henry Jsp 394
_____, Hicks Put 188
_____, Hodyah Put 183
_____, Ida Up 104
_____, Isaac W. Mor 253
_____, Isaac Tlb 344
_____, J. J. Har 184
_____, James Sr. Jsp 378
_____, James Jr. Jsp 394
_____, James New 54
_____, James B. Han 152
_____, James P. Jns 435
_____, John Tlb 326
_____, John Hry 202
_____, John Jns 468
_____, John Tlf 4
_____, John Wsh 269
_____, John A. Hry 211
_____, Jonthron B. Crf 411
_____, Joseph B. Twg 75
_____, Joshua Han 152
_____, Jesse T. Har 184
_____, Kinchin Scr 311
_____, Levi Jns 429
_____, Levin Han 152
_____, Levin H. Han 152
_____, Louisa Hry 216
_____, Major Wsh 246
_____, Martin T. Har 177
_____, Martin Jns 456
_____, Mary Bal 40
_____, Matthew G. Gre 294
_____, Miles Jks 338
_____, Moberry Up 108
_____, Nathan Bts 168
_____, Nathan Put 183
_____, Rhesa J. Twg 87
_____, Richard P. Pik 121
_____, Richard W. Bib 50
_____, Robert Wrn 213
_____, Shadrack Up 117
_____, Stephen Hal 101
_____, Stephen Hst 270
_____, Stephen Pik 121
_____, Thomas Gre 281

Ellis, Thomas Hry 20
_____, Thomas M. Bib 5
_____, Thomas Gly 26
_____, William Bal 4
_____, William Hry 20
_____, William New 5
_____, William Ogl 10
_____, William Ogl 10
_____, William Rab 22
_____, William Tlf
_____, William Wyn 28
_____, William J. Pik 12
_____, William P. Jns 42
Elliss, Hodyah Put 18
_____, John Jsp 38
Ellice, William Dec 1
ELLISON/ELISON/ELLISSON
Ellison, Benjamin Bke 13
_____, Benjamin Hab
_____, Christian Ogl 10
_____, David Hab 6
_____, Fran. Jks 32
_____, George Tlb 34
_____, Hamilton Hab
_____, Isom Put 19
_____, James Cht 25
_____, James Tlb 32
_____, John Tlb 32
_____, John A. Tlb 32
_____, Jonathan Hab 6
_____, Mary DeK 5
_____, Mathew Jks 34
_____, Robert Bke 14
_____, Robert DeK 5
_____, Robert Wal 13
_____, Samuel Wal 16
_____, Thomas Gwn 32
_____, Wade Mwr 16
_____, William Wal 15
_____, Zacharia Hab 6
Elison, Benjamin Hab
_____, Richard Gwn 36
_____, Samuel H. Fay 19
_____, William Hab
Ellisson, Charity DeK 4
_____, Henry DeK 3
_____, Jarrett DeK 5
ELLSWORTH, John Bib 5
ELMORE, Luke Ran 24
_____, Mark Ran 24
_____, Matthew Mon 22
ELROD/ELLROD/EROD
Elrod, Abram J. Hal 12

Name	County	Page
lrod, Abram Sr.	Hal	120
_____, Christoper	Hal	120
_____, George	Hal	120
_____, Jacob	Hal	114
_____, John	Hal	116
_____, Levi	Hab	51
_____, Nubery	Hab	51
_____, Samuel	Hab	51
_____, Samuel	Hab	51
_____, William	Hal	117
llrod, Jeremiah	Gwn	323
rod, John	Hab	10
LSEY (Indian)	Car	233
LTON/ELSTON		
lton, Abraham	Crf	408
_____, John	Wsh	257
lston, John	Hab	36
MANUEL, Amos	Lwn	86
_____, Benjamin T.	Bke	154
_____, Caswell	Dec	8
_____, David	Dec	12
_____, John	Dec	7
MBERSON, Henry	Hal	122
_____, John	Mor	241
MBRY/EMBREE		
mbry, Enoch	Pik	107
_____, Henery T.	Cow	381
_____, Reuben	Hal	109
mbree, B. H.	Col	352
_____, Hezekiah L.	Wil	295
MMERSON, John	Crf	406
_____, William Jr.	Jns	456
_____, Zachariah	Jns	445
MORY/EMMERY/EMRY/EMERY		
mory, Joel	Ogl	75
_____, John	Jks	342
_____, Wiley	Ogl	73
mmery, Hiram H.	DeK	49
_____, Merrel	DeK	49
mry, Bola	Jks	342
_____, Elijah	Clk	320
mery, Samuel	Jsp	388
NDSLEY, Jesse	Cow	389
_____, James	Cow	389
_____, John	Cow	389
NGLAND/ENGLIN		
ngland, Elisha	Hab	26
_____, John	Car	230
_____, Jonathan	Hab	65
_____, Joseph	Hab	64
_____, Martin	Hab	7
_____, Richard	Hab	64
_____, Thomas	Ogl	75

Name	County	Page
Englin, James	Hab	44
ENGLETT, Hezekiah	Crf	397
ENGLISH, Aron	Wrn	215
_____, Charles F.	Ogl	91
_____, Cornelius	Lwn	82
_____, Eli	Lau	23
_____, George	Han	152
_____, George L.	Ogl	91
_____, Green	Mon	212
_____, Haywood	Hab	48
_____, Henry	Gre	285
_____, Henry	Ogl	91
_____, James	Lwn	84
_____, James	Mar	141
_____, John W.	Frk	246
_____, John	Hab	35
_____, John	Hst	277
_____, John	Jns	442
_____, John	Rch	254
_____, Johnathan	Jns	442
_____, John	Wrn	218
_____, Joseph	Tat	373
_____, Lover W.	Lwn	83
_____, Mathew	Wrn	214
_____, Nancy	Ogl	90
_____, Reuben	Bry	87
_____, Sampson	Hst	292
_____, Sarah	Frk	246
_____, Stephen	Fay	185
_____, William	Bry	87
_____, William	Cpb	209
_____, William	Jns	442
_____, William	Wrn	214
_____, See INGLISH		
ENGRAM/ENGRAND		
Engram, Edward	Hst	271
_____, James	Hst	288
_____, Robert	Hst	262
Engrand, Thomas	Car	231
ENLOW, Winny	Lin	62
ENNIS, David	Jns	456
_____, Izra	Scr	309
_____, James	Lee	34
_____, John	Cam	189
ENOCH, Wamble W.	Up	108
ENSLEY, Robert	Hab	47
EPPERSON/EPESON/EPISON		
Epperson, Benjamin	Car	217
_____, John	Frk	244
_____, John	Hal	84
_____, Peter	Hal	100
_____, Samuel	Up	103
_____, Thompson	Frk	222

Name	County	Page
Epeson, Thompson	Hab	23
Epison, George	New	18
EPPINGER, James	Cht	249
_____, Jno.; Est. of	Cht	283
EPPS/EPP		
Epps, Daniel	Twg	73
_____, Grey W.	Pik	127
_____, James	New	33
_____, Joshua	Col	361
_____, Thomas	Clk	291
_____, William	Clk	294
_____, William	Clk	311
_____, Nathaniel	Clk	312
ERNEST/EARNEST		
Ernest, Ada E.	Bib	64
_____, Catherine	Eff	114
_____, Elisha	Clk	296
_____, George L.	Clk	291
_____, George Sr.	Clk	292
_____, Robert A.	Clk	300
Earnest, Henry	Wal	161
ERVIN/ERWIN		
Ervin, Eliza	Cht	242
_____, Greenberry	New	28
_____, Hugh L.	Hst	280
_____, James	Clk	298
_____, Mary	Cht	267
_____, Thomas	New	29
_____, Thompson	New	29
Erwin, Thomas B.	Jsp	352
ESAU, Abner	Mus	281
ESCO, George	Ogl	80
ESHAM, James	Col	353
ESKEW/ESKEY		
Eskew, William	DeK	63
Eskey, Richard L.	DeK	33
ESKRIDGE, John	Jks	313
ESPY/ESPEY/ESPRY		
Espy, James	Clk	314
_____, John	Clk	319
_____, Joseph	Clk	318
_____, Robert	Clk	319
_____, Thomas	Clk	316
Espey, Robert	Mor	257
_____, Samuel	Cow	371
_____, Thomas	DeK	52
Espry, Robert	Mor	258
ESTES/ESTIS/ESTERS		
Estes, Charles	Gwn	328
_____, Elisha	Har	186
_____, Joel	Gwn	360
_____, John G.	Cpb	205
_____, Joshua	Gwn	333

Name	County	Page
Estes, Osborn	Gwn	32
Estis, Thomas	Crf	39
Esters, Abram	New	2
ETCHISON/ETCHERSON		
Etchison, Allen	Mad	108
_____, John	Mad	10
_____, Nathaniel	Mad	10
Etcherson, William	Wal	16
ETHRIDGE/ETHERIDGE/ EATHERIDGE/ETHEREDGE		
Ethridge, Allen	Wks	33
_____, Caswell	Bts	16
_____, Edward	Wks	34
_____, Elijah	Mon	17
_____, Eliza	Bib	7
_____, Enoch	Wsh	27
_____, Gilford	Wal	15
_____, Lewis	Wks	348
_____, Mark	Bal	4
_____, Merit	Wks	33
_____, Richard E.	Mar	138
_____, Robert	Wks	35
_____, Sarah	Bib	7
_____, Shepherd	Gwn	36
_____, Thomas	Wks	34
_____, William	Bib	7
_____, William	Wks	35
Etheridge, Isham	Jns	46
_____, Mar.	Bal	4
_____, William	Jns	46
_____, William	Jns	47
Eatheridge, Reason	Jns	468
Etheredge, Aaron	New	2
_____, Lewis	New	2
ETRIS, Henry	Hab	1
_____, Joseph	Hab	1
_____, Samuel	Hab	
EUBANKS/EUBANK/EWBANKS		
Eubanks, Danill	Pik	11
_____, Elijah	Crf	405
_____, Elijah	Hal	126
_____, Elisha	Hal	126
_____, George Sr.	Bts	17
_____, Giles	Hal	126
_____, Isaac	Mar	14
_____, James	Fay	18
_____, John	Col	33
_____, Jonathan	Hal	11
_____, Joseph	Hal	10
_____, Littleberry	Bts	17
_____, Martin	Tfo	368
_____, Richard	Col	360
Eubank, Edward	Jns	442

ubank, John Han 152
_____, Nancy Han 152
_____, William Cow 388
wbanks, Thomas Jns 460
_____, also see HUBANKS
UGLIT, John Mar 137
_____, also see ENGLETT
UNICE, Ruth Ware 183
UNIER, Daniel App 13
_____, Hugh App 13
_____ Same as NUNEZ
USTACE, George Wil 308
VANS/EVINS/EVEANS/EVENS/
AVANS/EAVINS/EVAN
vans, Abraham Elb 145
_____, Anslam L. Jns 446
_____, Ansolin Crf 413
_____, Arch[d]. Gwn 331
_____, Arden Wil 314
_____, Benjamin Hal 126
_____, Boswell Y. Fay 200
_____, Cain Hal 92
_____, Carter Hal 109
_____, Charles Col 363
_____, Charles Mon 205
_____, Charles Mon 214
_____, Charles Mon 219
_____, Charles Scr 302
_____, Daniel Wal 148
_____, Daniel G. Bke 144
_____, Darcus Rch 284
_____, David Bts 170
_____, David Fay 200
_____, David Har 178
_____, David Jks 340
_____, David New 32
_____, David Rab 231
_____, Edward H. Mon 182
_____, Elijah Tfo 363
_____, Elizabeth Elb 154
_____, Elizabeth (w) Mor 244
_____, Elizabeth (w) Mor 267
_____, Frances Up 115
_____, George Gwn 329
_____, George Hal 92
_____, George Pul 151
_____, George W. Bke 120
_____, Gum Clk 299
_____, Henry Lin 69
_____, Henry Pul 151
_____, Hezekiah Ear 99
_____, Hezekia Scr 300
_____, Isaac Har 181
Evans, Isaac Pik 127
_____, Isham Jef 412
_____, Isham Twg 73
_____, Jacob Bke 141
_____, Jacob Wks 339
_____, James Mor 246
_____, James Dec 5
_____, James Jefferson DeK 62
_____, James W. New 46
_____, Jane New 40
_____, Jeremiah Mwr 168
_____, Jessee Col 349
_____, Jessee Jsp 393
_____, Jesse Wil 315
_____, John Bal 41
_____, John Clk 310
_____, John DeK 28
_____, John DeK 42
_____, John Gwn 328
_____, John Hal 106
_____, John Jks 340
_____, John Mon 173
_____, John Mon 192
_____, John New 32
_____, John New 51
_____, John New 53
_____, John Tlb 331
_____, John Tlb 337
_____, John Sr. Tfo 360
_____, John Jr. Tfo 354
_____, John A. Han 152
_____, John M. C. Rch 285
_____, John S. Cow 377
_____, John W. New 50
_____, Joseph New 48
_____, Joseph M. Mor 246
_____, Joshua Cow 377
_____, Joshua J. Hry 207
_____, Lee Tfo 366
_____, Llewellen Wil 305
_____, Madison Wal 128
_____, Martha Bts 175
_____, Martin Hal 72
_____, Mordeau Rch 283
_____, Peter Wsh 266
_____, Pleasant Jsp 391
_____, Rachel Mon 196
_____, Rebecca Ear 99
_____, Richard Sr. Bke 136
_____, Richard H. Bke 144
_____, Robert Tfo 364
_____, Robert H. Bke 144
_____, Rufus K. Bib 55

Name	County	Page
Evans, Samuel	Hal	106
______, Sarah Ann	Bib	58
______, Stephen	Wks	352
______, Stephen	Wks	353
______, Stokely	Fay	185
______, Sturling	Han	152
______, Thomas	Col	334
______, Thomas	Mon	190
______, Thomas	Scr	302
______, Thomas	Trp	45
______, Thomas C.	Mwr	153
______, Thomas M.	Mon	205
______, Timothy B.	Pul	143
______, Turner	Hry	228
______, Uriah	Twg	84
______, W. H.	Cht	272
______, William	Jsp	393
______, William Sr.	Tfo	359
______, William Jr.	Tfo	359
______, William B.	Gre	288
______, William E.	Bke	120
______, William G.	Bke	144
______, William G.	New	33
______, William G.	New	52
______, Winston	Gre	287
______, Zachery	Em	165
Evins, David	Mad	102
______, David T.	Ogl	99
______, John	Hab	49
______, Thomas Jr.	Mad	107
______, Thomas Sr.	Mad	102
______, Thomas	Gwn	340
______, William	Mad	99
______, William B.	Mtg	231
Eveans, Robert	Hal	113
Evens, John	DeK	62
Eavans, Elijah	Put	191
______, Martha	Put	218
Eavins, Jane	Fay	200
______, John	Fay	205
Evan, Peter	Tat	375
EVANSON/EAVONSON		
Evanson, George	Elb	158
Eavonson, William	Elb	145
EVE, John J.	Rch	271
______, Joseph Sr.	Rch	278
______, Joseph C.	Rch	276
______, William	Rch	278
EVENINGHAM/EVERINGHAM		
Eveningham, John	Cht	242
Everingham, Thomas Sr.	Rch	291
EVERHART, Jacob	Ogl	83
EVERETT/EVERITT/EVERTT/		

Name	County	Page
EVRETT/EVETT/EVIT		
Everett, Aaron	Tms	2
______, Aaron	Tms	2
______, Anthony	Eff	10
______, David	Wsh	27
______, Drury	Tlb	34
______, Hardy	Scr	29
______, James A.	Crf	39
______, Jesse H.	Han	15
______, John Sr.	Bul	9
______, John E.	Bul	9
______, Joshua	Bul	9
______, Josiah	Dec	1
______, Martha	Crf	404
______, Sarah	Bul	100
______, Thomas	Hst	27
______, Turner	Doo	8
Everitt, Sherwood	Hal	100
______, William	Ran	244
Evertt, William	Pul	163
Evritt, Samuel H.	Hal	71
Evrett, Samuel H.	Hal	100
Evett, James	Hab	35
______, Jese	Hab	35
______, Thomas	Han	39
______, William H.	Hab	39
Evit, John	Hab	61
EVERS, Gibson	Hst	286
______, Jasper	Mon	180
______, Jonathan	Bak	20
______, Serenith	App	5
______, Solomon	App	5
EVES, Levins	Car	215
EWING/EWIN		
Ewing, John	Han	152
______, Jonathan	Han	152
______, Samuel	Han	152
______, Thomas	Gwn	359
Ewin, Jane	New	10
______, Robert	Gwn	374
EXLEY, Elizabeth	Eff	113
______, James	Wal	127
______, John	Eff	114
______, John W.	Eff	108
______, Solomon	Eff	113
EXUM, Benjamin	Wks	331
______, James	Wks	334
______, Stanley	Wks	337
EZARD/EZZARD		
Ezard, John T.	Gwn	323
Ezzard, William	DeK	26
EZELL/EZEL		
Ezell, Catharine	Gwn	328

Ezell, Henry G. Ran 246
______, Jane Mon 180
______, Thomas Gwn 322
______, William Ear 93
______, William Gwn 328
Ezel, B. R. Jsp 363
______, John Hal 76
______, Mason Hal 76

FABER, Mrs. C. E. Rch 260
FACKLER, Samuel Jns 450
FAGAN, Enoch Hst 290
______, Thomas Crf 396
______, Thomas B. Hst 289
FAHM, Mary Cht 256
FAIL/FAILS
Fail, Jacob Trp 33
______, William Hst 279
______, William Hst 293
Fails, John Mon 217
FAIN/FANE/FANN
Fain, Abram DeK 37
______, Ebenezer Hab 8
______, Greenbery DeK 37
______, Jason Hab 8
______, Jesse DeK 34
______, Joel DeK 37
______, John Hab 64
______, Samuel Hab 64
______, Thomas P. Dec 11
______, Thomas Sr. Dec 5
______, William Sr. DeK 37
______, William Jr. DeK 37
Fane, John Elb 143
______, Robert Elb 143
Fann, Milley Bke 140
FAIR, Edmund Pul 140
______, P. Bal 43
FAIRCHILD/FAIRCHILES
Fairchild, A. T. Wks 356
______, Ely Wks 338
______, Eliz. Wks 357
______, L. Cht 267
______, R. Wks 335
Fairchiles, Mary Dec 18
FAIRCLOTH, Allen Bak 19
______, Ann Doo 79
______, Benjamin Bak 18
______, Benjamin Em 171
______, Benjamin Tms 20
______, Caleb Bak 18
______, Davis Bak 18
Faircloth, Dred Tms 22
______, Etheldred Doo 79
______, Frederick Lau 10
______, James Em 171
______, John Bak 18
______, John Dec 3
______, Joshua Tms 20
______, Kinchen Pul 143
______, Mathew Bak 16
______, Nancy Pul 142
______, Peter Bak 18
______, Redden Bak 16
______, Richard Tms 22
______, Robert Lau 19
______, Thelpheleas Pul 131
______, Thomas Bak 16
______, William Bak 18
______, William Pul 140
FAITH, Abraham Hry 221
______, James Hry 221
FALK/FAULK
Falk, Charles Gwn 328
______, Henry Elb 119
Faulk, Jason Bib 50
______, Jason Bib 64
______, Mark Twg 74
FALKNER, Benjamin Trp 36
______, James Hry 227
______, James Lwn 90
______, James L. Hry 223
______, Jefferson Fay 189
______, Jobe Fay 202
______, John Jks 329
______, John Trp 36
______, John M. Fay 186
______, Maston Hry 215
______, Peter Hry 223
______, Vincent Trp 36
______, William Elb 131
______, William G. Fay 203
______, William O. Elb 132
FALLIGANT, Louis Cht 255
______, R. A. Cht 268
FALLEN/FALLIN/FALIN
Fallen, Fleet Wil 294
______, John H. Jns 453
______, Sarah Up 110
Fallin, Charles Wil 293
______, Jesse Har 191
Falin, John Jef 402
FALLS, John S. Mor 255
FAMBROUGH/FAMBOROUGH
Fambrough, Alen G. Car 216

Name	County	Page
Fambrough, Anderson	Ogl	103
______, Robetson	Mon	178
______, Thomas	Gre	289
______, William	Gre	289
______, William	Mon	201
______, William L.	Mon	178
Famborough, Gadial	Clk	305
______, John A.	Clk	304
______, Joshua	Clk	315
FANNEL, Luke	Gwn	361
FANNIN/FANNING/FANING		
Fannin, A. B.	Cht	265
______, Benjamin	DeK	61
______, Benjamin	Elb	157
______, Catharine	Jsp	353
______, Col.	Rch	292
______, James W.	Mus	280
______, Jephthah	Mor	250
______, John	DeK	61
Fanning, James	Han	152
______, James W.	Trp	32
______, Laughlin	DeK	61
______, Richard	Tms	21
______, William	Wil	307
Faning, William	New	11
FARLESS, James	Hst	292
FARLEY, James	Jsp	379
______, John	Pik	124
______, Mathew	Put	205
______, Mathew C.	Put	204
______, S.	Cht	257
______, William	Har	184
FARMER, Ann	Scr	299
______, Daniel	Tfo	360
______, Elam	Frk	227
______, Elizabeth	Jns	460
______, Henry	Ogl	68
______, Isaac Sr.	Bke	155
______, Jacob	Hal	123
______, James	Bke	155
______, James	Hry	234
______, James	New	22
______, James	Tfo	362
______, Jesse	DeK	66
______, Joel	DeK	39
______, John	Bke	137
______, John	Elb	143
______, John Sr.	Hry	230
______, John Jr.	Hry	231
______, John	Jns	460
______, John	Tlf	3
______, Nancy (w)	Mor	238
______, Nathan	New	12
Farmer, Perry	Elb	13
______, Reuben	Hal	13
______, Samuel	Pik	12
______, Solomon	New	1
______, Thomas	Frk	23
______, Thomas	Ogl	6
______, Urial	Tfo	35
______, Verity	Bke	15
______, William	Hal	12
FARMINGTON, Sarah	Cht	25
FARNELL/FARNALL		
Farnell, Benjamin	Hst	28
______, Theresa	Bke	12
______, William	Hst	26
Farnall, Polly	Hry	21
FARNSWORTH, James	Wil	30
FARNUM, William N.	Twg	7
FARR, Catherine	Wrn	21
______, Caty	Wrn	21
______, Darkes	Wrn	21
______, Insel	Mus	29
______, Jeremiah	Cow	38
______, John	Cht	24
______, John	New	3
______, Sarah	Wrn	21
______, Thomas	DeK	2
______, William	Cow	38
______, William H.	DeK	2
FARRELL, James	Han	15
FARIS/FARRIS/FARRIES/ FAIRIES		
Faris, James	Gwn	31
______, James	Gwn	35
______, William	Gwn	32
Farris, John	DeK	6
______, John J.	Har	18
Farries, J. G.	Cht	25
Fairiss, Sam.	Rab	22
FARRORD, Francis	Clk	30
FARROW/FARRAR/FARRER/ FARROR/FARREAR/FAIRIOR		
Farrow, Abner	DeK	4
______, Fanney	Bke	12
______, Frances	Bke	12
______, George M.	Wal	12
______, Jane	Mwr	15
______, Hannah	Lib	4
______, Sheldon	Bke	12
______, Thomas J.	Wal	13
______, William	Hal	10
Farrar, Absalom	Hry	22
______, Elihu	Frk	23
______, James	Jef	41

Farrar, John	Frk	245
______, John A.	Hry	210
______, Nancy (w)	Mor	257
______, Richard	Frk	238
______, Stephen	Hry	231
______, Thomas	Mon	228
Farrer, John	Frk	238
______, Thomas	Lin	72
Farror, Richard	Hal	120
Farrear, Darcas	Cpb	196
______, James W.	Cpb	196
Fairior, Fredrick	Dec	8
FARRY, A.	Cht	269
FASHEE, Elisha	Hal	77
FASON, William	Han	153
FAUCH, Jonas	Gre	281
FAUGHTENBERRY, Jacob	Rch	282
FAUNT, Redden	Hry	201
FAVORS/FAVOR/FAVAURS/ FLAVOR		
Favors, Hiram	Put	196
______, Isaiah	Put	194
______, Reuben	New	220
______, Reuben	Tlb	332
______, Sanders	Trp	42
______, William	Put	194
Favor, Henry	Trp	42
______, Matthew	Wil	307
______, Thomas	Wil	307
Favaurs, H.	Mus	288
Flavor, Sarah	Wil	314
FEAGANS/FEAGAN/FEAGIN		
Feagans, William Sr.	Mor	266
______, William	Mor	265
Feagan, Uriah	Ear	94
Feagin, Henry	Jns	465
______, Michael J.	Jns	450
______, Samuel	Jns	456
FEARS, Absolemn	Wrn	212
______, Ezekial	Jsp	367
______, James	Mor	248
______, John	Jsp	367
______, Richard	Han	152
______, Robert	Jsp	367
______, Samuel	Jsp	391
______, William	Hry	206
______, William	Jsp	362
______, Zachariah	Mor	240
FEASTER, William	Cht	281
FEATHERSTON, Edw[d].	Mus	286
FEAY, S. H.	Cht	245
______, William T.	Cht	251
FEDRICK, Mary	Bib	55
Fedrick, Stephen	Put	179
FELDER, Charles	Cam	190
FELKER, Stephen	Wal	123
FELLINGEW/FILLINGEW		
Fellingew, Moses	Hst	284
Fillingew, Jarvis	Hst	262
FELPS, William	Mon	215
______, William D.	Mon	193
FELTENBURGER, John	Wal	145
FELTON, Grief	Car	219
______, Harrel	Car	219
______, Hezekiah	Car	219
FELTS/FELT		
Felts, Allen	Crf	410
______, Hartwell	Wrn	208
______, Jency	Elb	119
______, John	Put	174
______, Simeon	Put	174
Felt, J.	Cht	250
**FENDALL, Mrs. (slave)	Rch	269
______, Sarah	Rch	292
FENDER, David	Lwn	86
FENLEY, James	Gre	290
______, Jane	Gre	304
FENN, Eli	Wsh	251
______, Elijoe	Dec	12
______, Henry W.	Pul	138
______, Isaac	Han	153
______, Lovet P.	Pul	150
______, Jesse	Pul	146
______, John	Rch	277
______, John G.	Hal	102
______, Thomas A.	Hal	76
______, William	Clk	308
FENNELL/FENNEL/FENEL		
Fennell, Ephraim	Lau	23
______, Hardy L.	Up	111
______, Partrick	Lau	17
______, Stephen	Hst	264
Fennel, Dempsey	Tms	29
______, Margarett	Twg	78
______, Widow	Irw	302
Fenel, Ansel	Tms	21
FENTRESS, J. C.	Wsh	254
FERBUSH, Harris	Ogl	78
FEREBY/FERRBA		
Fereby, Jesse	New	25
Ferrba, Robert	Hab	33
FERGUSON/FERGERSON/FERGASON/FERGURSON/FORGASON/ FORGESON/FORGUSON/FOGINSON/ FURGERSON/FURGUSON/FURGASON		
Ferguson, Green	Up	95

Name	County	Page
Ferguson, Grief H.	Tlb	327
_____, Isaac	Mon	202
_____, James	Wal	123
_____, John	Mon	206
_____, Joseph	Hal	80
_____, Norman	Mon	183
_____, Unity	Tlb	324
_____, William	Trp	49
_____, William Ed.	Eff	104
Fergerson, Charles	Wal	126
_____, John	Lin	60
_____, John G.	Wal	166
_____, Rachel	Rch	288
_____, William H.	Bak	15
Fergason, Daniel	DeK	39
Fergurson, Benjn.	Bak	18
Forgason, Andesen	Hab	28
_____, John	Hab	41
Forgeson, Hugh	Hab	45
Forguson, Daniel	Hry	249
_____, John	Hry	250
_____, Johnson	Hry	232
_____, Lewis H.	Hry	214
_____, William	New	31
Foginson, Coleman	Hab	26
Furgerson, John Jr.	Lin	62
_____, Tabitha	Bts	178
Furguson, Lucy	Wil	315
_____, Sally	Gwn	325
Furgason, Malcome	Tms	25
FERNANDES, Samuel C.	Cpb	209
_____, William P.	Put	218
FERRELL/FERREL/FEREL/ FERRILL/FERRIL/FERILL		
Ferrell, Catherine	Wil	315
_____, Elizabeth	Jns	447
_____, Elizabeth	Put	175
_____, John	Wil	313
_____, Mickleberry	Jns	447
_____, Mrs. S.	Bal	43
_____, Susannah	Twg	88
_____, Thomas	Hry	251
_____, Thomas	Tlb	333
_____, William	Har	180
Ferrel, Benjamin	Scr	315
_____, Burton	Tms	21
_____, Hutchin	Tms	19
_____, Ludis C.	Tms	19
_____, William	DeK	66
Ferel, William	Jks	324
Ferrill, Franklin	Mon	190
_____, William	Mon	194
Ferril, John	Bts	162
Ferril, Macajah	Bts	15
Ferill, Williamson	Trp	4
FERRIS, Joab	Lib	4
FETTERS, John	Rch	29
FETZER, John G.	Eff	10
FEW, Albert	Mor	26
_____, Benjamin	Bke	14
_____, Benjamin	Wal	13
_____, Clement	Mor	26
_____, Emily	Bke	14
_____, Ignatas A.	Bib	5
_____, Leonidas	Jks	33
_____, Mary (w)	Mor	26
_____, William	Wal	16
FEYLE, John	Col	33
FICKETT, Alexander	Ogl	8
FICKLIN/FICKLAND/FICKLEN		
Ficklin, Fielding	Tfo	36
_____, Francis	Jns	45
Fickland, Jeremiah	Put	21
_____, Samuel	Bke	14
Ficklen, Burnard W.	Wrn	21
FIELDER, Elizabeth	Put	18
_____, George	New	1
_____, John	New	1
_____, John J.	Pik	10
_____, John Sr.	Wal	15
_____, Josiah	New	1
_____, Nancy	Trp	3
_____, Obediah M. B.	New	4
_____, Terrill	Mor	26
_____, Thomas	Mor	25
_____, William R.	Wal	15
FIELDING/FEALDING		
Fielding, Isham	Hal	10
_____, James	Hal	13
_____, Jonathan	Cow	37
Fealding, Samuel	Clk	32
FIELDS/FIELD		
Fields, Caleb	Cpb	19
_____, Dalila	Jef	40
_____, Elijah	Lee	2
_____, Elizabeth	Hab	1
_____, Elizabeth	Hry	23
_____, James	Hal	12
_____, James	Hry	20
_____, James	Jef	40
_____, Lewis	Gre	27
_____, Miles	Jef	40
_____, Sion	Hry	21
_____, William	Gwn	36
Field, Henry H.	Rch	26
FIFE, John	Har	18

Name	County	Page
IGS, Mary	Gre	301
ILES, Adom J.	Crf	401
____, David S.	Crf	393
____, William B.	Crf	395
ILLINGGAME/FULLINGAME		
JLLINGAN		
illingame, Abner	Ran	247
ullingame, Henry	Mor	263
ullingan, Nancy	Gre	283
ILYAW, Josiah C.	Doo	86
INCH, Allen	Bul	96
____, Bordeth	Ogl	87
____, Charity	Hal	91
____, Charles	Bul	93
____, Charles	Ogl	71
____, Eliam	Col	362
____, Freemon	Twg	75
____, Gabriel	Frk	234
____, Isaac	Hal	91
____, John	Mon	173
____, John E.	Ogl	87
____, Robert	Put	172
____, Thomas B.	Jks	322
____, William	Clk	304
____, William	Ogl	87
____, William	Ran	243
INCHER/FINCHUR		
incher, Benjamin	Hry	240
____, Elias	Gwn	348
____, Isaac	Crf	415
____, James	Up	119
____, Jemima	Hry	240
____, John	New	54
____, Johnathan	Fay	198
____, Joseph	Pik	119
____, Joseph	Trp	44
____, Joseph	Trp	55
____, Joshua	Fay	200
____, Micajah	Gwn	320
____, Patsey	Gwn	344
____, Thomas	Hry	240
____, William	Gwn	348
____, William C.	Hry	217
inchur, Benjamin	Jsp	387
INDER, Joseph	Cht	281
INISEE/FINNESEE/FINCHEE		
inisee, John	Har	192
innesee, John H.	Mon	209
inchee, Archibald	Bts	163
INLAYSON, Christian	Tlf	8
INLEY/FINLAY/FINALEY/		
INDLEY/FINDLAY/FINLY		
inley, Alfred	Jsp	390
Finley, Caney	New	40
______, Ezekel	Hab	54
______, George	New	
______, George W.	Gre	273
______, James	Hst	286
______, John	Bke	122
______, John	Trp	49
______, John	Wil	301
______, Nancy	Twg	84
______, Samuel P.	Ogl	104
______, Stephen	Em	177
______, William	Em	177
______, Zachariah	New	28
Finlay, John	Mon	196
Finaley, Mary	Gly	267
Findley, George	Mor	264
______, John F.	Fay	197
______, Mary	Mor	247
______, Samuel	Hal	93
______, William	Mon	194
______, William	Mor	247
Findley, Ryley	Jsp	389
Finly, Cullen	Mwr	166
FINNY/FINNEY/FINNIE/		
FENNEY		
Finny, Benjamin	Jns	453
______, Drury	Jns	430
______, Hezekiah	Jns	445
______, John	Lau	15
______, Murrel	Lau	15
Finney, Henry	Jns	445
______, James	Jns	445
______, Sarah	Bke	135
______, William H.	Pik	126
Finnie, James T.	Mor	242
______, Sterling	Mor	250
Fenney, Mrs. E.	Wsh	243
FISH, Calvin	Jsp	383
______, Joseph J.	Wsh	240
______, Nathan	Jsp	379
______, Richard	Bib	67
______, W.	Cht	271
______, William	Wsh	256
FISHER, Benjamin P.	Wil	314
______, Charles	Tlb	333
______, G. S.	DeK	26
______, Henry	Cht	251
______, John	Hab	64
______, John	Rch	256
______, Joseph	Cht	250
______, Metcalf	Wsh	248
______, William	Wsh	271
______, Williard	Cow	367

Name	County	Page
FITCH, Lewis	Bib	55
FITCHAW, Stephen	Wal	174
FITTEN, Isaiah C.	Tfo	369
FITTER, James	Gre	298
FITTS/FITZ/		
Fitts, John B.	Put	184
_____, William H.	Elb	123
Fitz, David	Wrn	194
FITZGERALD, Ambrose	Rab	223
_____, David	Irw	301
_____, David	Pul	160
_____, James	Hst	265
_____, John	Irw	301
_____, John	Pul	159
_____, Reubin	Twg	85
_____, Silas	Rch	281
FITZPATRICK, Alexander	Mor	240
_____, Benett	Mor	241
_____, Davis	Mor	240
_____, Elira	McI	131
_____, Hamner	Mor	240
_____, Jackson	Cow	381
_____, James	Mor	242
_____, Jesse	Mor	240
_____, John	Bke	117
_____, John	Cht	255
_____, John	Twg	64
_____, Joseph	Har	175
_____, Joseph	Har	189
_____, Joseph	Mad	104
_____, P.	Cht	266
_____, Perkins	Mor	248
_____, Raney	Bib	70
_____, Sarah	Mor	241
_____, Thornton	Mad	108
_____, William	Gre	273
_____, William	Twg	70
_____, William G.	Mon	192
FITZSIMONS/FITZSIMONDS		
Fitzsimons, John	Tlf	5
Fitzsimonds, Henry	Mor	249
FIVEASH, James	App	8
_____, Sion	Tms	20
FIZZEL, Jane	Wsh	268
FLACK, William	Hab	56
FLAHERTY, Thomas	Crf	410
FLAKE, John P.	Col	349
_____, Michael	Rch	291
_____, William	Scr	306
_____, William	Wrn	227
FLANDERS, Barnabas B.	Lau	20
_____, David	Bib	58
_____, Francis E.	Lau	8

Name	County	Page
Flanders, John	Em	
_____, Jordan	Em	
_____, Mark	Em	
_____, William	Em	
FLANIGAN/FLANGAN/FLANNAGIN/ FLANAGAN/FLANNIGAN/FLANEGAN/ FLANNAKIN		
Flanigan, Alex^{r}.	Gwn	
_____, Susan	Gwn	
Flangan, Gamueel	Col	
Flannagin, Thomas	Hab	
Flanagan, William	Hal	
Flannigan, John	Jks	
_____, Kenyon	Mon	
Flanegan, Sarah	New	
Flannakin, Lydia	Jno	
FLANNINGHAM, John	Tlb	
FLATON, Richard	Ran	
FLEETING, Margarett	Jef	
FLEETWOOD, Elizabeth	Elb	
FLEMING/FLEMMING/FLEMINGS		
Fleming, Allen	Twg	
_____, Caleb	Tlb	
_____, George A.	Cam	
_____, James	Jef	
_____, John	New	
_____, John	Tlb	
_____, Lard	Col	
_____, Margaret	Elb	
_____, Mark	Tlb	
_____, Mary	Col	
_____, Mrs.	Rch	
_____, Peter Winn	Lib	
_____, Robert	Col	
_____, Robert	Frk	
_____, Ryal	Ogl	
_____, Samuel	Jef	
_____, Samuel Jr.	Jef	
_____, William	Elb	
_____, William; dec'd. Estate of	Lib	
_____, William	Tlb	
_____, William B.	Lib	
Flemming, Elijah H.	Hal	
_____, Isaac N.	Hal	
_____, James	Lin	
_____, James	Har	
_____, Jincy	Gre	
_____, Joel F.	Lin	
_____, John	Cow	
_____, John	Pul	
_____, Oliver	Wsh	
_____, Robert	Lin	

Name	County	Page
lemming, Robert	Wrn	192
_____, Susan	Lin	72
_____, William	Hal	108
_____, William W.	Hal	108
lemings, James	Mon	177
LEMISTER, James	Jsp	385
_____, John	Jsp	380
_____, Lewis	Jsp	380
_____, William	Jsp	381
LETCHER, Allen	Wal	139
_____, Charles	Jsp	357
_____, Delila	Wal	174
_____, Elizabeth	Hry	233
_____, Ezekiel	Lin	70
_____, George	Lib	45
_____, James	Hab	8
_____, John	Jns	465
_____, John	Rch	253
_____, John	Tlf	8
_____, John	Wal	163
_____, John A.	Bul	95
_____, John T.	Pik	120
_____, John W.	Har	181
_____, Joseph	Irw	302
_____, Joseph L.	Em	173
_____, Liba	Har	177
_____, Martha	Cht	242
_____, Richard	Mon	221
_____, Thomas	Pik	111
_____, Thomas	Tlf	5
_____, William	Lwn	88
_____, Zachariah	Lwn	81
LEWELLEN/FLEWELLIN		
lewellen, Abner H.	Jns	465
_____, Ann	Bib	64
_____, Eaton	Jns	453
_____, Elizabeth	Bib	60
_____, Enos R.	Up	97
_____, Patsey	Mon	179
_____, Thomas	Up	103
_____, William	Jns	465
lewellin, Elizabeth	Wrn	194
LINCH, Margaret	Cpb	196
LINT, Aquilla	Col	344
_____, George W.	Col	363
_____, James	Col	344
_____, Robert F.	McI	127
_____, Thomas H.	Bib	50
LOOD, Jane	Gre	293
_____, Pamelia	Frk	247
_____, Samuel	Cam	182
LORENCE/FLORANCE		
lorence, David	Lin	59

Name	County	Page
Florence, John	Lin	69
_____, Joseph	Lin	64
_____, Obediah Sr.	Lin	58
_____, Obediah Jr.	Lin	58
_____, Thomas	Lin	58
_____, Thomas Jr.	Lin	58
_____, William	Lin	59
_____, Willis	Wil	321
Florance, Levi	Rch	269
_____, Seaborn	Up	100
FLOURNOY/FLOURNEY/FLORNOY		
Flournoy, Green	Tlb	324
_____, Josiah	Put	177
_____, L. Madison	Mon	173
_____, Marcus A.	Jef	401
_____, Obadiah	Wil	308
_____, R. W.	Cht	281
_____, Robert	Tlf	7
_____, Robert	Put	172
_____, Samuel	Wil	310
_____, Simeon	Wil	315
** _____, Thomas (slave)	Rch	276
_____, Thomas	Rch	268
_____, Thomas	Rch	285
_____, William	Put	216
_____, William	Up	95
Flourney, Smith W.	Mon	172
Flornoy, Annis	New	13
FLOWERS/FLOURS		
Flowers, Andrew	Hab	7
_____, Andrew	Gwn	336
_____, Charles	Lib	45
_____, Drury	Jsp	362
_____, Harrell	Jns	460
_____, James M.	Trp	44
_____, James	Gwn	362
_____, Jeremiah	Elb	128
_____, John	Bib	76
_____, John	Lib	45
_____, John M.C.	DeK	54
_____, Joseph	Jns	446
_____, Lewis	Elb	128
_____, M. B.	Bib	50
_____, Peter	Hab	9
_____, Sarah	Pul	139
_____, Theophelus	Jsp	365
_____, Thomas	Elb	147
_____, William	Wyn	281
_____, Wright	Lwn	83
Flours, William	Jsp	384
FLOYD/FLOID		
Floyd, Alexander	Mad	115
_____, Benjamin	Clk	316

Floyd, Clemant Ogl 95
_____, Dolphin Mon 198
_____, E. Cht 256
_____, Eli Lau 10
_____, Elijah Twg 75
_____, Galant Hal 72
_____, Goodwin Mon 180
_____, Jabus Mad 105
_____, James Ear 94
_____, James Mad 116
_____, Jason & Andrew Lib 45
_____, Jessee Lib 45
_____, John Bts 177
_____, John Cam 185
_____, John Ear 93
_____, John Hst 277
_____, John Mor 270
_____, John Ogl 72
_____, John Ogl 80
_____, John W. Mwr 163
_____, Lee Hal 91
_____, Lewis New 15
_____, Margarett Wil 317
_____, Mary Gwn 375
_____, Matthew Doo 87
_____, Mourning Pul 154
_____, Patenc Hal 122
_____, Prudence Ogl 62
_____, Rees Lib 45
_____, Richard New 36
_____, Robert Mad 99
_____, Silas Wsh 250
_____, Shadrack Lau 11
_____, Shadrack Pul 138
_____, Shadrick Gre 293
_____, Sol. Gwn 376
_____, Thomas Ear 98
_____, Thomas Mon 179
_____, Thomas Put 190
_____, William Ogl 75
Floid, Polly Hab 33
FLUKER, Isaac Wil 315
_____, Robert Wsh 263
_____, Sarah D. Bib 50
_____, William T. Tfo 360
FLURRY, Hendley Wil 314
_____, Henly Wil 316
_____, Thomas Wil 316
FLYNN/FLINN/FLIN/FLYN
Flynn, Geo. Wrn 219
_____, P. W. Mus 280
_____, Rebc[a]. Wrn 219
_____, William Gwn 332

Flinn, James Crf
_____, John Ran
_____, John B. Gly
Flin, Jane Wal
_____, William N. Gwn
Flyn, John Wal
FLYNT, Augustus W. Wil
_____, Sarah Wil
FOARD, Eliza Fay
_____, Ephraim Wil
_____, Joseph Fay
_____, Martha Hry
_____, Purley Hry
_____, Wyatt Bal
FOGATY, Cornelious New
FOGGERSON, James Twg
FOLDS/FOALS
Folds, David E. Put
_____, Eli New
_____, George Put
_____, Jacob Jsp
_____, John Bke
_____, John Jsp
_____, John B. Bts
_____, Richard Bke
_____, Thomas P. Bts
_____, William Bib
Foals, King T. Mon
FOLEY, Daniel Cht
_____, Edward Jef
FOLKER, Joseph Wsh
FOLKS/FOLK/FOKES
Folks, James Cht
_____, Solomon Doo
Folk, John Lau
_____, Needham Wks
_____, Porter Wks
Fokes, Amos Jef
_____, John Jef
_____, Winneford Jef
FOLSOM/FOLSUM/FOALSOM
Folsom, Benjamin Em
_____, Ebenezer Pul
_____, Elijah Lwn
_____, Elizabeth Em
_____, John Lwn
_____, Laurens Em
_____, Lawrence Lwn
_____, Penniwell Lwn
_____, Randal Lwn
_____, Sarah Lau
_____, Thomas Lwn
Folsum, Israel Lwn

Foalsom, William Irw 304
FOMBY/FORMBY
Fomby, Aaron Cow 376
_____, Moses Wal 155
_____, Nathan Wal 133
_____, Nathaniel Cow 385
_____, Pleasant A. Cow 376
_____, Thompson Cow 376
Formby, Aaron Jr. Mor 256
_____, Larkin Wil 313
_____, Mathew B. Mor 259
_____, Nancy Wil 314
_____, Nathan Mor 252
_____, Obedah New 25
_____, Richard Wil 314
FONDREN, George H. Hry 210
_____, James Cpb 207
FONES, Allvin T. DeK 33
_____, Daniel DeK 68
_____, Daniel R. DeK 40
FOOSE, Jesse Lee 29
_____, Moses Wsh 266
_____, Samuel Lee 30
FOOT, George DeK 50
_____, James DeK 43
FOOTMAN, Doc[tr]. R. H.
dec'd. Estate Lib 45
_____, Edward Bry 85
_____, William C. Bry 85
FORBES/FORBUS
Forbes, Benjamin Wsh 240
_____, Clement Trp 46
_____, John McI 128
_____, Margaret Hab 18
_____, Samuel Cpb 204
_____, Samuel Cpb 211
_____, Sidney R. Hab 18
_____, William Tlb 333
Forbus, Sidney Hal 103
FORD, Anna Wsh 261
_____, Arthur Twg 83
_____, Daniel Ogl 76
_____, Elisha Elb 131
_____, Hillory Wsh 261
_____, Isaac Elb 138
_____, Isaac Har 189
_____, J. S. Jks 321
_____, James Dec 17
_____, John Bib 60
_____, John Elb 146
_____, John Twg 75
_____, John J. Doo 87
_____, Joseph Jns 460
Ford, Keron Frk 230
_____, Merrick H. Hab 17
_____, Noah Trp 33
_____, Robert Lee 27
_____, Samuel Jef 418
_____, Samuel Mon 186
_____, Samuel Pik 129
_____, Sarah Hab 16
_____, Stephen Lau 12
_____, Thomas Jns 453
_____, Timothy Pik 120
_____, William DeK 42
_____, William Frk 212
_____, William Jns 438
_____, William D. Han 153
_____, William W. Wrn 192
_____, Zedock Gwn 315
FORDHAM, Benjamin Wks 345
_____, J. G. Cht 270
_____, William Lau 17
FOREHAND, Amos Jr. Doo 80
_____, Amos Jr. Doo 81
_____, Claibourne Scr 304
_____, David Doo 85
_____, Drewry Bke 128
_____, Nehemiah Pul 140
_____, Soloman Hst 287
_____, William W. Doo 80
FOREMAN, Isaac Pul 162
_____, James Ran 347
_____, William B. New 28
FORGANSON: see FERGUSON
FORREST/FORRIST
Forrest, Sugar Lau 16
_____, William Lau 19
Forrist, John Ran 242
FORRESTER/FORRETER/FORRISTER/
FORISTER/FORSTER/FORESTOR
Forrester, George B. McI 121
_____, Henderson Hab 47
_____, Hiram Hab 24
Forester, Jesse Elb 149
Forrester, Joel Gre 284
_____, John Hab 24
_____, Moses DeK 32
_____, William Gre 283
_____, William Hab 24
Forreter, Thomas Hab 57
Forrister, Benjamin Hab 47
_____, Gresham Gre 293
_____, James Hab 24
_____, Willis Gre 279
Forister, Amos Rab 234

Forister, George Wal 151
______, John Rab 228
______, Thomas Rab 228
______, Thomas Wal 151
Forster, John Up 116
Forestor, William Wal 134
FORSYTH/FORCYTHE
Forsyth, J. J. Cht 262
______, John Rch 285
______, Philip Han 153
______, Nancy Han 153
______, Nancy Han 172
______, William Hal 129
Forcythe, James Hab 23
FORT, Arthur B. Pul 159
______, Benjamin Put 217
______, Charles M. Jef 406
______, Elias Cht 252
______, Elizabeth Jef 406
______, James Wyn 285
______, John Twg 65
______, John Sr. Wyn 283
______, John Jr. Wyn 283
______, Moses Twg 61
______, Robert W. Bib 55
______, T. Bal 38
______, Thomas Twg 82
______, Tomlinson Twg 61
FORTH, Joel L. Bke 120
______, John T. Bke 120
FORTNER/FORTENEAR
Fortner, Ansel Lin 69
______, Benjamin Hal 129
______, Benjamin Jr. Hal 98
______, John Jsp 366
______, Rowland Bib 60
______, Sally Em 167
______, Willis DeK 45
______, Zach. Jsp 368
Fortenear, Joel Hab 60
FORTSON, Easter Elb 137
______, Elizabeth Elb 139
______, Richard Elb 136
______, Tavner W. Elb 139
______, Thomas Elb 146
FORTUNE, Buck Gwn 372
______, Richard Mad 113
______, Thomas Frk 231
______, William Gwn 352
FOSS/FOST
Foss, Alexander Mus 292
Fost, John Ogl 86
FOSSET/FOSETT
Fosset, George New 19
Fosett, Reuben Hal 118
FOSTER, Allen Put 188
______, Arkellis Hal 109
______, Arthor Col 335
______, Arthur Bib 70
______, Arthur Gre 287
______, Beaufort Hal 68
______, Benjamin Hry 214
______, Collier Mon 191
______, Cornelius DeK 59
______, David Jsp 386
______, David Rch 291
______, Elijah Gwn 310
______, Francis Mor 243
______, Fredrick Put 186
______, G. W. Jns 436
______, George Rab 222
______, George W. Gre 305
______, James Mon 195
______, James F. Gre 281
______, James F. Hry 233
______, James W. Bts 165
______, Jeremiah Mon 187
______, Joanah Pik 126
______, John Col 339
______, John Gre 304
______, John Gwn 330
______, John Rch 278
______, John F. Clk 306
______, John H. Wsh 249
______, John L. P. Jsp 370
______, John S. Elb 157
______, Joseph Gwn 314
______, Joseph Z. Wil 300
______, Joshua Col 339
______, Levy Clk 303
______, Lewis Mon 198
______, Ludwell Mwr 156
______, Rachel Hab 61
______, Ransom Hal 88
______, Richard Ran 246
______, Richard Rch 289
______, Robert Hab 60
______, Robert Tlb 335
______, Samuel Bke 143
______, Samuel B. Bal 37
______, Samuel C. Hry 237
______, Sterling Bke 140
______, Thomas Bts 169
______, Thomas Han 153
______, Thomas Rab 227
______, Thomas A. Pik 114

Name	County	Page
Foster, William	Bts	170
______, William	Cht	240
______, William	Elb	151
______, William; dec'd. Estate	Lib	45
______, William	Jef	422
______, William	Mon	198
______, William	New	36
______, William	Put	172
______, William H.	Gwn	327
______, William P.	Bts	172
______, William P.	DeK	44
______, Willis	Han	153
FOUCHE/FOSHEE/FORSHEE/ FOSCUE		
Fouche, Jonathan	Wil	290
______, Sarah	Wil	295
______, Thomas	Wil	312
Foshee, Joseph	Mwr	163
______, Wiley	Mwr	163
Forshee, John	Wsh	261
Foscue, Asa	Bak	20
FOUNTAIN/FONTAIN/FONTAINE		
Fountain, Amos	Pul	159
______, Brinson	Bke	126
______, E.	Wks	339
______, Green	Pul	159
______, Harmon	Hal	76
______, Isral	Wks	349
______, James	Cht	267
______, James	Cht	277
______, John	Wks	349
______, John	Gwn	334
______, John	Wks	349
______, John S.	Mon	183
______, Jonathan	Jef	421
______, Owen	Tms	23
______, Susannah	Lau	23
______, William	Tms	23
______, William	Pul	159
Fontain, William	Wsh	268
Fontaine, John	Wrn	192
FOURACRES, Jesse	Cam	189
FOURSON, William J.	Tms	21
FOWLER, A. C.	Rch	292
______, Arter	Gwn	346
______, Cody	Clk	305
______, David	Rab	229
______, Dennis	Fay	205
______, Drury	DeK	33
______, Eady	Fay	205
______, Elbert	Cow	379
______, Elizabeth	Rab	234
Fowler, George	Jef	410
______, J. W.	DeK	28
______, James	Hab	17
______, Jeremiah	Ear	97
______, Jeremiah	Rab	231
______, Jesse	Tlb	339
______, Joel W.	Wks	331
______, John	Gwn	372
______, John	Frk	248
______, John	Hal	82
______, John	Jef	410
______, John	Rch	287
______, John	Rab	228
______, John	Wsh	247
______, John D.	Wsh	266
______, Joshua	Jns	456
______, Lucinda	Gwn	363
______, Martha (w)	Mor	270
______, Miles	Gwn	366
______, Minta	Hry	238
______, Moses	Rab	225
______, Mourning	Hry	229
______, Nathan	Crf	408
______, Rachel	Elb	129
______, Richard	Hab	17
______, Ryal	DeK	30
______, Samuel	Hal	91
______, Stephen	Wrn	231
______, Theophilus	Mon	196
______, Thomas	DeK	52
______, Thornton	Ear	96
______, Wesley	Mon	215
______, William	Doo	81
______, William	Mon	181
______, William	Wrn	227
______, William T.	Frk	230
______, Wiley	Trp	33
______, Ziphamah	Wrn	228
FOX, Ann	Rch	261
** ______, Ann (slave)	Rch	273
______, Benjamin A.	Trp	55
______, Daniell	Cht	280
______, George	Wal	174
______, James	Hab	9
______, John	New	30
** ______, John (slave)	Rch	275
______, John	Rch	292
______, Nancy	Rch	257
______, Peter	Rch	270
______, Richard W.	Mor	240
______, William	Bry	85
______, Wilmuth	Put	209
FOY, George	Eff	110

Name	County	Page
Foy, Lewis	Bib	64
FOYL, Elizabeth	Jef	402
FRAIL, Richard	Wks	347
FRALEY, William	Han	153
FRALIX, Martin	Fay	189
FRANCIS/FRANCUS		
Francis, Cordial	Wsh	259
_____, James C.	Jef	406
_____, Reviere	Up	111
_____, Sarah	Bul	93
_____, Thomas	Bke	148
Francus (no 1st name)	Wal	173
FRANKLIN/FRANKLING		
Franklin, Abrahams	Hab	52
_____, Christopher	Gly	266
_____, Daniel	DeK	32
_____, David	Mon	175
_____, Esom D.	Hst	275
_____, Felix D.	Wrn	208
_____, Frances (w)	Mor	272
_____, George	Wsh	239
_____, Goodman	Mon	228
_____, James	Hab	9
_____, James M.	Wsh	248
_____, Jobe	Hab	29
_____, John	Hab	52
_____, John	Jsp	392
_____, John	Jsp	397
_____, John Sr.	Gly	265
_____, John Jr.	Gly	267
_____, Joseph	Jns	443
_____, Lewis	Har	178
_____, Richard	Hab	29
_____, Thomas	Hab	52
_____, Thomas	Wal	169
_____, Vashty	Wsh	258
_____, Wiley E.	Elb	159
_____, William	Cow	372
_____, William	Hab	57
_____, William	Trp	37
_____, William L.	Mwr	158
_____, Zephaneah	Wrn	206
Frankling, John	New	50
_____, Mary G.	Clk	324
_____, Singleton	Han	153
FRANKS/FRANK		
Franks, John	Cam	187
_____, Merriman A.	Frk	241
_____, Weston A.	Jns	465
_____, Wyley	Jns	443
Frank, Martha	Tfo	361
FRANY, William	Bib	76
FRAPP, Rachael	Bal	29

Name	County	Page
FRASER/FRASIER/FRAZIER/ FRAZER/FRASURE/FRESURE/ FRAZURE/FRASHER		
Fraser, Daniel; dec'd. Estate	Lib	45
_____, Elijah	Lin	60
_____, H. B.	Rch	258
_____, James	Rch	264
_____, John	Gly	264
_____, John E., dec'd Estate	Lib	46
_____, Simon	Lib	45
_____, William	McI	121
_____, William	Rch	284
Frasier, Daniel	Mon	198
_____, John	Doo	88
_____, John	Han	153
_____, John	Wal	156
_____, Joshua D.	Mwr	165
_____, Quail	Doo	86
_____, Samuel	Hal	76
_____, Thomas	Put	179
Frazier, C. M.	Cht	264
_____, Elizabeth	Mor	246
_____, Isaac	Wks	341
_____, Jeremiah	Wil	305
_____, John	Jef	420
_____, John H.	Wil	312
_____, Simon	Cam	192
Frazer, Allen	Lin	58
_____, James	Col	354
_____, John	Lin	58
_____, Nancy	Lin	59
_____, Robert	Lin	74
_____, Robert Jr.	Lin	58
Frasure, George	Tfo	362
_____, Susan	Bib	76
_____, Wilkinson	Wsh	268
_____, William	Twg	88
Fresure, Margarett	Wsh	276
Frazure, Thomas	Wks	357
Frasher, John	Ogl	64
FREDERICK, Joseph	Rch	263
_____, Martin	Rch	264
_____, Thomas	Eff	112
FREE, Bethuel	Hab	45
_____, Elizabeth	Wal	160
_____, Isaac	Crf	400
_____, Lewis	Hab	58
_____, Martin	Hal	123
_____, Peter	Mwr	168
FREELAND, Lewis	New	16
_____, Mary An	Hab	42

FREEMAN/FREMON/FREYNON

Name	County	Page
Freeman, A. B.	Bib	50
______, Anna	Gre	289
______, Bailey	Jsp	369
______, Bailey	New	47
______, Barna. C.	Hab	25
______, Benjamin	Jks	326
______, Boswell	Jns	444
______, Daniel	Jsp	373
______, Daniel	Mus	285
______, Delamare	Ear	95
______, Dred	Pik	120
______, Drury	Hry	202
______, Elizabeth	Jsp	386
______, Ferebe	Scr	313
______, Foster	Pik	132
______, Frederick	Frk	212
______, Friend	Tms	23
______, Gabriel	New	47
______, Garrett	Scr	317
______, George	Elb	155
______, George	Tlb	334
______, Hamlin	Bts	163
______, Hartwell	Frk	221
______, Hawkins	Jsp	380
______, Henry	Fay	199
______, Henry	Frk	258
______, Henry	Up	117
______, Hugh	Tlb	334
______, Isham	Bts	162
______, Isham A.	Fay	205
______, Jacob	Scr	317
______, James	Dec	14
______, James	Jns	473
______, James	Jsp	373
______, James	Mor	257
______, James	Put	212
______, Jeptha	Hab	8
______, Jerh. (Rev.)	Jsp	378
______, Jesse	Jsp	378
______, Jesse	Mor	258
______, Joel	Mad	100
______, John	Clk	316
______, John	Dec	9
______, John	Gwn	348
______, John	Hry	241
______, John Jr.	Hry	242
______, John	Hry	245
______, John	Jef	419
______, John	Frk	240
______, John	Jsp	373
______, John	Wal	158
______, John	Wal	162
Freeman, John	Wil	303
______, John Sr.	Wks	350
______, John Jr.	Wks	349
______, John S.	New	51
______, Jonah	Jsp	386
______, Johnson	Jks	333
______, Johnson	Mwr	152
______, Joseph	Tms	19
______, Joseph	Wal	167
______, Josiah M.	New	48
______, Josiah S.	New	37
______, Julia	Wil	315
______, Kyler	Tms	16
______, Lucy	Jsp	363
______, Matthew	Hst	291
______, Newton	Jsp	365
______, Noah	Hry	202
______, Noah	Scr	315
______, Richard	Frk	247
______, Richard	Tms	24
______, Robert	Cow	368
______, Robert	Hal	84
______, Robert	Ogl	98
______, Ruth	Doo	86
______, Samuel	Ogl	102
______, Samuel	Wal	163
______, Simeon	Cow	383
______, Thomas	Mon	200
______, Thomas	Mon	228
______, Thomas	New	29
______, Thomas	Ogl	73
______, Thomas H.	Dec	18
______, Wiley	Hab	54
______, William	Mon	203
______, William	Scr	315
______, William	Tms	22
______, William	Tfo	364
______, William	Wal	141
______, William H.	Wil	298
Fremon, Jacob	Hab	47
______, Nedom	Hab	47
Freynon, William	Frk	221
FREENY, E.	Bal	32
______, Fabian	Pik	130
FRENCH, Charles H.	Doo	87
______, Ellis	Bib	73
______, Elizabeth	Tlf	2
______, John	Bib	73
______, John R.	Mtg	233
______, William	Wrn	206
FRETWELL, Ann	Gre	273
______, Charles	Hst	268
______, Cullen	Gre	282

Name	County	Page
Fretwell, James	Pik	113
______, Leonard	New	16
______, Robert H.	Mor	241
FRIAR, Henderson	Tlf	3
FRICKS, Michael	Rab	229
FRIDDLE, Joseph	Wal	128
FRITH, Christopher	Mon	212
FROST, Eli	Bib	55
______, James	Wsh	269
______, Ruthy	Hal	117
______, S.	Clk	325
______, Sarah	Hst	282
FRUIN, James	Gly	267
FRUMAN, Tyre	Jns	453
FRY/FRYE		
Fry, Benjamin	Hry	248
______, Gilbert	Clk	303
______, J. M.	Cht	267
______, John	Crf	404
______, John G.	Cow	375
Frye, Philip	Hab	29
FRYER/FRYAR		
Fryer, Drewrey	Frk	220
______, E.	Cht	280
______, Fielding	Bke	139
______, John	Bke	142
______, Judah	Rch	270
______, Robert	Bke	150
Fryar, Zachariah	Pik	130
FRYERMUTH/FRIARMOUTH		
Fryermuth, Hannah E.	Eff	114
______, Moses	Eff	111
______, Peter	Eff	105
Friarmouth, D.	Cht	272
FUDGE, Benjamin	Hst	269
______, Daniel	Rch	254
______, David	Col	348
______, Jacob	Hst	293
______, Soloman	Hst	293
FUKUA/FUQUA		
Fukua, William	Gwn	334
Fuqua, Henry C.	Lau	4
FULBRIGHT/FULLBRIGHT		
Fulbright, Daniel	Frk	212
______, Henry	Hab	14
Fullbright, John	Frk	212
FULCHER, Ann	Rch	290
______, Austin	Jks	337
______, Daniel	Pul	146
______, Dillan	DeK	72
______, Francis	McI	121
______, James	DeK	29
______, Jesse H.	DeK	28
Fulcher, John	Bke	145
______, John	Rch	292
______, Polly	DeK	29
______, Rebecka	Mtg	235
FULGAM, Ephraim	Frk	251
______, Henry H.	Ear	97
______, Memory	Mor	252
______, Thomas	Ear	98
FULLALOVE/FULLILOVE		
Fullalove, Elizabeth	Clk	301
______, John	Ogl	95
Fullilove, Willis	Hry	212
FULLAM, Luke	Cht	268
FULLER, A.	Col	352
______, Abner	Mwr	169
______, Alphaus	Wrn	201
______, Amos E.	Hry	226
______, Benjamin	Mon	173
______, Benjamin	Wal	145
______, Benjamin Sr.	Wal	153
______, Benjamin F.	Gwn	326
______, Berry A.	Hry	230
______, Bryant	Pik	117
______, Charles	Col	344
______, Cooper B.	Frk	226
______, Crawford	Hry	217
______, David	Trp	33
______, Edmun	Col	348
______, Elanor	Hab	22
______, Eldridge	Jks	348
______, Elijah	Bts	169
______, Elizabeth	Col	349
______, Elizabeth	Gre	272
______, Ezekiel	Hab	55
______, Ezekiel	Wal	145
______, George	Up	99
______, Green	Tlb	331
______, Isaac	Bal	40
______, Isaac	Jns	472
______, Isham	Col	340
______, James	Wrn	193
______, James A.	Mwr	153
______, John	DeK	50
______, John	Wrn	216
______, John B.	Mwr	156
______, John C.	Wal	153
______, John M.	Hst	273
______, Jos.	Bal	40
______, Mrs. K.	Col	348
______, Matthew B.	Mwr	158
______, Paten	Gwn	329
______, Peggy	Wsh	273
______, Ransom	Hal	109

Name	County	Page
Fuller, Reubin	Lee	34
_____, Rutha	Col	351
_____, Samuel	'Bal	32
_____, Samuel	Wrn	208
_____, Simeon	Put	187
_____, Spivey	Put	188
_____, Spivy	Wrn	204
_____, Thomas	Mwr	169
_____, Uriah	Lee	29
_____, Washington	Mor	258
_____, William	Jks	315
_____, William	Mon	203
_____, William	New	30
_____, William	Trp	48
_____, William A.	DeK	50
_____, William A.	Tfo	357
FULLFORD/FULFORT		
Fullford, Jesse	Irw	303
_____, John	Lau	22
_____, Jordan	Lau	13
_____, Volentine	Lau	14
Fulfort, Council	Pul	143
FULLINGTON, Caleb	Pul	143
FULMER, Jacob	Cow	388
FULSOM, Benjamin	New	15
_____, Elisha	Mus	286
_____, John	Mus	289
FULTON, George W.	Bib	50
_____, James	Clk	320
_____, James H.	Hst	285
_____, John	Ogl	67
_____, John G.	Lib	45
_____, Sarah	Twg	74
_____, Silas	Lib	46
_____, Silas	Lib	51
FULWOOD/FULLWOOD		
Fulwood, Bryant	Bke	153
_____, Jane	Clk	324
_____, John	Hst	274
_____, Rachael	Bib	55
Fullwood, James	Ware	183
_____, Thomas	Ware	186
_____, Wilkins	Ware	188
FUNDERBURK, Abel	Tfo	365
_____, Anthony	Clk	305
_____, Anthony W.	Gwn	332
_____, Henry	New	29
_____, Jacob	Tlb	332
_____, Mary	Gwn	358
_____, Peter	Gwn	332
_____, Sarah	Twg	82
FURCRON, Cornelious	Ogl	97
FURGERSON: See FERGERSON		

Name	County	Page
FURLOW/FURLOUGH		
Furlow, Charles	Wal	144
_____, John	Cow	385
_____, John T.	Cow	386
_____, William	Wal	158
Furlough, David	Gre	290
_____, John	Put	184
FURMAN, William	Jns	443
FURNIE, Bartholemew	Pul	141
FURR/FUR		
Furr, H. W.	Jks	326
_____, James	Hal	71
_____, Paul	Hal	98
Fur, Andrew D.	Hab	36
FURTH, L. E.	Cht	244
FUSSELL, John	Irw	299
_____, Wallin	Irw	299
FUTCH, David	Bul	102
_____, Eli	Bul	99
_____, Isaac	Tms	26
_____, Jacob	Bul	102
_____, James	Bry	87
_____, Jane	Bul	95
_____, John	Bul	99
_____, Oneasimey	Bry	88
_____, Rowan	Bul	100
_____, Solomon	Bul	99
_____, Thomas	Lwn	89
FUTRELL/FUTRELLE/FURELLE/ FUTERELL/FUTRAL/FUTRILL		
Futrell, Micajah	Eff	115
Futrelle, Benjamin	Hry	207
Furella, John	Cht	252
Futerell, Joel	Bke	122
Futral, Allenson	Jef	407
Futrill, Abraham	Crf	406
GAAR, George	Elb	147
_____, William	Elb	136
GABBA, Andrew J.	Hab	59
GABRIEL, John	Cht	246
GACHET, James	Ran	247
GADDIS, Alexander	Frk	245
_____, Arcable	Hab	41
_____, Archabel	Hab	25
_____, Archabel	Hab	32
_____, Dennis	Hab	41
_____, Elijah	Hab	32
_____, Iredell	Hab	32
_____, James	Hab	28
_____, James	Hab	47
_____, John	Cow	387

Name	County	Page
Gaddis, John	DeK	47
______, Lewis	Hab	48
______, Sally	Hab	44
______, Thomas C.	Mon	223
GADDY/GADDEY		
Gaddy, James L.	Hry	221
______, Thomas	DeK	41
______, William	Cht	278
Gaddey, Jeremiah	Hab	11
GADIAN, Uriah	Hab	36
GAFFORD, Fanny	Twg	80
______, Fanny	Wil	294
______, Martha	Jns	472
______, Thomas	Tlb	338
GAGE, John E.	Trp	33
GAHAGAN, John R.	Rch	271
______, Larence	Bts	161
______, Mathias	Hry	251
GAHNAL, Joseph	Cht	251
GAILEY, Andrew	Hab	23
______, Andrew	Mad	109
______, Ezekel	Hab	24
______, James	Hal	113
______, Joseph	Hal	99
GAILLARD, Akin	Rch	276
GAINER, Joseph	Bib	55
______, Lazarus	Pul	141
______, Lemuel	Ear	98
GAINES/GAINS/GAINUS/GAIN		
Gaines, Duncan	Bke	122
______, Francis	Elb	122
______, George	Elb	122
______, Henry	Mon	223
______, Henry J.	Elb	125
______, James	Wsh	248
______, James H.	Mon	188
______, John P.	Frk	236
______, Ralph	Elb	158
______, Richard G.	Elb	122
______, Robert T.	Elb	123
______, Theophilus	Jef	414
______, Thomas	Gwn	317
______, William	Elb	158
______, William S.	Mon	188
Gains, Allen R.	Rab	229
______, Elizabeth	Rab	226
______, George G.	Dec	16
______, Henry S.	Rab	226
______, James	Rab	229
______, Mary	Hal	75
Gainus, Coopergur	Bke	138
______, John	Bke	138
______, Mary	Hst	294

Name	County	Page
Gain, Hiram	Rab	225
GAINEY/GANEY/GAINY/GAYNEY		
Gainey, John	Wks	340
______, Josiah	Wks	334
Ganey, Edmond	Tms	17
______, John	Twg	61
Gainy, Matthew	Wks	340
Gayney, Bartholomew	Lau	22
GAIRY/GAIREY		
Gairy, Van D.	Elb	122
Gairey, Alfred	Trp	32
GAITHER/GATHER		
Gaither, Eli	Wal	150
______, Henry	New	49
______, Mashack	New	27
Gather, Edward	Wal	124
______, Greenberry	Put	212
______, Shadrack	Cpb	195
GALE, Jane	Cht	257
______, William	Cht	253
GALINEAU, Rose	Cht	241
GALLEHER, James	Mad	99
GALLIAM, Edward	Pik	132
GALLMAN, Haney	Hry	209
______, James	Hry	199
______, John	Hry	232
______, John C.	Hry	219
GALLOWAY/GALLAWAY/ GALAWAY/GALIWAY		
Galloway, Henry	Mon	212
______, James R.	Pik	125
______, Thomas	Ogl	63
______, William	Hry	217
Gallaway, Thomas	Wal	127
______, William	Ogl	66
Galaway, Jourdin	Cow	389
Galiway, William F.	Rab	222
GALPHIN, Winney	Rch	270
GAMBLE, Charles M.	Jef	419
______, Hugh T.	Dec	11
______, Israel	Har	186
______, Jacob	Put	217
______, James	Bib	50
______, James	Hry	209
______, James	Scr	314
______, Rodger L.	Jef	402
______, Thomas	Put	218
______, William	Bib	55
GAMBLIN, Sion	Hal	121
GAMMAGE/GAMAGE		
Gammage, Alsay	Hst	276
______, James	Jns	431
______, Nathaniel	Hst	279

Name	County	Page
Gammage, William	Hst	279
Gamage, Thomas T.	Mus	280
GAMMELL/GAMIEL/GAMIL		
Gammell, James	Mon	202
______, William	Mon	179
Gamiel, John	Jns	438
Gamil, Ayres	Up	115
GAMMON, Joel	Mon	205
______, Joseph	Cht	245
______, Joshua	DeK	52
______, Samuel	Jns	437
______, Silas	Mon	172
______, Solomon	Bal	29
GANAS, James	Lau	21
GANDY, Ephraim	Wks	350
______, Leah	Mtg	236
______, Nancy	Twg	77
GANEY, Micajor	New	11
GANN, James	Clk	293
______, John Sr.	Clk	294
______, John Jr.	Clk	293
______, Luke	Wal	172
______, Micajah	Bts	169
______, Nathan	Car	214
______, Nathan	Clk	294
______, Nathan	Fay	181
______, Samuel	Clk	292
______, Thomas	Gwn	376
______, William Sr.	Clk	293
______, William Jr.	Clk	292
GANETT, Thomas	Crf	408
GANNON, Burt	Hab	27
GANT, Charlotte	Lin	60
______, Delila	Tlf	4
______, James	Up	105
______, Jane	McI	121
______, Jesse	Up	112
______, Jordan	Mwr	162
______, William	DeK	61
Ghant, Elizabeth	Put	206
GANTER, Joseph	Bke	140
GARBETT, Elisha	Bul	99
______, William	Eff	115
GARDNER/GARDINER/GARDENOR/ GUARDNER		
Gardner, Aaron	Em	169
______, Ann	Rch	255
______, Aron	Har	190
______, Asa	Pik	121
______, Catharine	Wyn	284
______, Christopher	Gwn	345
______, Elias	Jns	453
______, Elizabeth	Han	154
Gardner, Elizabeth (w)	Mor	251
______, Ezekial	Pik	117
______, Fredrick	Mon	176
______, Isham	Em	164
______, Jacob	Bts	174
______, James	Col	336
______, James	Rch	267
______, John	Cht	252
______, John	Clk	312
______, John	Mon	175
______, John	Tlb	346
______, John	Up	108
______, John E.	Wsh	264
______, John M.	Gwn	377
______, Joseph	Em	166
______, Samuel	Hry	240
______, Sterling	Wrn	193
______, Thomas	Bib	55
______, William	Har	189
______, William	Jsp	394
______, William	Mad	105
______, William W.	Jsp	378
Gardiner, Jason	Hst	278
______, Lewis	Hst	278
______, Thomas	Hst	276
Gardenor, Robert	Clk	312
Guardner, Harriet	Twg	80
GARLAND, Edward B.	Han	154
______, Henry Sr.	Up	109
______, Henry Jr.	Up	111
______, John	Jns	434
______, John R.	Mor	251
______, Patrick	Mon	207
______, William D.	Han	154
GARLICK, Judah	Bke	150
______, Edward	Bke	150
GARLINGTON, Ann	Bke	148
GARMON/GARMAN/GARMANY		
Garmon, Amy	Frk	244
______, George	Hal	109
______, Polly	Frk	244
Garman, Isaac	Cpb	207
______, Nancy	Mon	210
Garmany, Hamilton	Gwn	312
GARNER, Anna	Frk	253
______, Benjamin	New	52
______, Charles Jr.	Clk	299
______, Charles	Clk	313
______, Daniel	Mor	260
______, David	Frk	228
______, Elias	Mwr	151
______, Elizabeth	Wal	160
______, Francis	Wal	137

Name	County	Page
Garner, Gale	Clk	315
______, George	Frk	252
______, Henry	Wsh	256
______, Jacob	Wsh	274
______, James	Cow	387
______, James	Ear	91
______, James	Gwn	342
______, James	New	41
______, James	Wsh	265
______, Jesse	Clk	298
______, Jo. T.	Gwn	350
______, John	Gwn	342
______, John	Hry	246
______, John B.	Mor	251
______, Luke	Wal	145
______, Mark	Jsp	358
______, Margaret	Clk	315
______, Martin	Jks	315
______, Mary	Mon	209
______, Presley	Mor	260
______, Richard	Bke	124
______, Richard	Wal	148
______, Roderick	Cow	385
______, Samuel	Clk	313
______, Sarah	Clk	307
______, Stephen	Hal	72
______, Stephen	Jsp	359
______, Stephen J.	Trp	50
______, Sturdy	Frk	233
______, Sturdy	Gwn	342
______, Thomas	Gwn	367
______, Thomas	New	39
______, Thomas W.	DeK	57
______, William	Clk	297
______, William	Gwn	362
______, William B.	Cow	385
GARNETT/GARNET		
Garnett, B. A.	Cht	269
______, Major	Col	338
______, Nelson	Col	340
______, Rebecca	Col	339
______, Robert	Wks	337
______, S. M.	Rch	261
______, Z.	Rch	274
Garnet, Eli	Lin	71
______, Jabez	Lin	71
GARR, Benjamin L.	Mor	238
GARRARD/GARRAD		
Garrard, Jacob	Trp	33
______, Samuel	Hal	74
______, Wiley J.	Hal	72
Garrad, Jacob	Jks	332
______, James	Jks	332
GARRELL, Blake F.	Jns	435
GARRETT/GARRET/GARROTT/ GARROT		
Garrett, Abh^{m}.	Gwn	364
______, Allen	Wil	313
______, Benjamin	Fay	192
______, Benjamin	Jsp	384
______, Benjamin	Jsp	384
______, Blake F.	Jns	435
______, Blount	Up	116
______, Mrs. C.	Rch	258
______, Carney	Cam	189
______, Charles	New	38
______, Charles	Wal	137
______, Daniel	Hal	83
______, Elisha	Hry	247
______, G. B.	Mus	289
______, Hiram	New	52
______, James	Gwn	365
______, James	Twg	68
______, James	Up	104
______, Jesse	Frk	250
______, Jesse	New	38
______, Jesse	Up	95
______, John	Cpb	206
______, John	Jsp	384
______, John	Up	103
______, John	Wil	296
______, John	Wks	349
______, John H.	Mor	238
______, Johnathan	Cpb	194
______, Joseph	DeK	35
______, Josiah	Wal	164
______, Lewis	Mon	172
______, Mary	New	55
______, Miles	Up	105
** ______, Miss (slave)	Rch	262
______, Newton	Jks	340
______, Obediah	Cam	189
______, Samuel T.	Tlf	4
______, Seaborn B.	Fay	191
______, Stephen	Frk	252
______, Thomas	DeK	60
______, Thomas	Jsp	365
______, Thomas D.	New	49
______, Thomas L.	Hal	85
______, Tyre	Pul	138
______, Wells	Hal	85
______, William	Hry	230
______, William	Put	213
______, William	Tlb	326
Garret, Daniel	Han	154
______, Enoch	Wks	336

Name	County	Page
Garret, James	Wks	352
_____, John	Han	154
_____, Joseph	Han	155
_____, Sarah	Jks	345
_____, William	Wks	336
Garrott, Asa	Wsh	274
_____, Mary	Bke	140
Garrot, James	Har	181
_____, Richard C.	Har	189
GARRIS, Amos	Wsh	269
GARRISON/GARRASON/GARISON		
Garrison, Adam	Cow	389
_____, Ann	Hal	117
_____, Caleb	Car	222
_____, Colele	Cow	378
_____, Darius	Tlf	10
_____, David	Crf	410
_____, David	Frk	250
_____, James	Frk	222
_____, James F.	Car	227
_____, James H.	Frk	219
_____, Jedediah	Frk	256
_____, John	Fay	184
_____, John B.	Gwn	377
_____, Keziah	Frk	256
_____, Levi	Hst	263
_____, Levi B.	Frk	250
_____, Martin	Frk	223
_____, Mathias	DeK	35
_____, Nehemiah	Hal	87
_____, Samuel	Frk	223
_____, Sailesbury	Frk	222
_____, Thomas	Frk	256
_____, Thomas G.	Gwn	319
Garrason, Darius	Eff	110
_____, David	Ware	184
_____, Isaac	Eff	105
_____, Michael	Eff	110
Garison, Henry P.	Fay	190
GARTER, John	Rch	265
GARTMAN/GORTMAN/GIRTMAN		
GIRTMANS		
Gartman, Andrew	Jef	409
_____, Daniel	Tlf	4
Gortman, Danil	Hab	28
Girtman, David	Doo	82
Girtmans, William	Pul	159
GARTRELL/GATRELL/GATCHELL		
Gartrell, H.	Col	360
_____, Jeremiah	Hab	11
_____, Milton	Col	359
_____, William	Col	359
Gatrell, Joseph	Wil	305
Gatchell, Caroline M.	Pik	126
_____, Charles	Jns	474
GARVIN/GERVIN		
Garvin, David	Hal	112
_____, Ignatius P.	Bke	141
_____, James	Crf	403
_____, Richard	Frk	244
_____, Sarah	Rch	256
Gervin, John	Jef	411
_____, Rebecca	Jef	410
_____, Robert	Jef	410
GARY, Henry	Han	153
_____, John M.	Han	154
_____, Nicholas B.	Han	153
_____, Rebecca	New	29
_____, Richard	Han	154
GASKINS/GASKIN		
Gaskins, David	Tlf	2
_____, Fisher	Lwn	90
_____, George	Lin	72
_____, John	Lwn	90
Gaskin, Amos	Cht	277
GASSITE, William	Crf	412
GAST, Thomas	Gwn	378
GASTON/GASTIN/GASTING		
Gaston, Alexander	Gre	299
_____, Elizabeth	Jsp	373
_____, William	Cht	245
Gastin, Azeel	New	49
_____, James	New	13
_____, John G.	Gre	282
_____, Matthew	Gre	282
Gasting, Matthew	Bts	174
GATCHINS, Benjamin	Put	186
GATES, Benjamin	Mwr	163
_____, Bennett H.	Jns	460
_____, Charles Sr.	Gwn	352
_____, Federick	Trp	40
_____, Horatio	Ear	99
_____, James	Bib	60
_____, James	Jns	453
_____, James	Mon	181
_____, Joab	Hst	282
_____, John L.	New	29
_____, Joseph	Lwn	79
_____, Samuel K.	Mwr	163
_____, Thomas	Jns	446
_____, William	DeK	59
_____, William	Tms	27
GATEWOOD, Ainsworth D.	Put	180
_____, Frances	Put	180
_____, Philip	Cpb	198
GATHRIGHT, James C.	New	19

Name	County	Page
Gathright, Joel	Wil	296
_____, Mariah	Clk	311
_____, Osbern M.	Clk	325
_____, William M.	Jks	327
_____, Wilson	Mon	221
GATLIN/GATLEN/GATLING		
Gatlin, Alfeus	Mor	243
_____, Edward	Mor	243
_____, Furney F.	Pul	145
_____, Garrett	Gre	294
_____, John	Ware	186
_____, Stephen	Gre	300
Gatlen, Lemuel M.	Gre	276
_____, Wingate	Up	120
Gatling, James	Han	155
_____, Martin	Wks	340
GAULDING/GAULDIN		
Gaulding, Alexander	Elb	137
_____, Barnet	Elb	147
_____, William	Elb	139
Gauldin, George	Mus	291
_____, Jesse	Ogl	73
GAULT, Joseph	DeK	70
GAULTNEY, John	Tlb	346
GAUSE, Martha	Tat	376
GAWDY/GAUDRY		
Gawdy, George	Pik	114
Gaudry, John B.	Cht	257
GAWLEY, Robert	Har	181
GAWS, John	Hab	54
_____, Thomas	Hab	53
GAY, Abner	Cow	381
_____, Allen	Ear	92
_____, Barnabas	Jef	415
_____, Benjamin	New	48
_____, Elias	Cow	381
_____, Gilbert	Cow	374
_____, Gilbert	Fay	185
_____, Gilbert	Hry	202
_____, Imus	Bak	18
_____, Isaac P.	New	50
_____, Jacob	Lau	5
_____, James	Cow	373
_____, James	Elb	140
_____, James	Lee	27
_____, John	Bul	98
_____, John	DeK	72
_____, John Jr.	DeK	73
_____, John	Jns	440
_____, John	Lee	26
_____, John	Tlb	340
_____, Joshua	Car	221
_____, Joshua Sr.	Ear	94

Name	County	Page
Gay, Joshua	Ear	93
_____, Josiah	Lau	8
_____, Jourdan	Har	180
_____, Lewis	Ear	94
_____, Mathew	Em	174
_____, Nancy	Bke	119
_____, Nathaniel	Lau	13
_____, Reuben	Irw	301
_____, Samuel	Jns	435
_____, Sherrod H.	Jsp	388
_____, Simon	Lwn	82
_____, Solomon	Put	173
_____, T. T.	Rch	243
_____, Thomas	Jef	415
_____, Thomas B.	Fay	199
_____, William	Fay	192
_____, William	Jef	416
_____, William	Lwn	84
GAYDEN, John	Car	222
GAYER, Ernest William	Eff	104
GAZAWAY/GAZEWAY		
Gazaway, Enoch	Gwn	337
_____, John	Gwn	337
Gazeway, William	Hab	11
GEAN, Daniel B.	Cow	376
_____, John	Cow	384
GEARING, Robert	Hab	46
GEDIS, George	Wal	134
GEE, Drewry	Frk	247
_____, Henry	Mus	288
_____, Michael D.	Mon	201
_____, Samuel	Bts	166
GEER, Edmond	Mor	252
_____, Israel	Cam	184
GEESLING, Benjamin Jr.	Wrn	214
_____, Benjamin Jr.	Wrn	219
_____, Hiram	Wrn	229
_____, Richard	Wrn	193
_____, Samuel	Wrn	207
GEFFIS, Drury	Hab	33
GEIGER, Allen	Lib	46
_____, Cornelius	Wyn	284
_____, David	Bry	88
_____, Jeremiah	Eff	114
_____, John U	McI	121
_____, Martin	Wyn	284
_____, Mrs. Mary	Bry	88
_____, Philip	McI	121
_____, Sarah	Bul	99
GENKINS: see JENKINS		
GENOBLY/GINOOLE		
Genobly, Benjamin	Eff	107
Ginoole, John	Cht	257

Name	County	Page
GENTRY, Archibald	Gre	272
______, Burgess	Gre	280
______, Cornelious	Frk	221
______, Elisha	Fay	201
______, Harvey	Fay	201
______, Hesekiah	Ran	245
______, Jeremiah	Frk	232
______, John	Car	216
______, John	Ran	245
______, Martin	Car	225
______, Mason	Fay	201
______, Matthew	Frk	250
______, Matthew Jr.	Frk	233
______, Samuel	Gre	272
______, Seaborn	Hry	250
______, William	Twg	76
______, Wyatt	Cpb	208
GEORGE, Arthur	Rab	227
______, Benjamin	Cow	371
______, Brice	Apl	5
______, Britton	Lib	46
______, Daniel	Dec	16
______, Daniel	Gwn	329
______, David	Hry	228
______, Eli	Dec	6
______, Elizabeth	Jns	447
______, Federck	Jns	437
______, Henry	Jks	348
______, Henry	Jsp	372
______, Isaac	Rab	225
______, Isiah	Dec	6
______, J. B.	Cht	262
______, J. V.	DeK	28
______, J. V.	DeK	31
______, James Sr.	Jns	441
______, James	Rab	226
______, James B.	DeK	32
______, Jesse	Cow	390
______, Jesse	Hry	228
______, Jesse	Rab	231
______, John	Hry	229
______, Joseph	Cht	244
______, Mark	Mon	180
______, Travis	Cow	390
______, William	Gwn	350
______, William H.	Gre	275
GERDINE, John	Clk	318
GERKINS, John	Irw	299
GERMAN/GERMANN/GERMAND/		
GERMOND/GERMA		
German, William	Jsp	371
Germann, John	Rch	254
Germand, Mrs.	Rch	273

Name	County	Page
Germond, William	Rch	260
Germa, John	Cht	254
GERMANY, James	Col	334
______, James	Mwr	155
______, Robert	Pik	111
______, William	Pik	110
GERRALD, Irbay	Col	342
______, Isaac	Clk	291
______, Mary	Col	353
______, Susan	McI	123
GETER, Francis	Mwr	151
______: also see Jeter		
GETTS, William	Wrn	209
GHARST, Christopher	Car	224
GHOLSON/GHOLSTON		
Gholson, Joseph J.	Put	178
______, Zach.	Gwn	343
Gholston, Benjamin	Gwn	345
______, Leonard H.	Har	177
GIBBONS/GIBBON		
Gibbons, Henry	Lau	13
______, Jos.	Cht	278
______, Stephen	Rch	281
______, William	Cht	277
______, William	Cht	283
Gibbon, August	Cht	240
GIBBS/GIBS		
Gibbs, Fortson	Elb	138
______, Howell	Twg	85
______, John	Rch	278
______, John	Irw	299
______, Mathew	Mon	209
______, Samuel	Irw	300
______, Shaderick	Mtg	231
______, Thomas	Elb	136
______, Thomas	Irw	300
______, Thomas	Wal	159
______, Thomas A.	Wal	148
Gibs, Cornelius	Hab	64
______, Jeremiah	Hal	124
GIBSON, Abner F.	Jns	465
______, Andrew	Hry	248
______, Augustus	Wil	289
______, Churchwell	Mon	195
______, Clary	Cpb	204
______, David	Mon	182
______, Dicey	Wyn	283
______, Edward	Hab	60
______, Eliza	Col	343
______, Frances	Jns	465
______, George	Car	215
______, George	New	30
______, Henry	Col	362

Name	County	Page
Gibson, Henry	Jsp	384
______, Henry	Mon	176
______, Henry	Wrn	205
______, Henry B.	Ran	249
______, Henry B.	Wil	293
______, Gibson, Hugh	Hry	204
______, Isaiah	Hry	231
______, Jacob	Cpb	203
______, Jacobus	Gre	290
______, James	Cpb	204
______, James	Up	102
______, James	Wks	339
______, James F.	Hry	214
______, Jobe D.	Dec	8
______, John	Car	216
______, John	Gly	265
______, John W.	Bul	99
______, Jos. R.	Cht	283
______, Joshua	Jks	330
______, Littleton	Lin	73
______, Luke	Hry	204
______, Martha	Col	352
______, Mrs. Mary	Col	334
______, Michael	Hry	205
______, Mildred	Wil	294
______, Obedience	Hry	235
______, Ob. C.	Up	97
______, Patience	Up	111
______, Patrick	McI	126
______, Robert C.	Tfo	367
______, S. W.	Col	342
______, Sampson	New	51
______, Sarah	Bib	76
______, Sarah	Col	343
______, Shockley	Hry	235
______, Silvanus C.	Dec	13
______, Soloman	New	51
______, Springer	Har	191
______, Stafford	Hry	235
______, Susan	Mon	205
______, Sylvanus	Wil	308
______, Thomas	Wrn	194
______, Walter	Mon	205
______, Wesley J.	Jns	468
______, William	Cam	181
______, William	Cam	182
______, William	Lau	6
______, William T.	Lau	15
GIDDENS/GIDDONS/GIDDINGS		
Giddens, Abraham	Pul	162
______, George	Han	154
______, Isbin	Lwn	84
______, Moses	Pul	155
Giddens, Thomas	Lwn	89
______, Thomas	Pul	155
Giddons, Clarissa	Bul	101
Giddings, Erastus	Mus	280
GIDEON/GIDEONS/GIDION/ GIDEAN		
Gideon, Berry W.	Fay	202
______, Edward	Pul	156
______, Elizabeth	Wil	312
______, Francis	Lin	75
______, Hosia C.	Jks	311
Gideons, Isaac	Dec	12
______, Jesse	Dec	14
______, John	Pul	156
______, Moses J.	Pul	159
Gidion, Mims	Bib	60
Gidean, William	Mus	278
GIEKIE, James H.	Gly	268
GIFETH/GIFITH/GERFETH		
Gifeth, Benjamin	Hal	111
Gifith, Stephen	Hal	111
Gerfeth, Benja.	Hal	109
GIGGER, H. H.	Jsp	382
______, John J.	Jsp	393
GIGNILATT/GIGNILLIAT		
Gignilatt, Henry	Gly	268
______, John	Gly	265
Gignilliat, Norman	Gly	265
GILBERT/GILBIRT/GILBORD/ GIBLORY		
Gilbert, A.	Cht	255
______, A.	Mus	282
______, Allen	Han	155
______, Arther	Hab	64
______, Benjamin Sr.	Put	176
______, Bird	Twg	86
______, Caron	New	39
______, Darius	Han	155
______, Drury	Up	104
______, Edmund	Bib	70
______, Edward	Gwn	335
______, Elisabeth	Hab	60
______, Elizabeth	Frk	240
______, Esekiel	Har	184
______, Helkiah	Tlb	328
______, Henry	Cht	247
______, Instant	Mor	240
______, Isaac	Gwn	312
______, Jabez	Bts	161
______, Jacob	Gwn	320
______, Jacob	Gwn	369
______, James	Gwn	348
______, James	Hry	224

Name	County	Page
Gilbert, Jeptha	Dec	13
______, Jesse	DeK	42
______, Jesse	Jef	411
______, John	Cht	250
______, John	Cpb	207
______, John	DeK	53
______, John	Hst	288
______, John	Jks	347
______, John	Mad	99
______, John G.	Han	154
______, John M.	DeK	34
______, Joshua	Wal	163
______, Martha	Han	154
______, Mathew	Hry	224
______, Nancy	Gre	305
______, Richard	Wil	295
______, Robert	Lee	35
______, Robert	Put	184
______, Samuel	Car	228
______, Tamer	Gwn	369
______, Thomas	Han	154
______, Thomas	Hst	294
______, Thomas	Wks	341
______, Thomas W.	Jks	318
______, Wiley	Wal	266
______, William	DeK	64
______, William	Lau	13
______, William	New	24
______, William	Pik	111
______, William	Wsh	264
______, William P.	Twg	84
Gilbirt, James	Pik	114
Gilbord, Henry	Dec	14
Giblory, John	Cht	270
GILBREATH, James H.	Gwn	312
GILDEN, Richard	Cht	267
GILDER, GILDERS		
Gilder, Elizabeth	Twg	84
______, George	Mwr	155
______, Isaac	Twg	87
______, Senate	Mwr	162
Gilders, Jacob	Pik	124
GILDERSLEVE, Doctr. E.	Lib	46
GILES/JILES		
Giles, Alex[r].	Wsh	261
______, Andrew	Wal	172
______, David	Hst	292
______, Dempsey	Crf	409
______, Elijah	Hst	292
______, Jackson B.	Wal	124
______, John	Gwn	331
______, John	Han	154
______, John	Wsh	254
Giles, John	Wsh	270
______, Jeremah	Wal	143
______, Leah	Cht	252
______, Mary	Wsh	273
______, Nancy	Mon	211
______, Nathan	Wsh	272
______, Thomas	Wal	138
______, Wade H.	Bts	164
______, William	Bts	163
______, William	Wsh	254
______, William	Wsh	262
Jiles, James H.	Mor	266
______, Richard	Gwn	322
______, William	Wal	127
GILKEYSON, Margaret	Hry	217
GILL, Charity	Scr	315
______, Charles G.	Col	341
______, Dare	McI	131
______, Days	Bal	38
______, Edward W.	Ear	95
______, Hyram T.	Pik	122
______, James	Lwn	89
______, Jesse A.	Mor	271
______, John	Bul	100
______, John	Cht	271
______, John	McI	131
______, John	Mor	247
______, Joseph	New	41
______, Lucinda	McI	131
______, Peter	Jns	428
______, Robert	Mus	278
______, Robert	Wyn	282
______, Samuel	DeK	53
______, Thomas T.	Pik	122
______, Thomas Y.	Wil	322
______, W.	Bal	45
______, William	Wil	303
______, William H.	Col	341
GILLCOAT, John	Fay	199
GILLESPIE/GILLISPIE/GILLASPIE/ GILLESPY/GILLASPY/GILLASKEY/ GALISPI/GASASPIE		
Gillespie, David	Hry	246
______, Lowrey	Frk	222
______, William	Frk	229
Gillispie, James	Wal	166
______, James L.	Frk	223
Gillaspie, James B.	Pik	123
Gillespy, James	Ogl	98
______, Robert	Ogl	66
Gillaspy, Allen	Hal	105
Gillaskey, Ann	DeK	54
Galispi, John P.	Car	222

Name	County	Page
Galispie, Samuel	Bib	55
Gasaspie, William	Rab	223
GILLEY, Charles Sr.	Car	224
______, Charles Jr.	Car	224
______, George W.	Car	215
______, John	Car	227
______, Jordan	Car	214
______, Willis	Car	218
______, William B.	Car	224
GILLILAND/GILLELAND/ GILLELAN		
Gilliland, Lewellin	Trp	39
______, William Jr.	Fay	182
Gilleland, Allen	Rab	231
______, Elizabeth	Rab	229
Gillelan, James	Jks	318
GILLIS, Angus	Hry	209
______, Angus	Mtg	235
______, John	Mtg	234
______, Katharine	Em	170
______, Kenneth	DeK	63
______, Niel	Em	169
GILLUM/GILHAM/GILLION/ GILLIAN/GILLEN		
Gillum, Harris	Bts	168
______, Jacob	Ogl	87
______, John	DeK	33
______, Thomas	Ogl	88
______, William T.	Mad	99
Gilham, David G.	Hab	54
______, Ezekial	Ogl	100
______, Ezekial M.	Ogl	88
Gillam, Robert	Hry	234
Gillion, Hannah	Bak	16
______, Isaac	Bak	20
______, Isaac	Bak	20
Gillian, John	Cht	270
Gilian, Jesse	Hab	21
Gillen, James	Lib	46
GILMER, Archabald	New	23
______, Geo. R.	Bal	45
______, James	Ogl	62
______, John	Ogl	62
______, Peachy R.	Ogl	89
______, Robert	Ogl	89
______, Thomas S.	Wil	320
______, William	Frk	222
GILMORE/GILLMORE/GILMOR/ GALEMORE		
Gilmore, A.	Mus	287
______, Anthony	Mon	217
______, Dan.	Hal	100
______, Hugh	Doo	87
Gilmore, Hugh	Wsh	245
______, Humphrey	Mor	239
______, James	Doo	81
______, James	Hal	102
______, James	Hal	100
______, James	Mwr	156
______, James	Trp	54
______, James	Wsh	268
______, Jane	Hal	100
______, John	Hry	214
______, John	Mar	140
______, John	Wsh	268
______, Nancy	Pik	108
______, Obediah	Up	103
______, Samuel	Hst	266
______, Samuel	Jsp	394
______, Samuel	Mar	137
______, William	Hst	277
______, William	Mar	140
______, William	Mar	140
______, Wylye	Jsp	384
Gillmore, Francis	Fay	206
______, William	Bts	176
Gilmor, William	Hal	79
Galemore, John	Twg	70
GILPIN, Green	Col	346
______, Thomas	Put	202
______, William	Put	202
GILSON, Samuel	Mor	255
______, Stokeley	Gwn	370
GILSTRAP, Bryant	Jsp	380
______, Charles	Hst	293
______, Elizabeth	Pul	145
______, Henry	Bke	129
______, Lewis	Jsp	385
______, Wiley	Mwr	156
______, William	Bke	129
GINDRAT, Joseph H.C.	Put	174
______, Mary	Cht	242
GINKINS: see Jenkins		
GINN, Arthur	Mon	184
______, Elisha	Elb	159
______, Isaac	Elb	159
______, Jesse	Elb	120
______, Jordan	Gwn	326
______, Joshue	Elb	138
______, Luke	Elb	145
______, Ruffin	Rab	222
______, Sarah	Elb	134
______, Sherrod H.	Fay	183
______, Thomas	Rch	284
______, Wiley	Elb	134
______, William	Elb	145

GINNINGS: see Jinnings
GIPSON, Aggy Put 179
_____, Churchhill Trp 40
_____, William Trp 39
GIRARDEAU/GIRIDON
Girardeau, John Lib 46
_____, William P. Lib 46
Giridon, L. Cht 255
GIRLEY, Jacob Cow 372
GIVENS/GIVIN/GIVON
Givens, James Put 207
_____, Robert DeK 57
Givin, Stephen O. Hst 268
Givon, William P. Han 154
GIVITHY, Nehemiah Wal 138
GLADIN/GLADDEN/GLADDIN
Gladin, James Han 154
_____, Jonathan Han 154
Gladden, Genkins Pul 144
Gladdin, Solomon Wsh 253
GLADNEY, Rachel Hry 249
_____, Samuel Mwr 160
_____, William Hry 213
GLANTON, Abnor Mon 181
_____, Dempsey Up 105
GLASCOCK, E. B. Rch 263
_____, E. B. Rch 279
_____, Thomas Rch 263
GLASS, George Ogl 65
_____, James Jsp 361
_____, James Lau 15
_____, James New 30
_____, James Ogl 100
_____, John W. New 44
_____, Levi Tms 21
_____, Levi Jr. Tms 17
_____, Loueince Fay 183
_____, Manson Fay 191
_____, Manson New 41
_____, Pleasant M. Ogl 99
_____, Richard Fay 188
_____, Thomas Fay 183
_____, Thomas New 55
_____, Thomas Pul 143
_____, Thomas Tms 20
_____, Uriah Fay 190
_____, William Hal 104
_____, William Jsp 359
GLASSGOW/GLASGOW/GLASGO
Glassgow, Hy. Gwn 359
_____, Obadiah Gwn 352
Glasgow, William Mad 114
Glasgo, Miles DeK 73
Glasgo, Robert New 23
GLASSON/GLASON/GLAWSON
Glasson, Henry Clk 291
_____, James Clk 292
_____, John Wal 167
Glason, Jacob M. Hab 9
Glawson, David Bts 164
_____, Jesse Jns 444
GLATIGMY, John Cht 254
GLAUN, Susan Mon 219
GLAZE/GLASE/GLACE
Glaze, Grant Lin 64
_____, John M. Jef 401
_____, Joseph C. Hry 217
_____, Milly Lin 59
_____, Nancy Gwn 343
_____, Patcy Hal 68
_____, Patrick Jks 323
_____, Reubin Ogl 90
_____, Samuel Lin 58
_____, Susan Lin 64
_____, William Lin 58
Glase, Jacob Hab 43
_____, Joseph Hab 43
_____, Thomas Put 189
Glace, Nancy Hal 130
GLAZIER, Hiram Mwr 154
_____, John New 16
_____, William New 17
GLEATON/GLETON
Gleaton, William Hry 219
Gleton, Jos. Lee 35
GLENDINING, William Rch 284
GLENN/GLEN
Glenn, Bird Mor 270
_____, Franklin Frk 221
_____, George N. Gwn 319
_____, James Jks 346
_____, James Trp 51
_____, James Trp 51
_____, James W. Hry 212
_____, John DeK 34
_____, John Jks 332
_____, John Wsh 248
_____, John W. Jks 313
_____, Joseph New 41
_____, Joshua Wil 289
_____, Littlepage Jsp 393
_____, Mary Hry 234
_____, Mary Ogl 82
_____, Matthew New 36
_____, Mathew H. Jsp 360
_____, Nathaniel Frk 224

Name	County	Page
Glenn, Patience	Wsh	255
______, Radford	Ogl	83
______, Simeon T.	Elb	129
______, Thomas	Jns	468
______, Thomas A.	Gwn	320
______, Thomas M.	Elb	133
______, Wiley	Jks	322
______, William	Har	182
______, William	Frk	228
______, William	Jsp	392
______, William Sr.	Ogl	82
______, William Jr.	Ogl	82
______, William	Wal	159
Glen, George	Cht	263
** ______, George; slaves	Cht	282
______, John B.	Mwr	165
______, Mary A. J.	Hab	98
______, Thomas	Ogl	75
GLISSON/GLESSON/GLEASON/ GLOSSON/GLISTEN		
Glisson, Bryan	Lwn	82
______, Dennis	Bke	148
______, Evan C.	Bke	148
______, John	Ran	241
______, John B.	Bke	129
Glesson, Riley	Ear	92
Gleason, Joel	Ogl	97
Glosson, William	Hry	231
Glisten, Joseph	Tat	373
GLORE, Abram	DeK	33
______, Asa	DeK	31
GLOVER, A.	Wsh	263
______, Abel	Gwn	329
______, Allen	Wrn	229
______, Benjamin	Jef	413
______, Benjamin G.	Mor	270
______, Barbary	Frk	248
______, Drewry	Dec	16
______, Eli	Jsp	369
______, Foster	Lau	7
______, George	Bib	76
______, George	Lwn	87
______, Henry	Jsp	395
______, Isam	Lee	30
______, Jesse	Dec	16
______, Jesse	Jef	413
______, John	Crf	405
______, John	Twg	75
______, John	Wil	303
______, John	Wil	318
______, John P.	Crf	404
______, Joshua	Eff	108
______, Kelly	Twg	62
Glover, Larken	Wrn	230
______, Milton P.	Crf	405
______, Nancy	Mad	118
______, Nelson	Frk	236
______, Peter	Gwn	354
______, Preston H.	Gwn	349
______, Reuben	Gwn	329
______, Richard	Gwn	354
______, Seaborn	Har	191
______, Seaborn	Wrn	232
______, Thomas	Twg	74
______, Thomas W.	Crf	405
______, Washington	Har	178
______, Wilea	Gwn	321
______, William	Frk	240
______, William	Rch	264
______, William P.	Crf	404
______, Williamson	Bib	50
______, Wyley	DeK	63
______, Wyley	Jns	443
GNANN, Andrew	Eff	114
______, Benjamin	Eff	114
______, Christopher	Eff	114
______, Jacob	Eff	109
______, Jacob	Eff	116
______, Jonathan	Eff	114
______, Joseph	Eff	114
______, Joshua	Eff	105
______, Solomon	Eff	106
______, Solomon	Eff	114
______, Timothy	Eff	114
GOARE, Green	Jns	430
______, Henry	Jns	430
______, Pharas	Jns	430
______, Rachael	Jns	430
______, Talbot	Jns	430
GOBER/GOBOR/GOBERT		
Gober, Asa	Gwn	338
______, Daniel	DeK	45
______, George	Frk	223
______, Henry	Jks	342
______, Hiram	Gwn	338
______, John	DeK	45
______, John Sr.	Frk	224
______, John	Jks	336
______, John T.	Frk	230
______, Mary	Jks	336
______, Richard	DeK	42
______, Roley	New	13
______, Thomas Jr.	DeK	69
______, William	Jks	336
______, William	New	13
______, William C.	Mwr	162

Name	County	Page
Gober, William H.	Frk	240
______, William Y.	Gwn	338
______, Wyley	DeK	41
Gobor, Thomas	DeK	63
______, Wisdam	DeK	63
Gobert, Benjamin	Jef	413
GOBLE, Cornelius	Rab	228
______, John	Rab	228
GODBEE, Albert	Bke	147
______, Alfred A.	Bke	145
______, Drusilla	Bke	146
______, Henry Sr.	Bke	147
______, Henry Jr.	Bke	147
______, James	Bke	141
______, James	Bke	147
______, Margaret	Bke	147
______, Mary	Bke	147
______, Moses	Bke	147
______, Samuel	Bke	146
GODDARD/GODARD		
Goddard, Daniel	Mon	178
______, Frederick	Jns	444
______, John Sr.	Cpb	209
______, John Jr.	Cpb	208
______, Joseph	Pik	116
______, Mary	Jsp	373
Godard, Bailey	Bib	55
______, James	Bib	55
______, James	Jns	453
______, Joel	Jns	451
GODDEN/GODDIN/GODOWN		
Godden, Alexandria	Dec	6
______, Stephen	Dec	6
Goddin, David	Ran	246
Godown, Jacob W.	Jef	416
GODFREY/GODPHREY		
Godfrey, Aaron	Gwn	314
______, Ansel	Rab	227
______, George	Mwr	151
______, Francis H.	Bib	67
______, Sarah	Rch	288
______, Thomas	Mwr	151
______, Thomas	Rab	223
______, Thomas P.	Gwn	360
______, W. D.	Gre	290
______, William	Lau	5
Godphrey, Martha	Bke	149
GODISON, P.	Cht	244
GODLY, James	Jsp	398
GODSHEAR, H.	Cht	241
GODWIN/GODKIN		
Godwin, Arnold	Wks	350
______, Elias	Wsh	264
Godwin, Frances	Fay	204
______, Hardy	Lwn	81
______, Nancy	Bal	37
______, Rebecca	Lwn	80
______, Richard R.	Ware	188
______, Seaborn	Ware	188
______, Sim.	Bal	37
______, Sion	Doo	80
______, Wiley	Mtg	233
______, William	Mtg	232
Godkin, James W.	Gre	281
GOFF, Ellis	New	84
______, Garland	Jsp	362
______, James	Lwn	82
______, Malicah	Lau	18
______, Nathaniel	Jsp	362
______, Samuel	Irw	301
______, Sarah	Wsh	252
______, William	Lau	10
______, William C.	Lwn	82
GOGGINS/GOGGIN/GOGGANS		
Goggins, Alexander	Car	219
______, Thomas	Jns	439
______, Wesley	Hal	76
Goggin, John	Mon	174
______, Johnson	Mon	214
Goggans, Samuel	Jsp	357
GOIN/GOING/GOINS/GOYENS		
Goin, Basdal	Hal	116
______, Betsey	Hal	117
______, John	Hal	92
______, William	Hal	104
Going, Hugh	Bts	178
______, Martha	Lin	62
______, Moses	Lin	74
Goins, Dillard	Jks	321
Goyens, John	Up	96
GOLD, Sally	Hal	84
GOLDEN/GOLDING/GOLDIN/ GALDEN		
Golden, Andrew	Bul	98
______, Benjamin	Twg	80
______, Gilly	Wrn	215
______, John	DeK	25
______, John	Lee	31
______, Layton	Mar	139
______, Mark Sr.	Lin	66
______, Mark Jr.	Lin	65
______, Mark	Lin	66
______, Mary	Lin	67
Golding, Abram	Mon	192
______, Adam	Wil	292
______, Allen	Hry	236

Name	County	Page
Golding, Frances	Wil	292
______, James	Hal	126
______, Seaborn	Tlb	322
______, William	Hal	128
Goldin, Noah	Lee	30
Galden, Caleb	Wal	143
GOLDSMITH, Allen	Jsp	379
______, Ann	Cht	277
______, Benjamin	Cht	243
______, John	Mon	218
______, John T.	Har	189
______, Samuel	Cht	258
______, Simmons	Cht	272
______, William N.	Mon	218
GOLDWIRE, John	Eff	104
GOLEY, Caroline	Clk	324
GOLIGHTLY, James	Pul	160
______, Susannah	Wsh	250
GOLLEHAND, Samuel	Clk	327
GOLMAN, Francis	Lin	75
______, Henry	Wrn	219
GOLSON, John C.	Jsp	370
GORE, Manning H.	Mad	107
______, Nottey	Mad	106
GONDER, James	Han	154
______, Mark	Han	153
GOOCH, Tilman	Rab	230
GOODALL, Seabourne	Scr	312
GOODBREAD, John S.	Cam	190
______, Thomas	Cam	190
GOODE/GOOD		
Goode, Jesse	Jsp	373
______, John	Up	103
______, M.	Bal	31
______, Nicholas	New	51
______, Reubin S.	Cow	376
______, Robert	Hst	285
______, Thomas W.	Up	95
Good, Priscilla	Bib	50
______, Richard	Gwn	354
______, Thomas	Hab	64
GOODDY, George	Frk	255
GOODMAN, Aaron	Mwr	164
______, Daniel	Crf	400
______, G.	Lee	26
______, Gillum	DeK	27
______, Gillum	DeK	55
______, Henry	Bul	96
______, Henry	Crf	407
______, Isaac	Wks	357
______, James	Hal	107
______, John	Mad	110
______, John C.	Han	155
Goodman, Jesse	Lwn	82
______, William	Lee	27
______, William	Rch	250
GOODNOW, Thomas	Wal	164
GOODSON/GOOTSON		
Goodson, Abram	Wsh	264
______, Alexr.	Mon	199
______, Arthur	Mus	293
______, Charles P.	Put	218
______, Edwin	Wsh	260
______, Jacob	Bke	142
______, John	Wrn	193
______, Jordan	Fay	199
______, Josiah	Bry	85
______, Nancy	Hab	30
______, Nancy	Put	208
______, Thomas	Wsh	239
______, William	Hab	30
______, William	Wal	150
______, William	Wrn	219
Gootson, William	Wal	165
GOODWIN, Asa	Mwr	167
______, Ephrian	Hab	51
______, James Sr.	Bak	16
______, James	DeK	70
______, James	Gwn	356
______, James C.	Jns	451
______, James I.	Bak	15
______, Jesse	Bts	161
______, Jesse	Jsp	384
______, Jesse	Jns	436
______, John	Bke	133
______, John	DeK	29
______, John	Ear	99
______, John	Trp	55
______, Jonathan	Crf	412
______, Josiah	Crf	402
______, Lewis	Jns	456
______, Matthew	Bke	146
______, Micajah	DeK	30
______, Neelly	DeK	71
______, Richard	Hst	262
______, Sanford	Gwn	327
______, Shadrick	Jns	444
______, Sterling	Hal	131
______, William	Rch	289
______, William H.	Mon	203
______, Zachariah	Pik	130
GOODYER, James	Tfo	357
GOOLSBY/GOULSBY/GOOLSBIE/ GOULDSBEY/GOLDSBY/GLOOLSBY		
Goolsby, Allen	Ogl	80
______, Anson	Tlb	336

Name	County	Page
Goolsby, Carden	Jsp	365
______, Cealey	Ogl	63
______, Hezekiah	Tlb	335
______, Isaah	Ogl	62
______, Isaiah	Wal	136
______, James B.	Jsp	364
______, Jeremiah	Elb	129
______, Jesse	Wal	165
______, John	Jsp	371
______, Micajah	Ogl	85
______, Reuben	Elb	124
______, Richard	Ogl	80
______, Simeon	Ogl	80
______, Simion M.	Ogl	63
______, Tandy	Ogl	82
______, Wade	Jsp	365
______, William	Jks	328
______, William	Jsp	373
______, William	Ogl	81
Goulsby, John H.	Mwr	160
______, Kerby	Mwr	169
______, Mourning	Mwr	167
Goolsbie, Aaron	Ear	100
Gouldsbey, Charles	Cht	278
Goldsby, Pleasant	Up	120
Gloolsby, Isaac	Ogl	62
GORAN, James	Cht	271
GORCE, Amos	Bts	167
GORDON/GORDAN/GORDEN/ GORDIN/GORTON		
Gordon, Abraham	Hry	229
______, Alexander	Rch	255
______, Alexander J.	Har	177
______, Benjamin	Wsh	251
______, Charles	Gwn	368
______, Duncan	Bke	136
______, Elizabeth	Rch	259
______, Few	Gwn	318
______, George	Gwn	318
______, James Sr.	Bke	119
______, James Jr.	Bke	120
______, James	Gwn	368
______, James H.	Mon	195
______, James T.	Fay	188
______, Jo. B.	Gwn	363
______, John	Bke	142
______, John	Clk	299
______, John	Elb	128
______, John	Pik	126
______, John B.	Gwn	365
______, John W.	Jns	453
______, Louisa	Jsp	352
______, Mary	Cht	241

Name	County	Page
Gordon, Richard	Wsh	261
______, Richmond	Up	110
______, Sarah	Rch	270
______, Steven B.	Gwn	368
______, W. W.	Cht	250
** ______, W.W.; slaves	Cht	277
______, William	Gwn	315
______, William	Bke	122
______, William	McI	131
William	Jef	414
______, George	New	38
______, Henry	Jns	439
______, James	Jns	439
______, John	Jef	401
______, John W. G.	Jns	433
______, Nathaniel	Jns	439
______, Thomas H.	Jef	401
Gorden, Silas	Cow	369
______, Thomas	Trp	38
______, Thomas	Wrn	194
______, Thomas	Gwn	377
______, Vinson	Mad	105
Gordin, Ezekiel	Hry	221
______, James F.	Ogl	94
______, Thomas	Hab	35
______, Wrightman	Hry	239
Gordun, John	DeK	35
Gorton, Henry	Rch	268
GORDY, Elijah	Bke	127
______, Leonard	Up	104
______, Lott	Mon	183
______, Noah	Up	115
______, Peter	Bal	38
______, Thomas	Han	155
______, W.	Bal	38
GORE, James	Hry	225
______, James	Mar.	140
______, Thomas	Jsp	356
GORHAM/GORUM		
Gorham, Lazarius	DeK	63
______, Martin	Hal	102
______, Santford	DeK	63
______, William	Cht	248
______, Willis	Jef	419
Gorum, Henry	Trp	46
GORLEY, Mary	Clk	324
______, William	Put	213
GORMAN/GORMON		
Gorman, John	Bal	29
______, Thomas B.	Mon	196
Gormon, William	Cow	389
GORNTO/GRUNTO/GONTO		
Gornto, David	Lwn	84

Name	County	Page
Gornto, Mary	Lau	21
______, Nathan	Lwn	84
Grunto, Nathan	Lau	17
Gonto, James	Gly	268
GORTNEY, William	Frk	255
GORY, Joel	Jsp	379
GOSLIN, Barney	Tlb	341
______, James F.	Up	103
______, Sirman	Mus	292
GOSS, Benjamin	Hal	109
______, Charles S.H.	Har	178
______, Churchhill	Trp	43
______, H. F.	Mwr	154
______, Horatio J.	Elb	130
______, Isam	New	10
______, Jesse H.	New	31
______, Mathew	Hab	27
______, Miles	Cow	379
______, Nathaniel	Hal	108
______, Susanah	New	31
______, William	Cow	369
______, William S.	Tlb	333
______, Wyley	DeK	58
GOSSAWAY/GASSAWAY/GASAWAY		
Gossaway, Obedience	Rab	225
Gassaway, James	Tlb	322
Gasaway, John	DeK	37
GOSSETT, Jacob	Mad	109
______, James	Hal	72
______, John	Mad	113
______, John	Pik	116
GOSWICK, Mathias	Hal	111
GOTHARD/GOTHERD		
Gothard, Elias	Hal	134
______, Henry	DeK	59
Gotherd, George	Mwr	158
______, William	Hal	134
GOTT, Mary	Gre	295
GOUGH/GOUGE		
Gough, George	Bke	121
Gouge, Jo.	Gwn	327
GOULD/GOULDS		
**Gould, A. (slave)	Rch	275
______, John	McI	128
______, Thomas	Lib	46
______, Thomas R.	McI	126
______, William T.	Frk	223
______, William T.	Rch	257
Goulds, Jacob	Cht	280
GOULDEN, Jonathan	Lib	46
______, Layton	Mwr	156
______, Palmer; dec'd. Estate	Lib	46
GOULEY, Dr. John	Jsp	386
***GOURD, Rattling (Indian)	Car	234
GOVIE, Amos	Bts	167
GOW, Andrew	Cht	265
GOWDER, Frederick	Frk	220
GOYNE, Hiram	Tfo	358
______, Nancy	Tfo	362
Goyens, Noyal	Up	112
GOWEN/GOWIN		
Gowen, B. B.	Gly	264
______, Elias G.	Dec	12
Gowin, Nancy	Clk	312
GOZE, F. L.	DeK	65
GRACE, Allison	Wil	291
______, Bluford	Pik	107
______, Canon W.	Han	153
______, Elison	Jsp	391
______, George	Gwn	343
______, Hannah	Lin	66
______, Jeptha	Han	154
______, John	Pik	126
______, John	Tms	25
______, John B.	Crf	400
______, Joshua	Pik	114
______, Major	Tms	25
______, Matthew R.	New	7
______, Samuel	Hst	280
______, Silas	Han	153
______, Thomas	Tat	375
______, Thomas T.	Jef	419
______, William	Mus	284
______, William	Wrn	232
GRABIL/GRAYBILL		
Grabil, John	Han	154
______, Mary	Han	153
______, Micael	Han	154
Graybill, Philip	McI	121
GRADDY/GRADY		
Graddy, Frederic	Pul	147
______, James O.	Frk	241
______, John	Twg	87
______, Lavina	Hst	281
______, Winfrey	Hst	279
Grady, Dennis	Eff	109
______, Needham	Elb	135
______, William	Hal	69
GRADEN, Drewry	DeK	41
GRAGGS, William	Trp	41
GRAHAM/GRAYHAM/GREYHAM		
Graham, Alexander	Lau	10
______, Alexander	Tlf	10
______, Alexander D.	New	53
______, Andrew	Clk	327

Name	County	Page
Graham, Andrew	Dec	15
______, Armstead	Ogl	71
______, David	Doo	83
______, Duncan	Tlf	7
______, Duncan B.	Irw	300
______, Elijah	App	8
______, George	Lau	10
______, Green G.	Pul	160
______, Isaiah	Han	154
______, James	Em	165
______, James	Hab	51
______, John	App	6
______, John	Eff	111
______, John	Wyn	281
______, John W.	New	53
______, Jonathan	Frk	216
______, Kerrs	Rch	276
______, Leannah	Wal	167
______, Mary	Ogl	72
______, Moss	Jks	327
______, Nancy	Pul	160
______, Neill	Tlf	9
______, Robert	Up	107
______, Rubin	Col	342
______, Samuel	Jks	338
______, Samuel	Twg	75
______, Thomas	Mwr	164
______, Thomas	Hab	61
______, Thomas	Jks	340
______, William	Hry	216
______, William P.	Clk	323
______, Nindsor	Hry	238
Grayham, David	Mad	112
______, Edward	Lau	17
______, James	Lau	9
______, James	Mad	101
______, Jarusha	Lib	46
______, John	Lau	8
______, Joseph	Mad	108
______, William	Frk	226
______, William	Mad	112
Greyham, Jesse	Car	222
______, James	Car	222
GRAINGER, Absalem	Wal	139
______, Benjamin	Wal	128
______, John D.	Wal	135
GRANAD/GRANADE		
Granad, Adam	Wrn	211
______, James Jr.	Wrn	212
______, Martin	Wrn	212
______, Solomon	Tms	21
______, Stephen	Wrn	210
______, Timothy	Wrn	212
Granade, John	Jef	415
______, Patience	Jef	424
GRANBERRY/GRANBURY		
Granberry, George	Har	181
______, Samuel M.	Twg	66
______, Silas	Doo	83
______, Thomas	Doo	87
Granbury, Langley	Twg	65
GRAND, J.	Cht	255
GRANDEUR, Jack	Jsp	372
GRANNIS, Martin	Mor	242
GRANT, Charles	Jsp	398
______, Daniel	Clk	324
______, Daniel	Mwr	166
______, David	Jsp	372
______, Elisha	Hab	37
______, George	Rch	271
______, George R.	Jks	313
______, Giles	Mon	213
______, Gregory	Elb	139
______, Isaac	Rch	280
______, Isabelle	Cht	241
______, Izbel	DeK	37
______, James	Gly	266
______, James	Han	153
______, Jane	Cht	271
______, Jesse	Em	170
______, Jesse	Em	176
______, John	Hab	24
______, John O.	Tlb	325
______, Joseph	Col	334
______, Joseph	Han	153
______, Joseph	Mon	218
______, Martha	Jsp	372
______, Mary	Pul	152
______, Pricilla	Cht	240
______, Reuben	Lib	46
______, Robert	Gly	266
______, Sampson	Jsp	398
______, Samuel	Jsp	372
______, Stephen	Twg	87
______, Thomas	Gre	278
______, Thomas	Put	200
______, Thomas J.	Hab	23
______, William	DeK	46
______, William A.	Wil	288
GRANTHAM, Alfred	Scr	318
______, Daniel	Irw	301
______, Eady	Ear	99
______, Elijah	Irw	303
______, Henry	Ran	243
______, John	Irw	303
______, Joshua	Twg	61

Name	County	Page
Grantham, Nathan	Doo	79
_____, Thomas	Scr	309
_____, William M.	Rab	225
_____, Zadock	Pik	121
GRANTLAND, Seaton	Bal	45
GRAVES/GREAVES		
Graves, Ann	Wil	288
_____, Baydehal	New	54
_____, Benjamin	Lin	70
_____, Benjamin C.	Trp	43
_____, Catherine	Wil	292
_____, David	Fay	184
_____, Ellis	Col	341
_____, Iverson L.	New	27
_____, John Sr.	Fay	195
_____, John Jr.	Fay	184
_____, John B.	Put	183
_____, John J.	Elb	138
_____, John L.	New	27
_____, John W.	Clk	300
_____, Joseph D.	Tfo	356
_____, Lewis	New	54
_____, P.	Cht	257
_____, R. N.	Hab	11
_____, Robert C.	New	44
_____, Solomon Sr.	New	27
_____, Solomon Jr.	New	27
_____, William	Wks	346
Greaves, James	Mon	176
_____, Joseph	Mon	176
GRAVITT/GRAVAT/GRAVET		
Gravitt, Charles	Hal	133
_____, John	Hal	81
_____, Obadiah	Hal	81
_____, Robert	Hab	78
_____, Thomas	Hal	78
_____, William	Hal	78
Gravat, Obediah	Cpb	199
Gravet, James	Gwn	370
GRAY/GREY/		
Gray, Absalom	Gwn	372
_____, Absalom	Mwr	163
_____, Allen	Up	115
_____, Archibald	Tlb	346
_____, Barbary	Bke	143
_____, Benjamin G.	Mtg	234
_____, Benonis	Wal	149
_____, Daniel	Lin	68
_____, Daniel	Up	101
_____, David	Dec	10
_____, Elizabeth	Bts	174
_____, Elizabeth	Mwr	166
_____, Enoch	Wsh	269
Gray, Garrett	Frk	217
_____, George	Col	343
_____, George	Jns	445
_____, George	Ogl	67
_____, Gibson	Lau	19
_____, Greene	Jns	465
_____, Henry	Col	344
_____, Hezekiah	Frk	237
_____, Isaac	Cpb	201
_____, Isaac	Frk	254
_____, Jabez	Lin	67
_____, James	Col	351
_____, James	Cpb	208
_____, James	Hst	261
_____, James	Jns	453
_____, James	New	16
_____, James	Pik	109
_____, James	Twg	61
_____, James	Wrn	218
_____, Jeremiah	Clk	318
_____, Jeremiah	Hal	127
_____, John	Col	338
_____, John	Col	353
_____, John	Ear	95
_____, John	Elb	155
_____, John	Gwn	349
_____, John	Hst	271
_____, John	Lin	65
_____, John D.	Cam	187
_____, John H.	Dec	10
_____, John M.	Twg	82
_____, John W.	Cam	181
_____, John W.	Lib	46
_____, John W.	Trp	51
_____, Johnson	Frk	233
_____, Jonathan	Cow	375
_____, Joseph	Mon	225
_____, Joshua	Bke	132
_____, Joshua	Ear	91
_____, Mansfield	New	5
_____, Minchard	Dec	16
_____, Minchey Jr.	Bke	130
_____, P.	Cht	270
_____, Patrick	Mon	186
_____, Peter	DeK	55
_____, Rachel	Clk	319
_____, Rebecca	Elb	149
_____, Reese	Elb	151
_____, Samson	Hry	209
_____, Samuel	Hry	204
_____, Samuel Sr.	Mwr	168
_____, Samuel Jr.	Mwr	168
_____, Samuel	Wrn	216

Name	County	Page
Gray, Sar.	Wks	337
______, Sebron B.	Pik	109
______, Simon	Bib	60
______, Susannah	Elb	155
______, Thomas	Crf	397
______, Thomas	Gwn	329
______, Thomas	Gwn	355
______, Thomas	Lwn	90
______, Thomas	Trp	51
______, Thomas	Wks	333
______, Thomas J.	New	7
______, W. M.	Ran	249
______, William	Ear	94
______, William	Hry	215
______, William	Lin	67
______, William	Mon	217
______, William	Wks	333
Grey, Mrs. Ann	Bry	84
______, Richard	Mus	277
______, T. V.	Cht	244
GREAT, Mary	Cht	271
GREATHOUSE/GRATEHOUSE		
Greathouse, Absalem M.	Crf	413
______, Sarah	New	24
Gratehouse, Abram	Fay	202
GREEN/GREENE		
Green, Allen	Col	346
______, Allen	Jns	474
______, Amos	Mus	281
______, Aquilla	Lwn	88
______, Austin H.	DeK	34
______, Benjamin	Bke	124
______, Benjamin	McI	121
______, Burrel	Pik	115
______, Charles R.	Wil	320
______, Charles R.	Gwn	355
______, Daniel	Bke	124
______, Daniel	Cam	188
______, Daniel	Em	164
______, Daniel	Hal	125
______, Daniel	Han	153
______, Daniel	Ware	189
______, David	Wks	340
______, David E.	Bke	143
______, Eason	Lau	10
______, Edm[d].	Cpb	202
______, Eli	Mar	143
______, Elias	Jks	330
______, Elisha	Ware	189
______, Elizabeth E.	Bke	145
______, Enoch	Bib	60
______, George	Jsp	383
______, George	Wal	156
Green, Hannah	Up	120
______, Isaac	Cam	189
______, Isaac	Hal	125
______, Isaac	Pik	114
______, James	Col	345
______, James	Jks	329
______, James	Jns	445
______, James	Jsp	358
______, James	Mus	277
______, James	Trp	43
______, James D.	Col	348
______, James M.	Mor	247
______, Jason	Put	200
______, Jeremiah	Hst	261
______, Jese	Hab	58
______, Jesse	Lau	9
______, Jesse D. (unsettled)	Wrn	219
______, Jesse P.	Bke	143
______, John	Bib	60
______, John	Bul	98
______, John	Gwn	358
______, John	Hal	126
______, John	Lee	30
______, John	Ogl	62
______, John	Pik	122
______, John	Pul	151
______, John	Rab	235
______, John	Tms	27
______, John	Twg	85
______, John B.	Wil	290
______, John H.	Mon	180
** ______, John P.(slave)	Rch	277
______, John R.	Cpb	206
______, Joseph	Put	209
______, Joseph	Trp	43
______, Jos. B.	Bal	33
______, Joseph F.	Jns	444
______, Joseph P.	Hry	215
______, Larkin	Gwn	355
______, Lemuel	Har	175
______, Lewis	Bul	96
______, Lewis	Cpb	195
______, Lewis	Ware	189
______, Lovick	Lwn	88
______, Lydia	Pul	147
______, Martha	Eff	112
______, McKeen	Wsh	264
______, Miles	Bal	40
______, Miles	Mon	214
______, Moses	Lau	19
______, Moses	Scr	310
______, Moses W.	Trp	53
______, Peter	Fay	194

Name	County	Page
Green, Phillip H.	Trp	40
______, R. A.	Bal	38
______, Raleigh	Mor	269
______, Rebecca	Em	170
______, Rice B.	Gwn	311
______, Robert	Em	164
______, Robert	Mar	143
______, Robert	Hry	249
______, Robert	Twg	79
______, Roger	Hal	65
______, Samuel	Em	164
______, Samuel	New	18
______, Samuel A.	Ran	241
______, Sarah	Frk	211
______, Sarah	Hab	19
______, Shade	Gwn	349
______, Shadrack	Cpb	206
______, Shadrick	Wal	133
______, Shepherd	Jef	411
______, Tandy	DeK	43
______, Thomas	Bul	97
______, Thomas	Hal	125
______, Thomas	Jef	411
______, Thomas	Mor	238
______, Thomas	Wil	314
______, Thomas F.	Bal	29
______, Thornberry	Jns	435
______, Villet	Trp	44
______, William	Bal	43
______, William	Bul	98
______, William	Gwn	351
______, William	Gly	268
______, William	Hry	249
______, William	Jsp	383
______, William	McI	121
______, William	Mon	203
______, William	New	17
______, William	Mus	289
______, William	Ogl	63
______, William	Pik	123
______, William	Twg	85
______, William	Wal	132
______, William	Wsh	255
______, William H.	Mon	185
______, Willis	Gwn	352
______, Willis	Tfo	354
Greene, Augustus	Gre	282
______, B. Carter	Rch	286
______, Benjamin	Scr	313
______, Betsey	Gre	288
______, Charity	Wrn	194
______, David	Wrn	201
______, Duty	Scr	311
Greene, F. H.	Gre	28
______, Hartwell B.	Up	9
______, Henry	Put	17
______, John	Put	20
______, John	Tlb	33
______, Lemuel	Gre	27
______, Nancy	Jsp	35
______, Pleasant	Jsp	35
______, Samuel	Hry	21
______, Simon	Ear	9
______, Thomas Sr.	Jsp	35
______, Thomas Jr.	Jsp	35
______, Thomas	Scr	31
______, Thomas Jr.	Tlb	32
______, Thomas B.	Up	10
______, William	Gre	27
______, William	Han	15
______, William	Han	15
______, William	Hry	21
______, William	Scr	31
______, William B.	Bke	14
______, William G.	Han	15
______, Young	Wrn	19
GREENFIELD, Allen	Cht	27
GREENLEE, John R.	DeK	4
GREENWAY/GREENAWAY		
Greenway, Elijah	Elb	12
______, John	Bke	13
______, John H.	Elb	14
______, Samuel	Bke	13
______, William	Bke	13
Greenaway, Alexander	Hal	10
______, John	Hal	10
______, Thomas	Hal	10
***GREENWOOD (no other name)	Car	23
______, Benjamin L.	Mtg	23
______, Cary	Hab	1
______, Henry	Rch	29
______, John P.	Clk	31
______, Samuel	Mor	25
______, Thomas B.	Ogl	10
______, William	Ogl	10
GREER/GRIER/GREAR/GEER		
Greer, Abram	Gre	28
______, Anna	Gre	30
______, Aquilla	Gre	28
______, Archibald	Gre	27
______, Azquiller	Ogl	8
______, Conth	New	3
______, Francis M.	Mwr	16
______, George	Wsh	27
______, Gilbert	Mon	19
______, Gilbert D.	DeK	3

Name	County	Page
reer, Henry	Trp	50
_____, Henry H.	Gre	289
_____, James	Mwr	166
_____, James	Trp	36
_____, John	Jsp	355
_____, Joseph	Hal	98
_____, Martha	Gre	298
_____, Nathaniel H.	Trp	36
_____, Newton	Hal	131
_____, Robert	Trp	41
_____, Stephen	Gre	295
_____, Thomas	Jsp	355
_____, Thomas	Mor	252
_____, Thomas	Wrn	199
_____, Waters W.	Mwr	168
_____, William	Gre	281
_____, William	Hry	249
_____, William	Mor	253
_____, William	Trp	36
_____, William	Wal	125
rier, Aron W.	Wrn	198
_____, Aquilla	Fay	194
_____, Carlton	Wks	340
_____, David	Wsh	259
_____, Eli	Ran	247
_____, Elijah	Mon	227
_____, Elijah	Pik	130
_____, Elisha	Mus	288
_____, George	Mus	292
_____, James	Mon	227
_____, James	Ran	249
_____, John	Mon	187
_____, John G. W.	Mon	220
_____, Leonard	Mon	172
_____, Moses	Ran	248
_____, Richard	Mus	285
_____, Robert	Bts	159
_____, Robert	Wks	339
_____, Samuel A.	Ran	241
rear, Ann	Clk	309
_____, Aquilla	Clk	307
_____, Henry	Mon	179
_____, James	Clk	295
_____, John	Clk	312
_____, Joshua	Clk	295
_____, Marian	Clk	310
_____, Thomas	Clk	311
_____, William	Clk	297
eer, David	Gre	282
_____, William	Gre	285
REESON/GREASON		
reeson, Abraham	Wal	124
_____, James	Wal	151
Greeson, John	Wal	154
_____, William	Wal	168
Greason, Susannah	Wrn	208
GREGG/GRAGG/GREGGS		
Gregg, Israel	Twg	67
Gragg, John	Gwn	344
Greggs, Sarah	Gwn	344
GREGORY/GRIGORY/GREGREY		
Gregory, Abigail	Rch	267
_____, Charles	Pik	131
_____, David W.	Gwn	364
_____, Gorden	Clk	315
_____, Hardy	Jef	412
_____, Hardy	Put	184
_____, Jesse	Tlb	336
_____, John	Bke	117
_____, John	Pul	149
_____, John	Tms	28
_____, John A.	Rch	277
_____, Lewis	Ran	247
_____, Lewis H.	Bib	58
_____, Rachall	Tms	20
_____, Richard	Ogl	67
_____, Richard	Tms	20
_____, Sarah	Tms	28
_____, Thomas	Mon	223
_____, Thomas H.	Ear	97
_____, William	Wsh	239
Grigory, Samuel	Bak	19
Gregrey, Peter	Hab	11
GRENARD, Benjamin M.	Ogl	94
GRENVILLE, Mrs.	Rch	263
GRESHAM/GRISHAM/GRISAM		
Gresham, A. Y.	Mus	282
_____, Albert Y.	Clk	291
_____, Arch[d].	Tfo	356
_____, Charles	Wil	314
_____, David	Jsp	390
_____, David	Trp	54
_____, Davis	DeK	61
_____, Edmund	Wal	124
_____, Elison	Trp	46
_____, Elizabeth	Wil	322
_____, Fardinand	Jns	443
_____, Feli	Mon	215
_____, Frances	Jns	443
_____, G. M.	Gwn	320
_____, Isham	Trp	54
_____, James D.	Ear	100
_____, Job	Bke	155
_____, John	Ogl	90
_____, John	Pik	122
_____, John	Wal	142

Name	County	Page
Gresham, John	Wil	309
______, John	Up	99
______, John H.	Ogl	78
______, Kauffman	Wil	322
______, Lemuel	Har	188
______, Littleberry	Mon	212
______, Marmaduke	New	21
______, Martha W.	Ogl	72
______, Mary	Tfo	361
______, Merreba	Cow	372
______, Micajah	Wal	134
______, Pleasant	Tlb	347
______, Robert	Ogl	90
______, William	DeK	26
______, William	Trp	54
______, William	Wil	321
______, Young F.	Gre	305
Grisham, Edward	Jns	436
______, Isaiah	New	23
______, Jeremiah	Trp	54
______, Jeremiah	Up	119
______, Pleasant	Up	119
Grisam, William	Hal	76
GRIBB, Ezekel	Hab	15
GRIBBON, Jane	Cht	265
______, R.	Cht	269
GRICE, Delilah	Mwr	164
______, Demcy	Elb	144
______, Esther	Pul	153
______, Gary	Hry	202
______, Isaac N.	Rab	222
______, James	Twg	77
______, Jesse	Hry	199
______, John	Lau	16
______, Larry	Trp	50
______, Moses	Hst	269
______, Solomon	Jsp	396
______, Stephen	Hry	201
______, William	Tat	377
GRIDER, Benjamin	Mor	272
______, Jacob	Tms	17
GRIFFETH/GRIFFITH/ GRIFFIETH/GRIFFUTH		
Griffeth, David	Gwn	335
______, George Sr.	Tfo	367
______, James Jr.	Mad	118
______, James	Ogl	92
______, James L.	Clk	308
______, James R.	Mad	103
______, John	Mad	108
______, John	Tfo	367
______, John L.	Clk	307
______, Nathan	Ogl	91

Name	County	Page
Griffeth, Robert	Mad	11
______, William	Tfo	36
Griffith, Caleb	Hab	1
______, Henry W.	Jns	43
______, James	Bib	6
______, James	Mad	9
______, John	Mon	19
______, Jonathan	Jks	34
______, Mary	Mad	11
______, Morgan	Gwn	33
______, Oliver	Ran	24
______, Thomas	Ogl	9
______, William	New	2
______, William V.	DeK	6
Griffieth, David H.	Wal	14
______, Michael	Wal	16
______, Thomas D.	Wal	16
Griffuth, Joel	Wal	15
GRIFF/GREAFF		
Griff, Thomas M.	Pul	13
Greaff, Charles	Gwn	31
GRIFFIN/GRIFFEN/GIFFIN		
Griffin, Abner	Lwn	7
______, Allen	Hst	27
______, Anderson	Mon	17
______, Andrew	Cpb	19
______, Andrew	DeK	4
______, Andrew	Jsp	37
______, Archibald	Lau	1
______, Asa	Han	15
______, Asa	Hal	10
______, Asa	Irw	30
______, Benjamin	Dec	1
______, Benjamin	Irw	30
______, Beverly A.	Wal	16
______, Buckner	Wal	16
______, Burnett Y.	Bib	5
______, Charles	Wal	12
______, Comfort	Rch	28
______, Daniel B.	Bts	16
______, David	Em	17
______, David	Hry	20
______, Dempsey	Bry	8
______, Dempsey	Bke	14
______, Dempsey	Tms	1
______, Edward	Bib	5
______, Elijah	Frk	23
______, Elizabeth	Wil	29
______, Elizabeth	Gre	30
______, Enoch	Bal	2
______, Etheldred	Twg	7
______, Ezekial	Ogl	8
______, George	Bke	14

Name	County	Page
Griffin, George	New	43
______, George W.	Mwr	156
______, Gilford	Lau	20
______, Hardy	Lau	19
______, Henry	Hst	292
______, Henry	Mon	198
______, James	Dec	10
______, James	Scr	300
______, James	Irw	303
______, James	Ware	188
______, James	Bry	88
______, Jeremiah	Col	359
______, Jeremiah	Mor	269
______, Jesse	Frk	233
______, John	Bib	50
______, John	Crf	406
______, John	Fay	187
______, John	Han	154
______, John	Hry	236
______, John	Mus	290
______, John	Pik	111
______, John	Wal	143
______, John	Wal	150
______, John	Wil	304
______, John	Wrn	231
______, John C.	Rch	262
______, John C.	Scr	300
______, John C.	Wrn	206
______, John W.	Bib	64
______, Jonas	Wks	357
______, Joseph	Hry	203
______, Joshua	Irw	303
______, Kinchin	Wal	134
______, Larkin	Twg	62
______, Larkin	Wsh	242
______, Lenn	Dec	10
______, Leonard	DeK	45
______, Levi	Lau	16
______, Lewis	Bib	60
______, Lewis	Jns	456
______, Lewis	Tms	17
______, Lewis L.	Mon	175
______, Lunsford	Lau	10
______, Major	Tms	17
______, Mary	Bke	139
______, Mary Sr.	Bke	149
______, Mary Jr.	Bke	149
______, Micaja	Dec	9
______, Michat	Col	337
______, Moses	Bke	145
______, Murpha	Wil	292
______, Nancy	Lwn	81
______, Nancy P.	Twg	69
Griffin, Nathan	Bak	17
______, Nathan	Hst	295
______, Nathl.	Col	357
______, Noah	Irw	303
______, Noah	Irw	303
______, Owen	New	22
______, Patsy	Crf	397
______, Peter	Crf	397
______, Rebecca	Lin	72
______, Richard	Col	359
______, Richard	Frk	254
______, Robert F.	Gre	272
______, Samuel	App	10
______, Samuel	Cht	259
______, Sarah	Bke	148
______, Sarah	Wsh	261
______, Shadrack	Irw	299
______, Silas	Ogl	87
______, Solomon	Up	102
______, Stephen	Bke	139
______, Susan	Cow	387
______, Thomas	Har	186
______, Thomas	Wsh	272
______, Thomas	Fay	193
______, Thomas	Mus	287
______, Thomas E.	Rch	282
______, Thomas U	Bke	149
______, William	Bib	60
______, William	Bib	73
______, William	Dec	5
______, William	Frk	252
______, William	Hst	268
______, William	Hry	236
______, William	Jns	430
______, William	Twg	88
______, William	Wal	145
______, William	Wsh	255
______, William	Wrn	233
Griffen, Hardy	Elb	128
______, Jonathan	Elb	130
______, Leonard V.	Elb	129
______, Walden	Eff	107
______, William W.	Elb	136
Giffin, Robert T.	Hab	32
GRIFFIS/GRIFFICE		
Griffis, Charles Sr.	Ware	184
______, Charles Jr.	Ware	184
______, Henry	Crf	398
______, Joel	Ware	185
______, Matthew	Gre	276
______, Samuel Sr.	Ware	186
Griffice, Nancy	Hal	122
______, William	Han	154

Name	County	Page
GRIGGS/GRIGG/GRIGS		
Griggs, Bryant	Fay	183
______, Henry	Up	102
______, Hugh	Hry	205
______, James	Put	205
______, Jesse H.	Jns	451
______, Lynnah	Han	153
______, Milly	Han	154
______, Nathaniel	Han	154
______, R. S.	Wrn	207
______, Robert	Han	153
______, Robert	Han	153
______, Robert	Jsp	364
______, Samuel	Cht	270
______, Thomas	Han	155
______, Wesley	Put	205
______, William	Han	154
______, William	Har	180
______, William	Tfo	366
______, William W.	Han	153
Grigg, William	Bal	43
Grigs, John Sr.	Put	205
GRIGGSBY, James	Car	223
GRIMER, William C.	Jsp	391
GRIMES, Charles	Tlb	337
______, Gabriel	Wrn	214
______, Harbert	Wal	131
______, James	Hal	80
______, John	Han	153
______, John	Ran	242
______, Joseph W.	Gre	277
______, Josiah	DeK	58
______, Josiah	Mon	192
______, Morris	Jef	410
______, Peter	Gwn	373
______, Nathan	Twg	75
______, Thomas	Ran	242
______, Thomas W.	Gre	273
______, William	DeK	54
______, William	Em	173
______, William	Jef	411
______, William	Mad	117
______, William R.	Hst	275
GRIMMET/GRIMETT		
Grimmet, Robert	Bts	160
Grimett, Susanah	New	35
GRIMSLEY, Joseph	Ear	96
______, Lewis	Ear	96
______, Littleton	Mwr	158
______, Richard	Ear	95
______, Thomas	Twg	86
______, William	Lin	60
______, William	Twg	86
Grimsley, Zachariah	Lin	64
GRINAGE, Alvin M.	Har	192
GRINDEL/GRINNELL		
Grindel, James	Hab	9
______, John	Hab	40
Grinnell, Peter	Jsp	369
GUGLE/GUGEL		
Gugle, Daniel	Cht	258
______, F. A.	Cht	252
Gugel, David	Eff	104
GRINER/GRINDER/GRINNER		
Griner, Andrew	Eff	104
______, B. W.	Tat	375
______, James	Tms	16
______, John	Bul	102
______, Jonathan	Bul	102
______, Sarah W.	Bul	94
______, William	Scr	309
Grinder, John	Tms	16
Grinner, Emanuel	Lwn	91
GRINSTEAD, Martha	Lau	20
______, William	Pul	144
GRIST, Richard	Ear	97
GRISWOULD/GRISWALD/GRESWOULD		
Griswould, Polly	Gwn	377
______, Samuel	Jns	465
Griswald, Jesse	Car	218
Greswould, James	Gwn	327
GRIZZARD, Susannah	Wrn	226
GRIZZLE/GRIZEL		
Grizzle, Clement	Wrn	197
______, Elizabeth	Wrn	200
______, Lettuce	Wrn	198
______, Stephen	Wrn	201
______, Willie	Wrn	196
Grizel, John	Hab	43
GROCE, Bluford	Pik	107
______, Robert H.	Hry	241
GROGAN, Alfred	Gwn	316
______, Bartlett	DeK	36
______, Hannah	Gwn	34[illegible]
______, Joseph (Thomas written over Joseph; result illegible)	DeK	6[illegible]
______, Richard	DeK	4[illegible]
______, Thomas	DeK	6[illegible]
GROMET, Joseph	Eff	10[illegible]
GROOMS/GROOM		
Grooms, Ben.	Bul	9[illegible]
______, Benjamin	McI	13[illegible]
______, Colson	Bul	9
Groom, Council	Up	12[illegible]

Name	County	Page
Groom, Wiley	Tms	25
GROOVER, Daniel	Frk	234
_____, David	Bul	100
_____, Elias	Eff	114
_____, Enoch	Bul	100
_____, Jacob	Frk	241
_____, James	Hst	267
_____, James	Tms	18
_____, John	Frk	242
_____, John	Tms	18
_____, John	Tms	26
_____, Joshua	Bul	97
_____, Joshua	Eff	115
_____, Milly	Frk	249
_____, Peter	Frk	248
_____, Sarah	Bul	94
_____, Solomon	Tms	26
_____, William	Bul	99
GROSS, Edmund	Scr	309
_____, Elisha	Cow	379
_____, Harriott	Scr	310
_____, John	Scr	309
_____, John	Wks	343
_____, Mund Sr.	Jef	415
_____, Mund Jr.	Jef	417
GROVENSTEIN/GROVENSTINE		
Grovenstein, Henry S.	Eff	104
_____, Mary	Eff	113
Grovenstine, Christopher	Cam	182
GROVES, Mrs.	Scr	316
_____, James A.	Wil	287
_____, Robert	Mad	101
_____, Samuel	Mad	103
GRUBBS/GRUB		
Grubbs, Benjamin	Bib	70
_____, Benjamin	Wal	125
_____, Elisha	Jsp	388
_____, Hiram	Rch	253
_____, James	Bke	127
_____, John	Bke	125
_____, John	Gwn	316
_____, Thomas	Bib	70
_____, Thomas	Har	185
Grub, Silas	Jsp	385
GRUBER, John	Lib	46
GRUDEN, John	DeK	42
GRUINT, James	Trp	47
GRULL/GRUEWELL		
Grull, Joab	Pul	140
Gruewell, Robert T.	Cow	379
GRUMBLES, George	Bke	145
_____, John S.	Bke	144
_____, Levin	Bib	67

Name	County	Page
GUARD, Pleasant	Jsp	398
GUARDEAN, Phelps	Mus	282
GUERINEAU, William K.	Cht	251
GUERRY, Jacob M.	Har	180
_____, James	Hst	268
_____, James P.	Twg	67
_____, Peter V.	Hst	261
_____, Theodore	Hst	290
GUEST/GUESS		
Guest, Colbert	Frk	215
_____, David	Hal	78
_____, Elias B.	Tlf	8
_____, Elizabeth	App	8
_____, John	Frk	226
_____, Nancy	Tfo	361
_____, Sandford	Frk	243
_____, Sarah	Bke	146
Guess, James	DeK	33
_____, Moses	Frk	215
_____, Nathaniel	DeK	56
_____, Sophia	DeK	68
_____, William	Cam	191
_____, William	DeK	69
GUICE/GUISE		
Guice, Briton	Lin	61
_____, John Jr.	Lin	60
_____, John	Lin	63
_____, Joel	Lin	58
_____, Joseph	Wal	128
_____, Nicholas	Lin	60
_____, Peter	Lin	58
_____, William	Lin	63
Guise, Lewis	Tlb	328
_____, Moses S.	Tfo	357
_____, Samuel	Trp	39
_____, Thomas	Tlb	331
GUILDER, Irby	Hst	274
GUILFORD, Coulson	Hst	286
_____, Isaac	Hst	274
_____, John Sr.	Hst	273
_____, John Jr.	Hst	294
GUILL, Augustus	Ogl	92
_____, Buford	Gre	278
GUILMARTIN, John	Cht	257
GUILSON, John B.	Rch	261
GUIMAVIN, John	Rch	265
GULLATT/GULLET		
Gullatt, Charles	Lin	59
_____, Peter	Wil	312
_____, Peter Sr.	Lin	58
_____, William	Lin	59
Gullet, George M.	Mon	216
_____, Jese	Hab	63

Name	County	Page
GULLEDGE, Henry	DeK	65
GULLEY, John	Elb	125
_____, Richard	Elb	126
_____, Thomas	Elb	134
_____, Valentine	Elb	122
_____, William	Elb	126
GULLIVER, Edward	Pik	132
GUMM, Jacob	Bal	38
GUNBY/GUNSBY		
Gunby, George	Col	356
_____, Willam Sr.	Col	356
Gunsby, Mary	Cam	182
GUNN/GUN		
Gunn, Alexander	Pik	129
_____, Daniel	Jns	445
_____, Darcus	Pik	116
_____, David	Bke	144
_____, Eliza	Wrn	225
_____, Gabriel	New	31
_____, Green G.	Jns	439
_____, James	Jef	424
_____, James	Jns	433
_____, Jane	Twg	82
_____, Jesse Jr.	Wal	123
_____, Jesse T.	Bts	159
_____, John	DeK	55
_____, John	Jns	434
_____, Larkin R.	Tfo	357
_____, Moses	Jns	434
_____, Nancy	New	31
_____, Nich. P.	Up	103
_____, Rhadford	DeK	30
_____, Richard Sr.	Tfo	359
_____, Richard Jr.	Tfo	356
_____, Thomas	Jns	439
_____, Thomas G.	Bke	118
_____, William	Bke	144
_____, William	Tfo	359
Gun, Jesse	Mor	242
_____, John	Put	184
GUNNELLS/GUNNELS/GUNNALLS/		
GUNNELL/GUNNEL		
Gunnells, James	Jns	447
_____, Nathan	Frk	230
Gunnels, Augustus	Up	117
_____, Pitman	Mon	172
Gunnalls, Fielding	Wal	150
Gunnell, William	New	13
Gunnel, Stephen	Ogl	76
GUNTER/GUNTON		
Gunter, Allen	Elb	128
_____, Charles	Jks	338
_____, Fair	Mar	142

Name	County	Page
Gunter, Gideon	Jks	340
_____, Isham	Wal	129
_____, James	Wal	128
_____, John	Elb	149
_____, John M.	Hab	29
_____, Joshua	Mar	142
_____, Mary An	Hal	92
_____, Needham	Ware	183
_____, Olive	Crf	403
_____, Richard	Ware	187
_____, William M.	Wal	167
Gunton, Archibald	Eff	110
GUNTES, Rubin	Hab	48
GURLEY/GURLY		
Gurley, Thomas	Wil	294
_____, William	Cpb	207
_____, William	Hry	227
Gurly, John	Hab	53
GUTHERY/GUTHREY/GUTHRY		
GUTHRIE/GUTHREE		
Guthery, Leroy	Hal	85
_____, William	Cow	386
_____, William J.	Cow	376
Guthrey, David	Gwn	377
Guthry, William	Ogl	99
Guthrie, Benjamin	Trp	41
Guthree, Abner	Wrn	220
GUTHUARD, John	Hal	85
GUTTERY/GUTRY/GURTNEY		
Guttery, John	Hal	99
_____, John	Lwn	86
_____, William	New	9
Gutry, Nehemiah	Wal	174
Nurtney, Benjamin	Wal	151
***GUTTS (Indian)	Car	234
GUY, Ann	Cht	278
_____, Elizabeth	Rch	281
_____, Hillery	Col	349
_____, James	Col	349
_____, John G.	Col	350
_____, Lemuel	Tlb	335
_____, Mallachi	Col	349
_____, William	Col	349
GUYTON/GUITON		
Guyton, C. S. L. M.	Lau	4
_____, Joseph	Hal	90
Guiton, Joseph	Dec	19
GWINETT, Seaborn	Jsp	382
GWINN/GWYNN/GWIN		
Gwinn, Humphry	Wal	154
_____, Richard R.	Wal	153
_____, Seaborn	Wal	154
Gwynn, Dolley	Jsp	358

Name	County	Page
Gwynn, James	Jsp	353
_____, Minor	New	29
_____, Richard	New	29
Gwin, Ezekiel Ga.	Hst	269
_____, James	Doo	79
_____, John B. (slave)	Rch	277
_____, Mary	Put	189
HAASS, Henry	Lau	15
HABERSHAM, Harriet	Cht	246
_____, J. C.	Cht	249
_____, Jos.	Cht	264
_____, R.	Cht	264
_____, R. W.	Cht	265
_____, Sally	Cht	246
HACKETT/HOKETT/HOKIT		
Hackett, Olley	Hal	122
_____, Olliver	DeK	36
_____, Robert	Frk	254
_____, William	Frk	254
Hokett, Seriny	Jns	456
Hokit, Edmund	Bib	58
HACKNEY/HACKEY		
Hackney, Daniel	Wil	316
_____, James T.	Wil	301
_____, John	Gre	287
_____, Joseph P.	Tfo	364
_____, Richard	Fay	183
_____, Robert	Wil	301
_____, Sarah	Jsp	366
Hackey, Daniel	Wil	301
HADDAH, Nehemiah	Gwn	349
HADDEN/HADEN/HADON/HADDON		
Hadden, Benjamin	Jef	422
_____, Mary	Jef	410
_____, Samuel	Jef	421
_____, Thos.	Wrn	225
_____, William	Jef	420
Haden, Tunnel	Wks	350
Hadon, William	Ran	241
Haddon, Admiral	Jns	472
HADDAWAY, David	Jns	433
_____, James	Tfo	364
_____, John	Jns	434
HADDOCK, William	Hst	273
HADLEY/HEADY		
Hadley, Henry	Mus	284
_____, Simon	Tms	19
_____, Simon D.	Tms	24
_____, Simon P.	Tms	20
_____, Thomas	Har	188
Heady, George	Rab	233
HAGIN/HAGAN/HAGANS/HAGINS/ HAGEN		
Hagin, Absalom	Bul	94
_____, C. D.	App	6
_____, Edward	DeK	25
_____, James	Bul	94
_____, Jephtha	Bul	95
_____, Jesse	Bul	93
_____, Joseph	Bul	95
_____, Margaret	Bul	95
_____, Solomon	Bul	101
Hagan, Daniel	Cow	371
_____, Edward	Cpb	195
_____, Henry	App	8
_____, Hiram	Hst	286
_____, Isam	Mtg	235
_____, John	App	8
_____, John	App	10
_____, John	Put	196
_____, Stephen	Dec	7
Hagans, James	Dec	6
Hagins, Lucinda	Frk	244
Hagen, David	App	8
_____, Frances	App	8
HAGERMON, Harrison W.	Lin	73
HAGGARD/HAGWOOD		
Haggard, French	Jks	312
Hagwood, James	Wrn	220
HAGGER/HAGGIE/HEGGIE		
Hagger, John	Twg	65
Haggie, Thomas	Tlb	324
Heggie, Arch		
HAGLER/HAIGLER		
Hagler, Jacob	HRY	@@(
_____, Paul	Cpb	210
Haigler, Abraham	Trp	33
HAGUE/HAGUES		
Hague, Hiram	Rch	285
Hagues, Dr.	Cht	281
HAIR/HARE/HEIRS		
Hair, Carity	Lau	17
_____, Edmund	Bak	19
_____, Edmund	Dec	19
_____, Elija	Dec	18
_____, Joel	Lau	16
_____, John	Twg	85
_____, Thomas C.	Dec	19
_____, William	Dec	19
Hare, Mary	Wks	341
_____, William	Mar	139
Heirs, Moses	DeK	45
HAISTEN/HAIRSTON		

Name	County	Page
Haisten, Daniel E.	Fay	197
_____, James E.	Fay	186
_____, John	Fay	197
_____, John Jr.	Fay	193
_____, William	Fay	198
Hairston, James B.	DeK	46
_____, John	Up	116
_____, L. P.	DeK	61
_____, Sally	Jsp	368
_____, Thomas	Gwn	359
_____, Thomas	Jsp	360
_____, William	DeK	57
HALE/HAIL/HALES/HAILES		
HAILS/HAYLE/HAYLES		
Hale, Adam	Gwn	366
_____, Davis	Crf	409
_____, Edward	Car	214
_____, Elephalet	Wrn	192
_____, Elizabeth	Ogl	99
_____, Elizabeth	Wal	166
_____, John	Ogl	101
_____, John	Wal	153
_____, John H.	Cht	243
_____, Jonas	Wal	148
_____, Nancy	Put	197
_____, Nathaniel	Put	194
** _____, S. (slave)	Rch	276
_____, Samuel	Rch	256
** _____, Samuel (slave)	Rch	272
_____, Samuel	Rch	274
** _____, Samuel (slave)	Rch	274
_____, Samuel	Rch	285
_____, Samuel	Wal	154
_____, Tharpe	Bke	127
_____, Thomas	New	52
_____, Thompson	Gwn	343
_____, Thomas	Jns	469
_____, Thomas	Ogl	84
_____, William	Hst	263
Hail, Silas	Mor	265
Hales, Allen J.	Wal	166
_____, Andrew	New	33
_____, James	Hry	246
_____, John	New	33
_____, Salathiel M.	Tlb	325
_____, Samuel	Ogl	94
_____, William	Jks	346
_____, William	New	52
_____, William G.	Tlb	326
Hailes, Wiley	Clk	320
Hails, Joseph	Mar	143
_____, Mary	Mad	116
Hayle, James	Gwn	337

Name	County	Page
Hayles, Mary A.	Jef	4
HALEY/HALLEY/HALLY/HAILEY		
Haley, Ambrose	Hry	2
_____, Ambrose	Hry	2
_____, James	Frk	2
_____, James R.	Frk	2
_____, Joel	Frk	2
_____, John	Elb	1
_____, Luday	Frk	2
_____, William	Elb	1
_____, William	Elb	1
Halley, Samuel	Tlb	3
Hally, Nathaniel	Tlb	3
Hailey, James	Up	1
_____, John	Up	1
HALK, Thompson	New	
HALL/HAWL/HAUL		
Hall, Alex[r].	Mwr	1
_____, Benjamin	Bal	
_____, Benjamin	Rch	2
_____, Benjamin	Wks	3
_____, Benjamin B.	DeK	
_____, Caleb	Gwn	3
_____, Catharine	Elb	1
_____, Charles	Rch	2
_____, Cherry	Bry	
_____, Dancil	Rch	2
_____, Daniel	Mon	1
_____, Daniel Sr.	Wks	3
_____, Daniel M.	Wks	3
_____, David	Bke	1
_____, David	Cam	1
_____, David	Ogl	1
_____, David W.	Han	1
_____, Dempsey	Doo	
_____, Drusilla	Bke	1
_____, Edwin	Bke	1
_____, Eli	Bke	1
_____, Elihu	Gre	2
_____, Elisha	Wks	3
_____, Elijah	Irw	2
_____, Elizabeth	Col	3
_____, Erich	Hab	
_____, F. P.	App	
_____, Fenton	Cow	3
_____, Fewtral	Put	1
_____, Frank	Irw	2
_____, Geneper	Em	1
_____, George	DeK	
_____, George	Gre	2
_____, George W.	Hab	
_____, Hampton	Irw	2
_____, Hardy	Tlf	

Name	County	Page
Hall, Harvey	Mus	279
______, Henry	Mon	225
______, Henry H.	Bke	127
______, Henry T.	McI	121
______, Hiram	Bib	67
______, Hiram	Cpb	201
______, Hosia	Clk	299
______, Hugh	Gre	275
______, Ignatious	Tms	22
______, Instance	App	10
______, Instant	Lau	18
______, Irwin	Bke	127
______, Isaac	Mwr	169
______, Isaac	Wks	356
______, Isac P.	Pik	123
______, Isham	Hal	122
______, Jacob	Rch	279
______, James	Doo	88
______, James	Gwn	322
______, James	Han	156
______, James	Irw	298
______, James	Lau	18
______, James	Tms	20
______, James	Wil	289
______, James	Wks	334
______, James	Wrn	228
______, James A.	Bal	33
______, Joel	Clk	300
______, Joel	Wrn	227
______, John	App	8
______, John	Bib	70
______, John	Clk	300
______, John	Elb	141
______, John	Gly	264
______, John	Gre	274
______, John	Han	156
______, John	Hst	286
______, John	Jns	441
______, John	Lwn	81
______, John	Mad	118
______, John	Mon	225
______, John	Put	183
______, John	Tms	16
______, John	Wks	354
______, John C.	Gre	274
______, John C.	Tms	21
______, John D.	Fay	199
______, John W.	Up	97
______, Jonas	Clk	302
______, Jonathan	Har	180
______, Jonathan	Lau	4
______, Joseph	DeK	57
______, Joshua	Bke	146
Hall, Jourdan	Tms	22
______, Kindred	Tms	21
______, Lewis	Lee	35
______, Lacky	Jef	407
______, Leroy	Jns	431
______, Lewis	Tlf	3
______, Littleton G.	Lau	15
______, Luke	Mar	137
______, Martin	Han	156
______, Mathew	Clk	320
______, Noah	Clk	314
______, Morgan	Hst	289
______, Nancey	Mad	118
______, Nath[l].	Gwn	333
______, Obed.	Clk	320
______, Philo	Gwn	351
______, Red	Jef	407
______, Richard H.	Jns	465
______, Robert	Trp	32
______, Robert A.	Wal	125
______, Sally	Hry	229
______, Samuel	Gre	293
______, Samuel	Mon	176
______, Samuel	Wrn	227
______, Sarah	Cht	248
______, Sarah	Put	177
______, Sebon	App	10
______, Seon	Lwn	81
______, Toliafaro	Elb	133
______, Thomas	Elb	160
______, Thomas	Har	185
______, Thomas	Jef	412
______, Thomas	Ogl	101
______, Thomas	Tat	377
______, Thomas	Tms	21
______, Thomas G.	Rch	277
______, Thomas H.	Bal	39
______, Thomas L.	Tms	29
______, Unity	Hal	125
______, Uriah	Jks	325
______, Waid H.	Mar	143
______, Wiley	Mon	213
______, William	Em	164
______, William	Frk	250
______, William	Gwn	331
______, William	Hry	212
______, William	Irw	298
______, William	Jks	328
______, William	Jef	407
______, William	Jks	338
______, William	Jks	348
______, William	Lee	28
______, William	Mad	101

Name	County	Page
Hall, William	Tlb	329
______, William	Wsh	261
______, William A.	Wks	356
______, William G.	Pik	107
______, William K.	Pul	138
______, William Sr.	Wks	357
______, Zachariah	Put	203
Hawl, Nath[l].	Gwn	329
Haul, Amerger	Bak	20
______, Burrel	Bak	18
______, Daniel	Bak	20
HALLOW, James	Jks	346
HALLYBURTON, David	Hst	290
HALMARK/HOLMARK		
Halmark, David	Har	178
Holmark, George	Har	182
______, John	Har	182
HALSEY/HOLSEY/HOLSAY/		
HOLSY: also see Hulsey		
Halsey, Benjamin L.	Mon	193
______, Charles Sr.	Car	230
______, Gideon	Han	156
______, Susannah	Han	156
Holsey, Hopkins	Put	210
______, Martha	Pik	120
Holsay, James	Pik	122
Holsy, Nice	Scr	303
HALSTEAD, William C.	Twg	61
HALM, Jeremiah	Har	175
HAM, Aaron	Em	169
______, Elizabeth	Elb	133
______, Ezekiel	Rab	227
______, Ichabod	Twg	79
______, James	Elb	151
______, Jesse Sr.	Lib	47
______, Jesse J.	Lib	47
______, John	Mon	217
______, John	Twg	85
______, John V.	Lib	47
______, Levi	Twg	76
______, Littleton	Twg	85
______, Moses	Bry	85
______, Owin	Tms	23
______, Samuel	Hal	78
______, Samuel	Ogl	62
______, Smith	Crf	400
______, Stephen	Elb	124
______, William	McI	131
______, William	Mon	217
______, William	Twg	63
______, Williams	Hst	290
HAMBER, William	Hab	53
HAMBLETON, Erwin	Lee	33
Hambleton, Robert	Elb	154
______, William	Bts	164
HAMBRICK/HAMBRIC/HAMRICK/		
HEMBRICK/HUMBRICK		
Hambrick, Benjamin	Up	113
______, Briant	DeK	54
______, Hiram J.	Twg	79
______, James	Jks	340
______, James	New	16
______, John	DeK	62
______, John	Hry	220
______, John	Up	119
______, Joseph	DeK	54
______, Peter	Lin	73
______, Reuben	Wil	306
______, Robert S.	New	16
______, Thomas	Hry	226
______, William	Hab	13
______, William Sr.	Hab	17
Hambric, Clarissa	Pik	133
______, Hannah	Jns	461
Hamrick, Harrison	Mwr	169
______, Moses	Wil	304
Hembrick, Thompson	Hal	97
Humbrick, Andrew	Cpb	206
HAMBRIGHT, Lawson	Hab	29
HAMBY, Easther	New	37
______, Edmond	Trp	42
______, Edom	Hab	7
______, Esther	New	6
______, Frances	Frk	253
______, Henry	Car	228
______, Isaac	New	6
______, Jesse	Mor	254
______, John	Gwn	374
______, Lemuel	New	37
______, Micager	Hal	102
______, Rachiel	New	39
______, Samuel	Gwn	374
______, Samuel	Gwn	375
______, Sol.	Gwn	379
______, Thomas	New	39
______, William	Rab	228
HAMET/HAMIT/HAMAT/HAMMET		
HAMMETT/HAMMIT		
Hamet, Davis	Gwn	379
Hamit, James	Gwn	378
______, John	Gwn	378
Hamat, James	Car	218
Hammet, Thomas	Wrn	222
Hammett, William	Wil	315
Hammit, John	Wrn	225
HAMIL/HAMILL/HAMMILL/		

Name	County	Page
HAMELL/HAMMELL		
Hamil, Bryant V.	Bts	160
______, Clark	Bts	169
______, Hugh	Bts	172
______, William S.	Han	155
Hamill, George W.	Up	116
Hammill, John	Up	109
Hammel, George W.	Pik	129
______, James	DeK	31
______, James	Tlb	328
______, Simeon	Pik	129
Hamell, Patsey	Jns	461
HAMILTON/HAMMILTON		
Hamilton, Abegail	Gwn	354
______, Adin	Crf	393
______, Arch^{d}.	Gwn	332
______, Arc^{d}.	Gwn	352
______, Cader	New	26
______, Clarecy	Mtg	235
______, Cogdale	Jns	446
______, Daniel	Wrn	211
______, David	McI	128
______, David	Pik	109
______, Duncan	Wsh	266
______, Duke	Han	156
______, E.	Bal	36
______, Eleazer	Wal	124
______, George	Han	155
______, George K.	New	26
______, George W.	Wil	311
______, J. W.	Jns	451
______, James	Clk	297
______, James B.	Crf	402
______, James F.	Col	364
______, James; Estate of	Gly	264
______, John	Crf	412
______, John	Frk	243
______, John	Frk	257
______, John	Gwn	352
______, John	Hal	130
______, John	Jsp	366
______, John	Tms	23
______, John	Wal	153
______, John L.	Car	220
______, John L.	Gwn	370
______, Joseph	Gwn	357
______, Joseph W.	Hal	79
______, Josiah	Mtg	232
______, Mary	Wrn	211
______, Mary	Clk	311
______, Mary H.	Frk	222
______, Patience	Han	156
______, Reece	Ogl	73
Hamilton, Reubin	Clk	307
______, Robert	Gwn	353
______, Robert	Hal	114
______, Robert	Mon	216
______, Samuel	Cow	368
______, Samuel	Wsh	269
______, Simpson	Hal	130
______, Thomas A.	Jns	465
______, Thomas N.	Col	360
______, William	Gwn	308
______, William	Hab	18
______, William	Pul	151
______, William	Twg	62
______, William A.	Gwn	319
______, Zachariah K.	Crf	398
Hammilton, Mary	DeK	69
______, Moses	DeK	34
HAMLET/HAMBLET		
Hamlet, James	Mor	248
______, Richard	Mon	211
______, Robert	Clk	317
______, William	Bts	171
______, William	Wal	144
Hamblet, Sarah	Trp	54
______, William	Bib	59
HAMLIN/HAMBLIN		
Hamlin, Jethro	Mwr	168
______, John	Mon	190
______, Leonard	Mon	191
______, Robert	New	5
Hamblin, Thomas	Bib	61
HAMMETT, James	Frk	230
HAMMOCK/HAMMUC/HAMMAC/ HAMOCK/HAMACK/HAMMACK		
Hammock, Abel	Fay	206
______, Benjn.	Jsp	381
______, Benjamin	Wal	125
______, Charles	Hst	274
______, David	Wil	305
______, Edna	Hry	223
______, Emanuel	Tat	376
______, Harrison	Mar	139
______, Jackson	Doo	88
______, James	Bib	61
______, James	Twg	73
______, James L.	Wil	313
______, Jerimiah	Bib	50
______, Jesse	New	41
______, John	New	17
______, John B.	Lin	75
______, John M.	Jns	451
______, John M.	New	27
______, Johnston	Bib	50

Name	County	Page
Hammock, Johnston	Bib	55
______, Joshan	New	42
______, Joshua	New	17
______, Lewis	Bib	70
______, Lewis	Jns	451
______, Lewis M.	Jns	451
______, Mansil W.	Han	155
______, Marguritt	Wil	315
______, Paschal	Twg	68
______, Seaborn	Wil	313
______, Simeon	Crf	410
______, Stephen	New	16
______, Thomas	Doo	82
______, Thomas	Fay	199
______, William	Wrn	217
Hammuc, Jackson	Tlb	336
______, William B.	Tlb	334
Hammac, John	Tlb	335
Hamock, Elijah	Wks	357
______, Talbot D.	Crf	410
______, Willbourn	Crf	410
Hamack, Aaron	Cow	381
______, John	Tfo	355
______, Robert	Rfo	360
Hammack, John P.	Jns	428
______, John Sr.	Lin	74
______, Lewis W.	Jns	428
______, Thomas	Lin	74
HAMMOND/HAMMONDS/HAMMON/ HAMMONS/HAMONS/HAMANS		
Hammond, Abraham	Wil	311
______, Charles	Bts	171
______, Charles	Col	334
______, Daniel	Hal	77
______, Elijah	Cpb	194
______, Elijah	Gwn	369
______, Eliza	Hst	296
______, George	DeK	26
______, Jacob Sr.	Lin	59
______, Jacob Jr.	Lin	58
______, John	Frk	210
______, John	Hal	79
______, Johnathan	Lin	59
______, Leroy	Car	230
______, Mark	Hal	91
______, Reddick	Rch	258
______, Robert	Gre	303
______, S.	Bal	30
______, Samuel	Jks	337
______, Sarah	Rch	288
______, William	Gre	291
______, William	Frk	211
______, William	Rch	272

Name	County	Page
Hammond, William	Hal	78
______, William C.	Hal	91
Hammonds, Thomas	Mor	241
______, Thomas	Mor	241
Hammon, Charles	Ogl	63
______, Isaac	Pik	109
______, William	Ogl	63
Hammons, Alfred	Elb	125
______, Rolly	Ogl	78
Hamons, Henry	Lwn	79
______, Isham	Jns	441
Hamans, James	Irw	303
HAMNER/HAMER/HAMMER		
Hamner, Sarah	Put	194
______, Samuel	Wal	139
Hamer, Henry C.	Put	185
Hammer, Cynthia Y.	Crf	401
HAMPTON, Andrew	Lau	16
______, Andrew Y.	Lau	11
______, Benjamin J.	Trp	54
______, Benjamin W.	Lau	12
______, David H.	Mad	99
______, E. F.	Col	362
______, George	Mad	100
______, Hubbard	Mad	100
______, James	Bke	129
______, James	Jks	312
______, John	Crf	405
______, John	Hal	83
______, John	Jks	334
______, John	Trp	54
______, John M.	Lau	10
______, Joseph	Jks	311
______, Joseph	Jks	341
______, Reason	Mtg	235
______, Robert B.	Jks	326
______, Sally	Bke	129
______, Simeon	Bke	130
______, Thomas	Hab	21
______, Thomas	Trp	54
______, W.	Bal	42
______, Wade M.	Jks	334
HANAGAN, James	Hry	220
HANAM, --- (blank)	Cht	281
HANCOCK/HANDCOCK		
Hancock, Armstead	Put	214
______, Bennett	Tlb	327
______, Clement	Crf	407
______, Clement	Put	206
______, Enoch	Crf	407
______, H. W.	Tat	377
______, Henry	Put	174
______, Isaac	Hab	45

Name	County	Page
Hancock, Isham	Hab	37
______, Isom	Mwr	151
______, J. L.	Up	119
______, James	Tat	375
______, James	Up	113
______, Jane	Jks	348
______, James	Fay	182
______, Jesse	Bib	70
______, Joel	Mwr	158
______, Joel	Ogl	63
______, Joel	Up	118
______, John	Crf	396
______, John	Tms	25
______, John	Wrn	229
______, Joseph	Bke	142
______, Joseph	Hst	287
______, Leonard G.	Frk	227
______, Mary	Hab	33
______, Nancy	Mwr	169
______, Nero (colored)	Bke	140
______, Pleasant G.	Mwr	161
______, Rhoda	Ogl	81
______, Samuel	Clk	306
______, Shadrack	Tat	375
______, Thomas	Clk	310
______, Thomas	Wal	174
______, William	Hab	43
______, William	Jks	343
______, William	Jsp	366
______, William	Lwn	90
______, William	Tms	19
Handcock, Alfred	Wal	132
______, Cader	Lwn	91
______, Durham	Lwn	91
______, Herod	Wal	135
______, Jeremiah	Lwn	91
______, Jo	Wks	336
______, Joseph	Pik	107
______, Larkin	Pik	106
______, Richardson	Mad	98
______, Richardson	Mad	116
______, William	Wks	332
______, Willis	Pik	107
HAND, Bayard E.	McI	121
______, Edmund	Hry	207
______, Henry	Bal	37
______, Henry	Col	354
______, Henry H.	Hst	292
______, Isaac Jr.	Hry	243
______, Isiah	Hry	205
______, James	Hry	243
______, John	Bke	147
______, John	Car	226

Name	County	Page
Hand, John C.	Hry	205
______, Joseph	Hry	215
______, Joseph	Tlb	338
______, Lewis	Hry	204
______, Lucy	New	45
______, Mary	Ogl	95
______, Reubins	Hry	248
______, Simeon	Hry	205
______, Thomas	Col	354
______, Thomas J.	New	14
______, William	App	8
______, William	Hry	236
______, William	Col	356
______, Willis	Hry	207
HANDBY, Jarrett	Fay	183
HANDLEY/HANDLY/HANLEY		
Handley, Drewry P.B	Mad	112
Handly, James M.	Dec	13
Hanley, James N.	Cow	375
HANES/HANE/HAINES/HAINS/ HAYNES/HYNES/HAYNS/HAYNE/ HAMES		
Hanes, Edward	Hab	58
______, Henry	Hab	59
______, Irwin	Cow	369
______, Johnson	Hab	58
______, Permenus	Wal	143
______, Ransome	Wal	154
______, Reuben	Wal	123
______, William	Hab	58
Hane, John	Hab	58
Haines, David	Fay	192
______, Elijah	Fay	192
______, James	Fay	192
______, James Sr.	Fay	189
______, Joshua	Fay	192
Hains, Mathew	Mor	272
Haynes, Abram	Gre	278
______, Anthony	Col	342
______, Bythal	Wsh	253
______, Charles	Hal	122
______, Daniel	Pik	132
______, Elijah	Cow	380
______, Emerlia	Wsh	259
______, Ephraim	Car	220
______, Ezekeal	Pik	131
______, Frances	Col	345
______, Francis	Hal	96
______, Green B.	Wal	142
______, Harper	Hab	18
______, Henry	Hry	248
______, James	Elb	143
______, John	Gre	278

Name	County	Page
Haynes, John	Jks	341
______, John	Rch	270
______, John	Tlb	342
______, John	Wal	142
______, Jonathan	Car	214
______, Louisa	Wil	293
______, Martha	Mon	195
______, Mary	Elb	128
______, Moses	Elb	143
______, Nancy	Jsp	366
______, Nathan	Wsh	264
______, Parminas	Clk	295
______, Parmenins	Hry	248
______, Reuben S.	Elb	155
______, Richard	Lin	69
______, Richard	New	35
______, Robert B.	Cpb	208
______, Samuel	Tlb	342
______, Sarah	Elb	139
______, Smith	Tlb	339
______, Thomas	Elb	124
______, Thomas	Han	155
______, William	Elb	129
______, William D.	Elb	134
______, William P.	Wsh	239
Hynes, Churchwell	Wsh	253
______, G. W.	Wsh	251
Hayns, Lucy H.	Ogl	88
______, Robert	Ogl	88
______, William	Cow	383
Hayne, William	Bts	167
Hames, Joshua	Jsp	364
______, William	Gre	288
HANEY/HAINEY/HAYNIE/		
HAYNEY/HANNY		
Haney, Briggair	Cow	372
______, John	Jns	465
______, John	New	47
______, John	Tms	20
______, Joseph	Jks	320
______, Wilkens	Jks	343
______, William	Frk	235
______, William	Frk	254
Hainey, John	Gwn	312
______, John B.	Gwn	342
______, Jos.	Gwn	359
______, Jos^{h}.	Gwn	342
______, Peter	Jks	334
______, Tabitha	Mor	260
______, Thomas	Gwn	337
______, Thomas	Mad	104
Haynie, Francis	Up	102
______, James	Clk	297
Haynie, James D.	Rch	282
______, Warrington	Rch	287
Hayney, Charles	Ogl	80
______, Isaac B.	Gwn	342
Hanny, Mary	Cam	182
HANKINS, Martha	Pul	156
HANKS, John	Gwn	358
______, John	Hst	290
______, Thomas	Gwn	358
______, Thomas	Hst	295
HANNAH/HANNA/HANAH/HANDA		
Hannah, Alexander	Car	217
______, Margarett	Wal	170
______, Thomas	DeK	34
______, Thomas	Jef	420
______, William	Gwn	331
______, William	Gwn	348
Hanna, Eleanor	Mad	118
______, James	Mad	102
Hanah, Ham	Gwn	370
Handa, Nathanel	Hab	61
HANNON/HANION		
Hannon, George W.	Cpb	205
______, Henry	Wrn	206
______, John	Crf	395
______, Samuel	Wrn	205
Hanion, John	Lee	32
HANSARD, Jessey B.	Hab	8
______, John	Elb	152
______, Joseph	Hab	8
______, Thomas S.	Elb	132
HANSEL/HANSELL		
Hansel, Elija	Dec	17
Hansell, W. G.	Bal	33
HANSFORD/HENSFORD		
Hansford, Chs. P.	Up	119
______, George W.	Mon	215
______, John M.	Jsp	358
______, Sarah	Elb	148
______, Stephen	Mor	256
Hensford, Joseph	Hab	5[illegible]
HANSLEY, John	Elb	158
______, Reuben	Elb	15[illegible]
HANSON/HAMSON		
Also see Henson		
Hanson, Elizabeth	Wil	32[illegible]
______, Enoch	Mon	21[illegible]
______, George W.	Cow	38[illegible]
______, George W.	New	4[illegible]
______, H. E.	Col	33[illegible]
______, James	DeK	5[illegible]
______, James	Car	21[illegible]
______, James J.	New	4[illegible]

Name	County	Page
Hanson, Jesse	Fay	204
_____, Jesse	Mor	272
_____, John	Hal	117
_____, John	Mor	253
_____, John C.	Mor	252
_____, John M.	Wil	307
_____, Newton	Ogl	95
_____, Micheal	Wsh	255
_____, Reubin	Cow	381
_____, Richard T.	Ogl	99
_____, Richard W.	Mor	252
_____, Thomas	Cow	381
_____, Thomas	Fay	202
_____, Thomas	New	30
_____, Thomas	New	211
_____, Thomas V.	Cow	384
_____, William	Fay	202
_____, William	Mor	252
_____, William	Car	215
Hamson, Susan	Gly	265
HARALSON/HARALDSOM/		
HARRALSON/HARRELSON/		
HARILSON/HARRILSON		
Haralson, David	Trp	53
_____, Eli E.	Trp	43
_____, Elijah	Trp	41
_____, Henry	Wal	131
_____, Jugh A.	Trp	34
_____, Isaac	Trp	43
_____, Jesse	New	21
_____, Jesse B.	Trp	55
_____, Moses	Trp	40
_____, Vincent	Wal	128
Haraldsom, Herndon	Gre	282
_____, Jonathan	Gre	285
Harralson, Bradley	Mor	257
Harrelson, Rheubin	Mtg	231
Harilson, William	Lau	16
Harrilson, Hyram	Mor	261
_____, John	Hab	60
HARBERSON, John	New	47
HARBIN/HARBEN		
Harbin, Jesse	Hal	93
_____, John	Elb	120
_____, Nathanel	Hab	47
_____, Nathaniel	Hal	108
_____, Nathaniel	Jks	340
_____, Sarah	Elb	120
_____, Wiley	Hal	73
Herben, William	DeK	56
HARBOUR, Elizabeth	Frk	246
_____, Esaias	Frk	213
_____, John	Frk	231

Name	County	Page
HARBUCK, Barbary	Wrn	193
_____, Henry	Wal	168
_____, Jacob	Wrn	216
_____, James	Wrn	193
_____, John	Pik	126
_____, Mary	Wrn	193
HARCROW, Hugh Sr.	Elb	159
_____, Hugh Jr.	Elb	159
_____, James	Car	215
_____, Samuel	Car	225
HARDAGE/HARDANGE		
Hardage, Adam	Up	118
_____, James D.	Hal	96
_____, Joseph D.	Hal	97
Hardange, John T.	Hal	73
HARDAWAY/HARDEWAY		
Hardaway, Answorth	Mon	202
_____, Conner	Mon	204
_____, Fr[s].	Wrn	219
_____, Grief	Hry	217
_____, Robert	Mor	245
_____, Steth	Wrn	209
_____, Thomas C	Mwr	154
_____, Washing	Wrn	215
Hardeway, James C.	Bib	55
HARDCASTLE, John	Wrn	211
HARDEGREE, John	Clk	304
_____, Jonathan	Clk	305
_____, Pleasant	Clk	305
_____, William	Clk	303
HARDIMAN/HARDEMAN/HARDAMAN		
HARDIMON		
Hardiman, Felix	Jsp	386
_____, Frederick	Crf	403
_____, John	DeK	64
_____, Naman	DeK	28
_____, Robert V.	Jns	465
_____, William	DeK	63
Hardeman, Ann	Ogl	80
_____, Charles	Ogl	81
_____, John	Ogl	98
_____, Thomas	Put	217
_____, Ziller	Ogl	83
Hardaman, Uriah	Hry	246
Hardimon, Albert	Ogl	75
_____, Benjamin F.	Ogl	97
_____, Joseph	Twg	67
_____, Samuel	Ogl	75
HARDIN/HARDEN/HEARDIN		
Hardin, Adam	Mon	204
_____, Adam	Trp	32
_____, Ann B.	Hal	116
_____, Arabellah	Ogl	83

Name	County	Page
Hardin, Benjamin	Col	361
______, Benjamin	Wal	133
______, Benjamin	Wal	152
______, Benjamin Jr.	Col	362
______, Edward	Clk	302
______, Eda	Frk	256
______, Edward J.	Rch	268
______, Felix	DeK	66
______, Henry	Bts	177
______, Henry	Frk	238
______, Henry	Wal	124
______, Hudson	Ran	246
______, Isaac B.	Bke	153
______, Isaiah	Tat	377
______, James	Mon	204
______, John	Col	363
______, John	Trp	32
______, John	Twg	65
______, John	Wks	342
______, John T.	Wsh	276
______, Martin	Dec	18
______, Richard	Frk	238
______, Robert R.	Clk	322
______, Thomas	Hry	235
______, W. W.	Col	353
______, William	Hry	208
______, William	Wal	157
______, William C.	Trp	54
Harden, Adam	Put	177
______, Charles E.	Bry	84
______, Edward	Jsp	392
______, Henry	Gre	304
______, Jacob	Mon	186
______, James	Jks	338
______, James	Pik	130
______, James	Wrn	207
______, James M.	Jks	335
______, Joel	Mon	217
______, John	Hry	249
______, John	Wsh	249
______, Joseph E.	Lau	8
______, Levi	Tlb	337
______, Martin	Em	171
______, Mrs. Matilda	Bry	85
______, Milly	DeK	66
______, Thomas	Cht	242
______, Thomas	Col	338
______, William R.	Han	156
Heardin, Josiah	Wal	153
HARDISON/HARDESON		
Hardison, H.	Wks	342
______, William	Tlb	336
Hardeson, William L.	Wsh	248

Name	County	Page
HARDMAN, Allen	DeK	28
______, Isaiah	Bts	158
______, Joel	Elb	140
______, John	Mor	262
______, Robert T.	Ogl	62
HARDWICK/HEARDWICK/HARTWICK		
Hardwick, Andrew	Bke	152
______, Frizel M.	Mor	254
______, George W.	Col	336
______, James J.	Han	157
______, Judith	Jsp	396
______, Richard S.	Han	155
______, Thomas	Doo	84
______, William	Col	340
______, William P.	Wsh	248
______, William T.	Mor	244
Heardwick, David	Wal	135
Hartwick, Hezel	Mon	228
______, James	Mon	228
HARDY/HARDEE/HARDEY/ HARDIE/HARTY		
Hardy, Aaron	Lin	62
______, Allen	Wks	340
______, Arthur	Doo	87
______, Aquilla	Cow	388
______, Charles H.	Jks	324
______, Cornelius	Jsp	391
______, Harvy	Lin	61
______, Henry	Frk	238
______, James	Mwr	165
______, James	Trp	37
______, Joel	Wil	301
______, John	Jsp	379
______, John	Jns	457
______, John	Lin	66
______, John	Put	189
______, John C.	Lin	67
______, John Jr.	Lin	66
______, Lewis	Jks	312
______, Mary	Elb	149
______, P.	Cht	265
______, Preston	Jks	327
______, Robert	Twg	79
______, Susanah	Jsp	392
______, Sutton	Up	116
______, Thomas	Trp	55
______, Whitmill	Bib	73
______, William	Pik	126
______, William W.	Mon	226
Hardee, John	Cam	191
______, Jo. D.	Cam	190
______, Noble A.	Cam	185
______, Thomas	Wsh	266

Hardee, Thomas E. Cam 192
Hardey, Josiah Bts 163
Hardie, Martin L. Bib 76
_____, Robert Bak 16
Harty, Patrick Wrn 199
HARDWAYS, R. S. Mor 245
HARGAS, Philip Ran 241
HARGROVES/HARGROVE/
HARGRAVES/HAIRGROVE/
HAIRGROVES
Hargroves, Charles Ogl 66
_____, Hardy Hst 271
_____, Harmon Hst 289
_____, James Jks 336
_____, John R. Mor 264
_____, Joseph; dec'd.Est Lib 47
_____, Kinchen New 18
_____, Olive Rch 262
_____, Richard Ogl 66
_____, Samuel P. New 54
_____, Wiley Rch 276
_____, Zachariah B. New 14
Hargrove, Elvy Em 164
_____, Henry Bke 135
_____, Howell Bke 153
_____, Jacob Bke 135
Hargraves, Abraham Ware 183
_____, Benjamin Put 180
_____, George Wrn 194
_____, John Ware 183
_____, Lemuel App 11
_____, Thomas Ware 183
Hairgrove, William Trp 37
Hairgroves, John Dec 19
HARGUE, John M. Gre 291
HARKINS, John Hab 19
_____, John Fay 200
_____, Joseph T. Car 225
_____, Robert Cow 379
_____, Roger Mon 223
_____, William Cow 378
_____, William Jns 446
_____, William S. Crf 396
HARKNESS, Darcas P. Gwn 348
_____, George S. Mon 206
_____, James Bts 164
_____, Josiah Bts 176
_____, Robert W. Bts 163
HARLEY, Elizabeth Wil 309
HARLIN, James DeK 38
_____, Samuel Jks 318
_____, Valentine Jks 318
HARLOW, James Mon 184
Harlow, Mary Mon 184
_____, Southworth Bke 153
HARMON/HARMAN
Harmon, A. Cht 283
_____, Abram Lib 56
_____, Bartholomew Jns 435
_____, Frederic C. Wil 319
_____, H. M. Har 178
_____, Jacob New 15
_____, John Elb 160
_____, Merryman Mwr 163
_____, William Bts 164
_____, Wilson Mor 255
Harman, Isaac Rch 279
_____, William Jef 405
_____, William M. Mon 173
_____, Zach. Mon 227
HARN, John Bry 87
** _____, William (slave) Rch 269
HARNAGE/HARNEDGE
Harnage, Ambrose Gwn 374
_____, Isaac Lib 47
_____, Jacob Lib 47
_____, Jane Gwn 375
Harnedge, George Dec 6
HARNESBERGER/HEARNSBERGER
Harnesberger, Adam Lin 58
Hearnsberger, Stephen Z. Trp 46
HARNY, Isaac Jns 459
HARP, Collen Cow 388
_____, Dickson Up 106
_____, Edward Hry 208
_____, Green P. Crf 396
_____, James Cow 383
_____, James Lau 8
_____, John Hry 204
_____, Joseph Mwr 161
_____, Manuel Pik 132
_____, Releigh Hal 96
_____, Thomas Mon 219
_____, William Hry 202
HARPER, A. D. Jsp 366
_____, Andrew K. Frk 211
_____, Anslem L. Clk 293
_____, Bedford Elb 157
_____, Benjamin Han 156
_____, Benjamin Hry 249
_____, Benjamin Mor 258
_____, Brooks DeK 66
_____, Charles Lib 47
_____, Edward H. Wrn 200
_____, Elisabeth Har 187
_____, Elizabeth New 9

Name	County	Page
Harper, George	Cpb	199
_____, George	Jns	441
_____, George R.	Mon	214
_____, Grace	Elb	155
_____, Hannah	Jks	339
_____, Henry	New	22
_____, Henry	Rch	273
_____, Hiram M.	Hab	23
_____, Holcomb G.	Gre	280
_____, James	Hab	52
_____, James	Mon	213
** _____, James (slave)	Rch	269
_____, James	Rch	273
_____, James	Wyn	285
_____, James N.	Lin	62
_____, Jesse	Jns	457
_____, John	Bts	168
_____, John	Hab	23
_____, John	Lwn	88
_____, John	New	8
_____, John	Pik	125
_____, John J.	Har	176
_____, John W.	Clk	293
_____, Joseph	Clk	291
_____, Joseph	Cpb	195
_____, Joseph	Jns	456
_____, Josiah B.	Mor	269
_____, Leonard	Irw	303
_____, Lucy	Lin	62
_____, Lucy (w)	Mor	239
_____, Martha	Han	157
_____, Mary	Crf	406
_____, Mary S.	Cow	380
_____, Micajah	Mon	213
_____, Nancy	Wrn	228
_____, Nathaniel	Clk	291
_____, Nathaniel	Har	188
_____, Philida	Lin	60
_____, Pompey	Elb	155
_____, Prestley	Han	156
_____, Richard	Bts	158
_____, Robert	Cpb	200
_____, Robert	Cpb	205
_____, Roderick	Hry	213
_____, Samuel	Ogl	80
_____, Samuel	Ogl	82
_____, Sarah	Elb	155
_____, Sexton	Jks	339
_____, Sherrard	New	8
_____, Solomon	Cpb	195
_____, Solomon	Har	187
_____, Thomas	Hry	221
_____, Uel	Hry	219
Harper, Wilkins	Pik	124
_____, William	Bts	168
_____, William	Hab	40
_____, William	Hal	68
_____, William	Lin	64
_____, William	Pik	118
** _____, William (slave)	Rch	270
_____, William	Rch	273
_____, William A.	Crf	406
_____, William H.	Har	190
_____, Wyatt	Han	156
HARRARD/HARROD		
Harrard, William J.	McI	122
Harrod, James	Lau	24
HARRELL/HARREL/HARRALD/ HARROLD/HARROL/HARRALL/ HARRIEL/HARROLL/HERRELL		
Harrell, Abram	Wrn	217
_____, Anna	Twg	76
_____, Asa	Pul	151
_____, Cader	Twg	62
_____, Charles	Wrn	198
_____, Daniel	Pul	155
_____, David	Wsh	243
_____, David	Wrn	226
_____, Elisha	Bke	138
_____, Etheldred	Pul	151
_____, George	Hry	243
_____, Henry	Hst	292
_____, Holiday H.	Twg	63
_____, Hugh B.	Hry	251
_____, James	Gwn	346
_____, Jesse	Pul	151
_____, Jesse	Wsh	245
_____, Jethro B.	Hry	231
_____, John	Gwn	346
_____, John	Har	179
_____, John	Jns	457
_____, John	Twg	72
_____, John	Wrn	201
_____, John	Wsh	274
_____, Joseph	Hry	231
_____, Levi	Pul	151
_____, Lewis	Lwn	80
_____, Mary	Pul	154
_____, Mary	Gwn	346
_____, Miles	Hst	283
_____, Morgan	Hst	285
_____, Polly	Gwn	346
_____, Reubin	Wks	346
_____, Samuel	Twg	72
_____, Samuel L.	Fay	195
_____, Solomon	Wsh	245

Name	County	Page
Harrell, Susan	Twg	88
______, Stephen	Bke	152
______, Thomas	Bke	141
______, Thomas	Jns	451
______, William	Pul	151
______, William	Tlf	10
______, William	Wrn	197
______, Zachariah	Wrn	195
Harrel, Isaac	Dec	17
______, Jacob	Dec	9
______, Jane	Bib	73
______, John	Dec	8
______, Mary	Bib	61
______, Moses	Dec	8
______, Samuel	Jsp	364
______, Simon	Wrn	197
______, Thomas	Mus	288
______, Western	Mus	279
______, William D.	Dec	9
Harrald, Abner	Cam	191
Harrold, Hardy	Up	112
______, Hardy Jr.	Up	96
______, William	Han	155
______, William	Lin	70
Harrol, Alexander	Jef	415
______, Elijah	Jef	412
______, John	Tms	17
______, Zilphia	Jef	415
Harrall, Isaac	Tlb	327
______, Josiah	Tlb	326
______, Polley	Jsp	372
______, William	Tlb	322
Harriel, Dempsy	Dec	11
______, John	Dec	9
______, John	Lib	46
Harroll, Sarah	Jef	414
Herrell, Edward	Hal	128
HARREN, Edmond	Dec	10
______, Howel	Dec	11
HARRINGTON, Drewry	Fay	187
______, James J.	Gwn	312
______, John	Lib	46
______, John	Wsh	274
______, John H.	Jsp	397
______, Simon	Lib	46
HARRIS/HARRISS/HARIS		
Harris, Aaron	Wyn	283
______, Absolom	Frk	227
______, Absolum	Ogl	78
______, Agness (w)	Mor	270
______, Alsa	Ear	97
______, Alston	Mon	191
______, Ambrose	Mor	244

Name	County	Page
Harris, Amos	Wrn	214
______, Anna	Hal	133
______, Archibald	Gwn	348
______, Archelous	Wil	322
______, Benjamin	Lau	8
______, Benjamin	Mwr	166
______, Benjamin	Mor	241
______, Benjamin E.	Gre	296
______, Benjamin	Jns	438
______, Benjamin	Rch	290
______, Benjamin F.	Mon	209
______, Betsey	Gre	294
______, Braddock	Mwr	159
______, Britain	DeK	39
______, Buckner	Gwn	318
______, Cary	Trp	33
______, Charles	DeK	44
______, Charles	Har	178
______, Charles	Jns	451
______, Charles	Mor	270
______, Charles B.	Mor	271
______, Charles W.	New	26
______, Claiborn	Jks	320
______, Crecy	Gre	299
______, D. L. Mon	222	
______, Daniel	Trp	51
______, Drury	Mon	225
______, E.	Bal	35
______, Edmond S.	Trp	33
______, Edward	DeK	72
______, Edward	Hab	34
______, Edward	Wrn	223
______, Edward C.	Mar	140
______, Elbert G.	Wil	290
______, Elbrige	Hab	18
______, Elisha	Mar	137
______, Elizabeth	Bib	50
______, Elizabeth	DeK	64
______, Elizabeth	Han	156
______, Else	DeK	35
______, Else	DeK	72
______, Elsey	Wyn	282
______, Ephriam	Hab	32
______, Esther	Hry	244
______, Evans	Crf	414
______, Ezekial	Hal	76
______, F.	Cht	268
______, Fanney	New	21
______, Frances	Bib	51
______, Frances	Bib	51
______, Francis	Bib	51
______, Francis	Lib	47
______, George	Hab	53

Harris, Gideon G. Wrn 224
______, Giles Mad 107
______, Gillum Gre 289
______, Gray Put 185
______, Hampton App 9
______, Hannah Bib 67
______, Hardy Har 189
______, Henley Wal 145
______, Henry Han 155
______, Henry Wal 129
______, Henry Wrn 195
______, Henry A. Gly 266
______, Henry L. Mor 271
______, Hiram DeK 33
______, Isaac C. Jns 438
______, Iverson Bal 34
______, James DeK 71
______, James Hry 205
______, James Jns 429
______, James Jns 469
______, James Pik 111
______, James Trp 37
______, James Wrn 192
______, James J. Put 193
______, James W. Wal 151
______, Jane Hal 95
______, Jefferson New 12
______, Jephtha V. Elb 126
______, Jesse DeK 45
______, Jesse Doo 83
______, Jesse Tlb 329
______, Joannah Elb 125
______, John Dec 15
______, John DeK 72
______, John Elb 145
______, John Gwn 334
______, John Gwn 341
______, John Hal 83
______, John Mon 205
______, John Mor 270
______, John New 48
______, John Pik 125
______, John Trp 51
______, John Wrn 198
______, John B. Cam 192
______, John L. Rab 231
______, John N. Tfo 354
______, John R. Mor 271
______, John Sr. McI 128
______, John Jr. McI 128
______, John T. Bke 136
______, John W. Wrn 203
______, Jones Put 172

Harris, Joseph Jks 342
______, Joseph Mor 272
______, Joseph Wal 130
______, Joseph B. Hry 219
______, Joseph C. Han 156
______, Joshua Jns 469
______, L. D. Gwn 349
______, Leonard Pik 110
______, Lesly C. Trp 39
______, Levinah Ogl 85
______, Lewis Rch 291
______, Lucean B. Put 184
______, M. B. Gly 269
______, Madison Crf 411
______, Majors Pik 130
______, Mark Cpb 200
______, Martha Gre 289
______, Martha M. Jns 453
______, Mary Hal 88
______, Maryan Lib 46
______, Matthew Gre 298
______, Milley Bke 140
______, Moses Car 233
______, Moses Mon 220
______, Moses P. DeK 44
______, Moses S. Wyn 283
______, Myles G. Han 155
______, N. F. Wsh 239
______, N. W. A. Jns 445
______, Nancy Gwn 341
______, Nancy Pik 110
______, Nathan Ogl 84
______, Nathaniel Doo 87
______, Nathaniel Wal 126
______, Obadiah Car 222
______, Isborn Mor 271
______, Patrick H. Gre 302
______, Peter Hry 236
______, Rachael Wrn 211
______, Ransford Gwn 341
______, Raymond Lib 46
______, Rebecca Pul 158
______, Rhoda Wrn 224
______, Riddin Wal 134
______, Robert Up 114
______, Robert Wil 321
______, Roderick Tfo 369
______, Rubon DeK 28
______, Runnels Gwn 313
______, Samuel Mon 212
______, Samuel Mor 269
______, Samuel Wal 126
______, Samuel B. Clk 298

Harris, Samuel F. Mor 270
______, Samuel H. Han 156
______, Sarah Clk 324
______, Sarah Gre 299
______, Sarah Jns 438
______, Sarah Tfo 368
______, Seaborn Gre 289
______, Singleton Tfo 368
______, Stephen Cht 244
______, Stephen Gwn 365
______, Stephen Lee 35
______, Stephen Wil 321
______, Sterling DeK 53
______, Stogner App 5
______, Taliaferro Lin 71
______, Theophilus Mor 271
______, Thomas New 29
______, Thomas DeK 44
______, Thomas Gre 294
______, Thomas Hry 202
______, Thomas Hst 286
______, Thomas Tfo 362
______, Thomas D. DeK 71
______, Thomas M. New 8
______, Thomas O. Mor 271
______, Thomas P. Tfo 357
______, Thomas W. Hry 209
______, Thomas W. Wal 130
______, Thompson App 7
______, Tinsley Mad 100
______, Trecy Wsh 260
______, Tryon Elb 153
______, Tryon Elb 153
______, Tyre Wal 161
______, Virginia Clk 302
______, Vina Jks 342
______, Waid Bib 61
______, Walter Rch 291
______, Walton Jks 342
______, Walton B. Mwr 168
______, West Wal 166
______, West Wrn 197
______, Wiley Mus 278
______, Wiley J. Mon 180
______, William DeK 54
______, William DeK 63
______, William DeK 71
______, William DeK 72
______, William Frk 212
______, William Gre 275
______, William Gwn 374
______, William Hab 54
______, William Jns 438
Harris, William Jns 457
______, William Mwr 152
______, William Mon 221
______, William Mor 242
______, William Pik 118
______, William Wrn 209
______, William H. Clk 312
______, William O. Hal 93
______, William P. Bib 60
______, William T. Crf 396
______, Willie Wrn 194
______, Wilmott E. Gre 296
______, Winfred Put 210
______, Wyatt Gwn 315
Harriss, Alexander A. Bke 155
______, Benjamin Twg 67
______, Braddock Cow 385
______, Daniel Wsh 248
______, David Jsp 380
______, Elbert Cow 370
______, Emely Ogl 95
______, George Cpb 206
______, Gilford Fay 182
______, Greenbury Cow 371
______, Jacob Twg 82
______, James T. Twg 78
______, John Col 346
______, John Fay 183
______, John D. Ogl 94
______, Juriah Col 361
______, L. B. Cpb 207
______, Little Cow 376
______, Lunsford Cow 373
______, Mary Jsp 379
______, Micajah Cow 370
______, Morriss Fay 189
______, Nancy Cow 383
______, Rebecah Ogl 85
______, Robert Fay 207
______, Samuel W. Cow 386
______, Thomas J. Col 362
______, Tyn Clk 313
______, William D. Clk 313
______, William W. Cow 373
Haris, Archibald Gwn 341
______, Ben Gwn 343
______, Harison Gwn 365
HARRISON/HARISON/
HARRISSON
Harrison, Benjamin Bts 177
______, Benjamin Frk 217
______, Benjamin Wrn 210
______, Bennona Wrn 205

Name	County	Page
Harrison, Casity	Lau	24
______, Chaney	Lau	9
______, Charles T.	Hst	289
______, Charlotta	Jns	440
______, Colmon	Jks	314
______, David B.	Wrn	232
______, Eli W.	Fay	191
______, Elijah W.	Jns	461
______, Frances	Wyn	281
______, Gabriel	Wsh	254
______, George	Jns	441
______, George	Wrn	202
______, Gilbert	McI	128
______, Henry	Jns	439
______, James	Bts	173
______, James	Twg	62
______, James	Wal	158
______, James D.	Wil	296
______, Jefferson	Trp	53
______, Joel	Hab	14
______, John	Cam	190
______, John	Crf	412
______, John	Jks	316
______, John	Tfo	367
______, John B.	Frk	214
______, John H.	Hab	62
______, John H.	Tlb	335
______, John J.	Mtg	233
______, Jonathan	Crf	400
______, Joseph	Put	191
______, Joseph	Ran	246
______, Joseph	Tfo	368
______, Joseph	Wsh	246
______, Joseph	Wsh	267
______, Kinchin	Wrn	223
______, Larkin	Frk	213
______, Mary	Tlf	11
______, Moses	Wks	356
______, Nathaniel	Put	176
______, Oby (Obediah)	Jks	322
______, Reuben	Hal	97
______, Reuben	Har	180
______, Robert	Frk	212
______, Robert	Ogl	99
______, S.	Col	357
______, Sampson D.	Trp	52
______, Samuel C.	Tlf	5
______, Samuel W.	Col	346
______, Seaborn	Bke	151
______, Susannah	Col	350
______, Thomas	Frk	241
______, Thomas P.	Twg	67
______, Tilmon	Jks	322
Harrison, William	Bts	159
______, William	Cht	243
______, William	Cht	277
______, William	Hst	270
______, William	Jns	439
______, William	Mon	189
______, William	Tfo	354
______, William	Up	104
______, William C.	Twg	76
Harison, Benjamin	Dec	6
______, David	Mus	279
______, Hannah	Wrn	202
______, Thomas	Dec	6
Harrisson, Robert	Gre	297
HARRIST, Archibald	Trp	51
______, Hiram	Mor	271
______, Thomas M.	Trp	51
HARRY, John	Hst	264
______, William	Hry	231
HART/HARTT		
Hart, Allen S.	Lau	22
______, Allen T.	Mtg	235
______, Amos F.	Ran	242
______, Ann	Rch	288
______, Archebald	Ogl	69
______, Bain	Lau	22
______, Barnet	Wrn	221
______, Benjamin	Ran	250
______, Charles J.	Bry	84
______, Crawford	Twg	70
______, Eli	Tfo	366
______, Elisha	Hry	235
______, Elizabeth	Tlf	12
______, F.	Gwn	308
______, George	Wrn	216
______, Hardy	Gwn	319
______, Henry	Cht	241
______, Isaac	Tfo	359
______, Isaac Sr.	Wrn	221
______, Isaac Jr.	Wrn	221
______, John	Hry	208
______, John	Mon	190
______, John	Tms	23
______, Levi	Cht	260
______, Levi	Tms	24
______, Marmaduke	Twg	70
______, Nancy	Wsh	241
______, Patrick	Cht	245
______, Robert	Jns	451
______, Samuel	Tfo	357
______, Samuel	Wrn	221
______, Smith S.	Lib	46
______, Solomon	Har	183

Hart, Thomas Gre 280
_____, William Car 227
_____, William Lin 74
_____, William Wal 142
_____, William Wrn 223
Hartt, C. T. Lib 47
_____, Idenstell W. Lib 47
HARTFORD, James Rch 292
HARTLEY/HARTLY
Hartley, Burwell Wsh 246
_____, Hardy Wsh 241
_____, Hillery Wsh 255
_____, James Fay 201
Hartly, Michael Crf 403
_____, Pherraby Wsh 275
HARTLINE, George Hry 238
HARTNETT, Richard M. Cpb 202
HARTRIDGE, C. H. Cht 265
HARTSFIELD, Andrew Mus 289
_____, Andrew Ogl 72
_____, Godfrey Hry 210
_____, James Pik 106
_____, John H. Pik 106
_____, Moses Cpb 195
_____, Moses Hry 227
_____, Mary Bts 166
_____, Peter S. Crf 407
_____, Warren Pik 108
_____, Washington Ogl 75
_____, William Har 192
_____, William Ogl 73
_____, William A. Mon 201
HARTSMIZE, Pottis Bib 73
HARUP, James M. Gre 286
HARVEY/HARVY
Harvey, Albert Put 209
_____, Candecy Cht 247
_____, Daniel Wil 320
_____, Edmond C. Jsp 364
_____, Edward G. Clk 296
_____, Elijah Clk 301
_____, Elizabeth Bke 130
_____, Mrs. Elizabeth Bry 87
_____, Hamilton Hst 291
_____, Holden Mon 185
_____, Isaac Bry 86
_____, James Up 99
_____, James P. Put 210
_____, Jaris Pul 157
_____, John Bry 86
_____, John B. Mon 174
_____, John B. Wal 136
_____, Joseph A. Ogl 63
Harvey, Lindia Mon 185
_____, M. Bal 34
_____, Moses Put 207
_____, Pinkeshman Wal 149
_____, Richard Bry 86
_____, Robert Cht 279
_____, Steph Bal 33
_____, Thomas Hal 68
_____, Usula Put 209
_____, William Bry 87
_____, William Tlb 335
_____, Zephariah Jsp 363
Harvy, Caleb Lee 33
_____, Charles Pul 162
_____, John H. Pul 160
_____, Richard Crf 395
_____, Samuel Bry 88
_____, Thomas D. Lee 34
_____, William Pik 126
HARVARD/HARVERD
Harvard, Hardy Doo 78
_____, Stephen Doo 89
Harverd, Daniel Wal 155
HARVEL/HARVILLE/HARVILL/
HARVELL/HERVEL
Harvel, Needham Ran 244
_____, Ryal DeK 72
Harville, Nancy Wrn 212
_____, Samuel Lib 47
Harvill, Mark Ogl 77
Harvell, Ellis Wks 343
_____, Jackson New 30
_____, Richard New 30
Hervel, Habet Hab 51
HARVIANT, Peter Cht 247
HARWELL, Alexander J. Han 156
_____, Anderson Sr. Put 176
_____, Anderson Jr. Put 176
_____, Ishmael Mor 247
_____, James W. Cow 381
_____, John Crf 404
_____, Littleton P. Mor 246
_____, Mary Han 155
_____, Mary Jsp 397
_____, Ranson Jsp 395
_____, Samuel Har 179
_____, Samuel Trp 32
_____, Thomas Jks 339
_____, Vines Trp 47
_____, William Jsp 370
HASARD, John Dec 11
HASKINS, Joseph Hst 290
_____, Silas Crf 413

Haskins, Sylvamus Pul 143
HASLET, Andrew Gwn 308
HASLIP, Jonas Bke 123
______, Lott W. Bke 123
______, Loar B. Jef 410
______, Winney Jef 411
HASLOTT, John Car 222
HASSELL, Edward Col 341
HASTIN/HASTINGS
Hastin, Polly Wks 351
Hastings, Benjamin Up 107
______, Harison Mus 286
HASTY/HASTEY
Hasty, Hillory Twg 70
______, William Mwr 154
______, Willis Bke 117
Hastey, John Bts 168
______, Obediah Bts 168
HATCH, Isaac Ear 94
______, Paul Ear 94
HATHCOCK/HATCHOCK/HATHCOX/
HAITHCOCK
Hathcock, Hosea Elb 131
______, James Elb 120
______, James Frk 246
______, Middleton Frk 216
______, Nancy Mon 199
______, William Fay 204
Hatchock, Isaac Wks 336
Hathcox, E. B. Crf 414
Haithcock, Isaac Mon 194
HATHAWAY/HATTAWAY/
HATAWAY/HATTIWAY
Hathaway, David Gre 286
______, Henry B. Lau 7
______, Martin Cht 249
Hattaway, Baton Wrn 232
______, Irwin Wrn 231
Hataway, Levi Mor 262
Hattiway, Daniel Wsh 254
HATCHELL, John B. Gre 279
HATCHER, Ebanezer C. Elb 123
______, Edward Bke 145
______, Hamilton Mar 143
______, Henry Rch 284
______, Isham Jef 403
______, Jackson Bib 76
______, James Wks 334
______, James Wks 343
______, John Cam 186
______, John Col 334
______, John Crf 407
______, John Wks 331

Hatcher, John C. Bib 58
______, Josiah Jsp 367
______, Malony Jef 403
______, Martha Bib 67
______, Mary Rch 277
______, Master Jsp 363
______, Moses Wyn 285
______, Reuben Wks 351
______, Robert Wyn 285
______, Samuel Jsp 363
______, Sarah Bke 144
______, Uriah Jsp 366
______, William Hal 131
______, William Jsp 370
______, William Mwr 165
______, William Twg 71
______, William Wks 343
______, William G. Wks 333
HATCHET/HATCHETT
Hatchet, Edward Ogl 78
______, William Ogl 79
Hatchett, William Wal 150
HATCHWELL, John Col 334
HATELY, Henry Bts 161
______, James Mwr 168
______, Sherwood Hal 70
HATFIELD, Caleb Rch 264
______, James Wks 348
** ______, John (slave) Rch 258
______, John Rch 264
______, Richard Wks 348
______, Washington Hst 292
HATHHOUSE, Thomas Sr. Mon 199
______, Thomas Jr. Mon 199
HATIA, Solomon Cpb 209
HATHHORN/HATHORN
Hathhorn, Hugh Trp 52
______, James Trp 51
Hathorn, Eliz. Wks 348
______, William Mar 138
HATMAN, Thirson Col 349
HATTOX, Elijah Trp 54
______, James Trp 54
HATTEN/HATTON
Hatten, Peter Tlf 7
______, William Tlf 5
Hatton, James Col 337
______, John Har 180
HAUPT/HAWPE
Haupt, Henry Cht 268
______, John Cht 247
Hawpe, George Hal 70
HAVARD, Drury Doo 88

Name	County	Page
HAVILLE/HAVELL		
Haville, Dotson	Hry	249
Havell, John	Hab	27
HAVILAND, R. B.	Rch	276
HAVIN, Andrew	Tms	22
HAWK/HAWKS		
Hawk, Frederick	Mad	118
______, Jacob	Jsp	393
______, Peter	Jsp	383
______, Ursury	Jsp	384
Hawks, Henry	Ogl	77
HAWKINS, Allen	Put	213
______, Augustus C.	Mon	175
______, Benjamin	Up	114
______, Drewry	Wsh	254
______, Edmund	Hal	114
______, Edward	Put	175
______, Elias	Pul	143
______, Exey	Jsp	393
______, Ezekiel	Jns	469
______, Jesse	Pik	131
______, John	Put	199
______, John	DeK	31
______, John	Ogl	88
______, John	Put	175
______, John	Wal	139
______, John B.	Wal	150
______, John B.	Wal	165
______, Joshua	Up	113
______, Nathaniel	Hal	120
______, Nicholas	Put	199
______, Rebecca	Put	175
______, Soloman	Hal	120
______, Stephen	Doo	87
______, Thomas	Mus	287
______, Thomas	Put	213
______, William	Pik	132
______, William	Tfo	361
______, William K.	Wal	157
______, Willis A.	Wal	137
______, Zachariah	Hal	121
HAWS, Barnett	Jns	468
______, John	Col	354
______, John	Lin	70
______, Laton	Lin	71
______, Littleton	Lin	71
______, Nancy	Jns	469
______, Paten	Col	341
______, Richard	Jns	441
______, Samuel	Col	335
HAWTHORN/HAWHORN		
Hawthorn, Elias O.	Dec	8
______, John	Wks	348
Hawthorn, Jonathan	Dec	15
______, Nathaniel	Dec	19
______, William	Dec	15
______, William	Hst	274
Hawhorn, Mary	Wks	346
HAY/HAYS/HAYES/HAYSE/HAYZE		
Hay, Catherine	Wil	288
______, Chesley	Jsp	392
______, Gilbert	Hal	79
______, Howell	Wil	299
______, James	Lee	33
______, James G.	Wil	287
______, Laney	Fay	203
______, Mary	Wil	289
______, Ruben	Wsh	276
______, Samuel	Jks	319
______, William	DeK	40
______, William	Ear	95
______, William	Jsp	359
______, William	Wil	299
Hays, Alexander	Ear	98
______, Aley	Tlf	4
______, Arthur	Doo	82
______, Benjamin	Gwn	347
______, Calvin	Cam	184
______, Charles L.	Crf	394
______, David	Frk	257
______, Davis	Dec	12
______, Elias	Hal	75
______, Elizabeth	Hst	288
______, Estate	Eff	112
______, Etheldred	Ear	93
______, George	Gwn	321
______, George	Jks	331
______, George	Jks	349
______, George D.	Tlb	345
______, Hardy	Hal	75
______, Hiram	New	46
______, James	Ear	91
______, James	Twg	73
______, James	Gwn	374
______, Jessey	Jks	333
______, John	Ear	93
______, John G.	Tlb	340
______, Jonathan	Tlb	327
______, Joshua	Tlb	332
______, Lavis	Hry	234
______, Lemuel	Doo	82
______, Martin	Wks	353
______, Mary	Wil	320
______, Richard	Gwn	350
______, Robert	Trp	34
______, Robert P.	Tlb	348

Name	County	Page
Hays, Sarah	Tlf	9
______, Seabon	Ear	94
______, Thomas	Col	336
______, William	Gwn	308
______, William	Mus	280
______, William	Wal	161
______, Quney	Wsh	276
Hayes, Alfred	Clk	312
______, Ambrose	Wrn	213
______, Edmond	Wrn	218
______, George	Tms	19
______, James	Pul	144
______, James	Put	172
______, John	Jsp	372
______, John	Wrn	213
______, Jonathan J.	Frk	211
______, Leonard	Wal	150
______, Lorenzo D.	Wrn	210
______, Rachal	Cow	389
______, Thomas J.	New	33
______, William	Clk	301
______, William	Cow	375
______, William	Gre	287
Hayse, Ezekiel C.	New	34
______, George	New	34
______, James	DeK	67
______, John	DeK	41
______, Polly	Hab	44
______, Robert L.	New	32
______, Thomas	DeK	46
Hayze, Elijah	Hab	38
HAYCOCK, William	Crf	407
HAYDEN, James	Twg	88
HAYGOOD/HAIGOOD/HAGOOD		
Haygood, Aaron	DeK	58
______, Appleton	Hst	296
______, Asa	Hab	22
______, Benjamin	Hab	34
______, William	Clk	291
______, William	Hab	40
______, William	Hal	76
Haigood, James	Mor	253
Hagood, Benjamin Sr.	Mon	183
______, Benjamin Jr.	Mon	183
HAYMAN/HAYMOND		
Hayman, Stouten	Bry	86
______, William	Mon	205
Haymond, Elisha	Bke	141
______, Elizabeth	Bke	141
______, Stephen	Bke	141
HAYWOOD, Archabald	Wsh	270
______, Thomas	Hry	203
HAZE, Young	Har	175
HAZELLRIGGS, Benjamin	Gwn	341
HAZZLETT/HAZLETT/HAZELETT		
Hazzlett, Mary (w)	Mor	257
Hazlett, William	DeK	39
Hazelett, William	Mus	280
HAZZARD, Wm. G. T. F.	Gly	268
HAZZLEHURST, Robert	Gly	269
HEAD, Benjamin	Elb	123
______, Benjamin	Fay	195
______, Charles	Hal	121
______, Daniel B.	Fay	193
______, Edmond	Pik	111
______, George	Jsp	368
______, George W.	Bts	158
______, Henry	Mon	228
______, Isaac	Hal	115
______, James	Fay	197
______, James	Gwn	357
______, James	Hal	121
______, James A.	Hal	96
______, James Sr.	Mor	239
______, John	Bts	176
______, John	Gly	264
______, John	Jsp	368
______, John	Hal	96
______, John	Hal	124
______, John S.	Fay	190
______, John S.	Gwn	359
______, Margaret (w)	Mor	238
______, Marshal	Gwn	347
______, Polly	Gre	297
______, Richard	DeK	51
______, Richard	Hal	115
______, Samuel B.	Mus	279
______, Tarver	Fay	196
______, Thomas	Gwn	340
______, Thomas	Gwn	347
______, Thomas	Mor	263
______, Thomas	Put	199
______, William	Mon	227
______, William J.	Jsp	367
______, William R.	Fay	193
______, Willis R.	Bts	175
HEAL, Simeon	Trp	42
HEALY/HEALEY		
Healy, John	Pik	112
______, Michael M.	Jns	465
Healey, Michael M.	Jns	446
HEAN, John Sr.	Pul	157
______, John Jr.	Pul	157
______, William	Pul	159
HEARD/HERD		
Heard, Alen B.	Car	22[illegible]

Name	County	Page
Heard, Alexander H.	Fay	188
______, Barnard	Wil	316
______, C. M.	Jks	322
______, Charles	Bts	178
______, E.	DeK	33
______, Edmond	Rch	273
______, Elizabeth	Elb	156
______, Elizabeth	Jks	349
______, Elizabeth	Wil	291
______, Ephraim	Crf	413
______, Franklin C.	Rch	267
______, George	DeK	27
______, George	DeK	56
______, George	Gre	305
______, George W.	Elb	122
______, George W.	Trp	46
______, Hubard P.	Jsp	381
______, Hugh	Bts	176
______, James	Gre	281
______, James	Up	103
______, James Jr.	Mor	238
______, Jesse F.	Wil	324
______, John	Bts	167
______, John	Gre	287
______, John B.	Jks	322
______, John S.	Car	228
______, John W.	Rch	258
______, Joseph	Jks	333
______, Jubas C.	DeK	44
______, Mary	Cow	380
______, Mary	Elb	155
______, Mary (w)	Mor	247
______, Newsom	Rch	273
______, Rachel	Jks	334
______, Stephen	Fay	197
______, Stephen M.	Bts	176
______, Thomas	Gre	279
______, Thomas J.	Elb	136
______, William	DeK	45
______, William	Tfo	369
______, William S.	DeK	47
______, Woodson	Gre	281
______, Wyatt T.	Pik	130
Herd, Daniel	Mwr	156
______, George L.	Mor	246
______, Henry	Fay	200
______, John G. Sr.	Mor	260
______, Joseph	Col	359
______, Joseph	Mor	254
______, William	Mor	246
HEARN/HEARNE/HEARNES		
Hearn, Asa	Cow	387
______, Asa	Jsp	393
Hearn, Benjamin	Put	190
______, Charles	Put	204
______, Eleazer M.	Put	197
______, Elizabeth	Mus	291
______, Elizabeth Sr.	Put	197
______, Elizabeth Jr.	Put	197
______, Elijah	Tlb	331
______, Elijah	Up	109
______, Francis S.	Put	193
______, George	New	7
______, Fielding	New	44
______, Greenberry	Up	113
______, Isaac	Cow	386
______, Jacob	Cow	379
______, Jacob	Put	197
______, Jesse	Twg	74
______, Joshua	Frk	214
______, Joshua	Put	193
______, Lewis	Put	213
______, Lot	Put	196
______, Moses	Hry	205
______, N. J. P.	Up	120
______, Randal	Mon	186
______, Richard	Mrg	236
______, Samuel W.	Tlb	323
______, Stephen	Cow	379
______, William	Fay	196
______, William	Put	197
______, Zabud	DeK	34
Hearne, Thomas	Elb	157
Hearnes, Caswell	Hst	268
HEARNDON/HERNDON/HEARNDEN		
Hearndon, Benjamin	Jns	447
______, James	Wks	331
______, John P.	Put	217
______, William	Wks	342
Herndon, George	Wks	335
______, John	Wks	335
Hearnden, Walker	Jns	432
HEATH/HEETH/HETH		
Heath, Benjamin	Jns	432
______, Chappel	Jsp	386
______, Cowlson	Put	183
______, Dawson	Bts	161
______, Elizabeth	New	21
______, Gilford	Put	194
______, Henry	Bke	149
______, Henry	Tms	19
______, Hester Ann	Cow	385
______, James	Bke	146
______, James	Jns	438
______, John	Hab	60
______, John	Jns	436

Name	County	Page
Heath, John B.	Jns	438
______, Jordan Sr.	Bke	149
______, Jordan Jr.	Bke	149
______, Joseph	Jks	345
______, Lunsford	Put	175
______, Margaret	Put	180
______, Moses	Bke	147
______, Nancy	Hry	244
______, Nancy	Jsp	384
______, Nancy	Wil	293
______, Pleasant	Jns	465
______, Rigdon	Bke	133
______, Samuel	Bke	149
______, William	New	49
______, William B.	Mon	197
______, Winnefred	Em	173
Heeth, Abram	Wrn	201
______, Ambrose	Wrn	204
______, Daniel	Wsh	263
______, Hartwell	Wrn	204
______, Martha	Wrn	192
______, Rebecah	Wrn	202
______, Sarah	Wsh	268
______, Sarah	Wrn	202
______, Susan	Wrn	208
Heth, James	Mwr	162
HEATON/HEADEN/HEADIN		
Heaton, David	Hal	90
______, William	Hal	90
Headen, Rosea	Jks	348
Headin, Samuel	Frk	223
HECKLE, John	Rch	284
HECKLIN, R. N.	Wsh	363
HEDERICK/HEADRICK		
Hederick, Gasper	Hab	7
______, Gasper	Hab	8
______, George	Hab	7
Headrick, Henry	Car	224
HEERY, T.	Cht	255
HEFLIN/HEFLEN/HOFLIN		
Heflin, Cyrus	Hry	216
______, Wiley	Hry	240
______, Wiley J.	Hry	240
______, William	Pik	106
______, William	Put	205
______, Wyatt	Fay	185
Heflen, Sarah	Wrn	203
Hoflin, Wiley	Hry	250
HEFFNER, Ephrian	Hab	54
______, John	Hab	51
HEIDLEBERG, John	Doo	88
HEIDT/HEIGHT/Also see Hite		
Heidt, Abiail	Eff	105
______, Christian Jr.	Eff	104
______, Christian J. Sr.	Eff	107
______, George	Eff	105
______, Matthew	Eff	104
______, Samuel	Eff	115
Height, Christian	Car	219
______, Wiley	Jks	349
HEINEMAN, F. W.	Cht	249
HEISLAR, Samuel	Bke	123
HELLEM, Elizabeth	Hal	91
HELMLY, David Jr.	Eff	104
______, David Jr.	Eff	108
______, Joshua	Eff	107
HELSEBECK, Henry	Mor	271
HELTERBRAN/HELTERBRAND		
Helterbran, William	DeK	53
Helterbrand, Peter	Gwn	378
HELTON/HELDON		
Helton, Abraham	Ran	243
______, Abraham	Wal	154
______, Amos	Car	220
______, Elijah	Jns	454
______, Elisha	New	50
______, Ezekiel	Wal	163
______, George W.	Hry	240
______, Jacob	Hab	10
______, Jahial	Hal	99
______, James	Han	9
______, James	Ran	243
______, James C.	Hab	9
______, Joseph	Pik	128
______, Peter	Cow	376
______, Rebeca	Jns	446
______, Richard	Wsh	251
______, Thomas	Wal	170
Heldon, Pleasant R.	Hry	201
HELVERSON/HELVERSTON/HELVENSTON		
Helverson, James	Cam	185
Helverston, John C.	Bib	55
Helvenston, Joseph F.	Eff	109
______, Joshua J.	Eff	107
HEMBREE, Amariah	Hal	90
HEMPHILL, Alfonso	Mor	242
______, Charles	Jks	316
______, Elizabeth	Mor	240
______, Henryetta	Frk	211
______, James	Hal	123
______, James A.	Mad	110
______, Marcus	Mor	240
______, Patsey (w)	Mor	242
______, Philip W.	Jks	322

Name	County	Page
Hemphill, Robert	Frk	229
______, Robert J.	Mad	110
______, Sabra	Jks	332
______, Samuel	Mad	111
______, Thomas	Mad	100
______, Wade	Mor	240
______, William	Frk	228
HEMINGWAY, Wilson	Hst	263
HENCH, Mikel H.	Ran	243
HENDERSON/HENDISON		
Henderson, Alen	Hab	21
______, Andrew	Hry	205
______, Archibald	Gwn	366
______, Atha	Jks	348
______, Berrien	Ware	188
______, Bob	Clk	294
______, Charles	Jsp	390
______, Daniel	Bib	67
______, David	Jsp	393
______, Duncan	Ware	183
______, Edward	Rch	254
______, Elisha	Wal	137
______, Eliza	Cht	272
______, George E.	Bke	149
______, Greeville	DeK	41
______, Hannah	Twg	84
______, Henery	Cow	375
______, Hillary	Pul	144
______, Isaac P.	New	49
______, James	Bts	170
______, James	Elb	142
______, James	Gwn	324
______, James	Hab	48
______, James	Hal	80
______, James	Jsp	365
______, James	Trp	32
______, James B.	Put	190
______, James V.	Hal	133
______, Jane	Wil	315
______, Jese	Hab	38
______, Jeptha	Mus	289
______, John	Irw	301
______, John	Jks	340
______, John	Jsp	363
______, John	Jsp	373
______, John	Jns	469
______, John	Tms	16
______, John	Wal	132
______, John C.	Hry	218
______, John G.	Jks	340
______, Jones	Jks	338
______, Joseph	Bib	67
______, Joseph	Jks	341
Henderson, Joseph	Jsp	358
______, Joseph	New	5
______, Joseph	Wil	312
______, Kinney	Lwn	83
______, Lucy	New	51
______, M.	Jsp	382
______, M. A.	Bak	17
______, Martin	Cow	378
______, Michael	Scr	302
______, Milton	Jks	320
______, Mitchell	Hry	203
______, Nathanal	Hal	81
______, Nathaniel A.	Jks	325
______, Ned	Clk	326
______, Rd.	Up	101
______, Reason	Hab	46
______, Rice	Mus	289
______, Richard	Hry	200
______, Robert	Bts	170
______, Robert	Hal	76
______, Robert	Hal	85
______, Robert	Lin	65
______, Robert J.	Hry	206
______, S. R.	Jks	321
______, Samuel	DeK	40
______, Samuel	Hry	231
______, Samuel	Jsp	386
______, Samuel T.	Lwn	83
______, Simeon	Elb	137
______, Simeon	Elb	149
______, Simeon Jr.	Elb	122
______, Syrus H.	Hal	80
______, Thomas	Wal	150
______, Thomas	Wil	296
______, Widow	Irw	303
______, William	Doo	84
______, William	Elb	145
______, William	Gwn	373
______, William	Fay	181
______, William	Hal	117
______, William	Jsp	388
______, William	Mon	174
______, William	New	31
______, William	Ware	183
Hendison, Arch.	Col	342
HENDON, Andrew	Clk	307
______, Andrew F.	Car	230
______, Elijah	Car	222
______, Elisha S.	DeK	57
______, Hartsfield	Ogl	77
______, Isham	DeK	42
______, Isham	Gwn	331
______, Izrael	DeK	57

Name	County	Page
HENDON, Robason	DeK	66
_____, Roberson	Ogl	77
_____, Thomas	DeK	57
_____, William A.	Cpb	197
HENDRICK/HENDRICKS/HENDRIX/ HENDREX		
Hendrick, Asa	Mad	101
_____, Cornelus	Elb	125
_____, Drury	Har	177
_____, Eleas	Mad	114
_____, Emanuel	Hal	83
_____, Faxton	Mad	114
_____, Gustavus	Bts	167
_____, Hugh	Hry	213
_____, Isaac	Bts	175
_____, Jesse	Hal	128
_____, Joel	Mon	202
_____, John	Bts	158
_____, John	Cow	377
_____, John	Gwn	374
_____, John	Hal	131
_____, John	New	21
_____, John	Ogl	89
_____, Julias	Hal	82
_____, Luke	Hal	113
_____, Moses	Jks	340
_____, Seaborn	Tms	29
_____, Sion	Mon	198
_____, Thomas	Hal	77
_____, William	Frk	242
_____, William	Frk	245
_____, William	Hal	77
_____, William	Mad	112
Hendricks, Elisha	Wil	293
_____, Elizabeth	Gly	267
_____, Elizabeth	Wil	294
_____, Gideon	Wal	153
_____, Helory	Hal	122
_____, Isaac	Rch	265
_____, James	Elb	131
_____, James	Frk	236
_____, James	Hal	134
_____, James	Wks	340
_____, Jesse	Elb	135
_____, Jesse	Elb	140
_____, John	Gly	268
_____, John	Gwn	175
_____, Joshua	Wal	159
_____, Levi	Cow	379
_____, Milum	Elb	120
_____, Nancy	Gre	288
_____, Thomas	Hal	134
_____, Whitehead	Elb	119
Hendricks, William	Hab	18
_____, William	Hal	134
Hendrix, James	Bul	96
_____, John	Hab	22
_____, John	Scr	303
_____, John Sr.	Scr	303
_____, Joseph	Jks	341
_____, Wiley	Bul	97
_____, William	Bul	96
_____, William	Ear	93
Hendrex, Andrew	Jks	326
HENDRICKSON, J.	Cht	260
HENDRY, Charles	Elb	120
_____, John E.	Lwn	79
_____, Robert Sr.	Lib	47
_____, Robert Jr. Esq.	Lib	47
_____, Sampson J.	Mor	246
_____, William	Lwn	79
HENEDAL, Alexander R.	Har	183
HENIER/HENIOR/HINER/ HANNER		
Henier, John	Em	165
Henior, Adam	Bke	152
Hanner, James	Mwr	157
_____, Mary	Clk	292
_____, William	Clk	309
Hiner, John	Wal	169
HENLY/HENLEY/HENDLEY HENDLY		
Henly, Frances	Rch	254
_____, James	DeK	59
_____, James	Scr	311
_____, John	Crf	411
_____, John C.	Mon	196
_____, Lucy	Lin	64
_____, Micajah	Lin	60
_____, Stater	Mus	278
_____, William	Pul	149
Henley, Elmore	Em	175
_____, G.	Cht	270
_____, Horton	Pul	151
_____, Jas. C.	Up	116
_____, John	Em	174
_____, William	Em	174
Hendley, James	Wrn	208
_____, John	Pul	140
Hendly, William	Gwn	335
HENNINGHAM, Mitchell	Mon	218
HENNON, Sarrah	Pik	112
HENRY/HENERY		
Henry, Adam	Jks	326
_____, Alexander	Elb	142
_____, Alexander	Scr	300

Name	Co.	Page
enry, Alexander	Scr	302
_____, Amy	Wrn	206
_____, Benjamin	Mon	177
_____, Benjamin	Mon	191
_____, Benson	Har	190
_____, C. B.	Cht	248
_____, Daniel N.	Elb	132
_____, Daniel	Han	157
_____, David	Har	192
_____, David	New	47
_____, Dexter	Wil	302
_____, Ezekiel	Trp	48
_____, George	Trp	44
_____, George	Wal	162
_____, Henderson	Tfo	356
_____, Jacob P.	Cht	264
_____, James	Hry	216
_____, John	DeK	60
_____, John	New	39
_____, Joseph	New	36
_____, Joseph	New	47
_____, Mary	Han	157
_____, Mathew	Gwn	368
_____, Robert	Mus	291
_____, Sarah	Elb	120
_____, Thomas	DeK	60
_____, William	Bry	223
_____, Widow	Rch	256
_____, William Sr.	DeK	60
_____, William Jr.	DeK	60
_____, William P.	Mon	192
_____, William R.	New	46
lenery, William	Cow	373
ENSLEY/HENSLY/HENSLEE/		
ENSLOW/HINESLEY/HINESLY		
lensley, Enoch	Hal	129
_____, Maxfield	Car	230
_____, William	Trp	52
lensly, John H.	Pik	116
lenslee, David S.	Hry	230
lenslow, Benajah	Elb	136
linesley, Alford	Hry	242
_____, Robert	Jns	444
_____, Thomas	Car	219
linesly, John	Clk	297
IENSON/HINSON/HINCEN/		
also see Hanson		
lenson, Aaron	Frk	231
_____, Andrew B.	Rab	231
_____, Caleb	Twg	62
_____, Isaac	Rab	233
_____, James B.	Rab	232
_____, John P.	Pik	117

Name	Co.	Page
Henson, Joseph	Hab	27
_____, Joseph Jr.	Hab	48
_____, L.	Jsp	371
_____, Marann	Wal	173
_____, Richard	Hal	133
_____, Samuel	Hry	238
_____, Samuel	Tlb	326
_____, Thompson M.	Rab	233
_____, William	Col	339
_____, William	Hal	79
_____, William N.	Rab	231
Hinson, Charles	Han	156
_____, Elam	Twg	81
_____, George	Tfo	364
_____, James	Tlf	3
_____, James Sr.	Clk	306
_____, John	Clk	307
_____, Lowdon	Gre	274
_____, Samuel	App	12
_____, Tarpley	Clk	307
_____, Thomas	Tlf	4
_____, William	Hab	66
_____, William	Mon	220
Hincen, N.	Gwn	328
HEPBURN, Burt	Bal	39
HEPTINSTALL, William B.	Up	102
HERB, F.	Cht	256
HERBERT/HURLBERT/HUBART		
Herbert, G-orge B	Mwr	151
Hurlbert, Rosewell	Han	157
Hubart, John	Bal	43
HERNDON/HERNDEN		
Herndon, Dillard	Elb	157
_____, Edward	Elb	137
_____, Edward	Lau	5
_____, Elijah	Cpb	210
_____, Elisha	Clk	294
_____, Enoch	Cpb	210
_____, George	Lau	5
_____, James	Lau	10
_____, John	App	7
_____, John	Cpb	200
_____, Joseph	Wal	130
_____, Mereman	Wal	130
_____, Michael	Elb	137
_____, Reuben	Mwr	169
_____, Susannah	Elb	157
_____, Wiatt	Wsh	255
_____, William	App	7
Hernden, Joseph	Wsh	263
HERON/HERRON		
Heron, Alexander	Cpb	197
Herron, Granderson	Hal	71

Name	County	Page
HERREDGE, John	New	26
_____, William	New	9
HERRING/HERRIN/HERING/ HERREN		
Herring, Allen	Frk	226
_____, David	Wal	159
_____, Elisha	Hal	78
_____, Frederick	Wal	161
_____, Federick G.	Twg	64
_____, George	Bib	64
_____, Henry H.	Twg	64
_____, James	Cow	373
_____, James	Trp	34
_____, Jesse	Wal	165
_____, Jesse	Wal	169
_____, Joel	DeK	49
_____, John	Elb	136
_____, John	Mwr	155
_____, Jonathan	Mad	109
_____, Levi	Ware	184
_____, Stephen	Hal	77
_____, Stephen	Twg	77
_____, William	Fay	185
_____, William	Twg	61
Herrin, Aaron	DeK	36
_____, Abraham	Har	183
_____, Ephriam	Hab	24
_____, Isaiah	DeK	43
_____, James	Wyn	282
_____, John	Hab	24
_____, John	Har	181
_____, Joshua	Mar	144
_____, Peter	Fay	183
_____, Thomas	Fay	183
_____, William	Hab	24
Hering, Arthur	Trp	47
_____, Dorothy	Em	170
_____, Jacob	Crf	396
Herren, Gresham	Wal	149
_____, James M.	Wal	157
HERRINGTON/HERINGTON/ HERENDON/HERRENDEN/ HERONTON/HERRINGDINE		
Herrington, Alexander	Scr	313
_____, Ephraim	Doo	80
_____, Jeremia	Scr	316
_____, John	Jns	469
_____, John	Hst	269
_____, Mrs. Jobe	Scr	316
_____, Martin	Bke	135
_____, Moses	Em	172
_____, Richard	Scr	311
_____, Richard	Scr	315

Name	County	Page
Herrington, Stephen	Scr	3
_____, William	Twg	
Herington, Ephraim	Em	1
_____, James	Em	1
_____, Wiley A.	Hal	
Herendon, Benjamin	Hal	1
_____, Caleb	Hal	1
_____, Joel	Hal	1
Herrenden, Jacob	Hab	
Heronton, William S.	Hry	2
Herringdine, Silas	Han	1
HESAW, Absalom	Gwn	3
_____ also see Hoshaw		
HESTATI, James	Gwn	3
HESTER/HESTOR/HESTERS/ HESTON/HERSTIN		
Hester, Benjamin	DeK	
_____, Daniel	Wil	2
_____, David	Bke	1
_____, Elizabeth	Clk	3
_____, Henry	Lau	
_____, John	Wal	1
_____, Joseph	Clk	3
_____, Joseph	Eff	1
_____, Mathew	Mor	2
_____, Michael	New	
_____, Nancy	Lau	
_____, Robert	Mor	2
_____, Samuel	Clk	3
_____, Stephen	Mor	2
_____, Stephen B.	Lau	
_____, Stephen C.	Mor	2
_____, Thomas	Clk	3
_____, Thomas	Trp	
_____, William	Bke	1
_____, William B.	Up	1
_____, Willis	Ear	
_____, Wheeler	Han	1
_____, Wyatt	Pik	1
_____, Zachr.	Jns	4
Hestor, Stephen	Eff	1
Hesters, Allen	Mtg	2
_____, John	Dec	
_____, Thomas	Dec	
Heston, James Sr.	Mor	2
Herstin, Peter	Gwn	3
HESTERLY, Frances	Hal	
_____, John V.	Hal	
HEWELL/HUELL		
Hewell, James D.	Clk	2
Huell, William	Ogl	
HEWETT/HEWET/HEWIT/HEWITT/ HEWLET/HUETT/HULETT		

Name	County	Page
Hewett, Alex^{r}.	DeK	40
Hewet, Ezekiel	Jks	323
Hewit, Jackson	Mad	108
Hewitt, James	Jns	469
Hewlet, John	Mon	225
Huett, William	Jks	329
Hulett, Henry	Lwn	83
______, Henry	Tlf	8
HIATT, Isaac	Hal	87
HIBLER, Eldred M.	Car	222
HICKEY/HICKY		
Hickey, James	Bke	144
______, Joseph	Crf	409
______, William	Har	176
Hicky, Stephen C.	Pul	160
HICKMAN/HICKMON		
Hickman, Aaron C.	Up	101
______, Charles C.	DeK	46
______, Copeland C.	Cpb	202
______, Ed.	Wks	347
______, John	Mon	210
______, Josiah	Hal	69
______, Lewis	Mon	201
______, Mrs. Mary	Bry	87
______, Paschal	Bke	117
______, Stephen	Bke	146
______, Thomas S.	New	33
______, William W.	Elb	127
Hickmon, John	Bak	16
______, John	Bib	76
HICKS/HIX		
Hicks, Abner	Wks	352
______, Amos	Cow	378
______, Anderson	Cow	376
______, Anderson	Cpb	207
______, B.	Wks	336
______, Betsey	Rch	271
______, Betsey	Twg	88
______, Burton	Clk	322
______, Colly	DeK	62
______, Daniel Sr.	Crf	413
______, Daniel	Crf	404
______, David	Mad	104
______, David	Pik	111
______, Edmond	Col	343
______, Edward	Jsp	370
______, Edward G.	Up	100
______, Elijah	Crf	409
______, Elijah	Mon	216
______, George	Tms	22
______, George A.	Crf	394
______, Gillam	Tlb	339
______, Henry	Rab	233
Hicks, Henry D.	Mon	181
______, Hetty	DeK	62
______, Isaac	Hab	59
______, Isom	Hry	242
______, James	Cpb	211
______, James	Em	168
______, Jason	Hab	41
______, Jasper	Ran	250
______, Jese	Hab	47
______, John	Cow	368
______, John	Dec	17
______, John	Ear	98
______, John	Hal	71
______, John	Wrn	202
______, Johnson	Elb	140
______, Jonathan	Hab	58
______, Josiah	Frk	216
______, Lewis F.	Jns	454
______, Littleberry	Trp	39
______, Mark	Jsp	353
______, Martha	Em	168
______, Mary	Lau	21
______, Mathew	Hry	221
______, Nathaniel	Dec	16
______, Nathaniel	Mad	115
______, Ralph	Dec	8
______, Robert	Crf	393
______, Samuel	Col	335
______, Susannah	Up	117
______, Thomas	Cpb	207
______, Thomas	Hal	73
______, Thomas	Har	183
______, Tolifer L.	Cow	370
______, Toliver	Cpb	310
______, Wiley	Hab	16
______, William	Elb	119
______, William	Hry	219
______, William A.	Cow	368
______, Willis B.	DeK	50
______, Wyatt	Pik	114
Hix, John	Car	225
HICKSON/HIXSON		
Hickson, Seaborn	Wrn	213
______, Thomas	Jsp	364
______, William	Col	359
Hixson, Timothy	Wil	295
HIDE, Austin	Hal	128
______, Isaiah	Rab	223
______, Reuben	Rab	228
______, Saml.	Jsp	396
______, Steven	Gwn	326
HIDEN, A.	Col	354
HIGDON, Burrel	Em	165

Name	County	Page
Higdon, Charles	Lau	19
______, Charles Jr.	Lau	20
______, Daniel	Han	156
______, Elizabeth	Wrn	192
______, Robert	Em	172
______, Robert	Lau	19
______, Rutherford	Jks	326
HIGFIELD, David	Hab	24
HIGGESON/HIGGINSON		
Higgeson, Philip	Jsp	397
Higginson, Larkin	Pik	109
HIGGINTON, James J.	Elb	148
HIGGINGBOTHAM/HIGGINBOTHAM/ HIGGENBOTHEM/HIGINBOTHAM/ HIGENBOTHAM/HIGINGBOTHAM/ HIGGANBOTTOM/HIGNILOTHAM/ HICKOMBOTTOM/HICKENBOTTOM		
Higgingbotham, Bartley	Elb	157
Higginbotham, Ann	Mad	100
______, Elizabeth	Jsp	393
______, Elizabeth	Mad	117
______, Francis C.	Rab	224
______, George	Wal	157
______, John	Frk	216
______, Nelson	Mad	106
Higgenbotham, John G.	Elb	138
______, Sarah	Gly	269
Higinbotham, Oliver	Wal	137
______, Sanford	Wal	138
Higenbotham, Ephraim B.	Car	227
Higingbotham, Jacob	Elb	121
______, John	Elb	123
______, William	Elb	121
Higganbottom, Robert A.	Gwn	331
Hignilotham, Joseph	Wal	137
Hickombottom, Henry	Mor	250
Hickenbottom, Thomas	Mon	198
HIGGINS/HEGGINS/also see Huggins		
Higgins, Benjamin	Gwn	363
______, Benjamin	Hab	24
______, Burrel	Gwn	361
______, Charles	Bib	55
______, David	Bts	178
______, Enoch	Hab	22
______, Henry	Hab	22
______, James	Gre	290
______, John	Bts	178
______, John	Hab	45
______, Kaleb	Jks	337
______, Palmer A.	Bts	163
______, Reubin	Gwn	325
______, Reuben	Gwn	361

Name	County	Page
Higgins, Rubin	Hab	44
______, Sanford	Gwn	319
______, Starling T.	Bts	172
______, Thomas	DeK	73
______, William	Bts	162
Heggins, John	Hab	22
______, Newton	Gwn	366
______, Rubin	Gwn	366
______, Wiley J.	Mon	218
HIGGS/HIGS		
Higgs, John	Twg	78
______, Jessey	Mtg	232
______, Thomas	Hal	104
______, William	Mtg	233
Higs, Isaac	Tat	371
HIGH, John	Gre	278
______, John	Jsp	371
______, Samuel	Hst	262
HIGHERS, Joseph	Wyn	284
HIGHFIELD, Hamon	Wrn	203
______, Leonard	Cow	381
HIGHNOTE, Benjamin	Hst	269
______, Henry	Hst	292
______, Philip	Hst	292
HIGHSMITH, David	Wyn	282
______, Isaac	Wyn	283
______, Jacob	Wyn	281
______, John	Elb	127
______, Samuel	Em	178
______, Sarah	Wyn	282
______, Thomas H.	Elb	145
______, William	Wyn	282
HIGHT - see Hite		
HIGHTOWER, Aaron	Fay	184
______, Arnold G.	Trp	32
______, Charnd.	Hst	296
______, Daniel	Har	176
______, Echols	Lau	4
______, Elisha	Har	183
______, Ephraim	Lau	21
______, Gregory	Lau	11
______, Henry	Fay	187
______, Henry	New	35
______, Henry H.	Lwn	88
______, Isaac	Clk	309
______, Jacob D.	Put	218
______, James	Doo	80
______, James	Up	120
______, James M.	Up	105
______, Jesse	Fay	189
______, John	Fay	195
______, John	Lwn	87
______, John	Up	101

Hightower, John P. Wal 124
_____, Jonathan Clk 291
_____, Jonathan DeK 44
_____, Joshua Lau 21
_____, Joshua Wal 157
_____, P. R. Bal 35
_____, Presley Trp 35
_____, Rolla Hry 211
_____, Rolly Wsh 275
_____, S. J. Jns 433
_____, Stephen DeK 69
_____, Thomas Trp 34
_____, Thomas A. Put 215
_____, William Fay 195
_____, William New 48
_____, Winfield Lau 14
HILBURN/HILBERN
Hilburn, Lemuel DeK 27
_____, M. DeK 28
Hilbern, Samuel Car 218
HILELBURG, McLammy Ran 250
HILL/HILLS
Hill, Abner Wrn 200
_____, Abraham Elb 131
_____, Abraham Wal 157
_____, Abraham Wil 307
_____, Abram DeK 68
_____, Abram S. Ogl 98
_____, Alexander B. Jef 419
_____, Alex[r]. Jks 336
_____, Ambrose DeK 48
_____, Amos Hab 58
_____, Anderson Frk 223
_____, Archibald Mar 144
_____, Archibald M. New 11
_____, Asa Hab 18
_____, Asa Mus 289
_____, Bartholemew Bts 165
_____, Benjamin Ran 246
_____, Benjamin Wrn 200
_____, Benjamin K. Rch 272
_____, Berry Gwn 322
_____, Blanton M. Ogl 94
_____, Burwell P. Wil 319
_____, C. Col 348
_____, Caleb Frk 224
_____, Carter Wal 168
_____, Cathrine Jsp 395
_____, Daniel Lau 7
_____, Dar. B. Bal 40
_____, David Cpb 200
_____, David Hab 48
_____, Dempsey Cpb 202
Hill, Dempsey Cpb 211
_____, Dorothy Wrn 208
_____, E. Y. Jsp 370
_____, Elam Elb 119
_____, Eli S. Wal 137
_____, Elias New 5
_____, Elijah Bke 144
_____, Elisha Fay 191
_____, Enoch Mwr 156
_____, Fabrina Put 172
_____, Fanny Gwn 317
_____, Fielding Wrn 204
_____, Frances Wrn 198
_____, Francis W. Har 178
_____, Frederick Bke 143
_____, G. B. Jsp 363
_____, George Rch 271
_____, George A. Lee 27
_____, George W. Mwr 153
_____, Green B. Jsp 396
_____, Green B. Mon 208
_____, Gillium Bke 144
_____, Green Hst 262
_____, Green Lwn 83
_____, Green Pik 121
_____, Hampton W. Wal 125
_____, Hanah Dec 15
_____, Harbert Hab 27
_____, Hardy Mus 285
_____, Henry Mon 204
_____, Henry Wrn 204
_____, Henry Wrn 204
_____, Henry B. Bib 58
_____, Henry P. Ogl 86
_____, Hezekiah Jsp 390
_____, Isaac Clk 296
_____, Isaac Cpb 200
_____, Isaac Crf 396
_____, Isaac Jns 439
_____, Isaac Mon 219
_____, James Car 227
_____, James Frk 223
_____, James Mwr 153
_____, James Mon 214
_____, James Rch 288
_____, James A. Ogl 84
_____, James H. Mwr 153
_____, James J. Wsh 239
_____, James P. Gre 282
_____, Jeptha Mon 221
_____, Jeremiah Hal 97
_____, John Gwn 336
_____, John Han 157

Name	County	Page
Hill, John	Hry	222
______, John	Jks	328
______, John	Jsp	353
______, John	Jsp	370
______, John	Lwn	83
______, John	Mar	144
______, John	McI	124
______, John	Mwr	150
______, John	New	9
______, John	Pik	112
______, John	Wal	169
______, John	Wil	319
______, John O.	Frk	245
______, John W.	Mus	278
______, Jonathan	Rch	273
______, Joseph	Gwn	323
______, Joseph	Mon	175
______, Joseph	Wks	337
______, Joseph	Wrn	201
______, Joseph L.	Jsp	355
______, Joshua	Gwn	319
______, L.	Rch	265
______, Lewis	Elb	156
______, Lodowick	Wil	306
______, Mahala	Wal	123
______, Mark	Wrn	207
______, Martha	Col	352
______, Martha	Tat	373
______, Martin	Han	157
______, Mary	Bts	176
______, Mary	New	37
______, Middleton	Cpb	206
______, Miles	Ogl	93
______, Moses	Mar	144
______, Mountain	Cow	388
______, Nancy	DeK	67
______, Perry	Hst	288
______, Phillis	Rch	277
______, Richard	Wal	169
______, Richard A.	Cam	183
______, Robert	Har	175
______, Robert	Hry	244
______, Robert	Put	209
______, Robert	Wrn	198
______, Rubin	Col	343
______, S.	Gwn	309
______, S. B.	Cht	251
______, Samuel B.	DeK	61
______, Sarah	Ogl	65
______, Slaughter	Bib	64
______, Sion	Wal	169
______, Sion	Wrn	198
______, Sion L.	Jns	439

Name	County	Page
Hill, T.	Gwn	308
______, Theophillus J.	Wal	128
______, Theophulas	Wsh	249
______, Thomas	Cpb	203
______, Thomas	Cpb	209
______, Thomas	Frk	222
______, Thomas	Pik	121
______, Waid	Put	218
______, Waid	Trp	36
______, Whitmel C.	Mon	225
______, Wiley	Mar	144
______, William	Bry	85
______, William	Fay	200
______, William	Gre	304
______, William	Gwn	336
______, William	Jks	328
______, William	Jsp	390
______, William	Lin	63
______, William	Lwn	84
______, William	Mon	188
______, William	Wrn	197
______, William C.	Wrn	220
______, William M.	DeK	26
______, William M.	Mon	216
______, William R.	Bal	37
______, Wylie	Wil	308
Hills, Harriet	Cht	246
______, R.	Cht	252
HILLEY/HILEY/HELEY		
Hilley, Richard B.	Cow	377
Hiley, John	Hst	294
Heley, Barbary	Jef	401
HILLHOUSE, David	Wil	289
______, Elijah	Hal	86
______, Samuel	Hal	85
HILLIARD/HILLYARD/HILYARD/ HYLIAR/HYLLIARD		
Hilliard, Dennis	Lau	5
______, Francis	Lau	13
______, James	App	5
______, James	Doo	83
______, James	Ware	183
______, Kinchen	Lau	7
Hilliard, Silas	Ware	189
______, Thomas	Ware	183
______, Wiley	Mon	185
Hillyard, Richard	Wil	293
Hilyard, Gilas	Dec	12
______, William	Ran	249
Hyliar, W.	Wil	289
Hylliard, William	Wil	322
HILLISS, John	Bke	146
HILLMON/HILLSMAN/HILSMAN		

Hillmon, Caleb	Wrn	208	Hines, Thomas	Dec	18
_____, Mary	Wrn	213	_____, Thomas	Put	177
_____, Samuel T.	Wrn	207	_____, William	Bke	127
Hillsman, Micajah	Mor	264	_____, William	Cam	189
Hilsman, Bennet	Han	157	_____, William	Trp	37
_____, James Jr.	Han	155	Himes, John	Ogl	80
HILSON, John	Wrn	330	Heines, John W.	Put	177
_____, Lewis	Wrn	233	HINKLE/HINKEL/HINCLE		
_____, William	Wrn	232	Hinkle, George	Hal	107
HILTON/HYLTON			_____, Henry	Hal	107
Hilton, Elmsley	Gwn	329	_____, John	Hal	113
_____, Lawrence W.	Mon	183	Hinkel, Solomon	Hab	9
_____, Sarah	Jef	411	Hincle, Michael	Car	228
_____, Sterling	Clk	296	HINNARD/HINIARD		
Hylton, Thomas	Bul	100	Hinnard, John	Fay	203
_____, William C.	Bul	100	Hiniard, William	Fay	181
HILYER/HILLYER			HINSON: see Henson		
Hilyer, James	Mwr	168	HINTON/HUNTON		
Hillyer, John F.	Wal	123	Hinton, Allen	Twg	66
HINELY, Israel	Eff	108	_____, Bradford	Cpb	211
_____, John	Eff	108	_____, Fielding S.	Wil	323
_____, Joshua	Eff	107	_____, Hardy	Hry	224
_____, Solomon	Eff	109	_____, Henry	Wrn	215
HINESMAN/HINDSMAN			_____, Jacob	Cpb	204
Hinesman, Emanuel	Gly	265	_____, James	Mwr	159
_____, Peter	Hry	216	_____, James	Wil	317
_____, William	Hry	217	_____, James S.	Elb	125
Hindsman, Israel	Wil	315	_____, Jesse	Wil	318
HINES/HIMES/HEINES			_____, Joab	New	19
Hines, Charlton	Lib	46	_____, John	Clk	308
_____, Elias D.	Trp	43	_____, John	Cow	369
_____, Elizabeth	Jef	414	_____, John	Wks	334
_____, Henry	Doo	83	_____, John D.	Cow	367
_____, Henry	Mwr	157	_____, John L.	Elb	125
_____, Howell	Eff	115	_____, Lewis	New	10
_____, James	Jsp	360	_____, Lovit	Hry	210
_____, James	Mwr	157	_____, Noah	Wil	317
_____, James E.	Bke	129	_____, Peter	Elb	123
_____, John	Bke	124	_____, Robert	Elb	124
_____, John H.	Bke	123	_____, Robert	Tlb	331
_____, John Sr.	Bke	132	_____, Thomas	Elb	158
_____, Lewis	Bry	85	_____, William	Wal	152
_____, Lewis	Trp	34	_____, William	Wrn	223
_____, Martin	Clk	315	_____, Wood	Jks	322
_____, Nathaniel Sr.	Gre	303	Hunton, Charles	Clk	297
_____, Nathaniel Jr.	Gre	303	_____, John	Clk	298
_____, R. K.	Bal	44	HIPS, Joseph	Hab	53
_____, R. T.	Mon	216	HIRES, Anney	Lib	46
_____, Robert	Mon	180	HIRSTON, Hugh B.	Bts	163
_____, Samuel	Bul	92	HISLER, Daniel	Jns	442
_____, Sarah	Up	110	_____, George (Heisler)	Cam	187
_____, Starling	Dec	11	HITE/HIGHT		
_____, Stephen	Jef	410	Hite, Gab[l].	Gwn	334

Name	County	Page
Hite, Henry	Wrn	207
Hight, Howel	Wrn	206
_____, John	Twg	86
_____, Wyley	Wal	128
HITCHCOCK/HICKOX		
Hitchcock, Bedford	Ogl	76
_____, Daniel	Han	157
_____, Elizabeth	Scr	313
_____, James	Mus	280
_____, John	Cpb	209
_____, John	Ogl	76
_____, John	Wal	137
_____, Joseph	Eff	112
_____, Mesheek	Han	155
_____, William	Han	155
_____, William	Jsp	373
_____, William	Trp	34
Hickox, David	Ware	187
HITSON, Henry	Twg	86
_____, Joseph	Ogl	102
_____, Thomas	Ogl	103
HOBBS/HOBS/HOBB		
Hobbs, Berry	Lau	5
_____, Boling	Lau	4
_____, Charles	Bts	165
_____, D. H.	Col	350
_____, David	Wrn	225
_____, Elam	Mon	187
_____, George	Mon	216
_____, Gothrum	Wrn	221
_____, Henry	Bul	98
_____, Henry	Mar	144
_____, Ira T.	Hst	266
_____, Jacob	Har	191
_____, John	Wrn	223
_____, John Sr.	Up	120
_____, John Jr.	Up	120
_____, Larry	Hst	290
_____, Moses	Wrn	225
_____, Nathan	Gre	273
_____, Robert	Gre	280
_____, Robert	Up	106
_____, Solomon	Mon	216
_____, William	Mon	218
_____, William	Tlb	327
_____, William	Wrn	225
_____, William M.	Fay	204
Hobs, William	Mwr	162
Hobb, John	Bul	95
HOBBY, A.	Lee	28
_____, Francis J.	Pul	143
_____, Jesse	Irw	301
_____, M.	Lee	26
Hobby, M. Jr.	Lee	28
_____, William J.	Rch	267
_____, William Jr.	Rch	260
HOBDAY, Stark	Rch	269
HOBGOOD/HOPGOOD		
Hobgood, Henry	Hry	216
_____, Hezekiah	Hry	205
_____, Lewis	Hry	204
Hopgood, Josiah	Frk	250
HOBSON, James	Frk	234
_____, also see Hopson		
HODGES/HODGING/HODGE		
Hodges, Abel	Wsh	250
_____, Alfred	Pul	162
_____, Andrew	Bts	159
_____, Archibald	Tat	371
_____, Benjamin	Ear	97
_____, Dorothy	Bul	92
_____, Drury	Jns	435
_____, Edmund	Twg	84
_____, Edmund K.	Hst	273
_____, Elbert	Wsh	275
_____, Elias	Doo	89
_____, Elizabeth	Bke	118
_____, Mrs. Esther	Bry	88
_____, Foreman	Pul	162
_____, George E.	Har	176
_____, Hardy Sr.	Scr	299
_____, Henry	Wsh	268
_____, James	Hab	22
_____, James	New	26
_____, James	Scr	302
_____, Jane	Scr	306
_____, Jesse	Jns	436
_____, Jessee	Jsp	391
_____, John	Clk	293
_____, John	Doo	86
_____, John	Ear	97
_____, John	Eff	111
_____, John	New	25[illegible]
_____, John	Put	20[illegible]
_____, John	Wsh	24[illegible]
_____, John J.	Pul	15[illegible]
_____, John L.	Twg	6[illegible]
_____, John Sr.	Scr	29[illegible]
_____, Jordan	Wsh	27[illegible]
_____, Joseph	Bul	9[illegible]
_____, Joseph	Bul	9[illegible]
_____, Joseph	Clk	29[illegible]
_____, Mary	Lib	4[illegible]
_____, Matthew	Lau	1[illegible]
_____, Milly	Pul	15[illegible]
_____, Nathan	Lwn	8[illegible]

Name	County	Page
Hodges, Nathaniel	Bul	92
______, Rebecca	Pul	156
______, Redding	Wsh	245
______, Robert	Twg	63
______, Samuel	Doo	86
______, Samuel K.	Mus	279
______, Sarah	Wsh	259
______, Seth	Wsh	242
______, Wiley T.	Wsh	245
______, William	Clk	291
______, William	Eff	111
______, William	Tat	374
______, William	Tat	375
______, Willis	Twg	64
Hodging, Mary	Cht	266
Hodge, Allen L.	Mad	100
______, Alston	Gre	279
______, Alvey	Mor	242
______, Andrew F.	New	18
______, Archebald	Gre	282
______, David	New	33
______, Elisha	Dec	17
______, Hosa	Lee	33
______, James	Jks	342
______, James	Mor	239
______, James Sr.	New	34
______, James Jr.	New	19
______, John	Bal	35
______, John	Har	181
______, John	Lau	13
______, John E.	Har	175
______, Lemuel	Lee	33
______, Peachy B.	Tfo	355
______, Peggy	Up	118
______, Richard S.	Tlb	326
______, Samuel	New	18
______, Samuel	Scr	299
______, William	DeK	67
______, William	Mad	101
______, William	Mar	143
______, William	Trp	55
______, Wyly	New	51
HODNETT/HADNETT		
Hodnett, Henry W.	New	34
______, James	Trp	51
______, John	New	20
______, Lovit P.	Hry	223
______, Thomas	New	32
______, William	Trp	43
Hadnett, Benjamin	Hry	238
HODO, Baldwin	Wrn	209
______, Dyer C.	Tlb	329
______, Marquis D. L.	Tlb	328
Hodo, Nathaniel	Twg	73
______, Sarah	Wrn	209
HOGAN/HOGIN/HOGEN		
Hogan, Alexander	Car	223
______, Elijah	Hal	97
______, Elijah	Wks	337
______, Ellice	Car	223
______, Emsley P.	Car	220
______, James	Doo	80
______, James	Hab	26
______, James	Jef	415
______, James	Lin	71
______, James B.	Mon	202
______, John	Cht	259
______, John	Jks	339
______, Mary	Col	338
______, Matthew	Twg	81
______, Nancy	Jns	469
______, Ridgway	Jns	469
______, Sarah	Lin	71
______, Shadrack	Jks	340
______, Thomas	Car	214
______, Thomas	Wal	148
______, William	Cow	382
______, William	Jks	331
Hogin, Isham T.	Wal	156
______, James	Hab	37
Hogen, Dorcas	Bib	73
HOGG/HOGE/HOG/HOAG		
Hogg, Hugh	Gre	285
______, James V.	Bts	161
______, Jeter A.	Trp	42
______, John	Trp	41
______, Lewis	Mon	174
______, Mrs.	Cht	283
______, Samuel	Gre	285
Hoge, Jacob	Dec	8
______, Jesse	Hab	28
______, Nancy	Jns	465
______, William	Bib	70
Hog, Lucy	Put	185
______, William	Wks	340
Hoag, Stephen	Mon	200
HOGLY, Martha	Wil	318
HOGUE, Jacob	Cpb	194
______, Jacob B.	Mwr	163
______, Johnathan	Cpb	196
______, Jonathan	Gre	279
______, Solomon	Mwr	163
______, William	Clk	309
______, Willis	Wal	157
HOGWOOD, Benj[a].	Wrn	218
______, James Jr.	Wrn	228

Name	County	Page
Hogwood, Wiley	Frk	244
HOLBIL, Joseph	Lee	31
HOLBROOK/HOLEBROOK/HOLL-BROOK/HOLBROOKS/HOLEBROOKS		
Holbrook, Christopher	Frk	250
_____, Edy	Frk	249
_____, Jesse	Frk	252
_____, Jesse C.	Frk	250
_____, Samuel	Frk	250
_____, William	Frk	235
_____, William Sr.	Frk	234
Holebrook, Elender	Hab	24
_____, Fleming	Elb	126
_____, John	Hab	24
_____, Nathan	Ogl	93
_____, Thomas B.	Wal	139
Hollbrook, Green B.	Frk	212
Holbrooks, Alexander	Rab	222
_____, J. D.	DeK	27
_____, James H.	DeK	42
_____, John	DeK	38
Holebrooks, Jincy	Gwn	355
_____, Sally	Gwn	355
HOLCOMB/HOLCOMBE/HOLECOMBE/HOLCOLMBE/HOLECLOMBE/HOL-COM/HOLCOLUMBE/HOLCUMB/HOLECOME/HOCOMB		
Holcomb, Absalom	Hab	19
_____, Alfert	Hab	62
_____, Ansel	Hab	62
_____, Ezekiel	Frk	226
_____, George G.	Bal	32
_____, Hamton	Hab	33
_____, James B.	Mon	221
_____, James W.	Mon	187
_____, Jese	Hab	49
_____, Joel	New	6
_____, John	Frk	225
_____, John	Hab	49
_____, John	Hal	132
_____, John	New	6
_____, Richard	Gwn	326
_____, Samuel	Hab	20
_____, Sherwood	Hab	49
_____, Solomon	Frk	249
_____, William	Jks	340
Holcombe, Eliza	Cht	246
_____, George	Rch	273
_____, Henry B.	Rch	272
_____, James Sr.	Rch	280
_____, John C.	Rch	272
_____, John G.	Cht	269
_____, Joseph	Hab	15

Name	County	Page
Holcombe, Martin	DeK	41
Holecombe, Russel	Hab	15
Holcolmbe, John S.	DeK	73
_____, Ruben	DeK	70
Holeclombe, David	DeK	70
_____, Jonathan V.	DeK	69
Holcom, Henry D.	Hab	9
_____, Thomas	Jks	340
Holcolumbe, Henry	DeK	66
Holcumb, Jeremiah	Hab	33
Holecome, Dicksow	Wal	128
Hocomb, Isare	Hab	49
Halcomb, Henry	New	54
_____, Robert W.	New	25
HOLDEN/HOLDIN/HOLDING		
Holden, Isaac	Rab	233
_____, Jane	Tfo	365
_____, John	Col	363
_____, Joseph	Hab	45
_____, Thomas	Tfo	363
Holdin, Osias	Hab	42
Holding, James	Hab	46
_____, Lucy	Frk	220
_____, Richard	Hab	40
HOLDER, Abijah	Col	364
_____, Catherine	Clk	292
_____, James	Col	361
_____, Jesse	Col	364
_____, Jesse	Lin	74
_____, John	Wks	336
_____, John S.	Jef	409
_____, Lydia	Wrn	219
_____, Malichia	Trp	42
_____, Thomas	Wks	351
_____, Wiley	Pul	162
_____, William	Jef	409
_____, William	Wks	351
HOLDIDGE, James	Hry	227
HOLDNESS/HOLDERNESS		
Holdness, James M.	Hry	199
Holderness, James	Hst	276
HOLEMAN, Levy	Hab	40
HOLFURT, John	Hab	50
HOLLIDAY/HOLIDAY/HOLLADAY		
Holliday, Abner E.	Bke	126
_____, Andrew	Cht	280
_____, Ashley	Bke	127
_____, Bynum	Mor	245
_____, Dennis L.	Bke	126
_____, Elisha	Wrn	210
_____, Furney	Bke	128
_____, James	Jns	451
_____, John Sr.	Jns	451

Name	County	Page
Holliday, Latitia	Jns	451
______, R. J.	Col	337
______, Richard J.	Wil	305
______, Robert M.	Jks	325
______, Silas	Hry	227
______, Thomas	Bke	128
______, Thomas	Doo	82
Holiday, Catherine	Wil	289
______, H. J.	App	5
______, J. W.	Jks	324
______, Lucinda	Lin	75
______, Owen	Wil	294
______, Thomas	Wil	305
______, William	Put	174
Holladay, William	Twg	74
HOLIFIELD/HOLEFIELD		
Holifield, Wiley	Jsp	373
______, William P.	Bts	169
______, Willis	Bts	175
Holefield, Alsa	Jsp	371
______, George W.	Hab	62
HOLINRONSON, Thomas	Han	155
HOLLAND/HOLLAM/HOLLUM		
Holland, Abraham	Cow	382
______, Abraham	Jsp	386
______, Anna	Bke	147
______, Archabold	Hal	76
______, Benjamin	Lwn	83
______, Benjamin	Mon	174
______, Chesley	Hal	75
______, Civility	Bke	146
______, Daniel	Twg	68
______, Daniel S.	Doo	80
______, David	Hst	289
______, David	Tat	379
______, Elijah	Hal	103
______, Elisha	Clk	304
______, Elizabeth	Put	179
______, Frederick	Tat	373
______, George W.	Jsp	356
______, Haafrey	Jsp	367
______, Henry	Hal	75
______, Henry	Twg	75
______, Isaac	Mus	278
______, Jacob	Hst	289
______, James	Bke	147
______, James	Gwn	377
______, James	Hal	76
______, James	New	42
______, James	Mus	279
______, James	Pul	153
______, James H.	Fay	199
______, Jesse	Jks	341
Holland, Jethro	Doo	80
______, John	Gly	265
______, John	Jks	314
______, John	Hal	71
______, John	Mon	179
______, John	Put	217
______, John	Tat	374
______, John R.	Trp	46
______, Jonas H.	Jsp	356
______, Joshua	Pul	153
______, Lauson J.	Jsp	394
______, Lewis C.	Jsp	371
______, Lindsey	Fay	198
______, Lisha	Put	181
______, Margaret	Jsp	371
______, Mariah	Doo	84
______, Marragett	Wsh	253
______, Moses	Hry	219
______, Peter	Jks	320
______, Randolph	Pik	107
______, Rebecca	Fay	204
______, Robert	Har	191
______, Samuel	Mon	186
______, Tobias	Tfo	355
______, Widow	Wal	169
______, William	Gwn	353
______, William	Tat	378
Hollam, Austin C.	Hal	103
Hollum, William	Hab	63
HOLLINGEN, James	Gwn	376
HOLLIMAN/HOLOMON/HOLLOMAN/ HOLLEMAN/HOLIMAN/HOLLAMON		
Holliman, Harmon	Mus	280
______, John	Put	212
______, Sarah	Col	361
______, William	Cpb	194
______, William	Mus	292
Holomon, Abijah	Wrn	206
______, Eaton	Bib	76
______, John C.	Wrn	232
______, Samuel	Bak	15
______, Thomas	Wrn	202
Holloman, David	Col	361
______, Samuel	Col	361
______, Samuel B.	Col	361
Holleman, David Jr.	Put	179
______, David Sr.	Put	179
Holiman, David	Gwn	324
______, Richard	Gwn	361
Hollamon, Zachariah	Bib	67
HOLLIN, Archibald	DeK	56
HOLLINGSHEAD/HOLLINGHEAD/ HOLLENSHED		

Name	County	Page
Hollingshead, Hugh	Lin	66
Hollinghead, Jacob	Cpb	205
Hollenshed, John	Hal	109
HOLLINGSWORTH/HOLLENSWORTH/ HOLLINSWORTH/HOLANDSWORTH/ HOLLANSWORTH		
Hollingsworth, Aaron	DeK	64
______, Caleb	Lau	9
______, Cisca	Hab	60
______, Cornelius	Twg	78
______, Daniel	Ear	92
______, George	Lau	9
______, Isaiah	Hry	230
______, James	Bib	50
______, John	Bib	50
______, Joseph	DeK	54
______, Mary	Twg	80
______, Valentine	Irw	298
______, William	Doo	84
Hollensworth, Thomas	Gwn	358
Hollinsworth, Jesse	Fay	202
Holandsworth, Zebulon	Tat	374
Hollansworth, Joseph	New	22
______, Moses	New	22
**HOLLINSGROVES, R.(slave)	Rch	271
HOLLIS, James	Frk	228
______, James	Trp	53
______, John	Hry	223
______, John Sr.	Mor	267
______, John Jr.	Mor	265
______, Joseph	Cpb	194
______, Richard	Put	184
______, S.	Cht	253
______, Samuel	Gwn	368
______, Thomas	Mon	198
______, Thomas	Mor	265
______, Urias	Cpb	206
______, William	Trp	40
HOLLOMAN/HALLMAN/HOLLY- MAN/HOLMAN		
Holloman, Lewis	Up	115
Hallmon, George	Twg	80
Hallman, Nancy	Tat	379
Hollyman, William	Hst	286
Holman, Jacob	Rch	279
HOLLOWAY/HOLLAWAY/HOLAWAY/ HALLEWAY/HALLIWAY/HALLOWAY		
Holloway, Anthony	Put	177
______, Chesley	Jsp	380
______, Daniel	Jsp	361
______, David	Clk	304
______, Edward	Up	103
______, James	Bul	98
Holloway, James	Pik	121
______, Jeremiah	Hst	289
______, John	Hst	289
______, Mastin	Bts	177
______, Matilda	Bts	175
______, Mecklinberry	Bul	98
______, Norwell	Mon	211
______, Paul	Up	100
______, Patrick G.	Up	106
______, Peter	Up	100
______, William Sr.	Tms	27
______, William Jr.	Tms	27
______, Zachariah	DeK	57
Hollaway, Hubbard	Hry	220
______, Lacy	Cpb	195
______, Samuel	Cpb	208
______, Solomon	Cpb	203
______, William	Mon	213
Holaway, John	Car	226
Halleway, George	Wal	160
Halliway, Claraway	Wal	170
Halloway, David	Scr	316
HOLLY/HOLLEY		
Holly, Bricey	Hst	282
______, Editha	Elb	129
______, Eli	Bke	138
______, Elizabeth	Twg	81
______, Isaac	Twg	72
______, James	Hst	282
______, James H.	DeK	36
______, John	DeK	27
______, John	Mar	140
______, John	Pul	160
______, Mary	Lee	31
______, William	DeK	58
______, William	Hst	289
______, William Jr.	Hst	293
Holley, Francis	Elb	148
______, Frederick	Frk	211
______, Green Lee	Bts	166
______, Henry	Wsh	240
______, John J.	Wal	138
______, Nathaniel	Frk	213
______, Pleasant	Frk	216
______, Richard J.	Bts	175
______, Sarah	Frk	255
______, William	Wal	139
HOLMES/HOLMS/HOMES/HOMLES		
Holmes, David	Clk	312
______, Elizabeth	Cht	265
______, David	Mon	219
______, Elizabeth	Twg	85
______, Garnet	Car	216

Name	County	Page
Holmes, Henry	Twg	77
______, Ichabod	Wil	305
______, Isaac	Hst	264
______, Isaiah H.	Wks	339
______, J.	Jns	465
______, James	Bib	60
______, James	Car	215
______, James	Elb	136
______, James	McI	121
______, James	Up	104
______, James C.	Pik	113
______, James P.	Jsp	356
______, John	Jsp	392
______, John J.	Wsh	268
______, Jonathan	Mon	205
______, Joseph	Wil	295
______, Joshua	Cpb	203
______, Joshua	Elb	125
______, Josiah	Pik	127
______, Margaret	Lau	15
______, Mary	Wil	297
______, Richard	Hab	32
______, Richmond	Cow	375
______, Robert	Tlb	327
______, Shadrack	Elb	128
______, Tabitha	Frk	219
______, Washington	Clk	301
______, William	Tlb	328
Holms, John	Hab	38
______, Zekel	Hab	37
Homes, Burrel	Ogl	94
______, Charles L.	New	44
______, Findley	Bib	64
______, Frederick	Bib	64
______, Vivian	Gwn	320
Homles, Adam T.	Lib	47
HOLOWA, Rubin	Hab	49
HOLSENBACK/HELSABECK/ HOBSONBACK		
Holsenback, John	Gwn	324
______, Thomas	Gwn	312
Helsabeck, Frances	Gwn	356
Hobsonback, Jacob	Lin	70
HOLSOMBAKE/HOLSONBAK		
Holsombake, Matthew D.	Rch	283
Holsonbak, Lewis D.	Frk	228
HOLSON, Francis	Jks	311
HOLSTON, Asa	Mwr	151
______, Hiram	Mwr	151
HOLT, Anderson	Trp	55
______, Ann	Jef	406
______, Ann	Jns	469
______, Asa	Jef	402
Holt, Cicero	Clk	325
______, Elbert A.	Rch	291
______, Ellis	Wsh	269
______, Frederick	Cpb	205
______, Hallandsberry	Put	185
______, Harrison	Har	179
______, Henry	Put	185
______, Hines	Bal	42
______, Hines	Wal	152
______, James	Hst	290
______, James H.	Har	175
______, Joe (col[d].)	Bal	37
______, John	Hal	90
______, John	Har	176
______, John S.	Rch	285
______, Leroy	Wrn	198
______, Lewis	Jns	440
______, Mary T.	Put	176
______, Peyton	Put	205
______, Pulask S.	Put	219
______, Raugley	Put	172
______, Richard	Gwn	332
______, Samuell W.	Pul	151
______, Seabern	Hab	35
______, Simon	Put	185
______, Simon	Wal	132
______, Susannah	Wsh	269
______, Tarpley	Bib	64
______, Tapeley	Put	172
______, Thaddeus G.	Twg	60
______, William	Pul	161
______, William	Put	206
______, William	Trp	38
______, William W.	Pul	151
HOLTON/HOLTEN		
Holton, Elizabeth	Wsh	271
______, Francis T.	Em	171
______, Isaac	Bke	133
______, Josiah	Em	168
______, Martha	Em	171
______, Mary	Han	157
______, Nathaniel	Em	170
______, Robert	Hst	281
______, Samuel	Hst	284
______, Thial	Wsh	244
______, Thomas	Put	217
______, William	Wsh	265
______, William L.	Em	164
Holten, Gilleon	Dec	13
______, Sherrod		
HOLTZCLAW/HOLTSCLAW/HOLLS-CLAW/HOTTSCLAW		
Holtzclaw, Benjamin	Wil	290

Holtzclaw, Henry	Wil	323
______, Hosea	Wil	309
______, John G.	Gre	272
______, Mary	Wil	316
______, Sarah	Wil	309
______, Silas	Hry	222
______, Wilford	Gre	297
Holtsclaw, Harris	Tlb	325
Hollsclaw, Elijah	Ogl	90
Hottsclaw, Jane	Hry	251
HOLWELL/HOLLOWELL		
Holwell, John	Lwn	84
______, Theophilius	Scr	310
Hollowell, Joseph	Bak	19
HOLZENDORF/HOLRENDORF		
Holzendorf, J. L. K.	Cam	181
Holrendorf, Mahala	McI	122
HONAKER, Jacob	Cam	182
HONEY, John	DeK	62
______, Thomas	Mwr	161
______, William	Mwr	157
HONEYCUT/HONEYCUTT		
Honeycut, Henry	Put	203
______, Seth	Twg	79
______, William	Frk	234
Honeycutt, Edmond	Jks	324
______, Merick	Col	356
HOOD, Alexander	Crf	398
______, Allen	New	33
______, Andrew	Up	103
______, Benjamin	Lin	72
______, Burwell	Wil	296
______, Bynum	Hry	206
______, Elisha	Wal	128
______, James	Gwn	318
______, Jesse	Cow	389
______, Joda A.	New	49
______, Joel	Cow	382
______, John	Tms	26
______, Joseph	Hry	236
______, Joshua	Hry	243
______, Sally	Gwn	377
______, Sean	Wsh	245
______, Sherrod	Wsh	270
______, Stephen	Wil	324
______, Stephen W.	Wil	322
______, Viney	Gwn	377
______, William	Bts	171
______, William	Wsh	249
______, William C.	Frk	220
______, William W.	Frk	239
______, Z. S.	Jks	313
HOOKER, Jensey	Rch	286
Hooker, Nathan F.	Hst	274
HOOKS, A.	Wks	347
______, Asa	Pul	154
______, Bardin	Twg	61
______, D.	Lee	28
______, Dixon	Put	188
______, Hilery	Bak	18
______, Hillory	Wsh	268
______, James	Hst	295
______, Jesse	Wks	342
______, John	Mor	245
______, John	Put	189
______, John	Wks	342
______, John Sr.	Mor	246
______, Jonathan	Em	175
______, Jonathan	Wks	342
______, McKiney	New	26
______, Michael	Bke	126
______, Nathl.	Jks	329
______, Polley (W)	Mor	243
______, Sarah	Wsh	253
______, Thomas	Put	189
______, William	Em	175
HOOPER/HOPER/HOOPPER		
Hooper, Charles	Hal	128
______, James A.	Frk	229
______, Jesse C.	Frk	251
______, Johnson M.	Cpb	205
______, Joicy	Frk	251
______, Jonathon	Put	200
______, Joshua	Frk	232
______, Matilda	Hab	53
______, Matthew B.	Frk	229
______, Matthew B. Jr.	Frk	228
______, Richard Sr.	Frk	254
______, Richard	Frk	232
______, Rolly	Ogl	85
______, Sarah	Hal	128
______, Thomas	DeK	37
______, Thomas	Ogl	85
______, William	Hal	128
Hoper, Edward	Hab	65
______, James	Clk	316
______, John	Hab	43
Hoopper, James	DeK	70
HOOTEN, Henry	Up	113
______, James	Hry	244
______, James B.	Up	113
______, Littleton	Tlb	333
HOOVER/HOVER		
Hoover, Joel	Wks	350
______, John	Bul	101
______, John	Wks	333

Name	County	Page
Hover, A.	Cht	267
______, John	Cht	282
HOPE, James	Hal	84
______, John	McI	131
______, William Sr.	Lib	47
______, William C.	Hal	89
HOPKINS/HIPKINS		
Hopkins, B.	Mus	288
______, Benjamin	McI	126
______, Daniel	Trp	48
______, Dennis	DeK	39
______, Eucedas A.	Clk	296
______, Frances	Gwn	341
______, Green B.	Wil	302
______, Isaac	Wil	306
______, James	Wil	312
______, Jilson	Wil	305
______, Josiah	Mad	115
______, Lambeth	New	14
______, Levinia	Wil	316
______, Martha	Wil	312
______, Nancy	Ogl	99
______, Samuel	Tlb	340
______, Sarah	Clk	315
______, Sol	Gwn	339
______, Susannah	Clk	302
______, Timothy	Cam	187
______, William	Har	186
______, William	Lau	22
______, William	Rab	234
Hipkins, Susan	Cam	183
HOPPE, Jonathan	Ogl	85
HOPPING, Ephraim	Wil	298
HOPSON, Absalem	Wal	160
______, Caswell	Put	187
______, Green	Tms	20
______, Green B.	Bts	158
______, Hardy	Mon	220
______, Hardy	Wrn	207
______, Isaac	Hab	28
______, Warren	Mon	215
______, Warren A.	Tms	20
______, Wiley	Mwr	153
______, William	Trp	39
______, William	Wsh	243
______, Zachariah	Tms	22
______, also see Hobson		
HORN/HORNE		
Horn, Abisha	Twg	84
______, Abner	Up	101
______, Briton	Wks	352
______, Colin	Rch	254
______, Cullin	Hst	281

Name	County	Page
Horn, Ephraim	Pik	115
______, Elijah	Gwn	323
______, Evan	Wks	349
______, Franklin B.	Trp	32
______, Hellkijah H.	Tms	22
______, Henry	Wks	353
______, Howell	Jns	436
______, Howell	Up	104
______, Hugh	DeK	49
______, Isaac	Gre	291
______, Isaac	Hst	262
______, James	Bal	30
______, Jessee	Gwn	323
______, Jesse R.	Put	177
______, Joab	Twg	76
______, Joel	Jns	453
______, John	Gre	287
______, John	Gwn	378
______, John	Mon	186
______, Joshua	Trp	51
______, Josiah	Twg	69
______, Levi	Bal	30
______, Mary	Em	166
______, Michael	Har	181
______, Michael	Tms	22
______, Moses	Mwr	150
______, Nathan	Crf	393
______, Preston A.	Gre	274
______, Rebecca	Lau	15
______, Richard	McI	131
______, Roland L.	Tms	22
______, Sherrod	Pik	128
______, Sherrod H	Pik	128
______, Thomas	Mon	185
Horne, Elijah	Jns	454
______, Henry E.	Dec	8
______, Henry W.	Pul	141
______, Wiley	Dec	16
______, William	Bal	31
HORNBUCKLE, Nathaniel	Jsp	361
______, Richard B.	DeK	49
HORNIDAY, Isaiah	Mon	173
HORNING, Philip	Eff	114
HORNSBY/HORNBY		
Hornsby, John	Fay	201
______, John	Gly	268
______, Leonard	DeK	42
______, Moses	DeK	39
______, Noah	DeK	38
______, Rebeccah	Tms	28
______, Thomas	DeK	38
______, William	DeK	53
______, William	Gly	268

Name	County	Page
Hornby, James A.	New	8
HORSEBURG, John	Gwn	369
HORSLEY, James	Up	106
______, Joseph	Up	118
______, Thomas	Up	101
HORNSLEY, John	Mwr	162
HORTON/HORTEN/HORTIN'		
Horton, Abraham	Hab	51
______, Alfred	Cpb	205
______, Alfred M.	Han	155
______, David M.	Hab	7
______, Charles	Hab	7
______, Charles	Hab	8
______, Elizabeth	Elb	134
______, Edmund	Bal	36
______, F. K.	Wsh	243
______, Fletcher	Jks	331
______, Fred G.	Wsh	256
______, George W.	Wsh	243
______, Howel	Wsh	261
______, Hubbard	Lau	22
______, Isaac	Gwn	370
______, James	Crf	407
______, James	Elb	134
______, James	Han	156
______, James	Jks	346
______, Jeptha	Gwn	316
______, Jeremiah	Trp	39
______, Jesse	Gwn	348
______, Jesse	Jks	315
______, Jesse	Wsh	270
______, John	Jks	324
______, John	Jsp	354
______, John	Jsp	362
______, Joseph	Mon	190
______, Laben	Ran	247
______, Laborn	Wsh	261
______, Lott	Han	156
______, Memucan	Cpb	211
______, Nancy	Han	156
______, Proser	Jks	315
______, Remilisant	Bib	73
______, Robert	Mon	182
______, Samuel	Hab	27
______, Samuel	Trp	54
______, Thomas	Elb	132
______, Thomas	Hal	78
______, Thomas B.	Jns	472
______, Walker	Trp	38
______, Wiley B.	Wsh	270
______, William	Bib	67
______, William	Elb	142
______, William	Jsp	388
Horton, William	Pik	120
Horten, Anthony	Hab	44
______, Edwin	Hab	52
Hortin, Spencer	Hab	44
HOSEA/HORSEA/HAOS		
Hosea, Pedro	Gwn	374
Horsea, Drusilla	Frk	244
Haos, Albert	Hab	66
HOSHAW, Moses	Hab	50
______, see Hesaw		
HOSKINS, John	Jns	451
______, Lemuel P.	Jns	457
HOSTIN, Amos	Pik	112
HOTT/HOTE/HOTTE		
Hott, Richard	Tfo	368
______, Robert	Gre	303
______, William	Han	155
Hote, Beram D.	Hab	36
______, Larkin	Hab	37
Hotte, Ausbern	Hab	38
HOUGHTON/HAUGHTON		
Houghton, Alexandria	Bts	159
______, Earstley	Bts	178
______, James M.	Gre	284
______, John	Gre	293
______, John W.	Rch	257
______, Joshua	Gre	300
______, Matthew	Gre	281
______, Reuben	Gre	290
______, Willis	Put	215
Haughton, Elizabeth	Clk	324
HOUR, Littleberry	Jks	317
HOUSE/HOUZE		
House, Anderson	Car	228
______, Burrel	Ogl	77
______, Elias	Hry	242
______, Felix	Jks	324
______, Harris	Clk	310
______, Hiram	Ran	250
______, James	Cow	385
______, John	Hal	109
______, John	Jks	347
______, Lawrence	Jks	329
______, Lewis	Lin	65
______, Lot	Lin	65
______, Luston	Lin	64
______, Memory	Ogl	77
______, Pascal	Frk	218
______, Paschal	Hry	213
______, Richard	Clk	310
______, Samuel	Cht	243
______, Samuel	DeK	65
______, Sarah	Clk	303

House, Sehon Cow 367
______, Thomas Clk 303
______, Thomas Frk 212
______, Thomas Wrn 216
______, William Lin 64
______, William Trp 35
______, Willis Clk 311
______, Zachariah Tlb 340
Houze, Clabourn Tms 23
*HOUSEBUG (Indian) Car 233
HOUSELEY/HOUSLEY
Houseley, John Elb 137
______, William Rch 275
Housley, William Elb 140
______, William B. Col 350
HOUSTON/HUSTON/HOUSTAIN/
HOUSTOUN/HUSETON/HUSON
Houston, Alexander Elb 142
______, Frances Bke 147
______, George Cht 282
______, John Fay 190
______, John Har 181
______, John Har 186
______, Johnson M. Fay 185
______, Josiah Fay 186
______, Olliver Cow 390
______, P. Cht 282
______, Polly Cht 262
______, R.J., Estate of Cht 282
______, Robert McI 128
______, Samuel Fay 189
______, Tho. A. McI 128
______, William Cow 369
Huston, George DeK 36
______, Isaac Gly 265
______, Reuben Gwn 346
______, Sarah Gly 265
______, Susannah Wal 167
______, Thomas New 51
Houstain, John Cow 369
Houstoun, Dolly Cht 241
Huseton, David R. Wal 157
Huson, Frances A. Hry 209
HOUSEWORTH, Abram DeK 55
______, Philip DeK 55
HOWARD, Abalsom Car 214
______, Abner Bak 16
______, Alexander Mor 258
______, Asa Ogl 73
______, Benj. DeK 31
______, Benjamin Mus 285
______, Charles Tlb 329
______, David Fay 186
Howard, David Mon 222
______, Edward DeK 55
______, Edward Tlb 345
______, Elizabeth Clk 321
______, Elizabeth Wsh 268
______, Ellend Mus 278
______, Ezra S. Put 183
______, Greensberry Han 156
______, Groves Ogl 94
______, H. V. Bal 44
______, Hampton H. Hst 268
______, Hannon Lee 33
______, Hardy Jks 325
______, Harman H. Bib 64
______, Harriet Cht 282
______, Hawkins Clk 293
______, Henry Jsp 355
______, Henry McI 131
______, Henry Ogl 88
______, Henry Put 186
______, Hiram Up 114
______, Isaac A. Ogl 88
______, J. H. Bal 44
______, Jacob Lib 46
______, James Col 360
______, James Har 96
______, James Hal 109
______, James Lau 10
______, James Ogl 87
______, James Pik 112
______, James W. Har 182
______, James W. Wsh 253
______, Jane Clk 324
______, Jane Mus 290
______, John Gre 305
______, John Lib 46
______, John Lin 73
______, John Mwr 164
______, John Mon 187
______, John Mon 226
______, John Mor 254
______, John Put 200
______, John Rch 287
______, John H. Wil 302
______, John R. Wsh 276
______, John T. Lau 16
______, Jonathan Hal 112
______, Joseph Mon 193
______, Joseph Mor 255
______, Joseph W. Wil 316
______, Levi Mar 138
______, Mary Lau 22
______, Michael Pik 116

Name	County	Page
Howard, Moses	Scr	302
______, Nancy	Wsh	274
______, Nathaniel Sr.	Scr	305
______, Nathaniel Jr.	Scr	305
______, Nicholas	Mus	279
______, Pierce	Cht	260
______, Polly	Wsh	249
______, Ralph O.	Bib	64
______, Robert	Mor	241
______, Robert	Ogl	82
______, Ruthy	Fay	206
______, Samuel	Bak	15
______, Samuel	Doo	81
______, Samuel	Jsp	395
______, Samuel	Jsp	397
______, Sarah	Doo	81
______, Simon	Ware	188
______, Solomon	Har	188
______, Solomon	Wsh	269
______, Sterling	Mor	251
______, T. B.	Bal	44
______, Thomas	Bak	15
______, Thomas	Bib	67
______, Thomas	Lin	71
______, Thomas	Ogl	88
______, Thomas	Ogl	98
______, Thomas	Tlb	344
______, W.	Lee	28
______, William	Tlf	5
______, William	Up	102
______, William S.	Wil	303
______, Willis	Jef	415
HOWE, Elizabeth	Mon	212
______, Marian	Mon	183
______, Robert	Crf	414
______, Robert	Wyn	281
HOWELL/HOWEL		
Howell, Abel	Frk	221
______, Benjamin	Pul	141
______, Burrel	Bib	73
______, Bynum	Mor	245
______, Casper	Up	109
______, Charles	Cam	181
______, Daniel	Rch	289
______, Daniel W.	Trp	45
______, David	Hst	296
______, David	Mon	214
______, Dempsey	Mon	177
______, Elias	Crf	399
______, Ely	Hab	19
______, Etheldred	Hst	287
______, Etheldril	Pul	157
______, Evan	Gwn	361
Howell, Frances	Ogl	87
______, Henry	Rch	291
______, Hiram	Twg	68
______, Holliday	Mor	245
______, Hopkin	Ware	189
______, Hopkin	Lin	66
______, Isaac	Cpb	211
______, Jas.	Wks	349
______, Jesse	Hal	132
______, Jessee	Mon	212
______, Jesse F.	Frk	234
______, Jesse W.	New	45
______, John	Fay	193
______, John	Gwn	316
______, John	Wrn	210
______, John F.	Fay	199
______, Joseph	Cpb	211
______, Joseph	Han	157
______, Joseph	Tfo	368
______, Joseph	Wrn	217
______, Lewis	Lin	71
______, Lewis	Up	95
______, Mathew	Tfo	368
______, McKinney	Tfo	363
______, Mesheck	Han	157
______, Miche	Cpb	205
______, Mills	Han	156
______, Patrick	Frk	216
______, Pheoby	Wks	348
______, Phillip	Trp	52
______, Rachel	Han	156
______, Richard	Jef	429
______, Robert	Pul	141
______, S. A.	Bib	50
______, Samuel	Bib	73
______, Samuel	Scr	307
______, Samuel D.	Elb	151
______, Solomon	McI	131
______, Steven	Gwn	326
______, Stven	Gwn	330
______, Theoph.	Wrn	226
______, Thomas	Cam	190
______, Thomas	Frk	215
______, Thomas	Frk	240
______, Thomas	Hal	111
______, Thomas	Pul	157
______, Wiley	Tlb	325
______, William	Cow	384
______, William	Tlb	337
______, Wright	Hst	295
Howel, Arther	Dec	1[illegible]
______, David	Pik	12[illegible]
______, Even S.	Hab	[illegible]

Howel, Frances Car 226
_____, John Bak 16
_____, Jane Wal 170
_____, Joshua Car 225
_____, Joshua Wrn 214
_____, Lazarous Wrn 197
_____, Woodard Gre 303
HOWINGTON, William R. Mad 110
_____, Wilson Mad 104
HOWLAND, Stephen D. McI 128
HOWZE, Thomas Bib 64
HOXEY, Thomas Put 218
_____, William Wil 290
HOY, James Bib 61
_____, James C. Bal 28
_____, Mary Cht 256
_____, Quinton Bib 61
HOYATT/HOYT
Hoyatt, David Frk 248
_____, John Frk 235
Hoyt, James Hst 273
HOYLE, John J. Pik 119
_____, Spicer Pik 119
_____, William L. Up 105
HUBBARD/HUBARD/HUBBERT/
HUBERT
Hubbard, David DeK 28
_____, Elisha Mor 270
_____, Elizabeth Gre 292
_____, Harbert Ogl 85
_____, Henry Fay 187
_____, Irvin Ogl 86
_____, Jacob Wil 320
_____, James Gre 272
_____, James Hry 235
_____, Jeremiah Hal 119
_____, John Cht 246
_____, John Fay 191
_____, John Hal 105
_____, John Har 184
_____, John Mor 238
_____, John Ogl 84
_____, John Put 172
_____, Joseph Hal 119
_____, Joseph Ogl 84
_____, Joseph Tlf 11
_____, Joseph Trp 48
_____, Manoa Wks 349
_____, Mary Ogl 86
_____, Mary Wil 320
_____, Mathew Jsp 388
_____, Nancy Gre 288
_____, Peterson Fay 191

Hubbard, Phebe Pik 109
_____, Robert Ogl 84
_____, Royal Hal 120
_____, Sally Cht 269
_____, Stephen Tlf 10
_____, Timothy Cht 281
_____, Uriah Hal 132
_____, Warner Wal 168
_____, William Gre 297
_____, William Hal 123
_____, William Mor 254
_____, William Put 172
_____, William Wil 307
_____, William W. Pul 159
_____, Woodson Hry 202
_____, Zinos Jks 325
Hubard, Sarah Bal 35
Hubbert, Benja. Wrn 202
_____, M. H. Cam 182
_____, Wineford Cam 183
Hubert, Harmon Wrn 197
_____, Hiram Wrn 202
HUBANKS, Ormon Em 168
_____, William Em 168
_____, also see Eubanks
HUBART - see Herbert
HUCKABY/HUCKEBY/HUCKERBEY/
HUCKERBY/HUCKABEE/HUCABY
Huckaby, Felin Mon 207
_____, Isham Jsp 360
_____, James Hal 81
_____, James Jns 461
_____, Phillip Wil 293
_____, Seaborn Mon 190
_____, William Cow 370
_____, William Mon 205
_____, William Mon 219
Huckeby, Charles Pik 122
_____, David Pik 123
Huckerbey, John Wal 124
Huckerby, William Ogl 88
Huckabee, James Han 155
Hucaby, James Lee 28
HUDDLESTON/HUDDELSON
Huddleston, John Mor 239
_____, Susan Tfo 367
_____, William Cow 383
_____, Willis Mor 248
Huddelson, William B. Pik 125
HUDGINS/HUDGENS/HUDGEINS/
HUDGINGS/HEDGINS/HODGENS/
HUDGEON
Hudgins, Benjamin Cpb 207

Hudgins, Beverly Hal 68
_____, David Gwn 344
_____, Henry H. Mus 290
_____, John Bib 61
_____, John Hab 57
_____, Josiah B. Up 108
_____, William DeK 54
_____, William Up 102
_____, Zacheus Hal 68
Hudgens, Ambrose Mon 208
_____, John New 8
_____, Josiah Mon 189
_____, Richard B. Tlb 347
Hudgeins, James Hab 49
_____, Philip Hab 49
Hudgings, Ansel Col 358
Hedgins, Ansel Gwn 340
Hodgens, Hannah Wrn 214
Hudgeon, Martha Wks 351
HUDLER/HUDDLER/HUDLOW
Hudler, Penelope Fay 197
Huddler, Timothy Ear 92
Hudlow, Hampton A. Rch 290
HUDNAL/HUDNALL
Hudnal, Daniel (colored) Frk 234
_____, Jenard Tms 21
_____, Josiah Frk 254
Hudnall, John Lau 24
HUDMAN, Elizabeth Hry 233
_____, Garrett Hry 211
_____, Garrett Tlb 344
_____, John Hry 232
HUDSON/HUTSON
Hudson, Alfred Hal 133
_____, Andrew H. Lau 12
_____, Benjamin Elb 136
_____, Benjamin Jef 417
_____, Bird Mon 204
_____, Charles New 9
_____, David Elb 132
_____, David Har 188
_____, David Jns 461
_____, David New 9
_____, David B. Elb 136
_____, Elbert Jef 423
_____, Eli Jef 404
_____, Elijah Jef 413
_____, Elijah T. Jef 403
_____, Elizabeth Put 215
_____, Ephraim Mar 142
_____, Frederick Gre 280
_____, George W. Frk 220
_____, Granbury H. Jef 418
Hudson, Hall Lau 6
_____, Hamilton Bul 94
_____, Hilery Ran 241
_____, Irby Put 218
_____, Isaac Jef 420
_____, Isaac E. Mar 142
_____, Isham Jns 433
_____, James Cpb 211
_____, James T. Crf 403
_____, James T. Jef 413
_____, John Fay 198
_____, John Gre 289
_____, John Hst 265
_____, John Lau 4
_____, John Put 217
_____, John H. Mad 103
_____, John L. Hst 265
_____, Jonathan A. Mus 280
_____, Joseph Cpb 203
_____, Joseph H. Jef 414
_____, Joshua Frk 220
_____, Joshua Jns 474
_____, Lewellen W. Put 217
_____, Lucy Elb 153
_____, Madison Elb 149
_____, Mary Eff 113
_____, Mary Elb 148
_____, Mary Rch 284
_____, Peter New 42
_____, Richard Trp 41
_____, Richard Sr. Jef 420
_____, Richard Jr. Jef 414
_____, Richard D. Elb 136
_____, Robert Cow 376
_____, Robert Pik 113
_____, Rush Tlb 333
_____, Thomas Han 157
_____, Thomas Mon 188
_____, Thomas Trp 37
_____, William Bal 42
_____, William Elb 137
_____, William Han 155
_____, William Hry 209
_____, William Jns 451
_____, William Mad 116
_____, William Mad 117
_____, William Wal 174
Hutson, Ward Ogl 91
HUDSPETH/HUDPETH/HEADSPETH
Hudspeth, Jane Bts 167
_____, Mark Mwr 157
_____, William Cow 370
_____, William Wil 324

Hudpeth, Warren S. Ear 100
Headspeth, Costic Ogl 86
HUEY, James A. Har 175
_____, Robert D. Har 179
HUFF/HOFF/HOUGHF
Huff, Charles Ogl 85
_____, Charles Wal 136
_____, Clayton New 33
_____, Daniel Mwr 154
_____, Daniel Put 214
_____, David Wil 320
_____, Donalson Jns 440
_____, Drury Ogl 62
_____, George Gre 303
_____, Greene Han 156
_____, Hamblen Jsp 362
_____, Harrison Jsp 352
_____, Henry Clk 299
_____, Henry Hal 110
_____, James Har 175
_____, James Ran 248
_____, John Gwn 316
_____, John Wal 136
_____, Jonatha Wrn 225
_____, Leo M. Wrn 223
_____, Littleberry Clk 298
_____, Lundy Jsp 355
_____, Martha Wrn 225
_____, Needham Tlb 325
_____, Pressley Wal 172
_____, Ralph Bts 178
_____, Robert Ogl 82
_____, Tabitha Jsp 356
_____, Thomas Jsp 359
_____, Travis Put 205
_____, William Jns 439
_____, William Put 190
_____, William Wil 322
Hoff, Edmund Bal 36
Houghf, Daniel Mus 292
HUFFAKER, Michael Car 229
HUGELEY/HUGULY/HUGULEY/
HUGUELEY
Hugeley, Alley Wil 310
_____, Amos Wil 311
_____, George Wil 311
_____, John Wil 311
_____, Rebecca Wil 310
_____, William Wil 310
Huguly, Charles Lin 59
Huguley, Jacob Wil 310
Hugueley, Zachariah Mon 182
HUGENON/HUGENIN/HUGINEN
Hugenon, J. Cht 282
_____, John Cht 256
Hugenin, J. D. Cht 262
Huginen, Edward D. McI 128
HUGGINS/GUGINS: also
see Higgins
Huggins, Eli Cow 376
_____, Frances Rch 280
_____, Green Jks 327
_____, Isaac Lau 23
_____, James Tms 25
_____, John Hal 134
_____, John Tms 29
Hugins, James Hab 17
HUGHES/HUGHS/HUSE/HEWS
Also see Hews elsewhere
Hughes, Daniel DeK 49
_____, Edward Bke 154
_____, Eli Hry 222
_____, Elijah DeK 67
_____, George Tlb 331
_____, H. B. Col 362
_____, Hayden Twg 68
_____, Isaac DeK 43
_____, John Gwn 367
_____, John Twg 65
_____, Littleberry Twg 87
_____, Peter Mor 263
_____, Reddick Hst 293
_____, Samuel Frk 212
_____, Samuel Jsp 387
_____, Simon Trp 55
_____, Solomon Tlb 328
_____, William Frk 239
_____, William Gwn 320
_____, William Wil 291
_____, William W. Bke 155
_____, Willis Tlb 322
_____, Zophiah Tlb 329
Hughs, Benjamin Cow 387
_____, Benjamin Cow 388
_____, Carter Bul 99
_____, Dempsey Jef 418
_____, Emery Ogl 102
_____, Gabril B. Hal 102
_____, Hugh Mtg 232
_____, James Bib 67
_____, John Pul 160
_____, Jno. Wks 341
_____, John J. Mad 106
_____, John W. Hab 6
_____, Littleberry Jef 417
_____, Mathew Bib 70

Hughs, Micajah	Wal	166
_____, Phillip	Wal	154
_____, Samuel H.	Jns	474
_____, T.	Wks	347
_____, Thomas M.	Hab	8
_____, William	Hal	109
_____, William Esq.	Lib	47
_____, William	Wks	343
Huse, Elisha	Hab	46
_____, James	Hab	26
_____, Robert	Hab	22
_____, Samuel	Hab	56
Hews, Edward	Cht	269
_____, John	New	41
_____, Thomas	Lee	29
_____, William	Lee	32
HUGHEY/HUGHY/HUIE		
Hughey, Darkey	DeK	54
_____, Ephraim	Hry	237
_____, Henry	DeK	33
_____, James	DeK	43
_____, James T.	Mor	264
_____, John	App	13
_____, John	DeK	26
_____, John	DeK	47
_____, Joseph A.	Cow	374
_____, Joseph L.	Hry	228
_____, Seaborn	Car	227
_____, Thomas	Hry	224
Hughy, Mary	Wil	322
_____, Robert	Fay	200
Huie, Samuel	Mon	188
HULAN, John	Elb	147
HULIE, Joseph	Fay	200
HULING, Elizabeth	Wil	314
_____, James	Hst	275
_____, James	Wil	320
HULL, Asbury	Clk	324
_____, Daniel	Cpb	199
_____, Ezekiel	Bke	119
_____, Henry	Clk	327
_____, Joseph	Cam	192
_____, Nathaniel	Cpb	195
_____, Richard	DeK	50
_____, Thomas	Bts	158
_____, Thomas	Cpb	198
_____, Whitfield	DeK	54
_____, William	Bts	168
HULME, John T.	Elb	157
_____, Margaret	Elb	158
HULSEY/HULZA		
Hulsey, Addler Jr.	Hal	96
_____, Adler Sr.	Hal	124
Hulsey, Armsted	Hal	124
_____, Asa	Fay	194
_____, Charles	Hal	96
_____, Charles Jr.	Car	223
_____, Charles F.	Hal	129
_____, Elijah	Hal	116
_____, Henry	Fay	186
_____, Hiram	Hal	125
_____, James	Hal	122
_____, Jennings	DeK	54
_____, Jesse	Hal	127
_____, Joel	Hal	107
_____, Micager	Hal	127
_____, Pleasant	Hal	120
_____, Saltithal	Hal	127
_____, Sarah	Hal	119
_____, Vincent	Hal	130
_____, William	Fay	187
_____, William	Hal	117
Hulza, Sarah	Hab	43
HUMAN, Alexander	Mad	115
_____, Anna	Mad	118
_____, Jesiah	Mad	102
HUMBER, Robert	Bts	178
HUMPHLET, Asa	Wrn	217
HUMPHREY/HUMPHRY/HUMPHRYS/ HUMPHRIES/HUMPHRIS/HUMPH- REYS/HUMPRIS/HUMPHUS		
Humphrey, Alex. W.	Pik	114
_____, George W.	Ogl	90
_____, James	Scr	306
_____, James	Wrn	196
_____, John	Gwn	311
_____, Mathew	Han	157
_____, Robert	Wrn	197
_____, Thomas	Gwn	310
_____, Thomas	Han	157
_____, W. C.	Bal	29
_____, William	Gwn	321
_____, William	Gwn	365
_____, William	Hry	200
_____, William	Wrn	202
Humphry, Danul	Lwn	89
_____, Richard	Wal	170
Humphrys, James C.	Bal	35
Humphries, Amelia	Lau	16
_____, Benjamin	Car	225
_____, James	Gwn	378
_____, John	Hab	18
_____, John	Ogl	76
_____, John	Tms	27
_____, Nancy	Jns	457
_____, Salley	Wal	174

Name	County	Page
Humphries, Thomas J.	Jns	456
Humphris, George W.	Frk	230
______, James	Frk	230
______, Jonathan	Frk	233
______, Joseph	Wal	135
______, Nancy	Frk	230
______, Solomon	Bib	58
Humphreys, Elijah	Clk	294
______, H. P.	Bal	36
______, Nancy	Clk	305
______, Presley	Clk	305
______, William	Clk	322
Humpris, James	New	13
______, Uriah	New	47
Humphus, Solomon	Hal	104
HUNCK, Mary Ann	Eff	111
HUNT, Anderson	Cow	384
______, Anderson	Up	120
______, Daniel	Har	189
______, Daniel H.	Jns	451
______, Elizabeth	Hst	288
______, Eliza	Wrn	219
______, Garrett	Mon	173
______, George	Cow	378
______, George	Elb	137
______, George	Twg	81
______, Harris	Jns	451
______, Hellum	Hab	47
______, Henry	Jsp	398
______, Henry	Up	107
______, Henry	Wal	158
______, Henry H.	Mwr	168
______, Howel	Wrn	210
______, James	Bts	159
______, James	DeK	52
______, James	Elb	159
______, James	Han	156
______, Joel	Frk	212
______, John	Cpb	211
______, John	Gre	277
______, John	Hry	208
______, John	Hry	245
______, John	Jns	451
______, John	Jsp	358
______, John	Ran	245
______, John	Up	118
______, John	Wsh	247
______, John R.	Jsp	355
______, Judkins	Pik	125
______, Lewis	Hst	291
______, Littleton	Gwn	317
______, Lucinda	Wil	304
______, Lucy	Gre	277

Name	County	Page
Hunt, Martha	Col	345
______, Moses	Elb	121
______, Nancy M.	Elb	132
______, Nath.	Cht	277
______, Sarah	Gwn	366
______, Sion	Elb	127
______, Thomas	Hab	28
______, Thomas	Jns	443
______, Thomas	New	14
______, Timothy	Gre	293
______, Turner	Hry	222
______, Turner	Mon	180
______, Wilkins	Mon	196
______, William	Col	342
______, William	Hab	7
______, William	Jks	334
______, William	Jns	443
______, William	Mad	114
______, William	Twg	60
______, William	Twg	81
______, William	Up	107
______, William	Wal	156
______, William	Wsh	252
______, William	Wrn	229
______, William H.	Clk	324
______, William L.	Crf	406
______, Wyatt	Mon	172
HUNTER, Abraham	Scr	300
______, Alexander	Bts	162
______, Alfred	Jks	334
______, Archiebald	Han	157
______, Bryant J.	Wrn	233
______, David	Clk	294
______, David	Irw	298
______, David	Mon	214
______, Dempsey	Scr	300
______, Edwin W.	Gre	300
______, Elizabeth	Crf	401
______, Elisha	Gre	283
______, Ephraim	Scr	307
______, Hardy	Hst	270
______, Henry	Put	207
______, James	Cht	263
** ______, James (slaves)	Cht	281
______, James	Jsp	352
______, James	Lwn	85
______, James	Mon	213
______, James	Scr	307
______, James	Tlb	323
______, Jesse	Fay	182
______, Jesse	Scr	307
______, Job	Wrn	233
______, John	Cht	243

Hunter, John W. Rch 277
_____, Joseph Ware 183
_____, Joshua Jks 325
_____, Mary Jef 401
_____, Moses Hab 34
_____, Redin Irw 298
_____, Richard Pik 127
_____, Richard Rab 232
_____, Robert Rab 229
_____, Samuel Cam 190
_____, Samuel Jks 348
_____, Sarah Jks 334
_____, Seth Tlb 327
_____, Stockey Jks 323
_____, Thomas Gwn 365
_____, Thomas Irw 298
_____, W. J. Cht 263
_____, William Scr 300
_____, William A. Gre 283
_____, William P. Cht 252
HUNTINGTON, A. J. Rch 271
_____, Fred Cht 246
HUNTON - see Hinton
HURD/HERD
Hurd, William Har 192
_____, William Jef 406
Herd, James D. Hab 58
HURLEY, Howard Cpb 209
_____, Mary Hal 84
_____, Sarah Wil 309
HURNE, Peter Cht 278
HURSEY, George Tlf 3
_____, Thomas Tlf 3
HURST/HUST/HEARST
Hurst, Bryan Tms 29
_____, Daniel Tms 18
_____, David Tms 19
_____, Felix Eff 110
_____, Harmon Rch 290
_____, James Eff 112
_____, John A. Har 187
_____, Major Tms 19
_____, Miller Hal 85
_____, Nedum Scr 304
_____, Polly Car 218
_____, Samuel Hal 85
_____, Simon Gwn 367
_____, Stephen Doo 78
_____, Susannah B. Rch 292
_____, Thomas Tms 20
_____, Thomas Tms 24
_____, William Tlb 338
_____, William Eff 112
Hust, Harmon Bke 154
_____, Henry Wsh 242
_____, James Bke 134
_____, Jesse Bke 146
_____, John Bke 146
_____, William App 8
Hearst, Jesse DeK 68
_____, William Bts 175
HURT, Benja. Wrn 203
_____, Charles S. Put 211
_____, Henry Put 183
_____, Joel Ogl 91
_____, Joel Put 180
_____, Spencer Put 211
_____, William Han 156
_____, William Put 179
HUSH/HUSK
Hush, Mathew Wal 168
Husk, John New 21
HUSSEY, Levi H. Mwr 155
HUTCHINS/HUTCHINGS/
HUTCHENS/HUTCHIN
Hutchins, Anna Lau 21
_____, Burrel DeK 43
_____, Daniel Bke 124
_____, David DeK 43
_____, Edward Lau 16
_____, Elizabeth Bke 119
_____, Elizabeth Jef 403
_____, Furney DeK 25
_____, John P. Gwn 351
_____, Joshua Hry 239
_____, Littlebery Cow 386
_____, Nancy Bke 123
_____, Nathaniel L. Gwn 327
_____, Simon Jef 412
_____, Thomas Wal 124
_____, Widow Rch 277
Hutchings, Edward Han 155
_____, Robert Jns 453
Hutchens, Anthony Dec 3
_____, John New 7
_____, Littlebery Hab 85
Hutchin, Asa Dec 19
HUTCHINSON/HUTCHISON/
HUTCHENSON/HUTCHERSON/
HUTCHESON/HUCHERSON/
HUCHINSON
Hutchinson, Adam Rch 260
_____, Daniel Wrn 199
_____, Henry Tlb 336
_____, James Bke 141
_____, James Col 341

Name	County	Page
Hutchinson, James	Cow	367
_____, Joel	Elb	121
_____, John	Dec	14
_____, John	Em	179
_____, John	Em	179
_____, Joseph	Rch	292
_____, Moses	Elb	126
_____, Moses	Em	168
_____, Richard	Gwn	359
_____, Sarah	Cht	240
_____, Thomas	Em	170
_____, Thomas	Jsp	380
_____, Turner	DeK	30
_____, William	DeK	30
_____, William	Mon	219
Hutchison, David	Mor	260
_____, John	Pik	107
_____, John W.	Bib	67
_____, Samuel	Cpb	194
_____, William	Mwr	150
Hutchenson, Mary	Frk	250
_____, Nathaniel	Wrn	214
_____, Peter W.	Ogl	66
Hutcherson, Alford	New	25
_____, Hy.	Gwn	315
Hutcheson, John	Hry	214
Hucherson, Ambrose	Gre	291
_____, James	Gre	281
_____, John B.	Clk	305
Huchinson, William	Col	340
HUTSON, Archaba	New	21
_____, C. G.	Gre	294
_____, Charles	Jks	315
_____, Elizabeth	Jks	335
_____, Giles	Jks	335
_____, James	McI	126
_____, John Sr.	McI	124
_____, John Jr.	McI	126
_____, Sally	Clk	313
_____, Thomas	New	38
HUTTO, Benjamin	Tlf	8
_____, Eli	Bts	161
_____, George	Bak	18
_____, Henry	Bak	17
_____, John	Bts	160
_____, Martin	Bak	17
_____, Peter	Bak	17
HUZZA, Barbary (W)	Mor	257
HYDE, David	Hal	97
_____, David Jr.	Hal	100
_____, George	Frk	216
_____, Henry H.	Wil	299
_____, Micager	Hal	97

Name	County	Page
Hyde, William	DeK	52
_____, William	Hal	97
_____, Winifred	Wil	318
HYDLE/HYDRIL		
Hydle, Dyonnus	Mon	194
_____, John	Mon	194
Hydril, Powell	Lee	31
HYMAN, Henry	Wrn	197
_____, John	Wrn	196
HYMER, Samuel	Frk	213
IHLY, Mary Ann	Eff	109
ILEY/ILER		
Iley, John	Frk	241
_____, Richard	Frk	253
_____, Syntha	Frk	253
_____, William	Frk	252
Iler, William	Bul	96
INGE/ING		
Inge, Charles	Tfo	361
Ing, Jeremiah	Jsp	364
INGERSOL, S. M.	Mus	282
INGERVILLE, Henry	Gly	264
INGLETT/INGLITT		
Inglett, Abraham	Rch	281
_____, Andrew	Rch	281
_____, Jacob	Rch	283
_____, Martin	Rch	283
_____, Matthew	Rch	281
_____, William	Rch	283
Inglitt, Hugh M.	Rch	283
INGLISH, also see English		
_____, Martha	Bib	67
_____, Thomas	Bib	70
INGRAM/INGHAM/INGRAHAM		
Ingram, Abraham	Trp	37
_____, Barthelemew	Han	157
_____, Bartholomew Jr.	Han	157
_____, Council B.	Jef	317
_____, David	Lau	11
_____, Edmond	Cow	371
** _____, Elija (slave)	Rch	273
_____, Elizabeth	Put	208
_____, Etheldred	Jef	412
_____, Harmon	Hal	123
_____, Hugh	Dec	10
_____, Hughes	Lau	10
_____, James L.	Jef	411
_____, John	Cow	371
_____, John	Dec	5
_____, John	Hal	114
_____, John	Hry	212

Name	County	Page
Ingram, John Sr.	Put	187
_____, John B.	Put	187
_____, John R.	Hry	200
_____, John S.	Mon	176
_____, Little	Hal	97
_____, Martin	Hal	115
_____, Mathew	Up	98
_____, Presley	Bal	41
_____, Ruth	Hal	121
_____, Samuel	DeK	68
_____, Sarah	Bib	51
_____, Stith H.	Put	175
_____, Thomas	Han	157
_____, Thomas	Put	187
_____, Thomas	Up	101
_____, Thomas W.	Han	157
_____, Tilman	Hal	121
_____, William	Dec	10
_____, William	Mad	115
_____, William	Mon	176
_____, William H.	Jns	434
Ingham, And.	Wks	344
_____, David	Wks	358
_____, Joseph	Tlb	329
_____, Robert M.	Tlb	326
Ingraham, George	Har	191
_____, John	Tfo	368
_____, William	Rch	279
INMAN/INMON		
Inman, Alfred	Bke	126
_____, Allen	Bke	127
_____, Daniel	Bke	126
_____, Joel	Jsp	365
_____, John	App	9
Inmon, Elizabeth	Frk	247
INSLY, James	DeK	59
_____, John	DeK	59
INVALE, James	Tlb	346
INZER, H. W.	Gwn	321
_____, John	Hal	96
IRBY/IRBEY		
Irby, Abraham	Gre	299
_____, Constant	DeK	70
_____, Herod	Gre	299
_____, Maria	Jef	408
_____, Nancy	DeK	70
_____, William	Jef	418
Irbey, John S.	Bts	164
IRONS, William	Frk	221
IRWIN/IRVIN/IRVEN/ IRVINE/IRVING		
Irwin, Alexander	Hal	99
_____, Alexander	Wsh	248
Irwin, David	Mor	251
_____, Jane	Jef	424
_____, Jarred	Ran	241
_____, John	Hal	98
_____, John	Pik	109
_____, John R.	Tms	28
_____, Josiah	Jns	469
_____, Leander A.	Bts	165
_____, Obediah	Crf	401
_____, Thomas A.	Wsh	240
_____, William	Jns	472
Irvin, Catherine	Hab	44
_____, Christopher	New	12
_____, Francis	Cpb	211
_____, Hannah	Wil	314
_____, Isaiah	Wil	315
_____, James C.	Hab	45
_____, James S.	Hab	59
_____, John	Jsp	352
_____, Kirkham M.	Gwn	335
Irven, Absalom	Tlb	324
_____, Joseph	Tlb	324
_____, Joshua	Tlb	323
Irvine, Jane	Lib	47
Irving, Benjamin	Pik	108
ISAAC/ISAACS		
Isaac, Henry	Rch	267
Isaacs, Sarah	Cht	247
ISBEL, Daniel	Frk	253
_____, James	Frk	252
_____, John	Mon	177
ISDALL, J. J.	Col	362
ISHAM/ISAM		
Isham, Chas.	DeK	29
_____, David	DeK	30
_____, Reuben	Tlb	331
_____, Richard	Tlb	331
Isam, Jane	Jks	345
ISON, John	Pik	122
ISLANDS, Nancy	Lau	23
ISLER, John	Mad	114
ISREL, John	Dec	8
IVERSON/IVERSTON		
Iverson, Alfred	Jns	465
_____, Benjamin V.	Hst	261
_____, William	Hst	292
Iverston, George	Hab	29
IVERS, Isaac	Bib	70
_____, Reuben	Rch	292
IVIN, Archabald	New	17
IVY/IVEY/IVIE/IVYE		
Ivy, Adam	Wrn	195
_____, Barney	Hst	262

Name	County	Page
Ivy, Benj.	Gwn	351
______, Benjamin	Wrn	195
______, Charles	Clk	306
______, Denkins	Wrn	212
______, Elias	Wal	145
______, Elizabeth	Col	357
______, Elizabeth	Jks	344
______, Ephraim	Crf	406
______, Gutridge	Wrn	204
______, Henry Sr.	New	54
______, Henry Jr.	New	54
______, Henry	Wrn	213
______, James	Wsh	260
______, James S.	Pul	144
______, Jeremiah	Wal	156
______, John	DeK	66
______, John	Gre	297
______, John	Wrn	198
______, Lewis	Wrn	212
______, Mike	Wrn	219
______, Moses	Wrn	208
______, Myrick	Wrn	204
______, Owen	Wsh	260
______, Peebles	Wrn	195
______, Randolph	Wrn	209
______, Robert	New	54
Ivey, Anthony	Bib	61
______, Berryman	Up	119
______, Burney	Bal	41
______, Charles	Wil	322
______, E. P.	Col	352
______, George	Wal	150
______, Josiah	Wil	304
______, Jourdin	Bib	61
______, Mary	Col	356
______, Myrick	Mon	193
______, Robert	Bal	30
______, Robert	Tms	25
______, Thomas	Cam	188
______, Thomas	Frk	219
______, Wilson W.	Jsp	387
______, W. P.	Up	116
Ivie, John	Gwn	313
______, William	Gwn	313
______, William S.	Gwn	313
Ivye, William	Scr	300
IZLER/IZLA/IZLEY		
Izler, John	Wks	355
______, Nathan	Wks	333
______, Nathan	Wks	355
Izla, George	Gwn	330
Izley, Phillip	Gwn	357
JACK/JACKS		
Jack, James	Elb	140
______, Margaret	Clk	305
______, William H.	Elb	150
Jacks, Green B.	Clk	304
______, John	Clk	303
JACKSON, Aaron	Car	220
______, Abraham M.	Wal	132
______, Absalom	Mwr	167
______, Absolum	Wks	341
______, Sbsolum	Wks	343
______, Absalom J.E.A.	Ear	97
______, Alburtus	Mwr	153
______, Aldridge	Mor	240
______, Allen W.	Wrn	222
______, Amos	Hab	20
______, Archibald	Jks	314
______, Archibald	Mon	172
______, Aron	Mon	199
______, Aron	Wrn	198
______, Benjamin	Put	202
______, Booker A.	Gwn	322
______, Burwell	Bts	172
______, Candes	Wrn	201
______, Carey W.	Hal	73
______, Celia	Jsp	354
______, Charles C.	Gwn	349
______, Clarke	Ear	91
______, Clarke	Hab	12
______, Colby R.	Mwr	160
______, Cornelias	Hry	223
______, Cynthia	Wil	311
______, Daniel	Hst	270
______, Daniel	Mor	239
______, Daniel	Mor	257
______, Daniel E.	Wal	130
______, Daniel M.	Hry	241
______, David	Gre	274
______, David	Gwn	363
______, David	Hry	216
______, Delila	Frk	256
______, Duke W.	Ran	247
______, E.	Cht	283
______, Edmund	Gre	289
______, Edmund	Mon	206
______, Edmund	Tlb	325
______, Edward	Gwn	350
______, Edward	Hab	20
______, Eleanor	Wil	307
______, Elizabeth	Bke	148
______, Enoch	Jsp	385
______, Ephraim	Wil	314
______, F. R.	Cht	254

Name	County	Page
Jackson, Fielding	Up	98
______, G. B.	Jsp	368
______, Gabriel	Mus	281
______, George	Rch	264
______, George W.	Bib	64
______, Harda	Hab	53
______, Hardy R.	Mon	193
______, Harris C.	Wil	298
______, Hartwell	Clk	296
______, Hartwell	Wil	292
______, Henry	Bts	161
______, Henry	Clk	318
______, Henry	Crf	407
______, Henry	Han	158
______, Henry	Hst	271
______, Henry	Hst	278
______, Henry R.	Mwr	156
______, Hilliard J.	Mwr	165
______, Hiram	Hst	264
______, Isaac	Gre	276
______, Isaac	Han	158
______, Isaac	Mon	188
______, Isaac	Tfo	362
______, Isaac R.	Ran	249
______, Jabez	Jef	410
______, Jacob	Car	222
______, James	Clk	327
______, James	Cow	384
______, James	Frk	223
______, James	Frk	232
______, James	Gre	304
______, James	Gwn	346
______, James	Han	158
______, James	Han	158
______, James	Hry	235
______, James	Jef	407
______, James	Put	205
______, James	Tfo	362
______, James W.	Put	185
______, Jane	Wil	307
______, Jehiel	Hab	32
______, Jesse	Up	98
______, Job	Gre	292
______, Jobe	Han	158
______, Joel	Frk	212
______, John	Bib	67
______, John	Clk	309
______, John	Clk	327
______, John Sr.	Hry	232
______, John	Hry	232
______, John Sr.	Hry	249
______, John	Hst	275
______, John	Jns	428
Jackson, John	Lib	47
______, John	Scr	299
______, John Jr.	Scr	299
______, John	Gwn	323
______, John	Tms	25
______, John	Trp	49
______, John H.	Elb	144
______, John M.	Wrn	195
______, John P.	Mus	278
______, John R.	Mon	190
______, John W.	Wrn	197
______, John W. W.	Jef	416
______, Jordan	Fay	202
______, Jordan	Hry	235
______, Joseph	Hab	41
______, Jos.	Lee	33
______, Joseph	Put	202
______, Joseph	Wil	316
______, Joseph W.	Cht	252
______, Josiah	Twg	89
______, L. B. A. W.	Wsh	248
______, Law	Hry	246
______, Leonard G.	Tlf	2
______, Lewis	Wrn	197
______, Linson	Mar	143
______, Littlebury	Hal	113
______, Littleton	DeK	66
______, Lydia	Wks	331
______, M.	Wks	351
______, Mark Sr.	Gre	295
______, Mark Jr.	Gre	296
______, Mark	Up	109
______, Mark	Wrn	226
______, Mark P.	Mor	242
______, Martha (W)	Mor	261
______, Martha	Put	183
______, Mary	Jsp	395
______, Mary	Mon	191
______, Mary	Ogl	78
______, Moses	Gre	287
______, Moses	Up	109
______, Nathan	Hry	248
______, Nathan	Wks	345
______, Nathaniel	Har	178
______, Nimrod	Hst	269
______, Obediah	Clk	295
______, Owing F.	Ogl	77
______, Peter	Mor	247
______, Peter L.	Ear	95
______, Pheriba	Rch	254
______, Philip	Pik	116
______, Ralph	Hal	104
______, Reuben	Hry	21[illegible]

Name	County	Page
Jackson, Robert	Gwn	319
_____, Robert	Mor	259
_____, Robert	Up	108
_____, Rogis	Cht	259
_____, Roland	Pik	107
_____, Rosannah	Wsh	275
_____, Ruth	Tfo	366
_____, Rutha	Col	358
_____, Sampson	Hab	44
_____, Samuel	Frk	223
_____, Samuel	Wal	123
_____, Samuel W.	Mwr	158
_____, Sarah	Ear	97
_____, Sarah	Wil	307
_____, Seaborn R.	Wrn	221
_____, Shadrock	Fay	196
_____, Sol	Gwn	323
_____, Stephen	Clk	307
_____, Stephen	Gre	282
_____, Susan	Cht	248
_____, Thomas	Car	223
_____, Thomas	Hal	72
_____, Thomas	Han	158
_____, Thomas	Mar	141
_____, Thomas	Wrn	197
_____, Thomas	Wks	358
_____, Timothy	Mon	184
_____, Tyre	Hal	103
_____, Warren	Wsh	269
_____, Wilkin	Jns	438
_____, William	Bib	51
_____, William	Bke	129
_____, William	Car	223
_____, William	Cpb	204
_____, William	DeK	27
_____, William	Fay	193
_____, William	Gre	290
_____, William	Gre	297
_____, William	Gre	303
_____, William	Gwn	319
_____, William	Hab	45
_____, William	Hab	53
_____, William	Hal	103
_____, William	Han	157
_____, William	Jns	430
_____, William	Jns	442
_____, William	Jns	442
_____, William	Lin	61
_____, William	Mor	261
_____, William	Rab	222
_____, William (slave)	Rch	253
_____, William	Rch	258
_____, William	Up	118

Name	County	Page
Jackson, William	Wal	151
_____, William	Wsh	263
_____, William	Wks	358
_____, William F.	Dec	12
_____, William F.	Mon	192
_____, William H.	Clk	324
_____, Rev. William J.	Lib	48
_____, William M.	Ogl	78
_____, William P.	Clk	310
_____, William R.	Crf	396
_____, William S.	Up	98
_____, Woody	Mwr	160
_____, Woody	Ogl	88
_____, Wright	Hry	247
_____, Wyche	Wil	311
JACOBS, Elisha	Wal	168
_____, James	Jks	346
_____, Joseph	Lin	71
_____, Mordecai	Mon	208
_____, Morris	Jks	323
_____, Nancy	Twg	77
_____, Thomas	Wal	168
_____, William	Jks	347
_____, William	Twg	63
JAILLET, Peter	Bal	37
JAMES, Absalom	Tfo	362
_____, Archibald G.	Tfo	354
_____, Benjamin	Lib	47
_____, Charles	Cpb	202
_____, Daniel	Mar	137
_____, David	Hry	226
_____, David R.	Elb	136
_____, Edward	Tfo	356
_____, Elizabeth	Jns	461
_____, Fincher	Jsp	389
_____, George	Gwn	374
_____, Isaac	Elb	156
_____, James	Lib	47
_____, Jane	Gwn	332
_____, Joel H.	Tlb	332
_____, John	Bib	64
_____, John	Clk	311
_____, John	Cpb	209
_____, John	Gwn	364
_____, John	Jns	461
_____, John	Mon	191
_____, John	Ogl	82
_____, John	Rch	278
_____, John	Tat	376
_____, John B.	Mon	191
_____, Jordan	Rch	286
_____, Joseph	Clk	317
_____, Joseph	Hry	226

James, Joseph Sr.	Rch	285
______, Joseph Jr.	Rch	279
______, Joseph	Wal	140
______, Joseph W.	Wal	160
______, Mrs.	Scr	309
______, Orman	Tms	26
______, Samuel	Hab	22
______, Stephen	Cpb	202
______, Stephen	Mus	284
______, Thomas	Gwn	376
______, Vaughan	Up	111
______, William	Elb	148
______, William	Frk	248
______, William	Mor	266
______, William	Rch	284
JAMISON/JAMESON		
Jamison, Benj.	DeK	66
______, George	Tlb	334
______, John	Tlb	335
______, William	DeK	54
Jameson, David	Hst	266
______, George T.	Doo	79
______, James	Twg	82
JANES/JANAS/JONAS		
Janes, John	Tlf	9
______, William	Gre	272
Janas, Thomas G.	Gre	274
Jonas, David Z.	Pul	154
______, Joseph H.	Elb	126
JARNETT, Anslem R.	Hab	26
JARRELL/JARREL/JARRALD		
Jarrell, Claiborn	Up	96
______, Elisha	Gre	301
______, Georgw	Mad	101
______, Jacob	Gre	278
______, Nancy	Ware	188
______, Redden	Gre	301
______, William W.	New	45
______, Willis S.	Mad	108
______, Willis	New	41
Jarrel, Thomas	Gre	275
______, Thomas	Hab	34
______, Willis	Bts	162
Jarrald, James S.	Clk	308
JARRETT/JARRATT/ JARROTT/JARRATE		
Jarrett, Archelus	Jns	472
______, Alexander	Bal	29
______, Athel	Wil	301
______, David	Hab	44
______, Devericks	Hab	35
______, Howell	Jks	313
______, Ira	Jks	343
Jarrett, James	Hst	292
______, Nathaniel	Jks	313
______, Thomas	Hab	44
______, William D.	Bal	40
Jarratt, Elijah	Mon	180
______, Nicholas	Wil	315
______, Thomas	New	34
______, William	New	34
Jarrott, John	Hry	199
______, Peter	Hry	236
Jarrate, Jas.	Rab	224
JARVIS/JERVIS		
Jarvis, George Y	Trp	44
______, J.	Cht	241
______, John W.	Trp	44
______, Polly	Ogl	84
______, William	Clk	306
Jervis, Patrick F.	Jef	406
JARVIN, John	Up	116
JAY, Jesse	Hal	113
______, John	Hal	113
______, William	Hal	113
______, William	Pik	116
JEAN, Sherod	Jks	335
JEFFERS, Elizabeth	Bke	129
______, John	Frk	239
______, John	Scr	305
______, Jonathan	Bke	117
______, Samuel	Frk	238
______, Thomas	Bke	126
______, Thomas H.	Wil	298
______, William	Gwn	310
JEFFRIES/JEFFERIES		
Jeffries, Burkitt	Jsp	389
______, George	Tfo	356
______, Lee	Jsp	381
______, Thomas	Jsp	386
Jefferies, Thomas	Clk	291
______, William	Jsp	383
JEINACK, R.	Cht	281
JEMMERSON/JIMMERSON		
Jemmerson, Thomas	Up	103
______, William	Up	103
Jimmerson, Providence	Up	99
______, Thomas	Jks	324
JENKINS/JINKINS/JINKENS/ JINCKINES/GENKINS/GINKINS/ CHENKINS/JONIKIN		
Jenkins, Arthur	Wrn	229
______, Benjamin	Jsp	390
______, Benjamin	Pul	161
______, Catharine	Jsp	359
______, Catherine	Wil	299

Name	County	Page
Jenkins, Charles	Han	158
_____, D.	Lee	26
_____, Daniel	Ogl	99
_____, Drewry	Wsh	265
_____, Edmund	Jsp	359
_____, Elijah	Mor	239
_____, Eliz.	Wks	357
_____, Elizabeth	Jns	457
_____, Evens	Wsh	240
_____, Francis	Mon	227
_____, Fredrick	Mus	281
_____, George	Scr	310
_____, George W.	Mor	268
_____, Hezakiah	Wsh	250
_____, Isaitus	Bke	129
_____, James	Eff	112
_____, James	Gre	287
_____, James	Put	210
_____, James J.	Jef	411
_____, Jane	Col	349
_____, Jas. J.	Gwn	350
_____, John	Col	352
_____, John	Pik	126
_____, John A.	Tlb	322
_____, John J.	Jef	413
_____, Jonathan	Rch	263
_____, Joseph	Ogl	99
_____, Keseah	Lin	68
_____, Leroy	Wil	299
_____, Lewis	Wsh	269
_____, Martha	Wil	299
_____, Martin	Hst	265
_____, Mary	Gre	287
_____, Milly	Gre	287
_____, Nancy	Gwn	330
_____, Owen	Lee	26
_____, Reason	Hst	271
_____, Robert	Put	210
_____, Robert	Wks	336
_____, Robert	Wks	358
_____, Royal	Mor	269
_____, Ruth	Gre	287
_____, S. D.	Wsh	239
_____, Samson	Em	172
_____, Samuel	Bke	131
_____, Samuel	Elb	122
_____, Stephen	Bke	131
_____, Sterling	Bke	129
_____, Syrus R.	Mwr	167
_____, Thomas N.	Wsh	239
_____, Turner	Bry	84
_____, Uriah	Wsh	241
_____, W. S.	Bal	30

Name	County	Page
Jenkins, William	Gwn	361
_____, William	Scr	310
_____, William	Wrn	224
_____, William F.	Hst	265
_____, Willis C.	Wil	299
_____, Wilson	Hal	85
Jinkins, Charles D.	Frk	239
_____, David J.	Tms	20
_____, James M.	Frk	228
_____, Jesse	Frk	239
_____, Nicholas	Hab	17
_____, Shepherd	Frk	237
Jinkens, Charles C.	Em	171
Jinckines, William	Hab	48
Genkins, Abner G.	Cow	370
_____, William A.	Em	177
Ginkins, Ashford	Em	176
Chenkins, Thomas	Hab	37
Jonikin, Zaney	Tms	17
JENNINGS/JINNINGS/JENINGS/ JENNING/JININGS/JINNING/ JINNINS/GINNINGS		
Jennings, Allen	Fay	194
_____, Charles	Lin	68
_____, Creed N.	Wal	123
_____, Elijah	Ogl	69
_____, Elizabeth	DeK	34
_____, James	Ogl	78
_____, Jiles	Clk	292
_____, John B.	Hal	96
_____, Levy	Ogl	62
_____, Miles	Car	216
_____, Nancy	Lin	68
_____, Robert	Fay	196
_____, Robert	Ogl	78
_____, Sollomon	Ogl	62
_____, Thomas	Lin	58
_____, William	Fay	198
Jinnings, Coleman	Jks	319
_____, Gillian	McI	126
_____, Henry	Clk	312
_____, John	DeK	66
Jenings, George W.	Bal	38
Jenning, James	Lin	66
Jinings, Caleb	Clk	321
Jinning, James	Clk	316
Jinnins, Henry	Hab	8
Ginnings, Anthony	Cpb	199
_____, Nelson	DeK	45
_____, William	Cpb	199
JENTRY, Cornelius	Frk	256
_____, Mary	Gwn	332
_____, Rachal	Ogl	78

Name	County	Page
JEPSON, Lemuel	Mus	278
JERMAN/JERMON/JARMAN/ JARMIN		
Jerman, Clem	Ran	250
_____, William	Fay	186
Jermon, Reason	Bib	59
Jarman, Berry	Tlb	348
_____, Lewis	Ogl	91
Jarmin, Jarris	DeK	69
JERNIGAN/JERNIGIN/JERNAGAN/ JARNEGAN/JERNIGEN/JARNIGAN/ JERNAGIN/JURNEGAN/JOURNAGAN		
Jernigan, Alexander	Tlb	336
_____, D. S.	Bak	16
_____, Elias	Irw	301
_____, L. A.	Wsh	239
_____, Sarah	Mon	185
_____, William	Mon	179
Jernigin, Aaron	Cam	188
_____, Isaac	Cam	188
Jernagan, Aaron	Irw	298
Jarnegan, Needham	Car	215
Jernigen, Henry W.	Ran	241
Jarnigan, Elias	Hst	282
Jernagin, Albert	Gre	291
Jurnegan, Hardy	Han	158
_____, Jeptha K.	Han	157
Journagan, Franklin	Bak	15
JERRY/GHERRY		
Jerry, John	Cam	190
Gherry, George	Pul	161
JESSEME, William	Cht	245
JESSOP/JESSEP		
Jessop, James	Twg	80
_____, Samuel	Twg	80
Jessep, Young	Crf	405
JESTER/JESTURE		
Jester, Burges	Hry	248
_____, James	Bts	170
_____, Levi	Bts	170
_____, Nathan	Jsp	372
Jesture, William	New	38
JETER: also see Geter		
Jeter, Buck	Lin	67
_____, Charles	Mus	291
_____, Cornelius	Up	101
_____, Dudly	DeK	50
_____, James	Lin	68
_____, James	Mus	292
_____, James R.	Gre	290
_____, John	Mor	258
_____, Oliver	Mus	277
_____, Pressly	Lin	61

Name	County	Page
Jeter, Samuel	Lin	69
_____, Wiley	Lin	69
JETT, Bailey	DeK	31
_____, Daniel	Gre	297
_____, Ferdinand	Gwn	378
_____, Francis	Mor	262
_____, Hardy	Gwn	378
_____, James	DeK	69
_____, James A.	DeK	27
_____, John	DeK	69
_____, Stephen	DeK	44
JEWEL/JUELL/JUEL		
Jewel, Henry	Lau	21
_____, Moses	Em	167
_____, Umphrey	Em	167
_____, Zachariah	Em	168
Juell, William	Ogl	87
Juel, James	Ogl	93
JEWETT, Elijah	Mus	277
_____, Eliza	Cht	272
_____, George	Bib	55
JILES: see Giles		
JINKS/JENKS/JINCKS		
Jinks, Adam	Bts	168
_____, Burwell	Bts	167
_____, David	Ogl	82
_____, Irwin	Bts	171
_____, Isaac	Bts	167
_____, Matthew	Bts	168
_____, Thomas	DeK	58
_____, William	Hry	216
_____, Willis	Hry	230
Jenks, Garland	Trp	40
_____, William	Tlb	345
Jincks, Allen	Ran	250
JOHNS/JOHN		
Johns, Albert	Hst	267
_____, Booker	DeK	68
_____, Charles R.	Pik	118
_____, Daniel	Hst	290
_____, Enoch	Lau	18
_____, Ephraigm	Hab	7
_____, George	Cam	189
_____, Hetaville	Cam	187
_____, Jas. J.	Cam	191
_____, Jeremiah	Cam	191
_____, Jesse	Bke	117
_____, John	Cht	250
_____, John	Wal	131
_____, John M.	Hst	267
_____, Jonathan	Bke	125
_____, Levi	Cam	187
_____, Littleberry	Lib	4[illegible]

Johns, Mary E. Jef 405
______, Obadiah Mon 192
______, Silas Cam 191
______, Thomas Cpb 201
______, Thomas H. Han 173
______, William Cam 190
______, William Tat 373
______, William G. Hst 267
John, Bartlet C. DeK 48
______, Jas. H. Wks 350
______, L. Wks 358
______, Lewis Mon 185
______, Spanish Jsp 372
______, William Wks 354
JOHNSON/JONSON/JONSAN/
JONHSON
Johnson, A. App 12
______, A. M. Jsp 361
______, Aaron Hry 222
______, Abel Twg 71
______, Abner Pik 110
______, Abraham Jns 461
______, Abslom Dec 19
______, Abab Jns 431
______, Alan Tat 375
______, Alexander DeK 65
______, Alexander Elb 143
______, Alexander Frk 218
______, Alexander Wal 169
______, Alford Hst 269
______, Alfred Pik 117
______, Allen S. Gre 304
______, Amos Mwr 163
______, Amos Wrn 199
______, Andrew Gwn 342
______, Andrew Hab 56
______, Andrew Jsp 384
______, Anthony Jns 435
______, Archibald DeK 48
______, Aron Wrn 219
______, Arthur Mon 219
______, Asa Gre 303
______, Asa Lau 11
______, Bailey Trp 37
______, Barnabas Jks 323
______, Ben Gwn 321
______, Ben Gwn 327
______, Benjamin Car 234
______, Benjamin Hst 278
______, Benjamin Hst 287
______, Benja. Wrn 232
______, Benj. H. Gwn 318
______, Bonnitta Pik 127
Johnson, Bucy D. Wil 323
______, Burrel Hal 108
______, Bury Em 173
______, Bushrod Put 177
______, Calvin Wrn 229
______, Cary Wrn 209
______, Catherine Rch 286
______, Charles Hst 293
______, Charles H. Bul 98
______, Charlotte Ran 250
______, Chinia Wsh 275
______, Claborn Frk 222
______, Crawford Col 350
______, Daniel App 5
______, Daniel DeK 48
______, Daniel Sr. Elb 159
______, Daniel B. Dec 19
______, Daniel M. Elb 159
______, Darling Hst 265
______, David Hry 216
______, David Lwn 88
______, David New 32
______, David Ogl 77
______, David Wal 123
______, David Wks 342
______, David Wrn 224
______, Dempsey Cow 373
______, Dillan DeK 48
______, Duncan App 5
______, Earic App 7
______, Ed. Wks 346
______, Edmond Wrn 201
______, Edward Bal 29
______, Edward Bal 33
______, Edward Twg 68
______, Edward Wal 145
______, Edward Fay 182
______, Elam Mon 186
______, Elhannon Bke 137
______, Elijah Wsh 264
______, Elijah Wrn 222
______, Elisha Hry 209
______, Elisha Wrn 228
______, Eliza Put 194
______, Elizabeth Hry 235
______, Elizabeth Jns 469
______, Emanuel Rch 279
______, Ephriam Crf 488
______, Ephriam Hal 104
______, Esther Frk 219
______, Ezra Mon 183
______, Ferreby Jns 461
______, Francis Hab 7

Name	County	Page
Johnson, Fredrick	Gwn	365
______, Gabriel	Ear	100
______, Gamabel	Put	177
______, George	New	33
______, George	Tat	371
______, Heorge H.	Wrn	206
______, George W.	New	11
______, George W.	Wil	313
______, Gideon	Mon	181
______, Gilbert	Gre	295
______, Green	Lee	35
______, Green	Ogl	81
______, Green	Wrn	222
______, Greene	Put	186
______, Greene B.	Wrn	206
______, Mrs. H.	Col	346
______, Hardy	Em	167
______, Harris	Mon	208
______, Henry	DeK	56
______, Henry	Doo	80
______, Henry	Jks	316
______, Henry	Jns	461
______, Henry	New	29
______, Henry	Wsh	249
______, Henry S.	Wrn	203
______, Hiram	Dec	8
______, Howel	Col	356
______, Hugh	Rch	259
______, Hugh G.	Pik	119
______, Isaac	Jns	461
______, Isaac	Lwn	79
______, Isaac	Ogl	76
______, Isaac	Wsh	242
______, Isaac N.	DeK	26
______, Isaac W.	Ogl	77
______, Isham	Trp	50
______, Isreal	Wsh	266
______, J. C.	DeK	27
______, Jabez	Har	179
______, Jacob	Dec	7
______, Jacob	Wil	292
______, James Sr.	Car	229
______, James Jr.	Car	221
______, James	Elb	135
______, James	Em	169
______, James	Hab	28
______, James	Hab	32
______, James	Hry	201
______, James	Hry	235
______, James	New	20
______, James	Pik	131
______, James	Rch	262
______, James	Trp	51
Johnson, James	Wal	169
______, James	Wrn	215
______, James	Wks	341
______, James E.	Pik	123
______, James F.	Trp	42
______, James H.	Hry	200
______, James J.	Hab	51
______, James W.	Up	115
______, Janawa	Hab	46
______, Jane	Wrn	195
______, Jan^{t}.	Lwn	79
______, Jason	Wsh	276
______, Jeremiah	Trp	35
______, Jeremiah	Twg	70
______, Jesse	Dec	12
______, Jesse	Gre	295
______, Jesse	Hry	199
______, Jesse	Jsp	364
______, Jessey	Jks	328
______, Jesse	Jns	461
______, Jesse	Ran	242
______, Jesse	Rch	279
______, Joel	Gwn	317
______, Joel	Hab	34
______, Joel	Wal	154
______, Joel J.	Ran	247
______, John	App	6
______, John	Bal	37
______, John	Dec	4
______, John	DeK	47
______, John	Elb	145
______, John	Em	173
______, John	Em	174
______, John	Frk	235
______, John	Gre	285
______, John	Gwn	372
______, John	Hab	[illegible]
______, John	Hab	4[illegible]
______, John	Hab	6[illegible]
______, John	Har	17[illegible]
______, John	Har	18[illegible]
______, John	Hry	21[illegible]
______, John	Jsp	38[illegible]
______, John	Jks	34[illegible]
______, John	Lwn	8
______, John	Mwr	15
______, John	New	1
______, John	Ogl	8[illegible]
______, John	Pik	13[illegible]
______, John	Trp	3[illegible]
______, John	Wal	13[illegible]
______, John	Wal	16[illegible]
______, John	Wal	14[illegible]

Johnson, John Wsh 244
______, John A. Mwr 160
______, John A. Ware 185
______, John C. Wal 151
______, John C. Wal 163
______, John D. Har 176
______, John F. Jks 322
______, John G. New 10
______, John J. Wrn 202
______, John R. Gre 294
______, John R. Pik 132
______, Joicy Ogl 89
______, Jonathan Car 230
______, Jonathen Hab 58
______, Jonathan Mon 195
______, Joseph Sr. DeK 71
______, Joseph Put 180
______, Joseph Wal 170
______, Joseph B. Wil 305
______, Joseph C. Wrn 202
______, Joseph S. Fay 192
______, Joshua Gwn 373
______, Joshua Mad 115
______, Josiah DeK 72
______, Julius Rch 268
______, Kinclery Wil 321
______, Larkin Mon 227
______, Larkin New 17
______, Laughlin DeK 26
______, Leroy Mad 112
______, Levi Tms 16
______, Levi Up 101
______, Lewis Wrn 218
______, Lindsay Elb 134
______, Linsey New 25
______, Littlebury Bts 175
______, Littleton Wrn 202
______, Lucy Jsp 369
______, Macon Elb 130
______, Malcom App 10
______, Malcombe Car 218
______, Martha New 14
______, Martha Wrn 214
______, Martin Hst 282
______, Mary Bul 101
______, Mary Twg 78
______, Mary Ann Up 117
______, Matilda Mwr 169
______, Matthew Doo 80
______, Micajah Doo 83
______, Mical E. Ogl 77
______, Mordica Mwr 159
______, Moses Bke 137

Johnson, Moses Twg 67
______, Moses J. Har 176
______, Nancy Bts 165
______, Nancy Gre 294
______, Nancy Twg 69
______, Nancy Wsh 274
______, Nancy Wil 308
______, Nathan Crf 406
______, Nathan Gwn 369
______, Nathaniel Wal 148
______, Nathanl Wal 164
______, Nicholas Jsp 368
______, Nicholas Trp 33
______, Noel Wal 170
______, Oliver DeK 70
______, Penelope Lau 13
______, Perry G. New 37
______, Peter DeK 37
______, Peter Hry 214
______, Peter C. Gre 280
______, Philip Hal 121
______, Polly Wil 290
______, Polly O. Jsp 361
______, Posey Wal 124
______, Quinny Wsh 276
______, R. H. Rch 262
______, Rabun H. Ogl 103
______, Randall Wrn 216
______, Reese Wrn 216
______, Reubin New 7
______, Richard Hst 270
______, Richard Hst 280
______, Richard Jsp 368
______, Richard Wal 163
______, Robert Hry 234
______, Robert New 44
______, Robert New 54
______, Robert Wrn 202
______, Robt. D. Gwn 343
______, Robert P. Tfo 355
______, Rowan Em 174
______, Sampson Tms 16
______, Samuel Dec 6
______, Samuel Ear 96
______, Samuel Frk 219
______, Samuel Hry 209
______, Samuel New 19
______, Samuel Put 177
______, Samuel Ran 244
______, Samuel Tfo 363
______, Samuel Trp 51
______, Sanky T. Trp 51
______, Sarah Gwn 343

Name	County	Page
Johnson, Sarah	Jks	316
______, Scala	Jks	348
______, Seaborn	Em	166
______, Shadrick	Hab	33
______, Sherwood B.	Hry	206
______, Silas M.	New	18
______, Simon	Crf	415
______, Snelling	Jsp	352
______, Sol.	Gwn	322
______, Stephen	Doo	82
______, Stephen	Hst	293
______, Stephen	Wil	308
______, Stephen A.	Wil	289
______, Stidmon	New	38
______, Susan	Elb	157
______, Susannah	Twg	87
______, Sylvester	Up	98
______, Thomas	Bts	161
______, Thomas	Car	221
______, Thomas	DeK	60
______, Thomas	DeK	64
______, Thomas	Elb	158
______, Thomas	Hab	43
______, Thomas	Hry	234
______, Thos.	Jks	329
______, Thomas	Lee	30
______, Thomas	Mwr	163
______, Thomas	Mon	183
______, Thomas	Pik	112
______, Thomas	Put	172
______, Thomas	Wil	294
______, Thomas A.	Mon	192
______, Thomas B.	Hry	217
______, Thomas D.	Hry	209
______, Thomas J.	Hry	199
______, Thomas J.	Tms	22
______, Thomas T.	Hst	266
______, Timothy	Dec	4
______, Uriah	Tms	17
______, Vincent	Hal	68
______, Vincent	Wrn	201
______, Washington	Jsp	390
______, W.	Col	361
______, William	Bke	154
______, Wm.	Crf	412
______, William	Dec	6
______, William	DeK	32
______, William	DeK	67
______, William	Elb	138
______, William	Em	169
______, William	Gwn	366
______, William	Gwn	373
______, William	Hal	92

Name	County	Page
Johnson, William	Hry	216
______, William	Hst	266
______, William	Hst	280
______, William	Jsp	357
______, William Sr.	Jns	461
______, William Sr.	Jns	469
______, William	Lau	5
______, William	Mon	177
______, William	Ogl	77
______, William	Ogl	82
______, William	Tfo	360
______, Wm. Sr.	Tat	379
______, Wm.	Tat	379
______, William	Twg	74
______, Wm.	Wsh	247
______, Wm. Jr.	Wrn	219
______, Wm. B.	Gre	275
______, Wm. C.	Wsh	254
______, William L.	Lau	1
______, Wm. P.	Tfo	365
______, William W.	Rch	281
______, Willis	Trp	37
______, Willis	Wsh	26
______, Wilson	Wks	34
______, Zadock	DeK	6
Jonson, Thos.	Hab	3
______, Welborn	Mtg	23
Jonsan, Arthur	Mus	28
Jonhson, Anthony	Irw	30
JOHNSTON, Abagail	Jns	43
______, Abner	Cow	36
______, Albert	Bib	7
______, Alexander	Bib	7
______, Alexander	Lin	5
______, Allen	Bib	7
______, Alsa	Cpb	1
______, Amos	Han	1
______, Anna	Jns	4
______, Arnold	Bib	
______, Ashfield	Han	1
______, Barthelomew	Mor	2
______, Bedford	Ogl	
______, Benj. Sr.	Bak	
______, Benjamin Jr.	Bak	
______, Gary	Ogl	
______, Chandler	Mor	2
______, Daniel	Lau	
______, Daniel	Mor	2
______, David	Mar	1
______, Dempsey	Ogl	
______, Eli	Han	1
______, Elijah	Jef	4
______, Fred[k].	Gwn	

Name	County	Page
Johnston, George H.	Cht	250
______, George H.	Lib	47
______, Henry	Bib	61
______, Henry	Jef	413
______, Henry	Ogl	67
______, Isaac	Han	158
______, Isaac	Pul	161
______, Isaiah	Bke	127
______, Israel	Bak	19
______, Israel	Han	158
______, Jacob	Bib	67
______, Jacob	Han	158
______, James	Bry	84
______, James	Cam	181
______, James	Han	158
______, James Jr.	Han	158
______, James	Jsp	355
______, James	Jns	446
______, James	Lin	59
______, James	Mon	191
______, James	Mor	244
______, James	Ogl	72
______, James	Pul	144
______, James C.	Ogl	71
______, James C.	Ogl	73
______, James R.	Bak	19
______, James R.	Cht	265
______, Jared	Bke	127
______, Jesse	Cpt	211
______, Jesse	Cow	384
______, Jesse	Jef	416
______, John	Bib	67
______, John	Bib	73
______, John or Joel (written over)	Cow	378
______, John	Jsp	356
______, John	Jns	428
______, John	Mor	242
______, John	Rab	229
______, John C.	Bib	55
______, Jonas	Lau	13
______, Jonathan	Gwn	360
______, Jonathan	Gwn	360
______, Joseph	Hal	124
______, Joshua	Bib	67
______, Josiah	Bib	61
______, Josiah	Bib	61
______, Josiah	Cow	386
______, Kitty	Cht	271
______, Labon	Han	158
______, Lancelott	Mor	250
______, Laviell	Han	159
______, Lemuel	Lau	17

Name	County	Page
Johnston, Levi	DeK	40
______, Lewis	Cht	246
______, Liney	Bib	73
______, Littleton	Jsp	358
______, Luke	Bib	61
______, Luke	Hry	244
______, Luke Sr.	Ogl	67
______, Luke	Ogl	67
______, Malcom	Tfo	363
______, Martha	Pul	141
______, Martin	Cow	386
______, Martin	Han	159
______, Martin	Lee	31
______, Mathew	Jef	404
______, Micajah	Bib	61
______, Michael	Cam	183
______, Millington	Han	158
______, Molsey	Cht	270
______, Moses	Bry	88
______, Nathan	Jsp	355
______, Paul	Lib	47
______, Philip	Jef	405
______, Philip	Jns	440
______, Pricilla	Cht	242
______, Racheal	Cht	245
______, Rebecca	Cht	271
______, Richard	Jsp	358
______, Rily	Lee	31
______, Robert	Bib	67
______, Rolin	Hal	94
______, Samuel	Ogl	64
______, Samuel	Tlb	329
______, Solomon	Bry	89
______, Stephen	Bak	20
______, Stephen	Han	158
______, Stephen	Han	158
______, Thomas	Cow	377
______, Thomas	Jsp	357
______, Thomas	Pul	141
______, Thomas	Rab	222
______, Tim	Han	158
______, W.	Gwn	309
______, William	Bib	67
______, William	Bib	73
______, William	Bib	73
______, William	Bib	76
______, William	Cpb	207
______, William	Gwn	356
______, William	Han	158
______, William	Mor	250
______, William	Pul	153
______, William B.	Bib	67
______, William H.	Mon	215

Name	County	Page
Johnston, William H.	Mor	241
______, William W.	Bry	84
______, William W.	Ogl	73
______, Willis	Han	158
______, Young	Bib	55
______, Zachariah	Jns	433
JOINER/JOYNER/JYNER		
Joiner, Absolam	Mon	199
______, Absolemn	Wrn	232
______, Benajer	Bak	17
______, Benjamin	Pik	130
______, Benjamin	Put	180
______, Bennett	Hst	281
______, Curtis	Pul	161
______, Gibson	Pik	114
______, Guilford	Hst	280
______, Jacob	Pul	152
______, James	Pik	114
______, Jane	Hst	264
______, Joel	Doo	85
______, John	Doo	85
______, Jos.	Bal	40
______, Lewis	Doo	85
______, Malachi	Wsh	275
______, Mary	Mon	200
______, Mary	Wsh	252
______, Meredith	Hst	288
______, Moses	Pik	130
______, Sarah	Mar	138
______, Thomas	Bke	130
______, William	Rch	283
Joyner, Bennet	Lau	17
______, Charles	Wyn	284
______, Davis	Lau	13
______, E.	Crf	403
______, Jane	Cht	255
______, Jesse	Lau	13
______, John	Hry	249
______, Lawrence	Twg	62
______, Nathan	Lau	15
______, Rebecca	Twg	87
Jyner, Asa	Ran	249
JOINES, Edmond	Wsh	265
______, Ezekeil	Wsh	258
______, Jabeze	Wsh	245
______, James	Wsh	255
______, William	Wsh	258
JOLIFF, Joseph	Jns	465
JOLLY/JOLLEY		
Jolly, Asa	Crf	411
______, James	Bal	35
______, John	Bal	35
______, John	Frk	220

Name	County	Page
Jolly, Joseph	DeK	33
______, Joseph	Mon	174
______, Nimrod	Hal	92
______, William	Bal	36
Jolley, Jesse	Bts	164
JOLSON, Francis W.	Hst	261
JONAS: see Janes		
JONES, Aaron	Car	214
______, Aaron	Hry	230
______, Aaron	Ogl	78
______, Abner	Lwn	86
______, Abner	Trp	53
______, Abner W.	Ear	96
______, Abraham	Bke	128
______, Adam	Bul	96
______, Adam Sr.	Wrn	228
______, Adam Jr.	Wrn	227
______, Adam	Wks	340
______, Alexander	Ogl	71
______, Alexander	Ogl	97
______, Alfred T.	Frk	210
______, Allen	Bul	96
______, Allen	Col	358
______, Allen	Hry	225
______, Allen	Mon	185
______, Allen	Mor	262
______, Allen	Wks	333
______, Alvis	Dec	7
______, Ambrose	Han	157
______, Amos	Cow	369
______, Amos	Mon	190
______, Anthony	Wrn	196
______, Archwell	Hst	275
______, Arthur	Elb	139
______, Augustus S.	Scr	315
______, Balaam	Frk	255
______, Barnet	Frk	228
______, Barsheba	Jns	465
______, Bartlett	Frk	246
______, Bassel	Wsh	26[illegible]
______, Bazel	Bul	10[illegible]
______, Ben	Gwn	37
______, Benjamin	Clk	30[illegible]
______, Benj.	Gwn	32
______, Benjamin	Hab	1
______, Benjn.	Hab	5
______, Benjamin	Mon	20[illegible]
______, Benjamin	Put	20[illegible]
______, Benjamin	Tfo	36
______, Benjamin	Wsh	24[illegible]
______, Berry	Bul	9
______, Betsey	Jns	43[illegible]
______, Bruington	Ogl	[illegible]

Name	County	Page
Jones, Bryant	Jns	469
______, Burrill	Cam	189
______, Charles	Bib	70
______, Charles	Bke	139
______, Charles	Mad	110
______, Charles	Rch	256
______, Charles	Wal	156
______, Charles B.	Wrn	229
______, Charles E.	Lib	50
______, Chesley	Tlb	336
______, Clarissa	Frk	210
______, Claton	Lwn	86
______, Clemm	Trp	50
______, Cooper	Hst	289
______, Cullen	Mon	183
______, Dabney P.	Cow	371
______, Daniel	Wks	340
______, Daniel E.	Bul	94
______, Darling	Pul	143
______, David	Doo	82
______, David	Mon	190
______, Davis	Elb	139
______, Dickerson	Gre	272
______, Drucilla	Elb	151
______, Druery	Hab	15
______, Dudley M.	Mad	104
______, Due H.	Wal	135
______, Dr. E. W.	Col	352
______, Edmund	Bib	61
______, Edmund	Elb	139
______, Edward	DeK	55
______, Edward	Ogl	66
______, Edward	Wil	290
______, Eleana	Han	158
______, Eli	Wal	168
______, Elijah	Wrn	228
______, Elijah E.	Mor	249
______, Eliz.	Wks	336
______, Eliza	Col	334
______, Elizabeth	Eff	108
______, Elizabeth	Hal	83
______, Elizabeth (slave)	Rch	271
______, Elizabeth	Tms	22
______, Elizabeth	Wrn	194
______, Ellis	Col	356
______, Ephraim	Bib	70
______, Erastus W.	Mon	207
______, Evan	Wyn	282
______, Ezra B.	Bal	43
______, Fanney	Mar	143
______, Fletcher	Elb	153
______, Francis	Bke	125
______, Frank	Gwn	375
Jones, Frederick	Hst	277
______, G.	Col	344
______, G. W.	Gwn	320
______, Gabriel	Bib	76
______, Gabriel	Bib	76
______, Gabriel	Ear	91
______, Gabriel	Ogl	72
______, Gabril	Wks	354
______, Garland	Elb	144
______, Garland	Han	157
**______, George (slave)	Cht	280
**______, George (slave)	Cht	281
______, George	Frk	251
______, George	Gwn	339
______, Gilford W.	Ogl	68
______, Griffin	Wal	133
______, Hannah	Wrn	212
______, Hardy	Pik	116
______, Hardy	Trp	54
______, Harley	Ware	187
______, Harison	Gwn	335
______, Harrison	New	26
______, Harrowson	Ran	245
______, Hartwell	Jsp	360
______, Hartwell Jr.	Jsp	361
______, Henly	Wrn	229
______, Henry	Cam	185
______, Henry	DeK	70
______, Henry	Fay	186
______, Henry	Hab	15
______, Henry	Hal	127
______, Henry	Hst	286
______, Henry	Mon	218
______, Henry	Wal	160
______, Henry	Wsh	262
______, Henry	Wrn	227
______, Henry B.	Mwr	163
______, Henry P.	Bke	128
______, Henry P.	Crf	410
______, Henry P.	Ogl	83
______, Henry S.	Bke	128
______, Henry S.	Mon	178
______, Hesekiah	Put	183
______, Hez	Lee	31
______, Hezekiah	Ogl	71
______, Hiram	Elb	140
______, Hiram	Hal	77
______, Hiram	Rch	282
______, Hiram	Wks	354
______, Hiram B.	Mwr	156
______, Howel	Wsh	243
______, Isaac	Bib	76
______, Isaac	Mon	200

Name	County	Page
Jones, Isaac	Tlf	6
______, Isaac	Trp	49
______, J. L.	DeK	26
______, Jacob	Ear	100
______, James	Bal	33
______, James	Bul	103
______, James	DeK	33
______, James	DeK	53
______, James Jr.	DeK	54
______, James	Ear	95
______, James	Elb	128
______, James	Frk	255
______, James Jr.	Frk	249
______, James	Gly	269
______, James	Hal	133
______, James	Hst	281
______, James	Jks	347
______, James	Jns	437
______, James	Jns	446
______, James	Lau	18
______, James	Mon	184
______, James	Mon	210
______, James	New	23
______, James	Put	186
______, James	Put	192
______, James	Tlb	332
______, James	Trp	32
______, James	Trp	53
______, James	Twg	66
______, James	Wal	144
______, James (Slim)	Ware	187
______, James A.	Bal	29
______, James C.	Mor	266
______, James D.	Cow	387
______, James G.	Jns	451
______, James H.	Elb	144
______, James H.	Han	157
______, James Little	Ware	187
______, James M.	Rab	223
______, James N.	Car	217
______, James S.	Hry	208
______, James W.	Bke	152
______, James W.	Ran	244
______, Jane	Elb	151
______, Jane	Gwn	333
______, Jane P.	Gwn	364
______, Jemima	Tlf	6
______, Jempsey	Twg	85
______, Jeremiah D.	New	55
______, Jerre	DeK	64
______, Jesse	Cam	186
______, Jesse	Clk	306
______, Jesse	Clk	320
Jones, Jesse	Gwn	323
______, Jesse	Gwn	366
______, Jesse J.	DeK	47
______, Jesse S.	Wrn	205
______, Joab	Jks	320
______, Joel	Jsp	391
______, Joel Sr.	New	53
______, Joel Jr.	New	53
______, John	Bib	70
______, John	Bts	174
______, John	Clk	315
______, John	Col	347
______, John	Col	363
______, John	Dec	3
______, John	DeK	68
______, John	Gwn	323
______, John	Hal	132
______, John	Hst	267
______, John	Jsp	396
______, John	Jns	430
______, John	Jns	443
______, John	Lau	12
______, John	Lin	59
______, John Sr.	Lwn	85
______, John Jr.	Lwn	86
______, John	Mar	143
______, John	Mon	176
______, John	Mus	289
______, John	New	15
______, John	Ogl	102
______, John	Pul	162
______, John	Put	202
______, John	Tms	16
______, John	Wal	125
______, John	Wal	172
______, John	Wrn	197
______, John	Wil	296
______, John	Wks	354
______, John A.	Bal	39
______, John A.	Tlf	4
______, John B.	Jns	461
______, John C.	Gwn	352
______, John D.	Bib	70
______, John Floyd	DeK	73
______, John G.	Wal	173
______, John H.	DeK	53
______, John H.	Mwr	154
______, John H. R.	Hab	25
______, J. John	Bib	70
______, John J.	Tlb	347
______, John K.	Wrn	229
______, John M.	Bke	139
______, John M.	Han	159

Name	County	Page
Jones, John M.	Mor	261
______, John M.	Mor	263
______, John P.	New	26
______, John R.	Fay	185
______, John T. B.	Ear	92
______, John W.	Cpb	202
______, John W.	Mon	180
______, John W.	Wil	322
______, Jonathan	Lau	23
______, Jonathan	Pik	128
______, Jordan	Elb	155
______, Joseph	Clk	298
______, Joseph	Crf	409
______, Joseph Sr.	Gre	281
______, Joseph Jr.	Gre	294
______, Joseph	Lib	47
______, Joseph	Rab	224
______, Joseph	Wal	166
______, Joseph M.	Lib	47
______, Josiah	Dec	10
______, Josiah	Ear	93
______, Josiah	Rch	288
______, Landon	Jns	432
______, Lazarus	Gwn	339
______, Leah	Scr	300
______, Lemuel B.	Hal	87
______, Leroy	Wal	157
______, Levi	Up	100
______, Levice	Lau	13
______, Lewis	Frk	253
______, Lewis	Hab	24
______, Lewis	Put	185
______, Lewis	Wks	338
______, Lewis D.	Frk	224
______, Lewis J.	Elb	151
______, Lewis R.	Elb	150
______, Lucy	New	26
______, Lucy	Wks	352
______, Malechia	Hab	25
______, Margaret	Jef	403
______, Marshal	Elb	152
______, Martha	Bib	61
______, Martha	Clk	324
______, Martin	Car	228
______, Martin	Rab	223
______, Mary	DeK	62
______, Mary	Ear	96
______, Mary	Pul	139
______, Mary	Put	203
______, Mary	Tfo	362
______, Mason	Lin	64
______, Mason	Ogl	73
______, Matthew	Bke	125
Jones, Mathew	Dec	8
______, Matthew	Lib	47
______, Mathew	Mor	248
______, Micajah	Frk	213
______, Micajor	New	20
______, Milly	Hal	82
______, Moses	Lin	58
______, Moses	Ogl	73
______, Moses	Trp	46
______, Moses L.	Lib	48
______, Moses R.	Lin	74
______, Nancy	Fay	206
______, Nancy	Hal	127
______, Nancy	Jns	469
______, Nathan	Bib	70
______, Nathan	Mon	185
______, Nathan	Up	113
______, Nath[l].	Wrn	227
______, Neenna	Rch	253
______, Nelly	Rch	255
______, Nimrod	Hry	213
______, Noel	Pul	146
______, Nunery	Put	197
______, Obediance	Col	336
______, Oliver C.	Hry	239
______, Orin	Cow	378
______, Patience	Pik	126
______, Peggy	Put	197
______, Peter	Jks	341
______, Peter	Mon	204
______, Philip	Han	158
______, Pleasant	Ogl	96
______, Pleasant	Ogl	99
______, Pressley	New	9
______, Rev[d].	Col	347
______, Randal	Har	182
______, Randolph	Ogl	64
______, Rebecca	Put	202
______, Rebecca	Rch	276
______, Reese H.	Wrn	209
______, Reuben Sr.	Jsp	395
______, Reuben Jr.	Jsp	395
______, Richard	Frk	214
______, Richard	Jks	333
______, Richard	Mor	260
______, Richard	Wal	143
______, Richard H.	Tfo	360
______, Richard O. B.	Jns	432
______, Robert	Clk	306
______, RobertEsq.	Col	349
______, Robert Sr.	Col	349
______, Robert	Col	357
______, Robert	Dec	8

Name	County	Page
Jones, Robert	Em	164
______, Robert	Mus	280
______, Robert	Ogl	79
______, Robert	Put	203
______, Robert	Rch	253
______, Robert	Wal	143
______, Robert J.	Mwr	155
______, Ruben	Wrn	205
______, Russel	Jks	329
______, Russell H.	Mad	107
______, Russel T.	Frk	221
______, Samuel	Col	334
______, Samuel	Lau	22
______, Samuel, dec'd.Est	Lib	48
______, Samuel	Lin	73
______, Samuel	McI	131
______, Samuel	Ran	243
______, Samuel	Wrn	228
______, Samuel	Wil	300
______, Samuel F.	Crf	393
______, Samuel G.	Elb	155
______, Sarah	Bul	99
______, Sarah	Dec	8
______, Sarah	DeK	53
______, Sarah	Frk	239
**______, Sarah (slave)	Rch	257
______, Sarah	Twg	82
______, Sarah	Wal	151
______, Sarah R.	Jef	415
______, Seaborn	Jsp	360
______, Seaborn	Mus	290
______, Seaborn	New	9
______, Seaborn	New	20
______, Seaborn	Trp	37
______, Seaborn H.	Bke	152
______, Sealy	Bib	76
______, Selah	Tfo	356
______, Serena	Put	218
______, Simon	Lau	8
______, Simon	Wrn	228
______, Smith	Gwn	325
______, Solomon	Elb	155
______, Solomon	Lau	4
______, Stephen	Mor	253
______, Stephen	Put	208
______, Stephen	Twg	67
______, Stephen	Wrn	228
______, Stephen B.	Clk	306
______, Sterling	Wrn	192
______, Sugar	Gwn	323
______, Susannah	Wrn	206
______, T.	Col	345
______, Tandy C.	Jef	411
Jones, Tapley	Trp	33
______, Tempy	Put	189
______, Theophilis	Crf	403
______, Thomas	Bul	97
______, Thomas	Cow	369
______, Thomas Jr.	Cow	376
______, Thomas	Cow	390
______, Thomas	Elb	128
______, Thomas	Elb	136
______, Thomas	Gre	281
______, Thomas	Gwn	339
______, Thomas	Gwn	353
______, Thomas	Har	187
______, Thomas	Jsp	353
______, Thomas	Jsp	387
______, Thomas	Jns	428
______, Thomas	Mad	115
______, Thomas	New	20
______, Thomas	Put	203
______, Thomas	Tms	24
______, Thomas	Twg	82
______, Thomas	Wal	169
______, Thomas	Wrn	222
______, Thomas H.	Gwn	353
______, Thomas J.	Bke	138
______, Thomas M.	Hal	69
______, Thomas P.	Mor	255
______, Thomas P.	Wrn	205
______, Thomas W.	Col	356
______, Tignal	Frk	229
______, Tignal	Frk	255
______, Timothy	Cpb	196
______, Toliver	Lin	64
______, Uriah	Har	179
______, Vincen	Gwn	322
______, Vincen	Gwn	366
______, Vincent	Put	202
______, W.	Bal	40
______, Wade H.	Ogl	64
______, Walters	Col	342
______, Warrenton	Cpb	201
______, Welden	Wal	141
______, Widow	Pul	158
______, Wiley	Cow	387
______, Wiley	Mon	178
______, Wiley	Ran	245
______, Wiley	Wks	350
______, Wiley E.	Har	176
______, William	Bts	175
______, William	Cpb	199
______, William	Cht	245
______, William	Clk	297
______, William	Col	339

Name	County	Page
Jones, William	Elb	140
______, William	Em	176
______, William	Frk	239
______, William	Gwn	339
______, William	Hab	15
______, William	Hab	50
______, William	Hal	77
______, William	Han	158
______, William	Han	159
______, William	Hst	277
______, Williams	Hst	286
______, William Sr.	Jsp	393
______, William Jr.	Jsp	387
______, William	Jef	403
______, William	Jns	451
______, William	Jns	469
______, William	Lib	47
______, William	Lin	60
______, William	Lwn	84
______, William	Mon	184
______, William	Mon	193
______, William	Mon	218
______, William	Mon	226
______, William	Mor	241
______, William	Mor	266
______, William Sr.	Mor	268
______, William	Mor	271
______, William	New	43
______, William	New	52
______, William Jr.	New	53
______, William	Pik	116
______, William	Pik	124
______, William	Put	184
______, William	Put	203
______, William	Rab	224
______, William	Rab	225
______, William	Trp	47
______, William	Wrn	199
______, William	Wal	132
______, William	Wal	153
______, William	Wsh	274
______, William	Wil	288
______, William	Wks	344
______, William C.	Cow	377
______, William C.	Mon	228
______, William D.	Lin	66
______, William E.	Bul	102
______, William E.	Jks	313
______, William H.	Mor	268
______, William H.	Rch	256
______, William J.	Col	342
______, William M.	Twg	68
______, William P.	Wil	304
Jones, William R.	Pik	129
______, William S.	Fay	194
______, William S.	Jns	469
______, William S.	New	26
______, Williard	Jef	407
______, Willie	Rch	264
______, Willis	Jns	451
______, Willis	Mwr	155
______, Willis	Mor	262
______, Willis B.	Elb	149
______, Wily	Lee	31
______, Wright	Twg	69
______, Wyley	DeK	68
______, Wylie	Elb	132
______, Wylie B.	Wil	299
______, Zachariah	DeK	54
______, Zachariah	Trp	49
______, Zadoc	Mon	179

JORDAN/JOURDAN/JORDEN/
JOURDIN/JORDON/JOURDON/
JORDIN/JOURDAIN/JORDANS/
JURDEN

Name	County	Page
Jordan, Abner	Frk	247
______, Alvies	Pik	126
______, Asa	Wsh	263
______, Benjamin	Jsp	353
______, Benjamine	Wsh	256
______, Benj. S.	Bal	30
______, Burwell	Mor	242
______, Burwell	New	37
______, Charles	DeK	60
______, Charles	Hry	235
______, Charles	Mwr	168
______, Cornelious	Wsh	268
______, Daniel	Ware	189
______, Dempsy	Tfo	357
______, Demsey	Mwr	168
______, Derby	Wks	340
______, Edmond	Jsp	370
______, Edmund	Tfo	357
______, Elias	Hst	277
______, Elijah	Mwr	168
______, Elijah	Tfo	359
______, Elisha	DeK	68
______, Elizabeth	Jef	423
______, Elizabeth	Put	196
______, Emelin	Ran	244
______, Fountain	Elb	121
______, Gause	Jns	454
______, Green H.	Bal	28
______, Guilford	Hry	229
______, Henry	Mwr	159
______, Henry	Ogl	99

Name	County	Page
Jordan, Irby J.	Crf	401
______, Isaac	Elb	149
______, Isham	Irw	300
______, Jacob	Jns	461
______, Jacob	Wsh	254
______, James	DeK	33
______, James	Elb	125
______, James	Hal	113
______, James	Jns	457
______, James D.	Hry	206
______, Joanna B.	Frk	237
______, John	Bak	16
______, John	Har	181
______, John	Jns	451
______, John	Lwn	81
______, John	Pul	162
______, John	Wsh	257
______, John	Wil	319
______, John C.	Hry	206
______, John C.	Lin	74
______, John L.	Put	196
______, John M.	Hry	206
______, John W.	Tfo	356
______, Lovick P.	Jns	461
______, Margarett	Wsh	262
______, Mathew	Jef	423
______, Matthew J.	Bal	28
______, Nathan	Bak	17
______, Nathan	DeK	37
______, Obedience	Elb	120
______, P.	App	11
______, Reuben	Gwn	345
______, Reuben	Jsp	362
______, Samuel	Car	228
______, Samuel	Twg	60
______, Stephen	Elb	120
______, Thomas	Hst	264
______, Thomas	Mwr	168
______, Thomas	Wsh	268
______, Thomas G.	Jef	423
______, Thomas G.	Tlb	338
______, Mrs. W.	Wsh	257
______, Widow	Rch	276
______, Wiley	Twg	77
______, William	Bak	17
______, William	Ear	95
______, William	Elb	131
______, William	Jns	469
______, William	Tfo	362
______, William	Wsh	259
______, William D.	Wsh	249
______, William H.	DeK	61
______, William R.	Hry	235
Jordan, William T.	Jef	418
______, Willis	Ogl	96
______, Zacariah	Tfo	364
Jourdan, Asa	Hab	16
______, Benjamin	Trp	42
______, Chas. Sr.	Up	105
______, Chas. Jr.	Up	105
______, Edmund	Mon	184
______, Franklin	Hab	16
______, Jacob	Up	118
______, James	Up	113
______, John	Trp	43
______, John M.	Mon	207
______, John O.	Hab	18
______, Joseph	Hst	291
______, Josiah	Mon	205
______, Mathew	Mon	205
______, Membrance	Mon	200
______, Ruben	Hab	15
______, Siney	Hab	15
______, Warren	Jns	442
______, William	Doo	86
______, Willoughby	Hst	284
Jorden, Baxton	Mad	112
______, Edmond	Ogl	74
______, James	Mad	111
______, John	Mad	99
______, Peggy	Mad	117
______, Radford	Mad	111
______, Redding	Mad	114
______, Thomas	Mad	113
______, Thomas W.	Jns	451
Jourdin, Absalom	Bib	67
______, Benjamin	Cow	381
______, James E.	Bib	55
______, Joshua	Bib	61
______, Overoff	Bib	51
______, Zachariah	Bib	51
Jordon, James	Wsh	251
______, Jesse	DeK	57
______, Larkin	Crf	415
______, Mildred	Ogl	64
______, William W.	Crf	396
Jourdon, Abraham	Mar	138
______, Sarah	Cht	268
Jordin, Etheldred	Ogl	80
______, John Sealeofork	Ogl	62
Jourdain, John	Doo	86
Jordans, B. S.	Mor	243
Jurdin, Thos.	Mtg	233
JOSEPH, B.	Rch	260
______, Dennis	Rch	264
______, John	Cht	262

Name	County	Page
Joseph, Samuel	Pik	106
JOSEY/JOSE		
Josey, Henry	Wil	319
_____, Samuel	Jef	406
Jose, Sarah	Hst	292
JOSIAH, James	Hry	228
JOSLIN, William	Cam	188
JOY, Ephram	Wrn	197
JOYCE/JOICE		
Joyce, Gartner	Tat	378
_____, Henry	Ware	185
_____, James J.	Lwn	91
_____, John	Tat	380
_____, Washington	Lwn	91
_____, William	Lau	6
Joice, William	Tlb	331
_____, Mical	Dec	12
JUAKENNETT, Jacob	Jns	457
JUDDETH, James	Pik	128
JUDSON, Henry	DeK	65
JUHAN, Daniel B.	Jns	451
_____, Francis P.	Jns	461
_____, Isaac B.	Jns	461
_____, N. B.	Bal	38
JUNIOR, Anthony	Hry	245
_____, Silvester	Hry	245
JUSTIAN, Andrew	Gwn	359
_____, Noah	Gwn	359
JUSTICE/JUSTUS/JUSTIS/		
JUSTISS/JUSTUSE		
Justice, Aaron	Hst	263
_____, Alfred	Wks	356
_____, Appleton	Jns	465
_____, Archibald	Ear	92
_____, David	Dec	9
_____, Dempsey J.	Bib	64
_____, Isaac	Crf	401
_____, Isaac	Mon	188
_____, John	Doo	86
_____, John	Han	158
_____, Levi	Bib	64
_____, Lucretia	Wks	356
_____, Nancy	Mor	259
_____, Sarah	Wks	338
_____, Thomas	Hst	269
_____, Thomas	Mor	258
Justus, Allen	Jks	321
_____, Henry	Jks	320
_____, John	Jks	326
_____, Stephen	Jks	315
Justis, David	Jks	327
Justiss, William	Trp	35
Justuse, James	Pik	110

Name	County	Page
KAGLE: also see Cagle		
Kagle, Jacob	Hal	96
_____, Joseph	Hal	96
_____, William	Hal	96
KAGLER/CAGLER		
Kagler, John J.	Mar	143
_____, Margaret	Mar	143
Cagler, Henry	Jsp	382
KAHELY/CAHEELY		
Kahely, David	Jks	323
_____, Elijah	Jks	322
Caheely, Jacob	DeK	65
KAIN/KANE: see Cain/Cane		
KAKAGEE, Samuel	Mus	281
KALE, William	Bul	95
KALEN, David	Elb	124
KALIFF: see Califf		
KALLAHAND: see Callahand		
KANUP: see Canup		
KAPPELL, M. J.	Cht	245
KAPTO: see Cato		
KAUFMAN: see Kofeman'		
KAY/KAYS		
Kay, John B.	Bal	34
_____, Wiley	Rch	241
_____, William H.	Cpb	194
Kays, Michael	Twg	88
KEADLE/KADLE		
Keadle, John	New	11
_____, William	New	25
Kadle, Jeremiah	Mon	194
KEARLY, John	Crf	393
KEARNEY, Richard B.	Gre	304
KEARNS, Green	Hal	130
KEATING, Betsey	Rch	253
_____, Betsey	Rch	260
_____, John	Crf	394
_____, Richard T.	McI	127
KEATON/KEETON		
Keaton, Benjamin	Bak	15
_____, Kader	Bak	15
_____, Kader	Lib	48
_____, Rebecca	Put	215
_____, Samuel	Wks	331
_____, Sarah	Lib	48
Keeton, Bennona	Lee	29
_____, Joseph	Hal	132
KEEBLER, John	Cht	270
_____, Joshua Sr.	Eff	104
KEEGLER/KEEGLAR		
Keegler, David	Hry	226
_____, Jane	Cht	265
Keeglar, Margaret	Hry	229

KEEL/KELL/KILE		
Keel, Ardin	Tlf	7
_____, Gincy	Gwn	337
_____, Isaac	Wks	356
_____, John	Bak	17
_____, John	Lib	48
_____, Noah	Wks	356
_____, William	Bak	17
_____, William	Hab	12
Kell, F. S.	Cht	265
_____, Margery	McI	129
_____, Phineas	Bts	175
_____, William	Hal	102
Kile, Andrew	Gwn	331
_____, John	Hal	69
_____, Thomas	Gwn	331
KEELING/KEALLING		
Keeling, Leonard	Elb	123
_____, Thomas	Elb	143
Kealling, George	Col	360
KEENAM/KENAN/KENNEN/KENON/ KENNON/KENNOW/KENNUM/ KINION/KINYON/KANNON		
Keenam, Alexander	Cow	379
_____, John	Hal	108
_____, William	Hal	112
Kenan, Augustus Holmes	Bal	44
_____, Thomas Augustus	Bal	44
Kennen, John	Har	175
Kenon, Charles	New	16
_____, Richard Sr.	New	13
_____, Richard Jr.	New	14
_____, Selah	New	13
Kennon, Burwell	Bts	176
_____, Charles	Har	179
_____, Henry	New	32
_____, Lewis	Rch	268
_____, Owin H.	Cow	390
_____, Robert D.	Bts	175
_____, Spivey	Bts	176
_____, Thomas M.	Car	216
_____, William H.	Bts	160
Kennow, Thomas	Wal	130
Kennum, Lewis	DeK	68
Kinion, J. K.	Col	362
_____, James	Pul	140
Kinyon, Job H or A	Jsp	388
Kannon, C.	Wks	335
KEENER, Abraham	Rab	226
_____, John	Up	107
_____, Linson F.	Up	106
_____, Tilmon B.	Up	106
_____, William	Rch	270
KEEVA, William	Lee	29
KEFF, S.	Rch	254
KEIFFER, Ephraim	Eff	105
_____, Joel	Eff	106
KEITH/KEATH/KIETH		
Keith, Asa	Hal	132
_____, George	Hal	107
_____, Jer[h].	Jsp	395
_____, James	Hal	120
_____, James M.	Up	110
_____, John	Mer	166
_____, John	Wks	337
_____, John W.	Dec	3
_____, M. A.	Hal	109
_____, Mathew	Hal	118
_____, William	Hal	128
Keath, James	Mon	193
_____, James M.	Mon	193
_____, John	Twg	82
_____, Marshall	Col	335
_____, Martin	Hab	10
_____, Whitton	Bib	73
Kieth, Daniel	Mwr	155
_____, David	Mwr	155
KELLEBREW: see Kinnebrew		
KELLAM/KELLUM/CALLAM/ CALLUM		
Kellam, Amasa	Pul	144
_____, Celia	Pul	139
_____, Henry	Trp	34
_____, Willis	Trp	47
Kellum, Archibald	Tlb	322
_____, Elijah	Hry	212
_____, George	Tlb	329
_____, John	Ogl	69
_____, Russel	Lau	21
_____, Samuel	Ogl	69
_____, Seth	Lau	4
_____, Susannah	Lau	12
_____, William	Ogl	69
Callam, Absalem	Crf	414
Callum, James S.	Mon	219
KELLER/CALLER		
Keller, Mrs. Adam	Cht	278
_____, Godfrit	Jef	421
_____, Henery	Cow	367
_____, Paul	Cht	278
_____, Thomas	Hab	34
_____, Philip	Hal	107
_____, William	Hab	19
Caller, Joseph	Col	338
KELLOGG/KELLOG		
Kellogg, George	Hal	84

Name	County	Page
Kellog, Truman	Jks	314
KELSAL, Catherine	Mar	141
KELTON, John	Hal	95
______, Robert	Hal	95
KELLY/KELLEY/KELLET/		
Also see Calley		
Kelly, Abner	Han	159
______, Abraham	Bke	148
______, Alexander	Ran	247
______, Allen	Jsp	383
______, Amos	Gwn	339
______, Archobald	Ear	99
______, Barnabas	Elb	132
______, Benjamin U.	Twg	75
______, Celia	Put	218
______, Charles	New	18
______, Christopher	Tlb	334
______, Daniel	New	17
______, David	Fay	203
______, David	Rch	289
______, Deney	Cpb	197
______, Edward	Scr	310
______, Edward	Twg	69
______, Elizabeth	Scr	317
______, George	Hab	6
______, George	Rab	233
______, Giles	Crf	412
______, Greene	Put	218
______, Hiram	Hab	59
______, Hiram	Mus	287
______, Isaac	Trp	35
______, Jacob	Doo	81
______, James	Dec	15
______, James	Ear	96
______, James	Jsp	394
______, James M.	Hst	261
______, James W.	Elb	129
______, Janat B.	Jsp	381
______, Joel	Doo	81
______, Joel	Frk	251
______, John	Bak	18
______, John	DeK	72
______, John	Gre	291
______, John	Hst	262
______, John	Lwn	89
______, John	Rab	228
______, John	Rab	234
______, John	Up	119
______, John	Wyn	282
______, John L.	Rab	232
______, Joshua	Wil	291
______, Lemuel	Fay	190
______, Lloyd	Han	159
Kelly, Malakier	Dec	18
______, Margeret	Wks	357
______, Mary	Mus	278
______, Mathew	Twg	65
______, Mavel	Mwr	157
______, Mrs.	Rch	255
______, Ramey	Elb	134
______, Randolph	Ear	96
______, Robert	Rch	250
______, Samuel	Jns	451
______, Samuel S.	Wrn	226
______, Shadrick	Pik	108
______, Thomas	Hab	54
______, Thomas	Hab	54
______, Thomas	Har	175
______, Thomas	Lwn	88
______, Thomas Rev.	Rab	234
______, Thomas	Rab	234
______, William	Car	224
______, William	Clk	313
______, William	Dec	8
______, William	Elb	124
______, William	Elb	135
______, William	Rab	230
______, William	Wrn	187
______, William	Wrn	226
______, William W.	Dec	6
Kelley, Betsy	Rch	258
______, Edmon	New	41
______, James	Hal	86
______, James	Hry	210
______, James	New	16
______, James	Wrn	222
______, Jesse	Bts	169
______, Jesse	Wal	139
______, John	Cow	369
______, John	Wrn	200
______, John	Wrn	222
______, John	Wsh	243
______, Lewis	New	16
______, Lidia	Wsh	252
______, Matilda	Rch	270
______, Moses	Cow	372
______, Redic	New	44
______, Reubin	Hry	223
______, Robert	Hry	223
______, Thomas	Jks	328
______, Thomas	Wal	163
______, William	Hal	90
______, William	Hal	134
Kellet, John	Hab	27
______, Solomon	Hab	41
KAGLE: also see Cagle		

Name	County	Page
Kagle, Jacob	Hal	96
_____, Joseph	Hal	96
_____, William	Hal	96
KEMP, Alexander	Scr	312
_____, Benjamin	Hst	275
_____, Charles	Tlb	347
_____, Daniel	Frk	227
_____, David V.	Elb	138
_____, Delitha	Doo	83
_____, Elias	Dec	5
_____, Esther	Hal	87
_____, Folton	Doo	80
_____, George W.	Dec	6
_____, Henry	Gwn	313
_____, Hosea	Gwn	362
_____, James	Gwn	372
_____, John G.	Jns	457
_____, John Jr.	Jns	461
_____, John	Dec	3
_____, John A.	Em	175
_____, John S.	Hab	16
_____, Joseph	Up	106
_____, Joshua	Lwn	82
_____, Lewis	Wrn	199
_____, Moses	Gwn	326
_____, Moses Jr.	Gwn	365
_____, Peter	Tms	26
_____, Thoda	Wyn	283
_____, Simeon	Cpb	211
_____, Sol	Gwn	332
_____, Stephen	Hal	76
_____, Susannah	Hal	100
_____, Thomas	Cht	260
_____, William	Gwn	308
_____, William	Gwn	335
KENAS, B.	Rch	265
KENDALL/KENDAL		
Kendall, David	Up	108
_____, Eliza P.	Up	118
_____, Henry	Up	101
_____, Isaac	Fay	206
_____, Jeremiah	Fay	206
_____, Mary	Fay	206
Kendal, Elisha	Mwr	155
_____, William	Jsp	381
_____, William	Mus	289
KENDRICK/KINDRICK/KENRICK/ KENDRIK/KINDRECK/KINDRIK		
Kendrick, Alexander	Pik	121
_____, Brooks	Jsp	363
_____, Burwell	Hst	270
_____, Harvey	Hst	289
_____, Hezekiah	Bts	170
Kendrick, Harbert	Ogl	101
_____, Isam	Har	191
_____, Jacob	Wil	322
_____, James	Put	211
_____, James	Wsh	251
_____, John	Hal	102
_____, John	Put	213
_____, John D.	Gwn	330
_____, John W.	Trp	34
_____, Jonathan	Hry	225
_____, Jones	Put	209
_____, Jones	Wil	321
_____, Meredith	Put	210
_____, Nancy	Jsp	363
_____, Noel	Col	353
_____, Robert	Hal	74
_____, Robert	Ogl	102
_____, Samuel	Put	212
_____, Susannah	Hry	225
_____, Sylvanius	Mon	179
_____, William	Hst	273
_____, William	New	51
_____, William O.	Mon	178
Kindrick, Abel	Hal	90
_____, James C.	Mor	238
_____, William	Col	361
Kenrick, Elich	Rch	282
Kendrik, Hezekiah	Cow	377
Kindreck, John	Pik	132
Kindrik, Isaac	Jns	436
KEEN/KEAN/KENN		
Keen, Briant	Tlf	5
_____, David	Wrn	185
_____, George	Wyn	281
_____, John	Hry	228
_____, Theophilus	Wyn	188
_____, William	Wsh	255
_____, William H.	Wyn	285
_____, Young	Lau	13
Kean, Alexander	Cam	184
_____, James M.	Tat	374
_____, Josiah	Pul	151
_____, Robert S.	Wrn	208
_____, William	Pul	159
Kenn, George	Hal	80
KENEMORE, Michael	Tlb	333
KENLEY, James	Frk	214
_____, John	Hab	24
_____, John	Jks	324
KENNANNEN, James	Gwn	350
KENNEDY/KENNADY/KENADAY/ KENNEDA/KENEDY/KENNADAY/ KENNEDAY/KENEDAY/KENNIDAY		

Kennady, Absolam	Mon	204	Kenniday, Henry	Tlf	4
______, David	Hal	80	KENNETT, Isham	Gwn	346
______, Henry	Hal	107	KENNINGTON/KEMINGTON		
______, Huah	Hal	80	Kennington, Abso.	Wks	354
______, James	Hal	79	______, Edward	Hry	211
______, James	Hal	105	______, John	Wks	345
______, James	Hal	107	Kemington, James	Hal	113
______, Josiah M.	Jks	321	KENNY/KENNEY/KINNEY		
______, Margaret	Mon	196	Kenny, John	Gwn	313
______, Thomas	Jsp	361	______, M.	Cht	256
______, William	Hal	80	Kenney, Samuel	Wal	162
Kennedy, A.	Cht	257	______, William	Car	225
______, Alexander	Rch	282	Kinney, Jesley	New	41
______, Ann	Bul	95	KENNYHORN, Catherine	Rch	282
______, C. L.	Crf	395	KENT, Allison	Mor	241
______, Edmund	Rch	286	______, Asa	Mwr	159
______, Edward	Tat	375	______, Benjamin	Hst	261
______, Eli	Bul	95	______, Cane	Wrn	231
______, F.	Rch	274	______, Charles	Pik	111
______, James	Jef	420	______, Daniel	Em	173
______, Jessee	Gwn	336	______, Daniel	Pik	111
______, John	Crf	394	______, Edward	Gwn	363
______, John	Hal	80	______, Elijah	Ogl	79
______, John	Tat	374	______, Elizabeth	Clk	291
______, John	Up	117	______, Ezra	Cht	269
______, Lemuel	Gwn	337	______, Gilbert	Mad	100
______, Mary	Rch	275	______, Gilbert	Tfo	358
______, Solomon	App	6	______, Harvin	Ogl	88
______, Stephen	Tat	374	______, James	Hab	65
______, William	Jsp	391	______, Jesse	Ogl	99
Kenady, Ambrose	Hal	75	______, Jesse	Rch	264
______, David	Em	175	______, John	Col	349
______, John	Em	176	______, John	Twg	79
______, Jonathan	Gre	292	______, John	Wks	357
______, Joshua F.	Jks	333	______, Lewis	Ogl	84
______, Samuel	Em	176	______, Nancy	Ogl	86
______, William	Em	164	______, Patsey	Hry	241
______, William	Em	166	______, Price	Twg	73
Kenneda, David	Wsh	260	______, Rachel	Wil	298
______, Elizabeth	Wsh	258	______, Sampson	Ogl	86
______, John H.	Jns	447	______, Stephen	Wks	349
______, Leroy	Han	159	______, Thomas	Em	174
______, Samuel	Wsh	243	______, Thomas	Mus	290
______, Seth	Han	159	______, Thomas	Ogl	88
Kenedy, Elizabeth	Hry	231	______, Thomas	Twg	71
______, John C.	Hry	209	______, Thomas	Wrn	232
______, Nobl	Jks	347	______, Thomas W.	Wrn	230
______, Samuel	Gwn	363	______, Wiley	Pul	144
______, Thomas	Jef	412	______, William	Dec	17
Kennaday, John	Mon	223	______, William R.	Wrn	232
Kenneday, John	Gwn	314	KERBY/KERBEE/KERBO/KIRBA		
______, William	Frk	228	Kerby, Francis	Mor	256
Keneday, James	Har	186	______, Henry	Mor	254

Name	County	Page
Kerby, James	Elb	123
______, Noah	App	12
______, Moses	Em	177
______, William	Lwn	91
Kerbee, Willis	Elb	144
Kerbo, Solomon	Jks	347
Kirba, Joseph	Pik	117
KERN/KERNS: see Kearns		
KERNODLE, Richard	Mor	261
______, William	Mor	260
KERR/KER		
Kerr, Charles	Jsp	359
______, Hannah	Hal	79
______, James	Hal	77
______, James	Hal	86
______, John	Rch	276
______, Polly	Hal	79
______, William	Hal	94
Ker, James	Cht	265
KERSEY/KEARSEY		
Kersey, Ailsey	Bke	151
______, Charles	Hry	215
______, John	Em	176
______, Thomas	Em	176
______, William	Cow	373
______, William	Tms	18
Kearsey, Banister	Hst	290
KERSHAW, Alemintae	Lib	48
KESSLER/KESLER/KEESLER		
Kessler, David	Frk	257
______, Paul	Frk	257
Kesler, Valentine	Eff	106
Keesler, Henry	Frk	257
KESTERSON, Thomas	Doo	83
KETCHUM, Ralph	Rch	286
KETRELL/KITRELL/KITRAL		
Ketrell, Noah	Wsh	242
Kitrell, Joshua	Ogl	104
Kitral, Joshua	Ogl	103
KETTLE/KETLE/KETTLES/ KNETTLES		
Kettle, Jeremiah	Hal	97
______, Zachariah	Hab	12
Ketle, Jesse	Wal	153
Kettles, James	Scr	310
______, John	Scr	313
Knettles, Samuel	Dec	12
KETTLEY, Thomas	Wal	148
KEY/KEE/KEYS/KEES/KEYES		
Key, Abraham	Jsp	393
______, Benjamin	Wrn	221
______, Burwell P (or D?)	Jsp	391
______, Charles F.	Elb	139
Key, George W.	Jks	342
______, Henry	Mon	180
______, Henry	Wsh	251
______, Henry H.	Jsp	391
______, James	Col	342
______, James	Pul	140
______, Joseph	Bts	163
______, Joshua	Bke	154
______, M.	Gwn	371
______, Mathew	Gwn	366
______, Pierce	Frk	247
______, Tandy	Jks	312
______, Tandy W.	Hry	208
______, Thomas	Jsp	392
______, Thomas H.	Doo	78
______, Tolbert	Frk	246
______, Warren	Em	170
______, Warren	Pul	145
______, William B.	Elb	150
______, William W.	Jns	444
Kee, Charles	New	42
______, Stephen	New	36
Keys, Joshua	Hry	228
______, Moses	Wal	124
______, Thomas	Elb	156
Keyes, Moses	Wal	132
Kees, James O.	Frk	212
KIBBE, William	Rch	262
KICKLIGHTER, Andrew	Bul	95
______, Andrew	Bul	101
______, Thomas	Bul	102
KIDD/KID		
Kidd, Absolom	Ogl	85
______, Augustus	Bke	145
______, Christopher	Hal	90
______, Coleman	Hal	90
______, George W.	Jns	465
______, James	Jks	341
______, John	Hal	90
______, John	Ogl	73
______, Richard	New	31
______, Webb	Ogl	74
______, William Sr.	Ogl	74
______, William Jr.	Ogl	74
Kid, Abraham	Ogl	74
______, Zachariah	Ogl	73
KILBY or KELLY, Alex[r].	Ran	247
KILLCREASE/KILCREASE		
Killcrease, Arthur	Bts	176
______, Daniel	Bts	165
______, James	Gwn	333
______, Robert	Bts	177
Kilcrease, Elijah	Tlb	335

Name	County	Page
KILLGORE/KILGORE/KILGO		
Killgore, James	Wal	152
_____, John L.	Wal	125
_____, Matthew	Mwr	150
_____, Mira	Wal	169
_____, Robert G.	Wal	155
_____, Thomas F.	Gwn	324
_____, Theos. P.	Wal	164
_____, William	Wal	156
_____, William	Wal	161
Kilgore, Benjamin	Hry	247
_____, Charles	Bal	38
_____, J. T.	Mus	277
_____, John	Clk	301
_____, John	Put	197
_____, John V.	DeK	35
_____, Peter	Gwn	328
_____, Ralph	Wil	292
_____, William	Han	159
_____, William	Wil	310
_____, William	Wal	138
_____, Willis	Cow	367
Kilgo, Anna	Hal	70
_____, William	Hal	70
KILLINGSWORTH, Freeman	Rch	283
_____, John	Bib	70
_____, Randal	Wsh	250
_____, William	Wsh	250
KILLION/KILLEN/KILLIN		
Killion, Danel	Hab	45
_____, Daniel	Gwn	319
_____, H. T.	Gwn	315
Killen, James H.	Hst	264
Killin, William	Dec	5
KILLPATRICK/KILPATRICK		
Killpatrick, Adam	New	19
_____, J. H. T.	Bke	127
_____, James	Put	189
_____, John	New	50
_____, Joseph	Gwn	378
_____, Richard	Put	191
_____, Robert	Bke	140
_____, Sarah	Put	189
_____, Spencer	Bke	140
_____, Thomas	Put	186
Kilpatrick, David	Wsh	261
_____, James	Pik	112
_____, William	Cht	279
_____, William	Put	185
KIMBALL/KIMBLE/KIMBOL		
Kimball, Allen	Col	360
_____, Benjamin	Hry	243
_____, David	Bts	161
Kimball, Joseph	Put	202
_____, Joshua	Bke	134
_____, Mary	Hry	240
_____, Robert	Pik	123
_____, William	Bke	134
_____, William	Hry	241
Kimble, Peter	New	20
Kimbol, Christopher	Clk	317
KIMBREL/KIMBRAL/KIMBRIL		
Kimbrel, Charles	Hst	271
_____, Isham	Gwn	314
_____, Isham	Gwn	358
_____, John	DeK	73
_____, Littleton	Gwn	363
Kimbral, Gideon	Ogl	104
_____, John	Ogl	89
Kimbril, Peter	Wal	160
KIMBROUGH/KIMBRO/KIMBER/ KENNBROH		
Kimbrough, Bradley	Gre	303
_____, James	Hry	208
_____, James	Mon	175
_____, John	Bts	173
_____, John	Gre	274
_____, Thomas	Put	181
_____, Thomas	Put	187
_____, William H.	Har	181
Kimbro, Gordon	Wil	304
_____, Shad. K.	Jsp	385
Kimber, Brantley	Gre	291
Kennbroh, William	Wal	160
KIMMEY, John	Mar	141
_____, Lydia	Mar	142
KINARD/KINEARD		
Kinard, Daniel	Lwn	90
_____, John	Jsp	362
_____, Martin	Mon	217
Kineard, Barney	Hry	241
KINCHIN/KINCHLEY		
Kinchin, James	Lau	5
_____, Uriah	Lau	9
_____, William	Lau	22
Kinchley, Michael	Rch	264
KINDLE, Purnel	Hab	12
KINDER, David	Lin	68
KINEY/KINNY/KINNEY		
Kiney, Abs.	Up	116
_____, David	Clk	313
_____, James	Clk	314
_____, John	Clk	314
_____, Joseph A.	Clk	314
_____, Samuel	Clk	314
_____, William	Hab	48

Name	County	Page
Kinny, George	Hry	222
______, James	Lin	66
______, Thomas	Lee	34
Kinney, Jesse	Gre	286
KING, A. M. O.	Mon	192
______, Alexander	Gre	281
______, Alexander	Mon	184
______, Alfred	Mon	201
______, Alfred P.	Han	159
______, Ambrose B.	Hry	249
______, Amos	Har	192
______, Andrew	Mus	291
______, Benjamin	Hry	216
______, Benjamin	Jks	349
______, Benjamin	Lib	48
______, Benjamin (By Thos. Dunham)	Lib	48
______, Benjamin	Mon	196
______, Benjamin	Put	199
______, Benajah	Up	119
______, Berry	Frk	212
______, Betsey	Cam	183
______, Cason	Mad	112
______, Charles	Wsh	257
______, Charles C.	Wsh	240
______, Curtis	Gre	292
______, David	Hal	90
______, Dickson	Hry	245
______, Drury	Gre	300
______, Edmond (a man of colour)	Frk	219
______, Elephalet	Pul	143
______, Elihue	Hab	49
______, Elijah	Hab	30
______, Elish	Bal	34
______, Elisha	Wsh	260
______, Eliz.	Bal	39
______, Franklin T.	Mon	174
______, George	Clk	320
______, George	Frk	211
______, George C.	Jns	469
______, Geraldus	Jef	418
______, Green	Hal	94
______, H.	Cht	257
______, Henry	Doo	84
______, Henry	Pul	155
______, Henry	Trp	47
______, Henry D.	Tfo	356
______, Hiram	Hry	222
______, Hiram	Wks	341
______, Howel	Wks	346
______, Hy	Up	102
______, Isaac	Rab	228
King, Isaac W.	Pik	110
______, Jacob	Up	98
______, James	Bal	38
______, James	Bts	175
______, James	Cam	188
______, James	DeK	45
______, James Sr.	DeK	45
______, James	Frk	235
______, James	Gre	293
______, James	Hab	17
______, James	Mon	209
______, James	Mon	218
______, James	Pul	157
______, James	Wks	354
______, Jesse	Jns	461
______, Jesse	Ogl	97
______, Jesse	Put	217
______, John	Cht	257
______, John	Col	359
______, John	DeK	30
______, John	DeK	34
______, John	Gwn	340
______, John	Hab	29
______, John	Hal	102
______, John	Jef	403
______, John	Jks	312
______, John	Jks	314
______, John	Jns	469
______, John	Mon	184
______, John	Mon	216
______, John	New	43
______, John	Pul	157
______, John	Put	209
______, John	Rch	279
______, John	Tlb	332
______, John	Twg	67
______, John Jr.	Wsh	257
______, John Sr.	Wsh	273
______, John B.	Mad	103
______, John C.	Frk	252
______, John C.	Wsh	245
______, John G.	Clk	314
______, John H.	Fay	181
______, John M.	Jsp	355
______, John P.	Rch	174
**______, John P. (slave)	Rch	275
______, Jonathan	Jks	332
______, Joseph	Hry	243
______, Joseph	Twg	69
______, Josiah	Mon	174
______, Julius	Hal	119
______, Lewis	Jsp	372
______, Kinchin	Wil	293

King, L. B. Wil 287
______, Lamburt Hab 24
______, Lewis Jsp 372
______, Lewis Rch 255
______, Luraney Twg 87
______, Maria Jks 326
______, Martin Jns 432
______, Martha Jsp 393
______, Mary E. Cam 184
______, Mary Put 205
______, Mary Wsh 253
______, Mary Wil 297
______, Michael Bak 18
______, Michael Mwr 164
______, Mourning Twg 81
______, Nancy Tfo 369
______, Nathan Twg 69
______, Nehemiah Hst 295
______, Peter New 51
______, Polly Jsp 359
______, Ralph Cht 250
______, Reuben Lib 48
______, Reuben McI 122
______, Richard Jsp 353
______, Richard Pik 115
______, Robert Frk 246
______, Robert Hal 104
______, Roswell Jr. Gly 266
______, Roswell Jr. McI 124
______, Rufus Jef 417
______, Samuel McI 129
______, Sarah Clk 320
______, Silas Gwn 367
______, Solomon Hry 218
______, Sophia Hal 96
______, Stephen C. Gly 269
______, Stephen C. Wyn 281
______, Stephen H. Pik 117
______, Tandy D. Fay 182
______, Thomas Dec 17
______, Thomas Frk 210
______, Thomas Jsp 365
______, Thomas Jns 469
______, Thomas McI 129
______, Thomas Sr. Put 206
______, Thomas Wsh 264
______, Thomas B. Gly 269
______, Thomas G. Cow 373
______, Thomas H. Wsh 273
______, Thomas M. Put 209
______, Thomas S. Mor 248
______, Thomas W. Hry 220
______, W. Wks 355
King, Wesley Wks 341
______, Wiley Twg 71
______, William Elb 138
______, William Elb 146
______, William Eff 104
______, William Frk 250
______, William Frk 211
______, William Gre 300
______, William Gwn 340
______, William Hal 111
______, William Irw 303
______, William Jns 441
______, William Jns 469
______, William Mus 286
______, William New 42
______, William Ware 188
______, William C. Gre 299
______, William D. Pik 115
______, William D. Tfo 357
______, William J. McI 129
______, William J. New 36
______, William T. Mor 240
______, Willis Lwn 82
______, Woody Gre 299
______, Y. P. Gre 286
______, Zuriah Elb 143
KINGERY, Abram Wks 332
______, Daniel H. Wks 332
KINNEBREW/KELLEBREW/
KILLEBREW/KELEBREW
Kinnebrew, Edwin Elb 160
______, Henry Elb 160
______, Littleberry Ogl 79
Kellebrew, William Wrn 231
Killebrew, William W. Trp 47
Kelebrew, John Wrn 228
KINNINGHAM, Powel Jks 317
KINNINGTON, Edward Hry 237
KINSEY/KINGSLEY/KIMSEY
Kinsey, Elisha Hab 52
______, John Wrn 227
______, John Lwn 83
______, Joel Wrn 215
______, Robin Hab 48
______, William Hab 48
______, William Jr. Hab 52
Kingsley, Charles Tms 26
Kimsey, Peter Hab 25
KIRK, Anna Jns 444
______, George Gwn 365
______, Hudson Pik 106
______, Jep. Pik 106
______, John Gwn 326

Name	County	Page
Kirk, John	Hal	119
_____, John	Hry	242
_____, Joseph	Hry	202
_____, Levy	Jns	444
_____, Stephen	Frk	233
_____, William	Mus	286
_____, William	Ogl	70
KIRKAS, James	Gwn	320
_____, Thomas	Gwn	331
KIRKHAM, Michael C.	Jks	335
_____, Robert	Jks	337
KIRKLAND/KIRKLIN/KERLIN		
Kirkland, Aaron	Mad	103
_____, Abraham L.	Em	165
_____, Ambrose	Gwn	326
_____, Daniel	Hst	286
_____, Daniel	Mtg	234
_____, Jefferson	Hry	231
_____, John	Em	173
_____, John	Trp	38
_____, John S.	Em	172
_____, Joshua	Em	175
_____, Moses	Tlf	2
_____, O. C.	Bal	33
_____, Reubin	Ran	243
_____, Richard	Bul	92
_____, Sion	Em	173
_____, Snowden	Wil	287
_____, Tim	Ware	186
_____, William	Wal	135
Kirklin, Benjamin	Jks	347
_____, James	Cow	380
_____, Jesse	Tfo	366
_____, William	Tfo	366
Kerlin, John	Jks	331
_____, Peter	Tlb	325
KIRKPATRICK/KIRKPATTRACK/ KIRTHPATRICK		
Kirkpatrick, D.	Rch	254
_____, Elisha	Crf	412
_____, Hugh	Car	229
_____, James	Col	346
_____, James	Crf	394
_____, James	DeK	35
_____, James H.	DeK	26
_____, John	Bal	38
_____, John	Cow	380
_____, John	Rch	264
_____, John G.	Mon	196
_____, William	Hry	223
Kirkpattrick, John	Clk	325
Kirthpatrick, Ezekiel	New	44
_____, Hamon	New	45
KIRKSEY: also see Kersey		
Kirksey, Elisha S.	Bts	178
_____, Isaiah	DeK	44
_____, James	Tms	19
_____, John	Tms	21
_____, West H.	Bib	61
_____, William	Bts	177
KIRSH, Stephen	App	9
KIRTLEY, Jemma	Cpb	205
KIRWIN, J. H.	Mus	277
_____, Stephen	Mus	288
KISER/KIZER		
Kiser, James F.	Hal	92
_____, Joseph	Hal	91
_____, Joseph	Hal	92
Kizer, John	Cpb	201
KITCHENS/KITCHINS/KITCHEN/ KITCHINGS/KINCHEN/KATCHINS/ KITEENS/also see Catchings		
Kitchens, Bose	Wrn	217
_____, Boze Jr.	Wrn	226
_____, Charles	Hry	245
_____, David	Hal	103
_____, Eli	Bts	168
_____, George	Frk	247
_____, James	Wrn	223
_____, James	Wrn	224
_____, Jane	Frk	345
_____, Lawrence	Wrn	217
_____, Sarah	Wrn	217
_____, Wilie	Wrn	215
_____, William	Hry	245
_____, William Jr.	Wrn	218
_____, William H.	Frk	218
Kitchins, James	Hry	245
_____, John	Wrn	220
Kitchin, Benjamin	Hry	241
_____, John	Hry	241
_____, Ransom	Mwr	161
Kitchen, Charles	New	46
Kitchings, Gary	Jns	469
Kinchen, William	Hst	270
Katchins, Jacob	Put	209
Kiteens, James	Hab	32
KITE/KIGHT		
Kite, David	Fay	183
_____, David	Fay	192
_____, Henry	Jsp	396
_____, Hy	Gwn	358
_____, James	Lib	48
_____, Martha	Em	167
_____, Noah	Fay	200
_____, Samuel	Cow	377

Name	County	Page
Kite, Thomas	Tat	372
______, Vinety	Gwn	360
Kight, Joseph	Bul	95
KLINE: see Cline		
KLUTZ, Jacob	Clk	299
KNACK, Edward L.	DeK	67
______, William	DeK	67
KNAPP, David	Tms	18
______, H.	Cht	255
KNASH, Larkin	DeK	40
______, Larkin	DeK	41
KNER, Micheil J.	Wsh	262
______, Solomon Jr.	Wsh	244
KNIESS, F.	Rch	256
KNIGHT, Aaron	Cpb	209
______, Aaron	DeK	51
______, Abel	Jef	410
______, Abraham	Wyn	285
______, Alexander	Bul	94
______, Allin	Gwn	371
______, Asbury	Rch	258
______, Bethamy	Em	166
______, Carrington	Car	220
______, Calvary F.	Bts	169
______, Charles	Hry	204
______, Cofield	Doo	81
______, Daniel	Mor	260
______, Drucilla	New	49
______, Elisha	Jsp	388
______, Enoch	Rch	265
______, Enoch	Rch	279
______, Enoch	Tlb	348
______, George	Hst	273
______, George H.	Har	185
______, Henry	Wal	132
______, Henry D.	Bts	169
______, Isaac	Wal	168
______, James	Jsp	354
______, James	Wks	333
______, Jesse	Bke	143
______, Joel	Fay	194
______, John	Crf	397
______, John Sr.	Jsp	354
______, John Jr.	Jsp	353
______, John	Jef	408
______, John	Lwn	84
______, John	Mwr	160
______, John	Wks	336
______, John	Wks	355
______, Jonathan	Lwn	83
______, Jonathan	Lwn	89
______, Joseph	DeK	44
______, Kingsman	New	55
Knight, Levi J.	Lwn	84
______, Margaret	Bke	143
______, Martha	Pik	114
______, Mathew	Jsp	398
______, Mathew	Wal	159
______, Matthew	Car	215
______, Matthew	DeK	50
______, Nealy	Bke	119
______, Pressley	Car	216
______, Richard	Hry	242
______, Richard	Tfo	358
______, Robert	Bke	121
______, Robert	Crf	402
______, Robert	Doo	82
______, Robert Jr.	Doo	85
______, Robert	Wks	353
______, Rufus	Em	165
______, Saldkiel	Wks	357
______, Samuel	Lwn	89
______, Sarah	Doo	82
______, Seth	Tat	372
______, Spier	Lau	5
______, Thomas	Bib	51
______, Thomas	Bul	93
______, Thomas	Doo	82
______, Thomas	Wal	144
______, Thomas Jr.	Wyn	281
______, Tarlton	Tat	372
______, Walter	Rch	253
______, William	Lwn	89
______, William	Mon	178
______, William	Mon	212
______, William A.	Lwn	84
______, William C.	Lwn	85
______, Woody	Fay	203
KNOTT/KNOTTS/KNOT/NOT		
Knott, George	Wal	148
______, Jacob T.	Clk	323
______, James	Clk	323
______, John	Clk	306
Knotts, Nathaniel	Crf	407
Knot, Benjamin	Wal	131
Not, John	Wal	131
KNOWLES/KNOLES/KNOWLS		
Knowles, Daniel	Jsp	390
______, Emanuel	Irw	304
______, Henry W.	Jsp	354
______, Isaac	Han	159
______, James	Hry	246
______, James P.	Han	159
______, Parker	Tlb	323
______, R. P.	Jsp	355
______, Robert	Mon	199

Name	County	Page
Knowles, William	Gre	302
Knoles, Andrew	Bak	18
_____, Edmond	Fay	195
_____, Edmond	Fay	203
_____, James	Fay	195
Knowls, Britain C.	Gre	303
_____, Greene	Gre	276
_____, Thomas	Gre	302
KNOWLING, Anthony	Han	159
KNOX, Allixon	Lin	68
_____, David L.	Jks	313
_____, Edward	Cht	257
_____, George	Rch	284
_____, Hugh	Bib	51
_____, James H.	Hab	64
_____, John	Lin	66
_____, John A. P.	Frk	234
_____, Peter	Col	336
_____, Reddick	Wyn	282
_____, Robert D.	Wil	324
_____, Samuel	Frk	232
_____, Samuel Sr.	Jks	318
_____, Samuel Jr.	Jks	318
_____, William	Gwn	318
_____, William B.	Cow	382
KOFEMAN: also see Coffman		
_____, Morris	Mon	192
KOLB, Harman	DeK	57
_____, Harris	Jks	311
_____, James	Wal	148
_____, Martin	Cpb	207
_____, P.	Cht	270
_____, Peter	Jns	444
_____, William G.	Tlb	328
KOLLENDER, Jane	Lib	48
KOLLOCK, William	Cht	248
KOONER, Benjamin	Twg	77
KOPPELL: see Caple		
KORNEGA: see Cornege		
KRAATS, Elizabeth	Bib	51
KRAMER: see Cramer		
KRENSHAW: see Crenshaw		
KREWS: see Crews		
KURKINDOL: see Curkindol		
KYTE, Stephen	Mwr	151
LABUZAN, Charles	Rch	272
LACKEY/LACKIE/LACKLEY/ LOCKABY		
Lackey, Robert	Hry	215
_____, William	Wal	159
Lackie, Jonathan J.	Bts	167
Lackley, Samiel	Wal	156
Lockaby, James	DeK	73
LACREWK, Francis	Bib	51
LACY/LACEY/LACYEY/LACIER/ LICET		
Lacy, Benjamin	Bib	64
_____, John	Ogl	84
_____, John B.	Tms	25
_____, Pleasant	New	36
_____, Thomas	Mor	244
_____, William E.	Hal	99
Lacey, Philemon	Mon	206
_____, William	Mon	206
Lacyey, Thomas	Gre	280
Lacier, Lewis	Cam	184
Licet, Jorden	Lee	34
LADD/LAD		
Ladd, Hardy	Lau	7
_____, Jacob	Cht	241
_____, Thomas	Clk	317
Lad, William C.	Hab	50
LADEVIZE, Raymond	Rch	261
LAELL, Eleanor	Han	159
LAFEVER, Dianna	Jef	423
_____, John W.	Jef	419
LAFIELD/LAYFIELD		
Lafield, John	Han	160
_____, Josiah	Tlb	344
_____, Levin	Tlb	345
Layfield, William	Up	116
LAFILES, Armand	McI	122
LAFITTE, J. B.	Rch	277
LAFOY, John G.	Twg	66
LAIDLER, John	Hst	272
LAGIONE, Jacob	Crf	407
_____, John	Crf	407
LAKE, Abram	Mon	192
_____, Daniel	Wal	154
_____, Elisha	Wal	153
LAMAR, Benjamin B.	Bib	65
_____, G. B.	Rch	264
_____, George	Gwn	366
_____, George W.	Rch	265
_____, Haming	Col	345
_____, Henry G.	Bib	56
_____, James	Jns	474
_____, Jefferson J.	Jns	441
_____, Jeremiah	Mon	172
_____, John	Col	359
_____, John	Hry	213
_____, John	Jns	474
_____, John	Put	174

Name	County	Page
Lamar, John D.	Hry	202
______, John T.	Bib	51
* ______, John T. (slave)	Rch	253
______, L. Q. C.	Bal	29
______, L.	Bal	43
______, M. B.	Mus	281
______, Mary	Twg	88
______, Nathan	Irw	300
______, Peter	Lin	61
______, Philip	Mus	292
______, Thomas R.	Bib	64
______, Z.	Bal	43
______, Zachariah	Bib	51
______, Zachariah	Jns	474
LAMASTER, Ralph	Hab	28
LAMB, Arthur	Twg	86
______, Barnaby	Bke	152
______, Benjamin S.	Bry	84
______, Celia	Gly	266
______, Charity	Jef	419
______, David	Jef	401
______, Elijah	Bke	151
______, George A.	Tlb	346
______, Greene E.	Han	159
______, Hezekiah	Em	167
______, Isaac	Em	164
______, Isaac	Up	99
______, Isham	Dec	10
______, Jacob	Fay	191
______, Jacob	Mon	205
______, James	Crf	410
______, James	Jef	414
______, John	Gly	265
______, John	Jsp	367
______, Louis	Jef	404
______, Luke	Hst	281
______, Meda	Twg	74
______, Michael	Jef	422
______, Milley	Jef	417
______, Nancy	Tlb	347
______, Nicholas	Jsp	367
______, Reuben	Jef	409
______, Reubin	Twg	86
______, Sarah	Gwn	356
______, Taylor	Rch	262
LAMBERT/LAMBERTH/LAMBIRT/		
LAMBETH/LAMBROT/LAMBRIGHT/		
LAMBY/LUMBRY		
Lambert, Alexander	Jks	324
______, Allen	Cpb	194
______, Betsey	Cht	268
______, Blakely	Lau	12
______, Elijah	Cpb	199
Lambert, J.	Wks	345
______, James	Cpb	198
______, James	Dec	4
______, James	Pik	110
______, James	Scr	302
______, John	Car	223
______, John	Lau	12
______, John M.	Bke	122
______, John S.	Hry	211
______, Lewis	Put	194
______, Loviskey	Lau	12
______, Luke	Jsp	388
______, Noah	Dec	5
______, Sarah	Jks	329
______, Stokely	Jsp	398
______, Thomas	Bke	133
______, Thomas	Bke	143
______, William	Bke	149
______, William	Gwn	319
______, William	Scr	311
Lamberth, Edwin	Fay	183
______, Jess	Fay	190
______, John	Fay	190
Lambirt, John	Lib	43
Lambeth, William	Mor	269
Lambrot, Jeremiah	Hry	238
Lambright, James	Lib	49
Lamby, Levy	Frk	213
Lambry, Thomas	Wsh	271
LAMKIN/LAMPKIN/LAMKINS		
Lamkin, Ben H.	Gwn	314
______, George W. F.	Gwn	350
______, Jeremiah	Doo	83
______, John	Rch	287
______, John L.	Tlf	12
______, William M.	Lin	62
Lampkin, Augustas	Col	339
______, James	Col	339
______, John	Col	339
______, Lewis	Hal	72
______, Sampson L.	Ran	247
______, William	Ran	242
Lamkins, Lewis Ab. L.	Tlf	5
LAMNER, Jesse	Irw	302
LAMPEE, C.	Cht	282
LANCASTER, Benjamin	Mar	140
______, Cinclair	Pik	114
______, Hartwell	Hal	93
______, Henry	Fay	187
______, John	Hal	87
______, Laertas	Han	160
______, Lemuel	Put	180
______, Mahala	Trp	37

Lancaster, Samuel Gre 291
______, Thomas Han 160
______, Washington Pul 147
______, Wright Pul 146
LANCE, John Wrn 219
______, Martin Hab 25
LAND, Alexander Wil 301
______, Frederic Irw 301
______, Gidion Jks 338
______, Henry Twg 81
______, Jacob DeK 36
______, James Wil 292
______, Jeremiah Fay 187
______, Jesse Twg 81
______, Jonah DeK 28
______, Joseph DeK 36
______, Littleberry Tlb 329
______, Nathan Irw 302
______, Sarah Wrn 226
LANDERS, Claib. Bal 39
______, Elisabeth Hab 57
______, Hensley Col 338
______, Humphrey D. Gwn 347
______, James Gwn 376
______, James H. Crf 394
______, James O. Gwn 347
______, Jesse Wal 169
______, John DeK 36
______, John Mad 107
______, John C. Mad 110
______, John K. Frk 235
______, Lewis Mad 103
______, Mathew Clk 305
______, Richard Clk 310
______, Sarah Mad 118
______, Thomas DeK 36
______, Tyra Gwn 347
______, William Elb 159
LANDING, Benjamin Hry 241
______, John Bke 131
LANDINGHAM/LANNINGHAM
Landingham, Benjamin V. Dec 13
______, Peter V. Dec 13
______, Peter V. Dec 13
Lanningham, Mary Elb 139
LANDRETH, Thomas Put 212
LANDRUM/LANDRAM/LANAM
Landrum, Elias Tlb 334
______, Emmassa Mon 219
______, Hay T. Ogl 88
______, Jacob Wrn 214
______, James Hal 112
______, Jeptha Fay 183
Landrum, John Ogl 96
______, John Wil 302
______, John F. Hal 120
______, Joseph Jks 323
______, Joseph Ogl 99
______, Micager Hal 112
______, Samuel Hal 111
______, Thomas Sr. Ogl 99
______, Thomas Ogl 99
______, Thomas B. Ogl 96
______, Timothy Jsp 393
______, Whitfield Ogl 96
______, William Ogl 96
Landram, Elisha Jks 346
______, Larkin Fay 207
Lanam, Squier Dec 9
LANE/LAIN
Lane, A. W. Jsp 392
______, Abby Rch 267
______, Alexander Em 173
______, Alexander Jsp 379
______, Allen New 27
______, Asher Wil 303
______, Benjamin Em 173
______, Benjamin Wyn 284
______, Benjamin J. Twg 89
______, Bryan App 9
______, Bryan F. Bib 51
______, Bryant Hst 285
______, Bryant Wal 136
______, Bryant Wsh 348
______, Davis Mon 213
______, Edward Em 172
______, Edward J. Cpb 205
______, Edward W. Jsp 392
______, Elizabeth New 30
______, Etheldred Bke 131
______, Henry Sr. New 33
______, Henry Jr. New 27
______, James Hst 285
______, James R. Put 203
______, Jeffry Han 160
______, Jesse DeK 61
______, Joel Jsp 388
______, Joel Tlb 330
______, John Bke 128
______, John Car 230
______, John Frk 224
______, John Hst 266
______, John Tlf 10
______, Jonathan Car 228
______, Judeh Lib 48
______, Laban Mad 109

Name	County	Page
Lane, Lewis	Wil	303
______, Mark A.	Wil	287
______, Micajah A.	Wil	291
______, Phillip	Clk	317
______, Richard A.	Bul	99
______, Richard Q.	New	42
______, Robert L.	Frk	223
______, Samuel	Pik	112
______, Sander	Hst	285
______, Sarah	Ear	93
______, Sarah	Wal	160
______, Susannah	Doo	80
______, Thomas	Bke	129
______, Thomas H.	New	16
______, Turner	Frk	240
______, Wiley	Bke	128
______, Wiley	Hst	285
______, William	App	7
______, William	Bak	16
______, William	Cam	185
______, William	Jns	442
______, William	Mor	252
______, William	Wal	136
______, William	Wil	318
______, William M.	Mad	99
Lain, Garland	Hab	13
LANEY/LANY/LAMEY		
Laney, John Sr.	Hry	242
______, John Jr.	Hry	244
______, Joseph	Hal	101
______, Philip	Hry	244
Lany, Elizabeth	Han	160
Lamey, John W.	New	50
LANG/LAING		
Lang, Catherine	Cam	186
______, George	Cam	185
______, Henrietta E.	Rch	265
______, Isaac	Cam	186
______, John	Car	224
______, John C.	Hry	238
______, Margaret	Hry	223
______, Nancey	Cam	185
______, Nathaniel	Bul	102
______, Richard	Cam	187
______, Robert	Hry	226
______, Robert	Wil	292
______, Thomas G.	Hry	238
______, William	Car	217
Laing, David	Lib	48
______, James	Lib	48
______, Lydia	Lib	48
LANGDON, Dorothy	Tfo	365
______, Isaac	Wil	290
LANGFORD/LANKFORD/LANCEFORD/ LANSFORD/LANGSFORD/LANFORD		
Langford, Alen	Hal	91
______, Bezeleel	Clk	310
______, Bedford	Clk	294
______, Carter	Bib	51
______, Carter	Bib	56
______, Catharine (W)	Mor	240
______, Charles	Jks	345
______, Edmond	Up	108
______, G. A.	Mus	284
______, Garrot F.	Car	228
______, George	Mor	242
______, H. A.	Mus	284
______, Hilery	Wrn	210
______, James	Bib	64
______, James	Clk	293
______, John	Frk	233
______, John W.	Mor	241
______, Joseph	Bib	64
______, Josiah	Mor	256
______, Lewis B.	Bib	64
______, Richard	Tlb	330
______, Robert	Put	186
______, Seleta	Hal	108
______, Stephen	Cpb	205
______, William	Jks	343
______, Wyatt	Frk	234
Lankford, Aleron	Gwn	338
______, Edward	Wal	173
______, Jesse	Tat	377
______, John	Jns	470
______, Jonathan	Wal	128
______, William	Tat	371
Lanceford, Henry	Trp	49
______, James	Trp	49
Lansford, H.	Gwn	373
______, William	Fay	192
Langsford, John B.	Gwn	370
Lanford, Nicholas	Mon	225
LANGLEY/LANGLY/LAMPLEY		
Langley, Betsey	Hal	133
______, David	Gwn	344
______, Henry	Jks	333
______, Isaac	Mon	194
______, Isaiah	Jsp	378
______, James	Pik	123
______, John	Gwn	325
______, John	Gwn	355
______, John	Hal	131
______, Josiah	Mar	141
______, Lodge	Gwn	358
______, Miles	Gwn	328

Name	County	Page
Langley, Miles	Jks	326
______, Noah	Hal	133
______, Noel	Mar	143
______, Osel	Mar	141
______, Oswell	Gwn	362
______, Oswell B.	Gwn	327
______, Ozzy	Tlb	342
______, Thos.	Gwn	311
______, William	Gwn	311
______, William	Mon	182
______, William	Tlb	339
______, Zach.	Hal	132
Langly, James	Wrn	225
Lampley, Benja.	Jks	313
LANGHAM/LANHAM/LONGHAM		
Langham, Coleman	Wrn	194
______, Elizabeth	Up	110
______, Richard	Wsh	249
Lanham, Asa	Pik	125
Longham, Charles	Tfo	368
LANGSTON/LANKSTON		
Langston, Alexander	Frk	231
______, Asa	Frk	229
______, David	Ogl	66
______, Etheldred W.	Ogl	93
______, Isaac	Hry	220
______, Isaac	New	17
______, Jacob	Gwn	362
______, James	Cpb	210
______, James	Jks	335
______, Jason	Bib	68
______, Jesse	Elb	142
______, John	Frk	225
______, John	Rab	233
______, Samuel	Mus	288
______, William	Jks	331
Lankston, James	Col	356
______, John	Col	354
______, Willis	DeK	40
LANIER/LENEAR/LANAIRS		
Lanier, Aaron	Hst	284
______, Allen	Bul	93
______, Ben	Bul	95
______, David	Hst	284
______, David	Wal	136
______, Rev. Edmond	Tlb	323
______, Frederick	Bul	93
______, Henry M.	Han	159
______, James	Gwn	364
______, James	Mwr	158
______, James	Scr	299
______, James	Wsh	251
______, John	Bul	93

Name	County	Page
Lanier, John	Jsp	369
______, Lewis	Bry	87
______, Lewis	Bul	96
______, Lewis	Wsh	269
______, Louis	Scr	299
______, Mary	Jsp	396
______, Philip	Doo	78
______, Sarah	Bib	73
______, Sterling	Jns	470
______, Susan	Han	160
______, Thomas	Lib	48
______, Thomas B.	DeK	52
Lenear, George	Clk	294
______, Sampson	Gwn	359
Lanairs, Aron	Wks	350
LANSDELL, James	Col	345
LANSDOWN, David A.	Gwn	349
LANSING/LONSECY		
Lansing, Charles	Hry	243
______, Francis	Mwr	162
______, John	Hry	241
______, John Jr.	Hry	219
Lonsecy, Ann	Cht	247
LANTERN, Giddum	Col	341
______, John	Gwn	32[illegible]
______, Theophilies	Jks	34[illegible]
LAPROD/LEPRAD		
Laprod, Benjamine	Jns	43[illegible]
Leprad, John	Mon	17[illegible]
LARD, Archabald E.	New	[illegible]
______, Curtis	Hal	11[illegible]
______, James	Hal	11[illegible]
______, James Jr.	Hal	12[illegible]
______, Robert	New	3[illegible]
______, Samuel	New	3[illegible]
______, Thomas	Jsp	39[illegible]
______, William	Frk	24[illegible]
______, William	Gwn	36[illegible]
______, Zacheus	Wks	34[illegible]
LARECY, Moses	Scr	31[illegible]
LARGE, William	Bry	8[illegible]
LARK, James	Trp	3[illegible]
LARKIN/LARKLIN		
also see LIKENS		
Larkin, Joseph	Col	3[illegible]
Larklin, William L.	Col	3[illegible]
LARRY/LARY		
Larry, Leah	Rch	2[illegible]
______, Nathanl.	Mon	2[illegible]
______, P.	Rch	2[illegible]
Lary, Henchy	Mon	2[illegible]
______, Thomas	Mon	2[illegible]
______, Thomas	New	[illegible]

LARRYMORE/LOUROMOUR		
Larrymore, James	Tat	371
Louromour, Peter	Lib	48
LARUE, William	Hal	128
LAS, James	Hal	75
LASLIE/LASLEY/LASLEE		
Laslie, Charles	Tlf	10
_____, Daniel	Tlf	10
_____, James	Wks	347
_____, Lauchlan	Tlf	8
_____, Neill	Tlf	8
_____, Silas	Wks	340
Lasley, C.	Col	347
_____, Jane	Wil	294
Laslee, Hardy	Wsh	250
LASITER/LASSETER/LASSATER/ LASSITER/LASETER/LASSETTER/ LASATER/LACESTER/LASSAFER		
Lasiter, Barbary	Clk	297
_____, Elijah	Fay	188
_____, Jesse	Fay	192
_____, Joel	Wal	139
_____, John	Clk	327
_____, John	Mwr	156
_____, Sally	Clk	300
_____, Winny	Clk	300
Lasseter, Abraham	Wks	335
_____, David	Wks	335
_____, Henry	Wks	350
_____, Lemuel	New	26
_____, Lemuel	Pik	121
_____, Luke	Wks	336
_____, Solomon	Pik	125
Lassater, Britain	Mwr	159
_____, Hardy	Mon	178
_____, Mathew	Mon	207
_____, Robert	Mon	209
Lassiter, Ann	Jsp	392
_____, Jacob	Jsp	390
_____, Mary	Dec	13
_____, William	Bke	132
Laseter, George	Wrn	209
_____, Jesse	Wrn	195
Lassetter, Amos	Bul	98
Lasater, John	Mwr	165
Lacester, Benjamin	Cpb	197
Lassafer, Thos. J.	Mon	189
LASTINGER, James	Bul	94
_____, Seaborn	Lwn	86
LATHAM/LATHIM		
Latham, Amos	Cam	181
_____, George	Hal	105
Lathim, Anthony	Hal	105
LATHROP, Burrell	Cht	243
LATIMER/LATTIMER/LATIMON		
Latimer, Benjamin T.	Han	160
_____, Elizabeth	Han	160
_____, George	Ogl	96
_____, Henry W.	Han	160
_____, Joel	Han	160
_____, John B.	Han	160
_____, John S.	Han	159
_____, Patsy N.	Han	160
_____, Thomas L.	Han	160
_____, William	Han	159
Lattimer, Chas.	DeK	31
_____, Edward	Cow	384
_____, John	Ogl	64
_____, William	DeK	27
Lattimon, Samuel	Trp	39
LATTY, James	Hal	129
_____, John	Jks	339
LAUGHAM/LAUGHLIN/LAUGHREN		
Laugham, Benja.	Wrn	203
_____, James W.	Wrn	201
Laughlin, William	Hal	94
Laughren, Mary	Jns	457
LAUGHRIDGE/LAUGHRIGE		
Laughridge, Benjamin	Frk	233
_____, James	Gwn	332
_____, John	Frk	232
_____, Robert	Frk	231
_____, Susannah	Frk	254
Laughrige, William	Gwn	345
LAUGHTER, Henry	Wil	312
_____, John	Wil	291
_____, Robert	Wil	311
_____, Robert C.	Wil	312
LAUNIS, John	Mor	253
LAURISE, Seaborn	Han	160
LAVENDER/LAVINDER/LAVENTURE		
Lavender, Charles	Gwn	357
_____, George M.	Car	219
_____, James	Hry	234
_____, John	Wks	334
_____, John S.	Wks	358
_____, Levin	Wks	332
_____, Oliver	Wks	333
Lavinder, Mary	Cht	262
_____, William	Hry	215
Laventure, (no 1st name)	Rch	272
LAW/LAWS		
**Law, Dr. - slaves	Cht	282
_____, Charles	McI	129
_____, Charles R.	Hst	275
_____, Edmund	Jsp	361

Law, James Lib 48
______, John Hst 276
______, John R. Trp 34
______, John S.B. Mon 196
______, Col. Joseph, dec'd.
Estate by William
M.W. Maxwell Lib 49
______, Joseph Lib 48
______, Joseph Lib 49
______, Nathaniel Lib 49
______, Robert Jns 433
______, Rev. Samuel S.B. Lib 49
**______, William (slaves) Cht 281
______, William Ogl 72
Laws, Jesse L. Trp 35
______, John Gre 283
______, Joseph New 48
______, Light Put 178
LAWHORN/LAWHON
Lawhorn, Allen Har 188
______, David Gwn 377
______, Noah Lee 30
______, Simeon Up 120
Lawhon, John Wsh 241
LAWLESS.LAWLIS/LAWLACE/
LAYLESS
Lawless, Jacob Ogl 69
______, John Ogl 76
______, John Trp 55
______, Nancy Ogl 69
______, Thomas Mon 174
Lawlis, John Hal 76
Lawlace, Jones Mwr 158
Layless, Henry Twg 60
LAWREMORE/LOWREMORE/LOURMORE
Lawremore, Andrew Elb 124
______, Samuel Elb 141
Lowremore, James Elb 134
Lourmore, Sarah Elb 160
LAWSON/LAUSON/LAYSON
Lawson, A. B. Bke 122
______, Alexander J. Bke 151
______, Arthur Mon 213
______, Booker Trp 41
______, David Tlb 347
______, David Wks 344
______, David Wks 358
______, Devenport Crf 414
______, Elizabeth Up 113
______, Hugh Hst 284
______, Irwin Jsp 383
______, Ivey Hal 77
______, James Wks 341

Lawson, John Har 191
______, John Lwn 80
______, Jonathan Mon 190
______, Leathy Put 185
______, Matilda Jsp 383
______, Pleasant Tlb 327
______, Reuben New 48
______, Roger Twg 85
______, Shelton Tfo 367
______, Thomas B. Han 160
______, Washington Rch 267
______, William Mon 225
Lauson, Daniel Car 221
Layson, John F. Put 209
LAWRENCE/LAURENCE/LAWRANCE/
LARRENCE/LARRANCE/LOWRANCE/
LAWRENN
Lawrence, Abraham Bib 76
______, Abraham Tlb 332
______, Allen Put 210
______, Bennet Mwr 161
______, Britain Up 113
______, Diana Cht 241
______, David Put 202
______, Garret Rch 284
______, George Cpb 204
______, Hartwell H. Gre 274
______, Henry Pik 107
______, James Gly 266
______, James Gwn 346
______, James Put 202
______, James Trp 41
______, John Ear 100
______, John Gre 303
______, John Wsh 258
______, Joseph Frk 219
______, Lemuel O. Jsp 381
______, Mary (W) Mor 270
______, Michael Gre 302
______, Robert Hal 116
______, S. A. T. Cht 266
______, Seborn Crf 413
______, Thomas Mad 104
______, William Jsp 366
______, Zachariah Pik 123
Laurence, Ann Fay 202
______, Hugh Mor 270
______, Isham Jef 420
______, James Mwr 157
______, Jesse Pik 112
______, Joseph Pik 118
______, Malikiah Pik 106
______, Peyton Pik 106

Laurence, Richard Pik 124
_____, Thomas Crf 413
_____, Thomas DeK 69
Lawrance, John Gwn 313
_____, Rody Hab 25
_____, Thomas J. Ogl 86
_____, Zachariah Ogl 86
Larrence, George Dec 12
Larrance, Elizabeth G. Col 352
Lowrance, Samuel Trp 49
Lawrenn, James Lee 32
LAY/LAYS
Lay, David Fay 203
_____, Elijah Jks 348
_____, Elisha Jks 335
_____, John Gwn 377
_____, John H. Up 117
_____, William Gwn 377
_____, William Gwn 379
_____, Zachariah Jks 345
Lays, Sampson Mad 111
LAYTON/LATON/LAWTON
Layton, Hillary Lau 8
Laton, John Wsh 249
Lawton, Joseph Scr 313
LAZENBY/LIZENBY
Lazenby, Deborough Col 343
_____, Elias Col 364
_____, John Jsp 365
_____, John M. Wrn 211
_____, Joshua Wrn 209
_____, Richard Wrn 209
_____, Robert Wrn 206
_____, Samuel J. Col 357
_____, William Em 175
Lizenby, Elizabeth Wks 346
LEACH, Asa Wal 129
_____, B. W. Cht 262
_____, Burdit Frk 251
_____, E. Gwn 309
_____, John Gwn 339
_____, John Hal 113
_____, Louisa Mon 196
_____, William Gwn 321
LEACHMAN, Littleton Mon 188
LEAD, M. M. DeK 56
LEADFORD/LETFORD
Leadford, Curtis Hab 8
_____, John Hab 8
Letford, William Hab 55
LEAK/LEAKE/LECK
Leak, James Pik 125
_____, John Pik 114
Leak, Samuel Pik 114
_____, Thomas Pik 114
Leake, Garlington Jsp 388
_____, James Jsp 391
Leck, Robert New 49
LEALMON, Thomas Tlf 12
LEAPTROT, A. Wsh 261
_____, Bolin Wsh 261
LEARSON, Daniel W. Bts 176
LEARY, George Jns 454
_____, Malinda Jns 454
_____, Wilson Mon 188
LEATHERS, Abram Car 221
_____, Elizabeth Car 221
_____, Jobecom Hal 131
_____, Joel Car 220
_____, John Car 215
_____, John Wks 332
_____, Samuel Car 221
LEATHERWOOD, William Cpb 207
_____, William Hal 81
LECHARTIER, Placide McI 122
LECONTTE, Lewis Lib 48
LECROY, James Hab 19
_____, John Hab 19
_____, Lucas Hab 13
_____, William Hab 19
HEDBETTER/LEADBETTER
Ledbetter, Banks Put 199
_____, Daniel Hal 131
_____, Ephraim Trp 42
_____, Henry Jsp 384
_____, Isaac Trp 43
_____, James Rab 234
_____, James W. Tfo 368
_____, Jane Up 110
_____, John Hal 77
_____, Joseph Clk 319
_____, Mary Hal 77
_____, Sarah Put 200
_____, Silas Jns 454
_____, Washington Gre 286
_____, Williamson Clk 319
Leadbetter, James Pik 128
LEDLOW/LEDLO
Ledlow, Nancy Jns 429
Ledle, Abreham Clk 309
LEE/LEA/LEIGH
Lee, Abel Bul 100
_____, Abm. Up 101
_____, Abm. Up 103
_____, Alx. Wks 346
_____, Allen Put 193

Name	County	Page
Lee, Andrew	Cow	384
______, Andrew	Frk	238
______, Andrew	Gwn	331
______, Andrew	Lin	61
______, Arthenatious	Trp	52
______, Barney	Gwn	336
______, Benj. F.	Jks	319
______, Betsey	Gwn	347
______, Bryan	Mon	217
______, Bud	Fay	196
______, C. P.	Har	188
______, Charles	Tms	18
______, Charles B.	Ogl	97
______, Charles H.	Ogl	72
______, Daniel	New	20
______, Daniel	Wil	300
______, Drury	Gwn	337
______, Ebenezer	Dec	8
______, Edward	Hry	237
______, Elam	Ear	100
______, Elias	Jef	423
______, Elias	Wsh	247
______, Elijah L.	Mon	174
______, Federick	DeK	63
______, General	Bul	100
______, George	App	9
______, George H.	Elb	154
______, Henry	Bts	161
______, Henry	Bts	163
______, Henry	Twg	77
______, Henry B.	Tfo	364
______, Hy.	Gwn	334
______, Hy.	Wks	347
______, Irvin	Wal	142
______, Isham	Gwn	325
______, James	App	11
______, James	Bul	92
______, James	Bul	95
______, James	Cow	386
______, James	Pul	153
______, James	Scr	397
______, Jeptha	Cow	388
______, Jesse	Put	191
______, Jesse	Tms	27
______, John	Cam	182
______, John	Cow	389
______, John	Dec	5
______, John	Gwn	335
______, John Sr.	Pul	154
______, John Jr.	Pul	153
______, John	Put	193
______, John	Scr	302
______, John	Scr	310
Lee, John	Ware	185
______, John	Wil	292
______, John B.	Jef	416
______, Jordan W.	Twg	75
______, Joseph H.	Bib	51
______, Joshua	Crf	399
______, Joshua	Lwn	84
______, Joshua	Scr	307
______, L. B.	Wks	333
______, Levi	Tlf	2
______, Levi	Put	212
______, Lewis	Wks	347
______, Lovard	Wks	333
______, Mary	Hab	34
______, Milley	Wsh	276
______, Moses	Gre	275
______, Mrs.	Scr	307
______, Nancy	Har	189
______, Nathan D.	New	43
______, Needham	Bul	102
______, Needham	Bts	171
______, Needam	Jef	416
______, Rachel	Fay	200
______, Ransome R. G.	Wrn	227
______, Reuben	Cpb	205
______, Reubin	Scr	301
______, Samuel	Cpb	208
______, Samuel	Bry	231
______, Samuel	Wal	140
______, Sarah	Tlf	4
______, Silas	Ear	94
______, Simeon	Ogl	74
______, Sion	Put	191
______, Solomon	Cow	389
______, Solomon P.	Hry	227
______, Stephen	Gre	286
______, Stephen	Pul	153
______, Thomas	Bal	32
______, Vincent	Wyn	284
______, William	Bul	94
______, William	Bts	174
______, William	Cow	385
______, William	Gwn	337
______, William	Lau	5
______, William	Ogl	71
______, William C.	Fay	181
______, William G.	Cht	280
______, William H.	Crf	397
______, Woodson	Fay	187
______, Zachariah	Gwn	369
Lea, James	Clk	302
______, John	Clk	293
______, Jonathan	Clk	291

Lea, Joseph Clk 311
_____, Milton Mon 183
_____, Noah Wil 313
_____, Thomas Mon 177
_____, Wyatt Clk 310
Leigh, Anselm B. Wil 319
_____, Jas. J. Cam 188
_____, Mary Col 344
_____, Widow Rch 254
LEEDS, Mary Rch 257
LEEPER, David Hst 263
LEFSEY, Benjamin Mor 243
_____, Benjamin W. Mor 244
LEFTEWITCH, Hart Ogl 91
LEGG, Augustin Jks 327
_____, Lucy Jks 326
_____, Thomas Hry 233
_____, William Jks 312
LEGGETT/LEGGET/LEGGITT/
LIGGETT
Leggett, Allsey Hry 235
_____, David Bke 126
_____, Joshua Tlb 330
_____, Noah App 5
_____, Watson App 6
Legget, Benj. App 6
_____, Mathew Put 206
_____, Rebecca Put 210
Leggitt, Wilson App 6
Liggett, Thomas DeK 32
LEGRAND, George Frk 214
_____, Jesse Sr. Frk 214
_____, John N. Elb 119
_____, Sarah Frk 248
LEGRIELL, O. Cht 248
LEGURE, D. Cht 242
_____, J. Cht 266
_____, L. Cht 242
LeHARP, John Crf 414
LEITH, Mary Tlb 324
LEMMONS/LEMONS/LEMON
Lemmons, James DeK 35
_____, Robert DeK 63
_____, Thomas DeK 52
Lemons, Robert Mor 260
_____, William Mor 260
Lemon, Abraham Bts 159
_____, John Bts 162
LENOIR, Thomas Gwn 355
LEON/LEION
Leon, Lewis Rch 253
Leion, David Cht 259
LEONARD/LENIARD/LENARD/

LEONARD/LENIARD/LENARD/
LENNARD/LINEARD
Leonard, Elizabeth Twg 60
_____, Francis Tlb 330
_____, Isaac T. Hal 123
_____, Jos. Bal 37
_____, James Gre 285
_____, James Hal 130
_____, James Hab 62
_____, James C. Tlb 330
_____, John Bal 38
_____, John Gre 302
_____, John Lau 23
_____, John W. Hal 113
_____, Joseph Wrn 210
_____, M. Bal 38
_____, Patrick Mor 272
_____, Roderick Mor 272
_____, Van Mor 272
_____, W. P. W. Jns 439
_____, Willis T. Hab 62
Leniard, Johnson Hal 127
_____, Thompson Hal 132
Lenard, William Mwr 169
Lennard, John B. Wil 287
Lineard, Jonathan Hal 130
LEOPARD, Holland Fay 185
_____, John D. Fay 204
LEPTOYETT/LIPTOYETT
Leptoyett, Henry L. Cow 367
Liptoyett, Henry Cow 367
LESEUR/LUSEUR/LESIEUR/
LESUEUR/LESSUERU
Leseur, Cary S. Mon 179
_____, Jordan Mon 196
_____, Joseph Ogl 85
Luseur, Mede Mon 222
_____, Samuel Mon 224
Lesieur, Drury M. Bib 64
Lesueur, Samuel Elb 149
Lessueur, Charles Cht 253
LESLEY/LESLIE/LESSLEY
Lesley, James M. Mwr 162
_____, John Hal 92
_____, Jonathan B. Ogl 96
_____, Malcolm Mon 180
_____, Peter W. Mor 255
_____, William Ogl 96
Leslie, Catharine Har 181
_____, Moses Bib 61
_____, Moses Bib 68
Lessley, Thomas Wal 138
LESSELL/LEESSEL

Name	County	Page
Lessell, Aron	Bib	73
Leessel, Edon	Crf	403
LESTER/LASTER/LUSTER		
Lester, Abner	New	16
_____, Alexander	Ogl	66
_____, Alexander	Ogl	69
_____, Alfred J.	Pul	160
_____, Benjamin	Bal	43
_____, Daniel	Bul	94
_____, David	Jns	474
_____, Dennis	Jns	474
_____, Dorothy	Wal	157
_____, Edwin	Gre	295
_____, Elizabeth Jr.	Bke	131
_____, Ezekiel	Bke	131
_____, G. D.	Jks	325
_____, George	Ogl	66
_____, George W.	New	9
_____, Henry S.	Wal	153
_____, Hiram	Mon	212
_____, Isaac	Dec	10
_____, Isaac	Mon	216
_____, Jacob	Ogl	66
_____, James D.	Mon	183
_____, Jeremiah	McI	126
_____, John	Bal	44
_____, John	Mad	99
_____, John	Mon	181
_____, John E.	Jns	474
_____, John W.	Jks	318
_____, Jos.	Bal	33
_____, Joseph W.	Jks	329
_____, Lewis	Ogl	67
_____, Nathan N.	Pul	161
_____, Pleasant	Mad	104
_____, Richard H.	Gwn	320
_____, Robert Jr.	Ogl	69
_____, Salathiel A.	DeK	71
_____, Silas M.	Pul	159
_____, Thomas	Ogl	69
_____, Wade	Mwr	169
_____, William	Ogl	67
_____, William	Pul	149
_____, William R.	DeK	67
Laster, James	Clk	320
Luster, William C.	Dec	7
LESULF/LEEUF		
Lesulf, P.	Cht	257
Leeuf, William	DeK	26
LETSON, Robert	Bts	170
LETT, Hugh	Fay	188
_____, James	Jks	316
_____, Reuben	Jks	316
Lett, Robert	Han	160
LEUBY (?), Mary	Cht	250
LEVEL/LEVIL/LEVELL		
Level, Edward	DeK	65
_____, Richard	Mwr	152
Levil, John W.	Hab	47
Levell, Nancy	Col	338
LEVERETT/LEVERITT/LEAVRETT/ LEVRET/LEAVETT/LEVETT/ LEVRETT/LEVERICK		
Leverett, Abram	Put	187
_____, Absalom	Lin	68
_____, Buckner	Up	105
_____, Hardy	Lin	68
_____, Jeremiah	Put	190
_____, Joel P.	Gre	280
_____, Sarah	Bib	76
_____, Thomas	Put	189
Leveritt, Burwell	Jsp	392
_____, Jessee	Jsp	391
_____, John R.	Bke	135
_____, Maston	Bke	134
_____, Pherobe	Bke	146
_____, Robert S.	Har	179
Leavrett, John	Gwn	336
_____, John E.	Gwn	336
Levret, Duncan	Mwr	159
_____, Matthew	Mwr	154
Leavett, Ann	Wil	304
Levett, John	Cht	261
Levrett, Richard H.	Gwn	335
Leverick, James	Rch	265
LIVINEY, John	Mus	289
LEVINGSTON/LIVINGSTON LEVISTONES		
Levingston, Alford	New	42
_____, Aron	Mon	179
_____, Barna	Tlf	8
_____, Isaac	Mon	179
_____, James	Wal	152
_____, Jesse	Tlb	328
_____, John	Lau	24
_____, Jane	Pik	115
_____, Jones	Lwn	85
_____, Joseph	New	34
_____, Michael	Tlf	8
_____, Thomas	Jns	430
_____, Thomas	Rch	273
_____, William	Jef	405
Livingston, George	Rch	279
_____, John	Wil	293
_____, Joseph	Wal	148
_____, Martin	Pul	151

Name	County	Page
Levistones, C.	Cht	260
LEVINS/LEVIN		
Levins, Isaiah	Tlf	2
______, Jacob	Cow	384
______, Jacob	Tlf	2
______, James	Cow	384
______, James	Cow	384
______, Jesse	Cow	384
______, William	Ware	185
Levin, Jacob	Pik	126
______, William	Tms	28
LEVY/LEVI		
Levy, Lewis	Rch	271
______, Mary	Cht	244
Levi, Theadore	Mus	287
LEWALLEN/LEWALLIN		
Lewallen, John	Frk	235
______, Jonathan	Frk	216
______, William	Wal	129
Lewallin, Joseph	Hab	16
LEWIS, Abel	Bke	154
______, Abraham	Em	165
______, Aley	Bak	20
______, Amos	Gwn	372
______, Anthony	Col	334
______, Antony	Rch	288
______, Archibald	Ear	92
______, Asa	Hry	200
______, Austin	Bal	45
______, Benjamin	KeK	53
______, Benjamin	Hry	207
______, Benjamin	Hst	282
______, Carter	Gre	273
______, Catharine	Hry	250
______, Charles L.	Bib	56
______, Christian	Hry	245
______, Daniel	Bke	128
______, David	Ear	92
______, David	Hab	62
______, David	Hry	250
______, David	Hst	270
______, Durham Sr.	Lee	32
______, Durham Jr.	Lee	32
______, Edmond	DeK	69
______, Eleazar	Bke	126
______, Elizabeth	Bul	95
______, Elizabeth	Jks	321
______, Elizabeth	Put	216
______, Evan	Bke	153
______, F.	Bal	38
______, F.	Bal	38
______, Felix	Har	175
______, Francis	Pik	119
Lewis, Gabriel	Gre	302
______, George	Doo	78
______, George	Hab	31
______, George	Hry	240
______, George	Tat	380
______, Green	Ran	241
______, Hamlin	Han	159
______, Henry	Gre	299
______, Iras	Hry	238
______, Isaac	Hst	272
______, Jacob	Scr	317
______, Jacob	Twg	78
______, Jacob	Twg	87
______, James	Bak	20
______, James	Bal	33
______, James	Bke	130
______, James	Frk	218
______, James	Hst	267
______, James	Mor	265
______, James	Scr	317
______, James	Twg	65
______, James B.	Ogl	90
______, James C.	Jns	440
______, James F.	Up	101
______, James W.	Bul	96
______, Jephtha	Elb	162
______, Jeremiah	Elb	156
______, Jeremiah Jr.	Elb	158
______, Jesse	Crf	401
______, Jessee	Wyn	282
______, John	Bke	130
______, John	Cht	252
______, John	Cht	266
______, John	Elb	148
______, John	Hry	239
______, John	Rch	253
______, John C.	Bke	154
______, John E.	Jns	440
______, John H.	Han	159
______, John J.	Up	105
______, John L.	Jns	466
______, John W.	Ear	92
______, Jonathan	Bke	118
______, Jonathan	Crf	401
______, Lark	Hry	202
______, Laton	Twg	70
______, Martha	Han	160
______, Mary	Em	165
______, Michael	Cht	242
______, Mrs.	Bal	6
______, Nancy	Gre	277
______, Nathaniel	Cht	250
______, Nicholas	Gre	305

Name	County	Page
Lewis, Noah	New	22
______, Nowland R.	Tfo	357
______, Patsy	Em	166
______, Pearce A.	Jns	466
______, Phillip	Jsp	389
______, Prior	Tms	17
______, Ransom	Bke	133
______, Redding R.	Wsh	271
______, Ren	Hry	232
______, Richard	Clk	297
______, Richard	Gre	304
______, Richard	Wks	333
______, Samuel	Lib	48
______, Samuel	Lib	49
______, Samuel Sr.	Mwr	160
______, Samuel Jr.	Mwr	157
______, Samuel	Pik	108
______, Stephen	Em	173
______, Stephen	Tat	378
______, Theophilus	Fay	190
______, Thomas	Bke	127
______, Thomas	Hry	247
______, Thomas	Mwr	157
______, Ths.	Wks	337
______, Thos. B.	Dec	4
______, Ulysses	Mus	277
______, Walker	Gre	299
______, Wiley	Dec	4
______, William	Bal	34
______, William	Bke	135
______, William	Dec	14
______, William	DeK	62
______, William Sr.	Ear	92
______, William Jr.	Ear	92
______, William	Gwn	314
______, William	Han	159
______, William	McI	122
______, William	Mor	267
______, William H.	Gre	297
______, William W.	DeK	46
______, Worner	New	5
______, Zadoc	Tlb	340
______, Zebulon	Wal	161
LIDDLE/LIDDELL/LEDDLE		
Liddle, Moses	Gwn	312
______, William	Gwn	340
Liddell, James	Jks	321
Leddle, Daniel	Gwn	314
LIGHT, Jacob	Gwn	334
______, Obadiah	Hal	79
______, Ran^{s}. B.	Gwn	313
LIGHTBOURN, J.	Cht	282
LIGHTFOOT, Benjamin	Bek	117
Lightfoot, John A.	Tfo	364
______, Martha	Wsh	259
______, Philip	Crf	397
______, Robert	Wsh	257
______, Thomas	Jns	447
LIGON/LIGGAN/LIGGON/ LIGGIN/LEGIN/LEGAN/LEGUEIN		
Ligon, Branch	Har	180
______, David G.	New	20
______, Henry	Tlb	333
______, Rhoda	Rch	286
______, Robert	Clk	322
Liggan, Alexander	Mus	292
______, William	Mus	292
Liggon, John	Trp	43
Liggin, James	DeK	26
Legin, Robert	Hal	107
Legan, Marshal	Mwr	157
Leguein, Lott M.	Clk	297
LIKENS, Thomas M.	Mor	270
LILLY, Joseph	Han	159
______, Lewis	Rab	223
LINCH/LYNCH		
Linch, Asbury	Mor	245
______, Edlow	Mor	245
______, Elizabeth	Put	199
______, Ellison	Hab	17
______, Gilbert	Mor	245
______, George	Cow	389
______, Grief	Mor	245
______, Henry	Bke	124
______, John	Put	204
______, Lewis H.	Put	203
Lynch, Bailey	DeK	70
______, Berry E.	Pik	122
______, Christopher B.	Bib	51
______, George J.	Pik	122
______, James	Gre	293
______, Jarriott	Jsp	368
______, Letty	Gre	296
______, William	Tms	29[illegible]
LINDEN, John M.	Gwn	364
LINDER, George G.	Lib	48
______, Lewis	Lau	6[illegible]
LIDDIN, Jesse	Bts	163
LINDSEY/LINSEY/LINDSAY/ LINZEY/ LINDSY/LYNDSAY/ LYNSEY/LINLEY/LYNDLEY		
Lindsey, Archabal	Hal	13[illegible]
______, China M.	Gwn	36[illegible]
______, Clayborn	Gre	28[illegible]
______, Dolphin	Bts	17[illegible]
______, Elizabeth	Hst	29[illegible]

Name	County	Page
Lindsey, Hester	Lwn	89
______, Isaac	Hal	71
______, Jacob	Jns	439
______, Jacob	Trp	54
______, James	Jks	345
______, John	Bts	172
______, John	Lwn	90
______, Joseph	Trp	54
______, Nathan	Lwn	80
______, Parham	Bts	177
______, Robert	Lwn	90
______, Sally	Gre	293
______, Sarah	Wks	332
______, Thomas	Twg	79
______, William	Jks	313
______, William	Wks	335
Linsey, Adam P.	Han	160
______, Ann	Jef	408
______, Dennis	Wrn	233
______, Edward	Bak	20
______, John	New	16
______, Nancy	Hry	243
______, Widow	Irw	298
______, William	Doo	86
______, William	Mon	182
______, William	Mwr	160
Lindsay, Abram	Mon	200
______, Benj. F. H.	Tfo	356
______, David	Gre	284
______, H. W.	Up	117
______, James	Wil	299
______, John	Jsp	379
Linzey, David	Wsh	257
______, Mary	Em	169
______, Nelson	Wsh	257
Lindsy, Richard	Twg	61
Lyndsay, Jacob	Hal	73
Lynsey, Caleb	Wrn	221
Linley, Jonathan	New	23
Lyndley, James	Wal	142
______, Jonathan	Wal	142
______, Thomas	Wal	160
LINEBURGER/LINEBERGER		
Lineburger, Amy	Eff	114
______, John	Eff	114
______, Joshua	Eff	114
Lineberger, John C.	Tms	21
LINER, Christopher	Wal	160
LINGO, John R.	Twg	71
______, Peter	Bke	137
______, Pinkston	Ran	241
______, R. T.	Bal	33
LINK, Moses	Hab	50
LINSENBY, Samuel	New	33
LINTON, A. B.	Clk	324
______, John	Twg	73
LINVILLE, John	Fay	185
______, William	Lin	69
LIPFORD, H.F.M.M.	Clk	309
LIPHAM, David	Crf	407
______, E.	Mon	225
______, Frances A.	Wil	288
______, Henry	Clk	297
______, John	Trp	39
LIPP, John	Trp	35
LIPPET, Samuel C.	Mon	207
LIPSCOMB/LIPPSCOMB		
Lipscomb, Baker	Wil	307
Lippscomb, Nathan	Trp	48
LIPSEY, Amesa B.	Twg	79
______, Green H.	Wil	311
______, Hezekiah	Up	118
______, Levice	Scr	300
______, Rascoe	Jns	457
______, William	Bke	125
LIPTROT/LIPTROTT		
Liptrot, Elizabeth	Em	164
______, John	Hst	272
Liptrott, Hopkin	Bke	120
______, James	Bke	127
LISCOE, Celia	Hst	287
LISK, James	Bts	169
LISLE, Hezekiah C.	Car	231
______, James	Mjs	291
______, Martin B.	Gwn	327
______, Mathew	Trp	43
______, William A.	Trp	37
LISTON, Levi	Twg	85
LITTERAL, Richard	DeK	41
LITTLE/LITLE		
Little, Allen	Bal	39
______, Benja.	DeK	51
______, Brya	Hab	66
______, Daniel	Lee	31
______, Edmond	Wsh	268
______, Elizabeth	Put	182
______, Fanny	Scr	300
______, George	Hal	106
______, George	Twg	76
______, Henry	Cht	243
______, Jacob	Lee	31
______, James	Jef	415
______, James	Lee	31
______, James H.	Frk	231
______, Jesse	Put	177
______, John	DeK	64

Name	County	Page
Little, John H.	Lin	67
______, Joseph	Car	220
______, Josiah	Jks	314
______, Kinchen	Put	180
______, Little B.	Tfo	356
______, Mary	Lee	31
______, Mary	Tfo	368
______, Mathias	Hal	106
______, Merrit	Twg	87
______, Micha	Hab	19
______, Micajah	DeK	39
______, Nathum	Jsp	357
______, Robert	Jns	457
______, Sarah	Jef	413
______, Theophilus F.	Car	216
______, Thomas	Clk	325
______, Thomas	Han	159
______, Tomister	Jef	413
______, William	Bul	98
______, William	Car	220
______, William	Jef	423
______, William	Pul	144
______, William	Put	179
______, William	Tfo	354
______, Wyley	Jns	432
______, Zabud	Hry	199
______, Zara	Hab	12
Litle, Archibald	Wil	301
LITTLEBRIDGE, O.	Cht	266
______, Robert	Cht	279
LITTLEFIELD, John L.	Twg	75
______, Nathan	Cam	186
LITTLEJOHN, Abraham	Hab	11
______, Abram	Gre	303
______, James	Jsp	378
______, Thomas	Jsp	378
LITTLETON/LITTON		
Littleton, Enoch	Wil	298
______, John	Wrn	216
______, Mark	Hal	111
______, Southy	Mon	176
______, Susannah	Rch	253
Litton, John	Hab	7
LIVELY, Abel	Scr	306
______, Charles	DeK	63
______, Luke	Bke	146
______, Matthew	Bke	146
______, Rody	Ogl	72
LIVERMAN, Mrs. B.	Rch	256
______, James	Tlb	341
LIVES, George	Bal	30
LLOYD/LOYD/LLOYDS		
Lloyd, Also	Han	172
Lloyd, Betsey	Cht	271
______, Daniel	Wsh	240
______, Daniel	Wsh	269
______, James	Cam	189
______, James	Crf	399
______, James	Hab	7
______, James H.	Clk	294
______, Jehu	Tlb	322
______, John	Wsh	269
______, John E.	Tlb	324
______, John F.	Rch	287
______, JOseph	Tlb	324
______, Lucina	Cht	246
______, Richard J.	Tlb	322
______, William	Cht	247
______, William	Tlb	323
Loyd, Charles	Mor	261
______, Daniel M.	Put	205
______, Elijah	Mor	256
______, Ez. S.	Up	105
______, George	Hry	236
______, George	Mor	256
______, Isham	Jns	442
______, James	DeK	57
______, James	Fay	183
______, John	Wrn	217
______, Joseph	Mor	259
______, Polly	Gwn	345
______, Thomas	Fay	183
______, Thomas O.	Clk	302
Lloyds, Eliza	Cht	279
LOCK/LOCKE		
Lock, Ann	Lau	12
______, David	Mor	244
______, Elizabeth	Wrn	202
______, James	Lau	9
______, James	Pik	106
______, Leonard	Lau	18
______, Willis	Up	120
Locke, Rebecah	Wrn	197
LOCKETT/LOCKET/LUCKETT		
Lockett, Columbus	Tfo	361
______, Elizabeth	Tfo	365
______, George	Tfo	361
______, Greene	Wrn	215
______, James	Jns	442
______, James	Mon	225
______, Patsey	Mon	225
______, James R.	Tfo	360
______, John	Har	189
______, Mary	Tfo	361
______, Osburn	Wrn	230
______, Thomas	Wrn	216

Locket, Cullen Mon 185
______, Hugh Mwr 154
______, R. Bal 35
______, Solomon Wrn 201
Luckett, Francis Wil 293
LOCKHART/LOCKHEART/
LOCKHARD/LOCKART
Lockhart, Chestiny Wrn 230
______, David Tlb 337
______, David Tlb 345
______, Eliel Lin 70
______, Henry Wrn 192
______, J. A. Wrn 230
______, James Elb 125
______, James Lin 68
______, Jesse Han 160
______, John Lin 67
______, Lemuel Gre 286
______, Martha Crf 413
______, Mary Wil 299
______, Samuel S. Bul 96
______, Vincent Lin 68
Lockheart, Loel L. Har 176
Lockhard, Aaron Pik 107
Lockart, Aaron Cpb 205
LOCKLIER/LOCKLAR/LABALIER
Locklier, Elizabeth Mus 287
Locklar, Jesse Fay 202
Labalier, A. Cht 261
LOCKLIN, Samuel Wal 153
______, James Z. Wal 165
LOCKWOOD, William Crf 413
LODGE, John Bke 124
______, Simeon Bke 123
LOFLIN, Eady Put 188
______, George Lin 62
______, James Har 181
______, James T. Lin 70
LOFTES, William Elb 158
LOFTLY/LOFTLEY
Loftly, Wright Eff 110
Loftley, William Doo 82
LOFTON/LOFTEN/LOFFON
Lofton, James Bak 17
______, James Elb 137
______, John Bts 158
______, R. Y. Bak 17
______, Sarah Lau 15
______, William Lwn 81
Loften, Herin Wks 357
Loffon, Lewis Cht 266
LOGAN/LOGGINS/LOGGIN/
LOGGEN
Logan, Benjamin Wsh 276
______, James H. Gwn 338
______, John Bib 51
______, John Bts 177
______, Pleasant Hal 80
______, Sally Gwn 338
Loggins, Dickson Hal 100
______, James Hal 123
______, John Hal 123
______, Samuel Hal 123
Loggin, James Sr. Hal 129
______, Samuel Sr. Hal 129
Loggen, James Hal 129
LOGUE, Charles Wrn 231
______, Charles Sr. Wrn 233
______, James Han 160
______, Nancy Wrn 233
LOKEY/LOKAY/LOKY/LOUKER
Lokey, Dingley Wrn 212
Lokay, Benjamin Tlb 345
Lody, Benjamin DeK 48
Louker, William Mad 107
LOLLER, Betsy Cpb 208
LONDERRY, Ann Cht 247
LONG, Aaron Ear 96
______, Benjamin Hal 108
______, Blanchy Tlb 336
______, Crawford Han 160
______, David Jns 445
______, Davis Han 160
______, Eliza Wil 323
______, Elizabeth Bke 146
______, Fashaw Lib 48
______, George Bak 18
______, George Cam 183
______, George Hry 234
______, Henry Mon 190
______, James Crf 405
______, James Jns 446
______, James Mad 100
______, James M. Mor 261
______, Jane Car 222
______, Jesse Crf 405
______, John Car 215
______, John Han 160
______, John Tlb 338
______, John A. Jks 318
______, John J. Wsh 251
______, Jonathan Put 203
______, Louisa Bal 43
______, Lunsford Wal 165
______, Lyttelton Pik 109
______, Marcus Mor 259

Name	County	Page
Long, Mary	Mad	117
______, Mary E.	Cht	268
______, Mathew	Hal	75
______, Micajah	Gwn	319
______, Nimrod W.	Twg	66
______, Philip	Tlb	334
______, Richard	New	9
______, Sam.	Mad	114
______, Solomon	Car	229
______, Stafford	Bak	15
______, Thomas	Mad	106
______, Thomas	Mor	261
______, Thomas L.	Mor	262
______, William	Wsh	256
______, Zacheria	Scr	313
LONGINA/LONGENJER		
Longina, Hugh	Hry	201
Longenjer, Christopher	Trp	42
LONGSTREET, A. B.	Rch	292
______, Hannah	Rch	269
______, James	Rch	288
______, Wise	Hab	54
LOONEY/LOONY		
Looney, Adam	Frk	248
______, Joseph	Frk	233
______, Noah	Frk	217
______, Thomas F.	Frk	211
Loony, Dominick	Cht	242
______, Felin	Cht	272
LOOSER, John C.	Trp	51
LOOTS, George	Rab	229
______, Joseph	Rab	230
LOPER/LOOPER		
Loper, David	Cht	247
______, Messeek	Scr	316
Looper, Susannah	Cht	278
LORD, Abram	Lee	33
______, Baley	Gwn	371
______, H.	Cht	264
______, John	McI	122
______, John	Wsh	246
______, Joseph M.	Wks	352
______, Leandy	Wsh	264
______, Leon	Wsh	258
______, Levin	Wsh	258
______, Mary	Bke	135
______, Mathias	Clk	296
______, Robert	Clk	301
______, Samuel	Wks	352
______, Simon	Jks	319
______, W.	Bal	32
______, Major W.	Jks	319
______, William	Gwn	363
Lord, Wheatley	Wsh	246
______, William	Jns	336
______, William Sr.	Jks	336
______, William	Wks	351
LOTHER, Edward Thomas	Rch	266
LOTKEY, Sally	Jef	410
LOTT, Andrew	Hal	89
______, Arthur	Jef	418
______, Daniel	Tlf	2
______, Ellis	Cow	368
______, Hiram	Cpb	208
______, Jesse	Col	349
______, Jesse	Hal	69
______, Joel	Ware	186
______, John	Hal	68
______, John S.	Rch	272
______, Mark	Cpb	194
______, Mark	Tlf	3
______, Moses	Hal	70
______, Sarah	Cpb	208
______, William	Crf	406
LOUDE, Phillip L.	Wal	129
LOURHE, Lewis	Crf	404
LOVE, Andrew	Mon	181
______, Cathrine	New	14
______, Christopher	Hab	38
______, Daniel	Hal	133
______, David	Mor	244
______, Francis	Gre	286
______, Ingraham	Cpb	195
______, James	Cht	278
______, James	Cpb	209
______, James	Hry	210
______, James	Jsp	365
______, Jane	App	12
______, John	Em	164
______, John	Hal	109
______, John	Mon	176
______, John	Put	178
______, John	Tlb	332
______, John H.	Clk	315
______, Mary	Jns	440
______, Robert	Clk	300
______, Robert	Wsh	245
______, Thomas	Wsh	250
______, Wade	Fay	187
______, William	Clk	301
______, William	Cpb	199
LOVERN, John	Hal	96
LOVEJOY, Edward	Jsp	391
______, Eleazer	Jsp	386
______, Harrison	Jsp	396
______, John	Hry	22[illegible]

Lovejoy, John B. Hry 214
______, Samuel Car 226
______, Simeon Pik 111
______, William Jsp 386
LOVELADY, David Rab 232
______, Hiram Hry 203
______, John Hab 61
______, Thomas Rab 229
LOVELESS/LOVELACE/LOVE-
LASS/LOVLESS
Loveless, Allen DeK 27
______, James New 43
______, Solomon Rab 231
______, William DeK 35
______, William Pul 138
Lovelace, Allen Col 352
______, James Hry 205
______, Lucius B. Hry 204
Lovelass, Hazel Gwn 367
______, Love Gwn 316
Lovless, Barton Hal 121
LOVELL/LOVEL
Lovell, Isaac Rab 223
______, Lewis Rch 258
______, William Bke 144
Lovel, G. Col 364
LOVETT/LOVITT/LOVET
Lovett, Ahemale B. Twg 75
______, Allen Mar 144
______, Catharine Cht 269
______, David Bib 51
______, David Lwn 79
______, James Tms 27
______, John T. Scr 311
______, Joshua Ear 100
______, Lemuel Mon 211
______, Moses Twg 69
______, Rebecca Scr 311
______, Richard Wrn 229
______, Robert W. Scr 317
______, Thomas Scr 311
Lovitt, Benjamin Hry 216
Lovet, Joshua Mtg 234
LOVICK, James Col 363
LOVING/LOVINS
Loving, Elijah Fay 198
______, George Bib 64
______, James Hry 249
______, John Bib 51
______, Manuel W. Fay 202
______, Mastin Frk 222
______, Richard New 41
______, Samuel Fay 204
Loving, William Hry 225
Lovins, Martha Gre 288
LOVINGGOOD, Harmon Elb 151
LOW/LOWE
Low, Ann McI 129
______, Aron Jef 407
______, Basil Bts 162
______, Caleb Twg 63
______, Christopher Rch 269
______, David Gre 279
______, David Col 363
______, Edmund Hry 209
______, Elizabeth Wsh 272
______, George Jef 422
______, Isaac Col 363
______, James Jef 419
______, James P. Hry 221
______, Jesse Wal 166
______, John Cht 253
______, John Jns 461
______, John C. Gwn 329
______, Partin Gwn 370
______, Samuel Cam 184
______, Thomas Wrn 196
______, William Cht 245
______, William Gre 285
______, William Gwn 313
______, William Jr. Mwr 153
Lowe, Abraham Jns 470
______, Benjamin Jns 440
______, Curlis Wrn 206
______, Daniel B. Hst 272
______, Henry H. Har 182
______, James Mon 179
______, James P. Jns 457
______, Thomas Jns 457
______, Vincent B. Wil 299
______, William Han 159
______, William Jns 429
______, William Sr. Mwr 155
______, William Wrn 196
______, William H. Crf 404
LOWDEN/LODEN
Lowden, Robert Jef 408
______, Thomas Hal 93
______, William Hal 111
Loden, Mikeger Hab 36
LOWDER, J. Cht 267
LOWMAN, George Hab 22
LOWRY/LOWERY/LOWREY/
LOWRIE/LOWRY/LOURE
Lowry, Coonrod Wal 164
______, David Hal 127

Name	County	Page
Lowry, Edward	Gwn	371
_____, Edward D.	Gwn	371
_____, George W.	Bts	175
_____, Giles	Wal	174
_____, Jacob	Wal	160
_____, Jacob	Wal	164
_____, James	DeK	70
_____, James R.	Twg	88
_____, John	Hal	127
_____, Middleton	Hab	42
_____, Samuel	DeK	71
_____, Sol. R.	Gwn	352
_____, William	Hal	126
_____, William	Hal	127
Lowery, Andrew	Lau	16
_____, Christopher	Jef	424
_____, Charels J.	Hab	43
_____, David	Gwn	352
_____, Henry	Gwn	310
_____, John	Jef	420
_____, John R.	Twg	63
_____, John W. F.	Gwn	322
_____, Joseph	Jef	412
_____, Lydia	Jef	414
_____, Nathanel	Hab	42
_____, Sarah	Jef	424
_____, Shadrack	Gwn	355
_____, William	Jef	424
Lowrey, Amos	Frk	226
_____, Elisha	Frk	217
_____, James	Hab	26
_____, James	Pik	123
_____, John	Gwn	317
_____, John B.	Jks	314
_____, Simson	Bke	127
_____, Thomas	McI	129
Lowrie, Elizabeth	Tms	16
Loury, Levi	Jks	312
Loure, William	Gly	264
LOWTHER, Charles	Bal	100
_____, Hampton	Ware	197
_____, Samuel	Jns	466
LOYALL, Jesse	Jsp	369
_____, John	New	19
_____, Richard	New	36
LUCKIE/LUCKEY/LUCKY		
Luckie, Alexander F.	New	15
_____, Hezekiah	New	36
_____, James	Jks	321
_____, William D.	New	16
_____, William F.	Har	192
Luckey, James	Gre	297
_____, William	Col	350

Name	County	Page
Luckey, William A.	Bib	51
Lucky, John	Mon	225
_____, John	Put	191
_____, Samuel	Tms	28
LUFBURROUGH, M.	Cht	251
LUKE, Daniel	Irw	298
_____, Daniel	Irw	304
_____, Edward	Bke	117
_____, Henry	Clk	310
_____, James Sr.	Col	340
_____, James Jr.	Col	339
_____, John	Col	346
_____, John	Em	167
_____, Landers	Har	185
_____, Rubin	Col	339
_____, Thomas	Col	339
_____, William B.	Col	339
LUKER, Benjamin	Wil	312
_____, Martin	Cow	372
LUKROY, Jesse	New	24
_____, Thomas	Frk	223
_____, William	New	24
LULLERS, William	Col	350
LUMER, Micager	Hab	66
LUMPKIN/LUMPKINS/LUMKIN		
Lumpkin, Dickerson	Jns	431
_____, E. W.	Bke	122
_____, Edward	Clk	322
_____, Edmund	Mon	227
_____, Elijah	Ogl	93
_____, George	Hal	68
_____, George	Ogl	94
_____, Harrison	Jsp	380
_____, Henry H.	Mon	195
_____, Jack	Ogl	88
_____, James	Gre	274
_____, John	Up	114
_____, Joseph H.	Ogl	98
_____, Philip	Bke	153
_____, Polly	Jsp	381
_____, Samuel	Ogl	64
_____, Walter	Jsp	381
_____, William	Clk	326
_____, William	Hal	133
_____, William	Ogl	87
_____, William F.	Gre	277
_____, Wilson	Wal	142
Lumkin, George	New	25
_____, Thomas	New	25
Lumpkins, John	Ogl	88
_____, John C.	Cpb	203
_____, Joseph	Ogl	103
LUCAS, A. B.	Wks	33[illegible]

Lucas, Archabald M. Fay 191
_____, Arthur Twg 74
_____, Buck Mus 282
_____, Charles New 11
_____, Edwin Mus 280
_____, Isaac Col 339
_____, John Han 160
_____, John M. Eff 111
_____, Littleberry Mon 207
_____, Martha Bts 177
_____, Mary Mon 206
_____, Robert Mus 280
_____, Sina Twg 86
_____, Thomas J. Mor 238
_____, William New 11
_____, William D. Mus 278
LUCK, Frances Hal 104
_____, George Pik 125
_____, John Jks 330
_____, William Cow 390
LUCETTE, C. P. Lib 48
LUCINDER, Michael Cht 240
LUMSDEN/LUMDENS/LUNSDEN/
LUMSDELL
Lumsden, Jesse M. Jsp 395
_____, John G. Put 217
Lumdens, Jeremin C. New 14
Lunsden, Jeremiah Jsp 395
Lumsdell, Jesse M. Jsp 392
LUMUS/LUMBUS/LUMMUS
Lumus, James Frk 237
Lumbus, William New 48
Lummus, Robert Bts 159
LUNGINO, James Wal 126
LUNN/LUN
Lunn, John Dec 11
Lun, Peter Jns 436
LUNSFORD/LUNCEFORD/
LUNCFORD/LUNTFORD
Lunsford, Barbary Tfo 367
_____, Enoch Bib 56
_____, Hazel Mon 223
_____, Henry Tfo 367
_____, Jacob Wil 315
_____, James Elb 142
_____, James L. Twg 70
_____, John Tfo 367
_____, Joseph S. Hst 278
_____, Moses Jsp 367
_____, Peter Wil 313
_____, Reuben Elb 141
_____, Reuben Tfo 369
_____, Samuel Tlf 3
Lunsford, William Elb 145
_____, William Tfo 364
Lunceford, George Rab 222
_____, Lemuel DeK 41
_____, William Rab 225
Luncford, Stephen Tlb 339
Luntford, James DeK 35
LUNDY/LUNDAY
Lundy, Catharine Cht 278
_____, Henry Gre 301
_____, Susan B. Han 159
_____, Thomas Bib 64
_____, Williamson Han 159
Lunday, Maclin Scr 306
_____, Robert Scr 299
_____, Stephen Ran 249
_____, William Scr 306
LUPER, John Hst 289
LUSK, John Hal 120
LUTHER, F. S. Cht 252
_____, Godfrey Hal 89
_____, Jonathon DeK 25
LYBASS, Charles Wil 316
LYLE/LILES/LYLES/LILSES/
LYSLE
Lyle, David J. Jks 323
_____, Delmus Jks 337
_____, Delmus J. Jr. Jks 322
_____, Hugh Wil 301
_____, James Jks 327
_____, James Wil 301
_____, James G. Cow 367
_____, John Cpb 195
_____, John Fay 184
_____, John Hry 231
_____, Robert Wal 172
_____, Stephen Fay 194
_____, W. Jks 331
Liles, Akelly Twg 79
_____, Ephraim Twg 71
_____, Hiram Hal 87
_____, James Hal 87
_____, Jesse Hal 103
_____, Philip Hal 87
_____, Randolph Hal 103
Lyles, A. Wks 345
_____, Benjamin Wyn 283
_____, Charles Col 336
_____, Charles Cow 374
_____, Edmund Wyn 283
_____, Henry Wyn 283
_____, Stephen Fay 192
Lilses, Hampton Twg 71

Name	County	Page
Lysle, Pleasant R.	Gwn	357
LYNN/LYNES/LINES		
Lynn, Asa	Mwr	166
______, Ayres	Col	358
______, Charles	New	28
______, John	Col	358
______, John	Tat	374
______, John	Wrn	196
______, Solomon	Tat	374
______, William	Hry	200
______, William	Lin	74
Lynes, James	Col	335
Lines, Samuel S.	Lib	49
LYNUM, Charles	Tlb	344
LYONS/LYON/LIONS/LION/ LYENS/LYAN; also see Leion		
Lyons, Beersheba	Bke	138
______, Christian M.	Hry	212
______, Fanny	Col	338
______, James	Rch	291
______, James R.	Mus	278
______, Jane	Hry	222
______, Jeriah	Pik	132
______, John G.	Jef	405
______, John P.	Hry	211
______, Richard	Mus	288
______, Sarah M.	Hry	237
______, Squire	Hry	250
______, William	Jef	405
______, William F.	Bts	173
Lyon, David	Har	183
______, Edmund	Lin	71
______, Elizabeth	Bts	169
______, James	Mon	194
______, James M.	Har	177
______, John E. B.	New	22
______, Josiah M.	Fay	204
______, Thomas	Lin	73
______, Worner	New	9
Lion, Jesse	New	9
______, Milly	Lin	73
Lions, Napolean B.	Put	204
______, Nathan; Planta tion	Put	216
______, Nathan	Put	219
Lyens, Lucy	Col	341
Lyan, Jonathan	Wsh	242
McADAMS, Daniel	Hal	110
______, Thomas	Gwn	348
McAFEE, Arthur	Wsh	258
McAfee, Henderson	Hal	72
______, Hugh	Hab	49
______, James	Wsh	266
______, James T.	Gwn	352
______, John	Hal	74
______, John W.	Hab	10
______, Jorden	Hab	57
______, Joseph	Har	176
______, R. G.	Jsp	361
McALLISTER/McALISTER/ McALLESTER/McCALLISTER		
McAllister, John	Mwr	163
______, M. H.	Cht	260
______, M.H. Plantation	Cht	279
______, Samuel	Tlf	8
McAlister, Alexander	Jsp	383
______, Charles	Pul	146
______, James	Jsp	378
______, James	Rch	274
______, Laviney	Wrn	233
McAllester, Alexander	Elb	153
McCallister, George W.	Bry	84
McALLUM, William	Clk	298
McALPIN/McCALPIN/McKELPIN		
McAlpin, Andrew	Gre	288
______, Henry	Cht	263
______, Robert	Jks	332
McCalpin, Alexander	Mor	240
______, John	Mor	269
McKelpin, William	DeK	47
McANALLY, Catharine	Irw	300
McARTHUR, Charles	Tlf	5
______, Daniel	Mtg	235
______, Duncan	Mtg	235
______, John	Bib	74
______, John	Mtg	232
______, John	Tlb	332
______, Peter	Mwr	150
McARTY, Anthothy	Wal	154
______, Isaac	Wal	172
McARVER: see McIver		
______, James	Gwn	317
McAULEY, Auley	Tms	18
McAVOY, Michael	Wil	301
McBANE, James T.	Lau	4
______, Mary	Lau	9
McBEAN, Daniel	New	14
McBETH, James	Wsh	239
______, John C.	Pik	131
McBOG, Rachel	Jsp	365
McBRAYER, Joseph	Car	218
McBREER, John	Hal	71
McBRIDE/McBRYDE		

Name	County	Page
McBride, Andrew	Hry	251
______, Elizabeth	Hst	273
______, Henry	Cow	380
______, James	Fay	207
______, James	Jef	412
______, John	Bts	160
______, John Sr.	Crf	405
______, John Jr.	Crf	394
______, John	Wks	348
______, Mary	Hst	295
______, Samuel	Ran	248
______, Thomas	Jef	412
______, William	Fay	207
______, William	Jef	412
McBryde, Elizabeth	Jns	473
______, J.	Mon	218
______, John	Mon	224
______, Niven	Ear	93
McBURNETT/McBURNET		
McBurnett, Albert	Mor	263
McBurnet, Thomas	Mwr	158
McCAGHORN, Robert	Wal	135
McCALL/McCAUL/McCOLL		
McCall, A.	Gwn	372
______, Abraham	Irw	300
______, Charles	Tat	374
______, David	Tat	377
______, Eleazar	Bib	76
______, Elhannon	Tat	376
______, Elizabeth	Scr	306
______, Elizabeth W.	Lwn	83
______, Francis	Bul	93
______, George R.	Tlf	5
______, George W.	Tat	371
______, Jacob	Rch	262
______, James	Gwn	372
______, James B.	Eff	112
______, John	Irw	300
______, Joshua	Scr	307
______, Moses	Scr	307
______, Robert	Lwn	87
______, Rodger	Bib	52
______, Selaway	Irw	300
______, Stephen	Cam	186
______, Thomas	Lau	13
McCaul, Thomas	Rab	234
McColl, Nathaniel	Pul	158
McCALLA, Robert	Gwn	310
McCALLAM/McCALLUM		
McCallam, Hugh	Bts	179
McCallum, Patrick	Mon	207
McCAMICK, Nancy	Col	339
McCAMMON/McCOMMON		
McCammon, John	DeK	39
McCommon, Charles	Hry	242
McCANALISS, William	Gly	267
McCANDLER, Samuel	DeK	57
McCANN/McCANE/McCAIN/ McCUNE'		
McCann, Anna	Bke	137
______, Charles	Bke	138
______, Hugh	Tms	18
______, Joshua	Tms	29
______, Martin	Jks	330
______, Richard	Hal	78
McCane, William	Col	335
______, William A.	Bts	166
______, William D.	Gre	289
McCain, Alexander	Mon	221
______, James	Trp	33
______, William	Trp	37
McCune, Elizabeth	Bts	176
______, James A.	Bts	158
______, Thomas	Clk	293
______, William	Jsp	389
McCANT/McCANTS		
McCant, Delatha	Twg	86
______, Valentine	Twg	68
McCants, Alexander	Tlb	348
______, David	Hry	218
______, Sarah	Tlb	348
McCARDEL/McCARDELL		
McCardel, Charles	Bib	61
McCardell, William	Eff	111
McCARLEY, William	Gwn	351
McCARRA, William	Tlb	346
McCARROL, John	Wks	357
McCARTA/McCARTER/McCART		
McCarta, James	Frk	230
______, John	Frk	239
______, John H.	Frk	244
McCarter, Alexander	Frk	229
______, Matthew	Frk	231
McCart, John	Elb	155
______, William	Frk	241
McCARTHY/McCARTY		
McCarthy, Charles	Jns	466
______, Charles	Tlb	346
______, Dennis	Crf	415
______, Roger	Mon	208
McCarty, Alexander	DeK	66
______, Charles W.	Wrn	193
______, Cornelius	Car	216
______, Caniel	Bal	30
______, John	Jks	337
______, John	Wal	128

McCarty, John Wal 132
_____, Kesiah Wrn 213
_____, Margarette Rch 279
_____, Mary DeK 55
_____, Molly Wrn 213
_____, P. Mus 280
_____, Reese Wrn 213
_____, William Jks 344
_____, William Wks 349
_____, William Wks 350
McCASKEL, Robert Col 340
McCATHERIN, Malcum Cam 190
McCAULESS, John Hab 54
McCAUSON, William Hal 91
McCAW, Robert Cow 376
_____, Samuel New 40
_____, William New 39
McCAWLEY, James Hry 207
_____, William Hry 242
McCLAIN/McCLANE/McCLINE
McClain, A. D. App 11
_____, David Rab 222
_____, Ephraim E. Rab 223
_____, George Pike 118
_____, James Frk 244
_____, John Rab 222
_____, John Rab 222
_____, Samuel Pik 118
_____, Silas New 35
_____, Thomas New 38
_____, William Frk 244
_____, Zachariah D. New 34
McClane, Ephraim Hab 57
_____, John New 34
McCline, Andrew Rab 230
McCLANAHAN, James Elb 141
McCLEARY, James Hst 278
McCLARE/McLREAR
McClare, John Pik 115
Maclrear, Ashworth Cpl 208
McCLELLAN/McCLELAN/
McCLELLON/McCLELLAND/
McCLALLAND/McLELLON/
McLELLAN/McLELION/McLELAND
McClellan, Andrew Wyn 282
_____, Henry Tfo 363
McClelan, Abigal Scr 315
_____, John Scr 315
McClellon, James Gre 275
McClelland, James Hry 233
McClalland, Joseph Cam 190
McLellon, John Lib 49
McLellan, Thomas Gwn 367
McLelion, Martha Tat 380
McLeland, John New 46
McCLENDON/McCLINDON
also see McLendon
McClendon, Allen Jsp 367
_____, Andrew Hry 225
_____, Andrew Irw 304
_____, Burrel Bib 70
_____, Burrel Lau 15
_____, Charles Put 197
_____, Dennis Lau 15
_____, Dennis Pik 111
_____, Elizabeth Lau 22
_____, Enoch New 10
_____, Ezekiel Tms 26
_____, Frances Put 196
_____, Freeman Mwr 154
_____, Henry Hry 227
_____, Jacob Jsp 354
_____, Jacob Pik 112
_____, Jacob Put 196
_____, James Irw 304
_____, Jeptha Mwr 162
_____, Jeremiah Bts 165
_____, Jesse Bke 139
_____, Job Bak 18
_____, Job Put 193
_____, Joel Jsp 372
_____, John Bib 52
_____, Joseph Hry 205
_____, Judith Jsp 356
_____, Kenneth Tms 29
_____, Lewis Lau 9
_____, Lewis Put 196
_____, Mason C. Tlb 341
_____, Nancy Jsp 369
_____, Needham Lau 15
_____, Phoebe Jsp 366
_____, Rebecca Jsp 369
_____, Robert Mor 238
_____, Samuel Hry 227
_____, Simeon Up 112
_____, Simpson Jsp 362
_____, Stephen Jsp 358
_____, Thomas Cow 386
_____, Thomas Hry 239
_____, William Lau 10
_____, William Mwr 162
_____, William Tlb 330
McClindon, Joel Mon 218
McCLESKEY/McCLUSKEY/McCLESKY/
McCOSKEY/McCUSKEY/McLESKEY/
McLASKEY

McCleskey, Benjamin Jks 341
______, James J. Hal 73
______, James R. Jks 349
______, Thadeus H. Hal 71
McCluskey, Hiram Hry 230
______, John Hry 230
______, John J. Bib 56
McClesky, Asa Mon 178
McCoskey, James Hab 23
McCuskey, A. L. Wal 167
McLeskey, Benj. G. Hal 103
______, David G. Hal 94
______, David H. Hal 90
______, James Hal 91
______, Joseph H. Hal 91
McLaskey, John Mus 277
McCLOTHERING, James Lau 23
McCLOUD, Archibald Tms 25
______, Gilbert Bib 56
______, John Twg 80
______, Norman Tms 19
McCLUBHERD, Arnold Irw 302
McCLUNG, Charles New 23
______, Hiram Hry 232
______, John Tlb 343
______, Josiah Har 187
______, Ransom Up 108
______, Reuben Gwn 360
______, Robert Up 115
McCLURE/McCLEURE
McClure, David Hab 21
______, James Cow 388
______, James M. Jsp 361
______, John Bts 167
______, John Cpb 195
______, John B. Frk 251
______, Robert B. Hab 11
______, William Hal 131
______, William B Car 226
McCleure, Boley Hal 133
McCOLIN, Daniel Hab 52
______, John Hab 52
McCOLLUM/McCOLUM/McCOLLAM/
McCOLLIAM
McCollum, A. Bib 51
______, Archibald Mtg 234
______, Elizabeth Hal 121
______, George Hst 283
______, Harba Hab 60
______, Hugh Hab 13
______, Joab Hab 46
______, Joseph Bke 145
______, Samuel Frk 236
McCollum, Thomas Hst 283
McColum, Danil Hab 60
______, William Hab 54
McCollam, Abram Jsp 363
McColliam, David Hab 46
McCORMAN, James Mon 214
McCOMBS/McCOMBES/McCOOMBS
McCombs, Robert Bal 28
______, Robert Rch 253
______, Shildric Fay 198
______, William Fay 192
McCombes, Andrew Cow 377
**McCoombs, R. (slave) Rch 257
McCONNELL/McCONNEL
McConnell, James Hal 92
______, James Hry 211
______, John Hal 75
______, John Hry 240
______, Joseph Sr. Hry 237
______, Joseph Hry 211
______, Robt. E., Estate Lib 49
______, William Hry 216
______, Wm. P., doctor Lib 50
McConnel, Eli Gwn 377
______, William Wks 346
McCOOK, Daniel Han 162
______, Daniel Wks 354
______, Hamilton Bib 61
______, Joshua R. Mus 286
______, Othniel Bib 61
______, Robert Han 162
McCOOL, Creecy Tms 24
McCORD/M'CORD
McCord, Elisha Mon 220
______, James Lin 72
______, John Bts 161
______, John Lin 72
______, Robert DeK 68
______, William S. New 15
M'Cord, James Wal 163
______, Mary Wal 163
______, Nancy Wal 166
______, Polley Wal 167
McCORKLE/McCORCLE/McCORK-
ADALE/McCORQUODALE
McCorkle, Abram Hal 106
______, James M. Jsp 387
______, Robert Col 352
______, Samuel Mon 202
______, William Jsp 389
McCorcle, Archibald Lin 70
______, John Lin 71
McCorkadale, Daniel Wsh 266

Name	County	Page
McCorquodale, Duncan	Ear	92
_____, John	Ear	92
McCORMACK/M'CORMACK/ McCORMAC/McCORMICK/ McCOMUCK/McOMICK		
McCormack, George	Mor	238
_____, Hiram	Tfo	354
_____, Pollard	Bry	84
_____, Thomas	Tfo	359
_____, Matthias	Pul	158
McCormac, Alexander	Hal	88
_____, Angus	Hal	85
_____, Hecter	Hal	88
McCormick, John	Ear	93
McComuck, John P.	Hab	64
McOmick, James	Doo	81
McCORREY, Edward	Em	177
McCORTNEY, Barney	Fay	196
McCOWEN/McCOWAN/McCOWN		
McCowen, Duncan	Mor	253
_____, Greenbury	Mor	242
_____, John W.	Mor	241
_____, Robert	Jks	334
McCowan, Nancy	Bke	120
McCown, James	Ear	91
_____, John	Ogl	63
_____, Martha	Ogl	85
McCOY/McKOY		
**McCoy, Mrs. (slaves	Rch	270
_____, Abner	Up	100
_____, Alexander	Bke	121
_____, Alexander	Tat	377
_____, Ann	Wrn	205
_____, Benjamin	Mor	253
_____, Candace	Jef	405
_____, Charles	Hst	267
_____, Daniel	Trp	37
_____, Daniel	Wsh	243
_____, Danil	Hab	27
_____, David	Wrn	199
_____, Demroy	Wrn	217
_____, Edmond	Trp	55
_____, Henry	Bts	161
_____, Henry	Up	110
_____, Henry C.	Tlb	323
_____, Hugh	Bts	171
_____, Hugh M.	Mad	103
_____, Isaac	Hst	278
_____, Jacob	Up	101
_____, James	Hal	94
_____, James	Ogl	85
_____, Jane	Rch	265
_____, Jefferson	Trp	37
McCoy, Jerrimiah	Cow	369
_____, Jeremiah	Tlb	339
_____, John	App	11
_____, John	Bke	131
_____, John	Car	228
_____, John	DeK	41
_____, John	Hal	119
_____, John	Har	189
_____, John	Mor	266
_____, John B.	Tlb	326
_____, Leroy	Trp	55
_____, Mary	Hal	116
_____, Nancy	Wsh	262
_____, Neely	Bts	166
_____, Robert	Bke	152
_____, Robert	Wsh	261
_____, Sarah	Wrn	233
_____, Thomas	Fay	193
_____, Uell	Mor	266
_____, William	Up	121
McKoy, Alexander	Hal	89
Maccoy, Thomas	Cpb	196
McCRACKIN/McCRACKING		
McCrackin, Alexander	New	37
_____, William D.	New	14
McCracking, James	Hab	20
McCRANIE/McCRANEY/McCRANY		
McCranie, John Sr.	Lwn	90
_____, John Jr.	Lwn	90
_____, John	Tlf	7
_____, John R.	Wyn	281
_____, Malcom	Lwn	89
McCraney, Danul	Lwn	89
McCrany, W.	Wks	354
McCRAW/McCRAY		
McCraw, M. W.	Mon	226
McCroy, John	Mad	116
McCRARY/McCRAY		
McCrary, Asa	Wrn	227
_____, Bartley	Bal	28
_____, Evans	Wrn	201
_____, Ezra	Wrn	228
_____, Isaac	Twg	68
_____, Isaac	Wil	295
_____, James	Bal	28
_____, James	Hal	117
_____, John	Dec	19
_____, John	Tlb	348
_____, John	Wrn	226
_____, John T.	Twg	67
_____, Jonathan	Tlb	336
_____, Joseph	Hab	[illegible]
_____, Mathew	Mon	20[illegible]

Name	County	Page
McCrary, Mathew	Tlb	336
_____, Robert	Bal	32
_____, Robert	Hab	7
_____, Samuel	Hal	116
_____, Wiley C.	Crf	396
_____, William	Hab	38
McCray, Epafroditus	Han	162
_____, Marget	Wrn	229
_____, William	Rch	260
McCRAVY/McCRAVEY		
McCravy, Hezekel	Hab	27
McCravey, Micajah	Jks	324
McCREE/McCREA/MacCREAR		
McCree, William	Mon	224
McCrea, Gustavious	Twg	84
MacCrear, Ashworth	Cpb	201
McCRIEF, Samuel	Gre	294
McCRIMMON, Archibald	Tlf	8
_____, Duncan	Mtg	232
McCROAN/McCRONE		
McCroan, John	Tms	17
_____, Zilpha	Bke	153
McCrone, James	Twg	67
_____, Olly	Put	175
_____, Theophilus	Put	175
McCULLERS/McCULLAR/ McCULLARS/McCULLEH McCULLOAH/McCULLINS/ McCULLORS		
McCullers, Burwell	Jsp	395
_____, Charles	Hry	241
_____, Colson	Lau	23
_____, John Jr.	Bke	154
_____, John	Bke	154
_____, Jordan	Wrn	215
_____, Malcomb	Doo	88
_____, Matthew C.	Bke	125
_____, William Jr.	New	28
McCullar, Abagail	Wks	340
_____, Benjamin	Wks	331
_____, David	Wks	332
_____, George	Wks	348
McCullars, Hiram	Twg	72
McCulleh, Joseph	Hry	238
McCulloah, Joseph P.	Han	160
McCullins, Andrew	DeK	42
McCullors, William	New	28
McCULLOUGH/McCULLOCH/ McCULLOCK/McCALOUGH/McCULLO		
McCullough, Charles	Em	178
_____, Henry	Rch	289
_____, Jacob	Rch	291
_____, James, dec'd. Est	Lib	50
McCullough, Joseph	Em	177
_____, Sarah	Jef	402
McCulloch, John	DeK	46
_____, John J.	Jks	323
_____, Leonard P.	Ear	100
_____, Nancy	Ear	99
McCulluck, William	Clk	307
McCullock, William	Pik	122
McCalough, Sally	Em	164
McCullo, Mathew	Mon	223
McCURD, Elizabeth	Rch	255
McCURDY/McCURDEY		
McCurdy, James	DeK	62
_____, John S.	New	32
_____, Stephen	New	16
McCurdey, James	Mad	102
_____, John	Mad	101
McCURRY, Angus Sr.	Elb	130
_____, Angus	Elb	129
_____, John	Elb	143
_____, John	Elb	159
McCUTCHIN, Benj. R.	Hal	69
_____, John	Hal	69
_____, Joseph R.	Jks	331
_____, Robert	Hal	98
_____, Robert	Hry	200
_____, Samuel K.	Hal	98
_____, William M.	Trp	40
McDADE, David	Mon	196
_____, John	Gwn	328
_____, John Sr.	Rch	291
McDANIEL/McDANUL/ McDANEL/McDONIEL		
McDaniel, Alexander	Hry	250
_____, Alexander	Twg	64
_____, Allen	App	12
_____, Allen	Pik	132
_____, Andrew	Hab	15
_____, Arch.	Gwn	340
_____, Arch^d.	Gwn	359
_____, Arch^d.	Irw	302
_____, Bartlet	Tms	18
_____, Betsey	Gwn	375
_____, Buckner	Dec	4
_____, C.	Col	347
_____, Charles	Hry	237
_____, Charles	Jks	348
_____, Daniel	Dec	14
_____, Daniel	Hst	289
_____, Daniel	Jef	406
_____, Daniel	Jks	348
_____, Daniel	Tms	27
_____, David	New	46

McDaniel, David Rab 230
______, David L. Rab 226
______, Edward Wsh 239
______, Elizabeth Lau 23
______, Elizabeth Wks 331
______, Ennis Wks 356
______, Ennis Wks 357
______, Francis Up 119
______, Fredrick Jef 406
______, George Mwr 165
______, Isham Pul 146
______, James Col 347
______, James Wks 356
______, John App 12
______, John Dec 14
______, John Jks 345
______, John Jns 452
______, John Jns 457
______, John Lau 9
______, John Pik 127
______, John Tlb 324
______, Loshua Lau 4
______, Lee Han 162
______, Martha Mus 278
______, Milley Han 162
______, Normal Mwr 167
______, Samuel Fay 193
______, Samuel Up 110
______, W. Wks 337
______, William Bak 16
______, William Gwn 343
______, William Jks 348
______, William Tlb 347
______, Willie Han 162
______, Willis Hab 6
______, Wyatt Tms 25
McDanul, Absolum Pik 114
______, Benjamin Lwn 89
______, Mary Pik 126
McDanel, Loranza D. Hab 41
McDaniel, Daniel Lau 19
McDEARMON, Drury Put 216
McDEARMOT/McDERMONT/
McDERMETT/McKIRMIT/
McDURMENT/McDURMONT
McDearmot, Owen Jef 401
McDermont, Ballard Mor 271
McDermett, John Wil 300
McDirmit, Margaret Lwn 90
McDurment, Joseph Mad 100
McDurmont, Edward Wil 304
McDILDA, Elias Tat 378
McDILL, Elizabeth Gwn 344
McDill, George New 39
McDOLAND, James New 22
McDONALD/McDONOLD/
McDONNALL/McDONNALD/
McDONNOLD
McDonald, Alex McI 129
______, Alexr. Jsp 383
______, Alex[r]. Mon 175
______, Amy Frk 245
______, Archibald Frk 224
______, Barbara Fay 191
______, Cade Bib 61
______, Charles J. Bib 65
______, Donald Frk 224
______, George Gly 267
______, George McI 126
______, Giles Cam 185
______, Hiram Cow 370
______, Hugh Elb 126
______, Hugh Hal 127
______, Jacob Hal 89
______, Jacob Jns 439
______, James Bib 74
______, James Up 112
______, James Ware 187
______, James A. Jns 473
______, James A. Jns 474
______, James M. New 35
______, Jehiah Up 116
______, John Bib 73
______, John DeK 43
______, John Gwn 330
______, John Jef 411
______, John New 46
______, John Tat 377
______, John G. Wrn 222
______, Malcome Wal 134
______, Margaret Elb 130
______, Margaret McI 126
______, Mary Hal 89
______, Melton New 51
______, N. J. McI 124
______, Nancy Frk 220
______, Neely New 39
______, Randol Frk 219
______, Randol Lib 49
______, Richard Mon 176
______, Samuel Jns 436
______, Sarah Tat 379
______, Sar. Wks 334
______, Tilman Wal 145
______, William Hal 95
______, William Sr. McI 129

Name	County	Page
McDonald, William Jr.	McI	129
______, William A.	McI	124
______, William H.	Tlb	332
______, William M.	Crf	398
______, William R.	McI	129
McDonold, Andrew	Wrn	223
______, Daniel	McI	124
______, James L.	Wrn	210
______, John	Tat	374
______, John	Wrn	211
______, Sarah	Cht	242
______, Thomas	Gwn	376
______, William T.	Wrn	224
McDonnall, L. P.	Col	351
McDonnald, John	DeK	64
McDonneld, Joseph	DeK	64
McDONNOUGH/McDONOUGH		
McDonnough, James	Mad	103
______, Ransom	Mad	101
McDonough, James	Rch	261
McDOUGLE/McDOOGLE/		
McDOUGALD/McDOOGEL		
McDougle, Ananias	Mwr	164
______, Jonathan	Mwr	156
______, Samuel	Mwr	169
______, Thomas	Mwr	166
McDoogle, Ann	Wrn	225
______, Daniel	Frk	244
______, Matthew	Frk	244
McDougald, Daniel	Har	175
McDoogel, Sarah	Hab	53
McDOW, John	Hal	97
______, Samuel	Wal	150
McDOWELL/McDOWEL/McDOWALL		
McDowell, Isaac	Cow	374
______, James	Lwn	83
______, James	Har	191
______, John	Hry	239
______, John	Lin	62
______, Thomas	Tlb	331
______, Thomas C.	Tlb	328
______, William	Hal	112
McDowel, Charles	Pik	114
______, Daniel	Car	222
______, David	DeK	31
______, John H.	Mus	288
______, Mary Ann	Jsp	378
______, Nancy	Wrn	224
______, William	Jsp	378
McDowall, Danl.	Jsp	394
______, William	Hst	279
McDUFF, William	Bts	164
McDUFFIE/McDUFFEE/McDUFEE		
McDuffie, Alexander	Frk	242
______, Archibald	Tat	380
______, Archibald	Tlf	10
______, Daniel	Tlf	10
______, Daniel	Irw	298
______, Dougald	Tlf	10
______, James N.	Hst	276
______, John	Mus	287
______, John	Tlf	10
______, Malcom	Tlf	10
______, Murdock	Frk	242
______, Norman	Irw	298
______, Widow	Irw	298
McDuffee, Christia	Wsh	271
______, Duncan	Jns	435
______, James M.	Lee	31
McDufee, Duncan	Hal	93
McEACHIN/McEACHERN/McEACHEM		
McEachin, John	Tlf	7
______, Sarah	Tlf	7
McEachern, Peter	Tlf	5
McEachem, Archibald	Fay	189
McEARLY, Joseph	Wks	355
McELHANEY, William	Jsp	361
McELHANNON, Hugh	Jks	348
______, Jonah	Jks	331
McELMURRY, James R.	Bke	142
McELROY, Edward	Pik	121
______, Henry	Pik	122
______, Mark	Jsp	396
______, Nathan[1].	Har	182
______, Thomas	Har	182
______, Zachery S.	Pik	111
McELVIN/MCEVIN		
McElvin, Elias	Tms	21
McEvin, John	Jks	329
McEVER, Andrew	Hal	80
______, Brice	Hal	88
McEWIN/McEWEN		
McEwin, Isaac A.	Mad	117
______, Jos.	Mad	116
______, John N.	Mon	215
______, Thomas	Mad	116
McEwen, James H.	Mon	216
McFADIN, Mary	Bib	67
______, Mary	Bib	68
McFAIL/McPHAIL		
McFail, Eli	Lib	49
______, Fleming	Jsp	384
______, Isaac	Lwn	80
______, Judith W.	Lwn	79
McPhail, Dugal C.	Pul	153
McFARLAND/McFARLIN/		

McFARLANE/McFARLING/McFARLAN

McFarland, Charles	Mus	288
_____, John	Cht	268
_____, John	Frk	242
_____, John B.	Tat	381
_____, John J.	Mts	233
_____, Joseph D.	Tfo	354
_____, Peter	Jns	474
_____, Robert	Frk	228
_____, Sherod	Tfo	354
_____, Thomas G.	Mtg	233
McFarlin, Daniel C.	Cow	376
_____, John	Hab	47
_____, William	Hab	59
_____, William	Jns	433
McFarlane, Betsey	Rch	272
_____, William	Up	100
McFarling, Harvey	Bib	61
_____, Washington	Bib	62
McFarlan, Mary	Rch	264
McFERREN, Nancy	Frk	224

McGAHAH/McGAHA

McGahah, Benjamin	Jsp	363
McGaha, Michael	Jef	415
McGAINEY, McClendon	Dec	17

McGAR/McGARR

McGar, John	Rch	292
McGarr, Edward	Em	165
McGARITY, Gardner	Elb	136
_____, John	Elb	134

McGAUGHAN/McGUGAN

McGaughan, Joseph	Wks	342
McGugan, Duncan	Car	216
McGAULEY, Thomas J.	Wal	155

McGEE/MAGEE/McGHEE/MAGHEE/
McGEHEE/McGAHEE/MAGEEHEE

McGee, Alfred	Crf	405
_____, Ansel	Elb	127
_____, C.	Bal	44
_____, Davis	Crf	415
_____, Ephraim	Tlb	343
_____, Isom	Crf	412
_____, James P.	Hab	58
_____, Joseph	Crf	398
_____, Josiah	Crf	412
_____ Moret	Gwn	358
_____, Patrick S.	Hab	58
_____, Perry	Crf	405
_____, Sherrod	Mar	137
_____, William	Han	162
_____, William	Mon	210
Magee, John	Bke	122
_____, William	Wrn	201
McGhee, Abner	Put	186
_____, George W.	Trp	45
_____, John	Put	180
_____, John S.	Wil	319
_____, Levin	Trp	45
_____, Robert	Jns	439
_____, Thomas	Jns	433
_____, Thomas	Trp	55
_____, Thomas J.	Jns	439
_____, William	Put	174
Maghee, John	Col	349
_____, John	Col	354
_____, Laban	Bts	159
McGehee, David	Mwr	159
_____, Edward T.	Hst	261
_____, Esther	Jks	348
_____, Hugh	Elb	132
_____, Jacob	Up	103
_____, James	Bal	33
_____, James	Mor	269
_____, James	Irw	300
_____, John	Mor	253
_____, Thomas F.	Mwr	153
_____, William	Bal	33
_____, Willie	Mwr	157
McGahee, James	Wal	162
_____, Osborn	Mwr	153
_____, Thomas	Wal	165
_____, William	Wal	165
_____, William J.	Mwr	166
Mageehee, Nathan	Wsh	263
McGeehee, William B.	Pul	149

McGIBANY/McGIBENEY/
McGIBONY

McGibany, Erasmus	Gre	293
_____, William	Gre	301
McGibeney, William	Wal	162
McGibony, James C.	Put	174
McGILL, Archabel	Hab	31
_____, James	Gwn	322
_____, John	Cht	255
_____, John	Gwn	332
_____, Norris	Lin	66
_____, Peter	Mtg	233
_____, Robert	Lin	66
_____, Thomas	Lin	66
McGILLES, Hannah	Cam	182
McGILLIS, T. K.	Bry	86

McGINLEY/McGINLY

McGinley, Hugh	Rch	286
McGinly, John	Pik	124
_____, Thomas	Mon	189

Name	County	Page
McGINNIS/McGINIS/McGENNIS/ McGUINIS/McKINIS/McKINNIS/ McKANICE. Also see McInnis		
McGinnis, Alexander	Jks	321
______, James	Lau	20
______, John	DeK	36
______, John	Jks	319
McGinis, James Sr.	Gwn	310
______, James Jr.	Gwn	311
______, Stephen	Gwn	310
McGennis, Joseph	Cht	244
McGuinis, William	Jks	330
McKinis, John	Dec	14
**McKinnis, B. (slave)	Rch	257
McKanice, James	Jsp	356
McGINTY, George W.	Pik	129
______, Isaac	Mon	190
______, James	Mon	225
______, James	Wil	294
______, Josiah	Pik	117
______, Meshack	Jns	474
______, Robert	Han	162
______, Robert	Mon	225
______, Shaderick	Bib	65
______, William	Bal	37
______, William	Mon	177
McGIRT/McGUIRT/McGURTH		
McGirt, David	Mwr	167
McGuirt, William	Mwr	167
McGurth, Lawrence	Cht	256
McGLAMEY, George	Wrn	220
McGLAUGH, Joseph	Mon	209
McGLAUSON, Jeremiah	Bts	170
McGLAWN/McGLAUHORN		
McGlawn, Daivid	Jns	442
______, Hardy	Mon	174
______, Hardy Jr.	Mon	213
______, John	Pik	128
McGlauhorn, Luke	Jef	403
______, Susannah	Jef	483
McGONEGAR, F.	Cht	271
McGOUGH/McGOURK		
McGough, David	Gre	301
______, James	Mon	193
______, John	Gre	301
______, Robert	Mon	193
______, Thomas	Bts	162
McGourk, Evan	Hry	238
McGOWEN: also see Megowen		
______, Alexandria	Dec	12
______, Anthony	Dec	12
______, John, dec'd. Est.	Lib	50
McGowen, Joseph	Dec	11
______, Joseph Sr.	Lib	49
______, Joseph F.	Lib	50
______, Sarah S.	Lib	50
______, William	Wks	350
McGRADY/McGRADEY/McGRAWDY		
McGrady, Charles	DeK	40
______, Peter B.	Bib	70
______, Robert	Bts	178
McGradey, Archibald	Mad	105
McGrawdy, Silas	DeK	63
McGRATH, Roger	Mus	285
McGRAW/MAGRAW		
McGraw, C.	Wal	158
______, Cornelious	New	44
______, Ephraigim	New	27
______, George	Hab	9
______, James	DeK	32
______, John	Bib	71
______, John P.	Bib	52
______, Thomas	Rch	260
______, William	Hab	9
Magraw, Jesse	Wrn	212
McGREGGOR/McGRIGOR/McGRIGGER		
McGreggor, Rhesa	Gwn	329
McGrigor, Alexander	Bib	56
______, Charles	McI	122
McGrigger, Duncan	Mtg	233
McGRIFF, James	DeK	39
______, James	DeK	58
______, William	DeK	28
McGRUDER: also see Magruder		
______, Edward	Wal	134
McGUFFY, John Sr.	Hry	229
______, John Jr.	Hry	229
McGUIRE/McGURE/MAGUIRE		
McGuire, A. B.	Wal	149
______, Abner	Gre	275
______, Anderson	Elb	160
______, David	Gwn	334
______, Federick	Jks	311
______, Frances	Ogl	62
______, Frances	Trp	52
______, James P.	Gwn	336
______, John S.	Elb	153
______, Richard L.	Mor	244
______, Sam.	Jks	317
______, Shelton	Jks	343
______, Thomas	Elb	127
______, Thomas	Gwn	336
______, William D.	Elb	126
______, William S.	Rab	233
McGure, Zemima	Hal	80

Name	County	Page
Maguire, John J.	Rch	275
McGULLON/McGULION		
McGullon, Polly	Gwn	377
McGulion, Henry J.	Hal	111
McHARGUE, John	Up	103
McHENRY, John	Hst	278
McHUGH, Charles	Gwn	311
McINNIS/McINES; also see McGinnis		
McInnis, Ach[d].	Irw	299
______, Daniel	Tlf	10
______, John	Tlf	9
______, M.	Bak	19
______, Rody	Tat	373
McInes, Daniel	Irw	304
McINTIRE/McINTIER/McINTYRE/ McENTIRE/McENTYRE		
McIntire, James	Hab	56
______, John	Cht	254
______, John	Hab	55
______, Jonathen	Hab	48
______, Peter	Ware	189
______, Philip	Hab	49
McIntier, Hannah W.	Lwn	82
McIntyre, Archa. C.	McI	126
______, Daniel	Mtg	234
______, Hugh	Tlf	6
______, Robert	Put	202
McEntire, Joseph	Hab	10
McEntyre, James	Frk	249
______, Joseph	Frk	230
______, Thomas C.	Frk	231
McINTOSH, Alexander	Mtg	234
______, Alex. S.	McI	129
______, Daniel	Jsp	366
______, Daniel	Mor	261
______, Elsy	McI	129
______, Ishmael	Cht	249
______, James	Wil	305
______, Jesse	Mor	239
______, Jesse D.	Fay	193
______, John	Mon	189
______, John H.	Cam	186
______, John N.	McI	129
______, Lachlan	McI	129
______, Martha	Mor	239
______, Robert	Lib	50
MacINVALE, James	Cpb	200
______, James	Jns	429
______, John	Ran	247
______, John C.	Cpb	200
______, Robert	Jns	446
McIVER, A.	Rch	263
McIver, Alexander M.	Lib	50
______, Andrew	Mad	98
______, Daniel	Hry	211
______, John	Gwn	367
______, Zilpha	Bke	149
McJENKINS, John S.	Frk	227
McJUNKIN, David	Wil	298
McKANE/McKAIN		
McKane, Hugh	Har	184
______, Hugh	Mon	194
McKain, H. M.	Mon	223
McKAINEY, John	Jsp	379
McKAMER, James	Jsp	369
McKASTEL, Murdock	Wal	157
McKAY/McCAY/MacKAY		
McKay, Archibald	Tlf	9
______, Charlotte	Mon	218
______, Daniel	Mon	209
______, E.	Cht	251
______, Hugh	Jns	470
______, John	Tlf	9
______, Neill	Tlf	6
______, Thomas	Mon	217
McCay, George	Bke	148
**MacKay, Alexander (slave)	Rch	275
McKEE/McKEY/McKEES		
McKee, Allen	Jsp	360
______, Eliza	Hry	251
______, Elizabeth	Mad	117
______, Jacob	Hry	230
______, John	Mon	207
______, John	Mon	223
______, Louis	Jsp	383
______, Matthew	Wks	334
______, Thomas	Mon	188
______, William	Han	161
McKey, Jesse	Wks	351
______, Samuel	Frk	239
______, William	Hal	80
______, William	Wks	333
McKees, James	Jks	315
______, Ralph R.	Jks	335
**McKEEN, Mrs. (slave)	Rch	276
______, Van	Col	335
______, William F.	Tlb	333
McKEHEARN, Niell	Mwr	152
McKELER, Pter	Pik	126
McKELVY, John	Frk	230
McKENDREE, Thomas	Cam	185
McKENZIE/McKINSEY/McKINSIE/ McKINZIE/McKINZY		
McKenzie, Alexander	Rch	268
______, Carlos	Mon	212

McKenzie, Chesley Rab 224
_____, Eliza Cht 254
_____, Hardy Hst 277
_____, Henry Mus 291
_____, James Mon 210
_____, John Hst 277
_____, William Hst 282
_____, William Mon 201
McKinsey, Alexander Hal 73
_____, Benjamin Bib 76
_____, Duncan Col 346
_____, John Hal 81
_____, Sanders Hal 80
_____, Thomas Hal 127
McKinsie, Angus Har 184
_____, Nancy Wks 353
McKinzie, D. Cht 259
_____, George Jef 408
McKinzy, Daniel Dec 14
McKERLEY, Moses Elb 148
McKETHAN, Dougle Ran 243
McKIBBIN, Alexander Hry 242
_____, John Hry 243
McKIGNEY, Baley Jef 420
_____, James Jef 420
_____, Thomas Jef 418
McKINLY/McKINLEY/
MACKENDLESS
McKinly, Joseph Crf 415
_____, Robert Crf 414
McKinley, Chs. Up 106
_____, William Mon 204
Mackendless, Archibald D Ogl 96
McKINNEY/McKINNY/McKENNEY/
McKENNY/McKENEY/McKINNIE/
McKINNE/McKINNEE
McKinney, Benjamin Bib 74
_____, Charles Ware 187
_____, George Mon 188
_____, Eli Jns 433
_____, Hezakiah Bib 74
_____, Jeremiah Lin 74
_____, John Jns 474
_____, John Lin 75
_____, John Mon 222
_____, Moses Wrn 219
_____, Samuel Gwn 339
_____, Simeon Col 358
_____, Thomas Jns 474
_____, Travis Lin 73
_____, Travis Mon 188
_____, William Mon 187
McKinny, Caleb Bib 73
McKinny, Charles Jks 328
_____, Gresham Mon 188
_____, Joseph Bib 73
_____, Mikel Ran 249
McKenney, Charles Jks 327
_____, Hiram Car 218
_____, Justin Crf 405
McKenny, Mrs. Scr 312
_____, Joshua Up 106
_____, Julius Twg 71
_____, Robert Scr 312
McKeney, Thomas Rab 233
McKinnie, Abraham Hry 219
_____, John Hry 241
_____, William Hry 241
McKinne, Barna Rch 273
_____, Benjamin Hst 268
_____, George Wil 321
_____, Hansell Tlb 334
_____, Henry Tlb 336
_____, John Rch 286
_____, John Rch 287
_____, Mathew Tlb 335
_____, Sarah Rch 270
_____, William Tlb 347
McKinnee, Mardevai Wil 310
McKINNON/McKINON/McKENNON
McKinnon, Charles Tlf 9
_____, John Han 161
_____, John R. Cht 268
_____, Malcom Tms 26
_____, Neil Tms 19
_____, W. Cht 283
McKinon, Murdock Tlf 6
McKennon, John Mtg 234
_____, L. D. Wal 134
McKISSACK/McKISACK/
McKESSICK
McKissack, Jeremiah Up 100
_____, William Mwr 169
McKisack, John New 50
McKessick, Duncan Put 207
_____, John Put 207
McKNIGHT, Charles Wil 296
_____, James New 47
_____, Jane Wil 314
_____, John Cow 375
_____, Lydia Mad 116
_____, Thomas Hry 227
_____, William Trp 51
McLAUGHLIN/McLAUCHLAN/Mc-
LOCKLIN/McLOCKLAND/McGLAUGHLIN
McLaughlin, David Hal 134

McLaughlin, David Ogl 101
_____, David Wrn 200
_____, Duncan C. Elb 152
_____, Edward Wil 294
_____, James Hal 81
_____, James Ogl 64
_____, Thomas D. Wil 319
_____, William Wil 296
McLauchlan, Margaret Tlf 9
McLocklin, Nathaniel Clk 296
McLockland, Duncan Twg 79
McGloughlin, Ann DeK 44
McLARIN/McLERRON
McLarin, Harrison Cpb 210
McLerron, Estate of Cht 279
McLAWS, James Rch 266
McLEAN/McLAIN/McLANE/
McLEEN/McLIN/McLEON/also
see McClain
McLean, Allen Tlf 7
_____, Andrew Rch 258
_____, Augustus B. Jns 429
_____, Charlotte DeK 37
_____, E. R. Cpb 204
_____, J. DeK 26
_____, James Lin 64
_____, Jesse Jns 430
_____, John Ear 96
_____, John Fay 206
_____, John Mon 190
_____, Lauchlan Tlf 8
_____, Lemuel Wil 300
_____, Lucy Hst 294
_____, Oliver Fay 185
McLain, Hugh Har 176
_____, Samuel Ogl 91
McLane, Hugh Hst 272
_____, John Hst 271
McLeen, Margaret Cht 243
McLin, Hugh Bts 163
_____, John Bal 45
McLeon, Josiah DeK 61
McLeBERRY, Alden Bts 174
McLEMORE/McLIMORE
McLemore, Charles Trp 42
_____, Howel Em 171
_____, Wilson New 52
McLimore, Henry Hst 262
McLENDON/McLENDEN/McLENNAN/
McLANDON; also see McClendon'
McLendon, Beniah Car 222
_____, Bolen Lee 29
_____, Cassel Wal 149
McLendon, Dennis Jns 470
_____, Elizabeth New 40
_____, Gabl. Lee 27
_____, Gabriel Irw 302
_____, Hugh Jns 470
_____, Isaac Wil 317
_____, Joel Pul 162
_____, John Lee 28
_____, John Ran 249
_____, Jonathan Gwn 365
_____, Josiah Lee 28
_____, Lewis Jns 470
_____, Mary Wks 342
_____, Medad Lin 59
_____, Milly Crf 394
_____, Needham Ear 95
_____, Samuel Car 228
_____, Sarah Lin 65
_____, Silas Irw 302
_____, Simpson Wil 317
_____, Stephen Lee 29
_____, William Hst 295
_____, William Lee 27
_____, Willis Wil 318
_____, Zachariah Crf 394
McLenden, John Pul 143
McLennan, Kineth Mtg 231
McLandon, Amos Ran 242
McLEOD, Alexander Mon 227
_____, Angus McI 122
_____, Daniel Jns 470
_____, Daniel Ran 248
_____, Daniel Tat 374
_____, Duncan Han 161
** _____, F.H. (slaves) Cht 280
_____, James Lwn 82
_____, John Gly 264
_____, John Tat 377
_____, John S. Lwn 79
_____, M. Cht 283
_____, Mary Tlf 9
_____, Miley Lwn 82
_____, Murdock Mtg 234
_____, Murdock Pul 146
_____, Nancy Mtg 236
_____, William Tlf 9
_____, William L. Mtg 233
McLEROY/McKLEROY
McLeroy, Christiana Jns 470
_____, Henry Mad 102
_____, James Clk 310
_____, James Fay 181
_____, Jesse Jns 470

McLeroy, Jiles Clk 307
______, John Fay 188
______, John Jns 462
______, John Mad 99
______, John Mad 116
______, Mary Mad 106
______, Nedum Clk 308
______, William Clk 309
McKleroy, James DeK 58
______, John DeK 71
______, John Wal 164
______, Lewis Car 216
______, Samuel DeK 71
______, Thomas J. Car 228
McLESKEY: see McCleskey
McLUKES, James Wil 308
McLUNG, Jonas Gwn 318
MACMASTER, William McI 124
McMATH, Elijah Wrn 215
______, Eliza Wrn 219
______, Hackaliah Jns 439
______, John H. Jns 466
______, Philip Tms 25
______, William Jns 435
McMAHAN/McMAHON/McNAHAM
McMahan, David Mor 263
______, John Hry 199
______, John R. Bts 162
______, Robert Hab 19
______, Woodard Wal 163
McMahon, D. Cht 256
______, John Hab 20
McNaham, Barnett Wal 142
McMANUS, John Har 189
______, Leroy P. Bib 70
______, Mary Tlb 325
McMEEKIN, Elizabeth Wil 311
McMICHAEL/McMICAEL/
McMIKEL/McMICKEL
McMichael, Chs. Jsp 356
______, Elijah Bts 167
______, Elizabeth A. Bts 173
______, Ezekiel Crf 411
______, John Bts 162
______, John Jsp 371
______, John Tlb 346
______, Joseph Jsp 367
______, L. Mus 292
______, Matthew Bts 166
______, Samuel Crf 401
______, Shadrack Jsp 361
______, William Wal 137
McMicael, Seaborn Gre 281
McMikel, John Ran 247
McMickle, James Mon 214
McMILLON/McMILLAN/McMILLEN/
McMILLION/McMILION/
McMILLIAN/McMELLON
McMillon, Alex. Wks 354
______, Angus Mtg 232
______, Daniel Wks 354
______, Duncan Mtg 232
______, James Lin 61
______, Littleberry Gre 293
______, Mary Put 176
______, Micajah Twg 69
**McMillan, Mrs. (slave) Rch 262
**______, Mrs. (slave) Rch 272
______, Archibald Tlf 8
______, Archibald Tms 24
______, Daniel Han 162
______, Daniel Irw 302
______, Iver Ear 95
McMillen, Patrick Elb 128
______, William Gre 275
McMillion, Jesse Frk 228
______, John B. Frk 242
______, William A. Frk 212
McMilion, Elijah Hab 63
______, Loranzo Pul 150
McMillian, Duncan Lwn 91
______, Jeremiar Hab 49
______, William Har 180
McMellon, Amon Jns 443
______, Malcom Wsh 248
McMIN/McMEAN
McMin, Jese Hab 62
______, Robert Hab 62
McMean, Joseph Hal 84
McMULLEN/McMULLAN/
McMULLIN/McMULLINS
McMullen, Daniel Fay 203
______, George Jks 334
______, James Frk 254
______, James Fay 204
______, James Jks 315
______, James Lwn 82
______, Jeremiah Hry 249
______, Mary Jks 346
______, Peter E. Jks 321
______, William Jks 313
______, William Lwn 83
McMullan, Lewis Elb 144
______, Sinclair Elb 143
______, Thomas Elb 144
______, William Elb 143

Name	County	Page
McMullin, James	Twg	63
_____, John	Gwn	314
_____, Noel	Mon	202
_____, Sinclair	Up	104
McMullins, Mary	Crf	411
McMURPHY, Catherin	Rch	267
_____, Daniel	Rch	267
McMURRAY/McMURRY/McMURREY		
McMurray, James	Crf	411
_____, John	Mor	267
_____, William	Tlb	334
McMurry, David	New	38
_____, William	Crf	415
_____, William	Wks	333
McMurrey, Samuel F.	Twg	61
McMURRIN/McMURREN		
McMurrin, David	Bib	68
_____, James	Bib	65
_____, John	Bib	68
_____, Thomas	Bib	68
McMurren, Elizabeth	Lau	9
McNABB, Archibald	Tat	377
_____, Daniel	Tat	377
McNAIR/McNEAR		
McNair, Daniel	Dec	11
_____, Daniel	Hst	283
_____, Duncan	Jef	416
_____, Gilbert	Wks	337
_____, Gilbert	Wks	357
_____, James	Bke	145
_____, James J.	Har	189
_____, Louis L.	Jef	413
_____, Lusquil	Pul	143
_____, Martin	Rch	282
_____, Robert	Mon	226
McNear, Daniel	Col	348
_____, John	Wrn	225
_____, Robert	Wrn	225
_____, Samuel	Col	349
McNARIN, Alfert T.	Hab	52
McNAT, Robert	Put	177
McNEAL/McNEIL/McNEILL/ McNIEL/McNEEL/McKNEEL		
McNeal, Allen	Crf	397
_____, Daniel	Jef	402
_____, Henry	Hal	131
_____, James	Fay	190
_____, James	Jsp	387
_____, James	Wrn	232
_____, Nancy	Wrn	233
_____, Samuel	Tlb	330
_____, William	Tlb	330
McNeil, Cornelias	Tms	28
McNeil, John	Bal	44
_____, John	Frk	235
_____, John	Wks	35
_____, William	Frk	251
McNeill, Daniel	Lau	4
_____, Margaret	Mon	189
McNiel, John C.	Frk	250
_____, John T.	Mor	240
McNeel, Archibald	Bib	73
McKneel, John	Wal	172
McNEALY/McNEILY/McNEELY		
McNealy, Elenor	Jef	410
_____, Hugh	Jef	410
McNeily, Esther	Bke	120
McNeely, Jane	Em	165
MCNISH, Mrs.	Cht	282
McNORRELL, Henry	Bke	142
McNORTON, James	Mus	291
McPHAIL: see McFail		
McPHERSON/McPHEARSON		
McPherson, Archibald	Mar	140
_____, Arthur	Jns	470
_____, Calvin	Mon	181
_____, Huzza	Fay	186
_____, Martin L.	Jns	470
_____, Timothy	Jns	470
_____, William	Elb	122
McPhearson, Elijah	Car	223
McQUARTERS, Francis	New	27
McQUASH, Mary	Cht	271
McQUEEN/McQUEAN		
McQueen, Mrs.	Cht	281
_____, L.	Cht	266
_____, Rachel	Scr	313
_____, Sarah	Cht	248
McQuean, John	Mtg	232
_____, John D.	Mtg	231
McRAE/McREE/McREA/McRA		
McRae, Alexander	Tlf	8
_____, Alexander B.	Tlf	8
_____, Angus	Tlf	8
_____, Charity	Jsp	394
_____, Charity	Wsh	264
_____, Christopher	Mtg	231
_____, Daniel	Mtg	231
_____, Daniel	Tlf	8
_____, Duncan	Tlf	9
_____, Duncan	Tlf	10
_____, Farquhard	Mtg	231
_____, John	Tlf	7
_____, John	Tlf	10
_____, Noel	Mtg	231
_____, Norman	Mtg	236

Name	County	Page
McRee, Benjamin	Clk	298
______, Francess	Clk	298
______, John	Clk	297
______, Mary	Clk	315
______, Rowan	Hry	251
McRea, Archibald	Tlb	343
______, Daniel	Car	223
McRa, Christopher	Wal	128
McRIGHT, Blueford	Gwn	326
______, John	Gwn	334
______, Matthew	Cow	374
______, Mathew	Gwn	332
McROY/McRORY		
McRoy, Anderson	Ogl	76
______, Daniel	Hal	87
______, Sarah	Ogl	75
______, William	Ogl	70
McRory, John	Eff	107
McSWAIN, Alfred	Trp	44
______, Allen	Ear	98
______, Angus	Pik	128
______, Asa	Mor	260
______, Dennis	Mwr	157
______, Florida	Dec	14
______, Hiram	Mwr	159
______, Peter	Pik	129
McSWANN, Edmund	Cow	383
McSWINNY, Edmund	Tfo	365
McTARITY, Archabald	Elb	135
______, Delilah	Elb	135
McTERREL, John	Irw	303
McTYRE/McTYEIRE/McTEER		
McTyre, John	Rch	279
______, Kendall	Wrn	206
______, Robert	Put	202
McTyeire, Holland	Rch	278
McTeer, John	DeK	73
McURN, Edward	Wil	309
McVAY/McVEY		
McVay, David	Hst	284
______, James	Up	105
______, John	Han	162
______, John	Hst	284
______, John	Up	101
McVey, David	Wsh	242
McVEAL, Sarah	New	46
______, William	New	35
McVEES, William	Crf	400
McWADE, John	Scr	317
McWARTERS, William	Ran	250
McWATTY, Thomas	Jef	419
McWHIR, Rev. Wm. P.	Lib	50
McWHORTER/McWHORTOR/		
McWHERTOR/McWHERTER/		
McWHIRTER		
McWhorter, Alen M.	Car	227
______, George A.	Hal	92
______, Isaac	Cow	390
______, J. G.	Rch	256
______, John	Han	162
______, John	Ogl	91
______, Samuel S.	Han	161
______, William	Bts	171
______, William	Ogl	91
McWhortor, John P.	Bts	162
McWhertor, David	Hal	93
______, John	Hal	124
McWherter, James	Hal	72
McWhirter, Moses W.	Hry	222
MacWIER, Riley	Cpb	200
______, Thompson	Cpb	202
McWILLIAMS, Asa	Twg	79
______, Sally	Twg	80
______, Thomas N.	Hst	264
McWRIGHT, James	Hry	234

MABRY: also see Maybry

Name	County	Page
MABRY/MABERRY/MABERY/		
MABURY/MABEERS/MABREY		
Mabry, Alfred	Gre	305
______, Branch M.	Gre	300
______, Ephraim	Frk	227
______, Irvine	Gre	278
______, Joel S.	Frk	227
______, John	Gre	305
______, Joshua	Frk	226
______, Joshua	Gre	305
______, Mark	Frk	215
______, Robert W.	Gre	285
______, Solomon	Put	189
______, Thomas	Elb	141
______, Thomas	Gre	277
______, Thomas	Put	184
Maberry, Ephraigme	New	54
______, Ephraim M.	Up	111
______, James H.	New	36
______, Patrick	Hal	105
Mabery, Russel	Hal	105
Mabury, Allen	Wil	305
______, Jameson	Lin	75
Mabeers, Polly	Put	197
Mabrey, Daniel W.	Mon	195
MACA, Archabel	Hab	54
MACHAM, John	Pik	108
MACK, John	Wal	144
MACKEY/MACKY		

Name	County	Page
Mackey, Alexander	Pik	108
_____, Jonathan	Hry	240
Macky, Littleton	New	15
MACHITT, Joseph	Crf	407
MACON/MACKIN/MACKLIN		
Macon, Edwin H.	Gre	278
_____, Gideon	Up	100
_____, Henry	Har	188
_____, Pleasant	Har	175
_____, William G.	Han	161
Mackin, Bonaport	Gwn	320
Macklin, David	Cow	371
MADAMOISELLE (no other n)	Wil	301
MADDEN/MADDIN/MADIN		
Madden, David Jr.	Pik	112
_____, Michael	Hst	262
_____, Richard	Fay	201
_____, Samuel	Fay	205
Maddin, Abraham	Cow	390
_____, Dennis	Pik	124
_____, Eleas	DeK	49
_____, John	Rch	269
Madin, David Sr.	Pik	111
MADDOX/MATTOX/MATTOCKS/ MADDUX/MADOX/MATTOCK		
Maddox, Alexander	Put	202
_____, Ann	Hal	127
_____, Anthony	Gre	275
_____, Benjamin	DeK	30
_____, Benjamin W.	Gwn	362
_____, Chapman	Wrn	198
_____, Claiborn	Jks	315
_____, David R.	Lau	18
_____, Davis	Bts	171
_____, Edward	Hal	123
_____, Edward	Put	204
_____, Fieldings	Gwn	371
_____, George	DeK	59
_____, George	Jns	470
_____, Henry	Col	347
_____, Ira H.	Bts	174
_____, James	Trp	34
_____, Jesse	Bts	174
_____, Jesse	Tfo	361
_____, John	Gwn	328
_____, John	Jsp	385
_____, John	Lau	7
_____, John A.	New	6
_____, John C.	Put	202
_____, John G.	Jks	326
_____, John W.	Col	350
_____, Joseph	Clk	318
_____, Joseph	New	39
Maddox, Leutha	Up	104
_____, Lewis	Lau	7
_____, Martha	Gre	288
_____, Mary	Bts	174
_____, Nathan	Up	118
_____, Spencer	Bts	167
_____, William	Put	215
_____, William	Tfo	366
_____, William G.	Jns	434
Mattox, Aaron	Lwn	84
_____, Amelia C.	Wil	293
_____, David	Elb	140
_____, Elijah Sr.	Tat	374
_____, Elijah Jr.	Tat	381
_____, Hardridge	Mor	262
_____, Jesse J.	Jns	428
_____, John	Tat	371
_____, John Jr.	Tat	375
_____, John R.	Mon	215
_____, Michael M.	Tat	371
_____, Nathan	Elb	140
_____, Peter A.	Jks	320
_____, Samuel	Mon	217
_____, Seaborn	Mus	291
_____, William	Wil	292
_____, William S or G	Jns	435
Mattocks, Chandler	Hry	228
_____, Daniel	Gwn	345
_____, John	Gwn	345
_____, Lindsey	Gwn	320
_____, Patsey	Gwn	368
_____, William	Gwn	359
_____, William	Hry	227
Maddux, Jennet	Lau	24
_____, Patrick N.	Wrn	194
_____, Thomas	Wrn	192
_____, William	Tlb	328
Madox, Henry H.	Hal	119
_____, James H.	Mon	221
_____, Nathan	Pul	156
_____, Samuel	Mon	221
_____, Tabitha	Mon	221
Mattock, Stephen	Tat	380
MADRAY, George	Bke	117
MAELLOCK, Dicy	Col	334
MAFIELD, Obediah	Clk	301
MAGAHIRTY/MAGERITY		
Magahirty, Abner	DeK	43
Magerity, John A.	Wrn	205
MAGARE, William	Col	335
MAGBEE/MAGBY		
Magbee, Hiram	Bts	158
_____, Rachael	Bts	173

Magby, John Jks 341
_____, Suzannah DeK 29
MAGILL, Chs. Cam 183
MAGNES, Abner Hab 31
MAGNON, Elijah Jns 462
MAGOHED, William Col 350
MAGRUDER/MARGRUDER
ALSO see McGruder
Magruder, Archer Col 351
_____, George Rch 283
_____, John Bke 123
_____, Martha Col 344
_____, Sarah Col 352
_____, William Col 354
Margruder, Archie Col 346
_____, Benj. Col 344
_____, George Col 345
_____, Hez. Col 342
_____, William Col 342
MAGUOIRK/MAGOUIRK
Maguoirk, James Up 109
Magouirk, John New 29
MAHAFFY/MAHAFFEY/MEHAFFY
Mahaffy, Carter DeK 48
_____, James Hry 219
_____, Thomas DeK 61
Mahaffey, Ira Gwn 331
Mehaffy, Hiram Car 224
_____, John Jr. Car 224
_____, John Sr. Car 224
_____, Martin Car 224
_____, Thomas Car 222
MAHAR, John Wal 162
MAHARRY, Charity Rch 262
_____, J. P. Rch 263
MAHON/MAHONE
Mahon, Ellen E. Jns 444
_____, James Gwn 349
_____, William Put 184
Mahone, James Jns 470
_____, Nixon Tlb 345
_____, Peter F. Tlb 326
_____, Rowland Tlb 329
_____, Thomas Har 175
MAHONEY/MAHONY
Mahoney, James Lin 64
_____, George Lin 64
Mahony, William Col 342
MAINOR/MAINER/MAINNER/
MAYNOR
Mainor, Sarah Bke 129
_____, Willis Bke 117
Mainer, Hosea DeK 36
Mainner, Alford DeK 37
Maynor, Jesse Crf 397
_____, John D. Har 179
_____, William H. Har 186
MAIZE: see May/Mays
MAJORS/MAJOR
Majors, Daniel Clk 300
_____, Daniel Wks 345
_____, Eleanor Twg 79
_____, James Car 223
_____, Thomas Wks 345
_____, William Car 216
_____, Wright Car 220
Major, Richard Hal 69
MALCOM/MALCOME
Malcom, Alexander Wal 154
_____, Barnett Mor 263
_____, Ganaway Mor 264
_____, James Mor 264
_____, John Mor 264
_____, Mary Cam 188
Malcome, David Wal 129
_____, George Wal 165
MALLARD/MALLED
Mallard, John Bke 147
_____, John, dec'd. Est. Lib 49
_____, Lewis Lin 67
_____, Thomas Lib 50
Mallad, Elijah Wrn 204
MALLETT, Jessee Jr. Mon 202
_____, Jessee Sr. Mon 211
_____, Samuel Mon 201
MALLIGO, William Cht 267
MALLORY/MALLERY/MALLARY/
MALORY
Mallory, Henry Gre 274
_____, John Gre 272
_____, Lucy Wil 319
_____, Mary Wil 317
_____, Stephen H. Wil 317
_____, Thomas Bke 152
_____, Thomas Gre 303
_____, William Jks 338
_____, William Trp 33
Mallery, John Cht 249
_____, William Cht 265
Mallary, C. D. Rch 276
Malory, Horrace Mor 271
MALONE/MALONG
Malone, Allen Hal 88
_____, Burrel Pik 125
_____, Chs. Bal 41
_____, Christopher Hry 204

Name	County	Page
Malone, Clement	Gre	280
_____, Daniel	Jns	474
_____, Frances	Jsp	388
_____, Gilbert	Mwr	160
_____, James	Col	342
_____, John	Bts	163
_____, John	Dec	17
_____, John	Jsp	381
_____, John A.	Bts	168
_____, Jones	Pik	125
_____, Ludwell E.	Pik	116
_____, Mary	Mus	281
_____, Robert	Cht	251
_____, Robert	Dec	4
_____, Robert	DeK	28
_____, Robert	Mon	223
_____, Robert	Rch	283
_____, Thomas	Col	336
_____, Thomas	Mon	175
_____, William	Dec	17
_____, William	DeK	26
_____, William B.	Up	106
_____, William P.	Trp	33
_____, Young F.	Gre	288
Malong, William H.	Fay	198
MALONY/MALONEY		
Malony, S. M.	DeK	27
_____, William	DeK	44
_____, William	DeK	54
_____, William W.	DeK	48
Maloney, Robert	Gwn	353
_____, Samuel	Gwn	353
MALOY/MALAY		
Maloy, Jane	Hab	14
_____, John	Bib	59
_____, John V.	Trp	40
_____, William	Hab	33
Malay, John	Dec	16
MALPASS/MALPHURS/MALPHUS		
Malpass, John	Jsp	378
_____, John	Tlb	322
_____, Morris	Wsh	247
Malphurs, George U.	Cam	188
_____, John	Cam	188
_____, William A.	Cam	188
_____, William John	Cam	188
Malphus, Martha	Tms	16
MALTBIE, William	Gwn	365
MANARD/MENIARD/MINIARD/ MINYARD		
Manard, Stephen	Bib	56
Meniard, Thomas	Hal	101
_____, William	Hal	101
Miniard, John	Jks	322
_____, Thomas	Mus	291
Minyard, James	Frk	243
_____, Richard	Trp	33
MANCURS, Elijah	Crf	412
MANDECHI, Nicholo	McI	122
MANDERS, Samuel	Gwn	333
MANDEVILLE/MANDVILLE		
Mandeville, Mary	Rch	256
Mandville, Charles G.	Jns	441
MANE/MANES		
Mane, James	Wal	153
_____, John G.	Clk	312
_____, Lewis	Wal	137
Manes, Benjamin	Tlb	326
MANER/MANOR		
Maner, Elijah	Clk	310
_____, James	Clk	311
_____, William	Clk	310
Manor, George H.	Scr	310
_____, John	Scr	310
MANESON, L. B.	Wal	135
MANGHAM/MANGRUM/MANGRAM/ MAGHAM/MANGUM/MANGHON/ MANGHAN		
Mangham, Ann	Gly	265
_____, Bryant S.	Hst	272
_____, Henry H.	Mwr	165
_____, James	Jks	335
_____, James C.	Gly	268
_____, James M.	Bts	164
_____, James P.	Pik	113
_____, Jessy	Jks	335
_____, John C.	Pik	119
_____, John G.	Tlb	324
_____, Josiah	Tlb	342
_____, Robert	Tlb	337
_____, Sarah Ann	Pik	113
_____, Thomas	Up	112
_____, William	Hry	251
_____, Willie E.	Pik	113
_____, Willis	Pik	113
_____, Wylee	Pik	109
Mangrum, Arthur	Jks	332
_____, Howell	Frk	229
_____, Howell	Frk	256
_____, William	Jks	337
Mangram, James	DeK	49
_____, William	DeK	49
Magham, Thomas R.	Ran	244
Mangum, Samuel	Gwn	321
Manghon, Wiley A.B.	Mor	262
Manghan, Thomas	Jns	454

Name	County	Page
MANLEY/MANLY		
Manley, Isaac D.	Frk	236
______, John	Ran	249
______, Mary	Frk	248
______, Moses	Frk	236
______, Richard	Har	180
______, Sally	Frk	248
______, Temperence	Frk	248
______, Washington	Ran	249
______, William	Clk	322
Manly, A. P.	Tlb	333
______, Abner F.	Hry	217
______, David	Hry	217
______, John F.	Hry	217
______, Joseph P.	Hry	201
______, Winney	Ogl	82
MANN/MAN		
Mann, Allen J.	New	45
______, Asa	Elb	149
______, Baker	Wal	141
______, Daniel J.	Bry	88
______, David	Wks	348
______, David W.	Hst	265
______, Edmon	New	48
______, Henry	Gwn	338
______, Henry	Jks	314
______, Hiram	Hst	271
______, James	Gwn	334
______, James	Hry	199
______, James H.	New	48
______, James L.	DeK	46
______, James W.	New	48
______, Jeremiah	Elb	149
______, Jeremiah D.	Fay	186
______, Jesse	Fay	191
______, Jesse	Gre	280
______, Joel	Jks	322
______, Joel	Pik	131
______, John	Hab	12
______, John	Han	161
______, John	Lee	34
______, John	Mon	197
______, John D.	Fay	191
______, John H.	Rch	260
______, John R.	Elb	141
______, Jonathan	Fay	195
______, Judith	Rch	257
______, Luke	Bry	84
______, Mary	App	8
______, Nancy	Wil	309
______, Peter	Fay	203
______, Sarah	Lib	50
______, Stephen A.	Elb	147

Name	County	Page
Mann, Thomas	Lib	49
______, William	New	40
______, William	Tat	375
______, William B.	New	20
______, Young	Crf	413
Man, David	Wal	167
______, John	Put	188
______, John W.	Dec	7
______, Reubin	Mor	248
______, William	Wal	150
MANNING/MANING		
Manning, Benjamin	Hst	289
______, Britain	Trp	34
______, Cassander	Wsh	273
______, Elizabeth	Hal	104
______, Henry	Mad	104
______, Isaiah	Put	196
______, James	DeK	59
______, Jarvis	Twg	75
______, John	DeK	58
______, John	Pik	128
______, John	Wal	145
______, John B.	Jns	434
______, Joseph	Wyn	283
______, Littleton	Wal	172
______, Mark	Fay	205
______, Margiman	Hal	72
______, Martin	Wyn	281
______, Michael	Trp	34
______, Moses	Wyn	281
______, Osburn	Hal	72
______, Redrick	Fay	194
______, Reubin	Lau	23
______, Sarah	Lau	24
______, Thomas	Tlb	329
______, Walter	DeK	63
______, William	Mad	108
Maning, Alexander	Doo	88
______, Larry C.	Doo	88
______, Mathias	Cam	191
______, Richard	New	12
MANSEL/MANSELL/MANCIL/ MONSEL		
Mansel, Edward	Pul	146
______, George Jr.	Pul	162
Mansell, William	Ware	186
Mancil, Robert	Twg	82
Monsel, Seth R.	Put	191
MANSFIELD, Eli	Han	161
______, Federrick	Dec	18
______, Lucius	Jsp	369
______, William	Dec	18
MANSON, Frances E.	Hry	251

Name	County	Page
Manson, James	Wks	342
______, John	Hst	273
______, Margaret	Jef	413
______, Mary	Jef	413
MANTZ, P. H.	Rch	257
______, P. H.	Rch	275
______, William	Elb	128
MANUS, Nathan	Cpb	198
MAPLES, John	Frk	214
______, John	Tlb	345
______, Nathan	Bak	19
______, Thomas	Dec	12
MAPP/MAP		
Mapp, James	Tfo	369
______, Littleton	Han	162
______, Mary	Gre	277
______, Robert H.	Han	161
______, William F.	Bts	174
______, William F.	Wal	153
Map, John A.	Put	204
MAPPIN, Martha	New	23
MARABLE, Champeon	Mor	256
______, Christopher	Clk	306
______, George	Wal	126
______, Joel	Wal	154
______, John B.	Wal	123
______, Mathew	Wal	131
______, William	Ogl	102
MARBACH, Cathr.	Cht	264
MARCH, James	Em	175
MARCHANT, Joseph	Tlb	348
MARCHMAN/MARCHMANS		
Marchman, Albert	Put	191
______, Asa	Put	193
______, Ebee	Put	191
______, James	Put	212
______, John	Hry	247
______, Stephen	Put	190
______, William R.	Trp	44
Marchmans, Henry R.	Hry	246
MARCHMONT, John	McI	127
MARCUS, Hannah	Put	180
______, Mary	Jns	466
______, Peter	Mus	288
______, William E.	Put	180
MARCY, Joel	Mus	287
MARIDAY, John	Car	217
MARINER/MARONA		
Mariner, John	DeK	72
Marona, William	Car	225
MARKET, James E.	Up	118
______, John	Crf	409
MARKS/MARK		
Marks, Christian	Rch	274
______, Richard T.	Mus	280
______, Robert	Wrn	207
______, Samuel	Wrn	209
______, Stephen	Wrn	209
______, Washington	Har	186
Mark, Henry	Jks	326
______, J. Ann	Cam	183
______, Samuel	Jsp	397
MARKUM/MARCRUM		
Markum, Hurl	Jns	434
Marcrum, James	Mus	280
MARLEY, Eliot	Crf	400
MARLIN, Henry	Mar	139
MARLOW, George C.	Hry	223
______, John	Hal	75
______, John	Twg	68
______, P.	Cht	264
______, Paul	Eff	110
______, Ransom	Jks	338
______, Sarah	Pul	154
______, Stephen	Eff	111
MARLER, Thomas H.	Wil	288
MARQUAND, Tenab	Cht	260
MARR/MARS/MERR		
Marr, Lloyd	Mad	99
Mars, A.	Lee	29
______, Jacob	Cht	242
Merr, Dempsey	Pul	157
MARRIN, Ann	Mor	253
MARSH, John	Jns	432
______, John	Wrn	222
______, L. B.	Bke	119
______, Mulford	Scr	312
______, Nathan	Fay	200
______, Nathaniel	Wrn	224
______, Reuben	Irw	298
______, Robert	Wrn	230
______, Tarnor	Jns	474
______, William	Har	186
MARSHALL/MARSHAL/MARSHEL		
Marshall, Allen	Jns	429
______, Andrew	Cht	270
______, Asa	Crf	397
______, Benjamin	Tlb	340
______, Chesly	Crf	395
______, Daniel L.	Col	360
______, David	Jns	440
______, Elizabeth	Jsp	366
______, Frances	Clk	307
______, G. B.	Rch	277
______, G. B.	Rch	286
______, George Y.	Han	162

Marshall, Henry Irw 298
_____, J. O. Col 336
_____, James Cht 268
_____, James, Plantation Cht 279
_____, Jiles P. Col 343
_____, John Han 160
_____, John Jns 440
_____, John Rch 254
_____, Joseph Y. Col 360
_____, Levi Col 360
_____, Mathew Jns 429
_____, Nakor Put 177
_____, Stephen Put 172
_____, Stephen B. Put 172
_____, Susan Col 360
_____, William Cht 265
_____, William Jns 441
_____, William B. Har 175
_____, William S. Bke 122
Marshal, Ann Jef 411
_____, John Mon 184
_____, Joseph Jef 411
_____, Joseph Jef 409
_____, Joseph Jef 422
_____, Louis F. Jef 411
_____, Matthew Hst 270
_____, Mathew Jef 424
Marshel, Abraham Pik 125
_____, John Pik 118
MARSHBURN/MASHBURN/
MASBORN/MASBURN
Marshborn, Joseph Jsp 356
Mashburn, David Doo 78
_____, Nancy Jns 430
Masborn, Thomas Pul 161
Masburn, Daniel Pul 159
MARTIAL, Jesse S. Cow 388
MARTIN, Abel Wrn 224
_____, Abner Hab 33
_____, Abraham Gwn 347
_____, Abm. Jr. Gwn 315
_____, Abraham Hal 83
_____, Alexander Clk 319
_____, Alexander Hab 72
_____, Alexander Ran 247
_____, Alexander Rch 263
_____, Allen Gwn 310
_____, Allen Mon 187
_____, Andrew DeK 47
_____, Andrew Frk 253
_____, Angus Lib 49
_____, Angus Rch 292
_____, Arron D. Ear 98
Martin, Asa Put 193
_____, Austin DeK 47
_____, Austin Up 99
_____, Barclay Mus 281
_____, Bartley Jks 332
_____, Barton Bts 169
_____, Benjamin Hab 32
_____, Benjamin Hst 264
_____, Bennet Ogl 79
_____, Bird Wsh 246
_____, Catharine Bib 51
_____, Charles Jks 328
_____, Charles B. Jks 317
_____, Cheremiah Hab 30
_____, Clarke Ogl 68
_____, Crawford Jns 442
_____, Daniel Mwr 160
_____, Daniel Ware 185
_____, David Hal 73
_____, David Pik 117
_____, Edmund Rch 254
_____, Elias Bul 93
_____, Elijah E. Bul 95
_____, Elijah Hal 82
_____, Elijah Jsp 396
_____, Elijah Ogl 93
_____, Elijah Pik 108
_____, Elisabeth Ogl 63
_____, Elizabeth Wal 164
_____, Emanuel Bry 88
_____, Ewel Jks 342
_____, Frances A. Dec 7
_____, Francis S. Pik 120
_____, Gabrail Han 162
_____, George Gwn 376
_____, George Gre 291
_____, George New 18
_____, George W. Cow 390
_____, George W. Mor 245
_____, Green Bts 169
_____, Green Wsh 258
_____, Henry Jks 344
_____, Hezekiah Ogl 63
_____, Ira L. Fay 206
_____, Isaac Cow 372
_____, Isaac Wal 139
_____, Isabel Lib 50
_____, Israel Pik 116
_____, Jacob Hal 74
_____, Jacob Hal 80
_____, Jacob Jks 347
_____, James Bke 128
_____, James Cam 189

Name	County	Page
Martin, James	Cht	270
______, James	Em	176
______, James	Frk	240
______, James Jr.	Frk	249
______, James	Gre	297
______, James	Hab	61
______, James	Hal	82
______, James	Hal	99
______, James	Hst	281
______, James	Jsp	382
______, James Sr.	Mad	115
______, James (overseer)	Mor	239
______, James	Rab	229
______, James	Wsh	244
______, James	Wsh	258
______, James	Wrn	231
______, Rames B.	Elb	127
______, James B.	Mad	101
______, James B.	Tfo	354
______, James B.	Tfo	365
______, James C.	Gwn	369
______, James E.	Lib	50
______, James G.	Clk	296
______, James L.	Ran	242
______, James N.	Ran	243
______, James R.	Lee	27
______, Jeremiah	Hab	30
______, Jeremiah	Jns	457
______, Jesse	Bke	128
______, Jesse	Em	175
______, Jesse	Hal	73
______, Joe	Jef	402
______, Joel	Rch	292
______, John	Car	221
______, John	Crf	410
______, John	DeK	27
______, John	DeK	64
______, John	DeK	71
______, John	Hab	32
______, John	Hal	90
______, John	Hal	116
______, John	Hst	292
______, John	Jks	332
______, John	Jns	457
______, John	Lib	49
______, John	Mad	115
______, John	Mon	220
______, John	New	7
______, John	Pik	112
______, John	Rch	255
______, John	Tlf	10
______, John	Twg	80
______, John	Wsh	242
Martin, John	Wsh	266
______, John	Wsh	275
______, John F.	Gwn	364
______, John M.	Bul	95
______, John N.	Lau	21
______, John R.	New	6
______, John S.	Mon	175
______, John S.	Wrn	231
______, Jonathan	Hal	96
______, Joseph	Hal	79
______, Joseph	Twg	64
______, Joshua	Hal	82
______, Kinchin	Twg	64
______, Larry	Wrn	225
______, Levi	Pik	118
______, Levi	Tat	379
______, Lewis	Irw	304
______, Linwood	Col	344
______, Lorette	Lib	50
______, Lucretia	Gre	290
______, Lucy	Gwn	377
______, Mahala	Frk	247
______, Margaret	Hal	92
______, Marshall	Wil	320
______, Martha	Jsp	379
______, Martha	Ogl	82
______, Mrs. Mary	Bry	88
______, Mary	Pik	118
______, Mary	Rch	286
______, Melissa	Ogl	72
______, Micajah	DeK	36
______, Morris	Bal	43
______, Moses	Hal	83
______, Moses	Mus	282
______, Murdock	Hal	92
______, Nancy	DeK	47
______, Nathaniel	Lib	49
______, Nepthate	Mad	114
______, Nicholas	Bke	143
______, Noah	Lee	33
______, Oden	Wks	338
______, Oliver H.	Jsp	392
______, Patsey	Ear	9[illegible]
______, Peter	Frk	238
______, Peter	Hal	10[illegible]
______, Phillip	Hab	1[illegible]
______, Pleasant	Jks	33[illegible]
______, Randol W.	Clk	31[illegible]
______, Richard	Wsh	26[illegible]
______, Robert	Col	34
______, Robert	Cow	38
______, Robert	DeK	4
______, Robert	Hry	24

Martin, Robert	Jns	438	Mason, Gideon	Jns	430
______, Robert	Trp	47	______, Isaac (colored)	Bke	140
______, Robert	Twg	75	______, James	Tlb	343
______, Robert E.	Gre	273	______, Jehu	Hal	117
______, Samuel	Gwn	347	______, John	DeK	26
______, Samuel A.	Jks	311	______, John A.	Clk	317
______, Seaborn	Tlb	325	______, John C.	Put	218
______, Stephen	DeK	31	______, John M.	Han	162
______, Stephen	Hal	83	______, John W.	Bts	158
______, Stephen	Tlf	10	______, Laban	Jns	430
______, Thomas	Bib	65	______, Mary	Bts	160
______, Thomas	Em	175	______, Nancy	Gwn	367
______, Thomas	Hal	97	______, Squire	Frk	215
______, Thomas	Hry	246	______, Susannah	Clk	309
______, Thomas	Rch	289	______, Theophilus	Lau	18
______, Thomas	Wrn	210	______, Thomas	Clk	308
______, Thomas O.	Hry	246	______, Thomas	Han	162
______, Thompson	Mad	110	______, Thomas Jr.	Han	161
______, Vincent	Wks	338	______, Turner	Lau	5
______, Westly	DeK	25	______, Walker	Hal	95
______, Wiley	Mon	197	______, William	DeK	63
______, Wiley	Wks	338	______, William	Ear	96
______, William	Bul	97	______, William	Elb	160
______, William	Dec	5	______, William	Gwn	313
______, William	DeK	68	______, William	Gwn	343
______, William	Em	173	______, William	Har	178
______, William	Gre	289	______, William	Lau	18
______, William	Gwn	350	______, William L.	Lau	13
______, William	Gwn	365	______, Willie W.	Put	217
______, William	Jsp	396	MASSA, Aulston S.	Har	191
______, William	New	6	MASSENGALE/MASINGALE/		
______, William	Put	188	MASSINGALE/MASSANGALE		
______, William	Rch	270	Massengale, James	Mwr	164
______, William	Twg	80	______, Reddick	Trp	32
______, William	Wsh	250	______, Warren	Jns	428
______, William	Wil	295	______, Wright	Mwr	168
______, William	DeK	25	Masingale, Daniel	Col	362
______, William D.	Jks	313	Massingale, John	Gre	294
______, William D.	Mwr	154	Massangale, Nathan	Gre	304
______, William H.	Lib	49	MASSEY/MASSY/MASSAY/MASSIE		
______, William M.	Wrn	214	Massey, Abel	Wsh	271
______, Willis	Wrn	211	______, Abraham	Jns	466
______, Woody	Ogl	68	______, Abraham	Wsh	268
______, Wright	DeK	53	______, Andeson	Hab	57
______, Wright	Fay	184	______, Bardchian	Mus	292
______, Yearby	Jsp	366	______, Bennett	Wsh	242
MASES, John	Cpb	203	______, Berry	Hry	224
MASH, Henry	Tms	20	______, Cordy	Wsh	260
MASON, Andrew	Elb	160	______, David	Gwn	345
______, Benjamin	Jns	441	______, John	Ran	250
______, Churchill	Bts	160	______, John B.	Wsh	243
______, Ford	DeK	63	______, Reddick	Tlb	344
______, George	Wsh	276	______, Reubin	Mor	239

Name	County	Page
Massey, Ruth	Jns	457
Massy, Daniel	Twg	60
______, Elizabeth	Wsh	254
______, Needham	Hst	293
______, Prudence	Frk	256
______, Warren	Hst	293
Massay, Thomas	Hry	209
Massie, Peter	Gly	264
MASTERS, Levi	Elb	126
______, Mary	Elb	129
______, Robert	Crf	394
MASTIN, John	Har	184
MATCHETT, Holden	Irw	299
______, William	Irw	299
MATHER, Nathanel	Hab	60
______, Thomas	Hab	31
MATHERSON/MATHISON		
Matherson, Malcom	Ran	244
______, Philip	Ran	244
Mathison, Murdock	Bib	70
MATHEWS/MATTHEWS/MATHEW/ MATTHEW		
Mathews, Allen	Tlb	347
______, Andrew	Gwn	327
______, Archibald	Mon	198
______, Benjamin W.	Crf	396
______, Berry	Ogl	83
______, Burrell	Cpb	206
______, Charles	Jef	422
______, Coleman	Ogl	82
______, Daniel	Gwn	337
______, Edward	Wrn	215
______, Eliza	Wrn	219
______, Elizabeth	Jef	416
______, Enoch	Crf	399
______, Enoch	Pik	118
______, G. F.	Crf	400
______, Gabriel T.	Clk	319
______, Galba	Ran	244
______, Henry	Har	188
______, Isaac	Bib	68
______, Isham	Mar	142
______, James	Gwn	323
______, James	Jef	416
______, Jehu	Wrn	222
______, Jeminy	Wrn	212
______, Jesse	Jks	323
______, Jesse	Tlb	348
______, Joel	Up	100
______, John	Col	350
______, John	Crf	400
______, John	Crf	397
______, John	Hry	228
Mathews, John	Mon	202
______, John	Up	116
______, John	Wsh	265
______, John	Wsh	271
______, John	Wsh	273
______, John	Wrn	219
______, Johnathan	Bib	70
______, Joseph Jr.	Wrn	211
______, Josiah	Pik	129
______, Josiah	Tlb	339
______, Laban	Tlb	331
______, Loddiwick	Wsh	265
______, Loddrick	Tlb	327
______, Mary	Wal	163
______, Micajah	Crf	400
______, Milton	Jks	346
______, Moses	Pik	119
______, Nat.	Jns	436
______, Noel	Mus	282
______, Philip	Crf	395
______, Philip	Elb	149
______, Priscila	Hal	84
______, Rebecca	Cht	250
______, Rebecah	Wrn	204
______, Samuel J.	Crf	395
______, Sugar	Wal	152
______, Thomas	Ear	100
______, Thomas	Jef	419
______, Thomas	Tlb	328
______, William	Clk	320
______, William	Pik	115
______, William S.	Lau	13
Matthews, Abraham M.	Wil	298
______, Allen	Jks	321
______, Arthur	Up	95
______, B.	Wks	351
______, Ben	Wks	351
______, Cary	New	7
______, E., Estate	Gly	266
______, Frederick	Cow	386
______, Frederick	Jns	457
______, George G.	Gre	304
**______, H. (slave)	Rch	269
______, Isaac	Har	190
______, Isaac N.	Wil	323
______, Jacob	Ogl	65
______, James	Fay	196
______, James	Hst	29[illegible]
______, James	Jsp	360
______, James	Wks	35[illegible]
______, James	Wil	32[illegible]
______, Jarriott	Jsp	35[illegible]
______, Jeremiah	New	[illegible]

Name	County	Page
Matthews, Joel	Crf	394
______, John	Fay	196
______, John	Lib	49
______, John	Lin	63
______, Johnson	Hst	290
______, Jordan	Jns	462
______, Joshua	Lau	18
______, Juda	Jns	461
______, Lewis M.	New	7
______, Levi	Wks	341
______, Matthew	Jns	452
______, Morris	Pul	140
______, Naacy	Jks	347
______, Nancy	Jks	330
______, Peter	Bke	145
______, Phinias	Jks	327
______, Richard	New	11
______, Robert	Fay	186
______, Sally	Twg	87
______, William	Jks	329
______, William	Lin	60
______, William	Wil	312
______, William	Wks	349
______, William	Wks	354
______, Willis	Cpb	194
Mathew, Jesse	Crf	412
______, Mathias	Gwn	371
Matthew, Thomas	Mwr	155
MATHIS/MATTHIS/MATHIAS		
MATHUS/MATHES		
Mathis, And^{w}.	Gwn	340
______, Arch^{d}.	Gwn	340
______, Britan	Hal	83
______, Elijah	Bib	71
______, Elisha	Put	203
______, Ezekiel	Gwn	341
______, Francis	Gwn	339
______, Greene	Put	211
______, H. T.	Gwn	340
______, Howel	Doo	86
______, James	Dec	16
______, James	Gwn	366
______, James	Mon	199
______, Jane	Put	207
______, John	Doo	86
______, John	Gwn	339
______, John	Wsh	272
______, Liberty	Gwn	340
______, Littleton	Wsh	253
______, Mary	Put	206
______, Nelly	Put	191
______, Mrs. P.	Wsh	260
______, Thomas Sr.	Gwn	340
Mathis, Thomas	Gwn	341
______, Thomas J. J.	Gwn	341
______, William	Gwn	343
______, William	Put	175
______, William H.	Put	211
Matthis, Arthur	Mar	137
______, As.	Wks	334
______, David	Lwn	90
______, Edmond	Lwn	86
______, Gideon	Mwr	156
______, James	Lwn	91
______, John Sr.	Lwn	87
______, John Jr.	Lwn	84
______, Moses	Mon	224
______, Sarah	Doo	81
______, Thomas	Lwn	84
______, Tyre	Lwn	84
Mathias, Richard	Ran	241
______, William	Gwn	374
Mathus, Timothy	Bib	65
Mathes, William	Hab	50
MATSON, Sherrod	Jsp	381
MATTERSON, John	Jks	324
MATTY, Hamden D.	Fay	193
MAUK, Albert W.	Mar	139
______, Joel T.	Up	108
______, Matthias	Up	107
______, Samuel	Mar	138
______, Silas	Mus	290
MAULDEN/MALDING/MALDEN/		
MALDIN/MAULDIN		
Maulden, Andrew	Frk	220
______, James	Lib	49
______, Martha	Jns	438
______, Richard	Frk	217
______, Richard	Lwn	82
______, Tucker	Twg	74
Malding, Alexander	Hab	18
______, Elias	Bke	130
______, Fleming	Elb	126
Malden, Rucker	Gwn	360
Maldin, Wesley	Hab	51
Mauldin, Caleb	Bib	51
MAUND, Daniel C.	Put	205
______, Hardy C.	Bke	131
______, William W.	Bke	125
MAUPAW, L. N.	Cht	266
MAUR, Cyntha	DeK	57
MAXEY/MAXLEY		
Maxey, Barnabas	Ogl	103
______, Boze	Ogl	103
______, Edward H.	Clk	305
______, Edward R.	Trp	33

Name	County	Page
Maxey, Garland	Jsp	380
______, Hale	Ogl	103
______, James E.	New	34
______, Jeremiah	Bts	173
______, John G.	Clk	315
______, Josiah	Clk	299
______, Moses	Cow	369
______, Pouney	Jsp	367
______, Sarah	Clk	315
______, Thomas	Pik	106
______, William	Jsp	389
Maxley, Wilson	App	12
MAXWELL, Audley	Lib	50
______, Benjamin C.	Bry	85
______, Benson	Elb	148
______, Catherine	Wil	307
______, Felix	Wsh	258
______, Issabella	Cht	263
______, J.E.	Lib	50
______, James	Cpb	206
______, James	Hab	17
______, James	Mad	100
______, James H.	Jef	402
______, Joel	Elb	159
______, John	Elb	148
______, John	Mor	246
______, John	Mor	267
______, John J.	Bry	85
______, Mary	Cht	253
______, Nathaniel	Jsp	369
______, Reuben	Tlb	341
______, Robert	Ogl	96
______, Susan M.	Lib	50
______, Thomas	Elb	159
______, W. B.	Jsp	363
______, William	Elb	121
______, William	Elb	151
______, William	Lib	50
______, William	Twn	71
______, William A.	Bry	84
______, William M. W.	Lib	49
______, Wylie	Wil	306
MAY/MAYS/MAYES/MAIZE/MAZE		
May, Amasson	DeK	43
______, Becemb	Col	356
______, Benjamin	Bib	70
______, Bird	Gre	279
______, Daniel	Hry	237
______, David	Dec	11
______, Drury	Fay	186
______, Edmond	Wsh	268
______, Edm^{d}.	Wrn	233
______, George	Wsh	248
May, Isaac	Wal	144
______, James	Gly	265
______, James	Jns	472
______, James	Wrn	232
______, James A.	Rch	285
______, Jeremiah	Wrn	217
______, Jethro	Wsh	251
______, John	Cam	186
______, John	Hst	288
______, John	Wrn	233
______, John C.	Pul	158
______, John F.	Gly	265
______, Joseph	Tlb	333
______, Kinchin	Crf	401
______, Lery	Clk	320
______, Levi	Gre	284
______, Lucy	Wrn	213
______, Major	Gre	272
______, Mary	Wrn	233
______, Nathaniel	Mwr	150
______, Peter	Mar	138
______, Phillip G.	Cow	372
______, Richard	Mon	201
______, Rubin	Wrn	232
______, Saml.	Gwn	378
______, Samuel	Trp	41
______, Saml.	Wrn	230
______, Solomon	New	55
______, Talbot	Trp	37
______, Thomas	Gre	283
______, Thomas	Hst	294
______, Thomas	Wsh	253
______, Wyley	Jns	439
Mays, Allen N.	Frk	217
______, Benjamin	Lin	61
______, Benjamin	Pul	140
______, Edward	Hal	108
______, Harvey M.	Frk	222
______, James	Mon	220
______, James	Trp	39
______, James H.	Mon	198
______, John	Pik	127
______, John H.	Mon	204
______, Margarett	Frk	217
______, Richard R.	Bts	176
______, Robert F.	Hal	108
______, Stephen	DeK	47
______, Sterling	Jks	346
______, Thomas	Frk	23[illegible]
______, William	Har	178
______, William C.	Trp	3[illegible]
Mayes, Abney	Jsp	35[illegible]
______, Alfred	Wrn	21[illegible]

Mayes, John Wrn 194
_____, Thomas Hal 114
_____, William Wrn 216
Maize, John Pik 127
Maze, Rutherford New 46
_____, William Jks 336
MAYBANK, Andrew Lib 50
MAYBRY: also see Mabry
_____, Hinchia P. Car 226
_____, Parham P. Car 219
_____, Rezin E. Car 226
MAYER, Adrian N. Clk 326
MAYFIELD, Battle Gwn 353
_____, Briant Hal 103
_____, Edward W. Frk 232
_____, Elizabeth Frk 232
_____, Jacob Cpb 203
_____, James Gwn 350
_____, Jesse Car 219
_____, Philomon Frk 251
_____, Robert Bts 179
_____, Robert Wal 170
_____, Rubin DeK 69
MAYNARD, Elijah Mon 191
_____, Larkin Pik 107
MAYNOR: see Mainor
MAYO, Benjamin Wsh 266
_____, Burrel Wks 332
_____, David Wil 287
_____, Eli Wks 348
_____, Elisha Wal 141
_____, Ephraim Wks 349
_____, George Gwn 327
_____, Harmon Doo 87
_____, Jacob T. Bts 172
_____, James G. Bts 176
_____, Jesse Wks 349
_____, John Wal 151
_____, John Wks 346
_____, Micajah Gwn 350
_____, Richardson Bts 172
_____, William Pul 138
_____, William Wsh 247
_____, William S. Cow 374
MAZO, James Cam 191
_____, John Gly 266
MEACHAM/MEACHEM/MECHAM
Meacham, Barnett New 30
_____, Hendrick New 30
_____, Marcus New 30
Meachem, H. Bal 40
_____, John Up 103
Mecham, Henry Har 192
MEAD/MEADES
Mead, John Mad 103
_____, Minor Car 220
_____, Thornton Gwn 335
Meades, John Scr 314
MEADLEY/MEDLY/MEDDLEY
Meadley, Francis Wal 152
Medly, James Mus 290
Meddley, James Wal 156
MEADOWS/MEDDOWS/MEADOW/
MADOWS/MADOWES/MEDOWS
Meadows, B. B. App 10
_____, Baley Gre 305
_____, Barney Frk 223
_____, Christopher Frk 222
_____, Daniel Tfo 355
_____, Edward Put 212
_____, G. W. Wks 332
_____, Isaac Jks 336
_____, James Tfo 362
_____, Jedediah Frk 222
_____, Jesse Tfo 360
_____, Joseph Wks 333
_____, Miles Crf 400
_____, Riley Tfo 360
_____, Simeon Trp 38
_____, Vincent Tfo 361
_____, Wilie Tfo 362
_____, William Clk 305
Meddows, Benjamin Har 190
_____, Daniel Bke 125
_____, Jacob C. Ogl 77
_____, Jacob Ogl 77
_____, John New 28
_____, M. Lee 28
_____, Thomas Gwn 341
_____, William DeK 67
Meadow, Abraham Wal 155
_____, Abraham Wal 161
_____, Edward Wal 168
Madows, Isham Tfo 358
_____, William Sr. Tfo 355
_____, William Tfo 358
Madowes, Edward Tfo 356
Medows, James R. Em 166
MEALING/MEALY
Mealing, Henry Rch 265
_____, Henry Rch 280
_____, William E. Mus 284
Mealy, Stephen A. Cht 243
MEANS, Alexander Elb 136
_____, Alexander New 14
_____, Elizabeth Elb 125

Name	County	Page
Means, Hugh	Mor	239
_____, Jacob	Elb	121
_____, James	Up	111
_____, Johns S.	Wal	131
_____, Samuel	Gwn	378
MEARION, John	Col	346
MEARS, John	Hal	115
_____, William	Hal	114
MEASLES/MEASELS/MEAZLES		
Measles, William	Hst	278
Measels, Patience	Scr	303
Meazles, William	Jns	462
MECLENDER, Easther	New	33
MEDARIS, Thomas	Car	225
MEDFORD, William	Gwn	348
_____, William	Han	161
MEDLIN, Riley	Trp	45
MEDLOCK, Charles	Han	161
_____, Isham	Gwn	356
_____, James H.	Gwn	363
_____, John	Gwn	370
_____, John R.	Gwn	353
MEEKS/MEEK/MEAKES		
Meeks, Arch[d].	Gwn	332
_____, Blany	Gwn	333
_____, Britton	Gwn	333
_____, H.	App	11
_____, Jesse	Frk	219
_____, Josiah	Fay	198
_____, Littleberry	Gwn	331
_____, Littleton	Frk	217
_____, Littleton	Hab	14
_____, Scrven	Fay	187
_____, Shadrack	Har	191
_____, William	Hab	14
Meek, Allen	Em	168
_____, Arthur D.	Hry	219
_____, Charles	Em	167
_____, Jonas	Em	169
_____, Martin	Em	168
_____, Moses	Hry	214
_____, Robert	Hry	243
_____, Uriah	Jns	473
Meakes, Benjamin	Wsh	267
MEELROY, William	Dec	5
MEGAHA, Josiah	Hab	61
MEGANA, Reddic	Dec	9
MEGOWEN, Jacob	Dec	4
MEIGLES, Luke T.	Lau	7
MEIGS/MEIG/MEGS		
Meigs, John	Cpb	199
_____, Jonathan	Rch	285
**Meig, Jonathan (slave)	Rch	273
Megs, William	Mwr	155
MELAROM, Alex.	Cht	248
MELER/MEALOR		
Meler, Robert	Hab	21
_____, William	Hab	19
Mealor, Thompson	Jsp	352
MELICAN, James K.	Hab	56
MELL, John S. for estate of Wm. Osgood, dec'd	Lib	50
_____, Morgan	Lib	49
_____, T. S.	Cht	257
_____, William H.	Wil	289
MELLHORTER, Eli	Han	161
MELROSE, Kidd J.	Bib	56
MELSON, Appleton W.	Cow	386
_____, Canna	Jns	466
_____, Mary	Jns	437
_____, William P.	Mor	244
MELTON, Bauldy	Tlb	326
_____, Benjamin	Tms	18
_____, Benjamin	Wal	151
_____, Clem Sr.	Twg	64
_____, Clem Jr.	Twg	70
_____, Daniel	DeK	51
_____, Denson C.	New	10
_____, Henry	Tms	26
_____, James	Tms	18
_____, Jeremiah	Bts	158
_____, Jesse M.	New	8
_____, John	Cpb	197
_____, Jonas	Hab	61
_____, Josiah	DeK	66
_____, Moses	New	20
_____, Nancy	Tms	26
_____, Nathaniel	Tms	25
_____, Orah	Han	162
_____, Peter	Bke	139
_____, Robinson	Tms	18
_____, Roda	Wal	167
_____, Scynthia	Twg	82
_____, Seaborn J.	Put	196
_____, Tabitha	Clk	292
_____, Thomas	Mon	189
_____, Thomas S.	New	7
_____, William	Wal	149
_____, William D.	Crf	396
MELVILLE, Ann	Cht	250
MELVIN/MELLVIN		
Melvin, Daniel	Mar	144
_____, Thomas	Doo	80
Mellvin, Nathan	Bib	76
_____, Richard	Bib	76

Name	County	Page
MENIFEE/MENEFEE/ MENAFEE/MINIFEE		
Menifee, George	Hry	236
Menefee, William	Cow	373
Menafee, Charles	Tlb	341
Minifee, Tatum	Fay	196
MENZIES, Robert	Up	103
______, William J.	Jks	328
MEPHUIN, Daniel	New	10
MERACKINGE, David	Hab	13
MERCER, Asa	Trp	52
______, Benjamin	Bal	43
______, Christopher	Bry	87
______, Christopher	Doo	80
______, Colin	Ware	189
______, Francis	Ear	95
______, Henry	Wks	355
______, Hermon	Tfo	354
______, Hymerick	Twg	85
______, J.W.H.	Cht	250
______, James	Jsp	382
______, James	Jsp	397
______, James	Mad	98
______, Jesse	Pul	156
______, Jesse	Wil	289
______, Joel E.	Gre	283
______, John	Gre	278
______, Joseph	Jns	437
______, Joseph G.	Cow	384
______, Joshua	Hst	287
______, Joshua	Wil	306
______, Leonidas B.	Tfo	368
______, Levi	New	38
______, Mary	Pul	155
______, Merideth	Ran	245
______, Noah	Jns	437
______, Riley	Em	177
______, Samuel	Jsp	397
______, Silas	Tfo	354
______, Stephen	Bry	208
______, William	Bts	162
______, William B.	Jns	438
______, Williby	Lee	34
MERCHANT, C. S.	Rch	292
______, Isaac	Tlf	7
______, Jacob	Crf	404
______, Peter	Cht	277
______, William	Wks	355
MERCHERSON/MERKERSON		
Mercherson, James W.	Up	115
______, William	Up	115
Merkerson, John R.	Lau	21
MERCK/MIRK/MICK/MIROCK		
Merck, George	Hal	94
______, John Jr.	Hal	91
Mark, George	Jks	334
Mick, Reubin	Dec	4
Mirock, Anny	Twg	81
MEREAU/MERROW		
Mereau, Ed or	Cht	244
Merrow, Ed	Cht	244
MEREDITH/MERIDUTH		
**Meredith, Mrs. (slave)	Rch	276
______, Caty	Wks	353
______, James W.	Rch	254
______, John	Wks	353
______, Pleasant	Hst	270
______, Rebecca	Rch	262
______, Samuel	Wks	331
______, Tignal	Frk	232
______, Thomas	Twg	68
______, William	Mar	137
______, Wyat	Wks	351
Meriduth, Joseph	Wal	127
______, Nathan	Wal	145
______, William A.	Wal	131
MERIWETHER/MERIWEATHER/ MERRIWEATHER/MEREWETHER		
Meriwether, Alexander	Bib	59
______, Charles	Clk	298
______, Charles	Ogl	63
______, David	Jsp	378
______, Francis	Jks	321
______, George W.	Clk	298
______, James	Clk	326
______, Sarah T.	Clk	324
Meriweather, William	Col	339
Merriweather, James A.	Put	217
Merriwether, James	Cow	382
Merriwether, Thomas	Jsp	397
Merewether, Valentine	Ogl	82
MERONEY, John	Mad	111
______, Nathan	Mad	99
______, William	Mad	98
MERRICK, George	Rch	270
MERRILL/MERRELL/MERRILLIES		
Merrill, Benjamin	Car	218
______, Lemuel	Mwr	154
Merrell, Benjamin S.	Frk	235
Merrillies, Jane	Cht	251
MERRITT/MERRETT/MERIT/ MERRIT/MERET/MERITT/ MERRET/MERETT		
Merritt, Absalom	Crf	403
______, Abscilla	Bke	150
______, Barbara	Jsp	359

Merritt, Benjamin Jns 443
_____, Clarrissa DeK 36
_____, Comfort Bke 151
_____, Frederick Tlf 11
_____, Henry C. Hry 225
_____, Isham Frk 238
_____, James Mon 210
_____, Joshua Up 109
_____, Levi DeK 36
_____, Mickelberry Mon 210
_____, Rytto Crf 403
_____, Sherwood Hry 217
_____, Thomas Up 119
_____, Uriah Twg 65
_____, William Up 107
Merrett, Berryman G. Clk 313
_____, Bunnion Lwn 83
_____, Jesse Ear 97
_____, John B. Clk 311
_____, Stephen Wks 344
_____, Thomas Gre 286
_____, William Mon 186
Merit, Aaron Bul 92
_____, Frederick Irw 299
_____, Lucy Rch 265
Merrit, William Mar 139
_____, William Put 202
Meret, James Hab 6
_____, Loren Elb 120
Merritt, Alfred Irw 299
Merret, Burrell Irw 299
Merett, Lovet Gre 281
MERRY, Bradford Wil 287
MERSE, Mary Han 161
MERSHOW, Jeremiah Han 161
MESSER/MESSEUR
Messer, John W. Hry 246
_____, Malachi Bul 98
_____, William Bts 159
Messeur, Henry Lin 59
MESSICK/MESSEX/MESSUX
Messick, Jeremiah Tlb 344
Messex, Isaac Bke 153
Messux, George Wsh 266
METCALF/MEADCALF
Metcalf, Horace Car 226
_____, Isaac Doo 88
_____, T. S. Rch 275
_____, William Doo 78
Meadcalf, Henry DeK 42
_____, John DeK 40
METHORN, Ths. Wks 341
METTS/METZ
Metts, Fred Wsh 275
_____, Leven Wsh 266
_____, Lewis Wsh 275
_____, Nathan Lau 12
_____, Redden Tlf 2
_____, Wright Wsh 267
Metz, George Hry 212
_____, Joseph Hry 221
_____, Samuel Hry 221
_____, Zachariah Hry 221
METZGER, David Sr. Eff 111
_____, John J. Eff 113
_____, Solomon Eff 108
MICKLEJOHN, George Bib 51
_____, Robert Bal 29
MICKLER, Jacob Cam 185
_____, Peter Cam 188
_____, William Cam 182
_____, William Sr. Cam 188
_____, William Jr. Cam 188
MIDDLEBROOKS/MIDLEBROOKS
Middlebrooks, Anderson C. Mor 266
_____, Ann Jns 431
_____, David New 30
_____, Isaac Clk 318
_____, Isaac New 30
_____, Isaac R. Jns 444
_____, James M. Jns 435
_____, John Jr. New 31
_____, John New 31
_____, Robert Mon 189
_____, Silas Jns 437
_____, Sims Jns 437
_____, Talbot S. Mon 208
_____, Thomas Mon 208
_____, Thomas A. Jns 444
_____, William S. Jns 431
_____, Zere New 30
Midlebrooks, Alford Han 162
_____, Micajah Han 161
MIDDLETON, A. G. McI 132
_____, C. Cht 253
_____, Hugh Hst 285
_____, James Gwn 349
_____, James Lib 49
_____, James A. Gwn 349
_____, John Gre 304
_____, John Gwn 312
_____, John Mon 204
_____, Margaret Gwn 364
_____, Margaret McI 129
_____, O. Bal 36
_____, Robert McI 132

Middleton, Samuel Doo 89
______, Thomas Rab 224
______, William McI 132
______, William Put 201
MIFFLIN, D. (col[d].) Bal 36
______, Mrs. (Col[d].) Bal 45
MIKELL/MICHAEL/MICHEL/
MICKLE/MIKAL/MICHAELS
Mikell, James Bul 95
______, James Bul 96
______, John Bul 93
______, Thomas Bul 96
______, William Bul 96
Michael, Britton Hab 54
______, James Car 214
______, William Wal 162
Michel, John Ogl 94
______, John F. Put 201
Mickle, James Cow 384
______, William Mon 219
Mikal, Jacob Ogl 93
Michaels, William Tms 24
MILAM/MILUM/MILEHAM
Milam, Jordan Pik 112
______, Lewis Hst 176
______, Thomas F. New 49
Milum, Benjamin Har 180
______, Dudley Hry 246
Mileham, Wylye W. Jsp 389
MILBORN, Williamson Jks 339
MILES, Abraham Har 180
______, Augustus Mor 270
______, Briant DeK 36
______, Daniel Twg 83
______, David DeK 42
______, Drury Bib 51
______, Edward Col 353
______, Elija Har 192
______, Gillum Mon 176
______, Isaac Col 339
______, Isham J. S. Han 161
______, James Gwn 358
______, Jane Mon 224
______, Louis Cpb 201
______, Sally Rab 223
______, Sarah Bib 62
______, Thomas Bal 35
______, Thomas W. Hab 50
______, William Fay 181
______, William Hry 218
______, William Wks 345
MILLEDGE, Ann Clk 324
______, Ann Rch 292

MILLEN, George (col[d]_ Bke 150
______, George Cht 265
** ______, John (slaves) Cht 282
______, Lee Lee 27
MILLENDER, Hobson Jsp 389
MILLER/MILLAR/MILLA
Miller, A. C. Cht 244
______, Aaron Car 217
______, Ademia Frk 252
______, Alcy Ogl 83
______, Alexander Cow 369
______, Andrew Up 117
______, Andrew Rab 222
______, Andrew J. Rch 260
______, Anna Car 230
______, Asa R. Frk 248
______, B. B. Bke 153
______, Bazil Bal 30
______, Benajah Pik 115
______, Benson Wsh 264
______, Betsey Mon 208
______, Burrel Hal 85
______, Charles Bts 166
______, Charles Em 174
______, Charles Hry 247
______, Charles Jks 325
______, Charles F. Gly 268
______, Charles L. Bak 16
______, D. W. Gwn 315
______, Daniel Tlf 11
______, David Gwn 355
______, David J. Ware 183
______, David W. Gwn 370
______, Dempsey Gwn 355
______, Ebenezer G. Dec 13
______, Ebenezer Jks 331
______, Eli Car 226
______, Elias Hal 81
______, Elijah Ran 242
______, Elizabeth Doo 86
______, Elizabeth Hry 217
______, Emson Mon 197
______, Ephraim Eff 106
______, Ezekiel Wks 345
______, Francis Gwn 376
______, Francis Hry 209
______, Francis Trp 35
______, Frances Wsh 265
______, Frederick J. Eff 105
______, G. S. Cht 268
______, George Jns 474
______, George Ogl 65
______, Goodwin Wal 141

Miller, Green Jns 435
______, H. B. Wsh 259
______, Henrietta Cht 256
______, Henry Cam 190
______, Henry Hal 98
______, Henry Wal 132
______, Henry J. Mtg 232
______, Irwin Bal 28
______, Isaac McI 126
______, Isaac C. Doo 79
______, J. T. Wsh 251
______, Jacob Cam 182
______, Jacob Cht 262
______, Jacob Dec 16
______, Jacob Wal 160
______, James Bul 92
______, James Cow 369
______, James Ear 93
______, James Jks 341
______, James Jns 452
______, James New 18
______, James Ran 247
______, James Rch 258
______, James A. Crf 394
______, James H. Jsp 363
______, James J. Dec 13
______, Jedediah S. Elb 154
______, Jesse Cpb 203
______, Jesse Wrn 205
______, John Bal 36
______, John Bul 101
______, John Car 230
______, John Cow 368
______, John Cow 383
______, John Dec 15
______, John Sr. Ear 99
______, John Jr. Ear 91
______, John Gwn 372
______, John Hal 113
______, John Hry 242
______, John Jns 437
______, John Jns 452
______, John Mtg 232
______, John Mon 182
______, John Mon 197
______, John Wsh 245
______, John Wsh 250
______, John Wsh 270
______, John C. Eff 106
______, John C. Rab 222
______, Jonathen Dec 9
______, Jonathan Han 162
______, Jon A. Wks 352
Miller, Jordan Wsh 257
______, Joseph Frk 242
______, Joseph Irw 301
______, Joseph Mtg 232
______, Joshua Clk 299
______, Joshua Eff 110
______, Joshua Wsh 255
______, Leannah Han 161
______, Lewis Ear 91
______, Lewis Wsh 255
______, Marey Hab 9
______, Mark Gwn 337
______, Marlin Mwr 159
______, Martha Wrn 205
______, Martin Bak 20
______, Martin T. Ware 183
______, Mason Jns 452
______, Melberry Hal 125
______, Micajah Jks 333
______, Murry Cht 254
______, Nathaniel Lau 10
______, Nathaniel Lau 15
______, Nath. Wks 354
______, Nicholas Hry 216
______, Obadiah Gwn 350
______, Philip Rch 292
______, Prestin Hal 97
______, Raleigh Han 161
______, Rebeca Lau 7
______, Richard Hal 98
______, Richard Scr 313
______, Robert Cow 375
______, Robert Frk 210
______, Robert Gwn 323
______, Robert New 23
______, Robert New 39
______, Robert J.H. Cow 369
______, Roda Pik 126
______, S. J. Jsp 366
______, Samuel Cow 381
______, Samuel Ear 99
______, Samuel Eff 108
______, Samuel Lau 9
______, Samuel Mtg 235
______, Samuel Pul 150
______, Samuel Wal 151
______, Sarah Cht 242
______, Sarah Lib 49
______, Sarah Ann Bib 61
______, Satteler Frk 255
______, Solomon Han 161
______, Stephen Hry 242
______, T. G. Cht 265

Name	County	Page
Miller, Thomas	Bib	76
______, Thomas	Cam	192
______, Thomas	Gre	289
______, Thomas H.	Cam	181
______, Thomas V.	Tlb	341
______, Uriah	Frk	230
______, William	Bts	173
______, William	Dec	4
______, William	DeK	33
______, William	Em	174
______, William	Gwn	372
______, William	Hal	108
______, William	Han	162
______, William Sr.	Jks	317
______, William	Jks	333
______, William	Jsp	362
______, William	Mad	107
______, William	Mon	211
______, William	New	55
______, William	Up	105
______, William B.	Bul	98
______, William P. Jr.	Jks	334
______, Wily	Wks	333
______, Zealous	Bal	38
Millar, Izrael	DeK	68
______, James	DeK	55
Milla, Free	Jns	442
MILLFORD, Henry	Wal	167
MILLICAN/MILICAN/MILLIGAN/ MILIGAN/MILIGIN		
Millican, Allen	Jks	316
______, Andrew Sr.	Mad	114
______, Delila	Clk	309
______, Hugh	Pik	119
______, James	Jks	325
______, John Jr.	Mad	108
______, Levi	Jks	316
______, Robert	Pik	126
______, Robert	Wal	143
Milican, Andrew Jr.	Mad	106
______, John Sr.	Mad	108
______, Thomas	Gwn	360
______, Thomas	Mad	109
Milligan, James	DeK	39
______, Samuel	Col	354
______, Thomas	DeK	67
______, William C.	DeK	40
Miligan, Benjamin	Ran	246
______, Lemuel	Car	218
Miligin, William J.	Mor	242
MILLINER/MILNER/MILLNER/ MILLENOR		
Milliner, Dudly	Har	188
Milliner, Eliza	Pik	128
______, Obadiah	Har	191
______, P. M. S.	Pik	128
______, Pile W.	Pik	113
______, Willis J.	Pik	128
Milner, Jeremiah	Frk	244
______, John	Mon	195
______, John B.	Wil	298
______, John H.	Mon	177
______, Jonathan	Ogl	89
______, Pitt	Mon	179
______, Penelope	Jns	437
Millner, James	Pik	129
______, Joshua	Wal	131
______, Sidney H.	Car	215
Millenor, John	Lee	33
MILLING, Maria	Up	100
MILLIONS/MILLIRONS		
Millions, George	Put	212
______, Henry	Put	175
______, Henry C.	Put	212
______, Jesse	Put	210
______, John Sr.	Put	209
______, John Jr.	Put	202
______, Sarah	Put	210
______, Solomon	Put	210
______, William	Put	210
Millirons, Betsey	Jns	461
______, Hiram	Tlb	344
MILLS, Abraham	Pul	161
______, Allen	Pul	161
______, Anthony	Bke	135
______, Archibald	Bke	135
______, Asoph	Wsh	272
______, Berry	Gwn	367
______, Berry	Mor	268
______, Charles	Pul	144
______, Charles	Wsh	270
______, Charles C.	Wil	294
______, Chesley	Frk	215
______, Daniel	Wsh	270
______, David	Hal	121
______, Dial	Frk	215
______, Elijah	Lau	22
______, Elizabeth	Bke	135
______, Enich R.	Hab	40
______, Franklin M.	Mon	195
______, Fredirlc	Ware	184
______, Henry	Tlb	333
______, Hugh	Gwn	350
______, Jacob	Jns	445
______, James	Fay	181
______, James Sr.	Gwn	347

Mills, James	Wsh	243
_____, Jane	Scr	303
_____, John	Bak	19
_____, John	Gre	285
_____, John	Gwn	317
_____, John	Gwn	318
_____, John	Gwn	350
_____, John	Jef	424
_____, John	Scr	304
_____, John	Wal	159
_____, John	Wsh	263
_____, John B.	Cht	282
_____, John B.	Dec	5
_____, Joseph	Cam	190
_____, Levi	Pik	132
_____, Littlebury	Dec	5
_____, Mary	Up	112
_____, Mary	Pul	145
_____, Mathew	Wsh	256
_____, Moses	Fay	203
_____, Nancy	Frk	231
_____, Richard	Doo	87
_____, Robert	Col	354
_____, S. L.	Cht	268
_____, Seth H.	Mon	223
_____, Stephen	Scr	305
_____, Stephen	Web	263
_____, Susannah	Crf	399
_____, Thomas	Bul	94
_____, Thomas	Doo	84
_____, Thomas	Frk	215
_____, Thomas	Wsh	260
_____, William	Elb	147
_____, William	Mwr	160
_____, William	Mwr	162
_____, William H. C.	Bke	118
MILLSAPS/MILSAPS		
Millsaps, Ezekiel	Jks	327
_____, Fuler	Wal	127
_____, Jacob	Jks	328
_____, Jacob	Wal	139
_____, Larkin	Fay	186
_____, Marvel	Jks	322
_____, Reuben	Fay	201
_____, William	Fay	189
Milsaps, Hiram	Clk	308
MILLWEE/MILWEE		
Millwee, William	Frk	210
Milwee, Ambrose	Frk	228
MILTON, Algernon S.R.	Jef	412
_____, Benjamin	Ware	188
_____, Berry	Lau	19
_____, Elbert	Hst	276
Milton, Eliza	Jef	412
_____, Elizabeth G.	Rch	287
_____, Hannah	Mar	140
_____, Hannah E.	Bke	152
_____, John	Jef	417
_____, Matthew	Hst	278
_____, McKinne	Hst	278
_____, Solomon	Tat	376
_____, Stroud	Clk	292
_____, William	Hst	288
MILWOOD, Lettace	Hal	125
MIMS/MIMMS		
Mims, Calvin	Ran	248
_____, David	Tlf	11
_____, David	Tms	18
_____, David	Wrn	205
_____, Drury	Mus	293
_____, Gideon	Bib	70
_____, Henry	Tlb	335
_____, James	Pik	109
_____, John	Wsh	267
_____, John	Wks	347
_____, Joseph	Gwn	372
_____, Joseph	Hst	270
_____, Judith	Col	340
_____, Lawder	Hst	280
_____, Martin	Lee	31
_____, Needham	Bib	65
_____, Thomas	Doo	84
_____, William	Wsh	271
_____, Wright	Hst	264
Mimms, Benjamin	Lau	11
_____, Benjamin	Lau	19
_____, Charles E.	Mus	279
_____, David D.	Fay	198
_____, Elias	Lau	24
_____, Elizabeth	Cow	392
_____, George	Lau	17
_____, Leroy	Tfo	363
_____, Robert	Cow	374
_____, Williamson	Mon	207
MINCHEW/MINSHEW/MINSUE/		
MINCHEON/MINCHEY		
Minchew, Abram	Ware	188
_____, Calvin	Twg	69
_____, Joseph	Hst	295
_____, Nathan	Hst	291
_____, Philip	Twg	72
_____, Willoby	Wyn	285
Minshew, Isac	Ware	189
_____, Thomas	Mwr	168
Minsue, Aaron	Mar	139
Mincheon, P.	Cht	256

Name	County	Page
Minchey, Sarah	Bke	132
MINCY/MINCEY/MINSEY/MINCE		
Mincy, Isaac	Hab	32
_____, John	DeK	70
_____, John	Scr	303
Mincey, Aaron	Hab	43
Minsey, Aaron	Hab	41
Mince, James	Hab	64
MINGLEDORF/MINGLEDORFF		
Mingledorf, George	Cht	260
Mingledorff, John G.	Eff	105
MINICK, George	Cow	388
MINISH/MINIS		
Minish, Hardy	Jks	336
_____, Isaac	Jks	342
_____, John	Jks	319
Minis, Abby	Cht	264
_____, Isaac	Cht	265
MINOR/MINER		
Minor, Lazarus	Gwn	336
_____, Mastin	Gwn	333
_____, Nancy	Han	162
_____, Samuel W.	Hry	251
Miner, Richard	Gwn	364
MINTER, Abner H.	Up	108
_____, James	Wks	352
_____, John M.	Put	206
_____, Richard	Jsp	385
_____, Robert R.	Jsp	353
MINTON, Benjamin	Twg	72
_____, Henrieta	Wil	288
_____, Jason	Jks	348
_____, John	Lib	50
_____, John	Mor	252
_____, Jonathan	Lau	11
_____, Mills	Up	111
_____, Moses	Jef	423
_____, Nancy	Han	162
MIRANDA, Joseph	Rch	284
MIRAULT, Aspasia	Cht	252
MIRES, Abra.	Wks	340
_____, Elizabeth	New	42
_____, Elizabeth	Rab	226
_____, Elisebeth	Hab	33
_____, George	New	46
_____, Joshua	Wks	345
_____, Sally	Hab	33
_____, Sarah	Wks	340
_____, William	Wal	131
MITCHELL/MITCHEL/ MITCHELE/MITCHIEL		
Mitchell, Ann	Tms	21
_____, Asa	Mon	203
Mitchell, B. B.	Rch	263
_____, Batty H.	Cpb	194
_____, Benjamin	Wks	342
_____, Burrell	Frk	254
_____, D. B.	Bal	31
_____, Daniel R.	Trp	33
_____, Danville	Fay	187
_____, David	Frk	228
_____, Drury	Hst	279
_____, Ebenezer	Mwr	160
_____, Eldor	Wal	168
_____, Eliz.	Wks	349
_____, Elizabeth	Jsp	381
_____, Elizabeth	Jns	454
_____, Frances	Wal	155
_____, G. G. F.	Jns	432
_____, George B.	New	10
_____, Green	Clk	297
_____, Green	Han	161
_____, Hardy	Trp	38
_____, Hartwil	Mtg	231
_____, Henchey	Hry	238
_____, Henry	Fay	187
_____, Henry	Frk	253
_____, Henry	Gre	292
_____, Henry	Han	161
_____, Henry	Hry	239
_____, Henry D.	Tlf	7
_____, Henry J.	Frk	232
_____, Isaac	DeK	63
_____, Isaac	Trp	32
_____, Isaac	Wks	350
_____, Isaac G.	Elb	141
_____, J. C.	Jsp	389
_____, James	Frk	229
_____, James	Hry	233
_____, James	Hry	250
_____, James	Jks	344
_____, James H.	Wal	159
_____, James L.	Gre	292
_____, Jane E. (W)	Mor	257
_____, Jeremiah	Mon	215
_____, Jesse	DeK	30
_____, Jesse	Wal	155
_____, Joel	Jsp	398
_____, John	Bal	29
_____, John	Bke	130
_____, John	Frk	210
_____, Hohn	Hry	214
_____, John	Hst	290
_____, John	Jns	454
_____, John	Mar	144
_____, John	McI	122

Name	County	Page
Mitchell, John	Mon	202
______, John	New	43
______, John	Rch	288
______, John J.	Hry	229
______, John T.	Mad	104
______, Johnathan	Fay	195
______, Jonathan	Wal	153
______, Joseph	New	14
______, Joshua	Jns	432
______, Joshua S.	Hry	208
______, Josiah	Hry	212
______, Julius C. B.	Jns	454
______, Lucy	DeK	36
______, Mary	Elb	124
______, Mary	Gwn	370
______, Nathaniel R.	Tms	19
______, Peter	Bts	174
______, R. M. J.	Jns	432
______, Randolph	Har	190
______, Ransom	Jns	442
______, Reuben	Frk	214
______, Ricey M. J.	Hst	278
______, Richard	Hry	210
______, Richard	Tms	21
______, Robert	Frk	231
______, Robert	Han	161
______, Robert	Jsp	357
______, S.	Cht	267
______, Samuel	Pik	119
______, Stephen	DeK	71
______, Stephen	Pul	150
______, Stith	Up	100
______, Thomas	Clk	318
______, Thomas	Gre	295
______, Thomas	Wal	148
______, Thomas Jr.	Wal	152
______, Thomas G.	Tms	24
______, Thomas R.	Wal	132
______, U.	Cht	246
______, Wiley	Frk	253
______, Wiley M.	Frk	235
______, William	Bke	144
______, William Sr.	Frk	252
______, William Jr.	Frk	225
______, William	Frk	235
______, William	Jns	447
______, William	Mad	113
______, William	Mar	143
______, William	Tlb	327
______, William	Trp	38
______, William	Wks	341
______, William H.	Tlb	333
______, William L.	Clk	325

Name	County	Page
Mitchell, William L.	Clk	326
______, Wyatt	Hal	130
Mitchel, John	Car	218
______, Sally	Rab	12
______, William	Har	187
______, William	Mus	278
______, William F.	Gwn	349
Mitchele, John V.	Pul	149
Mitchiel, William	Cow	378
MITCHINER, William B.	Scr	316
MITCHUM/MITCHAM/MICHAM		
Mitchum, James	Trp	51
______, John	Trp	51
Mitcham, John	Mwr	159
Micham, Elijah	Mwr	163
MIX, Joseph R.	Bts	175
MIXON/MICON		
Mixon, Edward	Tlf	5
______, Elijah	New	44
______, George	Bke	143
______, James	Irw	304
______, Jessee	Hst	274
______, Jesse	Scr	315
______, John	Frk	357
______, John	Lwn	84
______, Michael	Bke	144
______, Michael	Twg	80
______, Mitchell	Ear	93
______, Noel	Mor	249
______, Sarah	Tlf	5
______, William	Bke	143
______, William	Tlf	6
______, William	Irw	300
______, William W.	Scr	317
Micon, William	Rch	265
MIZE/MISE		
Mize, Abner	Frk	223
______, Anderson	Cow	370
______, Claxton	Frk	224
______, Henderson	Up	100
______, Henry	Frk	240
______, Henry	Wal	126
______, Howel	Hab	20
______, James	New	24
______, James B.	Jsp	370
______, John J.	Frk	218
______, Joseph	Jsp	389
______, Robert	Frk	249
______, Samuel	Elb	160
______, Thomas T.	Jks	340
______, Warren	Frk	224
______, Wiley	Cow	377
______, Williamson	Hal	98

Name	County	Page
Mise, Henry	Hab	15
______, John	Hab	15
______, Sterling	Har	191
______, Zachariah	Hab	20
MIZELL/MIZZUL/MIZZLE		
Mizell, David	Cam	191
______, David	Mar	137
______, Griffin	Tlf	9
______, James H.	Ware	185
______, Joel	Tlb	344
______, Joshua Sr.	Cam	187
______, Joshua Jr.	Cam	187
______, Mary	Cam	187
Mizzul, Dickason	DeK	45
Mizzle, Mark	Wks	346
MOBBS, Jesse	Clk	299
MOBLEY/MOBLY		
Mobley, Benjamin	Bke	146
______, Burrell	Hry	226
______, Daniel	Dec	9
______, David	Hry	226
______, Eleazur	Bts	168
______, Ephraim	Hry	238
______, Isaac	Ogl	76
______, James	Bke	134
______, James	Scr	316
______, James H.	Scr	317
______, Jethro	Bts	168
______, Joel	Hry	226
______, John	App	12
______, John	Mad	108
______, John	Tat	376
______, John	Wal	156
______, John M.	Eff	112
______, Ledford	Wal	169
______, Lewis	Crf	410
______, Ludd	Irw	298
______, Nelly	New	50
______, Peyton	Wal	169
______, Sampson	Crf	411
______, Sarah	Bke	147
______, Solomon	App	12
______, Stephen	Jsp	355
______, William	Bke	148
______, William	Hry	216
______, William	Hry	226
Mobly, Edward	DeK	48
______, Nelly	Scr	316
______, Patience	Scr	303
______, Reuben	Har	179
MOCK, Andrew	Scr	308
______, George	Scr	308
______, Harmon	Pul	159

Name	County	Page
Mock, Joel	Pul	161
______, John	Pul	162
______, Joseph	Scr	308
MOCKMAN, Nancy	Gre	302
MODESETT/MODDISET		
Modesett, James	Jns	472
______, Samuel	Jns	474
______, William	Rch	292
Moddiset, John	Mon	176
______, Isabel	Mon	176
**MODERWELL, W. (slave)	Rch	275
MOFFETT/MOFFIT/MOFFITT/ MOFFUTT/MAFFETT		
Moffett, Gabriel A.	Clk	312
______, Gabriel A.	Clk	326
______, H.	Mus	284
______, John	Gwn	315
Moffit, James	Mon	214
Moffitt, Mary Ann	Lin	68
Moffutt, Jacob	Crf	401
Maffett, Samuel	Gwn	359
MOLDEN, Jaremiah	Hab	50
MOLDER, Daniel	Frk	214
______, Jacob	Hal	77
______, Lewis	Frk	243
MOLES, Joseph M.	Cht	282
MOLIER, Clement	Jsp	397
______, Matilda	Jsp	397
MOLLINEAUX, E.	Cht	267
MOLSBY, John	Bib	52
MOMAN, John	Wil	305
______, Thomas	Wil	305
______, William	Har	188
______, William	Wil	305
MONCRIEF/MUNCRIEF		
Moncrief, David	Bib	62
______, Isaac	Gwn	328
______, James	Lin	61
______, John	Lin	68
______, Laban	Gre	283
______, Nancy	Lin	74
______, Samuel	Jns	462
______, Wiley	Lin	66
______, William	Col	358
______, William	Gre	287
______, William	Lin	73
Muncrief, Arthur	Wrn	192
MONFORT/MONTFORD/also see Mumford		
Monfort, John	Gre	297
______, William S.	Gre	298
Montford, Joseph	Lau	23
MONGLANING, John	Crf	398

MONGLEHORN, Mitchell	Crf	405	Montgomery, Nancy (W)	Mor	248
MONK, Hamilton	Car	230	______, R.	Gwn	308
______, Hosey	Bib	70	______, Samuel	Hal	121
______, James	Mwr	167	______, Samuel	Lau	8
______, Jerusha W.	Lwn	90	______, Samuel	Wks	348
______, John	Bib	61	______, Simpson	Wil	302
______, John	Put	210	______, Thomas	Hab	51
______, John H.	Crf	394	______, Ulysses Mc	DeK	36
______, Malon	Lwn	91	______, W. W.	Rch	255
______, Merrell	Wrn	209	______, William	Dec	17
______, Silas	Ear	94	______, William	Gwn	359
______, Silas	Har	187	______, William	Jks	318
______, Simon	Crf	401	______, William W.	Jef	412
MONROE/MAROE/MUNROE			MONTZINGO, Giles	Hst	266
Monroe, David	Bke	123	______, Lewis	Hst	277
______, Dugal	Hal	70	MOODY, Anderson	Rch	263
______, Edward	Twg	84	______, Arel	Ogl	79
______, Jackson	Gwn	335	______, Benjamin	Pik	108
______, Jane	Tms	24	______, Daniel	Wsh	250
______, Jese	Hab	61	______, Gabriel	App	5
______, John	Ran	245	______, Granville	Wrn	200
______, John L.	Wal	134	______, Green	Bts	178
______, Joseph	Bke	126	______, Jabez	Jns	430
______, Lorenzo D.	Ran	245	______, James	Lib	50
______, Maria	Rch	268	______, Jarrat	Hal	105
______, Stephen	Bke	125	______, Jeremiah	Pik	128
______, Thomas	Gwn	376	______, Jeremiah	Wyn	284
Maroe, Ann E.	Lib	50	______, Jesse	App	10
Munroe, Neill	Lau	4	______, Joel	Up	116
MONTAGUE, Susan G.	Elb	160	______, John	Gre	273
MONTGOMERY, Ann	Jef	412	______, John L.	Mor	244
______, Bartley	Hal	82	______, John	Tlf	3
______, Benjamin	Jsp	386	______, John	Wrn	233
______, Charles	Gwn	322	______, John W.	Ogl	87
______, David	Jsp	396	______, Joseph	Wil	320
______, David	Pik	120	______, Josiah	Crf	406
______, David F.	New	21	______, Martin	Rab	234
______, Ezekiel B.	Wil	316	______, Perryman	Tat	378
______, Hezekiah	Wil	317	______, Robert	Gly	268
______, Hiram	Hal	120	______, Solomon	Gly	267
______, Hugh	Hab	42	______, Sylvanus	Tlb	325
______, Hugh	Jef	418	______, Thomas Sr.	Ogl	84
______, Hugh	Wrn	211	______, Thomas	Ogl	87
______, J. M. C.	DeK	25	______, William	Lib	49
______, James	Jks	312	______, William	Rch	254
______, James	Wil	323	______, William	Up	101
______, James H.	Jsp	396	______, William	Up	109
______, John	Hst	284	MOON/MOONE/MONE		
______, John	Mad	106	Moon, A.	Mad	105
______, Lewis	Doo	85	______, Mrs. Ally	Col	340
______, Margaret	Bib	71	______, Arch[d].	Jks	326
______, Mary	Twg	88	______, Bud	Mad	115
______, Mary	Wil	302	______, Edom	Wal	173

Name	County	Page
Moon, Elijah	Wal	133
______, George	Cow	381
______, George	DeK	32
______, Jacob	Trp	35
______, James	Han	161
______, James	Wrn	222
______, James B.	Mon	173
______, James W.	Bib	71
______, Jessee	Col	341
______, Jesse	Wal	134
______, John	Clk	311
______, John	Hry	230
______, John	Hst	278
______, John B.	Twg	65
______, John M.	Mad	102
______, John M.	Wal	173
______, John P.	Gwn	315
______, Joseph	Wal	173
______, Lewis	Wal	133
______, Robert	Jks	321
______, Robert D.	Ogl	96
______, Robert R.	Mad	101
______, Rudderick	Col	363
______, Sarah	Elb	119
______, T. P.	Jks	321
______, Tabitha	Elb	119
______, Thomas	Wal	135
______, Thomas B.	Wal	140
______, William	Trp	39
______, William H.	Twg	66
Moone, Charity	Put	200
______, John	Put	188
______, Lovid	Mad	116
______, Moses	Pik	121
______, Prudence	Mad	116
______, Richard	Mad	111
Mone, John	Pik	120
MOONEY/MOONIE/MOONING		
Mooney, Daniel F.	Cow	370
______, James	Hal	71
______, John	Hal	86
______, John	Hal	87
______, Jonathan	Hal	87
______, Lewis	Hal	87
______, Mely	Hal	86
______, Michael	Mor	254
______, Richard	Rch	285
______, Robert	Hal	88
______, Sarah	Tlf	9
Moonie, Isaac	Har	180
Mooning, James	Wks	335
MOONEYHAN/MOONIHAN/ MANNAHAN		

Name	County	Page
Mooneyhan, Kinchin	Wal	161
Moonihan, Stephen	Jns	452
Mannahan, James	Rch	253
MOONMAUGH, Emmanuel H.	Jks	312
MOORE/MORE/MOOR		
Moore, A. D.	Wsh	259
______, Abel	Jef	403
______, Abraham	Gwn	364
______, Abraham	Mus	282
______, Agnes	Hal	89
______, Alexander	Hab	10
______, Alsa	Clk	326
______, Andrew	Hry	224
______, Arbin	Cow	370
______, Arthur	Cam	185
______, Asa	Wks	338
______, Augusta	Rch	267
______, Augustus	Pul	160
______, Bart B.	Up	102
______, Benjamin	Bal	31
______, Benjamin	Bts	166
______, Benjamin	Col	347
______, Bishop	Jns	462
______, Brian	Jef	403
______, Burnet	Gre	289
______, Burwell	Wsh	270
______, Cason	Wsh	258
______, Caswell	Jef	483
______, Charles	Ogl	94
______, Charles	Tfo	357
______, Clement	Bts	162
______, Daniel	Hal	89
______, David	Wal	160
______, Ebenezer	Jns	457
______, Edward	Fay	181
______, Edward	Hst	261
______, Edward	Tat	371
______, Elbert	Jsp	366
______, Elijah	Gwn	351
______, Elijah Jr.	Han	162
______, Elijah	Han	162
______, Elisha	Wil	292
______, Elizabeth	Bib	68
______, Elizabeth	Hry	225
______, Elizabeth	Wil	294
______, Elizabeth	Wil	315
______, Ella	DeK	69
______, Frances	Clk	298
______, Francis Jr.	Ogl	93
______, G. W.	Cht	250
______, George	Crf	415
______, George	Gre	304
______, George W.	Clk	322

Name	County	Page
Moore, George W.	New	13
______, Gilly	Gre	303
______, Hannah	Ear	99
______, Henry	Mon	215
______, Henry O.	Pul	162
______, Hilery	Gwn	327
______, Hiram	Bal	33
______, Hiram	Hry	236
______, Hiram	Jsp	385
______, Hugh	Gre	298
______, Irwin	Lib	49
______, Isaac	Col	363
______, Isaac	Fay	192
______, Isaac	Hry	248
______, Isaac	Tfo	360
______, Isabella	Rch	258
______, Isham	Gwn	329
______, Israeal	Wal	140
______, Jackson	Gre	301
______, Jacob	Gly	265
______, Jacob	DeK	56
______, James	Cam	185
______, James	Em	172
______, James	Gre	300
______, James	Har	192
______, James	Hry	221
______, James	Hry	243
______, James	Mus	291
______, James	Scr	302
______, James	Up	102
______, James	Wil	292
______, James B.	Car	217
______, James J.	Wal	124
______, James R.	Ran	247
______, Jason	Lee	27
______, Jason	Wks	334
______, Jesse	Bul	93
______, Jesse	Crf	397
______, Jesse	Em	176
______, Jesse	Hry	205
______, Jesse	Tfo	362
______, Jesse	Wil	323
______, Joel	Frk	254
______, Joel	Tlb	343
______, John	Gwn	336
______, John	Hal	77
______, John	Hal	89
______, John	Hal	105
______, John	Hal	108
______, John	Hal	116
______, John	Hry	200
______, John	Hry	236
______, John	Jns	454
Moore, John	Lee	30
______, John	Lwn	81
______, John	Lwn	88
______, John	Mwr	151
______, John	Mon	199
______, John	New	55
______, John	Ogl	97
______, John	Pul	154
______, John	Rch	264
______, John Sr.	Scr	302
______, John Sr.	Scr	304
______, John	Wil	297
______, John	Wil	307
______, John	Wil	323
______, John	Wrn	192
______, John B.	Col	356
______, John H.	Tlb	347
______, John L.	Gwn	351
______, John H.	Wil	315
______, John M.	Hst	261
______, John R.	Jns	454
______, John V.	Tlb	336
______, Joseph	Jns	461
______, Joseph	Mor	251
______, Joseph	Gre	294
______, Joseph	Ogl	97
______, Joseph J.	Mon	190
______, Joseph J.	Ogl	67
______, Joshua	Bts	161
______, Joshua	Bts	175
______, Joshua	Gre	280
______, Joshua	Jsp	394
______, Joshua G.	Clk	322
______, Josiah	Wsh	263
______, Jourdan	Up	116
______, Lemuel	Jsp	353
______, Leroy	Bal	31
______, Levin	Jns	454
______, Lewis	Bts	167
______, Lewis	Wil	308
______, Lovel	Em	174
______, Marion F.	Hry	224
______, Martha	Bal	35
______, Martha	Col	345
______, Mary	Bal	33
______, Mary O.	Lau	22
______, Matthew	Jns	452
______, Mathew	Wsh	245
______, Memory J. D.	Clk	308
______, Michael	Cpb	194
______, Miles	Bal	34
______, Milly	Mon	200
______, Mooren	Hal	89

Name	County	Page
Moore, Mourning	Bke	145
______, N. B.	Rch	265
______, Nathaniel	Cow	386
______, Petty	Jns	461
______, Phillis	Cht	271
______, R. R.	Col	364
______, Rachel	Wil	308
______, Ransom	Bul	101
______, Readin	Jns	454
______, Reuben	Cpb	203
______, Richard	Cpb	198
______, Richard	Mad	111
______, Robert	Clk	321
______, Robert	Mon	212
______, Robert	Tfo	366
______, Robert	Wal	140
______, Robert H.	Clk	316
______, Robert W. P.	Hab	6
______, Rowland	Bke	121
______, Sampson	Jns	462
______, Samuel	Bib	56
______, Samuel	Col	347
______, Samuel	Hry	246
______, Samuel	Jef	403
______, Samuel	Jns	452
______, Samuel	Mon	199
______, Santford	DeK	50
______, Sarah	Gre	297
______, Sarah	Han	173
______, Sarah	Jef	402
______, Sarah	Jks	345
______, Seth	Tfo	362
______, Shaderick	Wsh	252
______, Spencer	Mon	198
______, Spencer	Tat	376
______, Susan	Har	184
______, Susannah	Wil	293
______, Thomas	Bts	177
______, Thomas	Clk	317
______, Thomas	Elb	146
______, Thomas	Hal	113
______, Thomas	Jef	407
______, Thomas	Lau	15
______, Thomas	Twg	74
______, Thomas C.	Cow	367
______, Thomas H.	Har	177
______, Thompson	Gwn	369
______, Tillman	Col	364
______, Toliver	Jks	334
______, Turner B.	Bke	150
______, Turner B.	Hal	112
______, Ussery	Tlb	345
______, W.	Lee	27
Moore, William	Bul	93
______, William	Bts	174
______, William	Clk	303
______, William	Gly	266
______, William	Gre	301
______, William	Gwn	322
______, William	Hal	102
______, William	Hry	246
______, William	Mwr	169
______, William	Mor	259
______, William	New	18
______, William	Ogl	64
______, William	Put	188
______, William	Ran	245
______, William	Rch	286
______, William	Scr	300
______, William	Scr	306
______, William	Tlb	331
______, William	Wil	304
______, William A.	Jsp	380
______, William C.	Elb	139
______, William F.	Tlb	330
______, William H.	Mon	200
______, William M.	Mon	186
______, William R.	Har	184
______, William S.	Elb	141
______, William Y.	Wal	164
______, Willis	Gwn	327
______, Willis	Hry	241
______, Winfield	Bke	128
______, Winnaford	Wsh	270
______, Woodward	Up	116
______, Wyet	Hal	112
______, Young	Gwn	313
______, Zachariah	Wal	161
More, Christopher	Gwn	313
______, Edward	Mtg	236
______, Eli	Rab	225
______, John	Han	161
______, John B.	Rab	231
______, Jordan	Rab	225
______, Levi W.	Dec	3
______, Mathew R.	Dec	3
______, Robert	Hab	21
______, Sarah W.	Lwn	85
______, Thomas	Dec	19
______, Thomas	Hab	47
______, William	Hab	48
______, William	Rab	232
Moor, Majinpery	Pul	157
______, Stephen	Mad	115
______, Wiley	Pul	157

MOORMAN/MORMAN/MOREMAN

Name	County	Page
Moorman, Benjamin	Lau	7
_____, Elizabeth	Lau	7
_____, William	Lau	8
_____, William B.	Lau	14
Morman, Jacob	Pik	125
Moreman, James	Up	107
MORAN/MORIN		
Moran, James	Bal	37
_____, Jesse	Bib	65
_____, Jessee	Mon	191
_____, John	Bal	31
_____, John B.	Put	213
_____, William	Bal	31
Morin, Peter	Cht	254
MOREL/MORRELL/MORREL		
Morel, Benjamin	Eff	111
_____, Bryan M.	Bry	84
_____, David J.	Hst	279
_____, John	Cht	245
_____, John H.	Cht	264
**_____, John H. (slaves)	Cht	282
_____, M.	Cht	264
_____, Sarah	Ogl	94
_____, W.	Cht	263
Morrell, Benjamin	Cht	255
_____, John	Cht	281
Morrel, John	Jef	406
MORELAND, Colson	Up	109
_____, Edward	Jns	470
_____, Frances	Jsp	364
_____, Francis	Mon	189
_____, Isaac T.	Jns	436
_____, Jesse	Wks	351
_____, John	Put	200
_____, John J.	Put	200
_____, Joseph T.	Trp	45
_____, Robert	Har	191
_____, Tabithia	Lau	24
_____, Turner	Put	200
_____, William	Jns	470
_____, William B.	Clk	314
_____, Wood	Put	200
MOREY, Alfred	Twg	66
_____, James	Twg	66
_____, Joel	Mus	287
MORGAN/MORGIN/MORGAIN		
Morgan, Arthur A.	Hst	261
_____, Bethal	Mad	104
_____, Charles	Jsp	373
_____, Charles	Lau	14
_____, Christopher L.	Eff	105
_____, Daniel	Ogl	79
_____, David	Mad	111

Name	County	Page
Morgan, David	Scr	300
_____, Duncan	Dec	18
_____, Ed. A.	Wks	345
_____, Eldridge	Rch	285
_____, Eli	Rch	264
_____, Elihu	Scr	311
_____, Elisebeth	Hab	29
_____, Ellis	Rch	287
_____, Ephraim	Wyn	282
_____, Gabriel	Lib	49
_____, George	Put	207
_____, George B.	Gwn	322
_____, Hardy	Jef	403
_____, Hardy	New	18
_____, Henery	Cow	389
_____, Henretta	New	51
_____, Henry	Fay	207
_____, Henry C.	Mwr	168
_____, Henry J.	Hry	218
_____, Hiram F.	Fay	199
_____, Hopson	Mor	224
_____, Hy	Gwn	322
_____, Hy	Gwn	334
_____, Isham	Elb	151
_____, James	DeK	30
_____, James	Frk	247
_____, James	Hry	200
_____, James	Rch	285
_____, James	Twg	81
_____, James	Wil	293
_____, James	Wks	332
_____, James B.	Mor	246
_____, James W.	Jsp	373
_____, Jeremiah	Gwn	347
_____, Jessee	Mon	182
_____, Jesse	Mor	259
_____, Jesse	Ran	245
_____, John	Dec	7
_____, John Jr.	Frk	222
_____, John	Jsp	385
_____, John	Jef	403
_____, John	New	52
_____, John	Put	197
_____, John C.	Clk	296
_____, John E.	Trp	34
_____, John J.	McI	126
_____, John M.	Cpb	206
_____, John R.	Eff	110
_____, John T.	Mon	222
_____, Jonathan	Frk	223
_____, Joseph	App	7
_____, Joseph	Gwn	316
_____, Joshua	Wal	161

Name	County	Page
Morgan, Joshua	Wil	292
______, Judith	Hry	232
______, Kendred	Elb	148
______, Kinchen M.	Crf	409
______, Lovey	Mon	186
______, Levy	Lib	49
______, Lewellin	Hry	222
______, Lewis	Ran	241
______, Lotte	DeK	28
______, Luke J.	Bib	65
______, Millington	Rch	286
______, Moses	Rch	287
______, Nathan	DeK	71
______, Nicholas	Cam	184
______, Nicholas	Mon	224
______, Peggy	Wrn	217
______, R.	App	9
______, Randal	Mon	222
______, Rebecca	Rab	233
______, Richard	Hal	106
______, Samuel	Frk	219
______, Samuel	Frk	224
______, Samuel B.	Wyn	282
______, Solomon	App	7
______, Spencer	Frk	222
______, Stephen	Jef	413
______, Stephen	Mon	224
______, Stokely	Jsp	391
______, T. L.	App	7
______, Thomas	Eff	110
______, Thomas	Elb	155
______, Thomas	Gwn	314
______, Thomas	New	21
______, Thomas B.	Trp	42
______, Thomas	Twg	87
______, William	Cow	383
______, William	Eff	106
______, William	Eff	109
______, William	Fay	198
______, William	Hal	125
______, William	Hry	237
______, William	Jks	327
______, William G.	Jks	344
______, William	Jsp	373
______, William	Mon	223
______, William	Mus	285
______, William	New	7
______, William	Tat	371
______, William C.	Mon	212
______, William N.	Gre	278
______, William W.	Gre	296
______, Wilson	Trp	38
Morgin, Elias	Hab	65
Morgin, John	Hab	53
Morgain, Reubin Sr.	Dec	18
______, Reubin Jr.	Dec	18
MORIAH (no surname; col'd)	Lib	56
MORICEAU, Caroline	Cht	268
MORLEY, Silas	Ran	244
MORNINGSTAR, Henry	Cht	269
MORRIS/MORRISS/MORIS		
Morris, Allexander	Jns	432
______, Andrew	Bts	164
______, Ann	Scr	304
______, Benjamin	Hry	251
______, Burrel	DeK	50
______, Burwell	Mon	227
______, Charles	Pik	125
______, Charles	Tfo	358
______, Chesley	Hry	228
______, Daniel	New	22
______, David L.	Hst	278
______, Drury	DeK	70
______, Elias	Hab	38
______, Elijah	Jsp	359
______, Elizabeth (W)	Mor	246
______, Elizabeth	Pul	146
______, Enoch	DeK	69
______, Frederick	Jef	403
______, Gabril	Hab	8
______, Garrett	Clk	303
______, George	Hry	240
______, George G.	Tfo	364
______, George S.	Rch	271
______, Grovers	Hab	47
______, Hansel	Pul	139
______, Henry	Bib	76
______, Isaac	Pik	123
______, Isham	Pik	125
______, Jack	DeK	34
______, Jacob	Wsh	274
______, James	DeK	31
______, James	Frk	210
______, James	Jks	315
______, James	Jks	330
______, James Sr.	Jns	457
______, James Jr.	Jns	457
______, James	Tlb	337
______, James	Tms	29
______, James S.	Bts	174
______, James S.	New	36
______, Jesse L.	Hry	226
______, John	DeK	49
______, John	Doo	88
______, John	Frk	226
______, John	Hry	233

Name	County	Page
Morris, John	Mon	218
______, John	Pik	127
______, John	Pul	139
______, John	Rab	225
______, John	Twg	88
______, John W.	Har	187
______, Joseph	DeK	69
______, Joseph	Hal	129
______, Joseph	Har	182
______, Joseph	New	36
______, Josiah	Mwr	166
______, Jourdan	Hab	8
______, Kinchen	Bal	45
______, Letty	Hab	20
______, Marian	Bke	152
______, Mary	Jsp	372
______, Milly	Mon	184
______, Moses	Car	230
______, Nancy	Jns	452
______, Nathaniel	Jns	429
______, Rachael B.	Tfo	368
______, Richard	Hry	213
______, Sally	Wil	321
______, Sarah	Gwn	313
______, Sarah	Han	161
______, Shadrack	DeK	41
______, Sherod	Elb	146
______, Simon Sr.	Tfo	358
______, Simon Jr.	Tfo	355
______, Spencer	Har	185
______, Spencer	Jks	347
______, Taylor	Jns	454
______, Temple	Hab	16
______, Thomas	Jns	454
______, Thomas	Mwr	167
______, Thomas	Mus	278
______, Thomas	Pik	129
______, Thomas	Rab	223
______, Waren	Jks	347
______, William Sr.	DeK	52
______, William	DeK	51
______, William	DeK	53
______, William	DeK	66
______, William	Gwn	356
______, William	Hal	101
______, William	Hal	130
______, William	Har	184
______, William	Hry	240
______, William	Hst	284
______, William	New	54
______, William M.	New	55
______, William	Rab	232
______, William A.	Tfo	359
Morris, William	Trp	40
______, William	Wil	321
Morriss, Austin	Fay	206
______, Benjamin	Mad	113
______, Burwill	Jsp	396
______, Ebedoh	Col	344
______, Hiram	Cow	390
______, Jesse Sr.	Col	344
______, Jesse Jr.	Col	352
______, Jesse H.	Col	344
______, John	Col	347
______, Joseph	Col	352
______, Nancy	Col	351
______, Phebe	Fay	205
______, William	Cpb	205
______, William	Fay	195
______, William B.	Mad	110
Moris, John	Hab	24
______, John	Jks	349
______, William	Gwn	363
MORRISON/MORISON		
Morrison, Alexander	Jks	319
______, Alexander	Put	208
______, Angus	Tms	22
______, Danil	Hab	58
______, Edward	Jks	311
______, Ezra	Mon	175
______, George	Cam	190
______, Hugh	Mar	140
______, James	Cht	249
______, John	Gly	264
______, John	Mtg	234
______, John	Rch	263
______, John Sr.	Wsh	265
______, John	Wal	139
______, Martha A.	Wal	157
______, Mary W.	Lwn	82
______, Norman	Mar	141
______, Polly	Wks	355
______, R. C.	Lwn	80
______, Samuel W.	Ware	188
______, Thomas	Elb	150
______, Washington	Elb	155
______, William,	Jns	443
Morison, Catharine	Mtg	232
______, Daniel	Em	169
______, Hugh	Em	169
______, Malcom	App	5
______, Rodrick	Lwn	90
MORROW/MORRO		
Morrow, Agnes	New	40
______, James L.	Jsp	352
______, Jesse	New	29

Name	County	Page
Morrow, John	Frk	213
______, Joseph	Gwn	367
______, Joseph	Mor	265
______, Nancy	New	20
______, Peter G.	Wal	129
______, Peter G.	Wal	162
______, Thomas	Gwn	367
______, Thomas	Gwn	371
______, William	Frk	239
______, William	Gwn	332
Morro, James	Hab	56
MORSE, Jacob	Rch	268
______, Oliver	Mon	172
MORTON/MOURTON/MOTON/ MORETON		
Morton, Allen D.	Hab	15
______, David	Scr	299
______, Henry	Put	193
______, Joel	Clk	318
______, Joel	DeK	25
______, John	Mar	143
______, John	Put	193
______, Joseph	Clk	295
______, Judith	Clk	318
______, Oliver H.	Jns	452
______, Silas	Scr	299
______, Thomas	Clk	316
______, William	Clk	297
______, William	DeK	54
______, William T.	Put	194
Mourton, Nelly	Hal	132
Moton, Duke	Trp	50
Moreton, Joseph	Mad	118
MOSELEY/MOSLEY/MOSELY/ MOZLEY		
Moseley, Alanson	Hry	225
______, Benjamin	Hry	220
______, Benjamin	Put	215
______, Daniel	Frk	227
______, David	Cow	373
______, David M.	Wal	161
______, Garland	Frk	257
______, Laban	Jsp	390
______, Lewis	Gre	293
______, Priscella	Put	193
______, Samuel	Frk	257
______, Samuel G.	Wal	161
______, Seaborn	Lin	70
______, Silas	Hry	213
______, Stephen B.	Mad	117
______, William	Hry	205
Mosley, Brantley	Mtg	235
______, Clemment T.	Mtg	232
Mosley, Elisha	Ran	241
______, Howell	Fay	199
______, James	Bib	61
______, Joseph	Bib	70
______, Mary	Clk	315
______, Osbourn	Mor	258
______, Thomas	Bib	62
______, Thomas	Gre	291
______, Thomas	Mtg	234
Mosely, Isaiah	Twg	84
______, Jesse	Lee	28
______, John	Gwn	374
______, John	Lee	26
______, Joseph	Wil	287
______, Matthew	New	36
______, Nany	Wil	309
______, Samuel Jr.	Frk	251
Mozley, David	Rab	229
______, John E.	Mon	223
MOSES, Henry	Ear	97
______, Jessey	Jks	322
______, Neal	Fay	185
______, Samuel	Gly	266
MOSS, Abraham	New	17
______, Alfred	Wal	125
______, Beverly	Mor	240
______, David	Fay	186
______, Elizabeth W.	Lin	65
______, Epps	Pik	115
______, Francis	Mor	255
______, Gabriel	Gre	303
______, Henry E.	Pik	124
______, Hudson	Hab	14
______, James	Lau	23
______, James	Pik	112
______, James	Rab	229
______, James C.	Jef	409
______, James S.	Mwr	158
______, John	Frk	227
______, John	Hal	124
______, John	Lin	64
______, John	Wil	299
______, John A.	Put	204
______, John D.	Ogl	66
______, Joseph	Wal	165
______, Lewis	Lau	23
______, Martin	Elb	158
______, Phoebe	Wil	315
______, Sally	Em	166
______, Thomas	Mon	187
______, William	Elb	132
______, William	Hry	227
______, William	New	31

Name	County	Page
Moss, William	New	40
MOTHERSHED, Levi	Wks	349
MOTLEY, Benjamin	Lin	63
______, James	Tlb	342
______, John	Trp	48
______, Littleberry	Col	353
MOTT/MOTE/MOTES/MOAT		
Mott, Drucilla	Hst	261
______, Hiram	Wsh	267
______, John	Hst	279
______, John	Mus	282
______, John E.	Crf	403
______, Joseph	Wsh	254
______, Nathan	Wsh	273
______, Randolph D.	Bib	56
______, Uriah	Jns	462
______, William A.	Bal	40
______, Zachariah	Hst	279
Mote, Allen	Wrn	224
______, Benjamin	Hal	114
______, Drury	Mwr	164
______, James	Col	358
______, Joseph	Col	358
______, Levy	Hab	26
______, Ripley	Mwr	166
______, Silas	Col	357
______, William	Wrn	223
Motes, Drewry	Frk	224
______, John	Hab	58
______, Thomas	Frk	246
Moat, John	Wal	165
______, Silas	Tlb	323
______, Simeon	Tlb	323
MOULTON/MOLTEN		
Moulton, John	Clk	322
Molton, Morrow	Mon	203
MOULTREY/MOULTRIE		
Moultrey, Brigs	Put	200
______, Joel	Put	203
Moultrie, Mrs.	Scr	308
MOUNT, Fanny	Rch	259
______, Mathias	Jns	470
MOUNTAIN, Thomas	JEF	422
MOWMAN, Silas	Hry	242
MOXAM, Thomas	Cht	240
MOXLEY, Addison	Rch	255
______, Benjamin	Bke	120
______, Daniel	Bke	122
______, J. W.	Gre	281
______, John	Bke	118
______, Matthew	Bke	119
______, Nathaniel	Ran	242
______, William Sr.	Bke	119

Name	County	Page
Moxley, William	Bke	119
MOYE/MOY		
Moye, Benjamin	Ear	99
______, Martha	Lau	23
______, Thomas	Ear	91
______, Turney	Scr	300
Moy, Duran	Wsh	252
______, George	Wsh	252
______, John	Wsh	252
MULLING, Isaac W.	Jef	403
MUBORN, Thomas	New	12
MUCKLEMEATH, Mich[l].	Cpb	206
MUCKLEROY, Andrew	Mon	185
______, John	Wal	126
______, Zacheus	Mon	216
MUD, Mary	Clk	311
MUFFETT, Nathan	New	46
MULDREW, Isaac	Ogl	84
MULER/MULIAR		
Muler, Christopher	Jks	333
Muliar, Thomas	Hab	51
MULFORD, William B.	Bke	135
MULGA, Hiram	Hab	37
MULGRIDGE, Charles	Scr	317
MULKEY/MULKA/MULKO		
Mulkey, Edney	Irw	299
______, Elisebeth	Hab	39
______, Elizabeth (W)	Mor	242
______, Homer	Bke	139
______, Isaac	Bke	149
______, John	Irw	300
______, John	Jns	443
______, Moses	Bke	141
______, Moses	Hab	36
______, Moses	Pik	117
Mulka, John C.	Hab	55
______, Phillip	Hab	55
Mulko, Mark	Hab	55
MULLALLY, Stephen	Rch	273
______, William	Mus	279
MULLET, Abraham	Eff	107
______, Hannah E.	Eff	109
______, Jeremiah	Eff	108
______, Susannah	Eff	108
MULLIGAN/MULLICAN/MULIGAN/ MULLAGAN		
Mulligan, Benjamin	Tfo	365
______, Berry	Gwn	361
Mullican, Susannah	Hry	232
______, Tandy	Hry	214
Muligan, Cary	Fay	205
Mullagan, Benjamin	Wil	311
MULLINAX, William	Frk	240

Name	County	Page
MULLINS/MULLENS/MULLIN/		
MULLEN		
Mullins, Austin	Mon	202
_____, Bud	Cpb	208
_____, Burton	Hal	74
_____, Clem	Cpb	199
_____, Elias	Cpb	203
_____, Jeremiah	Har	182
_____, Jeremiah	Jns	474
_____, Jesse	Mor	251
_____, John	DeK	73
_____, John	Hal	87
_____, John	Hal	113
_____, John	Tlb	334
_____, John	Wal	141
_____, John D.	Hal	71
_____, Levi	Jns	454
_____, Lewis	Tlb	345
_____, Malone	Han	160
_____, Nancy	Jsp	396
_____, Ozburn	DeK	72
_____, Pleasant J.	Jns	474
_____, Reuben	Hal	99
_____, Robert S.	Wal	125
_____, Salisbury	Cpb	196
_____, Samuel	Cpb	201
_____, Thomas	Tlb	333
_____, William Sr.	Cpb	198
_____, William	Hab	13
_____, William	Hal	68
_____, William	Wal	138
_____, William	Wal	154
ullens, Ausbern	Car	221
_____, Greene	Put	210
_____, James	Put	210
_____, May	Car	230
ullin, Ezekel	Hab	29
_____, James	Col	362
_____, John W.	Gwn	316
ullen, James	Rch	260
UMFORD/MUNTFORD/also		
ee Monfort		
umford, Robert	Lin	75
untford, Theodk(?)	Crf	412
UN, Edman	Lee	34
UNDAY, Reuben	Fay	195
UNDEN, William	Wyn	284
UNGAZER (only name)	Cht	282
UNKEY, David	Hab	34
UNKUS, Benjamin	Car	214
URAT, H.	Cht	259
_____, John	Cht	252
JRCHISON/MURCHERSON		
Murchison, John	Car	219
_____, William E.	Wsh	262
Murcherson, Colon	Up	108
MURDIN, Malichi	Tfo	361
MURDOCK, David	New	23
_____, Joseph H.	Hab	8
_____, John	Hal	99
_____, Miles S.	Pik	123
MURRAY/MURRY/MURAH/MURHEE		
Murray, Alanander	Hry	199
_____, Alexander or	Hry	199
_____, Daniel	Hst	294
_____, David	Hst	266
_____, David	Lin	64
_____, David S.	Lin	63
_____, Drury	Lau	19
_____, Ezekiel	Hst	294
_____, George	Rch	278
_____, George W.	Bal	29
_____, Henry	Bke	134
_____, Henry	Jsp	368
_____, Hilory	Lin	61
_____, James	Bke	134
_____, James	Frk	223
_____, James	Lin	63
_____, Jeremiah	Bke	134
_____, John	Gwn	376
_____, John	Hry	226
_____, John	Hst	291
_____, John	Lib	49
_____, Josiah	Frk	249
_____, Sylvester	Lin	60
_____, Thomas J.	Lin	61
_____, Thomas W.	Lin	62
_____, Timothy	Bke	134
_____, William	Clk	322
_____, William	Col	358
_____, William	Ware	184
Murry, Ann	Hal	85
_____, Bernard	Tfo	362
_____, James	Ogl	66
_____, John	Cow	385
_____, John	Hab	14
_____, Nancy	Wrn	226
_____, P. J.	Hal	74
_____, Thomas	Ogl	71
_____, Valentine	Hab	23
Murah, Mariah	Hab	63
Murhee, Edward	Wyn	282
MURRELL, Thomas W.	Cpb	211
MURROW/MURRER/MURREN		
Murrow, James	Clk	312
_____, John	Mad	115

Name	County	Page
Murrer, Woodson	Mad	106
Murren, Thomas	Clk	325
MURPHY/MURPHEY/MURFY/		
MURPHREE/MURPH/MURFRY		
Murphy, Absalom	Rch	285
_____, Cor.	Bal	34
_____, Dowry	Bal	53
_____, Drury	Han	161
_____, Elijah	Jks	334
_____, Elizabeth	Wil	312
_____, Felix	Jns	473
_____, George	Jks	331
_____, Ginny	Frk	255
_____, James	Twg	65
_____, Jessey	Jks	318
_____, John	Col	358
_____, John	Cow	388
_____, John	DeK	47
_____, John	Eff	109
_____, John	Hry	247
_____, John	Jef	401
_____, John	Up	117
_____, Jos.	Jks	327
_____, Leroy H.	Rch	283
_____, Lucy	Wil	311
_____, Malachi	Bke	119
_____, Malachi	Mwr	158
_____, Martha	Wil	305
_____, Martin W.	Up	108
_____, Mathew	Tlb	338
_____, Miles	Col	359
_____, Miles	Jns	466
_____, Moses	DeK	46
_____, Nicholas	Rch	281
_____, Robert	Lin	74
_____, S. B.	Wks	335
_____, Samuel	Wsh	272
_____, Sarah	Wks	335
_____, Sylvester	Scr	313
_____, Wiley	Tlb	343
_____, William	Hal	68
_____, William	Tlb	338
_____, William	Wsh	249
_____, William	Wil	307
_____, William	Wil	324
Murphey, Alexander	Bke	136
_____, Elizabeth	Han	162
_____, James	Fay	204
_____, John	Bke	122
_____, Mary	Fay	204
_____, Prury	Jef	402
_____, Sarah	Jef	421
_____, William	Bke	122

Name	County	Page
Murphey, William	Hab	60
Murphrey, Bartholomeus	Pul	144
_____, Willis	Ran	248
Murfy, James	DeK	73
_____, Malcolm	Lee	31
_____, Roger	DeK	68
Murphree, Josiah	Bke	126
_____, William	Bke	127
_____, Wright	Bke	126
Murph, George	Bal	40
_____, Jacob	Lin	66
_____, John	Lin	68
Murfry, Hiram	Dec	11
MUSE, George	Clk	319
_____, William P.	Wil	291
MUSGROVE/MUSGROVES		
Musgrove, Harreson	Col	335
_____, John	Bak	16
_____, John	Bak	19
_____, John S.	Em	167
_____, L. C.	Bak	16
_____, R. H.	Rch	267
_____, William	Bak	16
Musgroves, R.	Rch	271
MUSHONE, A. R.	Mus	287
_____, J. W.	Mus	289
MUSICK, David	Car	229
_____, George	Car	225
_____, Jonathan	Car	22
_____, Joseph	Car	22
_____, Major	Tlf	4
_____, Mills	Ware	18
MUSSA, Polley	Bke	12
MUSSELWHITE, James	Ware	18
_____, Lucy	Hal	9
_____, Leonard	Lau	1
_____, Leonard	Tlf	7
_____, R[rd].	Bal	3
_____, Thomas	Bib	5
_____, Thomas	Lwn	8
MUSTIN, Eli	Rch	27
MYERS/MYRES		
Myers, Abraham	Hal	6
_____, Absalom	Mor	26
_____, Ann	Mon	22
_____, David R.	Hal	6
_____, George B.	Elb	14
_____, James	Gly	26
_____, James	Lau	1
_____, John	Mon	17
_____, Lewis	Eff	1
_____, M.	Cht	2
_____, Mary	McI	1

Name	County	Page
Myers, Nicholas	Eff	113
______, Richard	Mor	260
______, Thomas	Wsh	257
Myres, David	Wal	140
______, John	Hab	40
______, Mary	Tlf	3
MYHAND, Alvin	Mor	240
______, James	Mor	239
______, Thomas	Mor	240
______, William	Mor	250
______, William	Tlb	329
MYRICK, David	Put	218
______, Evans	Mon	195
______, G.	Bal	44
______, James	Bib	65
______, John	Bal	44
______, John	Wks	334
______, John F.	Tlb	348
______, Josiah	Wrn	215
______, Mathew H.	Mon	205
______, Moses	Wks	332
______, Nathan T.	Mon	216
______, Richard	Pik	110
______, Robert	Bts	168
______, Septimus	Mon	205
NABB, William B.	Em	176
NAIL, Elizabeth	App	12
______, John	Hry	242
______, Reuben	Tat	376
NAILOR, Joseph	Hry	218
NALAN, Susannah	Frk	253
NALLS/NALL		
Nalls, Margaret	Hry	236
______, Middleton F.	Hry	205
______, Thomas J.	Hry	206
______, Wathan	Hry	236
Nall, Martin	Mon	195
______, Willis B.	Fay	206
NALLEAU, H. J.	Cht	260
NALLY/NALEY		
Nally, Henly	Lin	67
______, Joseph	Hal	125
Naley, John	Wks	349
NANCE, Ely	Hab	38
______, F. B.	Har	183
______, John	Clk	319
______, Nancy	Gwn	337
______, Nancy	New	35
______, William	Trp	44
______, William F.	Col	357
NAPIER/NAPPER/NAPPIER/NAPER		

Name	County	Page
Napier, Augustus	Col	360
______, Leroy	Put	199
______, Skelton	Put	174
______, Thomas	Col	343
______, Thomas	Mon	196
Napper, Drury	Wks	353
______, John	Wks	352
______, Shaderick	Twg	72
Nappier, Thomas	Bib	52
Naper, Caleb	Up	103
NAPP, John L.	Jks	337
NARAMORE, Eli W.	Hal	98
NARON, Eli	Cow	374
NARYMON, Sylvester	Har	183
NASH, Acton	Wil	315
______, Alice	Elb	151
______, Elijah	Jks	331
______, Gabriel	Mad	118
______, Henry E.	Elb	139
______, Jacob B.	Wil	314
______, James	Clk	319
______, James	Elb	151
______, James	Jks	336
______, James	Mtg	234
______, James E.	Trp	48
______, Jefferson	Mon	211
______, Jeremiah	Elb	155
______, John	Gwn	339
______, Katy	Mon	224
______, Micajah	Crf	409
______, Reubin A.	Twg	66
______, Robert B.	Gwn	342
______, Thomas J.	Mad	100
______, Stephen	Mtg	235
______, Thomas	Ogl	78
______, Valentin	Mon	212
NASON, James	Gwn	331
NASWORTHY, James	Mon	181
NATIONS/NATION		
Nations, Daniel	Pik	108
______, Ezzard	Cpb	202
______, John	Cpb	203
______, John	Hal	106
______, Thomas	Gwn	315
Nation, Esther	Hal	117
NAVES/NEVES/NAVERS		
Naves, C.	Bal	34
______, John	Bke	149
Neves, John	Ear	99
Navers, Tabitha	Rch	261
NAYEL, Vincent	Rch	256
NAYLOR, Dixon	Gwn	348
______, John	Gwn	374

Name	County	Page
Naylor, Josh	Gwn	312
______, Robert	Gwn	348
______, Stephen C.	Gwn	312
MEADON, Enoch	Wal	127
NEAL/NEIL/NEALL/NEEL/NIEL		
Neal, Basil	Col	360
______, Benjamin	Elb	128
______, Harrell	Wrn	216
______, James	Wks	336
______, James P.	Hal	114
______, Jeremiah	Jsp	368
______, Joel	Jks	346
______, Joel	Wrn	227
______, Joel	Wrn	229
______, John	Cow	381
______, John	Cow	389
______, John	Pik	119
______, John	Tlb	330
______, John M.	Frk	232
______, John R. M.	Ran	244
______, Jonathan	Ear	92
______, Joseph	Trp	46
______, Lindsay	Elb	129
______, McCormick	New	13
______, Mary	Mtg	235
______, Older	Gre	288
______, Reuben B.	New	38
______, Richard	Frk	246
______, Richard L.	New	13
______, Stephen	Frk	230
______, Tabitha	Frk	220
______, Thomas	Wrn	215
______, Thomas Jr.	Wrn	218
______, William	Frk	221
______, William	Frk	239
______, William F.O.	Hst	268
Neil, Alex[r].	Cpb	204
______, Elias	Tms	17
______, Elijah	Tms	26
______, Hamon	Dec	15
______, James T.	Dec	11
______, Thomas	Han	163
Neall, Jonathan	Hst	262
______, Peter L.	Jns	429
Neel, John M.C.	Hab	42
Niel, Mitchell	Em	166
______, Sarah	Em	169
NEELEY/NEELY/NEALY		
Neeley, David	Mor	266
______, Henry	Wal	143
______, John H.	Wal	143
______, Thomas	Ogl	66
Neely, Jackson	Bts	160
Neely, James	Jef	402
______, Thomas	New	37
______, Thomas	Wsh	268
Nealy, John	Up	116
______, William	Hal	93
______, William	Twg	87
NEASE/NEACE		
Nease, George	Eff	113
______, George	Eff	114
______, Godlieb	Eff	105
Neace, Manuel	Har	178
NEAVES/NEEVES		
Neaves, William	Ran	246
Neeves, C.	Bal	34
NEELAND, Solomon	Elb	154
NEICLER, Hugh	Clk	306
NEIDLINGER, Samuel	Eff	106
NEIGHBOURS, James	Jks	319
NEILSON, John	Rch	292
NELMS/NELMES		
Nelms, Chorrs	Tfo	355
______, Ezekiel	Rch	290
______, James	Elb	121
______, James	Gwn	375
______, Jordan	Elb	158
______, Thomas	Gwn	345
______, Thomas	New	7
______, William	Elb	141
______, William	Hry	209
Nelmes, Jesse	Elb	131
______, John	Elb	127
______, Nathaniel	Elb	146
NELSON/NELLSON		
Nelson, Abraham	Mor	258
______, Alexander	DeK	5
______, Alexander	Twg	6
______, Alfred	Twg	8
______, Ambrose	Wks	35
______, Andrew	DeK	4
______, Andrew	DeK	4
______, Anna	Bke	14
______, Archibald	Wal	15
______, Charles H.	Wil	28
______, Daniel	Cht	24
______, David D.	Bak	1
______, Ebenezer	Mus	28
______, Elizabeth	Pul	14
______, Gideon	Up	10
______, Henry	Put	18
______, Isaac	Cam	18
______, James	Wal	15
______, Jannett	Gwn	34
______, John	Bts	17

Name	County	Page
Nelson, John	Cow	385
______, John	Crf	408
______, John	Mon	188
______, John	Tat	375
______, John	Twg	62
______, John K.	Han	162
______, John S.	Gwn	374
______, Matthew	Rch	269
______, Mitchell	Rch	257
______, Moses	Jks	339
______, Nancy	Hal	87
______, Noah	Wal	155
______, Noah	Wal	158
______, Noah	Wal	163
______, Noel	Mor	261
______, Perry	Gre	301
______, Peter	Fay	205
______, Silvester	Jks	328
______, Stokely T.	Gwn	336
______, Tayler	Mor	255
______, Thomas	Jsp	354
______, Thomas	Mor	254
______, Thomas	Up	107
______, W.	Wks	339
______, Wade	Wks	352
______, Wiley	Elb	138
______, Wiley	Gwn	333
______, William	Fay	203
______, William	Jsp	353
______, William	Mon	188
______, William	Mon	201
______, William	Twg	82
Neilson, Eli	Mar	142
NELUMS/NELLUMS/NELAMS/ NELLEMS		
Nelums, Archabol	Hal	132
______, Curtis	Bak	18
Nellums, Presley	Mon	172
______, Shines	Lau	11
Nelams, David	Frk	249
Nellems, Joshua	Hab	38
NESBET/NESBIT/NESBITT/ NEISBET		
Nesbet, Alfred	Clk	327
______, Eugenious A.	Mor	249
______, James	Clk	327
______, John	Clk	325
______, John	Col	358
______, John Jr.	Clk	321
______, Samuel S.	Wks	331
______, William	Gwn	326
Nesbitt, Alex.	Wks	335
______, Jane	Wks	334

Name	County	Page
Nesbitt, Eleanor L.	Rch	264
______, James	DeK	35
Neisbit, James	New	52
______, Robert	New	52
______, William	New	39
NESMITH/NEESMITH/NESSMITH		
Nesmith, James	Bul	99
______, James	Scr	311
Neesmith, John	Bul	97
Nessmith, Charles R.	Bke	148
NESTER, Thomas	Eff	108
NESTRAND, George	Bul	99
NETHERCLIFT, A.	Bry	84
______, Dick	Cht	281
NETHERLAND, Isaac	Rch	289
______, James	Hst	268
______, James Sr.	Rch	289
NETTLES: also see Knettles		
Nettles, James	Gwn	363
______, Martin	App	7
______, William Sr.	App	7
______, William Jr.	App	6
NEUFVILLE, Rev^{d}. Ed.	Cht	253
NEVILL/NEVELL/NEVILLS		
Nevill, Hillman H.	Put	214
______, Jacob	Bul	100
Nevell, James B.	Rab	227
Nevills, Squire	Mon	186
NEW, Benjamin	Wal	158
______, Daniel	Wsh	263
______, Elijah	New	24
______, Henry	New	12
______, Jacob	DeK	58
______, Jesse	Mad	101
______, Joel	DeK	58
______, Samuel	Bts	163
______, William	New	24
NEWBERN, Archibald	Elb	141
______, Dread	Lwn	86
______, Hickman	Jks	344
______, John	Jks	343
______, John	Ware	183
______, Thomas	Elb	159
______, Thomas	Lwn	83
______, Thomas	Ware	184
______, William	Lwn	88
NEWBERRY/NEWBURY/NEWBERY		
Newberry, Isaac	Bib	68
______, James	Mar	138
______, James	Put	197
______, Joseph C.	Cam	188
______, Joshua H.	Hal	131
Newbury, John	Crf	408

Name	County	Page
Newbury, John	Dec	8
______, Robert	App	12
______, Sarah	Dec	15
Newbery, Nancy	Twg	60
NEWBY, Erum	Twg	69
______, James	Jns	430
______, Jesse	Ear	93
______, Jesse	Up	95
______, John	Jsp	360
______, Larken	Jsp	360
NEWCOMB/NEWCOMBE		
Newcomb, Lemuel	Bib	52
Newcombe, Ruben	Cht	254
NEWMAN/NEWMANS/NUMAN		
Newman, Daniel	Bul	99
______, Edward	Hst	281
______, Elwell	Wsh	270
______, Garrett	Wil	307
______, Hillary	Hst	281
______, James	Col	347
______, James A.	Tms	23
______, Jeptha	Cow	378
______, Jeremiah	Hry	236
______, John	Hry	206
______, John	Irw	303
______, John	Pul	161
______, John	Wrn	218
______, Lem	Mon	214
______, Samuel	Wrn	220
______, Thomas	Col	346
______, Thomas	Rch	281
______, William	Col	346
______, William	Col	359
______, William	Han	163
______, Wormley	Cow	388
Newmans, Charles	Tlf	4
Numan, Willis	Lwn	90
NEWSOM/NEWSOME/NEWSONE		
Newsom, A.	Bal	29
______, Amos	Col	349
______, Asa	Wsh	248
______, Catharine (W)	Mor	265
______, David A.	Mus	285
______, Elander	Dec	15
______, Hardy	Bib	76
______, Henry	Bib	62
______, James	Mar	138
______, Joel D.	Trp	32
______, John	Bul	92
______, John	Put	188
______, Jordy	Wsh	248
______, Joshua	Mar	143
______, Joseph W. H.	Jns	470
Newsom, Kinchin	Wsh	264
______, Nathaniel	New	53
______, P.	Bal	44
______, Ranzy	Wsh	251
______, Robert	Gre	283
______, Silas	Mus	292
______, William	Col	350
Newsome, Crawford	Wrn	224
______, Daniel W.	Wrn	193
______, Dicy	Wrn	220
______, Eliza	Wrn	224
______, Fig^{rs}.	Wrn	224
______, Gideon	Wrn	221
______, Greene	Wrn	221
______, Joel	Put	188
______, John Jr.	Wrn	221
______, John Jr.	Wrn	226
______, Polly	Cht	250
______, Rhoda	Wrn	226
______, Solomon	Wrn	220
______, Solomon Jr.	Wrn	222
Newsone, Batts	Pul	150
NEWTON, Ayres	Jsp	381
______, Bird L.	Tms	18
______, Ebenezer	Clk	327
______, Elezur L.	Clk	327
______, George	Scr	304
______, Giles	Fay	197
______, James	Tms	25
______, John H.	Jef	404
______, Josiah	Clk	325
______, Levy	Cow	370
______, Moses	Scr	302
______, Nathan	Hal	105
______, Philip	Em	173
______, Plantation	Cht	280
______, Samuel Sr.	Scr	301
______, Samuel Jr.	Scr	303
______, Thomas E.	Hal	116
______, William	Fay	200
______, William	Tms	23
______, William	Tms	26
NEWELL/NEWEL		
Newell, Catharine	Hry	234
______, Isaac	Bal	41
______, Samuel	Cow	379
______, Samuel	Frk	232
______, William P.	Trp	37
Newel, Simeon	Pik	110
NEYLAND, David O.	Hst	263
______, Mary H.	Bke	150
NEYLE, Affy	Cht	242
______, Sampson	Cht	248

**Neyle, Sampson (slaves) Cht 282
NIBLET/NIBLETT
Niblet, Abel Mwr 167
_____, Susanna Mwr 167
Niblett, Elizabeth New 24
_____, Tilman Gwn 370
NIBLACK, Thomas Jks 314
_____, Samuel J. Jks 311
NICHALOU/NICOLAU
Nichalou, Barnard Gly 267
Nicolau, Pascal Gly 269
NICHOLS/NICHOLLS/NICHOLDS/
NICKLES/NICKOLS/NICOLS/
NICHOLAS/NUCHOLS
Nichols, Ambrose Har 179
_____, Amelia A. Bke 121
_____, Archibald Bry 231
_____, Charles Bke 125
_____, David Bke 152
_____, David Hab 18
_____, David D. Irw 301
_____, Doeb Wil 323
_____, Elias Bul 92
_____, George Wrn 218
_____, Henry Hry 240
_____, Henry Wal 133
_____, James Crf 404
_____, James DeK 53
_____, John Cow 387
_____, John Hal 74
_____, John Hal 89
_____, John B. Hal 75
_____, Mathew Hab 29
_____, R. J. Bal 41
_____, Simon W. Jns 466
_____, Stephen Pul 138
_____, Thomas Cow 387
_____, Travers Fay 185
_____, Vincent Crf 404
_____, Wiley Hal 112
_____, William DeK 55
_____, William Ear 95
Nicholls, Abraham Frk 255
_____, Julius Frk 220
_____, Nathaniel Elb 133
Nicholds, Christopher Bts 171
_____, John O. Lin 62
_____, Nancy Ogl 78
Nickles, Ransom Clk 314
_____, William Clk 316
Nickols, Virginia Cow 380
Nicols, Johnathan Mwr 166
Nicholas, William S. Jns 459
Nuchols, Alexander Hal 81
NICHOLSON/NICHALSON/
NICHILSON/NICKELSON/
NICKERSON
Nicholson, Alford Hal 124
_____, Duncan Dec 14
_____, George Ogl 103
_____, James Dec 14
_____, James Hab 54
_____, James Put 218
_____, James Wal 124
_____, John Bib 68
_____, John Pik 115
_____, John Jr. Hal 98
Nicholson, John Sr. Hal 98
_____, Nath. Wks 354
_____, Rachel Hal 99
_____, Thomas Scr 314
Nichalson, George Ogl 102
Nichilson, William Gre 287
Nickelson, Dukin Ran 247
Nickerson, James Mon 198
NICOLL, John C. Cht 253
NIGHT, Elisha Trp 47
_____, Elizabeth Twg 86
_____, James Pul 159
_____, James Twg 68
_____, Jesse Wsh 241
_____, Lewis Wsh 267
_____, Mathew Wsh 269
_____, Silvanous Wsh 267
NILES, Henry New 5
NILSON, Drury Wrn 198
NIMMONS, William Cow 367
NIMS, Jo[h]. Gwn 364
NIPPER, Benjamin Pul 152
_____, Elijah Hst 289
_____, Elisha Hst 288
_____, John Pul 149
_____, John Ware 189
_____, Mary Irw 304
NIVIN, Daniel Jns 441
NIX/NICKS
Nix, Bishop Hab 27
_____, David New 5
_____, Edward Hal 111
_____, Edward New 52
_____, Edward Tlb 342
_____, George Frk 246
_____, George New 6
_____, George Pul 154
_____, Jacob Jks 334
_____, James Har 183

Name	County	Page
Nix, James	Hry	227
______, John	Gwn	350
______, John	Hab	31
______, John	Hal	111
______, John	Wal	139
______, Joseph	Hab	27
______, Nicholas	Har	184
______, Rebecca	Tlb	343
______, Thomas	Jks	325
______, Thomas	Tlb	342
______, Valentin	Hal	85
______, Washington	Twg	68
______, William	Hab	53
______, William	Hal	111
______, Williamson	Wal	139
______, Wiley	Hal	112
Nicks, Anderson	Wal	134
______, Aron	Hal	73
______, Elijah	Mwr	150
______, Jeremiah	Wal	137
______, Jeremiah	Wal	173
______, Jesse M.	Clk	314
______, John L.	Wal	172
______, Jonas	Hab	11
______, Joseph	Elb	160
______, Littleberry	Wal	170
______, Milly	Clk	305
______, William	Wal	172
NIXON/NICKSON		
Nixon, Henry	Clk	305
______, Honor	Doo	81
______, James	Mor	249
______, John	Frk	218
______, Robert	Doo	81
______, Samuel	Doo	81
______, Thomas	Jks	349
______, Travis	Jks	345
______, Washington	Bts	164
Nickson, Edmond P.	Fay	196
______, Joseph	Wal	162
______, William	Cow	384
______, William	Fay	204
NOBLES/NOBLE		
Nobles, Amos	Jns	433
______, Andrew	Twg	86
______, Edmund	Hst	268
______, Elizabeth	Scr	315
______, Hambleton	Lau	11
______, Hezekiah	Wks	343
______, John	Bib	74
______, John	Mar	142
______, John	Up	105
______, John G.	McI	129

Name	County	Page
Nobles, Joseph	Mar	142
______, Josiah	Hst	267
______, Luke	Up	108
______, Nathaniel	Ware	187
______, Rachel	Fay	186
______, Richard	Cam	190
______, Sarah	Wal	173
______, Solomon	Twg	76
______, Thomas	Cam	186
______, William	Twg	86
Noble, James	Tlf	5
______, Jesse	Tlb	342
______, Samuel	Pul	161
______, Wallace	Doo	87
NODE, Azarias	Gwn	345
______, James	Gwn	345
NOE, Bennett	Wal	167
NOLAN/NOLEN/NOWLIN/NOWLAN/ NOWLAND/NOLAND/NOLIN/ NOWLEN		
Nolan, James	Gwn	319
______, James	Wil	312
______, Thomas	Mor	268
______, Thomas F.	Up	100
______, William	Gwn	319
Nolen, Isaac	Bts	165
______, James	Hry	231
______, Joseph	Wil	299
______, Richard	Bts	165
______, Stephen	Bts	165
Nowlin, David	Jks	337
______, Sherod	Clk	314
Nowlan, Hannah	Eff	104
Nowland, William	Mor	266
Noland, Peyton	Cpb	194
Nolin, George	Hry	219
Nowlen, Briant W.	Jks	323
NOLES/NOWLS/NOLDS		
Noles, Charles	Hry	247
______, Ephraim	Bke	124
Noles, Rachal	Jef	411
______, Samuel	Frk	226
______, Thomas	Hab	29
______, Washington	App	9
______, William	Wks	353
Nowls, Elisebeth	Hab	52
Nolds, Benjamin E.	New	49
______, Dennis M.	New	44
NOLEMAN, Sarah	Ogl	98
NOLING/NOWLING		
Noling, Abner	New	47
______, Stephen	New	47
______, William Sr.	New	47

Name	County	Page
Noling, William	New	47
Nowling, Sharrard	Ran	249
NOLLEY, Daniel	Hry	220
NORMAN/NORMON		
Norman, A. B.	Tat	373
_____, Agyle	Wil	303
_____, Benjamin	Wil	303
_____, Benjamin	Wil	318
_____, Candace	Hry	250
_____, Charles	Car	219
_____, Elijah B.	Elb	145
_____, Elizabeth	Bib	76
_____, Elizabeth	Wil	308
_____, George W.	Car	217
_____, H. S.	DeK	26
_____, James M.	Lwn	90
_____, James S.	Mus	279
_____, Jesse	Wil	303
_____, John	Wil	302
_____, John	Wil	302
_____, Joseph, dec'd.Est.	Lib	50
_____, Joshua	Fay	192
_____, P. (col^{d}.)	Bal	40
_____, Samuel	Tms	18
_____, Wm., dec'd. Est.	Lib	50
_____, William	Up	96
_____, William A.	Lin	63
_____, William B.	Wil	289
_____, William B.	Wil	290
_____, William L.	Jks	344
_____, William S.	Bib	71
Normon, Isaac M.	Em	165
NONY, Hetty	Col	363
NORARD, Presley	Hal	84
_____, Thomas	Bak	20
NORRELL, Frances	Hal	106
_____, John B.	Hst	275
_____, Richard	Rch	255
_____, Thomas	Hal	106
_____, William	Gre	293
NORRIS/NORIS		
Norris, Abner	Wrn	216
_____, Alexander	Tfo	361
_____, Andrew M.	Hab	18
_____, Baldwin	Put	187
_____, Benjamin	Wal	150
_____, Cato	Cam	185
_____, Dennis	Bib	68
_____, Dennis	Hst	267
_____, Elisha	Jks	339
_____, Elizabeth	Han	163
_____, Frances	Tfo	365
_____, Gemima	Hal	122
Norris, Green	Hst	277
_____, Greene	Wrn	230
_____, Isaac	Hst	282
_____, Jacob	Gre	286
_____, James	Cht	280
_____, James	Hal	122
_____, James	Mon	181
_____, James	New	28
_____, Jas. (of Abner)	Wrn	219
_____, James of Jas. Jr.	Wrn	216
_____, James Jr.	Wrn	218
_____, James F.	Wal	131
_____, Jethero	Wal	148
_____, Jethraw	Wal	149
_____, Joel	Mon	181
_____, Joel	Wrn	215
_____, John	Gre	286
_____, John	Jsp	361
_____, Josiah W.	Mwr	166
_____, Littleton	Gwn	364
_____, Margaret	Ogl	69
_____, Mathew	Dec	17
_____, Morgan	Wrn	218
_____, Needham	Pik	121
_____, Noel	New	53
_____, Rebeca	Hal	130
_____, Robert	Bal	39
_____, Robert	Hab	55
_____, Robert S.	Hab	55
_____, Samuel	Gre	286
_____, Sanford R.	Hry	203
_____, Sarah	Cht	270
_____, Thomas	Hal	72
_____, Thomas	Wrn	220
_____, William	Bib	52
_____, William	Clk	301
_____, William	Crf	407
_____, William	Gwn	353
_____, William	Jsp	367
_____, William	Wrn	214
_____, William C.	Bke	146
_____, William P.	Mwr	157
_____, Young R.	Bts	170
Noris, William	Gwn	325
_____, Willis C.	Gwn	325
NORSWORTHY, Fredric	Mon	200
_____, William	Bke	125
NORTH, Abraham	Cow	382
_____, Anthony	Cow	368
_____, Chs. P.	Up	96
_____, John	Ware	185
_____, William	Ogl	64
_____, William B.	Ware	185

Name	County	Page
NORTHERN/NORTHON/NORTHAN/ NOTHERN		
Northern, Basset	Jsp	360
______, William	Crf	398
Northon, Peter	Jns	473
Northan, John	Ogl	82
Nothern, Polly	Tfo	361
NORTHINGTON, James	Ogl	78
______, Jesse E.	Wsh	239
______, William	Wsh	241
NORTON, Cornelious	Fay	187
______, Elizabeth	Cam	186
______, Isaac	Cht	261
______, Hiram	Hal	105
______, Jacob P.	Han	163
______, James	Ogl	99
______, James H.	Fay	193
______, John	New	14
______, John G.	Fay	184
______, Martin	Fay	192
______, Matthew	Har	187
______, Messer	Rab	229
______, Miles B.	Fay	182
______, Nehemiah	Hab	13
______, Robert S.	New	14
______, Silas M.	Wal	129
______, Thomas	DeK	60
______, William	Ogl	99
______, William	Wal	125
______, William G.	Fay	182
NOW, Martin	Cht	242
NOWEL/NOWELL/NOEL		
Nowel, Beasley	Ogl	101
______, Elisha	Wsh	257
______, Henry	Wsh	264
______, James	Ogl	72
______, James	Wal	162
______, John H.	Ogl	71
Nowell, Harris	Wsh	256
______, Luke	Mon	226
______, Thomas	Clk	320
Noel, Mrs.	Cht	263
______, Richmond	Car	218
NORWOOD/NORWARD		
Norwood, Blakely	Frk	218
______, Caleb M.	Tlb	327
______, James	Frk	246
______, John	Jsp	365
______, Joseph	Frk	247
______, Samuel	Car	221
______, William	Wks	315
Norward, Thomas	Han	162
NOYCE, P.	Cht	257

Name	County	Page
NULALLY, Benjamin F.	Har	190
NUNES, Chas. (colored)	Bke	140
______, Janet (colored)	Bke	140
______, Joseph (colored)	Bke	140
______, Robert (colored)	Bke	140
NUNEZ: see Eunier		
NUNGAZER, Joseph M.	Cam	190
NUNN/NUN		
Nunn, Charlton	Bib	65
______, Hiram	Bke	130
______, James	Gwn	371
______, Lemuel	Mad	102
______, Nimrod	Wrn	222
______, Samuel	Har	188
______, Thomas	Frk	239
______, William	Jks	336
Nun, Francis	Tlb	337
NUNNELEE/NUNNALLY/ NUNNELLY/NUNALLY		
Nunnelee, James F.	Elb	154
______, Walter	Elb	152
______, Walter	Tfo	354
Nunnally, Aaron P.	Clk	298
______, John A.	Clk	299
______, Sucky	Clk	300
Nunnelly, Josiah E.	Pik	118
______, Rubin	Hab	25
Nunally, William B.	Wal	142
NUNRY, Henry	Twg	88
NUTT, Andrew	Pik	129
______, Dianah	Ogl	91
______, Jane (W)	Mor	239
______, Jonathan	Cow	388
______, Samuel R.	Bts	162
______, William	Pul	160
______, William B.	Bts	168

Name	County	Page
OAKLEY, John	Fay	206
OAKMAN, William H.	Col	338
______, William H.	Rch	263
OAKS/OAKES		
Oaks, Jonathan	Wal	128
______, Rebecah	Ogl	89
Oakes, David	Rab	222
OATES/OATS		
Oates, Charles	Bke	122
______, J.	Cht	270
Oats, Richard W.	Cow	389
OBANON, B.	Wks	352
OBAR/OBER/OBARE		
Obar, Michael	Hal	71
Ober, Michael	Hal	71

Obare, Robert	Hab	42
OBENGEL, Sherwood	Hab	35
OBENYON/OBENION		
Obenyon, Green H.	Hab	35
Obenion, Benjamin	Hab	38
OBERY, James R.	McI	124
_____, John	McI	132
_____, Reuben	McI	124
_____, Solomon	McI	132
OBORN, William	New	53
OBUM, John	Clk	315
O'BRIEN/O'BRIAN/O'BRYAN/ O'BYRN		
O'Brien, Archa T.	Dec	10
_____, James	Bal	37
_____, Lewis	Dec	10
O'Brian, John	Gre	304
O'Bryan, Brepir	Tfo	356
_____, David	Dec	19
_____, Jesse	McI	129
_____, Susannah	McI	129
O'Byrn, D.	Cht	272
O'CONNOR/O'CONNER/ O'CONNERS		
O'Connor, Ed.	Cht	257
_____, Edward	Rch	274
_____, Thomas	Tlb	339
O'Conner, Patrick	Hal	72
O'Conners, Nancy	Clk	316
OCTWELL, Richard Y.	Trp	33
O'DANIEL, Wilson	Up	99
ODELL, Benjamin	Rab	223
ODENA, John	McI	122
_____, Peter	McI	122
ODINET, Charlotte	Cht	246
ODINGSELL, M. A.	Cht	244
ODLE, Polly	Clk	307
_____, Thomas	Hal	87
ODOM/ODUM/ODAM/ODEM/ODEN		
Odom, Archibald	Em	169
_____, Archibald	Pul	155
_____, Asa	Ear	96
_____, Christopher W.	Gwn	333
_____, Deldatha	Ear	96
_____, Elizabeth	Pul	155
_____, Ferdinand	Gwn	317
_____, Henry	Hab	55
_____, James	Em	170
_____, John	Lee	28
_____, Mildred	Crf	406
_____, Moses	Pul	154
_____, Susanah	Mad	110
_____, William	Pul	153
Odum, Abraham	Jns	457
_____, Bryant	Scr	315
_____, Celia	Bke	151
_____, Dempsey	Jns	457
_____, John	Har	189
_____, John	Mtg	231
_____, Laban	Bke	146
_____, Luriah	Doo	86
_____, Mary	Bul	102
_____, Sophia	Doo	84
Odam, Elkanah Jr.	Wal	156
_____, Elkaney	Wal	133
_____, Gedion	Hab	55
_____, John	Tat	373
_____, John P.	Wal	161
_____, Jordon	Clk	325
_____, Levingston	Wal	126
_____, William	Wal	127
_____, William	Wal	172
_____, Wilson	Cam	185
Odem, Dempsey	Wsh	259
_____, Elizabeth	Wsh	259
Oden, Allexander	Jns	436
OEMLER, A. G.	Cht	257
OFIELD, Elijah	Up	109
OFFUTT, Jesse	Col	342
_____, Joseph	Col	342
OGBURN/OGBERN		
Ogburn, Jacob	Wks	335
_____, James	Wks	334
Ogbern, L. B.	Crf	415
OGDEN/OGDON		
Ogden, Charles	Ogl	65
_____, Elisha	Ogl	79
_____, Isaac	Tms	29
_____, Jacob N.	McI	122
_____, Moses	Rch	260
Ogdon, Eliza	App	8
OGG, Thomas	Rch	289
OGLE, Herkelus	Hal	91
_____, John	Hal	87
OGILBY/OGELBY/OGILSBY/ OGELLEY/OGLESBY/OGLESBEY		
Ogilby, Benjamin	Ogl	96
_____, John	Ogl	74
_____, William	Ogl	74
Ogelby, Leroy	New	8
_____, Nancy	New	41
_____, Richard	Wal	132
Ogilsby, Hugh	Mor	251
Ogelley, Jesse M.	New	42
Oglesby, Ann	Cam	191
_____, Anthony	Cht	272

Name	County	Page
Oglesby, Anthony	McI	126
______, Daniel	Scr	311
______, Drury	Elb	119
______, Garrett	Wil	302
______, George	Elb	146
______, George L.	Wil	316
______, James	Elb	160
______, James	Em	174
______, James	Irw	302
______, James	Scr	311
______, Lewis	Irw	303
______, Lindsay	Elb	132
______, Richard	Scr	311
______, Robert C.	Elb	132
______, Sarah	Cht	268
______, Thomas	Bts	175
______, Thomas	Elb	119
______, William	Elb	146
Oglesbey, Benjamin	Twg	81
OGLETREE, Absalom	Fay	205
______, Gipson	Cpb	211
______, Hope H.	Fay	205
______, John	Tfo	360
______, John B.	Mon	179
______, John G.	Wil	300
______, Joseph	Mor	254
______, Littleton	Tfo	354
______, Philemon	Mon	179
______, Richard	Han	163
______, Samuel	Hry	204
______, Thomas	Up	112
______, Wiley	Mtg	233
______, William	Mon	180
O'HARRA/OHARROW		
O'Harra, James	Pik	111
______, Rebecca	Mwr	166
Oharrow, Andrew	Cpb	208
O'KELLY/O'KELLEY		
O'Kelly, Francis	Ogl	73
______, James	Mad	113
______, James	Ogl	67
______, John	Hab	41
______, Thomas	Ogl	73
______, Thomas D.	Hab	41
______, William	Hab	41
______, William J.	Tfo	362
O'Kelley, Charles D.	Wal	133
______, Francis	Wal	137
______, Francis D.	Wal	153
______, George W.	Ogl	75
______, James	Wal	136
OLCOTT, James L.	Eff	104
O'LEARY, Cornelius	Wil	294

Name	County	Page
OLER, John	Wal	136
OLLIFF, John	Bul	98
______, Joseph	Bul	97
OLIPHANT/OLEVENT		
Oliphant, John	Bak	18
______, Joseph	Jef	417
Olevent, Rebecca	Gre	301
OLIVE/OLLIVE		
Olive, Abel	Rch	283
______, Benjamin	Col	342
______, Benjamin	Hst	279
______, Herndon	Ogl	71
______, James	Lin	64
______, John	Ogl	72
Ollive, James	Col	350
______, John	Col	348
______, Thomas W.	Col	346
OLIVER/OLLIVER		
Oliver, Andrew	Jks	315
______, Apha	Rch	269
______, Asa	Wsh	267
______, Beryian	Elb	150
______, Billy	Rch	270
______, C. A. B.	Bul	93
______, Charles	Pik	127
______, Dyonesius	Elb	150
______, Elijah	Jks	313
______, Elizabeth	Frk	254
______, Frances	Clk	301
______, George	Cht	269
______, George W.	Lau	20
______, Henry S.	Elb	156
______, J. G.	Lee	26
______, Jackson	Elb	142
______, Jacob	Har	187
______, James	Cht	268
______, James	DeK	39
______, James	Elb	147
______, James	Hal	89
______, James	Mon	185
______, James	Mon	192
______, James	New	53
______, James	Pul	152
______, James	Twg	63
______, James	Wsh	241
______, James G.	Gre	272
______, John	Bib	76
______, John L.	Clk	300
______, John M.	Wsh	271
______, John Sr.	Clk	301
______, Lucrecia	Wrn	211
______, Luraney	Twg	83
______, McCarty Sr.	Elb	150

Name	County	Page
Oliver, Martin	Pul	161
______, Michael	Rab	226
______, Nancy	Elb	156
______, Oden	Wsh	264
______, Peter M.	Hal	90
______, Phinnihas	Hst	261
______, Roan	Wsh	263
______, S. H.	Rch	260
______, Sam	Gwn	376
______, Samuel	Bib	65
______, Samuel	New	11
______, Samuel K.	Hal	73
______, Shelton	Elb	151
______, Simeon	Elb	147
______, Simeon	Gwn	324
______, Sophin	McI	124
______, Thomas	Dec	14
______, Thomas	DeK	48
______, Thomas	Elb	136
______, Thomas H.	Elb	152
______, W. N.	Cht	278
______, Wiley	Twg	61
______, William	Em	177
______, William	Han	163
______, William	Mon	226
______, William	Twg	82
______, William C.	Up	112
Olliver, Benjamine	Jns	429
______, Jacob	Scr	315
______, John	Scr	316
______, Mathew	Jns	434
______, Thomas	Scr	317
______, William	DeK	34
______, William	Scr	317
O'NEAL/O'NEIL/O'NEEL/ O'NEALL/O'NAIL		
O'Neal, Aaron	Bts	173
______, Alfred	Up	115
______, Amy	Lin	75
______, Andrew	Mad	105
______, Benjamin	New	26
______, Britton	Hab	19
______, Britton	Twg	65
______, Bryant	Wal	150
______, Charles	McI	129
______, Cullen	Lau	21
______, Daniel	Dec	5
______, David	Col	340
______, Edmund	Put	199
______, Edwin	Tlb	328
______, Gerry M.	Mon	181
______, Gray	Gwn	368
______, Griffin	Mon	185
O'Neal, James		81
______, John	Tlb	329
______, Joseph	Wal	167
______, Masten G.	Lau	6
______, Phillip	Hab	23
______, Rebecah	Mor	266
______, Ross	Wrn	228
______, Sarah	Mor	248
______, Theophilus	Mon	185
______, Thomas	Mwr	160
______, Thomas W.	Put	199
______, Wooten	Gre	295
______, Zachariah	Bts	160
O'Neil, Harrison	Tfo	357
______, John	Wrn	283
______, Mary	Tfo	368
______, Mary	Wyn	282
______, Quinca	Tfo	356
O'Neel, Brittan Jr.	Hab	20
______, James	Hab	20
O'Neall, Henry	Jns	438
O'Nail, James	New	16
______, John	New	46
______, Wright	Mad	104
ONSTED, John	Gwn	317
OPRY, Joseph	Twg	77
O'QUIN/O'QUINN		
O'Quin, Allen	Wsh	247
______, Bryant	Wsh	261
______, John	Bal	37
______, John	Wsh	261
O'Quinn, Silas	App	9
ORAM/ORME		
Oram, Mrs.	Cht	252
Orme, R. W.	Bal	34
OREAR, Benjamin	Mon	202
______, John	Han	163
ORICK/ORIC		
Orick, Henry G.	Mwr	150
Oric, Celia	Put	211
O'RILEY, Michael	Wrn	200
ORIM, Thomas	Hab	66
ORMSBY, Ebenezer	Jns	466
ORR/OAR		
Orr, Abram	Gly	268
______, Andrew	New	39
______, Barrie	Pik	124
______, Christopher	Wil	308
______, Daniel	Pik	124
______, Dicy	Frk	223
______, James	Jks	313
______, James	Wal	123
______, Jesse	Hal	79

Name	County	Page
Orr, John	Jks	312
_____, John	Mon	198
_____, John	Wsh	263
_____, Mary	Frk	247
_____, Mathew	Pik	124
_____, Nancy	Jks	326
_____, Phillip	Cow	383
_____, Richard	DeK	49
_____, Robert	Hal	71
_____, William	Jks	326
_____, William	Wsh	247
Oar, Meshack	Jks	343
ORSON, Benjamin	Elb	128
OTWELL, James	Hal	80
OSBORN/OSBORNE/OSBON/		
OSBURN/OZBURN		
Osborn, Benjamin	Jsp	387
_____, Claiborn	Gwn	357
_____, Daniel	Mon	209
_____, George	Han	163
_____, George	Trp	32
_____, Green	Hry	248
_____, James	Jsp	398
_____, James	Gwn	350
_____, Jessee	Gwn	333
_____, Joel A.	Trp	32
_____, John	Cpb	210
_____, John	Han	163
_____, John	Mon	202
_____, John A.	Bal	28
_____, John M.	Jsp	388
_____, Margaret	Wrn	217
_____, Maria F.	Cam	183
_____, Nelson	Frk	211
_____, Pheby	Jsp	393
_____, Rubin	Wsh	264
_____, Thomas	Frk	256
_____, William	Hry	246
_____, William	Wsh	272
_____, William C.	Har	179
Osborne, Benjamin	Tfo	364
_____, Briton S.	Hry	232
_____, E.	Cht	252
_____, Elizabeth	Hry	232
_____, George	Har	177
_____, Irby	Hry	232
_____, James	Hry	248
_____, Rhoda	Rch	288
Osbon, William	Ogl	84
Osburn, George W. H.	Cow	372
_____, Samuel	Bts	170
_____, William K.	Fay	193
Ozburn, John	Wal	151
OSEMORE, Susan	Mor	247
OSGOOD, Rebecca	Lib	51
_____, William,dec'd,Est.	Lib	50
OSTER, Jacob	Har	186
_____, James R.	Har	190
OSLEY, Jesse	Elb	155
_____, Thomas	New	20
_____, Zachariah	Elb	150
OSLIN, Jesse	Hry	209
_____, John	Hry	249
_____, William W.	Crf	409
OSTEEN/OSTEN/OSTEAN/OSTIN		
Osteen, Allen	Ware	183
_____, James	Cam	189
_____, John	Ware	184
_____, John Sr.	Ware	189
_____, John Jr.	Ware	183
_____, William	Tat	377
Osten, John	Cpb	201
_____, Michael Sr.	Cpb	201
_____, Michael Jr.	Cpb	201
_____, Richard	Cpb	201
Ostean, Jessee	Mon	198
_____, Thomas	Mon	198
Ostin, J. C.	DeK	26
OSWELL, John S.	Jns	458
OTTERY, William	DeK	49
OTTMAN, John	Bib	74
OTWELL, Paul M.	Pik	108
_____, Saphira	Fay	205
_____, W. M.	Gwn	332
OUSLEY, Jesse C.	Tlb	338
_____, John	Tlb	334
_____, Newdagate	Mon	184
_____, Rebecca	Tlb	332
_____, William B.	Tlb	334
OUTLAW, Alexander	Em	168
_____, Alexander	Lau	14
_____, Edward	Em	168
_____, James	Wks	332
_____, Jane	Hst	261
_____, Jeremiah	Crf	399
_____, John	Twg	79
_____, Morgan	Wsh	255
_____, Nancy	Wsh	275
OVERBY, Freeman	Hal	133
_____, Thomas	Clk	306
OVERMAN, John	Jns	454
OVERSTREET, John	McI	132
_____, John D.	Wal	125
_____, McIllvay	Tat	371
_____, Martha	Em	165
_____, Moses	Bke	149

Overstreet, William App 5
______, William Bke 149
OVERTON, Abijah New 5
______, Ann Elb 151
______, Gilchrist Tfo 365
______, James Hry 203
______, John Cpb 201
______, John New 17
OWENS/OWEN/OWINS/OWINGS
Owens, Alexander Car 229
______, Anderson Gwn 357
______, Anderson Gwn 372
______, Ann Hst 296
______, B. M. DeK 27
______, Bathsheba Elb 151
______, Beacham Put 179
______, Benjamin New 43
______, Caleb Jef 416
______, Daniel Tlb 325
______, Edmund Put 179
______, Elijah Hab 58
______, Elisha Mor 243
______, Elisha Rch 253
______, George W. Cht 248
______, Geo. W. Plantation Cht 279
______, Isaac Rch 283
______, James Hab 45
______, James Mar 138
______, Jerimiah Clk 309
______, Jesse F. Rch 258
______, John Gwn 369
______, John Hry 248
______, John Lau 24
______, John D. Hab 21
______, John J. Hst 262
______, John N. New 21
______, John G. Bts 171
______, Jonathan Jns 470
______, Levi Dec 4
______, Lott Dec 18
______, Martha Jns 428
______, Martin Up 108
______, Mary Up 106
______, Mary Wil 312
______, Micajah Doo 88
______, Milley Wsh 273
______, Moorfield Gre 302
______, Owen Hab 58
______, Peter Jns 470
______, Philemon Jsp 392
______, Purnell W. Jns 470
______, Ransom Wal 136
______, Samuel Bib 65

Owens, Samuel Doo 78
______, Sarah Wil 297
______, Spencer Jns 470
______, Uriah Put 176
______, Wesley Put 179
______, Whitman Dec 18
______, William Dec 18
______, William Hab 64
______, William New 12
______, William Up 99
______, William M. Dec 18
______, William Sr. Up 99
Owen, Aron Mon 188
______, Brackett Jsp 353
______, David Jks 316
______, Davis Tfo 367
______, George Mwr 167
______, Glen Ogl 78
______, Griffin Wal 136
______, Hardiman Mus 286
______, Jacob Han 163
______, James Gwn 310
______, John Bke 117
______, John Bke 136
______, John Hab 21
______, John Trp 41
______, John Wil 303
______, John H. Mon 176
______, Joseph Hal 126
______, Mary Jsp 356
______, Obadiah Wal 129
______, Robert Jsp 355
______, Thadeus Hal 127
______, Thomas Hal 126
______, Thomas P. Bts 172
______, William Bke 138
______, William Gwn 310
______, William Hal 114
______, William Hry 250
______, William Rab 225
Owins, (Blank 1st name) Jns 458
______, John Clk 299
______, Lemuel Pik 120
______, William B. Pik 119
Owings, Samuel McI 132
OWENSBY, James Hab 7
______, Thomas Hry 221
OXFORD, David Hab 6
______, Edward Hry 201
______, Edward B. Hry 201
______, John Hab 6
______, Jonathan Hab 6
______, Tillman D. Jns 474

Name	County	Page
Oxford, William K.	Mon	186
OZLEY, John Y.	Wal	139
PACE/PAICE		
Pace, Mrs. B.	Col	334
______, Barnabas	Elb	120
______, Barnebass Sr.	New	6
______, Barnebass Jr.	New	7
______, Basil	Hry	200
______, Bryant	Hst	263
______, Clement	Put	185
______, Dredsel A.	Trp	43
______, Dreadzel	Elb	131
______, George W.	Bts	158
______, Hardy	DeK	29
______, Hardy	Hry	246
______, Hardy	Twg	75
______, James	Rch	258
______, James	Twg	66
______, James	Wrn	193
______, James H.	Pik	110
______, John	Elb	140
______, John	Hry	203
______, Kendred	Twg	62
______, Nancy	Ogl	83
______, Noel	Trp	39
______, Noah	Eff	110
______, Parris	Ogl	97
______, Samuel	Bib	74
______, Solomon	Pik	131
______, Stephen	Mus	286
______, Stephen Sr.	Hry	203
______, Stephen Jr.	Hry	203
______, Thomas	Bib	56
______, Thomas	Cpb	195
______, Thomas	Hry	246
______, Thomas	Rch	261
______, Trion	Eff	108
______, William	Fay	186
______, William	Har	186
______, William	New	34
______, William Sr.	Put	185
______, William Jr.	Put	185
Paice, Richard	Put	191
PACILLY, Francis	Cht	240
PACKER, Lewis	Up	110
PACKET, Ezekiel	Mon	212
PADGETT/PADGET		
Padgett, Abram	Hal	107
______, Asa	Hal	107
______, Elijah	Bib	62
______, Elijah	Tat	371

Name	County	Page
Padgett, Elisha	App	6
______, Henry R.	Fay	181
______, James	Lib	51
______, James W.	Fay	190
______, Jesse	Hal	107
______, John	Ware	186
______, Moses	Fay	181
______, Nelson	Hal	107
______, Rhoda	Wks	336
______, William	Har	189
______, William	Ware	185
Padget, John	Ran	245
______, Nathan	Hal	106
PADON, Panel	DeK	62
______, William	DeK	34
PADDLEFORD, E.	Cht	261
PAGE/PAGGED		
Page, Ashey	Mar	143
______, Benjamin	Jns	462
______, Benjamin	Mad	100
______, Britton	Wsh	269
______, Cary	Rab	225
______, David	Rab	227
______, Eliza	Cht	270
______, Elizabeth	Elb	127
______, Elizabeth	Twg	88
______, James	Doo	87
______, James	Up	120
______, John	Elb	134
______, John	Wsh	250
______, John	Wsh	252
______, Joseph H.	Wsh	253
______, Josiph J.	McI	122
______, Lavina	Doo	87
______, Level	Elb	136
______, Mary	Cht	257
______, Mary	Wsh	253
______, Modaniel	Mar	144
______, Solomon Sr.	Wsh	248
______, Solomon Jr.	Wsh	253
______, W. S.	Up	120
______, Watson D.	Elb	132
______, William	Gwn	335
______, William	Gwn	369
Pagged, Tresa	New	49
PAINTER, Ezekiel	Hab	106
PAIR, Henry	Frk	213
______, Ingram	Frk	239
______, James L.	DeK	73
______, Matthew	Frk	211
______, Richard	Frk	213
______, Thomas	Frk	230
______, William	Frk	248

Name	County	Page
Pair, William	Hry	250
PAYNE/PAINE/PAIN		
Payne, Absolom	Lau	22
______, Abslom E.	Lau	19
______, Asa	Frk	215
______, Benedict	Frk	237
______, Benjamin	Rch	257
______, Benjamin	Rch	269
______, Benjamin W.	New	26
______, Charles	Hab	49
______, Chesley	Frk	241
______, David	Frk	257
______, David Jr.	Frk	216
______, Edwin	New	16
______, Flemmen	Hal	124
______, George	Lau	20
______, James	Jks	330
______, James	Jks	345
______, John	Frk	215
______, John	Pik	121
______, John	Rch	286
______, John H.	Frk	216
______, John M.	Frk	216
______, John W.	Frk	215
______, John Sr.	Frk	210
______, Joseph	Frk	218
______, Joseph	Wks	332
______, Joseph	Wks	355
______, Landon	Frk	213
______, Lettice	New	30
______, Louisa	Gly	267
______, Mayfield	Frk	210
______, Mic	Wks	336
______, Middleton	Tlb	341
______, Olive	Bts	176
______, Peyton T.	Frk	237
______, Pollard	Bts	173
______, Ranson	Jks	332
______, Ranson	Wks	355
______, Reuben	Frk	237
______, Robert	Gly	265
______, Samuel	Wks	355
______, Samuel Sr.	Frk	252
______, Samuel T.	Frk	216
______, Thomas	Bts	176
______, Thomas Sr.	Frk	213
______, Thomas	Frk	211
______, William	Col	339
______, William	Frk	215
______, William	Gly	266
______, William	Lau	22
______, William	Rch	271
Paine, Alexander	Jks	334
Paine, Archabald	Hal	84
______, Charles J.	Hal	34
______, Ed.	Cht	257
______, Edward	Clk	291
______, Flail	Mon	211
______, Henry D.	Hry	216
______, Isaac B.	Hal	74
______, James	Wsh	246
______, John	Hal	84
______, Lindsey	Hal	84
______, Margaret	Hal	84
______, Nehemiah	Hal	95
______, Randolph	Har	190
______, Thomas	Hal	97
______, William	Hal	81
Pain, Ann G.	Pul	158
______, Larkin	Gwn	346
______, Thompson	Gwn	366
______, Thomas	Hab	6
______, Thomas	Ogl	89
PALEY, John M.	Hry	215
PALIN/PALEN		
Palin, James	Cht	244
Palen, James	DeK	56
PALHERION, Mary	Jef	414
PALMAN, David	Ogl	99
______, John	Ogl	99
PALMER/PALMOUR/PALMERE/ MALMORE		
Palmer, Amasa	Gre	272
______, Benjamin	Bke	138
______, C. H.	Jsp	357
______, Daniel	Han	163
______, David	Rch	281
______, Denison B.	Cow	381
______, Edmund	Bke	143
______, Edward	Cht	241
______, Francis	Gly	264
______, Grief	Hry	212
______, Hasting	DeK	45
______, Hezekiah	Wal	153
______, Israel	Han	164
______, James	Han	163
______, James	Lee	30
______, James	Put	213
______, James	Rch	281
______, Jared J.	Lau	19
______, Jesse	Bib	74
______, John	Eff	115
______, John	Gre	281
______, John	Gwn	331
______, John	Gwn	354
______, John	Gwn	370

Name	County	Page
Palmer, John	Wal	145
_____, Jonathan	Rch	282
_____, Martin	Gly	267
_____, Mildred	Lin	69
_____, Nancy	Gre	302
_____, Richard	Jef	411
_____, Samuel	McI	122
_____, Stephen	Hal	109
_____, Thomas	Han	163
_____, William	Bke	138
_____, William	Hry	220
_____, William	Rch	281
_____, William	Wal	145
_____, Silson	Wil	306
_____, Winefred	Wrn	194
Palmour, John	Hal	121
_____, Silas	Hal	132
Palmere, Elijah	Wal	153
Palmore, George	Tlb	348
_____, George H.	Hab	59
_____, Isaac	Col	349
_____, John	Fay	186
_____, John	Fay	194
_____, Simon	Hab	66
_____, Solomon	Hab	33
_____, Solomon	Hab	47
PALMES, George F	Cht	263
PANNEL, William	Cpb	201
PAPOT, Robert D.	Cam	181
PAPPERSON, Daniel	App	6
PARADISE, James	Lin	60
_____, John	Mus	277
PARAMORE/PARRAMORE/		
PARAMOUR/PARREMORE		
Paramore, Benjamin	Hal	98
_____, Redding	Mon	220
Parramore, Matthew E.	Tlf	9
_____, Noah	Tlf	5
Paramour, James	Hst	283
_____, Thomas	Hst	280
Parremore, James	Ran	249
PARHAM/PARAM		
Parham, Benjamin	Mon	188
_____, Dixton	Pik	113
_____, Elijah	Wrn	204
_____, Francis	Wrn	205
_____, Harrison	Elb	136
_____, Isham	Elb	138
_____, Isham Jr.	Elb	142
_____, John	Hry	240
_____, John H.	Har	188
_____, Math	Wrn	227
_____, Polly A.	Mon	226
Parham, Ransom	Dec	14
_____, Robert	Wrn	205
_____, Seth	Mor	249
_____, Theophelus	Jks	333
_____, William	Bak	15
Param, John	Put	175
_____, Jones	Put	175
_____, Robert	Mwr	166
_____, Susannah	Put	175
_____, Thomas S.	Mwr	166
PARIS/PARRIS/PARICE		
Paris, Emanuel	Wyn	285
_____, Hester	DeK	73
_____, M.	Gwn	377
_____, Parthena	Wrn	192
_____, Samuel L.	DeK	66
Parris, Henry A.	Bke	134
_____, Nathanel	Hab	63
Parice, Wyett	Dec	13
PARISOT, John F.	Cht	249
PARKER, Aaron	Hry	228
_____, Alexander	Tlf	9
_____, Allen	Cpb	196
_____, Allen	New	39
_____, Asa H.	Mon	206
_____, Ashford N.	Lwn	86
_____, Austin	Put	183
_____, Barney	Hal	111
_____, Caleb	Doo	80
_____, Charles	Hal	91
_____, Christopher	Mon	183
_____, Daniel	Up	111
_____, Danil	Hab	37
_____, David	Jns	462
_____, David	Up	100
_____, David C.	Up	98
_____, Elisha	Tat	377
_____, Elizabeth	Doo	80
_____, Elizabeth	Han	163
_____, Elvinton H.	Tfo	360
_____, Emanuel	Gre	304
_____, Emanuel	Put	182
_____, Enoch	Car	216
_____, Eunetta	Rch	266
_____, Gable	Lee	35
_____, George	Mus	287
_____, George P.	Fay	200
_____, George W.	Wks	350
_____, Gustavus	Rch	263
_____, Hannah	Hab	40
_____, Henry	Hry	219
_____, Henry	Twg	73
_____, Herly	Wsh	243

Name	County	Page
Parker, Hiram	Twg	63
______, Ica	Ran	249
______, Isaac L.	Jsp	380
______, Isaiah	DeK	68
______, Isaiah	Fay	181
______, Isaac A.	Mon	225
______, Israel	Hry	201
______, Jacob	Bke	122
______, James	Clk	295
______, James	Hst	282
______, James	Ran	242
______, James	Scr	305
______, James	Tlb	332
______, James	Wal	151
______, Jeptha P.	Mon	182
______, Jeremiah Cuyler	Lib	51
______, Jesse	Twg	73
______, John	Bts	172
______, John	Clk	307
______, John	Cpb	209
______, John from N.C.	DeK	53
______, John	Han	163
______, John	Mon	185
______, John	Pik	125
______, John	Twg	78
______, John	Wrn	226
______, John D.	Frk	249
______, John P.	Lee	29
______, John S.	DeK	51
______, John W.	Wal	151
______, Jonathan	Ear	95
______, Jonathon	Hst	290
______, Jonathan	Lau	11
______, Jonathan	Wsh	257
______, Joseph	Elb	134
______, Joseph Sr.	Twg	73
______, Joseph Jr.	Twg	64
______, Joshua	Mor	253
______, Joshua	Wsh	271
______, Kinchen	Har	182
______, Leah	New	21
______, Lemuel	Hry	218
______, Lewis	Han	163
______, Lewis	Jks	343
______, Luke	Wal	162
______, Marlow B.	Tlb	334
______, Mary	Em	164
______, Mary	Wrn	228
______, Miles	Pik	123
______, Moses	Jks	324
______, Nancy	Twg	83
______, Nathan	Bib	71
______, Penelope	Hab	17
Parker, Peyton	Tlb	340
______, Phebe	Jns	462
______, Porter	Lau	13
______, Richard	Bts	171
______, Richard	Tfo	365
______, Richard H.	Lib	51
______, Robert	Tlb	326
______, Robert	Wks	358
______, Samuel	Mwr	167
______, Sanders	Hry	204
______, Sarah	Ear	91
______, Sarah	New	46
______, Shutley	Jks	346
______, Simeon	Tlb	341
______, Simon	Bib	62
______, Starling	Tms	18
______, Stephen	Mar	139
______, Stephen	Mon	226
______, Stephen	Tlb	348
______, Syntha	Bib	68
______, Thomas J.	Up	104
______, Thopeles S.	Pik	130
______, Warren	Jns	466
______, West	Clk	297
______, West	Hry	212
______, William	Bry	89
______, William	Cht	245
**______, William (slaves)	Cht	281
______, William	Cpb	204
______, William	Em	170
______, William	Hab	39
______, William	Hal	88
______, William	Hry	238
______, William	Jef	416
______, William	Jns	462
______, William	Mon	220
______, William	New	52
______, William	Tlf	5
______, William	Tfo	362
______, William B.	Hry	228
______, William C.	Bts	173
______, William H.	Bts	172
______, William H.	Clk	291
______, William H.	Elb	134
______, William H.	Lib	51
______, Zeal	New	45
______, Zilpha	Bke	117
PARKINSON, Cordeal	Pul	151
______, Hening	Tfo	354
______, Jacob	Pul	152
______, John C.	Wil	305
______, Leaven	Wil	305
PARKMAN, Minter	Har	187

Parkman, S. B. Cht 264
PARKS/PARK/PARKES/PARKE
Parks, Ann Elb 156
_____, Benjamin Hal 110
_____, Benjamin Sr. Hal 112
_____, Bethalem Hal 131
_____, Bird Cow 383
_____, Eli Mon 217
_____, Elizabeth Bib 62
_____, Elizabeth Frk 221
_____, Elizabeth Hst 278
_____, Gabriel Mon 188
_____, Garret W. Jks 318
_____, Hannah Jks 344
_____, Henry Frk 237
_____, Jane Jks 344
_____, James Wks 341
_____, John Bib 62
_____, John Col 357
_____, Joshua Gwn 370
_____, Lewis Lin 66
_____, Mary Mad 116
_____, Mary Mon 177
_____, Mary Mon 217
_____, Moses Bib 62
_____, P. J. Mad 114
_____, Richard S. Mor 243
_____, Robert Wil 308
_____, Samuel C. Mon 198
_____, Welcome Jsp 372
_____, William Lin 60
_____, William J. Frk 231
Park, Andrew Mwr 155
_____, Baptest Jks 337
_____, Garret Jks 344
_____, George Mon 219
_____, James S. Gre 273
_____, John Gre 287
_____, John Jks 319
_____, John G. Gwn 369
_____, John J. Jks 343
_____, John T. D. Jsp 397
_____, Jones Crf 395
_____, Joseph Mwr 155
_____, Moses Crf 400
_____, Moses Wal 140
_____, Sarah D. Put 218
_____, Thomas J. Gre 293
_____, William Jks 339
_____, William T. Wal 157
Parkes, Abraham Elb 146
_____, Henry Hal 124
_____, James Elb 145
Parkes, John Rab 222
_____, Thomas Ogl 65
Parke, George Wal 127
_____, Isabiah Mor 243
_____, Wallace H. Mor 243
PARLAND/PARLIN
Parland, John Gly 269
Parlin, Bennet Gwn 326
PARMER, Charles Dec 17
_____, Elizabeth Jks 327
_____, David Jks 347
_____, George Crf 398
_____, Isabella Wsh 275
_____, William DeK 30
PARNALL/PARNELL
Parnall, Abraham Elb 125
_____, Edward Elb 125
_____, Moses Elb 147
Parnell, James Mor 257
_____, Jesse New 31
_____, Moses Up 106
PARR/PARS
Parr, Benjamin Clk 305
_____, Bridges Sr. Bts 170
_____, Bridges Jr. Bts 170
_____, Charles Clk 314
_____, Christopher Pul 141
_____, Margaret Clk 320
_____, Thomas Mor 247
_____, William L. Jks 337
Pars, Stephen Cht 263
PARRADES, William Wsh 252
PARRAMORE, John Tms 24
PARRISH/PARISH
Parrish, Absalom Bul 97
_____, Ansel Bul 98
_____, Ansel A. Lwn 90
_____, Bennet Cpb 206
_____, Charles Frk 222
_____, Harriss Fay 190
_____, Henry Lwn 89
_____, James Wsh 262
_____, John Col 347
_____, Jonethan Jns 466
_____, Richerson Jsp 380
_____, Robert N. Lwn 90
_____, William Ran 246
_____, William Wsh 261
Parish, Edward Eff 115
_____, Elizth Cam 191
_____, Elizabeth Wrn 196
_____, G. F. Rch 257
_____, Harris Hry 223

Name	County	Page
Parish, Henry D.	Em	173
______, Hezekiah	Em	174
______, John	Hry	226
______, John	Twg	69
______, John F.	Cht	249
______, Jonathan D.	Hry	214
______, Joseph	Fay	181
______, Moses	Han	163
______, Nathaniel H.	Gre	298
______, Prosser	Jef	417
______, Thacker	New	52
______, William	New	46
PARROT/PARROTT		
Parrot, Ansly	Lau	13
______, Jesse	Mwr	163
______, Tyra	Mwr	164
______, William	Lau	6
Parrott, Benjamin	Gre	302
______, Daniel	Gly	267
______, James	Twg	87
______, James D.	Elb	138
______, John	Gre	299
______, John	Han	163
______, John	Tms	20
PARSONS/PARSON		
Parsons, Harris	Hab	14
______, John	DeK	73
______, Samuel	Fay	206
______, Samuel P.	Fay	203
______, Thomas P.	Fay	190
Parson, Evan	Car	218
______, Henry	Rch	269
______, Wade	Hal	102
PARTEE, Albert	Mor	263
______, Walter A.	Mor	263
PARTIN/PARTEN/PARTAIN		
Partin, Bennet	Gwn	317
______, Charles	Tat	374
______, Hezekiah	Crf	407
______, Robert	Bry	88
Parten, Henry	New	34
______, Simeon	Tlb	340
Partain, Kindred	Lau	16
______, William	Wal	131
PARTRIDGE/PATRIDGE		
Partridge, Henry	Wsh	243
______, James	Up	117
______, Jesse	Up	104
______, Thomas	Mon	203
______, William	Mon	178
Patridge, Hartwell	Trp	46
______, Henry	Jef	408
______, John	Wil	315
Patridge, Nicholas	Jns	440
______, Nicholas	Ogl	64
PASCHAL/PASCAL/PASKELL		
Paschal, Asa	Col	358
______, Dennis	Wil	304
______, George	Ogl	96
______, Isaiah A.	Up	98
______, Samuel	Wil	305
______, Thomas	Lin	72
______, William	Lin	75
Pascal, Frances (W)	Mor	243
______, John	Elk	291
______, John	Mor	243
______, Joseph	Gwn	371
Paskell, Samuel	Cow	376
PASINGER, Elizabeth	Hry	238
PASS/PAST		
Pass, John	New	18
______, Mathew J.	Ogl	80
______, Nancy	Ogl	82
______, Thomas	Hal	127
______, Willis H.	Wrn	202
Past, William	Gwn	378
PASSMORE/PASMOORE		
Passmore, Alex	Wks	352
______, Cilvey	Tlf	2
______, John	Har	175
______, John	Jns	474
______, John	Tlf	2
______, Nathan	Jns	475
______, Samuel	Twg	85
Pasmoore, Josephus	Jns	442
PATE, Aaron	Hry	210
______, Bennet	Tms	28
______, Benjamin	Tlb	332
______, Charles	Cow	390
______, Charley	Dec	5
______, David	Jns	429
______, David	Wrn	195
______, Elias	Bak	15
______, Elijah	Fay	201
______, Hardy	New	50
______, Isham	Bak	15
______, James Sr.	Fay	197
______, James Jr.	Fay	193
______, James D.	Gwn	344
______, Jesse	Jks	322
______, Jesse	Wrn	195
______, Joel	Tms	28
______, John	Em	168
______, John	Fay	200
______, John	Trp	53
______, John	Wrn	214

Name	County	Page
Pate, John S.	Hst	294
_____, John W.	Wsh	252
_____, Johnston	Hal	83
_____, Jordan	Jns	446
_____, Mary (W)	Mor	241
_____, Miles	Wrn	199
_____, Redding	Wsh	246
_____, Robert W.	Jef	402
_____, Samuel	Tms	28
_____, Samuel	Twg	69
_____, Sarah	Wrn	213
_____, Seaborn	Fay	203
_____, Sterling J.	Wrn	197
_____, Thomas J.	Wrn	218
_____, William	Fay	188
_____, William	Hry	219
_____, William	Pul	151
_____, William Jr.	Hry	237
_____, Zachariah	Tms	21
PATENT, Robert	Wsh	268
PATMON, James B.	Ogl	68
_____, Susan	Ogl	96
_____, William	Ogl	96
PATRICK/PATTRICK/PARTRICK		
Patrick, Alexander	Hry	217
_____, Catharine	Put	193
_____, Elijah B.	Han	163
_____, Henry	Jns	438
_____, Hugh	Col	335
_____, John	DeK	58
_____, John H.	Frk	212
_____, John M.	Mus	285
_____, John N.	Clk	320
_____, Joseph	Wyn	284
_____, Josiah D.	Ogl	101
_____, Larkin	Hry	239
_____, Levi	Em	175
_____, Lewis A.	Jns	438
_____, Littleberry	Hry	217
_____, Luke	Hry	207
_____, Paul	Wal	165
_____, Robert	Mor	254
_____, Robert	New	32
_____, Robert A.	Tlb	327
_____, Roda	Wal	162
_____, Solomon	Car	227
_____, William	DeK	60
_____, William	Em	174
_____, William	Jks	317
_____, William	Jsp	386
_____, William	New	27
Pattrick, David	Ogl	102
Partrick, Paul	Wal	128
Partrick, William L.	Lib	51
PATTASHALL/PATTESHALL/ PATTISHALL		
Pattashall, John C.	Wks	346
Patteshall, Eliz.	Wks	339
Pattishall, Joshua	Hst	263
PATTERN, Benjamin	Ogl	80
_____, James M.	Lwn	85
_____, Silas	Wal	158
PATTERSON/PATERSON		
Patterson, Abner	Mwr	160
_____, Alexander	Lwn	91
_____, Alexander	Mwr	158
_____, Alexander	Wks	343
_____, Andrew	Elb	134
_____, Ann	Rch	291
_____, Charles	Bib	62
_____, David	Car	226
_____, Douglass	New	11
_____, Drury D.	Hab	35
_____, Drury S.	Bts	174
_____, Elizabeth	Hal	100
_____, Enoch	Hal	122
_____, Francis	Hry	204
_____, George	Frk	223
_____, George	Hal	124
_____, George	Rab	226
_____, George S.	Scr	318
_____, Henry	Ogl	69
_____, Henry S.	Cpb	204
_____, Herndon	Jns	454
_____, Hiram	Hal	125
_____, James	Crf	408
_____, James	Elb	128
_____, James	Hal	117
_____, James	Jef	415
_____, James	Mon	209
_____, Jeremiah	Hal	122
_____, Jesse	DeK	37
_____, Jessee F.H.	Jsp	394
_____, Job C.	Jsp	366
_____, John	Bke	122
_____, John	DeK	37
_____, John	Hal	114
_____, John	Rab	230
_____, John T.	Mon	187
_____, Joseph	Hal	124
_____, Joseph	Rab	234
_____, Maria P.	Eff	115
_____, Mark	Jns	429
_____, Mary	Bke	122
_____, Mary	Ogl	69
_____, Matha	Hab	62

Patterson, Merril Hab 47
_____, Miles M. Crf 400
_____, Nomrod Elb 135
_____, Robert Jef 413
_____, Robert Put 199
_____, Robert Wal 127
_____, Roley Rab 227
_____, Samuel Elb 145
_____, Samuel Wal 148
_____, Samuel W. Jef 416
_____, Sarah Cht 242
_____, Thomas Wal 131
_____, Thomas M. Jef 419
_____, Tryon Frk 243
_____, Wiley D. Elb 148
_____, William App 10
_____, William Bke 120
_____, William Elb 148
_____, William Frk 214
_____, William Jef 416
_____, William Hal 125
_____, William Mwr 156
_____, William Mon 193
_____, William B. Hab 35
_____, Willis Jns 452
Paterson, David Clk 319
_____, George A. New 12
_____, John Clk 304
_____, Robert New 27
_____, Robert H. Clk 314
PATTILLO/PATTILO/PATILLO
Pattillo, Harrison Col 360
_____, Henry Mor 258
_____, James Hry 215
_____, Leroy Wal 123
_____, Samuel Wal 172
_____, Wesley H. Hry 211
Pattilo, John Mor 255
Patillo, Charles F. Hst 265
PATTON/PATTEN
Patton, David Ogl 62
_____, Elijah Mad 101
_____, George Mad 112
_____, George W. Twg 64
_____, Jacob Ogl 62
_____, James Jsp 365
_____, John Mad 105
_____, Lydia Wil 320
_____, Margarite Bib 68
_____, Martha Bib 68
_____, Robert Y. Bib 52
_____, Samuel Mon 220
_____, William K. Hry 233
Patten, David Hst 271
_____, James Mad 102
_____, John Crf 404
_____, Robert Mad 1-2
_____, Samuel Mad 116
_____, Steven Gwn 339
PATY, Elijah DeK 25
_____, John DeK 28
_____, Miles DeK 28
_____, William DeK 26
PAUDWIN, John Jks 320
PAUL/PAULL
Paul, Andrew Bke 124
_____, Archibald Y. Hry 209
_____, Benjamin Wil 287
_____, Burton Jns 429
_____, James Mad 107
_____, James Twg 67
_____, John New 53
_____, John Twg 63
_____, Moses Jns 429
_____, Robert Jns 429
_____, Robert B. Jns 447
_____, William Jns 446
Paull, Samuel Col 351
PAULETT/PAWLET
Paulett, B. G. Doo 78
_____, Henry Cpb 204
_____, Richard Cpb 204
Pawlet, Jesse C. Wal 140
PAULK/PALK
Paulk, Micajah Wks 343
_____, Samuel Lwn 82
Palk, William Jns 429
PAULNOT, John Ogl 88
PAVARY, Catharine Eff 114
PAXTON, Martha Cam 191
_____, Martin R. Hal 98
_____, Milton Wil 299
_____, Robert Cam 191
_____, Samuel Hal 98
_____, William Hry 241
PAXON, James A. Wal 135
PAYLOR, John S. Jns 466
_____, William D. Jns 466
PEABODY, John Wsh 256
PEACE, Major Han 164
PEACH, James Clk 305
PEACOCK, A. Wsh 240
_____, Alexander Pul 154
_____, Allen Pul 154
_____, Ann Hst 294
_____, Asa Wsh 240

Name	County	Page
Peacock, Bryant	Pul	161
_____, Cullin	Pul	161
_____, Exum	Hst	279
_____, Harrisson	Pul	153
_____, Ihan	Tat	380
_____, Jesse	Wks	349
_____, John	Lee	34
_____, John	Tlb	346
_____, John	Ware	184
_____, John	Wsh	240
_____, John B.	Bib	56
_____, John B	Hst	294
_____, Jonathan	Tlb	330
_____, Jonathon	Hst	280
_____, Levi	DeK	38
_____, Mary	Twg	85
_____, Michael	Pul	155
_____, Moulton	Tlb	346
_____, Richmond	Lib	51
_____, Robert	Hst	270
_____, Samuel	Lib	51
_____, Seth	Hst	293
_____, Uriah	Wsh	240
_____, William	Jsp	360
_____, William	Wsh	240
_____, William	Wsh	241
_____, William Jr.	Wsh	240
_____, Willis	Wsh	262
_____, Wright	Tlb	346
PEAK/PEAKE		
Peak, Henry Jr.	New	54
_____, James M. L.	Put	186
_____, William	Put	187
Peake, Lewis	Hry	210
PEAR, Daniel W.	Car	216
PEARCE, James	Hry	202
_____: see Pierce		
PEARDSON, Jeremiah	Jsp	369
PEARMAN, Oran D.	Put	210
_____, Robert	Mor	240
_____, Whitnell	Clk	307
PEARNAL, Abraham	Wal	170
PEARRE, Elizabeth	Col	344
_____, John	Col	363
_____, Johnathan	Col	360
PEARSON/PIRSONS/PIERSON		
Pearson, Ben	Bul	101
_____, Benony	Tlf	2
_____, Chesley	Tlb	344
_____, Evan	Hab	43
_____, Francis	Hry	214
_____, James	Mon	178
_____, James	Tlb	341
Pearson, James	Twg	65
_____, James	Wrn	221
_____, Jeremiah	Har	191
_____, Jeremiah	Mon	193
_____, John	Scr	299
_____, John C.	Gwn	327
_____, Jonathan	Wks	332
_____, Josiah	Pik	108
_____, Little	Hal	100
_____, Littleton C.	Tlb	344
_____, Moses	Hab	54
_____, Peter	Wks	351
_____, Sarah	Mon	183
_____, Samuel	Put	212
_____, Stephen	Han	164
_____, Thomas G.	Tlb	339
_____, Vincent A.	Tlb	324
_____, W. C.	Wks	347
_____, William	Eff	116
_____, William	Mwr	158
_____, William	Tlb	345
_____, William	Twg	74
_____, Winlock C.	Mon	200
Pirsons, Thomas	Trp	48
Pierson, Benoni	Doo	84
_____, Samuel	Gwn	327
_____, William H.	Jsp	384
PEAVY, Abraham	Trp	44
_____, Elizabeth	Wrn	204
_____, Ezekiel	Wrn	227
_____, James	Hst	293
_____, James	Rch	270
_____, James	Trp	51
_____, James	Wrn	227
_____, Thomas	Hst	276
PEDAN/PEDEN/PEADEN		
Pedan, James D.	Gwn	362
_____, S. D.	Gwn	359
Peden, James	Pik	132
Peaden, James	Pik	132
PEDDY, Albert	Hst	262
_____, Albret	Wks	344
_____, Alexander G.	Up	118
_____, Bradford	Jns	431
_____, James	Jns	433
_____, Jarious	Wsh	251
_____, Jeremiah	Up	106
_____, John	Hst	286
_____, Lavins	Mon	193
_____, William	Trp	52
PECK, David	Mor	251
_____, Henry Sr.	New	54
_____, Ira	Twg	60

Name	County	Page
Peck, Jonathan M.	Hry	208
______, Michael	Gly	415
PEOPLES/PEEPLES/PEEBLES		
Peoples, Henry	Hal	101
______, Henry	Up	119
______, Hy	Up	116
______, Isham	Ogl	69
______, Joel	Ear	98
______, John	Gwn	324
______, John	Wal	139
______, Joseph	Wal	155
______, Thomas	Ear	94
______, Thomas	Mar	138
______, William	Gwn	362
Peeples, Benjamin M.	Mor	245
______, Mary (W)	Mor	241
Peebles, Albert	Hry	221
______, Ephrm.	Wrn	224
______, Henry	Jef	415
______, Isaac	Wrn	224
______, Mary	Wrn	194
______, Rufus D.	Trp	37
______, Thomas	Jef	415
PEED/PEID		
Peed, James	Tlb	340
Peid, John	Lin	72
PEEK/PEAK/PEAKE		
Peek, Hart C.	Gre	295
______, James Sr.	Tfo	360
______, John	Hst	279
______, John C.	Gre	298
______, Judith	Tfo	365
______, Leonard	Gre	301
______, Littlebury	Gre	298
______, Lockett	Tfo	360
______, Mary	Gre	291
______, Robert	Gre	298
______, Solomon	Elb	135
______, William	Tfo	358
Peak, James C. L.	Hab	9
______, Osborn	Han	164
Peake, Solomon	Hal	127
______, Thomas H.	Col	338
PEEL/PEAL		
Peel, David B.	Mon	199
______, James	Mus	279
______, John	Mor	266
______, John	Jef	415
______, Nancy	Jef	422
______, William	Rab	230
______, William	Har	178
Peal, Willis	Mon	191
PEELER/PELER/PEALOR		
Peeler, Abner	Elb	138
______, Cader	Elb	121
______, Jacob	Mwr	158
Peler, Berry	Gre	294
Pealor, Anthony	Jsp	368
PEEVY/PEAVY/PEEVEY		
Peevy, Eli	Han	163
______, Elihu	Ogl	97
______, Shaderick	Mor	259
______, Susannah	Tfo	365
Peavy, Dial	Cpb	195
______, Ely	Mwr	162
______, David	Mwr	162
______, Redmon	New	26
Peevey, Helton	Mor	260
______, Littleton D.	Bib	71
PELFRY, Joseph	Frk	242
PELHINGTON, William	Cow	375
PELLOMS, John	Lee	30
PELLUM, Uriah	Fay	203
PELOT/PILLOT		
Pelot, J. S.	Cht	260
Pillot, A. P.	Rch	268
PEMBERTON, A. H.	Rch	260
______, Alton	Bke	139
______, F.	Bal	44
______, James	Bal	36
______, Joshua	Trp	53
PENABLE, Robert	Jks	312
PENACORBY, John W.	Cow	367
PENCE/PONCE		
Pence, Abraham	Hab	31
______, Absalom	Hab	31
______, Elisabeth	Hab	31
______, John	Hab	31
Ponce, Dimas	Han	163
PENDARVIS/PENDERVIS		
Pendarvis, Joseph	Wyn	284
Pendervis, James	Cam	192
PENDER/PINDER/PENDRE/ PENTER		
Pender, Josiah	Put	200
______, Wright	Jns	462
Pinder, John	Gwn	374
______, William	Gwn	349
Pendre, John	Jef	422
Penter, Fleming	Hab	16
PENDERGRASS/PENDERGAST		
Pendergrass, Dolly	Gre	290
______, Hiram	Mor	257
______, Levi	Jks	349
______, Nathaniel	Jks	346
Pendergast, Oflin	Cht	271

Name	County	Page
Pendergast, P.	Cht	249
PENDLETON/PENELTON		
Pendleton, Thomas	Jef	422
Penelton, Coleman	New	52
PENDLY/PENLY		
Pendly, John	DeK	34
_____, Levi	Gwn	373
_____, Thomas	Gwn	365
Penly, John	Gwn	321
PENGREE, Thomas	Scr	313
PENETENTIARY CONVICTS 97	Bal	41
PENETENTIARY GUARDS 12	Bal	41
PENIX, Joseph	Mor	248
PENN, Benjamin	New	32
_____, Edmon T.	New	32
_____, Gabriel L.	Cow	372
_____, John	Elb	140
_____, John T.	Mon	182
_____, John T.	Ogl	90
_____, Mary	Elb	119
_____, Moses	Ogl	87
_____, Moses	Ogl	89
_____, Thomas	Elb	160
_____, Thomas H.	Elb	121
_____, Thomas L.	Ogl	91
_____, William	Elb	137
_____, William	Jsp	371
_____, William	Mon	194
_____, William M.	Mon	179
PENNELL/PINNELL		
Pennell, Green	Bts	177
Pinnell, Jonathan	Hal	93
PENNINGTON/PENINGTON		
Pennington, Elizabeth	Jef	401
_____, Elizabeth	Rch	282
_____, Ephraim	Fay	184
_____, Ephriam	Jsp	382
_____, Federick	Trp	43
_____, Henry	Elb	341
_____, James	Har	186
_____, John	Doo	81
_____, Letha	Jsp	383
_____, Mary	Jsp	393
_____, Ned	Jns	466
_____, Samuel	Mor	247
_____, Thaddeus	Jsp	382
_____, Thomas	Jsp	382
_____, William	Pik	107
Penington, Abraham	New	44
PENNY, Alfred	Hst	272
_____, Becroft	Cht	247
_____, James	Hst	272
_____, Malachi	Gre	299
Penny, Theophalus	Hst	272
PENROW, Ralph	Bke	119
PENROY, John	Rab	230
PENSON/PINSON/PINSEN		
Penson, Elijah	Hal	122
_____, Elizabeth	Wsh	259
_____, Joseph	Jks	327
Pinson, Boyd	Ogl	68
_____, Curtice	Rab	226
_____, James	Ogl	69
_____, Joseph	Ogl	67
_____, Joseph	Rab	226
_____, Mary	Ogl	68
_____, Mary	Wrn	211
_____, Moses	Hal	122
_____, Sterling	Frk	238
_____, Thomas P.	Ogl	68
Pinsen, Allen	Hal	119
PENTECOST/PENTICOST		
Pentecost, William	Jks	349
Penticost, George	Cow	387
_____, Richard	Jks	348
PEPPER/PEPPERS		
Pepper, Caroline V.	McI	123
_____, Daniel P.	Jns	454
_____, John	Mon	210
_____, John	Wal	168
_____, Samuel	Hry	239
_____, Sunsberrey	Wal	169
Peppers, Parker	Wal	150
PEPPERMAN, Benjamin	Ogl	72
PERCEL/PERCELL/PERSELL		
Percel, Ignatious	Frk	257
_____, Jacob	Frk	216
_____, John	Frk	243
Percell, John	Tat	372
Persell, David	Ogl	98
PERDUE/PERDEW/PERDIEW		
Perdue, Daniel	Gre	281
_____, Isaac	Mon	176
_____, James	Jef	418
_____, James	Mon	193
_____, John	Jef	415
_____, Judah	Jef	415
_____, Marshall	Mon	193
_____, Newton	Jef	418
Perdew, James H.	Mwr	152
_____, John D.	Bib	65
_____, Joseph C.	Put	215
_____, Thomas	Put	184
_____, William	Bib	71
Perdiew, Cidney	Mor	256
PERGUSON/PERGERSON		

Perguson, Demcy	DeK	52
______, John	DeK	56
Pergerson, Ancy	Clk	309
PERKINS/PURKINS/PERKENS/ PIRKINS		
Perkins, Abram	Gre	294
______, Alexander	Mon	180
______, Alford	Tfo	359
______, Allen	Pul	157
______, Brinson	Bke	131
______, David	Bke	130
______, Ebenezer J.	Tms	27
______, Edward	Tfo	358
______, H. W.	Jks	338
______, Henry	Tfo	355
______, Henry D.	Tfo	356
______, Hiram B.	Frk	251
______, James	Hry	207
______, Jane	Hal	130
______, Jesse	Gre	282
______, John	Bib	71
______, John	Jns	431
______, John	Jns	440
______, John	Tfo	360
______, John J.	Gre	302
______, John S.	Bke	128
______, John W.	Tfo	355
______, Josiah	Hry	206
______, Lewis H.	Pul	157
______, Linkfield	Wks	344
______, Moses	Hal	133
______, Newton	Bke	131
______, Newton Jr.	Bke	131
______, Polly	DeK	73
______, Reuben	Frk	216
______, Sarah	Jsp	353
______, Sessums	Pul	140
______, Thomas (colored)	Bke	147
______, Thomas	Mus	285
______, Uriah	Crf	398
______, William	Em	171
______, William H.	Twg	63
______, Wright	Up	110
Purkins, Elijah	Hab	50
______, Joseph	Wsh	257
______, Stephen	Wsh	243
______, William	Mor	252
______, William	Wsh	242
Perkens, Ezekiel	Gre	291
Pirkins, Benjamin	Mor	261
PERMENTER, John	Mon	212
______, John	Ware	185
______, Susannah	Bts	172
Permenter, William	Mon	175
______, Wright	Jns	459
PERNELL, Henry	Col	360
PEROST, Naiomi	Tat	379
PERRIN, John	Car	215
______, Samuel	Hry	202
______, Thomas	Hry	202
PERRITT, Nathaniel	Jns	458
PERRY/PERREY/PEARY		
Perry, Alford G.	Jks	334
______, Allen	Bak	20
______, Ambrose	Ear	91
______, Amos P.	Mon	215
______, Anne	Wal	156
______, Archibald	Bts	176
______, Archibald	Jns	436
______, Betsey	Gre	300
______, Bird	Wrn	208
______, Burwell	Car	228
______, Burwell	Clk	292
______, Doctor	Har	189
______, Dow	Trp	33
______, Dwight R.	Crf	395
______, Elias	Bry	85
______, Elizabeth	Bib	77
______, Ezekel	Har	189
______, George	Gwn	333
______, George S.	Bke	148
______, Hardy	Bke	141
______, Henry	Wsh	267
______, Henry H.	Twg	61
______, Hiram	DeK	31
______, James	Car	227
______, James	Frk	217
______, James	Jsp	390
______, James	Tat	380
______, James Jr.	Frk	246
______, James R.	Bib	68
______, Jeremiah	Wrn	207
______, Jesse	Wil	305
______, Joel W.	Ear	95
______, John	Crf	405
______, John	Frk	218
______, John	Lau	4
______, John	Wsh	274
______, John G.	Crf	397
______, Joseph L.	Doo	80
______, Josiah	New	39
______, Levy	Bal	36
______, M. W.	Mus	279
______, M. W.	Mus	292
______, Nicolas	Pik	113
______, Obed.	Har	184

Perry, Phillip Hab 21
______, Rathel Mus 290
______, Reddick D. Mon 193
______, Shade Mus 284
______, Richard Hal 112
______, Simeon Tlb 331
______, Terrell Twg 62
______, Thomas Gwn 317
______, Thomas Jks 327
______, Thomas A. Han 163
______, Thornton Twg 84
______, William Cpb 196
______, William Crf 397
______, William Hab 21
______, William Twg 82
______, William M. Mon 193
Perrey, Isaiah Wal 124
______, John Lib 51
______, John G. Wal 148
______, Oscar Wal 137
______, Silas Lib 51
Peary, Allen Jsp 355
PERRYMAN/PERRYMON
Perryman, Anthony A. Elb 138
______, Cornelius Tlb 325
______, David Put 189
______, David A. Tlb 330
______, David B. Twg 68
______, Edward D. Har 187
______, Elisha Put 191
______, Elisha Wrn 209
______, Harmon Twg 67
______, James Tlb 331
______, James G. Hry 205
______, James H. Gwn 318
______, William Mon 177
______, William G. Up 104
Perrymon, Elisha Jr. Wrn 221
PERSER/PURSER
Perser, James Wsh 257
Purser, Richard Hry 211
PERSONS/PERSON
Persons, C. W. Col 357
______, John Wrn 206
______, John W. Mon 184
______, Jones Up 120
______, Pinkney Up 118
______, Sarah Wrn 194
______, Thomas Trp 48
______, Thomas Wrn 201
______, Turner Cow 383
Person, Jeremiah Mon 183
______, Thomas H. Mon 190

PERT, William Hry 235
PESNEL/PESNELL
Pesnel, John Hab 35
Pesnell, Henry Hal 86
PETEETT, Choeneth Wil 313
______, John Wil 324
______, Simeon Wil 307
PETEGREW/PETIGREW/PETTEGREW/
PETITGREW
Petegrew, Edward Hal 111
Petigrew, Robert Cht 257
**Pettegrew, James (slaves) Cht 281
Pettigrew, Robert Han 163
PETELLO, John Gre 292
PETERS, Balaam Jns 435
______, Elizabeth Twg 89
______, George Fay 190
______, Jesse New 10
______, John Wal 144
______, John Sr. Wal 141
______, John Wal 145
______, Lewis Wil 311
______, Matthew Crf 405
______, N. Mus 277
______, Nancy Jsp 357
______, Nathaniel Gre 273
______, Nathaniel Hry 209
______, Robertson Pik 131
______, Samuel Fay 202
______, Sarah Pik 131
______, William Lwn 88
______, William B. Twg 76
______, William M. Wal 164
PETERSON, Angelina Han 164
______, Batt Jns 473
______, Daniel Hry 246
______, Daniel Mtg 234
______, Dolly Jns 452
______, F. Cht 270
______, James Tlf 2
______, John Hab 36
______, John Tlf 2
______, Malcom Mtg 231
______, Mary Bke 131
______, Seaborn H. Bke 129
______, Teabow Hab 38
______, Thomas B. Ear 95
______, William Ware 184
PETTIS/PETTUS
Pettis, Mary Twg 80
______, Mary Wil 295
______, Moses Crf 413
______, Moses Twg 80

Name	County	Page
Pettis, Stephen	Twg	71
_____, William	Trp	38
Pettus, Charles	Wil	295
_____, John	Wil	288
_____, Stephen G.	Wil	288
PETTIT/PETIT		
Pettit, B.	Col	362
_____, Caty	Gwn	378
_____, P.	Col	362
*Petit, Thomas (free col)	Car	234
_____, Thomas	Gwn	378
PETTY, Ambrose	Mor	267
_____, Edward	Irw	300
_____, George	Bib	62
_____, John	Cpb	207
_____, John	Ogl	102
_____, L.	Cht	262
_____, Littleton	New	13
_____, Luke	Har	192
_____, Mithridath	Ware	189
_____, Moses	DeK	37
_____, Stephen	DeK	37
_____, Thomas	DeK	34
_____, Zachariah	Fay	204
PETTYFOOT, Luois A.	Clk	307
PETTYJOHN, Abraham	Hab	43
_____, James	Jks	329
_____, William	Jks	329
PEUGH, Asa	Pik	124
_____, Jehu	Up	110
_____, Whitson	Up	97
PEURIFOY/PEUROFOY		
Peurifoy, Benjamin W.	Jsp	364
_____, Caswell	Hry	251
Peurofoy, Standley	Up	110
PEW, Alexander	Jks	341
_____, Ann	Jsp	383
_____, Eleanor	Jks	341
_____, Isaac	Jks	341
_____, John	Jks	341
_____, Shadrack	Tms	30
_____, Shedrack	Tms	30
PEYTON/PAYTON/PEYDON		
Peyton, Cornelius	Mad	103
_____, Moriah	Mad	118
_____, Moses	Elb	133
Payton, William	Cow	372
Peydon, John	Gwn	359
PHAGAN: also see Fagan		
_____, James	Hab	15
_____, Moses	Hab	15
_____, Philip	Jks	341
PHAROAH/PHARROW		

Name	County	Page
Pharoah, Joshua	Rch	282
Pharrow, David	Hab	12
PHARR, Alexander	Wal	163
_____, Edward	Jks	322
_____, Edward	Jks	333
_____, Samuel T.	Wal	148
PHELPS/PHILPS		
Phelps, Arthur	Pul	149
_____, Aquila	Jsp	359
_____, Aquila	Jsp	379
_____, David S.	Mad	116
_____, Glenn	Jks	321
_____, H. C.	Mus	281
_____, James	Pul	149
_____, James C.	Lib	51
_____, Joseph L.	Mus	279
_____, Sophia	Pul	150
_____, Thomas	Elb	132
_____, Thomas	Jsp	386
Philps, Augustus	Wsh	249
PHILBRICK, Samuel	Cht	254
PHIFER, Samuel	Hry	225
PHILIES, Zachariah	Car	217
PHILPOT, James	Car	221
_____, James	Rch	254
_____, John	Rch	261
_____, Peter	Rch	267
_____, Reuben	Car	228
_____, Richard	Car	221
_____, William	Car	221
PHILLIPS/PHILIPS/PHILIP/ PHILLUPS/PHILLIPPE/FILLEPS		
Phillips, Abner	Gwn	349
_____, Ambros A.	Mwr	162
_____, Ashley	Jef	410
_____, Benjamin	Bke	130
_____, Bengn.	Cam	189
_____, Benjamin	Scr	304
_____, Bluford	Jsp	392
_____, Burrell	Scr	300
_____, Charles	Har	175
_____, Charles	Hry	231
_____, Cleverly	Frk	248
_____, Daniel	Trp	52
_____, Daniel	Jsp	379
_____, Daniel E.	Ear	94
_____, David	Gwn	340
_____, Dawson	Jns	471
_____, Dennis	Frk	228
_____, Elbert	Mwr	152
_____, Elijah	Cow	371
_____, Elijah	Cow	390
_____, Elizabeth	Jsp	396

Name	County	Page
Phillips, George	Hab	45
______, George	Jns	474
______, George	Pik	110
______, George D.	Hab	10
______, George L.	Cht	247
______, Hardy	Wal	149
______, Hardy	Wal	157
______, Hillary	Jsp	387
______, Isaac	Hal	81
______, Isham	Ran	246
______, Isham	Tlb	332
______, Isom	Hry	245
______, James	Cow	386
______, James	Gwn	324
______, James	Hry	234
______, James	Jsp	380
______, James	Mor	264
______, James	New	17
______, James	Wal	152
______, James	Wsh	254
______, James	Wsh	260
______, James A. T.	Pik	111
______, James R.	New	32
______, Jeremah	Jsp	382
______, Jesse	Mor	269
______, Joel F.	New	20
______, John	Bts	160
______, John	Ear	94
______, John	Trp	40
______, John	Wsh	266
______, John	Wil	294
______, John H.	Har	186
______, Jonathan	Wil	319
______, Joseph	Hab	26
______, Joseph Jr.	Bke	120
______, Joshua	Mor	245
______, Joshua	Wal	150
______, L. B.	Jsp	393
______, Lucinda	Ear	94
______, Maryann	Gwn	310
______, Matthew	Jsp	371
______, Nathan	Hry	241
______, Nathan	Jsp	380
______, Nathan	New	14
______, Nathan	Wil	319
______, Onesieus	Eff	115
______, Pleasant	Jns	471
______, Polly	Frk	249
______, Rebecca	Mwr	159
______, Reuben	Tlb	333
______, Reubin	Cow	369
______, Richard	Gwn	367
______, Richard	Ogl	71
Phillips, Richard	Scr	299
______, Robert	Cpb	206
______, Robert	Hal	75
______, Robert	Hry	231
______, Samuel	Tlb	332
______, Samuel Jr.	Jsp	358
______, Solomon	Cow	390
______, Solomon	Crf	413
______, Solomon	Jef	411
______, Stephen	Frk	249
______, Stephen T.	Wil	290
______, Thomas	Frk	239
______, Thomas	Rch	254
______, Trustin	New	32
______, Warren	Jsp	393
______, Wiley	Frk	248
______, William Sr.	Ear	93
______, William Jr.	Ear	94
______, William	Gwn	340
______, William	Jsp	354
______, William D.	Jsp	393
______, William L.	Bts	159
______, William S.	Cow	374
______, Williamson	Frk	242
______, Wyley	Jsp	380
______, Yearby	Wil	307
______, Zachariah	Cow	369
______, Zachariah	Wal	127
______, Zacheus	Wal	129
Philips, Adam	Jks	311
______, Arrington H.	Lau	24
______, Benajah	Hst	272
______, Benjamin	Bib	76
______, Cloe	Wsh	276
______, Cynthia	DeK	34
______, Elias	Twg	78
______, Elijah	Mon	211
______, Ephraim	Em	169
______, George	Gre	280
______, Hardy	Gre	295
______, Hardy	Twg	77
______, Hawkins	Car	226
______, Henry H.	Lau	17
______, Isaac	Dec	7
______, J.	Col	350
______, James	DeK	31
______, James	Mon	201
______, James	Mon	224
______, James	Pul	138
______, Jesse B.	Gre	291
______, Joel	Mon	210
______, John	Em	177
______, John	Mus	288

Philips, John Wks 358
_____, John W. Mon 217
_____, Joseph Col 347
_____, Joseph DeK 73
_____, Joseph Mtg 234
_____, Joseph Wrn 231
_____, Larkin Car 227
_____, Leonard Cpb 210
_____, Levi Cpb 196
_____, Levi Jks 335
_____, Levi Put 189
_____, M. G. Wks 355
_____, Mark Em 177
_____, Micajar Mtg 232
_____, Obedeah Mon 195
_____, Prudence Pul 155
_____, Royal B. Em 169
_____, Spencer Mon 213
_____, Thomas Jks 332
_____, Thomas G. Pik 116
_____, Wilder Har 190
_____, Wiley Elb 134
_____, William Car 227
_____, William Col 348
_____, William Em 178
_____, William Mon 175
_____, William Mon 211
_____, William C. Mtg 232
Philip, Robert Rch 269
_____, Rubin Hab 58
Phillups, Mark Ogl 71
Phillippe, John DeK 43
Filleps, William Lee 34
PHILLMAN, Elijah Ear 94
_____, James Ear 98
PHILSON, Thomas McI 126
PHINIZY/PHINIZEE/PHINOZY
Phinizy, Harry Rch 270
_____, Jacob Clk 324
_____, John Rch 279
Phinizee, Hiram Mon 178
_____, William Mon 178
Phinozy, J. Ogl 89
PHIPPS/PHIPP
Phipps, Elbert Lin 58
_____, John Lin 67
_____, Martha Hry 227
_____, Milly Lin 60
_____, Sarah Jks 336
Phipp, Richard Fay 184
PHORBES, Adelia Cht 247
PICKARD/PICKERD
Pickard, Henry Mon 226
Pickard, Micajah Han 164
_____, Silas Mon 226
_____, Y. S. Cht 259
Pickerd, John New 51
PICKEL/PICKLES
Pickel, Michael Wks 333
Pickles, Jacib Bul 102
PICKENS, Ezerall Gwn 357
_____, John DeK 61
PICKERING/PICKRON/PICKREN/
PICKERN
Pickering, A. Aron Mus 290
_____, Nayman Lau 16
_____, William Rch 258
Pickron, John Tlf 4
_____, William Wks 351
Pickren, James Scr 302
Pickern, Elijah Doo 78
PICKETT/PICKET
Pickett, Isaiah Frk 221
_____, Jeptha Mad 107
_____, Robert Jns 475
_____, Thomas C. Jns 475
Picket, James Ran 248
_____, Seaborn B. Crf 412
PICKFORD, Henry Hab 47
_____, Namenel Hab 47
PICQUET, Antoine Rch 257
PIERCE/PEARCE/PEIRCE/
PIEERCE/PERCE
Pierce, Aaxim Mwr 150
_____, Allen Irw 298
_____, Austin R. Mor 264
_____, B. L. Bke 151
_____, Cader Bke 125
_____, Cullen Bak 17
_____, D. S. Wks 352
_____, E. Wks 356
_____, E. H. Bal 44
_____, Edm[d]. Gwn 344
_____, Elijah DeK 60
_____, Elijah Hst 277
_____, Elizabeth Gwn 355
_____, Elizabeth New 30
_____, Ezekiel Bak 17
_____, Gad Gwn 326
_____, George Tlb 323
_____, Isham Elb 120
_____, J. William DeK 68
_____, James Cht 282
_____, James Hab 21
_____, Jesse DeK 68
_____, Jesse Gre 298

Name	County	Page
Pierce, John	Bke	123
______, John	Hal	103
______, John	Jef	406
______, John	Jsp	360
______, John H.	Pul	161
______, John M.W.	Gwn	326
______, Joseph	Mwr	160
______, Lovick	Gre	304
______, Lovick	Gwn	327
______, Masten	Gwn	361
______, Mastin	Gwn	377
______, Matthew	Gre	298
______, Nancy	Gwn	339
______, Polly	DeK	62
______, Reuben	Hal	114
______, Robert	Rch	283
______, Seth	Jef	407
______, Thomas	Jef	410
______, Thomas	New	30
______, Thomas	Wks	357
______, W. A.	Wsh	244
______, Walton	Tlb	322
______, Wiley	Dec	15
______, Wiley	Gwn	329
______, Wiley	Hal	110
______, William	Bke	140
______, William	DeK	28
______, William	Hab	40
______, William	Tlb	331
Pearce, Agnes	Col	357
______, Aleson	Col	338
______, Alexander	Twg	76
______, Ann	Cam	188
______, Charlott	Twg	88
______, Fielding	Put	191
______, George W.	Bke	139
______, Jacob	Twg	71
______, Jacob Sr.	Twg	76
______, Jacob Jr.	Twg	61
______, James	Cam	186
______, James	Col	338
______, James	Hry	202
______, James	Twg	67
______, James	Up	101
______, John Sr.	Fay	193
______, John	Fay	196
______, John	Twg	63
______, John J.	Put	213
______, Lazarus	Twg	72
______, Nathaniel	Col	343
______, Samuel	Up	112
______, Theophelus	Twg	77
______, Thomas	Put	176
Pearce, William	Fay	207
Peirce, Abagail	Cht	248
______, Jacob W.	Hst	291
______, Jesse	Wks	343
______, John	Frk	233
______, John	Hst	284
Pieerce, James	Hal	68
Perce, Peter	Mar	141
PIE, James	Scr	310
PIGGOT/PIGGOTT		
Piggot, George	Wil	289
Piggott, William	Wil	288
PIKE, Daniel	Cow	374
______, Esaw	Bts	159
______, Ezekiel	Wal	134
______, Jacob	Cow	383
______, James	Bts	159
______, John	Cow	375
______, John	Lwn	81
______, Mary	Put	216
______, Stephen	Wal	133
______, W. T.	Bal	34
______, William	Trp	48
______, William	Wal	134
______, William F.	Dec	18
PILANT, Chistian	Jef	422
______, James	Jef	421
PILCHER, James	Wrn	232
______, Lewis	Mar	139
______, Wilkham	Lee	31
PILES/PILE/PYLE		
Piles, James	Hry	234
______, John	Gly	268
______, R. S.	Gly	269
______, Samuel	Hry	234
______, William	Crf	414
Pile, John	New	7
______, Samuel	New	7
Pyle, John	Fay	192
______, Peter	Fay	199
PILGRIM/PILGRAM		
Pilgrim, Greene	Put	204
______, Martin	Hab	52
______, Michael	Hab	27
______, Thomas	Hab	56
Pilgram, Thomas	Hab	46
PINCHARD/PINKARD		
Pinchard, James	Mon	220
______, John Sr.	Mon	216
______, John Sr.	Mon	221
______, Sarah	Mon	221
Pinkard, Payton	Cow	392
______, Thomas C.	Cow	377

Pinkard, William Mon 192
PINCKLEY, Fanny Rch 258
PINKSTON/PENKARTON/
PIKINGTON/PILKENTON/
PELKENTON/PINSTON
Pinkston, Felix Wil 296
_____, G. B. Mus 278
_____, John Han 163
_____, John S. Lwn 82
_____, Shadrack Wil 300
Penkarton, James Put 179
Pikington, John Hal 110
Pilkenton, Permenas Hal 127
Pelkenton, John Hal 127
Pinston, Henry Crf 398
PINNER, John Clk 316
PIPER/PIPPER
Piper, William M. New 37
_____, Zadoc New 19
Pipper, John F. Trp 53
PIPKIN/PIPKINS/PEPKINS
Pipkin, Harvey B. Jef 423
_____, Prudence Pul 141
_____, William Pul 140
Pipkins, Kenchen Hal 79
_____, Moses Pul 155
Pepkins, Asa Pul 146
PIPPIN/PIPPEN
Pippin, Bailey Up 118
_____, Isaac Jns 434
_____, Noah Tfo 367
_____, Sarah Jns 432
Pippen, Needham Twg 83
PIRKLE, Elijah Hal 78
_____, Isaac Hal 79
_____, Jacob Hal 79
_____, Jacob Hal 130
_____, John Hal 80
_____, Robert Hal 70
_____, William Hal 79
PITCHFORD, Eli Hab 45
PITMAN/PITTMAN/PITTMON/
PITMON
Pitman, Albert Pul 151
_____, Arthur Ware 189
_____, Daniel N. Gwn 366
_____, Daniel Hal 94
_____, Edward Hal 97
_____, Edward Tfo 355
_____, Elijah Mwr 161
_____, Frances Gwn 353
_____, Henry Tfo 359
_____, Hiram Col 342
Pitman, Jeffery Gwn 353
_____, Jeremiah Fay 192
_____, Jesse Doo 82
_____, Jesse Fay 200
_____, Jesse Jef 421
_____, Jessee Hst 293
_____, John Cht 267
_____, John Hry 222
_____, John Mon 189
_____, John Pik 116
_____, John Twg 63
_____, John G. Rch 272
_____, Micajah L. Tfo 358
_____, Phillip Ran 245
_____, Robert Jef 421
_____, Thomas Tfo 355
_____, Tilgham R. Fay 198
_____, Timothy Wal 125
_____, William Cht 267
_____, William New 37
_____, William A. Put 205
Pittman, Buckey Wks 350
_____, Jacob Tat 378
_____, James Sr. Bib 71
_____, James Mad 115
_____, James Tat 378
_____, James Wks 340
_____, James F. Jks 345
_____, Jesse Wks 350
_____, John G. Jks 312
_____, L. App 10
_____, Marshall Col 361
_____, Martin H. Jks 343
_____, Mary Cht 261
_____, Nimrod Wsh 265
_____, Pleasant O. Jks 336
_____, Sion Lee 31
_____, Stanling Crf 407
_____, William Lee 35
Pittmon, Isham Wsh 270
_____, Malechi Wsh 270
Pitmon, Etheldred Ran 245
PITNER, Elias Trp 52
PITTARD/PITARD
Pittard, Humphrey Clk 319
_____, John Clk 320
_____, Thompson Clk 320
_____, William Clk 320
Pitard, William Ogl 76
PITTIN, Elijah Gwn 371
PITTS, Alexander Jks 343
_____, Chaney Jns 433
_____, Coleman Mad 105

Name	County	Page
Pitts, Daniel	Hst	271
_____, Ebenizer	DeK	37
_____, Elihu	Trp	36
_____, Frederick	Tlb	348
_____, George	Pul	160
_____, Hardy	Wrn	194
_____, Henry	Hst	291
_____, Hezekiah	Mon	216
_____, Isaac	Jns	434
_____, James	Jns	435
_____, Jesse	Jns	431
_____, John	Jns	454
_____, John	Mad	104
_____, John D.	Wsh	253
_____, John G. W.	Eff	112
_____, John J.	Eff	113
_____, John W.	Bal	36
_____, Laban	Trp	36
_____, Lewis G.	Har	192
_____, Lunsford	Hst	288
_____, N. W.	Col	336
_____, Nancy	Jns	431
_____, Nancy	Tlf	8
_____, Nestor	Jsp	388
_____, Noel	Mon	213
_____, Martin	Pik	120
_____, Peyton	Jns	454
_____, Samuel	Wrn	194
_____, Stephen	Dec	11
_____, Walker	Mon	172
_____, Westley	Jns	433
_____, William	Tlb	322
_____, William C.	Wsh	253
_____, Willis	Bib	65
PLANT/PLAINT		
Plant, Jason	Dec	8
_____, Nancy	Wil	324
_____, William	Mwr	151
Plaint, Lewis H.	Jns	443
PLATT, David	Lwn	81
_____, James	Scr	317
_____, John	Lwn	80
_____, Joshua	Lwn	80
_____, Peter	Lwn	81
PLAYER, Samuel	Rch	257
_____, Thomas	Twg	67
PLEACTY, Andrew	Cam	184
PLEASANTS, Sarah	Rch	269
PLEDGER, James	Trp	44
_____, Joseph	Fay	205
_____, Murrel	Fay	205
_____, Thomas	Elb	138
_____, Thomas	Mwr	163
PLESS, Alexander	Tlb	328
_____, Andrew	Tlb	325
_____, Augustus	Trp	37
_____, Philip	Tlb	325
PLUMB, David	Wil	287
PLUMMER/PLUMER		
Plummer, Edward	Jks	332
_____, Joseph	Lau	11
_____, Thomas	Jns	437
Plumer, Ezekiel	Gwn	364
PLUNKET/PLUNKETT/PLUNCKETT		
Plunket, James	Gwn	316
_____, Joseph N.	Gwn	317
_____, Richard	Gwn	309
Plunkett, James	New	23
Plunckett, Silas	Han	163
POAGE, James	Clk	312
POE, Gilbert	Fay	201
_____, James	Car	215
_____, Jese	Hab	43
_____, John	Car	215
_____, John	Mon	172
_____, Jonathan	Trp	50
_____, Robert F.	Rch	261
_____, Samuel	Hab	47
_____, Stephen	Hab	33
_____, Washington	Bib	52
_____, William	Trp	50
POGUE/POGUGE		
Pogue, Alfred	Wrn	205
_____, James	Gwn	353
_____, John	Gwn	366
_____, John	Jns	429
_____, Reuben	Cpb	197
_____, William B.	Hal	87
Poguge, Azzariah	DeK	41
POINTER, John	Tfo	354
POLAND, John	Tlf	6
_____, William	Irw	302
POLHILL, Jas.	Bke	150
_____, John G.	Bal	40
_____, Nathaniel	Bke	137
_____, Rebeccah	Bke	137
POLK, Charles	Mad	107
_____, Daniel	Lwn	88
_____, Evan	Jks	314
_____, Ezekiel	Mad	110
_____, Jacob	Irw	304
_____, James	Irw	301
_____, James	Mad	111
_____, John	Irw	304
_____, Jonathan	Ran	24[illegible]
_____, Levi	Mad	11[illegible]

Name	County	Page
Polk, Micajah	Irw	303
______, Thomas	Irw	303
______, Urior	Ran	243
POLLARD/POLARD		
Pollard, Abner	Mus	291
______, Benjamin G.	Car	217
______, Fredrick	Fay	194
______, Irwin	Car	217
______, James	Gre	283
______, James W.	DeK	33
______, Johnson J.	Jks	314
______, Joseph	Jks	316
______, Mary	Tfo	367
______, Pew	Tms	25
______, Richard D.	Wil	301
______, Seaborn	Tfo	357
______, Thomas	Col	361
______, Thomas	Fay	189
______, William	DeK	35
______, William	Wil	300
Polard, Martha	Col	360
POLLEY, Robert	Cpb	202
POLLOCK, George	Scr	317
______, Jessee	Hst	288
______, John	Bak	19
______, John	Dec	19
______, Lewis	Hst	273
______, Maccullen	Scr	317
______, Martin	Hst	288
______, Morris	Hst	273
______, Thomas	Hst	271
POMEROY, Richard S.	Wyn	284
POMMIL, Dolly	Cht	268
POMPHREY, Redden	Tms	20
PONCELL, Michael	Gly	266
PONCHEIR/PONCHER		
Poncheir, John	Bry	87
Poncher, William	Lib	51
POND, Asa	Ogl	98
______, John	Rch	279
PONDER, Alexander	Mon	189
______, Amos	Mon	192
______, Benjamin R.	Ogl	67
______, Daniel	Mon	214
______, Dawson	Jef	423
______, Ephraim	Bke	137
______, James	Mon	228
______, Jese	Hab	57
______, John H.	Mor	261
______, John L.	Mon	214
______, John M.	Ogl	93
______, Margaret	Mon	215
______, Richard	Bke	138
Ponder, Silas	Mon	214
______, William	Hab	57
POOL/POOLE		
Pool, Adam	DeK	50
______, Aron	Jef	416
______, David V.T.	New	23
______, Dennis	Mor	241
______, Dicy	Gwn	336
______, Dicy	Gwn	369
______, Disa	Pik	109
______, Elijah	Tfo	363
______, Elizabeth	Wil	318
______, Hardy	Jef	418
______, Hardy	New	29
______, Henry	Hal	110
______, Henry	Wrn	223
______, Hy. P.	Wrn	220
______, James	Jef	418
______, James	Wks	351
______, James	Wrn	216
______, Jane	New	51
______, Joseph	Hal	112
______, Laban C.	Tlb	339
______, Martha	Hal	108
______, Martin P.	Hal	113
______, Middleton	Wsh	243
______, Nathan	Hal	115
______, Robert	Hal	112
______, Robert C.	Mon	215
______, Samuel	Ear	100
______, Samuel	Up	114
______, Samuel	Wrn	223
______, Seth	Mon	216
______, Silas	Gwn	337
______, Stoval	Wil	322
______, Susannah	Hal	112
______, Thomas A.	Mon	228
______, W. W.	Bal	29
______, Walter	New	28
______, Wiley	New	29
______, William	Han	163
______, William	Wil	303
______, William P.	Hal	109
______, Young P.	Gwn	311
Poole, Benjamin B.	Frk	222
______, David	Tfo	355
______, James S.	Frk	224
______, John	Wal	156
______, William	Frk	246
POOLER, R. W.	Cht	264
POOR, Aaron	DeK	25
POP, Adam	Mad	103
POPE, Abnor	Jef	418

Name	County	Page
Pope, Aleck	Rch	271
______, Alexander	Wil	289
______, Augustin B.	Tlb	333
______, B.	Ogl	93
______, Benjamin	Cht	264
______, Britton	Pul	141
______, Burrel	Ogl	93
______, Burwell	Mon	205
______, Cadmus	Jns	443
______, Cullen	Mon	226
______, Danl.	Hab	20
______, Daniel	Wsh	246
______, David	DeK	25
______, Elijah	Twg	68
______, Frederick	Lau	18
______, Hardy H.	Fay	195
______, Henry	Wil	324
______, Henry J.	Ogl	95
______, Henry N.	Hry	214
______, James	DeK	59
______, James	Twg	68
______, Jefferson	Put	205
______, Jesse	Fay	187
______, Jesse	Mon	172
______, Jesse	Twg	72
______, Joab	Jsp	391
______, John	DeK	25
______, John	Lau	18
______, John	New	45
______, John	Tlb	343
______, John	Up	105
______, John C.	Clk	296
______, John D.	Pul	152
______, John H.	Wil	289
______, John T.	Up	110
______, Jonah	Jsp	385
______, Margeritt	Wil	289
______, Mary	Wil	320
______, Mechall	Pul	150
______, Micajah	DeK	52
______, Middleton	Ogl	93
______, Nathaniel	Dec	11
______, Sarah	McI	124
______, Susan	Mon	223
______, Thomas	Pul	159
______, Thomas L.	Mon	224
______, Walter R.	Mon	223
______, Wiley	Clk	320
______, Wiley	Wsh	250
______, Wiley	Wil	320
______, William	Hal	92
______, William	New	45
______, William H.	Wil	289

Name	County	Page
Pope, Willis B.	Jns	454
______, Wilson	Gre	299
______, Wilson	Jns	466
POPHAM, Amaria	Hab	55
______, Ann	Hab	55
______, Elijah	Hab	49
______, John	Frk	245
POPLE/POPPELL		
Pople, Abraham	Jsp	393
Poppell, Gidion	Tat	378
POPWELL, George	McI	132
______, Robert	Lib	51
PORCH, Sherrod	Mwr	164
______, Thomas	Mwr	152
POREA, P.	Cht	248
PORTER, A.	Cht	262
______, Archibald	Hry	205
______, Benjamin C.	Eff	108
______, Boswell G.	Bts	167
______, Chs.	Wks	357
______, Chs.	Wks	339
______, Charles H.	Tlb	324
______, David H.	Hab	21
______, Drewry	Tms	29
______, Edward	Mad	110
______, Elizabeth	Col	364
______, Elizabeth	Jsp	391
______, Fayette	Tlb	328
______, Freedrick	Ear	97
______, H. B.	Col	364
______, Henry H.	Bib	59
______, Hugh	Hal	104
______, Hugh	Pik	113
______, Isaac	Wks	357
______, Isaac R.	Wks	358
______, James	Bal	28
______, James	Bal	32
______, James S.	Gwn	318
______, James S.	Gwn	365
______, Jeddetha	Jks	336
______, John	Ear	100
______, John	Jns	471
______, John	Jsp	391
______, John A.	Tfo	364
______, John L.	Bak	15
______, John R.	Hab	40
______, John S.	Hal	83
______, John W.	Mor	251
______, Johnson	Gre	282
______, Joseph	Hal	108
______, Joseph G.	Jns	470
______, Julian N.	Wks	334
______, Mary	Hst	261

Porter, Mary Wil 295
_____, Mathew Scr 311
_____, Nancy Col 364
_____, Nobles Hst 294
_____, Nobles Lee 34
_____, Oliver Clk 315
_____, Oliver Gre 287
_____, R. T. Wks 344
_____, Richard Jsp 392
_____, Richard T. Wks 339
_____, Robert Tfo 367
_____, Rose Wks 357
_____, Sarah Pik 122
_____, Thomas Bak 15
_____, Uriah Jns 470
_____, V. R. Up 118
_____, William Jks 316
_____, William New 45
_____, William Tfo 359
_____, William Wsh 270
_____, William Wrn 199
_____, William R. Jns 470
PORTERFIELD, Christopher Car 220
_____, David Mad 98
_____, James Mad 101
PORTERSIANT, John T. Dec 3
PORTERVINE, James Mus 292
PORTIN, Britum Crf 399
PORTIS, James P. Tlb 322
PORTRESS/PORTTRESS
Portress, Meredith Scr 306
Porttress, Tabitha Scr 309
PORTWOOD/PORTEWOOD
Portwood, Catharine Jsp 358
_____, Howard Ran 242
Portewood, Dempsy Tfo 355
POSEY, Abraham Mar 143
_____, Bennett Trp 53
_____, Benjamin Mar 144
_____, Daniel Car 219
_____, Drucilla Pul 146
_____, Green Har 185
_____, Hannah Wal 125
_____, Henry Wsh 244
_____, Hezekiah Car 219
_____, Humphrey Hry 224
_____, James Lin 60
_____, James Tlf 6
_____, James Trp 53
_____, John Tlf 6
_____, Marcus Wrn 204
_____, Mary Pul 160
_____, Micajah Pul 149
Posey, Peter E. Hal 98
_____, Richard Hry 228
_____, Richard Wsh 265
_____, Telfare Pul 160
POSNER, Sylvia S. Jef 402
POSS, Adam Mad 103
_____, Christopher Wil 306
_____, George Wil 306
_____, George W. Fay 101
_____, Henry Wil 298
_____, Jacob DeK 44
_____, Jane Ogl 81
_____, John Fay 199
_____, Nicholas Ogl 81
_____, William Wil 306
POST, Allen Cow 385
_____, John Fay 201
_____, Joseph M. Trp 43
_____, Lindsey M. Trp 39
_____, Martin Fay 198
_____, Sam[l]. Jsp 396
_____, Samuel B. Trp 39
*** _____, William (Indian) Car 234
POSTELL, Edward P. McI 129
_____, Jane E. Cht 263
POTCH, Solomon Jsp 372
POTMORE, Hannah Col 348
_____, William Col 348
POTTELL, John Cam 184
POTTER, James Cht 277
_____, James Crf 407
_____, Pleasant Bts 163
_____, Plummer Mad 103
_____, William Jks 347
POTTS, Henry Jks 328
_____, Hiram Hab 25
_____, Isaac Hab 52
_____, James Sr. Jsp 387
_____, James Jr. Jsp 387
_____, John Bib 62
_____, John Hab 53
_____, Jonathan Hry 226
_____, Moses Jks 325
_____, Moses Jsp 387
_____, Moses Ogl 101
_____, Peter New 5
_____, Samuel Hab 25
_____, Samuel Hry 228
_____, Samuel Ogl 87
_____, Shadrick Wrn 222
_____, Stephen Jks 319
_____, William Jks 329
_____, William Wks 332

Name	County	Page
Potts, William E.	Mon	176
POULSON/POLSON		
Poulson, Johnathan	Jsp	387
Polson, Mark	New	7
POULTAR, Thomas N.	Gre	296
POUNDS/POUND/POWNS		
Pounds, Jarrod	Col	353
_____, John	Gwn	338
_____, Merriman	Put	208
_____, Newman	DeK	56
_____, Richard	Har	176
_____, Robert	Col	343
_____, William	Tfo	367
Pound, Joel	Han	164
_____, Mary	Cht	256
Powns, John B.	Put	209
POWELL/POWEL		
Powell, Abraham F.	Tlf	11
_____, Absalom	Tlf	11
_____, Alexander	Tlf	11
_____, Allen	Tlf	11
_____, Allen B.	McI	129
_____, Ambrose	Doo	83
_____, Ann D.	Jef	401
_____, Anney	Lib	51
_____, Artemas	Bke	148
_____, Asa	New	7
_____, Austin	Hal	106
_____, Barnet	Mon	215
_____, Barnet R.	Mon	228
_____, Benjamin	Hst	282
_____, Benjamin	Lau	23
_____, Benjamin	Wil	299
_____, Benjamin M.	Gwn	369
_____, Bob (colored)	Bke	149
_____, C. W.	Jsp	391
_____, Cader R.	Bke	148
_____, Campbell	Cpb	198
_____, Chas.	Lee	34
_____, Charles	Pul	158
_____, Cirus	Jef	416
_____, Daniel	Doo	86
_____, Dorcas	Tlf	11
_____, Edley	Rab	222
_____, Elisha	Cpb	198
_____, Elizabeth	Bke	141
_____, Enos	Twg	61
_____, Evan H.	Jsp	365
_____, Frances	Elb	126
_____, Francis	Lin	60
_____, Francis	Wil	299
_____, George	Bib	74
_____, George C.	Crf	394
Powell, George C.	Dec	9
_____, George	Wsh	271
_____, George	Up	105
_____, Henry	Fay	198
_____, Henry	Gwn	311
_____, Henry	Wsh	266
_____, Hilliard	Doo	83
_____, Hiram	Tlb	337
_____, Isaiah	Doo	85
_____, J. Estate	Cow	368
_____, James	Doo	83
_____, James	Hab	8
_____, James	Hst	278
_____, James	Hst	286
_____, James	Lin	62
_____, James G.	Mon	190
_____, Jason	Jef	405
_____, Jefferson	Rab	223
_____, Jesse	Mon	174
_____, Jessee	Gwn	312
_____, Jethro	Doo	85
_____, John	Cow	374
_____, John	Doo	81
_____, John	Hal	117
_____, John	Hst	281
_____, John	Jns	471
_____, John	Jsp	363
_____, John	Pul	156
_____, John	Tlb	327
_____, John	Wsh	266
_____, John H.	Crf	402
_____, Johnson	Hry	206
_____, Joseph	App	6
_____, Joseph	Crf	393
_____, Jos. B.	Rab	223
_____, Lewis	Col	336
_____, Lewis	Doo	85
_____, Lewis	Hst	276
_____, Lewis F.	Bke	141
_____, Lewis R.	Hal	72
_____, Lewis R.	Hal	105
_____, Littleberry	Jef	416
_____, Lucas	Jsp	371
_____, Mark M.	Bts	173
_____, Margaret	Tlf	11
_____, Martha	Col	351
_____, Martha	Tat	373
_____, Mary	Bke	126
_____, Millington	Bts	168
_____, Moses	New	13
_____, Nancy	Wil	311
_____, Nathan	Doo	85
_____, Nathan	Pul	158

Powell, Nathaniel Cow 373
_____, Norborne Tlb 328
_____, Pleasant Rab 226
_____, Presley Hal 118
_____, Quinney Hst 276
_____, Rachael Doo 84
_____, Richard Lin 62
_____, Richard Rch 265
_____, Richard Wrn 230
_____, Rigdon Crf 413
_____, Rutha Gwn 331
_____, Sampson Hst 279
_____, Sarah Cam 189
_____, Sarah Col 349
_____, Sarah Gwn 369
_____, Silas Hst 282
_____, Sion Gwn 369
_____, Stephen Ran 247
_____, Thomas Cpb 211
_____, Thomas C. Mon 196
_____, Thomas W. Mon 184
_____, Thompson Bib 59
_____, Tilman Rab 225
_____, Viney Ogl 100
_____, William Dec 3
_____, William Fay 182
_____, William Fay 187
_____, William Hst 283
_____, William Mon 198
_____, William New 11
_____, William Wrn 222
_____, William Wrn 230
_____, William C. Bib 77
_____, William P. Elb 125
_____, Willis Elb 127
_____, Wright Wsh 271
Powel, Abraham Hab 43
_____, C. DeK 26
_____, Elijah Elb 130
_____, Frances Hab 31
_____, Frances Jks 347
_____, Isaac Mus 288
_____, Jane Hab 43
_____, Jas. Dec 17
_____, Joel Tms 23
_____, John Tms 23
_____, Larkin Car 216
_____, Oliver C. Elb 133
_____, Richard L. Hab 48
_____, Robert Pik 118
_____, Samson Em 167
_____, Sarah Col 346
_____, Seamore DeK 55
Powel, William Wsh 241
POWERS/POWER
Powers, Alexander Frk 237
_____, Ann Rch 261
_____, Clem Eff 112
_____, Edmund Car 228
_____, Hardy Pul 140
_____, John Dec 11
_____, John DeK 68
_____, John Eff 115
_____, John Gre 277
_____, John J. Gre 303
_____, Joseph DeK 42
_____, Joseph DeK 45
_____, Joseph Lwn 88
_____, Lovey Rch 264
_____, Mary DeK 30
_____, Robert Bts 177
_____, Samuel D. Lau 7
_____, Thomas Hal 99
_____, Zara Eff 110
Power, David Mad 105
_____, Frances Trp 33
_____, James Mad 105
_____, James M. Mad 105
_____, Jesse Mad 108
_____, John M. Mad 102
_____, Samuel Ogl 87
_____, William Hal 87
_____, William Jr. Mad 105
_____, William P. Mad 108
_____, William Sr. Mad 106
POWLEDGE, George Eff 104
_____, Gideon Bib 56
_____, John M. Bib 62
POYNER, John Hry 216
_____, John W. Hry 202
POYTHRESS, John C. Bke 150
_____, Joseph Trp 35
PRATER/PRATHER/PRATOR/
PRATO
Prater, Aron Hal 103
_____, John A. Up 106
_____, Joseph Hal 93
_____, Josiah Hal 103
_____, William H. Up 98
_____, William K. Elb 122
Prather, Benjamin Wks 310
_____, John S. Trp 34
_____, N. V. Col 350
_____, Richard Lin 63
_____, William Wil 310
Prator, John Hab 39

Name	County	Page
Prato, Busdel	Tfo	367
PRATT, Abm.	Cam	181
______, Alexander	Cht	246
______, Calvin	Hst	280
______, Daniel	Bal	33
______, Falkner	Cam	181
______, Harris S.	Cam	184
______, Hillory	Mon	173
______, James	Hst	275
______, John	Ogl	95
______, John	Tlb	345
______, Leonard	Wrn	194
______, Susan	Cht	253
______, Thomas A.	Mon	208
______, Vincent A.	Wrn	221
PRAY, M. B.	Wil	290
PRAYDY, Lemuel	Car	227
PRESCOT/PRESCUTT/PRESCOT/		
PRESCOAT/PRESKET		
Prescott, Benijah	Bke	146
______, George W.	Ear	98
______, James	Bke	126
______, James M.	Rch	274
______, Jesse	App	9
______, John	Bke	141
______, John	Wrn	224
______, John R.	Bke	153
______, Joshua	Tat	376
______, Moses	Bke	147
______, Nancy	Bke	147
______, Sarah	Bke	148
______, William	Twg	74
Prescutt, Hester	App	12
______, John	App	7
Prescot, Alvin	Put	191
______, Benjamin	Scr	311
______, Samuel	Bke	151
Prescoat, James T.	Dec	4
Presket, Milledge	Mwr	169
PRESLEY/PRESSLEY/PRESLY/		
PRESSLY		
Presley, Charles	Elb	142
______, David	Hal	97
______, Israel	Frk	256
______, Jane	Hal	99
______, Jas.	Jks	349
______, John	Hry	201
______, Moses	Fay	206
______, Moses	Put	191
______, Peter	Hab	23
______, Robert	Cpb	203
______, Samuel	Hal	83
______, William	Bts	175
Presley, William	Frk	247
Pressley, John	Up	108
______, Jonathan	Wal	158
______, Moses	Hry	201
Presly, Richard	Gwn	322
______, Thomas H.	Pik	125
Pressly, Calvin	Lin	61
PRESSNAL/PRESNALL		
Pressnal, Jacob	Car	228
Presnall, Jeremiah	Ear	91
PRESTON, Archibald	Wal	150
______, Gillum	Bts	172
______, Thomas	Wal	127
______, Washington	Crf	400
______, William	Jsp	383
PRESTRIDGE, John	Fay	189
PRESWOOD, Henry	Wks	353
______, James	Wks	353
______, Mrs.	Bal	44
PRETT, Alexander	Cht	246
______, John	Lee	30
PRETTY, Robt.	Lee	35
PREVATT, William A.	Cht	278
PREWETT/PRUETT/PREWIT/		
PREWITT/PRUIT/PRUITT/PRUET		
Prewett, Alexander	New	41
______, Davis	Fay	194
______, Henry	Up	111
______, John	Frk	237
______, Jonathan	Mad	101
______, Judah	Hal	125
______, Levi	Up	117
______, Martin	Fay	190
______, Michael	Hal	82
______, Robert	Frk	224
______, Russell	Up	104
______, Samuel	Fay	200
______, William	Up	105
______, Zachariah	Frk	224
Pruett, Ansel B.	Gwn	352
______, Ben	Gwn	320
______, Bird	Gwn	335
______, Itai	Gwn	359
______, Jacob	Jns	43[illegible]
______, James	Jns	44[illegible]
______, Joseph	Jks	341
______, Rhesa	Gwn	310
______, Thomas	Gwn	33[illegible]
______, Wilea	Gwn	31[illegible]
______, William T.	Jns	43[illegible]
Prewit, Adam	Mwr	15[illegible]
______, John	Elb	14[illegible]
______, Samuel	Gwn	37[illegible]

Prewit, William Elb 157
Prewitt, Davis Tlb 323
_____, Joshua Elb 121
_____, Samuel Frk 247
_____, Solomon Mon 172
Pruit, Bird Put 177
_____, Henry Trp 44
_____, John Jsp 394
_____, John S. Cpb 201
_____, Joseph Trp 44
Pruitt, Bailey W. Cpb 207
_____, Tilmon DeK 64
_____, William Cpb 206
Pruet, David Gwn 329
_____, Turner Put 182
PRICE, A. Bal 16
_____, Benjamin Car 218
_____, Bridges Wsh 269
_____, Charles Put 187
_____, Charles Sr. Jks 337
_____, Charles Jr. Jks 330
_____, Edward Jsp 364
_____, Ephraigm Gre 287
_____, Ervin Hst 293
_____, Ezekiel Jks 323
_____, Hansford Put 26
_____, James Clk 313
_____, James Em 168
_____, James Jks 311
_____, James B. Rab 226
_____, James E. Crf 393
_____, Jesse *
_____, John Jef 404
_____, John Jsp 391
_____, John Pik 132
_____, John B. Rab 226
_____, John C. Car 217
_____, Joseph Jef 404
_____, Joseph Jks 323
_____, Joseph R. Dec 5
_____, Joshua Wsh 242
_____, Lewis Lib 51
_____, Littleberry Wsh 269
_____, Lorenza D. Em 165
_____, Lorenza S. Em 165
_____, Lucas Crf 414
_____, Lucy New 48
_____, Lydia Bib 52
_____, Matthew Elb 138
_____, Mary Em 164
_____, Mary Em 172
_____, Rader Wks 331
_____, Rice Wsh 265
Price, Richard Jns 462
_____, Robert Jsp 398
_____, Rosen Hab 36
_____, Samuel Hry 240
_____, Stephen W. Hry 243
_____, Thomas Hst 294
_____, Thomas Jks 315
_____, Thomas E. Bib 62
_____, Wiley Put 186
_____, William Clk 313
_____, William Gre 273
_____, William Hal 119
_____, William Ran 243
_____, William H. Put 185
_____, Zachariah New 38
PRICKELL, Israel Frk 247
PRIDE, John Mus 277
PRIDGIN/PRIDGEN/PRIDGEON
Pridgin, David Bul 98
_____, Edwin Wsh 244
_____, James Bts 161
Pridgen, James Hry 240
_____, Robert Jns 462
_____, William Bts 163
Pridgeon, Matthew Cow 387
PRIDDY/PREDDY
Priddy, Benjamin Trp 55
Preddy, James J. Cpb 199
PRIEST, Aron Hal 120
_____, John Hal 120
_____, John Jr. Hal 119
_____, Thomas Hal 119
PRIM, Abraham Crf 414
PRIMROSE, George Mor 238
_____, James Rch 287
_____, James Tlb 342
PRINCE, Carey Hab 34
_____, Daniel Mor 260
_____, Even Rab 222
_____, George Wsh 256
_____, Hamilton Mus 284
_____, James Hab 20
_____, Jeremiah Wal 145
_____, John Gre 300
_____, John Hab 56
_____, Joseph Col 343
_____, Joseph Hab 56
_____, Joseph Jsp 392
_____, Noah Clk 314
_____, Noah F. Clk 314
_____, Samuel Mon 200
_____, Sylvanus Crf 396
_____, Willis Hal 121

* County and page inadvertently omitted from index card

Name	County	Page
PRINGLE, Coleman S.	Mon	203
______, James	Wyn	283
PRITCHARD/PRICHARD/ PRICTCHARD		
Pritchard, Isaac	Gwn	367
______, John B.	Gly	269
______, Joshua	Gwn	367
______, Robert	Gly	268
______, Wiley	Mon	187
______, William H.	Mon	186
Prichard, John	Col	357
______, Mary	Crf	404
______, Presley	Put	172
______, William B.	Put	172
Prictchard, Sion B.	Frk	223
PRITCHETT/PRICKETT/PRICKET/ PRICHETT/PRITHETT/PRITCHET		
Pritchett, Benjamin	Han	163
______, Delfa	Elb	127
______, Guilford	Bke	137
______, James	Gre	297
______, John	New	6
______, Nicholas	Elb	125
______, Philip B.	Jsp	364
______, Thomas	Elb	126
______, W. H.	Jsp	366
______, William	Clk	307
______, William	Mon	174
Prickett, David	Bib	71
______, Jacob	Frk	225
______, Jesse	Hal	79
______, John N.	Frk	240
Prichett, Josiah	Hal	105
Prithett, William	Cow	390
Pricket, Elijah	Rch	288
Pricket, Joel	Mwr	157
Pritchet, Rhodom	Em	165
PROCTOR/PROCTER		
Proctor, Abraham	Bke	152
______, Brady	Gwn	372
______, David	Mon	218
______, Francis	Wil	294
______, Hiram	Hab	61
______, Hiram	Hal	132
______, Jacob	Hab	20
______, Jonas	Em	174
______, John	Hab	20
______, Julian	Mus	281
______, Moses T.	Bke	137
______, Nathaniel	Mwr	162
______, Richard	Hab	61
______, Samuel	Bke	129
______, Sterling	Wrn	224

Name	County	Page
Proctor, Stephen	Mon	218
______, William	Em	175
______, William	Hab	60
Procter, Daniel	Cht	248
______, John	Bak	16
______, Joshua	Tms	16
______, William	Cam	185
PROPHETT/PROPHIT		
Prophett, Robert	Jsp	397
Prophit, James	New	50
PROSSER, Coney	Bal	34
______, Oty	Wsh	262
______, William	Bal	35
PROTHRO, George	Elb	129
______, Zilphea	Elb	129
PROUDFOOT, Hugh W.	McI	122
PROUTY, Chaney	Rch	265
PRUDON, Henry K.	Jef	410
PRYOR/PRIOR/PRIER/PIOR		
Pryor, John	Pik	109
______, John	Pik	109
______, Mary	Jef	424
______, William	Pik	107
______, Wyley	Jsp	388
Prior, Ann C.	Bal	28
______, Asa	Mor	251
______, Elizabeth (W)	Mor	267
______, John S.	Wks	343
______, Robert	Bke	123
______, Robert	Bke	155
______, Waid	Har	181
Prier, Felix	Col	359
______, Philip	Car	224
______, William	Mon	206
Pior, John	Jef	416
PSALMONDS, Elizabeth	Wil	318
PUCKET/PUCKETT/PUCKER		
Pucket, Alexander	Gwn	362
______, Alexander	Gwn	370
______, Edmond	Gwn	345
______, Edmund	Jsp	368
______, Elijah	Hal	81
______, Harris	Hal	76
______, J. B.	Gwn	37
______, John	Bal	2
______, John	Gwn	32
______, Richard	Bal	3
______, Richard	Gwn	33
______, Sarah H.	Gwn	34
______, Weseley	Gwn	37
Puckett, James	New	4
______, James D.	DeK	3
______, John	Hal	8

Puckett, John New 35
_____, Page Hal 76
_____, William Cow 372
Pucker, William Jsp 393
PUELL, John Hal 117
PUGELEY/PUGSLEY
Pugeley, Sydney Bke 154
Pugsley, Elenor Jef 416
PUGH, Abel Han 172
_____, James Hal 78
_____, Martin Hal 81
_____, Mary Hal 134
_____, Ney Bts 174
_____, Susannah DeK 36
_____, William Hal 81
_____, William W. Han 164
PULLEN/PULLIN/PULLUM/PULLING
Pullen, Allis New 44
_____, George New 48
_____, George Wil 317
_____, James Wil 317
_____, James Sr. Wil 303
_____, James Jr. Wil 303
_____, John Wil 298
_____, Joseph Wil 303
_____, Majors Wil 303
_____, Moses Lau 14
_____, Robert Gre 295
_____, Sanford Wil 316
_____, Silas M. Wil 303
_____, Thomas Car 219
_____, Thomas Lau 14
_____, Thomas Wil 298
_____, Tilmon New 37
Pullin, Asker Col 338
_____, Atheal New 16
_____, Elijah Hry 199
_____, Greevill DeK 70
_____, Guilford Lin 65
_____, Henry Em 168
Pullum, James Jns 458
_____, Richard Mor 245
Pulling, Henry Han 164
PULLEY: see Polley
PULLIAM, Benjamin Frk 238
_____, Edward Hal 88
_____, Matthew Elb 141
_____, Nelson Up 101
_____, Robert Frk 234
_____, Sarah Sr. Frk 225
_____, Sarah Jr. Frk 225
_____, Thomas Frk 212
Pulliam, William Elb 141
PULLINER, Edward Hal 72
PUMPHREY, Betsy Twg 84
*** PUMPKINPILE (Indian) Car 233
*** _____, Daniel (Indian) Car 233
PURCELL/PURSEL
Purcell, James Hab 10
_____, John Hab 10
_____, John Sr. Hab 10
Pursel, John Hab 40
PURDEE, Larkin Col 354
PURDON/PURDEN/PURDAM
Purdon, George S. Jns 474
Purden, John Hab 46
Purdam, Thomas Wyn 283
PURIFY, McCarrol Put 205
PURNELL/POURNELL
Purnell, Henson Pik 120
_____, Richard Hal 68
Pournell, John Wsh 253
_____, William F. Wsh 239
PURSER: see Perser
PURVIS/PURVES/PERVIS
Purvis, Alfred Wrn 223
_____, Bennet Doo 84
_____, Chesley Doo 84
_____, Jesse Jef 417
_____, John Doo 83
_____, Needham Jef 417
_____, Richard Em 172
_____, William Em 173
_____, William Jef 415
_____, William Gly 264
_____, Zilpah App 8
Purves, Daniel Lib 51
Pervis, Hamon Crf 398
PURYEAR, John Clk 314
_____, Jemima Clk 324
_____, Thomas C. Car 227
_____, William H. Clk 313
PUTMAN/PUTMON
Putman, David Hal 115
_____, Elias Hal 70
_____, Thomas Hal 114
Putmon, Mary Cow 380
PUTNAM, C. E. Gly 265
_____, Daniel Hal 68
_____, Ezekiel Hal 68
_____, Hosea Pik 117
_____, Malzie Hal 115
PYE, Allen Ogl 85
_____, Asa Jsp 370
_____, Benier Mon 203

Name	County	Page
Pye, Edward	Ogl	82
______, James	Jsp	367
______, James	Ogl	81
______, James	Ogl	85
______, Jesse	Ogl	80
______, Jesse	Ogl	85
______, Jesse	Put	176
______, Lewis	Jsp	371
______, Nancy	Mon	186
______, Theophilus	Jsp	356
______, William	Ogl	80
PYNCHON, Edward E.	Lib	51
PYRON, Charles A.	Pik	121
______, Drury	Pik	124
______, William	Gre	296
QUARLES/QUALLS/QUALS/ QUERLS		
Quarles, Eleazer	Trp	49
______, David	Rab	226
______, Robert	Rab	233
______, Thomas	Hal	98
Qualls, Hubbard	Rab	224
______, Purnell	Jks	334
Quals, John	Hab	45
Querls, David	Hal	116
QUARTERMAN, Elizabeth	Lib	51
______, John S.	Lib	51
______, Joseph	Lib	51
______, Patrick	Ear	99
______, Robert P.	Lib	51
______, William E.W.	Lib	51
QUEEN, Nancy	App	12
QUESENBY/QUEZENBERRY		
Quesenby, James	Col	364
Quezenberry, Thomas	Rch	257
QUICK, Eli	Fay	202
______, John	Fay	187
______, John	Hst	281
______, Nathaniel	Hst	263
______, William	Hst	280
______, Zachariah	Hst	282
QUIGLEY, Charles	Wil	288
______, John	Hst	275
QUILLIN/QUILLEN/QUILLIAN		
Quillin, Daniel	Hab	45
______, James	Hab	26
Quillen, Henry K.	Hab	45
Quillian, Clement	Hab	45
______, James Sr.	Hab	45
QUIMBY, Moses B.	Bry	84

Name	County	Page
QUIN/QUINN		
Quin, Ashbord	Hab	64
______, Blackburn	Hab	63
______, Calvin	Mtg	234
______, Charles	Rch	264
______, Edward	Rch	268
Quinn, C.	Cht	255
______, Henry	Rch	254
______, John	Lin	74
______, Rebecca	Mon	210
______, William	Bib	62
______, William	Wil	317
QUINNEY, Hinson	Jef	411
QUINTON, James	Gwn	315
______, Joseph	Car	214
______, Samuel	DeK	72
______, Samuel	DeK	72
______, William	DeK	72
RABADAN, Joseph	Ware	185
RABB/RABES		
Rabb, J.	Cam	188
______, John	New	42
______, Robert	New	41
Rabes, Jacob	DeK	33
RABURN/RABON/RABUN/ RABORN/RABER		
Raburn, Burwell	Jns	458
______, Daniel	Mor	245
Rabon, Charles	Twg	72
______, Ichabod	Twg	79
______, Joel	Twg	72
______, Littleberry	New	36
Rabun, Hodge	Car	218
______, Josiah A.	Hab	45
______, Mary	Han	165
______, Thomas	Car	224
______, William	Han	164
______, Willis	Car	214
Raborn, Ronson	Wrn	225
Raber, Deba	Hab	63
RACHAELS/RACHELS/RACHEL		
Rachaels, Burwell	Han	165
______, George	Han	165
______, John	Han	16
______, William	Han	16
______, Zadak	Han	16
Rachels, Ezekiel	Bke	14
______, Myles	Wsh	25
______, William	Bke	14
Rachel, William	Wsh	26

Name	County	Page
Rachel, Zedoc	Wsh	272
RACKLEY, Joel	Bke	134
______, Nathan	Dec	15
RADFORD/RADSFORD		
Radford, Bolen	Twg	66
______, John	Twg	85
______, John	Mor	268
______, Julia (W)	Mor	267
______, Robert	Twg	64
______, Robert	Twg	73
______, Reuben W.	Har	189
Radsford, Martha	Bib	52
______, Shadrick	Bib	56
RADIN/RADEN		
Radin, George	Ogl	90
______, Thomas	Ogl	90
Raden, James	Gre	273
RADNEY, John	Han	165
______, Sylvester S.	Tlb	346
______, William A.	Trp	55
RAFFIELD, William	Hst	265
RAGAN/REGGAN/REGAN/ REGANS/RIGGINS/RIGINS/ REAGAN/RAGIN/RAIGAN		
Ragan, A. B.	Mwr	154
______, Brice	Wks	333
______, Cinthia	Mwr	169
______, Nathaniel	Lin	75
______, Philip	Wks	343
______, Thomas	Lee	26
______, William	Wks	342
______, William G.	Lib	52
Reggan, Hamilton	Wal	135
______, Joseph	Wal	172
______, Mark	Wal	135
Regan, John	Wal	139
______, Mary	Pul	153
______, Roberson	Dec	13
Regans, Chas.	Dec	5
______, Daniel	Dec	14
Riggins, James	Pik	109
______, Thomas	Hst	272
Rigins, Buckner	Hal	119
______, James	Hab	60
Reagan, James	Elb	139
Ragin, David	Ogl	79
Raigan, Charles	Mad	112
RAGIS, Poline	Cht	247
RAGLAND, Burwell	Hry	208
______, Evan	New	6
______, F. W.	Jsp	369
______, John A.	Jsp	367
______, John S.	Mwr	161

Name	County	Page
Ragland, Nancy	Jns	441
______, Reuben	Put	209
______, Richard	Put	209
______, Thomas	Bal	40
______, William	Hry	208
RAGSDALE/RAGSDEL/RAGDALE		
Ragsdale, Elijah	New	12
______, Francis A.	New	13
______, Isaac	Gwn	376
______, John	Gwn	375
______, John	Jks	336
______, John W.	Gwn	328
______, Michael	Frk	223
______, Nathaniel	Cow	373
Ragsdel, Colton	Hab	62
Ragdale, Larkin	New	13
RAHFUS, Fred	Cht	241
RAHN, Hannah E.	Eff	114
______, James	Eff	105
______, John C.	Eff	106
______, Jonathan	Eff	105
______, Joseph	Eff	107
______, William	Cht	250
RAIFORD, A. G.	Rch	271
______, Baldwin	Jef	409
______, Isaac W.	Jef	401
______, John D.	Hst	273
______, Mathew	Up	120
______, Maurice	Jef	408
______, Robert	Rch	268
______, William H.	Hry	200
RAIGH/REIGH		
Raigh, Peter	Hab	30
Reigh, Job	Hab	34
______, John	Hab	25
***RAINCROW, Widow (Indian)	Car	234
RAINEY/RANEY/RAINY/ RAYNEY/RANY		
Rainey, Ann	Jsp	365
______, Benjamin L.	Bib	59
______, Daniel	Ogl	93
______, Edmond	Up	112
______, Fredrick	Put	200
______, James H.	Jks	311
______, John	DeK	41
______, John	DeK	69
______, John	Put	206
______, John	Put	215
______, Matthew	Jsp	360
______, Rubin	Mar	139
______, Thomas	DeK	40
______, William	DeK	69
______, William	Mon	195

Name	County	Page
Rainey, William	Wil	314
______, Woodson	Gwn	355
Raney, Isham	Ogl	65
______, Sarah	Tlf	8
______, Sabron	Lwn	80
______, Signal	Twg	60
______, Thomas F.	Ogl	65
______, Wootson	Clk	316
Rainy, Benjamin	Pul	152
______, C.	Bal	36
______, Eleanor	Rab	230
______, James	Rab	227
______, Thomas Sr.	Rab	227
______, William	Rab	227
Rayney, James	Col	354
______, Mathew	Ogl	89
Rany, Isaac	Rab	228
RAINS/RAINES/RAIN/ RAYNS/RAMES/REINS		
Rains, Alfred	Twg	73
______, Allen	Wsh	265
______, Cadwell W.	Bib	65
______, Edmond	Mor	267
______, James	Lee	26
______, John	Twg	73
______, John	Wsh	266
______, John G.	Bib	65
______, Nathaniel	Bib	65
______, Sarah	Twg	88
______, Thomas	Cow	377
______, Washington	Wsh	257
______, Winnifred	Wsh	276
Raines, Dabny	Elb	142
______, Frederick	Wal	154
______, Ignatious	Ogl	64
______, John W.	Elb	133
______, Sarah	Jns	452
Rain, Joshua Sr.	Crf	409
______, William K.	Cam	188
Rayns, Henry	Ogl	84
Rames, William	Trp	42
Reins, Gideon	Wks	353
RAINWATER, Burrel	Hal	118
______, Elisha G.	Han	165
______, John	Gre	287
______, Joshua	Hal	106
______, Solomon	Han	164
RAKESTRAW, Gainham L.	Wil	287
______, Robert	New	33
______, William	Cpb	205
______, William	Gwn	328
RALEY/RAILY/RAILEY		
Raley, Abner	Wrn	229
Raley, Charles	Hst	270
______, Charles	Wrn	232
______, Henry W.	Hst	262
______, James	Wrn	227
______, Jimsey D.	Hst	262
______, John	Twg	73
______, John	Wrn	226
______, Josiah	Twg	72
______, Rutha	Wrn	228
Raily, Asion	Lee	30
Railey, John	Up	99
RALPH, Hiram	McI	122
RALSTON/RAULERSON/ RAWLSTON/RAWSON		
Ralston, A. R.	Rch	261
______, David	Bib	56
______, John F.	Hal	111
______, Lewis	Frk	233
Raulerson, Herod	Wyn	285
______, Jacob	Ware	189
______, Nimrod	Ware	183
______, Noel	Ware	187
Rawlston, Lewis	Hal	132
Rawson, Chas. W.	Gwn	320
RAMAGE, Josiah	Wks	356
RAMBO, James	Har	181
______, Jessie	Gwn	317
______, Kinchen	Gwn	365
RAMEY/RAMY		
Ramey, Daniel	Clk	317
______, John	Cpb	195
______, Silas	Put	187
Ramy, John	Gwn	334
______, Milly	Gwn	323
______, Thomas	Rab	227
RAMHOUR, Benjamin	Bib	71
RAMONDO, L.	Cht	250
RAMSDALE, David	Jsp	397
______, Susan	Up	119
RAMSEY/RAMSAY/RANZEY		
Ramsey, Alexander	Doo	79
______, Alexander R.	Car	221
______, Alfred	Wal	127
______, Archibold	Elb	126
______, Benjamin	Lee	33
______, David B.	Elb	124
______, Drewry M.	Frk	216
______, Eli	Frk	239
______, Elizabeth	Wal	165
______, Foster	Elb	147
______, Francis	Cpb	209
______, George	Hry	244
______, George W.	Cpb	205

Ramsey, Isaac Col 336
______, Isaac Lau 8
______, James Col 341
______, James Frk 230
______, James Hal 123
______, James Har 177
______, James Jks 318
______, James H. Hry 201
______, John Hal 125
______, John Wal 127
______, Lewis J. Lau 16
______, Moses Doo 87
______, Rachel Frk 239
______, Randol Ogl 103
______, Randol Sr. Ogl 104
______, Randolph Lin 70
______, Seabum Clk 309
______, Susannah Hry 218
______, Thomas Doo 79
______, Thomas Elb 125
______, Thomas Lwn 85
______, Thomas Wal 164
______, Thomas S. Frk 215
______, William Frk 216
______, William Frk 215
______, William Jsp 360
______, William H. Har 180
Ramsay, R. H. Rch 292
Ranzey, William Wsh 259
RAN, Nancy Hab 45
RANDALL/RANDAL/RANDLE/
RANDOL
Randall, Arthur Hry 239
______, Edmund Han 165
______, James Fay 198
______, Patsey Wal 173
______, Wheeler Cow 367
Randal, Fedrick B. Mwr 162
______, J. B. Jsp 381
______, Jackson H. DeK 45
______, Newton DeK 31
______, Peter Mon 197
Randle, Charles Gwn 322
______, James G. Gre 292
______, John S. Put 217
______, Thomas W. Gre 293
Randol, John Frk 213
______, Oney Frk 249
______, William Mor 254
RANDHAN, Peter Hry 208
RANDLESON, Andrew Bke 119
RANDOLPH/RANDOLP
Randolph, Beverley Bke 128
Randolph, Jeremiah Hry 245
______, John Jks 312
______, John Jr. Jks 315
______, Richard H. Mor 250
______, Robert Col 353
______, Thomps. P. Wil 296
______, Wood L. Jks 315
Randolp, Dorothy Wil 288
RANKIN/RANKINS
Rankin, Adam W. Gre 277
______, Margaret Gre 283
______, William Cht 240
Rankins, David Dec 5
______, Elizabeth (W) Mor 257
______, John Dec 4
RANSOM/RANSOME/RANSON
Ransom, Benjamin Lin 60
______, Davis Crf 410
______, Dudley Wal 141
______, James Bts 165
______, James Bts 175
______, James Hry 202
______, Jeremiah P. Wal 143
______, John F. Hry 203
______, Reuben Gre 290
______, Reubin Clk 316
______, Reubin Wal 132
______, Samuel Cow 386
Ransome, Armstead Tfo 368
______, James Wrn 227
______, Jordan Wrn 196
______, Robert S. Wal 148
Ranson, Elijah Frk 232
______, John W. Tlb 329
RAPE/RAPP
Rape, Henry Hry 222
______, John Hry 209
______, Peter Hry 242
______, Samuel Hry 210
Rapp, C. F. Cht 263
RAPER, Joseph Car 221
______, Thomas Rab 227
RAPSHAW, John DeK 53
RASBURY, Mary Wal 126
RASCOE/RASCO
Rascoe, John Cht 279
Rasco, Lodawick Pik 133
RASH, James Hab 25
______, James Hab 56
______, Leevy Lee 30
RASOR, Garrington Tlb 340
RATCHFORD/RACHFORD/
RATSFORD

Name	County	Page
Ratchford, Ezekiel	Fay	197
_____, Jos. Sr.	Jks	317
Rachford, Joseph	Tlb	323
Ratsford, William	Cpb	201
RATCLIFF/RATLIFF/RADCLIFF		
Ratcliff, Bazel	Jsp	357
_____, J.	Gwn	308
_____, James	Gly	268
_____, James M.	Wyn	281
_____, Martha	Gly	267
_____, Moses	Jsp	356
_____, Richard	Gly	267
Ratliff, George	Mus	291
_____, James	Lin	62
_____, John S.	Mon	192
_____, Milledge M.	Frk	223
_____, Thomas	Lin	62
Radcliff, John W.	Mus	281
***RATTLESNAKE (Indian)	Car	233
***RATTLING GOURD (Indian)	Car	234
RAVEN/RAVENS		
Raven, David B.	Mon	219
_____, John	Hab	27
Ravens, James H.	Mwr	158
RAWLINGS, Elizabeth	Bke	134
_____, John	Pul	152
_____, Thomas W.	Pul	151
_____, William	Wsh	242
RAWLS/RALLS/RAWLES		
Rawls, Allen	Bul	94
_____, Arthur	Lau	14
_____, Benjamin	Dec	13
_____, Dempsy	Ear	99
_____, Honor	Put	188
_____, Isaac Sr.	Jks	327
_____, Isaac	Jks	311
_____, J. C.	Col	361
_____, Jessee	Hst	274
_____, John	Dec	13
_____, John	Pul	163
_____, Joseph	Dec	13
_____, Joseph	Twg	88
_____, Moses	Hst	283
_____, Robertson	Put	187
_____, Shadrack	Jks	330
_____, Silas	Doo	85
_____, Silas	Hst	274
_____, William	Crf	393
_____, William	Em	165
Ralls, Cintha	Gre	275
_____, John T.	Tms	20
_____, Sally	Gre	305
Rawles, Hosea	Bke	143
Rawles, Maria	Cht	247
RAY/RAE/REA/RHEA		
Ray, Alfred	Mon	198
_____, Ambros	Wsh	270
_____, Anderson	Clk	323
_____, Andrew	Wal	130
_____, Bathena	Wal	124
_____, Benjamin	Crf	406
_____, Benjamin	Trp	55
_____, Benjamin	Twg	66
_____, Chesley	Wil	293
_____, Coleman L.	Bts	160
_____, David	Wal	152
_____, Duncan	Bak	15
_____, Duncan	Tms	16
_____, E. M.	Col	359
_____, Eda	Twg	77
_____, Elijah	Mwr	156
_____, Elisha	Mon	179
_____, Elizabeth	Hry	234
_____, Emanuel	Gre	284
_____, Frederick	Hry	239
_____, George	Bal	40
_____, George	Up	113
_____, George	Wal	126
_____, George A.	New	35
_____, George W.	Wrn	210
_____, Hardy	Crf	402
_____, Howell	Mon	227
_____, Jacob	Wil	293
_____, James	Mon	210
_____, James	Put	215
_____, James	Twg	66
_____, Jerusha	Gre	280
_____, John	Crf	394
_____, John	Har	185
_____, John	Hry	210
_____, John	Hry	225
_____, John	Wal	134
_____, John H.	Gre	290
_____, John W.	Mus	282
_____, Mark	Mon	212
_____, Mary	Clk	303
_____, Neal	Put	194
_____, Nimrod	Gre	284
_____, Peter	Jef	403
_____, Phares	Put	174
_____, Polly	Hal	117
_____, Raymon R.	Mor	256
_____, Reubin	Bts	160
_____, Robert	Hab	10
_____, Silas	Hry	212
_____, Solomon	Mwr	157

Ray, Susannah Han 166
_____, Thomas DeK 35
_____, Thomas Frk 250
_____, Thomas Har 185
_____, Thomas Tfo 361
_____, W. Gwn 309
_____, William Bts 159
_____, William Elb 133
_____, William Frk 214
_____, William Frk 238
_____, William Hry 206
_____, William Jks 336
_____, William Mwr 152
_____, William Mus 288
_____, William Trp 42
_____, William Wal 131
_____, William D. Bal 29
_____, William G. Hry 211
_____, Willy Trp 44
_____, Wilson Col 342
Rae, Widow M. Pul 150
Rea, Robert Gre 282
Rhea, John A. Mwr 152
RAYFIELD, Willis Lau 17
RAYMOND, George Bib 52
RAYNER, Lucian Tms 20
READER, Cary Wal 124
_____, Jonathan Wal 143
REAMS, Azariah Mwr 167
REAMY, Jacob Hal 68
REASON, Elizabeth Gwn 336
_____, Sarah Cht 266
REBB, Lewis Rch 255
REDD/RED
Redd, Berry Rch 256
_____, Charles A. Gre 278
_____, John D. Gre 292
_____, William DeK 53
_____, William Gre 292
_____, William A. Trp 33
Red, Hiram Bke 143
_____, Holland Bke 140
_____, J. Gwn 308
_____, R. Gwn 308
_____, William Bke 144
REDDICK/REDDIK
Reddick, David Up 119
_____, John Bke 132
_____, John Cam 184
_____, Nicholas Bke 133
_____, Peter Scr 311
_____, Peter F. Cam 190
_____, Sarah Bke 133
Reddick, Sarah Scr 303
_____, Thomas Scr 306
Reddik, Thomas Bib 74
REDDING/REDDIN/REDDEN
Redding, And. Bal 37
_____, Anderson Mon 222
_____, Arthur Mon 224
_____, Ezekiel Mon 222
_____, Halcomb New 13
_____, James P. Mon 188
_____, John Hal 91
_____, John Mon 188
_____, John Pik 111
_____, John F. Bul 97
_____, Margery Bul 97
_____, Parhum Mon 188
_____, Robert C. Mon 222
_____, Rollin Bal 34
_____, Rutland Bib 74
_____, Thomas Mon 226
_____, William Hal 90
_____, William C. Mon 226
_____, William S. Bul 97
Reddin, Elizabeth Hab 39
_____, James Hab 49
_____, John Mwr 160
_____, John Trp 38
_____, William Mwr 161
Redden, David Jsp 354
REDDISH, Samuel D. Wrn 209
REDDLE, William Mon 210
REDDY, A. Bal 30
_____, Isham Bal 29
_____, Richard Ogl 98
REDLEY/REDLY
Redley, Archobald B. Ear 96
Redly, Jon Wks 358
REDLING/RIDLING
Redling, Moses Jks 317
_____, William Jks 341
Ridling, Jacob Jks 320
_____, John Jks 343
REDMAN/REDMON
Redman, Rachel Hal 99
_____, Richard Rab 226
_____, William Bts 177
Redmon, George W. Rch 285
REDWINE, Daniel Jks 343
_____, Jacob DeK 38
_____, Jacob Elb 134
_____, John Cow 379
_____, Lewis Frk 211
_____, Michael Gwn 355

Redwine, William Hal 87

REED/REID/READ/REEDS

Reed, Mrs. Cht 283
______, Albred B. Mon 173
______, Ann Cht 256
______, Benjamin G. Trp 46
______, Daniel Hal 111
______, David DeK 56
______, David DeK 71
______, David Frk 213
______, Davis DeK 70
______, Elias Cht 263
______, Elisha Put 186
______, Ezekiel Col 338
______, George Frk 241
______, Griffith Hal 69
______, Henry Gre 282
______, Henry Wks 358
______, Isaac DeK 44
______, Isaac Hal 86
______, J. B. Cht 251
______, Jacob Bak 17
______, Jacob Ogl 101
______, Jacob Wil 304
______, James Sr. Frk 231
______, James Hal 92
______, James C. Gwn 311
______, John DeK 32
______, John Hal 86
______, John Wal 138
______, John L. Frk 225
______, Joseph Hal 70
______, Josiah McI 129
______, Luke Rch 259
______, Margarett Mus 280
______, Michael Col 339
______, Murry Cht 264
______, Nancy DeK 39
______, Nathaniel DeK 44
______, Owen Hal 92
______, Samuel DeK 58
______, Samuel Jsp 370
______, Samuel Jsp 384
______, Samuel Trp 34
______, Stephen Hal 73
______, Thomas Col 358
______, Thomas New 27
______, W. O. Lee 34
______, William Crf 404
______, William Hal 131
______, William Mad 118
______, William O. Hal 71
______, William P. Elb 132

Reed, William P. Hal 110
______, Zachariah Hry 226

Reid, Alexander Put 185
______, Alexander Put 194
______, Andrew Put 193
______, Asa Gwn 320
______, Cullen Put 185
______, Edmund Put 186
______, Elender Tlf 7
______, Fred. Jsp 364
______, George Car 225
______, George Gwn 320
______, George R. Irw 300
______, Henry Car 217
______, Hy. Up 120
______, Jacob Gwn 353
______, James Cht 251
______, James New 35
______, James Tfo 365
______, James Up 99
______, James H. Cow 374
______, Jesse Doo 82
______, John Doo 79
______, John Lin 71
______, John Pik 122
______, John Pik 123
______, John Pik 131
______, John B. Pik 132
______, John Up 115
______, Joseph Wal 132
______, Margaret Rch 261
______, Mathew Car 224
______, Peter Twg 69
**______, R. R. (slave) Rch 263
______, Rhesa Gwn 314
______, Robert Rch 274
______, Robert A. Rch 275
______, Robert Raymond Rch 292
______, Samuel Gwn 357
______, Thomas Put 196
______, Tolliver Hab 40
______, William Bib 74
______, William Tfo 361
______, William H. Twg 81
______, William R. Lin 58
______, William S.C. Jns 466

Read, David R. Pik 112
______, Hiram Har 175
______, Joel New 20
______, John B. Jef 407
______, Josiah H. New 20
______, William Har 192
**______, Jacob's slaves Cht 277

Name	County	Page
Read, Oliver	Rch	256
______, William	Bts	170
REEDY, William	DeK	49
REEL, Low	Hab	12
REESE/REES/REECE/ REASE/REAS		
Reese, Benjamin	Mon	187
______, Britton	Wrn	214
______, Cuthbert	Jsp	352
______, David A.	Jsp	370
______, Ezekiel	Wrn	211
______, Harris	Wrn	215
______, Harrison	Wrn	220
______, Henry	Hry	246
______, Henry L.	Wal	135
______, Herrod	Put	185
______, Hugh	Mon	192
______, Hugh	Wrn	211
______, Isham	Mon	172
______, James	Han	164
______, James B.	Han	165
______, Joel	Put	179
______, Joel	Wrn	213
______, Jordan (Capt.)	Mon	191
______, Jordan	Mon	173
______, Joseph	Cow	385
______, Moses	Frk	242
______, Moses	Wrn	218
______, Redmond	Wrn	205
______, Richard	Put	213
______, Richard	Wrn	220
______, Rivers	Wrn	218
______, Rowell	Put	204
______, Susanah	New	24
______, Tolbert	Wrn	208
______, Wesley W.	Bke	131
Rees, Eben J.	McI	122
______, Elizabeth	Col	356
______, John	Mor	267
______, John	Rch	268
______, Joseph	Mor	250
______, L. E.	Col	362
______, Martha	Col	362
______, Michael	Col	340
______, Reuben	Crf	399
______, Simeon	Col	361
______, Thadius B.	Mor	272
______, Thomas	Ogl	64
______, Venson	Col	356
Reece, Daniel J.	Mus	284
______, E. S.	Lib	51
______, James	Bke	14-
______, John	New	43
Reece, Thomas	Mus	292
Rease, Francis	Wal	123
Reas, James	Pik	111
REEVES/REAVES/RIEVES/ REIVES/RIVES/REVES/REEVS/ REVIS/REEVE/REAVIS		
Reeves, Abner	Wil	320
______, Absalom E.	Han	164
______, Alford M.	Fay	203
______, Allen	Fay	199
______, Allen	Wks	351
______, Asa	Jsp	365
______, Avery	Jsp	392
______, Berriah B.	Wil	297
______, Burrel	Hal	118
______, Demcy	DeK	51
______, Drury	Tlf	6
______, Elizabeth	Fay	197
______, Frederick	Wal	145
______, Fred^k. H.	Mon	193
______, Green	Jsp	384
______, Henry	Tlb	344
______, Irwin	Han	165
______, Jeremiah	Jks	314
______, Jeremiah	Jns	445
______, John	Bts	166
______, John	Col	351
______, John	Han	164
______, John	Pik	131
______, John	Wal	142
______, John	Wil	311
______, John B.	Bts	160
______, John D.	Wil	310
______, Jonathan	Jsp	367
______, Joshua	Fay	203
______, Lovet	Bal	30
______, Malakiah	DeK	41
______, Michael	DeK	51
______, Sarah	Crf	403
______, Sidney K.	Wal	123
______, Spencer	Col	350
______, Spius	Bke	132
______, Stephen	Tlb	345
______, Thomas	Put	181
______, Thomas K.	Fay	193
______, Wilie	Fay	199
______, William	Fay	193
______, William	Gwn	367
______, William	Mon	176
______, William	Wil	308
______, Willis B.	Pul	140
Reaves, Asa	Hab	16
______, David	Hab	12

Name	County	Page
Reaves, Edmund	Cpb	198
_____, Greenberry	Cow	392
_____, Isaac	Hry	231
_____, Jesse B.	Pik	117
_____, Jonathan	New	32
_____, Lawson	Hry	221
_____, Nathan	Cpb	196
_____, Prier	New	54
_____, Ransom	Cpb	196
_____, Thompson	New	12
Rieves, Burger	DeK	32
_____, James W.	DeK	40
_____, John	DeK	32
_____, John	Scr	307
_____, John G. (minor)	Mor	250
_____, Jonathan	DeK	57
_____, Lucius	Put	191
_____, Richard	Scr	313
_____, Thomas Sr.	Hal	117
_____, Thomas	Hal	109
_____, William	DeK	31
Reives, Elijah	Up	104
_____, John E.	Hal	119
_____, Robert	Hal	118
_____, Ta.	Wks	348
Rives, George	Han	165
_____, Grant	Cht	262
_____, Joel	Wks	346
_____, Robert	Han	165
_____, Wyatt B.	Han	165
Reves, Coleman	Mus	281
_____, Lee	Wsh	246
_____, Loftin	Wal	152
Reevs, Isham	Dec	3
_____, Jesse	Wks	352
Revis, James	Hab	46
_____, John	Gwn	331
Reeve, Stephen	Bul	101
Reavis, William	Mon	191
REGAN: see Ragan		
REGISTER/REISTER		
Register, Abel	Wsh	260
_____, Abram	Ware	186
_____, David	Lau	8
_____, James	Lau	10
_____, Jesse	Doo	82
_____, John	Lau	4
_____, John	Wsh	260
_____, Samuel	Lwn	89
_____, William	Doo	82
_____, William	Ware	189
_____, Willyam	Wal	155
Reister, Jacob	Bal	28
REIFF, Matthew	Wks	354
REILLY/RELY		
Reilly, Elizabeth	Rch	257
_____, John	Rch	273
_____, Moses	Rch	276
_____, Thomas	Cht	272
Rely, Charles	Wks	331
REINHARD, Lewis W.	Hal	71
REISSER, David	Eff	114
_____, Matthew	Eff	113
REMBERT, James	Elb	154
_____, Samuel	Elb	154
_____, Scarborough	Hst	289
REMMINGTON, Edward	Tms	19
REMSHEART, John W.	Cht	254
_____, William	Cht	265
REMSON, Rem.	Lin	61
RENDER, James	Wil	323
RENEW, Timothy	Bib	74
RENFROE/RENTFROW/RENFROW/ RENTFROE/RENFRO/RENFO		
Renfroe, Elisha	Wsh	261
_____, Enoch Sr.	Wsh	249
_____, Enoch	Wsh	270
_____, James	Wsh	270
_____, Joel	Jns	458
_____, John	Wsh	250
_____, Nathan	Jns	447
_____, Nathan	Wsh	268
_____, Nathaniel	Har	189
_____, Samuel	Wsh	245
_____, Stephen	Jns	445
_____, William Sr.	Wsh	272
Rentfrow, Counsel	Fay	182
_____, David B.	Fay	183
_____, Henry	Fay	188
_____, James	Mor	250
_____, Stephen	Fay	182
Renfrow, Everitt	Crf	413
_____, John A.	Han	165
_____, Zachariah	Car	229
Rentfroe, Asahol	Lwn	81
Renfro, Ephraim	Tlb	345
Refo, S.	Rch	254
RENIA, Ben	Cht	271
RENNO/RENNEAU		
Renno, John Sr.	Hal	90
_____, John Jr.	Hal	90
Renneau, William T.	Pik	121
RENTON, William	Fay	183
RENTZ, George	McI	129
_____, Joshua	Bak	17
RESCUTT, Moses	Lwn	87

Name	County	Page
RESH, Sylvester	Hab	25
RESPASS/RESPESS		
Respass, Nathan	Up	114
______, Richard	Pik	117
Respess, Thomas	Put	213
REVIERE/REVERE		
Reviere, Herbert B.	Wil	321
______, Milton	Up	105
Revere, John K.	Wrn	194
REVELS/REVEL/REVILS/ REVILL/REVIELL/REVELL		
Revels, Edmund	App	13
______, Henry	App	13
______, John	App	13
Revel, Hardy	Rch	255
______, Mathew	Tlb	324
______, Micajah	Tlb	324
Revils, Randolph	Tms	21
Revill, Harrison W.	Mwr	168
Reviell, Matthew	Col	350
Revell, Claborn	Col	347
REYNOLDS/REYNOLD/REYNALD		
Reynolds, Ann	Hal	88
______, Anson	Car	216
______, Bartemius	Hal	102
______, Benjamine	Jns	441
______, Benjamin H.	Jns	475
______, Charles	Elb	130
______, Charles	Elb	144
______, David	Gre	285
______, Gabrael	Han	164
______, Gallens	Cow	388
______, George	Han	164
______, George	Up	111
______, George W.	Cow	390
______, Greenberry	Wal	151
______, Jacob	Jsp	371
______, James	Cow	390
______, James	Elb	130
______, James	Gre	300
______, James	Jsp	368
______, James	Lin	70
______, James	New	9
______, James	Put	174
______, Jane	Jns	452
______, Jefferson	Wal	130
______, John	Gre	295
______, John	Han	164
______, John Jr.	Han	164
______, John	Wrn	227
______, John W.	Bke	130
______, Joseph	Twg	79
______, Josiah	Hry	204

Name	County	Page
Reynolds, Larkin	Jns	441
______, Levi	Hry	215
______, Margarett	Wal	174
______, Marshall	Tlb	335
______, Martha	Hal	128
______, Meredith	Elb	143
______, Perry	Elb	144
______, Peyton	Twg	68
______, Robert	Lin	68
______, Rubin	Crf	409
______, Sarah	New	55
______, Sharp S.	Hal	95
______, Silas	Cow	367
______, Spencer	Hry	215
______, Thomas	Wal	136
______, Thomas P.	Bts	173
______, Walker	Wrn	207
______, William	Bke	131
______, William	Elb	130
______, William	Han	165
______, William	Jns	445
______, William Jr.	Jns	447
______, William	Lin	60
______, William	Tlb	334
Reynold, Ephraim	Em	166
______, Larkin	Jns	455
Reynald, John	Col	347
RHEA: see Ray		
RHEENY, Charles	Rch	281
RHODES/ROADS/RHODS		
Rhodes, Absalom	Rch	282
______, Allen	Tfo	356
______, Benjamin	DeK	30
______, Benjamin	Tlb	345
______, Byrum	Rch	257
______, Euestues H.	Lin	63
______, Hannah	Elb	130
______, Heflin F.	Gwn	352
______, Henry	Gre	299
______, Henry W.	Han	164
______, Isaac	Gwn	353
______, James	Doo	86
______, James	Mad	108
______, James H.	Hry	207
______, Jesse	Wrn	230
______, John	Mad	98
______, John	Tfo	354
______, John	Wil	289
______, Joseph	Lau	24
______, Lemuel	Mon	213
______, Lewis B.	Rch	281
______, Mercer	New	5
______, Nicolas	DeK	40

Name	County	Page
Rhodes, Patsy	Scr	305
_____, Reddin	Tfo	354
_____, Richard	Wrn	231
_____, Samuel	Hry	207
_____, Samuel	Wil	299
_____, Sarah	New	10
_____, Sarah	Tfo	364
_____, Thomas	Jsp	368
_____, William	Scr	305
_____, William	Tfo	354
_____, William J.	Rch	281
Roads, Horrace	Mwr	151
_____, James Smith Cr.	Ogl	86
_____, John F.	Twg	63
_____, Leroy	Twg	67
_____, William	Tms	26
Roades, Jesse	Cow	373
_____, Zachariah	Mor	267
Roods, Elicuna	Crf	394
Rodes, Danil	Hab	48
Rhods, Nathaniel H.	Wal	136
RHODY, John W.	Crf	408
RHONEY, Morris G.	Bke	143
RHYMES, Elizabeth	Wrn	196
_____, William	Mon	208
RIALS, James	Dec	15
RIAN, Redie	Lee	33
RIBERO, Jos. or Jas.	Cht	253
RICE/RISE/RIZE		
Rice, Aaron	Elb	135
_____, Aaron	Wks	333
_____, Anderson	Bib	77
_____, Benjamin	New	13
_____, Charles	Gwn	337
_____, Charles H.	Hst	261
_____, David L.	Wil	300
_____, Dempsey	Hal	111
_____, Ebenezer	Hal	111
_____, Evan	Hst	264
_____, Jacob	Wil	301
_____, James Sr.	Cpb	197
_____, James Jr.	Cpb	197
_____, James	Frk	237
_____, James	Hry	204
_____, James	New	5
_____, James	Wil	300
_____, John	Frk	252
_____, John	Gwn	337
_____, John	Ran	246
_____, John	Tms	27
_____, John L.	Cow	374
_____, Leonard	Elb	120
_____, Mary	Frk	236
Rice, Milly	Gwn	377
_____, Nathaniel G.	Wil	300
_____, Richard	Elb	158
_____, Richmond	Lee	27
_____, Robert	Wal	163
_____, Solomon	Hal	119
_____, Thomas	Cht	282
_____, Thomas	Gwn	316
_____, Thomas	Gwn	364
_____, Thomas	Hry	218
_____, Thomas D.	Tfo	356
_____, William	Elb	141
_____, William	New	5
_____, Williamson E.	Clk	381
Rise, Edward	Frk	224
Rize, Sophia	Cht	263
RICH/RITCH		
Rich, Anthony	Mar	140
_____, Charles	Hab	23
_____, Daniel E.	Em	165
_____, Elizabeth	Ware	189
_____, George W.	Dec	6
_____, James	Ear	98
_____, John	Dec	7
_____, John	Elb	151
_____, Richard	Wil	323
_____, Shaderic	Mus	288
_____, Stephen	App	6
_____, Stephen	Dec	8
_____, William	Elb	153
_____, Zilpha	DeK	35
Ritch, Archabald	New	9
_____, Solomon	Hab	8
RICHARDS/RICHARD		
Richards, Alexander	Bib	56
_____, Augustus	Put	174
_____, Burrel	Col	361
_____, Elizabeth	Mad	115
_____, George	Hry	211
_____, Henry	Ear	92
_____, Ivins	Cpb	197
_____, James	Mus	287
_____, James W.	Trp	49
_____, Jediah	Gre	298
_____, John	Car	230
_____, John	Cpb	199
_____, John	Ear	92
_____, John	Hab	36
_____, John R.	Hry	210
_____, Josiah Jr.	Gwn	323
_____, M. C.	Jsp	387
_____, Rachel	Elb	133
_____, Reuben	Mus	292

Richards, Terah Gre 276
______, Thomas Car 227
______, Thomas Hry 221
______, Thomas Rch 268
______, Thomas S. Trp 49
______, Uriah Pik 112
______, William Mor 256
______, William Mus 288
______, William Rab 227
______, William L. Twg 60
______, Willis Gre 282
Richard, A. P. Wks 345
______, Francis Car 223
RICHARDSON/RICHERSON/
RICKINSON/RICHISON
Richardson, Abraham Bul 100
______, Abram Han 165
______, Allen Ogl 71
______, Amos Elb 145
______, Amos Gwn 376
______, Armstead L. Jns 452
______, Benjamin Gre 302
______, Daniel Lee 33
______, David Trp 53
______, David L. Han 165
______, Ed. Cam 183
______, Elijah Tms 24
______, Elizabeth Em 164
______, Isaac Bul 100
______, Isabella Cht 267
______, Jacob Trp 52
______, James Mon 208
______, James Wal 131
______, James V. Elb 144
______, Jane Han 165
______, Jane G. Clk 317
______, Jesse Hab 6
______, John Hal 90
______, John Han 164
______, John Lee 26
______, John Mon 213
______, John Ogl 71
______, John G. Clk 312
______, John S. Hab 11
______, Jonathan Up 118
______, Joseph Trp 42
______, Larrance Col 348
______, Malge M. Elb 145
______, Mary Ann Hry 243
______, Moses Trp 50
______, Peter Crf 400
______, Priscilla Hry 230
______, Richard Clk 311
Richardson, Richard Gwn 346
______, Robert E. Mus 291
______, Thomas DeK 59
______, William Gwn 313
______, William Han 164
______, William Mon 215
______, William Scr 304
______, William Wal 172
______, William Wil 318
______, William M. Elb 155
Richerson, Armstead Put 218
______, Hardy New 26
______, James New 26
______, James New 26
______, John Mar 142
______, Levi New 24
______, Obadiah D. Put 196
______, Priscilla Mon 227
Rickinson, Gordias Col 334
Richison, William Bib 71
RICHES/RICHS
Riches, James Hab 17
Richs, Richard Lau 9
RICHIE/RICHEY
Richie, James Jns 430
______, Rebecha Hab 38
______, William R. Jns 435
Richey, James New 27
RICKELS, Elisabeth Ogl 96
RICKETTS, Patience Jns 452
RICKETSON, Allen Ware 186
______, Arthur Wrn 194
______, Benjamin Wrn 193
______, Benjamin Jr. Wrn 208
______, James Wrn 193
______, Jesse Wrn 194
______, Jesse Jr. Wrn 208
______, Serinia Ware 187
RICKEY, William Hab 37
RICKS/RICK
Ricks, Arthur Em 170
______, Daniel Lau 11
______, Edmond Cpb 207
______, Harris Dec 16
______, John Crf 401
______, John Dec 10
______, John Em 170
______, Patience Twg 72
______, Richard Em 170
______, Wilson Doo 89
Rick, Nancy Bul 102
______, Stephen Em 164
RIDDELSPIGER, Elizabeth Pik 118

Name	County	Page
RIDDLE, Anderson	Wsh	263
_____, Bradley G.	Bib	62
_____, David	Pik	123
_____, Gideon	Trp	44
_____, Lucy	Bal	42
_____, Sarah Y.	Wil	317
_____, Thomas	Up	95
RIDEN/RIDING/RIDLING/RIDON		
Riden, Elizah B.	Mad	99
Riding, John S.	Jks	344
Ridling, John	DeK	71
Ridon, Benjamin	Jks	342
RIDER, Christopher	Hal	115
_____, John	Hab	6
_____, John	Hal	118
_____, Johnson	Hab	33
_____, William	Hal	115
*RIDGE, John (free col)	Car	234
RIDGEDELL, John	Tms	23
_____, Lott N.	Fay	195
RIDGEWAY/RIDGWAY		
Ridgeway, Boyd	Trp	54
_____, Burrel	Elb	133
_____, James	Elb	119
_____, Samuel	Bts	170
Ridgway, Drury	Clk	308
_____, Nelson	Clk	308
RIDLEY/RIDLY		
Ridley, C. L.	Jsp	35
_____, Henry	Jsp	353
Ridly, Robert	Wks	331
RIGDON, B. S.	App	11
_____, Daniel	Bul	93
_____, Ephraigh	Dec	12
_____, Stephen	Crf	413
RIGEL, Wythel	Twg	61
RIGGINS: see Ragan		
RIGGS/RIGS		
Riggs, John W.	Bul	95
_____, Racheal	Bul	96
Rigs, Dempsey	Tms	29
RIGHT: see Wright		
RIGSBY/RIGBY		
Rigsby, Allen	Gwn	362
_____, Allen	Trp	39
_____, Allen	Wal	136
_____, John	Car	225
_____, Samuel	Wal	136
_____, William	Trp	38
Rigby, Enoch	Hst	293
_____, Jesse	Crf	415
**RIGUIL, S.A. (slave)	Rch	274
RILEY, David F.	Bib	71
Riley, Edward	Frk	221
_____, James	Elb	121
_____, James Jr.	Hal	100
_____, James	Mon	181
_____, Jane	Gre	298
_____, John	Hal	124
_____, John	Put	193
_____, John P.	Mon	182
_____, Joseph	Ran	241
_____, Joseph	Tlb	346
_____, Lent	Hal	121
_____, Nathan	Elb	129
_____, Patsy	Elb	124
_____, Peter	Gre	274
_____, Polly	Mon	183
_____, Rens	Hry	247
_____, Sebina (W)	Mor	242
_____, Spencer	Bib	56
_____, Thomas	Gre	289
_____, William	Bib	56
_____, William	Clk	292
_____, William	Jns	446
_____, William	Mar	139
RIMES/RIME		
Rimes, James	Bul	101
_____, John	Bul	95
_____, William	Bul	92
_____, William	Trp	41
Rime, Sophia	Cht	263
RINE, Elizabeth	Em	169
RING, Marshal	Wks	335
RINGOLD, John	Bal	41
_____, Sarah	Gly	266
RIPLEY, Lynman	Jks	311
RISE: see Rice		
RISON, Richard A.	Trp	51
RITTENBERRY, William B.	Han	165
RIVERSON, Manuel	Cam	184
RIVERS/RIVER		
Rivers, James	Jsp	355
_____, John	Pik	112
_____, John A.	Put	193
_____, Joseph	Rch	275
_____, Lewis	Ran	244
_____, Richard	Mus	286
_____, Robert T.	Jsp	364
_____, Sarah	Pik	125
_____, Thomas	Jsp	365
_____, Thomas	Wrn	222
River, Coleman	Mus	281
RIZE: see Rice		
ROACH, Benjamin	Hab	59
_____, Charles	Lau	11

Roach, David Pul 140
_____, Doctr. Ear 97
_____, Elisha Mon 183
_____, James Hab 62
_____, James Pul 140
_____, James Rab 227
_____, John Lau 5
_____, John Lau 16
_____, Jonathan Ear 97
_____, Mary Hal 134
_____, Molly Gwn 346
_____, Samuel Ear 97
_____, Stephen Pul 140
_____, Thomas Car 217
_____, Vallentine Ear 97
_____, William Cht 241
_____, William Ear 100
_____, William Em 175
_____, William Lau 6
ROADS: see Rhodes
ROAN/ROANE
Roan, Hugh Wal 158
_____, Leonard Bts 166
Roane, James Wal 145
ROARRY, David Trp 39
ROBBINS/ROBINS/ROBIN/ROBEN
Robbins, Alexander Hal 110
_____, Arthur Scr 309
_____, George Scr 309
_____, Jeremiah Trp 33
_____, John Gre 275
_____, Samuel W. Jef 401
_____, Sarah Gre 292
_____, Thomas Scr 309
_____, William Rch 280
_____, William S. Gre 292
Robins, B. Col 348
_____, Danil Hab 53
_____, Lenizier Wrn 217
_____, Thomas J. Hal 96
_____, William Hal 96
_____, Zach Col 354
Robin, John Pik 123
Roben, Benjamin Hab 22
ROBERTS/ROBERDS/ROBBERDS/
ROBERT/ROBETS
Roberts, Aaron DeK 39
_____, Aaron Jr. DeK 39
_____, Abel Hal 78
_____, Abraham Hst 264
_____, Absalom Bke 121
_____, Allen Gwn 336
_____, Armstead Jsp 353
Roberts, Avera Fay 198
_____, Barnett Frk 256
_____, Bartholomew Mor 254
_____, Benjamin Han 165
_____, Benjamin Scr 315
_____, Charles Mon 216
_____, Cooper B. Wal 152
_____, Cornelius Hal 82
_____, Daniel Lau 5
_____, David Hst 263
_____, David P. Gwn 335
_____, Delilah Bke 118
_____, Dempsey Jsp 373
_____, Drury Ear 93
_____, E. A. Cht 257
_____, Eli Em 166
_____, Elias Tms 27
_____, Elijah Hal 118
_____, Elijah Scr 315
_____, Eliza Lib 52
_____, Elizabeth Wil 309
_____, Emily Scr 315
_____, Emsley Hal 113
_____, George Col 341
_____, Giles T. Bts 159
_____, Gray Crf 397
_____, Gray S. Ware 186
_____, Green Bak 16
_____, Haywood Lin 71
_____, Henry Crf 409
_____, Henry Mon 185
_____, Henry Twg 83
_____, Hiram Hal 82
_____, Hues W. Ogl 82
_____, Isaac Gre 297
_____, Jacob Doo 87
_____, James Bke 137
_____, James Cht 269
_____, James Cht 277
_____, James Crf 410
_____, James Gwn 321
_____, James Gwn 326
_____, James Gwn 354
_____, James Hal 80
_____, James Scr 316
_____, James Sr. Up 115
_____, James Jr. Up 104
_____, James Up 118
_____, James Wal 131
_____, James H. Bts 158
_____, James W. Ogl 77
_____, Jeremiah Lin 74
_____, Jessee Col 341

Name	County	Page
Roberts, Jesse	Frk	256
______, Jesse	Mor	251
______, Jessee H.	Mon	228
______, John	Bke	118
______, John	Col	335
______, John	Col	354
______, John	Doo	87
______, John	Elb	120
______, John	Gwn	317
______, John	Gwn	340
______, John Sr.	Lwn	87
______, John	Rab	229
______, John	Ware	185
______, John (P.S.)	Ware	186
______, John	Scr	311
______, John A.	Bke	150
______, John A.	Fay	192
______, John G.	Tfo	360
______, John H.	Wrn	192
______, John M.	Scr	315
______, Joseph Sr.	Elb	131
______, Joseph Jr.	Elb	131
______, Joseph	Han	164
______, Joseph	Wal	134
______, Joshua	Jks	311
______, Josiah	Bke	137
______, Josioh	Col	338
______, Josiah	Doo	78
______, L.	Bal	44
______, Lewis	Jks	315
______, Lewis	Lwn	88
______, Lewis	Wal	169
______, Luke	Jns	458
______, Lydia	Put	203
______, Marcus	Gwn	360
______, Marmaduke	Frk	255
______, Martin	Hal	82
______, Mary	Em	177
______, Mary	Mwr	166
______, Mary	Rch	286
______, Mary	Wrn	205
______, Mary G. (W)	Mor	248
______, Mitchelle J.	Fay	200
______, Moses	Elb	135
______, Nancy	Lin	72
______, Nathan	Em	173
______, Peggy	Frk	248
______, Pleasant	Put	177
______, Presley B.	Elb	135
______, Reuben Sr.	Jns	458
______, Reuben	Jns	458
______, Richard	Hst	275
______, Robert	Cht	263
Roberts, Robert	Jks	311
______, Robert	Ware	186
______, Rollin	Scr	304
______, Sherwood	Col	363
______, Simeon	Col	354
______, Simeon	Doo	79
______, Step	Gwn	325
______, Tammey	Bke	147
______, Tharp	Em	175
______, Thomas	Mor	260
______, Thomas	Up	112
______, Thomas R.	Hab	15
______, Weley	Col	340
______, William	Ear	93
______, William	Frk	256
______, William	Jsp	357
______, William	Lau	15
______, William	Lib	52
______, William	Mon	174
______, William	Scr	315
______, William	Wal	143
______, William	Wks	344
______, William M.	Jsp	378
______, William P	Lwn	84
______, Willis	Elb	142
______, Willis	Wrn	208
______, Wootson	DeK	71
______, Zemma	Cow	378
Roberds, James	Cpb	197
______, Jesse	DeK	71
______, Mark	Doo	78
Robberds, John	Mus	277
Robert, Henry	Rch	268
Robets, John C. Jr.	Lwn	85
ROBERTSON/ROBERSON		
Robertson, Allen	Jns	436
______, Amos	Hal	106
______, Andrew	Hab	21
______, Charles	Mor	265
______, Clayborn	Gre	282
______, Daniel S.	Trp	34
______, Drury	Hab	23
______, Fredrick	Wrn	229
______, Frier	Clk	296
______, George	Har	178
______, Henry D.	Mor	241
______, Isham	Frk	250
______, J. J.	Har	180
______, Jacob	Frk	253
______, James	Mor	265
______, James H.	Pik	120
______, James P.	Gre	298
______, James T.	Gre	272

Name	County	Page
Robertson, James T.	Jsp	383
______, Jane	Frk	239
______, John	App	6
______, John Sr.	Cow	372
______, John Jr.	Cow	372
______, John	Frk	224
______, John	Hab	40
______, John	Mon	187
______, John	Tlb	326
______, Joseph	Hal	106
______, Joseph T.	Mon	190
______, Josiah	Dec	4
______, Josiah	Wyn	284
______, Margaret	Clk	317
______, Martha	Clk	300
______, Matthew	Frk	234
______, Moses	Hal	95
______, Patrick	Tlf	11
______, Peter R.	Gre	283
______, Randall	Cow	382
______, Rebecca	Tlf	11
______, Reden	Wal	132
______, Richard	Jsp	382
______, Robert	App	7
______, Rutha	Gwn	339
______, Samuel	Frk	220
______, Theodolia	Pik	117
______, Thomas	Clk	305
______, Thomas	Gwn	346
______, Thomas	Hab	23
______, Thomas W.	Wal	126
______, Turner	Tat	374
______, Willey	Mor	265
______, William	Bal	35
______, William	Elb	122
______, William	Frk	221
______, William	Gre	287
______, William	Gwn	325
______, William	Mor	239
______, William	Ogl	76
______, William	Pik	132
______, William Jr.	Rch	261
______, William	Wal	134
______, William C.	Mon	203
______, Willis	DeK	30
______, Willis	Gre	293
______, Zack	Bal	33
Roberson, Alexander	Hal	73
______, Allen	Put	209
______, Archibald	Car	217
______, George	New	52
______, George	Twg	88
______, George W.	Wal	137
Roberson, James	Lwn	90
______, James	New	49
______, James	Wal	157
______, James B.	Car	230
______, James C.	Jns	458
______, Jane	Car	220
______, Jesse	Car	227
______, John	Car	219
______, John	Dec	12
______, John	Jks	327
______, John	Jks	330
______, John	Jks	338
______, John	Put	205
______, John A.	Put	209
______, Jonathan	Jef	402
______, Joseph Sr.	New	45
______, Noah	Dec	11
______, Patrick L.	Wrn	192
______, Robert	Hal	128
______, Sutherlin W.	Hab	22
______, William	Hal	104
ROBINET/ROBINNETT		
Robinet, Wilson	Mon	228
Robinnett, Phebe	Hal	75
ROBINSON/ROBENSON/ROBBINSON		
Robinson, A. P.	Col	337
______, Abee L.	Bts	161
______, Alexander	Tlb	342
______, Anderson	Tlb	334
______, Andrew	New	48
______, Benjamin P.	Trp	40
______, Blake	Mus	277
______, Carrington W.	Up	111
______, Catharin	Han	165
______, Cornulius	Jsp	386
______, Cyrus	Tlb	333
______, Edward	Hst	274
______, Elberry	Up	114
______, Ephaphoditus	Gre	291
______, Henry	Rch	256
______, Henry	Up	119
______, Ignatious	Han	165
______, Isaac	Up	98
______, James	Bke	122
______, James	Fay	189
______, James	Ogl	78
______, James	Up	100
______, James H.	Jsp	392
______, James V.	Ear	98
______, Jane	Cht	262
______, Jemima	Jsp	398
______, Jeptha	Fay	195
______, Jeptha	Fay	197

Name	County	Page
Robinson, Jesse	Jef	402
______, John	Cht	255
______, John	Fay	183
______, John	Jsp	379
______, John	Lib	52
______, John	Up	119
______, Joseph	Mor	244
______, Joseph L.	Bul	94
______, Joseph W.	Wil	288
______, Julius M.	Eff	109
______, Lemuel	Bke	142
______, Luke	Hry	243
______, Luke	New	24
______, Michael	Jsp	358
______, Mordeca	Fay	189
______, Moses	Wsh	249
______, Nancy	Wsh	271
______, Osborn	Jsp	394
______, Philip Sr.	Bke	154
______, Philip Jr.	Bke	154
______, Pleasant	Ogl	71
______, Richard	Ear	95
______, Richard B.	Gwn	320
______, Ryons	Jsp	358
______, Samuel	Fay	191
______, Samuel	Wsh	243
______, Samuel C.	Hry	209
______, Sidney	Cpb	206
______, Silas M.	Wil	301
______, Sol	Bal	38
______, Thomas	Bts	167
______, Vann	Ear	91
______, Wilie	Fay	185
______, William	Cht	243
______, William	Cht	244
______, William	Col	350
______, William	Gwn	324
______, William	Hst	272
______, William	Tlb	342
______, William	Up	99
______, William	Wsh	255
______, William C.	Lib	52
______, William P.	Hry	210
______, William T. L.	Jsp	384
______, Y. L.	Cam	187
Robenson, J.	Gwn	372
______, Silas	Hab	23
Robbinson, Matthew	Twg	64
ROBISON/ROBESON/ROBASON		
Robison, Adam	Bib	68
______, Alex.	Wks	332
______, Edward	Mwr	159
______, Elizabeth	Mwr	161
Robison, Hardy	Mwr	156
______, Henry	Mwr	154
______, Jane	Bib	56
______, Jesse	Mwr	162
______, John	Wks	342
______, Legate	Mwr	153
Robeson, Alexander T.	Wks	331
______, Andrew J.	Hab	59
______, Benjamin	Mon	177
______, Beverly	Mon	207
______, David	Hab	59
______, John	Hab	59
______, L.	Wks	345
Robason, James B.	DeK	57
______, John	DeK	43
______, Wyley	DeK	31
ROBSON, James	Ware	183
______, James Sr.	Wyn	281
______, James Jr.	Wyn	283
______, John	Mor	250
______, Solomon	Wyn	281
______, Willie	Wyn	281
ROBUCK/ROEBUCK		
Robuck, Benjamin	McI	129
______, Elizabeth	Elb	158
______, John C.	Elb	148
______, Julias	Pul	144
______, Martha	Pul	141
______, William	DeK	27
______, William	Elb	145
______, William	Pul	140
Roebuck, Langdon P.	Wil	316
ROBY/ROBEY		
Roby, Archibald	Put	196
______, Elijah	Cpb	209
______, John N.	Put	196
______, Jordan	Mwr	155
______, Mathew	Put	200
______, Robert	Put	193
Robey, Nathan	Jsp	359
______, Timothy	Jsp	384
______, Williamson	Jsp	384
______, Williamson	Jsp	392
______, Williamson B.	Jsp	382
ROCK, Drury	Hab	61
______, John	Hab	61
ROCKENBAUGH, Jacob	McI	124
ROCKMORE, Alsey	Bib	62
______, James	Jns	446
______, John	New	39
ROCKWELL, C. W.	Cht	261
______, Lamb	Bal	42
______, Peter P.	Bib	56

RODDENBERRY, George Tms 23
______, John Tms 18
______, Richard Tms 23
______, Robert Tms 23
RODDY, Thomas Car 215
RODEN/RODDEN
Roden, Jacob Lw n 89
______, John Lwn 88
Rodden, James Pik 106
RODERICK, Joseph Pul 159
ROGERMON, Peter Jns 471
ROGERS/RODGERS/ROGGERS
Rogers, Abner Fay 181
______, Adam Frk 253
______, Andrew DeK 55
______, Balaam W. Hry 236
______, Bartlet M. Tlb 325
______, Benjamin Mon 187
______, Britain Mon 207
______, Charles Wsh 239
______, Collin Trp 32
______, Cullen Pul 156
______, Daniel Mus 284
______, Demsy Jks 344
______, Drury HRY 217
______, Edmund Lib 52
______, Edward Up 100
______, Edwin G. Hry 210
______, Eley Wks 338
______, Eli Tlf 9
______, Elisha Hry 220
______, Enoch Hal 124
______, Ephrem Wal 139
______, George DeK 55
______, George Fay 182
______, George T. McI 122
______, George W. Har 190
______, Harvy Wsh 250
______, Henry Hst 273
______, Henry Put 185
______, Henry Trp 32
______, Hezakiah Wsh 262
______, Isaac Mar 142
______, Isham G. Elb 128
______, Jacob Hal 123
______, James Col 356
______, James Hry 201
______, James Tms 26
______, James Wal 136
______, James Jr. Wrn 202
______, James Jr. Wrn 203
______, James A. Tlf 12
______, James P. Jks 344

Rogers, Jane Mon 207
______, Jobe Mus 280
______, John Bry 88
______, John Elb 129
______, John Hal 133
______, John Jks 317
______, John Jks 337
______, John Mon 220
______, John Mus 282
______, John Pul 150
______, John Tat 373
______, John Tfo 359
______, John Wrn 203
______, John L. Hry 223
______, Joseph Har 188
______, Joseph Ware 185
______, Martin D. Cpb 198
______, Mary Mon 224
______, Mathew C. Hal 126
______, Matthew Frk 210
______, Mesh. Bal 32
______, Mich^{l}. Wrn 215
______, O. C. Bal 32
______, Osborn Mon 207
______, Peter Crf 414
______, Peter Scr 303
______, Ransom Scr 303
______, Reuben Put 177
______, Richmond Put 191
______, Right Clk 325
______, Robert Mor 263
______, Robert Wal 174
______, Robert P. Mor 259
______, Roda Jks 321
______, Rubin Wrn 200
______, Sampson Ear 100
______, Samuel Twg 65
______, Simeon Up 96
______, Shadrack Han 165
______, Starkie L. Hst 273
______, Stephen Hst 276
______, Stephens Pul 158
______, Sutly Mwr 150
______, Theophilus Jks 320
______, Thomas Lee 26
______, Thomas Mus 281
______, Thomas Mus 290
______, Thomas E. Ran 243
______, Thomas P. Cpb 198
______, Uriah Tms 25
______, Wiley Mon 214
______, William Bal 36
______, William Bke 139

Name	County	Page
Rogers, William	Frk	211
______, William	Mor	249
______, William	Mus	284
______, William	Mus	290
______, William	Tat	373
______, William A.	DeK	47
______, William P.	Mor	250
Rodgers, Widow	Irw	302
______, Allen	Bke	154
______, Berry	Bib	56
______, Charles	Gwn	357
______, Charles W.	McI	126
______, Cornelius	Wrn	222
______, Edward	Bib	52
______, Enoch	Jef	414
______, George	Elb	139
______, Isaac M.	Elb	141
______, James	Bke	136
______, James	Gwn	367
______, James	Jef	417
______, James H.	Bib	52
______, Jethro	Jef	409
______, John	Bke	153
______, John	Gwn	374
______, John	Hab	43
______, John	Hry	217
______, John C.	Bib	52
______, Johnson	Gwn	374
______, Joseph	Gwn	374
______, Joseph	Pik	129
______, Morgan	Jef	411
______, Nancy	Jef	414
______, Pleasant	Jsp	368
______, Robert	Gwn	374
______, Ruben	Wrn	208
______, Simon	Pik	130
______, Wesley	Elb	142
______, William	Gwn	374
______, William B.	Bib	56
Roggers, James	Rab	228
______, John	New	30
______, Nathaniel	New	22
______, Neadom	New	8
______, Polley	New	21
ROGERSON, James	Cht	272
ROGUEMORE, Vincent P.	Hst	262
ROGUS, Anon	Wal	149
ROLLERSON, Nichabod	Lwn	85
ROLLINS/ROLLEN/ROLLINGS		
Rollins, Benjamin	Gwn	368
______, Berry	Gwn	328
______, J.	Gwn	309
______, John	Bke	120

Name	County	Page
Rollins, Lodwick	Mwr	167
______, Nicholas	Gwn	368
______, Redden	Tlf	7
______, Richard	Gwn	321
______, Robert	Cow	385
______, Roley	Bke	120
______, Thomas	Ran	246
______, William	Bke	119
Rollen, Marton	Mad	113
Rollings, Job	Cpb	205
ROLLS/ROLES/ROLL		
Rolls, William	Lin	73
Roles, Jese	Pik	110
Roll, Luther	Rch	260
ROLLY/ROLEY		
Rolly, Ann	Cht	261
______, Peter	Hal	104
Roley, Isaac	Wrn	230
ROMON, Samuel	Crf	413
ROMER, Peter	Hab	31
ROOKER, Alexander	Elb	151
______, John H.	Car	227
ROOKS/ROOK		
Rooks, Abel	Jef	419
______, Ann	Hst	296
______, Betsey	Jks	325
______, Daniel	Jks	349
______, Dennis	Mor	266
______, Fredrick	Wrn	222
______, Isaac	Scr	311
______, James	Jks	333
______, James	Jns	473
______, John	Wyn	281
______, Miley	Eff	112
______, Nancy	Jks	325
______, Pharaba	Tlf	4
______, Ruth	Scr	315
______, Seaborn	Eff	112
______, William	Car	225
______, William	Jef	415
Rook, Torrence	Wil	294
ROONEY/RONEY		
Rooney, Hugh	Rch	28
______, Joseph	Rch	29
______, M.	Cht	27
Roney, Benjamin	Cpb	21
______, Hugh	Tms	1
______, Thomas	Wrn	21
ROOT, Charles	Put	21
______, William	Mus	28
ROPER, Aron	Hal	11
______, Aaron	Han	16
______, Charles	Gwn	32

Roper, Charles Gwn 358
_____, Charles Gwn 366
_____, Harris Han 165
_____, James Gwn 327
_____, John Gwn 365
_____, John Han 165
_____, Lavina Han 165
_____, William Gwn 365
ROQUMON, James M. Trp 38
RORTEN, Clemont Gwn 370
ROSE, Amos Up 96
_____, Bailey Car 228
_____, Benjamin Car 216
_____, David E. Mwr 154
_____, Francis Car 222
_____, Hardy Frk 247
_____, Henry Wil 291
_____, Hudson Jef 402
_____, Hugh Cht 252
_____, Hugh F. Put 205
_____, Seaborn Em 164
_____, Simri Bib 56
_____, Susanna Jns 466
_____, Thomas G. Up 111
_____, Washington Put 212
_____, William Cht 265
ROSEBERRY/ROSEBERY
Roseberry, George New 48
_____, James New 40
Rosebery, Richard New 41
ROSEY, Gasper Cht 250
_____, William Lee 27
ROSS, Abraham Bul 102
_____, Absalem B. Wal 128
_____, Ann Rch 274
_____, Battle Tlb 331
_____, Catharine Jef 423
_____, Cudjoe Cht 271
_____, Daniel Mon 182
_____, David Mar 141
_____, David Put 184
_____, Edward Col 341
_____, Eliza Cht 266
_____, Etheldred Lin 59
_____, George Scr 304
_____, George W. Har 177
_____, Henry G. Bib 56
_____, Isaac Trp 44
_____, James Bke 123
_____, James Col 348
_____, James Hal 91
_____, James Mon 200
_____, James Wks 331
Ross, James L. Bib 77
_____, Jesse Jns 435
_____, John Mon 210
_____, John Wks 343
_____, John B. Put 182
_____, Jonathan Jef 419
_____, Joseph Cht 249
_____, Joseph Doo 87
_____, Levi Jks 340
_____, Luke Bib 52
_____, Riley W. Up 100
_____, Robert Bib 62
_____, Rolling Jns 436
_____, Samuel P. Hal 89
_____, Sarah Col 352
_____, Wiley Jks 319
_____, William Bke 124
_____, William Jsp 371
_____, William Mon 191
_____, William Sr. Wks 356
_____, William Wks 342
_____, Wiseman Mon 173
_____, Wyatt Hal 116
ROSSEN, Elijah Jks 320
ROSSER/ROSSOR/ROSER
Rosser, Benjamin Put 175
_____, James Put 184
_____, John Put 196
_____, Lewis W. Put 199
_____, Moses Hry 241
_____, Sarah Put 180
Rossor, Isaac Wal 127
Roser, Thomas Mwr 166
ROSSETER, Timothy W. Han 164
ROSSIGNOL, James Rch 262
_____, Paul Rch 256
** _____, Paul (slave) Rch 262
** _____, Paul (slave) Rch 272
ROTER, Elizabeth Rch 270
ROTH, Alfred Scr 316
ROUNCEVILLE, David Clk 314
_____, Robert DeK 55
ROUREEVILLE, Josiah DeK 54
ROUNTREE/ROUNDTREE
Rountree, Mrs. Scr 313
_____, Cader Fay 201
_____, Delila Em 174
_____, Francis Tlb 326
_____, George Em 176
_____, James Lwn 87
_____, Joshua Em 176
_____, Penelope Fay 206
_____, Wilie Fay 188

Name	County	Page
Rountree, William	Irw	304
Roundtree, Arthur	Jef	408
_____, Burwell	Hst	290
_____, Frances	Lwn	82
_____, George R.	Rch	265
_____, John	Up	102
_____, Moses	Tlf	10
ROUSE/ROUCE		
Rouse, Benjamin	Hal	93
_____, Benjamin P.	Mar	142
_____, Dennis	Hst	280
_____, Henry J.	Twg	75
_____, John	Hal	92
_____, Joseph	Hal	92
_____, Joseph	Hst	278
_____, Martin	Hal	74
_____, Mary	Twg	87
_____, Mills	Hal	92
_____, Redding	Hst	264
Rouce, Henry	Lee	34
_____, Jesse	Lee	34
ROUSSEAU/RUSSEAU/RUSEAU		
Rousseau, George	Pik	116
_____, Hiram	Mor	263
_____, Jephtha V.	Elb	129
_____, Travis	Pik	116
Russeau, John	Put	210
_____, William	Put	209
Ruseau, Henry	Put	210
ROUSSETT, Louisa	Cht	262
ROUTON/ROUGHTON		
Routon, John	Fay	207
_____, Mathew	Up	115
_____, Talbot	Up	116
Roughton, Enoch	Wsh	250
_____, William	Wsh	274
ROUX: see Rowe		
ROWAN, Abraham	Hry	240
_____, Robert Sr.	Hry	226
ROWDAN/ROWDON		
Rowdan, Laban	Gwn	341
_____, Lot	Gwn	341
Rowdon, Hubbard A.	Gwn	341
ROWE/ROE/ROW/ROUX		
Rowe, Adna	Rch	269
_____, Ann	Jns	434
* _____, Arch. (free col.)	Car	233
_____, Asa	Put	203
_____, Daniel	Crf	409
_____, Davis	Trp	39
_____, Fredrick	McI	127
_____, James	Mon	202
_____, James H.	Trp	38

Name	County	Page
Rowe, John J.	Put	203
_____, Joshua Jr.	Crf	410
_____, Martin	Mad	102
_____, Mathew	Crf	414
_____, Samuel	McI	130
_____, Samuel	Tlb	339
_____, Shadrac	Put	204
_____, Stephen	Mad	105
_____, William	Bul	101
_____, William	Mon	178
Roe, Asel	Hab	49
_____, Chloe	Han	166
_____, Daniel	Ear	97
_____, Edward	Ear	96
_____, Enoch	Ear	97
_____, James	Doo	80
_____, James	Wrn	228
_____, John	Cpb	204
_____, John	Cpb	207
_____, John	DeK	25
_____, John	Ear	97
_____, John	Han	164
_____, Joseph	Bke	150
_____, Joseph	Ear	97
_____, Martha	DeK	62
_____, Samuel	Frk	213
_____, Stephen	Han	165
_____, William	Ear	99
Row, Richard	Irw	303
_____, Thomas	Wrn	193
Roux, Josephine	Cam	182
ROWELL/ROWEL		
Rowell, David	Lwn	83
_____, Elizabeth	Bke	150
_____, Grace	Rch	280
_____, James	Cam	188
_____, Joab T.	Bke	130
_____, John	App	13
_____, John A.	New	35
_____, John J.	Frk	243
_____, Richard	Bal	35
_____, Richard J.	Elb	128
_____, Sarah	App	8
_____, William	Crf	414
_____, William	Frk	243
_____, William	Lwn	84
Rowel, Jesse	Elb	124
_____, John	DeK	48
_____, John	Em	17[illegible]
_____, Umphrey	Mus	29[illegible]
_____, William	Em	17[illegible]
ROWLAND/ROLAND/ROWLAN/ ROLAN/ROLLANDS		

Rowland, Daniel Col 351
_____, George Pul 154
_____, Hiram Gre 286
_____, Isaac Lau 20
_____, Isaac B. Bib 56
_____, James Col 348
_____, James Gre 276
_____, John Bib 74
_____, John Pul 153
_____, John T. Bib 57
_____, Jordan Jr. Gre 276
_____, Jordan Gre 294
_____, Merritt Rch 281
_____, Milley Col 351
_____, Nathan Em 168
_____, Nathan Hst 275
_____, Needham Em 168
_____, Peter Gwn 370
_____, Rebecca Mon 186
_____, Richard Pul 140
_____, Robert Crf 405
_____, Thomas Bib 74
_____, Thomas Hst 276
_____, Thomas Mwr 150
_____, Wiley Gre 303
_____, William Em 167
_____, William Gre 282
_____, William (slave) Rch 257
_____, Williamson Col 350
_____, Williamson Em 169
_____, Willis Gwn 362
Roland, Brantley Bts 163
_____, Elizabeth Bts 169
_____, Rhoda Gwn 333
_____, Sherrod Cow 369
Rowlan, Berry Gwn 364
_____, Samuel Sr. Gwn 364
_____, Samuel Gwn 368
_____, Willis Jr. Gwn 329
Rolan, William Gwn 325
Rollands, Nicholas Gwn 336
ROWSEY, Henslow Elb 148
_____, Stephen Elb 138
_____, William Elb 145
_____, William Hab 30
ROWTON, John Car 229
ROYAL/ROYALS
Royal, Alfred Doo 85
_____, Arthur Bke 154
_____, John Jks 342
_____, John Bke 146
_____, John Doo 85
_____, John S. Bke 148
Royal, Mary Bke 149
_____, Raiford Doo 84
_____, Samuel Bke 149
_____, Sarah Bke 146
_____, William Doo 85
_____, William Elb 155
Royals, Asa Hst 266
_____, Isaac Hst 291
_____, Stephen Hst 266
_____, Vincent Twg 76
ROYNALDS/ROYNOLD/ROYALDS
Roynalds, Mary Col 345
_____, Outten Col 345
Roynold, John Col 357
_____, Reubin Y. Col 357
Royalds, Martin Col 345
ROYSTON/ROYSTER
Royston, Richard W. Frk 237
_____, Solomon Bul 92
Royster, James W. Frk 214
ROZIER/ROZIAR/ROZAR/ROSIER
Rozier, Isham Fay 186
_____, Martha Wil 295
_____, Martha Wrn 223
_____, Mary Wyn 283
_____, Theophilus Jef 416
_____, Wiley Cam 182
Roziar, John Pul 155
_____, Marcam Pul 155
_____, Seaborn Pul 155
_____, Shadrick Pul 155
Rozar, Anderson Wks 338
_____, Robert Wks 338
_____, Robert Wks 344
_____, Samuel McI 132
Rosier, Charles Bry 88
RUARK/RUARKE: also see Roux under Rowe
Ruark, Beletha Wrn 212
Ruarke, Lemuel Mor 269
RUCKER, Ardain S. Mon 195
_____, Catharine Elb 123
_____, Fielding K. Wil 291
_____, George Frk 217
_____, Gideon Wil 320
_____, Godeon Wil 320
_____, John T. Pik 114
_____, Joseph Elb 123
_____, Katharine Frk 219
_____, Lemuel Elb 149
_____, Mary Elb 156
_____, Masten Jsp 354

Name	County	Page
Rucker, Parden	Elb	144
______, Richard B.	Tlb	346
______, Simeon B.	Frk	219
______, Tarvanna	Frk	239
______, William	Elb	127
______, Willis	Wil	299
RUDASOLE, John	Hab	51
RUDD, Pleasant	Mor	268
RUDDLE, Leana	Wil	287
RUDEBELL, Elizabeth	Tfo	368
______, John	Tfo	368
RUDOLPH, Francis	Cam	184
RUFF/ROFF		
Ruff, Alen	Car	219
______, Charles	Lin	71
______, Fanny (of Col.)	Wrn	223
______, John	Hry	239
______, Joseph Wood	DeK	67
______, Lemmon	Bke	120
______, Martin L.	Hry	211
______, Rachael of Col.	Wrn	198
______, Shadrack	Elb	119
______, William	Hry	212
Roff, Moses Jr.	Rch	265
RUFFIN, Richard V. C.	Hst	266
______, Thomas	Up	115
RUIS, James	Em	164
______, John	Tat	378
______, Patsy	Em	166
______, Polly	Em	166
RUMNEY, Edward W.	Jns	466
RUMP, Jacob	Gly	265
RUMSEY/RUMSAY		
Rumsey, John	Frk	250
______, Kelbern	Elb	128
______, Mary	Elb	128
Rumsay, Richard	Frk	249
RUNNELS/RUNALDS/RUNNELDS/ RUNNELLS/RUNELL		
Runnels, Charles	Hab	48
______, Edmond W.	DeK	29
______, Hermon	Tfo	363
______, James	Hab	34
______, James	Tfo	362
______, James	Tfo	365
______, James	Tfo	368
______, Nancy	Mon	210
______, Peter	Hab	28
______, Radford	Tfo	365
______, Reubon	Hst	282
______, Richard	Mon	183
______, Richard	Tfo	364
______, William	Dec	13
Runalds, Colman	Clk	315
______, John	Clk	325
______, Thomas	Clk	301
Runnelds, Jane	Ran	250
______, John	Gwn	358
Runnells, James M.	Wil	300
Runnell, Terry	Wil	312
RUNS, Joseph	Wks	356
RUNSLEY, William	Lin	69
RUNYAN, Hiram	Gwn	358
RUPERT, John	Ogl	97
RURPIN, Mrs.	Rch	263
RUSH, James	Mon	204
______, James M.	Hab	38
______, John	Jks	347
______, Lewis P.	Elb	143
______, Sarah	Hab	61
RUSHING/RUSHEN		
Rushing, Eli	Crf	402
______, John	Crf	402
______, Sarah	Wsh	271
______, William	Bul	95
______, William	Han	164
______, William	Tlb	346
Rushen, Ann	Scr	307
______, William	Scr	307
RUSHTON, Mary	Gwn	375
RUSK, David	Wal	163
______, John	Wal	150
______, Precilla	Wal	163
______, Thomas	Wal	162
______, Thomas J.	Hab	63
RUSKIN, John	Hst	278
______, Perinah	Bib	5
RUSS, David	Mar	14
______, David S.	Mar	13
______, Eleazer	Mar	14
______, Lewis	Mon	17
______, Simeon	Pul	16
RUSSELL/RUSSEL/RUSEL		
Russell, Alexander	Mon	19
______, Anderson	Col	33
______, Archibald	Hry	25
______, Benjamin	Bib	5
______, Booker	Jns	44
______, Edward W.	Lib	5
______, Elisha	Rab	22
______, Ethelbert	New	5
______, Forgus	Hry	22
______, George	Jns	43
______, George	Mad	11
______, George	Rab	23
______, Henry R.	Lib	[illegible]

Russell, Isaac Cht 281
______, J. H. Jks 336
______, James Bke 150
______, James Gwn 372
______, James Hry 251
______, James Lib 52
______, James S. Gwn 316
______, Jane N. Cht 246
______, Jesse Hry 224
______, John Cht 240
______, John Lau 20
______, John Mad 105
______, John New 33
______, John M. Hry 199
______, John R. Tlb 322
______, M. Bal 31
______, Martha (W) Mor 272
______, Rebecca Col 337
______, Samuel H. Han 164
______, Taliaferro Tlb 324
______, Thomas Hry 220
______, Thomas Wal 170
______, Thomas C. Hry 209
______, W. Gwn 308
______, Washington Lin 62
______, Wilkins J. Trp 45
______, William Bib 56
______, William Hry 214
______, William Hry 224
______, William A. Mon 209
______, William R. Tlb 325
______, William R. Up 103
ussel, Abel Jef 418
______, Hiram Hab 12
______, Ignatius Bts 166
______, James DeK 38
______, James Hab 23
______, James Hal 99
______, James Hal 103
______, James G. Bal 31
______, John Mwr 161
______, John Mus 278
______, John H. Hab 23
______, Marco Ogl 90
______, Nancy Frk 253
______, Osborn Frk 250
______, Robert W. Car 223
______, Stephen Hab 12
usel, John Hab 53
______, William New 36
STIN, Henery F. Cow 377
______, William Lib 52
TH, Eliza Bib 77
Ruth, Moriah Bib 59
______, William B. Crf 413
RUTHERFORD, A. Mus 282
______, Benjamin H. Mon 221
______, Clabourn Cpb 195
______, David Gwn 364
______, Franklin Wsh 253
______, Henry Pul 149
______, Hiram Cpb 197
______, Isaac Gwn 348
______, Col. J. Bal 43
______, James Gwn 344
______, James Irw 299
______, John Twg 81
______, John Wks 343
______, Mary Wsh 273
______, Rachael Bib 74
______, Thomas Gwn 348
______, William Bal 33
______, William Gwn 365
RUTLAND, B. B. Crf 402
______, Reddick Bke 150
______, Reddick Mon 199
______, Wiley Mon 181
RUTLEDGE, Ann Wil 316
______, Charles Hry 227
______, Dewit Gwn 369
______, Dewit Gwn 370
______, James Ogl 64
______, Joseph Gwn 369
______, John Bke 132
______, John Gwn 317
______, John Gwn 370
______, Joseph Gwn 367
______, Kiah Mor 261
______, Nancy DeK 66
______, Nancy Wil 315
______, Richard Mus 277
______, Samuel Pik 109
______, Thomas Clk 313
______, William DeK 33
______, William Hry 222
______, William Hry 251
______, William O. Har 188
RYALS/RYLE
Ryals, Abel Lau 10
______, Charles Eff 113
______, David Tlf 10
______, Eleanor Rch 262
______, Gillis Lau 5
______, Henry Sr. McI 132
______, Henry Jr. McI 132
______, Herbert McI 132

Name	County	Page
Ryals, John	McI	132
______, John B.	Mtg	234
______, Joseph	Mtg	233
______, Jurdan	McI	132
______, Lewis	McI	132
______, Travis	Lau	22
______, William	Mtg	234
______, William	Tlf	9
______, Wright	Tlf	9
Ryle, James	Fay	184
______, John	Wks	347
______, Joshua	Wks	339
______, William	Wks	345
______, William Jr.	Wks	345
RYAN/RYON/RYEN		
Ryan, Dennis L.	Wrn	204
______, Hampton	Crf	393
______, John R.	Col	364
______, Joseph	Wrn	193
______, Mary	Cht	254
______, Obedience	Jks	345
______, Philip	Jks	345
______, Risden	Han	173
______, Sarah	Jsp	383
Ryon, Fanny	Col	357
Ryen, Haynes	Col	363
RYE, Dunn	Wks	357
______, Elizabeth	Har	183
______, Jacob	Up	115
______, James	Up	102
______, John	Wks	338
______, Mary	Wks	338
______, Peggy	Lau	22
RYERSON, Thomas	Cht	254
RYLAND, Bennona	Wrn	230
______, Phillip	Wrn	231
______, Samuel	Mor	248
SAASBY, Elizabeth	Hab	55
______, Solloman	Hab	55
SABAL, A.	Rch	268
SACRAE, Thomas	Bib	77
SADLER, Benjamin	Jsp	390
______, Henry R.	Cam	181
______, James	Dec	14
______, James R.	Elb	128
______, John F.	Elb	125
______, Nathaniel	Put	200
______, Thomas	Mon	187
______, William B.	Elb	128
SAFFOLD, Adam G.	Mor	251
Saffold, Daniel	Jsp	368
______, Daniel	Twg	81
______, Isham H.	Mon	191
SAFFORD, William	Wil	318
SAGAR: see Seegar		
SAGE, Oliver	Bib	57
______, Polly	Hab	33
SAGGUS, John	Tfo	367
SAILORS/SAILER/SAILERS		
Sailors, Abner	Jks	342
______, Christopher	Jks	342
______, David	Jks	342
______, James	Jks	342
______, Jerimiah	Hry	229
Sailer, John	Mad	112
Sailers, William	Mad	117
ST. GEORGE, Edward	Lau	8
ST. JOHN, J. B.	Rch	277
______, James	Dec	19
______, James	New	29
______, Lewis	Dec	17
______, Martin	Tlb	339
______, Isaac	New	10
______, James	New	19
______, Thomas	New	10
______, William	Hst	292
SALES/SALE/SALLES		
Sales, Charity	Lin	65
______, Gideon	Bal	39
Sale, Leroy	Mon	201
______, Richard	Wil	323
Salles, David	Wrn	218
SALLER: see Sellers		
SALLEY/SALEY/SALLY		
Salley, Daniel	Cow	375
Salley, William	Cpb	198
Saley, Michael	Cpb	21[illegible]
*Sally (free negro)	Bal	4[illegible]
SALLIS/SALLAS		
Sallis, Ethelred	Up	11[illegible]
______, James	Wrn	21[illegible]
______, William	Ran	24[illegible]
SALSBURY/SALLISBERY/ SAULESBURY		
Salsbury, William	Mus	28[illegible]
Sallisbery, William	Cow	39[illegible]
Saulesbury, James	Ran	24[illegible]
SAMMONS/SALMON/SALMONDS/ SAMMON/SAMMONDS/SALAMOND/ Also see Psalmond		
Sammonds, Burwell	Elb	1[illegible]
______, Chales	Wrn	21[illegible]
______, Groves	Rab	2[illegible]

Name	County	Page
Sammons, Jeremiah	Elb	130
______, John	Elb	157
______, Lewis	Elb	130
______, Louis	Jef	404
______, Nancy	Jef	404
______, Richard	Mor	247
______, Samuel	Wrn	193
Salmon, Ephraim	Jks	349
______, Henley J.	Mon	222
______, J. J.	Rch	272
Salmonds, Hesekiah	Lin	65
______, Thomas P.	Lin	64
Sammon, John	Gwn	313
Sammonds, Whitfield	Mor	247
Salamond, Abraham	Tlf	4
SALTAS, Elizabeth	Eff	113
SALTENSTALL, Mary	Lau	14
SALTER, James	Lee	32
______, James H.	Mor	249
______, John	Lib	53
______, John	Wsh	252
______, Joseph R.	Wyn	282
______, Mary	Mon	184
______, Richard	Lee	32
______, Robert	Wks	337
______, Zadoc	Wsh	252
SAMPLE/SAMPLES		
Sample, James	Jef	421
______, John	Put	204
______, Nathaniel Sr.	Jef	424
______, Nathaniel Jr.	Jef	421
______, Patsy	Jef	403
______, Uriah	Put	200
______, William	Put	204
______, William M.	Put	204
Samples, Charles	Gwn	324
SAMPLER, Jeremiah	Cpb	199
______, Samuel	Ran	247
______, Tacy	Ran	249
______, William	Cow	371
SAMS, James	Hry	203
______, Joseph	Wal	138
______, Reuben	Gwn	348
SAMSON/SANSOM/SAMPSON		
Samson, Dolles	New	20
______, Jas.	Clk	300
______, Thomas	Clk	311
Sansom, Elizabeth	Wil	309
______, Micajah	Wal	138
______, Polly	Hry	249
______, William	DeK	26
Sampson, James	Up	96
SAMUEL, Benjamin	Lin	75
Samuel, Edmund	Lin	71
______, Elizabeth	Lin	75
______, Squire	Jsp	371
______, Thomas	Lin	71
SANDBRIDGE/SANDIDGE/ SANDEGE		
Sandbridge, Margaret	Han	168
Sandidge, John	Frk	231
______, Garrett L.	Frk	231
Sandege, Claiborne	Elb	121
SANDERLIN, Jesse	Lee	33
______, Robert	Rch	285
SANDERS/also see Saunders		
Sanders, Aaron	Frk	218
______, Alexander	Up	103
______, Alsay	Mar	138
______, Alsey	Up	107
______, Andrew	Gwn	375
______, Angalus	Mad	106
______, B. M.	Col	352
______, Benjamin	Doo	83
______, Benjamin	Mad	103
______, Bluford	Wks	350
______, Burwell	Wsh	251
______, Caleb	Hal	89
______, Calvin P.	Elb	130
______, Charles H.	New	14
______, Coleman	Lau	16
______, Coulson	Wks	352
______, Clark	Ran	246
______, Daniel	Frk	218
______, Daniel	Hst	271
______, Daniel	Wsh	260
______, Daniels	Jks	335
______, David	DeK	49
______, David	Hry	205
______, David	Gwn	375
______, Dempey	DeK	61
______, Dennis D.	Twg	62
______, Duncan	Hst	294
______, Durham H.	Hst	274
______, Edward	DeK	36
______, Elias	Elb	130
______, Elias Jr.	Frk	244
______, Elizabeth	Wsh	274
______, Ephraim Sr.	Jns	440
______, Ephraim	Jns	432
______, Ephraim	Up	96
______, George W.	Tms	17
______, Ginny	Gwn	375
______, Hardy	Jns	428
______, Harris	Jks	341
______, Henry	Hry	237

Name	County	Page
Sanders, Henry	Wks	349
______, Holloway	DeK	60
______, Isaac	Hal	116
______, Isaac	Rab	233
______, Isaac	Up	109
______, Jacob	Hal	94
______, James	Mad	99
______, James	Wrn	213
______, James	Wks	336
______, James H.	Han	166
______, James H.	Mad	113
______, Jesse	Hab	49
______, Joel	Frk	218
______, John	Crf	401
______, John	Cpb	196
______, John	Dec	19
______, John	DeK	60
______, John	Gwn	375
______, John	Hab	65
______, John	Hst	294
______, John	Jks	319
______, John	Jsp	398
______, John	Jns	447
______, John	Mad	98
______, John	Up	119
______, John	Wyn	285
______, John M.	Bib	65
______, Jonathan	Car	214
______, Jonathan	Mad	103
______, Jordan	Mon	192
______, Joseph	Mad	98
______, Julius	Wal	165
______, Lewis	Elb	130
______, Logan	Dec	13
______, Lovett	Han	166
______, Mal.	Wks	340
______, Martha	Put	196
______, Mary	Mwr	165
______, Mary	Wrn	213
______, Mary R.	Col	358
______, Micajah	Jns	432
______, Miles	Hst	295
______, Minyard	Frk	217
______, Moses	Frk	218
______, Moses	Jks	341
______, Nancy	Han	166
______, Nancy (W)	Mor	267
______, Nathaniel	Up	107
______, Nelly	Put	203
______, Payton	Ogl	97
______, Peter	Mon	188
______, Peterson	Mar	141
______, Reuben	Col	358

Name	County	Page
Sanders, Rite	Dec	17
______, Robert	Mor	252
______, Samuel	Hry	204
______, Samuel	Mad	98
______, Samuel	Wks	352
______, Samuel P.	Elb	130
______, Seaborn	Mor	268
______, Shepherd B.	Up	107
______, Simon	Wal	165
______, Solomon	DeK	60
______, Stephen	Mor	247
______, Sykes	Pul	149
______, Thomas	Doo	83
______, Thomas	Frk	245
______, Thomas	Tlb	341
______, Thomas J.	Han	166
______, Wade	Wks	349
______, Wat.	Gwn	375
______, William	Bib	66
______, William	Dec	13
______, William	DeK	36
______, William	Eff	106
______, William	Mad	98
______, William	Mor	246
______, William H.	Mwr	166
______, William L.	Crf	395
______, William S.	Jks	320
______, William W.	Lwn	82
______, Z. B.	Up	96
SANDERSON, John	Jns	429
______, Patience	Lau	13
______, Patience	Pul	147
SANDIFER/SANDIFOR/SANDIFN		
Sandifer, Harry	Wil	287
______, John S.	Crf	414
______, Robert	Mus	281
Sandifor, Thomas R.	Twg	85
Sandifn, Thomas	Crf	405
SANDS, John	Tat	379
______, Ray	Cam	181
______, Thomas B.	Har	192
SANFORD/SANDFORD/SANDIFORD/ SANKFORD/SANDERFORD		
Sanford, Abner	Hst	280
______, Allen C.	Pul	157
______, Asa	Hal	117
______, Benjamin	Jef	409
______, Benjamin	Put	201
______, Berkley	Put	216
______, Charles	Tlb	331
______, J. W. A.	Bal	43
______, Jesse	Hal	116
______, Joshua	Lib	53

Sanford, Keen Lau 12
______, Lear Frk 247
______, Raymond Hal 84
______, Thomas Car 215
______, Thomas Clk 323
______, Thomas G. Put 215
______, William Bal 28
______, William Hst 296
______, William Wal 143
Sanford, Hamilton Wal 160
______, Henry Gre 277
______, James M. Tfo 365
______, Jeremiah Han 167
______, John Wal 139
______, John M. Tfo 355
______, Paschael Wal 164
______, Thomas J. Up 120
______, Thornton Put 215
______, Vincent Gre 273
______, Vincent Jr. Gre 288
Sandiford, Anderson App 7
______, James A. Lib 53
______, Sarah Wal 159
______, William Bke 152
Sankford, John Sr. Lwn 81
______, John Jr. Lwn 81
Sanderford, James Put 217
SANGSTER, Susan Hst 288
SANKEY, William D. Gre 279
SANSBURY, Mordice Dec 9
SANDWICK, Thomas K. Lin 74
SAPP, Abram Twg 73
______, Addison Har 190
______, Aly Lwn 83
______, Benjamin Tat 374
______, Charles Bke 132
______, Dennis Bke 135
______, Dilson F. Hst 273
______, Elijah Tat 376
______, Enoch Tlf 4
______, Everitt Bke 135
______, Hardy C. Bke 135
______, Henry Lwn 86
______, Henry Tat 371
______, Henry Tat 378
______, Isaiah Bke 135
______, Jason Em 177
______, James App 7
______, James Bke 135
______, James Dec 16
______, John App 9
______, John Bry 87
______, John Bke 135
Sapp, John Tat 374
______, John G. Dec 7
______, Leonard Hal 128
______, Luke Bul 102
______, Luke Pul 146
______, Luke Tat 379
______, Margret Dec 15
______, Mathew Tat 376
______, Moses Twg 64
______, Phenicy Bke 135
______, Phillip F. Ran 241
______, Reuben Em 178
______, Riley Lwn 82
______, Shadrack Tat 374
______, Solem Tat 379
______, Theophilus Bke 135
______, William Bke 134
______, William Dec 9
______, William DeK 64
______, William Lee 34
______, William Lwn 86
______, William Pul 149
______, William Tat 373
______, Zilpha Bke 135
SAPPINGTON/SAPINGTON
Sappington, Caleb Wal 135
______, Henry T. Hry 227
______, John Wil 297
______, Peggy Car 224
______, Richard Sr. Hry 227
______, Richard Hry 227
______, William J. Wil 296
Sapington, Thaeons New 36
SARDIS, James Bke 124
SARCEMETT/SARCENUTT
Sarcemett, James Han 168
Sarcenutt, Joseph N. Han 168
SARTAIN/SARTIN
Sartain, Elisha Mad 114
______, James Mad 111
______, John Jr. Mad 114
______, Tapley Mad 114
Sartin, Joel Frk 246
SASSER, Bryant Lwn 83
______, Clara Scr 304
______, Howell Scr 304
______, John Scr 304
______, Thomas Scr 304
SATCHER, Samuel Bib 71
SATERFIELD/SATTERFIELD
Saterfield, Curla Hab 52
______, Dasher T. Hab 62
______, Edward H. Hab 52

Name	County	Page
Saterfield, John	Hab	66
_____, Larkin	Hab	52
_____, Thomas W.	Hab	50
Satterfield, Catharine	Hab	18
SATROUR, John	Cht	266
SATTERWHITE/SATERWHITE/ SATTAWHITE		
Satterwhite, Anderson	Jns	432
_____, David	Har	185
_____, David H.	Har	185
_____, Dawson	Jsp	387
_____, James	Elb	150
_____, James	Trp	53
_____, John	Har	185
_____, Milly	Col	360
_____, Obed.	Trp	45
_____, Ober.	Trp	53
_____, Stephen	Jns	431
_____, Stephen	Jsp	358
_____, Thomas	Crf	400
Saterwhite, William	Gre	298
Sattawhite, Thomas	Wal	156
SAUGER, Aven	Tlb	339
_____, Josiah	Ran	245
_____, William	Mon	177
SAULS, Cullin	Twg	87
_____, Freeman	Hst	291
_____, Jacob	Hst	266
_____, Meridith	Bry	84
_____, Reubin	Twg	69
_____, Theophilus	Twg	70
_____, Thompson	Twg	85
SAUNDERS: also see Sanders		
Saunders, Alexander	Bke	128
_____, Ambrose Sr.	Twg	78
_____, Ambrose	Twg	65
_____, Elizabeth	Twg	84
_____, James	Mus	287
_____, Jeremiah	Lib	53
_____, John	Bts	162
_____, Joseph	Mus	279
_____, Mary	Cht	254
_____, Mary	Twg	87
_____, Samuel F.	Bul	102
_____, Thomas	Cht	264
_____, Thomas	Col	358
_____, Thomas	Mus	287
_____, Thomas	Mus	287
_____, William	Twg	69
SAVAGE, Daniel	Rch	261
_____, Elizabeth	Rch	287
_____, James	New	17
_____, John	Hal	129

Name	County	Page
Savage, Mary	Cht	266
_____, Mary; Plantation	Cht	279
_____, Peter	Cht	260
_____, Robert	Pul	140
_____, Robert C.	Hst	274
_____, Sarah	Cht	269
_____, Thomas Sr.	Hal	129
_____, Thomas	Hal	129
_____, William	Bry	84
_____, William	Rch	263
_____, Williams	Hal	129
_____, Zachariah	Col	345
_____, Zebulen	Hal	129
_____, Zebulon Jr.	Hal	129
SAVOY, L.	Cht	247
SAWYER/SAWYERS		
Sawyer, Cader	Twg	61
_____, Charles	DeK	65
_____, Elanan	Crf	396
_____, Joseph	Twg	65
_____, John	Twg	65
_____, Lewis	Crf	401
_____, Mastin	Crf	408
_____, Patrick	Crf	401
_____, Rebecca	Crf	401
_____, Sarah	Cht	254
_____, William	Crf	408
_____, Zadock	Hry	199
Sawyers, Amos	New	40
_____, Frances	Put	197
_____, John	New	40
SAXON/SEXON		
Saxon, Archelaus	Hry	205
_____, Benjamin	Twg	84
_____, Benjamin Y.	Bke	121
_____, Henry	Twg	77
_____, Jemima	Bke	152
_____, John	Bke	122
_____, John M.	Elb	154
_____, Lewis W.	Elb	154
_____, Nancy	Frk	254
_____, Robert	Hal	69
_____, Solomon	Hal	125
_____, William	Bke	151
Sexon, William	Hab	48
SAXTON/SEXTON		
Saxton, John	Jks	346
_____, Soloman	Jks	346
_____, Zadock	Jks	339
Sexton, Henry D.	Jns	463
_____, Lucinda	Gwn	328
_____, Robert	Hab	40
_____, Roda	Jns	458

Name	County	Page
SAYE/SAYRES/SAY/SAYS/ SAYRE/SAYER		
Saye, James	Hal	90
______, John	Hal	90
______, Margarett	Mad	109
______, Richard	Gwn	345
______, William	Hal	114
______, William H.	Mad	100
Sayres, David	Gre	272
______, Fredrick	McI	124
______, James	Gre	284
______, James M.	Gre	272
Say, David	Hal	120
______, William	Hal	120
Says, David	Gwn	336
Sayre, Benjamin W.	Lin	61
Sayer, Martha	Frk	223
SCALES, Aaron	Elb	120
______, Joel	DeK	43
______, John	Elb	128
______, Thomas	Elb	128
______, William	Hal	79
______, Willis	Frk	235
SCARBOROUGH/SCARBROUGH/ SCARBORO/SHARBOROUGH		
Scarborough, Aaron	Pul	154
______, Adam	Pul	155
______, Anus	Twg	86
______, Avent	Mon	209
______, David	Doo	88
______, David	Lau	8
______, Fedrick	Mad	106
______, Fedrick Jr.	Mad	114
______, James	Em	175
______, James	Lau	10
______, Jesse	Em	173
______, Joel L.	Bak	19
______, John	Hry	249
______, Lewis	Mad	114
______, Miles	Hry	236
______, Moses	Pul	140
______, Noah	Hst	270
______, Reddick	Bke	127
______, Sarah	Bke	128
______, Silas	Bke	123
______, Turner	Bke	124
______, William	Bke	125
______, William	Clk	310
Scarbrough,	Dec	3
______, Comfort	Lau	21
______, Elizabeth	Lau	22
______, Hardy	Scr	305
______, Theophilus	Bul	103
Scarbrough, William	Cht	271
______, William	McI	122
Scarboro, J.	Wks	351
Sharborough, James	Tlf	9
SCARBROOKS/SCARSBROOKS		
Scarbrooks, Henry	Mor	244
Scarsbrooks, William H.	Put	189
SCARLETT/SCARLOTT		
Scarlett, Francis M.	Gly	264
Scarlott, Lewis D.	Rab	234
SCATS/SCATES		
Scats, Thomas	Mor	255
Scates, Thomas	Pik	106
SCEAF, Lary	DeK	50
______, William	DeK	50
SCETH, William	Hab	24
SCHLEY, George	Cht	253
______, John	Jef	415
______, O. William	Bke	126
______, P. T.	Wsh	239
______, William	Rch	279
SCHOONMAKER, L.	Clk	326
SCHWEIGHOFFER, Thomas	Eff	108
SCIERS, Vincend	Hab	45
______, Wyett	Hab	26
SCISSON/SISSON/SISSAN/ SCESSON		
Scisson, James	DeK	55
______, John Sr.	Jks	330
______, Obadiah	DeK	47
______, Richard M.	Jsp	381
______, William B. Sr.	DeK	47
______, William J.	DeK	47
Sisson, John	Trp	41
______, Starling	Gwn	328
Sissan, Charles	Hab	15
Scesson, James	Jks	328
SCOFFIL, Philip	Crf	402
SCOGGIN/SCOGGINS/SCROGGIN/ SCROGGINS/SCROGIN/SCRIGGANS		
Scoggin, Benja.	Jks	320
______, C. D.	DeK	25
______, Henry	DeK	36
______, James	Clk	317
______, James	Pik	109
______, Sanders	DeK	28
______, Sarah	Bal	34
______, W. D.	Bal	32
______, Yonge	Pik	121
Scoggins, Benjamin S.	Jks	337
______, Charles	Rab	231
______, Francis	Wal	159
______, John T.	Gre	284

Name	County	Page
Scoggins, William S.	Frk	215
______, Wright	Gre	284
______, Wyley	DeK	58
Scroggin, King Hiram	Trp	47
______, Manly	Trp	46
______, Obediah	Trp	43
______, Philip	Pik	108
______, Seaborn J.	Jks	313
______, Thomas	Trp	46
______, William	Trp	39
Scroggins, Humphry	Ogl	100
______, Josiah	Bib	68
______, Robert S.	Gwn	366
______, Thomas	Ogl	84
Scogin, Gresham	Trp	38
______, Millington	Clk	312
Scriggans, James	Jsp	357
SCOLES, Rachael	Tfo	365
______, Robert	Tfo	363
SCONIERS, Jehu	Bke	124
______, John	Bke	124
______, Noah	Bke	124
______, Richard	Bke	124
______, Richard B.	Bke	124
SCOTT/SCOT		
Scott, A.	Mus	286
______, A. C.	Gly	264
______, Abraham	Cow	370
______, Absalom	Bib	52
______, Adam	Col	357
______, Agrippa	Frk	240
______, Alexander	Lin	66
______, Alexander	New	24
______, Andrew	Bke	152
______, Andrew	Gwn	349
______, Archibald H.	Clk	323
______, Baptist	Pul	157
______, Ben	Cam	188
______, Benjamin	Han	168
______, Benjamin	Pik	132
______, Benjamin C.	Ran	245
______, Britton	Em	170
______, Charles	Bke	151
______, Council	Mus	288
______, Daniel	Jns	441
______, Daniel	New	52
______, Darius	Tlb	331
______, David	Hst	286
______, Drury	Scr	308
______, Ewell	Lin	67
______, Francis	Crf	406
______, Francis	Tfo	354
______, Frederick	Han	166
Scott, George	Cow	367
______, George L.	Han	167
______, Gustavus	Wil	294
______, Henry	Col	362
______, Henry P.	Gre	303
______, Hiram	Wsh	259
______, Ira	Mus	279
______, Jacob	Dec	16
______, James	Har	185
______, James	Jks	318
______, James	Jsp	355
______, James (RS)	Lib	53
______, James	Mad	98
______, James	Pik	118
______, James	Scr	307
______, James	Wal	140
______, James	New	26
______, James C.	Cam	188
______, James C.	DeK	62
______, Jane	Mon	206
______, Jefferson	Bts	168
______, Jeremiah R.	New	26
______, Joel	Mus	280
______, John	Bib	66
______, John	Bry	84
______, John	Mad	105
______, John	Mon	175
______, John	Wal	128
______, John	Wil	302
______, John P.	Gre	281
______, John R.	Bal	38
______, John S.	Ran	244
______, John W.	Han	166
______, Joseph	Pik	108
______, Joseph	Pik	115
______, Joseph	Pik	125
______, Joseph J.	Jks	311
______, Josia	Scr	317
______, Lawson	Elb	125
______, Mary	Jef	401
** ______, Mrs. (slave)	Rch	258
______, N. J.	Har	18
______, Nathaniel	Scr	31
______, Patrick	Mad	11
______, Patrick	Pik	11
______, Perry B.	Bal	3
______, Peter	Han	16
______, Polly	Frk	25
______, Robert	Cht	24
______, Robert	DeK	6
______, Robert	Ear	9
______, Robert	Frk	22
______, Robert	Pik	12

Name	County	Page
Scott, Samuel	Gwn	313
______, Samuel	New	25
______, Samuel	Ran	249
______, Samuel	Mon	204
______, Samuel S.	Bts	159
______, Stephen	Pik	123
______, Thomas	Frk	257
______, Thomas	Gwn	309
______, Thomas	Har	187
______, Thomas	Mon	175
______, Thomas E.	Hst	266
______, W. F.	Bal	31
______, William	Bib	65
______, William	Col	353
______, William	Dec	4
______, William	Frk	221
______, William	Gwn	344
______, William	Lib	52
______, William	Mon	206
______, William	Twg	69
______, William R.	Cht	277
______, Willis S.	Jns	473
______, Wilson	Pik	123
______, Zillah	Mon	228
Scot, James S.	Put	187
______, John	Put	186
______, John W.	Put	186
______, McCiney	Hab	36
______, Sarah	Put	215
______, Stephen P.	Put	199
______, William	Put	188
______, William	Wal	168
SCREWS/SKREWS		
Screws, Benjamin	Jef	409
______, Enoch	New	49
______, James	New	49
______, Jesse	Doo	78
______, John	Jsp	389
Skrews, Isaac	Ear	97
SCRIMSHIRE, William B.	Up	107
SCRIVEN, Rev. C.O., dec'd. Estate	Lib	54
______, Dr. James, slaves	Cht	281
______, James P.	Cht	253
______, John	Cht	261
______, John (slaves)	Cht	281
SCRUGGS/SCRUGS		
Scruggs, A.	Cht	255
______, (Ed)und G.(illeg)	Jef	414
______, Joseph T.	Scr	299
______, Richard	Scr	306
Scrugs, James	Rab	228
______, William G.	Wrn	221

Name	County	Page
SCRUTCHENS, Josiah	Bke	123
SCUDER/SCUDDER		
Scuder, Jacob	Hal	133
Scudder, William	New	14
SCUDDY, James	Put	181
SCULL, John	Frk	237
SCURLOCK, Daniel	Bal	33
______, Ind.	Bal	31
______, William	Bal	39
SEA/SEE		
Sea, Cyrus	Hal	115
See, Anthony	Han	167
SEABOLT, Abraham	Hab	9
______, Solloman	Hab	66
SEABORN/SEABON		
Seaborn, Bailey	Jns	462
______, Richard	Mon	223
Seabon, David	Jns	462
SEABROOK, Smilie	Jns	455
SEALS/SEALES/SEALE		
Seals, Anthony	Put	204
______, Anthony	Wks	345
______, Archebald	Wrn	202
______, Arnold	Har	183
______, Elizabeth	Han	167
______, James	Wil	300
______, Reuben	Rch	291
______, Spencer	Han	167
______, Thomas	Wrn	203
______, William W.	Cam	182
Seales, George	Elb	141
______, John	Bke	138
______, John	Ogl	62
______, Sarah	Lin	63
Seale, John	Tfo	357
______, Redman G.	Lin	64
______, Richard J.	Elb	159
______, William A.	Lin	65
SEALY/SEALEY/SHEALY		
Sealy, Garrett	Jns	458
______, Peter B.	Crf	394
______, Samuel	Jns	458
Sealey, John	Crf	407
______, Margaret	Lau	12
Shealy, Henry	Scr	311
SEAMORE/SEAMOUR/SIMORE/ CEMORE		
Seamore, Aaron	Wal	170
______, Elias	Jks	348
______, Roe	Gwn	333
______, Zachariah	Elb	119
______, Zachariah	Elb	142
Seamour, John R.	Bib	71

Name	County	Page
Simore, John L.	Wal	135
Cemore, Mary	Lib	44
SEARCY, Aaron	Bal	33
_____, Benjamin	Tlb	345
_____, William	Bal	41
SEARLES, Covington	Lin	65
_____, Robert	Lin	70
_____, Thomas	Lin	66
SEARS/SEERS/CEARS		
Sears, Alford	New	38
_____, Anderson	Tlb	344
_____, Bishop	New	38
_____, David	Ware	186
_____, Harison	Mtg	233
_____, Jane	Mon	185
_____, Timothy	Wks	345
Seers, Rollin	Hab	49
Cears, John	Irw	299
SEAT/SEATS		
Seat, Lugus	Trp	34
Seats, Willis	Har	189
SEATON, James	Hab	62
SEAVER, John	Scr	309
SEAY, David	Col	359
_____, Fanny	Col	353
_____, James	Mwr	155
_____, Josiah	Hab	46
_____, Lorenzo D.	Lin	65
_____, Thomas	Col	359
_____, William	Col	362
SECKINGER, Benjamin	Eff	113
_____, John D.	Eff	109
_____, John G.	Eff	109
_____, Jonathan	Eff	105
_____, Joshua	Eff	104
SEDETH, Alexander	Hal	125
SEEGAR/SEGARS/SAGAR/SEGAR/ SEGARES/SEGERS/SAGER		
Seegar, Benjamin	Bke	120
_____, Charles	Bke	120
_____, Samuel	Bke	120
Segars, John	Cpb	195
_____, John	Gwn	330
_____, Southward	Gwn	326
Sagar, Ann	Gre	286
_____, William	Gre	292
Segar, John	Frk	240
Segares, John	Wal	142
Segers, Abel	Frk	240
Sager, William	Hry	234
SEGO, Ann	Rch	289
_____, E. W.	Rch	264
_____, Middleton	Rch	290

Name	County	Page
Sego, William	Hst	268
SEGRAVES, Currel	Gwn	320
_____, Patsey	Mad	117
_____, Solomon	Pik	121
_____, William	Mad	111
SEIGLER/SEGLER/SEAGLER		
Seigler, John	Scr	310
_____, Solomon	Scr	305
Segler, Joseph	Cpb	194
Seagler, John	New	19
_____, Matthew	New	19
SELF/SELPH/SEELF		
Self, Chappell B.	Twg	66
_____, Charnick	Bul	101
_____, David	Crf	410
_____, Jese	Hab	41
_____, Jethrew	Up	115
_____, Job	Hab	7
_____, Lovick	Clk	298
_____, Samuel E.	Elb	143
_____, Sincler	Elb	159
_____, William	Han	166
Selph, Ezekiel	Lwn	79
_____, Thomas	Lwn	80
Seelf, Lewis	Hab	22
SELFRIDGE, John	Hry	249
SELLECK, Frederick	Rch	273
SELLERS/SALLER/SELERS/ SELLARS'		
Sellers, Abel	New	53
_____, Andrew	Hry	210
_____, Hiram	Trp	49
_____, Jacob	Bul	103
_____, James	Hry	210
_____, John	Bul	93
_____, John	Lwn	80
_____, Josiah	Lwn	79
_____, Major H.	Jef	415
_____, Simeon	Tms	17
_____, William	Tms	17
Saller, Peter	Pik	125
_____, William	McI	126
Selers, Samuel	Dec	17
Sellars, John	Fay	185
SELLS/SELLES		
Sells, Jonathan	Gwn	333
_____, Maolirg	Col	357
Selles, Silas	Jsp	397
SELMAN/SELLMAN/CELMON		
Selman, David	Wal	158
_____, John W.	Wal	152
_____, William	Pul	157
_____, William	Wal	151

Sellman, John S. Hry 212
Celmon, William Pul 157
SELVEY, Joel Rab 228
_____, William Hab 62
SEMPLER, William Wrn 226
SEND, Uriah Mar 137
SENIARD, Henry Hab 43
_____, William Hab 43
SENTELE/SENTELL/SENTEL
Sentele, John Wal 138
Sentell, Martin T. Wal 149
Sentel, Joseph Mwr 161
SENTON, Wilis Tfo 363
SERGANT/SERJANT
Sergant, John Hab 19
Serjant, William Har 190
SEROGAN, Robert Gwn 356
SESSIONS/SESSOMS/SEISSAN/
CESSIONS/CESSOMS; also
see Scisson
Sessions, Asa Pik 124
_____, Benjamin Wsh 247
_____, John Lee 29
_____, John Pik 116
_____, Joseph Wsh 244
_____, Joseph Jr. Wsh 241
_____, Lewe Wsh 247
_____, Robert F. Trp 36
_____, Sherrod Wsh 239
Sessoms, Edward Lee 29
_____, Nicholas Tlb 337
Seissan, William J. Gwn 357
Cessions, Thomas Mor 269
Cessoms, Patrick Bak 18
SESTRUNK, Jacob Mar 139
SETSER/SETZE
Setser, Jacob Frk 254
Setze, John P. Rch 268
SETTLE, John Mon 177
_____, John Ogl 62
SEVILLE/SEVILLS/SAVELL
Seville, Samuel B. Jns 455
Sevills, John B. Mon 189
Savell, William Jks 330
SEWARD, William Tms 19
SEWELL/SEWEL/SEWAL/SUEL
Sewell, Aaron Jks 311
_____, Asa Frk 241
_____, Christopher Frk 248
_____, Green B. Frk 250
_____, Green B. Jr. Frk 235
_____, Isaac Mor 259
_____, James Frk 214
Sewell, James Mad 110
_____, John Frk 220
_____, John Frk 252
_____, Joshua Frk 221
_____, Joshua L. Frk 241
_____, Nicholas Frk 214
_____, Samuel Frk 229
_____, William Frk 247
_____, William Mad 116
Sewel, Charles M. Dec 11
_____, Christopher DeK 49
_____, John DeK 38
_____, Samuel DeK 38
_____, Wingfield Mor 238
Sewal, John Mor 258
Suel, Moses Gwn 347
SEXTON: see Saxton
SEYMORE, Eralborn Gre 278
_____, Richard H. Put 205
SHACKELFORD/SHACKLEFORD
Shackelford, Asa C. Elb 137
_____, Cullen New 18
_____, Edmond Elb 123
_____, Edmund Han 167
_____, Frances Gwn 363
_____, Henry Elb 123
_____, James B. Tlb 341
_____, Mordecai Mon 193
_____, Richard Har 182
Shackleford, Lucindia Mor 263
_____, Philip E. Jks 328
_____, William Frk 227
SHACKELLARD, John Jks 319
SHACKLEY, Martha Gre 304
SHAD/SHED
Shad, S. Cht 281
Shed, John Rab 235
SHADDIN, Robert Cow 378
_____, John Mad 110
_____, Thomas Cow 388
SHADDIX/SHADDOX
Shaddix, William Fay 206
Shaddox, James Pik 131
_____, John Pik 131
SHADINGFER, Andrew Fay 198
SHADRICK, Nancy Bts 164
SHAFFER, Jacob Cht 268
SHAFNER, Henry Mus 286
SHAMBLEN, Ann Mus 291
SHANLEY, William Gwn 315
SHANK/SHANKS
Shank, Henry Wil 310
_____, John Lin 58

Name	County	Page
Shank, John	Wil	310
Shanks, James D.	Lwn	87
SHANKLE, Eli	Jks	330
SHANKLING, Robert	Col	354
SHANNON, David	Frk	231
______, Evans	Pik	120
______, James	Clk	327
______, Rev. James B.	Lib	52
______, John	Cht	272
______, Levicey	Wyn	284
______, Samerel	Frk	230
______, Thomas M.	Frk	230
______, William	Lin	68
______, William	Rch	274
______, William	Rch	280
SHAPLER, James	Cht	253
SHARES, Isaac	Dec	9
SHARLEY, Benjamin	Rab	224
SHARMAN, James	Up	107
SHARP/SHARPE		
Sharp, Abbarilla	Jks	345
______, Abeda	Bke	117
______, Cader	Bke	117
______, Cyrus	Mon	195
______, Dennis	Hal	75
______, Elias	Hab	60
______, Elizabeth	Bke	131
______, Fielding	Mus	285
______, Francis J.	Mus	280
______, Grove Sr.	Tat	380
______, Grove	Tat	377
______, Henry	Jks	311
______, Howell	Em	169
______, James	Bib	52
______, James	Jns	463
______, James	Tfo	364
______, John	Bal	30
______, John	Rch	264
______, John F.	Mwr	159
______, John H.	Mwr	165
______, Joseph	Mwr	150
______, Mathew	Lee	35
______, Nancy	Mwr	169
______, Nathan J.	Jks	343
______, R^{d}.	Wrn	219
______, Robert	Ran	249
______, Thomas	New	36
______, Thomas H.	Ran	244
______, William	Mon	214
______, William S.	Mwr	165
Sharpe, Easley	Bal	30
______, H. W.	Lwn	81
______, Hiram	Car	214
Sharpe, John	Tat	375
______, John T.	Tat	376
______, Joshua	Tat	378
______, Littleton	Tat	376
______, Parker	Tat	377
SHARPTON, Dempsey	Gwn	333
______, Dennis	Gwn	333
SHARVER, William	Wal	164
SHAVE, Ann	Lib	53
______, John	Lib	53
______, William	Lib	53
SHAVER/SHAVERS		
Shaver, Michael	Rch	255
Shavers, George	Clk	327
SHAW, A. J. C.	Cht	247
______, Abn.	Wks	339
______, Amas	Ogl	102
______, Angus	Tlf	6
______, Daniel	Cow	387
______, Daniel	Wrn	210
______, Daniel K.	Dec	6
______, David	Mor	271
______, Elijah	Jks	323
______, Elizabeth (W)	Mor	251
______, Ephraim	Mor	252
______, George	Jks	313
______, George	Twg	66
______, George	Wal	148
______, George W.	Clk	327
______, Gilbert	Jsp	383
______, Haily	DeK	72
______, Henry	Mor	252
______, Henry Jr.	Mor	270
______, Hiram	Gwn	355
______, Hubard	Mor	271
______, James	Clk	294
______, James	DeK	65
______, Jeremiah	Dec	6
______, Jeremiah	Lib	53
______, John	Bke	144
______, John Sr.	Gre	290
______, John	Gre	295
______, John	Hry	245
______, John	Lib	52
______, Joseph	DeK	27
______, Josiah W.	Hal	74
______, L. C.	Cam	181
______, Lucy	Cow	383
______, Margret	Col	347
______, Martin	Lwn	89
______, Mary	Col	347
______, Mary	Rch	273
______, Milton	Hry	245

Name	County	Page
Shaw, Murdock	Pik	128
______, Norman	Mon	213
______, Robert	Car	227
______, Ruthy	Hal	86
______, Sarah	DeK	33
______, Thomas B.	Lib	54
______, William	Clk	293
______, William	DeK	64
______, William	Hry	218
______, William	Jks	348
______, William	Jsp	394
______, William	Rab	231
______, William	Rch	291
______, William W.	Trp	54
SHAYRS/SHAY		
Shayrs, Thomas	Rab	228
______, William Sr.	Rab	228
______, William	Rab	234
Shay, David	Pik	110
SHEARER/SERA		
Shearer, Catharine	Cht	263
______, John L.	Bts	164
______, Rebecca	Cht	254
______, William	Wil	313
Sera, A.	Rch	264
SHEARMAN/SHEARMON		
Shearman, Clement	Wil	322
______, John	Wil	309
______, Samuel	Mor	251
Shearmon, Elie G.	Wrn	204
SHEEROUSE, Emanuel	Eff	105
______, Godlief	Eff	111
______, Gottlieb	Eff	108
SHEETS/SHEETZ/SHEATZ/ SHEATS		
Sheets, Robert	Col	352
______, Talton	Cpb	195
Sheetz, Charles	Cpb	203
Sheatz, Nicholas	Clk	294
Sheats, Linsey	Clk	295
SHEFFIELD/SHUFFIELD		
Sheffield, Arthur	Ear	94
______, Bryant	Cam	187
______, Elizabeth	Ear	93
______, Isham	Ear	93
______, John	Ear	91
______, John	Wyn	285
______, John C. Sr.	Doo	78
______, Jos.	Bal	39
______, Lucy	Bul	97
______, Pliney	Wyn	281
______, Reuben	Hry	235
______, Sherrard	Wyn	281

Name	County	Page
Sheffield, Simeon	Bul	100
______, West	Ear	100
______, West	Wyn	285
______, William	Bul	100
______, William Sr.	Pul	152
______, William Jr.	Pul	152
______, Wynn	Ear	97
Shuffield, Elizabeth	Jns	458
______, Isome	Hab	42
______, Jacob	Mor	257
______, James	Mwr	157
______, Jeptha	Han	167
______, John	Tms	26
______, Robert	Wrn	203
______, William	Han	167
SHEFTALL, A.	Cht	265
______, M. Sr.	Cht	265
______, M. Jr.	Cht	266
______, Mary	Cht	268
______, Moses	Cht	254
______, S.	Cht	283
______, Solomon	Cht	259
SHEHEE/SHEHE		
Shehee, Ellapair	Wsh	251
______, Sherrod	Pik	127
______, Thomas G.	Pik	131
Shehe, A. B.	Lwn	86
SHELMAN/SHELMON		
Shelman, Augustus G.	Jef	401
______, John	Cht	252
______, John	Pul	146
______, John M.	Bib	52
______, Robert B.	Bib	66
Shelmon, Michael	Jef	401
SHELNUTT/SHELNUT/SHELLNUTT		
Shelnutt, Henry W.	Wal	127
______, John G.	Wal	130
______, William	Wal	129
Shelnut, Elizabeth	Fay	196
______, William	Cpb	196
Shellnutt, Thomas	Fay	196
SHELL, Byron	Lee	30
______, Cornelius D.	Mor	243
______, Edward	Wal	158
______, George	Frk	249
______, Green	Han	166
______, Isham	Hry	251
SHELLY/SHELLEY/SHELLECY		
Shelly, Archibald	Hst	269
______, Lucinda	Wks	353
______, Malachi	Hst	267
______, Reuben	Hst	267
Shelley, Moses	Mon	180

Shellecy, Moses Cow 381
SHELTON, Allen Mor 255
______, Aaron Hab 38
______, Abselum Hab 38
______, Benjamin Rab 229
______, Charles J. Tlf 11
______, Dav. Bal 42
______, Henry Wrn 195
______, John Frk 246
______, Joseph Mor 260
______, Keziah Frk 255
SHEPHERD/SHEPPARD/SHEPPERD/
SHEPERD/SHEPHARD/SHEPARD
Shepherd, Bazzel Pul 149
______, Benjamin Jef 405
______, Benjamin Pik 127
______, Benjamin Trp 52
______, Cath. Wks 351
______, Elijah Jef 404
______, Frances Wks 351
______, Harvey Scr 306
______, Jacob Jef 405
______, James Bke 131
______, James Jef 421
______, James Mor 244
______, James Wal 129
______, John Clk 302
______, John Jef 404
______, John Mus 285
______, Joseph Wil 319
______, Josiah Mus 290
______, Lymoun Dec 4
______, Martha Scr 300
______, Mary Wil 288
______, Nathan Fay 195
______, Nathan Hal 110
______, Richard Fay 191
______, Samuel Elb 121
______, Talmon W. Mor 244
______, William Pik 129
______, William Scr 306
______, William Trp 50
______, William Tms 16
______, William Up 96
______, William B. Pik 130
Sheppard, Abraham Hry 207
______, Charles Wsh 257
______, David Wsh 267
______, Edward Lau 11
______, Frances Wsh 266
______, George Bib 75
______, George F. Hry 235
______, John Hst 264
Shepherd, John Lau 6
______, John Wsh 244
______, John Jr. Wsh 256
______, Lewis Wsh 261
______, Robert Hst 281
______, Thomas Wsh 269
______, William Hst 264
Shepperd, John Wal 149
______, John Sr. Mus 292
______, John W. Mwr 152
______, Thomas Jsp 395
Sheperd, John M. New 45
______, Richard New 46
______, Thomas New 50
______, William New 37
Shephard, Seabon Crf 403
______, Thomas J. Lib 52
Shepard, Nimrod New 37
SHERBERT, Warner Put 200
SHERIDAN/SHEREDAN/
SHERIDEN/SHERDON
Sheridan, Abner Frk 222
______, Dennis Gre 285
Sheredan, John Frk 219
Sheriden, George Frk 222
Sherdon, Abner Car 220
SHERMON/SHERMAN/SHURMAN
Shermon, James Put 197
______, Robert Wsh 255
Sherman, John A. Jsp 384
Shurman, Robert Jsp 372
SHERODINE, Simeon Gwn 356
SHERRARD/SHERARD/SHERROD/
SHEROD
Sherrard, Elizabeth Tlb 324
______, Haywood Tlb 324
______, Wright Tlb 324
Sherard, Benjamine Em 164
Sherrod, James Jef 405
______, John Pul 143
Sherod, Mary Bib 53
SHERRELL/SHERILL
Sherrell, David Hal 90
______, Elizabeth Gre 283
Sherill, Little Berry Har 179
SHERRER/SHERRAR/SHERROR
Sherrer, Milly Wks 334
Sherrar, James Hry 243
Sherror, John Cpb 209
SHERSON, Joel Lee 34
SHERWOOD, Adiel Gre 281
SHETLEY, Ann Cht 258
SHEW, John Jsp 383

SHEWBIRD, Robert Hal 106
SHICK, G. F. Rch 266
_____, George Cht 257
_____, John Cht 257
_____, Peter Cht 259
SHIELDS/SHEALS
Shields, Francis A. Mon 189
_____, George Jks 332
_____, Hosatia Put 184
_____, J. Jks 324
_____, James Col 357
_____, James Jks 311
_____, Jeremiah Jsp 383
_____, John Jks 324
_____, John O. Jks 348
_____, Samuel Mor 250
_____, Susannah Mad 117
_____, William Mad 117
_____, William Mor 270
Sheals, John Wrn 213
SHIFLET/SHOFFIT
Shiflet, James Elb 128
_____, Picket Sr. Elb 123
_____, Picket Jr. Elb 127
_____, Powel Elb 128
Shoffit, William Hab 41
SHINE, Daniel W. Twg 61
_____, James Hal 69
SHINHOLSTER/SHINHOLSER
Shinholster, George Wks 355
_____, Thomas Bal 40
Shinholser, James Jns 466
SHIP/SHIPP
Ship, Benjamin Trp 38
_____, David Tlb 338
_____, John C. Jr. Wal 133
_____, Nancy Tlb 336
_____, Pleasant Wal 132
_____, Ransom Trp 38
_____, Reden C. New 21
_____, Richard Wal 135
_____, Samuel W. Pik 120
_____, William Wal 133
Shipp, Daniel Lin 72
_____, James Lin 67
_____, John C. Wal 173
_____, Lemuel Gre 302
_____, Mark Lin 69
_____, Richard DeK 43
_____, Thomas Lin 70
_____, William Up 100
_____, Wilshire Cow 371
SHIPLEY, George New 23
Shipley, William Car 221
SHIPMAN, Wilson Hab 55
SHIPPY, John Cpb 210
_____, Joseph Gwn 354
SHIRLEY/SHEARLEY/SHEARLY/
SHERLEY/SHURLY/SHURLEY/
SHIREY/SHIRY/SHIRLY/SHIRAH
Shirley, Riley Hab 35
Shearley, Esther Hal 88
_____, Nath^n. Wrn 228
_____, William Wrn 227
Shearly, James Twg 79
_____, William Jef 409
Sherly, John Hab 30
_____, Mose Hab 30
_____, William Lwn 85
Sherley, Robert Jks 343
Shurly, Aaron Crf 414
_____, Edward Crf 395
_____, Nathaniel Crf 393
Shurley, Elizabeth Crf 399
Shirey, Charles Bib 75
_____, Josiah Bib 75
_____, Samuel Wsh 260
Shiry, Benjamin Wsh 244
_____, John N. Wsh 258
_____, Loney Wal 167
_____, William Wal 145
Shirly, William Lau 17
Shirah, John N. Mus 290
SHIRLING/SHERLIN/SHERLING
Shirling, Isaam Put 207
_____, Isham Jsp 365
_____, John Mon 210
_____, John A. Put 207
_____, William Mon 203
_____, William Mon 211
Sherlin, Richard Gre 303
_____, William B. Ran 244
Sherling, Richard Put 206
SHIVER/SHIVERS
Shiver, Abraham Pul 157
_____, Alijah Pul 157
_____, Asa Doo 78
_____, Burrel Lau 22
_____, Darcas Doo 87
_____, Demiel Pul 157
_____, Enoch Doo 81
_____, Elijah Lau 22
_____, Fleming Hst 281
_____, Jacob Doo 81
_____, James Sr. Doo 87
_____, James Jr. Doo 78

Name	County	Page
Shiver, John	Doo	78
_____, John	Hst	287
_____, Maning	Doo	81
_____, Obadiah	Han	167
_____, William	Han	166
Shivers, Barnaba	Han	169
_____, G. W. C.	Wrn	197
_____, James	Han	167
_____, James	Wrn	196
_____, John M.	Wrn	226
_____, Jonas	Pik	126
_____, Thomas W.	Wrn	211
_____, William	Han	168
_____, Wilson	Wrn	195
SHOCKLEY/SHOCKLY; also see Shottley		
Shockley, Aquila	Hal	128
_____, C.	Jks	318
_____, Gideon	Jks	332
_____, John	Mon	221
_____, M. L.	Mon	189
_____, Silas	Mon	224
_____, Thomas	Hal	130
_____, Thomas	Jks	314
_____, Thomas	Up	97
_____, William D.	Up	118
Shockly, William	Hal	79
SHOEMAKER/SHOEMAKE/ SHEWMAKE/SHOMACA		
Shoemaker, James	Mad	110
_____, Jeremiah	Mwr	159
_____, John	Mad	109
_____, Samuel	Mad	104
_____, Tarlton	Elb	123
_____, William	Mad	110
Shoemake, Rebecca	Rch	287
Shewmake, Joseph	Bke	133
Shomaca, Louise	Cht	244
SHOLDERS, David	Har	187
SHORN, Seaborn	Mus	284
SHORT, Archabald	Ogl	66
_____, Aron	Hal	119
_____, David	Wal	130
_____, Howell	Tlb	347
_____, Jesse	Trp	36
_____, John	Cpb	203
_____, John	Gre	275
_____, John	Hal	133
_____, John C.	Tlb	347
_____, Laban	Ogl	79
_____, Nancy	Hal	86
_____, Peter B.	Col	353
_____, Pleasant W.	Ogl	66
Short, Reuben	Gre	278
_____, Robert B.	Trp	36
_____, Tarpley	Clk	313
_____, William T.	Mon	210
_____, Young W.	Ogl	66
SHORTER, Eli S.	Put	217
_____, Henry	Tfo	356
_____, James	Tfo	357
_____, Reuben C.	Jsp	369
SHORES/SHORE		
Shores, Daniel	Put	215
_____, Duty	Hst	295
_____, Elijah	Hry	208
_____, Planner	Put	215
_____, Riley	Put	189
Shore, John	Hab	55
SHOTTLEY, John	Up	107
SHOTWELL, Jesse	Jks	326
_____, Nathaniel	Jks	321
SHOWS, H. W.	Wks	346
SHROPSHIRE, James W.	Jsp	352
_____, Joshua	Mor	263
_____, Spencer	Ran	248
_____, Wesley	Ogl	101
SHUBTRINE/SHIPTRINE/ SHIPTRENE		
Shubtrine, Israel	Eff	109
Shiptrine, Daniel	Pik	116
Shiptrene, William	Pik	115
SHUFFLE, Everett	Hal	132
SHUFTELL, Wiley	Lib	54
SHUMATE/SHUMATT		
Shumate, Berry	DeK	56
_____, Daniel	Wil	291
_____, Joseph D.	Car	218
_____, Mason	DeK	26
_____, William	Wil	303
Shumatt, Elizabeth	Lib	53
SHUMAN, Mrs. Faithey	Bry	86
_____, George H.	Bry	87
_____, John	Bry	86
_____, John M.	Bry	86
_____, Martin Sr.	Bry	88
_____, Martin	Bry	87
_____, Nancy	Han	169
_____, Samuel G.	Bry	86
_____, William	Bry	86
SHURETT, John	Hal	105
_____, Sarah	Hal	105
SHURLING, James	Wsh	257
SHUTE, Giles	Pul	141
SHUTLY, Peter	Gwn	351
SHY/SHI		

Name	County	Page
Shy, James	Han	168
______, James	Mor	255
______, John	Han	168
Shi, Samuel	Jsp	395
______, Seaborn	Jsp	395
SIBBALD/SIBBOLD		
Sibbald, Milly	Rch	275
Sibbold, Jane	Clk	324
SIBLEY, A.	Cht	257
______, Amory	Rch	266
SIDES, Charles	Wal	134
SIDWELL, John	Mor	244
SIKES/SYKES/SITES		
Sikes, Arthur	App	9
______, Mrs. Catharine	Bry	88
______, Daniel	Tat	373
______, Dire C.	Tat	373
______, Jacob	Bry	87
______, James W.	Fay	207
______, John	Tat	373
______, John B.	Bry	85
______, Joseph	Hst	270
______, Matthew	Hst	267
______, Samuel	Hst	265
______, Sarah	Col	356
______, William	Cam	187
______, William	Doo	89
______, Zachariah	Clk	310
Sykes, Alfred	Har	189
______, Arthur	Rch	282
______, Isaiah	Hst	269
______, James	Rch	290
______, John D.	Han	166
______, Thomas	Bke	132
______, William B.	Han	166
______, Winefred	Hst	278
Sites, Frederick	Hry	200
______, Joseph	Hry	200
SILLS, Edward	Wks	349
______, Nancy	Bke	137
SILMAN, William	Up	110
______, William P.	Car	219
SILVER, Sylvester	Cam	182
SILVY/SILVEY		
Silvy, Abreham	Clk	299
______, Drury	Cpb	200
______, Jane	New	9
______, William	Clk	315
Silvey, John	Wil	309
______, Stephen	Tfo	367
SIMINGTON, Ezekel	New	42
______, Felix	New	42
______, Moses	Pik	117
SIMMONS/SIMONS/SIMON/ SIMMOND/SIMMON/SIMMONDS/ SIMONDS		
Simmons, Abraham	Mad	107
______, Adam	Hab	8
______, Alford	Put	213
______, Allen	Pik	118
______, Allen G.	Crf	410
______, Asa	Up	107
______, Asa C. A.	DeK	54
______, Bela	Tfo	360
______, Benjamin	Han	166
______, Benjamin	Put	181
______, Beverly	Hry	203
______, Beverly A.	Pul	144
______, Caleb	Wil	294
______, Charity	Bib	53
______, Charles	Ogl	64
______, Charles	Wal	157
______, Charles H.	Ogl	81
______, David	Har	176
______, Deborah	Wrn	225
______, Dennis	Hal	118
______, Dudley	Put	181
______, Edward	Pul	143
______, Elizabeth	Ogl	76
______, Enoch	Scr	302
______, Frances	Mad	105
______, Greene	Put	212
______, Harvey M.	Mad	113
______, Henry	Crf	409
______, Hiram	Gwn	360
______, Holmon F.	Hal	74
______, Isaac	Mad	108
______, Isaac	Tlb	342
______, Ivy	Lwn	87
______, James	Doo	85
______, James	Han	167
______, James B.	Trp	34
______, Jesse	Han	168
______, Jesse	Hry	236
______, Jesse	Put	181
______, Jesse	Wil	293
______, John	Bul	95
______, John	Fay	186
______, John	Frk	220
______, John	Gre	300
______, John	Hal	94
______, John	Jns	463
______, John	Lin	64
______, John	Mon	206
______, John	Pik	132
______, John	Tlb	342

Simmons, John B. Han 167
______, John K. Mon 198
______, John P. Wks 336
______, John W. Mon 216
______, Joseph Pul 144
______, Joseph Tlb 329
______, Martha Jns 429
______, Martin Bib 57
______, Mary Lin 63
______, Moses Crf 393
______, Moses W. Frk 219
______, Polly Put 180
______, R. W. Mon 222
______, Rachel Jns 454
______, Reuben Mad 104
______, Robert Pik 124
______, Samuel Scr 302
______, Samuel Tfo 360
______, Sarah Put 173
______, Simeon D. Mwr 169
______, Solomon Crf 411
______, Stephen Gre 300
______, Stern Lin 63
______, Thomas Har 179
______, Thomas Lin 63
______, Thomas Put 213
______, Thomas Up 95
______, Valentine Fay 196
______, Vinson B. Mwr 164
______, William Crf 408
______, William Gwn 362
______, William Gwn 371
______, William Jns 462
______, William Mar 139
______, William Mon 204
______, William Tlb 342
______, William Wsh 242
______, William Wrn 229
______, William H. Pik 125
______, Willie J. Put 181
Simons, Henry Sr. Tlf 4
______, Henry Jr. Tlf 4
______, William B. Crf 411
Simon, Martin Pik 127
______, Old Lin 69
______, William Hab 58
______, William Mon 228
Simmond, David Wil 292
______, James Mor 270
Simmon, John Mad 103
Simmonds, Joshua Hal 101
Simonds, Chester Rch 284
SIMMONETT/SIMONET
Simmonett, A. Rch 265
Simonet, William Cht 248
SIMONTON, Rebecca Clk 317
______, Robert Wal 135
______, Robert Wal 165
SIMPSON/SIMPKINS/SIMESON
Simpson, Abner DeK 64
______, Alexander Doo 85
______, Ann Cam 182
______, Arthur Hst 271
______, Cain Fay 187
______, Christopher Pul 158
______, Charles Up 118
______, David Twg 84
______, Dicy DeK 67
______, Ephraigm New 29
______, Ezekeal Wsh 269
______, George Put 207
______, Hardy Tms 24
______, Jack Cht 268
______, James Hst 286
______, James B. Wil 311
______, John Bal 31
______, John DeK 27
______, John DeK 64
______, John Hst 287
______, Leonard DeK 47
______, Lucretia Han 168
______, Lydia Cht 256
______, Mary Elb 122
______, Nathan Wrn 233
______, Robert Wil 301
______, Rose Cht 268
______, S. Wks 347
______, Soloman Hst 291
______, Thomas Bal 30
______, Thomas Hst 271
______, Thomas Irw 300
______, William Mon 187
______, William Wil 302
______, William F. Cht 257
______, William S. Han 168
______, Wilson Trp 46
Simpkins, Benjamin Jks 344
Simeson, Asa New 36
SIMS/SIMMS/SIMMES/SYMMS/
SYMS
Sims, Alexander Mor 267
______, Allen Trp 46
______, Ann Rch 266
______, Anna J. Frk 229
______, Benjamin Rch 285
______, Benjamin D. Wil 288

Sims, Bennet Ogl 75
_____, Bennett Hal 110
_____, Burkley Mad 99
_____, Charles Mad 111
_____, Cullin Wal 143
_____, David T. Trp 34
_____, Elizabeth Hal 128
_____, Frederick Crf 400
_____, Gaz. Col 337
_____, George H. Hst 274
_____, Gresham Ogl 99
_____, H. Lee 26
_____, Henry Wal 156
_____, Hope Frk 226
_____, Hull Frk 239
_____, Jacob Bry 87
_____, Jacob Lib 53
_____, James Clk 316
_____, James Hab 21
_____, James Wsh 245
_____, James Trp 55
_____, James S. Ogl 98
_____, John Twg 60
_____, John Car 219
_____, John Dec 16
_____, John Jns 455
_____, John Ogl 69
_____, John Tlb 342
_____, John Up 98
_____, John H. Jns 455
_____, John H. Wal 159
_____, John L. Gwn 315
_____, John M. Ogl 85
_____, Joseph Bul 94
_____, Larkin Pik 112
_____, Leonard Pik 131
_____, Leonard Wal 166
_____, Lewis Cow 369
_____, Lorenzo D. Clk 315
_____, Lucy Put 194
_____, Mark Wal 144
_____, Martha Ogl 102
_____, Martin Pik 106
_____, Mary Wal 164
_____, Mrs. Mary P. Col 337
_____, Michael Hal 127
_____, Murry Ogl 75
_____, Nancy Clk 317
_____, Newton Wal 166
_____, Rachael Lin 59
_____, Ransom R. Mor 272
_____, Robert Clk 311
_____, Sandy Mwr 165
Sims, Susannah Cht 247
_____, Sterling Mor 247
_____, Sterling Put 196
_____, Theriba Twg 83
_____, William Clk 295
_____, William Lin 59
_____, William Trp 41
_____, William P. Wal 141
_____, Willis Gwn 370
_____, Zachariah Bib 53
Simms, Arthur L. Clk 302
_____, Benjamin DeK 67
_____, Benjamin C. Tfo 360
_____, Britton Han 168
_____, Elisha Cpb 200
_____, George New 47
_____, James Col 354
_____, James Han 166
_____, Jane DeK 34
_____, Joel Wal 157
_____, John Cow 386
_____, Marion Lau 20
_____, Mary Tfo 366
_____, Nathan A. New 31
_____, Phil. S. Han 168
_____, Reuben B. Up 109
_____, Richard Tfo 355
_____, Robert M. Hry 219
_____, Sarah Han 168
_____, Thornton DeK 43
_____, William DeK 44
_____, William Mus 287
Simmes, Andrew G. Wil 289
_____, Ignatius Wil 294
_____, Thomas Wil 293
Symms, Bartlet Mon 201
_____, William Mon 197
Syms, Joseph Rab 295
SINCLAIR, Elijah Wil 290
_____, Elizabeth Mon 198
_____, Jessee Mon 184
_____, John Up 107
_____, Robert D. Hst 274
SINGER, John Bib 65
_____, Joseph Rch 275
SINGLETARY/SINGLETERRY
Singletary, Duram Bib 64
_____, Elijah Pul 139
_____, John Bib 62
_____, Michael R. Pul 146
_____, William Pul 141
Singleterry, Thomas Tlf 6
SINGLETON, Abner Tlb 347

Name	County	Page
Singleton, Biggers	Hst	274
______, Gregory	Put	213
______, Hansel	Lwn	79
______, Henry	Mon	189
______, Henry	Rab	226
______, James	Cpb	199
______, James	Rab	234
______, James	Ran	246
______, John	Tat	379
______, Joseph J.	Jks	312
______, Leroy	Put	214
______, Martha	Hry	240
______, Richard	Wal	158
______, Samuel	Pik	108
______, William	Put	172
______, William	Rab	227
______, William K.	Tlb	347
______, Williams	Hst	288
______, Wyatt	Mon	221
SINQUEFIELD, Asa	Jef	405
______, James M.	Jef	405
______, Moses	Wsh	258
______, William	Wsh	258
SIRMON/SERMON		
Sirmon, Abner	Lwn	86
______, Benjamin	Lwn	86
______, Jethro	Ear	96
______, Jonathan	Lwn	86
______, Joseph	Lwn	86
Sermon, John	Pul	144
SISK, Elijah	Hab	48
______, Gabril Sr.	Hab	63
______, Gabril Jr.	Hab	48
______, Singleton	Hab	63
SISTRUNK, John	Lin	68
SITER, Moses	Hab	29
SITTON, Joseph	Hab	49
SIZEMORE/SIZEMOORE/ SISEMORE		
Sizemore, Abigail	Gwn	330
______, Gabriel	Rch	286
______, George	Gwn	316
______, Henry	Car	229
______, James	Gwn	330
______, Mazerea	Mtg	236
Sizemoore, W.	Gwn	309
Sisemore, Richard	Hab	22
SKAGGS, Henry	Elb	157
______, James	New	36
SKELTON, Jabez	Elb	126
______, Jeremiah	Frk	228
______, John Sr.	Elb	127
______, John	Elb	145
Skelton, Lee	Jks	323
______, Marten	Elb	130
______, Noel	Frk	245
______, Richmond	Elb	127
______, Robert	Lau	8
______, Samuel B.	New	34
______, Wiley	Elb	145
SKIDMORE, Cosby S.	Mor	241
______, Jett T.	Wal	159
______, Samuel	Mor	241
SKINNER/SKINER		
Skinner, Archibald H.	Hry	203
______, Charles	Bke	133
______, David	Wal	154
______, E.	Mus	287
______, Finny	Put	196
______, Henry	Bke	153
______, Isaac H.	Hry	232
______, Jacob	Bke	121
______, Jesse	Bke	119
______, John	Bke	133
______, John	Bke	153
______, John	Bts	158
______, John	Mus	289
______, John	Mus	290
______, John	Rch	286
______, Jonas	Bke	120
______, Julius	Mor	264
______, Levingston	Wal	166
______, Livingston	Rch	285
______, Outlaw	Bke	152
______, Pakerson	Put	191
______, Randal	Ware	185
______, Rebeccah	Bke	133
______, Robert	Bke	133
______, Robert	Hry	212
______, Rowland	Hry	247
______, Thomas	Rch	284
______, Uriah Sr.	Bke	151
______, Uriah Jr.	Bke	151
______, William	New	50
______, William	Rch	284
Skiner, Catharine	Han	167
______, Mary	Han	168
______, Nancy	Han	168
SKIPP, Turner H.	Hab	18
SKIPPER, Benjamin	Lau	12
______, Daniel	Wks	356
______, Elias	Lwn	87
______, Henery	Cow	378
______, Jacob	Bib	74
______, John	Cow	392
______, Wright	Cow	382

SKIPPY, Josh Gwn 372
SKRINE, William A. Wsh 250
SLACK, Jeremeah Dec 13
______, Jesse Wil 300
______, John Wil 300
______, John Wil 318
______, Joseph Mor 254
______, Joseph Wil 318
SLADE, Harris Tlb 346
______, M. D. J. Bib 57
______, Samuel Jns 437
______, Simon Pik 131
______, Thomas B. Jns 467
______, William Doo 86
______, William Wsh 239
SLAPPY, A. G. Crf 397
______, John Lee 26
______, John G. Crf 411
______, John G. Pul 139
______, Reuben H. Crf 393
______, Uriah Crf 397
______, William Wks 334
SLATE, Samuel Bib 52
SLATON/SLATEN/SLATTON/
SLAYTON/SLATHAM/SLATEHAM
Slaton, Ann Hal 124
______, Arthur Wil 292
______, Benjamin Frk 245
______, Cornelius Bts 174
______, Daniel Pik 123
______, Flemming Hal 127
______, Headen Jks 331
______, Joseph Jns 430
______, Littleberry Jks 347
______, Littleton G. Hry 240
______, Sabra Jks 347
______, Samuel Hal 130
______, Uriah Jks 349
______, Usupiss Jks 349
______, Wade Jks 324
______, Wade Jks 333
______, William Wil 300
______, Zachariah Gwn 378
Slaten, Enoch Hal 122
______, Martha Hal 94
______, Zebedee Rab 224
Slatton, George Hab 14
Slayton, John Mwr 152
Slatham, James Pik 111
Slateham, James Pik 111
SLATTER/SLATER/SCLATTER
Slatter, H. H. Crf 393
______, Horatio Bke 122
Slatter, James E. Crf 400
______, John J. Har 177
______, Lemuel D. Mar 137
______, Nancy Jns 467
______, Thomas Crf 415
______, William C. Mus 280
Slater, Burrel Tms 19
______, Elisha Col 347
______, James Scr 299
______, Jesse Tms 23
______, Samuel Bul 94
______, William Bul 96
Sclatter, James F. Bal 37
SLAUGHTER, Barney Jsp 363
______, Bradley Put 185
______, Gains Put 190
______, George Gre 302
______, H. P. Jsp 366
______, Henry Tlf 7
______, J. W. Jsp 366
______, James Jns 463
______, James Lau 17
______, James Put 185
______, John Bal 43
______, John Gre 280
______, John Lwn 80
______, John Tlb 336
______, John B. Jsp 359
______, John B. Mwr 153
______, John J. Mon 213
______, John R. Cow 384
______, Lawson Trp 53
______, Martin Mon 220
______, Moses Lwn 84
______, N. G. Jsp 364
______, Nancy Put 185
______, Noah Lau 18
______, R. J. Jr. Up 99
______, R. Sr. Up 98
______, Samuel Lwn 80
______, Sam. B. Up 118
______, Thomas K. Put 183
______, Thomas P. Han 167
______, Thomas W. DeK 47
______, William Gre 286
______, William Jns 462
______, William A. Put 206
______, Wilson Lau 19
SLAY, Alphery Mwr 155
______, Daniel R. Bts 169
______, Nathan DeK 69
______, Noah DeK 41
______, William Ear 95

SLAYTON, Thomas Cow 376
SLEDGE/SLEDG
Sledge, Alexander Mon 208
_____, Amos Up 120
_____, Bryant Hst 269
_____, Hamblin Bib 71
_____, Hiram Twg 79
_____, Mims Trp 41
_____, Richard Jns 428
_____, Shirley Put 181
_____, Whitfield H. Trp 34
Sledg, Charles Clk 325
_____, Isham Clk 327
_____, Wiley Clk 316
SLOCUMB/SLOCOMB
Slocumb, David Jns 462
_____, Jesse Jns 462
_____, John C. Jns 462
Slocomb, Joseph New 9
_____, William New 9
SLONE/SLOAN/SLOANE/SLAWN
Slone, Elizabeth Bib 52
_____, John Tms 28
_____, Marvel Irw 300
_____, Samuel Irw 299
_____, William Elb 137
_____, William Irw 298
_____, William Tms 28
_____, William Twg 69
Sloan, Allen Dec 7
_____, Benjamin F. Frk 253
_____, John DeK 36
_____, Sarah Bke 119
Sloane, John Rch 282
Slawn, John Tms 28
SLOVER, Jeremiah Hab 40
SMALLEY, James Col 359
_____, Michael Col 361
SMALLWOOD/SMALWOOD
Smallwood, Elijah Hal 123
_____, Elijah Jns 452
_____, Elisha Mor 243
_____, Elisha Wil 321
_____, Elisha Wrn 200
_____, Francis Dec 15
_____, John Mon 176
_____, Makenzey Car 230
_____, Marcus New 38
_____, Mark Fay 192
_____, William Wil 321
_____, William S. Hab 22
Smalwood, James Hal 130
_____, Judah Hal 129
Smalwood, Polly Hal 129
SMARR, William Mon 187
SMART/SMARTT
Smart, Daniel Hab 15
_____, Edmond Dec 6
_____, Francis Tat 379
_____, Nathan Tat 379
Smartt, Littleberry Jsp 354
_____, Osborn Jsp 354
SMAYRES, John Rch 281
_____, Perril Rch 284
SMEADLEY/SMEDLY/SMEDLEY
Smeadley, James M. Put 193
_____, Thomas Put 193
Smedly, John Cow 390
Smedley, John Wal 145
SMELTS/SMETS
**Smelts, Mary (slave) Rch 260
Smets, A. A. Cht 252
SMISSON, B. B. Crf 412
SMITH/SMYTH
Smith, A. Col 364
_____, A. R. Gwn 317
_____, A. S. App 11
_____, Aaron Han 167
_____, Aaron Mad 111
_____, Aaron Pik 120
_____, Aaron Tat 381
_____, Abdallamey Ran 248
_____, Abel Pik 109
_____, Abraham Clk 305
_____, Abraham Wil 300
_____, Absalom D. New 36
_____, Absalom D. New 52
_____, Alexander Cow 389
_____, Alexandria Fay 181
_____, Alexander Hab 38
_____, Alexander Hal 80
_____, Alexander Jsp 372
_____, Alexander Mwr 162
_____, Alexander Tat 379
_____, Alfred Jks 332
_____, Alfred Wrn 211
_____, Allen Frk 227
_____, Allen Wsh 248
_____, Allen Wsh 260
_____, Ambrose Hab 51
_____, Ambrose Tlf 4
_____, Amos Lee 31
_____, Ana Jks 345
_____, Anderson Har 191
_____, Andrew Cpb 208
_____, Andrew Hry 225

Name		County	Page
Smith,	Andrew L.	New	18
______,	Andrew O.	Tms	16
______,	Ann	Wil	311
______,	Anna	Wks	358
______,	Anthony G.	Crf	406
______,	Archibal	Scr	303
______,	Archabald	Cht	250
______,	Archibald	Fay	181
______,	Archibald	Lwn	80
______,	Archibald	Mon	217
______,	Archibold	Wrn	223
______,	Armstead	Cow	370
______,	Arthur	Bts	162
______,	Arthur	Put	204
______,	Arthur	Rch	286
______,	Arthur	Tlb	326
______,	Arthur	Trp	35
______,	Asa	Jsp	398
______,	Asa	Mor	265
______,	Augustus	Trp	42
______,	Austin	App	10
______,	Banister	Put	175
______,	Barnett	Up	113
______,	Baxter	Gly	264
______,	Bazel	Jsp	372
______,	Benager	Mwr	151
______,	Benajer	Wal	127
______,	Benjamin	App	8
______,	Benja.	Bak	17
______,	Benjamin	Bib	74
______,	Benjamin	Bke	154
______,	Benjamin	Elb	136
______,	Benjamin	Gwn	332
______,	Benjamin	Hst	274
______,	Benjamin	Jns	442
______,	Benjamin	Lau	11
______,	Benjamin	Mad	103
______,	Benjamin	Tlb	343
______,	Benjamin	Trp	53
______,	Benjamin	Wil	318
______,	Benjamin B.	Cpb	202
______,	Benjamin B.	Twg	76
______,	Bennet	Jef	406
______,	Bennet B.	Jef	406
______,	Betsey	Mad	117
______,	Bird	Wal	127
______,	Braxton P.	Fay	204
______,	Brinkly	Ogl	82
______,	Britan	Lee	32
______,	Britan	Wal	153
______,	Brittain	Cow	376
______,	Bryan	Wal	161
______,	Bugis	Hab	38
Smith,	Burrel	DeK	60
______,	Burwell	Put	190
______,	Caleb	Bib	74
______,	Caleb	Bib	74
______,	Carlton	Put	199
______,	Celia	Pik	114
______,	Chs.	Bal	44
______,	Charles	Hab	31
______,	Charles	Hab	31
______,	Charles Sr.	Hal	97
______,	Charles	Hal	129
______,	Charles	Jsp	392
______,	Charles	Mor	244
______,	Charles	Ogl	96
______,	Charles	Rch	285
______,	Charles	Wal	154
______,	Charles	Wil	296
______,	Charles Sr.	Wyn	284
______,	Charles Jr.	Wyn	284
______,	Charles H.	Lau	6
______,	Charles L.	Up	96
______,	Charles W.	Ogl	103
______,	Charles W.	Tlb	335
______,	Mrs. Christiana	Bry	89
______,	Claborn	Jks	329
______,	Coleman	New	11
______,	Collins	Hal	70
______,	Daniel	Bke	137
______,	Daniel	DeK	69
______,	Dan[l].	Jsp	385
______,	Daniel	Rch	286
______,	Daniel Sr.	Hry	200
______,	Daniel Jr.	Hry	201
______,	Daniel L.	Hal	91
______,	Daniel M.	Gwn	317
______,	Daniel N.	Gwn	317
______,	David	Bke	143
______,	David	Bry	88
______,	David	Car	225
______,	David	Clk	301
______,	David	Cpb	199
______,	David	Fay	206
______,	David	Frk	234
______,	David	Hab	59
______,	David	Har	178
______,	David	Mad	113
______,	David	Mor	246
______,	David	New	17
______,	David	Rch	253
______,	David	Wal	155
______,	David	Wal	170
______,	David	Wks	358
______,	David D.	Ear	100

Smith,	David M.	Frk	236	Smith,	Ezekiel B.	Jns	441
______,	David O.	Hst	289	______,	Ezekiel F.	Jns	441
______,	David S.	Wal	152	______,	Falby	Up	119
______,	David T.	Jef	420	______,	Fanny	Jsp	398
______,	Davis	Mon	197	______,	Federick	Bib	57
______,	Dorothy	Bib	66	______,	Ferdinan	Bts	176
______,	Dred	Jef	423	______,	Fielding	Elb	122
______,	Drewry	Fay	186	______,	Flora	Tlf	11
______,	Drewry	New	37	______,	Francis	DeK	27
______,	E. B.	Wsh	251	______,	Franklin	Hab	50
______,	Eady	Wrn	212	______,	Frederick	Ogl	82
______,	Eason	Hst	280	______,	Frederick	Ogl	98
______,	Ebenezer	Bts	165	______,	Frederick	Up	112
______,	Ebeneizer	Cow	383	______,	G. S.	DeK	33
______,	Ebenezer	Gre	299	______,	Gabriel	Hst	270
______,	Ebinezer	Wil	290	______,	Gabriel Sr.	Frk	251
______,	Eda	Jns	438	______,	Gabriel D.	Frk	243
______,	Edmond	Hal	101	______,	Gedion	Hab	30
______,	Edward	Hab	12	______,	General W.	Ware	187
______,	Edward	Hst	291	______,	George	Gre	289
______,	Edward	Ogl	98	______,	George	Jks	316
______,	Elam	Up	96	______,	George	Mor	265
______,	Elbert	Pul	158	______,	George	Mus	282
______,	Elbert	Wil	316	______,	George	Rab	234
______,	Eli	Mor	149	______,	George	Wal	167
______,	Elihu	DeK	62	______,	George	Wsh	274
______,	Elijah	Elb	120	______,	George	Wil	301
______,	Elija	Mtg	232	______,	George A.	Bib	52
______,	Elijah	Bts	173	______,	George G.	Wrn	224
______,	Elijah	Jef	423	______,	George L.	Mor	260
______,	Elisha	Frk	256	______,	George W.	Bts	172
______,	Elisha	Jef	420	______,	Gideon	Han	168
______,	Elisha	Lib	53	______,	Gideon	Wsh	254
______,	Elisha	New	17	______,	Gilbeard	Ran	246
______,	Elisabeth	Cow	380	______,	Green	Hry	207
______,	Elizabeth	Frk	256	______,	Green	Jsp	383
______,	Elizabeth	Hry	248	______,	Griffin	Doo	83
______,	Elizabeth	Hst	279	______,	Griffin	Trp	53
______,	Elizabeth	Lin	63	______,	Gullum M.	Wrn	196
______,	Elizabeth	Mon	200	______,	Guy	Mor	265
______,	Elizabeth	Mtg	236	______,	Guy	Wil	292
______,	Elizabeth	Pik	114	______,	Guy W.	Hry	208
______,	Elizabeth	Scr	309	______,	H. S.	Mus	279
______,	Elizabeth	Tfo	369	______,	Haley	Ogl	71
______,	Elizabeth J.	Wil	314	______,	Hampton	Rab	228
______,	Emanuel	Bts	158	______,	Hardy	Han	167
______,	English	Wsh	272	______,	Hardy	Har	180
______,	Enoch	Hal	95	______,	Hardy	Hry	238
______,	Enos	Trp	32	______,	Hardy	Lau	4
______,	Ezakel	Hal	94	______,	Hardy	Lau	18
______,	Esther	Lau	22	______,	Harrison	Up	97
______,	Ezekiel	Lau	17	______,	Harrison R.	Bib	65
______,	Ezekiel	Rch	288	______,	Herbert	Up	99

Name	County	Page
Smith, Henderson	Hab	36
______, Henderson	Ogl	81
______, Henry	Bib	74
______, Henry	Bke	143
______, Henry	Clk	305
______, Henry	Dec	14
______, Henry	Gwn	378
______, Henry	Jns	467
______, Henry	Lau	19
______, Henry	Mad	116
______, Henry	Mon	203
______, Henry	New	8
______, Henry	Ogl	78
______, Henry	Ogl	79
______, Henry	Put	174
______, Henry	Tat	376
______, Henry	Up	119
______, Henry	Ware	184
______, Henry Sr.	Frk	251
______, Henry A.	Frk	227
______, Henry A.	Tat	380
______, Henry G.	Trp	36
______, Henry G.	Wal	138
______, Henry G.	Wal	150
______, Henry H.	Bak	18
______, Henry T.	Jsp	386
______, Henry W.	Jsp	396
______, Hezekiah	Frk	228
______, Hezekiah	Jsp	397
______, Hill	Ogl	95
______, Hiram	Mar	137
______, Horace	Han	166
______, Howard	DeK	29
______, Hugh	Hst	263
______, Hugh	Rch	265
______, Hugh B.	Har	191
______, Hughs	Doo	83
______, Isaac	Bts	172
______, Isaac	Doo	83
______, Isaac	Fay	184
______, Isaac	Pik	107
______, Isaac	Tlf	2
______, Isaac	Wsh	265
______, Isaah	Fay	192
______, Isaah	Ogl	99
______, Isiah	Ogl	96
______, Isaiah	Hst	269
______, Isaiah	Hst	280
______, Isham	Lau	22
______, Isham Jr.	Lau	14
______, Isham	Wal	165
______, Isom	Hab	38
______, Ivy	Tat	376
Smith, J. D.	Cht	268
______, J. E.	App	6
______, Ja.	Wks	336
______, Jack	Rch	261
______, Jackson	Hry	224
______, Jackson	Ogl	67
______, Jacob	DeK	63
______, Jacob	Mon	205
______, Jacob	Twg	86
______, Jacob	Wrn	214
______, James	Bib	75
______, James	Col	345
______, James	DeK	51
______, James	DeK	60
______, James	DeK	62
______, James	Frk	225
______, James	Frk	226
______, James	Frk	243
______, James	Frk	255
______, James	Gre	294
______, James	Hab	28
______, James	Hal	123
______, James	Han	166
______, James	Jks	323
______, James	Jks	328
______, James	Jks	343
______, James	Jns	466
______, James	Jsp	373
______, James	McI	124
______, James	Lib	52
______, James	Mwr	166
______, James	Mon	174
______, James	Mon	184
______, James	Pul	155
______, James	Rab	230
______, James	Rch	289
______, James	Tat	380
______, James	Tlb	326
______, James	Trp	36
______, James	Up	99
______, James	Up	114
______, James	Wal	126
______, James	Wal	155
______, James	Wyn	284
______, James B.	Gwn	336
______, James B.	Mon	191
______, James B.	Wil	314
______, James C.	Hab	44
______, James F.	Doo	79
______, James J.	Bke	155
______, James L.	Mwr	164
______, James M.	New	28
______, James M.	Wal	161

Name	County	Page
Smith, James M.	Wal	162
______, James O.	Ogl	73
______, James P.	Mor	247
______, James R.	Frk	251
______, James R.	Mon	209
______, James W.	Wrn	199
______, Jane	Wil	318
______, Jane	Wrn	214
______, Jefferson	Wal	169
______, Jeptha B.	Mwr	161
______, Jeremiah	Bib	57
______, Jeremiah	Rch	282
______, Jeremiah	Tlb	346
______, Jeremiah B.	Hst	283
______, Jeremiah C.	Pul	159
______, Jesse	Bal	43
______, Jesse	Bib	62
***______, Jesse (Indian) (alias Jesse Beanstick)	Car	234
______, Jesse	Elb	135
______, Jesse	Frk	226
______, Jesse	Frk	255
______, Jesse	Gwn	379
______, Jesse	Mad	111
______, Jesse	Mon	190
______, Jesse	New	36
______, Jesse	New	52
______, Jesse	Trp	47
______, Jessee	Mon	199
______, Jessey	Hab	8
______, Hesse H.	Mor	262
______, Job	Hst	290
______, Job	Wal	142
______, Job	Wal	149
______, Joel	Wal	163
______, John	App	9
______, John	App	10
______, John	Bak	20
______, John	Bib	52
______, John	Bry	88
______, John	Bke	131
______, John	Cam	189
______, John	Cht	270
______, John	Clk	326
______, John	Clk	327
______, John	Clk	297
______, John	Cow	388
______, John	Cpb	209
______, John	Elb	135
______, John	Em	170
______, John	Fay	201
______, John	Gre	281
______, John	Gwn	319
Smith, John	Gwn	325
______, John	Gwn	342
______, John	Hal	70
______, John	Hal	83
______, John	Hal	106
______, John	Hal	123
______, John	Hal	130
______, John	Hry	224
______, John	Hry	250
______, John	Hst	278
______, John	Jks	338
______, John	Jsp	353
______, John	Lau	13
______, John	Mon	228
______, John	Mor	259
______, John	New	35
______, John	New	50
______, John	Ogl	102
______, John	Pik	113
______, John	Pik	129
______, John	Rab	224
______, John	Scr	312
______, John	Scr	317
______, John	Tlb	322
______, John	Tlb	339
______, John	Tms	29
______, John	Twg	73
______, John	Up	109
______, John	Wal	167
______, John	Wal	169
______, John	Ware	184
______, John	Wsh	240
______, John	Wks	343
______, John	Wrn	224
______, John A.	Hry	212
______, John B.	Cow	377
______, John B.	Hry	241
______, John C.	Bke	133
______, John C.	Col	353
______, John C.	Jsp	395
______, John E.	Han	166
______, John F.	DeK	66
______, John H.	Jks	312
______, John H.	Put	189
______, John H.	Tat	372
______, John H.	Tlb	336
______, John J.	Crf	401
______, John J.	Mus	287
______, John L.	Bib	65
______, John M.	DeK	38
______, John M.	Hst	275
______, John M.	Wks	343
______, John N.	Mor	259

Name	County	Page
Smith, John P.	Bib	57
______, John P.	Mor	242
______, John R.	Bal	32
______, John R. H.	Hry	221
______, John W.	Mwr	166
______, John Y.	Gly	267
______, Johnston T.	Frk	225
______, Jonathan	Cow	388
______, Jonathan	Frk	257
______, Jonathan	Har	188
______, Jonathan	Hst	271
______, Johnathan	Irw	300
______, Jordan	Fay	204
______, Jordan Jr.	Jef	407
______, Jordan	New	10
______, Jordan	Wsh	252
______, Joseph	Clk	306
______, Joseph	Clk	323
______, Joseph	Cow	375
______, Joseph	Frk	356
______, Joseph	Hab	59
______, Joseph	Har	180
______, Joseph	Rch	279
______, Joseph Sr.	Hry	202
______, Joseph	Hry	201
______, Joseph	Hry	224
______, Joseph	Jsp	385
______, Joseph	Lib	52
______, Joseph	Wal	170
______, Joseph	Wrn	224
______, Joseph M.	Cpb	203
______, Joshua	App	11
______, Joshua	Bry	87
______, Joshua	Hal	113
______, Joshua	Rab	235
______, Joshua D.	Hry	224
______, Josiah	Bib	71
______, Judah	New	7
______, Kilpatrick	Ogl	73
______, L. B.	Col	337
______, Larkin	Ogl	72
______, Lawrence	App	6
______, Lawrence	Har	182
______, Lawrencw	Trp	51
______, Lawrence	Up	96
______, Lennear E.	Lau	20
______, Leah	McI	122
______, Lemuel	Mon	176
______, Leonard	Hab	17
______, Leonard	Hab	63
______, Leonard	Up	112
______, Leonard S.	Pul	141
______, Levi	Tlb	335
Smith, Levi	Up	98
______, Levin	Bts	166
______, Levin J or L.	Bal	40
______, Levy E.	Ogl	64
______, Lewis	Hal	118
______, Lewis	Wsh	271
______, Lewis	Wks	336
______, Lindsay	Elb	142
______, Littleton	Scr	307
______, Lofton	Lau	10
______, Lovett	Jns	444
______, Lovett B.	Twg	78
______, Lucinda	Hal	83
______, Luke	Wal	161
______, Luke H.	Ran	245
______, M.	Bal	33
______, Macom	Mad	106
______, Margaret	Cam	184
______, Marget	Car	218
______, Margaret	Hal	100
______, Margarett	Mad	118
______, Margarett	New	18
______, Mark	Frk	255
______, Mark	Ogl	96
______, Marshall	New	26
______, Marth	Hal	39
______, Martha	Trp	32
______, Martha W.	Ogl	90
______, Martin	Wal	158
______, Mary	Bal	37
______, Mary	Bul	100
______, Mary	Hal	89
______, Mary	Jns	438
______, Mary	Lau	14
______, Mary Jane	Bib	62
______, Mat.	Bal	38
______, Mathew	Lau	6
______, Mathew	New	6
______, Matilda	Wsh	247
______, Michael	New	6
______, Michajah	Wsh	241
______, Micool	Dec	3
______, Miles	Ogl	82
______, Miles	Ogl	84
______, Milinton	Bul	93
______, Milton	Hry	206
______, Moriah	Jns	435
______, Morris	Bke	143
______, Moses	Frk	210
______, Moses	Hal	115
______, Moses	New	26
______, Moses	Ogl	84
______, Miss Mourning	Lau	16

Smith, Nancy Car 229
_____, Nancy Jns 431
_____, Nancy New 15
_____, Nancy Wrn 196
_____, Nancy C. Put 216
_____, Nathan Cam 189
_____, Nathan Gre 292
_____, Nathan Lwn 89
_____, Nathan Mon 221
_____, Nathan New 32
_____, Nathan New 32
_____, Nathaniel Elb 135
_____, Nathaniel Fay 188
_____, Nathaniel Hal 93
_____, Nathaniel Ogl 87
_____, Nathaniel Rch 283
_____, Nathaniel H. Ogl 97
_____, Needham Hst 287
_____, Needham Hst 281
_____, Needham Twg 73
_____, Neil Hst 263
_____, Newell L. Mus 289
_____, Nicholas Mor 259
_____, Nimrod Mus 289
_____, Noah Bke 136
_____, Noah Hal 114
_____, Obadiah Pul 138
_____, Oliver Wrn 198
_____, Orange Wal 160
_____, Otis Han 168
_____, P. P. Wsh 255
_____, Parks W. Hry 207
_____, Paris Elb 123
_____, Patch Hal 89
_____, Patrick Gwn 323
_____, Patrick Gwn 331
_____, Patrick Wsh 251
_____, Peter Hry 230
_____, Peterson Ogl 87
_____, Pharaba (W) Mor 246
_____, Polley Wal 170
_____, Polly Hal 100
_____, Polly Twg 81
_____, Presley Mon 217
_____, R. Wks 354
_____, R. L. Mus 284
_____, Rachael DeK 62
_____, Radford Jks 345
_____, Ralph Hab 42
_____, Ralph Up 104
_____, Ransom L. Fay 187
_____, Rebecca Tfo 365
_____, Reddick Har 184

Smith, Rederick Ogl 82
_____, Reuben Gre 299
_____, Reuben Wal 172
_____, Reuben Wil 291
_____, Richard Bke 121
_____, Richard Frk 236
_____, Richard Frk 242
_____, Richard Gre 300
_____, Richard Hst 266
_____, Richard New 46
_____, Richard Wsh 260
_____, Richard L. Up 96
_____, Robert Bib 71
_____, Robert Bts 158
_____, Robert Bts 159
_____, Robert Bts 177
_____, Robert Bts 178
_____, Robert DeK 26
_____, Robert Elb 120
_____, Robert Elb 126
_____, Robert Gwn 323
_____, Robert Han 167
_____, Robert Hal 119
_____, Robert Hst 292
_____, Robert Lau 7
_____, Robert Sr. Ogl 73
_____, Robert Rab 223
_____, Robert Wyn 284
_____, Robert F. Clk 297
_____, Robert K. Ogl 80
_____, Robert S. Ogl 72
_____, Robert W. Jns 436
_____, Rollin Mon 228
_____, Rowlen Jsp 364
_____, Russell W. Hry 206
_____, Salley (W) Mor 239
_____, Sally & G.B. Cow 380
_____, Sally Pul 154
_____, Sam Mad 110
_____, Sampson Crf 393
_____, Samuel Bal 32
_____, Samuel Crf 414
_____, Samuel Em 165
_____, Samuel Frk 227
_____, Samuel Gwn 349
_____, Samuel Gwn 366
_____, Samuel Hal 71
_____, Samuel Hal 94
_____, Samuel Jks 323
_____, Samuel Lee 34
_____, Samuel Sr. Mad 111
_____, Samuel Mwr 164
_____, Samuel Mor 255

Smith, Samuel Rch 270
______, Samuel Wsh 244
______, Samuel Wrn 197
______, Samuel Jr. Wrn 196
______, Samuel Wrn 212
______, Samuel R. Hst 272
______, Samuel T. Wsh 253
______, Sarah DeK 39
______, Sarah Fay 188
______, Sarah Hab 17
______, Sarah Hab 38
______, Sarah Jsp 385
______, Sarah Pik 120
______, Sarah Wsh 258
______, Sarah Ann Hal 82
______, Sarah T. Jef 423
______, Shadrick Tms 28
______, Shederick Ogl 71
______, Sidney Mar 141
______, Silas Jks 331
______, Simeon DeK 48
______, Simeon Up 119
______, Simeon S. Har 188
______, Simon DeK 60
______, Simon B. Jks 343
______, Sion Ogl 67
______, Solomon Bry 87
______, Sperious Cow 370
______, Starling Bts 177
______, Stephen Fay 185
______, Steven Gwn 342
______, Stephen Gwn 360
______, Stephen Gwn 366
______, Stephen Hab 29
______, Stephen Hal 121
______, Stephen Hry 222
______, Stephen Hst 264
______, Stephen Mad 115
______, Stephen Pul 155
______, Stephen Tms 23
______, Stephen C. Mwr 165
______, Sterling G. Bib 71
______, Sterling W. Jns 471
______, Susan Bib 77
______, Susan Bke 150
______, Susan Cht 243
______, Susan Mtg 233
______, Talcot G. Mon 212
______, Thomas Bak 19
______, Thomas Bib 74
______, Thomas Cht 247
______, Thomas Cpb 203
______, Thomas DeK 38
Smith, Thomas DeK 71
______, Thomas Han 169
______, Thomas Har 183
______, Thomas Hry 203
______, Thomas Hst 261
______, Thomas Jef 422
______, Thomas Jsp 387
______, Thomas McI 126
______, Thomas Tms 19
______, Thomas Mor 245
______, Thomas Twg 78
______, Thomas Wal 130
______, Thomas Wal 161
______, Thomas Wsh 260
______, Thomas A. Han 166
______, Thomas D. Gly 267
______, Thomas G. Jns 466
______, Thomas J. Wal 172
______, Thomas J. Wal 172
______, Thomas K. Up 107
______, Thomas M. Ogl 93
______, Thomas Peter Lau 18
______, Thompson Mtg 233
______, Timothy S. Lin 63
______, Turner Rch 275
______, Valentine Elb 132
______, Vincent A. Wrn 199
______, Vines Clk 313
______, W. G. Lee 26
______, Walter Cht 242
______, Watkins Han 168
______, Wells Hry 249
______, Wiley Gwn 353
______, Wiley Twg 79
______, W. Col 354
______, William Bib 71
______, William Bts 178
______, William Cht 249
______, William Col 340
______, William Clk 309
______, William Cow 368
______, William Cow 369
______, William Cow 369
______, William Cow 384
______, William Sr. Crf 412
______, William Crf 411
______, William DeK 28
______, William Doo 82
______, William Em 169
______, William Frk 210
______, William Frk 226
______, William Frk 229
______, William Sr. Frk 243

Smith, William Frk 257
______, William Gre 300
______, William Gwn 326
______, William Gwn 342
______, William Hab 8
______, William Hal 99
______, William Hal 121
______, William Hal 124
______, William Hry 206
______, William Hst 265
______, William Hst 279
______, William Hst 280
______, William Hst 287
______, William Hst 288
______, William Jks 329
______, William Jks 333
______, William Jns 463
______, William Lau 12
______, William Lau 20
______, William Lib 52
______, William Lwn 80
______, William Mad 109
______, William Mor 256
______, William Mwr 161
______, William Ogl 71
______, William Pul 155
______, William Rab 230
______, William Ran 242
______, William Scr 312
______, William Tlf 10
______, William Jr. Tlf 3
______, William Twg 81
______, William Wal 142
______, William Wal 163
______, William Wal 168
______, William Ware 184
______, William Wsh 252
______, William Wks 339
______, William Wks 343
______, William Wrn 195
______, William B. Bts 163
______, William B. Cow 386
______, William B. Em 167
______, William B. Mwr 157
______, William D. Jks 343
______, William E. Frk 227
______, William F. Hry 216
______, William G. Frk 215
______, William G. Jsp 386
______, William H. Bts 173
______, William H. Col 337
______, William H. Hab 30
______, William H. Ogl 97
Smith, William J. Wal 152
______, William R. Pul 154
______, William T. Hst 283
______, William W. Elb 134
______, William W. Hal 82
______, William W. Jsp 357
______, Williamson Bib 52
______, Willis Hal 100
______, Winston A. Mor 241
______, Woody D. Gwn 353
______, Young Jns 437
______, Zachariah Elb 136
______, Zodoc Wil 291
Smyth, Samuel M. Wil 292
SMITHHART/SMITHART
Smithhart, David Bib 68
Smithart, James Hst 294
SMITHSON, Burney Crf 411
SMITHWICK, Edmund Wal 144
______, Reubin Ran 248
______, Robert Jks 313
______, William W. Hab 56
SMOOT, Robert Up 95
______, Vernon Tlb 325
SMYLIE/SMYLEY/SMILIE
Smylie, Archibald Lib 53
______, James Sr. Lib 53
______, James Jr. Lib 52
______, John M. Lib 52
______, Rob Crf 407
Smyley, John G. Pik 116
Smilie, Thomas Scr 313
SMITHY/SMYTHY
Smithy, John Hal 97
______, Mary An Hal 130
Smythy, Isaac Hal 83
SNEED/SNEAD
Sneed, Dudly Lee 29
______, Elijah Hry 248
______, John Jns 475
______, John G. Jns 452
______, Leaston Bke 126
______, Mary Wil 288
______, Meridith Clk 325
______, Sarah Wsh 256
______, William Frk 217
______, William Wsh 252
Snead, Beuchamp Fay 184
______, Tilman Bal 39
SNELL, Amos Hst 278
______, Barnabas Em 168
______, Christopher Em 169
______, John Em 168

Snell, John W.	Bal	29
_____, William	Hst	278
SNELLGROVE, Edward	Lau	6
_____, Jesse	Ear	92
_____, Mark	Ear	92
_____, Solomon	Lau	4
_____, William	Bib	75
SNELLINGS/SNELLING		
Snellings, Alexander	Mor	264
_____, John	Elb	133
_____, John	Mor	246
_____, Samuel	Elb	150
_____, William B.	Bib	53
Snelling, Richard J.	Ran	243
_____, William	Tlb	335
SNELSON/SNELSSON		
Snelson, John	Mwr	165
_____, Nathaniel	Wil	323
_____, William	Wil	320
_____, William	Wil	324
Snelsson, Cathrin	Lee	30
_____, John	Lee	30
SNIDER, Anthony	Cht	242
_____, Barnett	Wrn	217
_____, Benjamin	Cht	257
_____, Christian	Hry	204
_____, Elizabeth	Wrn	217
_____, Jacob	Wsh	273
_____, John	Wrn	233
_____, John G.	Eff	106
_____, John G.	Cow	386
_____, Jonathan	Eff	107
_____, T.	Cht	259
SNIPES, Chesley B.	Up	106
_____, John T.	Up	98
_____, Mark A.	Up	99
_____, W. B.	Bal	32
_____, William	Up	108
SNOW, Edmund	Cpb	194
_____, Eli	New	24
_____, Fountain	Cpb	196
_____, George W.	Car	226
_____, Hannah	DeK	59
_____, Harris	Cam	181
_____, Isaac	McI	122
_____, Jeremiah	Cpb	194
_____, Jesse	New	51
_____, John P.	Clk	295
_____, Levi	New	35
_____, M.	Gwn	372
_____, Mark	Gwn	351
_____, Samuel	Clk	303
_____, Sarah	Wks	353
Snow, Thomas	Bib	68
SOASBY, Thomas	Hab	62
_____, William	Hab	25
SOASLON, Sampson	Hab	50
SOBLUS, William	Dec	11
SOCKWELL, James	Up	95
_____, Levin D.	Jns	471
_____, Thomas	Car	227
SOLLEY, Daniel	Mon	190
SOLLS, Isaac	Cht	267
SOLOMON/SOLMON		
Solomon, Abraham	Tlf	4
_____, David	Wsh	239
_____, Grace	Bib	74
_____, Henry	Twg	76
_____, James	Ware	183
_____, John	Tlb	347
_____, Johnathan	Lau	6
_____, Lazarus	Twg	72
_____, William	Twg	60
Solmon, James	Rch	278
SOMERSETT, Mary H.	Bke	132
SONDER, Mrs.	Scr	308
SORRELLS/SORRELS/SORREL/ SORRELL		
Sorrells, Charles	Wal	132
_____, Charles G.	Wal	150
_____, Charles S.	Wal	143
_____, William S.	Wal	155
Sorrels, Richard T.	Mad	101
_____, Richard W.	Mad	99
_____, William	Wal	161
Sorrel, Green	Mwr	163
Sorrell, Thomas	Hst	291
SORROW/SORROWS		
Sorrow, James	Ogl	81
_____, Jesse M.	Mad	99
_____, John	Ogl	81
_____, Mary	Ogl	81
_____, Randolph	Ogl	80
_____, Randolph	Ogl	81
_____, Sally	Mad	100
_____, William	Ogl	63
Sorrows, Elijah	Elb	150
SORTER, John	Hal	82
_____, Johnson	Hal	82
_____, William F.	Hal	82
SOUHALL, William	Twg	63
SOULLARD, Ed^{W}. A.	Wsh	239
SOUTH, Benjamin	Gwn	312
_____, William	Gwn	312
_____, William	Ogl	77
SOUTHERLAND/SOUTHERLIN		

Name	County	Page
SOUTHERLAND/SOUTHERLIN/		
SOTHERLIN/SOTHELAND		
Southerland, Daniel	Hab	14
______, John	Gre	272
Southerlin, William	DeK	47
Sotherlin, John	Hab	54
Sotheland, Danil	Hab	33
SOUTHWELL, Charity	App	7
______, John J.	Eff	105
______, Thomas	Tat	371
______, William	App	7
SOWELL, Ann	Scr	306
______, Ezekiel	Hry	219
______, James	Hry	219
______, James	Mor	251
______, Jesse	Jks	349
______, John	Crf	404
______, John	Hal	89
______, John	Hry	243
______, John	Scr	313
______, Isaac	Hal	89
______, Isaac	Hry	199
SPAIN, Benjamin	Mon	207
______, Elizabeth	Han	168
______, John	Mon	201
______, Matthew	Bke	127
______, William	Pul	138
SPALDING, Albert M.	Elb	154
______, Henry	Col	341
______, Isham	Cam	181
______, Thomas	McI	126
SPANN/SPAN		
Spann, H.	Cht	259
______, J. B.	Cht	259
______, John	Dec	18
______, John	Wsh	270
______, Richard	Ear	97
Span, Laney	Jef	424
SPARKS, Carter W.	Mor	271
______, Citizen	Fay	183
______, David	Cpb	206
______, Elihew	New	8
______, Elijah	Frk	255
______, Henry	Gwn	357
______, Hy. J.	Gwn	332
______, James R.	Hal	73
______, Jeremiah	Mor	271
______, John	Gwn	364
______, John	Har	175
______, John	Mon	196
______, Leonard	New	5
______, Levin	New	5
______, Marboro	Fay	191
Sparks, Marlin P.	Mor	272
______, Matthew	New	5
______, Robert	Put	200
______, Thomas	Frk	252
______, Thomas	Put	193
______, Thomas	Wsh	253
______, Thomas K.	Hab	37
______, Uriah	New	29
______, William C.	Cpb	207
SPARKMAN/SPARKSMAN		
Sparkman, E.	Cht	267
______, William	Fay	188
Sparksman, Jehu	Cam	189
SPARROW, Beggars J.	Pul	144
______, Christian	Pul	143
______, Daniel	Pul	144
______, Henry	Pul	144
______, John	Pul	144
SPEAKS, Hezekiah	New	52
______, Presley	Wrn	198
______, Richard	Bts	164
SPEAR/SPEARS/SPIER/SPIERS/		
SPEIR/SPEERS/SPEIRS/SPERS/		
SPERES		
Spear, Allison	Mon	213
______, David	Mor	247
______, Henry	Bib	74
______, James M.	Jsp	386
______, Jane	Jsp	372
______, Jesse	Jsp	359
______, John	Jsp	386
______, John	Mon	221
______, Joseph	Fay	199
______, Lewis	Jsp	359
______, Thomas M.	Mon	203
______, W. A.	Gwn	336
______, William	New	39
______, William Sr.	New	51
______, William A.	Gwn	365
______, Willis	Jsp	398
Spears, Allen	Tms	17
______, Anna	Cow	380
______, Archibald	Twg	82
______, Fran	Hab	46
______, Frances	Wsh	253
______, John Jr.	Jsp	393
______, John	New	41
______, John	Tat	37
______, Joseph S.E.	Wrn	19
______, Lewis	Wks	34
______, Mercer	Cow	38
______, Polly	Cht	24
______, Thomas	Pul	15

Name	County	Page
Spears, William	Jsp	387
_____, William	Tlb	324
Spier, James	Har	176
_____, James	Jef	407
_____, James	McI	126
_____, Robert	Lau	9
_____, William	Eff	109
Spiers, James	Lau	6
_____, John	Cht	281
_____, Miles	Lau	17
Speir, James	Up	96
_____, James	Wal	143
_____, John P.	Jns	467
Speers, Charlotte	Bke	147
Speirs, A.	Wsh	241
Spers, John	Hab	46
Speres, John	Mtg	231
SPEARMON, Edmond	Cow	377
_____, Gabriel F.	Cow	371
_____, John	Cow	385
_____, Robert	Cow	385
SPEARSE, Nathaniel	Mar	141
SPEED, Gerrel	Elb	136
SPEIGHTS/SPEIGHT/ SPIGHT/SPIGHTS		
Speights, Andrew	Han	168
_____, John	Han	168
Speight, Jonathan	Wsh	263
Spight, Christopher R.	Hst	292
Spights, Levi	Bal	39
SPELL, George	App	12
_____, Howell	Scr	309
_____, Reason	Lau	8
_____, William	Dec	12
SPELLINGS, Thomas	Cow	385
SPENCE, Bluford	Pul	160
_____, David	Gwn	362
_____, George	Mor	257
_____, Greenville	Bke	125
_____, Insel	Scr	302
_____, Isaac	Tms	16
_____, Isaac	Wrn	193
_____, James	DeK	65
_____, James	Doo	78
_____, James	Mor	258
_____, Jane	Ear	98
_____, Jeremiah	Em	165
_____, Jeremiah	Jks	322
_____, John	Gwn	341
_____, John	Har	180
_____, John	Mwr	161
_____, John	Mor	259
_____, John	Ran	249
Spence, Joseph	Bke	124
_____, Joshua	App	6
_____, Leaston	Em	172
_____, Littleton	Em	165
_____, Mary	Bke	127
_____, Nancy	Ear	97
_____, Richard	Hst	284
_____, Samuel	Mwr	166
_____, T.	Wks	354
_____, William	Lee	26
SPENCER, Alexander	Rch	285
_____, Amasn	Hry	222
_____, Benjamin	Gre	277
_____, Caleb	Hab	11
_____, Elizabeth	Hry	214
_____, George	Clk	300
_____, Griffith	Elb	151
_____, Henry A.	Pik	110
_____, James W.	Eff	115
_____, John H.	Gwn	349
_____, Levy	Lee	30
_____, Samuel	Lib	52
_____, William	Har	192
_____, William	Jsp	364
_____, William	Lib	53
_____, Zachariah	Twg	83
SPERGEN, Erasmus R.	Ear	100
SPHERS, John W. L. W.	Dec	4
SPICER, John	Lau	6
_____, John F.	Lau	5
_____, Rowan	Mon	174
SPIKES, Benjamin H.	Jns	458
_____, John	Ware	186
_____, Silas	Gwn	358
_____, Unity	Tlf	3
_____, William	Mtg	233
SPILLER/SPILLARS/SPILLIARD		
Spiller, Emily	Cht	262
Spillars, Cairy	DeK	69
Spilliard, Samuel	Han	167
SPINCKS/SPINKS/SPRINKS		
Spincks, Enoch	Mor	259
_____, Isaac	Jns	428
_____, Rolly	Jns	445
_____, W. C.	Jns	445
Spinks, H. W.	Jns	445
_____, Baker	Wal	148
_____, Polly	New	23
_____, William	New	23
Sprinks, Garrett	New	23
SPINHOLSTER, David	Lib	53
SPINLOCK, Samuel	Ear	94
SPIRES, H. P.	Col	347

Spires, William Jef 412
_____, William Lin 72
_____, William Pul 141
_____, Zachariah Lin 72
SPIVEY/SPIVY/SPYVY/SPIVA
Spivey, B. Col 353
_____, Caleb Put 183
_____, Jacob Col 354
_____, James Col 351
_____, James Hst 275
_____, Jethro B. Lau 18
_____, John Put 183
_____, Jonas B. Em 170
_____, Littleton Hst 288
_____, Mary Jef 409
_____, Sarah Tlb 341
_____, Wiley Col 354
_____, William Mtg 235
_____, William Put 184
_____, William Put 190
_____, William Tlf 5
Spivy, John Wal 170
_____, Moses Jr. Lau 21
_____, Solomon Lau 13
_____, W. L. Wks 339
_____, William Rab 233
Spyvy, Moses Car 228
Spiva, Leson Hab 44
SPOONER, Adam Dec 14
_____, Joseph Scr 302
_____, Zore Scr 302
SPURLIN/SPURLEN/SPERLEN
Spurlin, Andrew Hab 51
_____, Hugh Hab 51
_____, James Pik 110
_____, John Hst 293
_____, William Hst 290
_____, William Pik 110
Spurlen, James M. Jsp 368
Sperlen, John Jsp 361
SPURLOCK/SPULLOCK
Spurlock, James Jks 332
_____, James Jr. Jks 332
_____, James Mon 194
_____, John Mad 117
_____, Samuel Jef 413
Spullock, Solomon Twg 71
SPURS, William Frk 212
SPRABERRY, Benjamin DeK 57
_____, Hiram DeK 59
_____, James DeK 33
_____, John DeK 57
_____, Uriah DeK 31
Spraberry, Wiley Put 205
SPRADLEY/SPRADLY
Spradley, Manning Jef 420
_____, William Ware 188
Spradly, Sylvia Lau 22
SPRADLING/SPRATLIN/SPRATLING/
SPRADLIN/SPRATTIN
Spradling, David Fay 202
_____, Irwin Fay 183
_____, James Fay 207
_____, Joshua Fay 200
_____, Oliver Fay 205
Spratlin, Absolom Cow 386
_____, David Cow 386
_____, Henry Wil 307
_____, John Mon 201
Spratling, James Ogl 69
_____, Johnston Ogl 68
Spradlin, John Gwn 363
_____, William Pik 115
Sprattin, William Cow 374
SPRAGGINS, Orsamus Cow 373
_____, Thomas Har 179
_____, William Cow 373
SPRIG/SPRIGGS
Sprig, Gilead Frk 227
Spriggs, Shelomi Hab 37
SPRINE, Sarah Hal 69
SPRING/SPRINGS
Spring, George Tlf 7
_____, James Bib 74
Springs, Bartholemew Bke 138
SPRINGER/SPRINGOR
Springer, Ann Wil 287
_____, Thomas Wrn 218
_____, William G. Car 214
Springor, Jonathan Gwn 341
SPRINGFIELD, Elizabeth Bts 177
_____, Moses Bts 177
SPRUCE, Lucinda Put 172
_____, Thomas N. Trp 49
_____, William Hal 75
SPRUEL/SPROUELL/SPRUELL
Spruel, Stephen DeK 42
_____, William DeK 44
Sprouell, Gabriel Fay 189
Spruell, William Fay 207
SQUIRES, David B. Mus 280
_____, Harvey H. Jns 466
_____, James Crf 399
_____, Wiley Tlb 343
_____, Willis Har 176
STACY, Ezra Lib 53

Stacy, James, dec'd.Est. Lib 53
_____, John W. Lib 53
STAFFORD, Abel Hry 213
_____, Andleton Up 98
_____, E. B. Lib 53
_____, Ezekiel Tat 374
_____, Jane Wyn 281
_____, Joshua Tat 380
_____, Joshua Twg 62
_____, Robert Cam 181
_____, Sarah Ear 98
_____, William Ear 92
_____, William Lee 29
STAGLE, Jacob Jsp 385
STAGNEY, Rachel Jsp 378
STAHM, Jesse Wal 136
STALEY, Hukel Wks 346
STALLINGS/STALINGS/
STALLIONS/STALEN
Stallings, Elisha H. New 7
_____, Isaac N. New 6
_____, J. W. Jsp 362
_____, James Jns 435
_____, James New 30
_____, James G. Rch 288
_____, Jessee Mon 189
_____, John Bke 143
_____, Josiah New 51
*_____, Miss (slave) Rch 276
_____, Moses Ogl 78
_____, Rallisiah Mor 258
_____, Robert Rch 253
_____, Sampson Bib 71
_____, Sarah Mon 226
_____, Saunders Mus 285
_____, Simeon W. Jns 431
_____, William Mon 193
_____, William Mon 222
_____, William Mor 261
Stalings, Joseph Col 359
_____, Lovet Col 359
_____, Wilson Gre 286
Stallions, Lydia Gre 294
_____, Moses Gre 294
_____, William Gre 290
Stalen, B. App 11
STALLWORTH/STALLSWORTH
Stallworth, Edmund Hry 244
Stallsworth, Joseph Jns 452
STALNAKER, Benjamin Hry 199
STAMPER, Irby Pik 123
_____, M. W. Up 103
_____, Spencer Pik 122
STAMPS, Britton Ogl 75
_____, G. W. Gwn 363
_____, James Cow 375
_____, John Cow 373
_____, Moses Cow 381
_____, Moses W. Cow 378
_____, Thomas Hry 244
_____, Thomas J. Ogl 67
STANALAND/STANERLAND/
STANDLAND
Stanaland, Borz. Tms 25
Stanerland, Richard T. Tms 28
Standland, Dempsy Bul 92
STANCELL/STANSEL/STANCEL/
STANILL
Stancell, Bennett K. New 22
_____, Jesse New 25
_____, Joel New 51
_____, John W. New 25
Stansel, Ellinor DeK 55
_____, Richard B. Tms 21
_____, William R. Wsh 245
Stancel, Elijah DeK 71
_____, Irvin DeK 73
_____, John Hab 9
Stanill, David Hab 6
STANDARD, Benjamin Mon 228
_____, Daniel Wil 290
_____, John Mon 227
_____, Kimbro Wil 299
STANDIFER/STANDIVER
Standifer, Archibald Jsp 353
_____, Joshua Mad 99
Standiver, Young T. DeK 31
STANDRIDGE, Samuel Hab 32
STANESTREET, Richard Wrn 198
STANFORD/STANDFORD
Stanford, Daniel Col 345
_____, David Lwn 88
_____, David Sr. Col 342
_____, David Jr. Col 343
_____, Elizabeth Wsh 258
_____, Isaac Crf 410
_____, James Bal 37
_____, Jeptha M. Put 209
_____, Johnathan Doo 83
_____, Joseph Put 208
_____, Joshua Col 357
_____, Levi Crf 400
_____, Levi M. Mwr 150
_____, Levin Put 207
_____, Nathaniel D. Put 206
_____, Nehemiah Put 205

Name	County	Page
Stanford, Samuel	Bib	57
______, Thomas	Han	167
______, Thomas	New	43
______, Thomas F.	Frk	257
______, Tilmon	Ogl	67
______, William	Bul	92
______, William	New	43
______, William	New	51
______, William W.	Twg	65
Standford, Isaiah	Wrn	211
______, Jesse	Wrn	211
______, John R.	Wrn	211
______, Jonathan	Wrn	212
______, Robert	Wrn	212
______, Rubin	Wrn	212
______, William	Wrn	212
______, William D.	Wrn	212
STANFIELD/STANDFIELD		
Stanfield, Elizabeth	Hry	203
______, James	New	15
______, John	Mtg	234
______, Joseph	Hry	203
______, Littleton	Scr	306
______, Richard	New	5
______, Robert	Cpb	199
______, William B.	Hry	206
Standfield, Jehu	Tat	371
STANLEY/STANLY/		
STANDLEY/STANDLY		
Stanley, Abner	Mon	186
______, Ezekiel	Gre	296
______, Ezekiel	Mon	209
______, Ezekiel	New	50
______, Felix	Mwr	161
______, Leary	Hst	274
______, Lewis	Clk	309
______, Major	Hst	294
______, Martha	Gre	288
______, Samuel	Han	169
______, Sarah	Mar	141
______, Spirus	Han	167
______, Thomas	Clk	326
______, Wiley	Mus	282
______, William A.	Mwr	161
Stanly, Evret	Mwr	169
______, Hardy B.	Lau	19
______, Ira	Lau	12
______, James	Jks	347
______, James Rowel	Lau	14
______, James Sr.	Lau	20
______, James Jr.	Lau	14
______, Jesse	Hry	208
______, John	Hab	63
Stanly, John	Wks	348
______, William	Gwn	376
Standley, Hannah	Tat	380
______, Rebecca	Tat	380
Standly, Jacob	Fay	191
______, James	Tat	376
STANTON, Batt. S.	New	30
______, John J.	New	20
______, John J.	New	39
______, Samuel	Bib	52
______, William	Han	166
______, William	Jns	473
STAPLES, John	Hst	266
STANT, Simeon	Mon	209
STAPLER/STAPLEAR		
Stapler, Amos	Mad	107
______, Elizabeth	Col	353
Staplear, William	Col	352
STAPLES, Charles	New	22
______, Jethro	Lau	21
______, Robert	Jks	346
______, Ruth	Jks	344
______, Thomas	Elb	131
______, Thomas Sr.	Jks	333
______, Thomas L.	Jks	320
______, William N.	Jks	320
STAPLETON, A.	Wks	348
______, George Sr.	Jef	419
______, George	Jef	417
______, James	Jef	418
______, John D.	Jef	417
______, Thomas	Jef	418
______, William	Jef	418
STAPP, John	Mor	257
______, Solomon	Mor	257
______, Thomas	Mor	257
STARE, Elijah	Hab	26
STARK/STARKE/STARKES		
Stark, Abner	Hab	58
______, B.	Col	364
______, E. A.	Cht	257
______, Robert	Col	363
______, Samuel C.	Elb	154
Starke, John W.	Mor	246
______, William E.	Mor	245
Starkes, Benton	Clk	296
______, Thomas M.	Wal	131
STARKEY, Jesse	Ogl	90
STARLING, F. A.	Cam	186
______, Levi	Lwn	89
______, Richard	Cam	181
______, William	App	5
______, William	Lwn	89

STARNS/STARNES/
Starns, Fred Hab 23
_____, Green Hal 91
_____, John Hal 99
_____, Joseph Hal 122
_____, Sleghter Hal 86
_____, William Hal 99
Starnes, Aaron DeK 28
_____, Joel DeK 58
_____, Titus DeK 56
STARR/STAR
Starr, Benjamin Wil 301
_____, Charles H. Bry 84
_____, Fenton Hry 202
_____, Henry Hry 205
_____, Henry Rch 289
_____, John Rch 255
_____, John W. Hry 204
_____, Polley (W) Mor 239
_____, Samuel New 33
_____, Silas New 33
_____, William Cht 262
Star, James R. Trp 46
STARRET/STARRETT/STARRITT
Starret, James Hab 50
Starrett, William Cam 181
Starritt, Benjamin Frk 217
STATE, Wilkins Hab 54
STATHAM/STATON/STATHAN/
STATUM/STATEHAM
Statham, Augustus D. Wil 299
_____, Charles Wil 298
_____, James Irw 300
_____, Jane Lin 64
_____, John Wks 339
_____, Memory W. Gre 282
_____, Nathel Irw 301
_____, Pleasant Irw 300
_____, Thompson N. Irw 301
_____, William Hst 295
Staton, Arthur Gre 286
_____, Joseph Gre 276
Stathan, Barnet Lin 62
Statum, Martin New 38
Stateham, Anderson Clk 309
STAVELEY, Elizabeth Bke 137
STAY, William Cpb 201
STCHERDY(?), Mary Rch 274
STEAD, Philip Lin 75
STEADHAM, James Wrn 199
_____, Zachariah Cow 380
*STEAM BOAT CO. (slaves) Rch 261
STEARNE, Daniel Hry 238
STEED, Green Jks 348
_____, Lennard Col 352
_____, Thomas W. M. Tlb 338
_____, William P. Col 356
STEEDLY, William Elb 120
STEEL/STEELE/STEAL
Steel, Adam Gwn 356
_____, Alvah Cam 183
_____, Isam DeK 62
_____, John Gwn 331
_____, John Jns 433
_____, John Mon 221
_____, John Wal 124
_____, Joseph Wal 144
_____, Patsey Hry 251
_____, Richard Rab 229
_____, Robert Elb 134
Steele, James Jsp 396
_____, James C. Hry 208
Steal, Thomas Fay 192
STEEN, George Gwn 309
STEGALL/STEGAL/STEIGALL
Stegall, Ivy F. Hry 207
_____, Samuel Hry 232
_____, Spencer Gwn 334
Stegal, Benjamin Pul 162
Steigall, Phara Cow 376
STEGAR/STEGER
Stegar, Robert M. Hry 210
Steger, Alfred M. Hry 223
STELL, Benjamin Wal 125
_____, Dennis Gwn 340
_____, George Gwn 377
_____, Grizell Gwn 340
_____, John Gwn 340
_____, John D. Fay 181
_____, Robert Gwn 340
_____, Robert M. Fay 197
_____, William Gwn 314
_____, William Gwn 341
_____, William M. Wal 153
STEMBRIDGE/STEMRIDGE
Stembridge, Henry R. Han 166
_____, William Han 167
Stemridge, Andinor Crf 404
_____, John Crf 404
STEP/STEPP
Step, Jesse Hab 36
_____, Martha Gre 273
_____, William Hab 32
Stepp, John Gwn 344
STEPHENS/STEPHEN/STEPENS/
STEPHONS

Name	County	Page
Stephens, Abigal	Doo	86
______, Abner	Wal	128
______, Absalom	Hab	16
______, Alexander	Ogl	71
______, Allen R.	Bib	65
______, Balaam	Jns	436
______, Benjamin	Trp	48
______, Cader	McI	132
______, Caleb	Jef	421
______, Charles	Cht	250
______, Charles	Jef	402
______, David	Clk	293
______, David	Doo	88
______, David	Mor	238
______, David	New	27
______, Eady	Jef	424
______, Ebenezer	Lau	11
______, Edward	Put	212
______, Elijah	Crf	393
______, Elijah	Frk	253
______, Elisabeth	Ogl	63
______, Enoch	Han	167
______, Fielding	Bke	120
______, Green	Up	105
______, Hampton	Har	187
______, Harris	Clk	293
______, Henry H.	Elb	146
______, Hesekiah	Hab	14
______, Hiram	Hab	16
______, Holman	Twg	67
______, Inmon	Up	115
______, Isaac	Bal	29
______, Isaac	Bke	139
______, Isaac	Irw	298
______, Isaac	Wks	331
______, Isham	Tat	372
______, Jacob	Han	167
______, Jacob	Ran	246
______, James	Bib	52
______, James	Crf	415
______, James	Hal	109
______, James	Put	172
______, James	Wal	139
______, Jese	Hab	61
______, Jesse	Up	106
______, Joel	Hab	27
______, John	Bal	30
______, John	Bal	34
______, John	Bts	163
______, John	Gwn	323
______, John	Scr	306
______, John	Gre	301
______, John	Hab	27
Stephens, John	Hab	42
______, John	Han	168
______, John	Jsp	358
______, John	Jsp	390
______, John	Pik	131
______, John	Up	109
______, John	Wks	336
______, John	Wks	350
______, John D.	Put	172
______, John M.	Ogl	91
______, John W.	Crf	396
______, Jonas Sr.	Jef	402
______, Jonas Jr.	Jef	402
______, Joseph	Lin	62
______, Joseph	Ogl	80
______, Joshua	Clk	233
______, Joshua	Gwn	367
______, Joshua	Hry	240
______, Joshua	Lwn	87
______, Kimbol	Jks	317
______, Larkin	Hab	26
______, Lemuel	Hal	111
______, Levi	Cht	278
______, Lydia	Tat	378
______, Marshall	Jsp	364
______, Mary	Bib	62
______, Mary	Up	117
______, Mathew	Hab	40
______, Miles	Jsp	388
______, Miner M.	Ogl	63
______, Morriss	Cow	369
______, Noah	Hab	50
______, Orrin	Hst	280
______, Rebecca	Jef	421
______, Rebecca	Wal	174
______, Reddick	Gre	295
______, Reubin	Cow	369
______, Richard	Twg	82
______, Robert	Cht	278
______, Rob.	Lee	32
______, Robert F.	Cam	187
______, Ross	Wrn	202
______, Samuel	Hab	61
______, Samuel	Wal	132
______, Silas	Tlb	348
______, Sol.	Up	97
______, Stephen	Trp	48
______, Theophilus	Put	176
______, Thomas	Hal	99
______, Thomas	Ogl	63
______, Thomas	Wal	126
______, Thomas J.	Hry	228
______, Thomas P.	Ogl	62

Stephens, Whitfield Jef 403
_____, Wilkins Put 206
_____, William Cht 268
_____, William Put 200
_____, William Tat 371
_____, William Twg 69
_____, William Up 103
_____, William B. Jns 467
_____, William J. Bts 163
_____, William M. Hry 213
_____, Willis App 9
Stephen, Benjamin Lau 8
_____, Heard D. Up 108
_____, Henry Lwn 87
Stephens, Richard Wal 174
Stephons, Robert Jef 407
STEPHENSON/STEPHERSON
Stephenson, Alexander DeK 57
_____, Arthur Jns 458
_____, Council Lau 14
_____, Hardy Ran 248
_____, Henry Twg 88
_____, John Car 216
_____, John DeK 55
_____, Nancy Jns 458
_____, Thomas Up 104
Stepherson, Silas Ran 241
STEPTOE, John Bke 137
_____, William Pul 150
STERK, John Cht 251
STERLING, Abram Ware 185
_____, Caleb Bak 18
_____, David H. Wsh 269
_____, Elizabeth Rch 263
_____, James Mad 114
_____, John Wsh 251
_____, John G. Wsh 268
_____, Wiley J. Trp 40
_____, William Ware 184
_____, Wright Bal 30
STERRIN, Jesse Cow 389
STETSON, David Lib 53
STEVENS/STEVANS
Stevens, A. W. Bry 84
_____, Abigale Em 167
_____, Abram Wks 339
_____, Caleb N. Mad 111
_____, Edmund Mon 210
_____, Ezekiel Mad 98
_____, Harley Mad 113
_____, James Clk 292
_____, James Lib 52
_____, James Ogl 74
Stevens, James Pul 160
_____, James B. Pul 158
_____, John Lib 54
_____, John Mad 102
_____, John Wks 347
_____, John A. Gwn 344
_____, John C. Cow 382
_____, Jones Wks 344
_____, Joseph Mon 175
_____, Joshua Mad 113
_____, Josiah Wks 345
_____, Kornegay Pul 141
_____, Levi Ear 92
_____, M. Gwn 309
_____, Martha Mad 107
_____, Murther Tfo 354
_____, Oliver Lib 54
_____, Samuel Lib 54
_____, Stephen B. Mad 106
_____, Stephen W. Mad 118
_____, Steven Tfo 354
_____, Susannah Mad 118
_____, Thomas DeK 44
_____, Thomas Hry 227
_____, Thomas B. Pul 158
_____, William Em 164
Stevans, Samuel Wal 163
STEVENSON/STEVSON
Stevenson, Henry J. Gwn 311
_____, John Jef 410
_____, John Twg 63
_____, Samuel Hry 237
_____, Thomas Clk 314
_____, William Clk 318
Stevson, John New 22
STEWARD, Absalom DeK 60
_____, Cornelius Cpb 200
_____, Daniel Cpb 199
_____, David Twg 71
_____, Desin Twg 71
_____, Eli Jef 416
_____, Henry Put 179
_____, James Cpb 208
_____, James Jef 416
_____, James W. Cam 190
_____, John Lwn 82
_____, John New 45
_____, Joseph DeK 71
_____, Lorenzo Han 167
_____, Louis Jef 416
_____, Matthew New 19
_____, Robert DeK 72
_____, Sarah Cam 183

Name	County	Page
Steward, Selvenus	Put	197
______, Sylvanus	Jsp	382
______, William	Cpb	200
STEWART/STEWARTT		
Stewart, Alexander	Fay	186
______, Alexander	Lib	52
______, Alexander Sr.	Mor	266
______, Alexander Jr.	Mor	267
______, Alexander S.	Mor	266
______, Alfred	Clk	312
______, Andrew	Han	167
______, Archibald	Lau	14
______, Archibald	Mor	266
______, Benjamin	Mon	193
______, Charles	Mon	198
______, Charles	Mon	217
______, Charles	Scr	311
______, Charles	Up	115
______, D. M.	Gly	269
______, David	Bke	144
______, David	Scr	306
______, David	Up	114
______, Drusilla	Ran	242
______, Dugal	Lau	19
______, Edmond	Up	114
______, Eli	Jns	462
______, Floyd	Ogl	92
______, Frances	Pul	154
______, George	Mus	282
______, Gordon	Tlf	3
______, Hannah	Rch	253
______, Hiram	Wal	144
______, Hugh B.	Jsp	391
______, Ishmael	Ran	242
______, James	Fay	191
______, James	Lau	19
______, James	Hal	133
______, James	Mwr	151
______, James	Mon	181
______, James	Mon	197
______, James	Mon	203
______, James	New	23
______, James	Trp	38
______, James	Trp	49
______, James	Wrn	192
______, James G.	Fay	181
______, James	Gwn	359
______, Jerusha	Up	120
______, John	Doo	85
______, John	Em	175
______, John	Gwn	317
______, John	Mon	184
______, John	New	23
Stewart, John	Ogl	88
______, John	Pik	108
______, John	Pik	111
______, John	Pik	128
______, John	Pul	162
______, John	Tlb	337
______, John	Wal	162
______, John F.	Pik	131
______, John H.	Mon	201
______, John M.	Gwn	327
______, John S.	Pik	131
______, Joseph	Mor	266
______, Joseph	Tlb	324
______, Joseph B.	Mor	265
______, Josiah	Car	227
______, Lanier	Hst	276
______, Levy	Clk	301
______, Licinda	Cht	262
______, M. W.	Cht	243
______, Mary	New	39
______, Mary	Wsh	276
______, Milley	Bke	145
______, Morning	Ogl	90
______, Nancy	Mon	185
______, Nathaniel	Wsh	265
______, Peter	Bib	65
______, Randol	Bib	74
______, Riley	Ran	250
______, Robert	Car	221
______, Robert	Clk	308
______, S.	Gwn	373
______, Sally	Gwn	371
______, Samuel	New	23
______, Thomas	Jns	462
______, Thomas	Mon	175
______, Thomas	Mon	209
______, Thomas	Mor	266
______, Thomas	Pik	112
______, Thomas	Pik	131
______, Thomas	Rch	281
______, Thomas W.	Jns	455
______, Wainright L.	Tlb	322
______, Walter	Bts	168
______, William	Car	226
______, William	Fay	185
______, William	McI	132
______, William	Mon	215
______, William	Mor	267
______, William	New	19
______, William	Trp	38
______, William	Trp	48
______, William	Wal	170
______, William B.	Mon	218

Name	County	Page
Stewart, William C.	Cow	387
_____, William D.	Mon	196
_____, Winey	New	53
Stewartt, Margaret H.	Lib	52
STIBBENS, Catharine	Cht	257
STIDUM, John	New	22
STILES, B. E.	Cht	264
_____, Claeborn M.	Gwn	357
_____, Clarissa	Twg	80
_____, Edward	Bry	84
_____, John C.	McI	126
_____, Joseph	Cht	270
** _____, Joseph's slaves	Cht	277
_____, Joseph G.	Jns	463
_____, R.	Cht	252
** _____, Richard's slaves	Cht	277
_____, Sally	Jks	334
_____, Samuel	Bry	85
STILL, Thomas J.	Trp	45
STILMAN, Samuel	Clk	307
STILWELL/STILLWELL		
Stilwell, Allen	Tlb	343
_____, Green	Tlb	336
_____, Jane	Cht	249
_____, John	Mon	219
_____, Reuben	Trp	42
_____, Shadrack	Tlb	343
Stillwell, Jacob	Trp	38
_____, Jacob	Trp	42
STINCHCOMB, Absalom	Elb	137
_____, Levi	Elb	139
_____, Phillip	Clk	308
STINCHWOOD, Nathaniel	Fay	189
STINSON, Andy	Mwr	166
_____, George	Mon	218
_____, Isaac	Wks	334
_____, James W.	Up	97
_____, John	Hal	79
_____, John	Mon	176
_____, John	Tlb	337
_____, Joseph	Tlb	337
_____, Michael	Gwn	356
_____, Michael	Put	180
_____, Phoebe	Wil	290
_____, Thomas	Mon	194
_____, William	Bal	28
_____, William	DeK	51
_____, William	Fay	197
STITH, Dan[l]. of Col.	Wrn	216
_____, John	Wrn	205
STOCKDALE, Nancy	Bke	137
STOCKS, John	New	26
_____, Redding	Mor	247
Stocks, Susanna	Fay	202
_____, Thomas	Gre	282
_____, William	Mor	247
STOCKTON, Benjamin	Jks	337
_____, R. F.	Gly	264
STODGEHILL, Durret	Elb	123
STOE, Hudson	Frk	256
_____, Warren Sr.	Frk	223
_____, Warren	Frk	227
STOGDEN, J. B.	Rch	265
STONE, Aaron	Rab	227
_____, Abram	Han	167
_____, Daniel	DeK	28
_____, Edward	Frk	225
_____, Elizabeth	Hry	232
_____, Erastus	Crf	395
_____, F. M.	Cht	245
_____, Hardy	Wrn	233
_____, Henry	Bry	88
_____, Hillery	Frk	251
_____, James	Frk	233
_____, James	Jef	413
_____, James	Wal	164
_____, James O.	Put	200
_____, Jeremiah	Wal	152
_____, Jeremiah	Wal	164
_____, John	Col	358
_____, John	Jsp	396
_____, John R.	Ware	184
_____, Jonathan	Gwn	312
_____, Joseph Sr.	DeK	38
_____, Lemuel R.	Hab	32
_____, Leonard	Irw	298
_____, Michael	Put	202
_____, Milly	Clk	292
_____, Nancy	Wil	290
_____, Nancy H.	Put	202
_____, Neill	Car	214
_____, Rene	Wal	129
_____, Rolly	Cpb	201
_____, Thomas	Bts	165
_____, Thomas	Rab	227
_____, Thomas M.	Lib	53
_____, W. B.	Jsp	367
_____, W. W.	Col	359
_____, Walter	Tlb	330
_____, William	Frk	252
_____, William Sr.	Put	201
_____, William	Put	199
_____, William	Wsh	261
_____, William	Wil	289
_____, William	Wrn	199
STONECYPHER, Benjamin	Frk	226

Stonecypher, John Frk 252
_____, Jos. Rab 222
STONEHAM, Jane Jks 345
STONER, John Hab 26
STOKELEY, William Lwn 83
STOKER, Arnold Har 190
STOKES/STOKS
Stokes, Archibald Elb 154
_____, Armistead T. Lin 65
_____, Daniel Wil 303
_____, Fedrick R. Pik 126
_____, Gillum Cpb 210
_____, Henry Clk 303
_____, Ignatius Jsp 380
_____, James L. Trp 35
_____, Jeremiah W. Jns 475
_____, Joel Wsh 273
_____, John Up 104
_____, John Wal 131
_____, Joseph T. Clk 322
_____, Josiah Lau 4
_____, Levi Crf 410
_____, Mark Bke 130
_____, Mumford Cow 392
_____, Nancy H. W. Lin 63
_____, Polly Jsp 362
_____, Rebecca Tfo 366
_____, Redding Hst 284
_____, Rev. Dr. Rch 276
_____, Richard Lin 58
_____, Sarah Frk 252
_____, Sarah Wil 303
_____, Silas A. Bib 71
_____, Silvester Cht 280
_____, Susannah Wal 159
_____, Thomas M. Twg 70
_____, Warren Doo 80
_____, William Cpb 205
_____, William Trp 35
_____, William Wsh 246
_____, William C. Lin 65
_____, William S. Mor 244
_____, William W. Lin 63
_____, Young Mor 254
_____, Young Wks 351
Stoks, Samuel D. Twg 63
STORMANT, Henry Hry 240
STORY/STOREY
Story, Abigail Rch 271
_____, Anthony Cow 375
_____, Benjamin Mon 184
_____, Crista A. Jks 312
_____, David W. Pik 115
Story, Edward Jks 318
_____, Elias Fay 206
_____, Henry W. Cht 249
_____, James Har 184
_____, James Har 189
_____, James Pik 115
_____, James Tlb 329
_____, Jesse Wrn 211
_____, John Hst 269
_____, John Jsp 397
_____, John K. Jks 318
_____, John S. Cow 367
_____, Joseph Pik 114
_____, Mitchell Mon 208
_____, Samuel Doo 88
_____, Samuel Wrn 221
_____, Thomas Hry 235
_____, William Pik 113
_____, William F. Cow 370
_____, William M. Cow 375
Storey, Richard Irw 299
_____, Samuel Irw 299
STOTESBURY, John Cam 183
STOUBL, John Dec 17
STOUTAMIRE, Jane Gre 293
STOVALL, B. Crf 403
_____, David Frk 247
_____, Ferdinand Frk 241
_____, George Bib 65
_____, George Frk 234
_____, George H. Frk 213
_____, James Frk 233
_____, Jane Lin 60
_____, John Frk 212
_____, John Jks 312
_____, John M. Frk 232
_____, Jos. Bal 35
_____, Josiah Frk 210
_____, L. B. Gre 288
_____, Mary Gre 288
_____, P. Rch 274
_____, P. W. Gre 296
_____, Pleasant Rch 267
_____, Samuel Mor 262
_____, Stephen Lin 69
_____, Stephen Mor 264
_____, William Hry 231
STOVER, Jacob Hab 40
_____, Jeremiah Hab 52
_____, John H. Hab 65
_____, Joseph Hab 41
STOWERS, Benjamin New 22
STRAHAN/STRATHERN/

STRAYHAN/STRAWHORN
Strahan, Rachel Scr 300
_____, Samuel Bts 164
Strathern, John Gwn 324
Stayham, Niell Mwr 154
Strayhan, William Mwr 151
Strawhorn, Moses Gwn 339
STRAIN, James Hab 21
_____, Sarah Gre 286
STRANGE, Benjamin Hst 278
_____, Edmond DeK 67
_____, Gideon Wsh 245
_____, James Frk 210
_____, John Doo 88
_____, John Frk 222
_____, Seth Frk 244
_____, Seth Frk 250
_____, William Frk 223
STRATTON, Andrew Jsp 352
_____, Asa E. Jsp 353
_____, James Bts 173
STRAWBRIDGE, Elisha Jks 349
_____, John Bib 77
STRAWN, Absalom Fay 188
_____, Amos Elb 156
_____, David New 24
_____, Jackson New 24
_____, James Cpb 208
_____, James New 25
_____, Littleton New 25
STRAWTHER/STRAWDER
Strawther, Martin New 44
_____, Susannah Lib 53
Strawder, Richard Han 167
STREET, George McI 122
_____, George S. Mor 264
_____, Samuel Jks 336
_____, Thomas Jef 410
STREETMAN/STREATMAN
Streetman, Isaac S. Twg 69
_____, Jane Twg 76
_____, Jehu B. Mad 112
_____, John Mad 114
_____, John W. Jks 345
_____, Martin Mad 105
_____, Pearce Jks 336
_____, Samuel Twg 65
_____, Sarah Jef 422
_____, Walter Jks 326
Streatman, Amos L. Pik 106
STREETOR, Willey Trp 43
STREIGLE, Nicholas Scr 310
STRENGTH, Nancy Jsp 358
STRIBBLING/STRIBLING
Stribbling, Francis Wil 318
_____, Thomas Wil 318
Stribling, Robert Hal 71
STRICH, Richard App 9
STRICKLAND/STRICKLIN/
STRICKLAN/STRICKLING/
STRICLIN
Strickland, Aaron Tat 378
_____, Aaron Wyn 285
_____, Aaron B. Tat 371
_____, Abner Elb 125
_____, Abraham Lib 53
_____, Archibald Lwn 79
_____, Barnabas Hry 218
_____, Bedford HRy 215
_____, Bennett Jks 344
_____, Canery Jsp 390
_____, Carey Up 115
_____, Corlor Jks 343
_____, Cynthia Hry 218
_____, Drury Hry 230
_____, E. B. Jsp 384
_____, Edmond Jks 344
_____, Eli Hry 215
_____, Elisha Mwr 150
_____, Ephraim Hry 201
_____, Ephraim Mad 100
_____, Ezekiel New 20
_____, Ezekiel Put 201
_____, Gabriel Tat 371
_____, Gadi Tat 371
_____, Isaac Mad 107
_____, Hardy Jks 329
_____, Hardy Sr. Mad 112
_____, Hardy Jr. Mad 110
_____, Henry Eff 109
_____, Henry Mon 186
_____, Henry Tat 372
_____, Horatio G. Trp 48
_____, Irvin Cpb 202
_____, Isaac Hry 233
_____, Isaac Jsp 390
_____, Jacob Frk 221
_____, Jacob Mad 113
_____, Jacob H. Tat 379
_____, James App 5
_____, James Pul 151
_____, James Wyn 284
_____, Jeptha Han 168
_____, Jesse Hry 218
_____, Joel Wyn 284
_____, John App 9

Name	County	Page
Strickland, John	Lau	16
_____, John	Mar	141
_____, Joseph	Elb	125
_____, Josiah	Lau	23
_____, Kinchen	Mad	107
_____, Kinsbird	Pul	161
_____, Larkin	Trp	49
_____, Lazarus	Cpb	207
_____, Lewis	Tat	372
_____, Mark	Pul	139
_____, Mary Ann	Up	117
_____, Miller	Mad	106
_____, Niel	Dec	14
_____, Noah	Jks	345
_____, Oliver	Jks	329
_____, Peter	Bry	86
_____, Peter H.	Jks	344
_____, Reubin	Dec	14
_____, Richard	Jks	344
_____, Samuel	Mad	110
_____, Silas	Tlb	327
_____, Simon	Cpb	200
_____, Simpson	Lwn	79
_____, Solomon	Hry	201
_____, Solomon	Mad	107
_____, Temperance	Pul	161
_____, Thomas	Han	168
_____, Thompson C.	Mad	112
_____, Wiley	Hry	244
_____, Willis H.	Mad	98
Stricklin, Alsey	Tms	21
_____, David	Bul	99
_____, John	Tms	22
_____, Louis	Scr	307
_____, Mathew	Gwn	311
_____, Sampson B.	Ran	242
_____, Simeon	Tms	27
_____, William	Hal	77
Stricklan, Drury	Gwn	364
_____, Hardy	Gwn	349
_____, Henry	Gwn	355
_____, Simeon	Gwn	313
_____, Simeon	Gwn	364
_____, William	Gwn	350
_____, Willson	Gwn	348
Strickling, Brinkley	Hal	87
_____, Joseph	Hal	86
_____, Irvin	Hal	87
Striclin, John	Bul	99
STRINGFELLOW, Elizabeth	Gre	287
_____, George	Jsp	370
_____, Robert	Fay	186
STRINGFIELD, Archibald	Wil	290
Stringfield, Susan	Mus	282
STRINGER, Andrew B.	Rch	266
_____, Daniel	Tms	19
_____, Ervin	Tms	19
_____, John	Hal	93
_____, Martha	Har	186
_____, Willis	Cow	387
STRIPLING/STRIPLIN		
Stripling, Benjamin	Tat	375
_____, Benjamin	Up	96
_____, Benjamin O.	Mor	267
_____, David	Car	223
_____, James	Mon	203
_____, James B.	Tat	372
_____, John D.	Mon	181
_____, Mary	Car	223
_____, Moses	Jns	462
_____, Thomas	Mon	205
_____, William Sr.	Jns	452
_____, William	Jns	458
Striplin, Benjamin	Crf	405
_____, John	Crf	405
STROBART, Ann	Cht	242
_____, Mary	Cht	257
STRONG, Allen B.	Bib	53
_____, C.	Jsp	367
_____, Charles	Ogl	70
_____, Christopher B.	Bib	57
_____, Elisha	Ogl	93
_____, Ezekiel	Wal	158
_____, James M.	Clk	313
_____, John	Wal	156
_____, John B.	Trp	34
_____, Noah	Gwn	364
_____, Robert	Clk	317
_____, Robert	Mon	196
_____, William	New	21
STROTHER/STRODER		
Strother, Aaren	Fay	192
_____, David	Han	166
_____, James	Rab	228
_____, William	Crf	399
_____, William	Tlb	341
Stroder, John	Mad	110
STROUD, Eli	Mus	289
_____, Ethen	Trp	37
_____, Irby	Hry	245
_____, James	Car	225
_____, James	New	20
_____, James	Wal	155
_____, John	Cpb	194
_____, John	Mwr	150
_____, John	Rab	230

Stroud, Levi Mon 183
______, Malvra Pik 111
______, Mary Jsp 398
______, Martha Clk 302
______, Nancy Wal 141
______, Orm. Wal 124
______, Phillip Cow 384
______, Sherod Wal 170
______, Sherrard Ogl 102
______, Thomas Tm 166
______, William Clk 292
______, William Bts 158
______, William Jr. Bts 160
______, William Fay 202
______, William Hry 245
______, Wyley Car 225
STROUP, Adam Hab 28
______, Jacob Hab 21
STROZIER, Charles Mon 228
______, John Tfo 367
______, Margerett Wil 313
______, Peter Wil 313
______, Reuben Wil 296
______, Reuben Wil 307
______, William Jsp 378
STRUTHERS, Andrew R. Mor 259
STRUTMAN, William Crf 396
STUART, Alexander Hry 228
______, Amos Sr. Tfo 359
______, Amos Jr. Tfo 358
______, Charles Hry 233
______, Charles D. Gre 280
______, George Jns 441
______, George W. Ear 100
______, Henry Tfo 363
______, J. P. Rch 274
______, John Ear 91
______, John Hry 218
______, John Lin 62
______, Josiah Hry 220
______, Margaret Gre 295
______, Martha Jns 440
______, Nancy Hry 229
______, Owen Tfo 356
______, Reuben Gre 288
______, Samuel Jns 437
______, William Hry 211
______, William Lin 61
STUBBLEFIELD, ------ Wil 324
______, Colvin Wal 170
______, Mary Ogl 64
STUBBS/STUBS/STIBBS
Stubbs, Abner Bul 101
Stubbs, B. Wks 250
______, B. P. Bal 29
______, Gabrel Wsh 269
______, George Ran 246
______, John Frk 239
______, John Wsh 254
______, Peter Bib 74
______, Rowland Fay 181
______, Thomas Bib 74
______, Thomas Hry 234
______, Thomas D. Bal 41
______, William Fay 196
______, William Mus 285
Stubs, Francis Put 203
______, James Put 202
______, John Pik 131
______, Thomas B. Put 214
Stibbs, Ann Cht 243
STUCKEY/STUCKY
Stuckey, John Wks 338
______, Nancy Wks 353
______, Simon Wks 338
______, Simon Wks 357
______, Starling Wks 339
______, Starling Wks 357
______, William Ran 250
Stucky, Daniel Lee 32
______, Edward Rch 289
______, Hester Rch 289
______, Polly Rch 291
______, Sarah Rch 290
STUDDARD/STUDART
Studdard, Abraham Wal 173
______, James Wal 129
______, James Wal 144
______, John Mor 272
______, Samuel Wal 144
Studart, Ensley New 5
STUDLY, William E. Tat 378
STUDSTILL, Hustus Ear 94
______, John Lwn 89
______, William Tlf 6
STURDE, John Hab 57
STURDEVANT/STURDIVANT/
STERDIVANT/STURDIFANT
Sturdevant, Charlott Wrn 195
______, Daniel W. Put 175
______, Edward Ran 242
______, Edwin Jsp 381
______, G. Cht 267
______, Joel Jsp 357
______, Joel Wal 141
______, Robert Han 166

Sturdivant, Allen Trp 44
_____, Jesse Wal 141
_____, John Han 166
_____, John Wal 141
_____, Williamson Wal 154
Sterdivant, John Jsp 357
Sturdifant, William A. App 6
STURGIS/STURGES
Sturgis, Alfred Col 353
_____, Jos. Up 95
_____, Mary Clk 302
_____, Sarah Rch 263
Sturges, Martha Lin 72
_____, Samuel Bke 150
_____, Samuel Rch 271
STUTMAN, William H. Hab 18
STUWIN, Canon New 26
STYRON, William Gre 303
SUDDETH/SUDDUTH/SUDDITH/
SUDDATH
Suddeth, Ann Pik 132
_____, Charles A. Ear 100
_____, Jarred Clk 309
_____, William Gwn 330
Sudduth, Mary Lin 63
_____, Spencer Lin 68
_____, William Lin 64
_____, Willis Lin 63
Suddith, John Gwn 310
_____, Smith Fay 198
Suddath, James Wal 129
SUGGS/SUGS/SUGG
Suggs, Ezekiel Hst 265
_____, James Hst 271
_____, Lewis Hst 282
_____, Moses Lib 53
Sugs, John Hab 57
Sugg, Gray Pik 126
SULLINS, Josiah Hal 123
SULLIVAN/SULIVAN/
SULLIVANT/SYLLIVAN
Sullivan, Ann Lib 53
_____, Denis Cow 367
_____, Elijah Jns 473
_____, Michael Jns 466
_____, Thomas C. Pul 146
_____, William H. Elb 129
Sulivan, Cornelious Col 351
_____, John Em 177
_____, John McI 122
_____, Mary Em 170
_____, Sarah Col 343
Sullivant, Pleasant Elb 127
Sullivant, Spencer Mon 181
_____, Zachariah Mon 182
Syllivan, Samuel Lee 32
_____, William Lee 32
_____, William Jr. Lee 32
SUMEVILE, James Hab 34
SUMMERALL/SUMMERSALL
Summerall, David App 5
_____, Thomas Tat 380
_____, William Rch 286
Summersall, John Lib 54
_____, Stafford Lib 54
SUMMERFORD, Abr. Wks 342
_____, Henry Hst 263
SUMMEROUR/SUMMERROUR
Summerour, John Wal 142
Summerrour, Henry Wal 174
SUMMERLIN/SUMMERLAIN
Summerlin, Elisha Bul 98
_____, Henry Gly 268
_____, Henry Ran 247
_____, Jacob Bul 97
_____, John Wyn 284
_____, Joseph Bts 174
_____, Lazarus Car 229
_____, Mary (W) Mor 266
_____, Wiley Cow 376
_____, William Gly 265
_____, Zachariah Gwn 314
Summerlain, William Twg 82
SUMMERS, Daniel Clk 292
_____, Ellen Col 352
_____, James Jns 458
_____, John Clk 293
_____, Nicholas Jns 458
_____, Seaburn Clk 294
_____, Thomas Lin 71
_____, William Twg 64
SUMMERSETT, George Doo 87
_____, George Lee 32
SUMNER, Alexander Em 168
_____, Alexander C. Em 171
_____, Benjamin Car 228
_____, Clarissa Bke 141
_____, David Jns 463
_____, Elizabeth Bke 141
_____, James Jns 463
_____, Jesse Irw 302
_____, Jethro Wsh 245
_____, John C. Em 166
_____, Joseph Irw 302
_____, Mary Jns 463
_____, Richard Em 167

Sumner, William Irw 302
SURLS, Reymond Twg 69
SURRENCY, Jacob Tat 377
_____, Maryann Lib 52
_____, Samuel D. Tat 371
SURRELL, Etheldred Clk 302
SURTHETON, Patsey Hab 9
SUSART, John Cht 259
SUTHERLAND/SURTHERLING
Sutherland, Frederick Hal 109
_____, John Col 344
_____, William Hal 132
Surtherling, Edmon New 47
SUTLEY, Daniel Frk 246
_____, David Frk 211
_____, James Frk 211
_____, Michael Frk 238
SUTTLES, William Lau 4
SUTTON, Abel Em 167
_____, Abner Em 176
_____, Allen Hst 285
_____, Ambrose Rab 232
_____, Aron Mon 202
_____, Charles M. Mon 202
_____, David Ware 184
_____, Doshur Hab 56
_____, Ebinalig Em 175
_____, Elijah Doo 87
_____, Elijah Gwn 376
_____, Elisabeth Dec 18
_____, Frances Hab 23
_____, Hardy Doo 79
_____, Hiram R. Hab 15
_____, Irwin Doo 89
_____, Jacob Bak 18
_____, James D. Hab 10
_____, James M. Har 188
_____, Jesse Twg 75
_____, Joel Hab 15
_____, John Hab 63
_____, John Hst 271
_____, John Lwn 90
_____, John Ware 186
_____, John C. Bak 18
_____, Jordan Em 176
_____, Joshua Hab 59
_____, Moses Wil 317
_____, Moses Wks 336
_____, Nancy Wks 336
_____, Peter Twg 86
_____, Pheneas Mon 202
_____, Phillip Wks 358
_____, Sarah Put 189
Sutton, Seaborn Bts 172
_____, Stephen Wks 334
_____, Theophilus Doo 88
_____, Thomas Pul 141
_____, Wiley Jef 409
_____, William Ear 91
_____, William Frk 230
_____, Zachariah Doo 83
SWAFFORD/SWOFFORD
Swafford, Moses Hal 126
_____, Thomas Hal 126
Swofford, James Hal 129
SWAIN/SWAIM
Swain, Canneth Tms 27
_____, Eldred Em 167
_____, George Jks 322
_____, Hannah H. Rch 290
_____, Isiah L. Mtg 233
_____, James Wrn 197
_____, Jeremiah R. Wrn 213
_____, John Wal 164
_____, Josiah Up 111
_____, Morgan Tms 27
_____, Patrick M. Wks 346
_____, Steven Em 166
_____, Susan Tfo 364
_____, Thomas S. Tlf 5
_____, Tiney Put 185
_____, William C. Tlf 4
Swaim, Elle Scr 316
SWAN/SWANN
Swan, Archibald Tlb 327
_____, Bishop Cpb 199
_____, Cyrus Mor 256
_____, Edward Cpb 196
_____, Elijah Lin 67
_____, George Gre 292
_____, John Tfo 360
_____, Jonathan Gwn 368
_____, Joseph Up 118
_____, Joseph B. Up 112
_____, Margaret Tfo 369
_____, William Jef 414
Swann, Andrew Hry 247
_____, Elizabeth Mon 212
_____, Erasmus Mon 177
_____, Frances Mon 221
_____, James Lin 69
_____, James New 22
_____, Richard H. M. Mon 182
_____, William Har 190
SWANSON/SWANSTON
Swanson, A. Jsp 372

Name	County	Page
Swanson, John	Ogl	90
_____, John Sr.	Mor	245
_____, John Jr.	Mor	245
_____, Lemuel	Jsp	380
_____, Nancy	Gre	285
_____, Nathan	Trp	44
_____, Samuel	Fay	183
Swanston, Henry	McI	122
SWAY, George	Jks	314
_____, Susanna	Hab	26
SWEARINGEN/SWEARINGIN/		
SWEARINGIM		
Swearingen, Baley	Doo	78
_____, Benjamin	Doo	85
_____, Bolin	Twg	83
_____, Howell	Doo	85
_____, John	Pul	154
_____, Thomas	Doo	85
_____, Van	Mus	282
Swearingin, Martin	Hst	279
Swearingim, Edward	Bib	65
SWEAT/SWEET/SWET/SWETT		
Sweat, Abner W.	Bul	97
_____, Benjamin	Fay	202
_____, James	DeK	48
_____, James A.	Ware	188
_____, John	Lwn	85
_____, Mary	Cht	277
_____, Nathan Jr.	Ware	187
_____, Solomon	DeK	37
_____, William	Ware	188
Sweet, George D.	Cht	251
_____, Richard	Twg	72
Swet, Ephraim	Pik	113
Swett, Gilbert	Wal	167
SWEETMAN/SWEATMAN/SWEMAN		
Sweetman, Augustus	Gwn	362
_____, Nelly	Gwn	363
_____, William	Hal	109
Sweatman, Stephen W.	Tms	25
_____, William	Tms	23
Sweman, John	Scr	313
SWEOP, S. E.	Har	183
SWICORD, Daved	Dec	11
SWIFT, Catharine (W)	Mor	251
_____, John T.	New	48
_____, Sheldon	Mus	277
_____, Thomas	Mor	262
_____, Tyre	Frk	255
_____, William A.	New	14
SWIGOVER, Mary	Cht	241
SWILLEY/SWILLY		
Swilley, Kernick	Lib	53
Swilley, Reason	Lwn	87
_____, Samuel E.	Lwn	87
_____, Senos	Wsh	266
Swilly, Stephen	Pul	154
SWIM/SWIMS		
Swim, Enoch	Hal	116
Swims, Levi	Hab	11
SWIMER/SWIMMER		
Swimer, John	Cht	256
**Swimmer, Widow (Indian)	Car	233
SWINABLE, William C.	Wal	160
SWINDALL/SWINDLE		
Swindall, Ann	Gre	299
_____, Daniel P.	Gre	293
Swindle, Solomon	Mad	116
SWINNY/SWINNEY		
Swinny, Alfred	Bak	16
_____, Ellis	DeK	64
_____, Henry	DeK	56
_____, Henry	DeK	58
_____, Jesse	DeK	66
_____, Joel	DeK	32
_____ William	DeK	66
_____, William H.	Gre	296
Swinney, Edward	Twg	68
_____, Henry	Wal	132
_____, Jotham L.	Tlb	330
_____, Levi	Hry	203
_____, Theothey	New	48
_____, Wyley	Wal	130
SWINSON, Starkey	Lau	6
SWINT, Edmond	Wsh	255
_____, Frederick	Han	168
_____, James	Han	168
_____, John	Wrn	221
_____, William	Han	168
SWITZER/SWETSER		
Switzer, Bird	Mon	174
_____, Edwards	Put	178
_____, Price	Mon	221
Swetser, Williamson	Put	217
SWORDS, Elizabeth	Wal	172
_____, James	Wal	126
_____, John	Wal	127
SWORSEY, Nathanel	Hab	32
SYBERT, John A.	Lin	59
SYLVESTOR/SYLVESTER		
Sylvestor, Asbury	Lib	52
Sylvester, Augustine	Lib	52
SYRD, Robert S.	Han	166

Name	County	Page
TABB, Davis	Bke	139
______, Edward	Bke	143
______, John	Bke	145
______, Thomas	Bke	142
______, Thomas	Mon	195
TABOR/TABER		
Tabor, Adkinson	Frk	249
______, Elizabeth	Frk	249
______, Isaac	Frk	216
______, Wesley	Twg	83
______, William	Frk	215
Taber, James	Bib	57
______, Zachariah	Crf	414
TACKWELL, Jane	Clk	319
TADLOCK, Wiley	Jks	315
TAFF/TEFT		
Taff, James	Crf	396
______, Riard	Crf	399
______, William B.	Hst	293
______, Teft, J. K.	Cht	244
**TABNECULLEHEE (Indian)	Car	233
TAITOR, William	Lwn	87
TALANT, David	Hal	110
TALBOT, Elihu	Tlb	328
______, Green	Mwr	150
______, James	Wil	310
______, John	Wil	298
______, Joseph	Wil	296
______, Matthew	Wil	310
______, Thomas	Wil	321
TALIAFERRO, C. C.	Rch	265
______, Nicholas	Wil	302
**______, Pettis (slave)	Rch	253
______, Richard	DeK	50
______, William	Rch	271
TALLEY/TALLY		
Talley, Elish	Cow	385
______, Elisha Sr.	New	23
______, Henry	New	19
______, Henry	New	27
______, John	Mor	270
______, Littleton	New	23
______, Nathan	Gre	274
______, Thomas	New	50
Tally, Eleana	Trp	35
______, Eugina J.	Gre	286
______, Evan	Rab	228
______, James	DeK	35
______, John R.	Bib	53
______, Oration	Rab	228
______, Paton	Up	118
______, Prior	Hab	65
______, William	DeK	40

Name	County	Page
TALMAGE, John	Clk	325
TALNER, Thomas	Jef	411
TALTON, Abner	Pik	130
______, Cullen	Hst	265
______, William	DeK	65
TAMPLIN, John	Jns	458
______, John	Tlb	338
______, John	Tlb	346
______, Mary	Crf	415
TANBRIDGE, Thomas	Crf	405
TANKERSLEY/TANKESLEY/		
TANKERLY/TANKERSLY		
Tankersley, Absalom	Lin	58
______, Carter	Mor	256
______, Charles	Hab	22
______, Elizabeth	Mon	196
______, Fountain	New	41
______, George G.	Col	340
______, Henry	Hab	22
______, John	Lin	29
______, John	Lin	71
______, John G.	Col	357
______, Joseph	Col	360
Tankesley, John	Hab	23
______, Lemuel R.	Hal	68
______, Richard	Hab	22
Tankerly, Bennett	DeK	63
Tankersely, William	Col	340
TANNER/TANER		
Tanner, A. C.	Tat	380
______, Archibald	Wal	130
______, Eli	Hal	85
______, Gideon	Bts	178
______, Gray	Em	167
______, Hezekiah	Wal	160
______, James	Crf	393
______, Jesse W.	Gre	286
______, John Q.	Wal	154
______, Joseph	Gre	292
______, Joseph	Wsh	244
______, Lewis	Crf	413
______, Rebecca	Wsh	250
______, Sarah	New	48
______, Thomas	Bts	162
______, Thomas	Hry	230
______, Thomas	Wsh	263
______, Thomas L.	Cpb	200
______, Vincent	Wsh	250
______, Vincent	Wyn	284
______, William	Wsh	257
______, Wilson	App	11
Taner, Benjamin S.	Cow	379
TANT, Elizabeth	Rch	273

Tant, James Jks 347
_____, John Rch 257
_____, Rhodam Rch 262
_____, Thomas Rch 255
_____, William Jks 315
TAPLEY/TARPLEY
Tapley, Adam Mon 219
_____, Garret Mon 219
_____, James Em 167
_____, Joel Mon 209
_____, Jordan Mon 176
_____, Sally Em 166
_____, Wiley Bib 71
_____, William Bib 71
Tarpley, Archebald Gre 292
_____, Eveline Clk 323
_____, John Bts 162
_____, John C. Ogl 91
_____, Rachael Clk 317
_____, Robert W. Ogl 87
_____, William Ogl 89
TAPP, Mary Frk 219
_____, Willis Frk 218
TARBERVILLE, Nathaniel Jns 471
TARBUTTON, Benjamin Wsh 243
_____, Humphrey Hal 108
_____, Joseph Wsh 247
_____, William Sr. Wsh 242
TARVER/TARBER/TARVIN/
TAVERS
Tarver, Allen Bke 138
_____, Andrew New 40
_____, Benjamin Mus 281
_____, Elijah Up 113
_____, Elisha Tlb 332
_____, Etheldred Sr. Rch 282
_____, Frederick Har 189
_____, George Hst 266
_____, Henry Twg 71
_____, Hartwell H. Twg 89
_____, Jacob Han 170
_____, James Mon 215
_____, John Han 170
_____, John R. Rch 281
_____, Mark Bke 136
_____, Mary Jef 410
_____, Nancy S. Han 170
_____, Olevia (W) Mor 240
_____, Penny Wsh 275
_____, Ransom R. Hry 208
_____, Robert Bke 138
_____, Robert Wsh 243
_____, Ruffin R. Twg 86
Tarver, Samuel Rch 281
_____, Samuel B. Jef 406
_____, Stephen Wsh 247
_____, William Bke 136
_____, William M. Twg 89
Tarber, Benjamin Wsh 241
_____, Jeptha Cpb 200
Tarvin, H. Col 348
_____, Rebecca Twg 82
_____, Reddick Col 350
_____, William J. Gwn 374
Tavers, Boring Gwn 372
TATE/TAIT
Tate, Asa Hab 51
_____, Asa Hab 19
_____, Cooper B. Frk 255
_____, Enos Sr. Elb 153
_____, Enos Jr. Elb 153
_____, Jacob M. Elb 154
_____, James Elb 153
_____, James Frk 217
_____, James Frk 225
_____, James H. Elb 154
_____, John Elb 152
_____, John Frk 221
_____, John Hab 49
_____, Lemuel Put 213
_____, Licinda Hab 34
_____, Martha Put 201
_____, Permelia Elb 154
_____, Pheryman W or M Hab 28
_____, Polly New 11
_____, Robert Hal 110
_____, Robert L. Mad 112
_____, Samuel Frk 241
_____, Samuel Hab 66
_____, Sarah Dec 16
_____, Solomon Frk 246
_____, Thomas B. Put 200
_____, Thomas S. Hal 73
_____, William DeK 70
_____, William Hab 21
_____, William Hab 31
_____, William A. Elb 152
_____, Zimri W. Wil 302
Tait, Edward B. Elb 147
_____, James Jks 332
_____, Thomas M. Cow 380
_____, William Jks 348
_____, William Mon 223
TATUM/TATOM/TATAM/TATEM/
TATEHAM
Tatum, Abel Mon 178

Name	County	Page
Tatum, E. T.	DeK	72
______, Jesse	Elb	155
______, John M.	Mon	177
______, Milly	Mon	179
______, Peter	Ear	91
______, Peter	Put	213
______, Peter T.	Gwn	310
______, Sarah	Mus	292
______, William Jr.	DeK	72
Tatom, Jesse D.	Crf	412
______, John	Lin	64
______, Moore	Crf	398
______, Nathanul	Twg	66
______, Richard	Crf	399
______, Richard	Lee	31
______, Silas	Trp	33
______, William	Hry	212
______, Wiley G.	Lin	58
Tatam, Edward	Car	221
______, John	Car	221
______, William	Car	221
______, William	Hal	104
Tatem, John	Ware	185
Tateham, Thomas	McI	132
TAUNTON/TANTON		
Taunton, Henry	Mar	137
______, Newsom	Wsh	256
______, William	Wsh	254
Tanton, Henry	Wsh	274
______, Newsom	Crf	397
TAYLOR/TAYLER/TAILOR/ TAYLAR/TAELOR/TALOR		
Taylor, A. B. Jr.	Crf	395
______, Abner	Hab	38
______, Abraham	Gwn	311
______, Absalom	Bke	155
______, Albert R.	Tfo	356
______, Alexander B.	Crf	410
______, Ann	Rch	288
______, Aquilla	Cpb	202
______, Bartholomew	Dec	7
______, Baxter	Mwr	158
______, Benjamin	Jsp	364
______, Benjamin	Scr	309
______, C.	Bal	32
______, C.	Rch	256
______, Candy	Wks	356
______, Catharine	Bke	132
______, Catharin	Wks	347
______, Charles E.	Pul	144
______, Christopher	Mon	173
______, Clark Sr.	Ogl	86
______, Clark Jr.	Ogl	85
Taylor, Cornelius	Twg	81
______, Daniel	Mad	113
______, David Jr.	Bke	153
______, David	Tlb	324
______, David	Twg	63
______, Dempsey	Dec	4
______, Dory	Bts	160
______, Drewry	Wsh	274
______, Eaton	Mon	225
______, Edmund	Doo	89
______, Edward	Wrn	220
______, Elijah	Hal	90
______, Elizabeth	Bke	122
______, Elizabeth	Elb	122
______, Ephraigm	Mar	144
______, Frd.	Wks	341
______, Frances N.	Jsp	359
______, Francis S.	Lin	72
**______, Frank (slave)	Rch	270
______, Fredk.	Gwn	310
______, Friggers	Lee	35
______, George	Hab	52
______, George	Har	176
______, George	Mon	221
______, George	Twg	64
______, George L.	Mon	199
______, H.	App	10
______, H. S.	Wsh	257
______, Henry	App	11
______, Henry	Mor	258
______, Henry	Rch	281
______, Hiram	Hab	30
______, Isaac	Hst	264
**______, Isaac (slave)	Rch	257
______, Isaac	Rch	271
______, Isaiah	App	10
______, Jacob	Hst	288
______, James	App	10
______, James	App	11
______, James	Cht	253
______, James	Cht	260
______, Jacob	Twg	79
______, James	Cow	368
______, James	Gwn	367
______, James	Har	176
______, James	Hst	267
______, James	Mon	180
______, James	Pul	138
______, James	Scr	311
______, James	Trp	32
______, James	Tms	22
______, James C.	Jns	467
______, James H.	Gre	298

Taylor, James H. Tfo 363
_____, James N. Hst 275
_____, James W. Bke 136
_____, Jeramiah Hab 34
_____, Jeremiah Hab 37
_____, Jesse Tlb 330
_____, Jesse Elb 122
_____, Jesse Tms 18
_____, Jesse J. Mwr 157
_____, Job Sr. Mon 180
_____, John App 11
_____, John Cow 368
_____, John Har 176
_____, John Jks 349
_____, John Lau 11
_____, John Mon 208
_____, John Pul 138
_____, John Scr 309
_____, John Tat 380
_____, John Trp 46
_____, John Tlf 3
_____, John Up 114
_____, John Wks 340
_____, John Jos. Pul 144
_____, John M. Mon 222
_____, Jonathan Put 203
_____, Joseph Tms 16
_____, Joseph Tfo 366
_____, Joshua Bts 166
_____, Kesiah Eff 116
_____, Kinchen Cpb 194
_____, Kinchin Wsh 244
_____, Labon Cam 189
_____, Labra Wyn 281
_____, Lemuel Twg 64
_____, Levy Hab 37
_____, Lewis Cow 369
_____, Littleton Tfo 364
_____, Margaret Bke 142
_____, Mary Bke 132
_____, Maryann Frk 256
_____, Matthias C. Hst 295
_____, Nancy Hab 55
_____, Oran Wal 156
_____, Peter Trp 52
_____, R. Mor 248
_____, R. G. Cht 256
_____, Rebecca Wil 320
_____, Reuben Mwr 160
_____, Richard Tms 20
_____, Richard L. Em 175
_____, Robert Cht 265
_____, Robert Mon 181
Taylor, Robert Rab 234
_____, Robert N. Pul 159
_____, Roderick R. Cow 368
_____, Ruthy DeK 46
_____, Sally Lin 60
_____, Sampson Jns 434
_____, Samuel Hst 268
_____, Samuel Twg 71
_____, Sarah DeK 46
_____, Sarah Mon 207
_____, Sarah (W) Mor 270
_____, Seborn Irw 300
_____, Septimes Gwn 355
_____, Silas Car 218
_____, Simeon Hst 270
_____, Simeon Mon 224
_____, Silas Mar 143
_____, Simeon Mon 208
_____, Simeon M. Mon 208
_____, Sofia Wsh 274
_____, Soloman Hab 30
_____, Stephen Up 96
_____, Susannah Elb 122
_____, Susannah Jks 345
_____, Tekil Mar 144
_____, Tekie Mar 143
_____, Theophlus Hab 34
_____, Thomas Gwn 335
_____, Thomas Hst 264
_____, Thomas Jns 434
_____, Thomas Mar 144
_____, Thomas Twg 71
_____, Thomas Wks 349
_____, Thomas C. Jsp 356
_____, Uriah Ran 243
_____, Warren Wrn 211
_____, Wilie Tfo 368
_____, Sir William Bke 121
_____, William Cht 258
_____, William Cht 260
_____, William Crf 396
_____, William Dec 6
_____, William DeK 45
_____, William DeK 46
_____, William Hab 34
_____, William Hal 119
_____, William Hry 225
_____, William Hry 244
_____, William Mar 144
_____, William Pul 151
_____, William Rab 224
_____, William Scr 309
_____, William Wks 351

Name	County	Page
Taylor, William B.	Clk	325
______, William C.	Frk	247
______, William D.	Up	117
______, William F.	Hst	291
______, William P.	Bke	121
______, William S.	Wil	312
______, Willis	Crf	401
______, Willis	Elb	158
Tayler, Abel	Hab	37
______, Ely	Hab	39
______, George	Hab	27
______, James	Col	336
______, Theophilas	Hab	37
Tailor, Everet	Pik	128
______, Jeremiah H.	Dec	3
______, Joshua	Jef	407
Taylar, Thomas	Mon	180
Taelor, Abner	Pik	130
Talor, John	New	8
TEAGUE, Benjamin	Hal	76
______, Elijah	Gwn	354
______, Sam	Gwn	344
TEAL/TEEL		
Teal, Bradbery	New	54
______, Calvin	Ran	246
______, Emanuel	Hry	213
______, Mesheck	Jsp	387
______, Samuel	Hab	43
______, Thomas	Jsp	388
______, Washington	Hry	242
Teel, Calvin	Fay	198
______, Edward	Bib	71
______, Henry	Har	179
______, Jess.	Fay	198
______, Loderick	Har	179
TEASLEY/TEASLY		
Teasley, Benajah	Elb	143
______, Beverly A.	Elb	127
______, Isham	Elb	121
______, James	Elb	143
______, James S.	Frk	226
______, John A.	Elb	146
______, Joshua	Elb	141
______, Russel	Elb	125
______, Sarah	Elb	159
______, Silas	Elb	127
______, Thomas	Elb	144
______, William D.	Elb	137
Teasly, Thomas	Hab	65
TEAT, John L.	New	25
______, Oren B.	New	25
TEAVER, James	Trp	41
TEBEAU, Catharine	Cht	240

Name	County	Page
Tebeau, Fred	Cht	242
______, Manet	Cht	244
TEDDER/TEDER		
Tedder, Benjamin	Lau	10
______, George	Up	117
______, Henry	Hal	118
______, Littleton	Lau	5
______, Ranson	Hal	118
______, Samuel	Up	102
______, Solomon	Hal	118
______, Zack[h].	Wsh	248
Teder, Jesse	App	8
TEDLEY, William	Jsp	362
TEDVARD, Samuel	Jsp	391
TEICE, M.	Cht	247
TEKEL, John	Mon	177
TELL, William	Tlb	328
TELFAIR/TELFARE		
Telfair, A.	Cht	260
** ______, A. slaves	Cht	279
______, Margarett	Wil	289
Telfare (Estate)	Scr	317
TEMPLES, A. F.	Mar	137
______, Andrew	Mar	138
______, Frederick Sr.	Ear	93
______, Frederick Jr.	Ear	95
______, James	Ear	95
______, John	Ear	95
______, John	Frk	221
TEMPLETON/TEMPLEMON		
Templeton, Greenbury	Mor	245
______, Matthew	Bke	138
______, William	Rch	283
______, Zephaniah	Mor	248
Templemon, James	Hab	25
TENACK, Mary	Cht	244
TENNELLE/TENEL/TENNILL/ TINNELL		
Tennelle, F. T.	Wsh	243
______, Robert	Wsh	250
Tenel, William	Elb	125
Tennill, William A.	Wsh	247
Tennell, John	Jks	335
TENNISON/TENISON/TENESON		
Tennison, James	Rch	290
______, Lemuel	Mon	211
Tenison, Elizabeth	Em	175
Teneson, Mathias	Gwn	379
TENPIN, George P.	Rch	257
TERHUNE, C. D.	Jsp	371
TERLINGTON, Thomas	Wsh	248
TERRELL/TERRILL/TERREL/ TERRIL/TORRELL		

Terrell, Charles Cow 379
_____, Charles Hal 134
_____, David Gre 305
_____, David S. Gre 305
_____, Edmon New 12
_____, Henry Wal 124
_____, Henry Wil 289
_____, Kitty Put 186
_____, James C. Frk 210
_____, Joel Wil 294
_____, Joel W. Cow 368
_____, John Hal 131
_____, John Hry 221
_____, Lewis New 50
_____, Meriam Hry 213
_____, Nancy DeK 50
_____, Patience Lib 54
_____, Richmon New 34
_____, Susan H. Hal 100
_____, Thomas Wil 287
_____, Thomas D. New 20
_____, Thomas F. Hal 100
_____, Timothy Hal 100
_____, William DeK 50
_____, William Han 170
_____, William A. Cow 371
Terrill, David Crf 412
_____, James Mor 272
_____, Sarah Gwn 369
_____, Thomas Gwn 375
_____, Thomas Twg 74
Terrel, Britania Elb 149
_____, Ignatius Pik 124
_____, Sarah Elb 153
_____, Thompson Hab 16
Terril, John B. Jef 413
_____, Samuel Gwn 377
Torrell, Fraces W. New 48
TERRY/TEARRY
Terry, Hannah Wrn 221
_____, James Col 360
_____, James Gwn 351
_____, John Cow 368
_____, John DeK 57
_____, John DeK 61
_____, John Mor 242
_____, John C. Fay 184
_____, Joseph Elb 122
_____, Judith Fay 207
_____, Lewis Hab 28
_____, Macajah Wrn 207
_____, Richard Trp 54
_____, Stephen DeK 48
Terry, Stephen Gwn 366
_____, Thomas J. Mus 289
_____, William Bib 75
_____, William Cow 378
_____, William DeK 54
_____, William Gwn 311
_____, William Jks 320
Tearry, A. Cht 269
TERVIN, Ulisus Jef 411
TESSIER, Lewis P. Bke 147
TETSWORTH, Isaac Jks 327
THACKER, Echo Hal 98
_____, William Hal 97
THACKSTON/THAXTON
Thackston, James Sr. Gre 279
_____, James Jr. Gre 279
_____, Peter Ogl 79
_____, Simion Gre 284
_____, Thomas Ogl 101
Thaxton, William Mon 202
_____, Yelverton Bts 169
THAGGARD, William Mar 137
THAMES, Amos Ear 99
_____, John Tlb 336
_____, William Hry 248
THARP/THARPE/THORPE/
THORP/THURP
Tharp, Benjamin A. Hst 283
_____, Charnic A. Hst 281
_____, Charnick A. Twg 78
_____, Jeremiah A. Twg 78
_____, John Wsh 276
_____, John A. Bib 62
_____, Presley A. Hst 280
_____, Ruth A. Twg 78
Tharpe, Presley Mar 142
_____, Sarah A. Twg 78
_____, William A. or H. Pul 140
_____, William A. Pul 161
_____, William A. Twg 78
Thorpe, Charles W. McI 130
_____, Elias A. Mar 142
_____, Willis A. Mar 132
Thorp, Elizabeth Han 169
_____, Samuel J. R. McI 129
Thurp, Harry Lin 70
THREADCRAFT, S. G. Cht 269
_____, Sarah Cht 248
THEDFORD/THETFORD
Thedford, Walter Mor 238
Thetford, Elisebeth Hab 63
THERSEY, Haney Bke 129
THIESS, Peter DeK 41

Thiess, Peter Jns 436
_____, Peter Lin 69
THIGPEN, Bryant Wrn 201
_____, Charles Irw 302
_____, Claborn Wrn 220
_____, Cullen Wrn 230
_____, James Wsh 241
_____, Joseph Pul 159
_____, Joshua M. Twg 60
_____, Melanston Em 170
_____, Melus Lwn 79
_____, Randal Wsh 274
_____, Redding D. Lau 7
_____, Travis Tms 29
_____, William Em 170
_____, William Wsh 258
THOMAS, Absalom Bke 139
_____, Absalom E. Ware 186
_____, Adward New 17
_____, Alexander Ogl 97
_____, Amos Hst 269
_____, Archibald Lau 20
_____, Archibald Mwr 160
_____, Banner Ware 188
_____, Barbara Tms 22
_____, Benjamin Lee 31
_____, Blassengame Jef 403
_____, Bradley Jks 320
_____, Branham Hal 87
_____, Bud C. Dec 5
_____, Cesiceap (?) Dec 5
_____, Charles Hab 10
_____, Charles Mon 200
_____, Daniel Lee 28
_____, David McI 132
_____, David Ogl 76
_____, David K. Wks 339
_____, David T. Cow 374
_____, Dicey Wrn 218
_____, Drury Clk 296
_____, Eavan Put 196
_____, Edward Rch 272
_____, Edward Rch 274
_____, Edward B. Wil 324
_____, Edward L. Clk 310
_____, Eli DeK 72
_____, Elijah Mon 223
_____, Elijah Mon 224
_____, Elisha P. Han 170
_____, Elizabeth Mon 178
_____, Ellis Cow 382
_____, Etheldred Lau 6
_____, Euphama Wsh 250
Thomas, Evan Hal 83
_____, Ezekiel Elb 157
_____, Ezekiel Frk 233
_____, Frederick Han 172
_____, Gabriel Put 217
_____, George DeK 57
_____, George Har 187
_____, George W. Cam 186
_____, George W. Cow 367
_____, Gideon D. Hst 263
_____, Greenbury Tlf 3
_____, Gregsby E. Wrn 192
_____, Harrison Tlb 322
_____, Hincher Lin 73
_____, Ivy Lin 69
_____, J. L. Bal 32
_____, James App 10
_____, James Gwn 377
_____, James Han 169
_____, James Mon 213
_____, James Ogl 76
_____, James Trp 38
_____, James Up 97
_____, James Wks 338
_____, James L. Clk 295
_____, James R. Ware 188
_____, Jane Cam 186
_____, Jane Jsp 385
_____, Jesse Sr. Frk 233
_____, Jesse Jr. Frk 232
_____, Jess Gwn 311
_____, Jesse Hal 108
_____, Jesse Mor 248
_____, Jesse Ware 183
_____, Joel Frk 220
_____, John App 9
_____, John Bul 100
_____, John Clk 295
_____, John Em 166
_____, John Frk 233
_____, John Hab 6
_____, John Hab 14
_____, John Hal 70
_____, John Sr. Hry 239
_____, John Hry 230
_____, John Jns 438
_____, John Lau 4
_____, John Mon 224
_____, John Ogl 67
_____, John Pul 153
_____, John Put 199
_____, John Up 97
_____, John C. New 53

Name	County	Page
Thomas, John F.	Cht	258
______, John H.	Fay	204
______, John H.	Gre	300
______, John R.	Trp	50
______, John T.	Hry	239
______, Jonathan	McI	130
______, Jonathan	Put	191
______, Joseph	DeK	55
______, Joseph	Lee	31
______, Joseph	Mus	286
______, Joseph D.	Bke	141
______, Lewelling	Cow	390
______, Lewis	Dec	6
______, Lewis	DeK	71
______, Lewis	Ware	188
______, Lewis A.	Tms	21
______, Leven W.	Clk	307
______, Lydia	App	11
______, Martha	Gwn	372
______, Martin	Hal	100
______, Mary	Han	172
______, Mary	Ogl	95
______, Mary	Wal	168
______, Massa	Put	177
______, Merril	Clk	300
______, Micajah	Han	169
______, Michael	Mus	286
______, Michael L.	Wrn	195
______, Nancy	McI	132
______, Nelson	Lib	54
______, Patience	Fay	207
______, Patrick	Ware	183
______, Patrick M.	Pul	149
______, Patrick M.	Wks	244
______, Philip	Bib	62
______, Pleasant	Hal	113
______, Pleasant	Jns	471
______, Polly	Hab	36
______, Polly	Hry	245
______, Precilla	Cam	186
______, Rachel	Dec	18
______, Rachel	Hab	6
______, Reuben	Har	178
______, Richard	Bke	121
______, Richard	Har	181
______, Riley	Up	118
______, Robert	App	10
______, Roberts	Rch	287
______, Ryall C.	Bul	102
______, Samuel	Clk	296
______, Samuel	Jsp	395
______, Samuel	Tlf	2
______, Samuel	Ware	188

Name	County	Page
Thomas, Samuel B.	Han	169
______, Samuel H.	Mar	142
______, Sarah	McI	123
______, Seaborn J.	Tlb	339
______, Seno	Lau	17
______, Spencer	Pul	143
______, Stevens	Clk	326
______, Susanah (W)	Mor	254
______, T. F.	App	5
______, Thomas	Bts	178
______, Thomas	Crf	402
______, Thomas	Han	170
______, Thomas C.	Hab	24
______, Thomas L.	DeK	38
______, Thomas L.	Hab	14
______, Western	Rch	267
______, Wiley	Bib	62
______, William	Bak	17
______, William	Bul	102
______, William	Cht	244
______, William	Clk	296
______, William	Col	335
______, William	Frk	220
______, William	Hal	83
______, William	Lin	69
______, William	Mon	208
______, William	Ogl	76
______, William	Pul	160
______, William	Put	216
______, William	Wal	137
______, William B.	Hst	263
______, William G.	Trp	34
______, William L.	Lau	20
______, Witfield	Han	169
THINCEY, Absalom	Bke	129
THOMASON/THOMASSON/		
THOMMASON/THOMASSEN/THOMESSON		
Thomason, Absalom	New	8
______, Bartlett	New	8
______, Eleanor	Hry	233
______, George	Frk	210
______, John	Elb	145
______, John B.	Har	177
______, Levi	Jsp	389
______, Littleton	Hry	239
______, Solomon D.	Frk	228
______, Thomas L.	New	44
______, William	Frk	224
______, William	Jsp	379
______, William	Wsh	263
______, William T.	Frk	235
______, Young J.	Hal	115
Thomasson, George	DeK	29

Name	County	Page
Thomasson, Jonathon	Crf	396
______, Nelson	DeK	29
Thommason, William V.	McI	123
Thomassen, Zimrie	Hal	126
Thomesson, George	Jks	340
THOMASTON, Harmond	Hal	115
______, John	Hal	114
______, Martin	Wal	144
______, Rowling	Wrn	195
THOMLEY, Josiah M.	Hst	291
THOMPSON/THOMSON/TOMPSON		
Thompson, Aaron	Bke	135
______, Absalom	Hal	95
______, Adam H.	Hab	42
______, Alexander	Pik	123
______, Andrew	Hal	116
______, Anthony M.	Hst	291
______, Asa	Em	171
______, Auston	Lwn	86
______, Balis	Frk	257
______, Beatrix	Han	170
______, Benjamin	Bry	86
______, Benjamin	Jef	409
______, Benjamin	Twg	68
______, Benjamin	Wrn	210
______, Betsey	Hal	121
______, Bridges	Ogl	69
______, Burrel	Hal	95
______, C.	Cht	250
______, Caroline	Cht	261
______, Charity	Bke	134
______, Charles	Mor	271
______, Charles	Wal	165
______, Charles J.	Hab	18
______, Chesley	Jsp	357
______, Daniel	Bke	134
______, David	Jef	422
______, David	Twg	84
______, David	Wal	127
______, David	Wal	165
______, Drury	Bib	53
______, Easter	Gwn	338
______, Edy	Em	178
______, Elihu	Bke	130
______, Elijah	Up	109
______, Elizabeth	Clk	316
______, Elizabeth	Hry	212
______, Elizabeth	Lau	24
______, Elizabeth	Lin	61
______, Elizabeth	Pul	157
______, Ephriam	Gwn	357
______, F.	Cht	256
______, Flanders	Hry	232
Thompson, Fredk.	Gwn	335
______, Frederick	Wal	125
______, Gaines	Elb	142
______, George	Gwn	322
______, George	Hal	82
______, George	New	42
______, George L.	Bts	159
______, Glawn	Lin	62
______, Grandville	Hal	70
______, Green	Jks	318
______, Guy	Lau	9
______, Hannah	Wrn	225
______, Henry	Em	170
______, Henry	Han	169
______, Henry	New	15
______, Henry	Wrn	216
______, Henry B.	Tfo	365
______, Henry T.	Twg	72
______, Howell	Twg	75
______, Hugh	Frk	220
______, Isham	Rch	274
______, Isom	Han	170
______, Mrs. J.	Bry	87
______, J. E.	Mon	223
______, James	Bib	68
______, James	Bke	150
______, James	Bts	166
______, James	Clk	310
______, James	Cht	240
______, James	Dec	6
______, James	DeK	60
______, James	Gwn	326
______, James	Gwn	351
______, James	Han	169
______, James	Hry	210
______, James	Jsp	364
______, James Sr.	Mad	115
______, James Jr.	Mad	100
______, James	Mon	206
______, James	Mus	291
______, James	Wal	152
______, James	Wrn	206
______, James D.	Jks	323
______, James G.	Gre	294
______, James M.	Hab	30
______, James W.	Pik	131
______, James Y.	New	40
______, Jeremiah	Gre	280
______, Jeremiah	Hry	235
______, Jeremiah	Lin	61
______, Jesse	Hal	123
______, Jesse	Rch	261
______, Jesse W.	Elb	143

Name	County	Page
Thompson, Joel	Mad	111
______, John	Bul	97
______, John	Clk	302
______, John	Clk	310
______, John	Crf	411
______, John	DeK	60
______, John	DeK	73
______, John	Em	171
______, John	Gre	277
______, John	Gre	284
______, John	Gwn	327
______, John	Hal	95
______, John	Hal	132
______, John	Jns	463
______, John	New	40
______, John	Scr	307
______, John	Tms	25
______, John	Twg	75
______, John	Twg	87
______, John	Wal	169
______, John D.	Wil	296
______, John F.	Mor	261
______, John H.	Wsh	275
______, John M.	Gwn	351
______, John P.	New	15
______, Johnson	Gwn	374
______, Joseph	Gwn	330
______, Joseph	Gre	289
______, Joseph	Hal	95
______, Joseph	Jsp	382
______, Joseph	Mor	270
______, Joseph	Pik	108
______, Joseph	Ran	242
______, Joseph R.	Cht	263
______, Joseph R.	Gwn	324
______, Joseph G.	Crf	410
______, Josiah	Lee	32
______, L. M.	Tfo	355
______, Leslie	Cht	253
______, Littleberry	Jks	320
______, Marian	Ear	99
______, Maroney	Hal	68
______, Martha	Gwn	322
______, Mary	Jks	316
______, Mary	Lau	21
______, Mary	Pik	130
______, Mary	Twg	86
______, Mary	Wil	319
______, Mary	Wrn	223
______, Mary Ann	Rch	267
______, Merinder	Jef	415
______, Micajah	Wks	343
______, Middleton	Clk	294
Thompson, Moses	Jef	417
______, Nancy	DeK	61
______, Nancy	Rch	256
______, Nancy	Wrn	210
______, Nathan	Gre	288
______, Nathaniel	Wrn	212
______, Nelson	Dec	10
______, Nichodemus	Bke	134
______, Obediah	Ogl	69
______, Oliver	Hal	108
______, P. P.	Cht	262
______, Peter	Pul	149
______, Peter G.	Twg	70
______, Pledge W.	Pik	131
______, Portlock	Hst	287
______, Rebecca	App	9
______, Reuben	Em	171
______, Richard	Hal	93
______, Richard	Jks	314
______, Richard	Tat	377
______, Richard	Wal	159
______, Robert	Clk	302
______, Robert	Em	171
______, Robert	Gwn	338
______, Robert	Jks	312
______, Robert	Jsp	394
______, Robert	New	40
______, Robert	Wil	295
______, Robert C.	Clk	326
______, Sally	Hab	59
______, Salvado	Wal	145
______, Samuel	Fay	181
______, Samuel	New	15
______, Samuel	New	40
______, Samuel	Ogl	94
______, Samuel	Tfo	366
______, Samuel	Ogl	101
______, Samuel	Trp	55
______, Samuel	Wal	128
______, Samuel	Wil	295
______, Sarah	Mad	117
______, Sarah	Wal	163
______, Sarah	Wal	165
______, Sarah	Wsh	261
______, Shardrick	Jef	403
______, Sherod	Jks	313
______, Silas	Hal	116
______, Solomon	Bry	88
______, Stephen	Wrn	194
______, Sylvia	Twg	87
______, Tabitha	Bke	142
______, Thim	Pik	108
______, Thomas	Bry	88

Thompson, Thomas Col 339
_____, Thomas Gre 296
_____, Thomas Mor 271
_____, Thomas B. Bry 87
_____, Thomas B. Clk 323
_____, Thomas P. Mor 240
_____, Washington Twg 83
_____, Wells Gwn 343
_____, Wiley Elb 136
_____, William Bry 86
_____, William Bke 134
_____, William DeK 73
_____, William Ear 94
_____, William Gwn 338
_____, William Hab 20
_____, William Hab 48
_____, William Hal 108
_____, William Hal 123
_____, William Hst 287
_____, William Jef 405
_____, William Jks 319
_____, William Sr. Mad 107
_____, William Mad 111
_____, William Mon 220
_____, William Mus 284
_____, William New 40
_____, William New 40
_____, William Pul 144
_____, William Rch 262
_____, William Rch 273
_____, William Scr 317
_____, William Twg 72
_____, William Wal 131
_____, William Wal 166
_____, William Wrn 225
_____, William B. Han 168
_____, William C. Jks 341
_____, William L. Jsp 396
_____, William S. Bal 43
_____, Winney Mad 117
_____, Zach Gwn 322
Thomson, Argin Cam 188
_____, David Cam 181
_____, Isaac Mwr 153
_____, Joseph Car 219
_____, Ranson Car 219
_____, Robert Mwr 158
_____, Seth Mwr 152
_____, Thomas P. Mor 272
_____, William Mwr 158
_____, Zachariah Car 219
Tompson, Ann Wks 333
_____, James Wks 338
Tompson, John S. Put 204
_____, Joseph DeK 35
_____, Mathew Put 199
_____, Penelope Bib 66
THORN/THORNE
Thorn, Hezekiah Har 181
_____, Nicolas Pik 110
_____, William Bke 129
Thorne, Middleton Scr 304
THORNTON, Abel Mon 189
_____, Benjamin Sr. Elb 147
_____, Benjamin Jr. Elb 147
_____, Burdong Pik 113
_____, Charles T. Gwn 376
_____, Cullen Mon 178
_____, Daniel Elb 146
_____, Dicy Mon 176
_____, Dosier Har 184
_____, Dozier Frk 234
_____, Dozier Mus 284
_____, E. App 9
_____, Edward S. Tms 27
_____, Eli New 29
_____, Elijah Jks 335
_____, Elizabeth Bib 71
_____, Elizabeth Elb 159
_____, Elsey Elb 159
_____, Francis Elb 157
_____, George Hal 81
_____, Green H. Har 192
_____, H. A. Mus 277
_____, Harrod Fay 196
_____, Harrison L. Ogl 85
_____, Henry B. Trp 36
_____, Herrard Ogl 62
_____, Isaac App 8
_____, James Gre 283
_____, James Han 169
_____, James Har 190
_____, James Jsp 360
_____, James A. New 50
_____, Jerminah Elb 147
_____, John Elb 144
_____, John Ogl 62
_____, John Pik 114
_____, John Wil 305
_____, Jordan New 44
_____, Judith Jsp 363
_____, Linsey Har 182
_____, Lucy Elb 158
_____, Mager Tlb 330
_____, Mak Put 194
_____, Mark Jks 332

Thornton, Mark	Mwr	154
_____, Mark	New	46
_____, Middleton	Cpb	207
_____, Phillip	Wil	311
_____, Rachal	Ogl	85
_____, Rebecah (W)	Mor	243
_____, Reddick	Bul	99
_____, Reuben	Frk	229
_____, Reubin	Hal	131
_____, Richard	Har	189
_____, S.	Har	180
_____, Samuel Sr.	Elb	148
_____, Samuel	Ogl	65
_____, Sarah	Gre	284
_____, Thomas	Hal	74
_____, Thomas	New	44
_____, Thomas A.	Elb	138
_____, Thomas A.	Jks	319
_____, Vincent R.	Gre	278
_____, Walker R.	Frk	218
_____, Willie	Pik	118
_____, William	Em	174
_____, William	Tlb	340
_____, William	Trp	36
_____, William	Wil	304
_____, Wyley	Wal	141
_____, Yancy	Jsp	352
_____, Yancy	Mwr	160
_____, Young	New	24
THRASH, Andrew	Put	215
_____, Christerpher	Put	192
_____, David	Mon	222
_____, George A.	Trp	45
_____, Isaac	Mwr	154
_____, Jacob	Put	191
_____, Joseph	Trp	44
_____, Susannah	Bts	178
_____, Valantine	Mor	246
THRASHER, Barton	Clk	316
_____, David	New	42
_____, George	Frk	215
_____, George	Gwn	324
_____, Isaac	Clk	306
_____, Jessee	Gwn	324
_____, John	Clk	306
_____, John	Frk	253
_____, Sally	Frk	237
_____, Thomas	Hal	82
_____, William	Gwn	324
THRELKELD/THRALKELD		
Threlkeld, Delilah	Elb	160
_____, John	Elb	134
_____, Oliver	Elb	119
Threlkeld, William A.	Elb	135
_____, Willis	Elb	149
Thralkeld, Chancy	Elb	131
THRIFT, Robert F.	Wsh	250
THROWER, Benjamin	New	5
_____, Jesse	Wks	355
_____, Lewis	Wks	355
_____, Margaret	Pik	122
_____, Thomas	Cpb	197
_____, Thomas	Pik	117
_____, Willis	Scr	305
THURMOND/THURMON/THURMAN/ THIRMOND/TURMAN/TURMON		
Thurmond, Benjamin	Jsp	365
_____, Charles	Wil	302
_____, Elizabeth	Hal	75
_____, Fielding	Hal	129
_____, Harrison	Jks	329
_____, James	Wil	319
_____, John	Jsp	354
_____, John	Mor	267
_____, Micajah	Car	222
_____, Phillip	Bts	175
_____, Philip	Jsp	365
_____, Powhattan B.	Wil	302
_____, Sucretia	Wil	302
_____, Thomas J.	Hal	75
_____, William	Hal	130
_____, William	Wil	319
Thurmon, Bolton	Jks	344
_____, James	Frk	231
_____, Jefferson	Jks	344
_____, John	Jks	329
_____, John	Jks	345
_____, Mary	Ogl	68
_____, William	Jks	331
Thurman, David	Clk	316
_____, Harris	Clk	304
_____, Harris F.	Wal	154
_____, Phillip	Clk	319
Thirmond, Benjamin	DeK	51
_____, David	DeK	51
_____, Richard	DeK	51
_____, William	DeK	51
Turman, Abner T.	Elb	155
_____, Joel	Rch	290
_____, John	DeK	57
_____, Lucy	Wal	153
_____, Samuel	Elb	137
Turmon, Simeon	Frk	237
THURP: see Tharp		
THURSTON, L. H.	Bak	15
_____, Lydia	Hry	240

Name	County	Page
THWEATT/THWEAT/THREATT		
Thweatt, James	Mon	222
* ______, James (slave)	Mon	229
______, John	Up	117
______, Kinchen P.	Jns	442
______, Thomas	Jns	467
* ______, Thomas (slave)	Mon	229
______, W.	Bal	37
Thweat, Henry	Crf	397
______, John	Crf	398
Threatt, M. W.	Mus	281
TIDWELL, Benjamin Sr.	Mwr	150
______, Caleway	Har	186
______, Isaiah	Put	213
______, John	Hal	133
______, John	Mwr	164
______, Mathew	Hry	218
______, Millen	Twg	78
______, Polly	Car	230
______, Sarah	Hal	133
______, Wiley	Har	186
______, William	Cow	389
______, William	Har	186
______, William	Mwr	150
TIE, Samuel	Ogl	95
TIFNEY, Levy	Jef	423
TIGNER/TIGNOR		
Tigner, Hope H.	Mwr	152
______, John	Jns	444
Tignor, Young F.	Mwr	165
TILLAH, John	DeK	33
______, Stephen	DeK	70
TILLER, Burrel	Ogl	63
______, Elijah	Ogl	81
______, H.	Jsp	384
______, Martin	Ogl	82
______, Mason	Put	174
______, Muscage E.L.	Crf	395
______, Nancy	Ogl	81
______, Randal	Ogl	84
______, William	Ogl	82
______, Willis	Bts	171
TILLERY/TILERY/TILLORY		
Tillery, John	Bts	178
______, Thomas	Lin	73
______, Willeby	Jns	443
______, William	Pik	109
Tilery, John	Tlb	344
Tillory, Susannah (W)	Mor	272
TILLEY/TILLY/TILLIE		
Tilley, Isaac	Bke	133
______, James R.	Bts	162
______, John	Bke	141

Name	County	Page
Tilley, John	Mus	279
______, Joseph	Bke	142
______, Lazarus	Rab	231
______, Rachel	Rch	284
______, William	Bke	139
______, William	Ear	99
Tilly, George	Tfo	354
______, James H.	Wks	339
______, James H.	Wks	357
______, John Sr.	Ear	100
______, John Jr.	Ear	98
______, Nancy	Hab	39
Tillie, Tapley A.	Tlf	2
TILMAN/TILLMAN/TILMON/ TILLMON/TILGHMAN		
Tilman, David	Tlb	325
______, Drury	Lau	5
______, Henry	Mtg	235
______, Henry	Tlb	336
______, James	Pik	128
______, James	Wal	154
______, John	Cht	280
______, Joseph	Mon	195
______, Robert	Jef	409
______, Willis	Pik	129
Tillman, James	App	5
______, Joseph	Tat	375
______, Joshua	Lwn	80
______, Lazarus	Jns	434
______, Martha	Mad	116
______, Penna	Jns	431
______, Richard	Jns	430
______, Sarah	Bul	95
______, Stephen	Rch	267
Tilmon, Berry G.	Frk	221
______, Burgess	Up	102
______, John	Frk	248
______, John	Up	100
______, William	Up	101
Tillmon, Jeremiah	Lwn	80
______, John	Lwn	80
Tilghman, Aaron	Fay	181
TIMMONS/TIMMONDS		
Timmons, John	Bak	20
______, John	Cht	280
______, Levi	Bak	16
______, Mary	Bak	16
______, Noble	Gwn	376
______, Stephen	Cht	242
______, William	Mwr	163
______, Williams	Pul	152
______, Zach.	Gly	267
Timmonds, John D.	Mor	243

TIMS/TIMMS
Tims, Nancy Jks 338
_____, Stephen Tms 29
_____, Walter Jks 314
Timms, John Gwn 324
_____, William Gwn 323
TINBROOK/TENBROOK
Tinbrook, Emily Rch 258
Tenbrook, R. K. Cht 242
TINCKLEY/TINKLY
Tinckley, Fanny Rch 258
Tinkly, George W. Dec 6
TINDALL/TINDALE/TINDOL/
TINDOLE/TENDOL
Tindall, Ann Cht 277
_____, James Cow 384
_____, John E. Col 347
_____, Nancy H. Col 337
_____, Rachal Col 347
Tindale, James Sr. Bke 131
_____, James Jr. Bke 131
_____, Wiley Bke 131
Tindol, William Clk 297
Tindole, Samuel Mor 262
Tendol, Jacob Wsh 246
TINER, John Hst 270
_____, William Hst 265
TINGLE, Daniel Mon 213
_____, Purifoy Mon 217
_____, Solomon DeK 58
TINLEY/TENDLEY
Tinley, Ann Rch 289
_____, David Rch 290
_____, James Rch 289
_____, John Rch 289
_____, Philip Rch 290
_____, William Hal 119
Tendley, C. D. Jsp 371
TINNEY/TINNY
Tinney, Isaac Pik 115
_____, John Pik 115
_____, Rebecca Pik 129
Tinny, Isaac Gwn 310
_____, William Wks 353
TINSLEY/TINSLY
Tinsley, Catherine Col 344
_____, Green Dec 3
_____, Indiana Hab 45
_____, James Clk 327
_____, James W. Jns 433
_____, Jefferson New 12
_____, John New 9
_____, Martha Frk 254
Tinsley, Susannah Bak 20
Tinsly, Phillip Lee 28
TIOT/TEOT
Tiot, Charles Eff 108
Teot, S. W. Cht 258
TIPPER, Berry Pul 143
_____, James Ogl 84
_____, Wiley Hry 208
TIPPET/TIPPETS/TIPPETT/
TEPPET
Tippet, Samuel Lau 10
_____, William Pul 162
Tippets, Thomas Elb 159
Tippett, Susanna Gre 299
Teppet, William Gre 285
TIPPINS/TIPPIN/TIPPENS/
TIPPONS
Tippins, George Hal 80
_____, George U. Cam 188
_____, James Hal 81
_____, James A. Tat 374
_____, Penelope Tat 379
_____, William Tat 375
Tippin, Elijah Gwn 343
Tippens, John L. Gwn 358
Tippons, Berry Pul 143
TIPTON, Jonathan Wks 333
_____, Joseph Bke 129
_____, William Hab 28
TIRPIN, Elias Rab 233
_____, James Rab 226
TISARUE, Button Bib 57
TISDALE/TEASDALE
Tisdale, Randerson H. Jns 443
Teasdale, Mary Cam 183
TISINGER, George W. Up 97
TISON, A. Lee 26
_____, Ann Tms 26
_____, Cornelias Irw 303
_____, Elizabeth Lee 35
_____, Eson Dec 16
_____, Fred Wsh 241
_____, Fred Wsh 276
_____, Hiram Twg 72
_____, Jane B. Hry 241
_____, John Wsh 255
_____, Kinchen P. Up 99
_____, Moses Lee 26
_____, Noah Wsh 241
_____, Sidnah Gly 265
_____, Stephen Wsh 241
_____, Sterling Twg 78
_____, W. Lee 26

TITCOMBE, Samuel G. Cht 240
TITTER, Elisha Ogl 63
TODD/TIDD
Todd, Andrew Cow 390
_____, Benjamin Jns 440
_____, Benjamin G. Hry 205
_____, Edward D. Tat 372
_____, Elcany Wrn 232
_____, Henry B. Jef 405
_____, Henry W. Gre 274
_____, Jacob J. Bib 57
_____, James Wks 341
_____, James Jr. Wrn 220
_____, James E. New 21
_____, Job Wrn 233
_____, John Hry 235
_____, John Hst 291
_____, John McI 130
_____, John B. Jns 440
_____, Joseph W. Mon 197
_____, Maria Rch 255
_____, Richard C. DeK 48
_____, Susan Wsh 258
_____, Thomas Gwn 312
_____, William Fay 188
_____, William McI 130
_____, William Put 184
_____, William Tat 377
_____, William Wks 341
_____, William L. Put 207
Tidd, David Jns 445
TOLAND, James Hry 233
TOLBERT/TOLBOT/TOBBERT
Tolbert, Allen Mad 104
_____, James Mad 1-9
_____, Miles Mad 98
_____, Ozbon Mad 112
_____, Rollin Mad 112
_____, Samuel Hab 44
_____, Tapley B. Mad 113
_____, William Clk 305
_____, William Mad 106
_____, William Wal 154
Tolbot, John Ran 242
Tobbert, Washington Hal 127
TOLER/TOLAR/TOOLER
Toler, James Jks 328
_____, John Lin 63
_____, Robert Crf 402
_____, William Jef 405
Tolar, Lewis Hry 219
Tooler, William Lee 31
TOLLISON/TOLISON/TOLLESON
Tollison, Daniel Gwn 368
_____, Jesse Mon 217
_____, John DeK 61
_____, John Mon 217
Tolison, James Gwn 368
Tolleson, Hitson DeK 67
TOLLS, John Jns 430
_____, Manning Hst 276
TOLON/TOLEN
Tolon, Michael Mon 216
_____, Samuel Mon 216
Tolen, Jonathan Mon 179
TOLSON, Henry Bts 158
TOMBERLIN/TUMBERLIN/TUMBELIN
Tomberlin, Darcas Hab 33
_____, Jarrot Lee 33
_____, John Wks 338
Tumberlin, Isaac Hab 46
Tumbelin, William Hab 33
TOMLIN/TUMLIN/TOMPLIN/TUMBLIN
Tomlin, Jacob Mor 260
_____, James Up 113
_____, Jesse Wal 155
_____, John Bke 144
_____, John Wal 172
_____, L. L. F. Bke 139
_____, Martin Mor 259
_____, Mary Bke 140
_____, Owen Hst 292
_____, Pharao Up 118
_____, William New 7
Tumlin, Jami Gwn 312
_____, William Gwn 332
Tomplin, Reuben Han 169
Tumblin, Abram DeK 73
TOMLINSON, E. J. Wal 124
_____, George DeK 73
_____, H. Wil 297
_____, Harris Wsh 262
_____, Humphrey W. Hry 203
_____, James Mon 198
_____, John Hry 238
_____, John Hst 270
_____, John Lwn 85
_____, John Mon 228
_____, John F. Hry 209
_____, L. H. DeK 35
_____, Leonard Mus 289
_____, Lucas Put 207
_____, Mary Jef 424
_____, Moses Lwn 85

Tomlinson, Nathan Put 206
______, Sara DeK 35
______, William Jef 406
______, William Lwn 85
TOMMY/TOMME
Tommy, James Hry 235
______, Zilpha Hry 235
Tomme, Henry Up 120
______, Othmel Up 114
TOMPKINS/THOMPKINS/
TOMKINS
Tompkins, Frances Cam 185
______, Giles Put 190
______, Haris Mus 282
______, John Sr. Cam 187
______, John Jr. Cam 185
______, John Jef 412
______, John Mon 214
______, John Put 190
______, John Y. Wsh 242
______, John W. Bib 66
______, Mary Bal 41
______, Nicholas Put 190
______, Partin Jef 412
______, Rukin Wsh 244
______, Samuel Bib 66
______, Samuel Wsh 264
______, Samuel Wrn 231
______, William Mar 139
______, William P. Bib 66
Thompkins, Burwell Wsh 245
Tomkins, Parten Ran 244
TOMSTER, Baile Gly 266
TONDEE/TUÑDEE
Tondee, Charles Eff 110
Tundee, Thomas Bry 88
TONDER, Charles R. Wks 344
TONEY, Charles Frk 247
______, Harris Frk 220
______, Hedrick Frk 236
______, James Frk 216
______, John Frk 223
______, John Jr. Frk 224
TOOK/TOOKE
Took, Allen Ran 248
______, Isham Gre 283
______, Joseph Ran 243
______, William S. Pul 160
Tooke, James Jns 455
______, Jesse B. Wsh 239
______, Sterling Pul 139
TOOLE/TOOL
Toole, Buland Jns 458
Toole, James Jns 458
______, James Sr. Rch 285
Tool, George A. Col 338
______, James Col 338
TOOLY, Mary S. Jns 455
TOOMBS, Catherine Wil 324
TOOMER, Daniel Eff 110
TOOTLE, John Tat 372
______, Richard Dec 10
______, William Tat 375
TORBET/TORBIT/TORBERT
Torbet, Samuel Mor 252
Torbit, George T. Ogl 80
Torbert, James Up 99
TORRANCE/TORRENCE/TORENCE/
TARRENCE
Torrance, A. Bal 32
______, James Bke 128
______, Moris Bal 43
______, W. H. Bal 35
Torrence, Albert P. Mus 292
______, John Cpb 207
______, Samuel Wrn 198
______, Septamues Wrn 199
Torence, Ebenezer Gre 280
Tarrence, John W. Wrn 199
TOTMAN, Joshua Elb 127
TOTTY, Elizabeth Gre 299
______, John Clk 322
______, Thomas Gre 295
TOUCHSTONE/TUCHSTONE/
TECHSTONE/TETCHSTONE
Touchstone, Annis Lau 21
______, Henry App 6
______, Henry Jsp 358
______, James Lwn 88
______, William Hry 223
Tuchstone, Stephen Dec 6
Techstone, James Lwn 88
Tetchstone, Lavena Pik 125
TOURISLEY, Lott S. Wsh 258
TOWERS, Amos DeK 62
______, Benjamin Gwn 315
______, Easter Cht 248
______, Isaac DeK 26
______, John Gwn 347
______, Lewis DeK 55
______, Matilda Wrn 202
______, Nathaniel Hal 74
______, William DeK 47
______, William DeK 65
TOWLE, William Mwr 152
TOWLER/TOLLER

Name	County	Page
Towler, Alejak	Wal	150
_____, Benjamin	Ogl	93
_____, William R.	Ware	183
Toller, James	Up	118
_____, William	Put	175
TOWLS, James	Bry	86
TOWNS, Bartley	Put	199
_____, Benjamin	Clk	326
_____, Daniel	Mad	112
_____, Drury	Gre	284
_____, John G. C.	Jsp	354
_____, George W. B.	Tlb	335
_____, Gideon	Wil	304
_____, Henry C.	Trp	42
_____, Hocky L.	Bib	57
_____, James	Mad	115
_____, James	Tfo	369
_____, John	Frk	247
_____, John	Trp	49
_____, John W.	Tfo	358
_____, Rebecca	Tfo	363
_____, Sherod	Tfo	363
_____, Solomon	Wil	319
_____, William	Tlb	328
TOWNSEND/TOWSON/TOWNSEN/ TOWNSAND		
Townsend, Allen	Lwn	86
_____, Darrah	Bib	50
_____, Edward	Hab	9
_____, Eli	Hab	9
_____, Jesse	Lwn	88
_____, John	DeK	47
_____, John	Lwn	86
_____, Joshua	DeK	45
_____, Sarah	Jns	471
_____, Solomon	Hry	229
_____, Thomas	Hab	8
_____, Thomas Jr.	Hab	9
_____, William	Eff	108
Towson, Henry	Wsh	265
_____, James	Mor	246
_____, Thomas	Mor	246
_____, William	Mor	247
Townsen, Andrew	Hal	75
Townsand, John	Ogl	101
TOWNSLEY/TOUNSLEY		
Townsley, V. S.	Wsh	242
Tounsley, Lott S.	Wsh	258
TRACY, Edward D.	Bib	53
TRAIL, Abraham	Jks	340
TRAILOR, Edward	Up	109
TRAINUM/TRANUM		
Trainum, Elizabeth (W)	Mor	243
Tranum, George W.	Cpb	201
TRAMMEL/TRAMMELL/TRAMEL/ TRAMELL/TRAMMIL		
Trammel, Alfred B.	Pik	106
_____, Daniel	Lau	12
_____, Dennis	Jsp	367
_____, James	Lin	73
_____, John	Hab	64
_____, John	Lin	73
_____, John W.	Lin	74
_____, Peter Sr.	Lin	74
_____, Peter	Lin	29
_____, Redin	Lin	73
_____, Thomas	Cow	383
_____, William	Elb	131
_____, William	Lin	73
_____, William	Lin	74
_____, William	Rch	288
Trammell, David	Lin	74
_____, Drakeford L.	Up	110
_____, Elisha	New	11
_____, Farr H.	New	5
_____, John	Clk	299
_____, John	Wal	140
_____, Mary	Up	110
Tramel, Frances M.	Har	183
_____, Hamilton	Gwn	343
_____, Robert	Hab	65
Tramell, James	Hal	131
_____, Thomas	Col	341
Trammil, Hiram	Gwn	315
TRANCE, James	Wks	346
TRANTHAM, Absolum	Cpb	208
TRAPNELL, Elijah	Bke	119
TRAPP, Benjamin	Jns	467
_____, Marth	Bal	42
TRATONS, William	Cht	271
TRAUB, Charles	Rch	255
TRAVIS, Asa	Dec	17
_____, David D.	Bke	122
_____, Harbard	Fay	198
_____, James	Mor	248
_____, James	Pul	143
_____, Jesse	Hry	210
_____, John	Mor	247
TRAYLOR/TRAYLER/TRALOW/ TRAILOR		
Traylor, George	Jks	316
_____, Myamin	Hry	249
_____, Paschal	Ogl	85
_____, Tilman	Ogl	94
_____, Washington	Ogl	84
_____, Wiley	Trp	44

Name	County	Page
Trayler, Esther	Jsp	363
______, John	Trp	43
Tralow, William	Trp	34
Trailor, William	Put	190
TRAYWICK/TRAWICK		
Traywick, Anna	Han	170
______, Francis M.	Han	169
______, Fredrick	Han	169
______, George R.	Han	169
______, Henry	Crf	414
______, Jane	Han	170
______, Lunsford	Wsh	276
______, Moses	Har	191
______, Moses	Wsh	264
______, Shadrack	Han	169
______, William	Wsh	270
Trawick, George	Mus	282
______, James	Tlb	340
TREADWATER, Elijah	Gre	288
TREBLE/TRIBLE/TREBBLE/ TRIBBLE		
Treble, Pheareabea	Mad	117
______, Spelsbey	Mad	98
______, Thomas	Mad	100
Trible, Benjamin	Wal	133
______, William	Wal	132
Trebble, Wily	Wks	349
Tribble, Joel	Ogl	72
TREDAWAY/TREDEWAY		
Tredaway, Elis	Trp	38
______, John	Wal	153
______, Sarah	Hal	130
______, William	Rab	229
Tredeway, Thomas	Dec	10
TREDWELL/TREADWELL		
Tredwell, David	Wal	166
______, David	Trp	48
______, Hardy	Wal	128
______, Harvey	Wal	152
______, Isaac	Clk	309
______, Isaac	Wal	136
______, Jacob	Cow	383
______, James	Wal	166
______, John	Trp	49
______, Robert T.	Cow	379
______, Stephen	Trp	49
Treadwell, Admiram	Rch	258
______, H. R. D.	Tlb	323
______, J. L.	Bke	141
______, John	Hry	213
______, John Jr.	Hry	215
______, Stephen	Hry	223
TREMBLE/TRIMBLE		
Tremble, James	DeK	2
______, James	Jef	42
______, John	DeK	2
______, John	Mon	19
______, John	Mor	25
______, Joseph	DeK	7
______, Moses	DeK	3
______, Robert	Mor	26
Trimble, Elisha	New	3
______, James L.	New	
______, Moses	New	4
______, Moses	Trp	3
______, Phillip L.	New	2
TRENT, James	Hst	27
TRESPAR, Christian	Cht	24
TREUTLEN, Christian	Eff	11
TREZEVANT, Margaret J.	McI	12
TRICE, Charles	Crf	39
______, Chesly P.	Tlb	34
______, Elisha	Tlb	32
______, Thomas C.	Jns	47
______, W. A.	Gwn	32
______, William	Up	9
______, Winnifred	Jns	46
TRIGGS, John J.	Jef	40
TRIPLETT/TRIPLET		
Triplett, Jim	Rch	25
______, William	Wil	28
Triplet, Mary	Wrn	20
TRIPP/TRIPPE/TRIP		
Tripp, James	Pul	15
______, James A.	Mon	19
______, Patience	Han	16
______, Samuel	Tfo	36
______, William	Mon	19
Trippe, John	Put	19
______, R.	Up	12
Trip, Thomas S.	Han	17
TROONEY, John W.	DeK	7
TROTMAN, Blount	Wsh	24
______, Thomas	Wsh	26
TROTTER, Hezekiah	Up	11
______, Joseph	Mwr	16
______, Joseph	Ran	24
______, William	Jns	44
TROUP, George M.	Lau	1
______, James	Gly	26
______, James	McI	12
______, Robert L.	Mtg	23
TROUT, George	Hal	11
______, Gideon	Hal	11
______, Jackson	Jks	31
______, Jeremiah	Jks	31

Trout, Tilman Jks 317
_____, William H. Jks 337
TROUTEN, Thomas Jns 452
TROUTMAN, H. B. Crf 395
TROY, Elizabeth Hst 284
_____, Philip Lee 35
TRUCHELETT, M. Cht 252
TRUITT/TRUIT/TREWETT
Truitt, Morris Mon 174
_____, Nathan Wil 324
_____, Purnall Wil 314
_____, Purnall Jr. Wil 322
_____, Purnell Har 186
_____, Thomas Tfo 363
Truit, John Har 186
_____, Samuel Trp 52
_____, Thomas B. Jsp 356
Trewett, Samuel Fay 188
_____, William P. New 43
TRUKNETT, George A. Rch 289
TRULL, James Twg 83
TRULUCK/TRULOCK
Truluck, Bryant Twg 87
_____, James H. Dec 16
_____, John Twg 87
_____, Joseph Tms 20
_____, Naurel Twg 86
_____, Sutton H. Dec 17
Trulock, George Twg 87
TRUMAN, John Wks 350
TRUSSELL/TRUSSEL
Trussell, Daniel Jsp 397
_____, Richard Hry 247
Trussel, Charles A. Jsp 363
_____, Daniel T. Jsp 363
TUBMAN, Richard Rch 267
TUCK, Bennett Clk 320
_____, Claiborne Wil 297
_____, Ely B. Clk 314
_____, John B. Jks 312
_____, Joseph Clk 311
_____, Josiah Wil 297
TUCKER, Aron Mon 210
_____, Arrin D. Hst 273
_____, Barna Dec 19
_____, Bartley Fay 190
_____, Benjamin F. Bts 164
_____, Benjamin Frk 214
_____, Coleman Fay 191
_____, Crawford Hry 226
_____, Daniel Bib 66
_____, Daniel New 7
_____, Daniel New 15
Tucker, Daniel R. Wsh 272
_____, Davies D. Lau 15
_____, Dean Jks 339
_____, Dejarnett Mad 100
_____, Elizabeth Jsp 398
_____, Epps New 15
_____, Ethel Sr. Elb 157
_____, Ethel Jr. Elb 157
_____, Gabriel Cam 187
_____, Germin, dec'd. Est. Lib 54
_____, H. D. Elb 150
_____, Harberd Elb 125
_____, Harper Wsh 246
_____, Henry C. Wsh 257
_____, James D. Ogl 73
_____, Jemima Lwn 89
_____, Henry C. Lwn 79
_____, Isaac Cam 187
_____, Jeremiah Jsp 383
_____, Joel T. Wks 352
_____, John Jsp 381
_____, John Lau 11
_____, John Jns 471
_____, John Mon 213
_____, John Up 97
_____, John C. Fay 191
_____, John R. Wsh 253
_____, Jordin Lee 34
_____, Joseph Har 175
_____, Joseph Tfo 361
_____, Lewis Frk 230
_____, Littleberry Han 169
_____, Mary Ann Up 104
_____, McKindre New 15
_____, Nathan Lau 7
_____, Pointor Jsp 382
_____, Richard Irw 301
_____, Robert Fay 187
_____, Robert Mon 210
_____, Robert New 16
_____, Robert W. Elb 131
_____, Stephen C. Elb 152
_____, Stephen E. Ware 185
_____, Tarpley Ogl 73
_____, Thomas Cam 192
_____, Thomas Mwr 161
_____, Timothy Jns 469
_____, Whitefield Mor 249
_____, William Elb 157
_____, William Frk 243
_____, William Hal 107
_____, William Han 169
_____, William Mon 175

Tucker, William Mon 201
______, William New 18
______, William Wsh 258
______, William D. Crf 403
______, William G. Mad 109
______, William H. Hry 244
______, William L. Tfo 357
TUDER, John Col 337
______, Thomas Col 337
TUFFTS, Frances Jns 444
______, Mary Cht 259
TUGGLE, Charles Mad 118
______, George Ogl 89
______, Henry Ogl 89
______, James Gwn 361
______, John Sr. Hal 76
______, John Sr. Hal 76
______, Lee Mwr 167
______, Leonard Jsp 367
______, Loderich DeK 27
______, Ransom Hry 215
______, Robert Jsp 381
______, Thomas Jsp 366
______, Thomas H. Jsp 379
______, William Gre 283
______, William Jr. Gre 284
______, William L. Hry 210
TULL, Isaac Wsh 265
______, Lewis Hst 262
TULLIS/TULLOS
Tullis, Moses Mon 180
______, Moses Jr. Mon 213
______, Newell Trp 55
Tullos, Stephen Eff 112
TUNE, William Crf 398
TUNNEL/TUNNELL
Tunnel, John Jks 336
Tunnell, William Gre 287
TUNING, Ambrose DeK 41
TUNNO, John C. McI 125
TURK, Arrington Put 197
______, M. Ann Bal 38
______, Thomas Bal 44
______, William Frk 217
TURLEY, Patrick Wrn 199
______, William A. New 12
TURMAN/TURMON/ also see Thurmond
TURNER, Aaron Hry 235
______, Aaron Lee 29
______, Abednego Mon 203
______, Absalom Bke 130
______, Alexander Hry 211
Turner, Alexander Mar 141
______, Allen Lin 65
______, Andrew Hry 205
______, Anthony W. Jef 423
______, Archebald Gre 277
______, Asa A. Gwn 313
______, Barthemew New 29
______, Benney Hab 9
______, Benjamin Hry 224
______, Butler S. Hry 219
______, C. W. Cht 249
______, Cherry Fay 205
______, Daniel C. Cow 386
______, David Gwn 315
______, David Jns 458
______, David Tat 377
______, Edward Hry 244
______, Edwin C. Up 105
______, Eli Wal 133
______, Elias Hab 9
______, Elijah DeK 52
______, Elisha New 5
______, Elizabeth Clk 315
______, Elizabeth New 36
______, Elizabeth S. Han 169
______, Ellinder Bts 165
______, Emily W. Lwn 84
______, Ephraim Em 170
______, Esom New 36
______, Ezekiah Mon 187
______, George Jef 423
______, George Mon 214
______, George Wil 303
______, George Wrn 197
______, George S. Hry 225
______, George B. New 35
______, Greory Crf 398
______, Henry Bak 1
______, Henry Bke 121
______, Henry Gwn 379
______, Henry Hab
______, Henry Hst 27
______, Henry Hst 28
______, Henry Hst 29
______, Henry Scr 29
______, Henry Wil 30
______, Henry G. Jsp 35
______, Henry P. Jef 42
______, Hezekiah Hal 11
______, Hy. Gwn 37
______, Isaac Bul 9
______, Isham Mar 13
______, Jacob P. Put 17

Turner, James DeK 37
______, James Fay 182
______, James Fay 197
______, James Irw 301
______, James Mon 178
______, James Mon 212
______, James Tat 375
______, James Trp 33
______, James Up 99
______, James Wrn 198
______, James B. Lin 65
______, James R. Hry 236
______, James R. Jsp 398
______, James R. Put 186
______, James S. Cow 387
______, Jane Put 182
______, Jared L. Gre 277
______, Jarett Hab 11
______, Jehu Put 177
______, Jesse App 12
______, Jesse New 24
______, Jesse New 25
______, Jo. Gwn 351
______, John Jr. Bke 117
______, John Jr. Bke 117
______, John Bke 121
______, John Clk 311
______, John Cow 375
______, John Cpb 200
______, John Crf 400
______, John Gwn 314
______, John Gwn 323
______, John Gwn 331
______, John Hry 205
______, John Hst 285
______, John Lee 29
______, John Mar 142
______, John Mor 267
______, John Put 197
______, John Up 103
______, John B. Hal 71
______, John B. Pik 127
______, John C. DeK 66
______, John D. Mad 113
______, John M. Mon 212
______, John T. B. Mon 214
______, John W. Cht 247
______, John W. Jns 475
______, John W. Gly 268
______, John W. Lin 67
______, Jonathan Ham 169
______, Joseph Hry 216
______, Joseph Jks 341
Turner, Joseph Mwr 167
______, Joseph Put 178
______, Josiah Jks 340
______, Julius Crf 407
______, Larkin Car 223
______, Larkin New 5
______, Levi H. Hry 247
______, Levi Jns 473
______, Levin Mon 194
______, Lewis Frk 215
______, Lewis Hal 99
______, Lewis Lin 60
______, Luke Wil 296
______, Manson New 32
______, Margarett Jef 424
______, Mark Fay 203
______, Mary Cht 269
______, Mary Jef 423
______, Mathew Gwn 323
______, Mathew Up 105
______, Matthias DeK 38
______, Meshac Mon 179
______, Miles G. Mon 187
______, Moses T. Fay 187
______, Philip Han 169
______, Pleasant Mad 114
______, Pleasant H. Gwn 356
______, R. Lee 29
______, Reuben Bke 121
______, Reuben Hry 206
______, Richard Cht 253
______, Richard Jsp 386
______, Robert Fay 187
______, Robert Hab 16
______, Samuel Cow 377
______, Samuel DeK 38
______, Samuel Han 170
______, Samuel B. New 43
______, Samuel P. Put 204
______, Sarah Har 188
______, Shadrack Jsp 379
______, Shadrack Lin 61
______, Silas Fay 185
______, Stephen Doo 78
______, Stephen C. DeK 36
______, Thomas Elb 122
______, Thomas Fay 181
______, Thomas Hab 53
______, Thomas Pik 117
______, Thomas Put 177
______, Thomas B. Gwn 316
______, Thomas B. Gwn 351
______, Thomas B. Put 172

Name	County	Page
Turner, Thomas F.	Hal	122
_____, Thomas M.	Cht	253
_____, Wade H.	Hry	221
_____, William	DeK	63
_____, William	Em	176
_____, William	Hab	6
_____, William	Hal	126
_____, William	Hry	211
_____, William Jr.	Hry	247
_____, William	Lin	64
_____, William	Mwr	160
_____, William	Mon	179
_____, William	Pik	113
_____, William	Put	183
_____, William	Wal	143
_____, William R.	Cow	386
_____, William R.	Cpb	199
_____, Wilson	Han	170
TURNHAM, Thomas	Mon	175
**TURPIN, Alfred (slave)	Rch	261
_____, Alin	Hab	63
_____, William H.	Rch	279
TURRENTINE/TURENTINE		
Turrentine, James	Pik	106
_____, Samuel	Up	99
_____, William	Pik	106
Turentine, George W.	Cow	375
TURVAVILLE/TURVENILL		
Turvaville, James	Hry	234
Turvenill, Tapley	Fay	202
TUTLE/TUTTLE		
Tutle, Pherraby	Wsh	275
_____, Robert	Bke	144
Tuttle, Isaac S.	Rch	262
TUTT, William	Rch	262
TUTTON/TUTON		
Tutton, Elijah	Gwn	316
Tuton, Rigdon	Gly	268
TWEADLE, Jeremiah	New	53
TWEATY/TWITTY		
Tweaty, George	Fay	202
Twitty, Thomas	Clk	308
TWIGGS, George L.	Rch	289
TWILLY/TWILLEY		
Twilly, Elijah	DeK	28
_____, Elijah	Pik	128
_____, James	DeK	53
_____, James	Gre	272
_____, Polly	DeK	51
Twilley, William	Wsh	256
TYE, Daniel	Jns	452
_____, Jobe	Ogl	94
_____, Samuel	Ogl	94
TYLER, Alexander G.	Put	215
_____, Enoch	Mwr	161
_____, Francis	Lin	74
_____, Henry	Elb	129
_____, Jacob J.	Hal	74
_____, James	Jsp	382
_____, James	Jsp	397
_____, John	Twg	62
_____, Owen	Jsp	398
_____, Reuben D.	Elb	129
_____, Thomas	Jsp	395
_____, Thomas	Wks	351
_____, Wiley	Up	117
_____, William	Jsp	360
_____, William	Jsp	396
TYNER, Elijah	Eff	106
_____, Harris	Elb	121
_____, Jackson	Put	179
_____, John	Ear	100
_____, Jonathan	Eff	109
_____, Kirland	Bib	57
_____, Simeon	Eff	109
_____, Tolison	Elb	127
_____, William	Elb	127
TYRE, Cannon	App	7
_____, John	App	5
_____, Louis	App	7
_____, Reaves	Hry	207
_____, William	App	7
_____, William	Trp	36
TYSON, Aaron	Ear	95
_____, Calvin	Eff	106
_____, Cammel	Eff	110
_____, Eason	Lau	6
_____, Eugene H.	Clk	312
_____, Hugh	Wrn	214
_____, Leuther	Eff	109
_____, M.	Bal	35
_____, Martha	Cam	189
_____, Mary A.	Bke	125
_____, Moses	Lau	20
_____, Phillip	Ear	96
_____, Sarah O.	Wrn	210
_____, Thomas O.	Wrn	218
TYUS, Eliza	Han	169
_____, John	Mwr	154
_____, William G.	Jns	433
_____, William Y.	Han	169

Name	County	Page
UBANKS, Harriet	Lin	73
ULLIAM, Joseph	Elb	142
ULM, Harry	Lin	62
ULMER, Charles	Cht	277
______, J.	Cht	277
______, Philip	Eff	104
UMPHREY/UMPHRY/UMPHREE		
Umphrey, John	Dec	11
______, William	Cpb	204
Umphry, Jesse	Cpb	208
Umphree, Wright	Bke	126
UNDERHILL, Jerh.	Ware	183
______, Joseph	Ware	188
UNDERWOOD/UNDOWOOD		
Underwood, Benjamin	Hal	132
______, Benjamin	Wks	340
______, Daniel	Gre	298
______, Enoch	Bal	31
______, Eady	Wrn	227
______, Elizabeth	Doo	84
______, Elizabeth	Hst	296
______, Ezekuel	Elb	158
______, George	Wrn	222
______, Isaac	Put	200
______, James	Lau	14
______, James	Tat	372
______, Jarratt	New	36
______, Jehu	Wyn	282
______, John	Cow	368
______, John	Elb	144
______, John	Gwn	360
______, John	Mar	144
______, John	Twg	64
______, John J.	Lwn	87
______, Joseph	Elb	122
______, Josiah	Wrn	228
______, Lewis	Wrn	221
______, Mason	Crf	403
______, Reuben	Elb	125
______, Reuben	Wsh	257
______, Robert	New	40
______, Sarah	Mon	205
______, Thomas	Lib	54
______, Thomas	Wks	350
______, Thon.	Gwn	354
______, William	Col	335
______, William	Mar	144
______, William	Wrn	217
______, William H.	Frk	222
Undowood, Aaron	Gwn	351
UNUS, Samuel	Elb	131
UPCHURCH, Britton	Gwn	346
______, Charity	Hry	250
Upchurch, Charles	Hry	250
______, Clayborn	Han	170
______, Eaton	Hry	250
______, Gay	Hry	247
______, Keaton	Hry	222
UPDEGRAP, David	Wil	290
UPSHAW, Adkin	Wal	157
______, George	Elb	142
______, Haston	Elb	119
______, James	Elb	140
______, John	Elb	160
______, Leroy	Elb	141
______, Rebecca	Elb	139
______, Richard	Wal	158
______, Tinsley	Wal	157
UPTON/UPTAIN		
Upton, David	Mus	279
______, James	Car	223
______, Thomas	Hry	230
______, Tobias	Wrn	217
______, William	Col	344
Uptain, George	Cow	372
______, John A. T.	Cow	372
URQUHART/URQHUART		
Urquhart, Charles	Rch	271
______, David	Rch	258
______, David	Rch	292
______, D. O. Wm.	Bke	154
______, Henery	Cow	369
______, John	Bts	170
Urghuart, Neil	Pik	110
USALUM, Delila	Jns	429
USHER/USSARY/USSERY/URSERY/USERY/URSHER/USRY		
Usher, Able	McI	123
______, Henry	Rch	282
______, Thomas	Tms	23
______, William	Scr	301
Ussary, John	Jns	428
______, John	Wrn	220
______, John Jr.	Jns	435
______, Peter	Wrn	221
Ussery, Meredith	Lau	14
______, Thomas	Tlb	348
______, William	Tlb	347
Ursery, Carrol	Wks	356
______, Elizabeth	Bke	132
______, John	Wks	357
Usery, Levi	Wks	358
Ursher, S. A.	Jsp	372
Usry, John	Mar	139
UTLEY, Henry	Bke	140

Name	County	Page
VADEN, Martha	DeK	52
VALENTINE, Andrew	Wks	340
_____, John	Rch	270
_____, Thomas	Wks	340
VALKINGBURGH, A. G.	Gwn	351
VALLOTTON/VOLLENTON		
Vallotton, Francis	Bke	136
Vollenton, Benjamin	Lau	5
VANBIBBER, Henry	Pik	122
VANBRACKEL, John	Bry	87
VANCE, Arthur	Jef	421
_____, John	Mus	292
_____, John W.	Jef	421
_____, M. D.	Jsp	352
VANDAGRFF/VANDERGRIFT		
Vandagrff, Jarred	Hab	51
Vandergrift, John	Hry	214
VANDEFORD, Barzillar	Mad	110
_____, Nathan	Hal	121
_____, Richard	Clk	309
_____, William	Clk	309
VANDEVER/VANDIVER		
Vandever, L.	Bal	44
Vandiver, Matthew W.	Frk	211
VANDIKE, John	Hab	19
VANHORN, Benjamin	Hab	22
_____, John	Hab	22
VANLANDINGHAM, Elizabeth	Ogl	84
_____, John	Mor	251
_____, John	Wks	337
_____, Thomas	New	11
_____, William	Wks	350
VANN, Ansel B.	Wal	158
*_____, Charles (free col)	Car	234
*_____, David (free col)	Car	233
_____, David	Fay	194
_____, Henry	Wsh	275
_____, Isaiah	Wal	158
_____, Jonathan	Mar	141
_____, Nancy	DeK	70
_____, Rolan	Jks	324
_____, Samuel	Wsh	267
_____, Sanders	Trp	53
_____, Saunders	Twg	71
_____, Thomas	Wks	339
_____, William W.	Wsh	266
VANWRINKLE, Jesse	Hal	81
VAN ZANDT/VANZANT/VINZANT		
Van Zandt, Hannah	Rch	267
Vanzant, William	Ware	184
Vinzant, Garret	Jns	446
_____, William	Jns	446
VARDAMAN/VARDEMAN/VARNAMAN		
Vardaman, Edwy. L.	Mwr	159
_____, Joseph	Mwr	152
_____, William	Mwr	151
Vardeman, Henry	Mon	211
_____, Syl.	Mon	211
Varnaman, Thomas	Mwr	164
VARNER, Alexander	Mon	197
_____, Charles	DeK	44
_____, Edward	Jsp	364
_____, George	Hab	37
_____, Hendley	Hry	208
_____, John	Clk	309
_____, John W.	Hab	33
_____, Judy	Cow	389
_____, Marcus	Mwr	150
_____, Mathew	Ogl	102
_____, Samuel	Gwn	340
_____, William	Cpb	196
_____, William	Mor	265
_____, William	Put	217
VARNIDORE/VARNADOW		
Varnidore, Charity	Lib	54
_____, Nancy	Lau	23
_____, Nathaniel	Lib	54
Varnadow, John	Doo	84
_____, Joseph	Doo	84
VARNOM/VARNUM		
Varnom, Redin	Mar	143
Varnum, Asa	Jks	330
VASSER, John	Elb	119
_____, Mary	Han	170
_____, Micajah	Lau	5
VASON, John	Mor	247
_____, Joseph	Mor	253
VAUGHAN/VAUGHN/VAUGN/VAUN		
Vaughan, Alexander	Elb	160
_____, Benjamin	Frk	253
_____, David	Frk	242
_____, Elijah D.	Hry	214
_____, Hannah P.	Frk	212
_____, James	Frk	241
_____, John	Bke	121
_____, John	Bke	121
_____, John	Hry	234
_____, John R.	Mad	109
_____, Joshua	Frk	253
_____, Meriett	Bib	68
_____, Peter	Frk	242
_____, Sena	Frk	256
_____, Starling	Hry	234
_____, Sterling	Frk	248
_____, William	Elb	160
_____, William	Ogl	82

Vaughn, Alexander DeK 62
_____, Benjamine Cpb 195
_____, Benjamin Hab 19
_____, Benjamin Mtg 236
_____, Daniel Col 363
_____, Felix Frk 222
_____, Frederic New 27
_____, Henry Gwn 311
_____, Howell Mon 209
_____, Isaac Col 345
_____, James Col 363
_____, Jessey Mtg 235
_____, John Hab 17
_____, John Hst 295
_____, John Mon 197
_____, John Mon 209
_____, Lewis Col 338
_____, Mary Hst 295
_____, Nancy Wks 352
_____, Thomas Gwn 361
_____, William Hal 77
_____, William Jsp 359
_____, William Pik 122
_____, William Wks 353
Vaugn, Claiborn Gwn 337
_____, Nancy Gwn 321
_____, William New 28
Vaun, Lewis Jns 429
VAUGHTERS, James Frk 241
VEAL, Anderson New 51
_____, Burwell Twg 72
_____, David Trp 37
_____, Edward Wsh 261
_____, Francis Hab 39
_____, George Clk 320
_____, George Wsh 270
_____, James Mad 113
_____, James Put 191
_____, John DeK 58
_____, Joseph Put 191
_____, Lewis D. DeK 67
_____, Nathan Wsh 276
_____, Richard H. Wsh 272
_____, William DeK 62
_____, William Twg 83
VEASY/VEAZEY/VEASEY/VESEY
Veasy, Abner Hst 273
_____, Abner Put 172
_____, James Tfo 366
_____, Jesse Tfo 362
_____, John Trp 45
_____, John Tfo 368
_____, Mrs. Bal 51
Veazey, Caleb Gre 298
_____, Ezekiel Gre 301
_____, Honson Gre 301
_____, James L. Gre 297
_____, Jesse Gre 292
_____, John H. Gre 273
_____, Nancy Gre 304
Veasey, John Wrn 227
Vesey, Stephen Mon 218
VEAVRE, B. Cht 270
VEITOIS, Milton DeK 58
VELIM, John H. Wal 151
VELVIN, Robert Gwn 324
VENABLE/VENIBLE
Venable, John Gwn 315
_____, Nathaniel Jks 329
_____, Robert Gwn 349
_____, Thomas DeK 64
Venible, William Fay 205
VERDEL, John A. Elb 138
VERDERY, Augustus Rch 285
_____, B. F. Bke 143
_____, M. P. Bke 128
_____, Maturin Rch 278
VERDIN, Elizabeth Bib 77
_____, William Pik 131
VERMILLIAN, William Hal 75
VERNON, Frederick Ogl 75
_____, George Ogl 72
VERONEE, William Wil 289
VERSON, John Jr. Jns 458
VESSELS, Ellender Frk 257
_____, Thomas Hry 211
VESTEL, Jeremiah Hab 21
VESTAL, William S. Frk 210
VICARS, Elijah Put 196
VICK, David Mtg 233
_____, Jonathan Doo 80
_____, Moses App 7
_____, Simon Lau 17
VICKERS, Abraham Jef 407
_____, Absolem Clk 304
_____, Drew Lwn 90
_____, Duncan M. Hry 207
_____, Elijah Wsh 276
_____, Ferdinand Cow 371
_____, Gresham Ogl 94
_____, James Lau 20
_____, James Wal 139
_____, James M. Pul 160
_____, Jesse Irw 303
_____, Jesse Lwn 90
_____, John Clk 295

Name	County	Page
Vickers, John	Wal	132
______, John M.	Hry	243
______, Josiah	Trp	38
______, Marten	Clk	296
______, Nancy	Twg	86
______, Sarah	Han	170
______, Silas	Hry	232
______, Wiley	Irw	303
______, William	Bts	176
______, William	Wal	128
VICKERY/VICKORY/VICKRY/ VICKREY		
Vickery, Albert	Hab	8
______, Eli	Dec	11
______, Hetty	Gwn	374
______, James	Elb	130
______, Jesse	Dec	9
______, Joseph	Elb	144
______, Marmaduke	Hab	8
Vickory, Christopher	Hal	111
______, Hezekia	Scr	310
Vickry, Aaron	Elb	130
______, Aaron Jr.	Elb	135
Vickrey, Thomas	Wyn	283
VICTORY, John	Mus	286
______, Thomas	Gre	274
______, William	Cpb	203
VIGAL, George	Bib	53
VILIARD, John	Hal	106
VINCENT, Benjamin	Bal	42
______, Benjamin	Wsh	246
______, Casia	Wsh	261
______, David	Col	337
______, David	Rch	287
______, E.	Wks	345
______, Elinr	Wks	341
______, Elisha	Gwn	319
______, George	Hal	110
______, George	Wsh	246
______, H. H.	Wks	350
______, Henry	Crf	405
______, Henry	Put	205
______, Isaac Sr.	Clk	308
______, James	Clk	294
______, James	Twg	63
______, John	Jns	463
______, Josiah	Wsh	246
______, Nancy	Gre	301
______, Nathaniel	Put	207
______, Nimrod	Gwn	362
______, Obediah	Clk	293
______, Peyton	Mus	282
______, Thomas	Twg	69
Vincent, Wiley	Jns	463
______, William	Put	209
______, Winaford	Hal	101
______, Wingate	Har	181
VINES, Benjamin	Cow	380
______, Hiram	Bib	72
______, James	Cow	372
______, John	Hal	113
______, Joseph	Elb	135
______, Parnell	Cow	380
______, William	Cow	380
VINEYARD, Allen	Gwn	325
______, James Jr.	Mad	115
______, John	Cow	379
______, Joseph	Mad	115
______, William	Gwn	327
______, William	Jks	322
VINING/VINEING/VINYING		
Vining, Benjamin	Cpb	203
______, David	New	31
______, John Sr.	Jef	424
______, John Jr.	Jef	405
______, Nelly	Wrn	233
______, Reuben	Put	187
______, Shadrick	New	48
______, Simeon	Put	187
Vineing, Samuel	Cpb	207
Vinying, Samuel	Crf	405
VINSON/VINCEN		
Vinson, Aaron	Ran	243
______, Isaac	Hst	270
______, James	Han	170
______, James	Mon	211
______, Jinny	Hry	244
______, John	Han	170
______, Moses	Jks	342
______, Nathan	Pik	128
______, Nimrod	Hry	215
______, Selby	Hry	244
______, Susannah	DeK	61
______, Tully	Han	170
______, Wesley	Hry	217
______, West	Han	170
Vincen, Nancy	Jef	420
VINTERS/VENTERS		
Vinters, James	Bib	53
Venters, Stephen	Put	197
VIOLS, Ellison	Up	109
VISAGE, James	Crf	394
______, William	Rab	230
VOILS, James	Hal	96
______, Samuel	Hal	123
VOSEL, John	Cam	184

VOSS, Mary Put 194
VOTY, David Cht 254
VOWELL/VOWEL
Vowell, David Cow 374
_____, John Cow 374
Vowel, Mala Car 226
VOYACLE, Josiah Wrn 227
_____, Lewis Wrn 228

WABBINGTON, E. Gwn 316
WACESTER, S. A. Gwn 376
WADDELL/WADDLE/WADDEL
Waddell, Henry Jsp 360
_____, Jane Jsp 362
_____, Noel Mar 139
_____, William W. Clk 327
Waddle, James Wal 166
_____, Marget DeK 67
_____, Thomas Mor 263
Waddel, James P. Rch 262
WADE/WAID/WADD/WAIDE
Wade, Ann Frk 237
_____, Asa Gwn 314
_____, Charles Col 362
_____, David Hal 117
_____, Edward Col 359
_____, Edward Sr. DeK 53
_____, Edward Jr. DeK 53
_____, Elijah Gwn 344
_____, Elijah Scr 316
_____, Elisha Scr 315
_____, Elizabeth Jsp 383
_____, George W. Mad 117
_____, Hamlin L. Mon 219
_____, Henry Gwn 311
_____, Hezekiah Pul 132
_____, Hudson Mor 252
_____, Mrs. J. Col 362
_____, James Frk 235
_____, James Hab 39
_____, James Lwn 90
_____, James H. Scr 318
_____, Jane Cht 261
_____, Jeremiah Pul 151
_____, Jesse New 25
_____, Jesse Twg 87
_____, John Frk 237
_____, John Gwn 362
_____, John Hry 243
_____, John B. Frk 237
_____, John D. Mor 238
_____, Joshua Gre 295
Wade, Lucy Tfo 369
_____, Magruder Pul 152
_____, Nathaniel DeK 61
_____, Nathaniel Scr 317
_____, Paton Mwr 168
_____, Payton Hal 94
_____, Peyton Mor 261
_____, Peyton L. Scr 315
_____, Philip Hal 117
_____, Polly Hab 39
_____, Polly Hab 60
_____, Reubin Gwn 362
_____, Richard Hal 127
_____, Robert Col 362
_____, Sarah Wil 303
_____, Thomas Clk 298
_____, Thomas Clk 303
_____, William Cpb 204
_____, William Cpb 211
_____, William Hal 71
_____, William Scr 302
Waid, James Mar 138
_____, James P. Hab 44
_____, Zachariah Bib 57
Wadd, Samuel Hab 37
Waide, John Har 184
WADSWORTH, Archibald Pik 129
_____, Daniel Bib 63
_____, Elbert Hst 289
_____, Highacur Crf 409
_____, Hiram Hst 275
_____, Isaac Jns 463
_____, James Har 178
_____, James Sr. Jns 463
_____, James Jr. Jns 473
_____, James Mus 281
_____, John Mwr 157
_____, John Pik 127
_____, John Pik 127
_____, Thomas Lin 73
_____, Thomas Pik 131
_____, Waller DeK 35
_____, William Bib 72
_____, William Fay 204
_____, William Jns 463
_____, William Lin 66
_____, William Pik 129
WAFER, James T. Try 52
WAFFORD/WADFORD
Wafford, Absalom Jks 339
_____, James W. DeK 41
_____, John Mor 262
_____, Lucy Han 172

Wafford, Moses Jks 337
______, Sarah Han 172
______, Solomon Jks 319
Wadford, Alexander Trp 35
WAGES, Andrew Jks 315
______, Caleb Bts 159
______, Joel Wal 168
WAGGONER/WAGNER/WAGNON/
WAGNOR
Waggoner, Albert Cht 267
______, Amos Put 204
______, David Mad 103
______, George P. Put 183
______, Henry Wrn 198
______, James Put 174
______, James M. Wrn 207
______, Seaborn Ogl 95
______, William Gre 296
______, Zacheous Wrn 198
Wagner, Benjamin Trp 34
______, Henry Rch 258
______, Michael Rch 257
______, Simeon Bal 36
Wagnon, John Hal 117
______, Wiley V. Cow 379
______, William J. Crf 393
______, William P. Car 214
Wagnor, Thomas P. Gre 275
______, Nicholas Bib 59
WAINWRIGHT/WAINRIGHT
Wainwright, James Wyn 282
______, Joseph Wyn 282
Wainright, Joseph Bib 57
WAITERS, James Gwn 329
WAITS/WATES/WAITES/WAIT
Waits, Absalom Gwn 356
______, Benjamin Jsp 366
______, David DeK 38
______, Henry Trp 52
______, Jerre DeK 38
______, John DeK 39
______, John DeK 70
______, John Jsp 373
______, Mark Gwn 353
Wates, James Gwn 370
______, John Cow 378
______, Sarah Hal 88
______, Wade Hal 92
Waites, Samuel Cpb 203
Wait, Susan Cht 260
WAKEFIELD, John *
______, William Fay 196
WALCH/WALSH
Walch, John Put 179
Walsh, Thomas Lib 54
WALDBURG/WALDBUG
Waldburg, George M. Lib 54
______, Jacob Lib 54
Waldbug, Sarah Cht 264
WALEA, James Em 165
______, James Em 166
______, Severn Em 165
______, William Tms 22
WALDEN/WALDRON/WALDREN/
WALDIN/WALDON
Walden, Alex. Cow 369
______, Amos Wrn 232
______, Edward Jef 404
______, Eli Jef 421
______, Elijah Jsp 390
______, Green Hst 265
______, Elisha Jef 404
______, Henry Jef 404
______, James Cow 384
______, Jane Jef 404
______, Lemuel Pul 153
______, Mitchel Jef 422
______, Moses Jef 404
______, Peter Gwn 311
______, Reuben Pul 153
______, Richard Wrn 231
______, Samuel Jef 404
______, Samuel Twg 83
______, Sarah Jns 459
______, Tavner Hry 223
______, William H. Hry 248
Waldron, David Ware 188
______, Oliver Ware 189
Waldren, Benjamin S. Bry 87
Waldin, Martin Dec 9
Waldon, Daniel Hal 124
WALDHAUER/WALTHOUR
Waldhauer, Israel F. Eff 104
______, John Eff 107
Walthour, George W. Lib 55
WALDROUP/WALDROOP/WALLDROOP/
WALDRUP/WALDROP/WALDRIP/
WALDROPE/WALDRUPE/WALDREP/
WALTROPE/WARDROP
Waldroup, A. Gwn 308
______, Harmon New 23
______, James Fay 194
______, S. Gwn 308
Waldroop, Amos Hab 65
______, Benjamin Cow 383
______, Eli N. Mon 172

* County and page inadvertantly omitted from index card.

Name	County	Page
Walldroop, Joseph	Hab	58
Waldrup, Isaac	Fay	189
______, Mathew	Hry	234
______, William	Fay	195
Waldrop, John	Tlb	325
______, Mager	Tlb	342
Waldrip, David	Jsp	360
______, Solomon	Jsp	362
Waldrope, John	DeK	32
Waldrupe, George	Mar	142
Waldrep, Mary	Bts	177
Waltrope, Jesse	DeK	68
Wardrop, Greenberry	Har	186
WALKER/WAKER		
Walker, A.	Bke	153
______, A.	Bke	153
______, A. B.	Rch	270
______, Abraham	Clk	327
______, Allen	Gwn	315
______, Amos	Bke	136
______, Ann	Col	350
______, Ann M.	Rch	267
______, Arther	Hab	36
______, Aurelius	Gre	303
______, Benjamin	Hry	230
______, Benjamin	Up	109
______, Beverly	Har	180
______, Buckner	Hab	66
______, Burton	Wal	172
______, Charles	Pul	138
______, Charles B.	Mor	272
______, Churchill	Put	206
______, Clarissa	Car	220
______, Clement	Han	170
______, Daniel Sr.	Rch	285
______, Daniel Jr.	Rch	286
______, Daniel	Wal	124
______, David	Col	346
______, David	Gre	276
______, David	Hst	296
______, David	Pul	139
______, David	Wsh	264
______, Decker F.	Mon	192
______, Dorsett	Wsh	262
______, Edmond	Mor	255
______, Elathan D.	New	6
______, Eli F.	Tlb	339
______, Eli H.	Mor	172
______, Elias	Ware	184
______, Elija	Har	188
______, Elijah	Jsp	386
______, Elijah	Ogl	80
______, Elisha	Hry	225

Name	County	Page
Walker, Elizabeth	Hst	295
______, Elizabeth	Jef	406
______, Elizabeth	Wil	312
______, Elizabeth	Rch	288
______, Ezekiel	Bts	166
______, Felix H.	Gwn	315
** ______, G.A.B. (slave)	Rch	275
______, George	Pul	139
______, George	Tlb	323
______, George A. B.	Rch	278
______, George M.	Rch	261
______, George W.	Wal	152
______, George W.	Wrn	206
______, Hackey	Jsp	380
______, Handridge	Hab	23
______, Henry	Gre	282
______, Henry	Jef	405
______, Henry	Wsh	276
______, Henry	Wrn	204
______, Henry Tandy	DeK	43
______, Herman N.	Wrn	220
______, Hiram	Bib	57
______, Holly B.	Wrn	194
______, Isaac	Mor	255
______, Isaiah	Bke	154
______, James	Car	217
______, James	Cow	390
______, James	Hab	18
______, James	Har	187
______, James	Hry	239
______, James Sr.	Irw	300
______, James Jr.	Irw	300
______, James	Lwn	85
______, James	New	37
______, James	Rch	256
______, James	Tlb	327
______, James	Up	113
______, James	Ware	187
______, James	Wil	291
______, James C.	Lin	72
______, James R.	Har	183
______, James W.	Mor	262
______, James Y.	Tlb	342
______, Jane	Wrn	222
______, Jepthah F.	Up	111
______, Jeremiah	Hry	212
______, Jeremiah	Lin	65
______, Jeremiah	Mus	280
______, Jeremiah	Wal	151
______, Jeremiah	Wyn	282
______, Jeremiah S.	Jsp	359
______, Jesse	Lee	33
______, Jessee	Lin	72

Walker, Joel Gwn 345
______, Joel Hst 269
______, Joel Put 177
______, John Car 226
______, John Col 349
______, John Frk 218
______, John Gre 298
______, John Hab 12
______, John Har 182
______, John Hry 199
______, John Hst 268
______, John Lin 65
______, John Mon 228
______, John Sr. Mor 255
______, John Mor 249
______, John Rab 224
______, John Tlb 341
______, John Wsh 256
______, John A. Lin 75
______, John B. Mor 255
______, John H. DeK 41
______, John S. Mor 251
______, John S. Up 97
______, John W. DeK 51
______, John W. Mor 249
______, Johnson Gre 292
______, Jonathan Car 214
______, Jonathan Clk 327
______, Jonathan Irw 299
______, Joseph Col 358
______, Joseph F. Crf 393
______, Katharine Frk 220
______, Lee Ear 91
______, Lewis E. DeK 70
______, Levi L. Tlb 340
______, Littleberry Sr. Ware 187
______, Littleberry Jr. Ware 187
______, Lundy Fay 194
______, Malichi J. Lin 60
______, Margaret Rch 284
______, Martha Rch 284
______, Mary App 13
______, Mason Ogl 93
______, Mathew Pik 114
______, Matthew Gre 299
______, Memory Hal 114
______, Micager Hal 112
______, Moses Bke 154
______, Moses Jsp 358
______, Moses P. Cow 381
______, Nancy LIN 72
______, Nathaniel Put 213
______, Neil Hst 296
Walker, Noah Lau 22
______, Patsy Wil 302
______, Persons Wrn 194
______, Ransom Wil 309
______, Robert DeK 46
______, Robert Pik 124
______, Robert Pik 133
______, Robert T. Bke 136
______, Robert W. Tms 19
______, Rowland Pul 158
______, Ryley Car 214
______, Sackfield M. Lin 61
______, Samuel Bts 178
______, Samuel DeK 25
______, Samuel New 22
______, Samuel Put 190
______, Shadrick Wrn 225
______, Simeon Mor 249
______, Skeaugh Mar 139
______, Solomon Rch 279
______, Sylvanus DeK 43
______, Sylvanus Gre 282
______, Tarlton Frk 224
______, Thomas Jef 406
______, Thomas Mwr 164
______, Thomas Mon 220
______, Thomas New 53
______, Thomas Rch 256
______, Thomas D. Pul 139
______, Thomas P. Bke 122
______, Valentine Rch 279
______, Virgil H. Har 181
______, Walter Scr 302
______, Wells Wrn 206
______, Wesley Hal 132
______, William Car 220
______, William Gre 291
______, William Gre 294
______, William Hab 25
______, William Han 170
______, William Har 182
______, William Jsp 357
______, William Mar 139
______, William Ogl 103
______, William Wyn 283
______, William B. Mwr 153
______, William F. Gre 281
______, William G. Har 183
______, William H. Wsh 267
______, William L. Tlb 339
______, William L. Wal 151
______, William S. Mwr 159
______, William W. Trp 42

Walker, William W. Up 121
______, Willis Jef 406
Waker, Joseph Hab 24
WALL/WALLS
Wall, Adam Lin 61
______, Asa Jns 439
______, Claborn Wrn 215
______, Drewry Rab 228
______, Etheld Rab 233
______, Evan Jsp 382
______, Ezekiel Up 96
______, Frances Col 356
______, Henry Hst 287
______, Hugh Mus 286
______, Isaac D. Bke 136
______, James Hst 285
______, James Pul 162
______, James G. Twg 78
______, Jessee Hst 285
______, Jesse Pul 157
______, Jesse Rab 235
______, John Hst 273
______, John Sr. Lin 72
______, John Lin 73
______, John A. Fay 193
______, Joseph Twg 75
______, King D. Twg 82
______, Lydia Twg 75
______, Mary Cht 246
______, Robert Hst 286
______, Robert R. Bke 155
______, Samuel Cht 277
______, Shadrick Bak 18
______, Solomon Mar 137
______, Wiley Elb 152
______, William Rab 228
______, William D. Mtg 235
______, William E. A. Twg 64
______, Willis Elb 152
Walls, Birch Dec 16
______, Charles Gwn 360
______, Charles Jks 346
______, Edwin Gwn 361
______, George W. Mor 271
______, James Bts 169
______, Jeremiah Frk 243
______, Jesse Bib 75
______, Jesse Mus 286
______, John Fay 199
______, John Jks 346
______, John A. Gwn 367
______, Sally Frk 257
______, Solomon Rch 219
Walls, Thomas Rch 291
______, Thompson Up 117
______, William Jks 346
______, Williamson Jks 323
______, Zachariah Frk 227
WALLACE/WALLIS/WALACE/
WALIS
Wallace, Abram Lin 69
______, Adam Bke 131
______, Benjamin DeK 37
______, Benjamin Wil 300
______, Cargal Put 181
______, Charles Lin 68
______, Civil Irw 299
______, Elias Crf 404
______, Elijah Lee 29
______, Elizabeth Put 181
______, Epps Pul 143
______, George Doo 79
______, James Cht 277
______, James Irw 302
______, James Lin 67
______, James Lin 70
______, James A. Lin 66
______, Jesse DeK 65
______, Jesse DeK 70
______, John Bke 131
______, John Pul 143
______, John Put 177
______, Lorenzo Put 199
______, Martha McI 130
______, Peter DeK 33
______, R. G. Cht 244
______, Robert Lin 68
______, Stiring B. Bke 128
______, Susan Lin 70
______, Thomas Elb 120
______, Vinety Gwn 354
______, Wade DeK 65
______, William Bke 131
______, William DeK 64
______, William Hal 74
______, William Lin 66
______, William Wsh 264
______, William L. Lau 7
Wallis, Absalom Jks 325
______, Daniel Jks 317
______, David C. Bts 165
______, Enoch Crf 413
______, Fielding New 35
______, Fielding New 38
______, Gabriel New 5
______, Jane Jks 316

Wallis, John Hal 108
______, John Jks 314
______, John Mon 181
______, Joseph Hry 212
______, Josiah Jks 316
______, Josiah Jks 329
______, Luther Hal 119
______, Mary Mon 219
______, Mortimer R. Bib 53
______, Nicholas Clk 308
______, Rachel Jks 329
______, Reuben Clk 310
______, Richard Mon 173
______, Thomas Wal 136
______, Thomas New 7
______, William Hal 110
______, William New 22
______, William New 27
Walace, Augustus Gre 292
Walis, Julia Han 170
WALLER, Archilles Up 101
______, Charles R. Mon 217
______, Daniel Put 175
______, Edwards Wil 321
______, Ellis M. Han 170
______, Eliza Wrn 218
______, George Bul 99
______, Handy Put 174
______, Hiram Bry 87
______, James Wil 294
______, James B. DeK 72
______, James B. Tlb 346
______, Jesse Ware 185
______, Job Han 171
______, John Han 171
______, John H. Wsh 246
______, Joseph Up 117
______, Nathaniel Mon 191
______, Newbold Up 97
______, Nimrod Wil 303
______, Sibby Jks 334
______, Smith Mon 190
______, William Mon 225
______, William Pik 120
______, William Up 111
WALLEY/WALLEE
Walley, Sally Hab 15
Wallee, Thoms Doo 78
WALLRAVEN/WALDRAVEN/
WALRAVEN
Wallraven, Isaac Gwn 355
______, John Jks 341
______, Jonathan Jks 333
Wallraven, William Gwn 355
Waldraven, John DeK 73
Walraven, Archibald DeK 28
WALPOOL, John Crf 396
______, Thomas Crf 395
WALSINGHAM, Catharine Eff 111
______, Charles Eff 111
______, Rebecca Eff 113
______, William Eff 111
WALTERS, Jackson M. Frk 238
______, Jeremiah Frk 250
______, Jesse Sr. Twg 84
______, Jesse Jr. Twg 83
______, John C. Frk 241
______, Judah Frk 238
______, Mary Frk 253
______, Moses Frk 241
______, Peter Sr. Frk 252
______, Richard Wsh 265
______, Robert Frk 238
______, Robert Frk 243
______, Ward H. Frk 243
______, William Frk 226
WALTHALL/WALLTHALL
Walthall, C. F. Jsp 388
Wallthall, John H. Mwr 155
WALTON/WALSTON/WALTEN/
WALLSTON/WALTUM
Walton, Daniel Bke 121
______, Elizabeth Put 189
______, Enoch Jns 446
______, Harriet S. Lin 63
______, Henry W. Mon 223
______, Isaac R. Mor 248
______, Jesse Lin 65
______, Jesse Lin 69
______, John Bke 145
______, John Lin 69
______, John Up 118
______, John S. Jns 441
______, Joseph W. Mor 244
______, Lucinda Mor 248
______, Peter W. Mor 246
______, Robert Bke 142
______, Robert Lin 72
______, Robert Mor 240
______, Robert Put 187
______, Robert Rch 271
** ______, T. J. (slave) Rch 276
______, Thomas Jns 428
______, Thomas J. Rch 260
______, Thomas S. Lin 64
______, William Wil 317

Name	County	Page
Walston, Bennett B.	Jks	326
______, Henry	Jks	342
______, Henry	Trp	39
Walten, Jessee S.	Col	336
______, Sherwood	Col	343
Walston, William	Jks	342
Waltum, Jesse	Cow	387
WALTZ, Mary (W)	Mor	256
WAMBLE/WAMBEL		
Wamble, Little B.	Em	178
Wambel, James	DeK	56
WAND, Em[1]. Sr.	Cht	254
______, Ema[1]. Jr.	Cht	255
______, Matilda	Cht	261
WANSLY, Nathan	DeK	27
______, Thomas	Elb	148
WARD, Abner	Elb	152
______, Abner	Ogl	103
______, Abner	Put	181
______, Albritain	Put	214
______, Amos	Jsp	382
______, Amos	Put	186
______, Anderson	Put	183
______, Andrew	Clk	292
______, Benjamin	Wal	143
______, Benjamin	Put	214
______, Benjamin D.	Jef	416
______, Briant	Hal	132
______, Burrell	Fay	183
______, Charles	Bke	142
______, David	Doo	83
______, Elum	Clk	306
______, Enos	Gre	300
______, Ezekiel	Up	106
______, Francis	Bke	151
______, Frederick	Mor	244
______, George	Hab	13
______, George	Mar	143
______, H.	Col	338
______, Hannah	Jsp	385
______, Hardy	Hry	229
______, Harris R.	Cam	185
______, Henry	Col	340
______, Ignatus	Wks	347
______, Ira	Cpb	194
______, James	Bke	142
______, James	Bke	151
______, James	DeK	48
______, James	Hal	132
______, James	Hry	210
______, James	Wks	347
______, James P.	Tlf	2
______, James T.	Up	121
Ward, Jane	Elb	153
______, Jephtha H.	Elb	122
______, Jeremiah	Hab	13
______, Jesse	Pik	122
______, Joab	Ware	189
______, John	Bke	130
______, John Sr.	Car	214
______, John Jr.	Car	214
______, John	Clk	306
______, John	Fay	188
______, John	Gre	289
______, John	Jns	442
______, John	Pik	121
______, John	Rch	284
______, John B.	Elb	153
______, John L.	Gwn	332
______, Jonathan	Gre	300
______, Josiah	Hal	96
______, Leonard	Clk	298
______, Lenard	Cow	368
______, Lucy	Hab	65
______, Mark	Eff	114
______, Mary	Bke	142
______, Mary	Ogl	91
______, Mary	Put	184
______, Mary	Put	197
______, Miles	Fay	184
______, Nancy	Bke	145
______, Nancy	Mon	192
______, Nathan	Gwn	360
______, Nathan	Hab	25
______, Nathaniel	Gwn	342
______, Nathaniel	Hab	13
______, Obediah	New	16
______, Paschal E.	Put	196
______, Peter Z.	Hry	213
______, Peyton	Jns	441
______, Powel	Mwr	168
______, Richard	Hab	17
______, Richard G.	Put	196
______, Richard M.	Up	98
______, Ridley	Jns	440
______, Robert	Bke	142
______, Robert	Col	337
______, Robert P.	New	45
______, Samuel	Hry	203
______, Samuel	Ogl	103
______, Samuel	Trp	48
______, Sarah	Cam	185
______, Sarah	Elb	158
______, Sarah	Em	169
______, Solloman	Hab	20
______, Solomon	Pik	112

Ward, Stephen Gre 276
______, Stephen Put 194
______, Susanna Pul 141
______, Thad. Wks 347
______, Thomas Bke 150
______, Thomas DeK 50
______, Thomas DeK 67
______, Thomas Jsp 379
______, Thomas Lee 34
______, Thomas F. Mwr 156
______, Thomas S. Hab 18
______, Uriah Put 202
______, Wade Pul 138
______, William Bib 53
______, William DeK 46
______, William Elb 158
______, William Fay 185
______, William Hab 14
______, William Han 171
______, William, dec'd. Est Lib 55
______, William Ogl 101
______, William Pik 110
______, William Tms 28
______, William Wal 162
______, William J. Hal 94
______, William W. Clk 306
______, Willis Twg 60
______, Winny Gre 302
WARDEN, Samuel Frk 219
WARDLAW/WARDLOW
Wardlaw, Absalom Gwn 339
______, David L. Gwn 339
______, George B. Bib 83
______, Samuel Gwn 314
______, William Gwn 339
Wardlow, Cynthia Jns 459
______, James Gwn 351
WARDROBE, Harriet L. Cht 244
WARE, Abenezer New 41
______, Alexander Fay 206
______, Allen Jns 475
______, Ally Car 230
______, Bennett Mor 259
______, Col. Edward Mad 98
______, Elisha Mad 100
______, Ezakiel Gwn 352
______, Frances Elb 142
______, George Fay 194
______, Hammilton DeK 59
______, Henry H. Jks 320
______, Hudson T. Mor 245
______, James Mad 104
______, James Twg 62
Ware, James Wal 128
______, James M. Fay 182
______, Jameson Gwn 353
______, Jane Cht 261
______, Jane Elb 124
______, John Jks 337
______, John Wrn 222
______, John S. Bts 167
______, Joseph New 53
______, Mary (W) Mor 245
______, Molly Mad 117
______, Moss Mor 262
______, Robert Bal 34
______, Robert Lin 72
______, Samuel Clk 318
______, Thomas Col 336
______, Thomas Gwn 352
______, Thomas Wal 167
______, William Jsp 394
**WARING, Dr., slaves Cht 282
______, W. R. Cht 262
WARLICK, Hiram Trp 34
______, Solomon Mwr 156
WARNAN, Lot Hab 28
WARNER, A. Lee 30
______, Adam Cht 278
______, Christian Hry 236
______, Elizabeth Jef 405
______, Hiram Crf 395
______, Oliff A. Jef 401
______, Rebecca Bib 53
______, T. T. Mon 228
______, William Mon 208
______, William Wyn 282
WARNOLD, R. Lib 55
WARR, William Wrn 222
WARREN/WARRON
Warren, Allen Em 168
______, Allen Jef 404
______, Amos Em 177
______, Arthur Hal 109
______, B. H. Rch 259
**______, B. H. (slave) Rch 275
______, Bethana Gwn 360
______, Co. Wrn 215
______, Edmond Bul 102
______, Eli Lau 5
______, Elizabeth Han 171
______, Ezekiel Gwn 321
______, Frederick Hst 268
______, Harrison Hab 30
______, Isaah Fay 198
______, James Em 177

Name	County	Page
Warren, James	Gwn	340
______, James	Lau	8
______, James	Mwr	153
______, James	Wrn	231
______, Jeremiah	Han	171
______, Jeremiah S.	Elb	148
______, Jerulia	Pik	117
______, Jesse	DeK	66
______, Jessee	Hst	287
______, John	Doo	87
______, John	Gwn	360
______, John	Hry	217
______, John	Hry	219
______, John	Hst	273
______, John	Put	217
______, Joshua	Bib	68
______, Josiah	Em	177
______, Lott	Twg	60
______, M. W.	Rch	254
______, Martin	Wal	124
______, Mary	Cht	245
______, Nancy	Wal	126
______, Reuben	Gwn	334
______, Reuben	Lau	9
______, Robert	Hal	70
______, Sampson	Pik	116
______, Thomas	Hry	242
______, Valenten	Hal	113
______, Wallis	Car	226
______, Washington	Pik	117
______, William	Gwn	321
______, William	Han	171
______, William	Hry	213
______, William	Jks	339
______, William	New	23
______, William	Tat	371
Warron, Rebecka	Hab	33
WARRINGTON, Nelly	Cht	271
WARWICK, Allen	Frk	225
______, Jacob	Hab	45
______, Wily	Hab	44
WASDEN, Phillip M.	Jef	404
______, Thomas	Jef	404
WASH, J.	Gwn	371
WASHAM, Edmund	Put	176
WASHBURN, A.	Cht	258
______, David	Hab	20
______, Hiram M.	Tlb	335
______, John H.	Hal	122
______, Joseph	Bib	53
______, Samuel	Lau	24
WASHINGTON, Charles W.	Bib	57
______, George	Har	188
Washington, Hiram	Col	349
______, James	Col	348
______, John	Mor	260
______, John S.	Mor	255
______, R. B.	Bal	34
______, Robert B.	Bib	57
______, Sophia	Bke	138
**WATERMAN, A. (slave)	Rch	270
**______, A. (slave)	Rch	275
______, Asaph	Rch	256
WATERS/WATTERS/WARTERS/ WATER		
Waters, Abraham L.	Hab	49
______, Allen	Doo	86
______, Allen	Scr	300
______, Benjamin	Eff	115
______, Charles	Hab	51
______, Charles W.	Bke	140
______, David	Dec	9
______, Edward D.	Pul	143
______, Elanor	Hab	22
______, Elijah	Wal	134
______, Elizabeth	Hal	95
______, Erastus	Bul	93
______, George	Dec	17
______, George	Tms	16
______, Henry	Hal	125
______, James	Hal	95
______, Isaac	Scr	303
______, John	Cht	260
______, John	Cht	283
______, John	Hal	74
______, John	Hal	125
______, John	Tms	16
______, John E.	Hst	267
______, Lewis	Hab	35
______, Littleberry	Hst	273
______, Lucy	Elb	129
______, Michael	Scr	309
______, Moses	Hal	109
______, Nancy	Wil	309
______, Obediah	Hab	36
______, Philip	Lin	70
______, Stacy	Hal	76
______, Thomas	Bul	93
______, Thomas	Hal	94
______, William	Cht	257
______, William	Mwr	164
______, William	Tat	372
Watters, Abner	Frk	221
______, George M.	Bry	84
______, Henry M.	Elb	154
______, James	Col	342

Name	County	Page
Watters, James	New	46
_____, James	Wks	331
_____, John C.	New	46
_____, John R.	Hab	20
_____, Joseph	Frk	231
_____, Joseph	New	15
_____, Larkin	Frk	225
_____, William	Twg	77
_____, William B.	New	8
Warters, Isaac	Twg	61
_____, John	Twg	69
_____, William	Twg	65
Water, Henry	Hab	24
_____, John	Bul	93
_____, John	Scr	303
WATERSON, George	Hab	29
WATKINS/WADKINS		
**WAtkins, Mrs. (slave)	Rch	271
_____, Abner	Hab	42
_____, Alfred	Twg	80
_____, Ann	Hst	261
_____, Arthur	Jef	406
_____, Benjamine	Cpb	198
_____, Benjamine Sr.	Jks	338
_____, Benjamine Jr.	Jks	338
**_____, Beverly (slave)	Rch	262
_____, C. A.	Bke	150
_____, Catherin	Rch	267
_____, Catherine	Rch	279
_____, Cornelius	Mus	290
_____, Delaney	Bke	154
_____, Daniel	Wsh	241
_____, David	Gwn	343
_____, David	Hab	65
_____, Henry	Hab	42
_____, James W.	Bts	162
_____, Jason	Rch	292
_____, Jesse	Gwn	343
_____, John	Bke	152
_____, John	Hry	237
_____, John	Jef	406
_____, John	Jks	338
_____, John	Tlb	325
_____, Jonas	Wsh	250
_____, Joseph	Hal	107
_____, Mills	Jef	407
_____, Mitchell	Wsh	255
_____, Nisber	Hab	43
_____, Polly	Gre	305
_____, Polly	Rch	270
_____, Redding	Wsh	250
_____, Rees	Hab	39
_____, Rhoda	Bke	138
Watkins, Richard	Wsh	265
_____, Samuel	Han	171
_____, Sarah	Wks	347
_____, Thomas	Rab	234
_____, William	Wil	287
_____, Wright	Hst	289
Wadkins, Eliza	DeK	62
_____, Griffin	Hal	114
_____, Isom	DeK	59
_____, James	Hal	126
_____, Jessie	Col	335
_____, John	Elb	154
_____, John Sr.	Hab	13
_____, John Jr.	Hab	12
_____, John	Hab	13
_____, John D.	Ogl	97
_____, Laborn	Ogl	93
_____, Mathew	Hal	126
_____, Nancy	DeK	31
_____, Philip	Ogl	86
_____, Rees	Ogl	85
_____, Reese	Frk	249
_____, Wiley	Frk	241
WATSON/WASSON		
Watson, Abner	Elb	160
_____, Adam H.	Hab	58
_____, Alexander	Tlf	8
_____, Anderson	Up	109
_____, Anselem	Hal	106
_____, Arthur C.	Mar	139
_____, Asa	Lau	14
_____, B. M.	Jsp	365
_____, Benjamin	Col	356
_____, Benjamin	Crf	397
_____, Benjamin	Mon	203
_____, Bryant	Gre	291
_____, Calvin	Frk	212
_____, Cassandri	Cow	392
_____, Claiborn	Hst	287
_____, D. C.	Gre	296
_____, David	Hst	273
_____, David	Jns	442
_____, David	Mwr	155
_____, Demsey	Mtg	234
_____, Douglas	Mon	227
_____, Edward	Rch	278
_____, Elias T.	Mon	223
_____, Elijah	Col	336
_____, Elijah	Wsh	264
_____, Elisha	Wal	137
_____, Elizabeth	Frk	229
_____, Elizabeth	Hab	39
_____, Ellias	Gre	304

Name	County	Page
Watson, Evort	Crf	404
______, Frederick	Hst	285
______, George	Mar	139
______, George	New	32
______, Gideon	Hst	293
______, Gideon	Mad	101
______, Guilford D.	Mad	113
______, Hamilton	Jef	407
______, Henry	Gre	303
______, Hiram	Trp	49
______, Isaac	Col	351
______, Jacob	Jns	442
______, Jacob	Pul	160
______, James	App	12
______, James	Eff	104
______, James	Mon	180
______, James	Wrn	210
______, James A.	Col	351
______, James C.	Bal	35
______, James M.	DeK	46
______, James T.	Mon	179
______, Jane	Mon	178
______, Jehial	Tfo	356
______, Jesse	Col	351
______, Jesse	Gre	277
______, Jesse	Gwn	361
______, Jessee	Hst	273
______, Joh[b].	Gwn	364
______, John	Fay	190
______, John Sr.	Frk	228
______, John Jr.	Frk	236
______, John	Gre	300
______, John Jr.	Gwn	365
______, John	Hal	95
______, John	Hst	267
______, John	Irw	303
______, John	Mad	116
______, John	Mon	192
______, John	Ogl	80
______, John	Trp	39
______, John	Wal	135
______, John B.	Cow	387
______, Jonathan	Jns	455
______, Joseph	Gre	296
______, Joseph	Mon	184
______, Joseph	Tms	26
______, Joshua	Trp	39
______, Josiah	Jks	321
______, Kindred	Lau	12
______, Laban	Lau	12
______, Lemuel	Bib	75
______, Leroy	Bib	77
______, Lewis	Tfo	360
Watson, Magen	Rch	283
______, Margret	Hab	54
______, Martha	Wal	167
______, Mary A.	Tfo	366
______, Michael	Har	175
______, Michael	Hst	274
______, Milly	Col	350
______, Moses	Mad	108
______, Nathan	Mar	139
______, Nehemiah	Gre	302
______, Ordrary	New	18
______, Paris	Wal	133
______, Petsey	Hab	54
______, Rebeca	Col	351
______, Reddick	Tms	28
______, Reuben	Gre	300
______, Richard	Hst	264
______, Robert	Bal	32
______, Robert	Fay	184
______, Robert Sr.	Mon	220
______, Robert Jr.	Mon	220
______, Sanders	Frk	222
______, Sarah	Pik	112
______, Sarah	Rch	254
______, Sarah	Trp	32
______, Seth G.	Mon	204
______, Silas	Hst	285
______, Silas	Lau	13
______, Solomon	Em	170
______, Solomon	Gre	297
______, Tabitha	Jns	467
______, Thomas	Cow	384
______, Thomas	Fay	184
______, Thomas	Gwn	373
______, Thomas	Hab	61
______, Thomas	Hst	296
______, Thomas J.	Wrn	213
______, Thomas M.	Col	359
______, Tyre	Car	227
______, William	Col	357
______, William	Fay	190
______, William	Gre	290
______, William	Jsp	352
______, William	Wal	123
______, William	Wal	133
______, William C.	Mon	178
______, Zadock	Hst	286
Wasson, John F.	Gwn	326
WATTEY, Wiley H.	Mar	144
WATTHALL, John	Cow	379
______, Termon	New	45
______, William P.	Cow	379
WATTS/WATT/WATS		

Name	County	Page
Watts, Anna	Fay	204
______, Berry	Cpb	202
______, David S.	Gre	278
______, Edward	DeK	51
______, George	DeK	51
______, H. H.	Gre	279
______, Hampton B.	Bib	72
______, Hope H.	Gwn	346
______, Isaac	Jns	459
______, James	Lee	28
______, James E.	Mwr	154
______, Jane	Mon	227
______, John	Car	228
______, John	Jns	431
______, John L.	Jns	439
______, Jonathan	DeK	34
______, Joseph	Rab	231
______, Joseph H.	Mor	246
______, Jubal	Gre	283
______, Malica	Jns	428
______, Mary	Jns	431
______, Pascal M.	Mon	215
______, Pleasant	Mor	248
______, Pleasant	Rab	229
______, Reuben J.	Trp	55
______, Richard J.	Gwn	350
______, Spencer	Jns	430
______, Susannah	Han	171
______, Thomas	Har	185
______, Thomas	Mor	247
______, Thomas	Wal	138
______, Thomas B.	Cpb	198
______, W. H.	Gre	279
______, William	Fay	183
______, William	Har	183
______, William	Han	171
______, William	Lau	8
______, William	Ran	241
Watt, Alexander	Cht	272
______, Maddox	Lin	72
______, Mercy (W)	Mor	257
Wats, Ann	Hab	16
______, David	Hab	63
WAYNE/WAN		
Wayne, James M.	Cht	277
______, John	Hal	76
______, John	Hry	247
______, Richard	Cht	279
______, William	Scr	307
Wan, Malinda	Mad	113
______, Susan B.	Rch	266
WATWOOD, James	DeK	49
WAUGH, Robert	Hry	202
WAY, Edward	Lib	55
______, Graves	Lib	55
______, John	Jef	422
______, John	Lib	55
______, John, dec'd. Est.	Lib	54
______, Joseph	Lib	54
______, Moses W.	Lib	55
______, Quarterman	Lib	54
______, Rachel	Hst	282
______, William	Crf	411
______, William J. Esq.	Lib	55
______, William N.	Lib	54
WEAR, Edward	Cow	371
______, John M.	Cow	377
______, Phillip	Cow	371
WEATHERBY/WETHERBY		
Weatherby, Aaron	Frk	255
______, Arvel	Wks	356
______, Benjamin	Crf	398
______, John	Up	108
______, Septimas	Crf	396
______, Septemus	Put	202
______, William	Clk	306
Wethersby, Gideon A.	Hst	288
______, Stephen	Hst	294
WETHERFORD/WEATHERFORD		
Wetherford, John	Bib	63
______, Josiah	Ogl	69
Weatherford, James	Wal	155
WEATHERINGTON/WEATHERTON		
Weatherington, John	Twg	75
Weatherton, Jacob Y.	Cpb	206
______, Thomas	Cpb	208
WEATHERS/WETHERS		
Weathers, Daniel	Up	102
______, Elisha	Lin	66
______, Elizabeth	Pik	130
______, Isham	Fay	197
______, Joel	Pik	128
______, Sam C.	Lin	70
______, Soloman	Lin	70
______, Stephen	Cpb	197
______, Valentine	Wal	156
______, William	Up	102
______, William W.	Fay	197
Wethers, Alexander M.	Mwr	153
______, Samuel	Mwr	167
WEATHERSPOON, Charles	Jks	347
______, John	Jks	347
WEATHERLY/WETHERLY/WETHERY		
Weatherly, Septemus	Jns	473
______, Thomas	Car	220
Wetherly, Abner	Hst	268

Name	County	Page
Wethery, Alexander M.	Mwr	153
WEAVER/WEVER		
Weaver, Aaron	Col	350
______, Absalom	Ran	249
______, Andrew	Ogl	83
______, Arthur	Mwr	159
______, Asa	Gre	273
______, David	Put	187
______, Dawson	Wks	353
______, Edward	Bts	171
______, Edward	Tlb	347
______, Ira E.	Ran	246
______, Isom	New	47
______, J. J.	Cht	257
______, Jacob	Crf	394
______, Jacob	Ear	95
______, Jarrett	Wil	313
______, Jethro	Wks	336
______, Jethro B.	Lau	10
______, John C.	New	43
______, John H.	Crf	411
______, John P.	Ogl	83
______, Jonathan	Ear	98
______, Julius	Ear	98
______, Othniel	Ran	245
______, Peter	Hal	107
______, Pleasant	New	46
______, Reuben	Wal	154
______, Samuel	Cow	380
______, Samuel	Mon	204
______, Sarah	Wks	355
______, Simeon	Put	188
______, Susanah	New	44
______, Travis A.D.	Jns	467
______, Wiley	Wks	356
______, William	Hry	248
______, William	Ogl	86
______, William R.	Fay	191
______, William W. D.	Gre	280
______, Wilson	Mon	204
Wever, David	Clk	298
______, David	Hab	26
______, John	Hab	36
______, John L.	Hab	61
______, Koonrod	Rab	227
______, Martha	Rab	234
WEBB/WEB		
Webb, A.	Lee	26
______, Abdues	Jns	430
______, Abner	Elb	146
______, Alford	Gwn	379
______, Allen J.	Em	171
______, Archibald	Frk	234
Webb, Augustus	Hry	248
______, Austin	Wal	152
______, Austin Jr.	Wal	160
______, Benjamin	Hst	272
______, Benjamin	Ogl	75
______, Burrel	Elb	133
______, Cathrine	New	46
______, Charles	Jsp	381
______, Charles H.	Mwr	163
______, Clinton	Gwn	351
______, Cullen	Hst	275
______, Daniel	Pul	149
______, Dawson	Wks	337
______, Dawson	Wks	358
______, Disbon S.	Put	175
______, Edmund	Jsp	381
______, Elias	Har	181
______, Elijah	Elb	123
______, Ephraim	App	10
______, Etheldred	Wks	349
______, Ewell	Crf	414
______, Fortunatus	Elb	146
______, Hollan	Wsh	275
______, Homer	Crf	410
______, Horatio	Jks	313
______, Isaac H.	Mar	144
______, J. G.	Lee	26
______, James	Hry	242
______, James H.	Twg	70
______, Jeremiah	Rab	232
______, John	Jsp	394
______, John	Lee	32
______, John	Wsh	244
______, John	Wsh	255
______, John D.	Elb	123
______, Jordan	DeK	42
______, Lemuel	Tms	29
______, Levi	Em	171
______, Levi	Mon	227
______, Margaret	Elb	123
______, Mary	Hry	246
______, Mary	Jns	467
______, Perry	Lee	29
______, Pleasant	Ogl	75
______, Samuel	Hst	274
______, Samuel B.	Pul	146
______, Thomas P.	New	50
______, Urbin A.	Elb	131
______, Viney	Em	167
______, Viney	New	32
______, Walton P.	Elb	146
______, Wiley	Crf	404
______, William	Gwn	364

Webb, William Ogl 75
_____, William Wsh 256
_____, William J. Em 171
_____, Willis Jks 341
Web, Archable Hab 25
_____, Jonathan Hab 25
WEBBER, Joseph Hal 84
WEBSTER, Benjamin Ear 98
_____, Elizabeth Wil 321
_____, John Hal 102
_____, John Up 106
_____, Lewis Wsh 246
_____, Richard Wsh 256
_____, Seaborn Tlb 337
_____, William Har 192
WEDDINGTON, Zena Put 180
WEED/WEAD
Weed, John Gwn 363
Wead, James Pik 128
WEEKLEY, John Lau 18
_____, Thomas Tlb 337
WEEKS/WEEKES/WEAKS
Weeks, Anderson Jns 473
_____, Charles New 37
_____, D. L. Jsp 352
_____, G. A. Cht 257
_____, James Bib 57
_____, Luke G. Wks 352
_____, Noah Lau 23
_____, Thomas Bke 122
_____, William Jef 417
Weekes, Bartemew M. Ran 241
_____, John A. Mon 216
_____, Joseph C. Jsp 353
Weaks, Micajah Doo 88
WEEMS/WEMMS/WEEM
Weems, Joel Frk 212
_____, Lock Wil 307
_____, Redfearn Frk 211
_____, Samuel Hry 199
_____, Samuel R. Hry 231
_____, Thomas Gwn 340
_____, Thomas Hry 220
_____, Walter H. Wil 287
_____, Washington Frk 234
Wemms, Bartholomew J. Fay 201
Weem, Susannah Jef 402
WEIDT, John G. Eff 109
WEITMAN, Hannah Eff 104
_____, Israel Eff 114
_____, Lewis Eff 107
_____, Solomon Eff 104
WELLAFORD, William Dec 7
WELCH/WELSH
Welch, Asa Wsh 272
_____, David Hab 18
_____, David Wks 345
_____, Edmond Cow 368
_____, Edward Hst 261
_____, Edward Wrn 210
_____, Eliza Cht 256
_____, Elizabeth Col 350
_____, George Gwn 375
_____, George W. Twg 70
_____, Isaac B. Tlb 336
_____, James Clk 325
_____, James Col 348
_____, James Twg 72
_____, Jesse Col 348
_____, John Gwn 379
_____, Joseph Hab 12
_____, Joshua Gwn 336
_____, Lemarcus Mar 139
_____, Luke Mor 260
_____, Michael Crf 393
_____, Moses Up 119
_____, Nicholas New 19
_____, Richard Tms 17
_____, Robert Har 178
_____, Thomas Car 219
_____, Thomas Gwn 376
_____, Thomas Mwr 161
_____, Wesley C. Bts 160
_____, William Bal 43
_____, William New 10
_____, Wright Up 102
Welsh, Judah Hal 85
_____, L. Rch 256
WELDON/WELDING/WELDEN
Weldon, Absalom Car 226
_____, Andrew Jsp 355
_____, Isaac Car 229
_____, Isaac Jsp 357
_____, James Mon 228
_____, James Tlb 348
_____, John Mwr 152
_____, John C. Tlb 330
_____, Joseph Har 179
_____, Moses Sr. Jsp 355
_____, Moses Jr. Jsp 355
Welding, Isac C. Pik 106
_____, Isaac S. Pik 107
Welden, Samuel Han 171
WELLBORN/WELBORN/WELBOURN/
WELBERN/WELLBURN
Wellborn, A. Gwn 308

Wellborn, Abner Wil 306
_____, Carlton Hst 269
_____, Cordial T. Tfo 355
_____, E. A. Col 360
_____, Elias Col 361
_____, James Gwn 329
_____, James Jks 349
_____, John Wil 295
_____, Johnson Hst 261
_____, Mary Tfo 367
_____, Sarah Wil 305
_____, W. Gwn 308
_____, William Hst 262
_____, William J. Wal 141
Welborn, Gideon Jks 349
_____, Jack New 49
_____, James Gre 283
_____, James Up 118
_____, Margaret Hry 236
_____, Sanford New 16
_____, Thomas New 50
_____, William R. Frk 224
Welbourn, Burkett Mor 259
_____, Curtis Mor 239
_____, Josiah Mor 239
_____, Sanders Mor 258
Welbern, James Ogl 97
Wellburn, Alfred Mwr 165
WELLONS, William S. Jns 452
WELLMAKER/WELMAKER
Wellmaker, Felix Wil 311
Welmaker, John Pik 128
WELMAN, F. H. Cht 245
WELLS/WELS
Wells, Abner Gwn 368
_____, Abner Jks 343
_____, Abner Put 181
_____, Andrew Mor 265
_____, Berry Hst 264
_____, E. A. Wsh 275
_____, Elijah Tlb 333
_____, Elijah Tlf 9
_____, Elinor Cht 270
_____, Elizabeth Irw 299
_____, Everit Jef 409
_____, George Gre 303
_____, George Hal 103
_____, George D. Cpb 210
_____, Hanon Hal 69
_____, Henry Hst 293
_____, Henry M. Gwn 368
_____, Howell Tlb 343
_____, Hy. W. Gwn 335
Wells, Jacob Scr 307
_____, James Gwn 314
_____, James Lee 26
_____, James E. Jef 413
_____, Jeremiah Frk 232
_____, Jeremiah Tlf 11
_____, John Bry 87
_____, John Gre 274
_____, John Han 170
_____, John Jns 446
_____, John Lib 55
_____, John Mon 227
_____, John Wil 300
_____, John A. for mother Ogl 96
_____, Joshua S. Wil 313
_____, Josiah Jef 408
_____, Mary Mar 140
_____, Samuel Hry 214
_____, Sarah Clk 319
_____, Sarah Hab 13
_____, Sarah Ogl 98
_____, Shadrick Tms 28
_____, Stephens Crf 401
_____, Susan Bib 53
_____, Taliafero Wil 299
_____, Tavner Hst 266
_____, Thomas Clk 314
_____, Thomas New 11
_____, Thomas Wal 148
_____, Thomas B. Jef 423
_____, William Bry 85
_____, William Jns 463
_____, William Mar 137
_____, William Mar 140
_____, William Scr 303
_____, William A. Hry 203
_____, William H. Pik 110
_____, Willis L. Gwn 368
_____, Zacheriah Bry 85
Wels, Larkin Hab 61
WERLY, Pleasant Hab 25
WESLEY, Evans Em 166
_____, Lemon Em 166
_____, Sarah New 8
WESSON, William Fay 206
WEST, Allen Ware 184
_____, Andrew Mon 186
_____, Barney Hal 107
_____, Benjamin Hal 95
_____, Charles Hry 210
_____, Dr. Charles Lib 55
_____, David Rch 254
_____, Eliza Col 335

West, Ephraim Cow 382
______, Francis Gre 272
______, Gibson Bke 135
______, Henry Trp 50
______, Isham Twg 76
______, James Bal 40
______, James Hab 61
______, James Put 216
______, James Tfo 367
______, James Wal 173
______, Jeptha Hab 62
______, Jeremiah Hry 225
______, John Col 359
______, John Gre 273
______, John Hab 66
______, John Hst 264
______, John Jsp 378
______, John Jsp 397
______, John Q. Wil 322
______, Joshua Lau 14
______, Major Bal 30
______, Mary Cht 260
______, Mary Ann Wil 322
______, Rena Twg 80
______, Robert Mus 280
______, Ruben Hab 22
______, Rufus Jsp 387
______, Sampson Twg 63
______, Samuel B. Hab 54
______, Thomas Hab 18
______, Warren Hry 230
______, William Bke 119
______, William Dec 16
______, William DeK 56
______, William Hab 27
______, William Hst 277
______, William Hst 280
______, William Mon 201
______, William E. Gre 282
______, William L. Mor 238
______, William P. Mor 251
______, Willis Fay 196
WESTBERY, Josiah Lib 55
______, Moses Jr. Lib 55
______, Rev. Moses B. Lib 55
______, Noah Lib 55
WESTBROOK/WESTBROOKS/
WESBROOK
Westbrook, Ganey Fay 184
______, James H. Frk 240
______, John Jr. Frk 222
______, John Frk 244
______, Joshua Frk 252
Westbrook, Moses Fay 184
______, Reuben Frk 255
______, Stephen B. Frk 231
______, Steven B. Gwn 348
______, Thomas Frk 237
______, William Gre 274
Westbrooks, Abram Trp 33
______, John Hry 234
______, Mary Twg 76
______, Thomas S. Hry 216
Westbrook, Tilman New 29
WESTER, Aaxum Trp 49
______, Benjamin Cow 378
______, Daniel Cow 372
______, Edward Trp 48
______, Elias Dec 12
______, Richard Tat 376
WESTMORELAND/WESTMORLAND
Westmoreland, John Fay 206
______, Reuben Pik 107
______, Robert Fay 206
______, Robert Hab 49
______, Robert Pik 108
Westmorland, J. H. Mus 277
WESTON, H. Rch 275
______, Job Elb 123
______, John Cpb 206
______, Robert H. Wal 123
______, Stephen Put 181
WETHEAL, John Hab 63
WETMAN, Mathew Cht 260
WHALEY/WHALLEY/WHALLY
Whaley, Agrippa Gwn 342
______, Charles Fay 199
______, Ebenezer Tlb 324
______, Eli Wal 151
______, Elijah Up 106
______, Isaac Fay 199
______, James Clk 308
______, James Up 115
______, John Fay 200
______, John Hry 245
______, John R. Wks 358
______, Madison Fay 199
______, Samuel Wal 136
______, Thomas Han 171
______, William Mwr 165
______, William Mwr 165
______, William Mor 257
Whalley, James Pik 127
______, Simion A. Cow 378
______, William Jns 443
______, Wilson Jns 438

Whally, Isaac Trp 35
WHATLEY/WATLEY/WHATLY
Whatley, Archy Trp 36
______, Daniel Hst 276
______, David Mon 172
______, Elbert Crf 399
______, Elizabeth (W) Mor 263
______, Elizabeth New 40
______, Floyd Mon 224
______, James Jsp 398
______, John Cow 382
______, John B Mon 214
______, Martin Fay 193
______, Michael Hst 294
______, Pascal J. Clk 296
______, Robert Mon 177
______, Robert Mon 212
______, Sarah Tlb 345
______, Seabron Wal 156
______, Seaborn C. Tfo 362
______, Seabon J. Wil 293
______, Solomon Fay 194
______, Tailor Hry 206
______, Thomas E. Hst 289
______, Willis Clk 296
______, Willis Wil 294
______, Wilmouth Ran 247
______, Wilson Wal 138
______, Wyatt New 49
Watley, Maben Mus 287
______, Wiley H. Mwr 144
Whatly, Abner Har 185
______, Willis Trp 42
WHEAT, Harry Lin 73
______, Levi Put 190
______, Mary Lin 75
______, Moses Up 102
______, Wesley Cpb 204
WHEATLEY, Greenbury Wil 299
______, Jesse Ogl 64
______, Joseph Wil 300
WHEATON, Martha Mon 196
WHEEBELT, R. H. D. Cht 240
WHEELER/WHELER/WHEELEY
Wheeler, Alexander Hry 213
______, Allen Hst 284
______, Amy Twg 82
______, Ann Hst 282
______, Asa Lib 55
______, Avry Lee 34
______, Benjamin Hab 31
______, Benjamin Trp 39
______, Brinson Eff 106
Wheeler, Charles App 11
______, Charles Hab 30
______, Colin Put 205
______, Eli Wks 354
______, Eliza Wrn 224
______, George Hab 38
______, Green B. Tms 20
______, Henry Jks 341
______, Hesekiah Put 174
______, Isaac Bib 75
______, Isaac Elb 158
______, Isham Wrn 225
______, James Frk 243
______, James Jks 334
______, James New 37
______, James F. Tms 24
______, Jesse Eff 105
______, John Bak 17
______, John DeK 68
______, John Hal 77
______, John Hal 82
______, John Twg 62
______, John Wks 356
______, John S. Wil 299
______, Joseph Rch 272
______, Leroy Elb 158
______, Lewis Gwn 314
______, Lot Tms 24
______, Mary Frk 257
______, Mitchell Ran 241
______, Nancy Pul 144
______, Noah Twg 64
______, Palasiar Pul 143
______, Polly Cpb 211
______, R. Lee 28
______, Richard Hab 11
______, Robert M. Mon 219
______, Samuel Wks 335
______, Shadrick Bib 72
______, Thomas Clk 308
______, Thomas Wrn 196
______, Thomas B. Hab 29
______, Washington New 37
______, Whillis Em 168
______, William Doo 84
______, William Jr. Doo 86
______, William Eff 116
______, William Hal 79
______, William Hal 107
______, William Hal 121
______, William Jr. Hal 121
______, William A. Mon 195
______, William C. Put 207

Wheler, John Hab 24
_____, Robert J. Lib 55
Wheeley, Mathew Mon 206
WHEELLES/WHEELIS/WHEELUS/
WHEELESS/WHELESS/WHELUS/
WHEELEAS/WHELAS/WHEELAS/
WHEELAN
Wheelless, Lewis Mor 268
_____, Marlin Mor 269
_____, Marlin B. Mor 269
_____, Sion Mor 268
Wheelis, Burton Jns 434
_____, Henry Jns 435
Wheelus, Drury Mwr 158
_____, Edmond Up 121
Wheeless, Charlotte Put 201
Wheless, Hardy Tlb 337
Whelus, Abner Mwr 155
Wheeleas, Colebe Hab 38
Whelas, Miles Ogl 102
Wheelas, Sion Mon 207
Wheelan, Charles Jns 467
WHELCHEL/WELCHEAD
Whelchel, Davis Hal 122
_____, Frances Hal 110
_____, Frances Hal 122
_____, John Hal 70
_____, John Hal 113
_____, John (Dr.) Hal 122
_____, Moses Hal 123
_____, William Hal 116
Welchead, Thomas Col 350
WHICHARD, Phillip Mar 143
WHIDDEN/WHIDDON/WHIDDEON/
WHIDDION/WITDON
Whidden, John Dec 14
_____, William Dec 12
Whiddon, Rody Wsh 249
_____, William Wsh 252
Whiddeon, Mathew Dec 12
Whiddion, Eli Dec 4
Witdon, Lott Irw 302
WHIGHAM/WHIGAM
Whigham, John W. Jef 419
_____, Joseph Jef 420
_____, Letty Jef 424
_____, Thomas Dec 7
_____, Thomas Jef 424
_____, William Dec 3
_____, William Jef 422
Whigam, William Ear 97
WHIPPLE, Stephen Wks 342
WHISENHUNT/WHISSINGANT
Whisenhunt, Adam Car 224
_____, George Car 216
_____, Henry Car 215
_____, John Car 215
_____, Peter Car 217
_____, Philip Car 215
Whissingant, Jacob Frk 255
WHITAKER/WHITTAKER/WHITEKER/
WHITTICAR
Whitaker, Abraham Wil 315
_____, Abram Mad 106
_____, Benjamin Frk 222
_____, Burton Hry 248
_____, Daniel Cow 385
_____, David E. Jef 413
_____, Edn. Bal 40
_____, John Crf 395
_____, John Frk 212
_____, John Mor 259
_____, John B. Jsp 369
_____, Joseph J. Har 178
_____, Mark Jns 463
_____, Mary Mon 200
_____, Richard Wks 334
_____, Samuel Wsh 258
_____, Simon Fay 200
_____, Thomas Bib 57
_____, William Bal 41
_____, William Mad 101
_____, William Rch 281
_____, Willis Wsh 249
Whittaker, John Ear 96
_____, Samuel Ear 94
_____, William Ear 94
_____, William Hry 208
Whiteker, John Wal 133
_____, Littlebery New 38
Whitticar, Joshua Col 346
WHITAMORE, Howell Hal 103
_____, Hugh Hal 100
_____, James A. Hal 100
_____, Obadiah Gwn 312
_____, Raleigh Hal 100
WHITBY/WHITBIE
Whitby, Susan Clk 324
_____, William Jns 473
Whitbie, Asa Hal 79
WHITCOMB, William Col 334
WHITE, Aaron Bts 177
_____, Abda Hry 233
_____, Abejah Wsh 262
_____, Abram Han 171
_____, Allen Em 168

Name	County	Page
White, Allen	Jks	317
______, Allen	Wsh	255
______, Amey C.	Wks	341
______, Anderson	Mad	98
______, Andrew	DeK	42
______, Ann	Mon	209
______, Ann Elizar	Clk	324
______, Ann M.	Cht	245
______, Asa	DeK	45
______, B. A.	Bal	40
______, Banhaber	Jsp	396
______, Benedict	Rch	286
______, Benjamin	Crf	414
______, Benjamin	Mor	261
______, Benjamin H.	Frk	227
______, Buart	Hab	28
______, Burrel	Frk	237
______, Carter	Frk	227
______, Christopher	Bts	178
______, Christopher	Scr	307
______, Cyrus	Jsp	394
______, Daniel	Bke	144
______, Daniel	Har	191
______, Daniel	Put	176
______, Daniel	Up	121
______, David	DeK	37
______, David	Frk	232
______, David	Hry	233
______, David	Hst	272
______, Edward	Mon	201
______, Edward	Wal	173
______, Edmund	Gre	278
______, Elbert	DeK	37
______, Elisha	Doo	89
______, Eliza	Col	344
______, Elizabeth	Jns	439
______, Elizabeth	Up	110
______, Eppy	Elb	135
______, Ezkiel	Ran	247
______, Freedom	Twg	60
______, Gabriel	Hry	210
______, George	Cht	263
______, George	DeK	34
______, George	Hry	224
______, George	Mon	193
______, Granville	Doo	86
______, Green	Mwr	160
______, Henry	Bke	155
______, Henry	Clk	318
______, Henry	Dec	10
______, Henry	Dec	15
______, Henry	Eff	113
______, Henry	Elb	152

Name	County	Page
White, Henry	Gwn	350
______, Henry	Jsp	391
______, Henry	Tms	24
______, Henry P.	Mad	104
______, Henry P.	Pik	112
______, Hy. E.	Gwn	321
______, Isom	Hry	233
______, Jacob	DeK	28
______, James	DeK	34
______, James	Frk	237
______, James	Gre	281
______, James	Gre	297
______, James	Hab	6
______, James	Hry	221
______, James	Mon	209
______, James	Tlb	332
______, James	Wal	143
______, James E.	Hst	274
______, James L.	Gre	273
______, James M.	Mon	194
______, James O.	Ware	184
______, James T.	DeK	32
______, Jane	Jns	471
______, Jeremiah	Hab	53
______, Jesse	Clk	319
______, Jesse	Elb	129
______, Jiney	DeK	30
______, John	Clk	319
______, John	Dec	5
______, John	DeK	39
______, John	Elb	148
______, John	Gwn	318
______, John	Hal	78
______, John	Hal	99
______, John	Hry	232
______, John	Hry	237
______, John	Hry	249
______, John	Rab	232
______, John	Up	117
______, John	Wsh	252
______, John B.	New	6
______, John D.	Han	171
______, John E.	Wks	345
______, John F.	Gre	277
______, John H.	Elb	133
______, John L.	Mon	214
______, John M.	Wal	152
______, John S. W.	Trp	35
______, John W.	Elb	135
______, John W.	Elb	135
______, John W.	Elb	143
______, Johnathan	Mwr	154
______, Joseph	Hab	22

White, Joseph Jns 463
______, Joseph Mon 172
______, Joseph Ran 243
______, Joseph Trp 40
______, Joseph S. Cpb 205
______, Levey Wal 159
______, Levi Hry 215
______, Logan Frk 237
______, Luke Hab 7
______, Luke Mad 102
______, Margaret Hry 233
______, Martin Elb 131
______, Mary Bry 85
______, Mary Elb 129
______, Mary Frk 226
______, Mary Hal 78
______, Moses Mon 218
______, Nathaniel H. Frk 244
______, Nelson C. Jns 471
______, Obediah Frk 257
______, Pleasant Ran 243
______, R. Up 128
______, Richard Car 226
______, Robert Mwr 151
______, Robert Wal 159
______, Robert Wrn 211
______, Samuel Bal 28
______, Samuel Wal 148
______, Samuel Wks 338
______, Sarah Cht 248
______, Shelton Elb 132
______, Simeon Hal 131
______, Sion Frk 227
______, Stephen Elb 121
______, Stephen Mad 101
______, Stephens Wal 134
______, Stephen S. Up 97
______, Sterling Jks 318
______, Thomas DeK 54
______, Thomas Frk 214
______, Thomas Ogl 63
______, Thomas B. Jns 433
______, Thomas W. Col 362
______, Tilmon S. Ran 246
______, Timothy Mor 269
______, Timothy Wrn 201
______, Valentine Har 191
______, Waide Cpb 194
______, Washington Mwr 157
______, Wiley Hab 59
______, Willey Mor 270
______, William Bal 43
______, William Col 348
White, William Elb 147
______, William Fay 195
______, William Sr. Frk 217
______, William Frk 246
______, William Hab 36
______, William Hab 66
______, William Hry 223
______, William Hst 281
______, William Jsp 372
______, William Lin 74
______, William Mon 228
______, William New 24
______, William Rch 269
______, William Tlb 330
______, William Tlf 5
______, William A. Hry 208
______, William A. Pik 107
______, William H. Gre 300
______, William M. Han 171
______, William P. Wil 287
______, William S. Tlb 325
______, William V. Pik 111
______, William W. DeK 43
______, Wilson Tms 28
______, Wright Cht 244
______, Zacharah Eff 108
______, Zachariah Tlb 322
WHITEHEAD/WHITHEAD
Whitehead, A. W. Hal 108
______, Austin Hst 268
______, Benjamin Wal 127
______, Bennet Lau 5
______, Elizabeth Bke 151
______, Elizabeth Clk 303
______, Elizabeth Clk 303
______, George Bib 63
______, George Bib 72
______, Gideon Bts 165
______, Henry Jef 416
______, Hilliard Mon 209
______, Jacob Hab 37
______, Jacob Hal 107
______, James Bke 153
______, James Mon 209
______, Joel Ogl 75
______, John Bke 153
______, Joseph Hab 38
______, Lewis Hal 112
______, Martha Twg 86
______, Mastian Bib 72
______, Nancy C. Han 171
______, Peggy Clk 303
______, Peter Trp 53

Whitehead, Ransom Clk 303
______, Reason Clk 302
______, Richard Hab 13
______, Richard Twg 89
______, Robert Mar 141
______, Samuel New 50
______, Samuel Ogl 75
______, Thomas Cpb 206
______, Thomas Hal 110
______, Thomas Har 188
______, Warren W. Lau 19
______, Wiley Ogl 77
______, William (Plantation Put 214
______, William Put 217
Whithead, John Col 347
______, Vaslin Col 348
WHITEHURST, Bartley Tlb 330
______, Chs. Wks 346
______, Josiah Wks 345
______, Unity Tlb 324
WHITFIELD, Alexander Clk 294
______, Benjamin Put 190
______, Bryant Bke 139
______, Bryant Trp 50
______, Bryant Wsh 252
______, Elisha Hab 14
______, George Col 334
______, George B. Hst 279
______, Horatio S. Trp 44
______, James Jsp 370
______, James E. Jef 412
______, John S. Lwn 82
______, Lewis Sr. Bke 139
______, Lewis Bke 139
______, Martha Clk 310
______, Mathew Jsp 384
______, Myles Wsh 252
______, Reuben Wsh 244
______, Robert Clk 311
______, Robert Wsh 248
______, Thomas Clk 310
______, Sampson Cht 268
______, Samuel Lau 9
______, Silvia Cht 241
______, William Bke 139
______, William Put 190
______, William H. Doo 89
______, William T. DeK 40
WHITIER, Orandatus Put 210
WHITLEY/WHITELEY/WHITLY
Whitley, Jesse Wal 130
______, John Hry 229
______, John Jns 475

Whitley, Lewis Up 102
______, Nathan Wal 140
______, Nathan Wal 155
______, Nathan Wal 157
______, Thomas W. Col 349
Whiteley, Micajah Wal 129
Whitly, Stephen DeK 59
WHITLOCK, Armsted Hal 95
______, Beasley Mor 263
______, Charles DeK 64
______, Charles Hal 96
______, George Frk 241
______, J. W. Rch 274
______, Jas. Jks 340
______, Josiah Gre 284
______, Mary Tfo 366
______, Thomas Hal 129
WHITLOW, Boling Wal 164
______, James Clk 301
______, John Sr. Clk 300
______, John Jr. Clk 296
______, Thomas Frk 216
______, William Clk 301
WHITMIRE, Henry Jks 316
______, Michael Jks 316
______, Samuel Jks 316
______, Stephen Hal 131
______, Stephen Jks 332
WHITMAN/WHITMON
Whitman, John L. Clk 326
______, Nathan W. Clk 321
______, Thomas Col 351
______, William Elb 148
Whitmon, Christopher Fay 188
______, Henry Jks 318
______, John Jks 312
______, Marcus Jks 318
WHITNEY, Josiah Tms 27
WHITSEL, Ela Hab 28
______, George Ogl 66
WHITTINGTON/WHITTINTON
Whittington, Alexander Jns 463
______, Ephriam Col 335
______, Ephrain Crf 412
______, Irwin Crf 402
______, John Crf 414
______, John Jr. Crf 395
______, Richard Cow 372
______, Sarah Col 335
______, Sherrod Crf 402
Whittinton, Faddy Pik 118
______, Fady J. Pik 127
WHITTLE, Ambros Wsh 260

Whittle, Burrell	Hst	275
_____, Elisha	Crf	406
_____, John	Wsh	273
_____, Seborn	Wsh	259
_____, Watson	Pul	155
WHITTON/WHITTEN/WHITTION/		
WHITTIN/WHITIN/WHITINGS		
Whitton, Alsa	Clk	315
_____, Elisha	Lin	67
_____, George	Clk	315
_____, Inman	Cow	383
_____, Robert	Wal	162
_____, Robert H.	Clk	312
Whitten, George	Mon	210
_____, James	Hal	113
_____, James Sr.	Ware	185
_____, Levi	New	20
_____, Phillip	Mor	269
_____, William	Cow	387
_____, William	Mon	178
_____, Willoughby	Ware	185
Whittion, James	Ware	189
Whittin, Alvin E.	Frk	210
Whitin, Mary	Hab	39
Whitings, John	Wsh	252
WHITWORTH, Clanson	Hab	9
_____, John C.	Gwn	319
_____, Joseph S.	Frk	233
_____, Richard	Gwn	320
_____, Samuel	Mad	109
_____, Southerland	Frk	233
_____, Thomas	Hal	78
_____, William S.	Mad	100
_____, Winston	Frk	234
WHOOPPER, John	DeK	35
WHORD, William	New	44
WHORTON, Bartlet	Gwn	326
_____, Benjamin	Hal	69
_____, Elijah	New	55
_____, Elisha	Jsp	389
_____, Isaac	Hal	133
_____, Jacob	Hal	69
_____, John	Gwn	325
_____, Joseph	Jks	321
_____, Joshua	Frk	219
_____, Joshua	Frk	247
_____, Robert	Frk	219
_____, William	Gwn	328
WICKER, Alfred	Wsh	256
_____, Benjamin	Wsh	256
_____, James	Pik	118
_____, John	Bal	33
_____, John	Wsh	255
Wicker, Julius A.	Bal	39
_____, Mary	Wil	312
_____, Thomas	Wsh	254
_____, Wiley	Bal	31
WICKNEY, Sampson	Hab	53
WICKREY, Christopher	Hab	26
WICKS, Bartlett	Mus	286
WIDENER/WIDNER		
Widener, Isaac	Jks	324
Widner, Henry	Hry	228
WIER, Isaac	Mon	223
WIGGENTON, Isaac	Car	219
WIGGINS/WIGGENS/WIGINS/		
WIGGIN		
Wiggins, Allen	Hst	274
_____, Amos	Bke	136
_____, Baker	New	19
_____, Christopher H.	Hry	199
_____, David	New	42
_____, Elias	Jef	408
_____, Elizabeth	New	41
_____, Greene	Put	190
_____, James	Em	175
_____, James	Mor	257
_____, James	Ware	188
_____, Jesse	Crf	409
_____, Jesse	Em	172
_____, Jesse	New	19
_____, John	Bke	151
_____, John	Cpb	199
_____, John	Em	172
_____, John	Em	174
_____, John	New	38
_____, John	Rch	291
_____, Joseph	Gly	268
_____, Joseph	Wyn	281
_____, Joshua	Wsh	259
_____, Lewis	Gwn	348
_____, Michael	Bke	151
_____, Nancy (W)	Mor	267
_____, Osborn	Hst	263
_____, Owen	Tfo	354
_____, Richard	Wrn	233
_____, Sarah	Hry	216
_____, Stephen	Irw	301
_____, Whittenton	Gre	304
_____, William	Bke	145
_____, William	Gre	295
_____, William	Wsh	274
_____, Willis	New	19
Wiggens, Joseph	Bib	72
_____, Sarah	Put	207
Wigins, Jesse	Cam	187

Wigins, Peter Cam 187
Wiggin, Alfred Pik 125
WIGGS, Daniel Ran 249
WIGHTMAN, William J. Rch 265
WIGLEY/WIGGLEY/WIGLY
Wigley, Allen Hal 118
_____, James Cow 389
_____, John Hal 118
_____, Joseph Hal 118
Wiggley, Job Hal 80
_____, Joseph Hal 79
Wigly, Nancy Man Gwn 334
WILBANKS/WILLBANKS
Wilbanks, Gillum Frk 255
_____, Hiram DeK 57
_____, Marshall Frk 255
_____, Richard Frk 225
_____, William Frk 226
_____, William T. Frk 249
Willbanks, Bryan Jks 335
_____, Solomon Jks 319
WILBERN, John P. Cow 392
WILBORN, Levi T. Cow 367
WILBUR, A. H. DeK 30
WILLCOX/WILCOX
Willcox, George Irw 299
_____, James Irw 304
_____, John Rch 284
_____, John Tlf 6
_____, Lewis Tlf 6
_____, Mark Tlf 5
_____, Martin Rch 272
_____, Taliaferro Rch 258
Wilcox, A. Mus 285
_____, John Lau 23
_____, Lorha Pul 154
_____, Martha Rch 288
_____, Samuel H. Tlb 333
_____, Thomas Sr. Tlf 3
_____, Thomas Jr. Tlf 3
_____, Uriah Lib 55
WILLCOXIN, Levi Cow 367
WILDE/WILD/WILDES
Wilde, Ann Scr 299
_____, John W. Rch 287
_____, William Jns 455
Wild, Catherine Rch 259
** _____, R. H. (slave) Rch 268
Wildes, Alexander Mor 244
WILDER/WILDORE/WHILDER
Wilder, Charles Hry 206
_____, Charles Wrn 204
_____, Dred Wal 169
Wilder, Drid Crf 412
_____, Edward Jns 459
_____, Elizabeth Scr 310
_____, Elizabeth Mon 218
_____, Ezekiel Cow 375
_____, Green Bib 63
_____, Henry Lee 35
_____, James Mon 191
_____, John Mon 197
_____, Johnathan Bib 66
_____, Jonathan Gwn 344
_____, Joseph Jns 459
_____, Joseph Jsp 387
_____, Levi Mad 104
_____, Sampson Jr. Wrn 201
_____, Sampson Jr. Wrn 207
_____, Seabon Ogl 86
_____, Simeon Hry 220
_____, Soloman Wrn 207
_____, Ward Jns 459
_____, William Hry 217
_____, William Jns 459
_____, William Tat 380
_____, William Wrn 199
_____, Willis Jns 459
Wildore, E. Cht 260
Whilder, George Jks 324
WILEY/WILLEY
Wiley, Alexander Gwn 359
_____, Ann Bal 39
_____, Austin Jks 345
_____, Eleanor McI 132
_____, Enoch McI 132
_____, George Elb 146
_____, James R. Hab 19
_____, John McI 130
_____, John F. Hal 120
_____, Johnson Frk 246
_____, Leroy M. Bal 39
_____, Mary Ann Twg 83
_____, Moses Han 171
_____, Nicholas Wil 323
_____, Peter Hst 272
_____, Samuel B. New 53
_____, Thomas Gwn 345
_____, William Col 357
_____, William Hal 119
_____, William Har 183
_____, William Hst 273
_____, William S. Elb 142
Willey, Francis Bib 57
_____, Thomas Elb 143
_____, Thomas Mor 252

WILHITE/WILLHITE/WILWHITE
Wilhite, John Mad 117
______, John B. Mad 118
______, Joseph Y. Elb 141
______, Philemon Elb 119
______, T. Jks 320
Willhite, Mumford Mwr 162
______, Rex Put 207
Wilwhite, Meshack Jks 321
WILKERSON/WILKISON/WILKESON
Wilkerson, Abel Trp 41
______, Abner Mon 182
______, Allen Har 182
______, Duncan Har 191
______, Harrison S. Trp 54
______, Henry L. Trp 41
______, Jane Col 362
______, John Mor 250
______, John Put 173
______, John Twg 83
______, Lemuel Cpb 194
______, Mary Jks 325
______, Rarah Cpb 194
______, Reuben Har 186
______, Robert Gre 272
______, Sherwood Gre 278
______, Sidney Cpb 201
______, Thomas Gre 276
______, William R. Ogl 89
Wilkison, John Hab 64
Wilkeson, Riley Hab 64
WILKEY/WILKY/WILKIE
Wilkey, George Hal 87
______, John Pik 110
______, Mitchel Col 340
______, Samuel Mon 193
Wilky, Jiles Crf 400
Wilkie, Elizabeth Tlb 338
WILKINS/WILKENS/WILKINGS
Wilkins, Allen Jsp 366
______, Catharine Han 172
______, David Hry 206
______, David L. Cow 387
______, Drury Jsp 379
______, Elizabeth Hry 228
______, Henry Col 336
______, Henry F. McI 123
______, James Cpb 201
______, James Cpb 210
______, James Cht 264
**______, James (slaves) Cht 278
______, James Han 171
______, James Wrn 231
Wilkins, John Col 340
______, John Fay 204
______, John R. Hry 222
______, Mary E. Lib 54
______, Paul Cht 257
______, Paul H. Jr. (Dr.) Lib 55
______, Robert Hry 227
______, Samuel Fay 182
______, Samuel Frk 230
______, Samuel Hry 232
______, Thomas Col 346
______, Thomas P. Car 215
______, Whit Bke 140
______, William Cpb 199
______, William New 31
______, William Put 217
______, William Tlb 343
______, William A. Col 334
______, Young S. Jns 459
Wilkens, Clement Elb 131
Wilkings, David Mus 278
WILKINSON/WILLKINSON
Wilkinson, A. Bal 33
______, Alex. Jsp 384
______, Benjamin Han 171
______, Calvin Cow 374
______, Daniel Jef 421
______, Drury Bal 34
______, Edward Trp 50
______, Eldred Jsp 382
______, Elijah Ware 188
______, Elisha Frk 251
______, Eliz. M. Tfo 361
______, Francis Wil 293
______, Hugh Jef 415
______, Isaac Fay 194
______, James Bul 99
______, James Frk 239
______, James Pik 132
______, James Tlb 334
______, Jared Mar 137
______, Jeptha Jsp 382
______, Jesse Lee 30
______, John Hry 199
______, John Pul 138
______, John Rch 276
______, John Ware 189
______, John Wil 323
______, Leroy Wrn 212
______, Mary Wrn 212
______, Neill App 5
______, Reuben Mwr 156
______, Rowland Fay 202

Name	County	Page
Wilkinson, Samuel	Bts	171
_____, Smith	Bts	172
_____, Thomas	Wil	313
_____, Thomas H.	Lau	6
_____, William	Wal	165
_____, William H.	Wal	133
_____, William L.	Wil	295
_____, Willis	Bul	98
Wilkinson, Ozburn	DeK	48
WILKS/WILKES		
Wilks, Beniajah	Pik	118
_____, Elijah	Doo	82
_____, Elisha	Em	178
_____, Francis	Em	172
_____, Jesse	Em	177
_____, John	Em	169
_____, Osborn	Ogl	96
_____, Solomon B.	Doo	82
_____, William	Em	169
_____, William	Ogl	100
Wilkes, Aaron	Trp	34
_____, James	Mar	137
_____, John	Jsp	378
_____, John	Put	212
_____, Joseph	Put	214
_____, Silas	Put	208
WILLARD/WILLIARD		
Willard, John	Hry	244
_____, Royal	Bts	163
Williard, Elijah	Mor	261
WILLETT/WILLET		
Willett, Henry	Hry	247
_____, Isaac	Mus	290
_____, Joseph	Bib	77
Willet, Benjamin	Mon	194
_____, John	Mon	184
WILLIAMS/WILLIAM/WILIAMS		
Williams, A. B.	Fay	197
_____, Aaron	Bke	151
_____, Aaron	Har	178
_____, Aaron	Pik	132
_____, Abraham	Twg	80
_____, Absalom	Tfo	364
_____, Alfred	Gwn	319
_____, Alfred	Up	110
_____, Alie	Hab	61
_____, Allen	Hst	273
_____, Allen	Jks	319
_____, Allen	Trp	43
_____, Ammi	Car	218
_____, Amos	Hal	126
_____, Amos	Rab	227
_____, Anderson	Eff	111
Williams, And^{w}. C.	Up	96
_____, Anson	Mwr	150
_____, Arrington	Car	229
_____, Avington	Mwr	161
_____, B. S.	Cht	249
_____, Barry	Pul	146
_____, Bartenis	Bry	85
_____, Benjamin	Clk	292
_____, Benjamin	Har	177
_____, Benjamin	Hst	263
_____, Benjamin	Lee	28
_____, Benjamin J.	Fay	188
_____, Bennet	Gwn	318
_____, Bennett	Har	179
_____, Berien	Wal	136
_____, Betsey	Bul	100
_____, Betsy	DeK	73
_____, Britain	Har	177
_____, Bud	Mad	100
_____, Burrel	Doo	78
_____, C. T.	Col	343
_____, Charity	Lau	22
_____, Charles	Pul	149
_____, Charles D.	Rch	268
_____, Charles Sr.	New	17
_____, Clinton A.	Hry	243
_____, Crafford	Hab	20
_____, Cynthia	DeK	68
_____, Daniel	Cht	241
_____, Daniel	Tfo	359
_____, Daniel	Wsh	244
_____, Daniel	Wsh	273
_____, Daniel M.	Crf	409
_____, David	Bul	97
_____, David	Doo	88
_____, David	Gwn	313
_____, David	Irw	298
_____, David	Mwr	154
_____, David	Tlf	7
_____, David	Wsh	239
_____, David M.	Jsp	352
_____, Deloney	Frk	222
_____, Dosson	Mad	108
_____, Drury	Wks	346
_____, Duke	Gre	297
_____, Duke	Up	101
_____, Edward	Cam	192
_____, Edward	Hab	11
_____, Edward	Rab	226
_____, Elihu	Hal	126
_____, Elijah	Mad	110
_____, Elisha	Frk	256
_____, Elisha	Hal	125

Name	County	Page
Williams, Elisha	Put	198
______, Elisha Jr.	Frk	246
______, Elizabeth	Gly	265
______, Elizabeth	Hab	20
______, Elizabeth	Mus	278
______, Elizabeth (W)	Mor	248
______, Enoch	Har	187
______, Etheldred	Rab	227
______, Ezekiel	Bke	141
______, Fredic	Irw	298
______, Galiway	Rab	224
______, Garret	Bul	97
______, George	Frk	256
______, George	Har	184
______, George	Hst	283
______, George	Tlb	336
______, George	Wsh	240
______, Gilbert P.	Gwn	314
______, Godfrey	Bul	93
______, Green	Lee	27
______, Green	Wal	141
______, Harrisson	DeK	51
______, Henry	Cht	251
______, Henry	Mon	184
______, Henry	Wrn	209
______, Henry J.	Hry	201
______, Hiram	Wal	140
______, Hiram R.	Gwn	313
______, Holloway	Frk	240
______, Howell F.	Jns	467
______, Hubbard	Bts	179
______, Hubbard	Pik	123
______, Hyram	Har	182
______, Ichabod	Jsp	365
______, Isaac	Bib	53
______, Isaac	Jef	421
______, Isaac	Har	175
______, Isaac	Dec	6
______, Isaac	Lee	28
______, Isaiah	Doo	80
______, Isom	Jks	323
______, J.	Gwn	308
______, J. F.	Mus	282
______, Jacob	Jsp	370
______, Jacob	Mwr	157
______, Jacob	Tlb	334
______, Jala	Mwr	151
______, James	Bry	85
______, James	Clk	300
______, James	Col	363
______, James	Em	174
______, James	Frk	224
______, James	Gwn	356

Name	County	Page
Williams, James	Hal	123
______, James	Jef	421
______, James	Mad	109
______, James	Mor	272
______, James	Scr	309
______, James	Tat	377
______, James	Tlf	9
______, James H.	Fay	185
______, Jane	Bke	139
______, Jane	Up	108
______, Jefferson	Jef	421
______, Jeremiah	Gwn	363
______, Jeremiah W.	Jns	439
______, Jesse	Ear	99
______, Jesse	DeK	61
______, Jesse	Gre	291
______, Jesse	Pul	152
______, Jesse	Ran	241
______, Jesse	Twg	79
______, Jesse	Wil	299
______, Joel	Clk	300
______, Joel	Lau	10
______, Joel	Pul	160
______, John	App	5
______, John	Bal	28
______, John	Car	224
______, John	Clk	301
______, John	Cow	381
______, John	Crf	411
______, John	Doo	81
______, John Jr.	Doo	81
______, John	Ear	100
______, John	Fay	201
______, John	Frk	243
______, John	Gwn	357
______, John	Hab	39
______, John	Hal	105
______, John Jr.	Hal	72
______, John	Hry	201
______, John	Hry	205
______, John	Jef	419
______, John	Jef	421
______, John	Jns	441
______, John	Jns	475
______, John	Lee	29
______, John Sr.	Mad	113
______, John	Mad	107
______, John	McI	123
______, John	Mor	238
______, John	Pik	125
______, John	Rch	289
______, John	Tlf	5
______, John	Twg	67

Name	County	Page
Williams, John	Ware	186
______, John	Wsh	249
______, John	Wks	338
______, John	Wks	343
______, John	Wrn	225
______, John A. C.	Clk	297
______, John C.	Hal	70
______, John G.	Bul	96
______, John G.	Mor	260
______, John H.	Har	180
______, James H.	Hry	204
______, John H.	Pik	123
______, John L.	Hry	215
______, John M.	DeK	65
______, John P.	Hab	64
______, Johnston	DeK	43
______, Jonathan	Lee	28
______, Jonathan	Rab	227
______, Jonathan	Up	105
______, Jonathan	Jks	320
______, Joseph	Cow	367
______, Joseph	Doo	81
______, Joseph	Fay	205
______, Joseph	Rab	227
______, Joseph	Ran	241
______, Joseph Sr.	Tlf	5
______, Joseph Jr.	Tlf	9
______, Joseph	Wrn	223
______, Joseph J.	Trp	46
______, Joshua	Pul	155
______, Josiah	Ware	186
______, Jourdan	Doo	84
______, Jordon	Eff	111
______, Lamuel	Bib	53
______, Lavina	Twg	78
______, Leroy	Hab	56
______, Lewis	App	8
______, Lewis	Gwn	337
______, Lewis	Gwn	350
______, Lewis	Gwn	355
______, Lewis	Hab	12
______, Lewis	Mwr	156
______, Littleberry A.	Gre	276
______, Louis	Wsh	251
______, Lucy	Jks	335
______, Lucy	Ogl	91
______, Ludlow	DeK	62
______, Luke	Jns	443
______, Luke	Jsp	385
______, M.	DeK	56
______, Margaret	Bke	141
______, Mark	New	32
______, Mark	Wal	145
Williams, Marmaduke	Gre	288
______, Martha	Bib	53
______, Martha	Hst	282
______, Mathew	Put	193
______, Martin	Frk	227
______, Martin	Rab	231
______, Mary	Hal	75
______, Mary	Lee	35
______, Mary	Scr	306
______, Mary	Scr	309
______, Mary	Twg	81
______, Micajah	Bib	57
______, Moses	Fay	197
______, Munill	Crf	410
______, Nancy	Gre	287
______, Nancy	Lau	9
______, Nancy	Put	172
______, Nancy B.	Gre	284
______, Nathan	Dec	15
______, Nathan	Frk	236
______, Nathan C.	Frk	236
______, Nathan Sr.	Frk	249
______, Nathaniel Sr.	Gwn	330
______, Nathaniel Jr.	Gwn	330
______, Nathaniel	Har	187
______, Newton	Wks	339
______, Nicholas	Wrn	194
______, Nicholas B.	Mon	195
______, Paul	Wsh	276
______, Peggy	Cht	269
______, Permenia	Mad	114
______, Perry G.	Mwr	151
______, Peter J.	Bal	29
______, Phillip	Wsh	272
______, Pleasant	Mad	110
______, R. F.	Cht	257
______, Randon	Em	172
______, Rebeca	Jns	436
______, Rebecca	New	29
______, Reuben	Mwr	160
______, Right	Lee	33
______, Robert	Bul	102
______, Robert	Frk	215
______, Robert	Frk	242
______, Robert	Gwn	330
______, Robert	Rch	279
______, Robert	Scr	303
______, Robert	Trp	48
______, Robert	Tlb	340
______, Robert	Wsh	264
______, Robert Jr.	Mad	113
______, Robert O.	Hry	200
______, Robert Sr.	Mad	113

Williams, Robert Sr. Scr 302
______, Roland Pik 106
______, Rubin Bib 63
______, Russell Hry 206
______, Ruth Hab 20
______, S. B. Cht 243
______, Samuel Bul 92
______, Samuel Bul 94
______, Samuel Dec 9
______, Samuel Doo 79
______, Samuel Pul 152
______, Samuel Ran 250
______, Samuel Wal 124
______, Sally New 18
______, Sally Twg 86
______, Sarah Jef 422
______, Sarah Mon 206
______, Sarah Scr 309
______, Shaderick Wsh 262
______, Sheppard Bul 95
______, Sheppard K. Hry 217
______, Silas Doo 81
______, Simeon DeK 35
______, Simeon Jef 421
______, Solloman Hab 36
______, Solomon DeK 70
______, Solomon Lau 17
______, Solomon Wks 349
______, Stafford Jns 428
______, Stephen App 5
______, Stephen Cht 264
______, Stephen Cht 278
______, Stephen DeK 52
______, Stephen Pik 110
______, Stephen Put 183
______, Stephen Tat 376
______, Stephen Ware 186
**______, Susan (slave) Rch 274
______, Susanna Fay 195
______, Templeton C. Wal 164
______, Theophelus Mon 207
______, Theophilus Scr 302
______, Thomas Bke 125
______, Thomas Bry 89
______, Thomas Em 172
______, Thomas Gre 272
______, Thomas Gwn 368
______, Thomas Hab 19
______, Thomas Jns 459
______, Thomas Trp 41
______, Thomas Wil 313
______, Thomas Sr. Ran 247
______, Thomas Jr. Ran 244
Williams, Thomas H. Cht 270
______, Thomas M. Gre 275
______, Thomas W. Hal 110
______, Timothy Clk 296
______, W. Wks 347
______, W. A. Gre 292
______, W. T. Cht 262
______, Whitmel Tlb 338
______, Wiat C. Crf 414
______, Wiley Mar 140
______, Wiley Pul 159
______, Wiley Wks 339
______, William Bib 72
______, William Bul 92
______, William Bry 86
______, William Car 228
______, William Cht 263
______, William Col 337
______, William Dec 5
______, William Dec 15
______, William DeK 49
______, William Eff 107
______, William Elb 129
______, William Gre 291
______, William Gwn 370
______, William Jsp 361
______, William Mad 108
______, William Sr. Mar 140
______, William Jr. Mar 140
______, William Mwr 165
______, William Pik 126
______, William Put 194
______, William Put 200
______, William Sr. Rab 227
______, William Rab 226
______, William Scr 301
______, William Twg 60
______, William Up 114
______, William Wal 169
______, William Wal 169
______, William Wil 302
______, William B. Bul 102
______, William B. Wrn 223
______, William C. DeK 58
______, William H. Cht 269
______, William J. Ran 246
______, William J. Up 98
______, William O. Cht 251
______, William R. Hab 42
______, William S. Hal 85
______, William S. Jsp 392
______, William W. Bts 161
______, Willis Har 178

Name	County	Page
Williams, Wilson	Gre	276
_____, Wilson	Jks	343
_____, Wilson	Mon	220
_____, Wilson	Trp	32
_____, Winney	Twg	86
_____, Wright	Frk	235
_____, Wyatt	Ogl	90
_____, Wyett	Mwr	151
_____, Zachariah	Col	343
_____, Zelpha	Hal	99
William, Cason	Han	171
_____, Charles Jr.	New	17
_____, David	Hal	105
_____, Tinley	Rch	282
Wiliams, Absolum	Hab	61
WILLIAMSON, Adam	Jks	326
_____, Ann	Clk	323
_____, Benajah	Hst	289
_____, Benjamin	Scr	315
_____, Benjn.	Wsh	250
_____, Betsey	Mon	211
_____, Charles	Bib	57
_____, Cullen	Scr	310
_____, David	App	12
_____, David	Pul	143
_____, Edmund	Bal	28
_____, George	Fay	184
_____, George	Hry	199
_____, George	Jks	327
_____, George	Ogl	101
_____, Green	Jns	431
_____, Green B.	Jns	447
_____, Hardy	Hst	276
_____, Henry	Pik	124
_____, Isaac B.	Pik	124
** _____, J. P. slaves	Cht	277
_____, James	Fay	185
_____, James	Tlf	11
_____, James	Trp	42
_____, James G.	Gwn	365
_____, John	App	6
_____, John	Bak	15
_____, John	Bke	147
_____, John	Bts	174
_____, John	Crf	412
_____, John	DeK	39
_____, John	Em	177
_____, John	Gwn	318
_____, John	Gwn	343
_____, John	Hab	50
_____, John	Jks	326
_____, John	Jks	328
_____, John	Jks	331

Name	County	Page
Williamson, John	Mtg	234
_____, John	New	14
_____, John	Ogl	101
_____, John	Put	178
_____, John	Trp	53
_____, John P.	Cht	258
_____, John R.	Hab	41
_____, Jonathan	Jns	471
_____, Joseph	Put	174
_____, Littleton	Cow	377
_____, Malachi	Wsh	275
_____, Mary	Cow	377
_____, McAllister	Jns	431
_____, Micajah	Har	188
_____, Nancy	Doo	86
_____, P. G.	Wsh	241
_____, Paul	Scr	312
_____, Penelope	Mtg	235
_____, R.	Bal	43
_____, Reubin J.	Crf	393
_____, Richard	Scr	310
_____, Robert M. Sr.	Scr	313
_____, Robert M. Jr.	Scr	313
_____, Ruben	Mwr	150
_____, Thomas	Bts	169
_____, Thomas	Hry	251
_____, Thomas	Tfo	360
_____, Thomas E.	Clk	300
_____, Thomas W.	Har	178
_____, W. W.	Jsp	370
_____, Walker	Elb	144
_____, Wiley	Put	205
_____, William	Car	219
_____, William	Clk	322
_____, William	Cow	373
_____, William	DeK	30
_____, William	Jks	326
_____, William	Lau	5
_____, William	Mar	138
_____, William	Put	181
_____, William	Up	109
_____, William	Wsh	247
_____, Zachariah	Bib	66
_____, Zachariah	Jns	467
WILLIE/WILLY		
Willie, P.	App	8
_____, William C.	Tat	377
Willy, James	Em	174
_____, John	Rab	234
WILLIFORD/WILLEFORD/ WILLIFRED		
Williford, Benjamin	Mon	208
_____, Charles	Fay	189

Williamson, Hansel Mon 185
_____, Hardy Wrn 226
_____, John DeK 47
_____, John Hst 280
_____, King H. Fay 203
_____, Nathan DeK 36
_____, Stephen Cpb 204
_____, William W. Mad 102
_____, Winefred Wrn 233
Willeford, Joel Wrn 232
_____, Judah Mad 117
_____, Levy Wrn 220
_____, Samuel Mad 98
Willifred, William Cpb 208
WILLING, Eliza Cht 271
WILLINK, H. F. Cht 245
WILLINGHAM/WINNINGHAM
Willingham, Abner Gwn 352
_____, Archibald Har 175
_____, Archibald Trp 37
_____, Caleb Jns 431
_____, Cash Wal 133
_____, George Wal 126
_____, Hardiman New 43
_____, Henderson Jks 342
_____, Isaac Esq. Lin 70
_____, Isaac Lin 73
_____, James Up 117
_____, Jesse Mad 118
_____, Jesse Sr. New 43
_____, John Lin 72
_____, John C. Wal 133
_____, John G. Lin 75
_____, Joseph Col 361
_____, Joseph New 43
_____, Lydia Frk 249
_____, Mary Tlb 347
_____, Raleigh Wal 132
_____, Sarah Col 361
_____, Thomas Cpb 194
_____, Thomas New 55
_____, Troy Ogl 83
_____, William Jns 434
_____, William Jsp 356
_____, William Mon 218
_____, William New 10
_____, William Wal 133
_____, William Wal 133
_____, William T. Ogl 80
Winningham, A. Gwn 309
WILLIS/WILLES
Willis, Alexander Bry 86
_____, Anan Jns 431
Willis, Benjamin Irw 302
_____, Benjamin Wil 295
_____, Daniel H. Mon 199
_____, Dempsey Jns 455
_____, Edwin Mon 197
_____, Enos Wil 318
_____, Ephraim Em 177
_____, Farney Eff 110
_____, Gideon Eff 105
_____, Henry Hst 277
_____, Hosea Jns 431
_____, James DeK 66
_____, James Hry 240
_____, James Twg 68
_____, James D. Wil 298
_____, James L. Tlb 325
_____, Jane Frk 233
_____, Jesse Lin 65
_____, John Bib 57
_____, John Eff 115
_____, John Irw 301
_____, John Mon 228
_____, John Tlb 337
_____, John A. Frk 250
_____, John E. Mon 210
_____, Joseph Jef 405
_____, Joshua Gre 296
_____, Lowdon Gre 282
_____, Marget DeK 49
_____, Mary Lib 55
_____, Mildred Elb 123
_____, Moses P. Tlb 326
_____, Owen Mon 208
_____, Patr. Wks 338
_____, Paul T. Wal 125
_____, Reddin Wks 342
_____, Richard J. Wil 308
_____, Robert Eff 109
_____, Robert L. Jsp 395
_____, Ruth Mon 207
_____, Sally Jks 340
_____, Sarah Jns 432
_____, Susannah Wil 298
_____, Thomas Bal 28
_____, Thomas Hst 277
_____, Thomas Jns 431
_____, Thomas Lin 75
_____, Thomas Ran 247
_____, Thomas F. Elb 147
_____, William DeK 49
_____, William Hal 132
_____, William New 29
_____, William Pik 126

Name	County	Page
Willis, William Sr.	Tlb	338
______, William	Tlb	334
______, William Sr.	Up	110
______, William Jr.	Up	104
______, William M.	Hst	291
______, Zechariah	Pul	138
Willes, Henry	Gre	290
WILLMAKER, Israel	Lin	59
WILLOUGHBY/WILLOBY/ WILLOWBY/WILLOBEY		
Willoughby, Jesse	Bib	75
______, John	Bib	75
______, John	Hst	268
______, Lemuel	Bib	75
______, William	Hst	269
Willoby, David	Clk	315
______, James	Clk	304
______, Robert	Clk	304
______, Thomas	Clk	304
______, Thomas	Wks	343
Willowby, Aron	Mon	178
______, Thomas	Mon	178
Willobey, Willis	Clk	304
WILLS, Francis W.	Tlb	330
______, John	Cow	371
______, Joseph S.	Twg	64
______, William	Bib	77
______, William	Cow	371
______, William	Hal	95
WILMOT/WILMOUTH/WILMOTT		
Wilmot, William	Up	113
______, William	Up	120
Wilmouth, William	Hab	44
Wilmott, Ely T.	Frk	217
WILCHER/WILSHIR		
Wilcher, Eliza	Wrn	233
______, Jerimiah	Bib	66
______, Jeremiah	Wrn	231
______, Jinney	Jef	404
______, Jourdin	Bib	66
______, Larken	Wrn	233
______, William G.	Jef	404
Wilshir, Jourdin	Bib	66
WILSON/WILLSON		
Wilson, Abel	Jsp	379
______, Abram	Hal	119
______, Absolum	Bts	167
______, Alexander	Har	176
______, Alexander	Tlf	5
______, Alexander	Wal	159
______, Allen	Tms	25
______, Alva	Pik	119
______, Andrew	Bul	94
Wilson, Andrew	Jks	333
______, Ann	Wrn	212
______, Ansel B.	Jks	319
______, Augustin	Wsh	243
______, Barbary	Wsh	260
______, Benja.	Han	172
______, Benjamin H.	Hry	247
______, Bennett	Jks	338
______, Bolar	Jks	318
______, Charles	Clk	291
______, Charles	Hab	49
______, Charles	Hab	56
______, Daniel	Up	101
______, Daniel	Wsh	262
______, David	DeK	42
______, David	Eff	110
______, Edward	Ear	93
______, Elbert	Eff	107
______, Eleas	Wrn	209
______, Elias	Hry	207
______, Elihu	Eff	106
______, Elijah	Hry	200
______, Eliza	Rch	268
______, Elizabeth	Jef	405
______, Elizabeth	Tfo	369
______, Ephraim	Hst	290
______, Fennel	Jks	321
______, Fennel Jr.	Jks	331
______, Franklin	Scr	302
______, George	DeK	52
______, George	Hab	28
______, George	Hal	121
______, George	Mus	286
______, George A.	Wal	166
______, George W.	Jns	471
______, Gilbert	Mor	247
______, H. N.	Jks	317
______, Henry	Car	225
______, Henry	Crf	397
______, Henry	Mus	285
______, Henry	Tlf	12
______, Henry	Wrn	210
______, Hugh	Hal	86
______, Hugh	Hry	244
______, J. B.	DeK	27
______, J. G.	Cht	248
______, James	Cht	280
______, James	Clk	319
______, James	DeK	71
______, James	Eff	110
______, James	Elb	127
______, James, dec'd. Est.	Lib	55
______, James	Gre	291

Name	County	Page
Wilson, James	Hal	87
______, James	Han	171
______, James	Jks	342
______, James	Jsp	395
______, James Sr.	Mon	186
______, James	Mon	182
______, James	Pik	126
______, James	Scr	302
______, James	Up	107
______, James	Up	121
______, James	Wal	150
______, James	Wal	164
______, James D.	Pik	119
______, James D.	Tlb	330
______, James H.	Wal	132
______, James J.	Hal	79
______, James W.	Jsp	378
______, Jenkins	Jsp	388
______, Jeremiah	Wal	167
______, Jesse	Wrn	209
______, Jesse M.	Mor	256
______, Joel	Mwr	152
______, Joel A.	Up	98
______, John	Bal	28
______, John	DeK	44
______, John	DeK	49
______, John	DeK	62
______, John	Ear	94
______, John	Eff	109
______, John	Hal	86
______, John	Hal	88
______, John	Hal	102
______, John	Hry	214
______, John	Jef	415
______, John	Lau	22
______, John	Mad	111
______, John	Scr	302
______, John	Twg	79
______, John	Wsh	270
______, John	Wrn	203
______, John	Col	356
______, John F.	Frk	210
______, John M.	Ogl	72
______, John S.	Wrn	221
______, John Jr.	Gre	287
______, John Jr.	Gre	281
______, Joseph	App	7
______, Joseph	Bul	94
______, Joseph	Hal	102
______, Joseph	Har	189
______, Joseph	Jsp	381
______, Joseph	Tlf	7
______, Joshua	Mwr	167
Wilson, Josiah	Lib	54
______, Josiah N.	Han	172
______, Josiah S. Dr.	Lib	54
______, Julian A.	Lib	55
______, Larkin	Mon	215
______, Lenard	Jsp	380
______, Levi	Mtg	231
______, Lewis	Elb	144
______, Luke	Eff	107
______, Martha B.	Mon	218
______, Mary	Pul	156
______, Mathew	Hal	89
______, Michael Jr.	Jks	319
______, Michael	Jks	342
______, Moses	Bul	94
______, Moses	Clk	316
______, Nancy	Jns	452
______, Newman	Hal	77
______, Obadiah	Hst	292
______, Orpha	Hal	82
______, Peter	Frk	234
______, Redin	Crf	394
______, Richard	Clk	318
______, Richard	DeK	40
______, Richard	New	33
______, Richard C.	Tlb	327
______, Robert	Hal	86
______, Robert	Jks	331
______, Robert M.	New	47
______, Ryley	Wal	144
______, S.	Cht	272
______, Samuel	Bul	94
______, Samuel	DeK	45
______, Samuel	Gre	293
______, Samuel	Jef	423
______, Samuel	Jns	463
______, Samuel	Wrn	193
______, Samuel A.	Jks	323
______, Samuel D.	Fay	194
______, Samuel H.	Hal	86
______, Sarah	Ogl	97
______, Sarah	Scr	309
______, Selah	Wrn	213
______, Seth	Wrn	222
______, Solomon	Pul	149
______, Solomon V.	Ear	99
______, Stephen	Mon	226
______, Teniel	Crf	411
______, Thomas	Crf	409
______, Thomas	DeK	66
______, Thomas	Hal	86
______, Thomas Jr.	Hal	86
______, Thomas	Jks	330

Wilson, Thomas Jsp 392
______, Thomas Hst 275
______, Thomas Mon 200
______, Thomas Wrn 193
______, Thomas A. Eff 109
______, Thomas B. Gre 285
______, Thomas C. Hal 86
______, Thomas K. Tfo 359
______, Thomas R. Hal 87
______, William Cht 271
______, William Cow 389
______, William DeK 40
______, William DeK 70
______, William Ear 93
______, William Frk 211
______, William Hal 87
______, William Hry 244
______, William Hst 265
______, William Lib 55
______, William Mor 262
______, William Ogl 63
______, William C. Pik 129
______, William E. Hal 86
______, William L. Bts 172
______, William L. Han 171
______, William P. Fay 193
______, William R. Tms 29
______, William W. Eff 107
______, Winna Hal 88
______, Young M. Up 104
______, Zach. Jks 338
Willson, Allen R. Gwn 326
______, Arkillis Jsp 372
______, Ephraim Gwn 358
______, H. Jks 335
______, Isaac Put 181
______, James Bts 167
______, James Frk 211
______, James Put 181
______, James J. Jks 312
______, John Bib 63
______, John Jks 342
______, John S. Gwn 317
______, Joseph Bib 57
______, Joseph Bts 160
______, Joseph Put 212
______, Joshua Jsp 389
______, Nancy Bib 75
______, Risbin Lwn 90
______, Robert Rab 229
______, Robert B. Wyn 281
______, William Bib 66
______, William Jks 313
Willson, William Jks 331
______, William Jks 332
______, William Rab 222
WILTBURGER. Peter Cht 282
WIMBERLY/WIMBERLEY/WOMBERLY
Wimberly, Mrs. Rch 255
______, Abner Hst 295
______, David Wsh 243
______, F. D. Mon 224
______, Henry Hst 267
______, James Twg 88
______, James Sr. Twg 81
______, Jeremiah Twg 70
______, John Tlb 337
______, Joshua R. Twg 84
______, Judia Doo 80
______, Lewis Tlb 337
______, Perry Twg 62
______, William Sr. Twg 82
______, William Jr. Twg 63
______, Zach. Tlb 341
Simberley, Henry Bke 149
______, Isaac Bke 149
______, John Bke 147
______, Lewis Sr. Bke 145
______, Lewis Jr. Bke 145
______, Malachi Car 224
______, Needham Bke 149
______, Wiley Bke 145
______, Zachariah Bke 145
Womberly, Lewis D. Jns 467
WIMPEY/WIMPY/WINPEY
Wimpey, Daniel Rab 230
______, John Bke 143
______, Mathew Hry 247
______, Samuel Jns 436
______, William Hry 247
Wimpy, Archibald Frk 233
Winpey, Aaron Hab 48
WIMS, John Hab 26
______, Thomas Hab 26
WINBURN/WINNBORN/WINBORN/
WIMBERN/WIMBORN
Winburn, Henry Tlb 335
______, William Pul 149
Winnborn, David Gwn 321
Winborn, Sarah Gwn 363
Wimbern, L. Col 354
Wimborn, Presaler Col 354
WINBUSH/WIMBISH
Winbush, Alexander Elb 140
______, John Mon 221
______, William Bib 66

Winbush, William M. Mon 208
Wimbish, Benjamin Jsp 358
_____, John M. Jsp 357
WINCEY, James E. Wyn 283
WINCHEL, Albert Put 188
WINCHESTER, David Trp 52
_____, Jesse Trp 51
WINDERWRIDLE, Henry Hry 245
WINDHAM/WYNHAM/WINHAM
Windham, Abel Crf 398
_____, Isom Mus 289
_____, John Crf 398
_____, John Mar 144
_____, Mahaley Dec 16
_____, Nancy Lau 13
_____, Peter DeK 63
_____, Rubin Mar 144
_____, William Mor 256
Wynham, Allen Hst 294
Winham, Benjamin Lau 21
WINDSOR/WINDSER/WINZER
Windsor, Jesse Trp 48
_____, William Hal 123
Windser, Anderson Rch 284
Winzer, William Dec 12
WINENS, John Jns 435
WINFREY/WINFRY
Winfrey for dec'd. father Ogl 71
_____, George Jks 324
_____, John Col 358
_____, John New 34
_____, Reuben New 30
_____, Richard R. Hab 11
_____, William Ogl 71
Winfry, Sarah Col 359
WING, Edward Gwn 325
_____, John Gwn 313
WINGATE/WYNGATE
Wingate, Emanuel Mon 213
_____, M. W. Bal 35
Wyngate, Amos Hst 281
_____, Amos Hst 285
_____, Richard B. Hst 283
_____, William Hst 290
WINGFIELD/WINFIELD/
WINKFIELD
Wingfield, Charles Wil 288
_____, Garland Wil 290
_____, James Wil 289
_____, James L. Pik 131
_____, John Elb 132
_____, John Mor 249
_____, John L. Wil 300
Wingfield, Thomas Gre 305
Winfield, Matthew Gre 280
_____, Nathan Gre 273
Winkfield, William New 11
WINGO, Simpson C. Cow 372
WINKLE/WINKLES
Winkle, Stephen Bts 173
Winkles, John New 10
WINKLER, G. W. Cht 270
_____, S. Cht 259
WINN/WYNN
Winn, A. B. Gwn 361
_____, Clem A. Gwn 346
_____, Elisha Gwn 335
_____, Eliza Gly 267
_____, Frances Put 200
_____, Francis Cpb 209
_____, Gennebeth Jks 348
_____, Glowman Gwn 318
_____, Hamilton Hab 17
_____, Hannah Put 188
_____, Hinchey Wal 125
_____, James W. Lib 55
_____, Jefferson Lin 72
_____, John Gwn 346
_____, John Gwn 360
_____, John dec'd. Est Lib 55
_____, John Lin 73
_____, John Ogl 65
_____, John A. Jks 324
_____, John J. McI 131
_____, John P. Hal 85
_____, Joseph Put 186
_____, Joshua Bts 176
_____, L. D. Gwn 361
_____, Lemuel Wal 169
_____, Mary Put 177
_____, Mary Wil 319
_____, Peter F. Lib 55
_____, Richard Hal 85
_____, Robert Bts 162
_____, Thomas Gwn 319
_____, Thomas G. Gre 304
_____, Washington Lib 55
Wynn, Benjamin Elb 133
_____, Benjamin Wrn 203
_____, Burwell J. Han 170
_____, Charles R. Tlb 332
_____, Delilah Mad 116
_____, Frances Wrn 201
_____, Irby Wrn 208
_____, James Wks 351
_____, James Wrn 201

Wynn, John Wrn 203
_____, John Mon 227
_____, John Wks 349
_____, John C. Tms 18
_____, John W. Hst 283
_____, Lemuel B. Wil 310
_____, Lewis Har 181
_____, Littleton Har 177
_____, Patsey P. Mon 187
_____, Peter Wrn 203
_____, Robert Han 171
_____, Robert Mon 194
_____, Samuel B. Wil 312
_____, Terrell Har 177
_____, Thomas Mon 208
_____, Thomas Tfo 361
_____, Thomas Wrn 204
_____, Thomas H. Har 181
_____, William Wks 337
_____, William Wks 349
_____, William Wrn 203
_____, William L. Ran 248
_____, Williamson Mon 224
Wynne, Clement Tfo 364
_____, Lemuel New 6
_____, Mathew Gwn 341
_____, Robert W. W. Pul 138
WINSHIP, Isaac Mon 195
_____, Joseph Mon 196
WINSLET/WINSLIT
Winslet, Jonathan Put 176
_____, Randal Mon 201
Winslit, Samuel Mwr 155
WINSLOW, William Tlb 348
WINSTON/WINSTELL
Winston, Thomas Gre 296
Winstell, Peggy Gre 276
WINTERS/WINTER
Winters, Albert Frk 218
_____, Charity Jks 335
_____, George W. Jks 329
_____, James Rch 289
_____, Jeremiah Rch 290
_____, John DeK 41
_____, Leonard DeK 68
_____, Pietta Hab 14
_____, Thomas New 39
_____, Willis Jns 459
Winter, John Rch 263
_____, John G. Wrn 192
WISDOM, Bird Gwn 312
_____, Jesse Gwn 378
WISE/WYSE
Wise, Abejah Clk 295
_____, Abner Ogl 84
_____, Augustus Bts 161
_____, Barney Bts 164
_____, Burrel Bib 68
_____, Hugh Bts 164
_____, Isaac Bts 177
_____, Jacob Bts 176
_____, Joel Jsp 368
_____, John Bul 96
_____, John Cpb 197
_____, John Ogl 65
_____, John Ogl 84
_____, John Wsh 271
_____, John Wks 346
_____, Josiah Cow 383
_____, Mary Wil 320
_____, Nancy Wsh 259
_____, Paterson Clk 295
_____, Preston Bry 86
_____, Riley Bts 172
_____, Sherrad Ogl 85
_____, Waine Clk 291
_____, Waldin Clk 296
_____, Zach. Jsp 367
Wyse, Thomas Bke 136
WISEMAN, Charles K. Hry 222
_____, John Lin 65
WISENBAKER, Christian Eff 108
_____, Mary Eff 104
WISENHANT/WISEHUNT/WISEN-HUNT/WISENHENT/WISHARD/
also see Whisenhunt
Wisenhant, Nicholas Hab 27
_____, Thomas Hab 37
Wisehunt, Henry Hab 36
Wisenhunt, Adam Hab 36
Wisenhent, Nicholas Hab 29
Wishard, Joseph Mus 291
WISNER/WISENER
Wisner, Jesse Hal 129
_____, Joshua Hal 114
Wisener, Jeremiah Hal 119
_____, William Mon 184
WITCHER/WITHER
Witcher, Ambrose Mad 116
_____, Benjamin Ogl 75
_____, James Mor 271
_____, James New 48
_____, John New 55
Wither, Lucy New 48
WITHERFORD, John Bib 63
WITHERINGTON:

WITHERINGTON: also see Weatherington
Witherington, Curtis Lwn 89
_____, Dennis Lwn 89
_____, Peter Lwn 85
_____, William Lwn 89
WITHERSPOON: also see Weatherspoon
Witherspoon, Elizabeth Clk 319
WITMAN, Mathew Cht 260
WITT/WITTS
Witt, David Jks 313
_____, Jacob Wks 345
_____, Martin Wks 339
Witts, David Hab 34
WITTBURGER, Peter Cht 282
WITTER, James Clk 325
_____, William Clk 325
WITTICH/WITTUK
Wittich, Lucius L. Mor 249
Wittuk, Ernest L. Cow 367
WOFFORD, Absolum Bts 166
_____, Benjamin Hab 13
_____, Daniel Hal 127
_____, James Hal 93
_____, Jeremiah Cpb 197
_____, John Hab 13
_____, Nancy Hab 13
_____, William B. Hab 13
***WOH HOH ACHIE (Indian) Car 234
WOLDER, John A. Ran 250
WOLF/WOOLF
Wolf, Andrew Wil 310
_____, Andrew Jr. Wil 310
_____, Cary Mar 137
_____, George Wil 310
_____, Jacob DeK 49
_____, James Fay 187
_____, Lewis DeK 46
_____, Stephen Lau 5
_____, Thomas Cht 277
Woolf, John Eff 111
_____, Noami Cht 250
WOLLUM, Thomas Cow 387
WOMACK/WOMMACK/WOMECK/WOMICK/WOMMAC/WAMMACK/WAMACK/WAMAC/WARNOCK/WAMOCK/WAMACK/WARNICK
Womack, A. M. Up 114
_____, Abram Mon 224
_____, Digitchen Up 119
_____, Frederick Eff 116
_____, Jacob Mus 285
Womack, Jacob Mus 285
_____, Nancy Tfo 363
_____, Sarah Wsh 276
_____, William Wsh 241
_____, Willy Trp 42
Womack, Charles Mon 189
Womeck, James C. Hab 11
Womick, John Hab 33
Wommac, Mark S. Tlb 344
Wammack, Benjamin Tms 16
_____, Bird DeK 68
_____, Bird Gwn 309
_____, Elizabeth Rab 225
_____, Thomas J. DeK 68
Wamack, Eli Lau 9
_____, James Jns 438
_____, John Scr 306
Wamac, Edmund Put 205
_____, Josiah Put 179
_____, Thomas Put 199
Warnock, John P. Gre 289
_____, Littleberry Hst 285
_____, Sarah Bke 119
Wamock, Nathaniel J. Crf 413
Wamach, Thomas Scr 303
Warnick, John Em 176
WOMBERLY: see Wimberly
WOMBLE/WOMBLES
Womble, Allen Ran 242
_____, Daniel Pul 157
_____, Edmond Ran 244
_____, Elizabeth Wsh 263
_____, Reddin Ran 244
_____, Thomas Wsh 263
Wombles, Elisha Trp 51
WONDOVER, Adam P. Hab 30
WOOD/WOODS
Wood, Abraham D. Pik 106
_____, Abraham S. Frk 234
_____, Abram Hal 132
_____, Allen Gwn 356
_____, Allen Mon 185
_____, Andrew Hal 133
_____, Archibald B. Mor 268
_____, Argy Gwn 337
_____, Argy Gwn 343
_____, Augustus Cow 384
_____, Aristareus Mon 212
_____, Ballenger Jef 421
_____, Calep Jks 335
_____, Caroline Han 171
_____, Cary New 16
_____, Catharine (W) Mor 264

Name	County	Page
Wood, Cullen	Bal	35
______, Cyrus	Mon	220
______, David	Hst	276
______, David	Pul	161
______, David H.	Twg	72
______, Dempsey	Tms	18
______, E.	Cht	255
______, Edmond	Hal	103
______, Edward	Hry	248
______, Elizabeth	Clk	313
______, Elizabeth	Rch	258
______, Elliot	DeK	59
______, Ely	Hst	295
______, Erich	Hab	62
______, Everedge	New	54
______, Fountain	Mad	102
______, Frederick	Pul	140
______, George R.	Wsh	252
______, Green	Cow	379
______, Green	Gre	302
______, Harris	Lee	32
______, Henry	Jns	467
______, Henry	Mon	193
______, Henry	Rch	288
______, Henry	Wsh	259
______, Hezekiah	Pul	158
______, Horla	Hab	46
______, Ira	Cam	184
______, Isaac	Twg	65
______, J.	Bal	42
______, J. J.	Jsp	373
______, Jacob	Lib	54
______, Jacob	McI	125
______, James	Cow	384
______, James	Jks	333
______, James	Mon	201
______, James	Mon	202
______, James Sr.	Wks	340
______, James W.	Gre	290
______, Jarrod	Wsh	256
______, Jethro	Bib	63
______, John	Clk	317
______, John (farmer)	Cow	378
______, John (preacher)	Cow	378
______, John	Dec	14
______, John	Hab	47
______, John	Hal	103
______, John	Jsp	363
______, John	Mad	109
______, John	Pul	158
______, John M.	DeK	59
______, John T.	Up	102
______, Johnathan	Doo	87

Name	County	Page
Wood, Joseph	Bib	68
______, Joseph	Put	183
______, Lazarus	Hal	96
______, Lewis	Pul	149
______, Linney	Rch	283
______, Lorenzo D.	Hal	91
______, Margarett	Wal	138
______, Martin	Ear	95
______, Marvel	Hal	72
______, Mary	Pik	131
______, Mathew	Mor	264
______, Merritt	Clk	302
______, Michael C.	Hal	132
______, Miesels	Wsh	266
______, Nancy	Gwn	337
______, Nancy	Hab	46
______, Owin	Clk	315
______, Polly	Wsh	261
______, Pucket	Car	225
______, Richard	Wal	159
______, Richard W.	New	39
______, Robert	DeK	39
______, Robert	DeK	67
______, Robert	Hal	120
______, Robert	Pik	130
______, Robert	Rab	232
______, Robert	Trp	40
______, Samuel	New	6
______, Sarah	Jef	420
______, Sol. P.	Gwn	348
______, Stephen	Em	169
______, Stephen	Mwr	165
______, Sterling	Wrn	219
______, Tabitha	Trp	48
______, Thomas Sr.	Clk	299
______, Thomas Jr.	Clk	315
______, Thomas	Hal	78
______, Thomas	Jsp	364
______, Thomas	Mor	253
______, Thomas C.	Mor	261
______, Thomas M.	DeK	31
______, Wilie	Wrn	215
______, Wiley E.	Hal	122
______, William	Car	229
______, William	DeK	53
______, William	Hal	83
______, William	Hal	109
______, William	Hry	250
______, William	Jks	328
______, William	Mor	265
______, William	New	6
______, William	New	21
______, William	Ogl	67

Wood, William Wks 340
_____, Williard Col 334
_____, Willis Trp 48
_____, Winston Car 229
_____, Wyatt Jks 331
_____, Young Wal 141
Woods, Ann Scr 299
_____, Archibald Bke 118
_____, Charles Put 193
_____, Edward Bib 75
_____, Eli Frk 212
_____, Elizabeth Mad 118
_____, Frances Pik 107
_____, Henry Mor 260
_____, James Mor 252
_____, Jesse DeK 61
_____, John Jef 409
_____, John Mad 102
_____, John Mon 216
_____, John Mor 253
_____, John Put 183
_____, John C. Mor 243
_____, John G. Put 184
_____, Joshua Bul 92
_____, Mathew M. Jef 411
_____, Nancy App 12
_____, Robert Mad 103
_____, Robert Sr. Mad 112
_____, Samuel Gwn 369
_____, Thomas Bke 119
_____, Thomas Rab 230
_____, Thomas Tat 380
_____, Timothy C. Wal 130
_____, W. A. Tms 18
_____, William Lin 73
_____, William Lwn 80
_____, William Mor 250
_____, William Put 185
WOODALL/WOODAL/WOODELL/
WOODALE
Woodall, Abner Mon 194
_____, Archibald Jns 455
_____, Drewry Rab 224
_____, Elihu Hst 270
_____, Elizabeth DeK 44
_____, Jacob Bal 31
_____, James Up 111
_____, John DeK 30
_____, John Jns 475
_____, John Mon 213
_____, John P. Up 117
_____, Joseph Ogl 68
_____, Joseph Rab 225
Woodall, Martin Tfo 358
_____, Morgan Rab 224
_____, Philip DeK 44
_____, Robert Jns 475
_____, Thomas DeK 73
_____, Williamson Wil 305
Woodal, Tolbert Ogl 64
Woodell, Lewis Hry 201
Woodale, William Rab 224
WOODARD/WOODWARD
Woodard, Aaron Bts 169
_____, John Lau 4
_____, Jonathan Gre 304
_____, Mary Em 177
_____, Thomas Irw 302
_____, William Hry 222
Woodward, Abedea Bke 123
_____, Elizabeth Wrn 197
_____, Elizabeth Wrn 217
_____, John S. Mon 205
_____, Joshua Bke 124
_____, Kizzy Mon 206
_____, Young Lau 5
WOODCOCK, Jacob Bak 19
_____, John Bul 92
_____, Seaborn Bul 102
_____, William Bul 101
WOODDESS, Samuel Hal 128
WOODFIN, Joshua Hab 60
WOODFORK, Robert Col 337
WOODHAM, James Gre 294
WOODHOUSE, Robert Cht 241
WOODING, Edward Col 343
_____, John Col 345
WOODLEY, Andrew Mon 172
_____, Caleb Mon 173
_____, Clayton Mor 268
_____, Temperance Elb 150
WOODLIF, George W. Hal 88
WOODRUFF/WOODROUGH
Woodruff, Benjamin Wal 140
_____, Clifford Gwn 317
_____, Clifford Wil 310
_____, James Tfo 361
_____, James Wil 295
_____, Joseph Wal 135
_____, Lemuel Cpb 202
_____, Richard Car 218
_____, Richard Wil 318
_____, Wilburn Dec 4
Woodrough, Clifford Ogl 72
_____, Elish Ogl 72
_____, Larkin Ogl 72

Woodrough, Reuben New 41
WOODSON, Elizabeth Mon 203
_____, Jessee Mon 180
_____, Jonathan Mon 191
_____, Mary D. Hal 74
_____, Ruth Mon 203
_____, Susan Hal 73
WOODSWORTH/WODSWORTH
Woodsworth, Mordock McL Ran 243
Wodsworth, John Wsh 261
WOODWARD: see Woodard
WOODY, John Hab 32
_____, Samuel Ogl 73
WOODYARD, Felix D. Mor 242
_____, Littlebury T. Mor 241
_____, Robert Mor 238
WOOLBRIGHT, Barnabas Mor 249
_____, Daniel Wil 314
_____, Jacob Mon 211
_____, Jacob Wil 298
_____, John Lee 29
WOOLDRIDGE/WOODDRIDGE
Wooldridge, John DeK 63
_____, Lucy Mon 200
Wooddridge, Irma W. Clk 322
WOOLFOLK, Samuel Mus 286
_____, Thomas Bib 77
WOOLHOPTER, Sarah Cht 246
WOOLSEY, A. M. Rch 287
_____, Benjamin Bal 33
_____, Homor Put 175
_____, John M. Mon 186
WOOLY/WOOLLY/WOOLEY
Wooly, Bazzell New 25
Woolly, Riley G. New 21
Wooley, Riley G. B. Wal 158
WOOTEN/WOOTTEN/WOOTAN/
WOOTON/WOTTON/WOTIN/
WOTTEN/WOODTEN
Wooten, Benjamin DeK 26
_____, Branson D. Trp 41
_____, Briant Tlf 4
_____, Daniel Hal 124
_____, Henry Tlf 5
_____, Jesse Wal 149
_____, John Bts 177
_____, John Hal 99
_____, Joseph DeK 57
_____, Redden Tms 27
_____, Richard Tlf 6
_____, Richard B. Cow 368
_____, Simon Tlf 7
_____, William B. DeK 49
Wootten, Chaney Rab 227
_____, Charles H. Wil 290
_____, Dudley Rab 224
_____, Henry P. Wil 291
_____, James B. Wil 302
_____, Jerusa Bke 126
_____, John Hst 272
_____, John Rab 224
_____, John T. Wil 324
_____, Joseph Wil 319
_____, Lemuel Wil 320
_____, Mourning Bke 126
_____, Thomas S. Wil 319
Wootan, John Mon 172
_____, John Wks 339
_____, John R. Bal 28
_____, Mary Mon 204
Wooton, James Han 171
_____, William New 37
_____, William New 50
Wotton, Benton Cow 367
Wootin, Thomas DeK 59
Wotten, Aaren Hab 45
Woodten, John Hab 41
WOOZENCRAFT, Thomas Clk 299
WORD/WORDE/WHORD
Word, John B. Frk 216
_____, Joshua Frk 229
_____, Nathaniel Mor 254
_____, Polly Hab 65
_____, Samuel L. Rab 229
_____, Wiley New 14
Words, Sally Hab 65
Whord, William New 44
WORLEY/WORLY
Worley, Jacob Cam 188
_____, William Hab 18
_____, William Rab 222
_____, Wootson Hab 27
Worly, Pleasant Hab 54
WORMSLEY, Louis Scr 306
WORNUM, Charles Jns 437
_____, William Put 216
WORRELL/WORREL/WORRILL
Worrell, Simeon S. New 35
_____, Solomon New 14
_____, William New 35
_____, William G. New 35
Worrel, Alexander Jef 421
_____, Stephen Jef 421
_____, William L. Put 207
Worrill, Ransom Elb 136
WORREN, Dred New 54

Worren, Edward New 54
_____, Joseph New 54
WORSHAM/WOSHEN
Worsham, Appling Jsp 364
_____, D. C. Mon 222
_____, Daniel B. Bib 68
_____, David Crf 408
_____, J. G. Bal 36
_____, Jer. Bal 39
_____, John Jsp 364
_____, John Mon 204
_____, Lucinda Bal 30
_____, Ludwell Jks 325
_____, Mitchel Bts 160
_____, Nancy Bal 36
_____, William Car 218
_____, William Put 184
_____, William H. Gwn 354
Woshen, John S. Hab 35
WORSLY/WORSLEY
Worsly, Elizabeth Pul 155
Worsley, Sampson Wrn 231
WORTHAM/WORTHEN/WORTHING/
WORTHAN/WORTHIN
Wortham, James Wil 308
_____, Nancy Hry 242
_____, Samuel Mwr 156
_____, Theophilus Wil 308
_____, William Mwr 165
_____, William Mwr 165
_____, William Trp 54
_____, Zacharias Mwr 156
Worthen, Green H. Wsh 257
_____, Rebecca Wsh 272
_____, Richard Wsh 267
_____, William B. Wsh 254
Worthing, Elijah Han 172
_____, Elison Han 172
Worthan, Thomas J. Wsh 255
Worthin, Elishama Mon 173
WORTHINGTON, Julius Hst 295
_____, Rebecca Hst 295
_____, Robert Hst 271
_____, Toliver Hst 269
WORTHY, Anderson Put 199
_____, John Bib 72
_____, John DeK 30
_____, John Wal 159
_____, Leonard Pik 124
_____, Margaret Lau 21
_____, Robert Wsh 259
_____, Samuel DeK 30
_____, Thomas Gwn 352
Worthy, William DeK 30
_____, William Up 102
_____, Williamson Up 107
WRAGGSDALE, Mason DeK 67
WRAY, Albert Ogl 98
_____, Elisabeth Ogl 100
_____, John Ogl 73
_____, John S. Ogl 103
_____, Thomas Gre 305
_____, Thomas J. Rch 260
_____, William Cht 259
_____, William Ogl 98
_____, William M. Ogl 98
WREN, Elizabeth Jef 419
_____, John Jef 418
_____, George W. Put 209
_____, Thomas Jef 417
_____, Zebulon Car 227
WRICE/RICE
Wrice, Jesse Hab 31
Rice, Moses Hab 40
WRIGHT/RIGHT/RITE
Wright, A. S. Jns 432
_____, Abedenego Mwr 158
_____, Abel Lau 17
_____, Abel Pik 130
_____, Abram Mwr 161
_____, Abrose Jef 401
_____, Absalom Mwr 161
_____, Alexander Mus 289
_____, Amos Wrn 204
_____, Applewhite Wal 129
_____, Asa Put 212
_____, Asah Ogl 72
_____, C. W. C. Jsp 370
_____, Caleb Jef 416
_____, Charles Bts 158
_____, Chs. Wks 352
_____, Chn[t]. Gly 266
_____, Charlton Mon 201
_____, Chrst Gly 266
_____, Clabourn Cam 186
_____, Crawford Car 230
_____, David Clk 320
_____, David Cpb 194
_____, David New 34
_____, Editha Mwr 161
_____, Elias Jks 313
_____, Elisha Jns 428
_____, Elizabeth DeK 42
_____, Elliot Mon 182
_____, Ellis New 22
_____, Ezekiel Hst 292

Wright, George Pik 130
______, George B. Fay 185
______, Gillis Pik 130
______, Henry Doo 86
______, Henry Jns 455
______, Henry Ogl 72
______, Hiram Car 225
______, Huellin Han 172
______, Levi Tat 374
______, Isaiah C. Jns 429
______, Isam Put 183
______, Isham Hst 270
______, Jack Rch 289
______, James Fay 205
______, James Han 171
______, James Lau 4
______, James Put 174
______, James Wrn 204
______, James B. Bul 98
______, James B. Gly 266
______, James C. Mon 194
______, James M. DeK 50
______, James N. Car 227
______, James W. Mwr 154
______, James W. Put 193
______, Jesse Car 225
______, Jesse Crf 413
______, Jessee Hst 292
______, John Car 223
______, John Clk 299
______, John Cow 372
______, John Gwn 376
______, John Hry 229
______, John Jks 316
______, John Jsp 368
______, John Mwr 167
______, John Wil 313
______, John Wil 293
______, John Wil 314
______, John Sr. Doo 84
______, John Jr. Doo 84
______, John F. Bal 28
______, John L. Clk 313
______, John M. Wsh 247
______, John W. Gre 305
______, John W. Gwn 316
______, Joseph Bts 176
______, Joseph Gre 285
______, Joseph Wrn 193
______, Kenon Lau 8
______, Laban Cht 246
______, Lewis Jks 328
______, Lewis Wrn 207
Wright, Little Berry Har 177
______, Lorenzo Bib 68
______, Martha Mon 227
______, Mary Put 209
______, Mary Tat 381
______, Mary Wil 303
______, Matthew Jns 455
______, Matthew H. Cow 388
______, Milecent Wrn 206
______, Milton Ogl 91
______, Moses Fay 189
______, Moses Pul 152
______, Moses Ogl 74
______, Moses Ogl 78
______, Nancy Jef 424
______, Nancy Tlb 341
______, Nancy Wrn 194
______, Nathan Wil 304
______, Obediah Frk 253
______, Obediah Cow 373
______, Pleasant New 33
______, Pryor Bal 42
______, Randol Bts 166
______, Reuben Gre 289
______, Reubin Bak 18
______, Richard W. Put 177
______, Robert M. Han 171
______, Robert Sr. Gre 287
______, Robert Jr. Gre 287
______, Rubin DeK 65
______, Samuel Gly 266
______, Samuel Gly 266
______, Samuel Jks 326
______, Samuel Jns 475
______, Samuel Up 101
______, Sarah Col 341
______, Sarah Ogl 80
______, Sarah Rch 261
______, Sarah P. Jef 401
______, Solomon Jns 475
______, Stephen Gre 299
______, Stephen Jks 313
______, Stephen Sr. Jns 455
______, Stephen S. Crf 398
______, Susannah Mor 259
______, Thomas Bke 158
______, Thomas Gwn 310
______, Thomas Hst 294
______, Thomas Mor 247
______, Thomas New 44
______, W. Mus 288
______, Wiley Gre 298
______, William Bul 94

Name	County	Page
Wright, William	Bts	172
_____, William	Clk	299
_____, William	Col	352
_____, William	Crf	408
_____, William	DeK	65
_____, William	Hal	102
_____, William	Jns	439
_____, William	Jsp	372
_____, William	Lau	10
_____, William	Mwr	159
_____, William	New	21
_____, William	Ogl	75
_____, William	Wal	128
_____, William	Wal	149
_____, William D.	Mon	226
_____, William R.	Car	225
_____, William S.	Jns	445
_____, Willis	Ogl	73
_____, Winfield	Lau	8
_____, Wingfield	Wrn	193
_____, Zachariah	Mor	244
_____, Zachus	Gre	302
_____, Zebulon	Gre	298
Right, A.	Gwn	356
_____, Benjamin	Lin	59
_____, Cornelius	Jks	337
_____, E. S.	Col	363
_____, Isaac	Lin	60
_____, Isaac N.	Gwn	326
_____, Jesse	Jks	316
_____, John	Gwn	328
_____, John	Lin	70
_____, John W.	Hal	90
_____, Johnson	Jks	339
_____, Nathan	Lin	63
_____, Mahaley	Jks	327
_____, Rasberry	Jks	342
_____, Samuel	Lin	73
_____, Stith H.	Cpb	197
Rite, Catharine	Cht	270
WYATT/WIATT/WYETT/WYAT		
Wyatt, Elijah	Twg	75
_____, Elizabeth	Hry	250
_____, Hardy	Lau	9
_____, John	Cpb	207
_____, John P.	Hry	213
_____, Joseph M.	New	49
_____, Samuel	Hry	250
_____, Sarah	New	49
_____, Simmons	Cow	368
_____, Thomas	Mor	254
_____, Thomas B.	New	55
_____, William	Mon	172
Wyatt, William H.	Hry	216
Wiatt, John	Mor	257
_____, Robert	Cow	370
Wyett, William	Mwr	154
_____, Phillip H.	Mwr	157
Wyat, John	Hry	246
WYCHE/WYCK/WYCKE		
Wyche, Albert	Trp	53
_____, Alfred	Jns	437
_____, Littleton	Tms	17
_____, Henry	Jns	452
_____, Susannah	Jns	437
_____, Thomas	Tms	25
Wyck, George	Mtg	231
_____, John	Mtg	236
_____, Robert	Mus	289
Wycke, George	Elb	160
_____, Jeremiah	Hst	272
WYER, Henry O.	Cht	262
WYLEY/WYLLY/WYLIE/WYLY		
Wyley, Oliver C.	Hab	37
_____, Waringham	Hab	43
_____, William	Frk	222
_____, William C.	Hab	35
Wylly, Alex	Gly	269
_____, L.	Cht	249
_____, Thomas	Eff	113
Wylie, George	Ear	100
_____, Jacob	Ear	93
Wyly, Alex C.	Gly	268
WYNN/WYNNE: see Winn		
YAGER, Abner	Gwn	311
YANCY, Absalom	Frk	246
_____, Elisha	Gwn	361
_____, James	Cpb	210
_____, James	Gwn	358
_____, Levi	Gwn	323
_____, Lewis	Hal	103
_____, Lewis Jr.	Jsp	398
_____, Lewis D. Sr.	Jsp	390
_____, Means	Hal	72
_____, Richard	Cpb	203
_____, Thomas	Ogl	67
_____, Thomas	Ogl	71
_____, Wesly	Gwn	345
_____, William	Cpb	211
_____, William	Gwn	320
YARBOROUGH/YARBROUGH/ YARBER/YARBOR/YARBORO		
Yarborough, Benjamin	Tlf	3
_____, Elvey	Hst	295

Name	County	Page
Yarborough, George	Fay	192
______, Jeptha	Fay	198
______, John	Clk	327
______, John	Crf	400
______, John	Pik	115
______, Joseph	Hst	282
______, Josiah	Jsp	352
______, Lewis	Hst	263
______, Moses	Mus	285
______, Nancy	Han	172
______, Randall	Hst	283
______, Thomas	DeK	69
______, Thomas	Ran	242
______, William	Clk	293
______, William	Tlf	3
______, Wyatt	Mor	262
Yarbrough, Amon	Jks	339
______, Elizabeth	Jks	340
______, Groves	Frk	213
______, James	Put	173
______, James	Trp	34
______, John	Jks	340
______, Joseph	Dec	18
______, Joseph	Trp	37
______, Moses	Wrn	196
______, Nancy	Col	337
______, Nimrod	Trp	45
______, Nimrod B.	Trp	44
______, Reubron	Jks	340
______, Silas	Hry	212
______, Thomas	Hry	220
______, Wiley	Ogl	100
______, William	Col	344
______, William	Har	186
______, William	Hry	230
Yarber, John	Cpb	201
______, Richard	Crf	410
Yarbor, Isaac	Hab	57
______, Jeremiah	Crf	403
Yarboro, Jane	Jef	424
______, P.	Wks	337
YATES/YEATES		
Yates, Abram	Gre	280
______, Bennett	Han	172
______, Daniel	Wrn	218
______, Eli	Fay	203
______, Elijah	Fay	202
______, Irwin	Fay	195
______, James	Fay	195
______, James	Hst	283
______, Jesse	Twg	84
______, John	Fay	204
______, John	Wsh	254

Name	County	Page
Yates, Joseph	Frk	243
______, Matthew	Fay	190
______, Peter	Em	166
______, Stephen	Mon	219
______, William	Fay	203
______, Willis	Up	117
Yeates, James	App	11
YAWN/YOUN/YON/YONN/YARN		
Yawn, George	Lin	66
______, Isaac	Dec	16
______, John	Dec	9
______, Martin	Dec	13
______, Patrick	Dec	13
Youn, Allen	Tlf	11
______, James	Tlf	8
______, Joseph	Pul	152
______, Uriah	Tlf	7
Yon, Benjamin	Lee	30
______, Simon	Mtg	231
Youn, Anthony	Lau	12
Yarn, Sarah	Hst	296
YEARGAN, Andrew	Frk	258
______, Benjamin J.	Frk	227
______, Samuel	Frk	252
YEARN, Charles	New	24
YEARTY/YERTY/YERTA/YEATA		
Yearty, Abraham	Pul	153
______, Elsberry	Pul	153
______, Vincent	Pul	153
Yerty, Thomas	Wks	339
Yerta, Jacob	Pul	155
Yeata, George	Mor	267
YEARWOOD, Andrew	Hab	39
______, Perry	Hab	35
YELDELL, Robert	Ear	96
YELLOWEY/YALLALY		
Yellowey, Elizabeth	Cam	184
Yallaly, Thomas	Han	172
YELVERTON, Bryant	Twg	70
YEOMAN/YEOMANS/YOUMONS/ YOUMANS		
Yeoman, Martin	Jsp	371
______, Samuel P.	Tms	23
Yeomans, Henry	Tms	27
Youmons, James	Em	172
______, Redden	Em	172
Youmans, Harris	Em	172
YERBY, Burwell	Clk	318
YEW, Catharine	Elb	133
YOPP, Jeremiah H.	Lau	10
______, Samuel	Lau	11
YORK, Alen	Car	222
______, Archibald	Trp	45

York, Asa Frk 215
______, David Tlb 331
______, Elizabeth Gwn 364
______, Henry Hal 74
______, Isaac Gwn 314
______, James Lin 59
______, Jeffrey Rab 230
______, Jeremiah Rab 230
______, John Lin 62
______, John Tlb 331
______, John G. Frk 221
______, Joseph Cow 381
______, Josiah Car 224
______, Nancy Frk 243
______, Semore Rab 234
______, Singleton Tlb 331
______, Thomas Car 221
______, William Car 216
______, William Frk 224
______, William Hal 70
______, William Tlb 331
YOUBANKS, John H. Doo 79
YOULES, Walter Wyn 281
YOUNG/YONGE
Young, Alexander Bke 148
______, Allen (colored) Bke 140
______, Amos Jns 463
______, Andrew Mwr 152
______, Augustine DeK 39
______, Benjamin Jef 413
______, Chs. Wks 346
______, Charlotte Mad 109
______, Daniel Wrn 210
______, Danil Hab 39
______, David App 11
______, David Wal 148
______, E. L. Jsp 371
______, Elam Jef 422
______, Elija R. Dec 10
______, Elizabeth Col 344
______, Elizabeth Jef 417
______, Elizabeth Wsh 265
______, Enos Mon 223
______, Frederick Tlb 326
______, George Ogl 89
______, George Put 201
______, George Twg 77
______, George H. Ogl 98
______, George W. Mor 238
______, Giles Ogl 87
______, Henry Jef 417
______, Henry Mar 138
______, Henry Ogl 87
Young, Hez. Col 348
______, Isaac Twg 80
______, Isaac N. Gwn 351
______, Jacob Irw 301
______, Jacob Sr. Jef 419
______, Jacob Jr. Jef 418
______, Jacob O. Pul 151
______, James Bul 94
______, James Car 227
______, James Col 344
______, James DeK 51
______, James Gwn 375
______, James Hal 112
______, James Mor 238
______, James Wsh 267
______, James Wks 346
______, Jane Cht 251
______, Jane Cht 282
______, Jesse (colored) Bke 140
______, Jesse Hal 111
______, Jesse Wsh 275
______, John Car 223
______, John Car 229
______, John Col 344
______, John Elb 160
______, John Hst 279
______, John Jks 314
______, John Mon 180
______, John Sr. Twg 77
______, John Jr. Twg 66
______, John C. Hab 21
______, John T. Bts 162
______, John W. Up 115
______, Joseph Mon 225
______, Kearney Car 225
______, Leonard H. Tlb 327
______, Linney Gwn 373
______, Lucretia Lau 15
______, Martha Lau 21
______, Mary Bal 31
______, Mary Mwr 161
______, Michael Tms 29
______, Milus Gre 298
______, Moses Sr. McI 130
______, Moses McI 126
______, Moses W. Mor 268
______, Nicholas App 12
______, Ostin Gwn 357
______, P. R. (negro) Bal 42
______, Philip Hab 58
______, Pierson Lau 13
______, Pleasant Up 121
______, Redding Eff 116

Name	County	Page
Young, Robert	Hal	84
_____, Robert	Ogl	87
_____, Robert	Put	207
_____, Sarah	Twg	81
_____, Susan	Bke	149
_____, Sutton	Hal	115
_____, Thomas	App	9
_____, Thomas	Bal	35
_____, Thomas	Cht	268
** _____, Thomas slaves	Cht	277
_____, Thomas	Hry	249
_____, Thomas	Irw	298
_____, Thomas	Jef	418
_____, Thomas H.	Ogl	94
_____, Valentine	Jks	324
_____, W. W.	Twg	81
_____, Washington R.	Hal	85
_____, William	Col	354
_____, William	Col	361
_____, William	Dec	19
_____, William	Mad	116
_____, William	Tlf	2
_____, William	McI	130
_____, William	Mar	138
_____, William	Put	207
_____, William	Wsh	241
_____, William A.	Jef	418
_____, William C.	Put	189
_____, William U.	Jef	422
_____, Willie	Scr	299
_____, Wilson R.	Trp	48
Yonge, Philip R.	McI	123
_____, William P.	Up	112
YOUNGBLOOD/YONGBLOOD		
Youngblood, A. B.	Wal	158
_____, Abraham	Bke	154
_____, Abram	Mon	173
_____, Arthur	Han	172
_____, Bennett	Fay	183
_____, Gideon	Gwn	339
_____, H. D.	Lee	31
_____, Isaac	Han	172
_____, Isaacs	Han	172
_____, J. R.	Wsh	263
_____, Jacob	Tlb	337
_____, James	Han	172
_____, Joel	Bal	44
_____, Joseph	Upt	112
_____, Nancy	Col	348
_____, Nath	Bal	36
_____, Sarah	Mor	243
_____, Thomas	Han	172
Yongblood, Jacob	Pik	128

Name	County	Page
Yongblood, William	Pik	132
ZABER/ZUBER		
Zaber, Emanuel	Ogl	101
_____, John F.	Ogl	102
Zuber, Daniel	Ogl	103
_____, Williamson	Ogl	102
ZACHARY/ZACHRY/ZACHARY/ ZACHERY/ZACKERY/		
Zachary, Jesse	Put	202
_____, John S.	Jns	444
_____, Lewis	Car	229
Zachry, Daniel H.	New	38
_____, James	New	6
_____, James B.	New	7
_____, Zadoc L.	New	38
Zacachara, Abner	Mor	244
_____, Asa C.	Mor	245
_____, Clementious	Mor	243
Zachery, Benjamin S.	Fay	191
_____, John	Col	346
Zackery, A. L.	Col	336
_____, William	Col	337
ZANITY, Mary	Rch	262
ZEIGLER/ZEIGLAR/ZEGLER		
Zeigler, David	Eff	108
_____, David	Eff	109
_____, Miner	Crf	400
Zeiglar, William	Crf	408
Zegler, Isral	Dec	10
ZELLER/ZELLERS/ZELLARS		
Zeller, Nathaniel	Eff	105
Zellers, Solomon	New	55
Zellars, John	Lin	59
ZELNA/ZELLNER		
Zelna, Andrew	Mon	205
Zellner, John	Tlb	340
ZINN, Edward	Jsp	385
_____, Jacob	Jsp	385
ZIPPERER, Catharin	Eff	104
_____, Christian	Eff	104
_____, Emanuel	Eff	115
_____, Jefferson	Eff	116
_____, John M.	Eff	111
_____, Jonathan	Eff	111
ZITTENS, James	Hab	31
ZITTROUR/CITROWER		
Zittrour, David	Eff	104
_____, George	Eff	107
_____, Gottlieb	Eff	106
_____, Gottlieb	Eff	108
_____, Solomon	Eff	109

Name	County	Page
Citrower, Charles	Bul	96
ZOON, Daniel	Lib	56
ZORN, James	Up	105
_____, William	Up	107
ZOUCHS, David	Lib	56
_____, Henry	Lib	56
ZUBER: see Zaber		

NO SURNAME LISTED

Name	County	Page
*_____, Abby	Clk	301
*_____, Abram	Lib	56
**_____, Baxter & Wiley	Bal	39
*_____, Bellow & Rachel	Lib	56
*_____, Ben	Clk	293
*_____, Billy	Clk	304
*_____, Dolly	Clk	319
*_____, Jack	Clk	327
*_____, Jim & Sue	Lib	56
*_____, Jinny	Clk	298
*_____, John	Clk	313
*_____, Laurah	Clk	327
*_____, Marget & Molley	Lib	56
*_____, Mary Ann	Cht	266
*_____, Milly	Clk	319
**_____, Wiley & Baxter (32 slaves; no whites	Bal	39
*_____, York	Clk	304
_____, Zacriah (white)	Ran	245